Christmas Cookies and Candy

PORTLAND HOUSE

This 1997 edition is published by Portland House,
a division of Random House Value Publishing, Inc.,
201 East 50th Street,
New York, New York 10022

Printed and bound in Malaysia

ISBN 0-517-19013-3

8 7 6 5 4 3 2 1

Christmas Cookies

Christmas Cookies
Contents

Introduction	11
Baking the Best Cookies	12
Storing Cookies	13
Packaging Cookies	13
Mailing Cookies	14
Cutout Cookies	15
Painted Cookies	16
Christmas Wreaths	18
Lebkuchen	20
Stained-Glass Window Cookies	22
Gingerbread People and Things	24
Orange Butter Cookies	26
Drop Cookies	27
Pumpkin Cookies	28
Brown-Edged Cookies	30
Monster Peanut Butter Cookies	31
Chocolate Meringues	32
Oatmeal Lace Cookies	33
Pecan Clusters	34
Hermits	35
Walnut Rocks	36

Orange Drop Cookies 37
Coconut Cornflake Cookies 38

Bar Cookies 39
Holiday Layer Squares 40
Fudge Brownies 41
Spicy Molasses Bars 42
Pumpkin Shortbread Squares 43
Chocolate Chip Squares 44

Hand-Shaped Cookies 45
Chocolate Teddy Bears 46
Walnut Cookie Balls 48
Peppernuts 49
Spicy Chocolate Cookies 50
Pecan Spice Cookies 51
Chocolate Chocolate Cookies 52
Date Walnut Cookies 53
Chocolate Crackles 54
Sandies 55
Gingersnaps 56

Special Cookies 57
Spritz Cookies 58
Chocolate Spritz Ribbons 59
Pecan Pie Cookies 60
Christmas Fantasy Cookies 61
Miniature Fruitcakes 62

Introduction

Rich melted chocolate and fragrant vanilla, crunchy nuts and chewy dates, spicy cinnamon and ginger, tangy orange and lemon rind—these are the delights of Christmas, when the kitchen is warm with remembered smells and flavors and the cookie jar is always full.

Cookies and Christmas seem to be synonymous. Perhaps this is because cookies are so versatile. Packed in a bright tin, a basket, or even a patterned paper bag, they make a thoughtful gift for a neighbor or hostess. Cookies can be used as ornaments on the Christmas tree or as personalized labels on packages. A beautifully arranged platter of cookies is a wonderful addition to a buffet table, and no one can resist a cookie that accompanies an ice cream or fruit dessert. Best of all, most cookies are easy to make, and while they are baking they fill the whole house with a delicious aroma.

Here is a new collection of irresistible cookie recipes. There are instructions for baking bar cookies and drop cookies, hand-shaped cookies and cutouts. You'll find recipes for painted cookies and gingerbread people, pumpkin cookies and chocolate teddy bears, miniature fruitcakes and tiny pecan pies, orange drop cookies and chocolate meringues. You'll want to try them all— and keep your cookie jar filled not just for the holidays, but all through the year.

Baking the Best Cookies

Just follow these ten basic rules and you will always bake wonderful cookies:

🌲 Always read a recipe through from beginning to end before starting to bake. You will then be sure to have all the necessary ingredients on hand, as well as sufficient time.

🌲 Always use the best-quality, freshest ingredients available.

🌲 Measure ingredients accurately, using standard measuring spoons for small amounts, a fluid measuring cup for liquids, and graduated measuring cups for dry ingredients.

🌲 Follow recipes carefully. Use only the ingredients specified and add them in the order and by the method given in the recipe.

🌲 Always preheat the oven for at least 15 minutes at the required temperature.

🌲 Try to make all the cookies in a batch the same size and thickness so they will bake evenly.

🌲 It is best to bake only one sheet of cookies at a time on an oven rack in the upper third of the oven. If you must bake two sheets of cookies at a time, place the second oven rack as close as possible below the first and place the cookie sheets so that neither is directly above or below the other. To ensure even baking, reverse the position of the cookie sheets halfway through the baking time.

🌲 Always use a timer for accuracy.

🌲 Unless a recipe directs you to do otherwise, as soon as you take the cookie sheet out of the oven remove the cookies with a spatula and transfer them to wire racks to cool completely.

🌲 Before placing another batch of cookies on the cookie sheet, let it cool, then brush off any crumbs. It is not necessary to grease the sheet again.

Storing Cookies

Cookies keep well if they are stored properly. Consequently, they can be made several days in advance of the occasion at which they will be served. They are perfect as gifts and can even be mailed to faraway places. Here are some rules for storing cookies so that they remain as delicious as they are when they come out of the oven:

♣ Always allow cookies to cool thoroughly before storing.

♣ Store soft cookies in a container with a tight-fitting lid. To restore moisture to soft cookies that have begun to dry out, place a piece of bread or a wedge of raw apple in the container with the cookies for 24 hours.

♣ Bar cookies may be stored in the pan in which they were baked, tightly covered with foil or plastic wrap.

♣ Crisp cookies should be stored in a container with a loose-fitting lid. If they soften, put them in a 300°F oven for 5 minutes before serving.

♣ Store moist and crisp cookies separately. If they are stored together, the crisp cookies will get soggy.

♣ Cookies made from very buttery dough should be stored in the refrigerator in an airtight container.

♣ Baked cookies may be frozen in freezer containers or tightly closed plastic bags for up to 12 months. Thaw them at room temperature for 15 minutes before serving.

Packaging Cookies

Cookies make splendid gifts, and wrapped imaginatively they can be very special. Attractive tins and wooden or cardboard boxes make fine containers for cookies. And what could be a more appropriate gift container than a cookie jar?

When using a round wooden box or tin, line it with several layers of white doilies. Cut rounds of waxed paper a little smaller than the circumference of the box. Put several thicknesses of the paper between each layer of cookies. Put a piece of waxed paper, then a doily, on top. Tie a ribbon crosswise around the closed box.

A wide-mouthed glass jar that has a well-fitting lid can be neatly filled with an assortment of cookies. Wrap the jar using several layers of colored tissue paper. Gather the tissue paper at the top with curling ribbon.

Baskets make excellent containers for cookies. Line the basket with white paper doilies. Arrange the cookies in the basket; they'll look best if you cluster the same kinds of cookies together. Wrap the whole basket in cellophane and tie a bright ribbon around it.

Mailing Cookies

Soft, moist bar and drop cookies, brownies, and miniature fruitcakes travel best through the mail. Thin, crisp cookies tend to crumble easily and frosted cookies often become sticky.

Use a sturdy, heavy cardboard box and have on hand an ample supply of such filler material as bubble wrap, crumpled foil, waxed paper, tissue paper, or paper towels. Begin by lining the box with foil or plastic wrap. Then put a layer of filler in the bottom of the box.

Wrap cookies individually or back to back in foil or plastic wrap, then pack the cookies in neat rows with filler between the rows and layers. When sending an assortment of cookies, put the heaviest ones on the bottom. Be sure the box is full enough to prevent the contents moving when the box is closed and put a generous layer of filler on top of the top layer of cookies. Alternatively, pack the cookies in layers in a decorative tin, using lots of filler. Tape the tin closed, then put it into a well-padded box for mailing and wrap it securely.

Be sure to mark the package FRAGILE and PERISHABLE.

14

Cutout Cookies

Cutout cookies are always fun to make because there is such a variety of cookie cutters available and so many ways that the cookies can be decorated. The recipes in this section will give you lots of inspiration.

The dough for cutout cookies must be firm so it won't stick to the rolling pin or work surface. For this reason, it should be chilled in the refrigerator for several hours or overnight. For faster chilling, divide the dough in half, or even in quarters, and wrap each portion in foil or plastic wrap before putting it into the refrigerator. Roll out only one portion of the dough at a time and keep the rest in the refrigerator.

Roll the dough on a lightly floured surface using a floured rolling pin. Always roll from the edges to the center. Cookie cutters should be dusted with flour or confectioners' sugar so they won't stick. Cut out the cookies as close together as possible, then lift them with a spatula and place them on the cookie sheets.

Unless a recipe specifies otherwise, cutout cookies should be baked only until they are very lightly browned around the edges.

Painted Cookies

These cookies are decorated with brightly colored egg-yolk paint that is applied with artists' paintbrushes before the cookies are baked. The best effects are achieved when the paint is used as an accent, rather than as a covering for a whole cookie. This recipe can also be used to make cookie labels for presents. Follow the recipe, but roll out the dough to a thickness of $\frac{1}{4}$ inch. Cut out the cookies in rectangles. Before baking, make a hole on one side with a drinking straw. Then use the egg-yolk paint to decorate the labels and paint on the names. The labels can be tied to packages with thin ribbon or yarn.

Makes about 70 cookies

> 1 cup unsalted butter, at room temperature
> 2 cups granulated sugar
> 2 eggs
> 1 teaspoon lemon extract
> $\frac{1}{2}$ teaspoon baking soda
> 1 cup commercial sour cream
> 5 cups all-purpose flour
>
> Egg-Yolk Paint
> 2 egg yolks
> $\frac{1}{2}$ teaspoon water
> Food coloring

In a large mixing bowl, cream the butter until it is smooth. Add the sugar and beat until light and fluffy. Add the eggs, one at a time, and beat well. Beat in the lemon extract.

Combine the baking soda with the sour cream. Add the flour to the batter, $\frac{1}{2}$ cup at a time, alternating with the sour-cream mixture and mixing well after each addition.

Gather the dough into two balls. Wrap each in foil and chill in the refrigerator for 2 hours.

Preheat the oven to 400°F. Lightly grease cookie sheets with butter.

On a lightly floured surface, roll out half the dough to a thickness of $\frac{1}{8}$ inch. (Keep the rest of the dough chilled until needed.) Cut out the dough with a variety of cookie cutters. Reroll and cut the scraps. Place the cookies on the prepared cookie sheets.

To make the egg-yolk paint, using a fork, blend the egg yolks with the water. Divide the mixture into small bowls. Tint each portion with sufficient food coloring to color it brightly.

Paint the cookies as desired, using a separate paintbrush for each color. If the paint thickens while standing, thin it with a few drops of water.

Bake the cookies for 8 to 10 minutes, or until the edges are lightly browned.

Christmas Wreaths

These delicate, pretty cookies make wonderful decorations for the tree. Use tiny cinnamon candies or red gumdrops to make the holly berries.

Makes about 60 cookies

$\frac{3}{4}$ cup unsalted butter, at room temperature
1 cup granulated sugar
1 egg
1 teaspoon vanilla extract
3 cups all-purpose flour
1 teaspoon baking soda
$\frac{1}{2}$ teaspoon salt
   Red candies

Decorative Icing
1 pound-package confectioners' sugar
6 tablespoons water
   Green food coloring

In a large mixing bowl, cream together the butter and sugar, then beat until the mixture is fluffy. Beat in the egg and the vanilla.

Sift together the flour, baking soda, and salt. Add to the batter, $\frac{1}{2}$ cup at a time, blending well after each addition.

Gather the dough into two balls. Wrap each in foil and chill in the refrigerator overnight.

Preheat the oven to 350°F.

On a lightly floured surface, roll out half the dough to a thickness of $\frac{1}{4}$ inch. (Keep the rest of the dough chilled until needed.) Cut out the dough with a 3-inch round cookie cutter, then cut out the centers with a 1-inch round cutter. Reroll and cut the scraps.

Place the cookies on ungreased cookie sheets. Bake for 10 minutes, or until the cookies are lightly browned around the edges. Cool the cookies on wire racks.

To make the icing, sift the confectioners' sugar into a medium bowl. Add the water, 1 tablespoon at a time, beating until the mixture is smooth. Add a few drops of green food coloring and blend well. If the icing is too stiff, add a little more water, a few drops at a time.

When the cookies are completely cool, swirl the icing on them, then decorate with the red candies.

Lebkuchen

These spicy honey cookies have been part of the German Christmas tradition for hundreds of years. There are many recipes for lebkuchen. This is one of the best.

Makes about 90 cookies

1 cup honey
2 eggs
$\frac{3}{4}$ cup firmly packed dark brown sugar
1 tablespoon lemon juice
1 teaspoon grated lemon rind
$2\frac{3}{4}$ cups all-purpose flour
$1\frac{1}{2}$ teaspoons baking soda
1 teaspoon ground cinnamon
1 teaspoon ground allspice
$\frac{1}{2}$ teaspoon ground nutmeg
$\frac{1}{4}$ teaspoon ground cloves
$\frac{1}{3}$ cup finely chopped citron
$\frac{1}{3}$ cup finely chopped walnuts
2 tablespoons milk

Cookie Glaze
1 teaspoon cornstarch
$\frac{1}{4}$ cup confectioners' sugar
$\frac{1}{2}$ cup granulated sugar
$\frac{1}{4}$ cup water

In a small saucepan, heat the honey just until it simmers. Remove the pan from the heat and set aside to cool.

In a large mixing bowl, beat 1 egg until foamy. Add the sugar, $\frac{1}{4}$ cup at a time, beating well after each addition. Add the honey, the lemon juice, and the grated lemon rind and mix well.

Sift together the flour, baking soda, cinnamon, allspice, nutmeg, and cloves. Blend the sifted ingredients into the honey mixture. Add the citron and the nuts and mix well.

Divide the dough into four parts. Wrap each in foil and chill in the refrigerator overnight.

Preheat the oven to 400°F. Lightly grease cookie sheets with butter. Lightly beat the remaining egg with the milk.

Make the cookie glaze. Sift together the cornstarch and the confectioners' sugar. Set aside. In a saucepan, combine the granulated sugar and the water. Bring to a boil, stirring constantly until the sugar dissolves. Continue boiling until the mixture threads from the spoon (230°F on a candy thermometer). Remove the pan from the heat and gradually stir in the confectioners'-sugar mixture. Set aside.

On a lightly floured surface, roll out one-quarter of the dough to a thickness of $\frac{1}{4}$ inch. (Keep the rest of the dough chilled until ready to use.) Cut the dough using a 2-inch round cookie cutter. Reroll and cut the scraps.

Place the cookies 1 inch apart on the prepared cookie sheets. Brush each one with the egg and milk mixture. Bake for 10 to 12 minutes, or until no indentations remain on the cookies when touched.

When the lebkuchen are removed from the oven, immediately brush them with the glaze. (If the glaze crystallizes while brushing the cookies, warm it over low heat, adding a little water, until it is clear again.) Transfer the cookies to wire racks to cool.

Stained-Glass Window Cookies

These cookies are so lovely you may want to hang some of them on your Christmas tree. To make cookie ornaments, use a drinking straw to make a hole in the top end of each cookie before baking it. After the cookies have cooled completely, simply thread a piece of yarn through each hole, tying the yarn at the top to make a loop. The hard candy required in this recipe can be sour balls in assorted colors or you may use rolls of ring-shaped candy.

Makes about 40 cookies

6 tablespoons unsalted butter, at room temperature
$\frac{1}{3}$ cup shortening
$\frac{3}{4}$ cup granulated sugar
1 egg
1 tablespoon milk
1 teaspoon vanilla extract
2 cups all-purpose flour
$1\frac{1}{2}$ teaspoons baking powder
$\frac{1}{4}$ teaspoon salt
4 ounces hard candy

In a large mixing bowl, cream together the butter, shortening, and sugar. Beat until light and fluffy. Beat in the egg, the milk, and the vanilla.

Sift together the flour, baking powder, and salt. Add the sifted ingredients, $\frac{1}{2}$ cup at a time, to the batter. Beat until smooth.

Divide the dough in half. Wrap each half in foil and chill in the refrigerator for at least 3 hours.

Preheat the oven to 375°F. Line cookie sheets with foil.

On a lightly floured surface, roll out half the dough to a thickness of $\frac{1}{8}$ inch. (Keep the rest of the dough chilled until needed.) Cut with decorative cookie cutters. Reroll and cut the scraps.

Place the cookies on the lined cookie sheets. Using a sharp knife or tiny hors d'oeuvre cutters, carefully cut out one or more small shapes in the middle of each cookie.

Separate the hard candies by color and put them into plastic bags. Place one bag at a time in a dish towel and, using a hammer or the flat edge of a meat mallet, crush the candy into coarse pieces.

Spoon a little of the candy into the cutout centers of the cookies. Be sure to fill the holes to the level of the dough. (As the cookies bake the candy will melt into smooth windows.)

Bake the cookies for 7 minutes, or until the edges of the cookies are lightly browned and the candy has melted.

Let the cookies cool completely on the cookie sheet, then remove them carefully with a spatula.

Gingerbread People and Things

Boys and girls, Christmas trees and wreaths, stars and crescent moons—this recipe can be used to make whatever manner of cutout gingerbread cookie you choose.

Makes about sixty 6-inch cookies or ninety 3-inch cookies

5 cups all-purpose flour
1½ teaspoons baking soda
2 teaspoons ground ginger
1 teaspoon ground cinnamon
1 teaspoon ground cloves
½ teaspoon salt
1 cup shortening
1 cup granulated sugar
1 egg
1 cup molasses
2 tablespoons white vinegar

Decorative Icing
1 egg white
2 teaspoons lemon juice
1½ to 2 cups confectioners' sugar, sifted
Food coloring

Sift together the flour, baking soda, ginger, cinnamon, cloves, and salt.

In a large mixing bowl, beat the shortening until it is soft and smooth. Add the sugar and beat until the mixture is fluffy. Add the egg, molasses, and vinegar. Beat well. Add the flour mixture, ½ cup at a time, beating well after each addition. When the dough is smooth, divide it into quarters. Wrap each portion in foil and chill in the refrigerator for at least 3 hours.

Preheat the oven to 375°F. Grease cookie sheets with butter.

On a lightly floured surface, roll out the dough to a thickness of $\frac{1}{8}$ inch. (Use only one-quarter of the dough at a time and keep the remainder in the refrigerator until you are ready to use it.) Cut the dough with cookie cutters. Reroll and cut the scraps.

Place the cookies on the cookie sheets. Bake for 5 minutes, or until the cookies are very lightly browned around the edges.

Let the cookies cool on the cookie sheets for 1 minute, then transfer them to wire racks to cool completely.

To make the icing, in a small mixing bowl, beat the egg white, lemon juice, and 1 cup of the confectioners' sugar. Gradually add only enough confectioners' sugar to make an icing of piping consistency. When the consistency seems right, stir in a few drops of food coloring if desired.

To decorate the cookies, fill a decorating bag no more than half full of icing. Use a tip with a small opening. First pipe outlines on the edges of the cookies, then fill in the details.

Orange Butter Cookies

Use a variety of cookie cutters to make these delicious cookies.
Store them in airtight containers in the refrigerator.

Makes about sixty 2-inch cookies

> 2 cups unsalted butter, at room temperature
> $1\frac{1}{2}$ cups firmly packed light brown sugar
> 4 cups all-purpose flour
> $\frac{1}{8}$ teaspoon salt
> 2 large navel oranges
> 2 eggs
> 2 tablespoons water

In a large mixing bowl, cream the butter and sugar together.
Gradually beat in the flour, $\frac{1}{2}$ cup at a time. Add the salt and
mix well. Grate the rind of the oranges and mix it into the
dough.

Gather the dough into a ball, wrap it in foil, and chill it in
the refrigerator for at least 4 hours.

Preheat the oven to 350°F. Line cookie sheets with baking
parchment.

On a lightly floured surface, roll out the dough to a thickness
of $\frac{1}{2}$ inch. Cut out the cookies using a variety of 2-inch cookie
cutters. Reroll and cut the scraps.

In a small bowl, beat the eggs and water together. Place the
cookies on the prepared cookie sheets. Brush the egg mixture
lightly over the cookies. Bake for 15 to 20 minutes, or until the
cookies are a light golden brown.

Drop cookies are so named because spoonfuls of the soft dough are dropped onto the cookie sheet in mounds that spread when baked. There the similarity ends. Drop cookies may be crisp or chewy, plain, or full of fruit and nuts and other goodies.

Since the dough for drop cookies spreads as it bakes, always use cool cookie sheets to prevent excessive spreading.

It is helpful to use the tip of a table knife or another spoon to push the dough off the spoon onto the cookie sheet. Try to make all the cookies the same size so they will bake evenly.

Drop cookies are done when the dough is set, the bottoms are lightly browned (check by using a table knife or a metal spatula to lift a cookie so you can peek underneath), and the tops look dry rather than shiny.

Pumpkin Cookies

Delicately spiced and full of dates and nuts, these cookies are wonderful plain and even better when they are frosted with an orange icing.

Makes about 36 cookies

1 cup unsalted butter, at room temperature
1 cup granulated sugar
1 egg, lightly beaten
1 teaspoon vanilla extract
1 cup canned pumpkin puree
2 cups all-purpose flour
1 teaspoon baking powder
1 teaspoon baking soda
$\frac{1}{2}$ teaspoon salt
1 teaspoon ground cinnamon
$\frac{1}{4}$ teaspoon ground nutmeg
$\frac{1}{4}$ teaspoon ground cloves
1 cup finely chopped dates
$\frac{1}{2}$ cup finely chopped walnuts

Orange Icing
$\frac{1}{3}$ cup unsalted butter, at room temperature
2 cups confectioners' sugar
2 to 3 tablespoons orange juice

Preheat the oven to 350°F.

In a large mixing bowl, cream together the butter and sugar. Add the egg and vanilla and beat well. Beat in the pumpkin puree.

Sift together the flour, baking powder, baking soda, salt, cinnamon, nutmeg, and cloves. Add the sifted ingredients to the batter, $\frac{1}{2}$ cup at a time, mixing well after each addition. Stir in the dates and the walnuts.

Drop by teaspoonfuls, about 2 inches apart, onto ungreased cookie sheets. Bake for 12 to 15 minutes, or until the cookies are firm and the bottoms are lightly browned. Transfer the cookies to wire racks to cool completely.

To make the icing, in a large mixing bowl, cream together the butter and the sugar. Beat in the orange juice, 1 tablespoon at a time, until the frosting is of a spreading consistency.

Using a spatula, swirl the icing on top of each cookie.

Brown-Edged Cookies

These classic cookies are easy to make and always delicious. Pecans or candied cherry halves may be substituted for the walnuts.

Makes about 75 cookies

> 1 *cup unsalted butter, at room temperature*
> 2 *teaspoons salt*
> 1 *teaspoon vanilla extract*
> $\frac{2}{3}$ *cup granulated sugar*
> 1 *egg*
> $2\frac{1}{2}$ *cups sifted all-purpose flour*
> $\frac{1}{2}$ *cup light cream*
> *Confectioners' sugar*
> *Walnut halves*

Preheat the oven to 375°F. Lightly grease cookie sheets with butter.

In a large mixing bowl, cream together the butter, salt, vanilla, and sugar, then beat until the mixture is light and fluffy. Beat in the egg. Add the flour, $\frac{1}{2}$ cup at a time, alternating with the cream. Beat well after each addition.

Drop the batter by teaspoonfuls, about 2 inches apart, onto the prepared cookie sheets. Let stand for 3 minutes.

Dip the bottom of a glass into confectioners' sugar, then use it to press the cookies flat. Gently press a walnut half into the center of each cookie.

Bake for 8 minutes, or until the edges of the cookies are lightly browned.

Monster Peanut Butter Cookies

Kids are amused and delighted by cookies that are the size of small plates. They love to eat them and to make them themselves. This recipe makes twelve 6-inch cookies. Double or triple the ingredients to increase the number. Any favorite drop cookie recipe, perhaps for oatmeal or chocolate chip cookies, can be used to make "monsters." Just use $\frac{1}{3}$ cup of dough for each cookie.

Makes 12 large cookies

> 1 cup unsalted butter, at room temperature
> 1 cup granulated sugar
> 1 cup chunky peanut butter
> 2$\frac{1}{2}$ cups all-purpose flour
> Confectioners' sugar

Preheat the oven to 375°F. Liberally grease cookie sheets with butter.

In a large mixing bowl, cream together the butter and sugar, then beat until the mixture is light and fluffy. Beat in the peanut butter. Add the flour, $\frac{1}{2}$ cup at a time, and mix well.

Scoop up $\frac{1}{3}$-cup measures of the dough and drop on the prepared cookie sheets. (The dough will spread, so it probably will not be possible to bake more than four cookies on one sheet.) Dip the bottom of a pie plate in confectioners' sugar and use it to press each mound firmly so that it flattens into a 6-inch circle.

Bake the cookies for 15 minutes.

Let the cookies cool on the cookie sheets for at least 5 minutes, then use a pancake turner to transfer them to wire racks to cool completely.

Chocolate Meringues

Crisp and delicate, these little meringues melt in the mouth. They are a delightful addition to a platter of Christmas goodies.

Makes about 96 small meringues

>   1 cup semisweet chocolate chips
>   3 egg whites
>   1 cup granulated sugar
> $\frac{1}{3}$ cup graham cracker crumbs
> $\frac{1}{2}$ teaspoon vanilla extract

Preheat the oven to 350°F. Lightly grease cookie sheets with butter.

Melt the chocolate in the top of a double boiler over barely simmering water. Remove from the hot water and set aside to cool for at least 5 minutes.

In a large mixing bowl, beat the egg whites until they hold stiff peaks. Add the sugar, $\frac{1}{4}$ cup at a time, continuing to beat until the mixture is smooth and glossy. Fold in the melted chocolate, the crumbs, and the vanilla.

Drop level teaspoonfuls, about $1\frac{1}{2}$ inches apart, onto the prepared cookie sheets. Bake for 15 minutes, or until the meringues are dry and the bottoms are lightly browned.

Oatmeal Lace Cookies

These thin, lacy cookies spread a lot while they bake, so be sure to leave plenty of room around them on the cookie sheet. One tablespoon of dough makes a large cookie. If you prefer smaller cookies, drop the dough from a teaspoon.

Makes about 35 large cookies

1 cup unsalted butter, at room temperature
½ cup granulated sugar
1 cup firmly packed light brown sugar
2 eggs
2 teaspoons vanilla extract
¼ cup water
1 cup all-purpose flour
¼ teaspoon salt
½ teaspoon baking soda
2 cups quick-cooking oatmeal
1½ cups finely chopped walnuts

Preheat the oven to 350°F. Lightly grease cookie sheets with butter.

In a large mixing bowl, cream the butter and sugars together. Beat until the mixture is light and fluffy. Add the eggs and beat well. Beat in the vanilla and the water.

Sift the flour, salt, and baking soda together. Add the sifted ingredients to the batter, ¼ cup at a time, beating well after each addition. When the batter is smooth, stir in the oatmeal and the walnuts.

Drop the batter by rounded tablespoonfuls, about 4 inches apart, onto the prepared cookie sheets. Using a spatula, spread the mounds to a thickness of ¼ inch. Bake for 8 minutes, or until the cookies are golden brown.

Let the cookies cool on the cookie sheets for 2 minutes, then use a pancake turner to transfer them to wire racks to cool completely.

Pecan Clusters

A real confection, these cookies may be made with walnuts instead of pecans or with very coarsely chopped Brazil nuts.

Makes about 36 cookies

$1\frac{1}{2}$ ounces unsweetened chocolate
$\frac{1}{4}$ cup unsalted butter, at room temperature
$\frac{1}{2}$ cup granulated sugar
1 egg
1 teaspoon vanilla extract
$\frac{1}{2}$ cup sifted all-purpose flour
$\frac{1}{2}$ teaspoon salt
$\frac{1}{4}$ teaspoon baking powder
$1\frac{1}{2}$ cups pecan pieces
1 egg white
1 teaspoon water

Preheat the oven to 350°F. Lightly grease cookie sheets with butter.

In the top of a double boiler, melt the chocolate over barely simmering water. Remove from the hot water and set aside.

In a large mixing bowl, cream the butter and sugar together. Add the egg and the vanilla and beat until the mixture is light and fluffy. Add the melted chocolate and mix well.

Sift together the flour, salt, and baking powder. Fold the sifted ingredients into the batter. Fold in the nuts.

Drop heaping teaspoonfuls of batter, about 2 inches apart, onto the prepared cookie sheets.

In a small bowl, lightly beat the egg white with the water. Brush the cookies with the mixture.

Bake for 10 to 12 minutes, or until the cookies are firm.

Hermits

Full of raisins and nuts, these old-fashioned spice cookies improve with age. Store them in an airtight container for at least 2 weeks before serving.

Makes about 48 cookies

$\frac{3}{4}$ cup unsalted butter, at room temperature
1$\frac{1}{2}$ cups firmly packed dark brown sugar
2 eggs
2$\frac{1}{2}$ cups all-purpose flour
$\frac{1}{2}$ teaspoon baking soda
$\frac{1}{2}$ teaspoon salt
1 teaspoon ground nutmeg
1$\frac{1}{2}$ teaspoons ground cinnamon
1 cup coarsely chopped walnuts
1 cup dark raisins
1 cup golden raisins

Preheat the oven to 375°F. Lightly grease cookie sheets with butter.

In a large mixing bowl, cream the butter and sugar together. Add the eggs and beat until light and fluffy.

Sift together the flour, baking soda, salt, nutmeg, and cinnamon. Blend the sifted ingredients into the batter. Add the nuts and the raisins and mix well.

Drop teaspoonfuls of the batter, 2 inches apart, onto the prepared cookie sheets. Bake for about 10 minutes, or until the cookies are golden brown.

Walnut Rocks

Rocks are classic American cookies. They get their name from their shape, not their texture.

Makes about 50 cookies

$\frac{1}{2}$ cup unsalted butter, at room temperature
$\frac{1}{2}$ cup granulated sugar
2 eggs, separated
1 cup plus 2 tablespoons all-purpose flour
$\frac{1}{2}$ teaspoon ground cinnamon
$\frac{1}{2}$ teaspoon ground cloves
$\frac{1}{2}$ cup finely chopped walnuts
$\frac{3}{4}$ cup raisins
$\frac{1}{2}$ teaspoon baking soda
1 teaspoon boiling water

Preheat the oven to 350°F. Lightly flour cookie sheets.

In a large mixing bowl, cream the butter and sugar together. Beat in one egg yolk at a time.

Sift together the flour, cinnamon, and cloves. Add to the batter and mix well. Stir in the walnuts and the raisins. Dissolve the baking soda in the water, then stir it into the batter.

In a medium bowl, beat the egg whites until they hold stiff peaks. Fold them into the batter.

Drop teaspoonfuls of batter, about 2 inches apart, onto the prepared cookie sheets. Bake for 15 to 18 minutes, or until the outsides of the cookies are firm and the bottoms are golden brown.

Orange Drop Cookies

Speckled with grated orange rind, these simple cookies are very special.

Makes about 36 cookies

> $\frac{1}{2}$ cup unsalted butter, at room temperature
> $\frac{3}{4}$ cup granulated sugar
> 1 egg
> $\frac{1}{2}$ teaspoon baking soda
> $1\frac{1}{2}$ teaspoons baking powder
> $1\frac{1}{2}$ cups all-purpose flour
> 1 cup buttermilk
> 1 large navel orange

Preheat the oven to 350°F.

In a large mixing bowl, cream the butter and sugar together, then beat until fluffy. Add the egg and beat well.

Sift together the baking soda, baking powder, and flour. Add the sifted ingredients to the batter, $\frac{1}{2}$ cup at a time, alternating with the buttermilk. Beat well after each addition.

Grate the rind and squeeze the juice of the orange. Add to the batter and mix well.

Drop by teaspoonfuls, about 2 inches apart, onto ungreased cookie sheets. Bake for 10 to 12 minutes, or until the bottoms of the cookies are lightly browned.

Coconut Cornflake Cookies

Easy to make, these chewy cookies are an unusual combination of simple ingredients.

Makes about 60 cookies

$\frac{3}{4}$ cup unsalted butter, at room temperature
$2\frac{1}{2}$ cups firmly packed dark brown sugar
3 eggs
2 teaspoons vanilla extract
1 cup flaked coconut
2 cups coarsely chopped walnuts
$8\frac{1}{2}$ cups cornflakes

Preheat the oven to 375°F. Lightly grease cookie sheets with butter.

In a large mixing bowl, cream the butter and sugar together. Add the eggs and the vanilla and beat until light and fluffy. Stir in the coconut and the walnuts and mix well. Add the cornflakes and mix gently but thoroughly.

Drop teaspoonfuls of batter, 2 inches apart, on the prepared cookie sheets. Bake for 8 to 10 minutes, or until the bottoms of the cookies are golden brown.

Let the cookies set on the cookie sheets for 5 minutes before transferring them to wire racks to cool completely.

Bar Cookies

Bar cookies are the easiest kind of cookie to make because they are baked all at once and then cut into squares, bars, or strips—but the ease of preparation does not make these cookies less varied or delicious.

For best results, always use the size of pan specified in the recipe. The pan may be made of aluminum, metal, or ovenproof glass. Use a rubber spatula to spread the batter evenly in the pan.

Cool bar cookies in the pan on a wire rack. Cut them into the size and shape you want using a sharp knife rinsed in cold water. Remove a bar from one corner first. The rest can then be removed easily. If you are going to ice the bars, always do so before cutting them.

Bar cookies are the easiest kind of cookie to store, too. Simply cover the bars in the baking pan with plastic wrap. Then cover the whole pan with foil and seal the edges tightly. Store in the refrigerator, or in the freezer if you are going to keep them for more than a week.

Holiday Layer Squares

Easy to make, these cookies are full of everyone's favorite ingredients. They are guaranteed to disappear quickly.

Makes 24 squares

> 4 tablespoons unsalted butter
> 1 cup graham cracker crumbs
> 1 cup flaked coconut
> 1 cup semisweet chocolate chips
> 1 cup finely chopped walnuts
> 1 cup sweetened condensed milk
> 1 cup candied cherries

Preheat the oven to 350°F.

Put the butter into an 8-inch square baking pan. Put the pan into the oven for a few minutes until the butter melts. Shake the pan so that the bottom and sides are coated with the melted butter.

Spread the graham cracker crumbs evenly over the bottom of the pan. Sprinkle a layer of coconut over the crumbs. Next make a layer of chocolate chips, then a layer of chopped nuts. Pour the condensed milk over the layers. Arrange the candied cherries on the top.

Bake for 30 minutes. Cool in the pan on a wire rack. When completely cool, cut into squares.

Fudge Brownies

This recipe makes moist, chewy brownies. If you prefer cakelike brownies, bake them for 5 minutes longer. Walnuts may, of course, be substituted for the pecans.

Makes about 20 brownies

2 ounces unsweetened chocolate
$\frac{1}{3}$ cup unsalted butter
2 eggs
1 cup granulated sugar
1 teaspoon vanilla extract
$\frac{2}{3}$ cup all-purpose flour
$\frac{1}{4}$ teaspoon salt
$\frac{1}{2}$ teaspoon baking powder
$\frac{1}{2}$ cup coarsely chopped pecans

Preheat the oven to 350°F. Grease an 8-inch square baking pan with butter.

Combine the chocolate and the butter in the top of a double boiler. Cook over barely simmering water, stirring frequently, until the chocolate and butter are melted. Remove from the hot water and set aside.

In a large mixing bowl, beat the eggs until foamy. Add the sugar, $\frac{1}{4}$ cup at a time, beating well after each addition. Blend in the melted chocolate mixture and the vanilla.

Combine the flour, salt, and baking powder and add it to the batter. Mix well. Stir in the nuts.

Pour the batter into the prepared pan. Bake for 25 minutes. Cool the brownies in the pan on a wire rack, then cut into squares or bars.

Spicy Molasses Bars

Molasses is a traditional Christmas flavor, and in this recipe it is delightfully combined with spices, nuts, and fruit.

Makes about 24 bars

$\frac{1}{2}$ cup unsalted butter
1 cup all-purpose flour
$\frac{1}{4}$ teaspoon baking powder
$\frac{1}{8}$ teaspoon baking soda
$\frac{1}{2}$ teaspoon salt
$\frac{1}{2}$ teaspoon ground cinnamon
$\frac{1}{4}$ teaspoon ground ginger
$\frac{1}{4}$ teaspoon ground allspice
2 eggs
$\frac{2}{3}$ cup granulated sugar
$\frac{1}{4}$ cup dark molasses
$\frac{1}{2}$ cup diced candied cherries
$\frac{1}{2}$ cup finely chopped pecans
1 tablespoon grated orange rind

Preheat the oven to 350°F. Grease a 9-inch square baking pan.

In a small pan over very low heat, melt the butter. Set aside to cool.

Sift together the flour, baking powder, baking soda, salt, cinnamon, ginger, and allspice.

In a large mixing bowl, beat the eggs until light and foamy. Add the sugar and beat well. Beat in the molasses. Add the melted butter and mix well. Add the sifted ingredients and stir only until blended. Fold in the cherries, pecans, and grated orange rind.

Pour the batter into the prepared pan. Bake for 20 minutes, or until the top springs back when lightly touched. Cool in the pan on a wire rack, then cut into bars.

Pumpkin Shortbread Squares

These cookies have a shortbread base, a pumpkin and nut filling, and a crumb topping. They are delicious.

Makes 24 squares

> $\frac{3}{4}$ cup unsalted butter, at room temperature
> $\frac{2}{3}$ cup granulated sugar
> $\frac{3}{4}$ teaspoon vanilla extract
> 2$\frac{1}{3}$ cups all-purpose flour
> $\frac{1}{2}$ teaspoon baking powder
> $\frac{1}{4}$ teaspoon salt
> 2 eggs
> 1 cup firmly packed dark brown sugar
> 1 cup canned pumpkin puree
> $\frac{1}{2}$ cup finely chopped pecans

Preheat the oven to 400°F. Lightly grease a 13 × 9-inch baking pan with butter.

In a mixing bowl, cream together $\frac{1}{2}$ cup of the butter, $\frac{1}{3}$ cup of the granulated sugar, and $\frac{1}{4}$ teaspoon of the vanilla. Add 1 cup of the flour, $\frac{1}{4}$ cup at a time, and mix well after each addition.

Press the dough into the bottom of the prepared pan. Bake for 5 minutes. Remove the pan from the oven and reduce the oven temperature to 350°F.

Sift together $\frac{1}{3}$ cup of the flour, the baking powder, and salt. In a large bowl, beat the eggs until foamy. Beat in the brown sugar, pumpkin, and the remaining $\frac{1}{2}$ teaspoon of vanilla. Stir in the sifted ingredients and the nuts. Spread the mixture over the partially baked shortbread.

In a medium bowl, combine the remaining 1 cup of flour and $\frac{1}{3}$ cup of granulated sugar. Using a pastry blender or two table knives, cut in the remaining $\frac{1}{4}$ cup of butter until the mixture resembles coarse crumbs. Sprinkle over the pumpkin layer.

Bake for 25 minutes. Cool in the pan on a wire rack. When completely cool, cut into squares.

Chocolate Chip Squares

Faster to make than traditional chocolate chip cookies, these bars will disappear just as quickly.

Makes about 24 squares

   1 cup unsalted butter, at room temperature
   ¾ cup granulated sugar
   ¾ cup firmly packed dark brown sugar
   1 teaspoon vanilla extract
   2 eggs
   1¼ cups all-purpose flour
   1 teaspoon baking soda
   1 teaspoon salt
   2 cups semisweet chocolate chips
   1 cup coarsely chopped walnuts

Preheat the oven to 350°F. Liberally grease a 13 × 9-inch baking pan with butter.

In a large mixing bowl, cream the butter and sugars together. Add the vanilla and the eggs and beat until light and fluffy.

Combine the flour, baking soda, and salt and sift it into the batter. Mix well. Stir in the chocolate chips and the walnuts.

Spread the batter in the prepared pan. Bake for 25 to 30 minutes, or until the top is golden brown. Cool in the pan on a wire rack, then cut into squares.

Hand-Shaped Cookies

The dough for all the cookies in this section is molded into balls. Some of them are then rolled in nuts, or sugar, or cinnamon; others are flattened. All of them are sure to become part of your Christmas-cookie repertoire.

Cookies that are shaped by hand must be made from dough that will not stick to your fingers while you are working with it. If the dough seems sticky, it is a good idea to chill it for several hours. For fast chilling, divide the dough in half, or even in quarters. Wrap each portion in plastic wrap or foil before putting it into the refrigerator. Work with only a small amount of the chilled dough at a time and keep the rest in the refrigerator until you are ready to use it.

Hand-shaped cookies that are not flattened should be baked until the edges are firm and the bottoms are a light golden brown. Use the tip of a table knife or a metal spatula to lift a cookie so you can peek at the underside.

Chocolate Teddy Bears

Everyone loves teddy bears, and these cookies will be no exception. If you are giving these teddy bears as gifts, tie a bow of bright, thin ribbon around each of their necks.

Makes 14 cookies

$\frac{2}{3}$ cup unsalted butter, at room temperature
1 cup granulated sugar
2 eggs
2 teaspoons vanilla extract
$2\frac{1}{2}$ cups all-purpose flour
$\frac{1}{2}$ cup cocoa
1 teaspoon baking soda
$\frac{1}{4}$ teaspoon salt
   Raisins

In a large mixing bowl, cream the butter and sugar together, then beat until light and fluffy. Beat in the eggs. Add the vanilla and mix well. Combine the flour, cocoa, baking soda, and salt. Add to the batter, $\frac{1}{2}$ cup at a time, mixing well after each addition.

Gather the dough into two balls. Wrap each one in foil and chill in the refrigerator overnight.

Preheat the oven to 350°F.

Make the teddy bears one at a time. Shape dough into one 1-inch ball for the body, one $\frac{3}{4}$-inch ball for the head, six $\frac{1}{2}$-inch balls for the arms, legs, and ears, and five $\frac{1}{4}$-inch balls for the paws and nose.

On an ungreased cookie sheet, flatten the large ball so it is $\frac{1}{2}$ inch thick. Attach the head by overlapping it slightly on the body and then flatten it to $\frac{1}{2}$-inch thickness. Attach the legs, arms, and ears and flatten them slightly. Then place one of the tiny balls on the head for the nose. Arrange the remaining little balls on top of the ends of the arms and legs for paws. Gently press raisins into the dough to make eyes and a belly button.

Bake for 6 to 8 minutes, or until the edges of the cookies are firm. Cool for 1 minute on the cookie sheet, then transfer the cookies to wire racks to cool completely.

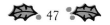

Walnut Cookie Balls

These cookies taste as good as they look. They add a festive touch to the holiday table—and they make a delicious gift.

Makes about 36 cookies

$\frac{1}{2}$ cup unsalted butter, at room temperature
$\frac{1}{3}$ cup honey
1 egg, separated
1 navel orange
$1\frac{1}{2}$ cups all-purpose flour
$\frac{1}{4}$ teaspoon baking soda
$\frac{1}{4}$ teaspoon salt
$\frac{1}{4}$ teaspoon ground nutmeg
$\frac{1}{2}$ teaspoon ground cinnamon
1 cup finely chopped walnuts
Green and red candied cherries, halved

In a large mixing bowl, beat together the butter and the honey. Beat in the egg yolk. Grate the rind of the orange and add it to the batter. Squeeze 2 tablespoons of the orange juice and add it to the batter.

Sift together the flour, baking soda, salt, nutmeg, and cinnamon. Add the flour mixture to the batter, $\frac{1}{2}$ cup at a time, and blend well. Cover the bowl and refrigerate overnight.

Preheat the oven to 325°F. In a small bowl, beat the egg white until foamy. Spread the chopped walnuts on a plate.

Shape the dough into 36 balls. Dip each ball into the egg white, then roll it in the nuts.

Place the cookies 2 inches apart on ungreased cookie sheets. Lightly press half a candied cherry on top of each cookie. Bake for 15 minutes, or until the edges of the cookies are firm.

Peppernuts

These little treats improve with age. Store the peppernuts in an airtight container for several weeks to allow them to ripen. Before serving, they may be rolled in confectioners' sugar.

Makes about 110 cookies

3 cups all-purpose flour
1 teaspoon baking powder
¾ teaspoon salt
½ teaspoon freshly ground black pepper
1 teaspoon ground cinnamon
½ teaspoon ground mace
1 teaspoon ground allspice
½ cup candied citron, finely chopped
¼ cup candied orange peel, finely chopped
1 teaspoon grated lemon rind
3 eggs
1½ cups granulated sugar

Preheat the oven to 350°F. Lightly grease cookie sheets with butter.

Into a large mixing bowl, sift together the flour, baking powder, salt, black pepper, cinnamon, mace, and allspice. Add the citron, orange peel, and grated lemon rind and mix well.

In another bowl, combine the eggs and the sugar. Beat until thick and lemon colored. Add to the flour mixture and blend well. If necessary, knead the dough with your hands.

Pinch off small pieces of dough and shape into ¾-inch balls. Place them about 1 inch apart on the prepared cookie sheets. Bake for about 15 minutes, or until the bottoms of the cookies are lightly browned.

Spicy Chocolate Cookies

Black pepper may seem like an unusual ingredient for a cookie. In this recipe it intensifies the flavor of the chocolate and of the spices.

Makes about 36 cookies

    $\frac{3}{4}$ cup unsalted butter, at room temperature
    $\frac{3}{4}$ teaspoon freshly ground black pepper
    $\frac{3}{4}$ teaspoon ground cinnamon
    $\frac{1}{4}$ teaspoon ground cloves
    1 cup granulated sugar
    1 egg
    $1\frac{1}{2}$ teaspoons vanilla extract
    $1\frac{1}{2}$ cups all-purpose flour
    $1\frac{1}{2}$ teaspoons baking powder
    $\frac{1}{4}$ teaspoon salt
    $\frac{3}{4}$ cup cocoa
    Confectioners' sugar

Preheat the oven to 375°F. Lightly grease cookie sheets with butter.

In a large mixing bowl, cream the butter with the black pepper, cinnamon, cloves, and sugar. Beat in the egg and the vanilla.

Sift together the flour, baking powder, salt, and cocoa. Add the sifted ingredients, $\frac{1}{2}$ cup at a time, to the batter, mixing well after each addition.

Shape the dough into 1-inch balls. Place them 2 inches apart on the prepared cookie sheets. Dip the bottom of a glass into confectioners' sugar, then use it to flatten the balls to a thickness of $\frac{1}{4}$ inch.

Bake for 12 minutes, or until the edges of the cookies are lightly browned.

Pecan Spice Cookies

Chopped walnuts, hazelnuts, or even Brazil nuts may be substituted for the pecans in this recipe. The addition of $\frac{1}{2}$ cup of raisins also makes a good variation.

Makes about 72 cookies

$\frac{3}{4}$ *cup unsalted butter, at room temperature*
$\frac{1}{4}$ *teaspoon ground cloves*
$\frac{1}{2}$ *teaspoon ground mace*
$\frac{1}{2}$ *teaspoon ground ginger*
$\frac{1}{2}$ *cup granulated sugar*
1 *cup coarsely chopped pecans*
2 *cups sifted all-purpose flour*
  Confectioners' sugar

Preheat the oven to 325°F.

In a large mixing bowl, cream the butter with the ground cloves, mace, and ginger. Gradually add the sugar and beat until the mixture is light and fluffy. Stir in the pecans. Add the flour, $\frac{1}{2}$ cup at a time, mixing well after each addition.

Shape the dough into 1-inch balls. Place them about 2 inches apart on ungreased cookie sheets. Bake for 20 minutes, or until the cookies are lightly browned around the edges.

Sift about $\frac{1}{2}$ cup of confectioners' sugar onto a large platter. While the cookies are warm, roll them in the sugar. Place them on wire racks to cool completely, then roll them in confectioners' sugar again.

Chocolate Chocolate Cookies

These rich chocolate cookies are marvelous at any time of the year, but they are particularly wonderful at Christmas because they are easy to make and keep extremely well in an airtight container.

Makes about 60 cookies

4 ounces German sweet chocolate
6 ounces unsweetened chocolate
1 cup unsalted butter, at room temperature
1 cup granulated sugar
1 cup firmly packed light brown sugar
2 eggs, lightly beaten
1 tablespoon vanilla extract
2 cups all-purpose flour
1 teaspoon baking soda
$\frac{1}{2}$ teaspoon salt

Combine the chocolate and the butter in the top of a double boiler set over barely simmering water. Cook, stirring frequently, until the chocolate and butter have melted. Remove from the hot water. Beat in the sugars, $\frac{1}{2}$ cup at a time. Then beat in the eggs and the vanilla. Continue to beat until the mixture is smooth, then pour it into a large mixing bowl.

Sift together the flour, baking soda, and salt. Gradually add the sifted ingredients to the chocolate mixture, stirring only until the flour is absorbed.

Cover the bowl and put it into the refrigerator for about 1 hour.

Preheat the oven to 375°F. Lightly grease cookie sheets with butter.

Form the dough into 1-inch balls. Place the balls about 2 inches apart on the prepared cookie sheets. Bake for 10 minutes.

Let the cookies cool on the cookie sheets for about 3 minutes before transferring them to wire racks to cool completely.

Date Walnut Cookies

Dates and walnuts are an unbeatable combination and these cookies are easy to make, too.

Makes about 60 cookies

$\frac{2}{3}$ cup unsalted butter, at room temperature
1 cup granulated sugar
1 cup firmly packed dark brown sugar
2 teaspoons vanilla extract
2 eggs
1 cup coarsely chopped pitted dates
1 cup coarsely chopped walnuts
3 cups sifted all-purpose flour
1 teaspoon baking soda
$\frac{1}{2}$ teaspoon salt
Confectioners' sugar

Preheat the oven to 375°F. Lightly grease cookie sheets with butter.

In a large mixing bowl, cream the butter and sugars together. Add the vanilla and beat until light and fluffy. Beat in the eggs. Add the dates and the nuts and mix well.

Sift together the flour, baking soda, and salt. Add to the batter, $\frac{1}{2}$ cup at a time, mixing well after each addition.

Shape tablespoonfuls of dough into balls. Place the balls about 3 inches apart on the prepared cookie sheets. Dip the bottom of a glass into confectioners' sugar, then use it to flatten the cookies.

Bake for 10 to 12 minutes, or until the edges of the cookies are lightly browned.

Chocolate Crackles

The tops of these chewy cookies are puffy and crackled. Be sure not to overbake them.

Makes about 50 cookies

4 ounces unsweetened chocolate
1 teaspoon vanilla extract
$\frac{1}{2}$ cup unsalted butter, at room temperature
$1\frac{3}{4}$ cups granulated sugar
3 eggs
2 cups plus 2 tablespoons all-purpose flour
2 teaspoons baking powder
$\frac{1}{4}$ teaspoon salt
$\frac{1}{2}$ cup confectioners' sugar

In the top of a double boiler, melt the chocolate over barely simmering water. Remove from the hot water and stir in the vanilla. Set aside.

In a large mixing bowl, cream the butter and sugar together, then beat until fluffy. Add the eggs and beat well. Add the chocolate mixture and beat until well blended.

Combine the flour, baking powder, and salt. Add to the batter, $\frac{1}{2}$ cup at a time, mixing after each addition only enough to blend the ingredients. Cover the bowl and chill the dough in the refrigerator for 2 hours.

Preheat the oven to 350°F. Lightly grease cookie sheets with butter. Spread the confectioners' sugar on a plate.

Shape heaping teaspoonfuls of dough into balls. Roll the balls in the confectioners' sugar then place them $1\frac{1}{2}$ inches apart on the prepared cookie sheets.

Bake for 10 to 12 minutes, or until the tops of the cookies are puffed and crackled.

Sandies

These buttery, nutty cookies are traditional Christmas favorites.

Makes about 48 cookies

> 1 cup unsalted butter, at room temperature
> $\frac{1}{3}$ cup granulated sugar
> 2 teaspoons water
> 2 teaspoons vanilla extract
> $2\frac{1}{4}$ cups all-purpose flour
> 1 cup finely chopped pecans
> $\frac{1}{4}$ cup confectioners' sugar

Preheat the oven to 325°F.

In a large mixing bowl, cream the butter and sugar together. Beat until light and fluffy. Beat in the water and the vanilla. Blend in the flour, $\frac{1}{2}$ cup at a time. Add the pecans and mix well.

Shape the dough into 1-inch balls. Place them about $1\frac{1}{2}$ inches apart on ungreased cookie sheets.

Bake for 20 minutes, or until the edges of the cookies are firm and the bottoms are lightly browned. Transfer the cookies to wire racks to cool.

Sift the confectioners' sugar onto a large plate. When the cookies are completely cool, roll each one in the sugar.

Gingersnaps

Crisp and spicy, these cookies are a wonderful addition to the Christmas cookie jar.

Makes about 48 cookies

$2\frac{1}{2}$ cups all-purpose flour
2 teaspoons baking soda
1 teaspoon ground ginger
1 teaspoon ground cinnamon
$\frac{1}{2}$ teaspoon ground cloves
$\frac{1}{4}$ teaspoon salt
1 cup firmly packed dark brown sugar
$\frac{3}{4}$ cup corn oil
$\frac{1}{4}$ cup molasses
1 egg

Preheat the oven to 375°F.

Sift together the flour, baking soda, ginger, cinnamon, cloves, and salt.

In a large mixing bowl, combine the sugar, oil, molasses, and egg. Beat well. Add the flour mixture, $\frac{1}{2}$ cup at a time, beating well after each addition. Continue to beat until the dough is smooth.

Shape the dough into 1-inch balls. Place the balls 2 inches apart on ungreased cookie sheets.

Bake for 10 minutes, or until the edges of the cookies are firm.

Special Cookies

Spritz cookies made with a cookie press, tiny pies, miniature fruitcakes, cookies made from dough that must be refrigerated overnight—these cookies are a little more difficult or time-consuming to make—but they are all well worth the additional time and effort.

Be sure to read each recipe through before beginning to bake, and then follow it exactly.

Spritz Cookies

These cookies require a cookie press, a piece of equipment no dedicated cookie baker should be without. Use whichever decorative blades you prefer.

Makes about 36 cookies

> 1 cup unsalted butter, at room temperature
> $\frac{2}{3}$ cup granulated sugar
> 1 egg
> 1 teaspoon vanilla extract
> $\frac{1}{2}$ teaspoon grated lemon rind
> $2\frac{1}{4}$ cups all-purpose flour
> $\frac{1}{4}$ teaspoon salt
> Colored sugar

Preheat the oven to 375°F.

In a large mixing bowl, cream the butter and sugar together, then beat until light and fluffy. Beat in the egg, then the vanilla. Add the grated lemon rind and mix well.

Sift the flour and salt together. Add it to the batter, $\frac{1}{2}$ cup at a time, mixing well after each addition.

Using one-quarter of the dough at a time, place it in a cookie press fitted with a decorative blade. Hold the press upright and force the dough onto ungreased cookie sheets, leaving about $1\frac{1}{2}$ inches between cookies. Sprinkle the cookies with colored sugar.

Bake for about 10 minutes, or until the cookies are golden.

Chocolate Spritz Ribbons

To make these rich cookies, a cookie press is required. And if you prefer rosettes to ribbons, it is easy to change the blade.

Makes about 50 cookies

   2 ounces unsweetened chocolate
   1 cup unsalted butter, at room temperature
   $\frac{2}{3}$ cup granulated sugar
   3 egg yolks
   1 teaspoon vanilla extract
   $\frac{1}{4}$ cup ground almonds
   $2\frac{1}{2}$ cups all-purpose flour, sifted

Preheat the oven to 400°F.

In the top of a double boiler, melt the chocolate over barely simmering water. Remove from the hot water and set aside.

In a large mixing bowl, cream the butter and sugar together. Add the egg yolks and the vanilla and beat until light. Blend in the melted chocolate.

Combine the almonds and the flour. Add to the batter, $\frac{1}{2}$ cup at a time, blending well after each addition.

Using one-quarter of the dough at a time, place it in a cookie press fitted with a decorative blade. Holding the press upright, force the dough onto ungreased cookie sheets in ribbons about 2 inches long and $1\frac{1}{2}$ inches apart.

Bake for 7 to 10 minutes, or until the cookies are set.

Pecan Pie Cookies

These miniature pecan pies are made in $1\frac{3}{4}$-inch mini muffin tins. They are unusual—a very special holiday treat.

Makes about 60 cookies

> 6 ounce package cream cheese
> 1 cup unsalted butter, at room temperature
> 2 cups sifted all-purpose flour

> Filling
> 4 tablespoons unsalted butter, at room temperature
> $1\frac{1}{2}$ cups firmly packed dark brown sugar
> 2 eggs
> 2 teaspoons vanilla extract
> $1\frac{3}{4}$ cups finely chopped pecans

Preheat the oven to 325°F.

In a large mixing bowl, cream together the cream cheese and the butter, then beat until fluffy. Blend in the flour, $\frac{1}{2}$ cup at a time, and mix to a smooth dough.

Put a small ball of dough into each muffin tin, then, using a thumb, press it into the tin so that it thinly lines the bottom and side, like piecrust. Set aside.

To make the filling, in a large mixing bowl, cream together the butter and the sugar. Add the eggs and beat well. Beat in the vanilla. Stir in the nuts. Fill the lined muffin tins half full. The filling will rise as it bakes.

Bake for 25 minutes, or until the top of the filling is lightly browned. Cool on wire racks, then remove the little pies from the tins, using the tip of a table knife to flip each one out.

Christmas Fantasy Cookies

These colored cookies are unusually pretty. The dough must be refrigerated overnight before baking.

Makes about 60 cookies

>   1 cup unsalted butter, at room temperature
>   1 cup sifted confectioners' sugar
>   1 teaspoon vanilla extract
>   1 tablespoon corn syrup
> $2\frac{1}{2}$ cups all-purpose flour
>   1 teaspoon salt
>   2 tablespoons milk
>   Red and green food coloring

In a large mixing bowl, cream together the butter and sugar. Beat in the vanilla and the corn syrup.

Sift together the flour and the salt. Add the sifted ingredients to the batter, $\frac{1}{2}$ cup at a time, blending well after each addition. Add the milk, a little at a time, but only as much as necessary to make a smooth, but stiff, dough.

Divide the dough into three parts. Add 6 drops of green food coloring to one part and 6 drops of red food coloring to the second part. Leave the third part uncolored. Blend the food coloring into the dough thoroughly. It will probably be necessary to knead it with your hands.

Mix the three pieces of dough together carefully so that each color remains distinct. The dough should have a marbled effect. Shape the dough into a roll about 2 inches in diameter. Wrap in foil and chill overnight in the refrigerator.

Preheat the oven to 375°F.

Using a very sharp knife, cut the dough into slices $\frac{1}{8}$ inch thick. Place the cookies about $\frac{1}{2}$ inch apart on ungreased cookie sheets.

Bake for 8 to 10 minutes. Do not let the cookies brown.

Miniature Fruitcakes

Great for holiday gift giving, these tiny fruitcakes are more confections than cookies. They will improve with age if they are stored for several weeks in airtight containers. Apple juice may be substituted for the brandy.

Makes 60 tiny fruitcakes

> $1\frac{1}{2}$ cups diced candied fruit
> 1 cup raisins
> $\frac{1}{2}$ cup currants
> 1 cup brandy
> $\frac{1}{3}$ cup unsalted butter, at room temperature
> $\frac{3}{4}$ cup firmly packed dark brown sugar
> 1 egg
> 1 cup all-purpose flour
> $\frac{1}{2}$ teaspoon baking soda
> $\frac{1}{2}$ teaspoon salt
> $\frac{1}{2}$ teaspoon ground allspice
> $\frac{1}{2}$ teaspoon ground cinnamon
> $\frac{1}{4}$ teaspoon ground nutmeg
> 1 cup finely chopped walnuts
> Red and green candied cherries

In a medium bowl, combine the candied fruit, raisins, and currants. Add $\frac{1}{2}$ cup of the brandy and mix well. Cover the bowl and set aside overnight to let the fruit marinate in the brandy.

Preheat the oven to 300°F. Line $1\frac{3}{4}$-inch mini muffin tins with foil baking cups.

In a large mixing bowl, cream the butter and sugar together. Beat until fluffy. Beat in the egg.

Sift together the flour, baking soda, salt, allspice, cinnamon, and nutmeg. Add to the batter and mix until well blended. Add the walnuts and marinated fruit and mix well.

Spoon the batter into the baking cups, filling them only three-quarters full. Press a candied cherry into the center of each one.

Bake for 30 minutes. Transfer the baking cups to wire racks and brush the top of each fruitcake with some of the reserved brandy.

Christmas Candy

Christmas Candy
Contents

Introduction   69
Making the Best Candy   70
Storing Candy   73
Packaging Candy and Other Confections   74

Chocolate Delights   75
Rocky Road   76
Chocolate Nut Truffles   77
Chocolate Rum Truffles   78
Milk Chocolate Truffles   79
Double Chocolate Delights   80
Chocolate Bourbon Balls   80
Chocolate Coconut Cups   81
Chocolate Walnut Drops   82

Divinity and Other Divine Candies   83
Divinity Kisses   84
Chocolate Divinity   85
Divinity Squares   86
Coconut Cherry Patties   87
Maple Pecan Candy   88
Pralines   89
Peppermint Creams   90

Fudge Favorites 91
Old-Fashioned Chocolate Fudge 92
Penuche 93
Fruit Fudge 94
Banana Walnut Fudge 95
Creamy Chocolate Pecan Fudge 96
Butterscotch Walnut Fudge 97
Mocha Fudge Slices 98

Christmas Confections 99
Popcorn Balls 100
Almond Pecan Popcorn 101
Walnut Treats 102
Fruit Chews 103
Walnut Date Slices 104
Taffy Apples 105
Candied Orange Peel 106
Candied Kumquats 107

Introduction

The marvelous confections of Christmas are surprisingly easy to make right in your own kitchen. In this new collection of recipes, you'll find a variety of scrumptious treats—luscious pecan pralines and creamy fudge, light fluffy divinity and nut-studded popcorn, bright candied fruit and crunchy spiced nuts, sweet taffy apples and sumptuous chocolate truffles.

Making candy is very satisfying, and homemade candy is especially delicious. Candy keeps well and travels well. Packed in a decorative tin, a pretty box, a beribboned jar, or, perhaps, a cut-glass dish, it makes a special gift, even for people who live far away. Homemade candy can be tucked into Christmas stockings. It is wonderful to nibble on while trimming the tree. And nothing is more fun during the holidays than making old-fashioned popcorn balls.

All of these recipes are easy-to-follow. (And, other than an inexpensive candy thermometer, no special equipment is required.) You can whip up a batch of old favorites like peppermint creams, chocolate truffles, pralines, rocky road, and butterscotch walnut fudge. Or try making such delights as candied kumquats and candied orange peel, fruit chews, walnut date slices, coconut cherry patties, and taffy apples. For entertaining and for special gifts, homemade candy is a welcome treat at any season of the year. You will enjoy rave reviews from your family and friends, for there is a recipe here to please every sweet tooth.

Making the Best Candy

Candy is not difficult to make. Some of the recipes in this book require little or no cooking. Others need only careful timing and adequate beating. For some types of candy, however, special care is necessary. Follow these basic instructions and you can become a successful and versatile candymaker.

🌲 Always read a recipe through from beginning to end before starting to cook.

🌲 Always use the best-quality, freshest ingredients available.

🌲 Measure ingredients accurately, using standard measuring spoons for small amounts, a fluid measuring cup for liquids, and graduated measuring cups for dry ingredients.

🌲 Follow recipes carefully. Use only the ingredients specified and add them in the order and by the method given.

🌲 To prevent sugaring, carefully follow directions about stirring and about covering the pan.

🌲 Use moderate or low heat, according to instructions in the recipe, so the syrup does not reach the boiling point too quickly.

🌲 Always use a saucepan large enough to allow space for the candy to bubble up when boiling. A 2-quart pan is large enough in most cases, but sometimes a 3-quart or even a 4-quart pan is preferable. A pan in which candy is made should be of heavy-gauge metal, which holds heat evenly and will prevent sticking.

🌲 Candymaking involves a lot of stirring and beating. Although an electric mixer may be used in some stages of preparation, such as beating egg whites for divinity, for most candy mixtures a spoon is best. A long-handled wooden spoon is preferable, since it will never get too hot to handle.

🌲 A candy thermometer that clips onto the side of the pan is almost a necessity for successful candymaking, since it is critical that the candy be removed from the heat at the moment it reaches the proper temperature. It is best to use a clearly marked, easy-to-read thermometer with a mercury ball that is set low enough to measure the temperature of the boiling syrup, but does not touch the bottom of the pan.

To use a candy thermometer, be sure it is at room temperature before putting it into the hot syrup. Lower the thermometer gradually into the candy mixture *after* the sugar is dissolved and the syrup has begun to boil.

♣ The cold-water test is an alternative to a candy thermometer. Many cooks still rely upon this test, although it is not as accurate as a candy thermometer. (All the recipes in this book specify a temperature reading as well as the cold-water test results, such as hard ball or soft ball.)

Temperature Tests for Candy

Temperature of Syrup	Test	Description of Syrup When Dropped Into Very Cold Water
234° to 240°F	Soft ball	Forms a soft ball that flattens on removal from water
244° to 248°F	Firm ball	Forms a firm ball that does not flatten on removal from water
250° to 266°F	Hard ball	Forms a hard ball that, on removal from water, remains hard enough to hold its shape, yet is pliable
270° to 290°F	Soft crack	Separates into threads that are hard, but not brittle, when removed from water
300° to 310°F	Hard crack	Separates into threads that are hard and very brittle

To water-test, use very cold, but not ice, water. Use a clean cup, spoon, and fresh water for each test. Remove the pan from the heat and drop a little of the hot mixture into the water. Use your fingers to gather the drops into a ball and feel its consistency. If the candy is not yet ready, immediately return the pan to the heat.

🌲 Avoid making candy on damp or rainy days. High humidity is the candymaker's enemy. If for any reason you cannot postpone a candymaking session, cook the candy 1 or 2 degrees higher on the thermometer than indicated in the recipe.

🌲 Altitude also affects candymaking. Temperatures given in recipes in this book are for sea level. At high altitudes the candy must be cooked about 2 degrees higher.

🌲 Be patient and always allow sufficient time. Most candy does take time to make, and there is no way to rush the cooking without disaster.

Storing Candy

One of the nicest things about homemade candy is that it can be eaten when it is at its freshest. In addition, it contains no chemicals, artificial flavoring, or preservatives, although the lack of preservatives does limit its storage capabilities. Most homemade candy, however, will keep well for several weeks if it is stored properly. (The exception is divinity, which gets stale quickly and should be eaten within two days of preparation.) Here are some rules for storing candy successfully.

♣ Sticky and chewy candies, like taffy, nougat, and caramels, and hard candies, like butterscotch, should be individually wrapped in waxed paper, plastic wrap, or foil.

♣ All candy keeps best in an airtight container in a cool, dry place. Some chocolate candies, like truffles, are best stored in the refrigerator.

♣ Do not store brittle candies in the same container with soft, creamy candies. The moisture from the soft candies may make the hard candies sticky.

♣ Candy freezes well. Place the candy, individually wrapped if appropriate, in a cardboard box or plastic container. Overwrap the container with freezer paper or foil. To thaw the candy, let it stand for several hours, or overnight, and come to room temperature before opening the container. This will prevent moisture from collecting on the candies because of the temperature change.

Packaging Candy and Other Confections

Homemade confections are a wonderful present for a neighbor, a host or hostess, or a friend. You can make the packaging itself part of the gift by using decorative tins, boxes, and gift bags. Or create your own unique container by covering a plain box or tin with fabric or paper. Try sponge-painting or stenciling. Let your imagination run free.

To pack your confections in a round container, first line it with several layers of white doilies. Cut several rounds of waxed paper, a little smaller than the circumference of the box. Arrange the candy on the doilies in the box, then place several thicknesses of waxed paper, then a doily, on top. Tie a ribbon crosswise around the closed box. This would be a nice way to present pralines or walnut treats.

Fudge squares are best packed in a square box. Each square can be put into a foil or paper candy cup. Use square doilies to line the box and several thicknesses of waxed paper between layers of the candy.

Candied orange peel or kumquats look attractive in a wide-mouthed glass jar with a well-fitting lid. Wrap the jar using several layers of colored tissue paper. Gather the tissue paper at the top with curling ribbon.

A shiny, decorative tin pail is an excellent container for popcorn balls or almond pecan popcorn. Pack the popcorn in a large plastic bag before putting it into the pail. Then put the lid on the pail, seal it with transparent tape, and tie a big, bright bow on top.

When packaging chocolate candies, such as truffles, bourbon balls, or chocolate walnut drops, put each piece into a foil or paper candy cup before putting it into a gift box.

Chocolate Delights

Chocolate bourbon balls, rocky road, chocolate walnut drops, a variety of truffles—these chocolate treats are exceptionally easy to make. Many of them need no cooking, and none of them requires a candy thermometer or cold-water test. Be sure, however, to use the best-quality chocolate available and when melting the chocolate to do so in the top of a double boiler over barely simmering water.

Rocky Road

Chocolate, marshmallows, nuts, and coconut combine to make this the richest and best-ever rocky road. If you are going to include this candy in a gift box, put each square in a foil candy cup.

> 2 cups semisweet chocolate chips
> $2\frac{1}{4}$ cups miniature marshmallows
> $\frac{1}{4}$ cup flaked coconut
> $\frac{1}{2}$ cup coarsely chopped walnuts

Line an 8-inch square pan with foil. Grease the foil with butter.

In the top of a double boiler, melt the chocolate over barely simmering water, stirring constantly.

Remove from the hot water and stir in the marshmallows, coconut, and walnuts.

Pour the candy into the prepared pan and, using a spatula, spread it into an even layer. Chill in the refrigerator for about 3 hours, or until the candy is firm.

Remove the candy from the pan. Peel off the foil and, using a sharp knife, cut the candy into 1-inch squares.

Chocolate Nut Truffles

The secret of successful truffles is the quality of the chocolate. Always use the best chocolate available. Truffles should be stored in a covered container in the refrigerator. They will keep for about two weeks. Serve them at room temperature.

> 8 ounces semisweet chocolate
> 6 tablespoons unsalted butter
> $\frac{1}{2}$ cup heavy cream
> 1 teaspoon vanilla extract
> $\frac{1}{2}$ cup finely chopped almonds

In the top of a double boiler, melt the chocolate and the butter over barely simmering water, stirring constantly. Remove from the hot water and set aside.

In a small, heavy saucepan, bring the cream just to the boil. Remove from the heat and pour the cream into the chocolate mixture. Mix well. Add the vanilla and stir until the mixture is smooth. Pour into a shallow bowl and set aside to cool, stirring occasionally.

Cover the bowl and chill in the refrigerator for about 4 hours, or until the mixture is firm, but not solid.

Spread the chopped nuts on a plate. Scoop up the chocolate mixture with a teaspoon and shape it into rough balls. Roll the balls in the nuts.

Chocolate Rum Truffles

These truffles are sinfully rich—and very satisfying. Grand Marnier or Kahlúa may be substituted for the rum. Store the truffles, covered, in the refrigerator. Let them stand at room temperature for about 30 minutes before serving.

> 2 *tablespoons heavy cream*
> 2 *tablespoons dark rum*
> 6 *ounces dark sweet chocolate, coarsely chopped*
> 4 *tablespoons unsalted butter, cut into chunks*
> $\frac{1}{2}$ *cup unsweetened cocoa powder*

In a small, heavy pan, bring the cream just to a boil. Remove the pan from the heat and stir in the rum and the chocolate. Cook over very low heat, stirring constantly, until the chocolate melts.

Remove the pan from the heat and quickly mix the butter into the chocolate mixture. When the butter has melted and the mixture is smooth, pour it into a shallow bowl and set aside to cool. Cover the bowl and chill in the refrigerator for about 2 hours, or until the mixture is firm enough to handle.

Sift the cocoa onto a large plate. Scoop up the chocolate mixture with a teaspoon and shape it into rough balls. Roll each ball in the cocoa.

Milk Chocolate Truffles

Lightly spiced with cinnamon, these milk chocolate truffles are sweet, rich, and creamy. Store them covered in the refrigerator, but serve them at room temperature.

6 *ounces milk chocolate*
$\frac{1}{2}$ *teaspoon ground cinnamon*
1$\frac{1}{2}$ *teaspoons unsalted butter, at room temperature*
$\frac{1}{2}$ *cup less 1 teaspoon sweetened condensed milk*
$\frac{1}{2}$ *teaspoon vanilla extract*
$\frac{1}{2}$ *cup chocolate sprinkles*

In the top of a double boiler, melt the chocolate over barely simmering water, stirring constantly.

Remove from the hot water and stir in the cinnamon and the butter. When the butter is melted and the mixture is smooth, add the condensed milk and the vanilla. Stir until well blended.

Pour the mixture into a shallow bowl. Cover the bowl and chill in the refrigerator for 3 hours, or until the mixture is firm enough to handle.

Spread the chocolate sprinkles on a large plate. Scoop up the chocolate mixture with a teaspoon and shape it into balls. Roll each ball in the chocolate sprinkles.

Double Chocolate Delights

This luscious candy is extremely easy to make. It should be stored in a covered container in the refrigerator.

   8 *ounces unsweetened chocolate*
   4 *ounces German's sweet chocolate*
   15 *ounce can sweetened condensed milk*
   1 *cup finely chopped pecans*

In the top of a double boiler, melt the chocolates over barely simmering water, stirring constantly. Add the condensed milk and stir until well blended. Remove from the hot water. Pour the mixture into a shallow bowl and set aside to cool.

Cover the bowl and chill in the refrigerator for 1 hour, or until the mixture is firm enough to handle.

Spread the chopped nuts on a large plate. Scoop up the chocolate mixture with a teaspoon and shape it into balls. Roll each ball in the nuts.

Chocolate Bourbon Balls

These delicious candies require no cooking and will keep well in an airtight container in a cool place. Whiskey, rum, or your favorite liquor may be substituted for the bourbon.

   1 *cup chocolate-wafer cookie crumbs*
   2 *cups coarsely chopped pecans*
   1 *cup confectioners' sugar*
   1½ *tablespoons light corn syrup*
   ¼ *cup bourbon*

In a blender or food processor, coarsely grind the cookie

crumbs with 1 cup of the pecans. Transfer to a large mixing bowl. Add the sugar, corn syrup, and bourbon and mix thoroughly.

Shape the mixture into 1-inch balls.

Spread the remaining 1 cup of pecans on a plate. Roll the balls in the nuts.

Chocolate Coconut Cups

These elegant candies couldn't be easier to make. After they are firm, they may be stored in an airtight container in a cool, dry place.

8 ounces bittersweet chocolate
1¼ cups flaked coconut

Put 25 foil candy cups on a cookie sheet.

In the top of a double boiler, melt the chocolate over barely simmering water, stirring constantly.

Remove from the hot water and add the coconut. Mix lightly until the coconut is completely coated with the chocolate.

Drop a teaspoonful of the mixture into each foil cup. Chill in the refrigerator until firm.

Chocolate Walnut Drops

These delicious candies are easy to make. They should be stored in an airtight container in a cool, dry place.

>   1 cup firmly packed dark brown sugar
> $\frac{1}{3}$ cup evaporated milk
>   2 tablespoons light corn syrup
>   1 cup semisweet chocolate chips
> $\frac{1}{2}$ cup finely chopped walnuts
>   1 teaspoon vanilla extract
>   Walnut halves

Line a cookie sheet with waxed paper.

In a heavy saucepan, combine the sugar, milk, and corn syrup. Cook over moderate heat, stirring constantly, until the sugar is dissolved and the mixture comes to a boil. Boil, stirring constantly, for 2 minutes.

Remove the pan from the heat. Add the chocolate chips, chopped walnuts, and vanilla and stir until the chocolate is melted and the mixture is slightly thickened.

Drop the candy by rounded teaspoonfuls onto the prepared cookie sheet. Press a walnut half on top of each mound.

Chill in the refrigerator for 30 minutes, or until the candies are firm.

Christmas Wishes

Divinity and Other Divine Candies

Light-as-air divinity, pecan-studded pralines, and classic pepper-mint creams are among the delights included here. None of these candies is difficult to make. Some don't require a candy thermometer or cold-water testing. Most of them are drop candies. When dropping these or any candies from a spoon, be sure to work quickly or the mixture may harden in the bowl. Do not attempt to make any of these candies on a humid or rainy day, because, even if the recipes are followed to the letter, the candy will not set properly.

Divinity Kisses

Light and sweet, divinity is a distant cousin of meringue. To make coconut divinity, substitute $\frac{3}{4}$ cup of flaked coconut for the walnuts and omit the cherries.

> $2\frac{1}{2}$ cups granulated sugar
> $\frac{1}{2}$ cup light corn syrup
> $\frac{1}{2}$ cup water
> $\frac{1}{4}$ teaspoon salt
> 2 large egg whites, at room temperature
> 1 teaspoon vanilla extract
> $\frac{1}{2}$ cup coarsely chopped walnuts
> Red and green candied cherries, halved

Spread a large piece of waxed paper on a work surface.

In a large, heavy saucepan, combine the sugar, corn syrup, water, and salt. Cook over moderate heat, stirring constantly, until the sugar is dissolved. Cover the pan and continue to cook over moderate heat until the mixture comes to a boil, 2 to 3 minutes. Remove the lid and continue cooking, without stirring, until the syrup reaches the hard-ball stage (265°F on a candy thermometer).

While the syrup is cooking, in a large mixing bowl beat the egg whites until stiff peaks form.

Pour the hot syrup into the egg whites in a fine stream, beating constantly and at high speed with an electric mixer. When the mixture becomes thick and heavy, it will be necessary to use a wooden spoon to beat it. Add the vanilla and continue beating until the candy just holds its shape when dropped from the spoon. Quickly stir in the nuts.

Drop the candy by rounded teaspoonfuls onto the waxed paper. Press a candied cherry half into each kiss.

Chocolate Divinity

No candy is as divine as divinity, and for the chocoholic nothing beats chocolate divinity.

    3 tablespoons unsalted butter
    ½ cup unsweetened cocoa powder
    2¼ cups granulated sugar
    ½ cup light corn syrup
    ⅓ cup water
    ¼ teaspoon salt
    2 large egg whites
    1 teaspoon vanilla extract
    ¾ cup finely chopped walnuts

Spread a large piece of waxed paper on a work surface.

In the top of a double boiler, melt the butter over hot, not boiling, water. Add the cocoa and stir until smooth. Remove from the hot water and set aside.

In a large, heavy saucepan, combine the sugar, corn syrup, water, and salt. Cook over moderate heat, stirring constantly, until the sugar is dissolved. Cover the pan and continue to cook over moderate heat, until the mixture comes to a boil, 2 to 3 minutes. Remove the lid and continue cooking without stirring, until the syrup reaches the hard-ball stage (265°F on a candy thermometer).

While the syrup is cooking, in a large mixing bowl beat the egg whites until stiff peaks form.

Pour the hot syrup into the egg whites in a fine stream, beating constantly and at high speed with an electric mixer. When the mixture becomes thick and heavy, it will be necessary to use a wooden spoon to beat it. Add the vanilla and continue beating until the candy just holds its shape when dropped from the spoon. Quickly blend in the cocoa mixture, then the nuts.

Drop the candy by teaspoonfuls onto the waxed paper.

Divinity Squares

These divinity squares are topped with chocolate and chopped walnuts—and they are very special.

$2\frac{1}{2}$ cups granulated sugar
$\frac{1}{2}$ cup light corn syrup
$\frac{1}{2}$ cup water
$\frac{1}{4}$ teaspoon salt
2 large egg whites, at room temperature
1 teaspoon vanilla extract
2 ounces semisweet chocolate
$\frac{3}{4}$ cup finely chopped walnuts

Grease an 8-inch square pan with butter.

In a large, heavy saucepan, combine the sugar, corn syrup, water, and salt. Cook over moderate heat, stirring constantly, until the sugar is dissolved. Cover the pan and continue to cook over moderate heat until the mixture comes to a boil, 2 to 3 minutes. Remove the lid and continue cooking, without stirring, until the mixture reaches the hard-ball stage (265°F on a candy thermometer).

While the syrup is cooking, in a large mixing bowl beat the egg whites until stiff peaks form.

Pour the hot syrup into the egg whites in a fine stream, beating constantly and at high speed with an electric mixer. When the mixture becomes thick and heavy it will be necessary to use a wooden spoon to beat it. Add the vanilla and continue beating until the candy just holds its shape when dropped from the spoon.

Spoon the divinity into the prepared pan. Using a rubber spatula, smooth it into an even layer.

In the top of a double boiler, melt the chocolate over barely simmering water, stirring constantly. Remove from the hot water and set aside to cool.

Pour the cooled melted chocolate over the divinity and spread in an even layer with a clean rubber spatula. Sprinkle the chopped nuts over the chocolate.

When the candy has cooled completely, use a sharp knife to cut it into squares.

Coconut Cherry Patties

Top these creamy patties with red and green candied cherry halves for a festive look. If you prefer, you can substitute pecan or walnut halves.

2 cups granulated sugar
½ cup milk
1½ cups flaked coconut
1 teaspoon vanilla extract
   Red and green candied cherries, halved

Spread a large sheet of waxed paper on a work surface.

In a heavy saucepan combine the sugar and the milk. Cook over high heat, stirring constantly, until the sugar is dissolved. Reduce the heat to moderate and cook, stirring constantly, until the mixture reaches the soft-ball stage (238°F on a candy thermometer).

Remove the pan from the heat and stir in the coconut and the vanilla.

Drop the candy by teaspoonfuls, about 2 inches apart, onto the waxed paper. With a spatula flatten each mound. Place half a candied cherry in the center of each patty.

Maple Pecan Candy

This luscious, creamy candy takes about 20 minutes to make—and it's so easy you don't even need a candy thermometer.

> 4 cups pure maple syrup
> 1 cup heavy cream
> $\frac{1}{4}$ cup unsalted butter
> 1 cup coarsely chopped pecans
> 1 teaspoon lemon extract

Liberally grease an 8-inch square pan with butter.

In a heavy saucepan, combine the maple syrup, cream, and butter. Cook over moderate heat, stirring constantly, until the mixture comes to a boil. Continue cooking for 9 minutes, stirring frequently.

Remove the pan from the heat. Stir in the pecans and the lemon extract. Stir for 5 minutes.

Pour the candy into the prepared pan. When it is completely cool, cut it into squares.

Pralines

A praline studded with pecans is a perennial favorite. If you like large patties, drop the pralines from a tablespoon. If you prefer them smaller, use a teaspoon. When the pralines have cooled completely, they may be stored in an airtight container between layers of waxed paper.

> 4 cups firmly packed light brown sugar
> $\frac{2}{3}$ cup half-and-half
> 2 tablespoons unsalted butter
> $\frac{1}{8}$ teaspoon salt
> 2 cups coarsely chopped pecans

Spread a large sheet of waxed paper on a work surface.

In a large, heavy saucepan combine the sugar, half-and-half, butter, and salt. Cook over high heat, stirring constantly until the sugar is dissolved.

Reduce the heat to moderate and continue cooking, without stirring, until the mixture comes to a boil. In the meantime, fill with water a pan into which the saucepan will fit. Bring the water to a boil, then turn off the heat.

When the mixture comes to a boil, begin stirring constantly. Boil for 4 minutes, then stir in the nuts.

Put the saucepan over the hot water while dropping the candy from a spoon onto the waxed paper.

Peppermint Creams

These creamy candies look quite pretty when red or green food coloring is added.

> 2 cups granulated sugar
> $\frac{1}{4}$ cup light corn syrup
> $\frac{1}{4}$ cup milk
> $\frac{1}{4}$ teaspoon cream of tartar
> $\frac{1}{2}$ teaspoon peppermint flavoring
>   Red or green food coloring

Spread a large sheet of waxed paper on a work surface.

In a heavy saucepan, combine the sugar, corn syrup, milk, and cream of tartar. Cook over low heat, stirring constantly, until the sugar is dissolved.

Increase the heat to moderate and continue cooking, stirring constantly, until the mixture reaches the soft-ball stage (238°F on a candy thermometer). Remove the pan from the heat and set aside for about 3 minutes to allow the mixture to cool slightly.

Beat in the peppermint and a few drops of food coloring. Continue beating until the mixture is creamy.

Drop the candy by teaspoonfuls onto the waxed paper.

Fudge Favorites

Everyone loves fudge, and here is a collection of marvelous fudge recipes. There's old-fashioned chocolate fudge, penuche, fruit fudge, an unusual banana walnut fudge, never-fail recipes for creamy chocolate pecan fudge and butterscotch walnut fudge, and a rich mocha fudge that requires no cooking.

When making any old-fashioned fudge, use a candy thermometer and be sure to watch the temperatures carefully. When the mixture reaches the boiling point, it becomes very sensitive to stirring and beating. Follow the recipes carefully and success is ensured.

Old-Fashioned Chocolate Fudge

This traditional, rich chocolate fudge is not difficult to make. Just follow the instructions carefully and be sure to use a candy thermometer.

> 2 ounces unsweetened chocolate
> 1 cup milk
> 2 cups granulated sugar
> 1 tablespoon light corn syrup
> 2 tablespoons unsalted butter, at room temperature
> 1 teaspoon vanilla extract
> $\frac{1}{2}$ cup finely chopped walnuts

Grease an 8-inch square pan with butter.

In a large, heavy saucepan, combine the chocolate and the milk. Cook over low heat, stirring constantly, until the chocolate has melted and the mixture is smooth.

Stir in the sugar and corn syrup. Increase the heat to moderate and continue stirring until the mixture comes to a boil.

Cover the pan and cook for 1 minute. Uncover the pan and insert a candy thermometer. Cook, uncovered, without stirring, until the mixture reaches the soft-ball stage (236°F on the candy thermometer).

Remove the pan from the heat and stir in the butter and the vanilla. Set aside until the candy cools to lukewarm (110°F).

With a wooden spoon, beat the fudge until it is thick and creamy and no longer glossy. Quickly stir in the nuts.

Pour the fudge into the prepared pan. Cool in the pan on a wire rack.

When the fudge is firm and completely cool, cut it into squares.

Penuche

A brown-sugar fudge studded with pecans, penuche has a creamy texture and caramel flavor.

2 cups firmly packed dark brown sugar
$\frac{3}{4}$ cup milk
$\frac{1}{8}$ teaspoon salt
$\frac{1}{4}$ cup unsalted butter, at room temperature
1 teaspoon vanilla extract
1 cup coarsely chopped pecans

Grease an 8-inch square pan with butter.

In a large, heavy saucepan, combine the sugar, milk, and salt. Cook over moderate heat, stirring constantly, until the mixture comes to a boil. Continue cooking, without stirring, to the soft-ball stage (236°F on the candy thermometer).

Remove the pan from the heat and stir in the butter and the vanilla. Set aside until the candy cools to lukewarm (110°F).

With a wooden spoon, beat the fudge until it becomes thick and begins to lose its gloss. Quickly stir in the pecans.

Pour the fudge into the prepared pan. Cool in the pan on a wire rack.

When the fudge is firm and completely cool, cut it into squares.

Fruit Fudge

This is an old recipe, but it is always successful. Candied cherries may be substituted for the mixed fruit.

2 cups granulated sugar
1 cup milk
$\frac{1}{4}$ cup unsalted butter
1 teaspoon vanilla extract
$\frac{1}{2}$ cup mixed candied fruit, coarsely chopped

Grease an 8-inch square pan with butter.

In a large, heavy saucepan, combine the sugar, milk, and butter. Cook over high heat, stirring constantly, until the sugar is dissolved. Reduce the heat to moderate and continue to cook, stirring constantly, until the mixture comes to a boil.

Cover the pan and cook for 1 minute. Uncover the pan and insert a candy thermometer. Cook, uncovered, without stirring, until the mixture reaches the soft-ball stage (236°F on the candy thermometer).

Remove the pan from the heat and stir in the vanilla. Set aside until the candy cools to lukewarm (110°F).

With a wooden spoon, beat the fudge until it is thick and creamy and is no longer glossy. Quickly stir in the fruit.

Pour the fudge into the prepared pan. Cool in the pan on a wire rack.

When the fudge is firm and completely cool, cut it into squares.

Banana Walnut Fudge

This firm fudge is nicely spiced with cinnamon. It is an old and unusual recipe. A candy thermometer will ensure success.

2 large, ripe bananas
2½ cups granulated sugar
½ cup firmly packed dark brown sugar
1 cup milk
½ teaspoon cream of tartar
2 tablespoons unsalted butter
¼ teaspoon salt
½ teaspoon ground cinnamon
1 teaspoon vanilla extract
1 cup coarsely chopped walnuts

Grease an 8-inch square pan with butter. Mash the bananas.

In a large, heavy saucepan, combine the mashed bananas, sugars, milk, cream of tartar, butter, salt, and cinnamon. Cook over moderate heat, stirring occasionally, until the mixture reaches 226°F on a candy thermometer. Then stir constantly until it reaches the soft-ball stage (236°F).

Remove the pan from the heat and stir in the vanilla. Using a wooden spoon, beat the fudge only until it starts to become creamy and is no longer glossy. Stir in the nuts.

Quickly spread the fudge in the prepared pan. Cool in the pan on a wire rack.

While the fudge is slightly warm, cut it into squares.

Creamy Chocolate Pecan Fudge

This creamy fudge never fails, and it is very easy to make. It will keep best well-covered in the refrigerator.

7 ounce jar marshmallow cream
1½ cups granulated sugar
⅔ cup evaporated milk
¼ cup unsalted butter
¼ teaspoon salt
3 cups semisweet chocolate chips
1 teaspoon vanilla extract
1 cup coarsely chopped pecans

Line an 8-inch square pan with foil.

In a large, heavy saucepan, combine the marshmallow cream, sugar, milk, butter, and salt. Bring to a rolling boil over moderate heat, stirring constantly. Boil the mixture, stirring constantly, for 5 minutes.

Remove the pan from the heat and add the chocolate chips, stirring until they have melted and the mixture is smooth. Add the vanilla and the pecans and mix well.

Pour the fudge into the prepared pan. Using a spatula, smooth the top.

Chill in the refrigerator for 2 hours, or until the fudge is firm. Then turn it out of the pan, remove the foil, and cut the fudge into squares.

Butterscotch Walnut Fudge

This butterscotch fudge is very easy to prepare. You don't even need a candy thermometer. The fudge will keep best well-covered in the refrigerator.

- $1\frac{1}{2}$ cups finely chopped walnuts
- 7 ounce jar marshmallow cream
- $1\frac{1}{2}$ cups granulated sugar
- $\frac{2}{3}$ cup evaporated milk
- $\frac{1}{4}$ cup unsalted butter
- $\frac{1}{4}$ teaspoon salt
- 2 cups butterscotch chips

Line an 8-inch square pan with foil. Spread $\frac{3}{4}$ cup of the walnuts in an even layer on the foil.

In a large, heavy saucepan, combine the marshmallow cream, sugar, milk, butter, and salt. Bring to a rolling boil over moderate heat, stirring constantly. Boil the mixture, stirring constantly, for 5 minutes.

Remove the pan from the heat. Stir in the butterscotch chips. Continue to stir until they have melted and the mixture is smooth.

Pour the fudge into the prepared pan and sprinkle the remaining $\frac{3}{4}$ cup of walnuts evenly on top. Using a rubber spatula, gently press the walnuts into the fudge.

Chill in the refrigerator for 2 hours, or until the fudge is firm. Then turn it out of the pan, remove the foil, and cut the fudge into squares.

Mocha Fudge Slices

This rich fudge requires no cooking. Store the slices, layered with waxed paper, in a covered container in the refrigerator. Let them stand at room temperature for about 20 minutes before serving.

> 6 ounces unsweetened chocolate
> 1 tablespoon instant coffee powder
> 2 teaspoons boiling water
> 8 ounce package cream cheese, at room temperature
> $\frac{1}{2}$ teaspoon ground cinnamon
> $\frac{1}{8}$ teaspoon salt
> $\frac{1}{4}$ cup coffee liqueur
> 5 cups sifted confectioners' sugar
> $2\frac{1}{2}$ cups finely chopped walnuts

In the top of a double boiler, melt the chocolate over barely simmering water, stirring constantly. Remove from the hot water and set aside to cool.

In a small bowl, dissolve the coffee in the boiling water.

In a large mixing bowl, combine the cream cheese, cinnamon, and salt. Beat until the mixture is smooth. Gradually beat in the liqueur and the coffee. Add the melted chocolate and beat until it is well blended. Add the sugar, 1 cup at a time, beating well after each addition. Add 1 cup of nuts and mix well.

Cover the bowl and chill the fudge in the refrigerator for 1 hour, or until it is firm enough to handle.

Spread the remaining $1\frac{1}{2}$ cups of nuts on a cookie sheet.

Divide the fudge into quarters. Working with one quarter at a time, place the fudge in the center of a 12-inch piece of waxed paper. Fold two opposite sides over the fudge. Roll the wrapped fudge into a log about $1\frac{1}{2}$ inches in diameter. Remove the waxed paper and roll the fudge log in the chopped nuts. Wrap each fudge log in plastic wrap and refrigerate overnight, then cut into $\frac{1}{2}$-inch slices.

Christmas Confections

Popcorn balls and taffy apples, candied kumquats and walnut treats, fruit chews and walnut date slices—most of the confections in this section are easy to prepare, and, packaged with imagination, they all make very special, edible gifts.

Popcorn Balls

Popcorn balls are fun to make, especially if there are kids around to help. Make tiny balls and heap them in a bowl. Make medium-size or large balls, wrap each one in cellophane gathered at the top with a red or green ribbon, and hang them on the Christmas tree. About $\frac{1}{2}$ cup of unpopped corn should make the 6 cups of popped corn called for in this recipe.

> 6 *cups popped corn*
> 2 *cups shelled peanuts*
> $1\frac{1}{2}$ *tablespoons unsalted butter*
> $1\frac{1}{2}$ *cups firmly packed dark brown sugar*
> 6 *tablespoons water*

Put the popped corn into a large bowl or pot. Add the peanuts. Mix well and set aside.

In a heavy saucepan, melt the butter over low heat. Add the sugar and water and continue cooking over low heat, stirring constantly, until the sugar is dissolved.

Increase the heat to moderate and boil the syrup, without stirring, until it reaches the soft-ball stage (238°F on a candy thermometer).

Slowly pour the hot syrup over the popped corn and peanuts, turning and mixing with a long-handled wooden spoon to coat all the kernels and nuts.

As soon as the mixture is cool enough to handle, shape it lightly into balls with buttered hands.

Let the popcorn balls dry thoroughly on waxed paper or a cookie sheet before wrapping them.

Almond Pecan Popcorn

This nutty popcorn has a light caramel glaze. It makes a wonderful gift, since it keeps well in airtight containers. A scant $\frac{3}{4}$ cup of unpopped corn should make the 8 cups of popped corn called for in this recipe.

2 cups pecan halves
2 cups blanched, whole almonds
8 cups popped corn
2 cups granulated sugar
1 cup light corn syrup
$\frac{2}{3}$ cup water
2 cups unsalted butter, at room temperature

Preheat the oven to 350°F. Lightly oil a large bowl or pot. Lightly grease two cookie sheets with butter.

Spread the pecans and almonds on an ungreased cookie sheet in one layer. Toast them in the oven for about 10 minutes, or until they are lightly browned.

Combine the toasted nuts and the popped corn in the bowl or pot. Mix well.

In a large, heavy saucepan, combine the sugar, corn syrup, and water. Cook over high heat, stirring constantly, until the sugar is dissolved. Reduce the heat to moderate and cook, stirring frequently, until the mixture comes to a boil. Cut the butter into pieces, then add it and continue cooking, stirring constantly, until the mixture reaches the hard-crack stage (300°F on a candy thermometer).

Slowly pour the hot syrup over the nuts and popcorn, mixing and tossing with a long-handled wooden spoon to coat the nuts and popcorn with the caramel. Spread half the popcorn mixture in a thin layer on each cookie sheet.

When the mixture is completely cool, break it into small pieces.

Walnut Treats

These sugary walnuts are flavored with lemon and orange. They will keep well in an airtight container.

1 cup granulated sugar
2 tablespoons water
2 tablespoons orange juice
2 tablespoons grated orange peel
2 tablespoons grated lemon peel
2 cups walnut halves

Grease a cookie sheet with butter.

In a heavy saucepan, combine the sugar, water, and orange juice. Cook over moderate heat, stirring constantly, until the syrup reaches the firm-ball stage (244°F on a candy thermometer).

Remove the pan from the heat and stir in the orange peel, lemon peel, and walnuts. Continue to stir until the syrup is creamy and the walnuts are well coated.

Spread the nuts on the prepared cookie sheet. Be sure they are all separated. Set aside until completely cool.

Fruit Chews

These chewy fruit-nut balls require no cooking and are full of good healthy ingredients. Store them in a cool, dry place or in the refrigerator.

1½ *cups raisins*
1 *cup dried apricots*
1 *cup pitted dates*
1 *cup flaked coconut*
1 *cup finely chopped walnuts*

In a food processor or blender, grind the raisins, apricots, and dates.

In a large mixing bowl, combine the ground fruit with the coconut and ½ cup of the walnuts. Mix well.

Shape the mixture into thirty 1-inch balls.

Spread the remaining ½ cup of chopped nuts on a plate. Roll the balls in the nuts, pressing the nuts firmly into them.

Walnut Date Slices

This chewy confection is quite easy to make. Pecans may be substituted for the walnuts. The slices keep best well-covered in the refrigerator, but serve them at room temperature.

3 cups granulated sugar
1 cup evaporated milk
1 cup finely chopped pitted dates
1 cup finely chopped walnuts

In a heavy saucepan, combine the sugar and milk. Cook over high heat, stirring constantly, until the sugar dissolves. Reduce heat to moderate and continue cooking, and stirring, until the mixture reaches the soft-ball stage (238°F on a candy thermometer).

Remove the pan from the heat and stir in the dates and the walnuts.

When the mixture is cool enough to handle, shape it into a roll, about 2 inches in diameter, using buttered hands. Wrap the roll in plastic wrap. Chill in the refrigerator overnight. Then, using a sharp knife, cut the roll into slices $\frac{1}{4}$ inch thick.

Taffy Apples

Commercially made taffy apples don't compare to the ones you make yourself. Be sure to use well-flavored, unblemished apples.

8 small or 6 large apples
2 cups granulated sugar
$\frac{1}{2}$ cup water
$\frac{1}{8}$ teaspoon cream of tartar
$\frac{1}{2}$ cup unsalted butter, cut into small pieces
1 teaspoon white vinegar
$\frac{1}{2}$ cup heavy cream

Push a lollypop stick or a skewer into the stem end of each apple. Liberally grease a cookie sheet with butter.

In a large, heavy saucepan, combine the sugar and the water. Cook over low heat, stirring constantly, until the sugar is dissolved.

Stir in the cream of tartar, butter, vinegar, and cream. Cook, stirring constantly, until the mixture reaches the soft-crack stage (290°F on a candy thermometer). Remove the pan from the heat.

Dip each apple into the syrup, then carefully place it on the prepared cookie sheet.

When the taffy has cooled completely, wrap each apple in plastic wrap.

Candied Orange Peel

This recipe makes a sugary, moist confection that keeps for many weeks in an airtight container. If you prefer candied grapefruit peel to orange, simply substitute the peel of 4 large grapefruits. Do not mix the peels in one batch. It's better to candy them separately.

> 8 *large unblemished oranges*
> 3 *cups granulated sugar*
> 1 *cup water*

Score the peel of each orange into eighths, then, using a blunt knife, pry the peel off the fruit. Scrape as much of the white pith (which can make the candy bitter) as possible from the inside of the peel. Cut the peel into strips.

Put the peel into a saucepan and add cold water to cover. Cook over low heat until the water comes to a boil. Remove the pan from the heat and drain the peel well. Repeat this process four more times, draining the peel thoroughly each time.

In a heavy saucepan, combine 2 cups of the sugar and the water. Cook over high heat, stirring constantly, until the sugar dissolves. Bring the syrup to a boil, add the drained peel, and cook over moderate heat, stirring constantly, until all the syrup is absorbed by the peel.

Turn the peel out onto an ungreased cookie sheet. Separate the peel. Let it cool.

Spread the remaining 1 cup of sugar on a large plate. Put a large sheet of waxed paper on a work surface.

When the peel is cool, roll it in the sugar, then put the pieces on the waxed paper to dry for about 2 hours.

Candied Kumquats

This sweet-sour little fruit has a unique flavor and makes a delightful confection. Use only firm, brightly colored kumquats.

> 4 cups kumquats
> 5 cups water
> $3\frac{1}{2}$ cups granulated sugar
> $\frac{1}{8}$ teaspoon cream of tartar

Wash the kumquats and, using a skewer or a tapestry needle, prick a hole in the stem end of each one.

Put the kumquats into a saucepan and add 4 cups of water. Cook over moderate heat until the water begins to boil. Reduce the heat and simmer the kumquats for 10 minutes.

Drain the kumquats in a colander, then spread them on paper towels to dry.

In a heavy saucepan, combine the remaining cup of water with 2 cups of the sugar. Cook over low heat, stirring constantly, until the sugar is dissolved. Stir in the cream of tartar. Increase the heat to moderate and cook, stirring constantly, until the syrup reaches the soft-ball stage (238°F on a candy thermometer).

Reduce the heat to low, add the kumquats, and let them simmer gently, stirring frequently, for 10 minutes.

Using a perforated spoon, remove the kumquats from the syrup and put them on wire racks to drain and cool.

Spread the remaining $1\frac{1}{2}$ cups of sugar on a plate.

When the kumquats are cool enough to handle, roll each one in the sugar. Return the kumquats to the wire racks to cool completely.

MORE PRAISE FOR NORMAN MAILER

AND

HARLOT'S GHOST

"Mailer writes with a power and sparkle not often seen these days. . . . This is a great book, the U.S. Cold War version of *War and Peace*."

David E. Anderson
San Diego Tribune

"The kind of intensely imagined world that only the very best novelists can create or sustain."

Wilfrid Sheed
The New York Review of Books

"Highly entertaining . . . Brimful of the most original anecdotes I've read in years."

Howard Frank Mosher
Chicago Sun-Times

"This is one of the best fucking novels [I've] ever read. . . . Whatever his faults, he is simply the best."

Blanche McCrary Boyd
The Village Voice

"Reads like an express train . . . Never has Mailer written more swiftly and surely, more vividly."

Publishers Weekly

"*Harlot's Ghost* is the most brilliant novel ever written about the CIA."

Paul D. McCarthy
Minneapolis Star Tribune

HARLOT'S

GHOST

NORMAN
MAILER

BALLANTINE BOOKS
NEW YORK

Portions of this work were
originally published in *Rolling Stone*.

Grateful acknowledgment is made to the following for
permission to reprint previously published material:
HARCOURT BRACE JOVANOVICH, INC.,
AND FABER AND FABER LIMITED: Five lines from
"The Waste Land," which appear on pages 27 and 28 of
Collected Poems 1909–1962 by T. S. Eliot.
Copyright 1936 by Harcourt Brace Jovanovich, Inc.
Copyright © 1964, 1963 by T. S. Eliot.
Rights throughout the world excluding the U.S.A. are
controlled by Faber and Faber Limited.
Reprinted by permission of Harcourt Brace Jovanovich, Inc.,
and Faber and Faber Limited.
THE NEW REPUBLIC: Excerpts from "Unofficial Envoy"
by Jean Daniel, December 13, 1963, and excerpts from
"When Castro Heard the News" by Jean Daniel, December 7, 1963.
Copyright © 1963 by The New Republic, Inc.
Reprinted by permission of *The New Republic*.

Library of Congress Catalog Card Number: 92-90052
ISBN: 0-345-37965-9

Text design by Holly Johnson
Cover design by James R. Harris
Cover photography by Armando Ysidro Reyes

Manufactured in the United States of America

First Ballantine Books Trade Paperback Edition: September 1992
10 9 8 7 6 5 4 3 2

TO JASON EPSTEIN

For we wrestle, not against flesh and blood,
but against principalities, against powers,
against the rulers of the darkness
of this world, against spiritual wickedness
in high places.

—*Ephesians, 6:12*

BELINDA: Ay, but you know we must return good for evil.
LADY BRUTE: That may be a mistake in the translation.

—SIR JOHN VANBRUGH
The Provoked Wife

Dark, dark my light, and darker my desire,
My Soul, like some heat-maddened summer fly,
Keeps buzzing at the sill. Which I is I?

—THEODORE ROETHKE
In a Dark Time

HARLOT'S

GHOST

OMEGA - 1

ON A LATE-WINTER EVENING IN 1983, WHILE DRIVING THROUGH FOG along the Maine coast, recollections of old campfires began to drift into the March mist, and I thought of the Abnaki Indians of the Algonquin tribe who dwelt near Bangor a thousand years ago.

In the spring, after the planting of corn, the younger braves and squaws would leave the aged to watch over the crops and the children, and would take their birchbark canoes south for the summer. Down the Penobscot River they would travel to Blue Hill Bay on the western side of Mount Desert where my family's house, built in part by my great-great-grandfather, Doane Hadlock Hubbard, still stands. It is called the Keep, and I do not know of all else it keeps, but some Indians came ashore to build lean-tos each summer, and a few of their graves are among us, although I do not believe they came to our island to die. Lazing in the rare joys of northern warmth, they must have shucked clams on the flats at low tide and fought and fornicated among the spruce and hemlock when the water was up. What they got drunk on I do not know, unless it was the musk of each other, but many a rocky beach in the first hollow behind the shore sports mounds of ancient clamshells, ground to powder by the centuries, a beach behind the beach to speak of ancient summer frolics. The ghosts of these Indians may no longer pass through our woods, but something of their old sorrows and pleasures joins the air. Mount Desert is more luminous than the rest of Maine.

Even guidebooks for tourists seek to describe this virtue: "The island of Mount Desert, fifteen miles in diameter, rises like a fabled city from the sea. The natives call it Acadia, beautiful and awesome."

Beautiful and awesome. We have a fjord in the middle of Mount Desert, a spectacular four-mile passage by water between promontories on either side. It is the only true fjord on the Atlantic coast of

North America, yet it is but a part of our rock-hewn splendor. Near the shore, peaks rise abruptly a thousand feet to afford sailing craft the illusion of great mountains, and our finest anchorage, Northeast Harbor, is in summer a dazzle of yachts.

Perhaps it is the nearness of our mountains to the sea, but silences are massive here, and summers have an allure not simple to describe. For one thing, we are not an island to attract people who follow the sun. We have almost no sand beach. The shore is pebble and clamshell strand, and twelve-foot tides inundate the rocks. Washed by incoming waves are barnacles and periwinkles, rockweed mussels, Irish moss, red seaweed, dulse. Sand dollars and whelks lie scattered in the throw of the surf. Kelp is everywhere and devil's-apron often winds around one's ankles. In the tide pools grow anemone and sponge. Starfish and sea urchins are near your toes. One walks with care over sharp stones. And the water is so cold that swimmers who did not spend childhood vacations in this icy sea can hardly bear it. I have lolled in the wild green above the reefs of the Caribbean and sailed over purple deeps in the Mediterranean, I have seen the inimitable mist of hot summer on the Chesapeake when all hues blend between the sky and the bay. I even like slate-brown rivers that rush through canyons in the West, but I love the piercing blue of Frenchman's Bay and Blue Hill Bay, and the bottomless blue of the Eastern and Western Way surrounding Mount Desert—indeed, one's affection for the island even shares the local accent. As decreed by the natives, one spells it Mount Desert, but the pronunciation is Mount Dessert. The view is as fine as sugar frosting to a New Englander's eyes.

I speak in hyperbole, but then who cannot on recalling such summer beauties as the astonishing color of our rocks at water's edge. They are apricot, then lavender, and pale green, yet in late afternoon they become purple over the whole, a dark royal violet is the color of the twilight shore seen from the sea. That is our island in August. Beach heather and wild rose grow near the salt marsh grass, and in our meadows white-throated sparrows spring from one decaying stump to another. The old hayfields smell of redtop and timothy, and wild-flowers bloom. The northern blue violet and the starflower, the wood sorrel and the checkerberry, painted trillium and wild geranium, golden heather and Indian pipe grow in our bogs and fields and on the sunny slopes of our mountains in the seams between ledges of rock. Down by the marshes are swamp candles and jewelweed. Once, when I was a boy (for I studied the names of wildflowers then) I found the white-vein orchid in some swampy woods; it was greenish-white, and lovely, and as rare as the moon entering eclipse. For all its tourist traffic come July, Mount Desert is still possessed of a tender yet monumental silence.

If one would ask how the monumental can ever be tender, I reply that such words recall us to the beautiful and awesome. So am I tempted, when caution deserts me, to describe my wife, Kittredge. Her white skin becomes luminous in any pale meadow; it also reflects the shadows of the rock. I see Kittredge sitting in such shadows on a summer day, and her eyes have the blue of the sea.

I have also been with her when she can seem as bleak as the March storms that strike this island. Now, in March, the fields are dun, and the snow, half-gone, will be stained in the morning with the stirring of the mud. In March, the afternoons are not golden but gray, and the rocks are rarely burnished by the sun. Certain precipices become as grim as the endless meditations of granite. At winter's end, Mount Desert is like a miser's fist; the dull shell of the sky meets a leaden sea. Depression sits over the hills. When my wife is depressed, no color stirs in my own heart, and her skin is not luminous but hooded in pallor. Except for snowy days, when island lights still dance off the frozen rock like candles on a high white cake, I do not like to live in late winter on Mount Desert. The sunless sky weighs over us, and a week can go by when we do not speak. That is loneliness kin to the despair of a convivial drinker who has not poured a glass for days. It is then that ghosts begin to visit the Keep. Our fine dwelling is hospitable to ghosts.

The house sits alone on an island, not ten acres of spread, just a stone's throw—literally one long throw—off the western shore of Mount Desert. Called Doane, after my great-great-grandfather, it is subject, I suspect, to visitations. While islands, according to my wife, are supposed to be more acceptable to invisible spirits than to such peculiarly apparent manifests as ghosts, I think we break the rule.

Out on Bartlett's Island, somewhat to the north of us, is the all-but-certified ghost of Snowman Dyer, an eccentric old fisherman. He died on Bartlett's in 1870 under the roof of his spinster sister. Once, as a young man, he had bartered five lobsters for a small Greek tome that belonged to a classics scholar at Harvard. The work was the *Oedipus Rex* and it had an interlinear trot. The old fisherman, Snowman Dyer, was intrigued so much by Sophocles' words in literal translation that he attempted to read the original Greek. Not knowing how to pronounce the alphabet, he contrived nonetheless a sound for each character. As he grew older, he grew bolder, and used to recite aloud from this unique tongue while wandering over the rocks. They say that to spend a night in the dead sister's house will bring Snowman Dyer's version of Greek to your ear, and the sounds are no more barbaric than the claps and groans of our weather. A corporate executive from Philadelphia, Bingham Baker, and his family now inhabit the house and seem to thrive on the ghost—at least, all the Bakers look pink-cheeked in church. I do not know if they hear the moan of winter in Snowman Dyer's voice.

Old Snowman may be the ghost of Bartlett's Island, but we have another on Doane, and he is not so agreeable. A sea captain named Augustus Farr, he owned and occupied our land two and a half centuries ago. There are allusions to his habits in an old sea-diary I have found in the library at Bar Harbor, and one voyage is cited "durying whych Farr ingaged in practize of piracie" and boarded a French frigate in the Caribbean, took its cargo of Cuban sugar, put the crew to sea in an open boat (except for those who would join him), and beheaded the commodore, who died in naked state because Farr had appropriated his uniform. Then Augustus was so bold in later years as to have himself buried on his northern island—now our island—in the Frenchman's dress apparel.

I have never seen Augustus Farr, but I may have heard his voice. One night, not long ago, when alone in the Keep, I came out of a dream to find myself conversing with the wall. "No, leave," I said boldly, "I do not know if you can make amends. Nor do I trust you." When I recall this dream—if it was a dream—I shiver in a way I cannot repeat at other times. My flesh shifts on my back as if I am wearing a jacket of lizard skin. I hear my own voice again. I am not speaking to the plaster in front of me but to a room I feel able to see on the other side of the wall. There, I visualize a presence in a tattered uniform sitting on an oaken and much-scarred captain's chair. An odor of corruption is in my nose. Out on the mud flats, or so I hear through the window—I do not dare to look—the sea is boiling. How can waters boil when the tide is out? I am still in my dream but watch a mouse streak along the floor, and feel the ghost of Augustus Farr on the other side of the wall. The hair stiffens on the back of my head as he descends the stairs to the cellar. I hear him going down to the Vault.

Underneath the cellar, it was originally a dugout built by my father after the Second World War when he still owned the Keep. He prided himself on being the first American to take in the consequences of Hiroshima. "Everybody needs a place where he can get under it all," said my father, Cal Hubbard, two years before he sold our property to his second cousin, Kittredge's father, Rodman Knowles Gardiner, who in turn gave it over to Kittredge on her first marriage. In the time Rodman Gardiner had it, however, he decided to go my father one further and was the first man, so far as I know, in this part of Maine to have a cinder-block fallout shelter complete with canned goods, bunks, kitchen, ventilation fans, and at the entrance, two corridors set at right angles to one another. What that ninety-degree turn has to do with keeping off nuclear radiation I cannot say, but there were curious fashions in early fallout shelters. It is still there for us; a family embarrassment. Up in Maine you are not supposed to protect your life that much.

I despised the shelter. I let it molder. The foam rubber of the bunk mattresses has gone to powder. The stone floor is covered with nothing less than an old slime. The electric light bulbs, long burned out, are corroded in their sockets.

Let this not give too false an idea of the Keep. The floor of the Vault—so the fallout shelter came inevitably to be named—is ten feet below the main cellar, which is, itself, a large, clean, stone chamber. The main floor and second story and full attic of the Keep are kept in reasonable order by a Maine woman who comes in every day the weather permits when we are there, and once a week when we are gone. It is only the Vault that is left untended. That is my fault. I cannot bear to let anyone go down to it. If I open the door, a mad dank odor comes up from below. It is no rarity for subcellars to be dank, but the odor of madness is another matter.

On the night when I emerged from my dream to encounter Augustus Farr, on that night when I became convinced I was not dreaming and heard him descending the stairs, I got up from bed and attempted to follow. This was not an act of bravery so much as a product of endless conditioning in the special art of converting one's worst fears to fortitude. My father told me once when I was an adolescent, "If you are afraid, don't hesitate. Get right into the trouble if that is the honest course." It was a hypothesis on the art of courage that I had to refine considerably in bureaucratic wars where patience was the card to play, but I knew when fear proved paralyzing that one had sometimes to force a move or let one's soul pay up. The honest course on encountering a ghost was clear: Follow him.

I tried. My feet as cold as a winter corpse, I started down the stairs. That was no dream. In front of me, doors slammed in a fury. "I will not return until I do," I thought I heard a voice cry. By the time I descended to the first cellar, my resolve had run out. At the entrance to the Vault a presence as malevolent as any dark creature of the sea seemed to be waiting below. My courage was now not large enough to take my legs down the last ten steps. I stood there unmoving, as if some part of honor would be safeguarded if I did not flee, but stood in place to accept the wrath of whatever it was. I will say it. I lived in the intangible embrace of that malevolence. Then, Augustus—I assume it was Augustus—withdrew into the depths of the Vault and I felt free to retreat. I went back to my bed. I slept as if drugged by the most powerful of tranquilizers. Since that time I have not gone to the Vault nor has Augustus come to me.

Nonetheless, the Keep was altered by his visitation. Possessions get broken now at an alarming rate, and I have seen ashtrays slide off tables. It is never so dramatic as in the films. Rather, it is sly. You cannot say to a certainty that your coat sleeve did not brush the object nor that the old floor does not have a tilt. It could all have happened through natural causes, or just about. Dealing with such phenomena is like trying to ascertain the facts when talking to a consummate liar. Things keep turning into other things. The wind outside our windows seemed quicker than ever to show its cardinal points: sinister, or saintly, soft or shocking. I never listened to the wind so much as after the visit of Augustus Farr, and the sound of oars would come to me although no boatman was visible. Still, I could hear oarlocks groaning, and bells rang out from chapels on the main island where, so far as I knew, no towers stood to hold the bells. I would listen to the gate swinging in a high wind and plaster falling behind the laths. Small beetles with shells as hard as 12-gauge shot came out of the sills. Every time I went through my books in the library, I could swear a few had moved, but of course the cleaning woman often passed through, or Kittredge, or even myself. No matter. Like a chill pool in a warm hall, Farr was about.

Yet, for all this, the Keep was not spoiled. A ghostly presence is not always dire. Kittredge and I, being childless, had space to let in so large a house. Farr was a mighty diversion, not unequal to living with a drunk or a crazy brother. If he remains as a phantom I cannot swear I have seen, still I would speak of ghosts as real. Some ghosts may be real.

EMBARKING A YEAR LATER, in March of 1984, on an overnight flight from Kennedy Airport, New York, to London, with a connection to Sheremetyevo Airport, Moscow, I kept reading and rereading the dozen pages of typescript that described my former home on Doane Island in Maine. I did not dare to cease. I was in a state of anxiety that gave promise of growing unmanageable. Those dozen pages were the first chapter of what I had come to call the Omega manuscript. I had another, an Alpha manuscript, which once took up twelve inches in a locked file cabinet next to my desk at the Keep, a work that could boast of more than two thousand typewritten pages, but it was formidably indiscreet, and so I had committed its bulk to microfilm, and consigned the original sheets to a shredder. The Alpha manuscript was with me now, all two thousand frames of microfilm on two hundred strips of ten frames each which, laid by sets into glassine sleeves, were packed snugly within an eight-by-eleven-inch manila envelope. I had concealed this slim, even elegant, package, not a quarter of an inch thick, in a recess of a special piece of luggage I had owned for years, said medium-size suitcase now riding in the cargo hold of the British Airways plane that was taking me on the first leg, New York to London, of my flight to Moscow. I would not see it until I was ready to unpack the bag in Russia.

My other manuscript, however, the Omega, a moderate one hundred and eighty pages, so recently written that I had not converted it to microfilm, still existed as typescript in the attaché case beneath my seat. If I had spent the first hundred minutes of this trip in limbo, which is to say, there in the middle of Economy, dreading my arrival in London, my change of planes, and, most certainly, my eventual terminus in Moscow, I felt unable to explain to myself why I had embarked in the first place. Like an insect rendered immobile by a whiff of poison spray, I sat in my chair tilted back all three inches of rearward slant available to the Economy tourist and read the first fourteen pages of the Omega manuscript one more time. I was in that half-stupor where one's legs are too massive to move. All the while, nerves jumped like light-up buttons in an electronic game. Nausea was my neighbor.

Due for arrival in London in another few hours, I felt obliged to read the rest of Omega, all of one hundred and sixty-six pages of typescript, after which I would tear up the sheets and flush away as many of them as the limited means of the British Airways crapper on this aircraft would be able to gulp into itself, then save the rest for the sturdier gullets in the men's room attached to the Transit Lounge at Heathrow. Visualizing the whirl of these shreds and strips of paper revolving into the hound's gurgle of a near-to-choking bowl came close to carrying me off on the good ship vertigo.

My anxiety was from pain of loss. I had spent my last year working on Omega. It was all I had to show for a twelve-month of inner turmoil. If I had reread Omega a hundred times during the months of advancing its chapters, page by slow and daily page, I would now be reading such work for a last time. I was saying good-bye to a manuscript which, in the past year, had accompanied me through hints and recollections of some of the worst episodes of my life. Soon, in but a few hours more, I would have to dispose of the contents, yes, paragraph ripped through the middle after paragraph, these pages, drawn and quartered, flushed into sewer pipes. If I dared not get drunk, I did order a Scotch from the stewardess, and swallowed it at a gulp while offering a toast to the last of Omega.

O M E G A - 2

ON THAT MOONLESS NIGHT IN MARCH, RETURNING TO THE KEEP, I took the road from Bath to Belfast, the road that goes by Camden. In every cove was fog and it covered one's vision like a winding sheet, a fog to embrace the long rock shelf offshore where sailing ships used to founder. When I could no longer see anything at all, I would pull the car over; then the grinding of the buoys would sound as mournful as the lowing of cattle in a rain-drenched field. The silence of the mist would come down on me. You could hear the groan of a drowning sailor in the lapping of that silence. I think you had to be demented to take the coast road on such a night.

Past Camden, a wind sprang up, the fog departed, and soon the driving was worse. With this shift in the weather, a cold rain came. On some curves the highway had turned to ice. Going into skids, my tires sang like a choir in a country church surrounded by forest demons. Now and then would appear a shuttered town and each occasional streetlight would seem equal to a beacon at sea. Empty summer houses, immanent as a row of tombs, stood in witness.

I was full of bad conscience. The road had become a lie. It would offer traction, then turn to glass. Driving that car by the touch of my fingertips, I began to think once more that lying was an art, and fine lying had to be a fine art. The finest liar in the land must be the ice monarch who sat in dominion on the curve of the road.

My mistress was behind me in Bath, and my wife awaited me near the island of Mount Desert. The ice monarch had installed his agents in my heart. I will spare you the story I told Kittredge about small transactions that would occupy me in Portland until evening and so cause my late return to Mount Desert. No, my business had been done in Bath, and in the merry arms of one of the wives of Bath. By acceptable measure, she did not have much to offer against my mate. The woman in Bath was agreeable, whereas my dear wife was a beauty. Chloe was cheerful, and Kittredge was—I apologize for so self-serving a word—distinguished. You see, Kittredge and I, while only third cousins, look much alike—even our noses are similar. Whereas Chloe is as common as gravy and heartening to taste. Buxom and bountiful, she worked in summer as a waitress in a Yankee inn. (Let us say: a Yankee-inn–type restaurant run by a Greek.) One night a week, on the hostess's night off, Chloe was proud to serve as *pro tem* hostess. I helped her funds a bit. Perhaps other men did, too. I hardly knew. I hardly cared. She was like a dish I was ready to consume once or twice a month. I do not know if it would have been three times and more a week if she lived just over the hill, but Bath was considerably more than a hundred miles from the backside (our word for the backshore) of Mount Desert, and so I saw her when I could.

A liaison with a mistress that is kept so infrequently tends, I think, to serve civilization. If it had been any marriage but my own, I would have remarked that a double life lived with such moderation ought to be excellent—it might make both halves more interesting. One could remain deeply, if not wholly, in love with one's wife. My occupation offered wisdom on such matters, after all. Did we begin by speaking of ghosts? My father commenced a family line that I continue: Spooks. In Intelligence, we look to discover the compartmentalization of the heart. We made an in-depth psychological study once in the CIA and learned to our dismay (it was really horror!) that one-third of the men and women who could pass our security clearance were divided enough—handled properly—to be turned into agents of a foreign power. "Potential defectors are at least as plentiful as potential alcoholics," was the cheerful rule of thumb we ended with on that one.

After so many years of work with imperfect people I had learned, therefore, to live a little with the lapses of others so long as they did not endanger too much. Yet my own defection from the marital absolute left me ill with fear. On this night of blind driving to which

I have introduced you, I was half certain I would soon be in a wreck. I felt caught in invisible and monstrous negotiations. It seemed—suspend all logic—that dreadful things might happen to others if I stayed alive. Can you understand? I do not pretend: I think something of the logic of the suicide is in such thoughts. Kittredge, who has a fine mind, full of aperçus, once remarked that suicide might be better understood on the assumption there was not one reason for the act but two: People may kill themselves for the obvious reason, that they are washed up, spiritually humiliated down to zero; equally, they can see their suicide as an honorable termination of deep-seated terror. Some people, said Kittredge, become so mired in evil spirits that they believe they can destroy whole armies of malignity by their own demise. It is like burning a barn to wipe out the termites who might otherwise infest the house.

Say much the same for murder. An abominable act which, none-theless, can be patriotic. Kittredge and I did not talk long about murder. It was a family embarrassment. My father and I once spent close to three years trying to assassinate Fidel Castro.

Let me return, however, to that icy road. There, if my sense of preservation kept a light touch on the wheel, my conscience was ready to crush it. I had shattered more than a marriage vow. I had broken a lovers' vow. Kittredge and I were fabulous lovers, by which I do not intend anything so vigorous as banging away till the dogs howl. No, back to the root of the word. We were *fabulous* lovers. Our marriage was the conclusion to one of those stern myths that instruct us in tragedy. If I sound like the wind of an ass in whistling about myself on such a high note, it is because I feel uneasy at describing our love. Normally, I cannot refer to it. Happiness and absolute sorrow flow from a common wound.

I will give the facts. They are brutal, but better than sentimental obfuscation. Kittredge had had but two men in her life. Her first husband and myself. We began our affair while she was still married to him. Some time after she betrayed him—and he was the kind of man who would think in terms of betrayal—he took a terrible fall in a rock climb and broke his back. He had been the lead, and when he went, the youth who was belaying him from the ledge below was pulled along. The anchor jerked out of the rock. Christopher, the adolescent killed in the fall, was their only child.

Kittredge could never forgive her husband. Their son was sixteen and not especially well coordinated. He should not have been led to that particular rock face. But then, how could she forgive herself? Our affair sat over her head. She buried Christopher and watched over her husband during the fifteen weeks he was in the hospital. Soon after he came home, Kittredge chose to get into a warm bath one night and cut each of her wrists with a sharp kitchen blade, after which she lay back and prepared to bleed to death in her tub. But she was saved.

By me. She had allowed no communication since the day of the fall. News so terrible had divided the ground between us like a fissure in earth that leaves two neighboring homes a gaping mile apart. God might as well have spoken. She told me not to see her. I did not try. On the night, however, that she took the knife to her wrists, I had (on a mounting sense of unease) flown up from Washington to Boston, then to Bangor, and rented a car to go on to Mount Desert. I heard her calling to me from caverns so deep in herself she was never aware of her own voice. I arrived at a silent house and let myself in through a window. Back on the first floor was an invalid and his nurse; on the second, his wife, presumably asleep in a far-off bed. When her bathroom door was locked and she did not reply, I broke in. Ten minutes more would have been too late.

We went back to our affair. Now there was no question. Shocked by tragedy, certified by loss, and offered dignity by thoughts we could send to one another, we were profoundly in love.

The Mormons believe that you enter into marriage not only for this life but, if you are married in the Temple, will spend eternity with your mate. I am no Mormon, but even by their elevated measure, we were in love. I could not conceive that I would ever be bored in my wife's presence either side of the grave. Time spent with Kittredge would live forever; other people impinged upon us as if they entered our room holding a clock in their hand.

We had not begun in so inspired a place. Before the disaster on the rock face, we were taken with each other enormously. Since we were third cousins kissing, the tincture of incest enriched the bliss. But it was—on the highest level—qualified stuff. We were not quite ready to die for one another, just off on an awfully wicked streak. Her husband, Hugh Montague—"Harlot"—took on more importance, after all, in my psyche than my own poor ego. He had been my mentor, my godfather, my surrogate father, and my boss. I was then thirty-nine years old and felt half that age in his presence. Cohabiting with his wife, I was like a hermit crab who had just moved into a more impressive carapace; one was waiting to be dislodged.

Naturally, like any new lover in so momentous an affair, I did not ask for her motive. It was enough that she had wanted me. But now, after twelve years with Kittredge, ten in marriage, I can give a reason. To be married to a good woman is to live with tender surprise. I love Kittredge for her beauty and—I will say it—her profundity. We know there is more depth to her thought than to mine. All the same, I am frequently disconcerted by some astonishing space in the fine workings of her mind. Attribute it to background. She has not had a career like other women. I do not know many Radcliffe graduates who went into the CIA.

Item: On the night twelve years ago when we first made love, I performed that simple act of homage with one's lips and tongue that a good many of our college graduates are ready to offer in the course of the act. Kittredge, feeling some wholly unaccustomed set of sensations in the arch from thigh to thigh, said, "Oh. I've been waiting years for that!" She soon made a point of telling me I was the next thing to pagan perfection. "You're devil's heaven," she said. (Give me Scotch blood every time!) She looked no older on our first night than twenty-seven, but had been married already for eighteen and a half of her forty-one years. Hugh Tremont Montague was, she told me (and who could not believe her?), the only man she had ever known. Harlot was, also, seventeen years her senior, and very high echelon. Since one of his skills had been to work with the most special double agents, he had developed a finer sense of other people's lies than they could ever have of his. By now he trusted no one, and, of course, no one around him could ever be certain Harlot was telling the truth. Kittredge would complain to me in those bygone days that she couldn't say if he were a paragon of fidelity, a gorgon of infidelity, or a closet pederast. I think she began her affair with me (if we are to choose the bad motive rather than the good) because she wanted to learn whether she could run an operation under his nose and get away with it.

The good motive came later. Her love deepened for me not because I saved her life but because I had been sensitive to the mortal desperation of her spirit. I am finally wise enough to know that that is enough for almost all of us. Our affair commenced again. This time, we made an absolute of love. She was the kind of woman who could not conceive of continuing in such a state without marriage. Love was a state of grace and had to be protected by sacramental walls.

She felt obliged, therefore, to tell her husband. We went to Hugh

Tremont Montague and he agreed to divorce. That may have been the poorest hour of my life. I was afraid of Harlot. I had the well-founded dread one feels for a man who can arrange for the termination of people. Before the accident, when he was tall and thin and seemed put together of the best tack and gear, he always carried himself as if he had sanction. Someone on high had done the anointing.

Now, stove-in at the waist, conforming to the shape of the wheelchair, he still had sanction. That was not the worst of it, however. I may have been afraid of him, but I also revered him. He had not only been my boss, but my master in the only spiritual art that American men and boys respect—machismo. He gave life courses in grace under pressure. The hour that Kittredge and I spent together on either side of his wheelchair is a bruise on the flesh of memory. I remember that he cried before we were done.

I could not believe it. Kittredge told me later it was the only time she ever saw him weep. Hugh's shoulders racked, his diaphragm heaved, his spavined legs remained motionless. He was a cripple stripped down to his sorrow. I never lost the image. If I compare this abominable memory to a bruise, I would add that it did not fade. It grew darker. We were sentenced to maintain a great love.

Kittredge had faith. To believe in the existence of the absurd was, for her, a pure subscription to the devil. We were here to be judged. So our marriage would be measured by the heights it could climb from the dungeon of its low beginnings. I subscribed to her faith. For us, it was the only set of beliefs possible.

How, then, could I have spent my most recent hours this gray March day slopping and sliding on the over-friendly breast and belly of Chloe? My mistress's kisses were like taffy, soft and sticky, endlessly wet. From high school on, Chloe had doubtless been making love with her mouth to both ends of her friends. Her groove was a marrow of good grease, her eyes luminous only when libidinal. So soon as we subsided for a bit, she would talk away in the happiest voice about whatever came into her head. Her discourse was all of trailer homes (she lived in one), how ready they were to go up in flames, and of truckers with big rigs who ordered coffee while sitting on enough self-importance to run the Teamsters. She told anecdotes about old boyfriends she ran into at the town lunch counter. " 'Boy,' I said to myself, 'has he been shoveling it in! Fat!' Then I had to ask myself: 'Chloe, is your butt that far behind?' I put the blame on Bath. There's nothing to do here in winter except eat, and look for hungry guys like

you," at which she gave a friendly clap to my buttocks as if we were
playing on a team together—the old small-town sense that you heft
a person's worth—and we were off again. There was one yearning in
my flesh (for the common people) that she kept at trigger-trip. Skid
and slide and sing in unison, while the forest demons yowl.

I had met her in the off-season in the big restaurant where she
worked. It was a quiet night, and I was not only alone at my table but
the only diner in my section. She waited on me with a quiet friendliness, much at home with the notion that a meal that tasted right for
me was better wages for her than a meal that tasted wrong. Like other
good materialistic people before her, she was also maternalistic: She
saw money as coming in all kinds of emotional flavors. It took happy
money to buy a dependable appliance.

When I ordered the shrimp cocktail, she shook her head. "You
don't want the shrimp," she said. "They've died and risen three times.
Take the chowder." I did. She guided me through the meal. She
wanted my drinks to be right. She did it all with no great fuss—I was
free to stay in my private thoughts, she in hers. We talked with
whatever surplus was in our moods. Perhaps one waitress in ten could
enjoy a lonely customer as much as Chloe. I realized after a while that
on pickup acquaintance, which was never my style, I was surprisingly
comfortable with her.

I stopped off again at the restaurant on another quiet night and she
sat and had dessert and coffee with me. I learned of her life. She had
two sons, twenty and twenty-one; they dwelt in Manchester, New
Hampshire, and worked in the mills. She claimed to be thirty-eight,
and her husband had broken up with her five years ago. Caught her
cheating. "He was right. I was a boozer then, and you can't trust a
boozer. My heels were as round as roller skates." She laughed with
enough good humor to have been watching her own pornographic
romp.

We went to her trailer. I have an ability developed, I believe, by
my profession. I can concentrate on what is before me. Inter-office
flaps, bureaucratic infringements, security leaks, even such assaults on
the unconscious as my first infidelity to Kittredge, can be ignored. I
have a personal instrument I think of as average, a good soldier, a dick
as vulnerable as any other. It throbs with encouragement and droops
with the oncoming of guilt. So it is testimony to the power of my
concentration and to Chloe's voluptuous exposures (call it a crime
against the public pleasure for her to be seen in clothes) that, consider-

ing the uniqueness and magnitude of my marital breech, there was only a hint of sag from time to time in the fine fellow below. I was starved, in truth, for what Chloe had to offer.

Let me see if I can explain. Lovemaking with Kittredge was—I use the word once more—a sacrament. I am not at ease trying to speak of it. Whereas, I can give all away in talking about Chloe; we were like kids in the barn; Chloe even smelled of earth and straw. But there was ceremony to embracing Kittredge.

I do not mean that we were solemn or measured. If it did not come to real desire, we might not make love for a month. When it happened, however, it certainly did; after all our years together, we still flew at each other. Kittredge, indeed, was as fierce as one of those wood-animals with claws and sharp teeth and fine fur that you can never quite tame. At its worst, there were times when I felt like a tomcat in with a raccoon. My tongue (once key to devil's heaven) was rarely now in her thoughts—rather, our act was subservient to coming together, cruelty to cruelty, love to love. I'd see God when the lightning flashed and we jolted our souls into one another. Afterward, was tenderness, and the sweetest domestic knowledge of how curious and wonderful we were for one another, but it was not in the least like getting it on with Chloe. With Chloe it was get ready for the rush, get ready for the sale, whoo-ee, gushers, we'd hit oil together. Recuperating, it felt low-down and slimy and rich as the earth. You could grow flowers out of your ass.

Driving that car, my heart in my teeth, and the road ice in my ice-cold fingers, I knew all over again what Chloe gave me. It was equality. We had nothing in common but our equality. If they brought us up for judgment, we could go hand in hand. Our bodies were matched in depth to one another, and we felt the affection of carrots and peas in the same meat soup. I had never known a woman so much my physical equal as Chloe.

Whereas, Kittredge was the former consort of a knight, now a crippled knight. I felt like a squire in a medieval romance. While my knight was off on a crusade, I entertained his lady. If we had found a way to pick the lock of her chastity belt, I still had to mount the steps. We might see lightning and stars, yet the bedroom remained her chamber. Our ecstasy was as austere as the glow of phosphorescent lights in Maine waters. I did not see Creation; rather, I had glimpses of the heavens. With Chloe, I felt like one more Teamster with a heavy rig.

On a night of driving so unsettled as this—sleet on the cusp of freezing—there was no way to meditate for long. Rather, thoughts jumped up before me. So, I saw that Chloe had the shape of a wife, and Kittredge was still my lady. In most affairs, a kiss can remind you of many a mouth you have known. It lubricates a marriage to have a wife who reminds you of other women as well. Many a connubial union is but the sublimation of orgies never embarked upon. With Kittredge, I had hardly been enjoying the promiscuity of making love to one woman who might serve as surrogate for many.

Once, about a month after we were married, she said to me, "There's nothing worse than the breaking of vows. I always feel as if the universe is held together by the few solemn promises that are kept. Hugh was awful. You could never trust a word of his. I shouldn't tell you, darling, but when you and I first began, it was such an achievement for me. I suppose it was the bravest thing I'd ever done."

"Don't ever be that brave with me," I said, and it was no threat. At the uneasy center of my voice, I was begging her.

"I won't. I won't ever." She would have had the clear eyes of an angel but for a touch of mist in the blue. A philosopher, she was always trying to perceive objects at a great distance. "No," she said, "let's make a pledge. Absolute honesty between us. If either of us has anything to do with someone else, we must tell."

"I pledge," I said.

"My God," she said, "with Hugh I never knew. Is that one of the reasons he clung to that awful name, Harlot?" She stopped. Harlot, whatever he was doing at this moment, was in the wheelchair now. "Poor old Gobby," she said. Any compassion she still held for him was in this nickname.

"Why is the name Gobby?" With Kittredge, there was a time for everything and I had never asked her before.

"God's old beast. That's his name."

"One name, anyway."

"Oh, darling, I love giving people names. At least, people I care about. That's the only way we're allowed to be promiscuous. Give each other hordes of names."

Over the years, one by one, I had learned a few of them. Hugh had a fine mustache, trim pepper-and-salt. It belonged on a British cavalry colonel. Kittredge used to call him Trimsky. "Just as bright as Leon Trotsky," she'd say, "but ten times as neat." Later I found out she was, this once, not original. It was Allen Dulles who first christened him thus. That was when Hugh was working for the OSS in London during the war. Apparently Dulles repeated it to Kittredge at her wedding. Kittredge had been mad about Allen Dulles ever since meeting him at a Georgetown garden party her parents took her to during the Easter vacation of her sophomore year in Radcliffe. Ah, the poor Harvard men who tried to spark Kittredge after Allen Dulles kissed her on the cheek for good-bye.

Following the nuptials, she took to calling Hugh Tremont Montague by Trimsky. He gave her monikers in return. One was Ketchum, for Ketchum, Idaho (since Kittredge's full pedigree was Hadley Kittredge Gardiner, first name taken from Hadley Richardson, Hemingway's first wife, whom Kittredge's father, Rodman Knowles Gardiner, met in Paris in the twenties and thought was "the nicest woman ever encountered").

It had taken its own good time for me to learn a few metamorphoses of my beloved's names. Ketchum, avoiding Ketchup, was transmogrified into Red—which was perfect, and stuck for a period, since Kittredge's hair was raven-black (and her skin as white as your best white marble). I also knew a lover's pain when Kittredge confessed that Hugh Montague, on notable nights, would call her Hotsky. Did people in Intelligence shift names about the way others move furniture around a room?

In any event, Gobby was the postmarital a.k.a.

"I hated," said Kittredge, "the idea that I couldn't trust Gobby's personal honesty. You do pledge, darling? We will have honesty between us?"

"We will."

My car went into a severe skid, much longer now in memory than it takes to tell. The wall of forest on one side stuttered up to me, and my front end yawed when I spun the wheel, whereupon car and I rushed viciously across the lane toward the other wall of pines at the far shoulder, now suddenly the near shoulder. I thought for a moment I had died and become a devil, for my head seemed put on backwards: I was looking down the road at the turn I had just come out of. Then, as slowly as if I were in a whirlpool at sea, the road began to revolve. Interminably. I could have been a spot of dust on a turntable. Presto!—car and I were moving forward again. I had skidded ninety degrees to the right, then had spun the other way through a full three-sixty counterclockwise, no, put on ninety more degrees to find myself going straight at last, a full one-and-a-quarter, four-fifty-degree turn. I was beyond fear. I felt as if I had fallen out of a ten-story window, landed in a fireman's net, and was now strolling around in a glow and a daze. *"Millions of creatures,"* I said aloud to the empty car—actually said it aloud!—*"walk the earth unseen, both when we wake and when we sleep,"* after which, trundling along at thirty miles an hour, too weak and exhilarated to stop, I added in salute to the lines just recited, "Milton, *Paradise Lost,"* and thought of how Chloe and I had gotten up from bed in her trailer on the outskirts of Bath a couple of hours ago and had gone for a farewell drink to a cocktail lounge with holes in the stuffing of the red leatherette booths. Just after the potions were brought, I knocked one over in a conversational sweep of my arm, and the glass shattered into intolerable little bits as if nothing much was holding together any longer. Whereupon Chloe and I both fell into an uncharacteristic brown spell, and were gloomy when we said good-bye. Infidelity was on the horror of the air.

Now I pondered those millions of creatures who walked the earth unseen. Did they whisper in Kittredge's ear as she slept, even as once they had called out to me on that long-ago day eleven years back when she grew ready to cut her wrists? Who ran the espionage systems that lived in the ocean of the spirits? A spy needed thoughts as narrow as lasers to rouse no stir. How did an agent making copies of secret papers week after week, year after year, keep from himself the awful fear that this spirit sea of misdeeds might seep into the sleep of the man who could catch him?

I passed a phone booth in a rest area and stopped the car. I was in a panic to speak to Kittredge. Abruptly it seemed that if I did not reach her at once, every last barrier between my mind and hers would be down.

What can be closer to the ages of old-ice than one corroded, pockmarked phone booth on a freezing highway in Maine? I had to raise the operator, and she had trouble repeating the number of my credit card. I was stamping my feet to keep warm before the machinery of the Bell Company was able to stir itself out of chilly sleep. The phone rang four, five, six times, and then I leaped with love at the sound of Kittredge's voice and, on the instant, recalled how my heart had once lifted equally with joy one dark night alone in a canoe in Vermont, when, behold! a galaxy of light lit up every ripple on the black waters of the pond as a full harvest moon rose exactly in the notch between two steep round hills. Druid certainties left their flush

then on my heart. I knew a curious peace. So did Kittredge's voice
now give ease to the stricken tunnels of my breath. I felt as if I had
never heard her voice before. Let no one say I did not love my wife
if after eleven years of marriage I could still discover her wonders.
Most speaking tones come into my ear through filters and baffles. I
hear people monitoring their larynx to purvey warmth and cold,
probity, confidence, censure, approbation—we are phony voices if
only by a little. After all, one's speech is the first instrument of one's
will.

Kittredge's voice came out of herself as a flower opens out of its
bud, except I never knew which bloom would be first. Her voice was
as amazing in anger as in love—she was never on guard for the turn
of her own feelings. Only those who walk about with the notion (it
can be modest) that they are an indispensable part of the universe can
speak with such lack of concern for how they sound to others.

"Harry, I'm glad you called. Are you all right? I've been full of
forebodings all day."

"I'm fine. But the roads are terrible. I'm not even to Bucksport."

"Are you really all right? Your voice sounds as if you just shaved
off your Adam's apple."

I laughed as madly as an embarrassed Japanese businessman. It was
her claim that I would have been as dark, tall, and handsome as Gary
Cooper or Gregory Peck if not for my prominent Adam's apple. "I'm
all right," I said. "I think I needed to talk to you."

"Oh, I need to talk to you. Can you guess what arrived today? A
telegram from our friend. It's demoralizing. After being nice for so
long, he's now in an absolutely deranged mood."

She was speaking of Harlot. "Well," I said, "it can't be as bad as
that. What did he say?"

"I'll tell you later." She paused. "Harry, promise me something."

"Yes." I knew by her tone. "Yes," I said, "what's your forebod-
ing?"

"Drive most carefully. There's a very high tide tonight. Please call
me when you get to the dock. The water's roaring already."

No, her voice concealed nothing. Tones were flying in many
directions as if she were working a dinghy buffeted by chop.

"I have the oddest thoughts," she said. "Did you just have a bad
skid?"

"Never a worse," I answered. The windows of my telephone

booth might be iced up, but perspiration was collecting on my back. How near to me could she get without encountering the real hurly-burly?

"I'm all right," I went on. "I expect the worst weather is over. It feels that way." I took a chance. "Any other odd thoughts flying around?"

"I'm obsessed with a woman," she said.

I nodded intently. I felt like a boxer who is not certain which hand of his unfamiliar opponent he should respect more. "Obsessed with a woman?" I repeated.

"A dead woman," Kittredge said.

You may believe I took relief.

"Is she family?" I asked.

"No."

When Kittredge's mother died, I woke on more than one night to see Kittredge sitting at the side of the bed, her back to me, talking with animation to the bare wall on which, with no embarrassment, she could perceive her mother. (How much this had to do with my warped dream—let us call it such—about Augustus Farr is, of course, anyone's good question.) On these earlier occasions, however, it was clear: Kittredge was in some sort of coma. She would be wide awake, but oblivious to me. When I would tell her in the morning of such episodes, she would neither smile nor frown. My account of her actions did not disturb Kittredge. It seemed fitting to the nocturnal fold that there would be occasions when those of the dead who had been near to you could still speak. Of course her son Christopher had never come back, but then he had been smashed. His death was different. He had fallen into the bottomless abyss of his father's vanity. So his demise had been rendered numb for all. In this fashion, Kittredge reasoned.

Kittredge had Highland blood both sides, and you have to know how Celtic a few Highlanders can be. Not all of the Scotch content themselves with devising controls for the law, the banks, and Presbyterian practice; some take a cottage on the interface between this world and the next. They do not blow those bagpipes for too little.

"Do you want to tell me," I now asked, "about this woman?"

"Harry, she's been dead for ten years. I don't know why she is trying to reach me now."

"Well, who is it?"

She did not reply directly. "Harry," she said, "I've been thinking about Howard Hunt lately."

"Howard? E. Howard Hunt?"

"Yes. Do you know where he is?"

"Not really. Someplace quiet, I guess, picking up the pieces."

"Poor man," she said. "Do you know I actually met him first at that party long ago when my parents introduced me to Allen Dulles. Allen said, 'Here, Kitty, meet Howard Hunt. He's an absolutely nifty novelist.' I don't think the Great White Case Officer had top powers in literary criticism."

"Oh, Mr. Dulles always went in for superlatives."

"Didn't he?" I had made her laugh. "Harry, he said to me once, 'Cal Hubbard would be the Teddy Roosevelt of our outfit if it weren't for Kermit Roosevelt.' Lord, your *father*. It *fits*!" She laughed again, yet her voice, honest as a brook full of the quick lights offered by moving clouds and pebble bed, was in shadow now.

"Tell me about the woman."

"It's Dorothy Hunt, darling," said Kittredge. "She's come right out of the woodwork."

"I didn't realize you knew her well."

"I don't. I didn't. Hugh and I had the Hunts once for dinner."

"Of course. I recall."

"And I do remember her. An intelligent woman. We had lunch a few times. So much more depth than poor Howard."

"What does she say?"

"Harry, she says, 'Don't let *them* rest.' That's all she says. As if we both knew. Whoever *them* may be."

I didn't reply. Kittredge's dismay, delicate but pervasive, leaped over the wire. I almost asked: "Did Hugh ever talk to you about the High Holies?" but I did not speak the thought. I trusted no phone entirely, certainly not my own. While we had said nothing to get any big wind up, still one did one's best to keep all conversation under some kind of damage control. So, now I merely said, "That's curious about Dorothy," and added no more.

Kittredge heard my shift of tone. She, too, was aware of the telephone. There was always, however, her perverse sense of the wicked. If there were monitors on this call, she would offer them a heaping plate of confusion. Kittredge now stated: "I didn't like the message from Gallstone."

"What did it say?" Gallstone—you may have guessed—was one more name for Harlot.

"Well, it was delivered. That awful handyman, Gilley Butler, was standing at my door this evening. He must have taken our dinghy and rowed across, then presented me the envelope with a raffish grin. He was awfully drunk, and acting as if the heavens would undulate should he ever smuggle me into a cave. I could see by his attitude that somebody paid him much too much to deliver it. The most awful emanation came off him. Superior and sort of sleazy all at once."

"What," I repeated, "did your message say?"

"Five hundred seventy-one days on Venus. Plus one on leap year. Eight months to do it all."

"He can't possibly be right," I replied, as if I had comprehended every word.

"Never."

We finished by telling each other that we missed each other, speaking as if it would be years rather than a couple of hours before we met again. Then we hung up. So soon as I was back in the car, I took a worn paperback of T. S. Eliot's poems out of the glove compartment. The eight months mentioned in the telegram referred to the fifth poem in the volume. We had agreed to add the number of the month—March was the third month—to the number of the poem. Venus was a garnish to distract attention, but 571 plus one, by our private convention of subtracting five hundred, gave me the seventy-first and seventy-second lines of the fifth poem, which was—dare I confess it?—"The Waste Land." To any qualified person who had the same edition of Eliot's selected poems, it would be no great work to break our code, but only Harlot, Kittredge, and myself knew which book was in our employ.

Here was Harlot's message—lines 71 and 72:

That corpse you planted last year in your garden,
Has it begun to sprout? Will it bloom this year?

He had done it again. I did not know what Harlot meant, but I did not like it. I had supposed we were enjoying a truce.

In the year just after my marriage to Kittredge, when ex-husband Hugh Montague lived through the nights of the long knives, he had sent off hideous telegrams from his wheelchair. On our wedding day came the first: "Lucky are you for the dice roll eleven. You must buss

each other 528 times plus two and save the sheets—A Friendly Heap"
translated into:

Your shadow at mornings striding behind you
Or your shadow at evening rising to meet you;
I will show you fear in a handful of dust.

That succeeded in coloring our wedding night. Now, after all
these years, he was sending personal messages again. Perhaps I deserved no less. My nostrils still reeked criminally of Chloe.

Of course, cruelty can be a cure for tension when visited on a
guilty man. (So says our penal system.) Harlot's message, sinister as the
fog—"that corpse you planted last year in your garden"—enabled me
to climb onto the same plateau as the difficulties of the weather. I was
at last ready for each little breakaway of the tires. I could think while
my reflexes did the driving, and given the fruits of our call, I had a bit
to go over. I was trying to decide whether Kittredge had a clue to the
High Holies. I had certainly not told her, and now it was reasonably
clear that Harlot hadn't either. Her voice had been too unknowing
about Dorothy Hunt. Kittredge certainly appeared to be wholly unaware that Harlot and I had joined forces.

Having all this much to go over in my mind, I obviously needed
the ruminative powers offered by an easier journey. So, I appreciated
the change in weather as I passed through Belfast where Route 1
joined Route 3. For now, the air was a crucial degree warmer, the
sleet had eased to rain, and the roads, if wet, were free of ice. I was
able to settle into my thoughts. In the special file on the High Holies,
Dorothy Hunt occupied a manila binder.

O M E G A - 3

SOUTH OF THE POTOMAC, JUST BELOW WASHINGTON, THE VIRGINIA
woods were not well treated by the profit-taking of the last ten years.
The wildland swamps had been drained and covered with asphalt,
quartered with superhighways, studded with corporate implants—I
speak of office buildings—and blindsided by molecule-like chains of
condominiums. The parking lots in summer are now as bilious as
natural gas. I was no lover of the development of the humid environs

where I had worked for so long. And the drive from the Langley gate out to Harlot's farmhouse was traffic-jammed for all fifteen miles. His place, a pre–Civil War small beauty which he purchased in 1964, used to stand alone on an old dirt road lined with maples, but now that the four-lane had been built, the house was left on an off-highway eyebrow just twenty yards from where the trucks blasted by. A depressing metamorphosis. It did not help that after his accident, the interior had had to be partially gutted to install a ramp permitting him to propel his wheelchair from the first floor to the second.

All the same, not many occasions in my life had been more momentous than the summer day in 1982 when Harlot had invited me to work again with him. "Yes," he had said, "I need your assistance so much that I will forgo my true innings." His knuckles, huge as carbuncles, fretted his wheelchair forward and back.

Harlot's call to new work was well timed. At Langley I had been in the doldrums. I was sick of walking the corridors. At Langley we had corridors not unreminiscent of the fluorescent pedestrian routes in a huge airport—we even had a wall of glass looking on the central garden. One could pass hundreds of doors on any corridor, all color-coded, leaf green, burnt orange, madder pink, Dresden blue, designed by a pastel-minded coordinator to bring cheer and logic to our cubicles. The colors were to tell you what kind of work was done behind the doors. Of course in the old days—let us say twenty and more years ago—a number of the offices were being run undercover, so the color of the door was misleading. Now only a few such doors were around. I was bored with that. My office door practiced no deception these days. My career (and my wife's) might just as well have been ended. In fact, as I will soon explain, Kittredge and I were not often in Washington anymore, not nearly so much as we stayed at the Keep. For a long time I had been walking a treadmill of no advancement under five Directors of Central Intelligence, no less than Mr. Schlesinger, Mr. Colby, Mr. Bush, Admiral Turner, and Mr. Casey, who, when he passed me in the hall either did not know me, or chose not to greet me by name (after more than twenty-five years in the Company!). Well, who could not see the shadow? Two former Chiefs of Station at two Third World republics, now back at Langley and ready for retirement, shared my office—what was left of my office. They served as my case officers—in this case, editors—for the books I oversaw and/or ghosted. They had reputations as burnt-out cases, much like me. Their reputations, unlike mine, were deserved. Thorpe was drunk at ten in the morning, and his eyes were like marbles, full of pep. They bounced, if they happened to meet your gaze. The other, Gamble, had a stone-dead expression and was of late a vegetarian. He never raised his voice. He was like a man who has flattened twenty years in a state penitentiary. And I? I was ready for a quarrel with anyone.

It was at exactly this time, when disaffection was collecting in my pores like bile, that Harlot summoned me to his rump office at the farmhouse in Virginia, much as he must have called in several other men like myself, still ambitious enough to know rage that their careers were in irons, yet old enough to suffer the knowledge that their best years were committed and gone. Who knows what Harlot cooked up for the others? I can tell you what he talked about with me.

We, at CIA, had gone through some considerable suffering on the exposure of the Family Jewels in 1975. Maybe a few bushmen in Australia had not heard how we labored to rub Fidel Castro out, but by the time the Senate Select Committee to Study Intelligence Activities was done inquiring, there were very few bushmen. The rest of the world had learned that we were ready to kill Patrice Lumumba as well, and had gone in for LSD experiments in brainwashing so exuberantly that one of our subjects, a Dr. Frank Olson (on government contract), had jumped out a window. We hid the fact from his widow. She spent twenty years thinking her husband was an ordinary suicide, which is onerous for a family to believe since there are no ordinary suicides. We opened mail between Russia and the U.S. and closed it again and sent it on. We spied on high government officials like Barry Goldwater and Bobby Kennedy; we had all of those activities advertised in the marketplace. Since we are, at CIA, a proud and secretive people, we felt not unlike a convention of Methodist ministers who are sued by a fine hotel for infesting the bed linen with crab lice. The Company has never been quite the same since exposure of the Family Jewels.

In its wake, many of our top men had to go. Harlot, however, could hardly be dismissed in these, the worst of times, since he had accumulated too much sympathy at Langley for his gallant perambulations down the hall in his wheelchair. He was allowed to stay and fish the eddies. He could work on matters that would attract no attention. Of course, it was generally agreed: Harlot, too, had been left to molder.

Seven years later, however, he was calling me to action. "I ask us, Harry boy," he said, "to forgive the spears we've left in one another.

There is a scandal forming that will prove worse than the Skeletons"—which was his term for the Family Jewels. "I'd estimate about as much worse as Hiroshima was an order of magnitude beyond Pearl Harbor. The Skeletons decimated our ranks; the High Holies, if not excised, will cut us right out of the map."

When he said no more, I stepped back. "I like the name," I said. "High Holies."

"A *good* name," he agreed. Whereupon he did a quadrille with his wheelchair, to and fro, wheel to one side, wheel to the other. He was in his late sixties by now but his eyes and voice belonged to a man who could still charge the troops.

"I vouchsafe," he said, "that few things ever perplexed me as much as Watergate. We had so many ducks in the White House pond. As you have reason to know, I put in one or two myself." I nodded.

"All the same," Harlot went on, "I wasn't prepared for Watergate. That was an extraordinarily dippy operation. Nothing adds up. I had to conclude we were being entertained not by one master plan, no matter how ill conceived, but three or four by different parties. All managed to collide. When the stakes are high, coincidences collect. Shakespeare certainly believed that. No other explanation for Macbeth or Lear."

He had succeeded in irritating me. At this moment, I did not wish to discuss Macbeth or Lear.

"Call the break-in at Watergate act one," he said. "Good first act. Full of promise. But no answers. Now comes act two: the crash, six months later, of the United Airlines plane 553 from Washington to Chicago. It's trying to land at Midway Airport and falls short in the most unbelievable fashion. The plane rips up a neighborhood of small houses not two miles shy of the airport, and in the process kills forty-three of the sixty-one people aboard. Do you know who was on board that plane?"

"I suppose I did once."

"The half-life of your memory retains no trace?"

"Obviously not."

"Dorothy Hunt is the most significant passenger to perish." He held up his hand. "Now, of course, Watergate had not yet cracked open. This is December 1972, a couple of months before Senator Ervin and his committee open shop, and quite a few weeks before our wallah, James McCord, is to sing his first note. Long before John Dean tunes up. Howard Hunt had, you must remember, been breaking a lot of noxious wind up White House way to the effect that, in his immortal words, he would not be a patsy, and Dorothy Hunt was certainly tougher than Howard. In a tight spot, you'd give her the pistol." I shrugged. The point was moot. I had worked for Howard Hunt. "Still!" said Harlot, "that's an awful lot of cannon to kill one bee. Scores of people dead. Who could have done it? Not the White House. They wouldn't mug an airplane. After all, the White House couldn't even give Mr. Liddy a fatal dose of the measles, not even at his invitation, nor did they put the fatal ray on Dean, nor on Hunt, nor on McCord. How, then, could they have given the go-ahead to something so *wholesale* as this plane crash? It *could* be sabotage. The White House is obviously aware of such a possibility. The same Butterfield who will later confess to the Ervin Committee that Richard Nixon taped everything but his trips to the loo is moved over to the Federal Aviation Administration, and Dwight Chapin of CREEP goes to United Airlines. The Nixon palace is obviously positioning itself against a runaway investigation. I think they also suspect us. Nixon, as an old China lobby hand, knows all about the plane that blew up years ago when Chou En-Lai was supposed to be on board. So he understands. We know how to sabotage a plane—they don't. It poses a frightful question. If flight 553 to Chicago was buggered in order to get Dorothy Hunt, then she had to be holding on to no ordinary piece of information. You don't demolish twoscore civilians in order to terminate one lady unless she is in possession of an ulti-mate."

"What do you say is ultimate here?" I asked.

He smiled.

"I always," he said, "refer to my own values when trying to solve these matters. What would get me up for that? Well, I reasoned, I would embark on such egregious slaughter if the target, Mrs. Hunt, knows who was behind the Kennedy assassination, and I cannot afford to let that get out. Or two, Nixon or Kissinger is a KGB mole, and target has the evidence. Or three, elements among *us* have managed to dip into the Federal Reserve pond."

"What has the Federal Reserve to do with Dorothy Hunt?"

"Good Harry-boy, take a look at who else was in the Watergate Office Building back there in June 1972. The Federal Reserve kept an office on the seventh floor just above the Democratic National Committee layout. What makes you think McCord was bugging the Democrats? He could have been using the ceiling of the sixth floor to put a spike-mike into the floor of the seventh. McCord is not merely a religious monomaniac, you know. He happens to be talented.

"Try to conceive then of how long I've been brooding on these matters. It's years since Dorothy's crash. Yet I do keep coming back to the Federal Reserve. If a few of us were tapping into the seventh floor then, maybe we are at it still. Advance information on when the Federal Reserve is going to shift the interest rate is worth, conservatively, a good many billions." He leaned forward. He whispered into my ear. Two good words. "High Holies," he said. Then he turned his wheelchair toward me. "I have loads of stuff for you to do."

We shook hands on it. We would be rogue elephants together. As I suspected, he was persona non grata in many an office where he needed a look at the files, and I still had access. Under one ghost's name or another, I was helping on a few pro-CIA spy novels which were not as popular as they used to be—not the *pro*-CIA jobs, anyway—as well as overseeing one or two scholarly works, not to mention dashing off an occasional magazine piece on the new invidiousness of the old Commie threat. Will it help to explain that under various names I dealt with commercial publishers as agent, author, freelance editor, and even had my pseudonym on several books I did not write so much as midwife for others? Of course, I did a few jobs as full ghost myself. If a prominent evangelist took a trip to Eastern Europe or Moscow, intermediaries called on me afterward to boil the sap of his taped meanderings into homiletic American for the patriotic subscribers of *Reader's Digest*. I mock my published work, and that is fair. My serious work had cost me more.

Indeed, I was by now my own semicomic legend at Langley. For years, ever since my return from Vietnam, I had been working, first at Harlot's behest, then—after the rupture—on my own, over a monumental work on the KGB whose in-progress title was *The Imagination of the State*. Great hopes had been attached to this book early by Harlot, and by others. The job, however, was never honestly begun. Too monumental. Notes proliferated, yet over a decade and more the actual writing hardly progressed. I was bogged down in confusions, lack of desire, and too many petty literary jobs. A number of years ago, in secret with myself—I did not even tell Kittredge—I gave up *The Imagination of the State* in preference to the literary work I really wished to do, which was a detailed memoir about my life in the CIA. This book progressed apace. I had already, in the couple of days I could give to it each week, been able to describe my childhood,

my family, my education, my training, and my first real job—a stint
in Berlin, circa 1956. I had gone on to cover my station work in
Uruguay and an extended stint in Miami during that period when we
were having our undeclared war with Castro.

I thought my memoir was reading decently (even if I was my only
critic), but I was tempted to call it a novel. It was impermissibly
candid. I had included material on several of our assassination attempts. Some of that was public knowledge, but a good deal remained
privileged. I felt much at sea. This very long memoir, call it my novel,
had not yet taken me to Vietnam, nor back to my work in the Nixon
White House during the early seventies. Nor did it include my affair
with Kittredge and our marriage. I had navigated my way across half
of a large space (my past) and if I put it in that fashion, it is because
I did not see how I could publish the manuscript, this Alpha manuscript as I called it—working title: *The Game*. Of course, it did not
matter how it was christened. By the pledge I had taken on entering
the Agency, it was simply not publishable. The legal office of the
Agency would never permit this work to find a public audience.
Nonetheless, I wished *The Game* to shine in a bookstore window. I
had simple literary desires. I even descended into depression at fash-
ioning in secret so massive a work. Was I to be one of the first to create
a manuscript that would have to be passed from hand to hand as a
species of American *samizdat*? Could I take such a plunge? For if I did
not, I was misrepresenting myself to myself. Such self-deception may
be analogous to looking in the mirror and not meeting one's eyes.

In any event, since my colleagues in the Company knew no more
than that my work on the KGB had not gotten off the ground, I was
being treated (and CIA is good at this) as one of the *sad people*. It is
equal to being an unproductive child in a large and talented family.
Indeed, I was encouraged to work on semi-sabbaticals at home in
Maine for weeks, sometimes months, at a time. Yet, if I was thick with
resentment on the one hand, it was joy on the other to be rid of those
low Virginia suburbs. Of course, I still pretended to be taking work
papers for *The Imagination of the State* back to Maine, back to the Keep,
but, oh, how many trips I had made lately to Langley, how many odd
memos I had been hunting down for Harlot along with files I needed
for purported legitimate intellectual burrowings. Administratively
speaking, my need to know was too complex to keep tabs on. I had
been around so long that they preferred to ignore me. Seen as a
self-absorbed nest-builder, I was able to get copies of hot stuff out in

my briefcase along with reams of papers I was entitled to withdraw. It was worth one's limbs to be caught on some of the high-temperature sheets I passed on to Harlot. The irony is that I journeyed all the way from Maine to Washington to pick up the consecrated bread, but delivered it just fifteen miles down the line from Langley to where Harlot still steered himself around in that small Virginia farmhouse once shared with Kittredge.

Yes, we were on a mission; the High Holies. And I could just about lose my neck for that—which is to say, my job, my pension, my freedom. Jail was conceivably on the horizon. Yet, not for anything could I trust Harlot's sentiments toward me. All the same, I had signed up with him as if he were fate itself. There are more metastases in guilt than in cancer itself. I remember muttering in my throat at the power of such a premise even as I drove along in Maine.

O M E G A - 4

THE TRUTH IS THAT AFTER THE STRAIN OF ALL THIS ICY TRACTION, I WAS now handling the car with such unholy ease I had to wonder at the felicity of my condition. The road was a riverbed to my thoughts, and carried me down the dark highway between Bucksport and Ellsworth. As I passed through Sears, the houses looked as white under my headlights as the bones of Indians long dead.

On I went past shuttered Doughnut Dairy Queens and the last outpost of McDonald's. The shopping mall at Ellsworth went by my windshield like light from a shattered glass, the oil-soak of the empty parking lot gleaming in new steams and mists. At twelve miles an hour I traversed the short bridge from Tremont to the island of Mount Desert and entered a cloud again. Once more, I could not see past the silver droplets of fog that danced before me in the car beams. I would have to crawl the last ten miles along the road that goes by Prettymarsh where the centerline is worn away.

The western half of Mount Desert does not offer such fine towns as Northeast Harbor, Bar Harbor, or Seal Harbor; our western half is not notable. In daylight, the road winds through miles of second-growth trees and thicket; our nearby mountains are wooded and offer few lookouts. Our marshes and ponds are likely to be covered with acid-yellow algae. Our villages—Bass Harbor, Seal Cove—are hardworking, the hamlets are poor. Often, no more than four or five trailers, two or three frame houses, and a cinder-block post office will squat by the highway. The routes are not often favored by a sign.

All the same, knowing every curve, I was ready for the unmarked right turn onto the two-mile dirt road that leads to the wharf where our dinghy is stowed. On I drove, past lobstermen's front yards full of old tires and rusted iron of every description. Everyone's lights were out. I passed a house I never liked—it consisted of two trailers connected by a shed. A father, Gilley Butler—the man who brought the envelope to Kittredge earlier today—and his son, Wilbur Butler, lived on the premises with their mates, whelps, and assorted oafs, cold categories of description, but the Butlers would have been hung as poachers three centuries ago in England, and put in stocks right here. Now, I will not say more than that the father had had a series of savage arguments with my father, and the son, Wilbur, had done as well with Hugh Montague. In recent years, Wilbur had been a familiar to the police and the courts—he had belted an old woman around pretty badly when she discovered him robbing her trailer. I did not even know as I passed whether Wilbur was still in the state penitentiary. I had heard rumors at the post office that he would soon be free, and I did not enjoy the possibility. On those separate occasions when his vehicle used to meet mine on our mutual dirt road, he always looked at me with a squint of such quintessential hostility that I also spent an hour in the Bar Harbor Library on the genealogy of the Butlers. They were an old Mount Desert family, paupers and near-paupers for fifteen generations, and half of the children were dubiously christened. So I could not satisfy the suspicion that would connect them by illegitimate blood to Augustus Farr, but I did find, at least, the diary of Damon Butler, first mate of Farr's crew, the one who wrote of Farr's "practize of piracie."

In any event, each time I drove by those two trailers linked by their slatternly shed, I was prepared for unpleasantness. The pall of old drunken nights and heavy-handed yard fights with crotch-shots, stomping boots, old blood, and old puke, hovered around the broken lobster pots. Beer cans empty as clamshells abounded.

It was two long miles to reach the wharf. Our back roads are rutted. Along my camp track are furlongs of bramble by either ditch, and you pass many a feverish profusion of weeds that have sprouted over old battle trenches—in this case, the foundations dug for cheap homes whose walls never went up. The miasma of insufficient funds pervades the space. Bottle-green horseflies as large as bumblebees harass you in summer, and loathsome winged slugs imperil your hair should you jog. Through March, if the snow melts, the ground looks like a Bowery beggar sleeping it off. A heavy thaw introduces you to the mud of World War I. There were times when I could not traverse the two miles from the highway to the wharf without winching our jeep forward a hundred feet of cable at a time, but tonight the mud was still crusted, the ice, mixed with gravel, gave a base, and I went down that deserted route past small and desolate barrens. In one raw clearing, the skeleton of an old boat trailer lay rusted in two. Even in the dark, I knew these sights. I knew them well, and was glad to reach the last delta of lanes and tracks that went off to different camps on the backshore.

At our wharf, I pulled into the car shed, but before I even shut my motor I could hear the bay water taking its churn through the channel. The roar was louder than it had ever been. I could have been listening to the ongoing growl of an earthquake. It was then I took off my topcoat and left it in the car. It would hardly be automatic to row the dinghy across the channel tonight.

I am used to living with fear, I suffer such occupational stresses the way a good businessman worries about cash flow and his breaches of government regulations, his lawsuits, his health, and where he should be buried. No, it is worse for me. I live with a prime fear. My specific professional assignment invariably becomes my first fear. There is also, however, what Harlot used to call *Queen-for-a-Day*. It is the old heart-in-throat on the day of battle.

I was now full of Queen-for-a-Day. I did not wish to row from the back side of Mount Desert over to Doane's—only a couple of hundred feet, as I have stated, but how often had the water looked this bad? The wharf planks shook. Out there was no chop, but a horripilative race. If the dinghy overturned, I might not survive for a minute in such freezing water. Could I swim even twenty yards before my lungs locked? So, I debated whether to retrace my route to the state road and drive on to Southwest Harbor, where I could find a motel for the night. The thought was unsatisfactory, but the dinghy might be worse.

I did not debate it long. Since I wished to see Kittredge now, I had to try the channel. Bless Harlot. If I made it, I'd feel a lot better. And if I never got to shore at all, well, cleanse my soul of Chloe, I might be absolved between the oarlock and the ocean ground.

Into our dinghy I got. We have several that are aged, wooden, leaky, and as seaworthy as an old sailor, but stowed on the wharf right now was our newest, a fiberglass with walnut seats and shiny fittings. While it had its vices, including the tendency of all plastic shells to bob like a bubblehead, it reacted quickly to the oars. Sometimes you need a handsome fool to take you through a storm.

I slid the boat off the wharf into the quieter churn on the lee side, leaped in myself to face the bow, slammed oars into locks, and, in a flurry, set out to cross the seventy yards of the channel without careening more than three hundred yards downstream. More than that, and Doane Island would be lost, the dinghy loose in the reaches of Blue Hill Bay, an impossible prospect on this night.

Let me say it was the purest example of rowing with one oar, blade to port, that I had ever tried. The starboard oar was hardly more than an outrigger. I bucked up and down like a Yankee on a Houston rodeo machine. A full splat of ice water, heavy as the tail of a ten-pound fish, smacked me across the face in the middle of a stroke. I kept rowing with my left arm. One misjudged pull and we'd be running downstream through the middle of the channel. The water came at me in a froth, slamming its imprecations against that stupid plastic shell. Speak of getting wet—I was drenched. I had a first premonition of drowning. The bow slammed down into a trough and up a wall of water, which shattered on my face, gorged my throat. I coughed, I rowed, I would have prayed but I heard a fisherman singing in Greek. It was no Greek I knew. More fearsome than Gaelic were the sounds. They turned my head. They twisted the bow. For the second time this night, I went into a spin and lost my oars, which is to say, for one stroke I lost all sense of which blade to use. I had reversed my inner switches—some fatal flaw within!—and went hurtling downstream, hurtling is the word, stern first downstream, and shipping water. Mad strokes with the starboard oar, both oars, port oar again—I came out of the spin. I was within ten yards of the shore of Doane, and had pushed through the channel. I was now between two large offshore rocks.

In that placid pool I rested. I had five more yards of water to cross, and but thirty yards left to me of the island of Doane. I was freezing and my lungs burned like a grass fire, but it would take one more effort. Sitting between the rocks, backing on the oars to keep position, how I heard the wind! I was coming back to Kittredge, to my good grass widow Kittredge, and in my mind I saw her features twist. A fury was on her face. "Go away, Harry," said the wind.

I laid hands on the oars. "Doane is where I am supposed to be tonight," I told myself with all the simplicity (and unaccountable confusion) one brings to a ticket window when purchasing a long-arranged journey, and pushed off, took five good strokes with the port oar and two with both before the bow banged into a dark ledge, caromed off, and lifted onto a strand of stone and pebble. The sound of those small rocks grinding under the weight of the bow was as satisfying to my ears as the crunch of a bone for a dog. I was on my land. The gamble had been eminent and worthwhile. I felt no less bombarded than the Prince of Wales after a night in World War I trenches, and felt no less a prince. I was also heaving, trembling, and soaked to the bone.

I pulled the boat out, dragged it up beyond the last fretwork of seaweed into the tall grass at the southern point of Doane's. Given the wind, I not only turned the dinghy over, but cached the oars beneath and tied the painter to a tree. Then I staggered up Long Doane, the main trail on the island, all of four hundred yards long, in the direction of the Keep, which sat in the waist looking westward across Blue Hill Bay.

If the barrens on the other side of the channel are blighted and marsh-ridden, Doane has beauty. Our small forest is favored with the deep velvet of many a mossy cave. Dark green is our prevailing color in spring, summer, and fall; our trails are red needle. Stands of spruce tower over hackmatack while pitch pines bend to the solicitations of the wind. They pray to the seas with one limb and raise a sword with the other. They undulate to the flight of gulls and shake with the passage of the geese. They stand with the mist on the edge of shore.

Considering that I had come so near to foundering in the dark, this must seem a calm description of our island by day, but then, it is the silences of an island that prevail. I had no more than to step ashore and my senses began to quiet. I could see the island as it would appear to me in daylight, and knew each green chamber I approached, each porch of ledge I passed along the shore. The island was like a house. We felt as if we inhabited a dwelling within a dwelling. I am near to exaggeration, I know, but the Keep with no one but Kittredge and myself in winter would have been cavernously large if not for Doane's surrounding embrace. To inhabit a circle within a circle is to enter a spell.

What do I attempt to say? In our era of heartless condominiums,

Kittredge and I still lived like a bankrupt count and countess. As real estate, the Keep was much too vast for two. Onto the first building, a stone farmhouse built as a fort for Farr, my great-great-grandfather, Doane Hadlock Hubbard, attached a barn. Other generations added plumbing and partitions. The barn served as a camp for family overflow in summer, and then there was the year when my mother brought her lavish taste to the property and managed to dragoon my father into hiring an architect to design us a long, blonde-wood, much-glassed living room that cantilevered out from the second floor to arch over Blue Hill Bay. When finished, we looked across the water to the west and could glimpse other islands rising luminous in the dawn or slipping away like ships down the horizon into the nocturnal mist; we saw tropical sunsets in Maine. This modern room was so reminiscent of a small first-class lounge on a well-appointed ocean liner that we came to call it the Cunard.

I was then returning to a house whose parts were so separately named as the Cunard, the Camp, the Vault, and the Keep (which last title denoted the original farmhouse, but, to preserve confusion, was employed equally for the whole). We dwelt in the Old Keep—what else could one title it?—by winter, and inhabited everything but the Vault in summer when Kittredge's cousins arrived and their children, as well as my cousins and their wives with their children. Then the rites continued as before. In boyhood, I used to spend two weeks each summer with my father on Doane. One trial of passage in adolescence had been to muster enough family madness to jump off the balcony of the Cunard into the waters of Blue Hill Bay below. That was a time-consuming plunge of thirty-plus feet which gave you ample measure of the eternal distance down. It took forever to reach the water (otherwise equal to a second and a half). It was pure happiness, however, to come bubbling up to the ice-cold surface again. What virtue hummed in your blood as you swam to shore! My cousins and I were heroes to ourselves on the memorable first day when we could break out of terror and take the leap.

That had now become the first feat of summer for another generation of children. How full of sound was the house as they came racing up the stairs for one more go! In winter, however, while Kittredge and I might occasionally use the fireplace in the Cunard and work on warm days by the afternoon light that came through its full windows, we kept for the most part to the rooms of the Old Keep, just the two of us, living in such calm and silence that each chamber became steeped in its own mood and could not have been more particular if it had had a signature. Sometimes I felt as if I knew my rooms in the way a farmer knows his livestock. But for fear that few would understand, I might suggest that I spoke to them, and they replied to me. Leave it at such. I make the point only to insist, for those who would believe us, that Kittredge and I were not lonely.

I, however, was still outside, and aware suddenly of how close I was to frostbite. The heat of rowing ashore, the glow of navigating Long Doane in the dark, was gone. Abruptly, I was running. I had plunged with no warning from inner warmth to spasms of cold, and I came up to the main door of the Keep with such stiff hands, I could hardly mate the key to the lock.

Once inside, I looked about for Kittredge, but no one answered my call. I could not believe that she was sleeping in our bedroom instead of waiting up for my arrival. As disappointed as a boy who is refused a dance, I did not climb the stairs but went wandering down the hall to a mud room off the pantry. There, I stripped my wet gray flannel suit, and put on an old shirt and gardening pants with a faint but unmistakable whiff of sweat and fertilizer, a mixed odor I would hardly applaud, but maybe I was full of the need to pay wages for the pleasure taken tonight. Or did I not wish to see Kittredge in the clothes I wore while with Chloe?

I put down a tot of Bushmills Irish, which required taking three steps from the mud room to the private stores in the pantry, and my shivering eased. I threw in another shot, and began to feel like a workable manifest of myself. Famous words, uttered by legions of Americans, came to my lips: Let's get it over with.

The fortitude of the whiskey was watered by the stairs. The hall began to seem as long as my childhood memory of it. The door to our bedroom was closed. I tried the knob softly. The door was locked. A bolt went through my heart equal to that moment when the accused is found guilty in court. I rattled the knob. "Kittredge," I cried aloud.

I heard a rustle on the other side. Or did I merely suppose I had? My ears were confused by the wind. It was pounding and blathering on the storm windows outside, chattering, chewing like birds on a corpse. "Kittredge, for God's sake," I called out and had an image, immediate and inerasable, of Kittredge in pale crimson bleeding waters. The bathtub, where I had found her once, was still the same tub.

I was ready then to break the door, but her voice spoke at that moment. I heard clear articulated vowels that might come from a neat old lady who is altogether dotty. She sounded exactly like her mother.

"Oh, Harry," she said, "do wait a minute. Oh, dear man, don't come in. Not yet."

If my body had suffered chills tonight, now my mind suffered the cold. Something was certainly wrong.

"Darling," she said, "I just heard frightful news. I can hardly tell you." Was it the wind? I did not know whether it was the wind. There seemed some lament in the air.

"Harry," said Kittredge through the door, "Hugh is dead. They killed him, I fear. Gobby is dead."

O M E G A - 5

I CRIED OUT: "KITTREDGE, UNLOCK THE DOOR." ON THOSE OCCA-sional but startling nights when she would speak to her dead mother, she would croon a tuneless lullaby. Right now she was making some such sound.

In the silence that ensued, I tried to descend into the fact. Harlot was dead.

"Kittredge, I implore you. Please talk to me."

"Harry," her voice was undeniably strange, "can you leave me alone?"

"Alone?"

"For just a little while."

If my knock had caught my wife in bed with a lover, her panic could not have been more evident.

There was no lover, however, behind that door. Just the presence of his death. My heart followed this recognition. Death was as inti-mate to her fine senses as Chloe's rut on mine.

"I can't leave you here," I said, "unless you tell me more." When she did not reply, I said again, "Tell me!"

"Hugh washed ashore in the Chesapeake. Shot." She came close to halting, but went on. "Security says it's suicide. That's what they are going to announce."

"Who gave you this information?"

When she offered no answer, I knocked on the door again. "You have to let me in."

"I won't. Never now." She said this with such determination that

I wondered whether she had heard about Chloe? But when? It could only be after our phone call.

"I'm not sure," I said, "how safe it is for either of us to be alone."

"Safe enough." Another tone was entering her voice—the limitless anger that stirs at the obduracy of a mate.

"Kittredge, let me in. Do let me in."

"Do let me in. Oh, do," said Kittredge.

I backed off. Harlot's death still seemed far away. He had inhabited my psyche since I was sixteen. But now he was dead. In a day or two, *they* would say Harlot was a suicide. Someone inside had to have made the call to Kittredge.

I went back to the mud room, picked up the wet gray pinstripe off the hook, and carried it and my sopping blue oxford shirt and underwear to the laundry on the other side of the pantry. I did not know much about these matters but obviously was not without an inkling that our dryer might flagellate the suit. No matter. I could not live much longer in gardening clothes. It was like sniffing the shovel used for the grave. May I submit that I took another tot of Bushmills. It is hell not to know whether you mourn a dead friend or are relieved that an implacable and/or treacherous superior is gone.

In truth, however, I was not having any pronounced reaction. What would you do if you received incontrovertible news that the Lord had died? You might continue making your breakfast. In ten weeks, or ten years, the edge of this knowledge could be as sharp as a knife, but now I was waiting for my suit, listening to its slap-tap going around in the dryer. Outside, in the open shed, some small animal, a raccoon perhaps, fresh from hibernation, was rattling the cans. The drip of the laundry sink came down, drop for drop. In the corner, undone by damp, a little plaster had crumbled to the floor. That dust, sad and pleasureless, caused me to think of Harlot's remains. Would he be cremated? Had he given instructions? Other unanswerable questions rose one by one, and fell in unison with the water tap.

I was trying to hold off the idea that I was in trouble. I did not know if my warning system had collapsed, but I did not have a sense that anyone was traveling toward me. Of course, how could anyone cross the channel tonight? Thinking this, I had to recognize my wits were asleep. Despite the chop, a good power boat would have no undue trouble reaching here from Bartlett's Island or Seal Cove.

A cobweb in the near corner of the laundry room began to claim my attention. On the spider's back was a species of yellow face, or at least some small markings like eye sockets, a spine of line for the nose, something close to a mouth and chin. I meditated upon these cosmic clues like a drunk who regards the wonders of a bashed-up fingernail while galaxies of the night's failure wheel about.

My suit had to be ready. Ready or not—I think the Bushmills was having its untoward effect—I opened the dryer door, pulled out shirt, underwear, vest, jacket and pants, all more muddled by now than fruit in an Old-Fashioned, and got dressed.

It was at this moment that my hand went up to my breast pocket. Only my desire to account for all the events of this night can oblige me to confess the next detail. My passport—soaked, doubtless, in the crossing of the channel—had been left in my breast pocket while the suit was being flung about in the dryer. Now its official pages, as I soon discovered, were all puffed up. I had a biscuit for a document. The print was barely visible. What a stupidity! I had been carrying this particular passport ever since I commenced the High Holies. Harlot had obtained it for me to use abroad should I have to decamp on short notice. William Holding Libby was the sweet alias Montague had bestowed—a god-awful name, but no matter. Should all go wrong, it was my trapdoor. I kept it on me. Now, standing on the bare wood floor of the laundry, wearing my still damp and battered suit, I seemed incapable of attaching myself to the immediate situation. That is detachment! I was in some exotic realm where the passage of time does not bring you back to any of your responsibilities.

All the same, I wasn't certain if I cared to knock on my bedroom door, no, not to be rejected again. Yet what other course was open? I felt no better and perhaps no worse than a man who is being asked by a superior to justify an outrageous expense account. How silent was the house as I climbed the stairs.

Our bedroom door was slightly ajar. Not opened, but cracked. Had Kittredge gone to look for me? It did not seem probable. More likely, she had had a small change of heart, enough to open the bolt. Of course, that did not mean I was welcome.

Before I stepped into the room, I could hear her speaking. I did not have to make out the words to know by her tone, loud and a bit abstract, as if addressing a deaf person, that she was talking to the wall. How I hoped it was her mother, hoped for it so devoutly I visualized Maisie Minot Gardiner before me with her white hair, strong white teeth, and the parrot's voice that gracious ladies often have (as if they would not dream of using a phrase that had not been uttered first by some more appropriate person—the tones coming out of Eleanor Roosevelt's throat were the first, perhaps, to draw attention to this phenomenon).

Kittredge's mother had eyes like the purple-blue of the hybrids that grew in her garden. I knew the names of wildflowers, but Maisie bothered only with brand-new species. She grew the tallest flowers, super-zinnias, four and five feet high and fabulously bright. If you put a Bonnard on an easel in her garden, the palette would have been dominated by Maisie's blooms. On warm days those blossoms swayed to their own mood, much like Maisie. She was notoriously perky in her opinions. "Harry, don't be a fool about the French," she could say, "they are simply not to be trusted."

Yes, I prayed Kittredge was speaking to Maisie, but knew she was not.

"I will," I now heard my wife say, "follow you nowhere."

The door opened at my touch. It was exactly as I expected. That is to say, it was a good deal worse than my hopes. Kittredge sat in a chair facing the wall. She wore a white nightgown, no whiter than her skin, which made her look both nude and draped at once. Her hair had never seemed darker or more lustrous, and her eyes were no longer full of mist. They glowed. It is not common for blue eyes to glow in a modestly lit bedroom, but I could have sworn that the light came from within. She was certainly oblivious to me.

"Hugh, I warned you," she said aloud. "I prayed for you. Now I am free. I will not accompany you out of this house."

On that occasion, not long after we were married, when I first heard her talking to her mother, I made the mistake of telephoning from Doane's all the way to McLean, Virginia, where a psychiatrist, on CIA contract, kept his office. Kittredge had come close to not forgiving me. Ignore the damage done to her career (and mine) now that such an episode had been implanted in her file; this was the least of my error. What she could not forgive was the simple lack of respect. "I love my mother," she said to me, "and it's a grace that I am able to talk to her. Can't you see? That was an overbearing thing to do—phone a doctor. Harry, I will think we are not suited for one another if you try such a barbarism again. You were calling my gift an infirmity."

She did not have to repeat herself around me. I did my best to mend the broken link. I had, after all, spoken to the psychiatrist but once. When he called again, on follow-up, I implied that Kittredge and I had gotten very drunk together—a highly uncharacteristic state of affairs for us, I said, and her acts under intoxication had not quite squared with mine. That was how I put it, and added, "After all, Doctor, a person's got a right to veer off their bearings by a quadrant or so when a parent dies."

"Call it a quart or so," he said, and we both made a point of laughing, first in harmony, then in counterpoint. Why is phony laughter musically more structured than the real stuff?

Career loss for my wife was limited to a notation in her 201 file: *Psychiatric aid solicited on May 19, 1975.* Given the number of alcoholics, divorcées, and discovered homosexuals among us (no worse, I would warrant, than in a high-pressure corporation), I hoped the listing would not do real damage. I knew, however, that the slopes were getting slippery. Our marriage had been an in-house scandal comparable to a general's wife running away with a major.

All of this may help to explain why I now walked around Kittredge's chair as if I circumnavigated a holy man. Be certain, I did not fetch water to wash her face, nor chafe her feet, nor think to shake her, or even touch her. With all the habits of a life trained to take hold of things, there was nothing to do but sit down.

She remained still for a long time. Then she began to nod her head. She said to the wall, "Gobby, you never could bring yourself to admit the truth to a soul. But you can tell me. If you think it's important, darling, perhaps you should."

It was like a conversation on a roof when someone is ready to jump and the police look to dissuade him. I suspect the dialogue on such occasions comes to seem natural. Kittredge spoke to the wall as if, no question, Harlot was there. I confess it soon began to seem less exceptional to me. Our bedroom, too ascetic for my taste, too much like an upstairs chamber in a good New England inn—even the white flounces on the counterpane were professionally chaste—was put in no disarray by the intensity of Kittredge's words. When she ceased speaking, the room took up its white pervasive silence.

"Harry, get the fuck out, will you?"

Through our years together, she rarely used the word. But then I was not certain she had spoken. Could that have been Harlot's voice issuing from her larynx?

Kittredge arched forward in her chair. "You are covered with seaweed," she said aloud. "Oh, Gobby, pull it off. You look like you're wearing a wig." She laughed loudly in what was nearly a man's voice, and then as the laugh continued, the tone became unmistakably hearty. Some men laugh as if even the embers in a fireplace, and the wrapper leaves of a good Havana, are part of the splendid service that surrounds them. My God, I thought, she is laughing just like my father. Then her features took on an expression to remind me of Allen Dulles, equally as departed as my father.

Once in Vietnam, after a carouse through the *Department Store* (our name for the largest brothel in Saigon), I ended in a hotel room with a young and tiny Vietnamese prostitute who procured me opium. I smoked it with a great sense of sin, and vomited up my dinner with a whole sense of redemption. Afterward, the peace of the pipe came to me, and I began to hallucinate. The face of the whore became the face of my mother, and then the face of Kittredge whom I was in love with from afar. After a while, I was able to turn the features of this Vietnamese prostitute into any woman I chose.

In our bedroom, however, I could not select the face I wished to see next, nor did I have any happy confidence that I was afloat on misty clouds of controllable hallucination. Rather, each set of features came forth as if someone was there to work her flesh. Upon Kittredge's delicate upper lip appeared to sprout the rough pepper-and-salt brush of Harlot's mustache. His wire-rimmed spectacles were on her nose, her full head of hair became his half-bald dome, and he stared at me. Next, he spoke. It came through Kittredge's mouth, but it could as well have been his voice. "You'll find out, Harry. She's a consummate liar."

The mustache faded with the spectacles. Her mane of black hair belonged to her again. Kittredge began to weep.

"Gobby, take me with you. I'm lonely here." Her grief soon passed. Like a child declaring a quick end to the previous mood, a new expression moved over her features, a leer. It was the private look that only Chloe could offer, her come-into-my-domain leer. You would not see that turn on Chloe's mouth until you were naked against her and the fiend was parting the insulations of the flesh; the baubles were ready to gleam. Released at last!

I was feeling odd impulses. To be walking on the avenue and feel an abrupt inclination to go down a side street is not an uncommon impulse. Presumably it comes from oneself. Here, I had no doubt. The suggestions coming to me were not my own. I was like an iron filing skittering about on a plate as magnets are shifted beneath. Pow-

erful as gods are those magnets. Whatever compulsion delivered me
periodically to the door of Chloe's trailer was now on the prowl for
my wife. A wash of lust, pure as wild goat, came into my loins. The
screw-grease heats reserved for Chloe were over me again. I cannot
bear to confess my next thought. Colder than Harlot was my heart:
I wanted to bring Kittredge to the Vault.

But I had invoked Harlot's name. That gave up the game. I broke
into a sweat. Was it Harlot who was coaxing me toward the Vault?

Leaving Kittredge in her chair, I went down to the first floor of
the Keep. There I lit the fire in our den. It was the warmest room we
had. When other lights were out, and the fire was well along, the
stained wood of the old barn planks enriched the walls with the color
of bourbon and brandy. One could summon the illusion that one's
marriage and profession were not without their liaison to the universal
hearth.

Now, however, my thoughts were as livid as the obsessions of an
insomniac. I sprawled into an old leather chair and studied the fire. I
did my best to empty my mind. I had gifts for meditation; techniques,
as you may suspect, to restore detachment. I needed peace in the way
an exhausted general needs sleep. After twenty minutes of seeking to
compose myself, I received instead the poor coin of the substitute:
apathy.

It was at this moment that the telephone on the end table began
to ring. That was not common at this hour. Ten years ago, calls
sometimes came from Langley in the middle of the night, but not
lately. At this moment, however, what impressed me most was my
quiet expectation that the phone was going to ring. Then it did.

O M E G A - 6

I KNEW THE VOICE BEFORE I COULD UTTER THE NAME. "CHLOE," I SAID.

"I hate to call you like this," she began. A full amateur's pause
followed, as if only now had it even occurred to her—"Can we talk?"
she asked.

Was guilt still skewing my senses? I had the notion that Kittredge
was stirring in the bedroom. "Yes, we can talk," I said. But my voice
was low enough to assure her we could not.

"I've got to see you. I wanted to call you hours ago, but I didn't know if it was okay."

"How is the weather back in Bath?" I make no excuse for saying this. I might have said anything to purchase a moment. Then, I added, "Aren't the roads bad?"

"My four-wheel-drive happens to be a big fat lemon on the ice, but it will be all right. Harry," she said, "something has happened. I've got to see you. Tonight."

"Well," I said, "there's nothing open now."

"I want to come to your place."

"Yes," I said. "You're certainly welcome, but you could never find it."

"Oh," she said, "I know your place. I know the road. I lived near Doane one winter."

"You did?"

"Sure," she said, "I was shacked up for a while with Wilbur Butler. I lived in the double trailer down the highway."

I saw those car carcasses rusting in the front yard.

"How is it I never had a sight of you then?"

"I just lived with Wilbur for a couple of months. He never let me out of bed. I used to watch through the window when you drove by. 'Boy, he's cute,' I used to say to Wilbur. Did he get to hate you!"

I thought again of the malevolence in Wilbur's eye when we passed on the road. "I guess he did," I answered. I could hear her breathing. "Chloe," I said, "it is not at all a good idea to come here tonight."

"You're spinning your wheels," Chloe said. Her voice showed the same anger she brought to carnal junction. "Now!" she always said at such times. "Harder, you son of a bitch! Harder!" Yes, the echoes were there. "Harry, it's got to be tonight," she said.

"Why? Why tonight?"

"You're not safe." She paused. "I'm not safe," she said. She paused again. "Have they gone through your house?" she asked.

"No."

"They went through mine."

"What?"

"While I was out having that last drink with you. They went through every last thing in the trailer. They cut open the stuffing in the furniture. They broke into my picture frames. They took apart my gas stove. They slit my mattress. They dumped the bureau drawers."

She began to cry. She cried like a strong woman who has just received news that a relative was maimed in an accident. "Harry, I sat there for an hour. Then I went through what I own. I was prepared for the worst, but they didn't steal a thing. They even put my costume jewelry in a neat pile on the bed. And my bikini panties. And my red and black bra. Right next to it, what do you think? They laid out one roach. I toked a little marijuana last New Year's Eve and hid the roach at the bottom of my drawer. They laid it right next to my costume jewelry. I hate them," she said.

"*Them?*"

"If it had been thieves, they would have taken my TV, my microwave, my stereo, my clock-radio, my Winchester with the walnut-burl stock, my chain saw. These have to be cops." She thought about it. "Special cops." She asked, "Harry, what were they looking for?"

"I don't know."

"Is it connected with you?"

"I don't know that either."

"What kind of work you do?"

"I told you. I write and edit."

"Harry, come on. I'm not dumb." She dropped her voice. "Are you in secret work?"

"Not at all."

This mistruth set her weeping again. I felt one pang of pure sympathy. Chloe's things poked and grabbed, tossed about; here was I lying to her.

"Wilbur's father, Gilley, used to say, 'The Hubbard family may be in the CIA, but that don't make them better than you or me.' If he was drunk, he would say that. Every time you drove by."

It had never occurred to me that our Maine neighbors had any notion of what we did. "I can't talk about it, Chloe."

Now her voice began to rise. "Do you have any understanding of me at all, or am I just one more suck-and-fuck?" Yes, her voice was on the rise.

"The mark of how much I feel for you," I said as slowly as I could, "is that I love my wife, do you understand, I do love her, yet I still see you."

"That's elegant," she said. "I'll keep the change."

Are not all such conversations the same? We went on for five more minutes, and then another five, before I could hang up, and when I took my hand from the phone, I was full of misery. Any shield of detachment I had managed to fashion about my double life had been smashed by the phone call. It was now crucial to go back to our bedroom, to Kittredge, and I suffered this thought with so much intensity that I had to wonder if something I could not yet name had come near, so near that I raced up the stairs by twos and threes to the upstairs hall. Outside our bedroom, however, my will turned in on itself, and I began to feel as weak as a man sitting up with a fever. I even had one of those fantasies that appear to rise from our limbs themselves when they are aching with illness but curiously happy. I was able to conceive of Kittredge asleep in her bed. She would be in deep slumber—so went my thought—and I would ensconce myself in a chair and watch over her. With all the care incumbent on maintaining such an image, I took the last steps to our bedroom door, looked in, and indeed she was asleep even as I had conceived. What relief to possess this much of my wife; her unspeaking presence was superior to the loneliness of being without her. Could I take that as a sign? For how many years had no more than the sight of her freckled forearm holding a tennis racquet been my passport to happiness?

I stared at her as she lay on the bed, and enjoyed the first sense of relief since I had come home, as if in truth I was again virtuous. I loved her again, loved her as I had on the first day, no, not on the first day of our affair, but in the hour I saved her life.

That was the most notable achievement of my life. During a bad day, I would wonder if it was the only achievement. I had, when all was said, a simple notion of grace. I never saw love as luck, as that gift from the gods which put everything else in place, and allowed you to succeed. No, I saw love as a reward. One could find it only after one's virtue, or one's courage, or self-sacrifice, or generosity, or loss, had succeeded in stirring the power of creation. Therefore, if I felt love now, I might not be wholly unredeemed. The apathy I had suffered before was but a clue to the great fatigue of my soul. I was not a burnt-out case so much as a wholly belabored one, my own morphine for holding off loss. I was not, however, void of grace, no, not if my love for Kittredge still lived in that rose arbor where sorrow rises from the heart.

I dimmed the lights so she could sleep, and sat beside her bed in the near dark. How long I was there I cannot say—a few minutes or was it more?—but a tapping on our picture window intruded at last on the simple gathering of my peace, and I looked over at the smallest and most astonishing sight. A white moth, its spread no more than the width of two fingers, was fluttering against the pane. Had I ever seen a moth outdoors before on a March night? Its wings on the other side of the glass were as white as Melville's whale.

I crossed to the desk, picked up a flashlight, turned it on, and held it against the glass. The moth attached itself to the other side of the pane as though to absorb the small warmth offered by the bulb. I looked at its trembling wings with the respect one gives a true creature, whatever the size. Its black pupils, each comparable in diameter to the head of a pin, looked back at me with the same bulging intensity of expression one finds in the eyes of a deer or a lapdog, yes, I could have sworn the moth was staring back at me, creature to creature.

I slid my flashlight along the picture window and the moth followed the light. When I came to a casement that I could open, I hesitated. The prize was a moth, after all, not a butterfly. Like a maggot was its white body, and its antennae were not filaments, but brushes. I let it in all the same. There was such entreaty in that beating of wings.

Once inside, like a bird studying the place where it will alight, it circumnavigated the room before descending into a fold of Kittredge's pillow.

I was about to go back to my chair, but had the impulse to place my flashlight against the window again, and by the movement of its beam along the ground, there out in that silvery penumbra between the last of the light and the dark of the woods, I saw nothing less than the figure of a man. He darted so quickly behind a tree, however, that I, in my turn, stepped back quickly, and turned off the flash.

O M E G A - 7

IT WAS PECULIAR. THERE WAS AN UNHOLY EXHILARATION ABOUT IT. IF I had felt oppressed for the last hour by the conviction that I was being watched, this much confirmation was relief: I began to gulp in whole swallows of breath as if a stocking had been removed from my head. Indeed, I was close to happy. I was also on the edge of unruly panic.

In childhood I had always thought of myself as the feckless son of a very brave man, and I could tell the story of my life by the attempts I have made to climb out of the pit. If you think of yourself as a

coward, the rashest course usually proves to be wise. My father's
Luger, captured by him during OSS days, and in his will bequeathed
to me, was in a case in my closet. I could get it out and do a little
reconnoitering.

I rebelled. I was hardly prepared to go into the woods. I would
have to, yes, get ready. An occupation so exorbitantly professional as
mine obviously develops a few personal powers even when one is,
oneself, far from extraordinary. On occasion, I could force my mind
into preparing for a near impossible situation. Of course, this ability
was a curiously exaggerated faculty. One could also have been a
contest winner on one of those television shows where you had to
find the answer to a riddle while hell was popping forth on the stage
and the audience roared. To clear my mind and focus my will, I
confess that I liked to use a certain text from the Book of Common
Prayer.

Let me admit that the words were hardly said in prayer. If I now
repeated to myself the Collect for Fridays—*Lord Jesus Christ, by your
death you took away the sting of death: grant to us your servants so to follow
in faith where you have led the way, that we may at length fall asleep peacefully
in you*—I was trying not to shrive myself for battle so much as to return
my agitations to the deep. Repeating this prayer, if need be, ten times,
my prep school years would always appear before me, and the fatal-
drowse-in-chapel, as we used to call it at St. Matthew's, would also
return. I would "fall asleep peacefully" in someone, or in something,
and awaken, after a five- or ten-second cut-out, to face in the direction my mind wished to follow. Every man to his own mnemonic! I
came out of these ten seconds with the recognition that I must not sit
beside Kittredge and keep guard until dawn. It might be prudent to
sit in this chair and take care of my life, but it would lose my love.
That is an outrageously romantic equation, yet I saw it as the logic of
love—which usually reduces itself to a single equation. Love is outrageous. One must endanger oneself to preserve it—a likely reason why
so few people stay in love. I was *obliged* to discover who the prowler
might be.

I removed my father's Luger from its case and slipped a loaded
9mm magazine out of the side pocket, inserted the clip into the
handle, drew back the slide, snapped it forward, heard the round go
home to the breech. To the gun lover, that is a satisfying sound (and
I was a gun lover at this moment). Next, I stepped to our bedroom

door, opened it, locked it, pocketed the key, and, weapon in hand, strolled down the hall.

My father used to say that the Luger was Germany's most dependable contribution to gracious living. In profile, his captured Luger is as handsome as Sherlock Holmes, and its heft in one's palm can make you feel like a good shot in much the way a fine horse will offer suggestions to your seat that you may yet become a good rider. I felt ready.

The Keep is a house with seven doors, a mark, we often say, of the luck it is ready to bestow. We have a front door on the old house, and a back one, as well as a side entrance for the Cunard (which gives on a stairway to the beach at low tide), a door at each end of the Camp, plus the pantry exit to the woodshed and a cellar hatch.

I took the pantry door. There was no illumination from nearby windows, and the wind was loud enough, I figured, to overpower any grating of the hinges or the bolt. So it proved. I emerged with no loud announcement.

Outside, the darkness was massive, a cavern. I took comfort that the ground was wet, my steps were stilled. I had not felt so alive (in just this way) since a sojourn near to fifteen years ago in Vietnam—in truth, I had not taken ten silent steps before I was back to whatever I learned on the few patrols where I went along with a platoon on a search-and-destroy. There is much to be said for feeling alert in one's toes and fingertips, in one's eyes, nostrils, ears, even to the taste of the air on one's tongue.

Yet, in the time I spent emerging from the open end of the shed, and slipping into the woods, it was evident that I was as likely to bump into some unknown party on guard as to slip up unheard on whoever might be observing our house. The night, as I say, was black, and the wind was strong. When it blew at its best, I could take ten quick strides and never hear my steps on the wet pine carpet, nor, for that matter, the whipping of a branch. So I saw soon enough that to learn anything, I would have to circle the house at a distance, then, every forty or fifty paces, work back to the lights. If sufficiently careful, I ought to be able to come up on anyone from behind, assuming, that is, that *they* were stationed in place. Or were they prowling like me? Did I have to watch my back? I traveled in circles more ways than one.

I must have been out for a full twenty minutes before I came across the first guard. Sitting on a stump was a man in a poncho with a walkie-talkie in his hand. I saw him from fifty feet away, his attention fixed on my front door, his body revealed in silhouette by the light above our entry, and his posture attentive, although not enormously so, no different from a hunter who has been waiting in a blind for a deer. By the posture of his body, I suspected that his assignment was to report on his walkie-talkie so soon as anyone was sighted.

I passed through a moment when I was tempted to shoot him. Raising the Luger, I lined up the dark object of his head, dramatically back-lit in my front sight, and knew I could do it—legally and spiritually. I can never remember feeling so sure of myself with a handgun; in truth, it was fifteen years since I had fired one in anger and that had been in Vietnam in the middle of a sudden and ferocious firefight where everyone was shooting off all they had, and I, as unbalanced and blind as any grunt on war fever, emptied a .357 Magnum into a bush whose looks I did not like, although in contrast to the war movies I had seen, no Oriental with a dazed look tumbled out of the foliage, rather the bush was blasted away. Magnum force!

That had been combat mania laced with considerable funk (and pot!) and connected to little else in my life, but this impulse now came from the center of myself as cold and implacable as the desire to carry Kittredge down to the Vault. I felt—in a word—evil, and enjoyed it, and took pride in the way my hand did not quiver. I had never held a pistol as steadily in training. Yet I also knew it would not be wise to shoot him. He had to be part of a team. I would explode a situation I did not yet comprehend. Besides, the situation did not feel dangerous, not in these familiar woods, not now. The night seemed pendant, as if both of us, guard and myself, were waiting for a further event.

So I stepped back from that man with his walkie-talkie, and continued my tour around the house. I felt balanced, cool, dangerous to others, and attuned to the wet aromatic of the evergreens about me. In such a splendid state, I must have gone fifty paces around the larger perimeter I had drawn for myself before stealing in again toward the hub, but this time saw no one near the Camp, not by either door. On the next approach, however, moving in toward the Cunard where the beach stairs descended to the rock shelf, I could detect a bit of movement that seemed to belong more to a man than a shrub. Then I heard a poncho flap. The sound was as loud as a mainsail catching the wind. Another guard.

I could hardly discern him. He was but a darkness within other darkness. The Cunard, as described, projected in cantilever above the

house to give a view of Blue Hill Bay. I was hidden at this moment
in the inky invisibility of the rock shelf beneath the cantilever. To go
forward could reveal me. I retreated therefore. I was hardly out from
underneath, however, before a light went on in the long living room
of the Cunard, and from my angle, I could look up through our
picture window to see the head and shoulders of a man I knew but
could not yet name. I could swear all the same that he was good
Langley kin. Yes, this was one of *us*.

I returned to the woodshed, keeping my distance from the first
guard. I was not in any particular fear for Kittredge. The stranger in
the Cunard—familiar to me in that one quick look—had not appeared
threatening so much as gravely concerned. Indeed, I was sufficiently
sure of this perception to put the Luger in the drawer of an old
cupboard in the pantry, as though everything would be set needlessly
askew if I walked forward, gun in hand. The reconnaissance I had just
undertaken in the woods, while of mixed returns for my ego (since it
had been good to do it, but once done, of limited value), had succeeded nonetheless in honoring my anxiety. I had determined who
the visitor was—the glimpse of his face had come into focus. He was
a high official from the Office of Security, and I knew him. I knew
him well. Arnie Rosen. Reed Arnold Rosen. Now, in the time I had
consumed in coming back to the house, he had moved from the
Cunard to the den, and it was there that I came in on him sitting in
my favorite chair, smoking a pipe. Reed Arnold Rosen, once Arnie,
then Ned, now *Reed* these days to friends and coworkers. I qualified,
probably, as both. Arnie Rosen and I had gone through training
together at the Farm, and seen much of each other soon after as
assistants to Harlot. Was it twenty-seven years ago? Yes, I knew Reed
and he knew me. It was just that by the measure of our careers, he had
prospered more than myself.

All the same, I had an unholy impulse to use the old nickname,
Arnie.

"Hello, Reed," I said.

"Harry, you're looking fit."

I knew I was not appearing fit in his eyes. "I'm a mess," I said,
"but then it's wet in the boondocks."

He nodded. "I was out a little earlier." His three-piece suit hardly
showed it—English worsted and a London tailor had taken him equably through the damp.

If human beings had pedigrees as finely nurtured as dogs, our best people (whether born as Scotch-Irish, Ukrainian, Italian, or Lithuanian) would have put the ethnicity behind—we look to be one breed. We are what our vocational environment has made us: American Intelligence. It grated on me a little that I, who belonged to a pretty good kennel, had, at this point, with my professional life awash (not to dwell on my muddied clothes), less of the look than Rosen. His neat, medium-sized body and close-cropped gray hair, short sharp nose, tight upper lip (which always looked as if it were being squeezed against his capped front teeth), even his silver-rimmed eyeglasses fit the gray suit he was wearing about the way a foxglove sits in the sconces of its stalk.

All the same, I was glad to see him. To find that my inquisitor (whom I must have been awaiting for months) was as civilized a top cop as old Ned Rosen, allowed me to feel—there is no end to the logic of these organizational matters—back in the Company again.

"It was a bit of a jaunt to get to your woods," he said.

How he had improved since the old days. When we trained together, Rosen, who had been Phi Beta Kappa at Columbia, Mensa, et cetera, had also been—in a word—adenoidal. His nasal intelligence kept boring forward. He was a fellow to be rejected by in-groups before they even formed.

Now, he was married to a nice gray Episcopalian lady with whom, in fact, I had once had a memorable date in Montevideo, and he had obviously learned a lot from her. The nasality had metamorphosed into the resonance of a high government official.

"Yes," he said, "you look damp, and I'm not dry."

Enough of the warm-up, however.

"Did you telephone Kittredge tonight?" I asked.

He took his pause, more in decorum than caution. "About Hugh Montague?"

"Yes."

"Harry, I didn't telephone her. I brought the news."

"When?"

"A while ago."

He must have arrived not long after I had made my call from the Bell Telephone icebox on the coast road. So he had been here when I came back. His walkie-talkie people had heard me approaching through the woods, had heard, conceivably, how my teeth were chattering with cold as I tried to find the key for my door. They would have reported this to the small button he kept in his ear.

I got up to stir the fire and was able to verify that, yes, in his right ear was a buff-colored ear-piece.

"What have you been doing since you arrived?" I asked.

"Trying to think."

"Where were you doing this?"

"Well, for the most part—in one of the guest bedrooms." He took a puff on his pipe.

"Are those your ladies-in-waiting outside?"

"One would hope so."

"I counted two."

"In fact," said Reed, "there are three of us out there."

"All for me?"

"Harry, it's a complicated business."

"Why don't you invite them in?" I asked. "We have other guest rooms."

He shook his head. "My men," he said, "are prepared to wait."

"Expecting more people?"

"Harry, let's not play ping-pong. I have to discuss a situation which is *out of hand*."

That meant no one at Langley had a clue what to do next.

The tour I had made, Luger in fist, was still working like a spansule, calming to anxiety. I felt as if my wits had returned. Clear and overt danger was the obvious prescription for my spiritual malformations.

"Ned," I asked, "would you like a drink?"

"Do you keep Glenlivet?"

"We do."

He chose to go on about its merits. That was annoying. I did not need to hear any of the palaver he had picked up while motoring about Scotland and its distilleries one summer vacation with his gray Scotch bride. Withdrawing a bottle from the den cupboard, I served our Glenlivet neat—screw him if after all that praise he secretly wanted ice. Then I said, "Why are you here?"

I could see he wanted to enjoy the fireplace and the Scotch a little longer.

"Yes," he said, "we have to get to it."

"I'm honored that they sent you," I told him.

"I may be dishonored in the morning," he replied. "This trip is on me."

"Not authorized?"

"Not altogether. You see, I wanted to arrive quickly."

"Well," I said, "we won't be playing ping-pong, will we?"

It was out of character for him not to cover his delicate behind; no one knew better than Rosen that we can be the most paper-haunted bureaucracy of them all. So there are times when we pay a lot of attention to getting the right paper. We feel happier when unorthodox actions can be traced to a piece of the stuff. If, from time to time, we are obliged to move without a program, statute, directive, memo, or presidential finding, it is a naked feeling. Rosen had no paper.

"I hope you are prepared to get into it," he said.

"You can start up," I said.

As a way of assent, he gave a grin. Since he was keeping his pipe in his mouth, it resulted in a grimace. "Did Kittredge," he inquired, "provide any details about what she heard vis-à-vis Harlot?"

"I'm afraid my wife was not coherent."

"Harlot," said Rosen, "left his house three days ago, went out alone in his boat, which, as you may know, was not uncharacteristic of him. He was proud of his ability to skipper that boat solo, physical disability and all. But he did not return. This morning, the Coast Guard found the craft drifting, checked its registration, and called us. Would you believe it? The boat papers listed the Langley personnel office extension as the telephone number to ring for next of kin! Meanwhile, the body of a man in a considerable state of disrepair washed up on a mudflat in Chesapeake Bay. Coast Guard was notified, and soon after my office was on the scene. Just before lunch today."

"I understand you're calling it a suicide."

"We will probably call it that. Hopefully, the press could decide that's worth no more than an obituary."

"Is it murder?"

"Can't say. Not yet."

"How did you get here?" I asked. "Did you fly to Bar Harbor Airport?"

"In my plane. I have added a pilot's license to my small assortment of virtues."

"There's always something new to learn about you, Reed."

My praise, you would think, was edged, but he couldn't keep from showing his pleasure. Once after Richard Helms had rescued a few of Hugh Montague's less savory chestnuts from a congressional inquiry, Harlot, in recognition of the debt, was quick to offer the Director a large compliment. "You, Dick," Harlot had said, "are so aptly named. One small craft after another to skipper through the fearful breeze." That was a little thick, I thought, but Helms, who looked as much to the point as an ice pick, and was certainly on guard around Harlot, still couldn't keep from beaming at such homage to his now masterly moniker. Later, Harlot remarked, "Depend on it, Harry, the vanity of the high officeholder never bottoms out."

Ergo, I had gone my way to put Rosen on automatic feed. I was thinking to catch him while he was munching.

"As you were flying up here," I inquired, "you didn't stop off in Bath, Maine, did you?"

He went so far as to take his pipe out of his mouth. "Most certainly not." He took his pause. "I must say," he added, "the thought occurred to me. We *are* on to your friend Chloe."

"Was it the FBI who paid her a visit tonight?"

"Not by way of *us*."

"How about the DEA?"

"Ditto. I could swear."

"Who, then, ransacked her trailer?"

"What?" He seemed genuinely surprised.

"She called me. In panic. By her description, it was a thoroughgoing, insulting, highly professional job."

"I'm at a loss."

"Why are you interested in her?" I asked.

"I don't know that I am. Is she relevant?"

"Ned, if we are to speak of my so-called *friend Chloe*, work with the facts. I happen to have coffee with her sometimes when I pass through Bath. And Chloe and I have no carnal knowledge of one another. Not at all. But, Ned, I'm desirous to know"—yes, the Glenlivet (after the Bushmills, after the Luger) was having an unanticipated effect; the good Scotch was making me testy—"yes, tell me, pal, what the hell has Chloe got to do with anything? She's just a waitress."

"Maybe yes, maybe no."

I was coming around the buoy a bit late. "Did you *opera lovers* tap the phone here in this den? I did have a phone call from her tonight. So what?"

He held up his hand. I realized I was too angry. Was guilt getting into my voice? "Ease off, Harry," he said, "ease off. Presumably your phone call with Chloe is on tape one place or another. I just didn't have the means to tap into you directly. Nor," he added, "the desire. I didn't come here to strap you to the table and whip out the procto-scope."

"Although you wouldn't mind a conversation in depth."

"I'd like to go equal to equal."

"Do you know what is in the back of my mind right now?" I asked.

"The High Holies."

Rosen was showing how unequal we were after all.

"Reed," I told him, "I don't know all that much about the High Holies."

"Not by yourself, you don't." But we both knew: Much that was meaningless to me might be a gift for him. He sipped the last of his shot glass, and handed it over. "Let me drink a little more of this splendid Scotch," he said, "and I'll get into kilts."

I managed to smile. It took a considerable rearranging of the local passions in my mouth.

"This has to be a hellish occasion for you," he said. "Whether you believe it or not, it's a hellish occasion for me."

Well, now we were talking about the same thing. He must have some idea of how much paper I had carried out of Langley. I had an impulse to tell him it had not proved bothersome to that complex fellow, my conscience. In truth, it was amazing. While there might be a day when I would have to pay up on these accounts, I virtually looked forward to the occasion. I have a lot to tell you, Ned, I nearly told him now, of my feelings in this matter: I feel righteous.

Instead, I chose to be silent. Rosen said, "Harry, you've been mad as a boil for years. Maybe with reason. When a marriage breaks up, I think one has to say, 'Don't judge. Only God can apportion the fault.' We're all married to the Agency. If you're ready for a separa-tion, I'm not the one to sit in judgment. Not on you. Over the years, you've done work that would put us all to shame. Such bold and well turned stuff."

I was trying to conceal my unprecedented pleasure. "Bold and well turned" had left me outrageously agog. Just as vain as a high official.

Rosen followed up by saying, "I'll tell you in confidence that whatever lifting you've done, and I believe we have pretty good track on these rampages by now, still, fellow—" his voice had never been more resonant—"on my word, the sins are *venial*."

It was his way of telling me to cooperate. Rosen over the years must have supplied Harlot with a good deal of stuff the Office of Security preferred to keep for themselves. Venial sins went on all the time. Information slipped through the cracks between State and *us*, Defense and *us*, NSC—yes, especially NSC—and *us*: we were merely good Americans who had invested in *Leak Gardens*.

Mortal sins were another matter. Mortal sins delivered papyrus to the Sovietskys, an incomparably less humorous business. While Rosen could not be absolutely certain that I was on the lower end of the venial-mortal scale, he was nonetheless making covert promises. Resignation from the service might be in order, he had all but said, rather than trial and/or discharge. Obviously, he needed my help. The questions surrounding Hugh Montague's death were going to be orders of magnitude more vital than any of my peccadillos.

Perhaps it was just as well that I would have Ned for my interlocutor rather than some high-ranking Security baboon who would not know how many generations of Hubbards it had taken to shape the dear, shabby quiddities of the Keep.

O M E G A - 8

THE LIGHT FROM THE FIREPLACE WAS REFLECTED IN HIS EYEGLASSES. I even saw the logs flicker as I spoke.

"Let's take it for granted," I said, "that my separation from the service will be equitable." I do not know if my voice sounded inadmissably smug in its assessment, or if Rosen had been playing me with a well-chosen fly, but now I could feel him taking in slack.

His thin lips took on the severity of a bureaucrat about to land his trout.

"Let us assume," he said, "that concerted cooperation will permit separation on equitable terms so far as relevant guidelines allow."

Not everyone could speak bureaucratese. I nodded scornfully. I realized I was drunk. That didn't happen often these days no matter how much I drank, but you do get to feel competitive about your command of the tongue after more than twenty-five years in the government.

"Subject," I told him, "to appropriate conjunction, we will engineer a collateral inquiry out of the competing contingencies."

I said this to get that highly domiciled little smile off his face, but he merely looked sad. I realized that Rosen was as full of liquor as myself. We had been running a small rapids on the great river of booze. Now the drop was over. The river was calm.

He sighed. I thought he was about to say, "How could you have done it?" but instead he murmured, "We're not ready to make deals."

"Then where are we?"

"I'd like your overview."

I took a sobering swallow of Scotch. "Why?"

"Maybe I need it. We're in the middle of a disaster. Sometimes you see things more clearly than me."

"All right," I said.

"I mean it," he said. I began to think he did.

"What do we have?" I asked. "You are holding a body that is Harlot's body?"

"Yes," he said, but reluctantly, as if ready to deny his own affirmative.

"I assume," I said, and I took another sip of Scotch before bringing my voice down this gravel path, "the remains are damaged and swollen by water."

"The body, ostensibly, belongs to Harlot."

We were silent. I had known it would not be routine to speak of Harlot's death in any fashion, yet was still surprised at the engorgement of my throat. Sorrow, anger, confusion, and a hint of hysteria at my own confusion were all groping alike for a safe spot in my larynx. I discovered that it helped to look at the fire. I studied a log as it glowed into incandescence before collapsing softly upon itself, and I began to mourn Harlot—along with all else! Yet mortality, we learn from every sermon, is the dissolution of all matter, yes, all our forms flow down to the sea, and Harlot's death was entering the universe. So, too, did my throat feel less impeded.

I discovered I did want to talk about Harlot's death. No matter how much had taken place this evening—or was it precisely because of all that had happened?—I felt as if I had finally retreated to the middle of myself, to the clear logical middle of myself, and if my emotional ends had been consumed, so was the middle stronger. If drunk ten minutes ago, I now felt sober, but then drunkenness is the abdication of the ego, and mine had just surfaced like a whale. I felt a considerable need to recognize all over again just how sane I could be, which is to say, how lucid, how logical, how sardonic, how superior to everybody's weaknesses, including my own. Did Rosen look for analysis? I would give it to him. Something of the old days was coming back to me—the sense the two of us used to share of being Harlot's best and brightest. And certainly his most competitive. It did not matter any longer how tired I was, I felt tireless in the center of my brain.

"Ned, the first question is whether it's murder or suicide."

He nodded.

To myself I thought: Suicide could only mean that Harlot had been playing for large stakes and lost. The corollary was that the High Holies were mortally disloyal to the Company, and I was, therefore, in no small trouble.

"Keep going."

"If, however, Harlot was murdered," I said, and stopped again. Greater difficulties commenced here. I chose an old CIA saw: "You don't lance a boil," I told him, "without having some idea where the drainage will go."

"Of course," said Rosen.

"Well, Reed, if Harlot suffered a hit, do the sluiceways point east or west?"

"I don't know. I don't know whether to look for the King Brothers or closer to home." He exhaled from the tension of having carried this by himself all these hours.

"It can't be the King Brothers," I said.

He tapped the stem of his pipe against his teeth. It would be the next thing to mutual kamikaze if we and the KGB ever began killing each other's officers. By unspoken covenant we didn't. Third World agents, perhaps, and an occasional European, but not each other. "No, not the Russians," I said, "unless Harlot was working a double game with them."

Rosen sighed.

"On the other hand," I proposed, "it could be us."

"Would you expatiate on that?" Rosen asked.

"Harlot was riding one hypothesis fairly hard. He had decided there was an enclave among us using our most classified information as a guide to buy, sell, and invest all over the world. By his estimate, these covert finances are larger by now than our entire budget for Operations."

"Are you saying, then, that Harlot was killed by Agency people?"

"They stood to lose billions. Maybe more."

I was partial to the thesis. For Harlot's sake and for my own. If he was the good sentinel on guard against massive internal corruption, then to have worked with him might cast an honorable light on me.

Rosen, however, shook his head. "It's not productive to go in this direction yet," he said. "You don't know the worst-case scenario. There's a hell of a roadblock in front of your thesis."

I poured a little more Scotch for both of us.

"You see," said Rosen, "we are not, in fact, sure it's Harlot's remains. Not what washed up in the Chesapeake."

"Not sure?" I could hear the echo in my voice.

"We have what *purports* to be Montague's body. But the labs can't give 100-percent probability to the cadaver. Although the specificities are respectable. Good fit for height and weight. On his third finger, left hand, a St. Matthew's ring. The face, however, is no help at all." Rosen's pale gray eyes, usually unremarkable, now looked awfully bright behind his eyeglasses.

"I couldn't get myself to tell Kittredge," he continued. "The face and head were blown off. Shotgun muzzle pressed against the palate. Probably a sawed-off shotgun."

I did not wish to contemplate this image longer than I had to. "What about Hugh's back?" I asked.

"There is a severe back injury on the body. No perambulative functions would be possible." He shook his head. "We can't be positive, however, that it's the Montague injury."

"Surely you have Harlot's X-rays on file?"

"Well, Harry, you know Harlot. He had all records transferred from his hospital treatment center to us. He would never allow information about himself to repose anywhere out of the domain."

"What do his X-rays tell you?"

"That's the roadblock," said Rosen. "The X-rays can't be found." He took his pipe out of his mouth and scrutinized the progress of the char in his bowl. "We have a first-rate headache."

O M E G A - 9

I COULD ANTICIPATE ROSEN'S NEXT QUESTION: HAVE YOU, HARRY Hubbard, removed Harlot's X-rays from the file?

The trouble was, I couldn't give an answer. I had no recollection of ever bringing anything to Harlot from his medical file. My powers of on-demand recollection, after thirty years of drinking, could show a gaping hole or two. It was not impossible that I had forgotten.

More likely someone else had done the lifting. I could have been merely one of a number of mules carrying bales of papyrus from Langley out to Harlot. For that matter, the loss of the X-rays could be attributed to FMWP—pronounced as *foam-whip*—our in-house acronym for *Files Mislaid Within Parameters*. The CIA had been expanding for close to four decades in spite of—or was it due to?—*foam-whip*. One could never assume a missing file to have been filched in mortal sin. The removal was more likely to be venial—plucked to protect some officer's self-interest, or assigned to the wrong department on its way back to the nest, or, for that matter, a young file clerk, distracted over a dubious romance, could have plunked the papers into the wrong folder, the wrong box, or now that we were computerized, down the chute on an off-key. The user-friendly computers employed by our common folk were as ready to take you off the road as the steering wheel of a fat old four-door sedan.

In short, Harlot's X-ray files were not now available.

"We're also having some trouble locating his fingerprints," Rosen now told me. "Although that may not matter. The fish got to the ends of his fingers. Which is interesting. There is a substance, some equivalent of catnip, but solely for fish, that could have been painted on the fingertips. Which got the catfish nibbling in the desired place. On the other hand, fish do nibble at extremities. So it could be for natural reasons."

He dipped into an attaché case he had sitting beside him on the floor, and handed over two eight-by-ten glossies respectively of a left hand wearing a ring, and a right hand. "Would this be recognizable?" Perhaps it was the pallor of the black-and-white tones in the photograph, but the hands could have belonged to anyone, they were identifiable only as the puffed-up mitts of a man who had been in water much too long. And the tips of the fingers were indeed frayed to the bone.

"I asked Kittredge if she could make any identification from this, but she became distraught," Rosen said.

Yes, distraught. The moment when I begged her to let me into the bedroom came back in all its rags of woe. How she must have suffered at the sight of those enlargements. Harlot's hands—once so deft. Kittredge's grief became a little more comprehensible to me. It was—cruel paradox—that her torment had nothing to do with mine: Her suffering had a separate existence. This occurred to me in the way that a physicist might encounter a new and offensive proposition in his field: It did not matter how much I loved Kittredge, no guarantee was returned that she could love me. That was the offensive proposition. Did Einstein, facing the quantum theory and a universe of chance, feel any more of an unholy stir?

I am a professional, however. It is the operative word. It was time again to remind myself. One's body must be in the appointed place. Hung over or well rested; friendly or boiling with bile; loyal or treacherous; fit for the task or conceivably incompetent; one is, none-theless, a professional; one shuts off the part of one's mind that is not appropriate to the task. If what is left does not have enough to manage the job, one is still professional. One has shown up for work.

"Harry," said Rosen, "not all of the face is lost."

I could hardly follow him. Then I did. "What was left for us?"

"The right lower jaw. All the teeth on that side are absent. Except for the last two molars. That checks out. Harlot used to wear a bridge on his right lower jaw anchored to the same two molars."

"How do you know about this bridge?"

"Well, my friend, we may not have his general medical records, but the dental file was found. On those X-rays, one of the two molars shows a small gold inlay. So does the cadaver. In fact, the filling on the dead man matches astonishingly well to the Montague X-rays."

"Astonishingly well? Why not assume you have Hugh Mon-tague's funeral to prepare for?"

"Because it doesn't feel right to me." He put out his hands in apology as if he had been debating this through the afternoon with technicians in the laboratory. I realized he might be alone in his suspicions. "I can't help it," he said. "I don't like the product."

He filled his pipe and lit it. I did not care to speak while he was refueling. I suppose I have been annoyed by pipe smokers all my working life. We do not have as many now in the Company as in Allen Dulles' day when the Director's old Dunhill became part of the role model for a good many of us, but how many of my hours have been spent inhaling a colleague's pipe?

"Can you tell me why," he asked at last, "it doesn't feel all that good?"

"It's the only path through the evidence," I said. He knew it. I knew it. Harlot had taught us: Partial evidence which leads to but one conclusion is to be distrusted. Categorically distrusted.

"I think," he said, "that a cosmetic deception may have been brought off."

"Can we put the ball back on the playing field?" I asked, and had the passing thought—my mind seemed afflicted now by passing thoughts—that it was, after all, amazing how so many of us still spoke the way advertising people used to carry on twenty and thirty years ago. I think we are equal in some way—we, too, may not know whether an assertion is true or egregiously fraudulent. Run it up the mast and see if it waves. Many of our ventures were dependent on metaphor.

I digress, but I did not wish to engage the enormity of Rosen's suggestion. There was no alternative, however. I tasted my Scotch. I said, "Ned, are you proposing that a dental technician worked on another man's mouth skillfully enough to convert those two molars into facsimiles of Harlot's? And did it in advance of his death?"

"Not impossible." Rosen was excited. Harlot might be over the horizon, but the game was before him. "This," he said, "is what we have so far. Hugh Montague's dental X-rays were done a couple of years ago. At his age, teeth grind down and shift. So it isn't as if someone had to find a man of the exact age and size who also had two molars identical to Harlot's. You just need molars that are *close*. Obviously there would be no great problem in producing a precise copy of the gold inlay."

"Would the dentist be working for the King Brothers?"

"Yes," he said, "it would have to be. We could lock in on some person whose physical specifications are near enough to be satisfactory, but we could hardly deal with the rest of the job. I postulate that we have been presented with a highly worked-up KGB special."

"Are you," I asked, "really claiming that they found some seventy-year-old Soviet prisoner and proceeded, after much dental work including possibly the extraction of all the other teeth on that half of the lower jaw, to go ahead and very carefully break the old fellow's spine in just the right place, and then mend him back to health, smuggle him into this country, take him down to Harlot's boat, carefully shoot off his head to leave no more than the two facsimile molars, and then consign him to Chesapeake Bay long enough to puff up the rest of the remains, while they hang around through it all to be able to nudge him back to shore? No," I said, answering my own question, "I'd rather believe Harlot is dead, and you are holding the remains."

"Well," he replied, "it *would* be a demanding operation. Even for the KGB. With all their patience."

"Come," I said. "It's worthy of Feliks Dzerzhinsky."

Rosen stood up and poked the fire. "They would never go to such lengths," he said, "unless the stakes were very large. Let's go back to the worst-case scenario. Suppose Harlot is in the hands of the King Brothers?"

"In the hands of the King Brothers and alive?"

"Alive and *happy*," said Rosen. "Happy and on his way to Moscow."

I certainly didn't wish to give Rosen any help at this point. Where could this thesis leave me? Yet, my mind with all its conditioned reflexes for twisting a hypothesis until it broke or took on form—we treated hypotheses not unlike the way Sandy Calder used to bend wire—now bent Rosen's line of thinking into the next turn, and did so, I suspect, for no better reason than to improve on his scenario. The need for superior acumen is also an uncontrollable passion. "Yes," I said, "what if Harlot is alive and happy and on his way to Moscow, and doesn't want us to be able to conclude whether he's alive or dead?"

I had gained a step on Rosen. We did not even have to speak of it. For Harlot to defect was as huge a one-man disaster as the CIA could conceive. Even Bill Casey might recognize that it was larger than Nicaragua. Yet if it took a good many qualified people a year or more, we could still assess the damage—call it the meltdown—of the mess that would leave us in. If, however, we did not even know whether he was actually dead or, to the contrary, was educating the King Brothers about *us*—which would be the education of the century!—then we were condemned to live in a habitat where the keys would fit the locks until they didn't. This had Harlot's signature. It would be exactly in his style to leave us a tainted corpse. How often had he instructed Rosen and myself in the principle. "Americans have to have answers," he told me once. "The inability to reply to a question drives us mad, and Russians look for control before they even have the answer. Both courses breed the same unmanageable anxiety. Find the answer! Neither CIA nor KGB can tolerate ambiguity. It's to our advantage, therefore, in many an operation, to leave behind just a bit of our spoor—just a trace. The spoor will consume a thousand hours of investigation for every hour they gain by the product. Not at all routine to bring off, Harry, but demoralizing to the opponent."

O M E G A - 1 0

ROSEN AND I SAT IN THE AURA OF THE FIRE. EVEN AS A SILENCE IS composed of small sounds—the gossip, to put it so, of unseen events— so did the hearth prove equal to a blazing forest. I was giving attention to the transmogrifications in burning wood. Universes curved toward one another, universes exploded; ash thickened from a membrane to a shroud. I could hear each fiber spit its curse into the flames.

Rosen was slumped morosely in my favorite chair. I thought of a joke that had made the rounds of CIA just before the expected summit meeting in 1960 between Eisenhower and Khrushchev, the one that never took place because Gary Powers' U-2 plane was shot down over Russia. Khrushchev said to Eisenhower, "I love you."

"Why do you love me?" asked Eisenhower.

"Because you are my equal. You are the only equal I got in the whole world."

Rosen was my equal. Harlot was a manifest of the Lord, and we had known him together. "How could he have done it?" Rosen exclaimed.

"I know," I murmured, which is to say, I did not.

"He literally carried me into Christianity," said Rosen. "I converted because of Hugh Montague. Do you know what it means for a Jew to convert? You feel like a Judas to your own people."

I tried to search my starched soul—starched, I had to recognize, in its likes and dislikes—to determine whether I had been over-hard on Rosen. I had always assumed he converted to advance certain professional pursuits. Did I do him an injustice? Had I remained censorious over all these years merely because I had once felt so superior to him? In the old days of slavish training at the Farm, our

group of *stunts* (as we called ourselves, in comparison to Marine Corps
grunts) used to look upon Rosen as a bagel-baby from the middle-
class purlieus of the Bronx. I, however, used to be grateful he was
there. Luck of the draw, Rosen and I had been assigned to a training
platoon with an undue allotment of heavy-duty stunts. Half of them
could climb a twelve-foot wall somewhat faster than I could look at
it. With Rosen present, they could laugh at him instead of me. That
is a good fellow to have around. Of course, they might also have
laughed because he was their token Jew doing gentile's work, and I
think that burned his soul. I know I suffered with him, since I had
something like an eighth of Jewish blood by way of my mother, just
enough never to know quite what to do about it. At this moment,
however, Rosen was my only equal in the world. Had Harlot defected? How could one ever seize the meaning of that? As soon plunge
one's hand into water and seize a minnow.

Sitting before the fire, I was living with the memory of Harlot as
he used to look in full health, not yet fifty, equal in trim to his
mustache. Over how many years at Langley had I sat next to him
while a projector threw up the faces of KGB men on a screen? The
opponent looks astral when magnified so. I had seen faces four feet
high whose light of eye seemed to go inward as if one were shining
a flare down the dark halls of their deeds. So did Harlot's face appear
to me now in the fireplace, four feet high and full of force.

Out of the silence, Rosen asked, "Do you think it would be
possible to talk to Kittredge?"

"Now?"

"Yes."

"Can it wait?" I asked.

He took his time considering this.

"I suppose it can."

"Ned, she knows nothing about the High Holies."

"She does not?" He seemed surprised.

It was the quality of surprise that disturbed me. He seemed at an
odd loss.

"You find that peculiar?" I asked.

"Well, she has been in Washington a good deal lately to see
Harlot."

"Just old chums," I said.

Like wrestlers whose bodies have become so slippery with exertion that they can no longer hold a grip, so were we at this moment sliding around each other.

"Do you really believe he told her anything?" I asked.

I had had no inkling she was seeing Harlot. Every few weeks she would leave me to visit her father, Rodman Knowles Gardiner, now approaching the magical age of ninety, magical I say because such common events of the day as slumber, evacuation, and alimentation could be accomplished only by charms, spells, and the endlessly repetitive rituals of the old. "What did you say your name is, girl? . . . oh, yes, Kittredge . . . that's a nice name . . . that's the name of my daughter. What do you say your name is, girl?"

I had once been on a visit to Oneonta, New York, Dr. Gardiner's birthplace, and now the site of his abode in a rest home. That solitary occasion was sufficient for me. There were always enough tolls to pay in marriage without the drear surcharge of watching a senile father-in-law whom one has never liked nor been liked much by, as he takes an endless meander through the last of his time. Somewhere in the reservoirs of aged animal cunning, I believe old Dr. Gardiner was trying to decide just which of the seven doors of death he would choose to go through. Numbers can be as ambivalent as disturbed beauties, and none more so than seven, the seven doors of the Keep for good luck, and the seven doors of death, or, at least, that is how I saw it: termination by such natural causes as cancer, heart attack, stroke, hemorrhage, suffocation, infection, and despair. I speak like a medievalist, but not wholly in jest—it did seem natural to me to be able over the course of a slow demise, to be able to choose one's exit, to perish, for example, by way of the liver or the lungs, the brain or the bowels. So, no, I did not wish to watch Dr. Gardiner continue to deliberate before the too-patient doors of death while his daughter had to cross those great reaches of apathy between one quotidian burp and the next in a very old man, five senses just about gone, the sixth weaker than ever.

I commiserated in spirit with her each weekend she was away, and was grateful she had not requested me to go along nor even suggested that she really needed my company for so dreary a voyage. (Mount Desert, Maine, to Oneonta, New York, is, by any mode of travel, a time-squandering trek!) And I, in my turn, loved her while she was gone, missed her, and on the one or two occasions I had profited by her absence to take a trip to Bath, felt such guilt over Chloe as to put the profit on Kittredge's side; never did I feel more devoted to my wife than after biting into the wild garlic of treachery. No wonder I never sniffed it on her. Not if I was eating of it myself!

Now, however, her telephone calls came back to me. She was the one who always rang in from Oneonta—"It's easier that way"—but, then, she did not phone that much. What, after all, was there to talk about—the lack of change in her father's condition?

At this point, I could keep, however, from unpleasant questions no longer. Was she seeing Harlot because her love for him was ineradicable? Or was it from pity? No. She would not make fortnightly visits, full of matrimonial deceit, for the sake of pity. Was she, then, part of the High Holies and did not share the fact with me because Harlot did not want either of us to know of the other's participation? (Unless she did know—another question!) I felt like some rebellious slave caught in the building of the pyramids, each new question a heavy stone laying a further cruelty on my back: For what is cruelty but pressure upon the piece of flesh that aches the most, even as confusion is intolerable to a tired mind. I would throw down all the stones. I could not tolerate another question. "If you wish," I said to Rosen, "I'll go upstairs for Kittredge."

He shook his head. "Let's wait a minute. I want to be sure we're ready."

"Why? What now?"

"Can we look at our case again? From the viewpoint that it may be Harlot's body after all."

I sighed. I sighed truly. We were not so different from two midwives examining the birth of a monster—to wit, a large and ugly obsession. What is obsession but the inability to know whether the strange object that has just entered our lives is A or Z, good or evil, true or false? Yet it is certainly there, and right before us, an inescapable gift from the beyond.

"I don't think it's Harlot's body," I said.

"Just take up the possibility," he said. "Please."

"Which mode? Murder? Suicide?" I must have barked this forth.

"Suicide seems dubious to me. On the facts," said Rosen. "He was used to swinging himself around the boat by the use of his arms, but, still, he would have had to get into position on the railing without the aid of the lower spine and thighs. I believe it would have required holding on to a stay with one hand, while firing the sawed-off shotgun with the other. Then he would have had to fall over backward into the water. Why commit suicide from so awkward a position?"

"In order not to mess up the boat with your blood."

"That's a telling point. We could move from a 10-percent possibility of suicide to 20 percent."

"Every bit helps," I said. I was wretched. The drinks had turned on me again. I could feel the first warnings issue from another monster. Once or twice a year, no more, I would come down with a prodigious headache, royal cousin to a migraine, which would leave me next day with a short-term case of amnesia—I would be unable to remember the last twenty-four hours. Some such storm seemed to be mounting now in the tropics of my brain. Tropic of Cerebrum. Tropic of Cerebellum. "The key thing, Arnie," I said, "is to keep your medulla oblongata clean."

"Harry, you're a class act. It's what you have to offer. Please don't go off on tangents."

"The English," I said, "have one test for vulgarity. It is: Do you descend the steps properly? Glenlivet, old pal?" I poured the Scotch. Screw the oncoming headache. Some hurricanes blow out to sea. I took the drink in two nips, filled my shot glass again. "All right. Murder. Murder by our people."

"Don't dismiss the KGB."

"No, let's talk of murder by our good people. It's been on your mind, hasn't it?"

"I keep coming back to what you said," Rosen now told me.

Yes, I could feel how real it had been for him ever since I said it. "Billions," I said. "Somebody who stands to lose a billion bucks and more."

"When the sums of money are that huge, individuals don't get killed," Rosen said.

"Not individuals. Indians. Twenty or forty Indians. All gone." Was I thinking of Dorothy Hunt?

Something had happened, however, to Rosen. I thought he was having an outsize reaction to my last remark, until I realized someone was speaking to him from a walkie-talkie outside. His right hand pressed against the buff-colored earplug and he nodded several times, then reached into his breast pocket, pulled out a black wireless microphone the size of a fountain pen and said, "Are you certain?" listened, then said, "Okay, out."

Now Ned started to speak to me. His voice was not merely small in volume, but close to inaudible. He had begun to rattle the stem of his pipe against his whiskey glass in a disconcerting tattoo, a time-honored method for jamming any state-of-the-art electronics that might be tapping into the room.

Why, however, had he begun to do it now? It seemed likely to me that one of the guards out in the rain would have brought along additional electronic gear to detect any unscheduled approaches. Rosen had just been fed an alert. That seemed the simplest explanation for his behavior. Certainly his voice emerged in a thin whistle as if weighty forces had descended on his chest. Finally, his speech became so impoverished that he took out a notebook, wrote a sentence on it, held it up to me to read, then threw the paper in the fire.

"There is one man I can think of," Ned Rosen had written, *"who has acquired the kind of fortune you name while working with us. However, he's not on board anymore."*

I stood up to poke the logs. I felt timeless in my heart. Each beat of blood seemed to take its great and deliberate pause. I could feel the bellows of my lungs on their rise and on their fall. The confirmation of a hypothesis is one of the richest emotions left to our modern temper.

There was one man Ned could name, but he was not about to. His breath would not permit it. The hound of fear was in his lungs. And I could not name the man, not yet. My memory bore too much resemblance to those old brass tubes which once carried the cash and change for one's purchase up and down floors in department stores. The name might be already inserted in its tube and on its way, but, oh, my brain!—there were floors and floors to climb.

Then the name of the man did come to me, and sooner than expected. There was an undeniable pop-out in my head.

I reached for Rosen's note pad. *"Are you thinking of our old friend on the Farm?"* I wrote.

"PHENOMENAL!" Rosen printed in capital letters.

"Can it really be Dix Butler?" I wrote.

"How long since you've seen him?" asked Rosen aloud.

"Ten years."

He picked up the pad. *"Have you ever been to Thyme Hill?"*

"No," I said aloud, "but I've heard of it."

Rosen nodded, threw the page into the fire, and as if fatigued by the weight of this transaction, lay back in his chair.

I wondered at his travail. It is an odd word, but I think appropriate. He was reacting as if engaged in hard labor. It occurred to me that he must be carrying more than one full weight of anxiety. Until now, however, he had not shown the burden. Not until now. The significance of the three men in the woods redefined itself. They were not there for me. They were waiting for someone to arrive.

Rosen sat up, nodded as if to assure me that all was well—what was well?—and then removed a silver pill box from his breast pocket, took out one white pill so small I assume it was nitroglycerine for his heart, and lay it under his tongue with a certain tenderness as if he were handing a small, carefully trimmed morsel of food to a pet. Then he closed his eyes to absorb it.

Probably he had been waiting for Dix Butler all night. Why else would he write: *PHENOMENAL!*

PRIMITIVE, I should have replied. Who was to say we do not receive messages from each other without signing the receipt? Had I begun to think of Dix Butler because Rosen was preoccupied with him?

We sat there, each to his own, and who could know what was shared? *Millions of creatures walk the earth unseen.* The interval of silence lengthened once more.

O M E G A - 1 1

I COULD SENSE MYSELF RAISING A BARRIER AGAINST EVERY FEAR THAT Rosen was communicating. I needed none of that. I had to be able to think about Butler. There was more than enough to contemplate. Butler had always been the most impressive man, physically speaking, of any group you found him in. He was powerful; he was—no other word—handsome. In training, instructors used to tell him that he had come to the wrong place, he should have taken his whack at Hollywood. He didn't disagree. His arrogance was ready to agree. He had, after all, given up professional football after two seasons of injuries (linebacker, fourth-round draft, Washington Redskins) to join CIA. At the Farm, we had been assigned to the same group of thirty, and he had, of course, been a good distance ahead of us on all physical levels. Since he was also intelligent, he went on to blaze a career trail in the Company. I had run with Dix Butler in Berlin in 1956, and saw him in Miami in 1960 when Howard Hunt and I were helping to train exile Cubans for the Bay of Pigs, and I had an adventure or two with

Dix in southern Florida in 1962 when the local Cuban community was riddled with Fidelista spies. One of our jobs was to weed them out. Questioning suspects, Butler was not above using the toilet bowl to prime a confession. "It's the condign procedure for that kind of Cubano," he said. "Different chokes for different folks."

Now I was attempting to recall what I had heard about him over the last ten years. He had left the Company and gone into business for himself, several kinds of business. That much I knew, not much more. If the gossip in large corporations is analogous to a river, then our whispering gallery is an underground river. Sometimes it even reaches the surface and talk flows freely among us about the marital difficulties of colleagues, or of a caper in Kinshasa that crashed so badly they were still scraping the egg yolk off the safe-house walls. But we knew when not to talk. Then the stream went into a cave and did not come out.

Dix Butler cut his swath through the Company and came back from Vietnam a legend. After which, he gave his resignation to CIA, and made a fortune. Envy alone would have been sufficient cause to talk about him forever, but we didn't. We weren't too sure of what we were talking about. The news received could be naught but cover. He purported to be detached from us; he could be doing contract work: God knows what we really had him doing. Talk was, therefore, *sensitive,* just as sensitive as a tooth that will strike up a spasm if touched. So we were silent. We were tribal. Out in the great prairie (of the common-folk cafeteria at Langley) where the gossip blew, we knew to distinguish the north wind from the south.

It was acceptable, however, to speak in general terms of how successful he had become. He had purchased a bluegrass horse farm some hundred miles into Virginia, and raised Appaloosas there, or, at least, the stud-farm equipage working for him did, and Thyme Hill expanded over the years. One heard of ten thousand acres more often now than of one thousand acres, and once I listened to talk of a training center for mercenaries somewhere in his trees. Ten thousand acres, went the argument, was fifteen square miles, just about the size of Camp Peary, our old Farm. It was a weak argument. There might be a few of his favorite tiger-people from Nam housed out in those woods, but no power on American earth would dare to train a small army one hundred miles from the capital, no.

Other stories seemed to reach us just long enough to go underground again. There were weekend parties on his grounds that owed more to the kind of whing-dings we used to give in Saigon than to diplomatic Washington. Lobbyists, senators, hot congressmen, hot industrialists, hot corporate raiders were joined by hot ladies. In Washington, enterprising people might give parties for corporate and congressional powers, but not with hot ladies. As a credible description of any reality I could comprehend, tales about Butler entertaining the right people and thereby amassing uncountable sums would have gone better on one of those honey-and-tycoon TV dramas that live it up for an hour a week by exploiting the true physics of gossip. That science calls for *low specifics in the scenario,* otherwise known as fairy tales for the horny. I was wise enough to know that the accumulation of money was too consuming a pursuit to be distracted by sex. Sex was but a sidebar for the young and cocaine-inclined. While there appeared to be no shortage of cocaine out at Thyme Hill, and some of the ladies, doubtless, were young, the scenario was wrong. If Butler was giving the wildest parties within a hundred miles of Washington, D.C., it was not to make deals, but to cover something larger.

A *symphony* might be in the works. You could calibrate its size by the gossip at Langley. The gossip kept stopping short. No real nuggets came back with the stories. That was the telling clue. While speculation had Dix Butler running a gargantuan *Venus flytrap,* I did not see that as the prime operation. A Venus flytrap might be out there, but what was Dix putting behind it? Certainly, he was capable of anything. In Saigon, he had recruited his own small army of Vietnamese for improvisational hits on the Vietcong; that army had waged a few drug wars as well. One night, very drunk, under a Southern Hemisphere moon, Butler claimed to have started an enterprise or two with the profits. These monies, he assured me, would go back to the Company. That was important.

"What is coming up?" he asked me solemnly. "I'll tell you. Harry, this war is going to undress the CIA. Sooner or later they are going to rip off all our band-aids, and there won't be blood for the great American public to look at."

"Yes? What will there be?"

"Batshit. All the batshit we've been hiding. The great American public, and their elected cocksuckers, the Congress of these Disgruntled and Disunited States, are going to cut the CIA's balls off when they discover all those tons of batshit. So we got to get ready. We need covert money, honey. Secret money nicely put away. Take a good look at me." He showed his teeth. "I'm going to be the Agency *banker.*"

Whether he had or had not become our covert banker, a Venus flytrap to catch key politicians in covertly photographed positions was still not likely. Not only was sexual blackmail illegal by our charter, it was also close to anathema for those fifteen thousand ribbon clerks, typists, experts, analysts, and programmers, all that human tonnage who made up 90 percent of our CIA personnel; they were as conventional as Pentagon folk. High-profile sex shops were not the soup of choice for good Company people who went to church on Sunday, read *National Review,* and believed we were the clean-living in the land, no, you could not have such people processing paper from Butler's peephole operation, and besides, such a peephole sounded as large as a tunnel entrance. What, then, was going on? Why Thyme Hill?

I looked across at Rosen. I do not know if it was the slow pace of my thoughts or the calm with which I waited—I had drunk enough Glenlivet by now to be calm at my own funeral—but he, too, seemed to be back in some facsimile of composure. He scribbled a line on a piece of notebook paper, tore it off and held it up for me.

"I've been out to Thyme Hill," was what I read.

"Did you like it?"

"I've never been to the Playboy mansion," he wrote, *"but Thyme Hill must make Hugh Hefner look like a spinster having a few lady friends in for tea."*

He gave a wan smile and consigned such information to the fire. I gave a wan smile back. In those awful hours when you wonder if you have spent half your life in the wrong occupation, it was usually my estimate that much of our work would seem ludicrous to an impartial observer. Of course, we did our work on the assumption that God had small use for impartial observers.

The fact is that we were in need of a high-level sex shop. The Intelligence services of other nations took such instruments of the trade for granted. Harlot had inveighed for years against our domestic bonds. In the U.S., we couldn't begin to do what we needed to do. All too many delicate but local counterintelligence operations had to be handed over to the FBI, and they, from our point of view, were egregious bunglers. Their power, if you believed Harlot, had been maintained less by their proficiency than by J. Edgar Hoover's special files. Hoover loved *tidbits.* He collected them. It had given him a wrestler's lock on Congress and the presidency. J. Edgar, after all, kept encyclopedic files on every cabinet officer and senator who had anything to do with a woman not his wife, and should the wife go in for comparable excursions, Hoover was ready to have photographs of her navel as well. No president ever took him on. J. Edgar had already supplied them with too good an insight into the maverick inclinations of previous presidents. When it came, therefore, to reducing J. Edgar's power at home, and increasing ours, his private files made the difference.

We had tried to lessen the gap. We bestowed a few extra duties on our Office of Security. The O of S had access to the files of the Metropolitan Police in Washington, D.C., who had an officer, one Captain Roy E. Blick, who had a pipeline into a call-girl operation in a Washington hotel (the Columbia Plaza, if you would have the name). Blick had caught his share of significant folk in extremes of gay apparel, degradation, subjugation—I heard about such from Harlot in the days when he still maintained a clandestine but monitorial function over Rosen in Security. Poor Ned—not yet Reed—had to put in his hours with Captain Blick, which meant he had to do his best to keep Blick from sharing all the spoils with Hoover. "Ah, those names," Harlot once exclaimed. "I tell you, Harry, people who work on the margins of propriety seem to have been given their monikers by Charles Dickens." As if he were an outback tribesman repeating a sound he did not understand, he added, "J. Edgar Hoover. Roy E. Blick. J. Edgar Hoover. Roy E. Blick." Then he sighed for Rosen. "Poor Ned. They do give him sorry jobs at Security. Catering to Blick!" And Harlot gave his wink. After all, Rosen, before moving to Security, had once been in charge of Harlot's special files. Limited they might be, but as a point of professional pride, Harlot separated himself from Hoover's grab-bag of slurs, innuendos, and Polaroids, and instructed Rosen not to pick up every piece of gumbo that landed on the beach. Content had to be evaluated.

Still, Harlot had powers of anticipation. A friend of Kittredge's, Polly Galen Smith, the former wife of a senior officer in one of our divisions, had begun a *VIP affair* with President Kennedy. (VIP affair is a descriptive of the prevailing arrangements: time allotted for entering, doffing clothes, taking one's jump into bliss, showers, clothes back on, saying good-bye, is twenty minutes—"You don't become VIP for too little," remarked Harlot.)

A year and a half, however, after the President's assassination, Polly Galen Smith was beaten to death on the towpath of a Potomac canal. A possible assailant was found, tried, and acquitted. While her murder seemed to have no relation to us, the conclusion that we were not involved was not obvious in the immediate hours after the assault. Whom had the lady been taking to bed, after all, *since* Jack Kennedy? Harlot proceeded at once to her house, and—as an old family friend— was able to console the children. Rosen, whom he had brought along, thereby managed to slip up to the master bedroom where he lifted Polly Galen Smith's diary from a small drawer in her kneehole desk and removed the *sneaky* Harlot had installed in the baseboard back of her bed. Montague had seen it as his direct if disagreeable duty to monitor the lady. At worst, there could have been hanky-panky with attractive Soviet officials in Washington.

Relatively speaking, all that had been the petty improvisation of pioneering days. Now, in the eighties, by the thrust, at least, of the overmuted gossip, the question was whether we had constructed a Venus flytrap that would be the envy of the FBI. Or was that too unbalanced an assumption? It begged the question whether Dix Butler was still a loyal son of the grange. He could have made separate arrangements with the FBI and/or the DEA. Or, if they could afford it, the SIS, SDECE, and the BND (which, for those who would inquire, are respectively English, French, and German intelligence).

I reached for the pad.

"*Did Harlot go out to Thyme Hill?*"

"*On occasion.*"

"*Do you know what he did there?*"

"*No.*"

"Zero return?" I asked aloud.

"Well, Harry, you could be making too much of it. A lot of people went out there. Sunday afternoon was not Saturday night."

I did not want to ask the next question, but need was greater than pride. I took the pad. "*Did Kittredge accompany Harlot?*"

Rosen looked at me. Then he nodded.

"How many times?" I asked.

Rosen held up his extended hand. Five times, said his fingers. He was looking at me with compassion. I did not know whether to feel insulted or to admit that I was sufficiently bruised to accept his concern. I was certainly taken all the way back to a fistfight I had one summer in Maine with a cousin two years older, age eleven, and too large for me, really, to fight. He had landed a roundhouse on the side of my nose which sent a star rocketing from one end of my inner firmament to the other; the star so dislodged my balance that I went down to one knee. Drops of blood, heavy as silver coins, plopped from my nose to the ground. The recollection added old pain to new. I had to see Kittredge.

When I got to my feet, Rosen looked miserable. That may have been what I needed. Irony is the armature to keep one erect when everything within is falling. I held fast to the irony that Rosen, who had wanted me to fetch Kittredge, could not now bear to be left alone. I saw the fear in his eyes.

On the pad, I wrote, *"Are you expecting Dix Butler tonight?"*

"I can't be certain," he managed to say.

"Will your three men prove enough?"

"I can't be certain of that either."

I nodded. I pointed upstairs.

"I'd like you to remain in earshot," Reed Rosen said.

"If Kittredge is feeling well enough, I'll come down with her."

"Please."

I left him by the fire, climbed the stairs to our bedroom, and took out my key. When I reached for the knob, it turned freely in my hand, and so I was not caught completely by surprise that Kittredge was neither in bed nor in the bedroom.

O M E G A - 1 2

LOOKING AT THE LONG, LIGHT HOLLOW WHERE SHE HAD LAIN ON THE coverlet, I knew where she had gone. Once Kittredge gave me a great start by confessing she would, on occasion, visit the Vault.

"I detest the place," I told her.

"No, when I'm alone in the house and begin to wonder if I can't possibly become any more lonely, I go there," she said.

"Tell me why."

"I used to be so afraid of what is in this house. But now I'm not. When I go down to the Vault I feel as if I've gotten to the center of my loneliness, as if there's a bit of land, after all, in the midst of absolutely endless seas. Then, when I come up, Harry, the rest of the house seems less unpeopled."

"Nothing bothers you down there?"

"Well, I suppose if I allowed myself," Kittredge said, "I could hear Augustus Farr rattling his chains, but, no, Harry, I feel no vengeance in that place."

"You really are a lovely girl," I replied.

Now, I was obliged to remind myself how near I had come this night to carrying her down to the Vault. It gave me a sudden glimpse of myself—one of those rare views returned by the mirror when we are not in any degree loyal to ourselves and so pass cruel and immediate judgment on the apparition in the glass only to realize in the next instant that it is our own face we are condemning. Drunk, miserable, hollow as a gourd, I could hear the silences where unseen judges gather.

The cry of an animal came through the night. It was no ordinary sound. I could not tell from how far away, but the howl came to my ear like the lonely moan of a wolf. There are few wolves in these parts. The cry came again. Now it was as full of suffering and horror as a lacerated bear. There are no bears near. The cry had to have been stirred by my commotion.

Twenty-one years ago, on the dirt road leading from the highway to our back shore, a tramp had been found, partially devoured, in the thicket near Gilley Butler's house. I am told he lay there with the most frightful expression of fear on what was left of his mouth. Could the shriek of the animal I had just heard be equal to the mutilated silence of the tramp? Who could know? Twenty-one years ago came down to early spring of 1962, a time when some of us were looking to locate a plane to spray poison on Cuban sugar fields. Had there been a year of my working life that had not offered one smothered howl?

Standing in our empty bedroom, my thoughts collided face to face with Damon Butler, the long-dead relative of Gilley Butler—Damon Butler, first mate to Augustus Farr, two and a half centuries dead. This unholy surprise visited me at this moment neither as a ghost nor a voice, but as an image so deep within my mind that for an instant I felt occupied by another presence: I saw what he had seen.

I made prodigious efforts not to see anything at all. I stood in the middle of the bedroom, and made—yes, I call them prodigious efforts although I did not move—made a most fervid attempt to decide that what I now saw in my imagination was neither a gift nor an invasion, but the simple delayed result of an afternoon I had spent ten years ago in the Bar Harbor Library reading Damon Butler's ship journal, an honored artifact among local library treasures. So, I tried to tell myself that the vision before me now had been put together from no more than the first mate's papers: bills of lading, shoals negotiated, sloops for sale. The execution of the French commodore that I was witnessing was but the gory essence of Butler's journal; it was just that I had not allowed it to come back to my thoughts until now. What a formidable incarceration of memory! It all came back. Like a knock on the door before the door flies open.

His ship gone, his men butchered, the French commodore was stripped of his uniform. Naked, arms pinioned, the victim spit, none-theless, into his captor's face. In reply, Farr raised his cutlass. The blade was sharp. The commodore's head flew off like a cabbage. Like the thump of a cabbage striking the deck—so goes Damon's account. Other crew members were to swear that the corpse, neck spurting, bound limbs straining, sought to rise to its knees until Farr, in a frenzy, kicked it over. There the body lay on the deck, feet twitching. But the head, off to the side, kept moving its mouth. All agreed its mouth was moving. To that, adds Damon Butler, he heard speech issue from those bloody lips. To Farr was said: *Si tu non veneris ad me, ego veniam ad te.*

On that night, years ago, when I followed whatever or whoever was in my dream all the way down to the Vault, I did not think of the speech that came forth from the decapitated head. Now I did. The Latin was clear: "If you do not come to me, I will come to thee." An intimate curse!

To be out of earshot of Rosen, I took the back stairway. In the cellar, one of the casement windows showed a small pane broken. Through the gap came night air, and its odor was not native to the island. If the nose is a link to memory, then I was sniffing the stale waters of a canal off the Potomac; the muggy fens of the old George-town swamps were redolent on the Maine air. I thought of Polly Galen Smith and her attacker; I shuddered. I had just brushed into a cobweb, and its touch, sticky and intimate, remained in my hair. Now I was less certain of what I breathed. Was it the effluvia of the mud flats on the old Chesapeake and Ohio Canal? Even as the whoops and cries of a drinking party can travel immaculately through a fog, to be heard a league away on a stranger's porch, so I wondered if the bay marsh that had witnessed the death of the man who might or might not be Harlot could be dispatching its scent hundreds of miles north to me. In what a malodorous place had the body first washed ashore! The dank smell I used to fear at the bottom of the Keep must have been the first herald of such a horror. Now the wooden steps to the Vault were rotted and loose. It was so long since I had used them that I had forgotten how they could cry out. I might as well have been walking into a ward of men maimed by war. Each step had its own bottomless lament.

There were no lights in the Vault. The bulbs, as I recounted, were long burned out. Only the open door provided a shaft of illumination. My shadow preceding me, I worked my way down, feeling as if I pushed my limbs through palisades of oppression merely to reach the cubicle where Kittredge slept. It was only when I stood in the near-to-complete darkness of the inner room, light from the cellar above much reduced by the right-angle turn off the entrance, that I could dare to recognize it had been years since I ventured here. How decomposed were the bunks when I touched them.

One foam mattress had gone to powder less than the others, and, on it, Kittredge was lying. There was almost no light in the Vault, but by reflection, her pale skin was white. I could see that her eyes were open, and when I approached, she turned her head ever so slightly to indicate that she was aware of me. Neither of us spoke, not at first. I thought again of that moment years ago when the full moon rose over the horizon from the bottom of the notch between two black hills, and the surface of the dark pond on which my canoe floated was alive with a pagan light.

"Harry," she said, "there's something for you to know."

"I expect there is," I said gently. The anticipation of what she would say reverberated in my head before her words. I experienced that pang one feels so rarely but so precisely in marriage—alarm in advance of the next irremediable step. I did not want her to go on.

"I've been unfaithful," she said.

In every death is a celebration; in every ecstasy, one little death. It was as if the two halves of my soul had just exchanged their places. My guilt for every moment spent with Chloe was, on the instant, relieved of weight; my woe at the new space opened between Kittredge and me rushed in on a flood. The hurricane I had been awaiting in the Tropic of Cerebrum was here. Its first blow to my head came down with the long sullen smash of an ugly swell against an old wooden hull.

"With whom?" I asked. "With whom were you unfaithful?" and the royal observer in myself, untouched by hurricane, earthquake,

fire, or storms at sea, had time to notice the rectitude of my grammar—what a peculiar fellow was I!

"There was an afternoon with Harlot," she said, "but it wasn't
quite an affair, although it was—awful." She stopped. "Harry, there's
someone else."

"Is it Dix Butler?" I asked.

"Yes," she said, "Dix Butler. I fear I'm in love with him. I hate
the very thought of it, but, Harry, I may be in love with that man."

"No," I said, "don't say that. You must not say that."

"It is," she said, "a different feeling."

"He's a bold man, but not a good one," I told her, and my voice
came out like a verdict rendered from the center of me. No, he was
not a good man.

"It doesn't matter," she said. "I'm not a good woman. No more
than you are really a good man. It is not what we are," she said. "I
think it is what we inspire. Do you know," she added gently, "I like
to believe that God is present when we make love. It was certainly
true with Gobby, and just as true with you. It was just that God was
there in the guise of Jehovah. He was over us, and full of judgment.
So harsh. But with Dix Butler, I can't explain why, I feel very close
to Christ. Dix is far away from any kind of compassion, but Christ
chooses to come close to me then. I have not felt such tenderness since
Christopher died. Do you see, I no longer care about myself." She
took my hand. "That was always my dungeon—to live entirely within
myself. Now I think of how beautiful it would be if I could give Dix
some conception of the compassion I feel. So, you see, it just doesn't
concern me whether Dix, by your lights or anyone else's, is deserving
or not deserving."

As I stood before her, one awful image came near. It was myself
in my car, a livid vision: I had crashed against a tree. My face looked
out at me from the back of the head of the man who was smashed.
Was it only an illusion that I had driven away from that endlessly long
skid?

Then the bottom fell away. I plunged into my true fear. With the
force of an infection that bursts an organ wall to race through the
body, had the haunting of this Vault broken out?

"No," I said, "I will not give you up." As if I were in a trance
where one climbs higher and higher into the rigging of one's soul in
order to dare the leap down, I said, "Dix is on his way here, isn't he?"

"Yes," she said, "he will be here, and you must leave. I cannot let you be here." Tears were just visible in this light. She wept silently. "That would be as awful as the day you and I told Hugh that he must give me a divorce."

"No," I said again, "I have been afraid of Dix Butler since the day I met him, and that is why I am obliged to remain. I want to face him. For myself."

"No," she said. She sat up. "It has all gone wrong, it is all a mess, and Hugh is dead. It is hopeless for you to remain. But if you go away and are not here to be found, then Dix can take care of me. I think he will be able to. Harry, I tell you, there is no way to measure how many ways it will go wrong if you are still here."

I was no longer certain whether she spoke of love, or of peril, but then she answered the question.

"Harry," she said, "it will be a disaster. I know what you have been doing for Hugh. I was working with some of that myself."

"And Dix?"

"Dix knows enough to keep a lot of people in place. That is why you have to leave. Otherwise, I will be pulled down with you. We will both be destroyed."

I embraced her, I kissed her with that whole mixture of love and desperation that is the only force available to ignite the cold engine of matrimony when passion is lost. "It is all right," I said. "I will leave if you think it is necessary. But you must leave with me. I know that you do not love Dix. It is just an affair."

That was when she broke my heart altogether. "No," she said, "I want to be alone with him."

We have come to the last moment of this night that I can recount as a witness. I have some recollection of picking up my heavy manuscript of *The Game* and making my exit by the pantry door to take a silent promenade in the darkness down Long Doane. I passed around one of the guards, and I recall putting the boat back into the channel, but the tide was low and I crossed without difficulty to a neighbor's camp a quarter of a mile south of where I parked my car. I remember driving to Portland, and emptying our bank account in the morning, per Kittredge's suggestion, as if, our marriage gone, the umbilical of property still existed. "Harry," she had said at the end, "take the money that's in Portland. It's twenty thousand and more. You'll need it, and I have the other account."

So I emptied what was there, and flew to New York, and here I do not know if I can go on with even this much summary, for as I learned a day and a half later (in the full seizure that accompanies personal and unendurable news when it comes to you by way of the media) our Keep had burned at dawn and the body of Reed Arnold Rosen had been found. There was no word in any of those reports of Kittredge, Dix, or the guards outside.

That night now exists for me in a darkness equal to the void which comes over a cinema palace when the film is savaged by the claw in the gate and tears, the last image dying with a groan as the sound rolls off the sprocket. A wall arises within my memory as black as our incapacity to know where death will lead us. I see the Keep in flames.

For the next months in New York, I obliged myself to give an account of my last night at the Keep. It was an act, as you may expect, of no ordinary difficulty, and there were days and nights when I could not write a word. I believe that I clung to sanity by an expedition into madness. I found that I kept returning to the moment when my car was turning through its skid and time seemed to divide as neatly as a deck of cards cut in two. I began to have the certainty that if I returned to that hairpin turn where the wheel whipped out of my hands, why then I would not see an empty road, but an automobile smashed against a tree, and behind the windshield would be my shattered person. I saw this mangled presence with such clarity that I was convinced: I had *gone over*. The idea that I was still alive was an illusion. The rest of that night had taken place in no larger theater than the small part of the mind that survives as a guide over the first roads chosen by the dead. All recollection of myself driving a car, headlights prancing forward like the luminous forelegs of a great steed, was no more than the unwinding of such expectations. I was merely in the first hour of my death. It was part of the balance and the blessing of death that all uncompleted thoughts existing in our mind at a moment of sudden extinction would continue to uncoil. If I had been feeling a touch unreal on my return to Doane, why, that might be the only clue that I was on the pathways of the dead. In the beginning, such roads might hardly diverge from all one knew. If the night had ended with the disappearance of my wife, had it really been my own end that I was mourning? Was Kittredge still waiting for me to return to the Keep on this stormy night? By such means did I keep my sanity through a year in New York. A dead man has less reason to go mad.

IT IS A MEASURE of the life I led in hiding through that year that I did not do anything about the peculiar condition of my passport. Out of the question was any attempt to replace it. Looking like a small layered pastry, this passport was now being held aloft by the Soviet guard in the glass booth, and he had an incredulous look on his face. Was I proposing to enter the U.S.S.R. by way of Sheremetyevo International Airport, Moscow, holding such water-soaked credentials? Worse. He did not yet know that the name of William Holding Libby referred to an imaginary life which would not bear up under serious interrogation.

"Passport," said the fellow out of his glass cage, "this passport! . . . Why?"

His English was going to prove no more useful than my Russian.

"River," I tried to say in his tongue, helping to suggest that one had fallen into the river with the passport. I was not about to admit I had consigned the document to a laundry room dryer. "River," I thought I was saying, but later, studying phrases for tourists in my guidebook, I came to recognize that I had used the words for arm and rib and fish (respectively ruka, rebro, and ryba). Doubtless I was telling him that I had stuck my passport up my rib and lost my arm to the fish—God knows it was enough to leave my Sovietsky critically befuddled. Like a good stubborn dog, he kept saying, "Passport—no good. Why?" After which he would draw himself to full height and eyeball me—they were obviously groomed to do that. I was perspiring as profusely as if I were wholly innocent, which in some degree I was. How, I kept asking myself, could I have failed to anticipate the consternation this puffed-up torte of a passport would arouse under examination?

"Not good," he said. "Expired."

I could feel the line of passengers waiting behind me.

"No. Not expired. Please," I said to him, "pozhaluysta!" and reached out my hand. He gave the passport over in great suspicion and I turned with caution the faded crinkled leaves. There! I had found the proper page. My passport had not expired. I pointed out the date and handed it back to him.

The Soviet guard might have been a Minnesota farmboy. He had blue eyes, high cheekbones, and close-cropped blond hair: I don't think he was twenty-five. "You," he fixed me with his finger, "you—waiting," and walked off to come back immediately with an officer, a man of twenty-eight, dark hair, a mustache, the same dull green soldier's tunic with tight collar and braiding.

"Why?" said the new one, pointing to my passport as if it were a wholly execrable object.

I found the separate words for ice and water. They came into my mind like a pas de deux. "Lyod," I said, "bolshoy lyod. Much ice." I spread my hands as if I were smoothing a tablecloth. Then I gave to the horizontal plane just fashioned in the air one good karate chop. I made a cracking sound. Hopefully, it might sound like an ice-pond breaking up, and I plunged my hand toward my feet. "Voda. Bolshaya voda—lots of water, isn't that so?" I waved my hands in desperate strokes. A frozen swimmer.

"Ochen kolodno," the first guard said.

"Ochen kolodno. Right. Ice-cold, very cold."

They nodded. They studied the passport back and forth, they looked at my visa which was clean and had the stamps it needed. They fumbled with my name aloud. "William Holding Libby?" It came out: "Veelyam Haul-ding Leeboo?"

"Yes," I said, "that's it."

They studied some names on a hit list. Libby was not on it. They stared at each other. They sighed. They were not dumb. They could feel something was wrong. On the other hand, should they take me off for further questioning, they would have papers to fill out, possibly a lost evening. They must have had plans to go out after work, for the blond guard now stamped my papers. He gave a big kid's grin. "Pardone," he said, attempting to give it a friendly Italian-French spin. "Pardone."

The rest of the way through Arrivals showed me Sheremetyevo, a concrete airport built as a showcase for the 1980 Olympics: Welcome to the U.S.S.R. (Note that our Soviet walls are gray!) My bags went through Customs. The microfilm of Alpha, stowed in my secret compartment, attracted no notice—the suitcase had been designed to take confidential papers through routine inspections. I passed the last gate and encountered multilingual signs that told me to look for the Intourist guide. Instead, a cabdriver approached, a snarling New York–type cabdriver who reminded me of Thomas Wolfe's dictum that people in the same profession tend to be the same all over the world. My man wanted twenty dollars to take me to the Metropole, a hotel which a travel agent in New York had assured me was a piece of good luck to get into, the Metropole being almost as difficult to snag as the old National. "I can slip you into the new National," the travel agent had said, "but you don't want that. It's all tourist groups."

"Yes," I had said, "I don't want tourist groups." Had something been obvious about me? Of course, I had popped in on the agent, paid cash, asked for speed in processing my visa (on the assumption he had connections sufficient to rush one through occasionally), and he did, and I tipped him for getting the permissions in a week although it had probably meant putting William Holding Libby on a KGB list which went under some unappetizing category like Individual Tourist, Special. Now, before I was even settled into my cab seat, the driver announced in his black-market English that he wished to buy American dollars from me. His rate, three rubles for a buck, was almost four times better than official exchange.

It could be a trap. I didn't like him. I certainly didn't trust him. The authorities could have me jailed for dealing in rubles on the black market.

Indeed, the driver was demanding so much of my attention that I was hardly looking out the window. I was not taking in my first impressions of Russia. Travel in a state of nerves is like passage through a tube. The racket of the car—we were in some kind of Soviet mini-flivver—impinged on me more than the landscape. The driver's voice, "All right, you tell me, hey, how many dollars you got, come on," gargled in my ear.

We passed expanses of clean snow, dirty snow, and melted fields about as sprightly as the mud in the Jersey flats. Bits of Moscow began to appear, funky little gingerbread shacks by the side of the road, built in rows but yawning individually, paint peeling. Then came palisades of high-rise housing projects, dirty white for the most part in the dirty white snow. They looked as if the plaster had cracked on the lower floors before they put the trowel to the top ones: What a misery was this land. The March sky was as gray as the concrete walls in the Sheremetyevo Airport. Communism was irritating me personally at this point, equal to the cabdriver, pushy, dirty, depressed, eager for loot, out of date. Of course, the driver might be some outrigger of the KGB. Was I being encountered?

A banner stretched across the superhighway. A legend in Russian. I saw Lenin in the words. Some bouquet, doubtless, of homiletic language. Over how many roads in how many mean and outrageously underequipped Third World countries would you see these banners? Zaire for one. Ditto Nicaragua, Syria, North Korea, Uganda. Who could care? I couldn't even come out of my tunnel. Moscow streets began to appear, but the side windows of my car were mud-spattered, and sights to the front were only visible through the slip-slop of two overworked wipers that kept drawing striated salt fans on the glass. The driver was as sullen as heavy weather in August.

Now we were on a large boulevard without much traffic. Solemn old

*buildings—government departments and specialist institutes—peram-
bulated by the side windows. There were few pedestrians. It was Sunday.
This was downtown.*

*We came to a stop in a public square before an old green six-story
building. Its sign read* **RUSSIAN**. *I was at the Metropole. My home
away from home.*

*I gave the cabdriver two dollars for a tip. He wanted ten. He had his
own peculiar psychic force. Some weak nerve in me was pinched, for I gave
him five. My nerves, we can repeat, were not what once they were.*

*A stocky, wide-jawed old boy, equal to a retired Mafia soldier of the
lowest rank, was the doorman. He had a decoration on the lapel of his gray
coat—a hero of the Great War. He would not be about to show cordiality
to a stranger.*

*Nor was he in a rush to help me with the bags. His function was to
keep people out. I had to show him the travel-agency voucher in order to
get through the door. Inside, the lobby was grim. The palette passed from
cigar-butt brown to railroad-coach green. The floor was an aged parquet that
buckled like cheap linoleum when you stepped on it. I felt as if I had landed
in one of those unhappy hotels on the side streets of Times Square that sit
in old cigar smoke, waiting to be demolished.*

*Was this the famous Metropole where, if my historic recollections
proved correct, the Bolsheviks used to gather before and after the Revolution? A huge marble stairway spiraled upward in right-angle turns around
an elevator shaft faced in wrought iron.*

*The woman at the registration desk was wearing a sweater and had a
nose cold. She wore eyeglasses, was plain, and pretended not to notice me
until I seized her attention. Her English had an unhappy accent reminiscent of such tortures to the spirit as ballet lessons for unpromising girls. The
elevator operator, another decorated old war hero, was gruff, and the
concierge on the fourth floor was a heavy blonde of about fifty with a beehive
hairdo and a big tough Russian face—she looked like a mate for the
doorman. She sat behind a little glass-topped desk facing the elevator, kept
a rose in a small vase, and scowled at the task of looking for my key, which
was large and bronze and as heavy as a pocketful of change.*

*The route to my room led down one long dark corridor and then turned
a right angle to another old shellacked floor. It was parquet with a considerable number of gaps in which squares of plywood had been inserted. A
narrow, red carpet, half a football field in length, went down the first
corridor, then half a football field down the other to my door. Since the floor*

buckled every step of the way, I had the sensation—if I may allude to
frozen water once more—that I was hopping from one ice floe to the next.

My room was eleven feet by fourteen and had a ceiling twelve feet high.
The window looked on a gray court. I had a chest of drawers and a narrow
bed with a thin, European mattress laid upon a larger mattress. At the head
was a bolster as heavy as a water-soaked log. Plus a TV set!

I turned it on. Electronic snow, pulses of wave-over. Black-and-white.
A show for children. I turned it off. I sat on my narrow single bed and put
my head in my hands. I got up. I closed the curtains to the courtyard. I
sat down again. I was here, and—assuming I had entered without attracting official attention—I could stay here for a week at least, and sort some
questions into categories. I had so many questions that I no longer looked
for answers. Only for categories.

The rigors of remembering a life that had, in many ways, terminated
in the middle of one long night had me proceeding, as you may imagine,
through states of peculiar delicacy. A director once told me how, after one
of his films was wrapped, he had not stopped living with the camera crew
and actors. They had departed, but he would awaken from every sleep with
fresh commands. "Bernard, we have to reshoot the market sequence today.
Tell Production it's a hundred extras at least." He would be out of bed and
shaving before he could say to himself: "The movie is over. You have gone
mad. You cannot shoot any more." But he had, as he explained to me,
stepped through the looking glass. The film was more real than his life.

Was I equal to that director? For a year, hiding out in a rented room
off an airshaft in an apartment house in the Bronx, I had worked to raise
a wall between my last memory of Kittredge and myself. Sometimes a
month would go by without incident, and I would sleep through the night
and work through the day putting one word onto another as if I were
spinning a thread to guide me out of the caves.

Then, without warning, love for her would strike. I felt like an epileptic
on the edge of grand mal. One misstep and seizures would come. After
many months, the Bronx became untenable for me—I had to move.

Besides, they would be looking for me. That was certain. The longer
I did not surface, the wider would become their frame of reference. They
would have to wonder if I had moved to Moscow. How I laughed—in those
paroxysms of silent laughter with which one entertains oneself in the
pit—that all the while I was living in the Bronx, they were thinking of me
in Moscow.

Yet out of a logic of separate steps that seemed altogether rigorous to me—although I could not specify the steps, I had come to the conclusion that I had to take a trip—for the first time—to the U.S.S.R. I did not know why. I was in profundities of trouble if they ever ran me down in Bronx County, New York, but to be found in Moscow by the KGB? With my extended memoir in microfilm? Why, that would be unforgivable even to myself. What if, despite safe passage through Customs, the Russians knew of my arrival? If Harlot had defected, my present alias might be sitting in Soviet files. That supposition, however, belonged to the world of common sense. I was living in a domain of subterranean logic. Which told me to take along the microfilm of Alpha. Who knows how the boxcars of obsession are shuttled through the freight yards of sleep? I did not feel insane, yet, there was a schedule to madness I seemed to obey. I clung to my writings as if they were body organs. I could never have left Alpha behind. Indeed, the old Jewish lady in whose apartment on the Grand Concourse I had rented a room was aware that I was a man who was writing a book.

"Oh, Mr. Sawyer," she said when I told her of leaving, "I'm going to miss the sound of your typewriter."

"Well, I'm going to miss you and Mr. Lowenthal."

He was an eighty-year-old arthritic; she, a seventy-five-year-old diabetic—we had entertained not much more than passing conversations for most of a year, but I was content with that. Bless them—I knew their lives were bound to be, should I know them better, boring to me. I could feel the worm of condescension stirring when we spoke. It was hard for me to take people seriously who had spent their lives being good thrifty middle-class people. While I expected they would be curious enough about my past, I did not have the heart to regale them at length with the fictitious careers and possible marriages of one Philip Sawyer—a name I employed in order to leave no trail for William Holding Libby, but then there was not much flimflam with the Lowenthals. We made occasional conversation when we met in the hall, and that was it. They were able to supplement their retirement monies with my rent (paid, happily, for both parties, in cash) and I could keep my privacy relatively intact. I stayed in my room except when I grew tired of soup on a hot plate and went out to eat or see a film. I wrote slowly and painfully.

The writing of Omega, however, had gone as well as could be expected, considering how slowly it did go. There were days when I felt neither haunted nor invaded. Nonetheless, I knew I was a boulder on the edge of a cliff. Sooner or later, it would fall. It did. Moscow blinked in my mind like a lit-up billboard. I saw the travel agent, made preparations, tried to study Russian, and said farewell to the Lowenthals. I told them I was going to Seattle. Mrs. Lowenthal said in reply, "Will you have a finished book for your family to read?"

"Yes," I said.

"I hope they like it."

"Well," I said, "I hope so too."

"Maybe you'll even get a publisher."

"Conceivably."

"If you do, please mail me the volume. I'll pay for it. I want you to autograph my copy."

"Oh, Mrs. Lowenthal," I said, "I'd be delighted to send you a free copy."

It was exactly the sort of conversation she would never forget. If they ever found this lair in the Bronx, they would learn from her that I had done some typing.

I got off the bed of my room in the Metropole, opened my valise and started to unpack. I took out everything but the envelope containing Alpha. I was hardly ready to begin reading. It was four now, Sunday afternoon, Moscow time, which was eight o'clock in the morning for me. I was sleepy, I was exhausted. I had left at eight in the evening from Kennedy, lost eight hours to the clock, and ten to the flight (with the transit stop at Heathrow) and had landed at 2:00 P.M. Moscow time which was 6:00 A.M. New York time. My nerves, long out of synchronization, were upside down. Since it was 8:00 A.M. now in New York, no wonder I felt full of the false vigor that comes in the morning after a night of false sleep. I had to get out of the room for a while.

I took a walk. My first steps in Moscow. If forty years of American media was enough to bring anyone to the conviction that Communism was evil, I had had my stints of special scholarship. Communism might well be evil. That is an awesome and terrible thesis, but then the simple can reign over the complex. Perhaps evil was to be comprehended in the grand thesis that Communism was evil.

My first steps, therefore, on Moscow streets were hardly routine to me.

I felt not unlike a prisoner let out of jail after twenty years. Such a man does not know the world he is entering, does not, for example, know how to walk into a store and buy a pair of pants. He has been issued pants for twenty years. Now, I did not know what was allowed me here. I was not certain I could leave the hotel and go out on the street without some proper paper being stamped. I hung about the lobby to observe the comings and goings, but soon felt uneasy. My continued presence might become suspect. So I took a chance, walked to the entrance, stepped out, and was met by a scowl from the doorman—it would take me a while to realize that because he had not placed me yet as a checked-in hotel guest, he was scowling.

At any rate, I was on the street. Cabdrivers, parked at the hotel curb, yelled at me as a prospect, passersby took their glances. I just walked. I made no moves to determine if anyone was following, for I did not wish to show any knowledge of evasive tactics, but, then, for the little it was worth, I did not feel as if I were being followed. I had put on an old jacket and wore a black knit hat pulled over my ears like a merchant seaman. It was all right. I felt like giving a great whoop.

A square away from the hotel would be, I knew, a statue to Feliks Dzerzhinsky, founder of the Cheka, "Sword of the Revolution," great-grandfather of the KGB. Back of him would be the infamous Lubyanka. From books, photographs, and debriefings, I knew that place better than any American prison—I had listened a hundred times in the imaginary auditorium of my ear to the screams of the tortured in the cellars of the Lubyanka, and I did not know if I wanted to go near it now, but, thus debating, went directly from the Metropole to Dzerzhinsky Square. Before me was an edifice, a late nineteenth-century seven-story morgue of an office, the Lubyanka, once a prerevolutionary business palace for czarist insurance companies. It still had white curtains on the windows, and highly polished brass fittings on the entrance door, but its exterior wall was a soiled khaki-yellow, a dismal, old-fashioned building in and out of which on this late Sunday afternoon came and went a few men wearing officer's uniforms. The air was as cold as a New England forest in winter, and all the while I heard no screams. This Lubyanka—conceivably my future home—failed to stir adrenaline.

I wandered away through side streets, gray in the light, near to black in the shadows, "the old streets of the merchants"—a phrase from my guidebook. Had these enclaves of gloom ever lifted? It was nearly agreeable to discover depression this palpable, and I had a moment in which I understood the comforts of gloom—was this my first real thought in a week? For even as the acceptance of one's own poverty might be the first protection against corruption of the soul, so was gloom a fortress in which one could live encapsulated from insanity. Yes, the protective if heavy resonance of gloom would not be hard to find in Moscow, and thinking this, I came out of one more side street onto Red Square, a shock as nice as stepping from a Roman alley into the great plaza of St. Peter's, except here was no

Vatican but a field of cobblestones near to half a mile long and hundreds of feet wide spreading out to the walls of the Kremlin. On the gray horizon were early signs of a lavender twilight, but Russians were still waiting to see the tomb of Lenin and his body, preserved below, in its vault. Two thousand people, two by two, were in that line, and perhaps twenty people entered the tomb each minute, suggesting that the last man in the queue would have to wait one hundred minutes in this cold, a reasonable mortification for a pilgrimage.

I began to pay attention to these Russians on the street. They all looked middle-aged. Even the young had an air of relinquishment that speaks of middle age. All the same, Red Square was a cheerful scene. To my astonishment, it was cheerful on this late Sunday afternoon. There was a shimmer to the air, a conviviality to the faces red with cold. Busloads of tourists—native Russians—were leaving, others were yet arriving. Hundreds of others walking through the Square were showing the simple happiness that comes to hardworking people when they are transported to an important place. These could have been Mormons, or Jehovah's Witnesses, on a ferry to the Statue of Liberty.

How much like a film it appeared to be. The center of Red Square rose higher than the corners, which left people in the distance only visible above the knee. Their feet had disappeared beneath the cobblestone horizon. Everyone seemed to bounce, therefore, as they walked, even as heads bob when a crowd is perambulating toward a telephoto lens. I did not know the history of Red Square, which is to say, didn't know what old great events had produced this bouquet of the spirits, but my own were up—I felt delivered from the iron clangor of the Bronx and the walls of Moscow. I was ready, for one irrational instant, to celebrate, I hardly knew what. Maybe it was only the joy of coming to the end of a trip.

I went back to the Metropole, received an increment more of greeting from the doorman, the elevator man, and the dezhurnaya (my floor lady), returned to the room, sat on my bed, sat on the chair next to the bed, took down my valise, looked at the neatly concealed Velcro seam to the false compartment where I kept the microfilm, put the valise up in the closet again, and realized abruptly how tired I was. I was weary from the cold outside, the scrambling of the hours, my whippings-about of mood, the rigors of the walk—everyone in Moscow seemed to stride along at top pace, and I, good American, had stepped it up to stay with them. Now I was tired with the real desolations of my mood. I did not know if I had ever felt so alone on a quiet day.

I went downstairs to eat, but it was not much better. I was seated among strangers at a table for eight with a rumpled tablecloth, not dirty exactly, but no more immaculate than a shirt that has been worn for a few hours. The only dish available was chicken Kiev, a rubber chicken fit for a routine political banquet with a gusher of butter that tasted like lubricating oil mixed with some sour sorrow emanating from the kitchen. The kasha was overcooked, the dark bread was coarse, the fresh vegetable was a thin slice of tomato. Then came one cookie and a cup of tea. The waitress was a heavy, middle-aged woman with weighty personal concerns. She sighed a lot. It took all of the little attention she could give to the world outside herself to keep level with her job.

After I left the table, I realized that I had supped in the equivalent of the hotel's coffee shop, an eating hall, so to speak, exclusively for guests. The real restaurant, designed for a more prosperous gang, was entered by two glass doors off the lobby. Here black marketeers and bureaucrats, accompanied by their wives, waited on line. Inside, a dance band as full of pep as some of the prom bands that used to work the dances at Yale was hacking away, a weird, bouncy band whose sound reverberated through the glass doors.

I went back to the elevator. I needed to sleep. I hoped I would get to sleep. At the landing, as I got off, my dezhurnaya with the blond beehive gave a real smile when she handed over the key. I understood. Already I gave every evidence of going by her desk many times a day, of being a regular customer. The comings and goings of her keys were her liveliest transactions. True hell. Homage to Sartre.

I locked my door, undressed, washed my face, dried my hands. The sink was cracked, the soap was gritty, the bath towel was small and coarse. So was the toilet paper. This was one of the ten best hotels in Moscow. I was furious suddenly at I knew not what. How did these people presume to be our greatest enemy on earth? They did not even have the wherewithal to be evil.

Then I got into bed. Sleep did not come. There was every intimation the High Holies were on their way. I decided to get up again and read Alpha. Will it tell you something of the year I spent in that rented room in the apartment of the Lowenthals that I knew the first pages by heart? But then, I knew much of the material by heart. It had taken me through many a night when I could not work on Omega. Yes, even when Kittredge appeared in these pages, Alpha was endurable. My actual love affair with Kittredge had not begun, after all, during the period I covered in Alpha.

Besides, as I projected the microfilm, I would sometimes whisper the words aloud. That held off certain thoughts. Even as we and the Soviets had spent years jamming each other's radio broadcasts, so would I recite the manuscript of Alpha whenever Kittredge became too alive. Such observances did not always work, but when they did, I could turn the corner. The ghosts of long-gone deeds would not appear, and I could live with Kittredge. Alpha was all I had of her now. I began, therefore, to recite my first sentences aloud, slowly, quietly, intoning the words; the sounds themselves came forward as forces in the unseen war of all those silences in myself that rode to war when I slept.

Alpha commenced. I read by microfilm even as I whispered some of the words aloud. It was half of my past, expressed in what style I could muster after years of ghostwriting, but it was a good half of my past: "A few years ago, in disregard of the discretionary contract I signed in 1955 on entering the CIA . . ." That is how the Foreword to Alpha begins. (Of course, a two-thousand-page manuscript is always in need of a foreword.)

So I was back in the book again, reading with my white hotel-room wall for a screen, moving my microfilm manually through my special flashlight equipped with its filmgate and lens, reading about the early career in the CIA of Harry Hubbard, a name that sometimes seemed as separate from myself as the name one repeats on shaking hands with a stranger just introduced in a room full of other strangers whose names one will also repeat. I felt as near and as removed from my original pages as if I were looking at old photographs attaching me imperfectly to the past.

FOREWORD

A FEW YEARS AGO, IN DISREGARD OF THE DISCRETIONARY CONTRACT I signed in 1955 on entering the CIA, I embarked on a memoir that looked to present a candid picture of twenty-five active years in the Agency. I expected the work to be of average length, but my account proliferated until it may now be the longest reminiscence ever written by anyone within the Agency. Perhaps I was captured by Thomas Mann's dictum that "Only the exhaustive is truly interesting."

This attempt, then, to follow the changes in my character and outlook from 1955 to 1965 (for indeed I have managed to carry my account no further as yet) is not to be read as a memoir. It is rather a *Bildungsroman,* an extended narrative of a young man's education and development. Any sophisticated reader of spy novels picking up this book in the hope of encountering a splendidly plotted work will discover himself on unfamiliar ground. As an Agency officer, I certainly encountered my fair share of plots, initiating some, concluding others, and serving as messenger for many, but I was rarely able to see them whole. By bits and pieces they passed before me. It is even a reasonable conclusion that this is the way of life for nearly all of us in CIA. One learns to live with the irony that we who spend our lives in intelligence usually read spy novels with the wistful sentiment, "Ah, if only my job could turn out so well shaped!"

Nonetheless, I hope to offer my private insight into the nature of our daily lives and our intermittent adventures. They are sometimes exceptional for the complexity of the inner experience we encounter while spending our professional years on the team that plays this unique game.

PART ONE

EARLY YEARS, EARLY TRAINING

1

LET ME OFFER THE PRIMARY FACT. I AM A HUBBARD. BRADFORD AND Fidelity Hubbard arrived in Plymouth seven years after the *Mayflower* and branches of the clan are to be found today in Connecticut, Maine, New Hampshire, Rhode Island, and Vermont. To my knowledge, however, I am the first Hubbard to make public admission that the family name is not quite as impressive as our share of lawyers and bankers, doctors and legislators, one Civil War general, several professors, and my grandfather, Smallidge Kimble Hubbard, Headmaster of St. Matthew's. He remains a legend to this day. At the age of ninety, he still managed on warm summer mornings to get into his single shell and row one hundred strokes out into Blue Hill Bay. Of course, one stroke missed and over he would have gone into cold Maine waters, a near-fatal proposition, but he died in bed. My father, Boardman Kimble Hubbard, known to his friends as Cal (for Carl "Cal" Hubbell the New York Giants pitcher, whom he revered), was equally exceptional, but so divided a man that my wife, Kittredge, used him as a source of private reference for her work *The Dual Soul*. He was a swashbuckler and yet a deacon; a bold, powerful man who showered in cold water with the same morning certainty that others used to feel while eating eggs and bacon. He went to church each Sunday; he was a prodigious philanderer. During the time shortly after World War II, when J. Edgar Hoover was doing his best to convince Harry Truman that the proposed CIA was not necessary and the FBI could take over all such jobs, my father went on a save-our-outfit mission. He seduced a few key secretaries in the State Department, thereby picking up a flood of in-office secrets which he then passed to Allen Dulles, who promptly sent such product on to the White House with a cover story to protect the secretaries. It certainly helped to convince the White House that we might need a separate Intelligence body. Allen Dulles was fond of Cal Hubbard after that, and said to me once, "Your father won't admit it, but that month with the secretaries was the best time of his life."

I loved my father outrageously and thereby had a frightened childhood, worried, strained, and cold within. I wished to be the salt of his salt but my stuff was damp. Much of the time I came near to hating him because he was disappointed in me and I did not hear from him often.

My mother was a different matter. I am the product of a marriage between two people so quintessentially incompatible that they might as well have come from separate planets. Indeed, my parents were soon separated and I spent my boyhood trying to keep two disjointed personalities together.

My mother was small-boned, attractive, and blond, and she lived, but for summer at Southampton, in that social nucleus of New York which is bounded by Fifth Avenue on the west, Park Avenue to the east, the Eighties to the north, and the Sixties to the south. She was a Jewish Princess but the emphasis can be put on the second word. She could not have told you the difference between the Torah and the Talmud. She brought me up to be ignorant of every Jewish subject but one: the names of prominent New York banking houses with Semitic roots. I think my mother thought of Salomon Brothers and Lehman Brothers as ports of call in some future storm.

It was sufficient that my mother's great-great-grandfather was a remarkable man named Chaim Silberzweig (who had his name streamlined by immigration officials to Hyman Silverstein). He came over as an immigrant in 1840 and rose from a street peddler to the clear-cut status of a department-store owner. His sons became merchant princes and his grandsons were among the first Jews tolerated in Newport. (The name by now was Silverfield.) If each generation of my mother's family was more spendthrift than the one before, it was never at a catastrophic rate: My mother was worth about as much in real money as the first Silverstein had left for his immediate heirs—and she possessed about a quarter of his Jewish blood. The Silverfield men married golden gentile women.

That is my mother's family. Although I saw more of her when young than of my father, it was my paternal grandfather with his single shell that I deemed to be true kin. My mother's side I tried to ignore. A man on death row once said: "We owe nothing to our parents—we just pass through them." I felt that way about my mother. From an

early age I did not take her seriously. She could be charming and full
of interesting follies; she was certainly a lot better than average at
giving merry dinner parties. She was also, unfortunately, the owner of
a terrible reputation. The Social Register dropped her a few years after
Jessica Silverfield Hubbard became an ex-Hubbard, but it took another ten years before her best friends stopped seeing her. The reason,
I suspect, was not her succession of affairs so much as her propensity
to lie. She was a psychopathic liar, and finally her memory became her
only lasting friend. It always told her what she wished to remember
about the present and the past. In consequence, you never could
know what anyone was up to if you listened to her. I make this point
because my mother equipped me, I believe, for counterespionage, a
field where we do, after all, attempt to implant errors in our opponent's knowledge.

At any rate, I can hardly pretend that I ended as any good fraction
of a Jew. My only kinship with "that herring baron," as my mother
referred to great-great-grandfather Chaim Silberzweig, is that anti-
Semitic slurs made me tense. I might as well have grown up in a ghetto
for the size of the fury aroused in me. For I would then feel Jewish.
Of course, my idea of feeling Jewish was to be reminded of the strain
on people's faces in the rush hour on the New York subway as they
stood prey to harsh and screeching sounds.

I had, however, a privileged boyhood. I went to the Buckley
School and was a Knickerbocker Gray until asked to withdraw, a
reflection of my serious incompetence at close-order drill. While
marching, I would generate headaches of such intensity that I would
fail to hear commands.

Of course, the bad reputation of my mother may have been
another factor, and I take confirmation for this suspicion by the
manner in which my father had me reinstated. As a cold-shower
warrior he was not inclined to ask for favors for his progeny. This
time, however, he called on people one saves for emergencies. The
Hubbards had well-placed friends in New York, and my father took
me to meet a few alumni of the Grays. "It's unfair. They're blaming
the boy for *her,*" was part of what I overheard, and it must have done
the work. I was reinstated, and managed to soldier my way thereafter
with fewer headaches, although I never knew one relaxed breath as a
cadet.

I suppose people who were happy when young may recall their
childhood well. I remember little. Summary disposes of the years and

I collect memories by subjects. I can always answer such absurd essay questions as "What was the most important day you spent with a parent?" I would reply: "When my father took me to Twenty-One for lunch on my fifteenth birthday."

Twenty-One was the perfect place to take me. While my father did not know "one superior hell of a lot"—his phrase—about boys, he knew enough to be standing at the bar waiting for me.

I cannot swear in all confidence that the downstairs dining room has not been altered since 1948, but I might bet on the possibility. I think the same model toys are still suspended from the low dark ceiling, same steamships, 1915 Spad biplanes, railroad locomotives, and trolley cars. The little coupe with its rumble seat and spare tire in the white slipcover is still above the bar. Above the bottle cabinet hang the same hunting horns, cutlasses, elephant tusks, and one pair of boxing gloves small enough to fit an infant. My father told me that Jack Dempsey gave those gloves to the owner of Twenty-One, Jack Kriendler, and while I would hope the story is true, my father did not mind polishing legends of his own devising. I think he had concluded that good feeling was always in danger of being wiped out; ergo, he gilded the stories he told. He had, by the way, a degree of resemblance to Ernest Hemingway—he was at least equally vivid in presence—and he cultivated the same large dark mustache. He also had Hemingway's build. Sporting relatively spindly legs for a man of strength, he often said, "I might have made first team All-American fullback if not for my pins." He also had a great barrel of a chest which bore a distinct likeness to the antique bronze cash register on the bar at Twenty-One. My father's heart beat with pride.

Of course, the pride was for himself. If I state that my father was vain and self-centered, I do not wish to demean him. While he carried the complacent look of a successful college athlete, his fundamental relation to others was a reflection of his concealed but endless negotiations with himself: The two halves of his soul were far apart. The deacon and the swashbuckler had miles to walk each night before they slept; I think his strength was that he had managed to find some inner cooperation between these disparate halves. When the headmaster's son, impacted with Cromwellian rectitude, was able to hook up with a venture that the conquistador could also applaud, well, the energy poured forth. My father, while not uncommonly reflective, did say once: "When your best and worst motive agree on the same action, watch the juices flow."

On this day in December 1948, my father was dressed in what I would come to call his "battle tweeds." That once had been a suit of light brown Scotch tweed (light in hue, but as heavy and hard to the touch as a horse-blanket). He bought his suits from Jones, Chalk and Dawson on Savile Row, and they knew how to outfit a horseman. I had seen this same suit on him for ten years. By now, patched with leather at elbows and cuffs, and become more malleable, it could still stand on its legs when taken off. It fit him, however, with a comfortable surround of dignity to suggest that these two materials—his manly flesh and that iron cloth—had lived together long enough to share a few virtues. In fact, he no longer owned a business suit and so had nothing more formal to wear until you got to his black velvet dinner jacket. Needless to say, on such nightly occasions, he was a lady's vision. "Oh, Cal," they would say of him, "Cal's *divine*. If only he didn't drink so much."

I think my father would have broken relations with any friend who dared to suggest Alcoholics Anonymous was waiting for him, and he could have been right. His contention was that he drank no more than Winston Churchill and held it as well. He never got drunk. That is to say, his speech never slurred and he never staggered, but he did move through moods powerful enough to alter the electromagnetic fields through which he passed. It is a way of remarking that he had charisma. He had no more than to say "Bartender" in a quiet tone, and the man, if his back were turned, and had never heard my father's voice before, would nonetheless spring around as if starting a new page in his bar accounts. My father's emotional temperature seemed to rise and fall as he drank; his eyes, by the shift of the hour, could blaze with heat, or install you in a morgue; his voice would vibrate into your feet. Doubtless I exaggerate, but he was my father, and I saw him so seldom.

On this day, as I came in, he and his battle tweeds were sheeted in anger. For practical purposes, I was not unlike one of those little wives who are married to huge sea captains: I could feel his thoughts. He had been busy on some serious job before lunch, and had nearly cracked its difficulty; now he was putting down his first martini with all the discontent of interrupted concentration. I could imagine how he said to some assistant, "Damn, I've got to see my son for lunch."

To make matters worse, I was late. Five minutes late. When it came to promptitude, he was always on the mark, a headmaster's son. Now, waiting for me, he had had time to finish the first drink and review in his mind an unpromising list of topics about which we might converse. The sad truth is that he invariably gave off gloom on those rare occasions when we were alone with each other. He did not know what to talk to me about, and I, on my side, filled with my mother's adjurations, injunctions, and bitch-fury that I was going to see a man who was able to live in whole comfort apart from her, was jammed up. "Get him to talk about your education," she'd say before I was out the door. "He's got to pay for it, or I'll take him to law. Tell him that." Yes, I would be in great haste to tell him. "Watch out for his charm. It's as real as a snake," and, as I was going out the door, "Tell him I said hello—no, don't you tell him that."

I gave a nod with one quick bob of my head and got onto the barstool next to him. Naturally, I scrunched my larger testicle by too abruptly lowering my butt to the seat. Then I sat there through the small wave of discomfort this brought on and tried to study the signs above the bar.

YO, HO, HO, AND A BOTTLE OF RUM, said one old wooden placard. 21 WEST ZWEI UND FÜNFZIGSTE STRASSE, said a painted street sign.

"Oh," I said, "is that German, Dad?"

"Fifty-second Street," he told me.

We were silent.

"How do you like St. Matthew's?" he said.

"Okay."

"Better than Buckley?"

"It's tougher."

"You're not going to flunk out?"

"No, I get B's."

"Well, try to get A's. Hubbards are expected to get A's at St. Matt's."

We were silent.

I began to look at another sign hanging over the bar. It obviously enjoyed its misspelling. CLOSE SATURDAYS AND SUNDAYS, it said.

"I've had one superior hell of a lot of work lately," he said.

"I guess," I said.

We were silent.

His gloom was like the throttled sentiments of a German shepherd on a leash. I think I was something of a skinny version of him, but I believe he always saw every bit of resemblance I had to my mother during the first five minutes of every one of our meetings, and I even came to understand over the years that she might have done him a real damage. There was probably never a human he wished to kill more with his bare hands than this ex-wife; of course, he had had to forgo such pleasure. Blocked imperatives brought my father that much nearer to stroke.

Now he said, "How's your leg?"

"Oh, it's recovered. It's been all right for years."

"I bet it's still stiff."

"No, it's all right."

He shook his head. "I think you had your trouble with the Grays because of that leg."

"Dad, I was just no good at close-order drill." Silence. "But I got better." The silence made me feel as if I were trying to push a boat off the shore and it was too heavy for me.

"Dad," I said, "I don't know if I can get A's at St. Matthew's. They think I'm dyslexic."

He nodded slowly as if not unprepared for such news. "How bad is it?" he asked.

"I can read all right, but I never know when I'm going to reverse numbers."

"I had that trouble." He nodded. "Back on Wall Street before the war, I used to live in fear that one bright morning my touch of dyslexia would make the all-time mistake in the firm. Somehow, it never did." He winked. "You need a good secretary to take care of those things." He clapped me on the back. "One more lemonade?"

"No."

"I'll have another martini," he said to the bartender. Then he turned back to me. I still remember the bartender's choice of a keen or sour look. (Keen when serving gentlemen; sour for the tourists.) "Look," my father said, "dyslexia is an asset as well as a loss. A lot of good people tend to have dyslexia."

"They do?" Over the past term a few boys at school had taken to calling me Retardo.

"No question." He put his eyes on me. "About ten years ago in Kenya we were going for leopards. Sure enough, we found one, and it charged. I've hit elephants coming at me, and lions and water buffalo. You hold your ground, look for a vulnerable area in the crosshairs, then squeeze off your shot. If you can steer between the collywobbles, it's as easy as telling it to you now. Don't panic and you have yourself a lion. Or an elephant. It's not even a feat. Just a measure of inner discipline. But a leopard is different. I couldn't believe what

I saw. All the while it was charging it kept leaping left to right and back again, but so fast I thought I was watching a movie with pieces missing. You just couldn't get your crosshairs on any part of that leopard. So I took him from the hip. At twenty yards. First shot. Even our guide was impressed. He was one of those Scotsmen who sneer at all and anything American, but he called me a born hunter. Later I figured it out for myself: I was a good shot because of my dyslexia. You see, if you show me 1-2-3-4, I tend to read it as 1-4-2-3 or 1-3-4-2. I suppose I see like an animal. I don't read like some slave— yessir, boss, I'm following you, yessir, 1-2-3-4—no, I look at what's near me and what's in the distance and only then do I shift to the middle ground. In and out, back and forth. That's a hunter's way of looking. If you have a touch of dyslexia, that could mean you're a born hunter."

He gave my midriff a short chop with his elbow. It proffered enough weight to suggest what a real blow would do.

"How's your leg?" he asked again.

"Good," I said.

"Have you tried one-legged knee raises?"

The last time we had been to lunch, eighteen months ago, he had prescribed such an exercise.

"I've tried it."

"How many can you do?"

"One or two." I was lying.

"If you're really working at it, you would show more progress."

"Yessir."

I could feel his wrath commencing. It began slowly, like the first stirring of water in a kettle. This time, however, I could also sense the effort to pull back his annoyance, and that puzzled me. I could not recollect when he had treated me to such courtesy before.

"I was thinking this morning," he said, "of your ski accident. You were good that day."

"I'm glad I was," I said.

We were silent again, but this time it was a pause we could inhabit. He liked to recall my accident. I believe it was the only occasion on which he ever formed a good opinion of me.

When I was seven, I had been picked up at school one Friday in January by my mother's chauffeur and driven to Grand Central Station. On this day, my father and I were going to board the weekend special to Pittsfield, Mass., where we would ski at a place called Bousquet's. How the great echoes of Grand Central matched the reverberation of my heart! I had never been skiing and therefore believed I would be destroyed next day flying off a ski jump.

Naturally, I was taken over no such towering jump. I was put instead on a pair of rented wooden slats, and after a set of near-fiascoes on the long rope-tow up, attempted to follow my father down. My father had a serviceable stem turn which was all you needed to claim a few yodeling privileges in the Northeast back in 1940. (People who could do a parallel christie were as rare then as tightrope artists.) I, of course, as a beginner, had no stem turn, only the impromptu move of falling to either side when my snow plow got going too fast. Some spills were easy, some were knockouts. I began to seek the fall before I needed to. Soon, my father was shouting at me. In those days, whether riding, swimming, sailing, or on this day, skiing, he lost his temper just so quickly as first returns made it evident that I was without natural ability. Natural ability was closer to God. It meant you were wellborn. Bantu blacks in Africa, I came to learn in CIA, believed that a chieftain should enrich himself and have beautiful wives. That was the best way to know God was well disposed toward you. My father shared this view. Natural ability was bestowed on the deserving. Lack of natural ability spoke of something smelly at the roots. The clumsy, the stupid, and the slack were fodder for the devil. It is not always a fashionable view today, but I have pondered it all my life. I can wake up in the middle of the night thinking, What if my father was right?

Soon he grew tired of waiting for me to get up.

"Just do your best to follow," he said, and was off, stopping long enough to call back, "Turn when I turn."

I lost him at once. We were going along a lateral trail that went up and down through the woods. Going uphill, I did not know how to herringbone. I kept getting farther behind. When I came to the top of one rise and saw that the next descent was a full-fledged plunge followed by an abrupt rise, and my father was nowhere in sight, I decided to go straight down in the hope such a schuss would carry me a good way up. Then he would not have to wait too long while I climbed. Down I went, my skis in a wobbly parallel, and almost at once was moving twice as fast as I had ever traveled before. When I lost my nerve and tried to switch to a snowplow, my skis crossed, dug into the soft snow, and I wrenched over in a somersault. There was no release to the bindings in those days. Your feet stayed in the skis. I broke my right tibia.

One did not know that at first. One only knew more pain than ever felt before. Somewhere in the distance my father was bellowing, "Where are you?" It was late in the afternoon and his voice echoed through the hills. No other skiers were coming by. It started to snow and I felt as if I were in the last reel of a movie about Alaska; soon the snow would cover all trace of me. My father's roars were, in this silence, comforting.

He came climbing back, angry as only a man with a powerful, sun-wrinkled neck can be angry. "Will you rise to your feet, you quitter," he cried out. "Stand up and ski."

I was more afraid of him than the five oceans of pain. I tried to get up. Something, however, was wrong. At a certain point, my will was taken away from me completely. My leg felt amputated.

"I can't, sir," I said, and fell back.

Then he recognized there might be more than character at issue here. He took off his ski jacket, wrapped me in it, and went down the mountain to the Red Cross hut.

Later, in the winter twilight, after the ski patrol had put on a temporary splint and worked me down to the base in a sled, I was put in the back of a small truck, given a modest dose of morphine, and carried over some frozen roads to the hospital in Pittsfield. It was one hell of a ride. By now, well into the spirit of the morphine, the pain still rasped like a rough-toothed saw into my broken bone each time we hit an evil bump (which was every fifty yards). The drug enabled me, however, to play a kind of game. Since the shock from every bump shivered through my teeth, the game became the art of not making a sound. I lay there on the floor of the truck with a wadded ski jacket under my head and another beneath my leg, and must have looked like an epileptic: My father kept wiping froth from my mouth.

I made, however, no sound. After a time, the magnitude of my personal venture began to speak to him for he took my hand and concentrated upon it. I could feel him trying to draw the pain from my body into his, and this concern ennobled me. I felt they could tear my leg off and I might still make no outcry.

He spoke: "Your father, Cal Hubbard, is a fathead." That may be the only occasion in his life when he used the word in reference to himself. In our family, fathead was about the worst expression you could use for another person.

"No, sir," I said. I was afraid to speak for fear that the groans would begin, yet I also knew the next speech was one of the most important I would ever make. For a few moments I twisted through falls of nausea—I must have been near to fainting—but the road became level for a little while, and I succeeded in finding my voice. "No, sir," I said, "my father, Cal Hubbard, is not a fathead."

It was the only time I ever saw tears in his eyes.

"Well, you silly goat," he said, "you're not the worst kid, are you?"

If we had crashed at that moment I could have died in a happy state. But I came back to New York in a cast two days later—my mother sent chauffeur and limousine up for me—and a second hell began. The part of me that was ready to go through a meat grinder for my father could hardly have been the poor seven-year-old boy who sat home in New York in his Fifth Avenue apartment with a compound fracture surrounded by a plaster cast that itched like the gates of sin. The second fellow seethed with complaints.

I could not move. I had to be carried. I went into panic at the thought of using crutches. I was certain I would fall and break the leg again. The cast began to stink. In the second week the doctor had to cut the plaster off, clean my infection, and encase me again. I mention all this because it also cut off my father's love affair with me nearly as soon as it had begun. When he came over to visit—after an understanding with my mother that she would not be there—he would be obliged to read the notes she left—"You broke his leg, now teach him to move."

Allowing for his small patience, he finally succeeded in getting me up on crutches, and the leg eventually mended, just a bit crooked, but it took too long. We were back in the land of paternal disillusion. Besides, he had more to think about than me. He was happily remarried to a tall, Junoesque woman absolutely his own size, and she had given him twin boys. They were three years old when I was seven, and you could bounce them on the floor. Their nicknames—I make no joke—were Rough and Tough. Rough Hubbard and Tough Hubbard. Actually, they were Roque Baird Hubbard and Toby Bolland Hubbard, my father's second wife being Mary Bolland Baird, but rough and tough they promised to be, and my father adored them.

Occasionally I would visit the new wife. (They had been married four years but I still thought of her as *the new wife*.) It was just a trip of a few blocks up the winter splendor of Fifth Avenue, that is to say, an education in the elegance of gray. The apartment houses were lilac-gray, and Central Park showed field-gray meadows in winter and mole-gray trees.

Since finding myself on crutches, I no longer ventured from my apartment house. In one of the later weeks of convalescence, however, I had a good day, and my limb did not ache in its cast. By afternoon, I was restless and ready for adventure. I not only went down to the lobby and talked to the doorman but, on impulse, set out to circumnavigate the block. It was then the idea came to me to visit my stepmother. She was not only large but hearty, and succeeded at times in making me think she liked me; she would certainly tell my father that I had visited, and he would be pleased I was mastering the crutches. So I decided to attempt those five blocks uptown from 73rd to 78th Street and immediately went through a small palsy the first time I put my crutches out from the curb down six inches to the gutter. This small step accomplished, however, I began to swing along, and by the time I reached their apartment house, I was most talkative with the elevator man and pleased with how much pluck I was showing for a seven-year-old.

At their door a new maid answered. She was Scandinavian and hardly spoke English, but I gathered that the nurse was out with the twins and "the Madame" was in her room. After some confusion the new girl let me in and I sat on a couch, bored by the wan afternoon sun as it reflected on the pale silk colors of the living room.

It never occurred to me that my father was home. Later, much later, I would gather that this was about the time he had given up his broker's slot in Merrill Lynch to volunteer for the Royal Canadian Air Force. To celebrate, he was taking the afternoon off. I, however, thought Mary Bolland Baird Hubbard was alone and reading, and might be as bored as I was. So I hopped across the living room and down the hall to their bedroom, making little sound on the pile carpet, and then, without taking the time to listen—all I knew was that I did not wish to return home without having spoken to some-one, but would certainly lose my nerve if I waited at the door—I turned the knob, and, to keep my balance, took two big hops forward on my crutches. The sight that received me was my father's naked back, then hers. They were both pretty big. They were rolling around on the floor, their bodies plastered end to end, their mouths on each other's—if I say *things,* it's for want of remembering the word I had then. Somehow I had an idea what they were doing. Importuning sounds came out of them, full of gusto, that unforgettable cry which lands somewhere between whooping and whimpering.

I was paralyzed for the time it took to take it all in; then I tried to escape. They were so deep in their burrow they did not even see me, not for the first instant, the second, nor even the third as I backed my way to the door. Right then, they looked up. I was nailed to the door frame. They stared at me, and I stared at them, and I realized they did not know for how long I had been studying them. For heavens, how long? "Get out of here, you dodo," my father roared, and the worst of it was that I fled so quickly on the crutches that they thumped like ghost-bumpers on the carpet while I vaulted down the hall. I think it was this sound, the thump-thump of a cripple, that must have stayed in her ears. Mary was a nice woman, but she was much too proper to be photographed by anyone's memory in such a position, let alone a slightly creepy stepson. None of us ever spoke of it again; none of us forgot it. I remember that in the time it took to reach my mother's apartment, I generated a two-ton headache, and it was the first of a chronic run of migraines. This pressure had been paying irregular visits from that day. Right now, here at lunch, I could feel it on the edge of my temples, ready to strike.

Now, I cannot say that these headaches were responsible for the ongoing fantasy of my childhood, but it is true that I began to spend many an afternoon after school alone in my room making drawings of an underground city. It was, as I look back on it, a squalid place. Beneath the ground in a set of excavations, I penciled in clubhouses, tunnels, game rooms, all connected by secret passages. There was an automat, a gym, and a pool. I giggled at how the pool would be full of urine, and installed torture rooms whose guards had Oriental faces. (I could draw slant eyes.) It was a warren of monstrous and cloacal turns, but it brought peace to my young mind.

"How are your headaches?" asked my father at the bar at Twenty-One.

"No worse," I said.

"But they don't get better?"

"They don't, I guess."

"I'd like to reach in and pull out what's bothering you," he said. It was not a sentimental remark so much as a surgeon's impulse.

I shifted the subject to Rough and Tough. They were now Knickerbocker Grays, and doing well, he told me. I was tall for my age, almost as tall as my father, but they gave every promise of outstripping me. As he spoke, I knew there was some other matter on his mind.

It was his inclination to pass me tidbits about his work. This presented curious debits to his duty. In his occupation, you were supposed to encapsulate your working life apart from your family. On the other hand, he had formed his reflexes for security, such as they were, working for the OSS in Europe during World War II. Nobody he knew then had been all that cautious. Today's secret was next week's headline, and it was not uncommon to give a hint of what one was up to when trying to charm a lady. Next day, after all, an airplane was going to parachute you into a strange place. If the lady were made aware of this, well, she might feel less absolutely loyal to her husband (also away at war).

Besides, he wanted to fill me in. If he was not an attentive parent, he was at least a romantic father. Moreover, he was a team man. He was in the Company and his sons ought to be prepared as well: While Rough and Tough were a foregone conclusion, he could hardly swear on me.

"I'm all riled up today," said my father. "One of our agents in Syria got shot on a stupid business."

"Was he a friend of yours?" I asked.

"Neither here nor there," he replied.

"I'm sorry."

"No, I'm just so goddamn mad. This fellow was asked to obtain us a piece of paper that wasn't really needed."

"Oh."

"I'll tell you, darn it all. You keep this to yourself."

"Yes, Dad."

"One of those playboys at State decided to be ambitious. He's doing his Ph.D. thesis on Syria over at Georgetown. So he wanted to present a couple of hard-to-get details that nobody else has. He put through a request to us. Officially. From State. Could we furnish the poop? Well, we're green. You could grow vegetables with what they scrape off our ignorance. We try to oblige. So we put a first-rate Syrian agent on it, and there you are—lost a crack operator because he was asked to reach for the jam at the wrong time."

"What'll happen to the fellow in the State Department?"

"Nothing much. Maybe we'll slow down a promotion for that idiot by talking to a guy or two at State, but it's horrifying, isn't it? Our man loses his life because somebody needs a footnote for his Ph.D. thesis."

"I thought you looked upset."

"No," he said quickly, "it's not that." Then he hoisted his martini, stepped off the stool, raised his hand as if calling a cab, and the captain was there to bring us to our table which was, I already knew, in his favored location against the rear wall. There my father placed me with my back to the room. At the table to my left were two men with white hair and red faces who looked like they might have gout, and on the right was a blond woman with a small black hat supporting a long black feather. She was wearing pearls on a black dress and had long white gloves. Sitting across from her was a man in a pencil-thick pinstripe. I mention these details to show a facet of my father: He was able, in the course of sitting down, to nod to the two gentlemen with gout as if, socially speaking, there was no reason why not to speak to one another, and freeze the man in the pencil-stripe suit for the width of his stripes while indicating to the blond lady in black that she was blue ribbon for blond ladies in black. My father had a gleam in his eye at such times that made me think of the Casbah. I always supposed a Levantine would come up to you in the Casbah and give a flash of what he had in his hand. There!—a diamond peeked out. That made me recollect Cal Hubbard rolling with Mary Baird on the carpeted floor, which in turn caused me to look down quickly at my plate.

"Herrick, I haven't seen a superior hell of a lot of you lately, have I?" he asked, unfolding his napkin, and sizing up the room. I wasn't too happy being placed with my back to everyone, but then he gave a wink as if to suggest that he had his reasons. It was incumbent on his occupation, as he once explained, that he be able to *eye* a joint. I think he may have picked up the phrase from Dashiell Hammett, with whom he used to drink before word went around that Hammett was a Communist. Then, since he considered Hammett smarter than himself, he gave up the acquaintance. A loss. According to my father, he and Dashiell Hammett could each put down three double Scotches in an hour.

"Well, there's a reason I haven't seen a lot of you, Rick." He was the only one to call me Rick, rather than Harry, for Herrick. "I have been traveling an unconscionable amount." This was said for the blond woman as much as for me. "They don't know yet whether I'll be one of the linchpins in Europe or the Far East."

Now the man in the pencil-stripe suit began his counteroffensive. He must have put a curve on what he said, for the woman gave a low intimate laugh. In response, my father leaned toward me across the table and whispered, "They've given OPC the *covert* operations."

"What's covert?" I whispered back.

"The real stuff. None of that counterespionage where you drink out of my teacup and I drink out of yours. This is war. Without declaring it." He raised his voice sufficiently for the woman to hear the last two phrases, then dropped back to a murmur as if the best way to divide her attention was to insinuate himself in and out of her hearing.

"Our charter calls for economic warfare," he said in a highly shaped whisper, "plus underground resistance groups." Loudly: "You saw what we did in the Italian elections."

"Yessir."

He enjoyed the *yessir.* I had broadcast it for the blond lady.

"If not for our little operation, the Communists would have taken over Italy," he now stated. "They give the credit to the Marshall Plan but that's wrong. We won in Italy in spite of the money that was thrown around."

"We did?"

"Count on it. You have to take into account the Italian ego. They're an odd people. Half sharp, half meatball."

By the way in which the man in the pencil-stripe reacted, I suspected he was Italian. If my father sensed that, he gave no sign. "You see, the Romans themselves are civilized. Minds quick as stilettos. But the Italian peasant remains as backward as a Filipino. In consequence, you mustn't try to motivate their self-interest too crudely. Self-esteem means more to them than filling their bellies. They're always poor, so they can live with hunger, but they don't want to lose their honor. Those Italians really wanted to stand up to us. They would have derived more pleasure spitting in our face than sucking up to us with their phony gratitude. Nothing personal. The Italians are like that. If Communism ever takes over in Italy, those Red wops will drive the Soviets just as crazy as they're driving us."

I was feeling the wrath of the Italian man next to me. "Dad, if that's what you think," I blurted out, scurrying to save the peace, "why not let the Italians choose their path? They're an ancient and civilized people."

My father had to ponder this. Allen Dulles may have said that the happiest week of Cal Hubbard's life was spent seducing secretaries, but I expect no period could have been equal to the year he spent with the partisans. If Italy had gone Communist in 1948, my father would probably have gone right over to form an anti-Communist underground. In recesses of his brain so secret he could not even reach them in his dreams, I believe he would have enjoyed a Communist takeover of America. What an American underground he could have helped to set up then! The thought of dynamite Americans waging an underground war up and down our countryside against an oppressive enemy would have been a tonic to keep him young forever.

So my father may have been on the edge of saying "You bet," but he didn't. Instead, he answered dutifully, "Of course, we can't afford to let the Russians in. Who knows? Those guineas might get along with the Russians."

We had an interruption here. The man next to us suddenly called out for his check, and my father immediately stopped our conversation in order to look appreciatively at the blond lady.

"Weren't we introduced at Forest Hills this fall?" he said to her.

"Nah, I don't think so," she answered in a muffled voice.

"Please tell me your name," said my father, "and I'm certain I'll recollect where it was."

"Think of nowhere," said the man in the striped suit.

"Are you trying to give directions?" asked my father.

"I heard of people," said the man, "who lose their nose by poking it around the corner."

"Al!" said the blond lady.

Having stood up abruptly, Al was now putting money on the table to cover his tab. He dropped each new bill like a dealer snapping cards, signally upset that one of the players had called for another deck. "I've heard of people," repeated Al, and now he looked sideways at my father, "who stepped off the curb and broke a leg."

Into my father's eyes came that diamond of the Casbah. He, too, stood up. They each took a long look at the other. "Buster," said my father in a happy, husky voice, "don't get tough!"

It was his happiness that did the job. Al thought of replying, then thought better. His jaw did not work. He folded his napkin as if folding his tent, looked for the opportunity to throw a sneak punch, did not find what he was looking for, and gave his arm to the blond lady. They left. My father grinned. If he couldn't have her, he had at least broken a couple of eggs.

Now my father began to talk a good deal. Any victory over a stranger was kin to triumph over rival hordes. Al was out there with the Russians. "There are six million soldiers in the Red Army," said my father, "and only a million of us. That's counting NATO. The Russians could take all of Europe in two months. It's been true for the last three years."

"Then why haven't they?" I asked. "Dad, I read that twenty million Russians were killed in the war. Why would they want to start one now?"

He finished his drink. "Damned if I know." As the waiter sprang for the refill, my father leaned forward: "I'll tell you why. Communism is an itch. What does that mean, to have an itch? Your body is out of whack. Little things take on large proportions. That's Communism. A century ago, everybody had their place. If you were a poor man, God judged you as such, a poor man. He had compassion. A rich man had to pass more severe standards. As a result, there was peace between the classes. But materialism came down on us. Materialism propagated the idea that the world is nothing but a machine. If that's true, then it's every man's right to improve his piece of the machine. That's the logic of atheism. So, now everybody's ears are being pounded to bits, and nothing tastes right anymore. Everybody is too tense, and God is an abstraction. You can't enjoy your own land so you begin to covet the next guy's country."

He took a long, thoughtful swallow from his drink. My father could always bring a cliché to life. Many have been described as taking long thoughtful swallows of their drinks, but my father drank like an Irishman. He took it for granted that real and true spirits were entering with the fire of the liquor. He inhaled the animation around him and could breathe back his own excitement. Emotion must never be wasted. "Rick, keep clear on one matter. There's a huge war brewing. These Communists are insatiable. We treated them as friends during the war and they'll never get over that. When you're older, you may have the bad luck to get into an affair with an ugly woman who happens to enjoy what you offer but has never been on daily terms with a man. She's too ugly. Fellow, you're going to have trouble on your hands. Before long, she's insatiable. You've given the taste of the forbidden to her. That's the Russians. They got ahold of Eastern Europe; now they want it all."

He did not halt long at this place. "No," he said, "it's not a good analogy. It's really worse than that. We're in an ultimate struggle with the Russians, and that means we have to use everything. Not only the kitchen sink, but the vermin that come with the sink."

My father was interrupted at this moment by the two white-haired gentlemen seated on his right. They were getting up to leave and one said, "I couldn't help hearing what you were explaining to your son, and I wish to say, couldn't agree more. Those Russians want to crack our shell and get all the good meat. Don't let them."

"No, sir," said my father, "not one knuckle will they get," and he stood up on that remark. The rich compact that comes from a common marrow guarded us all. Honor, adventure, and sufficient income was in the air of Twenty-One. Even I could prosper there.

When we sat down again, my father said, "Keep this most strictly to yourself. I'm going to trust you with a weighty secret. Hitler used to say, 'Bolshevism is poison.' That idea is not to be rejected out of hand just because Adolf said it. Hitler was so awful that he ruined the attack on Bolshevism for all of us. But the fundamental idea is right. Bolshevism *is* poison. We've even come to the point"—and here he dropped his voice to the lowest whisper of the lunch—"where we've got to employ a few of those old Nazis to fight the Reds."

"Oh, no," I said.

"Oh, yes," he said. "There's hardly a choice. The OSO is not all that competent. We were supposed to put agents in place all over the Iron Curtain countries and couldn't even seed it with birdfeed. Every time we built a network, we discovered the Russians were running it. The great Russian bear can move his armies anywhere behind the Iron Curtain, and we don't have an effective alert system. If, two years ago, the Soviets had wanted to march across Europe, they could have. We would have gotten out of bed in the morning to hear their tanks in the streets. No reliable intelligence. That's fearful. How would you like to live blindfolded?"

"No good, I guess."

"It came down to this: We had to use a Nazi general. I call him General Microfilm. I can't reveal his name. He was top intelligence man for the Germans on the Russian front. He would weed out the most promising of the Russians captured by the Germans and manage to infiltrate them back behind Russian lines. For a while, they honey-combed the Red Army, even worked a few of their boys into the Kremlin. Just before the war ended, this general, prior to destroying his files, buried fifty steel boxes somewhere in Bavaria. They were the microfilm copies of his files. A voluminous product. We needed it. Now he's dealing with us. He has built up new networks all through East Germany, and there isn't much those East German Communists don't tell his West German agents about what the Reds are planning to do next in Eastern Europe. This general may be an ex-Nazi, but, like it or not, he's invaluable. That's what my business is about. You work with the next-to-worst in order to defeat the worst. Could you do that?"

"Maybe."

"You might be too liberal, Herrick. Liberals refuse to look at the whole animal. Just give us the tasty parts, they say. I think God has need of a few soldiers."

"Well, I believe I could be a good one."

"I hope so. When you broke your leg, you were a great soldier."

"Do you think so?" This moment alone made the lunch superlative for me. So I wanted him to say it again.

"Not in question. A great soldier." He paused. He played with his drink. His free hand made a rocking motion on the table from thumb to little finger. "Rick," he announced, "you're going to have to pull up your gut again."

It was like coming in for a landing. My focus moved closer to my father's with every instant.

"Is it medical?" I asked. Then answered myself. "It's the tests I took."

"Let me give you the positive stuff first." He nodded. "It's operable. There's an 80-percent likelihood it's benign. So when they take it out, they've got it all."

"A benign tumor?"

"As I say, they are 80-percent certain. That's conservative. I believe it's 95-percent certain."

"Why do you think that?"

"You may have bad headaches but the powers that be aren't ready to lift you from the board. It makes no sense."

"Maybe the whole thing makes no sense," I said.

"Don't you ever believe that. I'd rather you took a dump right here in public, right in the middle of my favorite restaurant, than that you descend into that kind of sophomoric nihilism. No, look at it this way. Assume the Devil made a mistake and put all his eggs in one basket concerning you"—again my father was whispering as if any

loud statement of Satan's name could summon him to your side—
"and we're going to remove him all at once. Excise him. Rick, your
headaches will be gone."

"That's good," I said. I was ready to cry. Not because of the
operation. I had not realized an operation was this near, but it had
been part, certainly, of my inner horizon. I had been taking tests for
three months. No, I was ready to cry because now I knew why my
father had taken me to lunch and favored me with professional secrets.

"I convinced your mother," he said. "She's a very difficult
woman under any and all circumstances, but I got her to recognize
that one of the best neurosurgeons in the country is available for this.
I can tell you in confidence he also works for *us*. We've talked him
into putting his toe in the water for some studies we're doing on
brainwashing techniques. We need to keep up with the Russians."

"I guess he'll learn a little more about brainwashing with me."

My father gave a half-smudged smile for the joke. "He'll give you
every chance to become the man you want to be."

"Yes," I said. I had an awful feeling I could not explain. There
was no doubt in my mind that the tumor was the worst part of me.
Everything rotten must be concentrated there. I had always supposed,
however, that sooner or later it would go away by itself.

"What if we don't have surgery? I can keep living with my
headaches," I said.

"There's a chance it is malignant."

"You mean when they open my head, they could discover cancer?"

"There's one chance in five."

"You said 95 percent. Isn't that one chance in twenty?"

"All right. One in twenty."

"Dad, that's twenty to one in our favor. Nineteen to one, actually."

"I'm looking at other kinds of odds. If you're debilitated with
headaches during all the formative years to come, you'll end up half
a man." I could hear the rest. "Shape up" were the words he was
inclined to speak.

"What do the doctors think?" I asked at last.

I had given up the game by asking this question. "They say you
must have the operation."

Years later, a surgeon would tell me that the operation would
have been elective, not mandatory. My father had lied. His logic was

simple. He would not manipulate me or any other family member who was arguing a point out of his own feelings; if third parties, however, were consulted, then the debate had become a recourse to authority. Since I asked what the doctors said, my father was ready to substitute himself as final authority.

Now he got out his wallet to pay the check. Unlike Al, my father did not snap his money down. He laid it like a poultice on the plate.

"When this is over," he told me, "I'm going to introduce you to a dear friend of mine whom I've asked to be your godfather. It's not customary to have a brand-new godfather at the age of fifteen, but the one we gave you at birth was a friend of your mother's and he's dropped out of sight. The guy I'm bringing in is wholly superior. You'll like him. He's named Hugh Montague, and he's one of us. Hugh Tremont Montague. He did wonderful stuff for OSS while on liaison with the Brits. During the war he worked with J. C. Masterman—I can tell you that name. An Oxford don. One of their spymasters. Hugh will fill you in on all of that. The English are such aces in this kind of work. In 1940, they captured a few of the first German agents sent over to England and succeeded in turning them. As a result, most of the German spies who followed were picked up on arrival. For the rest of the war, the Abwehr was fed the niftiest disinformation by their own agents in England. And, oh, how the Brits got to love their German agents. Just as loyal to them as to their favorite foxhounds, yes, they were." Here my father began laughing heartily. "You have to," he added, "get Hugh to tell you about the code names the English gave their little Germans. Perfect names for peachy dogs. CELERY," said my father, "SNOW, GARBO, CARROT, COBWEB, MULLET, LIPSTICK, NEPTUNE, PEPPERMINT, SCRUFFY, ROVER, PUPPET, BASKET, BISCUIT, BRUTUS. Is that, or is that not, the English?"

For years, I would fall asleep surrounded by men and women holding brass nameplates in capitals: BRUTUS, COBWEB, TREASURE, RAINBOW. As I grew ready in the last of this lunch at Twenty-One to lose a part, forever, of the soft meats of my brain, so were old spies with the code names of hunting dogs filing one by one into the cavity waiting for them.

2

In adolescence, I had only to say "God," and I would think of my groin. God was lust to me. God was like the image of the Devil offered to us at St. Matthew's. Chapel was daily and devoted to Christ, but once a week on average we might hear of the temptings of a somewhat legendary master-ghost named Satan. Chapel kept God and Satan well separated, but I, unlike other Matties, kept mixing them up. I had my reasons: I was introduced to carnal relations during my first year in the school by an assistant chaplain of St. Matthew's who *glommed*—I choose the word to convey the sensation of that rubbery, indefatigable seal—my fourteen-year-old penis in his tight, unhappy lips.

We were in Washington, D.C., on a school trip. Maybe that is one more reason I dislike our subtle, oppressive capital, that broad, well-paved swamp. Boredom and bad memory are at the root of many an oppression, I would suppose, and that night I was sharing a double bed with the assistant chaplain in an inexpensive hotel not far from H Street, NW, and was unable to sleep and feeling full of apprehension just about the time that the chaplain came out of a millrace of stentorian snoring, murmured his wife's name several times, "Bettina, Bettina," and proceeded to embrace my hips and strip my bewildered young privates of their primeval dew. I remember lying there with a complete sense of the sixteen other members of my class who were also on the trip and in the hotel. I visualized them, two by two, and four by four, in all the other six bedrooms where they had been placed. On this annual trip to Washington the assistant chaplain was our guide, and since I had not succeeded in my first year at the school in being associated in anyone's mind with anyone else, and was marked as a loner, the assistant chaplain, a sympathetic fellow, had assigned me to his room.

In the other cubicles, who knew what might be going on? At St. Matthew's, they used to call it "kidding around." Since my memory was seared with images of the two-backed beast of my father and stepmother (it was a two-backed beast long before I ever encountered the phrase in *Othello*), I stayed far apart from such gang play. All of us knew, however, that there were goings-on all up and down the dorm. Boys would stand side by side and stroke themselves into erections to see who was longer. It was the age of innocence. Being wider was not even a concept to us, for it would have suggested penetration. The nearest any of the boys came to that was by mounting a sweet, fat little creature named Arnold; we called him St. Matthew's Arnold. Even at the age of fourteen, literary wit was not discouraged among us, and St. Matthew's Arnold (in no way to be confused with Reed Arnold Rosen) used to drop his pants and lie on a bed, buttocks exposed. Six or eight of us would watch while two or three of the more athletic of our skulk would take turns slapping their brand-new instruments onto the crack between St. Matthew's Arnold's cheeks. "Ugh, you're disgusting," they'd say, and he'd whine back, "Aaah, shut up. *You're* doing it too."

It was never homosexual. It was "kidding around." Once done, it was not uncommon for the budding jock to leap off the body, wipe himself, and say, "Why can't you be a girl? You look just like a girl." Which was true—Arnold's cheeks were cousins to the moon—and Arnold, having his own male dignity to defend, would reply, "Aaaah, shut up." He was smaller than the boys who did it to him, so they barely cuffed him for being rude.

I would, as I say, merely watch. I was not up for studies in comparative phallitude. I was electrified by them, but even at fourteen I had already acquired some of our Hubbard insulation. I didn't show a spark.

My own relation to these sports and circuses was revealed to me, however, by the sweet-edged shudder which the chaplain's mean little lips pulled from me. When it was over, and I had been given an adolescent's peek into the firmament, he swallowed all the nourishment offered the parching of his mouth and began to sob in shame. Deep sobs. He was not a weak man physically, and his strength, like my father's, was in his upper body. So his sobs were strong.

I felt injected with ten tons of novocaine. Except, that is not true either. Two rivers were flowing in me, although to opposite directions. I felt relief I had never known before in my limbs, yet my heart, liver, head, and lungs were in a boil. This was even worse than seeing Mary Bolland Baird and my father in their roll-around. I knew myself to be the compliant apprentice of a monster.

After his sobbing, the man began to weep. I knew he was worried about his wife and children. "Don't worry," I said, "I'll never tell." He hugged me. Gently, I disengaged myself. I did it gently out of no noble funds of generosity, rather in the fear he would turn angry and grow rough. I think my secret instinct knew he wished me to have, in turn, a thirst I would slake on him. If I had none (and I did not), well, went his unspoken imperative: Generate some! You damn well better generate some.

How the poor man must have been hung between his lust for one good, reciprocal suck on his charged-up end and the horror of knowing that he was inching out along the precipice of his career. When I remained still and did not move at all, his sobbing finally ceased and he lay still as well. I did my best to picture him officiating at a High Mass in school chapel, white silk surplice over white linen cassock, his ritual gestures a talisman I could employ against him. It may have been a real magic. After an interval of silence, equal in weight to the darkness of our hotel room, he gave a sigh, slipped out of bed, and spent the rest of the night on the floor.

That was the extent of my homosexual experience, but what a bend it put into the shape of my psyche. I stayed away from sex as though it were a disease. I had bog-and-marsh dreams where I was Arnold and the chaplain released streams of the foulest suppurations over me. In turn, I would awaken to feel infected. My sheets were wet, sprayed with nothing less than the pus, I was certain, of my unholy infections. The headaches grew worse. When the boys got ready to kid around, I took off for the library. I believe I finally accepted my father's desire to have an operation on my head because I could not overcome the part of me that was certain there was awful matter in the brain to be cut out.

Conceivably, something may have altered. When I went back to St. Matthew's in the fall of 1949, after my summer of convalescence, the school seemed at last a reasonable place. Our soccer teams (it was the first prep school I knew to take soccer seriously), our football scrimmages at every class level, our Greek, Latin, daily chapel, and prayers before meals, our ice-cold showers from October to May (lukewarm in June and September), our button-down shirts and school ties for all occasions but sports (starched, white collar and shirt on Sundays) had now become an agreeable order of the day. My dyslexia seemed to wane after the operation. (As a result, my case was written about in neurosurgical papers.) I felt more like others, and stronger for average tasks. I had a B-plus average.

Left to myself, I think I might have ended like most of my classmates. From Yale, where many a good Mattie went in those days, I would have continued on to Wall Street or the Bar. I probably would have made an acceptable, even a good, estate lawyer, my experience with the chaplain keeping me alert to the pits of horrible possibility in the most proper affairs, and like many another not quite notable prep school product, I might even have improved with the years. The odds are favorable if you can hold your liquor.

Hugh Tremont Montague intervened. My father, who always kept his promises, if late by many a season, finally arranged for the meeting a year and a half after our lunch at Twenty-One. My operation had come and gone, as well as my convalescence. I was now a senior, and a responsible figure to my younger cousins and brothers in the summer frolics at Doane, curious frolics—the eight-hundred-yard swimming race around the island, four hundred with the current, four hundred back in the channel against it, and the all-day hike that commenced at The Precipices south of Bar Harbor at eight in the morning, went over Cadillac Mountain to Jordan Pond at noon, then up to Sargent Mountain and down all the way to Somesville; next, Acadia Mountain descending to Man of War Creek. We ended at the dock in Manset by eight in the evening. There a lobster boat came to meet us for the trip by water around the Western Way, up to Blue Hill Bay and Doane. A platoon of Marines would have complained of a twenty-mile march over hills like that, but we were rewarded by explorations in the lobster boat over the next few days to islands scattered around the bay, islands so small their names were in dispute, and their topography eccentric—great grass meadows on one, guano-encrusted sea ledges on another, forests with unearthly trees warped by long-lost winds. We would feast on lobsters boiled over driftwood fires and clams baked in the coals—even the charred hot dogs tasted as good as wild game caught with bow and arrow. To this day, Kittredge and I are visited in summer by cousins who have shared these Hubbard gymkhanas. No great tennis players ever came out of such a regimen, but our family life was our social life.

When Hugh Tremont Montague came up one weekend with my father in a light chartered plane from Boston, it was, therefore, an event of the first measure. We had a much spoken-of visitor. I might have heard of my anointed godfather for the first time during lunch at Twenty-One, but his name seemed present everywhere thereafter at school. A new file in my personal history had been opened. He was, as I now discovered, one of the myths of St. Matthew's. All through my first year at school, teachers must have spoken of him, but the name never entered my ear. Once my father inscribed his importance on my attention, however, accounts of him popped up everywhere.

One spoke of him now as if he had been headmaster. By actual record, he was coach of the soccer team and founder of the Mountaineering Club. A graduate of St. Matthew's, '32, and of Harvard, '36, he taught at the school until he joined the OSS. Instructor in English and in Divine Studies, he installed his own dicta in our dogma and lore. At St. Matthew's I had heard of the Egyptian goddess Maat before I ever heard of Hugh Montague. Maat had the body of a woman and a large feather for her neck and head. As the Egyptian Goddess of Truth, she embodied a curious holy principle: In the depths of one's soul, the difference between a truth and a falsehood weighed no more than a feather. St. Matthew's tended to equate this weight to the presence of Christ, and Montague was the determined author of that addition. St. Matthew's had always taken Divine Studies seriously, but after Montague's influence on us, we felt we had a greater contribution to make than any other school of our ilk in New Hampshire or Massachusetts, or, if one is to lower the bars, Connecticut. We were closer to God than the others and Mr. Montague had given the clue: Christ was Love, but Love lived only in the Truth. Why?—because one's ability to recognize the presence of Grace (which I always saw as a leavening in the region of the chest) could be injured by a lie.

Harlot left other precepts at St. Matthew's. God the Father—awesome, monumental Jehovah—was the principle of Justice. Mr. Montague added that Jehovah was also the embodiment of Courage. Just as Love was Truth and there could be no compassion without honesty, so was Justice equal to Courage. There was no justice for the coward. There was only the purgatory of his daily life. Did a student feel despair? Look to the root. A cowardly act had been committed, or a lie told. Somewhere in the school pamphlets sent out to increase St. Matthew's endowment, there are a few lines quoted from an address Hugh Montague gave on a special occasion to a senior class in chapel. "The first purpose of this school," he said, "is not to develop your potentialities—although some of you do indeed bear the unruly gift of quick mentality—but to send out into American society young men keen to maintain their honesty and sense of purpose. It is this school's intention that you grow into good, brave young men."

I will say it for Mr. Montague and St. Matthew's. Our theology was more complex than that. There was the special temptation of evil for the good and brave. The Devil, Montague warned, employed his finest wits to trap the noblest soldiers and scholars. Vanity, complacency, and indolence were a curse, since bravery was an ascending slope and one could not rest on it. One must succeed in rising to every challenge except the ones that would destroy us needlessly. Prudence was the one amelioration God allowed to the imperative of Courage; Love, on fortunate occasions, could offer support to Truth.

Competition on the playing field became, therefore, an avatar of Courage and Prudence, Love and Truth. On the playing field, one could find the unique proportions of your own heart. Later, properly prepared, out in the world, one might be able to deal with the Devil. Although it was never stated so at St. Matthew's, we all knew that women—as opposed to mothers, sisters, cousins, and ladies—had to be one more word for the world.

Since Mr. Montague had been gone for six years before I entered, I had no notion of the dialectical niceties of his mind. Only the precepts came down to us in strong doses imparted by instructors who lived with the conclusions. So hypocrisy also abounded at St. Matthew's. We were all smaller than our precepts. Indeed, the assistant chaplain who minted my adolescent glans was a disciple of Hugh Tremont Montague, even a rock climber, although I heard he was not a good one.

Rock climbing, after all, was the objective correlative of Virtue, which is to say, the meeting of Truth and Courage. I was soon to find out. That night in the summer of 1949 when Hugh Montague came to the Keep for the first time, he was thirty-five and I was seventeen, and much as I expected, he looked half a British officer with his erect posture and mustache and half an Anglican clergyman by way of his wire-rimmed eyeglasses and high forehead. Let me say that he could have been taken for a man of forty-five, but continued to look no older for the next twenty years, right up to his dreadful fall.

On shaking hands, I knew immediately why Christ was Truth not Love for Mr. Montague. He had a grip to remind you of the hard rubber pads that are put on vise-jaws to keep them from injuring any object in their grasp. Heaven help me, went my thought, this man is a real prick.

Accurate was my instinct! Decades later, over the seasons of my marriage to Kittredge, I learned the innermost secrets of Harlot's young manhood even as he had confessed them one by one to her; what other gift could measure his profound love for Kittredge? He had indeed been a prick, and of the worst sort. His personal devil had been a great desire to ream young pits. There was hardly a good-looking boy in his instruction whom he had not wanted to bugger. According to Kittredge, he never had: at least, not if he was telling the truth—which was always the question—but he avowed that until he met her, this impulse was the ongoing daily torment of his years at Harvard, then later at St. Matthew's where he ground his teeth in sleep. Indeed, he had not entered the ministry for fear that he would, one good day, dive deep into his impulses and betray his church. The sexual energies, in consequence, were in-held. As he took my hand on introduction and stared into my eyes, he was a force and I was a receptacle: He was clean as steel and I was a punk.

I remember how my father, forty pounds heavier than Hugh Tremont Montague, circled nonetheless around our introduction like an anxious relative, a facet of Cal Hubbard's personality I had never seen before. I not only realized how much this meeting had to mean to my father, but even why it had taken so long to arrange—Cal Hubbard's expectations would suffer a dull return if it did not work.

I describe our meeting as if there were no one else in the house. In fact, something like seventeen of us, Mary Bolland Baird, Rough, Tough, cousins, fathers and mothers of cousins, aunts, uncles, numerous Hubbards were there. It was our last summer in that period at the Keep. My father was in the process of selling the place to Rodman Knowles Gardiner, Kittredge's father, and we were all taking a long farewell to our summer house. There might have been five people present when we were introduced, or ten, or we could have been alone. All I remember is that my father circled Mr. Montague and me, and my father was soon gone. I have some recollection that we then went down to the den to have a talk. That comes to me with clarity.

"You're out of the dyslexia, your father says."

"I think so."

"Good. What are your subjects at St. Matthew's?"

I named them.

"Your favorite?"

"English," I said.

"What's the best novel you've read this year?"

"*Portrait of a Lady*. We had it assigned, but I liked it a lot."

He nodded sourly. "Henry James is a quince pie as large as the Mojave Desert. It's a pity. Put Hemingway's heart in him and James would have been a writer to equal Stendhal or Tolstoy."

"Yessir," I said. I was such a liar. I had gotten an A for my paper on *Portrait of a Lady,* but I had merely parroted a few critical appreciations. *The Young Lions* was what I had enjoyed most last year. Noah Ackerman, the Jew, had appealed to me.

"Let's go out tomorrow," he said. "Your father wants me to take you on a climb. I hear there's dependable rock suitable for beginners over at a place called Otter Cliffs. We'll pick a route that's feasible."

"Yessir." I was hoping that what he called Otter Cliffs was some other Otter Cliffs than the one I knew. That was black rock and dropped a straight eighty feet down to the sea. Sometimes on the rise of the tide, there was a heavy roll of surf in Frenchman's Bay, and I had heard the growl of black waters on black rock at Otter Cliffs. Indeed, the fall was so steep I could never look over the edge.

"Guess I haven't done any rock climbing," I said, and regretted the remark on the instant.

"You'll know a little more tomorrow than you know right now."

"Yessir."

"Your father asked me to be your godfather."

I nodded. My quick fear at the thought of tomorrow had already commandeered the lower register of my voice. If I said "yessir" one more time it would come out like ship's pipes.

"I have to tell you," he said, "I was inclined to refuse." He fixed me front and center with his stare. "One must have a close personal interest to be a godfather."

"That's true, I suppose." I croaked it forth.

"I don't like close personal interest."

I nodded.

"On the other hand, I have regard for your father. No one will ever know how good his war record was until the secrets can be told."

"Yessir." But I beamed. Absolutely unexpected to myself, I experienced such happiness at this confirmation of my father's qualities that I knew the value, on the spot, of family pride and could have been filled from head to toe with well-nourished blood.

"Some day," he said drily, "you must try to equal him."

"Never," I said. "But I intend to try."

"Harry," he said, giving me back my name for the first time, "you're fortunate to be carrying that kind of burden. I don't tell people often, but since you and I are obviously embarked on a special venture, at least personally speaking, I choose to inform you that a father one admires extravagantly may be less of an impost than growing up without one. Mine was killed in Colorado in a shooting accident."

"I'm sorry to hear that."

"I was eleven when it occurred. I must say I didn't have to grow up altogether without him. He was always a presence in my life."

It took a few more years before I was to learn from Kittredge that David Montague, Harlot's father, had been shot by Harlot's mother, Imogene, as David entered the master bedroom one night. It was never clear whether he had lost his keys and was climbing through the window or walking through the door. There was too much blood on the floor. Either he had traveled on his belly, mortally wounded, from the window to the door, as was her claim, or had been dragged by Hugh's mother from the door to the window, then back to the door, to support the story that his unexpected entrance by the window caused her to believe he was an intruder. I understand Ty Cobb's father was shot under similar circumstances and there are some who believe it accounts for the tigerish rapacity of Ty Cobb on the base paths. If that is the formula for generating ungodly determination, I see no reason why it could not apply to Harlot.

Next day, true to his promise, he drove me out to Otter Cliffs. In anticipation, I spent a sleepless night. First I hoped it would rain, then that it would not. I was certain Mr. Montague would say the essence of rock climbing was to accept the given. If the rock was slippery, we would still have a go. So I began to pray it would not rain.

It was misty at 6:30 in the morning, but I knew the weather on Mount Desert well enough to see that the sky would be clear by eight. To avoid a family breakfast, we had fried eggs and coffee at a hash-house (no granola for outdoorsmen then!) and I ate my food in all somber duty, the yolk and biscuits going down like sulphur and brimstone, after which we took the Park Drive along the eastern shore of Mount Desert. As we drove I named for him places long familiar to me, the Beehive, Sand Beach, Thunder Hole, Gorham Mountain, a guide leading the way to his own terminal hour. Or so I was convinced. Rock climbing was familiar to me, if only in sleep. I always knew when a dream had become a nightmare, for there was I clinging to a wall.

We parked. We walked along a wooded trail for a hundred yards, and suddenly had, all to ourselves, the precipice of a cliff. Our view was open to the boom and hiss of the Atlantic pounding on rocks below. I took a quick glimpse down. It proved no easier than standing on the edge of a roof seven stories high that had no railing. My impulse was to ask Mr. Montague if this was, for certain, the right place.

He was scouting, his boots six inches from the lip. He strode along, frowning and clucking, weighing one ascent against another while I sat beside his pile of climbing gear, nerveless, and for all I knew, limbless. The stone on which I perched was pale pink and friendly, but the straight rock-fall below was dark gray, and black at the bottom. Years later, in the Department Store in Saigon, I was to have an outrageous attack of anxiety one night while staring at a Vietnamese prostitute's outspread legs. Her open vagina looked as sinister to me as an exotic orchid. Only then did I realize that the contrast of her pink petals and near-black overleaves had brought me back to the fearful minutes I waited for Harlot to take the measure of where to commence my instruction.

Finally he settled on the right place. "This will do," he told me, and unstrapped his gear, took out two coiled nylon ropes from the tote bag, and tugged on a few trees near the edge. "We'll rappel down," he said. "It's easy. Beginners like it. I, however, confess to you—it terrifies me."

Somehow, that was reassuring. "Why?" I managed to ask.

"You're dependent on things external to yourself," he answered, as if that were the only reply. "There's no sure means of knowing when a little tree like this gives way."

He was taking precautions. I will not try to describe all that he did, but I could see that he anchored one end of the rappel rope not only to the tree, but to an adjacent rock through the agency of a long sling of webbing. These various ties converged through an oval chromium ring smaller than my palm, which I knew was called a carabiner.

"Are you going to use pitons?" I asked, trying to give a warrant of knowledgeability.

"Oh, no need," he said. "Not for this."

Old as he was, we were acting as if both of us were seventeen. Which made it worse—he was vastly superior.

"All right, you wait here," he said when done, "and I'll go down, look it over, and come back. Then you'll do it."

I found it hard to believe that he was going to make a voyage up and down that cliff as casually as taking reconnaissance of a few floors

on an elevator, but indeed, he gave one mighty yank on the anchor
of his rappelling rope, and satisfied with such security, stood on the
edge of the cliff, back to the sea, the rope wound once around his
waist, and stated, "You'll find this the hardest part of the rappel. Just
slack off some rope and consign your butt to the void. Then, sit back
on the rope." Which he did by placing the sole of his shoes on the lip
and leaning backward, until his extended legs were in a horizontal line
with the ground. "Now," he said, "just walk down, step by step.
Keep your legs stiff, your feet against the rock, and give yourself slack
when you need it."

He made a few moves slowly, simulating the step-by-step technique a beginner should employ, the performance going on for five
or six steps of descent. After which, bored with the sluggishness of this
method, he gave a little whoop, shoved off with his feet from the rock,
and slackened ten feet of rope in a rush. When he bounced, toes first,
back into the wall, he was a good piece further down already, and with
three or four more such springs out from the wall, there he was below,
standing on a ledge of flat, black, wet stone.

He slipped the rope from around his waist, called to me to pull it
up. Then he climbed right after. It seemed to take him no longer than
he would have spent on five or six flights of stairs.

"Nice rock," he said. "You'll have a good time."

I did not say a word. I thought of every excuse I could make. I
had had no sleep. My operation left me dizzy at unexpected times. I
would like to approach this more slowly: Could we warm up on a trail
that did not require ropes? Below, tolling loudly on the rocks, the surf
reverberated among my fears.

I said nothing. My own destruction was by now superior to
whimpering out of this situation. Since I could find no excuse to
survive, I stood as passively as a martyr before faggots and flames, but
I was only a numb body suffering the rope to be fastened about me.
Later there would be much sophistication of apparatus, but on this
occasion, he merely knotted one end of a mountain cord around my
waist and dropped the rest of the coil on the ground beside him. He
took another rope, doubled it, and slipped it through the carabiner
attached to the tree, after which he passed it through two carabiners
linked onto my harness at the waist, these carabiners to serve as brake,
he explained, during the rappel. Then he ran this double rope under
my thigh, passed it diagonally across my chest, and around my back

to the other arm. So holding each end of its snakelike embrace of me, one hand guiding the slack, the other out for balance, I prepared to go off the lip.

To put one's heels on a ledge and lean backward into space, holding only to a rope, is equal to the wail one hears in childhood on falling out of bed. One discovers the voice is one's own. My first few steps, feet pressed flat against the vertical rock, were as clumsy as if my legs were concrete posts.

It was only after I descended five or six steps that I began to comprehend that the act of rappelling could actually be accomplished; indeed, it was a good deal easier than learning to use crutches.

How intimate was the surface of the rock, however! Each pock before me was an eye-socket; each large crack, a door ajar. Faces of intricate benignity and malevolence looked back at me from the lines and knobs of the rock. I felt as if I were lowering myself around the flank of Leviathan. Yet such was my relief at being able to perform these acts that before I reached the bottom, I actually gave a few thrusts out with my legs and tried running off slack through the double carabiners at my waist, these tentative efforts not dissimilar, I am certain, to the first stir of the lower throat that a six-week-old dog will make in preparation for barking.

I reached the ledge. The surf was steaming just below, and the wet, black stone under my sneakers felt as oily as a garage floor. I released the double rappel rope from the double carabiner and only then realized I had been attached all the while by my harness itself to the coil of cord Mr. Montague had held. If all had gone wrong, and I had lost balance on the rappel, Mr. Montague would have been there to support me by the second connection. Now my initial fear felt absurd to me. I was commencing to learn that fear was a ladder whose rungs are surmounted one by one, and at the summit—as Mr. Montague would probably say—lay Judgment itself.

He now plummeted down in three long swoops to stand beside me on the wet ledge. "This climb will test you," he said. "However, it's not unreasonable. Just a matter of learning a new vocabulary."

"What do you mean?" I murmured. I now had had my first good look at the ascent, and fear returned.

He gave the smallest smile—the first he had been ready to offer since his arrival. "You'll find I picked a climb with a few buckets."

Unattached to any rope, he started up. "Try to recall my route when you're here," he called down from fifteen feet above, "but

don't fret if you lose it. Part of the fun is to come on your own finds."
Whereupon he mounted the face in one continuous series of easy
moves and was at the top before I became aware again that the rope
attached to my waist was still very much in place, and its other end
was tied to some tree above the lip and out of sight. Mr. Montague
appeared on the edge, some eighty agonizing feet above, sitting on the
brink in all comfort, his feet dangling over, my rope—the rope, that
is, with which he would belay me—wound casually, and only once,
around his waist.

"Won't I pull you with me if I fall?" I asked. My voice emerged
in a reasonably clear little croak, but the effort was analogous to
putting the shot.

"I'm anchored to the tree." He beamed down on me. "Get
started. I'll send you clues by carrier pigeon." I was beginning to
understand what animated him. The air of funk in others can taste, I
suppose, like caviar.

How to speak of the beauty that rises from one's fear of the rock?
I was shriven. I understood the logic of God: The seed of compassion
is to be found in the harsh husk of the demand.

As I started up the wall, I could not believe how vertical was the
ascent. I thought there might be some slant in my favor, but no.
Vertical. True, the rock was cracked and scarred and nubbled and
pitted, a raw acne of surface that you could certainly get a grip on.
Feeling a friendly knob of a hold at the top of my reach, and seeing
a small slot for my foot, I stepped in, reached up, and pulled myself
one foot off the bottom ledge. I knew something of the emotions of
the first great day at Kitty Hawk then. Yes, this was as good as the
virgin jump from the balcony deck into Blue Hill Bay. To fortify me,
Mr. Montague pulled slightly on my harness. "If you need a little
help," he yelled down, "call: 'Tension,' " on which, by demonstration, he pulled harder so that I felt somewhat less than my own full
weight and more inclined to climb. I found another grip and foothold
just above, took the move, took another, and another, glanced down.
I was eight feet above the ledge. Splendid! I found another knob and
just above my knee was one of the buckets of which he spoke, a hole
about as large as a pool-table pocket in which I could rest my foot.
There I halted, catching my breath. The rock felt alive. It had odors,
grooves filled with dirt, overhanging elbows, armpits; it had pubic
corners. I do not wish to exaggerate, but I was not prepared for the
intimacy of the activity. It was as if I were climbing up the body of

a giant put together of the bones and flesh and pieces and parts of a thousand humans.

Now, soon enough, I entered a more difficult portion of the ascent. About halfway up, I came to a place where I did not know how to continue. There were no good grips to reach with my hands, and not a quarter inch of rock-wrinkle to support the next push with my foot. In deadlock, straddled, I encountered the agonizing indecision of the rock climber. All the while that one's limbs are burning from expenditures of anxiety, one does not know whether to try to continue up or look to descend a few feet in order to veer onto another route. Frozen on the rock, my voice scorched in my throat, the open depths below were falling away into the unrecoverable past. I stared like a pawnbroker at the dubious possibilities presented by each ripple in the rock. I think half of all I ever learned about rock climbing came from these first five minutes on Otter Cliffs; I was given a quick introduction to the great social world of vertical stone. There the smallest bit of irregularity can prove an immensely useful friend, a treacherous if conceivably employable associate, a closed door, or an outright enemy. I had by now managed to maneuver myself into a coffin's corner just beneath an overhang.

There I rested, sobbing for breath, altogether bewildered what to do next. The more I squeezed myself into this perch, which accommodated only a part of my body, the more I had to consume the strength of my arms in unhappy holds. I heard Montague call out, "Don't build your nest there. It's no place to breed."

"I don't know what to do," I said.

"Back down a few feet. Work to your right."

Here I discovered the curious nature of one's own virtue. That is so inaccessible to us on normal occasions that we are doomed to become more intimate with our vices. Even as I took my first step in retreat, eyeing already the potentialities he had suggested on the right, I saw what might be a quicker way around the overhang if I tried a route to the left. It was riskier. To the right, I had his word at least, whereas to the left I could see one good move and then another, but there appeared to be a straddle ten feet above—a smooth rock face with two vertical cracks five feet apart—perhaps a grip or two, I could not tell. What appears to be a hold from below can prove only the shadow of a bulge; what promises an edge for one's foot comes out to no more than a striation in the stone.

I took the option to the left. It was mine. It had not been given to me and so could become my virtue. Such was the state of my logic. Panting for breath as unashamedly as a woman in labor (which image I account for by my adolescent, film-sophisticated understanding of how a woman acts in labor), I could feel my religious education advancing by leaps. Virtue was grace. The impossible could be traversed by the intuitions of one's heart. Scaling off to the left, I had to make moves I would not have attempted before. Desperate to prove my choice, I had to include one fancy scrabble from one welt of rock up to another, neither step of which could have held me for more than a second, but I did it all in one continuous move as if I were Montague, and in reward found myself able to stand and rest on the small ledge above the overhang.

Montague called down, "Three cheers, boy. You're past the crux."

It came on me. I had gotten through the worst. I continued on to the top in a state of elation that was potentially as dangerous as an all-out funk. "Perfect," he said when I joined him. "Now we'll try you on tougher stuff," and began packing the gear for the drive to the next step.

3

ONE'S FEARS ON THE ROCK SOON GAIN PROPORTION. IF ONE DOES NOT take the lead like Montague, but is belayed from above by a good climber, it soon becomes clear that you can afford on occasion to fall. Unaware my first time up of such relative security, I made every move as if a mistake might be my death. It took a second ascent that afternoon on a vertical column in The Precipices to make me aware that I was living in comparative safety. For when one move I made did not work and I slipped from a fractional foothold, I plunged but a couple of feet, suffering no more than a scrape to my knee. The rope was belaying me from above.

I made progress after that. Mr. Montague had accepted my father's invitation to take his two-week summer vacation at Doane. So for two weeks I went out every day with him. (And often in the rain.) Once, he took along two of my cousins, but I took no pleasure in their fears. I felt—rare emotion—like a veteran.

Mr. Montague and I preferred to be alone. Each day he took me

over a different kind of hazard. I was introduced to finger jams and
pressure holds. I learned how to *smear* smooth rock with the heel of
my hand. Lie-back holds and crack-backs were shown to me, foot
jams and chimneys. He took me up squeeze chimneys and over slabs,
gave me problems in mantling and hand traverses. Forgive me, but I
mention these techniques to keep track of the different rock faces on
which we spent our days. There were nights when the proper placement of pitons and bongs clanged in my head as I went to sleep, and
I heard the hiss of the rope as Mr. Montague, on the lead, tugged it
through the carabiner above me.

I had fallen in love with the illimitable skill of the rock climber.
Clumsy, using my arms more than my legs, and my will as a substitute
for wisdom, I scratched my way up many a face, growing filthy with
the effluvia of the stone. For those two weeks of summer, I did not
have a finger, an elbow, or a knee that was not raw, and my thighs and
shins acquired a hundred bruises, but I was happy. I expect I was more
happy than not for the first time in my life, and thereby, at the age of
seventeen, grasped a truth some choose never to go near: Happiness
is experienced most directly in the intervals between terror. As each
climb he led me to was, in general, more difficult than the one before,
so did I rarely have a day in which I was not washed in sweat. I spent
time with fear as intimately as a body down with flu knows fever. I
learned the implacable law of fear. It has to be conquered or it collects,
then invades one's dreams. There were days when I could not complete a climb and had to go down. In rock climbing, it is harder,
however, to descend than to climb—one's feet have to search for the
holds, and they see less well than the fingers. So I slipped often, and
dangled on the rope, and sweated, and knew myself doubly abject, and
could not sleep that night for confronting my terror: I would have to
return next day and do it properly. A compelling transaction. One is
raising at such times all the ships that sank in childhood from loss of
courage, yes, hoisting them up from the sea bottom of oneself. I felt
as if all the childhood fears that weighed me down had begun their
ascent to the surface—I was being delivered from the graveyard of
expired hope. But what a chancy operation! Each time I failed to
complete a climb, the fear I was hoping to cure was not consumed but
turned corrupt.

Yet each time I succeeded, I received my dependable reward. For
an hour, or for a night, I was happy. On the best day I had in those
two weeks, which was next to the last day, Montague brought me

back to Otter Cliffs and told me to take the lead. Notwithstanding all
I had learned, going up first on the same ascent where I had begun
proved several times more difficult. Taking the lead, I had to hammer
in my pitons as I went, my arm in such a catalepsy of controlled panic
that it would cramp after every few raps of the hammer. Now the
prospect of a fall was serious again. On the lead, I tried to put a piton
in every five feet, knowing each prospective fall could double the
length since one might plummet from five feet above the last piton to
five feet below. And that ten feet would double again should the
lower piton pull out. Facing such a prospect, easy climbs became
difficult.

Once I did fall. It was for ten feet, no more. My piton held, but
I bounced on the end of the rope, then took a mean swing into the
rock. Scraped, bruised, and feeling as shattered as a cat who has been
plunged into a pail of ice water, I held my breath against the long
temptation to whimper, took a full minute to call back the wide-flying
streamers of my will, and, hard to believe that I was exacting this on
myself, took on the climb again and searched for a way through the
crux. It happened to be the same overhang as on the first day, but now
I was dragging a rope behind me rather than being encouraged from
above. Two weeks of newly acquired knowledge made the difference.
I worked my way to the lip without another fall.

Those two weeks did more for me than any operation on my
skull. I had new standing in the family. My cousins gave way to my
opinions in passing squabbles, and my father took me out for a night
of drinking in the modest bars of Bar Harbor. Toward the end of the
evening, I was feeling as relaxed as a piece of spaghetti cooked in wine,
and my male parent, giving, as usual, no more sign of drink than his
massive emanations of good or bad will, said—he was obviously in a
splendid spirit—"Hugh Montague has a good opinion of you. That's
the accolade, Harry. He doesn't have three words to say for any ten
people."

"Well, I'm glad," I said. I felt so corny I was ready to cry. Instead,
I laid in a good swallow of bourbon. The flush it inspired told me for
the first time how rich my father's insides must feel.

"Hugh's going to take you for a lobster dinner tomorrow," he
told me. "Hugh says you're worth a good-bye party all to yourself."

In the event, Hugh Montague had a great deal to say to me. By
the first drink, I had begun to babble—the intoxication of having
encountered this vocation which was a sport, a skill, and an open-air

monastery for the soul, augmented by my successful lead that very afternoon, not to mention my felicitous connection with bourbon the night before, as well as the great (if hitherto unadmitted) release of knowing that Mr. Montague, fearsome godfather, would be gone tomorrow, had me nattering. I was ready to take vows never to betray the new discipline, but Mr. Montague cut me off.

"Harry, I'm going to tell you something that will hurt. I advance it, however, for your benefit. I have kept a high opinion of you over these two weeks. You are going to make a good man, and I respect that doubly in your case because you were dealt paltry cards in childhood. I gather your mother is tiny."

"Yes."

"And not wholly dependable, according to your father."

"Not wholly."

"Men work to develop their evil skills. Women—it is my belief— merely summon them." When he saw my adolescent eyes were not within a hundred miles of the peak of this observation, he shrugged, and said, "When we know each other better, we might trade a few anecdotes about our respective mothers"—he came to a full stop as if startled by himself—"although, don't count on it."

"Yessir."

"From now on, when we're alone, you and I, I want you to call me by the name my associates employ. That name is Harlot. Not to be confused with Harlow, Jean Harlow, but *Harlot*."

"Yessir."

"One of the most persistent little questions over at Foggy Bottom is why Montague chose such a point of reference. Sooner or later, they all make the pilgrimage over to my good side and have the touching simplicity to ask directly. As if I were in haste to tell! Should we become exceptional friends, I'll spill the beans. In twenty years."

"Yes, Harlot." I stopped. "It doesn't sound right."

"Never fear. You'll get used to it." He picked up the knuckles of a claw, twisted them apart without getting his fingertips caught on the spurs, and proceeded with his lobster fork to pluck forth the meat.

"Harry, I'll present you with the worst first." He fixed me with his eyes. There would be no sliding off. "I want you to give up rock climbing."

He could as well have struck me in the face.

"Oh," I said. "Golly."

"It's not that you are bad. You are better than your physical skills. You have innate moxie. Of ten beginners one might instruct, I say you would probably come in second or third in the lot."

"Then why do I have to stop?" I paused. I dropped my voice. "Would I kill myself?"

"Probably not. Hurt yourself, certainly. But that's not my reason. It's more particular than that. Only the best of beginners should ever dream of going on. It's more than just a sport, you see, for brave ones like yourself." This was the first time anyone had ever called me brave.

"No," I said, "why? Why do you want me to quit?"

"It's an activity that insists on excellence. Harry, if you went on, it would take over your life. You could not rest. Whenever you failed on a climb, the memory would overpower every thought until you succeeded. Even among good people, that can be a terribly debilitating process. An addiction. One ends as a coward, a victim, or a mediocre monomaniac. It is like being an ex-alcoholic. One is able to contemplate nothing else."

I was sufficiently agitated to say to him, "I don't understand what you're saying." My voice must have been rude-edged for I could feel his annoyance. His disciplines as a pedagogue may have saved me from a few thrusts of his temper.

"All right then," he said, "we will go further. A man who acquires high competence in rock climbing is able to become the instrument of his own will. That's what we try to arrive at. That's what we're encouraged to desire from the year one. A child is taught not to soil his pants. His bowels become the instrument of his will. And as we grow older, we often feel emotions that are as low and obstreperous as the embarrassing necessity, if caught in public, to take a *drop*." He used the word as though that were the only acceptable synonym ever to employ. "Nonetheless, we say to our good sphincter, so much the creature of our will, 'Tighten up, you fool.'

"Obviously rock climbing firms the upper regions of the will. But it's quite a process. And just as dangerous as black magic. For every fear we are ready to confront is equally open, you see, to the Devil. Should we fail, the Devil is there to soothe our cowardice. 'Stick with me,' he says, 'and your cowardice is forgiven.' Whereas, rock climbing, when well done, pinches off the Devil. Of course, if you fail, his nibs returns twofold. If you are not good enough then, you spend half your days getting the Devil out. That is marking time. And so long as we stay in place, Satan is more than satisfied. He loves circular, obsessive activity. Entropy is his meat. When the world becomes a pendulum, he will inhabit the throne."

"Maybe," I said, "I would know what I could climb and what I couldn't, and just stick with that."

"Never. You are half your father. That half is not going to rest. I could see from the first day that by one measure you were equal to the best rock climbers. You understood it. You knew you were in one damned awesome church, indeed the only one where religion comes close enough to Our Lord to give a little real sustenance."

"Yessir."

"There's a story I was told about some farfetched, terribly intense sect of Jewish people called Hasidim. They used to inhabit village ghettos in Russia and the Ukraine. It seems that one of their folk, a rabbi, was so devotional that he prayed to God forty times a day. Finally, after forty years, the rabbi grew impatient and said, 'God, I have loved You for so long that I want You to reveal Yourself to me. Why won't You reveal Yourself to me?' Whereupon God did just that. He revealed Himself. How do you think the rabbi reacted?"

"I don't know."

Harlot began to laugh. I had never heard him give a full laugh before. It gave a clue to why he had chosen his name. Inside him were more people than one would have thought. His laugh was all over the place. "Well, Harry, the good fellow dived right under the bed and began to howl like a dog. 'Oh, God,' the rabbi said, 'please do *not* reveal Yourself to me.' That, Harry, is a useful story. Before all else, God is awesome. It's the first thing to know. If Christ had not been sent to us, no one would ever have gotten out of the cave. Jehovah was too much for all of us. There would have been no modern civilization."

"What about Egypt, or Greece and Rome? Didn't they take us out of the cave?"

"Harry, those cultures marked time. They were perfect examples of the obsessional. Devil's abodes, all three, Egypt, Greece, and Rome. Don't be impressed by how beautiful they were. The Devil, you must never forget, is the most beautiful creature God ever made. Spiritually, however, those cultures did not choose to emerge from Plato's cave. It took Christ to come along and say, 'Forgive the sons for the sins of the fathers.' That's the day, Harry, that scientific inquiry was born. Even if we had to wait a millennium and more for Kepler and Galileo. So, follow the logic: Once the father begins to believe that his sons will not suffer for his acts of sacrilege, he grows bold enough to experiment. He looks upon the universe as a curious place, rather than as an almighty machine guaranteed to return doom for his curiosity. That was the beginning of the technological sleigh ride which may destroy us yet. The Jews, of course, having rejected Christ, had to keep dealing with Jehovah for the next two millennia. So they never forgot. God is awesome. 'Oh God, do not reveal Yourself to me. Not all at once!' "

He paused. He ordered another drink for each of us, Hennessey for himself, and Old Harper's, I recollect, for me. "Let us have an Old Harper's for Young Harry," he actually said to the waitress, and went right back to his disquisition on the awesome: "I suspect that God is with us in some fashion on every rock climb. Not to save us—how I detest that tit-nibbling psychology—God saves!—God at the elbow of all misbegotten mediocrities. As if all that God had to do was preserve the middling and the indifferent. No, God is not a St. Bernard dog to rescue us at every pass. God is near us when we are rock climbing because that is the only way we get a good glimpse of Him and He gets one of us. You experience God when you're extended a long way out beyond yourself and are still trying to lift up from your fears. Get caught under a rock and of course you want to howl like a dog. Surmount that terror and you rise to a higher fear. That may be our simple purpose on earth. To rise to higher and higher levels of fear. If we succeed, we can, perhaps, share some of God's fear."

"His fear?"

"Absolutely. His fear of the great power He has given the Devil. There is no free will for man unless the Devil's powers were made equal on this embattled planet to the Lord's. That is why," he said, "I don't want you to continue rock climbing. The brute fact is that you don't have the exquisite skills that are necessary. So you will keep finding a little courage and losing it. You could end up like one of those monumentally boring golfers who work for years to improve their swing and never stop talking about it. Orotund blobs of narcissism."

"Okay," I said. Now I was angry. Awfully hurt but clearly angry.

"All this is not in disrespect for your feelings, but in true respect. I believe there is a place for you. It will make demands upon your courage, your intelligence, your will, and your wit. You will be tempted by the Devil at every turn. But you can, in my modest opinion, serve God. In a far better way, I propose, than as a rock climber."

Formidable were his gifts of transition. I had been shifted from the pits of an unexpected wound to a pitch of interest. "Are you saying what I suppose you are saying?"

"Of course. Your father asked me to spend my vacation looking you over as a prospect. Nothing less. I had other plans for these two weeks. But he said, 'More than anything, I want the boy to come aboard with us. Only, however, if you think he's right. It's too important a matter to be judged by my desires and affection.'"

"Did my father speak that way to you?"

"Most definitely."

"You told him I could come aboard?"

"Yesterday. By now, I know you better than your father does. You have nice gifts. I'll say no more. Your father is an enthusiast, and overextended, therefore, on occasion, in judgment, but I pride myself on a cold eye. You have qualities that your father, for all his splendid stuff, is lacking."

I was tempted to say, "There is nothing special about me"—is that not the most painful cry one can utter in adolescence?—but now I was gifted with judgment. I kept my mouth shut.

"You're planning to go to Yale?"

"Yessir."

"I'd say, short of a collapse on entrance exams, it can be taken for granted you will get in. Yale is perfect. I call it Uncle Eli's Cabin."

I laughed.

"Oh, yes," said my new associate, Harlot, "part of the underground railway. One of the stations on the route. At least for a few." He made a face. "As an old Harvard man, I don't like to say this, but Yale is a touch niftier to our purposes. Harvard gets quiffy about recruitment. It's a stinking irony since half of our real people did happen to go there. Well, as I always say, trust a good fellow so long as he doesn't matriculate at Princeton."

Harlot held up his glass. We would drink to that. One knew all the merriment of drinking to the health of Annapurna as opposed to Nanda Devi. Then we shook hands and drove back to the Keep. In the morning, Harlot left. He would drop me a letter on a point of advice from time to time, but I was not to be in the same room with him again for several years.

4

THE ROCK CLIMBING LEFT ITS INHERITANCE. IN MY SENIOR YEAR AT ST. Matthew's, I went from second shell to first on the 150-pound crew and rowed against St. Paul's and Groton. I passed my Entrance Boards with good marks and one full leap ahead of my now domiciled dyslexia. I won the one fistfight I had in my three years at prep school. I even worked out at wrestling which was difficult for me since I was still expunging from my brain every trace of the glom-job by the assistant chaplain (who always nodded when we passed). My loins no longer felt impacted with pus. And I did get into Yale. I had had, as one would suspect, a sense of future mission all through my last year at St. Matthew's and it continued in college. I entered Yale with the full expectation that some official at one of the freshman inquiry desks would lead me over to my undergraduate CIA unit, but as I soon learned, the Agency did not go in for college cells. No raps sounded on my door at midnight.

At Harlot's suggestion, I did join ROTC. "You'll be dealing with idiots," he told me, "but there are requirements for military service that have to be satisfied before you can join the Agency, and ROTC takes care of that. After Yale, you certainly wouldn't want to face two years in the armed services before coming to us."

I did close-order drill over the next eight semesters and managed to get good enough to air out any dank memories of left-foot-club-foot with the Knickerbocker Grays. I discovered a vein of optimism in myself. As one grew older, the traumatic impasses of childhood could actually dissolve.

Harlot would telephone from time to time and prove interested in which courses I chose. Usually it was to push my interests toward English. "Learn your mother tongue and you'll appreciate the others." Before sophomore year he sent me what he saw as a great gift, a first edition of Skeat's *Etymological Dictionary of the English Language,* and truth, it wasn't bad. There was a time when I could not only locate the roots of a word in Latin and Greek, but enjoy the exotic yams and tubers that come to us from Scandinavian and Celtic. I learned of English words derived from Italian by way of Latin, as well as of Portuguese from Latin (*auto-da-fé* and *binnacle*), and French out of Portuguese from Latin (*fetich* and *parasol*), and French out of Spanish from Latin, and Portuguese out of Spanish and Dutch derived from

Latin (*cant* and *canal* and *pink*), and German from Latin, and French from Late Latin, and German out of Hungarian from Serbian from late Greek from Latin, all to be tapped for *hussar*. I learned crossbreeds of French out of Spanish from Arabic from Greek—*alembic* is one reward—and I will not go on at length about English that came to us from Low German, Dutch, Slavonic, Russian, Sanskrit, Magyar, Hebrew, Hindustani. Harlot, by his lights, was getting me ready for CIA. The theory? Why, look to the tendrils of other tongues that had grown their way into English. Thereby one might develop a taste for the unspoken logic of other lands.

Of course, I saw it all as preparation. For the next four years, my courses and the friends I made, were all there to contribute to my mission as a CIA man. If I had any conflict over my future occupation, it was on spring nights in New Haven, after an occasional and frustrating date with a girl, when I would tell myself that I really wished to become a novelist. Brooding upon this, I would also inform myself that I did not have sufficient experience to write. Joining CIA would give me the adventures requisite to working up good fiction.

I was certainly single-minded. I see myself in junior year before the Yale-Harvard game, drunk at Mory's with my peers, holding the silver bowl high. I was obliged to keep drinking Green Cup for as long as my table would continue to sing, yes, how I drank and how they chose to sing. The song was long, and I would not quit until the last bar of music was sung, and sung again.

Words I have not thought of in thirty years come to me out of the pale, sunlike glare of the interior of that large silver punch bowl. I quaffed Green Cup at Mory's and around me in a ring of ten illuminated voices, the song cried on:

> It's Harry, it's H, it's H makes the world go round.
> It's Harry, H, that makes the world go round.
> Sing Hallelujah, sing Hallelujah,
> Put a nickel on the drum,
> Save another drunken bum,
> Sing Hallelujah, sing Hallelujah,
> Put a nickel on the drum,
> Save another drunken bum,
> Put a nickel on the drum,
> And you'll be saved.

They paused for breath but I had to keep drinking.

> Oooh, I'm H-A-P-P-Y to be F-R-double-E,
> F-R-double-E to be S-A-V-E-D,
> S-A-V-E-D from the bonds of S-I-N,
> Glory, glory Hallelujah,
> Hip, Hooray, Amen.

And I, drinking that sweet, potent, noxious, liquor-hallowed Green Cup, swallow into swallow, giving my soul to finish the bowl, knew that angels watched me as I drank, and if I drank it all before the song was done, we would beat Harvard tomorrow, we would serve our team from the stands. We would be there to offer our devotion, our love, our manly ability to booze with the gods at Mory's. Only gods drank to the depths of a silver bowl. We would ring Yale Bowl with the might of our mission at Yale, which was to defeat Harvard tomorrow. God, didn't I guzzle it down, and the score next day, in that November of 1953, was Yale 0, Harvard 13.

5

I WAS INTRODUCED TO KITTREDGE TOWARD THE END OF JUNIOR YEAR at Yale. Just before Easter vacation, a summons came by telegram: COME MEET MY FIANCEE HADLEY KITTREDGE GARDINER. SPEND EASTER AT THE KEEP WITH KITTREDGE AND JEAN HARLOW.

Back to Doane. I had not been to the island since my father, in need of the money a couple of years ago, had pushed and cajoled his two brothers and single sister into agreement on the sale. Why his funds needed replenishment remained one more family mystery. Among the Hubbards, windfalls, disasters, and outright peculation were kept at a greater distance from the children than sexual disclosure; all we knew (and it was talked about in whispers) was: "A damn shame. Got to sell the Keep. Boardman's idea." My father walked about for two weeks that summer with a mouth as tight as a South American dictator under palace arrest. I hardly cared. I loved the Keep less than the others, or so I thought. It was only over the next summer, which I spent at loose ends in Southampton with my mother, getting drunk with new, rich friends I did not like, and banging tennis balls through August days, that I came to understand what it was to lose the splendor of afternoon silences over the Maine hills.

The call to go back to the Keep was then agreeable; the opportunity to see Harlot spoke of more. I was still like a girl who fell in love with a man who went away to war. If he had not come back for three years, no matter. The girl went on no other dates; she did not even accept telephone calls from nice boys.

I was in love with CIA. I am one of those types—is it one in ten, or one in fifty?—who can give up just about all of life for concentration upon a part of life. I read spy novels, made island hops from word to word in Skeat, attended foreign-policy forums at Yale, and studied photographs of Lenin and Stalin and Molotov, of Gromyko and Lavrenti Beria; I wanted to comprehend the face of the enemy. I eschewed political arguments about Republicans and Democrats. They hardly mattered. Allen Dulles was my President, and I would be a combat trooper in the war against the Devil. I read Spengler and brooded through my winters in New Haven about the oncoming downfall of the West and how it could be prevented. Be certain that under these circumstances I sent Harlot a telegram that I was on my way, signed it Ashenden (for Somerset Maugham's British spy), and drove my car, a 1949 Dodge coupe, up from New Haven all the way to the back side of Mount Desert, where I found the house not at all as it used to be.

I do not know if I care to describe the changes. I would need to add a treasures-in-trash catalogue to the insights of a geologist: Generations of Hubbards had left their strata. We used to have oak whatnots in corners, and blonde-wood Danish in the Cunard; one fine old drafting table at the Camp had come down to us from Doane Hadlock Hubbard (who also left us punctilious drawings of a proposed lookout tower one hundred feet high that he once planned to build on the southern head of the island). Along the walls were hordes of washed-out framed photographs, spotted, glass-cracked, oak-mitred, come down to us from the 1850s on. Then there were the color prints, long sun-faded, of Matisse, Braque, Dufy, Duchamp—all introduced by my mother. They had been kept, even if she never came back. Once up on a wall, things remained; it was a summer house. No wars of selection went on—merely an accommodation of accumulation. The beds were a disaster area, summer-cottage pallets. Lumpy, broken-spring mattresses with old ticking, wooden bureaus with thick paint scored by fingernail scrapings to attest to hot bored summer after-noons; spiderwebs on casement windows, birds' nests under the eaves, and mouse droppings in many an unused room were the price we paid for that much spread of house.

Rodman Knowles Gardiner and his wife fixed it up when they bought it from us. Kittredge's father, being a Shakespeare scholar (distantly related to the famous Shakespearean George Kittredge, also of Harvard), knew enough about the unwinding of plots to stipulate later in the deed of transfer to the couple for a wedding present that in the event of Kittredge's divorce from Hugh Montague, she was to own the Keep without impediment. Which is how I returned to living in it. By way of Kittredge. But that was in time to come. Now in the Easter of my junior year at Yale, more than two years after the closing with the Hubbards, Dr. Gardiner and his wife had certainly spruced up the Keep. Retired from teaching, they moved some of their best Colonial furniture from their Cambridge home to Maine. There were drapes on the windows now and the walls bore Dr. Gardiner's collection of nineteenth-century Victorian paintings. The bedrooms had new beds. At first sight I hated it. We now looked like a New England hostelry of the sort that keeps the temperature too high in winter and screws down the windows.

I spent a difficult two hours after my arrival. Neither Hugh Montague nor his fiancée were there—instead, I was received by the eminent Shakespearean and his wife, Maisie. They endured me; I suffered. He was a Harvard professor of a variety that may no longer exist. Dr. Gardiner was so well established that there were tiers to his eminence. Stages of his personality, much like assistants in a descending chain of command, were delegated to conversation. We spoke of the Yale and Harvard football teams of the previous fall, then of my category in squash—I was a B-group player—and of my father, whom Dr. Gardiner had last seen with Mr. Dulles at an annual garden party in Washington: "He looked very well indeed—of course, that was last year."

"Yessir. He still looks well."

"Good for him."

As a tennis player, Dr. Gardiner would not have let you enjoy rallies during the warm-up. He'd drive your innocent return cross-court and leave you to trot after it.

Maisie was not conspicuously better. She spoke of the flower garden she would put in this May; she intoned in a dreary if nonetheless dulcet voice against the unpredictability of spring weather in Maine. She mentioned the hybrids she would plant; when I offered mention of some wildflowers to look for in June and July, she lost much interest in me. Conversational pauses expanded into extensions of silence. In desperation, I tried to charge into Dr. Gardiner's center of strength. I expatiated on a term paper (for which I had received an A) on Ernest Hemingway's work. The consciously chosen irony of the later style showed, I said, that he had been enormously influenced by *King Lear,* particularly by some of Kent's lines, and I quoted from act one, scene four, "I do prefer . . . to love him that is loved, to converse with him that is wise and say little, to fear judgment, to fight when I cannot choose, and to eat no fish." I was about to add, "I can keep honest counsel, ride, run, mar a curious tale in telling it, and deliver a plain message bluntly," but Dr. Gardiner said, "Why concern yourself with the copyist?"

We sat. After a stretch, Kittredge and Hugh Montague came back in the twilight. They had been—it was a very cold Easter—ice climbing on parts of the lower trail of Gorham Mountain. Nice stuff, Kittredge assured me, and she looked full of red cheeks and Christmas.

She was lovely beyond any measure I had for a woman. Her dark hair was cut short like a boy's, and she was wearing pants and a windbreaker, but she was the most wonderful-looking girl. She could have been a heroine out of her father's collection of painted Victorian damsels, pale as their cloisters, lovely as angels. That was Kittredge— except that her color today after the afternoon's ice climb was as startling as a view of wild red berries in a field of snow.

"It's wonderful to meet you. We're cousins. Did you know that?" she asked.

"I suppose I did."

"I looked it up last evening. Third cousins. That's no-man's-land if you get down to it." She laughed with such a direct look (as if to speak of how very attractive a man younger than herself might be if she liked him) that Hugh Montague actually stirred. I knew little enough yet of jealousy, but I could feel the wave that came over from him.

"Well, I must tell you," she said, "all the while Hugh was taking us up this dreadful pitch, I kept saying I wouldn't marry him until he promised never to do such a thing to me again, whereupon he said, 'You and Harry Hubbard are in the same boat.' He banishes us equally from his grubby art."

"Actually," said Hugh Montague, "she's a little better than you, Harry. All the same, it's hopeless."

"Well, I should hope so," said Maisie Gardiner. "Fool's play to risk your neck on ice."

"I love it," said Kittredge. "The only thing Hugh would bother to explain was, 'Ice won't betray you until it does.' What a husband you'll make."

"Relatively secure," said Hugh.

Rodman Knowles Gardiner had a coughing fit at the thought of his daughter in marriage.

At precisely that moment Kittredge said, "I believe Daddy thinks of me as Desdemona."

"I don't see myself," said her father, "as a blackamoor, nor espoused to my daughter. You have rotten logic, darling."

Kittredge changed the subject.

"Never did any ice climbing?" she asked of me. When I shook my head, Kittredge said, "It's no worse than the awful thing they do to you at the Farm when you have to leap out of a mud ditch and scramble up a link fence in between sweeps of the searchlight." She stopped, but not in caution, more to calculate when I would be eligible for that chore. "I guess you'll be getting into it year after next. The fence is modeled on the Grosse-Ullner barrier in East Germany."

Hugh Montague gave a smile with no amusement in it. "Kittredge, don't practice indiscretion as if it were your métier."

"No," said Kittredge, "I'm home. I want to talk. We're not in Washington, and I'm tired of pretending through one blah–blah cocktail party after another that I'm a little file clerk at Treasury. 'Oh,' they say, 'what do you file?' 'Oodles of stuff,' I tell them back. 'Statistics.' They know I'm lying. Obviously, I'm a madwoman spook. It stands out."

"What stands out is how spoiled you are," said her fiancé.

"How could I not be? I'm an only child," said Kittredge. "Aren't you?" she went on to ask.

"By half," I said, and when no one responded, I felt obliged to give a summary explanation.

She appeared to be fascinated. "You must be full," she said, "of what I call ghost-overlays." She held up a marvelous white hand as if she were playing traffic cop in a skit at a charity ball. "But I promised everybody I would not theorize this weekend. Some people drink too much. I never stop theorizing. Do you think it's a disease, Hugh?"

"Preferable to drink," he offered.

"I'll tell you about ghost-overlays when we're alone," she declared to me.

I winced within. Hugh Montague was possessive. If she smiled nicely at me, he saw the end of their romance in her smile. Ultimately, he was right—it is just that lovers condense all schedules. What would take us more than fifteen years looked like immediate danger.

On the other hand, he was bored. Carrying on a conversation with Rodman and Maisie Gardiner was equal to taking dinner in a room where light bulbs keep going off and on. Most of the time we talked as if there were rules against logical connection. During drinks I kept track of a few remarks. Ten statements were uttered over ten minutes. Three belonged to Dr. Gardiner, two were by Maisie, three by Harlot, one from Kittredge, one from me. There are limits to memory. I offer a reasonable substitute.

Rodman Knowles Gardiner: "I've got Freddy Eaves at the boatyard looking out for a new spinnaker."

Maisie: "Why do the royal purple zinnias slip into blight so much more readily than the cosmos zinnias?"

Hugh Montague: "There was word of a major avalanche yesterday in the Pyrenees."

Kittredge: "If you would give the purple zinnias a bit less mulch, Mother . . ."

Maisie: "Is Gilley Butler a reliable handyman, Mr. Hubbard? Your father, Cal Hubbard, says to watch out for him."

Myself: "I should listen to my father."

Montague: "They weren't carrying avalanche cords so the bodies are not recoverable."

Dr. Gardiner: "The spinnaker ripped in the Backside Regatta. I had to finish with a jenny. Half as much headway."

Montague: "Three cheers for making the honor roll again, Harry."

Dr. Gardiner: "I'm going to fill the martini shaker."

Kittredge and I had, nonetheless, one hour alone. She demanded it. On Sunday morning, coming back from Easter Mass, with an hour to wait for Maisie's cook to serve us Sunday dinner, she forced the situation. "I want Harry to show me the island," she said to Hugh. "I'm sure he knows the nooks and crannies." A lack of plausibility quivered in the air. It would not require a guide to find nooks and crannies on our small island.

Hugh nodded. He smiled. He held out his hand like a pistol, thumb up, forefinger extended. Wordlessly, he fired a shot at me. "Keep those nasal passages clean, Herrick," he said.

Kittredge and I walked in kelp and sea wrack on the pebbled shore. Near us reared the unseen presence of Harlot, a stallion over the field of our mood.

"He's awful," Kittredge said at last and took my hand. "I adore him but he's awful. He's *raunchy*. Harry, do you love sex?"

"I would hate to think I didn't," I said.

"Well, I would hope you do. You are as good-looking as Montgomery Clift, so you ought to. I know I like sex. It's all sex with Hugh and me. We have so little else in common. That's why he's jealous. His Omega is virtually void of libido and his Alpha is overloaded."

I did not know as yet that she had been consorting with these two principalities, Alpha and Omega, ever since the concept first came to her four years ago. Now I heard of them for the first time. I would encounter those words again over the next thirty years.

"What makes it worse," she said, "is that I'm still a virgin. I think he is too, although he won't offer a conclusive word about it."

I was twice shocked, once at these astonishing facts, and again that she would tell me. She laughed, however. "I take a True Confession pill every night," she said. "Are you a virgin, Harry?"

"Regrettably," I replied.

She laughed and laughed. "I don't want to be," she confided. "It's absurd. It isn't as if Hugh and I don't know each other's bodies rather well. In fact, we know them perfectly. We're very much naked together. That kind of truth binds us. But he insists on waiting for marriage to consummate the last part."

"Well, you'll be wed soon, I guess."

"In June," she said. "We were supposed to gather up a few final plans this weekend, but Daddy and Hugh when put together are hopeless. Worse than two relics in an old folks' home trying to make conversation with each other's dentures."

It was my turn to laugh. It went on for so long that in embarrassment I sat down. She sat beside me. We perched on the southern head of the island and looked down Blue Hill Bay to the cold Easter sun shining over the remote Atlantic.

"Hugh may be the most complicated person I've encountered," she said, "but this weekend he's ridiculously simple. He's in a thundering grouch because we can't get together at night. Daddy insisted on putting me in the room next to Mother and him. So Hugh is falling apart. He's outrageously priapic, you see. Back in Washington he's on me all the time. I hope you don't mind hearing this, Harry. I've got to talk."

"Yes," I said. I didn't know what she was talking about. The facts seemed to contradict each other. "How can he be on you," I asked, "if you're both virgins?"

"Well, we go in for what he calls 'the Italian solution.'"

"Oh," I said. I didn't know anymore. Then I did. It was physically painful to contemplate what she allowed him to do. Nor could I conceive how it connected with all her soap and sunlight.

"Actually," she said with the quick, rising zephyr of a Radcliffe girl, "I love it. It's debauched. To be a virgin and yet feel so wanton. Harry, it's opened a purview on the Renaissance for me. Now I see how they could observe the Catholic forms and yet live in such near-mortal violation of so much. That's not the unhealthiest approach, you know."

"Do you talk this way to everyone?" I asked.

"Heavens, no," she said. "You're special."

"How can that be? You don't know me."

"I only needed one look. Before it's over, I said to myself, I'm going to tell this man everything. You see, Harry, I love you."

"Oh," I said. "I guess I love you too." I did not have to pretend. The thought of Hugh Montague as a satyr hot on her back left me feeling criminally wounded. I might as well have been the cuckolded lover. I hated how her confidence had reached so easily to the very center of me.

"Of course," she said, "you and I are never going to do anything about it. We're cousins, and that's what we'll always be. Dearest friends. At worst, kissing cousins." She gave the littlest example of such a kiss to my lips. That too went all the way in. Her mouth had the scent of a petal just separated from the flower. I had never been near a nicer breath. Nor one with more surprises. It was like picking up a great novel and reading the first sentence. *Call me Ishmael.*

"Someday," she said, "after Hugh and I are tired of each other, maybe you and I will have an affair. Just the passing kind to give a lot of naughty pleasure."

"Kissing cousins," I replied hoarsely.

"Yes. Only now, Harry, I need a good friend. I need one like pure stink. Somebody I can tell everything to."

"I'm incapable of telling all," I confessed, as if I had numerous adventures meticulously secreted away.

"You *are* buttoned up. It's what I brought you out of the house for. I want to talk about your ghost-overlays."

"Is that phrase from your psychological theories?"

"Yes."

"My father told me you're a genius. Allen Dulles says so."

"Well, I'm not," she said petulantly as if the stupidity of the supposition doubled every likelihood of great loneliness. "I have a brain that's marvelously empty when I'm not using it. So it allows thoughts to enter which other people would sweep away. Don't you think the heavens often reach us with their messages just as fully as dark forces below tickle our impulses?"

I nodded. I would not have known how to argue with this. But then, she was not looking for a debate. By her change in tone, I could sense that she was in a mood to expound.

"I've always found Freud uncongenial," she said. "He was a great man with bushels of discoveries, but he really had no more philosophy than a Stoic. That's not enough. Stoics make good plumbers. The drains go bad and you've got to hold your nose and fix them. End of Freud's philosophy. If people and civilization don't fit—which we all know anyway—why, says Freud, make the best of a bad lot."

She had obviously given this speech before. She must have to explain her thesis often on the job. So I took it as a mark of friendship that she was willing to outline it for me. Besides, I liked listening to her voice. I felt she would give this lecture because she wanted us to be closer. And felt a pure pang of the nicest kind of love. She was so beautiful, and so lonely. Wildflowers in her hair, and blue sneakers on her feet. I wanted to hug her, and would have, if not for a sense of the prodigiously long shadow of Hugh Montague.

"Philosophically speaking," she went on, "I am very much a dualist. I do not see how one can not be. It was all very well for Spinoza to postulate his Substance, that wonderfully elusive, meta-physical, metaphorical world-goo he employed to bind all opposites together and so be able to declare himself a monist. But I believe he was scuttling the philosophical bark. If God is trying to tell us any-thing, it is that every idea we have of Him, and of the universe, is dual. Heaven and Hell, God and the Devil, good and evil, birth and death, day and night, hot and cold, male and female, love and hate, freedom and bondage, consciousness and dreaming, the actor and the observer—I could add to such a list forever. Consider it: We are conceived out of the meeting of one sperm and one ovum. In the first instant of our existence, at the moment of our creation, we are brought to life by the joining of two separate entities; how very much unalike they are. Immediately, we start to develop with a right side and a left side. Two eyes, two ears, two nostrils, two lips, two sets of teeth, two lobes to the brain, two to the lungs, two arms, two hands, two legs, two feet."

"One nose," I said.

She had heard this before. "The nose is only a work of flesh surrounding two tunnels."

"One tongue," I said.

"Which has a top and a bottom and they're awfully different." She put her tongue out at me.

"Five fingers on each hand."

"The thumb is in opposition to the others. The big toe used to be in opposition to the foot."

We began to laugh. "Two testicles," I said, "but one penis."

"It's the weak link in my theory."

"One navel," I went on.

"You're awful," she said. "You're implacable."

"One head of hair."

"Which you part." She ruffled my hair. We almost kissed again. It was delicious to be flirting with a third cousin who was a couple of years older than me.

"Try to be solemn," she said. "There's really more evidence for duality than singularity. I decided to take the next step. What if there are not only two nostrils, two eyes, two lobes, and so forth, but two psyches as well, and they are separately equipped? They go through life like Siamese twins inside one person. Everything that happens to one, happens to the other. If one gets married, the other is along for the ride. Otherwise, they are different. They can be just a little different, like identical twins, or they can be vastly different, like good and evil." She stopped for a nearer example. "Or optimism and pessimism. I'm going to choose that because it's somewhat easier to discuss. Most things that happen to us have optimistic overtones, and pessimistic possibilities. Suppose Alpha and Omega—for those are the two names I've finally applied to these two psyches—one has to offer them some kind of name, and A and Z is much too cold to live with—so, Alpha and Omega. It *is* pretentious, but one does get used to it."

"You were going to give me an example," I said.

"Yes. All right. Let us say that Alpha tends to be optimistic in most situations, whereas Omega is inclined to pessimism. Each experience that comes their way is interpreted with different sensitivities, so to speak. Alpha picks up what might be positive in a specific situation; Omega anticipates what could be lost. That divided mode of perception operates for any duality you wish to invoke. Take night and day. Let me propose that Omega is a little more responsive to nocturnal experiences than Alpha. In the morning, however, Alpha is better at getting up and going off to work."

As if to prove the presence of Alpha and Omega within herself, her intimacy, so innocent and audacious at once, had by now drawn back, and the pedant had appeared. One would have to win both sides of this woman. It also occurred to me that I was not being very loyal to Hugh Montague, but what the hell, that might be my Omega. "I just don't see," I said, "why the two must react differently all the time."

"Remember," she said, holding up an instructor-like finger, "Alpha and Omega originate from separate creatures. One is descended from the sperm cell, Alpha; Omega from the ovum."

"You are saying we have a male and a female psyche inside ourselves?"

"Why not? There's nothing mechanical about it," said Kittredge. "The male side can be full of the so-called female qualities, whereas Omega can be an outrageous bull of a woman just as virile and muscular as a garbage collector." She gave a merry look as if to show the return of her Alpha. Or was it Omega? "God wants us to be as various and faceted as kaleidoscopes. Which looks to the next point: Hugh and I agree on this: The war between God and the Devil usually goes on in both psychic entities. That's as it should be. Schizophrenics tend to separate good and evil altogether, but in more balanced people, God and the Devil fight not only in Alpha, but in Omega as well."

"There seems to be endless capacity for strife in your system."

"Of course there is. Doesn't that fit human nature?"

"Well," I said, "I still can't see why the Creator desired such a complicated design."

"Because he wished to give us free will," she said. "I agree with Hugh on this as well. Free will amounts to giving the Devil equal opportunity."

"How can you know that?" I blurted out.

"It's what I think," she said simply. "Don't you see, we have a true and real need for two developed psyches, each with its own superego, ego, and id. That way, one can feel some three-dimensionality, so to speak, in our moral experience. If Alpha and Omega are quite unalike, and, believe me, they often are, then they can look upon the same happening from wholly separate points of view. It's why we have two eyes. For the same reason. So we can estimate distance."

"Account for this," I said. "When our eyes become too different from each other, we need glasses. If Alpha and Omega are awfully different, how can a person function?"

"Look at Hugh," she said. "His Alpha and Omega must be as far apart as the sun and the moon. Great people, and artists, and extraordinary men and women have dramatically different Alpha and Omega. Of course, so do the feebleminded, the addictive, and the psychotic."

Something in the certainty of her voice was making me dogged. "How do you account, then," I asked, "for the difference between an artist and a psychotic?"

"The quality of inner communication, of course. If Alpha and Omega are incredibly different, but can manage all the same to express their separate needs and perceptions to each other, then you have an extraordinary person. Such people can find exceptional solutions. Artists, especially. You see, when Alpha and Omega don't communicate, then one or the other must become the master or there's a standstill. So the loser becomes oppressed. That's a desperately inefficient way of living."

"Like totalitarianism?"

"Precisely. You do see what I'm talking about."

I was awfully pleased to hear that. Encouraged, I asked: "Would a healthier person have an Alpha and Omega about as different, say, as Republicans and Democrats? Agree on some things, disagree on others, but work it out?"

She beamed. I had brought out her better side. The wicked light was in her eye again. "You're wonderful," she said. "I do love you. You're so direct."

"You are making fun of me."

"I'm not," she said. "I'm going to use your example with some of those dummies I have to give explanations to."

"Don't they love your ideas? I can see where Alpha and Omega tell us a lot about spies."

"Of course. But so many of the people I work with are afraid to trust it. I'm just a girl to them. So they can't believe that this could prove the first reliable psychological theory to explain how spies are able to live with the tension of their incredible life-situations, and in fact, will not only bear up under such a double life, but indeed, go looking for it.

I nodded. She had termed me direct, but I was wondering if her mode of presentation might not also be somewhat too unadorned. Most of the intellectuals I had met at Yale seemed obliged on first meeting to fire off an artillery barrage of great and/or esoteric authors they had presumably absorbed. With Kittredge, however, one citing of Spinoza plus one reference to Freud seemed to take care of it. She had not sent out a cavalry of esteemed authorities to turn my flank. She pursued her thoughts; they were enough. I thought she showed the forceful but innocent head of an inventor.

Well, we went on talking. We never came to ghost-overlays, but before we were done with our hour in the nooks and crannies of Doane, I was somewhat offended that she could take as much pleasure in exposition as in our flirtation. Before we went back to the house, therefore, I tried to tease her. I asked her to confess: Who was her own Alpha, her own Omega?

"Oh," she said, "others perceive such things better than oneself. Tell me your impressions of how they shape up in me."

"Oh," I said in imitation of her voice, "I think your Alpha is full of loyalty and your Omega is as treacherous as the tides. Alpha is surfeited with chastity, and Omega is unbalanced with sacrilege. You're a spontaneous child on one side and an empire-builder on the other."

"You're a devil through and through," she said, and gave me another kiss on the lips.

Nothing will ever tell me for certain whether Harlot saw that small embrace or merely sensed it. As we walked back, hand in hand, we came on him standing above a rock. He had been holding a view of our approach. I have no idea how long he had been there, but some constraint in the pit of my heart seemed confirmed. He certainly did not alter his manner, but intimacy between Kittredge and me was *singed* by his presence. The word is just. When we came near, my eyebrows felt like ash: I wondered if I would pay for my hour with his fiancée when I joined the CIA.

What I have next to relate is painful. That Easter Sunday evening, Dr. Gardiner gave vent to the buried furies in his throat, and honored his guests: By the light of the fire in his den, he read Shakespeare aloud to us.

He offered an early work: *Titus Andronicus.* An odd choice. I would not recognize how bizarre until I knew the family better. While Dr. Gardiner did not belong to the school of scholars who thought Shakespeare had not written *Titus Andronicus,* he did consider it, he told us, one of the Bard's poorest plays. Uninspired, and much too dreadful. Yet Dr. Gardiner read from it on Sunday night with a voice full of passion, choosing the terrible speech where Titus tells Chiron and Demetrius that in consequence of their vile acts on his family—they have severed his hand and cut off both hands of his daughter, Lavinia—he, Titus, will now revenge himself.

> *Hark, wretches! How I mean to martyr you,*
> *This one hand yet is left to cut your throats,*
> *Whilst Lavinia 'tween her stumps doth hold*
> *The basin that receives your guilty blood.*
> *Hark, villains, I will grind your bones to dust,*
> *And with your blood and it I'll make a paste;*
> *And of the paste a coffin I will rear;*
> *And make two pasties of your shameful heads.*
>
> *And now prepare your throats. Lavinia, come,*
> *Receive the blood, and when that they are dead,*
> *Let me go grind their bones to powder small.*
> *And with this hateful liquor temper it;*
> *And in that paste let their vile heads be baked.*
> *Come, come, be everyone officious*
> *To make this banquet, which I wish might prove*
> *More stern and bloody than the Centaurs' feast.*

He recited it in the full sonority of a renowned lecture voice, gave it all the Elizabethan hullaballoo due vowels and consonants grappling with one another over hurdles and down falls: How he relished the conjunctive sinews of these words. Hair stood on my neck. I knew then what a sixth sense was hair.

"I do not approve of the play," said Dr. Gardiner when he was done, "but the bile of the ages is in the boil of this fabulous stuff."

Maisie had fallen asleep while he read. Her head was to one side, her mouth was open, and I thought for a moment she had suffered a stroke. She had merely taken her nightly jot of three Seconals; soon Dr. Gardiner walked her up to bed. It would also take years before I learned—how many little confessions was Kittredge eventually to make!—that Dr. Gardiner had a preferred means of connubial union: It was to investigate Maisie while she slept. Kittredge discovered her father's habit when she was ten. She peeped and saw it all. In sleep, Maisie, a wanton of Morpheus, made cries like a bird.

Husbands and wives have been known to discover that their separate childhoods are curiously linked: Kittredge and I had both seen our parents in the act of love. Or, more to the fact, we had, between us, seen three of our four parents. Titus and Lavinia, taken together, had lost three of their four hands. The allusion is meaningless, I am certain, except that numbers command their own logic, and Augustus Farr may have been on a promenade that night while Dr. Gardiner and his somnolent Maisie were transported to those underworlds that dwell beneath the navel.

6

I RETURNED TO THE KEEP IN JUNE FOR THE MARRIAGE OF HADLEY Kittredge Gardiner to Hugh Tremont Montague. My father and stepmother, my brothers, my uncles, aunts, and cousins, were there in the gathering of good Maine summer families. The Prescotts and the Peabodys came, the Finletters and Griswolds, the Herters, and the Places. Even Mrs. Collier from Bar Harbor together with half of the Bar Harbor Club took the crooked twenty-mile journey west across the fifteen miles of the island to the back side. Contingents were present from Northeast Harbor and Seal Harbor, and David Rockefeller attended. Desmond FitzGerald was in view, and Clara Fargo Thomas; Allen Dulles flew up from Washington with Richard Bissell and Richard Helms, Tracy Barnes and Frank Wisner, James Angleton and Miles Copeland. One of my cousins, Colton Shaler Hubbard, who liked to see himself as the operative definition of a wag, was heard to say, "Drop a bomb on this shindig and U.S. Intelligence is gone to smithereens."

It is no part of my intention to expatiate on the floral arrangements chosen by Maisie, nor the sober character of our Episcopal church, St. Anne of the Trinity in the Woods (which has been quietly criticized since the turn of the century for its penurious Presbyterian air), and I am certainly not equipped to describe the niceties of the wedding-gown brocades. I speak of the nuptials because they confirmed my suspicion that I was in love with Kittredge, and that proved to be the most inexpensive, self-sustaining, and marvelous love a young man could attach himself to. For a long time, it cost me no more than the luxurious enrichment of my self-pity, which was promoted on the day of the wedding from the spiritual equivalent of a sigh to the deepest mahogany melancholy. I was in love with a beautiful, brilliant girl who was married to the most elegant and incisive gent I had ever met; there was no hope for me but, oh, the love was beautiful.

Mr. Dulles seemed to agree. Soon after we assembled back at the Keep for the wedding party, he stood up and (very much in his function as Director of CIA) gave the first toast. I still remember how delicately he held his glass yet with what a sense of gravity.

"The Greco-Roman concept of the healthy mind in the healthy body is personified by our good and brave colleague, Hugh Tremont Montague," were Dulles' first words. "Indeed, if it were not for the one prodigality he shares with me—no, let me say in which he surpasses me—at squandering the once rich crop of his hair, we could speak of the perfect fellow." Polite but happily unweighted laughter passed gently through the room. "For those few of you who are not connected to the legends of his heroic exploits in OSS during the war, let me say that you must take it on faith. His feats, for the present, remain in the bailiwick of the highly classified. For equally good cause, I cannot begin to describe the work he does now except to hint that he is always threatening to become indispensable before he is even properly middle-aged." Sweet, light laughter. "Nonetheless, for all his sterling attributes, he is still the luckiest fellow in the world. He is marrying a young lady of incommensurate beauty who, if I dare to grow portentous on so festive an occasion, has also become by dint of inspiration, talent, and study, a psychological theorist of a power and persuasion to inspire all Jungians and confound all Freudians. When she was still an undergraduate at Radcliffe, I happened to be shown her senior thesis and it was a wonder. I break a little confidence by saying I was quick to tell her, 'Kittredge, your thesis is a marvel and I can promise you that some of us just might need it. You, Kittredge, are coming aboard.' How could a young lady, confronted by such admiration, not give assent? I, holding this cup for the toast, raise high my heart as well. God bless you both. May He sanctify your marriage, handsome, half-bald Hugh Montague, and our own Hadley Kittredge Gardiner, here with us, yet remaining on such close terms with the divine."

Afterward, I had been introduced in a rush as the Director was leaving, and there was time to receive no more than a foursquare handshake and the friendliest smile. "Your father is one whale of a fellow, Harry," he said with eyes to twinkle at all the rich findings between the lines. Mr. Dulles, I decided, might be the nicest man I met at the wedding. My impatience to hook up with CIA was hardly less lively.

Of course, I was also feeling the presence of many men whose names had been legends to me ever since my father began to speak of them in the intimate tones reserved by a god for fellow gods; such names as Allen and Tracy, Richard and Wiz, Dickie and Des, were already installed in an amphitheater of my mind. While none of these personages was as handsome as my father, many were as tall, or as forceful; their persons offered the suggestion that one should not impinge on them for too little. They had *bottom*. "Something in me," said their presence, "is inviolable."

I gave up the last semester of my senior year at Yale, making a quick decision right after the wedding to enroll immediately in summer school so that I could graduate at midterm in January and thereby apply to the Company six months earlier. It was a sacrifice, the first conscious one I had made, for I was comfortable at Yale, liked my rooms, and still had the idea from time to time that I might want to spend a year after college writing fiction. I even had the means to write late at night for I had carefully chosen no classes that began before 10:00 A.M. I also had friends of all the shades and affiliations you make after three years at a good college, and was otherwise ensconced. I even had some small chance of making the Varsity Eight after slaving at crew the last three seasons. By my lights, I was giving up a lot. Yet I wanted to. If I wished to serve my country, I could start best by making a sacrifice. So, I went to summer school, and was graduated eight accelerated months later onto the slushy streets of Washington in early February, a midyear diploma-holder, a bear cub without hair. But I was proud of my sacrifice.

I will not describe the tests I took for admittance. They were numerous, and classified, but then, given the Agency officers who may have been enlisted in support of my application, I suppose I would have had to do poorly not to get in.

Of course, you were expected to do well. Only a few out of every hundred who applied were able to make it all the way through the IQ tests, the personality tests, the lie-detector, and the security question-naire. I remember that in the Personal History Statement, there was the question: *On a scale of 1 to 5, how would you rate your dedication to this work?* I put down a five and wrote in the space allowed for comment: *I have been brought up to face ultimates.*

"Explain yourself," said the interviewer.

"Well, sir," I said, and I had been waiting to make this speech, "I feel that if I had to, I could stand trial before an international tribunal." When my interlocutor looked at me, I added, I thought not un-adroitly, "The point I'd like to make is that although I am a moral person, I am ready to get into activities where I might have to stand trial for my country, or, if it ever came down to it, die for ultimate purposes."

I had more trouble with the lie-detector. It was the test to dread. Although we were warned not to talk about it with applicants who had already taken it, we met with them as soon as possible after the drear event; usually they said as little as they could and consumed prodigies of beer.

I still see my polygraph interview in transcript. It is an imaginary transcript. What the interviewer and I said to one another at the time cannot be what I now remember. I offer a false memory, then, but it is imprinted. The face of the interviewer has, in recollection, become long-jawed and bespectacled; he looks as gray as a personage in a black-and-white film. Of course, we were installed in a dingy-white cubbyhole off a long crowded hall in an edifice called Building 13 off the Reflecting Pool, and much of my memory of those wintry days is, indeed, in gray and white.

I offer what I recollect. I do not vouch for anything in this reconstructed transcript other than its ongoing psychological reality for me.

INTERROGATOR: Ever had a homosexual experience?

APPLICANT: No, sir.

INTERROGATOR: Why are you having such a large reaction?

APPLICANT: I didn't know I was.

INTERROGATOR: Really? You're giving the machine what we call a *flush*.

APPLICANT: Couldn't the machine make a misinterpretation?

INTERROGATOR: You are saying you are not homosexual.

APPLICANT: Certainly not.

INTERROGATOR: Never?

APPLICANT: Once I came close, but held off.

INTERROGATOR: Fine. I can read you. Let's move on.

APPLICANT: Let's.

INTERROGATOR: Get along with women?

APPLICANT: I've been known to.

INTERROGATOR: Consider yourself normal?

APPLICANT: You bet.

INTERROGATOR: Why am I getting a flutter?

APPLICANT: You're asking me to volunteer a response?

INTERROGATOR: Let me rephrase it. Is there anything you do with women that community consensus might consider out of the ordinary?

APPLICANT: Do you mean—unusual acts?

INTERROGATOR: Specify.

APPLICANT: Can I be asked a specific question?

INTERROGATOR: Do you like blowjobs?

APPLICANT: I don't know.

INTERROGATOR: Overlarge response.

APPLICANT: Yessir.

INTERROGATOR: Yessir what?

APPLICANT: Yes, to the blowjob.

INTERROGATOR: Don't look so unhappy. This won't keep us from accepting you. On the other hand, if you were to lie in this test, it could hurt you a lot.

APPLICANT: Thank you, sir. I understand.

I get a whiff of the old perspiration. I was lying to the lie-detector: I had still not lost my cherry. Even if two-thirds of my class at Yale could probably say the same, anything was better than such confession. How could a CIA man be a virgin? Down the line, I would learn that many another applicant lied to protect the same green secret. That was all right. The tests were looking to screen out men who might be vulnerable to blackmail. Well-raised college graduates, however, claiming more amatory experience than they'd earned could be accepted just as they were.

During those weeks of testing, I lived in the YMCA and shared meals in drugstores with other applicants. They, for the most part, had come from state universities and had taken their majors in government, or football, or languages, in foreign affairs, economics, statistics, agronomy, or some special skill. Usually, one of their professors had had an exploratory conversation with them, and if interest was there, they received a letter that spoke of an important government career with foreign duties, and were told to reply to a post office box in Washington, D.C.

I pretended to have been approached like the others, but given my lack of gov, ec, pol-sci, or applied psych, I pretended to have made some studies in Marxism instead. None of my new acquaintances knew much about that. I got away with it until I met Arnie Rosen, whose father was a third cousin of Sidney Hook. Rosen, in homage, perhaps, to this family tie, had read Lenin, Trotsky, and Plekhanov in his adolescence, not, he assured me, to become an advocate of such ideas, but to set himself up as their future antagonist. As he put it to me one morning over pancakes and sausage, "From the word go, I knew the cockamamie elements in V. I. Lenin." Yes—Rosen, Honors, Phi Beta Kappa, Columbia. I disliked him to the quick.

For those four or five weeks, my life in junction with other applicants was spent in promenade from one processing building to another in the I-J-K-L complex, a set of four long buildings in a row that ran from the Lincoln Memorial for more than a quarter mile along the Reflecting Pool toward the Washington Monument. On gray and barren winter mornings those buildings looked not wholly unlike pictures I had seen of Dachau, same long, two-story sheds that went on forever. We were jammed into quarters thrown up for government offices during the Second World War. Since we had other facilities dispersed over many a side street, and in many a fine old house, special bottle-green government buses took us from building to building in Foggy Bottom. We filled out questionnaires and walked in self-conscious groupings, obviously inductees.

All the while, I pretended, as I say, to be just like my new friends. In truth, so dislocated was this existence from all I had known at Yale that I felt myself a stranger in my own land. Such feelings were most likely to come over me in the course of listening to a lecture in one of our ubiquitous classrooms with its beige walls, blackboard, American flag in a stand, and its dark gray stain-compatible carpet and portable lecture chairs with their small one-arm writing tables attached. My classmates showed the same good American crew cut as myself (good for at least 80 percent of us), and if our collective demeanor was somewhere between the YMCA and the Harvard Business School, it did not mean I was yet like anyone else. I was discovering how little I knew about my countrymen, at least those who were trying like me to get into CIA. Nor did I feel altogether real to myself. That, on reflection, was a familiar wind in my lonely harbors.

Occasionally I voyaged out to the canal house in Georgetown which Kittredge and Harlot had bought in the first year of their marriage, and such evenings were full of stimulation for me. Some of their dinner guests were grand. Henry Luce was there one night, and he took me aside long enough to inform me that he knew my father. Mr. Luce had white hair and hugely heavy black eyebrows. His voice turned husky as he said to me, "It's a wonderful life you're going to have. Momentous decisions, and the best of it is that they will count! I've worked on occasion on endeavors much larger than myself or my own interests, and I can tell you, Harry, since we share the same diminutive, whether from Herrick or Henry, that there's no comparison. Doing it for the larger dream is what it is all about, Harry!" Like a reverend, he did not release me until he took his hand from my shoulder. Nor could I pretend to myself that I was ungrateful for the speech, since after evenings at the Montagues, I would go back to my brother dogs at the Y to find them worrying where the next bone was going to be thrown. I, however, would feel like a radioactive dog. I would glow within. I had seen the Company, and it was there. The CIA was not merely long, shedlike buildings, or the dead-tank smells of people crowded into impossibly small office spaces, nor leering inquisitors who strapped belts and instruments to your body; no, CIA was also a company of the elegant, secretly gathered to fight a war so noble that one could and must be ready to trudge for years through the mud and the pits. Ah, those evenings at the canal house! Indeed, it was Harlot who was the first to tell me I was in, certified and in, on the day after my last test. My roomies at the Y would have to wait three more days to obtain as much knowledge, and I suffered with the secret I could not relate to them, and so discovered that holding a confidence when one wishes to let it out is comparable to thirsting for a shot of liquor on an awful day.

After acceptance, we reported one morning for our orientation lecture. Perhaps a hundred of us were taken by bus from the 9th Street Personnel Pool to an old five-story house with a Queen Anne roof behind the State Department. There we crowded into a small basement auditorium. A man sitting up on the stage whom I would have taken for an Ivy League professor stood up to welcome us and said, "In case any of you are wondering, you will now be working for CIA."

We laughed. We applauded. He strode across the stage to an easel on which a cloth was draped. Whisking the sheet away, he revealed the first of our scrolls—an organizational chart. With a pointer, he informed us that the Agency had three Directorates which could be envisaged as analogous to three sister corporations, or three regiments of a division: "The Directorate for Plans oversees covert action and gathers intelligence. It directs spies. Learn a new word. Plans *runs* spies, even as you would run a business." Since espionage and counterespionage were Harlot's province, and covert action belonged to my father, the Directorate of Plans was nine-tenths of CIA for me.

Then he went on to speak of the Directorate for Intelligence, which analyzed the material gathered by Plans, and the Directorate for Administration, "which keeps in order the management of the first two directorates." Needless to say, I had no interest in either.

"Gentlemen," he continued, "you one hundred and three men"—he looked about—"or, if I avail myself of the indispensable tool of precision, you one hundred and one men and two women have been chosen for the Directorate of Plans. That is a fine place to be."

We cheered. We stood up and cheered him, but not for long because next, Allen Dulles, now Director of Central Intelligence, came through the curtains to speak. On this day, Mr. Dulles had a genial, courteous, even benign warmth of the sort that would enable you to believe in any establishment with which he was associated, whether bank, university, law firm, or branch of government. Dressed in old tweeds with leather patches for the elbows, a nifty bow tie, his pipe in hand, his spectacles as bright with reflected light as intelligence itself, he was quickly successful in giving all one hundred plus of us the same impression he had given me at the wedding.

"Being with you here at the beginning, I can all but promise that you will have lively, worthwhile, exciting careers." We applauded. "Winston Churchill, after Dunkirk, could only offer the gallant British people 'blood, sweat, toil, and tears,' but I can promise you dedication, sacrifice, total absorption, and—don't let this get out—a hell of a lot of fun." We whooped.

"You are all in Plans, an uncommon group. You will live, most of you, in many countries, you will doubtless see action, you will—no matter how tired and weary—never lose sense of the value of your work. For you will be defending your country against a foe whose resources for secret war are greater than any government or kingdom in the history of Christendom. The Soviet Union has raised the art of espionage to unprecedented heights. Even in times of so-called thaw, they wage their operations with unflagging vigor.

"In order to catch up, we are in the process of building the greatest agency for Intelligence the Western world has seen. The safety of this country depends on no less. Our opponent is formidable. And you, here, have been chosen to be part of the great shield that resists our formidable foe."

You could feel the happiness in the room. No matter the small basement stage with its American flag to one side, we shared, at this moment, the warmth of a venerable theater as the curtain descends to a momentous conclusion.

He was hardly finished, however. It was not Mr. Dulles' style to end on a major note. More agreeable was to remind us that we had been accepted into a fellowship; our privileges entitled us to hear a story at the expense of the leader.

"Years ago," he said, "when I was as young as most of you, I was posted by our foreign service to Geneva during World War I, and I remember one particularly warm spring Saturday in 1917 when I was on watch for the morning duty. There was little to do in the office, and all I could think about was tennis. You see, I had a date for tennis that afternoon with a young lady who was lovely and comely and beautifully composed . . . a veritable knockout!"

Who else could speak in such a way? In this pre–Civil War basement which might, more than ninety years ago, have heard cannonading to the south, Allen Dulles was telling us of Geneva in 1917.

"Just before midday my phone rang. A most heavily accented voice was on the line," said Allen Dulles, "a man who wanted a *responsible* American official to speak to. *Verantwortlich* was the word he

used. He gave his speech in the worst German. One of those impor-
tuners, I decided. Someone with a tale of petty woe bound to tell it
in the worst accent possible.

"Now, the only American official at the Embassy that morning
who happened to be remotely *verantwortlich* was myself. Was I going
to play tennis with a lovely English girl, or was I going to eat sauerkraut with some Russian emigré?"

He paused. "Tennis won out. I never saw the fellow."

We waited.

"Too late I learned who the man happened to be. The voice with
the dreadful German accent, frantic to talk to a responsible American
official, was none other than Mr. V. I. Lenin himself. Not long after
our phone call, the Germans sent Mr. Lenin across Bavaria, Prussia,
Poland, and Lithuania in a sealed train. He arrived at the Finland
Station in Leningrad to bring off in November of the same year
nothing less than the Bolshevik Revolution." He paused, giving us
sanction to become hilarious at the size of Allen Dulles' miscue.

"Al," a voice cried out, "how could you do that to the team?"

It was my first glimpse of Dix Butler. His face was unforgettable.
His head, his massive jaw and neck, his full mouth were as strongly
formed as the features in a Roman bust.

Dulles looked pleased. "Profit by my error, gentlemen," he said.
"Reread your Sherlock Holmes. The most trivial clue can prove the
most significant. When you are on duty, observe every detail. Do the
damnedest fine job you can do. You'll never know when the shovel
turns up an unexpected gem."

He canted his pipe back into his mouth, parted the stage curtains,
and disappeared.

Our next speaker offered business. Burns, Raymond James "Ray
Jim" Burns, case officer: Japan, Latin America, Vienna. He would be
our instructor in an eight-week course on World Communism. He
was also captain of the pistol team at Plans. He would, he told us,
welcome anyone interested in improving his aim.

A man of medium height, he was there for us to study. He had
short, reddish-brown hair, a trim build, and regular features with an
unforgiving twist. His mouth was a short straight cut. He was wearing
a brown jacket, a white shirt, a narrow brown tie, light pink-khaki
trousers, and sunglasses shaded brown. His belt had three narrow
horizontal stripes, brown, tan, and brown. His shoes were brown and
cream and as pointed as his nose. He wore a heavy ring on his left hand

and clicked it on the podium for emphasis. He had one decoration, a maple-leaf pin in his buttonhole, a spot of gold. I was feeling full of Mr. Dulles' adjuration to observe each detail.

Ray Jim hated Communists! He stood on the podium and pinned us with his eyes. They were bullet brown, a deep lead brown, near to black, a hole impinging on you. He looked us over, one by one.

"There's a tendency these days," said Burns, "to give a little leeway to the Communists. Khrushchev is not as bad as Stalin; you're going to hear that. Of course Khrushchev was called the Butcher of the Ukraine in his earlier days, but he's not as bad as Stalin. Who could be as ruthless as Iosef Djugashvili, alias Joe Stalin, the purge-master? In the U.S.S.R. they have a secret police that has no parallel to us, no comparison. It's as if you boiled the FBI, the Agency, and the state and federal prison systems into one big super-equivalent of the CIA, but lawless, unrestrained, ruthless! Their police—some of whom are even supposed to be in Intelligence—are kept busy purging millions of their own poor citizens, sending hordes of them by the million out to Siberia to die under forced labor and near starvation. Their crime? They believe in God. In the Soviet Union, you can slice up your grandmother before they'll rate your crime on a par with believing in the Lord Almighty. For the Soviet think-police know how the force of God stands in their way, resisting all those Red dreams of world conquest. To that purpose the Red devotes his evil genius. You can't begin to conceive of what we are up against, so don't try to understand Communists by the measure of your own experience. Communists are ready to subvert any idea or organization which is a free expression of the human will. Communists look to invade every cranny of every person's private activity, and seep into every pore of democratic life. I say to you: Be prepared to fight a silent war against an invisible enemy. Treat them like a cancer loose in the world body. Before you are done with this orientation course, you will be on the road to *de*fusing their attempts to *con*fuse world opinion. You will be able to counterattack subversion and brainwashing. You are going to come out of your training as different men"—he peered about—"and, seeing as they rationed me to one joke, two different women."

We laughed that he had been good enough to release the tension, and then we stood up to cheer him. He was one of us. He was not, like Mr. Dulles, a little above the fray, but one of us. Since Ray Jim was dedicated, we too could aspire to such clarity of purpose.

Of course I was not taking close account of myself. Mr. Dulles was much nearer to my understanding. Ray Jim came out of that vast middle of America which goes from west of the Hudson out to Arizona, that huge tract which, in comparison to the neatly tended garden of my education, was a roadless desert, but I did not wish to say to myself that I did not know my own country.

In the heat of the standing ovation we gave Mr. Burns, we were administered the Vow. Standing under the grand seal of the CIA in the center of the proscenium arch, our hands upraised, we were inducted formally and legally into the Agency, and swore not to speak without permission of what we learned, *now and forever.*

That is a solemn vow. I have been told of Masons, inactive for years, who will nonetheless impart not one detail of the rites of the fraternity, not even to their sons. Some equivalent of that fidelity must have entered us. My fear of retribution was lashed at that moment to my sense of honor. I might just as well have been commingling my blood with another warrior's. A sacred (and sweet) pang of emotion came to me on this instant of induction. If not for the perils of hyperbole, I would say that my will stood to attention.

This vow was not diminished by our training. It constrains one's mind to describe the awesome loyalty that soon developed. To give away our secrets was to betray God! A mighty syllogism! I must say this oath still retains some of its essence after close to thirty years in the Agency. Of my own actions, I recognize that I am obliged to tell a good deal. I will break through—if need be—but I still feel inhibition at discussing our seminars in the use of such agents of influence abroad as could be found among native lawyers, journalists, trade unionists, and statesmen.

I will, however, describe our tradecraft as it was then. Most of these methods have been superseded, so it is relatively safe to go on about such matters. They are the stuff of spy novels. Besides, I may as well confess, it is what I enjoyed the most at the time. Courses in economics and administrative procedures made me fearfully drowsy. I got my marks, and was able to spout the stuff back, but my true love was tradecraft. I was not in the CIA to become a bureaucrat but a hero. So if this memoir is a tale of development, my purpose may be served if I relate my instruction in picking a lock and all the other wonderfully amoral techniques of my profession.

All the same, I must take one more pass at our instruction in the evils of Communism. Such studies may have lacked the zest of trade-craft, but they managed to convince me that any mischief we could work on our evil opponent left us clearly on the right side. I think that was the allure of tradecraft. Is there any state more agreeable than living and working like a wicked angel?

Well, I had far to go. Let me demonstrate.

7

ABOUT FOUR WEEKS AFTER I TOOK THE VOW, I HAD BECOME SO MA-rooned in the repetitions of Raymond James Burns' course in World Communism that I made the mistake of yawning in class.

"Hubbard, am I boring you?" Ray Jim asked.

"No, sir."

"I'd like to hear you repeat what I've just said."

I could feel my father's temper stir in me. "Look, Mr. Burns," I said, "I'm not bored. I get it. I know the Communists are treacherous, and double-dealing, and use *agents provocateurs* to try to subvert our labor unions and work double-time to befuddle world opinion. I know they have millions of men in their armies getting ready for world domination, but I have to wonder one thing . . ."

"Shoot," he said.

"Well, is every Communist a son of a bitch? I mean, are none of them human? Isn't there one of them somewhere down the line who likes to get drunk just for the fun, say, of getting drunk? Must they always have to have a reason for what they're doing?"

I could feel by the shift in the class that I was by now marooned in Harry-Hubbard-Land, population: 1. "You've told us," I went on, "that the Communists condition people to the point where they can only receive *approved ideas*. Well, I don't really believe what I'm going to say next, but for the sake of argument"—I was obviously preparing for a graceful exit—"would you say that we're receiving something of the same nature, although different in degree, and, of course, demo-cratic, because I can speak in freedom without reprisals."

"We're here," said Ray Jim, "to sharpen your instincts and your faculties of critical reasoning. That is the opposite of brainwashing. Specious political reasoning is what we're on the lookout for. Find it and uproot it." He was striking the palm of one hand on the back of the other. "Now, I like your example," he said. "It shows critical faculties. Just carry them further. I'm willing to accept the idea that there's a dedicated Communist here and there who might get a hard-on without Party approval, but I'll tell you this. Before long, he's got to decide. Is it his career, or his dick?"

The class laughed with him. "Hubbard," he stated, "you can put all of the Soviet people into three categories. Those who have been in a slave camp, those who are in a slave camp now, and those who are waiting to go."

I now rejoined the fold by saying, "Thank you, sir."

One night, visiting the Montagues at their canal house, I brought it up with Hugh. He didn't take long to reply. "Of course the question is more complex than good stalwarts like old Ray Jim would have you know. Why, we're debriefing a Soviet defector right now who's obsessed with one fellow he destroyed, a silly drunk whom he'd encourage to booze up in some black hole of a bar in Siberia. So much anti-Soviet sentiment was milked out of the drunk that not only the poor wretch but all of his family were sent off to a camp. All of them harmless. But our defector had a quota of arrests to make, in the same way New York police are given parking tickets to hand out. It revolted him. A human Communist, so to speak."

"Let me ask a stupid question," I started. "Why are Communists so awful?"

"Yes," he said. "Why?" He nodded. "It's very Russian to be awful. Peter the Great once beached a small fleet of his on the bank of some large lake in Pereslavl. Then he didn't go back to the place for thirty years. Of course, his beautiful boats had just about rotted out on the muddy lakeshore. Peter's rage is captured in a formal document. 'You, the governors of Pereslavl,' went his pronunciamento, 'shall preserve these ships, yachts, and galleys. Should you neglect this obligation,' "—here Harlot's voice rose in imitation of his idea of Peter the Great—" 'you, *and your descendants,* will stand to answer.' "

He nodded. "Extreme, would you say?"

I nodded.

"Normal. That is, normal to the pre-Christian view of things. Christ not only brought love into the world, but civilization, with all its dubious benefits."

"I don't follow you."

"Well, as I seem to recollect telling you, Christ adjured us to forgive the son for the sins of the father. That's amnesty. It opened the scientific world. Prior to this divine largesse, how might a man dare to be a scientist? Any error which proved an insult to nature could bring disaster down on his family. The Russians are spiritual, as every Russian will rush to tell you, but their Greek Orthodoxy gagged on that gift from Christ. It would have wrecked the tribal foundations. Forgive the sons? Never. Not in Russia. The punishment must remain greater than the crime. Now they want to march forward into technology land, and they can't. They're too spooked. Deathly afraid of terrible curses from Mother Nature. If you sin against nature, your sons will perish with you. No wonder Stalin was a total paranoid."

"In that case," I said, "the Russians ought to be easy to overcome."

"Easy," said Harlot, "if the retarded parts of the Third World have a true wish to enter civilization. I'm not sure they do. Backward countries may dream of cars and dams, and rush to pave their swamps, but it's halfhearted. The other half still clings to pre-Christian realms—awe, paranoia, slavish obedience to the leader, divine punishment. The Soviets feel like kin to them. Don't sneer altogether at Bullseye Burns. It *is* awful over there in the Soviet. Just today a paper crossed my desk about a sect of twelve poor Doukhobors who were rounded up in some alley of an outlying town in some poor half-forgotten province. The present Soviet leaders know the potential power in a dozen starved clerks and workers. Lenin and Stalin and Trotsky and Bukharin and Zinoviev, all of that top layer, were also a ragtag circle once of impoverished clerks. In consequence, the KGB doesn't cut down the sapling, it looks to extirpate the seed. That has huge effect. Suppose I hand you a six-chamber Colt with one round in it, spin the barrel, and say, 'Now for Russian roulette.' The chances in your favor are five to one as you pull the trigger, but in your heart it will feel no better than even money. Indeed, you probably expect to die. Ditto with extreme punishment. Let it fall on twelve individuals, and twelve million will shiver. Bullseye Burns is not so far off the mark."

8

After eight weeks of Mr. Burns' course in the Recreation and Services Building on *The Communist Party: Its Theory and Tactics,* I could offer exposition on the organization and tactics of the Comintern, the Cominform, the Cheka, the GPU, the NKVD, and the KGB

in each of its twelve directorates. If the material required memoriza-
tion of long, inhospitable lists, be certain I devoted the same concentration a medical student gives to his lectures out of the unholy fright
that should he fail to store away one item, a future patient might
perish. It was tough. Burns stuffed us like sausage. Word passed
through the class that he had once been a counterintelligence man in
the FBI. No surprise if we had to store away such memorabilia as
"The Eleventh Directorate of the KGB, also called the Guard Directorate, is responsible for safeguarding the security of the Praesidium of
the Central Committee of the Communist Party in the U.S.S.R." I,
who had never found it routine to pay attention while suffering
instruction, was now trying to reorganize my nervous system.

We were also introduced to the machinery for routing messages
through the hierarchy of our offices, and learned how to write in
government language (no small matter!). We took instruction in how
to compartmentalize an agent's dossier, biographical material in one
file, reports on his activities in another. We, too, in future, would be
given our separate cryptonyms for different transactions. Harlot had,
at one time, as he later confided to me, eight, one of which was
DEUCE. Running an operation in Africa, the tag became LT/
DEUCE, LT to indicate that Africa was the theater. Another job in
Vienna would list him as RQ/DEUCE, RQ for Austria. Later, during
the Austrian endeavor, for one or another reason, he might metamorphose into RQ/GANTRY. Like a lazy body after a week of stiff
workouts, my mind, imbibing all this input, felt stiff and sore and livid
with new sensation. I thought the change of name itself ought to be
enough to alter one's character—ZJ/REPULSE should call for a different personality than MX/LIGHT—my thoughts took sensuous
turns. Perhaps it was due to my sexual virginity, but I was now so
pervasively libidinous that I could even take pleasure in such courses
as *Locks and Picks, Flaps and Seals,* or *Reversibles.* Best of all was the
mnemotechnic we were provided for recalling telephone numbers.
Intimations of buried wealth streamed into strange corners of my
psyche.

I was very young. I loved, for example, *Flaps and Seals,* that is,
unsealing letters. Methods ranged from the use of a teakettle spout all
the way over to highly classified chemical swabs. By whatever means,
I enjoyed the moment when the flap, supposedly protecting inviolable
contents, relaxed its grip. The small sound elicited by that act produced what I thought was a private reaction, but the instructor was

ahead of me. "Ever hear of the chorus girl who was horny?" he asked our class. "She did a split and stuck to the floor." We moaned at our own merriment.

Then came *Reversibles.* In preparation for shadowing a man, we practiced quick changes. We would dart into a vestibule off the classroom, doff our raincoat, turn it inside out, and reappear (eight seconds allotted) in a tan Burberry rather than a blue waterproof, a simple enough matter, but even as shifting one's cryptonym called forth a new potentiality for oneself, so was there a shiver of metamorphosis in this alteration of appearance.

I could say, to stretch a point, that we were being schooled in minor arts of sorcery. Are not espionage and magic analogous? I took unholy enjoyment in the stratagem for memorizing a phone number once that process was mastered. Of course, no immediate gratification was found at first, since there was much stress on the need to concentrate. We would stand at the front of the class and an accomplice walking past us would whisper a telephone number, and move on. Another trainee would come up from the other side to offer one more number. As the exercise grew more demanding, we built to as many as five telephone numbers at once. Finally, we were put into competition: Our winner managed to retain nine of ten numbers. (I was, by the way, that winner—which still provides a freshet of recollected glory.)

The point, from which I digress, is that this technique, so full of tension in class, became agreeable on the edge of sleep. The seven digits of a telephone number became a boudoir.

That may be worth expounding upon. We were assigned a specific color for each number. White represented zero; yellow was 1; green equaled 2; blue, 3; purple, 4; red, 5; orange, 6; brown, 7; gray, 8; black, 9.

Next, we were asked to visualize a wall, a table, and a lamp. If the first three digits of the telephone number were 586, we were to picture a red wall behind a gray table on which was sitting an orange lamp. For the succeeding four numbers, we might visualize a woman in a purple jacket, green skirt, and yellow shoes sitting on an orange chair. That was our mental notation for 4216. By such means, 586-4216 had been converted into a picture with seven colored objects. Today, in training, the area code has to be added. Now, the room has a window to look out on sky, water, and earth, a woe my class did not suffer. I think of brown sky, red water, and blue earth for the area code

753, an interesting day for Gauguin! We, however, had to visualize no more at the sound of 436-9940 than a purple wall, a blue table, and an orange lamp. Our lady—Yolanda was the name we gave her—sat in the purple room with the blue table and the orange lamp; she was wearing a black jacket, black pants, and purple shoes as she installed herself on her white chair: 436-9940. It seems like the long way around, but I became so proficient at these equivalents that I saw hues so soon as I heard numbers.

We can skip over lock-picking. Those simple but elegant swages we employed are still marked SECRET, and for a Junior Officer Trainee like myself, able to find sexual stir in the flap of an envelope, what was to be said for cracking a door? That was primal stuff. Each lecturer took entitlement to one off-key joke, and for this course, our instructor was there to tell us: "If you can't figure out a way to get this little pick into this old lock, well, fellows, I don't know what you'll do when you get older."

I never did use lock-picking until 1972 when I had all but forgotten the techniques. Then I used it in the White House, and twice in five minutes, once to open a door, once to open a desk, but that is down the road. Codes is next on my list, but I do not care to get into Codes either, for its study took up a good many hours during winter and spring in Washington, and it is certainly too technical a subject. I will say that it was so sealed a curriculum that even the cryptographic labs were an introduction into the logic of real security: barred windows on either side of the hall; credentials necessary in every section; receptionists and armed guards; even food-servers for the special pre-packaged sandwiches in the cryptographer's cafeteria were chosen because they were blind and so could never identify any of the workers in Codes by photographs if, perchance, the KGB turned one of them.

Let me move to a more agreeable discipline. Anyone who has read a spy novel is familiar with *dead drops,* but active instruction in the practice is another matter. All twenty-three trainees in my class left our homeroom, and filed down the corridor past the bulletin board notices to the men's lavatory where, predictably, ritual jokes were offered to the lone woman in our group; she, in ritual repayment, was good enough to blush. For that matter, I felt my cheeks reddening. I was uncomfortably aware of the unabashed odor coming up from the open urinals, but then 1955 is a long time ago.

Our first dead drop! The instructor took a handful of paper towels out of the metal dispenser by the sink, removed a roll of 16mm Minox film, the size of a thimble, from his vest pocket, put it in the dispenser, and replaced the towels. In turn, to much laughter, each of us repeated the act. The laughter derived, I believe, from how quickly a few of us could accomplish it and how slow were the others. Soon the paper towels were hopelessly mangled. Admonished to practice on our own, we were then shown other possibilities to be extracted from this same rest room, including the cardboard cylinder at the core of the toilet-paper roll. Such dead drops, we were assured, were only suitable when the contact could make rendezvous soon after. *Brush drops,* therefore, were preferable. You did not have to worry whether the agent had found your parcel.

To become familiar with brush drops, we were taken on a field tour to the aisles of a Washington, D.C., supermarket. Having en-riched my shopping basket with a can of Campbell's Tomato Soup and a pound of Armour's Hickory Smoked Bacon, I bumped into my assigned mate, and in the course of such collision, managed to drop a roll of film into his basket, after which, exchanging apologies, we moved on.

It must have looked odd to any housewife buying food. The aisles, invariably empty at mid-morning, were now packed with a platoon of men bumping vigorously into one another and whispering loudly, "No, you hacker, it's my turn." What can I add? The *brush* was electric. One waited for sparks to jump from basket to basket.

Later that night we were taken on a tour of a private estate beyond Chevy Chase and given further instruction about dead drops in more rural areas. If, for example, the agent liked to take daily walks, we looked for a loose brick in a garden wall, or a split in a dead elm. I became aware all over again of the cavernous recesses in a tree trunk. Groping about in the dark of the estate forest, my crevice seemed hairy. What a transaction! I could not find the film at first, and when I did, whipped my hand out so quickly as to draw a remonstrance from the instructor, "Casual, buddy, keep the thing casual."

On our last night, Bullseye Burns threw a party for our class in his small apartment in a newly built four-story complex of middle-cost housing in the outskirts of Alexandria, Virginia. He had three kids, all boys, all towheads, and I learned on this night that he and his wife were high school sweethearts from Indiana. Mrs. Burns, plain-faced, slab-shaped, served us the casserole dish of cheese and tuna and hot dog relish that had been her party fare for twenty years. (Or, as she

called it, her "main-eventer.") It was obvious that she and Ray Jim
barely bothered to speak to each other anymore, and I must say I
studied them like a foreign student looking for insight into American
customs of the Midwest and the Southwest. I concluded that people
like Jim Ray did not quit their marriages until they were feeling
inclined to take an ax to their mate.

So I was surprised at how good the casserole tasted. Somehow, it
did. We were eating in the fold of the Vow and drinking what Ray
Jim called "my favorite Italian red ink. It's my favorite because it's
cheap."

A Junior Officer Trainee named Murphy started to gibe at Bullseye Burns. "All right, sir," he said, "for eight weeks you have given
us JOTs a lot of hints about how you guys dispose of spooks. In special
circumstances, that is."

"Yessir," said Ray Jim, but the arm holding his glass became as
stiff as erectile tissue.

"Well, sir, to satisfy our ravenous class curiosity, did you ever
personally pull the plug on a double-crossing foreign individual?"

"Decline comment."

"Never had to call on your Browning?" asked Murphy. "Not
even once?"

"Policy is against drastic termination," Burns stated. "Individual
solutions cannot be, however, disallowed." He made a point of staring
straight ahead.

"I get it," said Murphy, making a pistol of his forefinger and fist.
"Ping, ping," he said, offering two shots. I was one of the men who
made the mistake of laughing.

We were not to get away unmarked. After supper, Burns took out
a tin box from which he extracted bits of note paper one by one. "I
collect doodles," he said, "from the work desks of the Junior Officer
Trainees. I recommend their study." He held one up, squinted, and
said, "This is Murphy's. Shows he is impulsive, and self-destructive."

By now, a lot of us were drunk on vino tinto, and we jeered at
Murphy, who had a habit of punching hallway walls in the YMCA
when he got drunk.

"This doodle is Schultz's. Schultz, are you ready?"

"Yessir."

"You are showing me what I know already."

"Yessir. What is it, sir?"

"You, Schultz, are tight as a tick."

It was my turn.

"Hubbard, your doodle is one hell of a dilly."

"Yessir."

"It shows that you are up to something difficult."

"What, sir?" I made the mistake of asking.

"You are engaged in the noble attempt to fly up your own asshole."

I think he had time to offer his kind verdict on ten more of us before my normal pulse came back to me. To the Farm!

9

ON THE WEEKEND LEAVE BEFORE THE COMMENCEMENT OF FIELD TRAIN-ing at Camp Peary, I went up to New York on Friday night to see a Mount Holyoke girl who was in town for Easter vacation, had a routine date that would spark no memories for either of us, and took my mother out to lunch on Saturday at the Edwardian Room of the Plaza.

I do not know if it is a reflection of how complex was our relation, or how superficial, but my mother and I were not close, and I never confided in her. Yet she had that delicate power which immaculately groomed blond women can always exercise. I was constantly aware of pleasing or displeasing her, and such critical emanations began with the first glance she took of my person. She could not bear unattractive people; she was generous to those who pleased her eye.

On this noon, we were off to a bad start. She was furious; she had not heard a word from me in two months. I had not told her I was in the Agency. Her animosity toward my father, a dependable reac-tion in a loose and caterwauling world, suggested that I not advertise how closely I was following his example. In any case, I was not supposed to inform her. Theoretically, one's wife, one's children, and one's parents were to be told no more than that one did "government work."

Since she would see immediately through such a phrase, I pre-sented her instead with vague talk of an importing job I had taken on in South America. In fact, I was actually looking forward to using some of the Company's more exotic mail-routing facilities for sending her an occasional postcard from Valparaiso or Lima.

"Well, for how long are you planning to be there?" she asked.

"Oh," I said, "this import stuff could keep me terribly active for months."

"Where?"

"Everywhere down there."

I had made the first mistake of the lunch. When around my mother, I always made errors. Did I like to think of myself as razor-keen? Her powers of detection sliced my intelligence into microscopic wafers. "Darling," she said, "if you're going to South America, don't be bland about it. Tell me the countries. The capitals. I have friends in South America."

"I don't want to visit your friends," I muttered, calling by habit on the old sullenness with which I used to greet her men friends when I was an adolescent.

"Well, why not? They're wonderfully amusing people, some of them. Latin men are so concentrated in their feelings, and a Latin woman of good family might be just what you need for a wife—someone deep enough to bring out the depths in you," she murmured half caressingly, but for the other half, most critically. "Tell me, Harry, what sort of importing is it?"

Yes, what *sort* of case officer would I make when I had not even developed my cover story? "Well, it's precision military parts if you want to know the truth."

She put her head to one side, her cheek resting against one white glove, her blond hair all too alert, and said, "Oh, my Aunt Maria! We're traveling to South America for *precision* military parts! Herrick, you truly think I'm blissfully stupid. You are joining the CIA, of course. It's evident. I say, three cheers. I'm proud of you. And I want you to trust me. Tell me it's so."

I was tempted. It would make this lunch considerably easier. But I could not. That would be transgression of the first injunction given us. Worse, she would let every one of her New York friends in on the secret—only-for-your-ears! Might as well drop an announcement in the *Yale Alumni Magazine*. So I stuck to my story. Well, I told her, she might have her dear friends in South America, but I happened to be a far less contemptuous person than she about the Latin people's potential economic possibilities. When it came to casings and gun-powder, quite a few Southern Hemisphere nations could bid most competitively with our own bullet folk. There was money to be made. I wished to make money, I told her. For my sense of pride and self, if nothing else. I was speaking with enough indignation to convince my own ear, but her eyes filled, and in complete disregard of the damage to her highly crafted eyelashes, a tear ran down, depositing mascara in its train. The misery of her life sat on her stained cheek. "I think of all the people I've loved, and, do you know, Herrick," she said, "none of you have ever trusted me."

Lunch went on, but that was the true end to it, and I left New York on the first train I could catch, and returned to Washington and went down the next day, which was Sunday, to the Farm.

That involved a bus to Williamsburg, Virginia, and a cab to drop me and my luggage at a fresh-painted shed and gate in an endless chain-link fence beside a sign that read: CAMP PEARY—ARMED FORCES EXPERIMENTAL TRAINING ACTIVITY. In answer to a phone call made by the sentry, a Jeep finally arrived driven by a drunken Marine who kept wheeling his head up and down or from side to side while he steered, as if his shaven skull happened to be a small craft. Sunday was obviously the day to get drunk.

Down the twilight we motored along a narrow road between tidewater pines, passing fields of thicket full of thorny scrub that spoke of ticks and poison ivy. It was a long two miles to reach a parade ground. Around it were wooden barracks, some buildings that looked like hunting lodges, a chapel, and a low cement-block structure. "The Club," said my driver, speaking at last.

I dropped my bags on an empty cot in the barracks I had been told to report to, and since nobody was about except for one fellow sleeping in the upstairs dormitory, I headed over to the Club. My classes would begin in the morning, and all day people in my group had been arriving. Dressed in clothing suitable for Washington on Sunday, we stood out as rookies. Not yet issued camouflage fatigues and combat boots and cartridge belts like the veterans around us (first rule of the military I learned was that a veteran has a week of seniority on you), we did our best to show our mettle by slugging down mugs of beer. Men at the pool tables and ping-pong tables set up a counter-din to the far end of the bar, which was being used for parachute landings. Veteran trainees in camouflage uniforms would hop up on the mahogany, shout "Geronimo," and drop the yard and a half to the floor, feet together, knees bent, as they rolled over.

Others were discussing explosives. Before long, those of us who had just come in were attaching ourselves to technical discussions: Could you blow a lap-butt box-girder joint weld with C-3 plastic? I gave appropriate nods and gobbled beer like a wolf let loose on wounded game. The Green Punch at Mory's could not have gone down faster.

Later, as I fell asleep in the upstairs dormitory of my new barracks, my cot turned into a gondola and carried me along mysterious canals. I had an epiphany. I was reminded of those distant relatives of mine, the Jews, who believed in twelve just men. Once, at Yale, a lecturer in Medieval History had spoken of the ancient ghetto belief that the reason God, whenever He became enraged at humankind, did not destroy the universe, was because of His twelve just men. None of the twelve had any conception that he was unique, but the natural and unwitting goodness of each of these rare men was so pleasing to God that He tolerated the rest of us.

In my half-sleep, I wondered if something of the same divine phenomenon had not been taking place in America ever since the Pilgrims landed. Were there not forty-eight just men for the forty-eight states I had grown up with? (For that matter, would the sum change when we went to fifty?) In any event, America had God's sanction. Out in Camp Peary, on my first night at the Farm, I wondered if I might be one of America's forty-eight just men. My patriotism, my dedication, my recognition that no one could love America more, put me—was it possible?—among such anointed innocents. Yes, I, lacking conspicuous talents and virtues, could be a true lover all the more. I adored America. America was a goddess. Washed by beatific rhapsodies, I fell asleep on my half-gallon of beer.

In the morning, I was queasy at stomach and owned a pile driver for a head. Taken by our drill instructor to the supply room for fatigues, we promptly christened them by jogging two miles out to the gatehouse and two miles back. In those days, jogging was looked upon as bizarre—about as many people practiced it as do hang gliding now, but then everything that first day was alien. As was the rest of the week. We took most of our courses in two-hour labs, and our curriculum was exotic to me. It was like sitting down in a restaurant to discover that you had never tasted anything on the menu before: roast of peccary, cassowary stew, anteater steak, breast of peacock, lumpwort salad, passion-fruit pie, bisque of kelp.

Owing to the Agency's success in 1954 in Guatemala, priorities at the Farm had gone back to covert action. While we still had clandestine photography, surveillance, border crossing, interrogation techniques, clandestine radio communication, advanced use of dead drops, the real emphasis over the next sixteen weeks was focused on aiding resistance groups to overthrow Marxist governments. We had courses in parachute jumping, map reading, wilderness survival, unarmed special combat (dirty fighting), silent strikes (murdering without noise), physical conditioning, obstacle courses, and the assembly and disassembly of foreign and domestic pistols, rifles, submachine guns, mortars, bazookas, grenades, grenade launchers, TNT, C-3, C-4, dynamite and classified explosives with an accompanying variety of pressure release, push–pull, delay, slow fuse, and other varieties of detonators for the demolition of bridges, generators, small factories.

Compared to the real difficulties, our sixteen weeks, we were soon told, was an overview. After all, you wouldn't attempt to become a good courtroom lawyer in sixteen weeks. Still, it had purpose. The alumni who came back to St. Matthew's to deliver an evening exhortation in chapel were fond of remarking over tea how strenuously tough it used to be in the old days. Invariably, they would tell us in confidence, "My years at St. Matt's were the worst of my life, and the most valuable." Say something of the same for the Farm. I went in as a young man not properly graduated from college, a stranger to his own nature, not ready, but for his rock climbing, to pin any merit badges on his soul, and came out in the best physical condition of my life, ready for a street fight, ready for glory. I was also one hell of a patriot. I would have trouble falling asleep if I began to think of Communists; murderous rages rose in me, and I was ready to kill the first Red who came through the window. I was not brain-washed so much as brain-fevered.

I also made friends in large numbers. Were there thirty Junior Officer Trainees in our group? I could devote a chapter to each—if, that is, we have, as I suspect, chapters for those who come close enough to color our emotions. Yet the irony is that we formed these deep alliances like actors who are together in a play for sixteen weeks and love and detest each other and are inseparable and have nothing to do with one another again until meeting once more on a new job. If I speak of Arnie Rosen or Dix Butler, it is because I saw a lot of them later.

Camp Peary, however, could have turned out badly. I had been put, by the luck of the draw (unless my father's hand was present), into a training platoon of ex–football players and ex-Marines. If I did well in the more sedentary classwork, and Rosen even better, our physical tests were severe. While I was adequate at weapons, found map reading a piece of cake and forty-eight-hour survival treks in the forest around Camp Peary, offering, after summers in the Maine woods, no undue demand, I found myself hopelessly inhibited at silent strikes. I could not throw myself into the state of mind required to tiptoe up behind a trainee while I whipped a ribbon (in substitute for a wire garrote) around his neck. When it was my turn to serve as sentry I'd flinch before the cloth even touched my skin. My Adam's apple, a prominent Hubbard pride, was in its own panic at getting crunched.

Dirty fighting went better. It was not difficult to simulate breaking a man's fingers, stamping on his feet, cracking his shin, sticking three fingers into his larynx, one finger into his eye, and biting whatever was available. After all—these were dummy moves.

Boxing was done on our own time at the gym, but we all felt the unspoken imperative not to avoid it. I hated being hit on the nose. One blow was enough to switch me over to all that was wild-swinging in my makeup. Besides, I was afraid. Whenever I caught my opponent with anything harder than a tap, I'd blurt out, "Sorry!" Who was fooled? My apology was to hold the other man off. I could not learn a left hook, and my jab flew out with no force, or left me lunging off balance. My straight right was as round as a pork chop. After a while, I accepted the inevitable, and proceeded to mill as best I could with men who were something like my own weight, and learned to take punishment everywhere but on my nose, which I so protected that I was always getting hit on the brow. Boxing left me with headaches equal to college hangovers, and my worst humiliation was with Arnie Rosen, who was as scrappy as a cornered and wholly frantic cat. Nothing he bounced off my head and body made a dent into the hard envelope of my adrenaline, but it was infuriating to realize that he might even have won the round.

One night at the Club, I ended up drinking with our boxing instructor, who had the odd name of Reggie Minnie. He was the only one of our teachers that we found impressive. The verdict in our training group had soon gone around: Good men in the Agency were too valuable to use for teaching. We received the culls. Minnie, however, was special. He fought in a stand-up classic stance, and had been a Navy boxing champ during the war. He had also been married to an English girl who was killed in a car accident, a fact to mention because he was the driver. His sorrow was complete; it was as if he had been dipped into a tragic rue. This loss permeated every pore and organ cell, left him, indeed, a complete man, all of one piece, one whole tincture of loss. He spoke in a gentle voice and listened to every word that everyone said, as if words were as much of a comfort as warm clothing.

While he sipped his one beer and I had three, while we drank in the twilight and explosions still kept going off in the woods while men on a twenty-four-hour exercise dashed in for a quick shot and dashed out, I complained about my ineptitude at defense as if it were a peculiar phenomenon, some hopeless relative to my body.

He then made a remark I never forgot. "You have to learn how to hit," he said. "It'll give you more of a sense of when the punch is coming at you."

I thought a good deal over the next few days of the cousin who had knocked me down to one knee when he was eleven and I was nine, and how I had not risen to fight him back but merely watched blood fall from my nose to splash down on the ground, and with each drop, wished for it to be his blood. Now in the gym, when I worked on the heavy bag, something of that vast and near to long-lost rage came back to me, and I tried to embody a bit of such hatred into each punch I gave the bag.

How well it worked, I do not know. I got better as time went on, but then, so did everyone. I may have gained a few strides on the rest. At the least, I began to handle Rosen with ease. What did more for me was parachuting. From the day they first brought us to the thirty-eight-foot tower, I was ready. Four stories above the ground, I would leap through a mock-up of a C-47 hatch—our instructor called it the "open-door policy"—and jump into space with my parachute harness (no parachute) attached to a spring cable. I was back to leaping off the balcony in Maine—when STOP! the cable and harness jerked us to a halt, and we swung above the ground. Some of the ruggedest men in our class would throw up before making their jump.

It was even better when those few of us considered best in these exercises were allowed to practice accuracy jumping at a nearby airport. I found that I was relatively free of fear, even of the fear I might have packed my chute incorrectly. I thought it was not unlike sailing: Some understood it, some never did. In Maine, I used to show what the family called a spiffy nostril for the yaw of the wind to port or starboard, but the signs were subtler passing through air. Still, the pullulation of the trees gave a clue to the wind vector, and I became enough of an adept to steer my parachute onto a target during night drops. The sky could be black and the whitewashed landing circle below appear no more phosphorescent than the minuscule presence of a barnacle on a rock deep underwater, but I made the circle as often as any man in our group.

Veteran covert-action officers kept coming back to Camp Peary for this special parachute training, so I cannot make the claim that I was the best in our class, but I was among the best, and the first of my pleasures was to be clearly superior to Dix Butler. He had the fastest time on the obstacle course, was unapproachable at dirty fighting, surprisingly silent as a putative assassin, and a beast at boxing. Nobody but Minnie could work with him. He was also the unofficial arm wrestling champion at Camp Peary, and once succeeded in taking on everyone in the Club at the time, twenty-two men was the count, instructors and heavies among them, and it did not take long.

I could top him every time, though, when it came to hitting that parachute target. It proved unbelievably grievous to his idea of himself. Rage came off him like a ground wave.

The irony is that he ought to have been proud of his parachuting. He began with a large fear of airplanes. Later, after we knew him better, he explained it one night in the Club. While he usually did his drinking in a group, for he liked a quorum to give resonance to his stories, Rosen and I were his pets, and on occasion, he drank only with us. I expect his motive was clear. Rosen and I were invariably first and second at book work. Butler, surprisingly good in the classroom, could nonetheless recognize our superiority there. I think he saw us as members of the Eastern establishment which, from his point of view, was running just about everything in the Company. In consequence, Rosen and I became the field studies available. On the other hand, he was hardly without contempt for us. He loved to tell us how to live. "You fellows would not be able to comprehend it. Big strong man, ha, ha. Why is he so afraid of flying? Horseshit. I have what I call superior-athlete fear." He stared at us hard, then without warning, grinned, as if to feint us off our feet. "Neither of you can comprehend what goes on in an athlete's skull. You think like sportswriters. They observe, but do not comprehend. The clue to a superior athlete is that he is telepathic." Butler nodded. "Some of us also have the power to hypnotize moving objects, no, not hypnotize—the appropriate word is *telekinesize*. When I am properly keyed, I can not only read which play is next in my opponent's mind, but I can telekinesize a football."

"Divert it in its path?" asked Rosen.

"By one foot at least on a long pass. And when a punt hits the ground, I can affect the bounce."

"You're crazy," said Rosen comfortably.

Butler reached forward, took Rosen's upper lip between his thumb and forefinger, and squeezed. "Cut that," Rosen managed to cry out through the grip, and to my surprise, Butler let go. Rosen had an odd authority, not unlike the way a spoiled but very self-assured young boy can command a fierce police dog. Up to a point.

"How could you do that?" Rosen complained. "We were just having a discussion."

"They don't teach it here," Butler said, "but that's the treatment for quieting an hysterical woman. Grab her upper lip and squeeze. I have used it in motel rooms from the time I was sixteen." Another toke of beer. "Goddammit, Rosen, don't you people in New York have the foggiest conception of manners? An hysterical woman calls me crazy, not a man talking to me."

"I don't believe your claims," said Rosen. "It's delusional. Telekinesis cannot be measured."

"Of course it can't. Heisenberg's Principle of Uncertainty applies."

We laughed. But I was not unimpressed that Butler could cite Heisenberg's Principle of Uncertainty.

"My fear of airplanes," said Dix Butler, "derives from the fact that I am always looking to raise the ante. The first time I got on a plane, it was a ten-seater with no partition between the pilot and the passengers. I tell you, I just had to play some games. Before long, there is old Dix putting his mind into the pilot's fingertips, and thereby getting the plane a bit whippy. Well, the pilot overcame that in turn by his will. You can move other men's matter just so much with your mind—it's a highly inefficient interpersonal mode," and here he looked at us across the table, his yellow-green eyes as childlike and solemn as a lion in a tender moment, full of a poet's sweet awe at the wondrous equations of movement, and said, "All right, what do I do now that this pilot's hand is on guard, why, I start to listen to the plane. It's old, and its two motors are wheezing out their lungs with every buck and tuck—man, my ears get into the vitals of that ship. I know how little it would take to set the motors on flame or crack the wing at the root. Nothing is holding that flying machine together but the mental strength of every one of the passengers and the pilot praying to keep hold of their paltry existence. And there I am, in the middle, a maniac.

My existence is larger than myself. I've been in car wrecks, been shot at. There's a no-man's-land out there between the given and the immense, and it has a set of rules very few can follow. All I know is that I am not sufficiently afraid of death. It is a transcendental experience that calls to me right through the foam of this piss-taster's brew. Can rational shit-heads like the two of you comprehend that? I tell you, the mad scientist in me was ready to experiment. I wanted to wreak a mischief on the inner machinery of that plane. You better believe that the desire was powerful. Why, the little washed-out idiots sitting around me in their passenger seats were so fearful of losing what they never had, an honest-to-God life, that I had to pull myself back from exercising my powers. I could truly visualize those plane motors catching fire. I still believe that by my mental efforts, I could have started such a blaze. In another moment, I would have. But I pulled myself back. I saved the plane from myself. Gentlemen, I was sick from the effort. My forehead had sweat on it the size of hailstones, and my liver might just as well have been stomped on by a platoon of Marines. I had to crawl off that misbegotten flying flivver when we landed. And I have been afraid of planes ever since. Afraid of my inability to restrain my evil impulses." Beer. A pause. Another swallow. One could visualize the stately flow of the beer down his gullet, equal in solemnity to the sure sweep of a conductor's baton.

I had no idea if he was serious or had merely been telling one of his tales, always and dependably extreme, but I suspect it was the truth, for him at least, since I believe he told it to purge himself, in much the way I had given my confession to Reggie Minnie. Next day, he began to make progress in his parachuting techniques, even as I began to move up in boxing until I even dared to get into the ring with Dix, and mustered enough character not to mumble as I put in my mouthpiece, "Take it easy, will you, Butler?"

It was an interesting three minutes. We were using headgear and fourteen-ounce gloves, but his jab was heavier than a straight right from any other trainee, and the first left hook I caught sent me half-across the ring.

I was in a panic. Only the sight of Reggie Minnie in my corner made me stay in with Butler and accept the bombardment to my ribs; I felt brain cells blinking out in full banks each time his jab rammed my forehead. When, once or twice, he chose to catch me with a straight right, I was taught all I needed to know about electricity. The voltage discharged in my brain would never be discharged again. In the middle of it, I began to understand for the first time what a serious athlete must feel, for I had reached a place where I was ready to live in the maelstrom. I no longer wished to quit. I had found peace in combat. Blessed feeling! Damn the damage! Whatever little futures were being wrecked in me forever were not going to count against this fortification of my ego.

Of course, I knew the bell would ring, and the three minutes would be over. My vast determination to take whatever onslaught the gods would loose was attached to a three-minute contract. Just as well. Another three minutes and I might have been in the infirmary. Later, watching Butler blast away at the trainee closest to him in weight, I was appalled at the power of his punches. Had Butler been hitting me that hard? I made the mistake of asking Rosen.

"Are you kidding?" he said. "He carried you."

I offer that in partial explanation for my dislike of Rosen.

10

OUR TRAINING FOR THE LAST TWO WEEKS WAS GIVEN OVER TO *FUN AND GAMES*. Introduced to surveillance, we were formed into three-man teams that practiced tailing an instructor (our Target) through the streets and stores of Norfolk. This involved a good amount of fast walking, and a great deal of standing in front of windows that could offer a clear reflection of the street. Our leader, the Point, was supposed to stay close to the Target while Liaison and Reserve watched alternate exits in buildings. We had signals to direct each other back and forth: Stop, Go right, Go left, Speed up, Slow down, were indicated by such actions as removing our hat, leaning against a wall, stopping by a fire hydrant, blowing one's nose, tying one's shoe, and—the abominable favorite—cleaning your ear with a forefinger.

Our signs broke down. Before long, we were waving at one another, and running at a half-trot. Rushing into a department store behind Target, we invariably lost him to an elevator. If Point did manage to sight Target again, Liaison or Reserve had been lost on one of the turns. When, sooner or later, Target would finger Point, the game was over. Every hour on the hour, we returned to the steps of Norfolk City Hall to take on another Target.

That night at the Club, drinking turned into a spree. Practical jokes abounded. Dix and one of the detonation experts set up a compressed air cartridge in the toilet connected by a wire to their end of the bar. There was a fifteen-minute wait for *in-phase resolution,* but when Rosen finally went to the toilet to take, as he made the mistake of announcing, "an ungodly dump," Trigger flicked the switch. Cartridge went off. Geyser splashed Target clear off the seat. Rosen's clothing was so drenched that he cut back to his barracks for a change of denims. "Surveillance is working at Camp Peary," became Dix's battle cry.

Meanwhile, more bona fide explosions went off on night demolition exercises in the woods, and night parachutists landed, and men with blacking on their faces rushed in, quaffed a beer, rushed out. Years later, on my way to Vietnam, I was invited to a movie set by an old Yale classmate, now a producer, and so was able to watch a battle being filmed. It was a bit of preparation for Vietnam, and it certainly reminded me of the Farm. War consisted of special effects going off from time to time; that was more in the nature of the event than death. "Death is the price you pay for enjoying a real war," one of our more hard-bitten instructors said, and I thought of that on nights when I was having a good time in Saigon.

Now I felt like a kid on one of those endless August evenings when the late fever of summer games keeps one running into the house and slamming the door on the way out. Our surveillance exercise might have been nerve-wracking, humiliating, and just about wholly unsuccessful, but the hysteria peculiar to the work was erupting now. We had, after all, been active in the next thing to an honest-to-God movie. Shadowing a man felt as odd as a dream.

Another victim walked into the bathroom of the Club, sat on the throne, and came out soaking wet. We laughed, and something in that commotion of waters got into the rest of the night. Rosen joined us again in dry clothes. Drunk on beer, he made the mistake of saying to Butler, "That was a crazy thing to do to a buddy. You're lopsided."

"Punk," said Butler, "spread your cheeks. I'll teach you lopsided."

He said it within the hearing of everyone around. Rosen, who usually presented a small but iron face to his persecutors, hovered on the edge. "Dix, you are not quite human," he managed to say, and with something like dignity, walked out of the club. Butler shook his head. "Hubbard, I was just treating him like a brother," he said.

"I wouldn't want to be your brother," I said.

"Hell, my older brother used to corn-hole me until I hit him up side of the head with a rock. I was fourteen. What did your older brother do?"

"I only have younger brothers."

"Corn-hole them?" Dix asked.

"No."

"Weren't man enough?"

"My brothers are twins. It's confusing."

He laughed. He clapped me on the back. He had a light in his eye that put perspiration into the palms of my hands. To my surprise, however, he sighed. "Oh, well, Arnie will recover. The question is: What about me? I'm getting too old to be a legend."

I don't know how much of this scene with Butler carried over, but things did go wrong with Rosen on the night we tried to cross the East German border (Camp Peary version). For one thing, it had rained through the day. The woods were muddy, the air swarmed with midges. Our night sky was clouded. We had to proceed by compass alone, a slow procedure prone to error.

We were working on a well-prepared scenario. If there was a climax to training at the Farm, and one course that received superior instructors and good preparation, it was *Escape and Interrogation*. Over the last three weeks, each of the trainees in my group had been given the role of a West German agent infiltrated into East Germany. We had each had to absorb our own West German biography, then add a detailed East German cover story. This second biography we were obliged to memorize even as a West German agent would have had to if he were infiltrating into East Germany. We were, in consequence, prepared to speak of the jobs we had held in East Germany, of family and school history including those of our near relatives killed in the Second World War, and we were supplied with the dates corresponding to major Allied bombing raids on our alleged hometown, Männernburg. Rosen and I, renamed Hans Krüll and Werner Flug for the exercise, had been memorizing hundreds of details over the last few weeks.

At this point in time—so went the prearranged scenario—our West German principal sent out an alert to us in East Germany: Transmissions from our radio were being picked up. We had to make a run for the West German border. The last two miles would traverse an East German wood which happened to correspond to our own Virginia thicket. If we succeeded in getting over the fence unobserved, then our cover stories would not have to be used (although we were still expected to volunteer for an interrogation as if we had been caught—in order not to miss the experience!). Any chance to use this more gracious option, however, was unlikely. We were not expected to make it over the fence. Few did.

I wanted to. I had gathered from Harlot that not only were grades at the Farm put into one's 201 file, but also a five-letter code grouping that had much critical bearing on the future career. While you might have a fair idea of how well you had done at the Farm, the five-letter group could advance or exclude you from exceptional posts. The highest marks, I was just about certain, would be given for getting over the fence: There would be another concealed rating, no doubt, on how well one did in the interrogation.

Rosen and I did not get off to a good start. By the time we reached the ditch adjacent to the East German fence, our fatigues were imbued with a noxious muck. Filthy and unmanned, we had to duck every thirty seconds as a searchlight swept the dirt road and fence in front of us. Every minute or so, a Jeep went by in one direction or the other. During one of these irregular intervals, we were supposed to scramble up the mudbank, climb the fence, go over the barbed wire at the top, and drop fourteen feet down to the other side. *There,* by the rules of our game, was freedom!

Rosen seemed demoralized. I think he was desperately afraid of the barbed wire. "Harry, I can't do it," he muttered. "I can't make it." He was sufficiently frantic to infect me with his fear.

"You goddamn Kike, get your ass over," I shouted. It was a half-throttled cry, pulled back even as I was saying it, but it was there between us forever, a small but permanent dent in my view of myself as an essentially decent fellow. The searchlight went by. Sobbing from fatigue, we scrambled up the vile mud bank, hit the fence, started to climb, and were transfixed—also forever—in the glare of the searchlight as it returned, stopped like the angel of death, and rested on us. In but a few seconds, an armed Jeep with two guards drove up, its machine gun trained on our bodies. We had flunked. So, for that matter, would most of the class. Even the Big Ten jocks. The exercise was not designed to make East European agents of us, but to give insight into the kind of horrendous experience some of our future agents might undergo.

Since the guards were wearing East German uniforms, the Jeep proved to be the only element in the charade that did not seem authentic. We were manacled and driven at high speed along the border road to a whitewashed cinder-block building. Inside, was an aisle down the middle and a series of windowless interrogation cells on either side, each cell about eight feet square and containing no more than a table, a couple of chairs, and a strong lamp with a reflector that would soon be directed into our eyes. The interrogator spoke English with such an intense German accent that, willy-nilly, one found oneself copying him. I had never seen any of these men at the Farm, and learned only later that they were professional actors on contract work to the Company; this contributed to disrupting one's anticipations; everything was becoming more real than I expected.

Since the interrogators moved from room to room questioning other trainees as they were brought in, one was left by oneself for longer and longer periods. Given the alternation of intense interrogation and glaring white-walled silence, I began to feel a sense of dislocation as the night went on. My cover story felt awkwardly lodged, a mind jammed into my mind. During questioning, the cover story became nearly all of me. I learned that a role could become more vivid to an actor than his own life. Why hadn't I realized how quintessential was preparation? Each detail in my imaginary life upon which I had failed to meditate sufficiently now became an added weight. For I could recall certain details only by an act of will. In contrast, every item I had been able to meditate upon in advance became alive to me. My cover story had put me in the vocational school at Männernburg near Leipzig right after the Second World War, and I had been able to imagine the pervasive stench that came through the school windows from the rubble of charred humans, dead rats, crumbled stone, and garbage—my voice sounded good to me when I spoke about my studies there.

"What was the name of the school in Männernburg?" my interlocutor asked. He was dressed in a black Volkspolizei uniform and held an impressive sheaf of papers. Since he was also dark in complexion and had a shock of heavy black hair and a dark beard, I found it difficult to think of him as German until I remembered that the Nazi Rudolf Hess had also had just such an iron-blue pallor to his shaved cheeks.

"Die Hauptbahnhofschule," I replied, "was my school."

"What did you study there?"

"Railroad trades."

"Graduate?"

"Yessir."

"How did you get to school, Werner?"

"I walked."

"Every day from your home?"

"Yessir."

"Remember the route?"

"Yessir."

"Name the streets you took."

I recited them. Not only was the map clear in my mind but I knew from photographs taken soon after the war how the streets ought to look.

"On your route, Herr Flug, it was obligatory to take the Schön-heitweg?"

"Yessir."

"Describe the Schönheitweg."

I could see it before me as I spoke. "It was our grand avenue in Männernburg. The Schönheitweg had an island of grass between the two directions of traffic."

"Describe this island."

"It had trees."

"What kind of trees?"

"I do not know the names."

"Were any of these trees cut down?"

"Yessir."

"Why?"

"I don't know," I said.

"How many traffic lights on the Schönheitweg?"

"Maybe two."

"Two?"

"Yessir, two."

"Near which traffic light did they cut the trees?"

"The second light on my way to school."

"In which year did they cut down the trees?"

"I don't remember."

"Think, Werner, think."

"Before I graduated in 1949."

"You are saying they cut down the trees in 1947 or 1948?"

"Probably."

"Do you recognize this picture?"

"Yes. It is of the intersection at the second traffic light on the

Schönheitweg. Before they cut down the trees."

He pointed to a building near the intersection. "Do you remember this?"

"Yessir. Postwar. The Männernburghof. A new government building."

"When did it go up?"

"I don't know."

"You don't remember the construction?"

"No, sir."

"You passed every day on your way to school, but you don't remember the construction of the only new government edifice in your town?"

"No, sir."

"But you saw it every day on your way to school?"

"Yes, sir."

"Was 1949 your last year at school?"

"Yessir."

"In 1949, the Männernburghof had not yet been constructed."

"It hadn't?"

"No, Werner."

"I am confused."

"It was erected in 1951. And the trees were cut down in 1952."

I was in a panic. Was the memory I had developed for my East German biography at fault, or was the interrogator lying to me?

He now inquired about my work in the railroad yards. Again, I was presented with small but definite discrepancies in the names and faces I had memorized: A locomotive repair shop to which I had been sent as clean-up man was located not at the east but the south end of the yards, and when I insisted it had to be in the east because I could remember the sun coming up in the morning, my interrogator left me alone for half an hour before coming back to ask the same question again.

Fortified by every photograph I had studied, I formed a picture of the town of Männernburg in my mind, but it was incomplete. As in a painting by Larry Rivers—whose work, after this interrogation, never failed to fascinate me—there were blank spaces to my Männernburg. As the hours of questioning went by, edges began to blur.

"Why were you climbing the border fence, Werner Flug?"

"I did not know it was the border."

"Despite the barbed wire at the top?"

"I thought I was in a government park. Me and my partner were lost."

"You were in a forbidden area. Did you know that?"

"No, sir."

"Männernburg is only five kilometers east of the border."

"Yessir."

"You are aware of that?"

"Yessir."

"Yet you walk through the woods that lie to the west of Männernburg and are surprised to find a fence."

"Me and my partner thought we were walking to the east, not the west."

"Werner, you were found with a compass on your person. You were not lost. You knew if you could climb the fence, you would be in West Germany."

"No, sir."

"Where would you be?"

"It was a prank, sir. We bet each other who would be the first to get over."

"You are a stupid fellow. Your story is sickening." He stood up and went out.

In chess, if one studies openings carefully enough, one can play on equal terms with a far superior opponent for the first eight or ten or twelve moves, for as long, that is, as the opening has been analyzed. After that, one is, as they say in chess, "out of the book."

I was out of the book. I had an acquired background and an acquired biography, but I did not have a good explanation of why I had tried to climb the border fence in the middle of the night.

My interlocutor came back, and began to question me as if our first colloquy had not taken place. Once more I was asked which year the trees were cut down on Der Schönheitweg. Again, I was interrogated on my claim that the railroad foundry was in the east yard. Each of my errors began to seem larger. I do not know if the act of confirming false details was responsible, but I began to feel as if his questions were related to a dentist's drill, and soon the nerve would be touched. To my horror, I began to contradict myself. Now I tried to claim that I must have blundered by error into West Germany. I must have gone across a portion of the border that had—could it be?—no fence, then had wandered through the woods wanting to return to East Germany, and so had climbed the fence on the Western

side, and was descending on the East German side in order to go back
to work in the morning like a good citizen of the German Democratic
Republic "just when the soldiers found us."

"Your sweat stinks with your lies. When I come back, Flug, I
want the truth or I will give you a couple of hot ones." He was
holding a rubber truncheon, and he slapped it against the table. Then
he left.

Outside my eight-by-eight-foot white cement-block room, a
prison din was building. The interview cells along the corridor had
filled, and the most curious condition began to prevail. I do not know
if the tempo of these interrogations was accelerating in anticipation of
the arrival of the dawn we could not see through the windowless
walls, but even as my questioner left me with the suggestion of dire
remedies, so did I become more aware of cries from other cells.

One captive was cursing audibly, "I don't know, I don't know.
You've got me deranged," he shouted. Another was whispering, but
so loudly I could hear: "I am innocent. You have to believe I am
innocent," and from the farthest room down the corridor, one of the
policemen was whipping his truncheon against the table. "No more,
no more," someone cried out.

Then I heard Rosen. "This is outrageous," he was saying in a
clear voice. "I do not care what my partner claims. You have confused
him and terrified him. We only climbed the fence to be able to see
the lights of Männernburg and thereby find our way back. That is my
story. You may have shaken my partner, but you do not faze me. You
cannot intimidate me with threats of violence. Never!"

The *thwap* came back from the cell at the far end of the corridor.

"Confess," said Rosen's interrogator. "You are not a citizen of
the German Democratic Republic."

"I am Hans Krüll," said Rosen, "born in Männernburg."

"You are a piece of filth. Tell the truth or we will use the filth that
comes out of you to stuff your nose. Why did you try to climb the
fence?"

"I am Hans Krüll," Rosen repeated.

Now two truncheons were being used, one at each end of the
corridor.

My sense of reality had not disappeared, but it was frayed. We
were in Camp Peary, not East Germany, but I did not feel safe. Even
as a casual vacation trip can remind one that death, too, is a journey,
so did I now feel as if insanity did not exist across the sea from reality,

but could be visited on foot. It was down the road.

My ears had never seemed more acute. I could hear Rosen arguing in his irritating, supercilious, nasal whine. Yet I could also hear his enormously developed sense of self-importance, ugly as gross riches, but nonetheless his kind of strength. "You are trying to throw me off the track," he was saying, "and it will not work. I submit my case to the legal guarantees substantiated by Order of Law 1378, Division Three, Chapter B, in the new Constitution of the German Democratic Republic. Look it up. It is there. My rights are being transgressed."

Yes, he had risen to the occasion! What a diversion! Now the interrogator was out of *his* book! Later I would learn that Rosen, in preparation, had gone to the Farm library three nights earlier to study the new Constitution of East Germany, thereby picking up enough to offer this exceptional gambit.

My interlocutor came back. Again, he began to question me from the beginning. I was led from detail to detail about the year the trees were cut down on Der Schönheitweg. Again, we passed through the railroad foundry and the aborted climb of the chain-link fence.

"It was because we were lost," I said, "and I wished to look for the lights of Männernburg."

"Your partner has told that story already. We have disproved it."

"I am telling the truth."

"Earlier you claimed that you did not know it was the border."

"I knew it was the border."

"You lied to me before?"

"Yessir."

"Why?"

"I was frightened."

"You claim you blundered into West Germany through an unfenced portion of the woods, and were now climbing back into East Germany."

"Also a lie."

"And now you are climbing the fence to look for the lights of Männernburg?"

"That is the truth."

"You have confessed to lying, but now you tell the truth?"

"Yessir."

"In fact, you are a liar, and an agent of the West German government."

A siren went off. It resounded through the corridors and cells of the building. My interrogator gathered his papers and sighed.

"It's over," he said.

"It is over?"

"I wish I'd had another fifteen minutes." He looked angry. Indeed, he still looked like a policeman.

"Well, it's been weird," I said.

"You did all right," he said.

"I did? How do you know?"

"I could kill you. When you make me feel like a cop, you've been good."

I stood up.

"Yeah, you can go," he said. "There's a truck to pick you up."

"I think I'll walk back to camp. Is that okay?"

"Sure. You've got the day off now."

"I think I need the walk."

"You bet."

We shook hands.

I did the two miles back to the parade ground and the barracks. New trainees were taking their first jumps through the mock-up of the C-47 door on the thirty-eight-foot tower. In another six hours my training would be over and I would go back to Washington to work in the I-J-K-L by the Reflecting Pool; then, presumably, I would be assigned overseas. As I made my way to the cafeteria for breakfast, I felt an epiphany near. I had passed through a dark wood full of midges and ticks, was captured in fatigues filthy with the slime of a border ditch, my fingers raw and newly scabbed from the chain-link fence, my eyes aching from the glare of the reflector lamp in an eight-by-eight-foot cell, and I had told lies all night in the face of prodigies of attack on a contrived memory, yet I felt clean and full of the virtue that greets one at the end of a rite of passage. It had been the most exciting eight hours I had spent in CIA; I had never been so happy. Something in these hours of interrogation confirmed my training. I had found the realm where I could spend my working life. To labor every day for the security of my country appealed to every breath that was deeded over to one's sense of the responsible and the appropriate. As for the other side of me, not yet worldly enough to go seeking for spiritual explorations and carnal adventures, it could be fascinated all the same by the arts of deception and the war against evil. It was certainly intrigued with games and the no-man's-land of those who were ready to play such games. So it was also in accord. I had my epiphany. Happiness was that resonance one knows in the heart when the ends of oneself come to concordance in the morning air.

11

THE CANAL HOUSE PURCHASED BY HUGH MONTAGUE AFTER HIS WEDding to Kittredge was situated on the bank of the old Chesapeake and Ohio Canal that passes through Georgetown. This waterway, if I recall correctly, was a thriving artery in 1825, floating down its fair load of coal from Appalachia to the Potomac, the barges then towed back with a cargo of such assorted sundries as flour, gunpowder, bolts of cloth, and axes. After the Civil War, however, the canal could no longer compete with the railroads. The mills on the riverbanks had long been empty, the locks were still, and the canal bed was a trickle.

Hugh's house, built as a stable for tow mules, was also graced with a second-floor loft where bargemen could sleep in the hay. The little building, already renovated by successive owners when the Montagues purchased it, had something like seven or eight rooms, and had become a modest but charming house for those who could abide child-sized chambers and low ceilings. One would have assumed that Hugh and Kittredge were too tall for the place, but the canal house revealed a side of them I might not otherwise have perceived. The nature of their separate professional tasks had this much in common: Their labors were often lonely, and rarely void of anxiety. So they tucked themselves into their canal house which they called—no great surprise—the Stable, and if there was a century-old effluvium of straw and mule-balls embedded in the floorboards, why, the better. Coziness was their connubial marrow. Since they were both, as I soon discovered, tough with a dollar, I think it helped that their little find had cost but $10,000. (Late in 1981, in a stroll one afternoon in Georgetown, I discovered that the house, sold by them in 1964 and several times again by subsequent owners, was now up to nothing less than an asking price of $250,000. That had to inspire some sour reflections on the changes in our American republic these thirty years.)

It also provided a half hour of melancholy. The Stable came back to my memory as it used to be in 1955.

I used to love their small living room, small dining room, and very small study for Hugh. In those former mule mangers, Kittredge showed something of her father's inclination for collecting antiques. Given a childhood in Boston and Cambridge, she had to perceive Washington as a Southern city. Why, then, not look for rare originals by colonial cabinetmakers from Virginia and the Carolinas? Listening to her speak of her acquisitions, I became half-familiar with names I had never encountered before, and was not to meet often again: Such colonial artisans as Thomas Affleck, Aaron Chapin, John Pimm, Job Townsend, Thomas Elfe, went in and out of her conversation until I did not know who had designed what, nor from where. I could hardly be concerned whether her cherrywood dining table and handwrought chairs with doe feet (which were, indeed, touchingly carved), her poplar sugar chest, her planter's table, her candlestand, were choice samples from North or South Carolina. It was enough that they had pedigree. Like show dogs, these pieces were not the same as other beasts. In the dining room on a panel between the mantel and the fireplace was a scene, neatly painted, of woods and houses and the canal; whiskey taken by the fire, then fortified with her pâté, could taste awfully good.

Harlot's study was another matter. Kittredge had furnished it to his choice, and I, feeling a pang at how well she understood his desires, suffered sentiments of disloyalty to Hugh in the midst of all my honest feelings. Since there were no two people I cared for more, I had an insight into the true attraction of treachery. It felt as bright as a spring leaf. Treachery helps to keep the soul alive—a most awful thought! What if it is true?

Harlot's study consisted of not much more than a massive dark oak desk and a leviathan of a chair. Victorian furniture, circa 1850, obviously satisfied Harlot's idea of a companionable style. A taste for the substantial gave solemnity, Harlot would explain, to the subterranean and lewd endeavors of the period. That is a large thought for one piece of furniture, but his grand seat was of mahogany and nearly five feet tall. The top of the chair-back was framed by a gothic arch full of quatrefoil fretwork. When you consider that this chair-back had been added to a sturdy Chippendale design for the arms, seat, and legs, the result was as baroque as a cathedral rising from an English manor.

The other rooms I never saw. Let me correct myself. The kitchen was an old pantry off the dining room with its share of cast-iron pots and trivets, and I was in there often, chatting with Kittredge while she

cooked for the three of us, but Harlot had an upstairs library I was
never asked to enter, and they had two or three bedrooms where the
loft used to be. I was not invited to stay over. Perhaps they had a finely
honed householder's fear that if I achieved entrance upstairs, I might
work up some way to live with them.

What evenings we had! While I never went over without telephoning first, and there were more than a few nights when they were
out, or had company they did not choose to have me meet, I still
encountered an odd collection of people at their small dinners. (Indeed, I was too young to know how curious and mutually unsuited
some of their dinner guests were.) The columnist Joseph Alsop, for
one, proved to be overpoweringly patriotic, even for me, and I must
say he breathed heavily whenever military or Company matters were
discussed. The thought of young American men in such pursuits was
obviously moving to him. Alsop also proved prodigious in his snobbery. I was paid no attention until he discovered that Boardman
Hubbard was my father, and then Alsop asked me to dinner, an
invitation which I, suddenly acting much like Cal, took pleasure to
refuse.

Actually, I was lonely on those evenings when I did not have a
welcome at the Stable. Graduated from the Farm, I had been bunking
with four other Junior Officer Trainees in a furnished apartment in
Washington. One or another roommate was invariably preempting
the living room in an attempt to seduce his date, usually a secretary
from the I-J-K-L, and I, looking to think a few things through, took
long walks at night.

No wonder, then, if invitations to the Stable meant much to me.
I felt not unlike an unemployed curator who, once or twice a week,
is permitted to visit the museum's private collection. There was no
doubt Harlot knew extraordinary people. Since many of them had to
do with OSS, I never judged by appearances. One hard-looking man
with a limp and an off-accent who talked about horses all night turned
out to have been one of the guerrilla leaders of the Chetniks—the
Mikhailovitch group that lost to Tito. I was impressed with his Balkan
manners. When he toasted Kittredge—which he did frequently—he
not only raised his glass but curved his knee, as if the good leg were
a bow and he was flexing it. Another guest was a formidable old lady
with a grand manner, porcelain blue eyes, and white hair, a half-
Bavarian, half-Italian countess who had run an underground safe

house in Rome for Jews during the Occupation.

Twice Kittredge had a girl there for me, each the younger sister of Radcliffe classmates, and both young ladies proved no better than I at petting on a couch somewhat later that night in my crowded apartment. We got awfully drunk to do it, and roommates would come through the door or go out, and my romances were without wings. I was becoming seriously concerned about the intensity of my sexual dreams compared to the lukewarm manifestations of it I was able to offer the dating world.

One evening the Montagues had a guest who most certainly brought out the best in Harlot. Given the size of the dining table, they never sat down to more than six, and this night we were four, but it looked like five. Their guest was a red-faced British general six feet seven inches tall, of magnificent bearing, with four rows of ribbons six inches wide on his chest, and he sat at his quarter of the table and drank all night and nodded wisely to all Harlot said. It seemed he had been in the SOE, and served on sister missions with the OSS, parachuting into France with Harlot. After which they became, as he put it, "good fellow sots" in London. Since the General contributed no more than his immaculate and immense presence, his lineage—which went back eleven hundred years—his title, Lord Robert, and his remarkably impressive uniform which he wore, he murmured, "in Kittredge's honor," conversation was left to Harlot. He did not flag. I had never known anyone to speak as well on so many matters; if Harlot had a conversational vice, it was his preference for monologue. Sir Robert suited him. "What," the General asked, after listening to other matters for a half hour, "is the history of this place? Looks quaint. What do you call it? *George*town? Has to've been named after one of the kings, hope not the Third." That was Lord Robert's longest speech of the night. Harlot reimbursed his guest with a disquisition on Georgetown after the war—the Civil War. "Nothing but camps and government corrals and a few bone factories. An awful lot of the horsemeat put into tins for the Union troops was processed just a few streets down. You can still smell dead animals in the fog."

"Hugh, you can't," said Kittredge.

"Darling, I can sniff them out," said Hugh, the reflections on his eyeglasses dancing from the candlelight.

"It must have been an awful place for a little while," admitted Kittredge. "Full of diphtheria and brothels."

I had the distinct impression that Lord Robert perked up. Dead horses one hundred years gone might not waken much appetite, but old brothels did!

"All the same, it was a thriving work town," said Hugh, "full of flour mills and corn mills, and hammers hitting the adze in the coopers' shops, a good sound."

"Good," agreed Sir Robert.

"Saws and planing machines," Hugh went on, "anvils dinging away. Such stuff. On a still night, I can hear echoes. Raucous bars. Canalmen fighting. A few of those taverns have made it all the way down to our time, and boys like Herrick, who work in the government, go to drink there now."

"What did you say your name was?" asked Lord Robert.

"Herrick Hubbard, sir."

"His father is Cal Hubbard," said Harlot.

"Yes, a man of very strong opinions, your father," said Lord Robert, as if mental life on his own promontory six feet seven inches high offered few people who would voice their opinions up to him.

"Hugh has got it wrong," Kittredge said. "Georgetown used to be, for the most part, a darling place. The houses had porticoes and gabled dormers. Slathers of gingerbread in the eaves."

"Kittredge, you miss the essence," said her husband.

"Do I?"

Two spots of anger showed in her cheeks, an unhappy color. It was the first time I had seen her looking harsh. It gave me a sense of the reason they did not invite me to sleep over: They would need the space to raise their voices.

Hugh, however, was not about to go to war with the General and myself as linesman and judge. "She's right," he said, "so am I. We happen to be talking about opposite ends of the town."

"Never knew a place that didn't have its up street and its down," Lord Robert said.

"Yes. Funny story. I was reading about Georgetown last night in a local history." Hugh began to laugh. His mirth was powerful enough to suggest that a good deal of anger had just been packed away. "Quotes a newspaper account from 1871. A resident of this town, Thaddeus Atwater, walking down Q Street one March morning, slips on the ice. His cane flies out of his hand and hits a hog strolling by"—a look at Kittredge, who put her tongue out at him and took it back so quickly that the General, if he had seen it, might have thought his eyes were up to tricks—"whereupon the injured pig roars like a bull and bolts into the nearest open cellar door. That happens to be a carpenter shop with shavings on the floor. It's filthy dark down there, and they've set a candle on a stand which, of course, the beast knocks over into the shavings and so starts one hell of a fire. Enter Red Hat . . ."

"Red Hat?" inquired Lord Robert.

"The local firehorse. A giant steed. Red Hat is pulling the Henry Addison fire wagon in unison with his mate, Dora Girl. The firemen drop hose into an adjacent brook, begin to pump, and manage to quench the fire, although they are all the while slopping so much water over Q Street that it soon becomes a frozen pond. By evening, the townspeople are out to try their ice skates. I enjoy that period," said Harlot.

"Yes," I said, "I guess events had more influence on other events, then."

"Yes," he said, "you're not a dull boy, are you? You see the metamorphoses."

"Just so, metamorphoses," Lord Robert remarked. He seemed to be coming out of the trance Hugh's story had left him in. "Do you know, there's talk of sending Philby to Beirut. Going to give him a journalist's job."

"Oh, no," said Harlot. "It'll play like hell over here. Do your best to stop it. It's hard enough to keep the FBI off MI6, without your people giving Philby a plum."

"Be bad for you personally, won't it?"

"No," replied Harlot, "all is forgiven."

"Hope so. I used to think it was your Waterloo."

"Not at all," said Kittredge. "They need Hugh much too much."

"Good to hear that."

"The mark of a great man is that his mistakes are also great," Kittredge declared.

"Well, damn Philby, I say," said Lord Robert. "Let's drink to his damnation."

"To Philby," answered Harlot, holding high his glass. "Damn him for eternity."

I had no idea what they were talking about. Yet its importance permeated the room. The shadow of things unsaid was on our evening. Once again I was content with my profession and the mysteries it would yet disclose. Philby. I was even stirred by the way they said his name; they could as well have been speaking of an old fort where drear losses had been taken.

One night there was a small gentleman at dinner named Dr. Schneider who, I was informed, had achieved some recognition in Europe as a concert pianist. He remained determinedly vague about whether he was Austrian or German, but was quick to express the most extreme monarchist opinions: Hitler, he insisted, might have been able to win the war if he had only been wise enough to restore the Hohenzollerns. "After all," Dr. Schneider said, "the monarchy could have underwritten the crusade against Bolshevism."

Dr. Schneider wore dark glasses and had large, pointed ears. He sheltered himself behind a thick, gray mustache. His hair was white, and he looked to be more than sixty. Given his opinions, he must have gone through some fancy footwork when the war ended, since he now spoke of giving recitals in the Soviet zones of Germany and Austria. I wondered if he had been a spy for Harlot. All the same, I found him unsavory and wondered why the Montagues treated him with respect. On second examination, I could detect that Dr. Schneider was wearing an expensive white wig, well placed on his head, but I had my mother's eye for masquerade and so was intrigued with his desire to present himself as an older man. I hardly knew how I felt about sitting at table with what might be a crypto-Nazi.

After dinner, Harlot sat down to a game of chess with Dr. Schneider, and I decided that Hugh liked to enjoy people by their pieces and parts. "Watch the play," Harlot confided to me. "Schneider is phenomenal in the endgame. He falters occasionally with openings, but unless I'm two pawns up after the middle game, I'm far from home."

The pianist would rub his hands and croon or moan after every one of Harlot's moves. "Oh, you are a devil, Mr. Montague, you are a clever fellow, the trickiest, aren't you, oh, oh, oh, you have me in a pickle, you do, si-, a fiend with your knights you are, yum, yum, yum, yessir," after which, nodding his head, albeit still groaning, "*Punkt*," he would say, and move a pawn. As Harlot predicted, Dr. Schneider did well in the endgame and brought off a draw. It was the only time I ever saw him at the Stable.

After he left—and I did notice that he and Harlot shook hands at the door like old comrades—Harlot asked me to stay. While Kittredge was doing the dishes (with which I usually helped her, although, on this night, by Harlot's insistence, signally not) he took me into his study, pinned me down on a small wooden chair to face his presence in the Cathedral Chippendale, and proceeded to give the first reasonably full deployment of his mind that I had received since the night he told me to give up rock climbing.

I was ready to talk to him about an unhappy situation at my new work (about which he had never made one inquiry) but, then, I did not dare. What if he had no interest?

At this moment he said, "Your father is coming back. We'll go out to dinner, the three of us."

"That sounds terrific." I kept myself from asking where my father had been. No word had come from him in months, so I did not see how I could inquire.

"Do you find CIA a large place?" Hugh Montague inquired.

"Enormous."

"We weren't always so big. In fact, the baby almost didn't get born. J. Edgar Hoover did everything he could to stop us. Didn't want his FBI put in competition. Hoover may be the most fear-ridden man in Christendom. We refer to him, by the way, as Buddha, J. Edgar Buddha. If the fellow you're talking to doesn't follow, then he is not one of us."

I nodded. I didn't know whether *us* now referred to all of CIA or but a small part.

"What with Foster Dulles owning Eisenhower's mind, Allen has us in good shape. We're certainly expanding."

"Yessir."

"To do what?" he asked. "What is our purview?"

"To supply the President with intelligence, I suppose."

"Do you have a vision of what that intelligence ought to be?"

"Well, first to catch up with the KGB."

"We can do that. We may have to do a little better than that. It is not just the Russians, you see. We can probably work their mainspring loose, disembarrass them—even if it takes a half-century—of their Marxism, but the war will go on. Right here. Right here, it's taking place. Across all the face of America. The secret stakes keep going up. The active question is whether this Christ-inspired civilization will continue. All other questions fade before that."

"Including the bomb?"

"It's not the bomb that's going to destroy us. If it ever gets down to the nuclear people, then we're merely incinerating the corpse of all that's been destroyed already. The bomb can't be used unless civilization dies first. Of course, that can happen. Our continuing existence depends on not falling prey to false perceptions of reality. The rise of Marxism is but a corollary to the fundamental historical malady of this century: false perception."

What a man of the cloth he would have made! The value of his words was so incontestable to himself that he did not question the size of his audience. I could have been one parishioner or five hundred and one: The sermon would not have altered. Each word offered its reverberation to his mind, if not to mine.

"It's sad," he said. "For millennia, every attempt at civilization foundered because nations lacked the most essential information. Now we lurch forward, overburdened by hordes of misinformation. Sometimes I think our future existence will depend on whether we can keep false information from proliferating too rapidly. If our power to verify the facts does not keep pace, then distortions of information will eventually choke us. Harry, are you beginning to have some concept of how much our people here have to amount to?"

I managed to mutter, "I'm not sure I see where you're heading."

"You just don't welcome it." He swallowed his brandy. "Our real duty is to become the mind of America."

I nodded. I had no idea whether I was ready to agree with him, but I nodded.

"There's absolutely no reason," he said, "why the Company can't get there. Already, we tap into everything. If good crops are an instrument of foreign policy, then we are obliged to know next year's weather. That same demand comes at us everywhere we look: finance, media, labor relations, economic production, the thematic consequences of TV. Where is the end to all we can be legitimately interested in? Dwelling in an age of general systems, we are obliged to draw experts from all fields: bankers, psychiatrists, poison specialists, art experts, public relations people, trade unionists, hooligans, journalists—do you have a good idea how many journalists are on contract to us?—do observe a little *hush-hush* on that one. Nobody knows how many pipelines we have into good places—how many Pentagon pooh-bahs, commodores, congressmen, professors in assorted think tanks, soil erosion specialists, student leaders, diplomats, corporate lawyers, name it! They all give us input. We're rich in our resources. You see, we had the great good luck to start all at once." He nodded. "For a bureaucratic organization, that is usually a disaster, but it happened to work for us. Not only were we seeded with some of our best OSS people, but we attracted good ambitious men from all over the place, State, the FBI, Treasury, Defense, Commerce—we raided them all. They all wanted to come to us. That created a curious situation. Organizationally speaking, we were set up in a pyramid. But our personnel, as measured by their skilled experience, gave us the shape of a barrel. Enormous amounts of talent in the middle ranks. And they had no way to rise. After all, the people at the top were also young. Relatively young, like myself. So a good many of the men who rushed to join our ranks five years ago had to sign out again. Now, they're all over the place."

"All over Washington?"

"All over America. Once you've been in the Company, you don't really want to quit it altogether. It's tedious to work in those financial worlds and business worlds. I tell you, we have liaison into every game that's going on in this country. Potentially, we can give direction to the land." He smiled. "Feeling tired?"

"No, sir."

"Didn't wear you out with the size of the mural?"

"I'll be up all night."

"Good for you." He smiled. "Let's have one more drink before you go. I want you to understand something. I don't get confidential very often, but from time to time, I will. You see, Harry, everyone in this Pickle Factory has a weakness. One fellow drinks too much. Another screws around heedlessly. A third is a closet queer—either he brazened it through the polygraph, or turned queer later. A fourth smokes marijuana on the sly. My vice, old Harry Hubbard, old before your years, is that I tend to talk too much. So I'm obliged to choose people I can trust. One does get the feeling, speaking to you, that it all goes down into the deepest vault you've got. So, yes, I'll tell you a thing from time to time, and Heaven help you if you don't keep it to yourself."

He took a full draw on his Churchill and let the smoke surround him. "What did you make of our Dr. Schneider?" he asked.

I had the sense to be brief. "I would," I said, "read him as an ex-Nazi in a wig. I think he must be ten years younger than his false white hair, and he may know less about concert recitals than dead drops."

"It's tempting," said Harlot, "to tell you more. But I'm afraid I can't let you in."

"Despite what you just said?" I was as suddenly hungry for secrets about Dr. Schneider as a hound called back from his food.

"Well," said Harlot, "there's no remedy. Perhaps you'll discover him for yourself one of these days." He took a puff again. He was enjoying my frustration. "Harry," said Harlot, "keep the faith."

12

LET ME DESCEND FROM THE HEIGHTS OF HARLOT'S CONFIDENCE IN ME to the low information of how I spent my working day. If I had finished training with high hopes for my immediate future, having spent many a night at the Farm discussing the best station to be sent to; if the merits of Vienna and Singapore and Buenos Aires and Ankara and Moscow, Teheran, Tokyo, Manila, Prague, Budapest, Nairobi, and Berlin had been weighed for their qualities as the most lively spot for commencing one's career, I, in common with most of my class, was assigned to a job in Washington, D.C.

Then came another disappointment. I was not selected for any of the foreign desks. That was the usual prelude to getting an overseas post. An assistant to the Iran Desk in Washington could assume he was learning the ropes for Teheran. Ditto for the Congo Desk and the Japanese, the Polish Desk, and the Chilean. It was generally agreed among Junior Officer Trainees at the Farm that if you had to begin in Washington, Assistant to the Desk Officer was the best job.

Now, I was not an ambitious young politician, but I had enough of my mother's social sense to know I had been invited to the wrong party. I landed in the Snake Pit, also known as the Boiler Room and/or the Coal Bin. On an unrewarding job, synonyms proliferate. In a huge room whose fluorescent lights droned away under a relatively low ceiling, in the very small draft of a few modest air conditioners situated in little windows on a far-off wall, we bumped and maneuvered around one another down aisles that were always too narrow for their human traffic. It was hot, unseasonably hot for October. On either side, six feet high, were old-fashioned wooden cabinets with shelves and file boxes.

We had a Document Room next door, a large chamber stuffed with stacks of papers as yet unfiled. The stacks grew to the ceiling. The names encountered in each pamphlet, station report, agent report, magazine reference, newspaper reference, trade journal, or book were supposed to be set down on a card with a summary of the information contained. After which, the card could be filed, and the document stored more permanently. The theory at the core of such labors was to be able to look at all the information available on any person the Company might be interested in. By such means, telling profiles could be formed.

It was chaos, however. Documents accumulated faster than we could card them. The Western Hemisphere Division was soon six months behind their tower of paper in the Document Room; Soviet Russia was four months back; China (given the difficulty of ideograms) a year and a half. For West Germany, to which I was assigned, only three months were in arrears. It was enough, nonetheless, to bring stress to every endeavor. I spent much of my time squeezing my way down aisles, or wiggling my fingers into a file box. Once in a while, there was honest panic. One morning, for instance, the Chief of Base in West Berlin sent a cable requesting vital information on one VQ/WILDBOAR. Since hordes of such requests came in, and the turnover of personnel at my low level was considerable, such chores were assigned by lot—you took the cable on the top of the pile at the Incoming Queries Desk.

Then you worked your way through traffic, doing your best not to collide with the body, its nose in a file, that was blocking your path down the aisle. The odor of sweat was ubiquitous. It might as well have been summer. The air conditioners had small lungs, and each one of us clerks—were we better, for all our training, than clerks?—was carrying his own anxious stir. It was not enough to find WILDBOAR for Chief of Base, Berlin; one had to find him quickly. The cable had been frantic: NEED ALL RECENT ENTRIES ON VQ/WILDBOAR. URGENT. GIBLETS. Yes, the Chief of Base had signed it himself.

I had had to wait in Records Integration Office down the corridor to obtain access to the *PRQ-Part I/Part II/201-File Bridge-Archive,* which hopefully was up to date and so could tell me who VQ/WILDBOAR might be. On this morning, VQ/WILDBOAR did translate into Wolfgang-from-West-Germany, last name unknown, last address Wasserspiegelstrasse 158, Hamburg. That, at least, was a start. Back in the Snake Pit, I could continue my search through the two file boxes—each twenty inches long, each containing something like eighteen hundred index cards, stuffed with Wolfgangs who had been sufficiently inconsiderate to provide us with no last name. Wolfgangs who offered the courtesy of a last initial, a Wolfgang F., or a

Wolfgang G., took up another three file boxes. Wolfgangs with a whole last name occupied ten. I did not know that so many Wolfgangs were interesting to us in West Germany!

Then I discovered they were not. My Wolfgang-from-Hamburg had been entitled to one card in the Snake Pit for the occasion on which he was arrested in 1952 after heaving a brick during a street demonstration in Bonn. Yet he had nothing less than fifteen such entries, carded from fifteen separate West German newspapers which reprinted the same West German wire service story. Absolutely invaluable stuff on my Wolfgang might well be lying somewhere in the Document Room at the other end of this interminable shed, but it had not yet been carded. I was, by now, irritable. In the lunch break, I sent back a cable to the office of Chief of Base, West Berlin. NOT ABLE TO SATISFY REQUEST FOR RECENT ENTRIES RE: VQ/WILDBOAR. SEND BETTER ADDRESS. KU/CLOAKROOM. It was my first cable out. My first use of my own cryptonym.

At end of day, an answer was routed back to me. CABLE 51— (SERIES RB 100 A). TO KU/CLOAKROOM: MOST RECENT, REPEAT AND UNDERLINE, MOST RECENT INFORMATION ON VQ/WILDBOAR IS OF THE ESSENTIAL, REPEAT, ESSENTIAL. FILE-RAT, ARE YOU INEPT? COME UP WITH YOUR OWN BETTER ADDRESS. VQ/GIBLETS.

The Chief of Base in Berlin was famous for his short fuse. Yet I had no idea where to look. If I didn't respond to his cable, I could conceivably receive a Notice of Censure. It left me full of unspoken rage at Harlot. Why had I been left at the Snake Pit? Others in my training group were sited already at some of the best desks in Washington. Rosen was in Technical Services, a supersecret plum—was that due to his performance on the night of interrogation? Worse, Dix Butler, as I learned by way of Rosen, was actually operating out of West Berlin.

Just when my mood felt condemned to brood through the night—where is Wolfgang, and what would I do tomorrow?—I received a phone call from my father. Heading up something big and unnameable in Tokyo, as I learned from his first remarks, he was reporting back to Washington after a visit to stations in Manila, Singapore, Rangoon, and Djakarta. "Join me for dinner," he said right off. "We'll celebrate your release from the Farm. Montague will be there."

"Terrific," I said. I would have preferred to see my father alone.

"Yes," he said, "watch Hugh tonight. He knows I've got the jam on a lot of doings in the Far East. He'll be dying to know. Keep an item away from Hugh, and he carries on like you're picking his pocket."

Well, we had a rich dinner at Sans Souci, and a good deal of maneuvering did go on between Cal and Harlot. I could hardly follow the shoptalk about Sumatra, and SEATO, and the rigors of getting a little intelligence out of Singapore without ruffling the Raj. When Harlot asked, "How do you plan to hold Sukarno's feet to the fire?" my father leaned forward, touched my elbow with his, and replied, "Hugh, that's just what we won't get into."

"Of course not. You'll listen to some total fool out there who's covering every base and hasn't idea one on how to proceed, but you won't take a chance with me."

"Hugh, I can't."

"I see where it's leading. I sniff it. You're going to try to photograph Sukarno in one of his circuses."

"Throwing no stones," said my father, "he's certainly got a few going."

"You're on squander-time. It's madness. You can't trap Buddhists with sex. They place it somewhere between eating and evacuating. Part of the comedy of what goes in and comes out. You'll need more than photographs to get Sukarno into your pouch."

"The only alternative is the Colonels," said my father. "I don't know that they're honest dinner guests."

Such talk went on. I certainly couldn't swear to what they were contesting, but I thought it wonderfully interesting. Before too many years went by, perhaps I, too, would carry on such conversations.

Of course, I was not enjoying the evening altogether. I was still in dread of tomorrow's search for Wolfgang, and my stomach was raw. Harlot and Cal had taken, after the smallest acknowledgment, no further recognition of my last six months of training, and my graduation from the Farm. Nor had they given me room to talk about my present condition. After three martinis, I had begun to pack veal roulade into my gorge with a red burgundy whose nature seemed more complex than my own. Add Hennessey, and the attempt to smoke a Churchill with panache, and what I had hoped would be a party of celebration (and possible explanation for why I had been marooned in the Bunker) was now becoming a long march of gastrointestinal fortitude. I lost interest in Sukarno and how they would hold his feet to the fire.

Beneath it all, I was feeling the same sure resentment my father always stirred. Sad cry: He had no desire to see me for myself alone. I was his adjunct to business, pleasure, or duty. So, despite my physical discomforts, heavy as thunderclouds, I felt the same rush of love my father could also stir in me when he said at last, "I'm really waiting to hear about you, boy."

"There's not much to tell."

"He's in the Snake Pit," said Harlot.

By my father's pause, I could tell this came as unexpected information. "Well, that's a hell of a place to have him."

"No. It's advisable."

"You put him there?"

"I didn't keep it from happening."

"Why? Did he do that badly at the Farm?"

"No. He landed in the top quarter of his class."

"Good."

"Not good, adequate."

All this, of course, was being said in front of me.

"Then why do you have him in Files?"

"Because it's a holding tank, and I plan to send him to Berlin. That's an interesting place right now."

"I know all about Berlin. I agree. But why isn't he working at West German Desk?"

"Because it can be fatal to young fortunes. Four promising kids have come and gone from that slot in the last three months. Harvey chews them up before they have time to learn."

My father nodded. He puffed on his cigar. He sipped his brandy. He took this much time to say in effect that he was a Far Eastern hand and did not know all that much about what was closer to home.

"I want," said Hugh, "for you to write a letter to Harvey. A puff for Harry. Tell him what a great son you've got. Harvey respects you, Cal."

This Bill Harvey, I could recognize, was the same Chief of Base, West Berlin, who had called me a file-rat. Why did Harlot think I should work for him? I was, despite the last full lecture imparted at the canal house, not without suspicions.

Perhaps my unhappy stomach could not hold its own bad news much longer. I told them of Harvey's cable.

"I'm no longer," I said, "exactly anonymous. He knows there's a guy named KU/CLOAKROOM who didn't produce what he wanted on VQ/WILDBOAR."

They laughed. They could have been brothers for the way they laughed together.

"Well," said Cal, "maybe KU/CLOAKROOM ought to disappear."

"Exactly," said Harlot. "We can drink to the new fellow. Got a preference in the christening?"

"KU/RENDEZVOUS?" I proposed.

"Much too salient. Get over into the gray. Let's start with KU/ROPES."

I didn't like ROPES any more than CLOAKROOM, but I discovered it didn't matter. It was explained to me that just as laundered money grew cleaner with each new bank, so did each change of cryptonym remove you farther from the scene of a fiasco. My new cryptonym would soon be altered from KU/ROPES to DN/FRAGMENT, then, over to SM/ONION. Last stop: KU/STAIRS. Harlot jotted down these names with little self-congratulatory clicks of the tongue, while my father chuckled in approval. They were cooking a dish.

"I don't know how it works," I protested.

"Worry not. Once I get this through, odds against discovery will go up to something like ten thousand to one," said Harlot.

It still seemed to me that all it would take for Mr. William Harvey, Chief of Base in West Berlin, to find out who KU/CLOAKROOM was, would be to ask the West German Desk in Washington to get my real name over to him in a hurry.

No, my father assured me, it couldn't happen that way.

Why?

"Because," said Harlot, "we are dealing with bureaucrats."

"Harvey?" I asked.

"Oh, no. The people between Harvey and you. They won't see any reason to violate their rules of procedure. If West German Desk here at Headquarters is asked to furnish the identity of KU/CLOAKROOM to Chief of Base, West Berlin, they must apply first to Bridge-Archive, who, in turn, will reply that KU/CLOAKROOM has just been given a shift to KU/ROPES. Well, that means delay for West German Desk. Any alteration of cryptonym invokes a seventy-two-hour elapse before *translation* can occur. This protective regulation is a perfectly good one, by the way. Such a change took place, presumably, for some valid purpose. At this point, West German Desk probably decides to wait the required three days. It's a minor search, after all. They're just accomodating Harvey. He's over in Berlin, and West German Desk is working for West German Station in Bonn."

"Doesn't Base in West Berlin have priority over West German Station in Bonn?" I asked my father.

"Don't know about that. Bonn does have the Soviet Russia Division." He frowned. "Of course, Berlin, on balance, could be more important. Only we're not talking about real clout. We're dealing with bureaucracy, and that's a whole other kingdom."

"Count on it," said Harlot. "If Bill Harvey insists on immediate processing of his request, which is highly unlikely, because he's bound to be mad at somebody else by tomorrow—it's another day, after all—West German Desk still won't be able to satisfy him directly. They will have to go a step higher to Bridge-Archive:Control. Right there, they will meet a STOP. I will have put it in. STOP will say: 'Wait your seventy-two hours.' If they don't want to, they have to take it up even higher, to Bridge-Archive:Control—Senior. Now, that is a committee. Bridge-Archive:Control—Senior meets only for emergencies. I happen to be on the committee. One never presumes on Bridge-Archive:Control—Senior unless one can prove extraordinary need to know."

He puffed with complete happiness on his Churchill. "Obviously, you're safe enough for seventy-two hours. In the interim, we will switch your cryptonym from KU/ROPES to DN/FRAGMENT. That means West German Desk, far from discovering who KU/CLOAKROOM is, will have to recommence the process to learn the identity of DN/FRAGMENT. They're still not near anything, you see."

"DN," said my father, "is the digraph for South Korea."

"Yes," said Harlot. "KU/ROPES has gone to South Korea and become DN/FRAGMENT. On paper, at least. Of course, an overseas cryptonym puts a two-week hold on Bridge-Archive. By then, Harvey, we can predict, will be well on to other things. Nonetheless, as a matter of pride, I believe in carrying these matters out properly. If Harvey, for any reason, becomes obsessed with finding out who you are, which is always a possibility, and waits out the two weeks, I promise that at the end of such interval, you will be shifted over to London as SM/ONION. Still on paper, of course. A fortnight further down the road, we will bring you figuratively back from London to the U.S., which, dear boy, you have not left in the first place. But we'll have you back working as KU/STAIRS. Total write-off for Harvey at that point. He will see that a *signature* is on this business. It will tell him to lay off. He's obviously tampering with something. No ordinary file-clerk gets three cryptonyms in one month including junkets to South Korea and London with protective STOPS from Bridge-Archive:Control. So it's our way of saying to Bill Harvey: Bug off. Big guns are in place."

It seemed clear enough to me. I would be safe. But why go to such pains?

My father must have been enough of a parent to read my cerebrations. "We're doing it because we like you," he said.

"And because we like doing it," said Harlot. He nudged the ash from his cigar onto a clean plate as carefully as he might roll an egg with his forefinger. "I'll also have to get," he remarked, "KU/CLOAKROOM expunged from your 201. Then there'll be no record at all."

"I appreciate the troubles you're taking on," I said, "but, after all, I committed no crime. It's not my fault if the Document Room is buried in backlog."

"Well," said Harlot, "the first rule in this place, if you value the size of the future contribution you want to make, is to protect yourself when young. If some mogul sends a request for information, supply it."

"How? Do you tunnel through ten thousand cubic feet of un-carded documents?"

"Wolfgang was a student in a street gang, and he moved around a lot. You could have made up a report that kept him moving a little more. Send him to Frankfurt, or over to Essen."

"Maybe," said my father, "Rick should still do that."

"No," said Harlot. "Too late. It won't work now. Too much attention will be paid to the false information. But the point for my godson to recognize is that in the beginning Harvey was not asking for a serious inquiry."

"How can you be certain of that?" I asked.

"If Chief of Base in West Berlin is not aware of the frightful condition of the Snake Pit, he is incompetent. William King Harvey is not incompetent. He knew, given the chaos, there would be nothing up to date on VQ/WILDBOAR. I would say he sent the cable,

and put his name to it, mind you, to scorch some of his people in
Berlin. They probably lost contact with Wolfgang. It's a slap in the
face for them if our file system here has to do the job when they are
in place over there. If you had provided some fiction for Wolfgang's
travels, Harvey could have used it to stir up his principals and their
agents. 'See,' he would tell them, 'Wolfgang has gone back to Frankfurt.' 'Impossible,' they might answer. 'He's too recognizable in
Frankfurt.' 'All right,' Harvey could have answered, 'get cracking and
find him.' "

I could not keep myself from saying, "What if it was urgent to
find Wolfgang? What if he"—I showed, I fear, a wholly callow
spirit—"what if he was about to pass some nuclear secrets on to the
Russians?"

"It doesn't matter," said Harlot. "We've lost it at that point.
We're lumbered. The world ends because the Document Room is an
impacted mass."

My father took a long look at Hugh Montague and something was
exchanged between them. Harlot sighed. "In fact," he said, "there is
one larger-than-life secret in West Berlin, and I may have to let you
in on it before you go over. If you don't have any idea of what it is,
you could get in Harvey's way." He sighed again. "It's a thousand to
one that Wolfgang has nothing to do with larger-than-life, but if he
does, we'll know about it soon enough."

"How?"

Hugh sniffed another measure of that air of the judicious and the
corrupt which is common to courtroom corridors and cigars, and said,
"We'll get you out of the Snake Pit tomorrow, and on to intensive
training in German." That was all the answer provided.

13

AFTER DINNER, MY FATHER PROPOSED THAT I STAY WITH HIM FOR THE
night. He was living, he told me, at a friend's apartment off K Street
and 16th, "an old hand in an old apartment," my father said in passing,
and when we went up, I was struck with how shabby were the
furnishings. It spoke of small income for an old hand without private
funds; it also reminded me of how pinch-fisted we Hubbards could
be. My father was certainly able to afford a decent hotel, yet chose to

bunk here instead—I hardly knew if he was saving expense money for the CIA or himself. On second look, however, I realized his story was not true. The spartan lack of amenities—one gray sofa, two gray chairs, one old carpet, one pitted metal ashtray on its own stand, no drapes, and a bureau with cigarette burns, a refrigerator, as I soon discovered, with three beers, a tin of sardines, a box of crackers, and half-empty old jars of mustard, ketchup, and mayonnaise—was enough to tell me that no one was living here. There was no personal clutter. Not one picture or photograph. This couldn't be a friend's apartment. We were in a safe house. I was visiting my first safe house. Naturally my father would choose to stay in one. It fit the loneliness he liked to wrap around himself whenever he was not back in his Tokyo home with warm reliable Mary Bolland Baird Hubbard.

My father now waved me into one of the two dusty armchairs, and brought forth from a kitchen cupboard a half bottle of cheap Scotch which we drank with water, no cubes. He had turned on the refrigerator, however, and it was humming loudly enough to discourage any microphone hidden anywhere about. I was, at this point, highly sensitive to the possible presence of *sneakies,* inasmuch as one of the courses back at the Reflecting Pool had been in electronic surveillance, and I wondered if my father's quick tapping of his fingernails against the end table by the side of his chair came from nervousness, fatigue, or his long-trained habit to send out sufficient noise to discourage any but the most advanced listening devices. Of course, I had even less idea whether I was being too paranoid or insufficiently so.

"I want to talk to you about Hugh and Bill Harvey," said my father. "Hugh means a good deal to me, but I have to tell you—he's not perfect. It's damnable, because he's almost perfect, if you know what I mean."

"I don't."

"Well, when people get up to 98 percent, it hurts out of proportion if they can't reach those last two points. Hugh may be the best man we have in the Company. He's the most brilliant, and certainly one of the more scholarly, and he has guts. He's a real cross between a panther and a mountain goat. Don't get him angry, and don't dare him to leap."

"Yessir," I said, "I have a very high opinion of him."

"I don't mind if he takes his own leaps, but I'm not sure he isn't asking you to go along with him on this one." My father threw up his hands as if to apologize for not being able to tell me more.

"Does any of this concern the larger-than-life secret?" I asked.

He coughed heavily with an unhappy subterranean sound. A considerable mucus must have been ravaging his powerful chest. My father was still in his late forties, but the sound of this cough, filled with the gravel of booze and nicotine, seemed to have come from a much older man concealed within that powerful body. "Yes," he said. "Hugh should not have brought the matter up. I know I won't tell you, and I wouldn't even if I could because I don't want you to bear the responsibility of holding such a weighty secret, a true secret of state. Tell me, then, why Hugh figures he can feed it to you as part of your orientation?"

There was obviously no answer to that.

"He will certainly tell you," my father went on. "Don't repeat this to a soul, but he lets more secrets out than anyone in his position ever should. It's as if he's making a bet on his own judgment. I suppose it gives him the grandest feeling."

I think my father may finally have had his fill of drink, for I could feel him meandering away from me in his mind. Then he sat up with a jerk. "The point is, Hugh has no right to trust anyone. Not after Philby. You've heard about Kim Philby?"

"A little," I said. I was trying to recall Lord Robert's comments on the subject.

"Philby came very near to being Hugh's nemesis. Philby was so thick with Burgess and Maclean. Ever hear of them?"

"Wasn't it a newspaper story? They were British Foreign Office stationed over here, weren't they?"

"Damn right," said Cal. "When Burgess and Maclean pulled their disappearance back in 1951 and ended up in Moscow, everybody here divided into camps. Did Philby tell Burgess and Maclean to decamp, or did he not? Old friends weren't speaking, not if one thought Philby was guilty and the other didn't."

"Which camp were you in?"

"Pro-Philby. Same as Hugh. Kim Philby was a friend of Hugh's, and he was a friend of mine. We used to drink together in London during the war. You'd swear Philby was the peachiest Englishman you ever met. Had a stammer. But very funny when he could get the words out. Which he could, when drunk." After which my father suddenly went silent.

I waited, but he said no more. Then, he yawned. "I'm ready to turn in," he said. "I caught this bug in Djakarta—a hellzapopper of a bug. I wonder what it looks like under the microscope." He smiled in superiority to his own physical defects, and added, "Let's not get into Kim Philby now. It's too depressing. The point is, Hugh ended up looking pretty bad when it was over. The anti-Philby people clearly won out. That was Bill Harvey's doing. When Hugh tells the story, and I think he will if you ask him, he'll pretend to be half-fond of Harvey. He has to. By now, we're just about certain that Philby was working for the KGB. So Hugh has to say half-decent things about Harvey. Don't believe him. He hates Bill Harvey."

Then why am I being sent to Berlin? I wanted to ask.

"All the same," said my father, as if I had in fact spoken aloud, "Berlin's a good idea. I *will* write that letter. You could use some roughing up. Bill Harvey's the man to give it to you."

With that, I was left to turn in for the night. There were two single beds in the next room and sheets and blankets of a sort. I lay there listening to my father cry out from time to time in his slumber, a short barking sound, and I finally slept in a half-coma which commenced with visions of Bill Harvey through Kittredge's eyes. She had certainly described him once. "We know a man in the Company, awful person, who carries a handgun in a shoulder holster even when he comes to dinner. Isn't that so, Hugh?"

"Yes."

"Harry, he's built like a pear, narrow shoulders and a relatively thick middle. His head's the same way. Pear-shaped. He has goggle eyes. An absolute frog, this man, but I couldn't help noticing—he has the prettiest little mouth. Small and nicely curved. Very well shaped. A glamour-girl's mouth in a toad's face. That sort of thing gives even more clues to Alpha and Omega than the right and left side of the face."

Had it been Bill Harvey who confronted me at the edge of sleep? I had a curious experience that night, and it was far from wholly unpleasant. I felt West Berlin coming nearer to my life. My first foreign tour awaited me. Even this grim safe house with its olfactory echo of old cigarettes and wet cigar butts, its memories of men waiting for other men to arrive, was a harbinger of the years to come. My loneliness could serve much purpose. The mean appurtenances of our gray apartment, spectral by the streetlight that came through the window shades, as brown by now as old newspapers, gave me a sense of why my father chose to stay here rather than at a hotel. A safe house was the emblem of our profession, our monk's cell. Perhaps that was why my father had produced the transparent fiction that this was a friend's apartment. In the act of penetrating his cover story, I would see a safe house with eyes of discovery. Many a rendezvous in West Berlin would look like this, I supposed, and I was to prove right.

Let me describe the bizarre vanity of the meditation that followed. Lying in this habitat, I felt equipped to travel through dark spaces and engage in deeds not free of the odor of burning sulphur. A few feet away was my father's troubled body, and I, sensitive to the specters that would bring a man as strong as himself to cry out in barking sounds as though to warn off nocturnal enemies, thought of my old taste for caverns, including that underground city of excavated rooms whose plans I had drawn as a boy. That brought me to contemplate once more the cavern in my own head. It had been left in place of whatever half-formed monsters of harsh tissue or imperfect flesh had been uprooted from my brain. Did that unfilled volume now draw me toward many a strange situation I would yet encounter?

At that moment I thought of Harlot with whole admiration. He believed that our work could shift the massive weight of historical drift by the only lever our heavens had given us, the readiness to dare damnation in our soul. We were here to challenge evil, negotiate its snares, and voyage out into devious activities so far removed from the clear field of all we had been taught that one could never see the light at the end of such a crooked tunnel. Not when one was in the middle.

On just this thought, I fell asleep. I did not know that my reverie had produced a kind of revelation. The larger-than-life secret of West Berlin alluded to on this night was nothing less than a fifteen-hundred-foot tunnel dug in holy secrecy, under Harvey's supervision, into East Berlin for the purpose of tapping Soviet military headquarters' long telephone lines out to Moscow.

14

I WAS TO HEAR MORE ABOUT BILL HARVEY BEFORE I LEFT. HARLOT NOT only provided me with a full account of the fateful party in Washington that Kim Philby threw for Guy Burgess, but entrusted me—even as my father had predicted—with all the fathoms-deep hush-hush about William King Harvey's tunnel. That, I thought, was a true farewell gift: Harlot was taking me into the inner house of the Company.

I flew from Andrews Air Force Base to Tempelhof in West Berlin on a Douglas C-124. A fat, four-motor Globemaster called "Old Shakey," it shook like an old radiator. You mounted this plane from a ramp in the rear, and those twenty of us who were on our way to Europe, Air Force personnel for the most part, were sent up into the cargo well, forward of the vehicles and crates that would be loaded on after. Strapped into our seats, we faced to the stern and looked down on cargo whose neatly packed contents took up considerably more room than ourselves, and seemed, by comparison, more respected in treatment.

The flight took nine hours to Mildenhall, in England, where we stopped for another nine hours before moving on to Mannheim and Berlin. I was on that plane, or waiting for it to go up again, a total of twenty-four hours, and the interior was unheated, and had no view. I stared at electrical cables on the cabin walls. It was the longest trip.

After attempts to read in the poor cabin light had failed, and conversation with men on either side of me had ground down (for I was discovering again how circumscribed was conversation with people who were not in the Agency), I reached at last, somewhere in the middle of the night, an island of contemplation sufficiently removed from the grinding of the airplane's motors and the vibration of the cabin to allow me to dwell on my last memory of Washington, a farewell dinner with Harlot, again at Sans Souci.

He told anecdotes all night, filling me in on what he obviously considered the true flavor of the Company. Yes, Herrick, went his presentation, you have discovered after all that training with motley instructors, and demoralizing days on the files that, yes, we plod, we mess up, we go in circles, we expand too quickly here, and are out of it there, but it's the people who count, the one hundred, two hundred, at most five hundred people, who are the active, lively *nerve* of the Company. All those thousands of others are but the insulation we need, our own corps of bureaucrats there to keep the other Washington bureaucracies away from us. At the center, however, it can be splendid.

"The only real problem," he said, looking into his brandy, "is to spot the Devil when you see him. One must always be on the lookout for someone like Kim Philby. What a devil! Have I ever given you the go on Harvey's night at Philby's party?"

He knew he hadn't. He was launching another anecdote. It may
have been the Hennessey, but a vein in Harlot's forehead began to
throb prominently. "I don't know," he said, "if any Englishman who
came over here from MI6 or the British Foreign Office was ever more
popular than Kim Philby. A good many of us got to know him around
London during the war, and we took up the friendship again when he
arrived in 1949. We used to have the best lunches. He was shy with
strangers because of that frightful stammer, but such an agreeable man.
Something *sandy* about him, the hair, the jacket, the old speckled
pipe. He drank like a loon, never showed it. You have to respect that.
It suggests an intensity of purpose when you can handle all that drink.
Harry, I forswear sentimental exaggeration, but Kim Philby had a
quality the English do produce in many of their best people. It's as if
their own person embodies everything that's first rate about their
country. And, of course, we had the word. Kim Philby was bound to
head up MI6 one of these days.

"Now, it wasn't altogether as good-fellow as that. During the
war, MI6 used to treat us as if we OSS were good-natured oafs who
did well to kneel at the feet of British savvy. They gave us a hard,
snobby time. 'You chaps may be the plutocrats, but, don't you know,
we still have this.' And they would lay a finger to their temple. We
were awfully in awe of them. We were so young at Intelligence.
When Philby came to Washington in '49, it was still like that. We
were expanding the Company every day, and it was obvious the
British were going to end up in our shadow, but, oh, that little nod
of the head, that paper-thin smile. They had it. I used to study Kim
Philby. Such filigree. There was his poor country to our wealthy one,
and him stammering half the time, yet even the best of us felt a
competitive minus when we had to go face to face.

"The thing about Kim—my God, just in saying his name I discover I'm still egregiously fond of Philby—is that he was audacious.
True wit resides in audacity. You have to know when to break away
from the book move. After the British Foreign Office sent Guy
Burgess to Washington as First Secretary, Philby invited Guy to move
in with him. Now, looking back on it, I still don't comprehend how
the Russians dared to work with Burgess. He had to be the most
improbable KGB asset. He was, as you may have heard, a holy, roaring
mess, a homosexual of the worst sort, a bully on the prowl for slender
fellows ready to turn queer. 'I'm going to *plunder* you,' is the kind of
look that came off Guy Burgess. You did not measure his drinking by

glasses, but by bottles. He also smoked like a Rube Goldberg filthy-nicotine machine. Besides which, he wore white clothes considerably clotted with his last half-dozen meals. He was half as grand as Randolph Churchill, and had manners absolutely as *bad*. One has to expect Englishmen from good families to be awful with waiters. I think they are seeking to pay back all those Scotch nannies who used to shovel porridge into their mouths. But Burgess was the worst. 'See here, you bloody fucking fool,' he would bellow at the nearest waiter, 'are you a cretin, or merely presenting yourself as hopelessly inadequate?'" Hugh, imitating Burgess, spoke loudly enough to have embarrassed us if Sans Souci had been empty, but dinner clamor was our security.

"Philby would always reassure us, 'Guy has been suffering through the most frightful aftereffects of his car accident, poor Guy.' Philby would say, 'Guy is talented, but his head is b-b-b-banged-up, you see.' Philby made it sound like a war wound. The loyalty of one Brit for another!

"Well, enter Bill Harvey. He had the curious luck to be invited to Philby's one night in spring 1951 for a large dinner. Everybody was there, Harvey, Burgess, hoards of us and our ladies. J. Edgar Buddha almost came, but then he heard about Harvey's being invited and did not show. Bill Harvey, to bring you a little more into the picture, was at that time very much en route to becoming our in-house pet. Since then, he's become considerably more than a toy. But at that time, we loved him. We'd taken him up. His handshake was even clammier than his pistol butt, but he was our FBI man. To get started in business, we had, of course, done our best to raid the Bureau, and signed on a few of their agents, among whom Harvey was the cream. You know, he'd helped snag the Rosenbergs. J. Edgar Buddha never forgave him for quitting the marble halls of Justice to come over to us. Then to make matters worse: Harvey, what with old contacts at FBI, was obtaining a lot of back-drawer information from the Bureau that we could use. FBI deserved no less. They had been poaching on CIA jurisdictions in six or seven countries along about then. In fact, they were hoping to kill us in our infancy. It was inhumane! Why, Allen Dulles could hardly get through to Buddha on the phone. 'Tell me,' he once asked Hoover, 'what is CIA doing to offend you so?'

" 'Mr. Dulles,' J. Edgar replies, 'tell Bill Harvey to quit pinching our stuff.'

"Well, that puts Harvey into our graces. Naturally, Philby invites Bill and his wife, Libby, to dinner. Bill Harvey was married to Libby then. I could have warned Philby not to give such an invitation. I was not sanguine about the social prospects. When you put a *plain* like Bill Harvey alongside a *fancy* like Guy Burgess, Heaven may not be able to help.

"Well, we all start drinking. Harvey can go round for round with Burgess. So can Libby. Harvey's wife is out of Indiana or Kentucky, some agricultural *seat,* a sexy-mousy girl with no presence at all, I fear, except for a huge horse-laugh that's so bad it could only belong to a duchess. No scullery maid would ever be allowed to *guffaw* in such fashion. Whoopee! We all get five yards under. It's a revel. Harvey has been boasting up and down Foggy Bottom that he has had sexual intercourse every day of his life since some such tender age as twelve. So help me. If it can't be his wife, he implies, it might be *yours*. And Libby is not only kissing everyone at the party—'Here's mud in your eye,' she keeps yelling—but is also carrying on with, of all people, Guy Burgess. Guy even takes his hands off the boy he's towed along to play bumper-cars with her rump. Under it all, is this desperate, pervasive wash of what I call *social sorrow*. It's insufficiently recognized as one of the major passions. Harvey and Libby are full of *social sorrow* because in relation to the rest, they know damned well that no amount of rump-bumping is going to lower the real barriers.

"Burgess starts to brag about his powers as a caricaturist. 'Draw me,' asks Libby. 'Oh, I'll do that, darling,' says Burgess. He makes a sketch of Libby. Shows it to me first. I pride myself on keeping a few wits together—but I tell you, Harry, I wasn't able to say a word. Burgess drew Libby too well. There she is in an armchair with her legs apart, skirts up, her fingers right where they'll be—he's even drawn her pubic hair with detail. An expression on her face you can't mistake. It's how she must look at avalanche time. Burgess is a percipient devil!

"Now, just as I take this drawing in, Burgess whips it from my hand, and passes it around. Most people are decent enough to pop no more than a quick peek, but no one, by now, really wants to bury it. We've put up with a lot from Bill Harvey. We are, in fact, surprisingly ready to witness his woe. He walks across the room, intercepts the drawing, and—I thought his heart would burst. I also passed through an instant when I expected him to draw his gun. I could feel the impulse clear across the room. Holding on to himself with an effort of will worthy of a boa constrictor's embrace, he seizes Libby's hand— by now, she's seen the drawing, too, and is *wailing*—and walks out with her. I have never witnessed any look of hatred equal to the bolt Bill Harvey threw at Burgess. 'I wish,' says Bill, 'I wish . . .' He can't get it out. Then he does. 'Choke on a nigger's cock,' says Bill Harvey, and is out the door.

" 'The man has just given his blessing,' says Burgess.

"A month later Burgess is called back to London. From there he quickly decamps with Sir Donald Maclean for parts unknown, but, of course, it can be no place but Moscow. Maclean, also stationed in America, has had the most god-awful high clearance at Los Alamos. So, the question now was Philby. Could he possibly be working for the Soviets? We can't believe that. I tell you, he's too nice. I am hardly prepared, I'll confess to you. I even got out a three-page memo more or less to exonerate Philby. Noblesse oblige. I was less witting then. My memo also spoke of Burgess: I related that Guy joined us at lunch one day in a soiled white British naval officer's uniform, wholly unshaven, and proceeded to carry on about 'the damned exaggerations and over-claims in the technical data on American Oldsmobile's blood-sucking new Dynaflow transmission!' Burgess knows a lot about automobiles; he tells me as much. Also, Burgess brags of having been to bed on countless occasions with Philby's male secretary. It's virtually an FBI memo, those three pages. Gossip, no grit. But Philby, on balance, comes through my audit with more credits than debits.

"At this point, if not for Wild Bill Harvey, Kim might have weathered the storm. Possibly, given a few years, he could have worked back into MI6's good graces. Who, after all, ever heard of the KGB allowing two of their agents to live in the same house? Kim must be innocent of everything but bad judgment.

"Harvey, however, had his own memo to write. He had been putting together fifteen- and twenty-hour stretches on the files. That's always the other side of Harvey. Hard work. He was also pulling in whatever he could obtain from the best FBI counterintelligence. FBI had cracked a few Russian codes they were not about to share with us, but, old FBI buddies being what they are, Harvey did obtain one Soviet intercept that J. Edgar had been keeping under his monumental seat, and it made reference to a high British mole. The specifications fit Kim Philby well enough for the powers to accept Harvey's version rather than mine. 'Take back your Philby and try him,' CIA tells MI6. Which they now had to do, much as they hated the prospect. Philby got a draw at his MI6 hearing. No incarceration, but was obliged to resign. Poor Kim. I say 'poor Kim,' and yet, if he's guilty, he's the worst of all. In fact, I've come to the most reluctant conviction that he was KGB all the while."

Harlot took bitter savor of the Churchill before adding, "I'm afraid it was generally accepted that Harvey had proved superior to me on this case. Do you know, it wasn't long before he accused your honorable godfather of being a Soviet agent. It's Alger Hiss time, don't forget. Joe McCarthy is getting his good start in life. The nicer your family antecedents, the worse, I must say, you now look. So I was asked to take a lie-detector test, and am fluttered all over the place, but pass. No incurable heart disease. And Harvey becomes one of our larger people. Why do I tell you this story?"

"I'm not sure I know."

"Because I wish to remind you one more time: The Devil is the most beautiful creature God ever made. Drink to Kim Philby, a consummate swine. Drink to your new Chief, God's own wild boar, King William, I do mean, William King Harvey. He's no Devil if beauty is the criterion."

PART TWO

BERLIN

1

Dix Butler came by in a Jeep to pick me up at Tempelhof Airport. Once again I would share accommodations with four Junior Officers, and Dix was one of them. A few blocks off the Kurfürstendamm, in what must have been a substantial neighborhood before the war, our apartment was on the fourth floor of a six-story edifice, the only habitation still standing on its side of the street. In the stairwell, elaborate moldings full of cracked plaster gave way to plasterboard walls at the higher landings. Parquet floors showed swatches of lino-leum. It was in accord with my first impression of Berlin—dusty, heavy, half-patched, gray, depressed, yet surprisingly libidinous. I felt depravity on every street corner, as real to me as vermin and neon lights.

I do not know if I can afford even one more reference to my sex life (which was still an empty ledger) but these days I was reacting to the presence of sex like a devil's imp in a sealed cylinder. As I came off the landing ramp from "Old Shakey," I had a unique experience. My first sight of the close-packed working-class streets surrounding Tempelhof produced an erection in me. Either the air or the architec-ture was an aphrodisiac, and panoramas of West Berlin went flying by the window like wartime newsreels of bombed cities. I saw buildings in every stage of restoration or demolition, half-destroyed, or going up in rubble-cleared lots that revealed the sheared-off backs of build-ings from the next street. Billboards, bulldozers, cranes, trucks, mili-tary vehicles, were everywhere. It seemed one year after the war, not ten.

As we drove along, Dix was discursive. "I like it," he said. "West Berliners have the quickest minds I ever ran into. New Yorkers are nothing compared to these people. I was trying to read a German newspaper on a park bench the other day, and this small neat dude in a pinstripe suit, professional type, is sitting across from me. He speaks up in perfect English, 'See that policeman over there?' I look. It's a cop, one more hefty Kraut. 'I see him,' I say. 'What's it to you, pal?' 'I bet,' says the stranger, 'that cop shits like an elephant.' Then he goes back to his newspaper. *Berlin,* Hubbard. They can tell you how the cop squats. Compared to them, we are sparrows picking seeds out of the horse-balls, and the horse manure is everywhere. It's all ex-Nazis. General Gehlen who runs BND for the West Germans is one. He used to be financed by us."

"Yes," I said, "I know that." Was it ten years ago, sitting at lunch at Twenty-One, that my father had spoken of a German general who had been able to strike an agreement with U.S. Army Intelligence after the war? "Yes, I heard of him," I said.

"He also," said Butler, "got the word out to all the fellow ex-Nazis who worked with him on the Russian front. A lot of those guys jumped at the chance to find a good-paying job in postwar Germany. After all, the work is easy now. Anybody in your family who finds himself in the East Zone can furnish you information. But that's all right. Analyze the SSD, and you'll find East German Communists running it at the top, and half the Gestapo underneath. It's all bullshit, friend, and I'm having the time of my life."

Butler did not offer a word on what my work might be. I was left to discover such details bit by bit. For my first few days in Berlin I was occupied with obtaining accreditation for my cover job, and a cryptonym: VQ/STARTER. Considerable time was left to spend in our once-grand and now cavernous apartment. The furnishings depressed me. The bed in which I slept had a monumentally heavy mattress, as damp as an old cellar, and the pillow bolster could have been mistaken for a log. I could see why Prussians had stiff necks. The substantial if leaky throne in the bathroom was two-tiered, offering a flat shelf within the bowl. Not since infancy had one been obliged to pay so much attention to what one had just accomplished, a testament, I decided, to the love of civilized Germans for primitive studies.

My cover job proved so clerical I hesitate to describe it—I had a desk in a Department of Defense supply unit and was expected to show up once a day to make certain that no papers requiring real administrative disposition had by any mischance been routed through me. The quarters were cramped, not so cramped as the Snake Pit, but tight enough for my relatively empty desk to look inviting to more legitimate workers. Before long they began to take squatter's rights.

By the second week, not only my drawers but my tabletop was being appropriated. Warned in advance that CIA personnel working in State Department or Department of Defense offices inspired resentment, I was still not ready for the intimacy of the irritations. By the end of the second week, I made a point of sweeping from my desk all the unauthorized paperwork, and dropping it into one large carton which I left in the aisle when I went out to lunch. There was a hush in the room as I returned.

That afternoon, a committee of three approached me. Following a twenty-minute conference on the merits of the situation, my desk was divided, by mutual agreement, into zones as fully demarcated as Berlin under four-power occupation.

Our treaty probably worked better than most, but no one in this office was ever at ease with me again. It hardly mattered. I needed no more than a place where people whom I could not inform of my real work might get in touch by phone or mail.

My more legitimate labors were performed *Downtown*. That was the name of a shed surrounded by barbed-wire fence, one of the numerous Company offices. The rest were located, by no particular logic I could untangle, all over the city, including Chief Harvey's home, a large white stucco house which not only doubled as an office but, under heavy sentry guard, was fenced about and sandbagged. Its machine-gun emplacements trained fields of fire down the neighboring streets. The place was certainly a redoubt, and might have kept the flag flying for a few hours if the Russians came over from East Berlin.

I spent my first week on the telephone at Downtown, aspiring in my intensely crammed German to pick up surveillance reports from the doorman, the barman, the headwaiter, and the *portier* of each leading hotel. In the beginning, it had not been routine for me to make a phone call on the basis of a quick orientation by a colleague— at last, I had colleagues!—and begin true spy work. So, for a time it was fun. Yes, the doorman at the Bristol, or the Kempinski, or the Am Zoo would tell me (usually in English considerably better than my German) yes, of the four people whose activities he had been asked to watch, Karl Zweig, for one, had stopped by in his Mercedes to pay a visit to room 232. The doorman would have the name of the occupant of room 232 when I called again that afternoon. Heady stuff. I felt as if I had, at last, entered the Cold War.

After a few days of checking twice daily through my long list of headwaiters and barmen for their pieces of information, the task brought my early enthusiasm down to the sober responses we bring to a chore. Nor could I always divine whether Karl or Gottfried or Gunther or Johanna was East German or West German, one of ours or one of theirs. If the barman had overheard a conversation of interest, I had to dispatch a memo to the appropriate desk. A case officer with more experience than myself would be sent out to debrief the bartender. Indeed, I did not even know yet whether this was done by way of a drink, or both men repaired to a safe house. Be it said that Dix Butler was doing such work. My new ambition was to get off the telephone (where I was beginning to feel like a man who sold space for classified advertising) and get out, be a street man.

On I stayed, however, at my telephone for ten days, until a call came for me to report to FLORENCE at VQ/GIBLETS. VQ/GIB-LETS, I knew already, was Base Chief William King Harvey's home, the white stucco fort I had heard so much about. Harvey, as my colleague on the next telephone informed me, thought of this well-guarded house as Little Gibraltar, or Giblets, and FLORENCE was "C.G."—Clara Grace Follich was her name. She was William King Harvey's new wife.

"Wonder what it's about?" I asked.

"Oh, you're on the Ivory Soap trolley," he said. "C.G. gets around sooner or later to all the new people on base. Looks them over."

I learned quickly enough about the trolley. C.G. had been a major in the WACs and administrative assistant to General Lucien Truscott. Now married and semiretired, she watched over the maintenance of the safe houses. She and I took a tour of Berlin that day in a modest van with no identifying flag or marks, and I carried towels and sheets and toilet paper and caustic cleansers, plus beer and wine and bread and sausage and cartons of cigarettes and boxes of cigars up flights of stairs or in and out of old elevators with clanging gates, and took out soiled towels and sheets (leaving food remains and trash and empty bottles for the chambermaid), and so serviced something like seven safe houses in as many neighborhoods. If three of them were new and clean with Swedish blonde-wood furniture and picture windows in new apartment houses, four looked just like the seedy stained-carpet hideout my father had taken me to in Washington.

C.G. was not a woman with much small talk, but then you were rarely in doubt of where her mind might be. She had a practiced hand at taking inventory of what was left in each safe house, and I noticed that she gave a different knock to each entrance door before inserting her key, presumably to alert any case officer inside who might be debriefing an agent. At no place, however, on this day was there a response. Seven safe houses, empty of occupants, were in this fashion processed.

"I know what you're thinking," she said when we were done. "That's a lot of safe houses to be lying idle."

"I guess I was telling myself something like that."

"When we need them, we really need them."

"Yes, Major."

"You didn't see any chambermaids today, Hubbard?"

"No, ma'am."

"If you had, you would have noticed that they are not spring chickens. Can you tell me why?"

"Well, if one of our agents has to hole up for a few days, and the chambermaid is young, he might get into a relationship."

"Please expand on that."

"Well, suppose one of the KGB agents who are trained lovers"— we had been given orientation about such KGB agents—"was to exercise a hold on the chambermaid, why, the KGB could obtain all kinds of access to the safe house."

"Believe it or not," she said, "you're one of the few juniors to understand that right from the get-go."

"Well, I think I've had more than the average background," I volunteered. "My father is an old OSS man."

"Hubbard? Not *the* Cal Hubbard."

"Yes, Major."

"My husband knows your father."

"My father has a lot of respect for your husband." All the while, I was wondering if Cal had sent his letter. I decided he had. There was something in the way she said, "Not *the* Cal Hubbard."

"I'm going to talk to my husband about you," C.G. added.

No call to visit the Chief came back over the next week. In compensation, my work grew more interesting. Another Junior Officer came to us from the States. Since I was senior to him, if only by two weeks, he was soon on my telephone, and I was moved to agent traffic, where I kept a log on which Communist officials were traveling back and forth from Poland, Czechoslovakia, and East Germany to East Berlin. This involved using agents' reports, and so offered a good picture of our network of observers in East Berlin: taxi drivers, newsstand operators off the Unter den Linden, the Friedrichstrasse, and the Stalin Allee, our East Berlin police—how many Vopos were in our pay!—our East Berlin hotel personnel, even a towel boy in the one important East Berlin brothel. This variety of input was fortified by daily reports from just about every established madam in West Berlin. In 1956, there was as yet no Berlin Wall, and so officials from the Eastern bloc were always crossing over for an evening of adventures in the West!

These were passive networks. Any recruiting of new agents was beyond the purview of my job: I could not even say whether the information we collected went back to Washington and the Document Room, or whether our people in West Berlin were already implementing new actions because of what was learned that day.

A call came through at last. VQ/BOZO wished to see me. VQ/BOZO was William Harvey. As was VQ/GIBLETS-1. As was VQ/COLT. The cryptonym changed with the place where you were going to meet Mr. Harvey. VQ/GIBLETS-1 was the private office in his home; VQ/BOZO his main office off the Kurfürstendamm; and VQ/COLT was the turnaround in back of his house. He had had the tennis court paved in asphalt to provide a quick turnaround for vehicles and limousines. Should the message be signed off as VQ/COLT, one had to be ready to tear up in one's Jeep, jump out, and leap into Harvey's moving (and armored) Cadillac. Of course, that did not always happen. I had heard stories about juniors like myself who dashed over to the tennis court on the call from COLT, whipped out of their vehicle on arrival, jumped into his Cadillac, and then waited forty-five minutes for Chief to saunter out of GIBLETS (which villa, I add, even bore a physical resemblance to him when he wore, as he usually did, his bulletproof vest). Still, there could be that one time when you came roaring up twenty seconds late.

Today, in the main office at BOZO, it would be easier. Many were scheduled to see him. How many was another matter. Installed in a private cubicle, the size of a walk-in closet, you waited in isolation until your call came; then you were led by a secretary down an empty corridor to his door. The idea, presumably, was that none of us, new arrivals, case officers, American officials, and/or West German officials were supposed to get a look at one another.

Waiting in that cubbyhole, I tried to prepare myself. I had been warned that Mr. Harvey would probably be sitting behind his large desk with his coat off, the butts of his two revolvers poking from his shoulder holsters. It was also legend, however, that he would never appear in public without his jacket, no matter how hot the day. Sweat might lave his cheeks like water on a horse's belly, but FBI training gave you decorum forever; he was not about to expose those shoulder holsters to the public.

I had also been warned that soon after meeting him, he might take out either gun, spin the cylinder, remove the bullets, pull back the hammer, aim in your direction, and click the trigger. My father had remarked that only an ex-FBI man could be party to such opera.

On the other hand, we were all, by Mr. Harvey's orders, obliged to carry firearms when out on an operation, no matter how minor. The Russians, it was estimated, had pulled off twenty kidnappings in West Berlin over the last year. Of course, the victims were Germans. The KGB had not abducted any Americans, no more than we had trafficked with them, but if the Soviets were going to break this rule, it seemed to be Harvey's assumption that he was the man they would choose.

I was not old enough to know how pervasive such a fear could become. All I felt, when led into his office, was his power to intimidate. There were enough firearms on the wall to fill a gallery in a museum. Harvey sat at his desk, a phone to his ear, vest unbuttoned, the butts of two revolvers growing like horns out of his armpits. Wide in the middle, he looked heavy enough to waddle when he walked, and he reeked of gin and Sen-Sen tablets.

Nonetheless, he gave an impression of strength. Rage came off him. He hung up the phone and looked at me with one full wad of suspicion. I had the instinct to guess that he looked at each new man in the same way. We knew more than we were supposed to know, and he wanted to find out what it was.

Of course, he was right. A moment later, I knew exactly how much knowledge was too much. I had been told of the Berlin tunnel, and I knew about Guy Burgess' drawing of his ex-wife, Libby. I had once been KU/CLOAKROOM. I had reason to feel uncomfortable.

Harvey nodded. A cop has his preferences, and one of them is to meet people who are aware of his force. By looking uneasy, I had just passed the first test. From those small, well-curved lips, advertised in advance by Kittredge, issued his voice, a low, resonant burble. I had to lean forward in my seat to hear Base Chief Harvey speak.

"My wife says you're okay," he stated.

"Oh, she's a fine lady," I answered quickly. Too quickly. His suspicion of me was in order: My instinctive reflex was to lie to William Harvey. C.G., I had already decided, was from the Midwest, and there is a prejudice buried as deep as a taproot in the Hubbard fold. Midwesterners can have their share of virtues, but the fine ladies are all accounted for by the time western Massachusetts reaches New York State.

All the same, C.G. had approved of me. I was enough of a slop to think it was one of the best things about her. Then I took a second look into Harvey's protruding bloodshot eyes. I was dealing with no ordinary husband. Jealousy was as natural to him as bread and butter.

It was ill founded. For all her friendliness, C.G. sent out one clear instruction: She was a married woman. Of course, I was not about to try to tell him this. I had just noticed on top of each of the three large safes in this office three prominent thermite bombs. At his right hand was a panel with many buttons. Within his drawer must be other buttons. On the desktop were a red phone and a black-and-white-striped phone that looked not unlike a landing craft just come in from Mars. I did not know which one of these buttons and instruments could trigger the thermite bomb device, but it was evident to me that the room could be set ablaze in two-fifths of a second.

"Yeah, kid," he said, "she likes you." He breathed a bit heavily, his eyes fixed on me with the intentness that accompanies a man who wants to take a drink but is holding off. "She don't like many."

"Yessir."

"Do not say 'yessir' around me unless you're feeling insubordinate. 'Yessir' is what people say when they think you're full of shit, but are still ready to put their tongue up your ass."

"Okay," I managed to get out.

"I called you in here for a talk. I need a couple of juniors to do a couple of jobs for me. But I'd rather find such capability in one amateur, not two."

I nodded. I had never wanted to say "Yessir" so much in my life.

"C.G. seems to think you can do it, so I looked up your 201. The training grades are respectable. For me there's only one beeper in your file. You went from training to Technical Services but no *saddlebags* come with your 201." That was the fearful word I had been awaiting. Saddlebags were cryptonyms. "What the hell did you do at Technical Services?" he asked.

"Well, Mr. Harvey, I didn't get an assignment, so in a short while

I was transferred to the course in Intensive German. There was never a need for me to pick up a cryptonym."

"It's off-chart to land in Intensive German before you even know where you're going to be assigned. I'd hate to dive into Kraut-talk and end up in the Philippines." He burped. "In fact, language is not the initial necessity here at Base. Let's remember that we won the war, not the Heinies. You can get along with *poco* German. I do."

He did. I may have just met him, but for the last two weeks the pool had been informing me: Harvey's German was one of the best jokes at Base. He held up the revolver for the first time, and aimed to the left of my ear. "Seems to me, you knew you were coming here."

"Well, Mr. Harvey," I said in reply, "I had reasons to think so."

"What allowed you to know more about your future than Personnel?"

I hesitated, but only to make the point. "I was given the idea by my father."

"The old family fix?"

"Yessir."

" 'Yessir?' You're feeling insubordinate, huh?" he chuckled. The sound was raspy and full of phlegm, like an automobile starter kicking around. "Let me hand it to your father," he declared. "The Oh-So-Socials may not run as much of the Company as they used to, but your father hangs in. I guess he can still get his son assigned where he wants."

"He seemed to think Berlin was where I should be."

"Why?"

My cheeks were red. I hardly knew what turn to take. "He said that's where the action is."

"Hubbard, did your father tell you anything about VQ/CATHETER?"

"I don't know who or what that is." I didn't, which was just as well. Bill Harvey seemed to receive one's verbal output with as much close metering as a polygraph machine.

"I don't believe you do," he said. "Good."

In the next moment, however, I divined that VQ/CATHETER might be a cryptonym for the Berlin tunnel. It was not considered good procedure to go in for analogical or poetic connections between the operation and the cryptonym, but I could see where VQ/CATHETER would be exactly to King William's taste.

Whereupon, he looked me over once more, and said, "Is your

yap able to maintain itself within allowable parameters?"

"I'm closemouthed. My cousins accuse me of being a bit of a clam."

He broke out the revolver beneath his left arm, opened the chamber, removed the bullets, rotated the cylinder, replaced the bullets, closed the breech, and stuck it back in his holster. The butt of the handle looked out at me again from his armpit. He had done it all with an easy delicacy, as if it were the equivalent of a tea-pouring ceremony.

"I'm going to use you," he said. "You're not smart enough yet for the street, but I've perused some of the stuff you've done on our hotel people. You show a sense of network. Not everybody has that."

"Check."

"You can say 'yessir' if you want to."

"Yessir."

"When it gets on my nerves, I'll let you know."

"Righto."

"What did they tell you Downtown? About what I need?"

No one had told me anything. I had the feeling, however, that I would do well to reply. "They said you needed a gofer. A good gofer."

"I need a great one, but I'll settle for a good fellow."

"If you're thinking of me, I'll do my best."

"Listen to a job description first. My gofer doesn't go out for coffee. He goes along for the ride."

"Sir?"

"He sits next to me in my bulletproof ultra-high-steel-alloy Cadillac, which, when it comes to resisting Soviet armor-penetrating XRF-70s, is no more bulletproof than ultra-high-alloy wet newspaper."

"Yessir."

"You can get killed sitting next to me. Those Soviet rockets do the job. And their look-alike for our bazooka does not look like us at all. Their bazooka telescopes down into a cylindrical case about the size of a 300mm telephoto lens. Read me?"

"I think so."

"Expatiate."

"A terrorist could dress himself up to look like a photographer. At an intersection, he could open his case, extend his bazooka, and hit your car."

"With you sitting next to me."

"Yessir."

He began to chuckle. Once again phlegm revolved in his throat. Despite myself, I thought of the taffy you see in an amusement-park mixing machine. When it was up to texture, he hawked it neatly into a handkerchief and lit a cigarette. His hands were the equal of his delicate mouth, and cupped the cigarette with finesse, two fingertips bringing the moist end to his cupid's-bow lips which pursed forward to suck in a full measured heartbeat of smoke.

"When the car door is opened," said Harvey, "you will not always step out before me. Sometimes I will go first. Why?"

"I don't have an answer."

"The flunky gets out first. The sniper, if there is one, will be waiting for the second man. What do you say to that, Hubbard? Are you afraid of buying an explosive bullet in a vulnerable area?"

"No, sir."

"Take a good look at me. Do I appear to be the kind of man you want to die sitting, or standing, next to?" He said this so quietly that I was, indeed, leaning across the desk.

"You wouldn't believe me if I told you it was an honor."

"Why?" he persisted.

"Given your achievements, Mr. Harvey, the personal sacrifice would not be meaningless."

He nodded. "You're twenty-three?"

"Yessir."

"You get down to essences fairly well for a kid. If you want to know the truth, I told my wife to take a look at you because I liked the way you wrote your reports. You're not getting this job because my wife likes you, but because I think you can help me. You can finish up what you're doing Downtown, then take the junior who came in after you, groom him into what you've been carrying, and figure to start with me next Monday, at this office, 9:00 A.M." He put a finger on either side of his nose as if to center his thoughts. "Drop your German course. Put your time for the next few days into hand-gun work. We have an arrangement with the Army to use their pistol range in the NCO Club. Get in some hours before Monday." He stood up to shake hands with me, then lifted his leg and farted. "The French got a word for it," he said.

2

I GROOMED MY REPLACEMENT SO CONSCIENTIOUSLY THAT BY THE END of the week, he was carrying out my old tasks as well as myself. Perhaps better—his German was better. Religiously, I went each morning to pistol practice, and began to believe that I might yet become a decent shot. I had fantasies that Mr. Harvey would run into an ambush from which he would be rescued by the path cleared to safety through the ice-cold aim of my pistol.

Nine A.M. on Monday morning I reported to Base Chief's office in BOZO, ready for the job, but I did not ride out in his black Cadillac that day. No call came. I stayed at my new desk, which was as innocent of work papers as my first desk at the Department of Defense; the next glimpse I had of Mr. Harvey was not until Tuesday afternoon when he passed in the aisle, saw me, grunted in displeasure, as if to say, "What in hell will we do with you?" and moved on quickly. Wednesday, I did not see him at all. I found myself on the phone talking to my replacement about the networks in East Berlin. I was homesick for Downtown.

Thursday afternoon Mr. Harvey came along at a hard fast rolling gait down the hall, saw me again, wagged a thumb for me to follow, and I sat beside him at last in the rear seat of the Cadillac. There had been no time to pick up my overcoat, and the February air was cold whenever I had to get out of the car to walk with him into another office.

He was having a vendetta with the State Department, and so had taken every opportunity to spread our Base functions into more and more abodes around West Berlin. While we still had a substantial wing at the Consulate, where the bulk of our administrative work was done (which meant that most of our employees were still there), his contempt for the place was in the code name he used, the Ukraine. "Tell the top asshole over in procurement—what's his name?"

"Ferguson," an assistant would say.

"Tell Ferguson to get going on that tape order."

Besides the Ukraine, we had Downtown, and BOZO, and GIBLETS, and seven safe houses, and a translation mill off the English Garden called CRUMPETS, and one out at Tempelhof Airport in a warehouse near Customs labeled SWIVET (in recognition, I suppose, of how something was always going wrong at Customs). We also had more than a dozen subsidiaries to visit. Everything from an import-export bank to a sausage exporter. We got around. Traveling with Chief Harvey was close to my idea of what it must have been like to ride around with General Patton. Maybe George Patton lived in Bill Harvey's mind as well. My father told me once that Patton could measure the fighting morale of an outfit by driving his Jeep into their perimeter. On one occasion, visiting a field hospital, he had slapped a soldier who he believed was a malingerer. Something in the whine of the invalid's voice suggested to the General that the man was a carrier for a spiritual disease that would yet undermine the Third Army. "Patton had his instinct and was bound to act on it," my father said.

Harvey could always pick out what was wrong in an office. It might be a broken-down cable machine, a telephone switchboard, a secretary indisposed, or a section chief who was getting ready to resign, but Harvey took it in. "I want you to sign on for another two years in Berlin," he would say to the section chief, "we need you," and give the secretary an afternoon off as he was leaving. He would kick the cable machine, and sometimes it would start. He would pass eight juniors working in a corridor at eight jammed desks, stop at one, pick up a cable that had just come in, nod, say, "This operation is going to heat up in a couple of days—keep an eye on it," and move on. He was God, if God was not too tall, thick in the middle, and had goggle eyes. For that matter, God drank like a fish and hardly slept.

It took me a while to realize his virtue was often his vice. He was not efficient. If unable to decide a matter instinctively, he might never decide it. But what an instinct! One day in the Cadillac, he said to me, "I had a job to give you when I told you to come aboard. Now I've forgotten it." He stared at me, he blinked those bloodshot eyes most carefully, then he said, "Oh, yes, KU/CLOAKROOM."

"KU/CLOAKROOM, sir?"

"A loose end. It's been bothering the hell out of me. I need a bright young fellow to chase it down." He held up his hand at the look of full perplexity I was doing my best to offer.

"Let me fill you in," he said.

As I had discovered on the first ride, Mr. Harvey was depending on more than my pistol for his firepower. The driver had a shotgun on a mount between the front seats, and the security man in the passenger slot next to him held a Thompson submachine gun. I would hear more than once that a tommy gun was, for close range, Mr.

Harvey's weapon of choice. "Part of my FBI heritage," he would inform you. Now, as if he had already said too much in hearing of the others, Chief Harvey pressed a button to raise the glass divider behind the front seat, then murmured in his low voice, "We have what could be a security problem. I'm putting you to work on the preliminaries."

"Terrific," I said.

"Just paper-chasing," he said. "Here's the summary. A Berliner named Wolfgang, a student, a Bohemian, one of our petty-fry, organized some street riffraff a couple of years ago to throw a few stones at the Soviet Embassy in Bonn. It made the wire services. Since then we assume that Wolfgang's been doubled."

"By the East Germans, or the KGB?"

"Probably East Germans. Half the Krauts on our payroll are also feeding the SSD. Take that for granted. It's all right. Half their Vopos are working for us. It's no big deal either way. A thousand small-fry cost more, if you try to check out all their stories, than the information is worth."

"I see." I was thinking of the work I had been doing the last few weeks.

"They're like insects," he said. "In quiet times, they feed in all directions. It's not worth watching. But if a swarm of insects suddenly start moving in unison, what do you deduct?"

"A storm is coming?"

"You have it, kid. Something big and military is on the way. If the Russians ever decide to take us out of West Berlin, we'll know in advance. That's what the small-fry are for—big clambakes." He reached forward, took a cocktail shaker out of an ice bucket, and poured himself a full martini. It was hard not to watch the way he held it, for his wrist reacted to every bump in the road with more subtlety than the car springs. The glass never lost a drop.

"All right," he said, "we keep in loose touch with Wolfgang, and he checks in periodically with us. As I say, petty-fry. I do not go to sleep at night thinking about Wolfgang. Not, that is, until we have a flap. VQ/CATHETER, as you've gathered, is our most sensitive area of security. I won't even allow the men who work on it to buy a chunk of strange."

"Chunk of strange?"

"A piece of ass. Too risky, security-wise. If any of them get into a one-night stand, they are on order to furnish a detailed report to Security in the morning. Well, there's one law of bureaucracy you can count on: The more you protect yourself against an eventuality, the more it will eventuate. One of our kids turns out to be a closet homosexual. He comes to us and admits to having sex with a German fellow. Name of the chunk: Franz. What does Franz look like? Young, insignificant, slim, dark. That description narrows it down to about four hundred East Berlin agents, West Berlin agents, and known double agents. We can muster photographs of most of this group. That's a large number of photographs to make our sissy-boy go through. We need him back at work. He's a specialist and we can't afford to lose his time. Except now he confesses to a little more. 'Yes,' he tells us, 'Franz did inquire about the work I do. Naturally, I wouldn't tell him a thing, but Franz wanted to know if my job had anything to do with VQ/CATHETER! Then, Franz says it's okay to talk to him because he has clearance from the Americans. He, too, is working with them!' "

This was worth a serious sip of the martini. "You better believe," said Harvey, "that we put our specialist through a sweat. He must have looked at three hundred photographs before he narrowed it down to Wolfgang. Wolfgang is Franz. So we pored through our log of the Thirty-Day Back-Index, and our Thirty-One-to-Sixty-Day Back-Index, and then the Sixty-One-to-One-Hundred-and-Twenty, and there's not one report has come in to us lately from Wolfgang. That can hardly be. Wolfgang used to be an active little punk. He liked being on retainer. Now, all we have are some chits which we have not yet paid because he's sent them in from Hamburg. Not Berlin. What develops, on examination, is the kind of administrative nightmare you're always fearing. Our files grew so quickly that we used up the space allotted for them. So some intermediate-level asshole at the Ukraine decided to fly the contents of the Thirty-, the Sixty-, and the Hundred-and-Twenty-Day Back-Index to Washington. All we had to do was rent one more building here, and we could have kept the stuff on hand, but the little lords of the budget do not allow that. Building rentals are local. Budgetarily speaking, you can't spend two dimes on rental when there's only one in the cup. Air freight, however, is another matter. Air freight is tucked into the Air Force budget, not ours. Air Force doesn't care what we spend. Billionaires do not make a count of their dishwasher's pimples. In consequence, a lot of files were sent off at one stroke of a pen by some incompetent in the Ukraine who did not check with my office. All he knew was that he had to find new file space for BOZO. He must have thought he was doing me a favor. Can you believe it? Whole branches and bags of potentially crucial material were air-freighted over to the Document Room back at Cockroach Alley in order to obtain a little more room here."

Another sip on the martini. "So we have to find Wolfgang. That faggot in CATHETER could have given more away to Wolfgang than he now cares to remember. Only Wolfgang can't be found. Is he dead, or underground? He does not contact his case officer. He responds to no signals. Maybe Wolfgang has slipped over to the East with news about CATHETER? It's a long shot, but I send a cable to the Snake Pit. Maybe they can find something on Wolfgang. Lo and behold, I get back a snotty reply. Just what I needed. 'Owing to conditions in the Document Room, et cetera . . .' Whoever sent it obviously did not realize the significance of a cable signed by a Chief of Station. I may be Chief of Base, not Station, but find me one Station in the world that counts for as much as Berlin Base. We are in the front line of the Cold War, except they don't seem to know that back in Foggy Bottom. They don't alert the newcomers to that fact. I am obliged to deal with bureaucratic backbiting in the shape of some indescribable turd named KU/CLOAKROOM. Ergo, I get ready to gun a few motors. I decide to blow KU/CLOAKROOM off the pot he is sitting on."

"Wow," I said.

"Nothing to what's on the menu next, kid. I ask West German Desk in Washington to supply me with the identity of this KU/CLOAKROOM and they come back with the news that Bridge-Archive will be *anti-forthcoming* for seventy-two hours. You count them. Seventy-two hours. It's due to a change in cryptonym. That son of a bitch CLOAKROOM knows he is in fucking trouble. I tell West German Desk to get Bridge-Archive to kick over the Seventy-two-hour Elapse and furnish *Immediate Translation*. Desk has to know I am angry. They send back a cable: WILL CONCUR. Only they can't. They can't concur. By procedure, they have had to move up to Bridge-Archive:Control, and someone there has put in a STOP. I can't believe it. I'm facing *forces*. Wolfgang is in hiding, his records are buried in the Document Room, CATHETER is conceivably endangered, and somebody who may just turn out to be a mole has put STOP on my search. I don't think there are twenty men in the Company who have sufficient clout to put STOP on me. Yet one of them has. Eighteen of those twenty, at the least, have to hate my guts for the best reason in the world. My family may not be quite up to the elevation of theirs (although it's good enough stock, thank you) but, God, kid, my brain works faster,"—and he emptied his martini glass and turned it upside down—"yes, STOP, when expanded properly, reads: STOP HARVEY."

He exhaled heavily. He glared at me. "Well," he said, "you have to know when the other side has won the first round. Whether it was done to frustrate me, to protect Wolfgang, which is the extreme and worrisome possibility, or to safeguard CLOAKROOM, who may be some kind of intermediary, I can see one thing: CLOAKROOM is now my target. Other answers will be obtainable once I get my hands on him." He sighed. "The trouble with being Chief of Base is that each week you get caught up in the crisis of the week. Other matters got me sidetracked. Besides, I know enough not to go up against Bridge-Archive:Control—Senior with half a deck. One needs to collect a few high cards. For one thing, if forces are protecting CLOAKROOM, they'll take him through two or three cryptonyms. In that kind of shell game, you have to be able to concentrate on your objective. I don't have the time. You do. As of now, you are promoted from gofer to junior troubleshooter."

I hesitated to speak. My voice might not be faithful. I nodded.

"We'll use a two-pronged attack," he said. "First, you crank up the West German Desk at the I-J-K-L. They're still on the titty. Total bureaucrats. They can't wait for spring to paper-bag their lunch around the Reflecting Pool. Those people are soft as plop. They respond to unrelenting pressure. Get them on the trail of CLOAKROOM's shift of saddlebags. It'll take time. They will want to drag their feet. So, you keep shoving it up their ass. Give a poke every couple of days. I'll throw in a nigger-dick from time to time. Bridge-Archive:Control may be able to lay a Seventy-two-hour Elapse on each new cryptonym for good old CLOAKROOM, but sooner or later they'll run out of holds."

"But as you said, won't they put it into Bridge-Archive:Control—Senior?" I had a moment of panic, wondering if he would think I was picking this up too quickly, but he was moving on.

"They will. Bridge-Archive:Control—Senior is inevitable. But by then, we ought to have some funny facts. We may lose at Senior— that's one committee I have minimal input with—but, all the same, we will have dropped a very bad smell in those marble halls. One egg-shaped fart, in fact, will be floating around in the perfumery. I'll teach those guys to fuck with me."

"Sir, may I speak frankly?"

"Save time. Just talk."

"If I understand, you are saying you will never obtain the name of CLOAKROOM. Whoever managed the changes is, you believe— as I follow you—a member of Senior. He will also be on the warpath by then. Is it okay for you to have a determined enemy when you can't even find out who it is?"

"Hubbard, you miss the point. Senior is not composed of cretins. They'll have a good idea at their end of who might be playing their game for them. And whoever it is will lose a few inches of height to his peers. That's my payback."

"Won't you lose also?"

"Kid, I invite anybody to trade punches with me. We'll see who's standing at the end."

"I have to hand it to you, Mr. Harvey. You're not timid."

"Working under Hoover, you pinned a little fear on your heart every morning when you went in to work. I got tired of that."

"What kind of man is J. Edgar Hoover?"

"A low, cowardly, ungrateful son of a bitch. Excuse me, I'm speaking of a great American." He burped and filled his martini glass again. "All right," he proceeded, "I said we were going to have a two-pronged attack. From one side, pressure all the way up to Senior; on the other, let's see how good your own network is."

"Sir?"

"I have a hunch that KU/CLOAKROOM is a recent trainee. He has to be. His cable was that stupid. You might even know him. I want you to get in touch with a few members of your training group at the Farm. Before long, you ought to be able to pick up a description of who was assigned to the Snake Pit."

I could feel perspiration starting behind my ears.

"I can obtain a couple of names," I said, "but will I be able to request their cryptonyms from Bridge-Archive? That looks like an odd request for a junior to put in."

"Candidly, it's not even comfortable for me to ask for too many cryps from Bridge-Archive. Not unless we score. And, of course, I don't know that in advance. I certainly don't want to attract beaucoup attention on a dud mission. But, kiddo, we won't go to Bridge-Archive. We'll use the Bypass."

"I'm not familiar with the Bypass," I said.

"You're not familiar with the name," he said, "but you're probably part of the process. None of you juniors ever admit to revealing your saddlebags to each other, yet half of you go around collecting them like autographs. Studies show: Half of the Americans in combat in the Second World War couldn't fire at an enemy soldier. Too much of the Ten Commandments in their nervous system. And half the new people in this cockeyed Company can't keep their own secret. Treachery comes with mother's milk." He reflected. "And father's bullshit." That was worth a sip. The martini glass did a dipsy-doodle over some bumps. "Just call in your favors," he said. "Get those saddlebags from your friends." He nodded. "By the way, what was yours?"

"You know that, Chief. It's VQ/STARTER."

"I mean, what was it in TSS? Don't keep trying to tell me that you didn't have one."

"I'm sorry, sir. I can't reveal it."

He nodded. "Wait'll we torture you," he said.

3

BERLIN, SEEN THROUGH THE DARK WINDOWS OF CHIEF HARVEY'S Cadillac, provided at high noon a vision of late afternoon shadow. The pale lots cleared of rubble, and the amputated backs of buildings presented themselves in hues of lavender-gray, the official tone for tinted glass in bulletproof limousines. It might be a sinister view of the world, but on this particular morning, I saw little enough of it. I was giving too much attention to each word Bill Harvey uttered.

As Mr. Harvey finished laying out those procedures I was to use for a venture that could only produce success by the final entrapment of myself, the voice to come out of my throat, if hoarse, did not betray me further. I felt not unlike the way I would soon feel on being able to get into bed with a woman for the first time. It might be strange, but sex was an activity I had been waiting to engage in for a long time.

A part of me told myself: "I was born to do this. Being a double agent is natural for me."

I was under no illusion that I was anything better. Hugh Tremont Montague and William King Harvey might serve the same flag, but I was already a different person for each of those men; that was the essence of the condition. To be a double agent working for West Germans and East Germans might be more dangerous, but whether BND against SSD, or Montague versus Harvey, one's balance was still equal to one's wit. An unholy stimulation.

Of course, my inner life had its ups and downs. Back at my desk, outright rage at the unfairness of things passed through me so intensely that I had to go to the men's room and pat cold water on my face. Yet in the mirror above the sink no strain showed. Looking back at me was the seamless Hubbard expression. My older cousin, Colton Shaler Hubbard, custodian of the family legends, once said, "With the exception of Kimble Smallidge Hubbard, and possibly your father, there's nothing particularly special about the rest of us. We're just about down there with *l'homme moyen sensuel*. Except for one faculty, Herrick. We Hubbards never show a thing. It's a bossy advantage, I tell you."

For practical purposes, he was right. In the midst of all this perturbation, an alert young man looked back at me from the mirror, life in my eyes, optimism on my mouth. I thought of other occasions when I had felt calm within, rested, and full of life, but my reflection appeared sullen, as if yesterday's fatigues were still on my skin. Could I assume that the agreeable face I now presented to the mirror was protective coloration? One did well to look lively when exhausted.

That night, ready to step away from a few of these concerns, I went out with Dix Butler. We made the rounds of his nightclubs. Over the last couple of weeks, I had traveled with him at night often enough to pick up a sense of how he worked. He had a contact in every club we visited. Of course, he had not recruited them, he had not been in Berlin long enough, and his German was inadequate for such a purpose, but his job put him on the scene. He served as a cutout between two of our case officers at BOZO and those of our German petty agents who could speak English. If Dix enjoyed full cover from one of our business subsidiaries, presenting himself to the natives as an American executive from an import brewery—"Just call me a beer salesman, Putzi,"—the staff at the clubs we visited had small illusion clouding their clear Berlin minds that Dix Butler, cover name Randy

Huff (for Sam Huff, the New York Giants linebacker), was anything but one more species of CIA man.

The axiom that intelligence officers and agents must be kept apart, inculcated in me throughout training, did not, as Dix warned, seem to apply in this milieu. Not only was he highly visible, but anyone who talked to him would come under suspicion from Germans who were anti-American. Since his agents did not seem to mind, I was certain most of his people had been doubled by the SSD.

Dix, however, was without concern. "It oughtn't to work, but it does," he said. "I get more information from my boys than any other officer, CIA or BND, working these streets."

"It's tainted."

"You'd be surprised. A lot of agents are too lazy to lie. They end up telling more than they're planning to. They know I can shake it from them if I have to."

"Dix," I began.

"Huff," he said, "is the name. Randy Huff."

"Everything you get from them is, at the least, steered by the BND."

"Put away the book. My people are earning a living. They're street stuff. Of course the BND runs them. You don't think West German Intelligence would encourage us to get down and dirty with any Kraut that didn't belong to them first? It's a comedy. Everybody is paying for information, the British, the French, the West Germans, the Soviets. We happen to be paying the most, so our job is the easiest. Take the subway and go over to East Berlin, to Café Warsaw. That's the place where they all hang out—agents, informers, contact men, cutouts, couriers, principals, even Russian and American case officers. Rodents go scurrying from table to table looking for the best price. West Berlin may be a spy market, but East Berlin is a bigger joke. Everybody is doubled and tripled. You can't even remember if they're supposed to be yours or theirs, and you know, buddy, it doesn't matter. They make up the stuff if they don't have it."

"Aren't you concerned that the SSD is polluting your input?"

"The SSD can't begin to pay what we do. Besides, I know who's working for them, and I know what to feed them." He was bored with this, just as bored as any lawyer giving legal information to his friends on Sunday. "Forget it, Charley Sloate,"—which happened to be my cover name at the Department of Defense desk—"just look at that redhead over there!"

We were in the Balhaus Resi at a corner of Grafenstrasse, and I am afraid it is exactly that legendary place where telephones sit on every table. You can call a woman across the room by dialing her table number. The process worked equally well in reverse, and our phone kept ringing. Women wished to speak to Dix. He was executive and cut off any female who could not converse in English. For those able, the advanced course was waiting.

"Angel," he would say, "wave your hand, so I'm certain I know whom I'm speaking to."

A blond lady across the room would now wag her finger into the smoke.

"You're fabulous," he would tell her. "Don't thank me. It's the truth." All this while, he would be drumming his knuckles on the table. "Helga. A nice name. And you say you are a divorcée. Good for you. Could you answer a question for me, Helga?"

"Yes?"

"Would you care to fuck?"

"Don't you get slapped a lot?" I asked him once.

"Yes," he said, "but I get laid a lot."

If Helga hung up, he would shrug, "One dried-up wildcat."

"What if she'd said yes?"

"I might have lubricated her screech."

Women did not always say no. He made dates for later. Sometimes he kept such dates. Sometimes his mood turned bitter at the very idea of women. He'd get to his feet and we would move to another club. At Remdi's, on Kantstrasse, the categorical imperative was to obtain a ringside table and use the fishing poles furnished by the management to lift pieces of loose clothing from the stripteasers. Homage to Immanuel Kant! We'd drop into the Bathtub on Nürnberger Strasse, a cellar pit for jazz, then on to the Kelch in Prager Strasse. There, a great many men dressed as women. I hated that, hated it with all the Puritanism lurking in the family blood, but Butler enjoyed it. Then we would move on. He was always in conversation, a hand on a girl's hip, a piece of paper going into his pocket from a waiter, a whisper from the hatcheck girl, a quick notation in his pad which he ostentatiously tore off to send to the bartender. Seeing how displeased I was at his technique, he began to laugh. "Go back to the manual on black propaganda," he said. "That bartender is working for the East Krauts. Pure SSD. I want to embarrass him."

So it went. One night out offered enough excitement to fire my fantasies for a month. Yet I went along on his rounds several times a week. I had never had such a sense of ferment in myself. I did not know if we were in a cellar or a zoo. Life was promising precisely because life had become dark and full of evil. We were in West Berlin and surrounded by Communist armies on all sides—we might live for a day or a century, but vice twinkled like lights in an amusement park. One night a middle-aged waiter said to me, "You think this is something now?" I nodded. "It is nothing," he said.

On impulse I asked, "Was more going on when the Nazis were here?"

The waiter looked at me for quite a while. "Yes," he said. "It was better then."

I was left wondering how it was better. At far-off tables, people might be depressed, but around us, a fever was rising. Dix's physical presence was never more overpowering than at 1:00 A.M. in a Berlin club. His features, merry and cruel, his blond hair, his height, his physical force, his clear-cut lust for plunder must have spoken to that other, victorious time when the dream of godlike power imbued with pagan magic lived in many a Berliner's mind. Dix always looked as if he had never been in a better place at a more appropriate time.

One might have supposed that with the number of women who came his way, I would have caught some of the overflow, but as I soon discovered, I was not ready. I had never been in so many situations to point out how terrified I was of women. I had always thought it was the best-kept secret of my life. I had even managed to hide it from myself. Now I was obliged to recognize that I was afraid of young ladies who looked no more than fourteen, and of women remarkably preserved at seventy, and we need not speak of the spectrum between. To know that some of these working girls, divorcées, single women, and wives on the loose wanted me aroused the same kind of panic I used to feel in my first years at the Buckley School when I did not know how to fight, and so believed I might be seriously injured for too little. Now it seemed to me as if sex were the fiercest human transaction of them all; one gave away large parts of oneself in order to receive one knew not what, and the woman could walk off with your jewels. Your spiritual jewels. I exaggerate my fear in the hope to explain it. When a woman sat next to me on those nights, I felt the most abominable, if well-concealed, panic. Something in my soul seemed about to be stolen. I might give away secrets God had entrusted to me. This was even more devout, I must admit, than the

Episcopalianism imbibed at St. Matthew's on the true force of Christ, courage, and responsibility.

On the other hand, I still felt competitive toward Dix Butler. I don't know if it was the cold showers of prep school, or the sinews in the family synapses, but it irked me not to be able to enter the lists against him on the field of female conquest. I wanted to be able to boast that I would yet be more of an artist at making love than Mr. Randy Huff, but the Hubbard common sense was also in my way; one reason I had until now been able to evade these terrors was due to the simple fact that in college I had spent my time paying attention to girls who for one reason or another were never available. This ironic light was now obliged to be cast as well on my love for Kittredge. A trapdoor had been opened to my dungeon. I hardly wished to come face to face with the depth of the problem now; it defaced the portrait I liked to keep of myself as a well-balanced young CIA officer.

I had to put some face, however, on this obvious rejection of all the women who came my way. Any tale I might offer to the effect that I wished to stay faithful to a girl back home would open me to every harassment in Dix Butler's book, so I told him I had a venereal disease. Clap, I muttered.

"You'll be all right in a week."

"It's a strain resistant to penicillin."

He shrugged. "Every time I caught a dose, I'd get evil," he told me. "I used to love sticking it in a woman, drip and all." He fixed me with a look. There was, as always, an extraordinary light in his eye when he talked about how low he was. He never looked more splendid than at such times. "You know, that was when I would try my damnedest to get into respectable women's pants. I loved the idea I was passing on my infection. Do you think I'm crazy?"

It was my turn to shrug.

"I attribute it," he said, "to the fact that my mother left my father and my brother and me when I was ten years old. My father was one hell of a drunk. Used to beat the bejesus out of us. But when we got older, we would count up how many of Dad's bitches we fooled around with behind his back. I hated those bitches for never providing me—when you think of all the women resident on this earth—with one good mother. Old King Bill, over on his little hill in GIBLETS, is the nearest I ever came to having a decent mother. Only, don't tell him I said that. He'll start to look at the overruns on my per diem. Don't want to get into that."

Dix mixed pleasure with official rounds and charged off his personal bar bills. When he offered to put in for my expenses as well, I refused. The rules he broke were not there for me to bend. From the attitude of the more sober officers I had worked with Downtown, it took no wise man to see that unauthorized use of one's expense account would be a bad debit to get listed on one's 201. We were signed up to cheat enemies, not our own folk.

Dix acted, however, as if his status were privileged. He showed more disregard for rules than anyone in CIA I had encountered so far. On the night I spent with my father in Washington, I had talked about Dix, but Cal was not impressed. "One like him comes up every month from the Farm," he remarked. "A few get through. Most go down in flames."

"He's exceptional," I told my father.

"Then he'll end up running a small war somewhere," Cal replied.

I was interrupted from thinking of this conversation when Dix remarked, "What's on your mind tonight?" I was not about to confess it was the assignment to unmask KU/CLOAKROOM. I merely smiled and looked around the Balhaus Resi. What a polyglot of human resources! I had never seen so many people with odd faces. Of course, to be a Berliner was not unequal to having one's features set at a slant—the collective physiognomy was reminiscent of the sharp edges on a cabinetmaker's tools (not to speak of the entrepreneurial glint you could find in the dullest eye). The band at one end of the dance floor had the mien of musicians who have played through the burning of the Reichstag, the death of von Hindenburg, the rise and fall of Adolf Hitler, the Allied bombardments, the Occupation, the Berlin Airlift, and they had never had to change expression. They were musicians. In ten minutes the set would be over and they could smoke or go to the bathroom—that was more meaningful than history. Now, having played their way through such American hits as "Doggie in the Window," "Mister Sandman," and "Rock Around the Clock," which last succeeded in chasing even the most libidinous of the bourgeoisie off the floor—I was thinking that only prosperous Germans with stiff collars could bring to vice the dignity of a serious pursuit—the band moved on to an oompah waltz with a tuba. That, in turn, swept all the wildly dressed young criminal element back to their tables, plus all the younger women with pink and purple wigs.

The telephone rang at our table. An American girl across the room wanted to talk to Dix. She had dialed his number on the assumption that he was German. "Hello, honey," he said. "You got it wrong. I'm an American, but that's all right. We can still fuck."

"I'm coming over. I want to learn what kind of yo-yo talks like you."

She was big and fair, with large features and a rangy body. By any gross measure of animal husbandry—were the shades of Nazi nightlife dictating my thoughts?—she would have made an appropriate mate for him. Her name was Susan, Susan Blaylock Pierce, and she had gone to Wellesley and was working in the American Consulate. In addition to the beer-import enterprise, Dix had cover from State, but when he chose to speak of working there, Susan Pierce needed no more than five minutes to poke through his qualifications. "Well, Randy Huff, or whatever your name is, I will tell you, somebody over at the Consulate must be sick and tired by now of looking at your empty desk."

"I'm just a field hand, ma'am," he said. I could see she was his choice for tonight. She had a horsey laugh and argued doggedly about the merits of English saddle over Western. "Who wants to look at some big slob slumped over a horse?" she said.

"Some people need an animal for work, instead of to show off their ass, lady."

"You," she said, "should have been a little ogre with warts."

He loved that. Marks of status rang in his mind like a cash register. I heard the bell sound for Wellesley, and for Susan Blaylock Pierce.

He surprised me by his next gambit. "Would you care to hear a long story about me?" he asked.

"No."

"Lady, cut some slack. This story is special."

"All right, but not too long," she said.

"At the age of fifteen," Dix declared, "I was in excellent shape. I lied about my age to get into the Golden Gloves in Houston, and I won my weight division. Sub-novice. I hardly drank. I ran six miles a day. I could do one-arm chin-ups, one-arm push-ups. Susan, name me a feat, I could perform it. I could have run for president of my sophomore class in high school if I wasn't from the wrong end of everything you ever saw. But I was happy. I was going with a blond girl who had blue eyes and fifteen-year-old plump little turn-up tits." When Susan Pierce showed her annoyance, he said, "Don't be offended. They were innocent, those tits. Weren't even all sure what they were there for. I loved that girl, Cora Lee, and she loved me. It was beautiful." He took a sip of his drink.

"One night I broke training to take Cora Lee to our big dance hall, Laney's, to show her off. She had to be the prettiest girl there. Laney's was always jammed with the best riffraff. Funky place. You could no sooner leave your girl alone than put a piece of meat on a plate and ask somebody else's dog not to look at it. But I didn't mind if I had a fight, and I sure wanted a beer. I hadn't had a drink in a month. Training. So I was thirsty. I placed Cora Lee on a bench and said, 'Honey, don't let any man sit down next to you. If they want to give trouble, tell them to watch out for Randy Huff.' Then I left her and went to the bar and bought two cans of beer. Since I had my own church key, I told the bartender not to open them. I brought those cans back ice-cold. Hard as rocks. I was saving them until I could sit next to her, and feel her sweet little thigh nuzzling mine when the first sip of beer went down.

"What did I see instead? A fellow with his arm around her. Cora Lee was looking at me in pure panic.

"He was huge. I was big, but this old boy was huge. He had a face you could put up against the bumper of a flat-bed truck and the face alone could push the truck uphill." Susan began to chuckle. "I was not demoralized, you understand. I was boss of my own equipment, thank you. So I said, 'Fellow, I don't know if you are aware of this or not, but that happens to be *your* arm on *my* girl.'

"'Well,' he said, 'what are *you* planning to do about it?'

"I smiled. I gave a dumb country-boy grin like I had nothing to do but get lost. Then I hit him in the face with the bottom end of the full beer can, him sitting down, me standing up. I hit him with the right arm that did those one-arm push-ups. The end of the beer can indented a circle from the top of his nostrils to the middle of his forehead. It broke his nose and laid vertical cuts over both eyebrows. He looked like a cross between a bat and a hog."

We were silent before this memory recollected in tranquility.

"How do you think the fellow responded?" Butler asked.

"How?" asked Susan.

"He sat there. He didn't blink particularly, and he didn't move. He just smiled. Then he said, 'You want to play? Let's play.' What do you think I said?"

"I don't know," she said. "Tell me."

"I said, 'Fellow, you can have her. You can have her.' I started running." Full pause. "I started running and I haven't stopped since."

Susan Pierce laughed as if something very far within had just caught on fire. "Oh, golly," she said, "oh, golly." Then she kissed his cheek. "You're cute. You're such a fool, but, do you know, you're cute." Proprietary lust for him appeared in her face.

After a few minutes, it was obvious there was nothing more for me to do than say good-night. On my way to bed I could find no explanation why his story had appealed so greatly to her. It impressed me, however, that he had told the same story once to a group of us at the Farm, and it had had a totally different ending. He had hardly run away. He had stayed in and taken the beating of his life against that huge old boy, but afterward he had made love to Cora Lee for all of July and August.

I was depressed. I had had dates with girls like Susan Pierce all through college and we would drink beers together. Nothing much more. Now he was going to seduce her in one night. Was it Berlin? I did not believe girls like Susan would make love that quickly back in America. On such thoughts, I fell asleep.

4

At 4:00 a.m. a gallon of German beer took the ride of the Valkyries through my urinary tract. Awake, after two hours of unconsciousness, I felt marooned in a neon desert of the night—sober, cold, wholly electrified. The reality of my situation came down on me again, and the hours I had spent slogging away at beer with Huff-Butler lay on my heart like a mustard plaster. William Harvey was on the trail of KU/CLOAKROOM.

I did my best to calm this panic. Before I left for Berlin, Hugh Montague had succeeded in taking my cryptonym through its first, second, and third transmogrifications. In the course of sending me the length of the Reflecting Pool over to Intensive German, he had also managed to expunge any paper trace of Herrick Hubbard's presence in the Snake Pit. My 201 now put me in Technical Services Staff for the same period, and Technical Services was mined, layered, and veneered with security. My immediate past had been effectively laundered.

All this Harlot bestowed on me as a farewell present. Now, none of it seemed that substantial. I was suffering from the worst form of paranoia a man in my profession can undergo—I was suspicious of my protector. Why had Montague chosen such a convoluted path? What in Heaven was I escaping from? My inability to satisfy an impossible task in the Document Room could certainly have resulted in a disagreeable letter being put into my 201 from Chief of Base, Berlin, and that would have done my future advancement no good. How could such harm compare, however, to the damage of discovery now? Harlot could weather a flap—it would all go into the portfolio of his commodious achievements—but I, if not asked to resign, would certainly have to live under a professional shroud.

I dressed and took the U-Bahn to the Department of Defense. I had clearance there to the key for a secure phone. Staring out upon the last of the night, the Department of Defense all deserted around me at that hour, I made a call to the secure phone that Harlot was authorized to keep at the canal house in Georgetown. It was midnight in Washington. Looking down the long hall of this empty office, I heard the sound of his voice, scrambled electronically, then reconstituted—which gave it the hollow timbre of words heard through a long speaking tube.

Quickly I explained my new assignment. His reassurance was firm. "You, dear boy, hold the strings, not King William. It's droll to be put on the trail of oneself. I wish that had happened to me when I was your age. You'll use it in your memoirs, supposing we ever get permissive about memoirs, that is."

"Hugh, not to disagree, but Harvey is already starting to ask what I did for four weeks at Technical Services."

"The answer is that you did nothing. You have a sad story. Stick to it. You were never assigned. You never met anyone but the secretary who guards the first waiting room. Poor boy, you were on the edge of your seat waiting to be assigned. It happens all the time. Some of our best trainees expire in just that manner over at TSS. Say . . ." He paused. "Say that you spent your hours ducking out to the reading room at the Library of Congress."

"What did I do there?"

"Anything. Anything at all. Specify something. Say you were reading Lautréamont in preparation for taking a good whack at Joyce. Harvey will pursue it no further. He is not interested in reminding himself how devoid he is of culture. He may bully you a bit, but in his heart he will know that people like Harry Hubbard do just such left-handed things as delve into Lautréamont while waiting for assignment at TSS."

"Dix Butler happens to know I was in the Snake Pit."

"Whoever this Dix Butler is, give him some definite impression that the Snake Pit was your cover. Don't say it. Let him come onto the idea himself. But I promise, you are worrying needlessly. Harvey is much too busy to pursue your activities down into the drains. Merely furnish him a bit of progress each week on the search for CLOAKROOM."

He coughed. It made a barking sound over the hollow center of the secure phone. "Harry," he said, "there are two choices in this Company. Worry yourself to death, or choose to enjoy a little uncertainty." He seemed about to hang up.

I must have laid one harsh note, however, on the empyrean of his calm, for next he said, "You remember our conversation concerning VQ/CATHETER?"

"Yessir."

"That project is the most important thing in the world to Harvey. If he starts pressing you on CLOAKROOM, nudge him back to CATHETER."

"I'm supposed to know nothing about CATHETER but that it's a cryptonym."

"Bill Harvey is broad-gauge paranoid. Such people think associationally. Speak of the Holland Tunnel, or of Dr. William Harvey. Bill must certainly know that the noble namesake charted the circulation of the blood back in 1620, but if by any chance our Base Chief is ignorant of the greater Harvey—never expect too much from an FBI man and you will never be disappointed—why, get him to think of blood vessels. Arteries. Before long his thought will slide back to the tunnel. You see, Harry, Bill Harvey believes that one day he will be running the Company, and VQ/CATHETER is his ticket to Top Desk. He won't get there, of course. He will certainly self-destruct. His paranoia is too high octane. So just divert him."

"Well, thank you, Hugh."

"Don't feel sorry for yourself. If you're obliged to take a few chances before you're ready, all the better. You'll be twice as good on your next job."

I got through the day. I sent a cable to West Berlin Desk in Washington, notifying them that Chief of Base wished to readdress

the cryptonym of KU/CLOAKROOM through Bridge-Ar-
chive:Control. I even wondered for the first time if Control was a
person, an office, or a machine. Then I called Dix Butler and arranged
to go out with him that night. So soon as we met, he told me in
passing about Susan Pierce. "It was a wall-banger," he said. "I figured
she would go for my tale."

"Is that why you told it?"

"Of course."

"Was that the real story? You told another version at the Farm."

"Don't stare at me in judgment. I steer an anecdote to suit the
scene."

"Why? Does it work? Is there a psychology of women?"

"Your dick is sixteen years old." He hooked my forearm with his
first two fingers. "Hubbard, admit it. You don't have a dose."

"I might."

"What if I conduct you to the men's room for an examination?"

"I won't go."

He began to laugh. When he stopped, he said: "I wanted a piece
of Susan Pierce. But I had to recognize that my initial approach was
laden with error. I was presenting myself as too sure of myself. You
don't make it with that kind of girl unless she can feel some superiority
to you. So I tried to make her feel sorry for this dude."

"How did you know she wouldn't be disgusted?"

"Because she's arrogant. Shame is one emotion that girl never
wants to feel. She has compassion for that. Like, if you fear blindness,
you usually develop some feeling for blind people."

I had a closer question I wanted to ask: "How was she in bed?"
The inhibiting hand of St. Matthew's, however, was at my throat. The
cost of continuing to see oneself as appropriately decent is that such
inquiries are not permissible. I waited, all the same, for his account.
On some nights, after listening to a slew of sexual particulars, all
forthcoming from him to me, I would return to the apartment while
he went off on one or another meeting. It was then I could not sleep.
My loins were stuffed with his tales.

On this night, Dix did not say any more about Susan. Was it
because he felt close to her or because it had been unsatisfactory? I was
discovering how much of an intelligence man I was becoming—
curiosity leaned on my gut like undigested food.

All the same, Dix stayed away from revelations. He was in a state
of exceptional tension tonight and repeated more than once, "I need

action, Herrick." He rarely called me by my full first name, and when he did, the ironies were not attractive. I could hardly explain to him that an old family name was reinvigorated when given to you as a first name and could even prove fortifying when you filled out a signature. So I said nothing. While I would never have to suffer being grabbed by the upper lip like Rosen, there might be some other price. To-night, he was drinking bourbon neat rather than beer.

"I'm going to fill you in, Hubbard, about me," he said, "but don't you pass this on or you'll be sorry. Fucking sorry."

"Don't tell me," I said, "if you don't trust me."

He was sheepish. "You're right." He stuck out his hand to shake. Again, I felt as if I sat next to an animal whose code of behavior rested in no good balance on his instincts. "Yes," he said, "I paid for running away from that dude with the beer can. I paid, and I paid. I used to wake up at night sweating. I stank. No beating is ever as bad as the depths you plumb in a *nadir* of shame." He used the word like a new acquisition. "I have learned the resonance of verbal surprise," I half expected him to add.

"I felt so bad inside," he said instead, "that I started to stand up to my father. And he was one man I had always been afraid of."

I nodded.

"He wasn't a big man. He was blind in one eye from an old fight, and he had a bad leg. But nobody could take him. He wouldn't permit it. He was a bad old dog. He'd use a baseball bat or a shovel. Whatever it took. One night he got abusive to me and I laid him out with a punch. Then, I tied him to a chair, stole his handgun and a carton of ammo, put all I owned in one cardboard suitcase, and was out the door. I knew just as soon as he worked himself loose, he would come at me with a shotgun. I even took his car. I knew he wouldn't report that. Just wait for me to come back.

"Well, dig it, Herrick, I entered on a life of crime. Fifteen and a half years old, and I learned more in the next year than most people acquire in a life. The war was on. The soldiers were far from home. So I became the stuff women looked to. I could have passed for nineteen, and that helped. I would hit some new good-sized town in the morning, and drive around until I could pick the store to hit. Then I would choose the bar that was right for me. I'd hang in with all those good soaks drinking their lunch until I'd found the right girl or woman, depending on my state of mind. Did I want to learn from a wise and greedy older person, or was I hankering to instruct young

pussy in the art of lust? Depended on the day. Sometimes you just
took what you could get, but I did leave a countless number of
satisfied women behind me in Arkansas, Missouri, and Illinois. I was
mean and sweet, and that is a difficult combination to improve upon.

"I couldn't have enjoyed life more. I'd pick up a girl or a woman,
and then I would park the car on a side street, ask the lady to wait
while I visited a friend for some money, and I would walk around the
corner, get into the first car whose door was unlocked, jump the
ignition, drive over to the store I'd selected, slip a stocking on my face
just as I walked in the door, and would hold up the proprietor and
empty the cash register. The best time to do it was two o'clock. No
lunchtime customers then, and the cash register full of the noontime
sales ready to go to the bank. In one minute, I'd be back in my stolen
car, face mask off, and two minutes later, I was depositing the stolen
car back around still another corner from my own car, at which point
I'd return to my daddy's heap, get in, and tell the new friend, 'We're
fixed for money now, honey.' Sometimes we'd even hear the sirens
going around the business district as we left town. 'What's that?' she
would ask. 'Beats me, Mrs. Bones,' I would tell her. I'd choose a
tourist cabin camp before I was ten miles away, and I'd hole up with
the female for twenty-four hours, or whatever interval she could
manage. Six hours or forty-eight. We'd eat, drink, and fornicate.
Those robberies were equal to injections of semen. You're raking in
the goodness from people when you stalk right over to their holding
and take it from them.

"I never tried to save any of that money. Once I got so lucky I
walked out with eight hundred dollars from a single cash register, and
there wasn't any way to spend such a sum on a girl and drink, so I
bought a good used Chevy, and sent my father a telegram. 'Your car
is parked on 280 North Thirtieth Street in Russelville, Arkansas. Keys
under the seat. Don't look for me. I'm gone to Mexico.' I giggled like
a looney-bird writing that telegram. I could see my old man on his
gimp leg searching for me in Matamoros and Vera Cruz, every low
bar. One of his teeth was like a broken fang."

There were more stories. Robbery followed robbery, and each
girl was described for my benefit. "I don't want to get your clap
stirring around too much, Hubbard, in your poor detumescent young
nuts, but this lady's pussy . . ." He was off. I knew everything about
female anatomy except how to picture it truly. A grotto of whorls and
looplets glistened darkly in my imagination.

Then his life altered. He lay over in St. Louis for a few months and lived with a couple of newfound buddies. They would have parties, and exchange girlfriends. I could not believe their indifference to questions of possession. "Hell, yes," he would say. "We used to take turns putting our dicks through a hole in a sheet. The girls would then give samples of oral technique. You'd have to guess which girl was on the chomp. Not easy. Leave it to chicks. They could mix their styles. Just to confuse us."

"You didn't mind that your girl was doing such things to another guy?" I admit to asking.

"Those chicks? Incidental. Me and my buddies did jobs together. We shared a half-dozen houses we thoroughly looted. I can tell you—there's nothing like home-burglary. Better than robbing a store. It ticks off crazy things. Cleans out any settled habits you might believe you have. For example, one of these dudes always used to take a shit right on the middle of the carpet in the master bedroom. I tell you, Herrick, I understood it. If you'd ever entered a medium-sized house in the middle of the night, you'd know. It feels large. You are aware of every thought that's ever passed through those walls. You might just as well be a member of the family. Me and my two buddies had a bond that was closer than any girlfriend." Now he fixed my eyes by staring into them, and I was obliged to nod. "None of this is to be passed on—you hear me?" I nodded again. "People ask about me," he said, "tell them I served in the Marines for three years. It's true. For fact, I did."

"Why?"

"Why?" He looked at me as if I were impertinent. "Because you have to know when to make your move. Hubbard, in years to come, keep an eye on my path. I talk a lot, but I get it done. Sometimes people who brag the most are the ones who accomplish the most. They have to—they'll look like fools if they don't. Since the Company is a clam-bar, I expect to have enemies up to here," he said, raising his hand well above his head, "but I will prevail. Comprehend why? Because I commit myself wholly to an endeavor. Yet I also know when to move. These are contradictory but essential favors. The Lord grants them to few. We were being pulled in," he went on without transition, "every week by the police. They had nothing on us, but they kept putting us into lineups as cannon fodder. It is no picnic to be in a lineup. The people who are trying to recover their memory as to who robbed them on their own street corner are often hysterical. They could select you by mistake. That was one factor. The other was my sixth sense. The war had just ended. Time to move. So I got drunk one night and enlisted in the morning. Lo, I was a Marine. Three years. I'll tell you about that sometime. The rest is history. I got out, went to the University of Texas on the GI Bill, played linebacker from 1949 to 1952, and thereby—help of certain alumni—was able to avoid being called up as a reserve for Korea, to which I could have gone and come back in a coffin or as a hero—I know such things—but I had my eye on professional football. I finished college and tried out for the Washington Redskins, but I smashed my knee. Whereupon I followed Bill Harvey's advice and signed up with my peers—you and the rest of the intellectual elite."

"Is that when you first knew Bill Harvey?"

"More or less. He liked my style of play on special teams. I got a letter from him when I was still with the Redskins. We had lunch. You could say he recruited me." Butler yawned suddenly in my face. "Hubbard, my attention is wandering. My tongue is turning dry." He stared around the room, his restlessness licking at my calm. Then he signaled, and we left for another bar. If the evening proved in the end to be without incident, I attribute it to the wisdom of the Germans. They knew when to leave him alone. I found it a very long night. I could not get away from the knowledge that the search for KU/CLOAKROOM was going to be with me through every drinking bout and hangover for quite some time.

5

CABLES WERE SENT BACK AND FORTH. I WAS ABLE TO INFORM MR. Harvey that KU/CLOAKROOM had been changed to KU/ROPES. Now we had to decide whether to wait seventy-two hours to pick up the next shift of cryptonym, or put a push on Bridge-Archive:Control. Harvey told me to wait. Three days later, I was able to inform him that we were in South Korea, courtesy of DN/FRAGMENT.

"That is going to hold us up for two weeks," he said.

"I can," I offered, "hit Bridge-Archive hard." Already, I was beginning to count on a contrary reaction to every move I proposed.

"No," he said. "I want to mull this one around. Just initiate a

request for DN/FRAGMENT. With all we've got to do, two weeks
will pass before we can turn around."

It was the truth. There was a lot to do. If, for the first few days,
my role as aide-de-camp to William King Harvey had meant not
much more than waiting for him to get into BLACKIE-1 (our bullet-
resistant Cadillac), the job soon expanded to on-hand note-taker,
intraoffice communicator of unhappy orders from the boss, plus monitor of the wastebasket product of significant hotel rooms in West and
East Berlin delivered by chambermaids on retainer. There was also
covert bookkeeping of our disbursements for special operational expenses, and various other payoffs that case officers passed over to me
as chits with code names. I do not wish to suggest that I was on top
of any of it. I had a little to do with a great many things, but most of
the time I could give no close account of what was going on; it made
more sense to recognize that we had a large-sized factory operation
spread over the 341 square miles of West and East Berlin, and information of all varieties came in as raw material, was processed in our
various intelligence shops and mills, and went out as product via cable
and pouch to Headquarters back at the Reflecting Pool and other
relevant offices in Washington. I was comparable to a clerk in the
superintendent's office who could brag that he had a desk near the
boss. It was no boon. Harvey worked as hard as any man I ever met,
and, much like Harlot, saw sleep as the interruption of serious activity.
Daily, he would go through the hundreds of cargo manifests that had
come in the day before at Schönefeld Airport, and since he could
hardly read German, this cost us the output of a couple of translators
who had to work through the night at CRUMPETS to number the
apples and rifles. Harvey could make out flights, time and place of
departure and arrival, and the amount of product; he knew the German words for cartons and cases, containers, and off-category loads;
he had a vocabulary for kilograms and cubic meters. That was his
linguistic limit. Because he could not recognize the names of the
variety of different arms and commodities flown into East Berlin from
Moscow, Leningrad, the Ukraine, Czechoslovakia, Poland, Rumania,
Hungary, et al., he had ordered his translators to assign a number to
each kind of item. Since this included, as I say, everything from apples
to rifles, and there were ten kinds of apples and several hundred
varieties of small arms, Harvey had put together a vest-pocket code of
several thousand numbers. In lieu of a dictionary, he kept a private
black book with each number listed, but he did not have to refer to

text often. He knew his numbers. Riding in BLACKIE, sipping on his martini, his other hand, one stubby finger extended, would be guiding his eye down a cargo manifest to which the translator had affixed the required numbers. Sometimes, when he wished to take notes, he would put the martini glass in its holder, or worse, pass it to me, and with his color-coding pen underline items in red, blue, yellow, or green, so that on the second pass through these pages, relations between various Soviet forces stationed in Berlin would start to speak to him. At the least, this is my supposition. He never explained any of it, but he certainly hummed like a handicapper reading the racing form. His mutterings sputtered in my ear with the agreeable sound of cracklings in a frying pan. "Twenty-six eighty-one, that's got to be some kind of Kalashnikov, but I'll look it up"—over came the martini to my hand, out came his black book—"damn, it's a Skoda, not a Kally, should have known that 2681 is the Skoda Machine-Pistol Series C, Model IV. Wasn't that discontinued?" He looked up. "Hubbard, take a note." As I fumbled for my notebook and pen with my free hand, while holding his martini in the other, he took back his glass, drained it, set it in the holder, and dictated: "Sovs either dumping outmoded Skoda Series C, Model IV on Vopos and ilk, or starting up Model IV again. Or, option three, preparing a caper. Latter most likely. Only ninety-six Skodas in shipment." He filled his martini glass from the shaker. "Put it in the Womb Room," he said.

That was an extra large closet the size of a jail cell off his office at GIBLETS. The sides had been covered in cork to give him a four-wall bulletin board. On it he tacked every unanswered question. Sometimes he would taper off from a sixteen-hour working day by snooping around in that cork cavern, dwelling among his enigmas.

My day, then, was generally lived within parameters. I had a desk adjacent to each of Mr. Harvey's offices at GIBLETS, BOZO, and Downtown, and I traveled with him, gathering together—if I could anticipate when he was ready to saddle up—all the papers I was working on, stuffed them, file folder and all, into my flunky-bag (the term he delighted in applying to my attaché case), and sprinted down one or another corridor after him. Off we went in BLACKIE, arsenal-style, driver, bodyguard riding shotgun, second shotgun (myself), plus Chief, and if he wasn't working on the radio-telephone, or extracting the essence from another swatch of papers, he would tell stories.

I once dared to remark to him that every leader I had known in the Company told stories. While the vast experience backing this remark was limited to Mr. Dulles, my father, Harlot, and Dix, Mr. Harvey did not ask for substantiation, but contented himself with replying: "It's biologically adaptative."

"Explain that, would you, Chief?" I was managing at last not to use "sir."

"Well, the work assigned to the kids in this particular army is unnatural. A young stud likes to know what's going on. But they can't be told. It takes twenty years to shape a trustworthy intelligence operative. Twenty years in America, anyway, where we all believe that everybody from Christ—our first American—on down to the newspaperboy is trustworthy. In Russia or Germany it takes twenty minutes to get a new operator ready to trust nothing. That's why we go into every skirmish with the KGB under a handicap. That's why we even have to classify the toilet paper in the crap house. We must keep reminding ourselves to enclave the poop. Still, you can't put too many limitations on the inquiring mind. Hence, we tell tales. That is the way to pass a big picture down in acceptable form."

"Even if the stories are indiscreet?"

"You've put your finger on it. We all have a tendency to talk too much. I had a relative who was an alcoholic. Gave it up. Never touched the stuff. Except once or twice a year, he'd break down, go off on a toot. It was biologically adaptative. Something worse would probably have happened to him if he didn't break out and drink. I guess I believe that in the Company it's good once in a while if a secret gets told over a drink."

"Do you mean that?"

"Now that I've said it, no! But we are living in two systems. Intelligence and biology. Intelligence would permit us to tell nothing unauthorized. Biology suffers the pressure." He nodded at his own words. "Of course, there are discernable variations in our top men. Angleton is a super-clam. So is Helms. Director Dulles may talk a little too much. Hugh Montague, way too much."

"How would you classify yourself, sir?"

"Clam. Three hundred and fifty days a year. Magpie for two weeks in summer." He winked.

I wonder if this was not a prelude to informing me about VQ/ CATHETER. I think he was beginning to find it difficult to live next to me every working day yet not be able to brag about his number-one achievement; besides, I was developing a need to know. My presence certainly got in the way of CATHETER-related conversations on the car radio. So there came a day when I was given clear-ance, and a new cryptonym, VQ/BOZO III-a, to classify me as an assistant in the high-clearance shop of BOZO himself.

It took another week to get to the tunnel. As I had surmised, Harvey made his visits at night, and often with visiting military celeb-rities, four-star generals, admirals, members of the Joint Chiefs of Staff. Harvey did not bother to restrain his pride. I had not seen such pleasure in an achievement since my father introduced me in 1939, at the age of six, to William Woodward, Sr., whose stable had won the Kentucky Derby with Omaha in 1935. Four years later, Mr. Wood-ward was still glowing at the mention of Omaha's name.

In turn, Harvey was not about to downgrade the beauty of his operation. I heard him describe it for the first time on an evening which commenced with me riding shotgun in the front seat of BLACKIE. We had a three-star general in the rear (who was, so far as I could make out, on a tour of NATO facilities for the Joint Chiefs) and Mr. Harvey took pleasure in interrupting our drive on a side street of Steglitz. We pulled into a parking shed, changed the Cadillac for a bulletproof Mercedes, and took off again with Harvey now behind the wheel, his driver riding shotgun, myself in the rear with the General. "Finger the turns," said Harvey, and his driver thereupon took up the duty of giving directions; we drove quickly through the outskirts of Berlin with much doubling back on side streets to make certain there was no tail. Twelve kilometers soon became twenty, and we passed through Britz and Johannisthal twice before coming to Rudow and its open fields.

All the while, Bill Harvey kept telling the General about problems faced in the building of the tunnel, sending this monologue over his shoulder. I was hoping the General's hearing was good. Familiar with Harvey's voice, I could barely pick up his words. Since the General managed, however, to share a rear seat without giving any acknowl-edgment that I was present, I soon began to enjoy his difficulties with this muffled orientation. The General reacted by helping himself to the martini pitcher.

"This was the only tunnel to my knowledge that had a sister tunnel built at the White Sands Missile Proving Ground in New Mexico to a length of four hundred and fifty feet, as opposed to our fifteen hundred feet, and for one reason," said Harvey nonstop. "The soil bears comparison to the white-pack sand soil we were facing in Altglienicke. The softness was the problem, said our soil engineers.

What if you dig the tunnel, putting in one steel ring after another to support it all the way, but the disturbance to the earth produces some small depression on the surface? That could appear as a rogue-line in a photograph. We can't have an unaccountable phenomenon showing up in the Soviet's aerial surveys. Not when we're tunneling into East Berlin."

"There was a lot of concern about that at the Joint Chiefs," said the General.

"You bet," said Harvey, "but, what the hell, we took a chance, didn't we, General Packer?"

"Technically speaking, it's an act of war," said the General, "to penetrate another nation's territory whether by air, sea, land, or in this case, from below."

"Isn't that a fact?" said Harvey. "I had a selling job here to Christmas. Mr. Dulles said to me, 'Can we refer to this behemoth as little as possible in writing?' " Harvey kept talking and driving, pushing his tires through many a tight turn with as much aplomb as a symphony man clashing his cymbals in a well-timed accord.

"Yessir," said Harvey, "this tunnel demanded special solutions. We had close to insuperable problems of security. It's one thing to build the Taj Mahal. But how do you slap it together in such a way that your next-door neighbors have no clue? This sector of the border is heavily patrolled by the Commies."

"What was it that somebody did with the Taj Mahal?" asked the General in a half-voice as if he could not decide whether it would prove more embarrassing to be heard or unheard. Having set down his glass, he then, on reflection, picked it up again.

"Our problem," said Harvey, "was getting rid of the immediate construction product—tons of soil. To dig the tunnel we had to excavate approximately fifty thousand cubic feet of dirt. That's more than three thousand tons, equal to several hundred average truckloads. But where do you dispose of that much earth? Everybody in Berlin has 360-degree vision. Every Kraut can count. Heinie is looking to supplement his income through the power of his observations. Okay, say you spread your dump all over West Berlin and thereby reduce the amount visible in any one place, you still have the truck driver to contend with. Ten truck drivers are ten highly vulnerable security packages. We came up with a unique solution: We would not truck tunnel dirt away from the site. Instead, we built a large warehouse right near the border of Altglienicke in East Berlin, and put a parabolic antenna on the top. 'Ho ho,' says the SSD, 'look at those Americans pretending to build a warehouse, when they have an AN/APR9 on the so-called warehouse roof. And, look, Hans, the warehouse is heavily protected by barbed wire. The Americans are putting up a radar-intercept station. Ho hum, one more radar-intercept station for the Cold War. That makes no big history.' Well, General, what the East Germans and the KGB didn't know is that we built this large warehouse with a cellar that happens to be twelve feet deep through-out. Nobody worries about any dirt we cart away while we're build-ing the cellar for the warehouse. Not even the truck drivers. Everybody knows it's a radar station pretending to be a warehouse. It's only when we're done with the trucks that we commence excavating the tunnel. Our cellar space proved adequate to receive the fifty thousand cubic feet of dirt we had to dig out. That, General Packer, was an elegant solution." He whipped around a car, cut back in the face of an oncoming truck.

"So all that dirt has just been sitting in the warehouse cellar all this time?" asked the General.

"Well, it's no worse than burying the gold at Fort Knox," said Harvey.

"I get it," said the General. "That's why the dig was called Operation GOLD."

"It's policy among us," Harvey said primly, "not to discuss cryp-tonym nomenclature."

"Right. I find that a reasonable stance."

"We're here," said Chief. At the end of a long, empty street that passed between empty fields on either side, we could see a large low warehouse in silhouette, back-lit by automobiles passing along the belt highway on the East German side. The warehouse had its own small floodlights around a barbed-wire perimeter and sentry lamps at a few windows and doors, but in the night it merely looked well guarded and somewhat inactive. I was more intrigued with the passing sounds of the cars and trucks on the Schönefelder Chaussee beyond. Their hum rolled through the night like ocean surf, and yet those vehicles knew nothing. Our warehouse would attract no more attention than one gives to any building at night on a desolate highway.

The sentry opened the gate, and we parked two feet from a small door to the warehouse. Harvey darted from his seat right into the building. "Apologies for running ahead of you," he said to the Gen-eral once we had followed, "but our E and A folk back at Headquarters say I'm the most recognizable CIA operative in the world. Except, of course, for Allen Dulles. So we don't want the Commies wondering why I come here. Might start up their mental motors."

"E and A? Estimates and Assessments?"

"A, actually, is for Analysis."

"You fellows are as much in the alphabet soup as we are."

"Just so the mail gets through," said Harvey.

We walked down a corridor with a few partitioned offices on either side, most of them unoccupied at this hour, then Chief opened another door to a large windowless room with fluorescent lights overhead. For a moment I thought I was back in the Snake Pit. At endless rows of worktables, recording machines were stopping and starting. Up on a dais, lights blinked from a console the size of a pipe organ. Half a dozen technicians, seated before it, were studying their local configurations of signals, while other technicians trolleyed shopping carts of tapes and cartridges to the machines. The sound of 150 Ampex tape recorders—Mr. Harvey provided the number—moving in forward or reverse, electronic beeps signaling the conclusions or commencements of telephone conversations produced an aggregate of sound that stirred me in the same uneasy fashion as some of the more advanced electronic music I had listened to at Yale.

Was there one telephone dialogue between the East German police and/or the KGB and/or the Soviet military that was not being captured at this moment on one or another Ampex? Their humming and whirring, their acceleration and slowdown, were an abstract of the group mind of the enemy, and I thought the Communist spirit must look and sound like this awful room, this windowless portent of Cold War history.

"Everything here is just a small part of the operation," Harvey said softly. "It's quiet now." He led us to a huge sliding door, pulled it back, and we strode down a ramp into an even more airless space, barely lit by an occasional overhead bulb. I could sniff the faintest odor of contaminated earth. What with the ramp, the minimal illumination and walls of dirt impinging on either side, I felt as if we were descending to the inner passage of an ancient tomb.

"Damnedest thing," said the General, "how you get to notice the sandbags after you buttress a dugout. Some sandbags smell good; others, you hold your nose."

"We had troubles," said Harvey. "Fifty feet into the tunnel-dig we encountered earth encumbered with stench. It scared the constitution out of us. There was a graveyard just south of the projected tunnel which we certainly had to avoid since the Sovs would make *mucho* propagandistic hay out of Americans defiling German graves if there was discovery. So we aimed to pass to the north, although the graveyard offered more suitable soil."

"Yet even so, there was a stink you had to get rid of," said the General.

"Nope." I do not know if it was my presence, but Harvey, if technically outranked by the General, was in no manner going to say "No, sir."

"What did you have to get rid of then?" insisted the General.

"We could live with the stink, but we had to divine the source of the odor."

"That's right. You guys in Intelligence ought to know how to work your way into a stench or two."

"You bet, General. We located it. A typical engineering nightmare. We discovered that we had invaded the draining field of the septic system built for our own warehouse personnel."

"C'est la vie," said the General.

We were on the lip of a cylindrical hole about twenty feet across and curiously deep. I could not estimate the depth. Looking down, one seemed to be studying the fall from a ten-foot diving board, but then it seemed more, a long dark plunge to the duckboards below. I felt an hypnotic vertigo, not so much disagreeable as magnetic—I had to go down the ladder that led to the base.

It descended about eighteen feet. There, at a cupboard on the floor, we exchanged our shoes for boots with heavily cushioned soles and put all our loose change away. A finger to his lips, as if he would draw all errant echoes into himself, Harvey led us along the duckwalk. The hypnotic, magnetic—I now called it the *honorable*—vertigo continued. Lit by an overhead bulb every ten or twelve feet, the tunnel stretched out before us to the vanishing point. I felt as if I were in a room of mirrors whose repeating view took us to infinity. Six and a half feet high, six and a half feet wide, a perfect cylinder, nearly fifteen hundred feet long, the tunnel took us down a narrow aisle between low walls of sandbags on either side. Amplifiers, set at intervals on the sandbags, were wired into lead-sheathed cables that ran the length of the tunnel. Harvey whispered, "Carries the sap from the tap to the bucket."

"Where's the tap?" whispered the General back.

"Coming attractions," Harvey replied as softly.

We continued to walk with one carefully weighted step after another. "Do not stumble," we had been warned. Along the route, we passed but three maintenance men, each isolated on his own watch. We had entered the domain of CATHETER. It was a church, I told myself, and immediately submitted to a chill on the back of my neck. CATHETER had its indwelling silence; one might as well have been proceeding down the long entrance to a god's ear. "A church for snakes," I said to myself.

Our path proceeded not much more than a quarter of a mile, but I felt as if we had been walking along the tunnel floor for the best part of a half hour before we came to a steel door in a concrete frame. A maintenance man accompanying us brought forth a key, turned a lock, and pressed four numbers on another lock. The door opened on silent hinges. We were at the terminus of the tunnel. Above us was a vertical shaft rising some fifteen feet into the dark.

"See that overhead plate?" whispered Harvey. "Right above, is where we made our connection to the cables themselves. That was one delicate deal. Our sources told us that the KGB sound engineers at Karlhorst sealed nitrogen into their cables to guard against moisture and had attached instruments to monitor any drop in nitrogen pressure. So, just about a year ago, right up above us, you would have been able to witness a procedure comparable in delicacy and tension to a world-famous surgeon going in for an operation never before attempted." Standing next to him, I tried to conceive of the immaculate anxiety experienced by the technicians when the tap went into the wire. "At that instant," said Harvey, "if the Krauts had been checking the line, it would have shown up on their meters. Just like a nerve-jump. So, ultimately, it was a crapshoot. But we brought it off. Right now, General, we are connected into 172 such circuits. Each circuit carries eighteen channels. That's more than twenty-five hundred military and police phone calls and telegraphic messages that we are able to record at once. You can call that coverage."

"You fellows," said General Packer, "are getting good marks for this back home."

"Well, I'm glad to hear the level of appreciation is rising."

"The Joint Chiefs won't be handed anything but good stuff from me."

"I remember," said Harvey, "when the Pentagon used to say, 'CIA buys spies to tell them lies.' "

"No, sir, not anymore," said General Packer.

On the ride back, Harvey sat in the rear with him, and they shared his pitcher of martinis. After a while, the General asked, "How do you handle the take?"

"The bulk of transmissions are flown back to Washington."

"That much I know already. They took me on a tour of the Hosiery Mill."

"They took you *there*?"

"Room T-32."

"No right to open it up to you," Harvey said.

"Well, they did. They gave me clearance."

"General Packer, no offense intended, but I remember a time when high clearance was given to Donald Maclean of the British Foreign Office. Why, in 1947 he was issued a *non-escort* pass to the Atomic Energy Commission. J. Edgar Hoover didn't even rate such a pass in 1947. Need I remind you that Maclean was part of the Philby gang and has been reliably reported to be making his home in Moscow these days. No offense intended."

"I can't help it if you don't like it, but the Joint Chiefs did want to know a few things."

"Such as?"

"Such as how much of the take is kept here for immediate processing and how much goes back to Washington. Are you in a position to give us twenty-four hours' notice if the Soviet army is ready to blitz Berlin?"

I heard the soundproof window partition going up behind my ears in the Mercedes. Now I could not hear a word. I leaned toward the driver to light a cigarette, and managed a look at the rear seat. They both appeared considerably more choleric.

When we stopped at the parking shed to switch cars again, I heard Bill Harvey say, "I won't tell you that. The Joint Chiefs can kiss every square inch of my ass."

Now, reinstalled in BLACKIE-1, two new martinis poured from the Cadillac decanter, Harvey kept his partition raised. I was able to hear no more until the General was dropped off at his hotel, the Savoy. Harvey immediately lowered the glass to speak to me. "There's a general for you. General Asshole. Stays at the *Suh-voyyy*." He said it as if he were trundling an English accent over a notable bump. "I once was taught that generals were supposed to stay with their troops." He belched. "Kid, you seem to be the troops. How do you like little old CATHETER?"

"I know how Marco Polo felt discovering Cathay."

"They sure teach you juniors what to say in those New England schools."

"Yessir."

" 'Yessir'? I guess you're telling me I'm full of shit." He belched again. "Look, kid, I don't know about you, but time-servers like that General scratch my woodwork. I didn't happen to be in uniform during World War II. I was too busy chasing Nazis and Communists for the FBI. So the military dogs irritate me. Why don't we wax the floor with some serious booze and recuperate?"

"I never turn down a drink, Chief."

6

ONCE WE WERE BACK IN GIBLETS, AND INSTALLED IN HIS LIVING room, Mr. Harvey's fatigue offered its manifest. He would fall asleep as we were talking, the glass undulating in his hand like a tulip in a summer breeze. Then he would awaken with a well-timed swoon of his wrist to compensate for the near spill of his liquor.

"I'm sorry my wife couldn't stay up tonight," he said, as he came out of a ten-second snooze.

She had greeted us at the door, made our drinks, and tiptoed out, but I could feel her moving about upstairs, as if, after my departure, she would come down to steer him to bed.

"C.G.'s a wonderful woman. Top of category," he said.

The injunction not to say "Yessir" cut off the easiest response to many of his remarks. "I'm sure," I said at last.

"Be double sure. Want to know the kind of individual C.G. is? I'll give you an idea. A woman living in the Soviet sector left a baby on the doorstep of a Company officer down the street. Right outside his home! I won't tell you the fellow's name because he went through a lot of flak. Why did this East German woman pick a CIA man? How did she know? Well, you can't clear yourself on a crazy drop like that, so let's forget his side of it. What's essential is that the woman left a note. 'I want my child to grow up free.' Enough to turn your heart-strings, right?"

"Right."

"Wrong. You don't take anything for granted. Not in our work. But my wife says, 'This baby could have been dropped on us from Heaven. I won't let her go to an orphanage. Bill, we have to adopt her.' " He shook his head. "Just the night before, I was sitting with C.G. looking at an East German TV newsreel to see if I could pick up a couple of clues about their order of battle from the outfits who were in their military parade—never feel superior to your source, no matter how mundane—and one of their bands went by. An entire platoon of glockenspiels. I looked at the ribbons they put on those glockenspiels—real Heinie froufrou—and I said to C.G., 'Why don't they hang prison-camp skulls on these instruments, ha, ha,' and next day, she picks me up on it. If I hate the Sovs all that much, she informs me, then it's my duty to adopt the baby." He burped, gently, sadly, fondly. "Make a long story short," he said, "I have an adopted baby daughter. Phenomenal, right?"

"Right," I said. I did not wish to echo him in order to be contradicted again, but he just grinned and said, "Right. My daughter is lovely. When I get to see her." He stopped. He looked at his glass. "Fatigue is your mother in this kind of work. You'd think it was a waste of time with the General, but it wasn't. You know why I was selling CATHETER so hard?"

"No, Mr. Harvey."

"The Director asked me to. I received a call from Allen Dulles just this afternoon. 'Bill, fellow,' he said to me, 'give their three-star General Packer the tour. We need to fluff a few feathers.' So I dedicated myself this evening to selling CATHETER to General Asshole. Do you know why?"

"Not yet, exactly."

"Because even the Joint Chiefs' flunkies live high on the military hog. They have battleships to visit and nuclear warning systems. It's hard to impress them. They're used to touring underground facilities as huge as a naval station. Whereas, we have just a dirty little tunnel. Yet we're picking up more intelligence than any operation in history. Any nation, any war, any espionage endeavor ever. Got to remind them of that. Got to keep them in their place."

"I could hear some of the things you said in the car. You were certainly keeping him at bay."

"It wasn't hard. The fact of the matter is that he didn't really want to know what we're picking up. Right here in Berlin we don't spot-check more than one-tenth of one percent of our total take, but that's enough. You can re-create the dinosaur from a few bones in the tibia. What we know, and the Pentagon hates to hear this, is that the state of the railroad tracks over on the Sov side of the line through East Germany, Czechoslovakia, Poland is execrable. Only word for it. And their rolling stock is worse. The Russians just don't have the choo-choo trains to invade West Germany. There's not a blitzkrieg in sight for years. Well, I hate to tell you how tight the Pentagon would sit on that news. If Congress ever got wind, it could strip the Army of billions of dollars in tank contracts yet to be allocated. And General Packer happens to be in tanks. He's touring NATO scared. Of course Congress won't even get wind unless we break a little over in their direction, and we won't fart unless the Pentagon goes out of their way to insult us. Because the bottom line, Hubbard, is that it's highly improper that Congress be given any inkling. They're too malleable to public reaction. And it is a mistake to reveal any Russian weakness to the American public. They do not have the appropriate background in Communism to appreciate the problem. Do you perceive, then, the parameters of my double game? I have to scare the Pentagon into thinking that we might shoot their future budget ducks right out of the water, when actually, I'm prepared to protect said ducks. But I can't let them know I belong to their team, or Pentagon won't value us. Anyway, it may be academic, Junior. The Hosiery Mill that General Asshole was talking about is already two years behind in translating the gross product we send them from CATHETER, and we've only been in existence one year."

He fell asleep. The life in his body seemed to move over into his glass, which perambulated further and further out to the side until the weight of his extended arm woke him up.

"Which reminds me," he said. "How are we doing with CLOAKROOM? Where is he now?"

"In England."

"From Korea to England?"

"Yessir."

"What's the new cryp?"

"SM/ONION."

Harvey sat up straight for a moment, put down his drink, grunted, reached over his belly to his ankle and raised his pants leg. I saw a sheath knife strapped to his ankle. He unhooked it, drew it, and began to pare his fingernails, all the while looking me over through bloodshot eyes. It had been a couple of weeks since he had put me to squirming in his presence, but now I could not say if he was friend or foe. He grunted.

"I guess," I said, "SM/ONION may be a way of telling us to keep peeling the layers."

"Fuck that noise." He set down the knife to knock back half of a new martini. "I don't intend to wait another two weeks to discover that this son of a bitch has still another cryptonym. Either he's a heavyweight, or somebody's in total panic of me. I smell VQ/WILD-BOAR in the woodshed."

"Wolfgang?"

"You bet. Do you think Wolfgang could be with ONION in London?" He mused on this long enough to snort. "All right. We're going to tie you in to a couple of our effectives in London. Tomorrow morning, you start calling them. If KU/CLOAKROOM assumes that he can hide in London, he is going to learn what a ream-job is all about."

"Yessir."

"Don't look so unhappy, Hubbard. Hard work never killed an honest intelligence operator."

"Check."

"See me here for breakfast seven o'clock."

With that, he put the knife back in its sheath, picked up his glass, and fell asleep. Sound asleep. I could be certain of this because the hand that held his martini did a quarter-roll of the wrist and emptied out his drink on the rug. He began to snore.

7

IT WAS CLOSE TO MIDNIGHT. I HAD SEVEN HOURS BEFORE THE RITES OF execution would commence. On leaving GIBLETS, I made a quick decision to find Dix Butler and drink the night through, and the first half of this proposition took considerably less time than the second. Right off, I came upon Dix in a small club we frequented off the Kurfürstendamm, a place called Die Hintertür. There was a girl in this Back Door who would dance and drink with you, and a lady bartender whom Dix liked. She had jet-black hair, not an everyday matter in Berlin, even if it was dyed hair, and offered a look of exceptional sophistication for a small bar with one waiter and not an agent in sight. I judge it was the luxury of being able to drink without an eye on business that brought Dix here, plus Maria, the bartender. He was uncharacteristically polite with her and never tried any more Herculean approach than to ask occasionally if he might see her home, to which she invariably responded with a mysterious smile as a congenial way of saying no. The other girl, Ingrid, had dyed red hair, was available for a dance, or for sitting with you and hearing your troubles, an office nicely complemented most evenings by one or another glum German businessman in from Bremen or Dortmund or Mainz. Dependably, such a fellow would buy Ingrid's time for a couple of hours of slow dancing, perfunctory conversation, and heavy silences. She would hold his hand, she would tell stories, and occasionally make him laugh. I was invariably impressed with the balance between supply and demand. Almost never was Ingrid free, but such was the tempo of the Back Door, seldom were two businessmen seeking her company at the same hour.

By now Ingrid was my pal. We flirted between customers, danced a little—she was encouraging to the idea I might improve—and alternately practiced German and English with each other. Occasionally she would ask, *"Du liebst mich?"*

"Ja," I would reply. In a foreign language, it was not difficult to agree that one loved somebody when one did not. In turn, her sharp mouth, primed with all the trade wisdom that love is a gritty condition, spread into a wide and slightly maniacal smile. *"Ja"* she repeated, and held up her thumb and forefinger an eighth of an inch apart. *"Du liebst mich ein bisschen."* She had a gutty voice which I enjoyed, for she employed it with precision, laying each German word like a template on my cloudy understanding.

I eventually learned that Ingrid was married, lived with her husband and child plus a few cousins and brothers in her mother's apartment, and wanted to get to the United States. Dix told me as much. "She's looking to hook an American." All the same, I enjoyed her occasional kiss of congratulation when I showed a little rhythm in my dance. Nor would she take remuneration from me. I was described to the German businessmen as her *"Schatz."*

Now that I had become the official sweetheart, I was entitled to hear gossip. Ingrid informed me that Maria was kept by a rich protector. When I relayed this to Dix, he promptly returned a dividend.

"The gent that Maria shares her apartment with," he said, "happens to be a rich middle-aged woman. That's why I can't score."

"Why do you try?"

"I'm asking myself."

His restlessness ratcheted up another notch. I was deciding that Die Hintertür was too quiet for him tonight, when the door opened and Freddie and Bunny McCann came in. Freddie (middle name Phipps, Princeton, '54) was my replacement Downtown, precisely the fellow who had learned my job so quickly, and all because—I sometimes thought—he was *nice*. He had put himself in my hands. He had trusted me. It is not difficult to instruct when there is no unhappy question about your motives. So I liked him and his manners. He was even taller than me, but weighed somewhat less, and if he had a shortcoming for certain kinds of Agency work, it was that he was too obviously an American official.

His wife, however, would be even more visible. She had a mane of beautiful dark hair and the loveliest face. Her eyes were blue. I confess, she reminded me of Kittredge.

In any event, they were much too well-suited a couple to impinge on Dix Butler at this hour. I could see by the tentative look on their marital face as they came over to sit with us that they were disappointed by the lackluster air of the joint, the empty tables, the absence of vice. It was my fault. Freddie had called during the working day to ask if I could recommend a *boîte* for quiet drinking, "a place with a little authentic Berlin mood." Assuring him that no such entity existed—"they're all circuses or morgues"—I came around to suggesting the Back Door, "where you can, at least, breathe and speak. The lady bartender might be a novelty, and the girl who's available for dances," I was low enough to brag, "pretends to have a crush on me."

"Well, it certainly sounds authentic. We've been cooped up. Bunny's cousin, Bailey Lawton, is in the Consulate here, and he's just about trapped us on the banquet list. Solemn stuff. When it comes to vulcanizing a chicken, the Germans are quite our equal."

"The Back Door might amuse you," I said.

"I thought you said it was Die Hintertür."

"It is," I told him, "but they also repeat the name in English. Right on the sign."

I wish that had warned him off. Never did my favorite, if dim, watering hole look so third rate.

"What did you say your name was?" Dix asked as soon as Freddie's wife sat down, and repeated, "Bunny Bailey McCann." It was not unlike the way he would say Herrick.

"What does Bunny stand for?" he asked.

"Actually, it's Martita."

"Martita Bailey McCann. A nice name," he said.

"Thank you."

"Good to-and-fro in the consonants."

"Are you a writer?"

"Actually, I'm a poet," Dix said.

"Do you publish?"

"Only in magazines that look for doggerel."

"Oh."

"Oh."

Freddie laughed. I did a bit to join him.

"What are you drinking?" asked Dix.

"Scotch," said Freddie. "Water, side."

"Two Scotches," Dix called out to Maria. "Make it the Scotch from Scotland."

"Thank you," said Freddie. "I suppose they put flavoring in grain alcohol and serve it up if you let them."

"I don't know," said Dix. "I can't drink the stuff. I don't understand Scotch."

"That's an odd remark," said Freddie.

"The liquor we put into ourselves is called spirits. I like to know which spirits I'm putting into myself."

"Terrific," said Fred McCann. "I've used the word all my life, and never thought about it once. Spirits."

"I think about it a lot," said Dix.

"Good for you," said Bunny.

He looked at her. "Actually, I learned about Scotch the other day. In this place. From the bartender over there. Maria. I asked her, 'What is it about guys who drink Scotch?' and she said, 'You do not know?' I said, 'I do not know.' 'Oh,' she said, 'that is not so hard. Guys who drink Scotch have *given up*.'"

There was a pause.

"I suppose the shoe fits," said Freddie McCann.

"Nonsense, darling," said Bunny, "you never give up. Not if it's something worthwhile." She looked at me. Her eyes were clear. They were lovely eyes and they were asking, "Is this your *good* friend?"

"Well, I don't know," said Freddie, "that I throw a large amount of weight."

"You're beautiful, Mrs. McCann," said Dix. "Your husband must be lucky."

"Would you believe it if I told you I'm just as lucky?"

"I wouldn't," said Dix, "believe it for a minute."

Freddie laughed. "Hear, hear."

"Here's the Scotch," said Bunny, and drank half of her glass at a gulp. "I think you may as well bring another," she said to the waiter.

"Yes," said Freddie, "another round."

"In fact, I would go so far," said Dix, "as to say that your husband is bloody fortunate."

"I would suggest," said Bunny, "that you shut your trap."

Dix knocked off the rest of his bourbon. We sat in silence.

"Yes, ma'am, you bet," he said into the silence. When no one replied, his unanswered presence began to use up more of our oxygen.

"You bet what?" she said.

He was not about to give up. "I bet you and me," he said, "could drink those two under the table."

"I would bet the heaviest drinkers in the world come out of Dartmouth," Freddie said. I had to honor him for trying. "I met one fellow in Hanover at the Princeton-Dartmouth game my sophomore year who used to drink so much that I don't believe he had any mental faculties left, except, that is, for the more basic motor functions. His fraternity brothers used to take exams for him so he could remain in school and win bets when they got into drinking contests with the other fraternities. I saw him again last year, and he was *gone*."

"Pal," said Dix, "you've written your letter. Mail it."

Freddie McCann did his best to laugh. I could see he still had some outside hope that Dix might be part of the authentic ambiance in this bar.

"Would you mind if I danced with your wife?" Dix asked.

"I believe it's up to her."

"She'll say no," said Dix.

"You're absolutely right," said Bunny.

"No, fellow, your wife doesn't want to dance with me. It could become a habit."

"Now, what are you trying to tell me?" said Freddie at last.

"That you're fucking fortunate."

"Enough," I said.

"No, Harry," said Fred, "I can speak for myself."

"I don't hear you very well," said Dix.

"This is becoming a little implausible," said Fred McCann. "I ask you to remember. There are Germans here. We are supposed to set an example."

"I think your wife has the most gorgeous hair," said Dix, and he ran his hand, not quickly, but not so slowly that she could react in time, from her brow to the nape of her neck.

I stood up. "All right," I said, "you can apologize. To my *friends*." It is odd, but at that moment, there seemed no physical punishment I might have to suffer which could prove equal to watching Dix Butler beat Fred McCann half to death.

Dix stared at me. He stood up and a body-wave of heat came off him. It altered the light in the room. At that moment, I would have testified to the existence of the human aura. His was three separate hues of red. With all I had been taught about hand combat in the last year, there was, right now, so little I knew in comparison to him. If he decided to hit me, he would. The only question was whether he would. If we die in violence, does a demon come to greet us in the same red light?

Now—and I may as well testify to this as well—the light ebbed to green, a dull and burned-out green. The air felt scorched. I heard a voice stirring in Butler's throat before speech came forth. "Are you telling me that I have been out of line?"

"Yes."

"And owe your friends an apology?"

"Yes."

"Tell it to me again," he said.

I hardly knew if this was a challenge or a request to save him some fraction of face. "Dix, I think you owe my friends an apology," I said.

He turned to them. "I'm sorry," he stated. "I beg the pardon of Mr. and Mrs. McCann. I was out of line."

"It's all right," said Fred.

"Grievously out of line," he said.

"It's accepted," said Bunny Bailey McCann.

He nodded. I thought he was going to salute. Then he grabbed me by the arm. "Let's get out of here." He called to Maria, "Put their drinks on my tab," and propelled me toward the door. I had a last clipped vision of Ingrid looking at me with wise and tender concern.

8

I CANNOT COUNT HOW MANY ALLEYS WE TRAVERSED. THE GHOSTS OF
long-gone buildings rose out of every bombed-out plot. Here and
there was a light in a window. In some schoolboy year, I might have
brooded with adolescent melancholy on the life to be revealed in each
such room. A couple fighting, a child ill, a man and a woman making
love, but now in this hooded city of sewers and empty spaces, where
intelligence was forever for sale, I saw instead behind each illumined
window shade an agent in transaction with another agent, BND with
SSD, SSD with KGB; and there, in the far building to the left with
its one light, was that a safe house that belonged to us? Had I helped
to stock it on the day I made the rounds with C. G. Harvey? I do not
know if the emanations of the dead had altogether ceased to stir
beneath the Berlin rubble, but I had never been more aware of the
bones compacted in this city.

Butler did not say a word. Walking along at his quick pace, I felt
him coming to some decision, but what it was I had no idea until I
recognized that our route was coming about and we were returning
in a long circle to the Kurfürstendamm. I now felt tied to him in all
the protocols of violence. He would not injure me provided I accompanied him, but I must convoy him through the night.

Six or eight blocks from the lights of the Ku-damm, he turned
into another alley. "Let's look up one of my sources," he said. He
spoke beneath a streetlamp, and there was a smile on his face I did not
like, as if the first of my payments had commenced. It was the most
peculiar smile, evil, I thought, yet he had never looked so young.
"Get set," he muttered, and banged on a heavy wrought-iron gate in
the wall of a small building. A doorman in a black leather overcoat and
a black leather cap came out of a room on one side of a short arched
tunnel behind the gate, took a look at Butler, slid the latch, and
opened the door to a passageway on the other side of the arched
tunnel. The doorman did not look happy to see Butler. We walked
down some stairs to an empty cellar room, crossed it, opened another
door, and were in a bar. It was the way I had envisioned it would be
if I ever got into night combat. You might be running across a dark
field and then all the world would come to light at once. Men in every
kind of costume were walking around. Some were flushed, some were
pale, and many were sweating profusely. More than half were stripped

to the waist, and a few were walking around in a jockstrap and boots. The odor of ammonia was everywhere, harsh, sour, and fierce as disinfectant. I thought a bottle of Lysol had broken, but the smell had too many properties of the flesh. The odor, I realized, was urine. The presence of urine prevailed. It stood in puddles on the floor and in a gutter at the end of the bar. Beyond was a wooden rack, and two naked men, about five feet apart, were pinioned there. A fat German in an undershirt, his pants hanging low by his suspenders, his fly open, was urinating over one of the men. It was a long urination. The man in the undershirt had a cigar in his mouth and a half-gallon of beer in one hand, his penis in the other. The flush of a heavenly sunset was on his face. He urinated upon the body and face of the fellow at one end of the rack as if he were watering every flower in the garden. Then he stepped back to give a little bow to the sounds of approval from those who watched. Two other men came forward, each to urinate in concert on the other naked man. I could not cease looking at the two humans harnessed to that frame. The first was a wretch, ugly, scrawny, and craven. He winced as the fat man pissed on him, he shivered, he trembled, he closed his mouth and ground his teeth as his lips were deluged, but then, doomed to betray himself, he suddenly gaped his mouth wide, drank, sputtered, choked, began to sob, began to snicker, and to my horror aroused a stirring of cruelty in myself as if he were supposed to be there for urinating upon.

His partner, equally in bonds, did not look like a wretch, but a creature. Caught in the crossed streams of two dark, intent young Germans who appeared to be sharing one black leather costume (since the first wore nothing but the jacket, and the second, the pants), this other naked figure was blond and blue-eyed, with a Cupid's mouth and a deep cleft in his chin. His skin was so white that his ankles and wrists chafed in his bonds. He gazed at the ceiling. He seemed delivered from all the people who pissed on him. I felt as if he lived in that place where humiliation has ceased to exist. Something of the tender concern Ingrid had bestowed in her last look on me now came forward into my drunken stirrings. I wished to wipe this young man off and set him free, or at least I had such thoughts until I came back to myself long enough to recognize that this cellar existed—it actually did exist! I was not alone in some theater of my mind. In the next moment, I was full of the panic to flee. I felt as if I must, absolutely must, decamp from here, and immediately, but even as I looked for Dix, he came into view beside the male couple who formed the complementary halves of the one black leather outfit, moved them two feet to the side by the fact of his presence, unzipped his fly, and urinated on the blond boy's thighs and calves without spleen or lust, perfunctorily, like a bored priest whose fingers have ceased to feel the immanence of the holy water; then, Dix's presence intimidating the German couple to put up their waters altogether, he now bent forward, watchful that neither his body nor his clothing touch the blond boy, and whispered in his ear, inclined his own ear to listen, and when there was no reply, the creature off in some rapture of the pits, Dix slapped him professionally, once, then twice, repeated his question, and when there was still no answer, said, "Next time I'll fry your ass, Wolfgang," and stepped away, walking like a show horse between the puddles, hitched a thumb at me, and we departed. "Damned drug-assed bastard," he said as we hit the air. "Totally senseless tonight."

"You know him?" I asked.

"Of course. He's my agent." Some part of me was ready to ask more questions, but I could not go on. I felt as if I had taken a bad fall.

"I don't believe what I saw," came out in a hoarse little croak.

He began to laugh. His mirth echoed in the small canyon of the alley, the back of six-story buildings close upon us from either side. We debouched into a street, and his laughter went caterwauling away from him on the wind. "The goddamn people I'm associated with," he said aloud, but if I thought he was referring to the cellar bar, his next few words removed the error. "Are we supposed to conquer the Russians with personnel like you and McCann?"

"I'm not a street man," I said.

"That's where the war is fought."

"Yes. In that bar."

"Half of our agents are queer. It comes with the profession."

"Do you pretend to be one of them?" I found the courage to say.

"I use them," he told me shortly. We did not talk for a while. We walked. When he spoke again, he had come back to the subject. "I don't think you received my point, Herrick," he said. "Agents lead a double life. Homosexuals lead a double life. Ergo"—had he picked up *ergo* from me?—"agents are often homosexual."

"I would judge that homosexuals are just a small part of it."

"You would judge," he jeered. "You choose to believe what you want to believe."

"What are you telling me?" No blow taken in boxing at the Farm had left me as numb in so many junctions of the mind. I needed a drink, but not to relax, rather to return to myself again. I was chilled in my mind, chilled in my heart, and not without the beginnings of some lively disturbance below. The nearness of sex to urine and feces seemed a monstrosity, as if some mongoloid of the Devil had been there at the Creation dictating nether anatomy. The smell of drains, prevalent in these nocturnal Berlin streets, was in my nose.

"What are you telling me?" I repeated. My discomfort kept shifting as if we were playing at musical chairs and one of my better views of myself had just lost his seat.

He stopped at a door, took out a key, let himself into a small walk-up apartment building. I did not care to follow, but I did. I knew where we were. It was one of C. G. Harvey's safe houses.

Once inside, installed in our chairs, holding glasses of bourbon neat, he looked at me and rubbed his face. He did this slowly and carefully for several minutes as if domiciling his temper.

"I've never talked to you," he said.

"You haven't?"

"Not as a friend. I've merely offered facets of myself."

I made no reply. I drank. It was as if I were starting to drink all over again. The liquor set loose a coil of thought in me, and I began to ponder the creature named Wolfgang whom Butler had promised to fry. Was Wolfgang, beatific Wolfgang, the same fellow known as Franz? Described by Mr. Harvey, he had been slim and dark. Of course, hair could be dyed.

"One difference between you and me," said Butler, "is that I understand our profession. You have to be able to turn yourself inside out."

"I am aware of that," I said.

"You may be aware of it, but you cannot do it. You get stuck in the middle. Your asshole is tight."

"I believe I'm ready to drink up and leave."

"Your asshole is tight," repeated Butler. He began to laugh. Of all the times I had heard him laugh tonight, none sounded so full of warring parties to his own balance. "They're crazy in this fucking Company," he said. "They give a polygraph test to all of us. 'Are you homosexual?' they ask. I never met a closet homosexual who couldn't lie to a polygraph. I'll tell you what they need in this Company. An initiation rite. Every Junior Officer Trainee ought to be ordered to pull down his pants on graduation day. Get his asshole reamed by a wise superior. What do you think of such a thesis?"

"I don't believe you would submit to it yourself," I said.

"I've had my initiation. Didn't I tell you? My big brother used to corn-hole me. From the time I was ten till I was fourteen. Then I knocked him down, and he stopped. That's what they mean by white trash, Herrick. Now, I do not believe there is any man in the Company who could stick it up me against my will. No one has the physical force."

"What if they had a gun?"

"I would die first." He smiled at me. "All the same, taking it up the ass, out of one's own free God-given choice, may be another matter. Call it the next thing to yoga. Frees the associations. Readies you for the street."

"Maybe I'll never be ready," I said.

"You dumb, smug, superior son of a bitch," he said. "What if I were to push your face into the carpet, and manhandle your cherry pants off your cherry ass? Do you think I'm strong enough?"

It was not routine to speak. "I think you're strong enough," I said, and my voice was weak in my ear, "but you don't want to."

"Why?"

"Because I might kill you."

"With what?"

I was silent.

"With what?"

"With whatever it took."

"How long," asked Butler, "would I have to wait?"

"Till whenever. Till I would do it."

"Do you know, I think you would."

I nodded. I could not speak. Too much fear was in me. It was as if I had already committed murder and did not know how to escape.

"Yes," he said. "You could shoot me in the back afterward." He pondered this. "Or even in the front. I'll say that for you. You might shoot me if I took away the only thing that is yours. The poor little cherry in your asshole. I wish you had something more to hold on to—you might not be so desperate."

If my father had uttered those words they could not have been more painful. I wanted to explain that I might be better than that. I believed in honor, I wanted to tell him. Certain kinds of honor could not be lost without demanding that one consecrate oneself thereafter—no matter how unsuited and unprepared—to a life of revenge. I knew, however, that I could not express this aloud. The words would never survive in open air.

"Well," he said, "maybe old Dix is not going to go in for breaking and entry. Maybe old Dix is wrong and ought to apologize." He weighed this. He weighed his glass. "I was wrong," he said. "I apologize. I apologize for the second time tonight."

But he looked as intent and full of ungovernable tension as ever. He took a long swallow of his bourbon. I took a short one of mine, happy for its heat.

Now Butler stood up. He undid his belt buckle, opened his pants, and stepped out of them. Then he dropped his jockey shorts. He was swollen, but without an erection. "There's two kinds of sexual behavior between men," he said. "Compulsion and mutual regard. The second does not exist until the first is attempted. So I decided to frighten you into putting out for me. But that don't work. So, now I can respect you. Come," he said, and he reached forward and took my hand, "take off your clothes. We'll do some good things to each other."

When I did not move, he said, "You don't trust me, do you?" In answer to my silence, he smiled. "Let me be the first," he said, and he bent over nimbly, put his fingertips to the floor and then his knees, and raised his powerful buttocks to me. "Come on, fuck-head," he said, "this is your chance. Hit it big. Come in me, before I come back in you." When I still made no move, he added, "Goddamnit, I need it tonight. I need it bad, Harry, and I love you."

"I love you too, Dix," I said, "but I can't."

The worst of it was that I could. An erection had risen out of I know not what, from puddles of urine on a cellar floor and a fat German slobbering his beer, from the buried loves of my life, from bonds of family and friends and all the muffled dreams of Kittredge, from naked-ass locker rooms packed into the constrictions of my memory, and the recollection of St. Matthew's Arnold, except here were no fat sweet buttocks, but two clumps of powered meat belonging to my hero who wanted me up his ass, yes, I had an erection. He was right. It was my chance to hit it big. I could steal something of his strength. And knew that if I did, I might live forever on this side of sex. But he had told the truth. I was too timid to live in such a way. He could leap from woman to man to woman, on top, on bottom, or hang from his heels. He was pagan, an explorer of caverns and columns, and I happened to be the piece of human work he wanted inside himself tonight. For what, I hardly knew. Was it a fiber from the spine of New England? Something he had missed? I felt for him. I walked around in front, knelt, kissed him once on the mouth, stood up quickly, stepped to the door, unhooked the chain, and felt an obligation to turn around and look at him one more time, as if in salute. He looked back at me and nodded. He was sitting on the floor.

Out in the street, wind flayed the cheeks of my face. I walked along quickly. I knew I had not gotten out unscathed. "I love you, Dix," were the words that would come back to me, and I writhed at the squalid echo they would soon acquire.

Instinct took me to Die Hintertür. Stalking night streets with a full erection must have served as my vector. An empty taxi passed, and although I needed to walk, on impulse I hailed him and thereby arrived at the nightclub just as the steel shutters were coming down, and Ingrid, small pocketbook held in one of her square hands, short and ratty fur coat on her shoulders, was shivering on the curb in the 4:00 A.M. winds. Without a tremor of hesitation, and the most perfect smile on her face as if this coincidence of our meeting was but the first note in a romantic symphony whose composer could only be Herr History, she came right into the cab, gave an address, and offered the full seal of her lips to mine. I went all the way back in my mind to the prep school instructor who had *glommed* me, but this was the night for such recollections to turn in their foundation. I was all over her in the back of the cab and could not stop kissing. "Oh," she kept saying in some mixture of English and German, "maybe you love me more than a little," and the repetition of *ein bisschen* (so much like "ambition") kept one small part of me in a state of standoff amusement while the rest was taking in the iron-corded fatigue of her legs and shoulders after a night of dancing, absorbing all of her pent energy, good and ill, into my fingers and my hands. We were necking and petting and gripping and grabbing and nipping one another like two exercise machines set loose upon one another. Since my education into the interstices, locks, and patents of a girdle was only now commencing at the age of twenty-three (Ingrid may have been slim, but she was German—in consequence, she wore a girdle), I was making frantic calculations whether to mount some central attack in the back of this cab, or to countermand the address she had given and take her to my apartment, my bed, and the inevitable waking up in the morning to the hung-over embarrassment of having to stumble through the cover names of my fellow CIA men. Already I could hear their guarded good-morning while they debated the dubious wisdom of bringing in this outside source (female) and sitting her down *en famille* at the linoleum-covered breakfast table. I was still running such calculations through the decision mill of my bourbonified brain when we pulled up at the address she had given to the cabdriver and it was an all-night food mill in full view of the street, two blocks off the other end of the Kurfürstendamm.

In that place, I quickly received one more education on Berlin and its nightlife. Half the people in this place were familiar to me. I had seen them in one nightclub or another over the last week. Now they were having coffee and American hamburgers, or schnapps, or cognac, or beer, or pig's knuckles and sauerkraut, or applesauce and potato pancakes, or gin and tonic, or Coca-Cola, or patisserie, or pastrami, or roast duck—a hell of an unlikely place, and brightly lit. I saw again some of the starched businessmen who had been dancing at Remdi's and the Bathtub and the Kelch, their collars wilted now. Prostitutes who were familiar, plus a few of the all-night divorcées like Helga were there, and to my disbelief, nothing less than the fat German I had seen not more than an hour ago whose pants had hung from his suspenders. He was neatly powdered now, having gone, I suppose, to just the kind of all-night barbershop that would complement this all-night emporium of food and drink, and, indeed, in the next moment, I saw *the wretch.* He, too, was bathed and powdered. Dressed in a gray suit and vest, he wore steel-rimmed spectacles, and looked like a clerk with spavined cheeks and a large appetite: He was devouring a plate of beans.

Ingrid, all the while, was hugging her fur coat and my body as one, proclaiming to everyone who watched that she had bagged an American. Ingrid was also eating an enormous "Grilled American" of Westphalian ham, tomatoes, and Muenster cheese. I sat beside her in twitchy detumescence while she slogged down a vast mug of beer, thereby communicating to me in twenty minutes how profoundly one might, over twenty years, come to dislike the eating habits of a mate. Poor Ingrid. The Back Door, as she put it to me with a toothsome grin, never allowed their help enough of food and drink to produce more than a goat turd for the other back door. On this night, therefore, in which my own sphincter had almost played a prominent role, insight came over me at last: I was in the presence of German humor. Die Hintertür. I got it. A nightclub for assholes.

She finished her meal. We found cabs waiting outside. We took one to another address she gave. It proved to be a cavernous cheap hotel in another bombed-out working-class quarter of Tempelhof, and the night clerk took an unconscionable time studying my passport and hers, and finally returned Ingrid's with a muttered German insult I could not catch. I begged her to explain, and in the rise of the self-service elevator which took us up at a creak and a hitch past one plaster-dusted floor after another she managed to translate. "American whore-bitch fucker" was something like how it went, but if there is a universal harmonium of consonants and vowels, it certainly sounded worse in German.

It affected her mood. We came to our floor and walked down an echoing cavernous hall. She took the key, whose prominent handle was the size of a phallus itself, and opened the door to a room as cold and damp as the night outside. The overhead bulb in the ceiling may have offered twenty-five watts. One standing lamp offered another such bulb, and the bed presented a coverlet in the full palette of entropy. That may be described as not-brown, not-gray, not-green, and it was long enough to wrap around a bolster as heavy as a rolled-up rug.

We started to kiss again, but with less fever, and she shivered. "You have *zwei Mark*?" she asked. When I found a coin, she put it into a gas meter, came back to me for matches, lit it, and stood by a fire which came up in a blue whispering flambeau behind artificial logs. I felt the weight of the city. All of Berlin was now contained for me in the image of a gargoyle straining to move a boulder up a slope—no vast originality at this hour!—and then I embraced her again, and we shivered with that side of our bodies which was not toasted by the fire.

I did not know how to proceed. The girdle seemed more formidable than ever. Sobering up, I was all too near to nothing at all, but my erection, holy prime factor, was intact. It had been waiting for years. I felt as if long-dead Hubbards were gathering about. In this ghostly room, so much more suited for laying out a corpse than lying on a living body, a filament of desire rolled around in me, hot and isolated as a wire in a heating coil. Yet it must have warmed some minimal ardor in her because now she was kissing me back, and after a moment, with a muted reluctance as grave and stately as a formal procession, we moved the four steps to the bed, and she lay down on the edge of it, gave, presto, a few deft snips and snaps to the yoke of the girdle, unhooked her garters so that each falling stocking inspired one more thin filament of desire—these unkempt stockings reminiscent of a pornographic daguerreotype, circa 1885, which had lain all through my boyhood in some old tin box of my father's up in Maine. Maybe my father had guarded it through his boyhood. One more family log to throw on the fire.

By the light of the twenty-five-watt bulbs, I saw revealed, without preliminary, my first vagina. As if I were robbing a house and did not wish to tarry, I opened my pants, to which she gave a grunt of pleasure at the readiness of my erection. I, however, taking another look at that repository of female secrets, was tempted to drop to my knees and pay homage until my eyes were sated of their formidable curiosity, but, child of good decorum, I did not really dare to look too long, and was certainly afraid of this vagina's superior relation (what with all its folds and recesses) to secrets of human state I could not even contemplate. Therefore, I placed the head of my cock where I thought it should go, shoved, only to hear another grunt, now of reproach, on which she took me by her hand, and guiding me with two deft fingers, put her other hand against my chest as I started to plunge. "No, Harry, *verwundbar!* I'm sore. Go easy, go easy. You are *mein Schatz, liebster Schatz*—soldier boy." And she opened her brassiere which had a catch at the front I had never thought to look for, and at the sight of those breasts, which were a little depleted but, all the same, *breasts,* the first naked ones ever seen so near to me, I plunged, and came back, and plunged again, and had a picture, as I now entered the land of sex (where far-off universes of the mind will, I suppose, implode) had, yes, a picture of Allen Dulles talking before us on the day of our initiation about a girl on a tennis court. Then I plunged and came back, and plunged again, and realized I was inside a cunt. It was another world, and all at once: The inside of her belly was one's first station in heaven, but another part of me was offended. What mean auspices—what a foul initiation! I hardly liked the odors in this stale cold room. A thin avaricious smell certainly came up from her, single-minded as a cat, weary as some sad putrescence of the sea.

So I hovered between, half a lover entering the hypnotism of love, and half an onlooker doomed to observe myself in the act of love. On I sawed, back and forth.

Soon she was moist and did not wince each time I plunged, or was it that she winced less? I must have made love at ferocious speed because the powers of displeasure were certainly growing—this wretched room and yes, this poor and hungry girl who loved me from the outside first—America first! I moved in two worlds at once, in pleasure, and in lack of pleasure, and it kept me moving. I did not dare to stop or all erection could be gone; then there came a few minutes when the sweat stood on my neck. In this chill half-heated icebox of a chamber, standing, feet on the floor, while a strange young woman was laid out before me on the bed, no heat gathered in my loins. I was lost in a perpetual-motion machine, I was in the purgatory of desire, and I humped and I pumped beneath a pall, on and on, until the image of Butler's knotted buttocks came back to me again, and the perpetual motion machine staggered, took a loop, then a leap, and the filaments of heat began to revolve in me and my body to quake with the onset of the irreversible. Pictures of her vagina flickered in my brain next to images of his ass, and I started to come, and continued to come, and to come from the separate halves of me, and had a glimpse of the endless fall that may yet be found on our way into the beatitudes.

We shared a cigarette. I was feeling a good bit better now. Achievement was my portion. Gloom might still reside in the outer reaches, but half the world was better than none. I adored Ingrid, and did not feel a thing for her. At the end, I had been all alone in myself. Now, she nuzzled my nose with her fingertip as if we were newly-weds and she was examining the features to face her in years to come. Then she spoke: Tomorrow at work she would inform Maria. That was the sum of her first speech. Ingrid was filing territorial rights.

"What will you tell her?" I asked. Maria, in secret, was my preference, and it occurred to me that if Ingrid spoke well of me, perhaps Maria would take another look.

"If she asks, I will say"—and she intoned the next words with special clarity—*"schwerer Arbeiter, aber süsser,"* and Ingrid offered a kiss.

It did not seem to me that the mysterious Maria would be particu-larly intrigued by a hard worker who was sweet.

The dawn was coming at the window. Ingrid would now go back to her husband, to her child, her mother, her brothers, and her cousins, and I would have time to change, take a bath, and go to work.

9

I NEVER DID GET TO SLEEP NEXT DAY. A TAXI RIDE AT DAWN DROPPED
Ingrid off at the shabby seven-story apartment house where she lived,
then a stop at my apartment, a shower—I was off to my job.

If I had hope that Bill Harvey could have forgotten his last conversation with me, it was at once dispelled. Before I filled my coffee mug
from the urn, the buzzer rang, and Chief's low voice reverberated in
my ear. "Start the London push with these fellows," he said, and
furnished me three cover names: Otis, Carey, Crane. "Approach
them in that order. Otis is an old friend. Has the clout to do the job.
Carey's a hard worker and will produce. Crane is less experienced but
a go-getter."

"Chief, do you want me to put all three on the job?"

"Hell, no. Take the first one who is available. Tell him it's worth
a couple of Brownie points." He hung up.

I had by now developed enough sense of Company security to
anticipate the difficulties. If Berlin Base wished to speak to Station in
London, or in Paris, or, for that matter, in Japan or Argentina, such
telephone traffic had to be routed through the hub in Washington. It
was out of bounds to go around the rim. If the procedure was time-
consuming, I undertook it nonetheless with no disdain. Exposure to
the shenanigans of the cellar bar had led me to see why foreign
outposts of the Company were not encouraged to communicate directly with each other. Given the amount of deviant behavior in the
world, communications along the rim could become damnably exposed—far safer to feed all messages into the hub and out again.

So I was soon engaged in the webwork of prearranging telephone
calls from Berlin to Washington to London, and spent the morning
putting in requests to speak at specific times that afternoon on secure
phone installations at London Station with Otis, Carey, and Crane.

By early afternoon, I reached cover-name Otis in London.

"What the hell is this," he asked, "and who are you? My boss is
pinning donkey tails on my ass. He thinks I'm looking to transfer to
Berlin."

"No, sir, it's not like that at all," I told him. "Big BOZO, Berlin,
needs a helping hand in London. On a minor matter."

"If it's minor, why didn't Bill use a fucking pay phone and call me
at my apartment?"

I was uneasy that Harvey's first name was used so freely, but then this was a secure phone. I replied, "The matter, when all is said, may not be minor. We don't know."

"What's your name?"

"Sloate. Charley Sloate."

"Well, Charley boy, tell me, what made Harvey think of me?"

"I don't know, Mr. Otis. He said you were an old friend."

"Bill Harvey doesn't have old friends."

"Yessir."

"Who are you, the flunky?"

"A rose by any other name," I managed to say.

Otis began to chuckle. "Charley boy," he said, "do me a favor. Walk Bill Harvey's little project around the corner and kick it in the ass."

"Yessir."

"I'm going to break a rule of two months' standing and have a martini before five."

"Yessir."

"Bill Harvey. Jesus!"

He hung up.

While I did have some idea that SM/ONION was not going to be found in London, I still had to proselytize Carey or Crane into working on our request; otherwise, I could face Base Chief Harvey with a report that I had nothing to report.

I prepared, therefore, to speak to Carey, the man described as able to produce. I told myself that Carey would not know the rank of Charley Sloate and I must address him as an equal. I had certainly been too meek with Otis.

It was a firm preparation, but Mr. Carey was not in London. His secretary, however, was pleased to be talking over a secure phone. "This," she said, "is the first time for me, Mr. Sloate. I hope you won't take it personally, but you sound like you're down in a well. Do I sound sort of ghoulish too?"

"We will improve on closer acquaintance."

"You're funny."

"Thank you."

"May I say whatever I want to over this phone?" she asked.

"It's safe."

"Well, Mr. Carey is in America. Can he assist you from there?"

"I don't believe so. When's he coming back?"

"Oh, it's at least a couple of weeks. He and his wife are getting a divorce, and he's over there to divide the property. It's a difficult time for him."

"Could you do something for me?" I asked.

"I'd be glad to."

"We're trying to locate a Company man who's been assigned to London. All we have is his cryptonym."

"Mr. Sloate, I'd love to be of help, but that kind of access is closed to me."

"Yes, I thought it might be."

"In fact, I received a reprimand from Mr. Carey because I wasn't careful enough. You won't repeat this?"

"No."

"Well, once or twice, I let slip his real name while talking to his colleagues, and that is a negative mark. I knew they were aware of the selfsame real name, so I wasn't as properly careful as I should have been about cover."

"I have trouble with such stuff too," I said.

"You're nice." She paused. "Will you ever get to London?"

We chatted about whether I would ever get to London. She assured me that it was a good place for Americans.

I was down to Mr. Crane, the go-getter. On the assigned time for ASTOR (Approved Secure Telephone Rendezvous), I encountered the voice of the man who would indeed help me.

"Yes," he said, "Crane on the line. I've been waiting. How is big BOZO?"

"Well, he's fine. Working hard."

"Great man. You tell him I said I would do anything he wants, and this is before I even know what it is."

"He'll enjoy your trust in him."

"Tell him I've learned a little more about poker since he took me down to my BVDs."

"Is that a warning not to get into a game with him?"

"Mr. Sloate, you'll learn at the feet of a master. And you will pay for it." He cleared his throat. Over the secure phone, it sounded like a motorcycle starting up, and I thought of the myriad of electrons scrambling and unscrambling themselves to the sound. "Hit me with the task," Mr. Crane said. "Harder the better."

"Person in question has been trying to locate one of our people, a Junior Officer Trainee, who's been recently assigned to London. His cryp is SM/ONION. We don't know his cover name or names."

"That should be the adverbial duck soup." He laughed at his own qualifier. Given our instant amity, I laughed with him. Now, we sounded like two motorcycles riding around in a large barrel.

"Need it today?"

"Preferably."

"Did you pick up any refills on this umbilical?" he asked.

"Yes. We have Repeat-Access at 1800 to ASTOR."

"Way to go. I'll call on the minute at 1800."

It was now a quarter to four. I had time to reach Harlot. To enter his secure telephone, there would be no need for ASTOR. I would be speaking directly to Washington. At BOZO, however, one still had to log in every secure telephone call, and I did not want to use William King Harvey's logbook for such a call. It would be necessary, therefore, to take a trip over to the Department of Defense where I still kept my desk even if I had not approached it in three weeks. On the other hand, DOD was half across the American sector from BOZO, and we were almost in the rush hour. Moreover, their phone might be in use. I decided to carry this operation as far as I could on my own.

Crane came back on the line at six. "I won't," he said, "give you definitive returns until tomorrow, but we don't seem to have an SM/ONION. Nor a scallion. Nor a rutabaga. Not in London town."

"Does London include all of Great Britain?"

"You don't think the Brits invite the Agency into every village with a mill, do you? London is about all of it. We've got a Consulate slot in Manchester." He stopped. "Plus Birmingham. A bloke in Edinburgh. Ditto Glasgow." He grunted.

"I appreciate your effort," I said. "I hope our troubles didn't impinge on your afternoon."

"Well, I thought I was going to have to stand up my golf four-some, but this is London. The drizzle turned into a downpour. No golf. Nothing lost."

"That's swell," I said.

"Charley Sloate, let me tell you. Our check-out will continue tomorrow, but BOZO's target is not going to be found on teacup liaison to some one-thousand-year-old color guard in Edinburgh. Target ought to be right here in London. However, we've pursued such inquiry already. Negative."

"Check."

"Where does that leave us?"

"My principal still wants SM/ONION," I said. "After all, ONION can't have an SM unless he's in England."

"Technically, he can't."

"Technically?"

"We're secure on the penmanship, right?"

"You mean this phone?"

"I mean this is *ex officio*. You're not memo-ing any of our palaver, I assume."

"I wasn't intending to."

"All right. Hear this: Cryptonyms can develop a life of their own. But, I never said that, Charley Sloate."

"I follow you."

"How important is all this, anyway?"

"I can't tell you because I really don't know."

"Inform our friend that I am ready to step up the search. We can keelhaul our files with search vouchers into the defunct cryptonyms of personnel who are still with us in London. That's a big load of wash. London Chief may query Headquarters, D.C., as to why Berlin Base has a meatball up its giggie. Does His Bigness want the onion that much? I'm happy to do the work if he does."

"I'll see him tonight."

"Good. Hear from you in the morning."

"By the way," I said, following an inspiration I had not owned even an instant before, "is there some possibility that SM/ONION is on detached duty to the English?"

"You mean Liaison to MI6?"

"Well, something of that order."

"Can't be Liaison," said Crane. "All the saddlebags at Liaison were checked out today."

"Might ONION be in a more committed activity?"

"Special duty?" He whistled. Over the secure phone, it sounded like a bear wheezing in a cave. "I don't know if we can penetrate such cover. Yet, that could be the answer."

In the evening, I had five minutes with Bill Harvey. He was taking C.G. to the opera. He was also swearing as he finished troweling his studs into a starched and pleated shirt.

"Total tap-out, you're telling me," he growled.

"No. Mr. Crane did have one interesting lead. He thinks ONION may be on special duty with MI6."

"Fearsome," said Harvey. He started to shake his head. His phlegm came up. Extracting a wet-tipped stub of a cigarette from his lips, his hand wobbled over to a standing ashtray and released the butt. His torso shook from the cough. The taffy machine started. He hawked his product into the ashtray to follow the cigarette, and like a leech it slid its way down the standing tube to the cuspidor at the bottom. His suspenders hung to his knees. I mention such details because in Harvey's presence it took that much to make you aware of anything more salient than the workings of his mind.

"This is a true son of a bitch," he said, "if it has real wings." He nodded. "Sit down. C.G. and I may just have to get to the opera a few minutes late. I have to think it out. Look at what this scenario signifies. First, an alleged file clerk is shifted all around Washington, then is shot out to Korea, slipped back to London, and now is placed on special duty to MI6. We could be talking about a bang-and-bust specialist they had tucked onto a siding in the Snake Pit for a couple of weeks. Why not? A demolition expert hidden in the Snake Pit? But what did he blow up so imprecisely that they have to send him flying around the world? What is his connection to me? Why is he now in England working for MI6? Could it have any tie-in to Suez? Shit! I happen to like Wagner, believe it or not, and I'm not going to hear much *Lohengrin* tonight. Are you free to meet me here after the opera?"

"I'll be on hand."

"SM/ONION assigned to MI6. I have a lot to kick around."

So did I. I descended to my cubbyhole office in GIBLETS, put all my papers on the floor, set the alarm for 11:00 P.M., and went to sleep on my cleaned-off desk.

This evening nap allowed me to recover from my hangover, and I awoke with good appetite and a desire to see Ingrid. I had hardly time, however, to make myself a sandwich from the icebox in GIB-LET's kitchen before I could hear the motor of BLACKIE-1 coming back to the paved turnaround in the rear of our sandbagged villa. By the look on Mr. Harvey's face as he came into the galley, his bow tie off, his dinner jacket open to show the handles of his revolvers, I gave up any notion of getting over to Die Hintertür in the next hour or two.

"Well, we arrived so late we had to promenade down the aisle just before the overture commenced," he said. "C.G. is plenty irked. She hates running that kind of gauntlet. Those Krauts hiss at you. The damnedest sound. Little pissy noises. *Psss! Psss!* I had to squeeze by an old biddy in a diamond tiara, and she was *sssss*-ing away, so I whispered, "Madame, we are the sons and daughters of Parsifal."

I was obliged to return him one blank look.

He grinned. "When in doubt, sow confusion. Strategies of Poker, Volume One."

"I heard today about your rep in poker."

"Which unqualified son of a bitch let you on to that?"

"Mr. Crane."

"He means well, but he can't play. If I claim any edge at the game, it is that occasionally I can read a mind." He burped. Mr. Harvey's gut utterances were like guided tours to his alimentary canal.

"Hubbard," he now said, "I like my mind to be clear. I hate impedance."

"Yessir."

"This situation with CLOAKROOM. It's lodged in my brain. Is it or isn't it penny-ante?"

"I suppose that's what we're trying to find out."

"The worst obsessions," he said with some gloom, "begin with the smallest things. Hell, the brain even has the same hue as an oyster. By which logic, every obsession is a putative pearl. All the while I was listening to the music, I was also running down my options. I've given up on any big American bang-and-bust man whom the Brits are grooming for Cairo. The Brits would never accept the idea that we have better technical personnel than they do. Too much pride."

"Where does that leave us?" I asked.

"Ready to do it by the numbers. I broke my own rule tonight. In these matters, you weigh hypotheses, you don't juggle them. You don't start with your largest possibilities. You paw over your small scenarios first. Check?"

"Check."

"All right. The very smallest. Let's say the whole thing is a fiasco from day one. It involves no more than some poor asinine kid who has a rabbi. Some rabbi high enough upstairs to know the ropes. KU/ROPES. Was somebody trying to tell me something right from the start?" He paused, he took a beat just long enough for my heart to lose its beat, and then went on. "Let's assume, if this is the case, that CLOAKROOM's poor performance on the cable concerning Wolfgang was an accident. I took to this possibility for a while because it was simple. I'm a great believer in Ockham's Razor. Did they teach you that at Yale?"

I nodded. Before I could offer my contribution, he stated, "The simplest explanation that covers a set of separate facts is bound to be the correct explanation. Check?" he asked.

"That's about it." Actually, Ockham's Razor, as I remembered it, went: *Pluralites non est ponenda sine necessitate*—excess cannot exist without necessity—but I wasn't about to substitute my erudition for his.

He burped ruminatively. "Our simplest scenario does not, however, manage to tell us why so much effort has been put into protecting CLOAKROOM. So I reject it. Too small. Something else is going on. Is CLOAKROOM part of a team? If so, what kind of rig are they rolling? First subhypothesis: They are the Let's-Give-the-Shaft-to-Bill-Harvey gang. Larger subhypothesis: One of our kingfish in D.C. is working a Berlin caper and it involves Wolfgang. I'm excluded. That makes me nervous. Wolfgang is one loose end, and I may be the other. Let's say it's time for a drink."

He got up, went to the icebox, took out the makings, and mixed a batch of martinis: He filled his shaker with ice, poured in a quarter inch of Scotch, poured it out, then loaded the pitcher with gin. "The best Chicago hotels make it this way," he informed me. "The bar at the Ambassador, and the one at the Palmer House. You have to use good gin. The Scotch adds that no-see-um flannel taste you're looking for. Slips the job down your gullet." He drank off his first fill, gave his glass another, and passed me one. It did slide down. Smooth fire, sweet ice. I had the disconnected thought that if I ever wrote a novel I would call it *Smooth Fire, Sweet Ice*.

"To resume. You enter my mental life this afternoon with Mr. Crane's hypothesis. SM/ONION may be in MI6. Ingenious. That certainly explains why we can't locate him at London Station. But it slings me off into my worst vice: premature intellectual ejaculation. I get too excited by hot hypotheses. If I ever went to a psychiatrist, he'd discover that I want to fuck an elephant. I have fucked, parenthetically speaking, everything else. Female, that is. But these martinis will have me writing my memoirs before long. It's the passing blaze when the gin hits your system. I am not off the track, Mr. Hubbard, merely taking on steam. Those Heinies were awful at the opera, *psss, psss*."

He lay back for a moment and closed his eyes. I did not dare to hope. I knew if I put all my mental efforts into concentrating upon his need to fall asleep, and failed to hypnotize his spirit, I would be good for not much more once he opened his eyes.

"Very well," he said, "I reject the idea of a demolition expert on loan to MI6. For all I know, the British are now planting bombs under Nasser's balls, but, as I say, they would not use one of our men for that, and, in addition, it takes us further away from Base Berlin. So, all through *Lohengrin* I was marching myself in the other direction. Since I can't explain what kind of CIA man could be inserted so far up into MI6 that he's untraceable by us, I employ an old Hegelian trick I acquired back in law school: Turn the premise upside down. What if this slippery slime-ball Señor Cloakroom-Ropes-Fragment-Onion is a young undercover operator for the English who has managed to bore his way into the CIA?"

"A mole? A mole working for the English?"

"Well, they just about managed that once with Burgess and Maclean. I don't even want to get into Mr. Philby. It'll ruin these martinis."

"But those men weren't working for the English. They were KGB."

"All Europeans, if you scratch them, are Communist. Amend that. Potentially Communist. There is no emotion on earth more powerful than anti-Americanism. To the rest of the world, America is the Garden of Eden. Unmitigated envy, the ugliest emotion of them all."

"Yessir."

He took another refill from the martini pitcher. "Let us suppose a group in MI6 was able to insert a small self-contained network into our ranks." He burped tenderly, reflectively, as if his stomach might be entering a regime of peace. "Go ahead," he said, "play devil's advocate."

"Why would the English go to such lengths?" I asked. "Don't we continue to pool some information with them? I think they have more to lose if such a venture were ever exposed than they could possibly gain from infiltrating us."

"They're still in pretty bad odor with Washington. We can't forgive them for building a royal pavilion to cover Philby's ass. Why, it was their way of saying, 'Our worst Englishman means more to us than your best detectives.' At present, we have stuff they need to know that we won't trust them with. We can't. Not so long as they are fatally inept at spotting KGB penetrations into their highest places. If I hadn't been there to sniff out Philby, he could have climbed all the way to the top. He was penultimate level already. The Russians

have demonstrated this ability time and again to recruit young Englishmen for lifetime jobs. The best young men. It's as if you, Hubbard, had been *made* by the KGB back in college, and joined the
Agency precisely to work for the Russians. Ugly to conceive, isn't it?
For all we know, it's going on right now. This much, I do postulate.
The tricky Brits have the motivation to get into our fanciest plumbing. It would give them a way of expressing themselves. Creative
bastards. Even if such an English mole is only loyal to Britain and
never to the Soviets, we're still hanging by our fingernails. Because let
there be one KGB agent working near the top of MI6, and he will get
wind sooner or later that they have a mole in our midst. He will find
a way to obtain the product and pass it on to the Sovs."

I was appalled how my inspired suggestion to Mr. Crane that
SM/ONION might be attached to MI6 had now been transmuted
into a threat to the West.

"Fearsome," repeated Harvey. "Awesome. But I'll find out.
There are a couple of Brits in this town who owe me beaucoup
favors."

"I don't see it," I said. "If the British have placed a mole in the
Company, why would they call him back to MI6?"

"Oh, they can slip him out again. Keep one step ahead of us—as
they have already. I expect they panicked. Once I got on the trail, they
decided to tuck him back into MI6 for safekeeping."

"As of now," I said, "this is your leading hypothesis?"

"As of now." He stopped in the middle of sipping his martini.
"But what do we do next?" he asked.

"That's what I don't know."

"Why, we return to the old hypotheses. We plod through them
again. One by one. From the simplest to the most elaborate. Only an
empty hypothesis fails to improve on second look."

"Check."

"So I, Hubbard, am going back to the smallest. Do you recall it?"

"Yessir."

"Expatiate."

"Whole thing a fiasco from day one."

"And?" he asked.

"Involves some poor kid who has a rabbi on high."

Now he looked me in the eye. Over the last few weeks, I had
been waiting for this. He was renowned for his ability to look at you
as if he were already dead and you would soon be. His gaze offered

no light, no compassion, no humor—just the dull weight of even-handed suspicion.

I bore up under this examination, but by the time he looked away, my hangover had returned. The gin so recently added to my blood had gone bad. Nonetheless, I took another drink. "Yes," I said, "that was your first hypothesis."

"Right. I asked you to separate out any juniors you knew who went from the Farm to the Snake Pit. Then, I told you to acquire their cryps through the Bypass."

"Yessir."

"Have you done that?"

"I may have been remiss."

"All right. I know how busy you've been. We're all remiss. Tomorrow, however, you get on the talk-box to Washington, and bring me back names."

"Check."

"Did you ever set foot in the Snake Pit?"

Was this the crux? Some instinct told me to say "Yessir."

"Yes," he said, "I've heard you were seen on those precincts."

"Well, I barely set foot there," I said. "I guess we can start, however, with me."

"What was your cryptonym on the days you went into the Snake Pit?"

"Don't you remember, sir? I told you that I can't reveal that saddlebag. It's from Technical Services."

"Nonetheless, you walked into the Snake Pit with your cryptonym."

"Yessir."

"Would they have a record of that?"

"I have no idea. I did sign an entrance book."

"I could probably triangulate your cryptonym from that. But let's save time. Unreel your last set of remarks, will you?" His eyes were now as calm and open as window glass.

"Well, sir, all the while I was waiting for clearance at Technical Services, I was instructed to use the Snake Pit for job cover. My roommates in Washington were under the impression that I went there to work every day. In fact, to implement such cover, I was given a pass to enter Snake Pit premises, and for a couple of mornings I did try to look busy. I'd take out a file, walk it down the corridor, take it back. I guess it was analogous, you could say, to my so-called job here at the Department of Defense."

"Which of your fellow trainees did you happen to run into on these excursions?"

"That's what I can't remember. I've been racking my brain. I don't recall a soul." That, at least, was true. I was the only one from my training platoon to be sent there.

"But you yourself did no real work in the place?"

"No, sir. None."

"All right. Let's call it a night."

"Yessir."

"Make those calls to Washington in the morning."

"Done."

I started to leave. He held up a hand. "Hubbard, at present, I subscribe to the MI6 hypothesis. But I still am going to take a hard look at you. Because this is the first occasion on which you've told me that you expended a little shoe leather in the Snake Pit."

"I'm sorry about that, sir. Will you believe me. It was so minor, I never thought about it."

"Well, don't stand there looking like Judas Iscariot. You've worked at your job for me. I don't turn on people for too little. Only when they flunk a lie-detector test."

"Yessir."

I got out of the room without rattling the knob. My inclination to look for Ingrid had disappeared. It was Harlot I needed. There was no choice now but to get myself over to the Department of Defense, and use the secure phone. For the first time since taking a course at the Farm, I employed evasive tactics, riding a taxicab from GIBLETS up to Charlottenburg where I got out and walked for half a mile before doubling back on my route in another taxi, which took me within a few blocks of Defense. It was, I discovered, impossible to be certain that one was not being followed. An empty street took on shadows, a taxi ride at night was dazzled by the reappearance of certain cars. I made the determination that I was 80-percent certain I had not been followed, even if my emotional state was ready to put it at even money.

Harlot, whom I had the luck to reach with no delay, was home for dinner. He listened to my account, paying particular attention to the episode with Butler and Wolfgang, then to my conversation with

Crane, and my distorted confession to Bill Harvey about the Snake Pit. I considered telling him about Ingrid as well since it was unlikely she would not occasionally have information to sell, but I chose not to. First things first.

"All right," he said when I was done, "Harvey is obviously paying attention to the largest and smallest scenarios, MI6 and you, dear boy."

The "dear boy" brought its own metallic hum to the secure phone.

"Yes," I said, "I've come to that conclusion, too." My voice must have been croaking its way through the Scrambler-Descrambler like a squall of gulls.

"I'm going," said Harlot, "to tip the scales in favor of MI6. I have a friend there. He'll come through for me. Harvey will be pointed toward our British compeers for the next couple of days."

"What will happen when he can't find out who it is?"

"He'll come back to you."

"Yessir."

"I'll tap into Bridge-Archive, meanwhile," said Harlot, "and obtain a few cryptonyms you can claim to have picked up from the Bypass. Just a few harmless Snake Pit drones. We'll choose types who are more or less your contemporaries, so as to keep Harvey convinced you're taking care of his assignment. Do you, by the way, happen to know anyone's cryptonym?"

"I do," I said, "but is that fair? A friend's career could be injured."

"It's never going to get to that. I have just made a decision. You are in this bouillabaisse because of me. Since I have legitimate Company business in Berlin, with Mr. Harvey no less, I'm coming over."

I did not know whether to take this news as a promise of succor or the guarantee that my fortune had just slipped a little further into peril.

"For the nonce," he said, "do get Mrs. Harvey to talk about her husband's decision to move from FBI to CIA."

"She wasn't married to him then," I said.

"I certainly know that. I just want to obtain a notion of the story Bill Harvey told her. Try to keep the lady close to the details. Install a sneaky on your person."

"I don't know if I could feel right about that," I said. "She's treated me well."

"You sound like the little sister I never had," said Harlot.

"Hugh, with all due respect, and I respect you . . ."

"Harry, you're in a hard game. As of this moment, I would hope you cease whimpering. Your conscience led you to this profession. Now you are discovering that your profession will oblige your conscience to see itself all too often as deplorably used, contemptible, atrocious, mephitic."

"Mephitic?"

"Pestilential. I would not be in the least surprised if iron, assuming iron has sentiments, feels much the same way when it is obliged to consign its sulphur to the furnace in the course of being annealed."

"I'll do it," I said. I did not know if it was a matter of steeling my conscience, or whether I was privately pleased by the assignment. Something new seemed to be stirring.

"Get the details," said Harlot. "The more details, the better."

"She's a closemouthed woman."

"Yes, but she does love her husband. Or so, at least, you tell me. Every injustice visited on him, therefore, must be packed into her memory. Once the closemouthed start to speak, you can find yourself on the face end of a cataract. Since J. Edgar Buddha seems to have been his usual gracious self in the manner he told Bill Harvey to get lost, do work on her sense of outrage."

"Please give my best to Kittredge," I said.

"Of course."

"Hugh?"

"Yes?"

"What if I were to locate Wolfgang? Assuming that the cellar-bar fellow was Wolfgang."

"Good point, Harry. Prepare the ground. I may want to look him over myself."

"When will you be here?"

"Figure on a week at the outside."

As we hung up, it occurred to me that the situation could come to issue in much less time.

No matter. I was too excited to sleep. Instead, I went in search of Ingrid, but it was her night off, and Die Hintertür was empty. I sat at the bar and flirted with Maria who, in turn, teased me about Ingrid. She had obviously received her report.

"That's all right," I said, "I'd rather be with you."

Maria returned her mysterious smile. I do not know what amused her, but two days later, along with everything else, I came down with a dose of gonorrhea.

10

AT THE MILITARY INFIRMARY WHERE I WENT FOR TREATMENT, I SAW Dix Butler. It was the first time I had encountered him since our night on the town, and he offered a quick guide to sexual etiquette: No reference was made to the episode in the safe house. For social purposes, it did not exist. Instead, he offered a joke about our mutual ailment, and I was relieved that he took it lightly. I didn't. I had hesitated to come to an American infirmary because my name would be recorded. On the other hand, our regulations carried serious demerits for failure to report a venereal disease. Ostensibly, no notation of this visit would go into my 201, but I was dubious.

If I did choose the official route, it was due to the medical orientation given Junior Officers on reaching Berlin. We were told it was inadvisable to seek out a West Berlin doctor since one never knew when such a person might not also be an East German agent. The SSD kept an up-to-date list of State Department and Agency personnel. Since local doctors had to report all venereal diseases to West Berlin health authorities, and since such files might as well be regarded as open to the East German police, your case could end in the hands of the SSD. They could blackmail you because of the failure to report your infection to the Agency facility in the first place. That proved to be one convincing argument.

All the same, it violated a sense of privacy to introduce CIA to my infected member. I wanted to be alone in all my shame and pride (it was, despite all, a manly disease!) and I did not wish to offer the particulars of my night. At the infirmary, moreover, I was asked to name the woman who had passed it on to me. "I don't know," I replied. "There've been a few."

"List them."

I delivered a few names—an imaginary Elli, Käthe, Carmen, Regina, Marlene—and located them in different bars.

"Better slow down with your sex life," said the medic.

"You're only young once."

"You come back venereal again, and it goes on your 201. Second time puts the tag in the file."

"Check."

I was tired of saying "Check." Dix Butler's presence reassured me. He had come to the infirmary, too, and knew presumably how to act in this sort of matter.

"Did you ever mention to Bill Harvey that I was at the Snake Pit?" I asked as we were sitting in the waiting room.

"I did."

"When?"

"Three, four days ago. Uncle Bill phoned to ask me."

"You know, I was only over at the Snake Pit to establish cover."

"Is that a fact? What were you covering?"

"You won't repeat it?" I said.

"Not unless there's another inquiry. I'll tell you, boy, I take my lead from Uncle Bill. He picked me for this slot over a bagful of other trainees."

"Well, I was over at Technical Services."

"With Rosen?"

"I never saw Rosen."

"I keep getting letters from Rosen. Long as manuscripts. He goes on about his work. It's certifiably insane. He spent time watching a whore in San Francisco through a one-way mirror. She had to slip different drugs into johns' drinks to see which drops would get the dupe to blab the most."

"Would you let me look at Rosen's letters?"

"If he's fool enough to put it in writing, why can't I show it to you?"

And, presumably, since I was fool enough to tell Dix about my job at Technical Services, he would see no reason not to repeat it to Harvey. I felt as if I had brought off a nice pocket-sized maneuver.

I was encountering a few changes in myself. If I had fallen from favor with King Bill, I did not feel weak so much as the possessor of a peculiar kind of strength. I do not know if the annealing of my conscience from iron to steel was already well begun, but I felt not unlike a soldier who has trained with considerable trepidation for a year, is now in combat, and finds it, to his surprise, a superior life. One could be dead in a day, or in an hour, but one's worries, at least, were gone. One's senses were alive. Small relationships took on meaning. I might never see Ingrid again, but the urge to protect her was instinctive. Combat, I was discovering, left me close to laughter, and full of sorrow for the brevity of my life (in this case, my career) but I was feeling cool.

Harvey had established my new status on the morning after my last nocturnal telephone conversation with Hugh Montague. "Kid," he told me, "I'm putting a crimp in your access."

"Yessir."

"Can't say how long this will ride. I hope it's resolved soon. There is one piece of luck for you, anyway."

"Sir?"

"Crane was on the line at eight this morning. He spent the last two days arguing with MI6. At first they gave no return. Then they assured him there was not one drop of onion juice on the floorboards. Six hours later, 6:00 A.M., London time, they woke him up with a phone call to his home. 'Hold off,' they told him, 'it's complicated. Can't say more.'"

"So SM/ONION is in MI6," I said. At a minimum, Harlot had made one crucial phone call.

"Looks like it, don't it?" Harvey said.

"Well, sir, I'll hang out in chancery as long as you want me to, but I can't see—"

"Kid, hold your water."

"Mr. Harvey, if there's nothing more forthcoming from MI6, and there probably won't be, I could be out on a limb for keeps. You might as well saw it off now."

"Don't estimate what I can and cannot determine."

I had an inspiration. "May I advance a guess?"

"You probably won't get an answer."

"You're going to put MI5 onto MI6." Of course. He would know any number of people in MI5 from his days in the FBI.

"I may take a reading or two," he confessed. I was amazed, given his new suspicions, that he would tell me this much, and yet I felt as if I understood him. He liked me. I had been a good pupil. If he was forever asking me to *expatiate*, the truth was that he did a good deal of it himself.

By late afternoon, Harlot moved again. A cable came to me from Washington listing the names of three people who worked in the Snake Pit. Their cryptonyms accompanied them. It decoded as QUALITY EQUALS SMITH, RUNDOWN EQUALS ROWNTREE, EASTER EQUALS O'NEILL. KU/CHOIR.

KU/CHOIR was one of my old Washington roommates, Ed Gordon. I was appalled at the open nature of Harlot's message and the effectiveness of the move. Ed Gordon, if queried, would of course deny that he had sent the cable, but, indeed, who would believe him? Supposing he had satisfied my request for a few Bypass cryptonyms, could he admit it? Poor Ed Gordon. I had never liked him much. He was half-bald at twenty-eight, had a deep blue shadow from a heavy beard, shaved twice a day, and had spent a lot of time at Villanova debating whether to apply to CIA or FBI. He was also pedantic and refused to lose an argument. Poor Ed Gordon. His testicles could be lost in this argument. Yes, I felt as hard-nosed as a combat veteran. And good. I had food to feed King Bill before concluding work for the day. He looked over the three cryptonyms, and grunted. "How did this stuff reach you?" he asked.

"Sir, you don't want to know."

"Maybe I don't." He handed them back. "Can you get any more?" he asked.

"Not from my primary source."

"Try for a secondary. My Washington people can eyeball a couple of these boys after we vet their files. But since the real actor looks to be over at MI6, it will have to wait. I'm taking off tonight to see a man in southern Germany."

I had the notion that Bill Harvey was going to Pullach, just below Munich, where General Gehlen kept the BND Headquarters.

"You won't be airborne for long," I said.

He shook his head. "I'm driving. It can be done at night under five hours, checkpoints and all, but you have to keep to 150, 160 kilometers most of the way. The martinis don't hurt. A little sleep, and I'll be ready for my man in the dawn."

"I wish I could go with you," I blurted out.

"Kid, let's not get delirious."

"Who do you have for my replacement?"

"There's one backup I always count on."

"C.G.?"

"She's coming along." He made a point of shaking hands with me. "See you in a couple of days. Have some product for me."

"Mr. Harvey?"

"Yessir?"

"Please don't tell C.G. that I'm persona non grata."

"Kid, you're a fucking prize," he said.

I left him at his desk under the thermite bombs. They were now as familiar to me as the expressions of lugubrious relatives.

I had not, however, been back at my apartment for more than a few minutes when the phone rang. It was Harvey. "Pack a bag," he said. "You're coming."

I started to thank him, but he cut me down. "Hell, no," he said, "it's not me. It's the fellow I'm going to visit. He requested that I bring you along. Says he met you in Washington."

"He did?" Now I couldn't conceive of who it was. Might it be Harlot? Had he arrived and gone directly to BND Headquarters? Was he, in effect, declaring our liaison? Harvey's next speech, however, took this supposition away.

"How you met him is more than I can figure out," he said. "The Kraut don't get to Washington that often."

11

WE DIDN'T LEAVE UNTIL MIDNIGHT. THERE LOOKED TO BE DIFFICULTIES in refueling. Harvey did not wish to use any of the U.S. Military gas stations on the route since some—particularly at night—were manned by civilian Germans, nor did he take to the idea of an impromptu stop at some army base where we'd have to wake up one or another Supply Sergeant to get the key to the storage tank. "Last time, I lost an hour that way," he grumbled. "The goddamn key was in the Sergeant's pants, hanging on a hook in a whorehouse."

"Bill, must you make a history out of everything?" asked C.G.

The problem was that we couldn't fit enough five-gallon jerricans into the trunk of the Cadillac, and Harvey wouldn't strap any to the outside of the car. "A sniper could hit us with an explosive bullet."

"Bill, why don't we go by airplane?" she asked.

"We have a couple of German mechanics at the air base. It's too easy to sabotage a plane. I ought to know."

Maintenance welded a bulletproof auxiliary tank into the trunk, and with two hours lost to that, and an hour waiting out some last-minute papers, we took off with Mr. Harvey riding shotgun, while C.G. and I were in the rear.

It was, as he had promised, a fast-moving trip. The checkpoint on the Brandenburg Autobahn offered no trouble to our entering East

Germany, nor did the second checkpoint an hour later when our southern route took us back into West Germany. We drove through flat black fields while he drank his martinis and told a tale of a captured Soviet agent who had a microdot message installed beneath a gold inlay filling. "I was the one to spot the son of a bitch," he informed us. " 'X-ray the lying bastard,' I said, and sure enough there was the faintest line between the inlay and the bottom of the cavity. 'Either the dentist is no good,' I told my gang, 'or the microdot is there.' So we unplugged the fellow's filling. Eureka: the microdot. The Russians never stop working at this job. Ever hear of their prussic-acid pistol? Shoots a spray. Nifty. The operator comes up to you on the street, fires it in your face, and *blap*! You're dead. Delay the autopsy even a few hours, and there are no signs of poison. That's why I won't walk the streets of Berlin. I want my friends to know I was terminated by the Sovs, rather than have them wondering if I popped a blood vessel from too much booze." He refilled his martini glass. "The antidote for this kind of attack, Hubbard," he said, "assuming, that is, that you are expecting some such take-out maneuver on your person, is to swallow a little sodium thiosulphate before going out. Look up the dose in the Medical Shelf at GIBLETS, Classified Manual 273-AQ, or, which is more likely, because you do have ten or fifteen seconds at your disposal before nepenthe welcomes you, is keep some amyl nitrate capsules handy in your jacket pocket. Pop them fast as you can after an attack. I always keep a few handy," he said, punching the glove compartment open, pulling out a bottle and pouring a handful. "Here," he said, passing back a dozen capsules to C.G. and to me, "keep these around. Hey, watch for those wagons, Sam!" he added to the driver without missing a beat, "give a wide berth to any wagon you see," and Sam swerved to the left at one hundred miles an hour to keep a good distance between us and a horse and wagon trundling along, step by step, on the shoulder. "I don't trust any farmer out on these roads at 2:00 A.M. with a cart," he stated, and went back to the poison pistol. "I saw a demonstration of it once down at Pullach, which is where we're going, Hubbard, in case you didn't guess."

"I guessed."

"The Heinies killed a dog for our benefit. The BND man performing the stunt just walked up, fired, and out the door. The dog did a four-legged split. Dead inside a minute. All behind glass."

"I'd like to get to the people who killed the dog," said C.G.

"One poor dog less, okay," said Harvey, "but one image seared on our retina forever. No length the Sovs are not prepared to go."

"The BND enjoys that sort of thing too," C.G. insisted.

"Now wait a minute," said Bill Harvey, "you're maligning Mr. Herrick Hubbard's friends who invite him down to Pullach for the weekend."

"Chief, I swear to you, I don't know what it's all about," I said.

"Here, take a look at this," he said, passing over a five-by-seven index card covered front and back with single-spaced typing. "This is the way I want my research presented in case I ever drop a comparable assignment on you. Skip the heavy history. Just the nuggets. Quick things. Like a box in *Time* magazine."

By the illumination of the rear seat light in the Cadillac, I read:

REINHARD GEHLEN

Now President of BND formerly known as the Org. Head-quarters in Pullach, on the banks of the Ysar, six miles south of Munich. Originally a small compound of houses, huts, and bunkers. Built in 1936 to house Rudolf Hess and staff. Later the residence of Martin Bormann. After WWII U.S. Military Intelligence appropriated it for Gehlen. General established his combined office and abode in "The White House," a large two-story edifice at the center of the original estate. In the ground-floor dining room of the White House, wall murals are unchanged from Bormann-Hess era. Big-bosomed German ladies braiding ears of corn into garlands. Sculptures of young men in gymnastic stances surround the fountain in the garden.

At present, Pullach has added many modern buildings. 3,000 officers and personnel work there at present.

Gehlen is 5′7″, nearly bald. Appears slim in earlier photographs. Now putting on weight. Often wears dark glasses. Has very large ears. Wears noiseless rubber-sole shoes. Is highly family-oriented.

Cryptonyms: The only one available to us is *Dr. Schneider.* No first name available. Gehlen is reputed to wear various wigs when traveling as Dr. Schneider.

Could this be the man I had met at the canal house? Dr. Schneider? The little man with the large ears who had crooned over

Harlot's every move on the chessboard? My mind was agog. Now, I knew the meaning of agog.

"Gehlen's boys used to have a swan," said Harvey, "who was trained to swim toward an ultrasonic signal. Under its wings, the Org sewed a couple of waterproof plastic pouches. The swan would glide across Glienicker Lake from Potsdam to West Berlin, carrying papers in the pouch, take on new instructions, and sail back under an East German bridge where the Russian sentries used to toss it pieces of bread. That's what I call a courier."

"Love the story," said C.G.

"On the other hand," said her husband, "in the old days when Gehlen's Org was expanding every month, the Krauts suffered from chronic lack of funds. Gehlen used to cry big tears to us. He'd claim he'd given up all that U.S. Military lucre to sign a contract with CIA, and now we weren't forking over the gold fast enough to suit him. Well, in fact, we were paying out a fortune, but it wasn't enough. Greedy bastard. Not to enrich himself, you understand, but to build up the Org. So, Gehlen got word out to his General Agencies."

"What are they?" I asked.

"About the equivalent of our Stations, only situated in every major German city. 'Enrich yourselves,' Gehlen told the General Agencies, and then he would get on the phone with some of his old friends in the U.S. Army. When it comes to a study of American corruption, go back to the chicken and the egg. Which came first? The U.S. Army or the U.S. Mafia? Anyway, Gehlen and our boys cook up this fiduciary maneuver. The General Agencies hand over a couple of petty SSD agents to the American Military Police who otherwise wouldn't know an enemy spy if he was confessing. Now, in return for feeding our boys with a few doormen on the Soviet payroll, the MPs pay back the local General Agency with truckloads of American cigarettes. The Org promptly sells these cigarettes on the black market to get the funds to meet their Friday payroll. Then, as soon as the Org has walked off with the cash, the MPs confiscate the truckload and return the cigarettes to the Org, who promptly sell them again to other black marketeers. The same ten thousand cartons of Camels get resold five or six times. That, my friend, was in the late forties, before I got here. The good old days."

"Tell the story about General Gehlen and Mr. Dulles," said C.G.

"Yeah." He grunted and was silent. I could feel him resisting the impulse to tell me one more tale. Had he just remembered that I was in disfavor?

"Tell it," repeated C.G.

"All right," he said. "Did you ever hear of Major General Arthur Trudeau?"

"No, sir."

"Trudeau was the head of U.S. Army Intelligence a couple of years ago. When Chancellor Adenauer visited Washington in 1954, Trudeau managed to get a word with him. He unloaded on Gehlen. Trudeau had the moxie to tell Adenauer that the CIA should not be supporting a West German organization run by an ex-Nazi. Should it hit the world press, that could be very bad for all concerned. *Ja,* says Adenauer. He's no lover of Nazis, he tells Trudeau, but in German politics, you can't make a three-egg omelette without one being rotten. One of Adenauer's people now passes this conversation on to Gehlen who thereupon complains to Allen Dulles. Our Director takes it over to the White House and informs President Eisenhower that General Trudeau is kicking American interests in the chops.

" 'I hear,' Eisenhower tells Dulles, 'that this Gehlen of yours is a nasty job.'

" 'Mr. President, there are no archbishops in espionage,' says Allen. 'Gehlen may be a rascal, but I don't have to invite him to my club.'

"Well, a battle royal ensued. The Secretary of Defense and the Joint Chiefs of Staff were on Trudeau's side. Yet, Allen won. John Foster Dulles always gets the last word into the President's ear. Trudeau was sent out to some fly-boy command in the Far East. I think it put a scare into Gehlen, however. He must have concluded that German money was safer than American. A year later, he convinced the Adenauer people to put the Org into German service. Now we have the BND. End of tale. Enough of enriching your mind. Tell me, kid, what do *you* know about our pal?"

I had been waiting for the question through each of these anecdotes. He had a habit of telling a good story with all the contained force of a lion sitting on his paws. Then—swipe!—you were part of the meal.

"I don't know much about the man at all," I said, but through the ensuing silence was obliged to add, "I'll give you any details I have."

"Yes," said Harvey. "Details."

"I met him at the house of a friend of my father's. He was called

Dr. Schneider. I hardly talked to him. He played chess with the host. I'm amazed that he remembered me."

"Who was the host?"

"Hugh Montague."

"Is Montague a good friend of your father's?"

"I don't know how friendly they really are."

"But friendly enough to invite you to dinner?"

"Yessir."

"What did Montague talk to Schneider about?"

"Not much. Schneider presented himself as a concert pianist. He played one recital, he claimed, for Wilhelm Pieck, the East German President. He said Pieck was a barbarian with low tastes. He liked to leave his official residence in the castle—I don't recall the name."

"Schloss Niederschön-something?"

"Yes."

"Good."

"Pieck would leave the official Schloss and go to a room in the servants' quarters where he would take off his shoes, put on slippers and old workingmen's clothes, and cook his evening meal. Old cabbage soup, cold noodles, pudding for dessert. He'd eat it all off the same tin plate, the pudding mixed up with the noodles. I remember wondering how Dr. Schneider could learn all this by playing an official concert for Wilhelm Pieck."

"What else did Montague and Gehlen talk about?"

"Chess."

"By the way, here's a verified photograph of Gehlen." He passed me a photostat of a snapshot. "Just to make certain that Schneider equals our man."

"He was wearing a white wig that night, but, yes, I would make a positive identification."

"One hundred percent?"

"I'll go one hundred."

"Good. Gehlen and Montague talked about chess in your presence. Nothing else?"

"I spent most of the evening talking to Mrs. Montague."

"Kittredge?"

"Yessir."

"What about?"

"Chitchat."

"Expatiate."

"Sir, if I may say, I feel more comfortable with Mrs. Montague than with her husband. We talk about everything under the sun. I think we were laughing together in the kitchen because of the funny noises Dr. Schneider, I mean, General Gehlen, was making while he played chess."

"How long have you known Montague?"

"I met him at his wedding to Kittredge. She was close to my family, you see. Her father bought my family's summer house. Since then, I've seen Mr. Montague socially once or twice."

"What do you think of him?"

"An iceberg. Nine-tenths under."

"Oh, isn't that true," said C.G.

"Well, we now," said Bill Harvey, "have a general picture that fails to explain why Gehlen asked me to bring you along to Pullach."

"Kittredge and I are third cousins," I said. "If she mentioned such a family relationship to Gehlen, he may wish to reciprocate the courtesy. Your briefing says he's very family-oriented."

"Are you saying Kittredge requested that he invite you?"

"No, Chief. Just that Gehlen must know who's working for you at GIBLETS."

"On what basis do you come to that conclusion?"

"It's my impression that everybody knows everything in Berlin."

"Son of a bitch, yes."

For whatever reason, that caused him to cease speaking. He had the ability to end a conversation as effectively as if he had turned off a light. We drove in silence while he drank alone from the jug of martinis. Flatlands gave way to rolling country but the highway curved little and there was no traffic. At Braunschweig we left the Autobahn and drove along two-lane roads, the driver reducing his speed to ninety miles an hour on the straight, seventy through the curves, and down to sixty through each village we traversed. Gonorrhea and fast car trips, I was discovering, did not accommodate each other. Yet my desire to urinate was overcome by my lately acquired knowledge of the price. Near Einbach we picked up the Autobahn again and went along at one hundred and twenty miles an hour. At Bad Hersfeld, the back roads began once more, and an endless series of turns in hill and forest and village took us to Würzburg where a better road went on to Nürnberg and the beginning of the last stretch of Autobahn to Munich. There, at an all-night gas station, 4:30 in the morning, Bill Harvey spoke again. "I need a pit stop," he said.

We parked in the shadow behind the gas station.

"Check out the men's room and the ladies' room, Sam," he told the driver. When Sam came back, and nodded, Harvey got out and motioned to me. "How about you?" he asked C.G. "Long trips never bother me," she said.

He grunted. His breath came across the night air on a riser of gin. "Come, kid," he said heavily, "just you and me and the shit-house walls." He picked up his attaché case and handed it to me.

Although Sam had presumably scouted the premises, Harvey withdrew one of his guns from the shoulder holster, turned the knob on the bathroom door and threw it ajar with one smooth pass, sighted in from that angle, crossed the open door space too quickly to be hit by any but the fastest trigger, sighted from the reverse angle, and satisfied, now entered, wheeled, squatted to scan the floor, threw open the stall doors, then smiled. "Sam is good at checkout, but I'm better." He did not settle, however. He carefully lifted the cover on each water tank, peered into the inside, took a coiled wire from his pocket, ran it a foot up the flush tunnel of each bowl, and finally let out his breath. "I have one bad dream," he said as he washed off the wire. "I'm trapped in the men's room when a satchel bag full of demo goes off."

"That's a bad dream."

He burped, unzipped his fly, turned his back to me and unleashed a urination worthy of a draft horse. I took the next stall, waited like a dutiful inferior for my own laggard waters to enter their small sound against his heavy one, and did my best not to wince as a hot wire went up my urethral passage in compensation for the pus-laden stream going out. I do not think the paucity of sound accompanying the urine I ejected was lost on him.

"Kid," he said, "your story is weak."

"It's weak because it's true." I almost cried out from the pain of my urination. My member was swollen abominably.

"That's one hell of an instrument you have there," he said over his shoulder.

I did not explain why it was twice its normal size.

"Speak softly and carry a big stick," he said.

"Theodore Roosevelt," I replied. "I believe that was his foreign policy."

"I happen to have a little dick," said Harvey. "Luck of the draw. But, boy, there were years when I knew what to do with it. Guys with little dicks try harder."

"I've heard about your rep, sir."

"My rep, hell. I was merely a cunt-lapper of the most diabolical sort." But before I had time to be prodigiously embarrassed by this, he said, "It's *your* reputation I want to know about. Did you ever fuck Kittredge?"

"Yessir," I said, lying right through the pain of wire-thin piss.

He lifted his free hand and clapped me on the back. "I'm glad," he said. "I hope you gave it to her good. Was she a cockeyed wonder in bed?"

"Fabulous," I muttered. My gonorrhea served me an undeniable lightning bolt.

"I might have had a whack at her myself if I hadn't given up on all that. Loyalty to C.G. mit lots of hard work—that's how the operation runs these days. So, I'm glad you laid the wood to her good. I hate that son of a bitch Montague."

I was discovering the secret of an escape route. You found it by making the effort to escape. "I hate him too," I said. To myself, I added, "Forgive me, Hugh." I did not, however, feel that much disloyalty. Harlot, after all, had encouraged me to find my own route through the crux.

"Have you talked to Kittredge lately?" Harvey asked.

"Yes."

"When?"

"A few days ago. After you lost confidence in me. I guess I called to complain about my troubles."

"That may be forgivable." He gave a last thwack to his penis, put it back in his pants, even as I was concluding my small torture, and said, "Do you think she could have been the one to call Gehlen?

"It might be," I said. "Dr. Schneider certainly acted like he was crazy about her."

Harvey yawped suddenly. That is to say, he belched emptily. Under the dangling light bulb, his skin had gone pale, and he was full of perspiration. I think it was an honest spasm of his much abused system. He went on speaking, however, as if physical discomfort were an element of the given, like heavy air in a railroad coach. He nodded. "If she called him, it makes sense. Gehlen would probably do anything for her. Yes, I can live with this one." Now, he seized me by the arm, and dug each one of his stubby fingers, strong as iron bolts, into my triceps.

"Are you loyal to Gehlen?" he asked.

"I don't like the fellow," I said. "Not from what I saw. I assume if I get to know him well, I will like him even less."

"And me? Are you loyal to me?"

"Chief, I'm ready to take a bullet for you."

It was true. I was also ready to die for Harlot, and for Kittredge. And for my father, conceivably. I was ready to die. The thought of sacrificing myself was still as large an emotion as I could find. The proctor in my personality, however, that young dean of probity installed by the canons of St. Matthew's, was horrified at how easily I could succumb to large acts of lying, and outrageous expressions of excessive emotion.

"Kid, I believe you," he said. "I'm going to use you. I need stuff on Gehlen."

"Yessir. Whatever I can do."

He bent over, his breathing heavy, and opened the attaché case. "Take off your shirt," he said. Before I had time to question his purpose, he removed a small plastic tape recorder.

"This is the best sneaky we've got," he said. "Here, let me tape it on."

In two minutes, his fingers fast and deft, he taped the recorder to the small of my back. Then he installed a switch through a small hole he slit in my pocket and ran a wire through a buttonhole in my shirt to which was attached a small white button which was, I realized, a microphone. He handed me an extra tape. "You've got a total of two hours, one hour each tape. Get everything Gehlen says once we're there."

"Yours, Chief."

"Now leave me alone. I got to throw up. It's nothing personal. Vomit once a day, you keep the doctor away. But leave me alone for that. Tell C.G. I'll be back in ten minutes. Maybe fifteen. I got to take my time with this. Oh, Jesus," he groaned as I went out the door, and I heard the first caterwaulings come up from his belly.

Back at the car, Sam was overseeing the transfer of gas from the reserve tank to the main, and C.G. was alone in the rear seat.

"How long did he say?" asked Sam.

"Ten minutes."

"It'll be twenty." Sam looked at his watch. "Every time we go down to Pullach he wants to break the record, but we're going to miss tonight. It's a shame. No ice. No fog. No delays for construction. No detours. He's going to ask why we didn't cut any minutes off our last time. I can't say it's 'cause he fucks around in the pit stop."

That was the longest speech I ever heard from Sam.

"Well," I said, "it's a crazy night."

"Yeah," said Sam, "tell it to the Marines." He strolled over to the door of the men's room and stood guard outside.

Back in the rear seat with C.G., it occurred to me that if luck was a current in human affairs, one had to ride on its tide. My hand went into my pocket to activate the switch to the sneaky.

"Is Bill all right?" she asked.

"He will be in a few minutes," I said.

"If people knew how hard he worked, they would understand his eccentricities," she told me.

I wanted to warn her not to utter a word; I was eager to manipulate every speech she offered. Bright was the inner light of the last martini on my moral horizon.

"I guess he's never been understood well enough," I said.

"Bill has so many gifts. It's just that the Almighty never provided him with the simple talent not to make needless enemies."

"I suppose he's taken on his share," I said.

"You may well believe that."

"Is it true," I began. "No," I said, "I won't ask."

"You can. I do trust you."

"I'm going to ask it then," I said.

"I'll answer if I can."

"Is it true that J. Edgar Hoover did not like your husband?"

"I would say Mr. Hoover didn't treat him very fairly."

"Yet Bill Harvey worked hard for the FBI." When she did not reply, I added, "I know he did."

Her silence was only to control her indignation. "If it hadn't been for Bill babysitting Elizabeth Bentley all those years," C.G. said, "you would never have heard of Alger Hiss and Whittaker Chambers and Harry Dexter White, and the Rosenbergs. The whole slew. Bill had a lot to do with exposing that gang. That, however, did not warm Mr. Hoover up toward him. J. Edgar Hoover likes to let his best people know who is the boss. His secretary, Miss Gandy, who is certainly no more than her master's voice, is perfectly capable of sending a Letter of Censure to a top operator if he happens to come into the Director's

Office with one spot of dust on his shoes. This, mind you, after ten days out in the field."

"Did that ever happen to Mr. Harvey?"

"No, but it did to two of his friends. With Bill it was worse. Inhuman, I would characterize it. The Company doesn't ever treat its people the way the Bureau did."

"Did Mr. Hoover actually fire Mr. Harvey?"

"No, Bill could not have been fired. He was too well regarded. Mr. Hoover wanted to put him in purdah, however, and Bill was too proud. So, he resigned."

"I don't believe I've ever heard the story properly."

"Well, you have to understand that Bill was sort of depressed in those days."

"About when was this?"

"The summer of 1947. You see, Bill had put in an immense amount of work trying to penetrate the Bentley network, but no dramatic success, so to speak. It would all come out later and Joe McCarthy would get the credit, but in the meantime, Bill was burning the candle at both ends. Which I attribute to his deep unhappiness with his wife Libby. They married awfully young. Bill, you see, was the son of the most esteemed attorney in Danville, Indiana, and Libby was the daughter of the biggest lawyer in Flemingsburg, Kentucky. I know only what Bill tells me, but that marriage, according to him, did contribute to his woes."

"Yes," I said. I was beginning to appreciate Montague's remark that closemouthed individuals, once under way, do not stop talking.

"Bill's critical troubles with Mr. Hoover go right back to one specific night in July 1947. Bill went to a stag party out in Virginia with a few FBI friends and had to drive back after midnight in a heavy rainstorm. He slowed down for a large puddle in Rock Creek Park, and a vehicle passing in the other direction was inconsiderate enough to race by. Bill's car was deluged with so much water that his motor conked out. He did manage to coast to the curb, but there was a foot of water all around him, and he was exhausted, poor man. So he fell asleep at the wheel. It was his first good sleep in weeks. He didn't wake till 10:00 A.M. And no police car bothered him either. Why should they? He was parked properly, and the puddle had receded. Since his car was able to start, he just drove home to Libby. But it was too late. Libby had already phoned FBI headquarters to tell them that Special Agent William K. Harvey was missing. She was hysterical

enough, or mean enough, or scared enough—I won't judge her—to
hint at suicide. 'Bill has been so despondent,' she told the Bureau. Of
course, that went right onto the record. When Bill phoned in a little
later to tell the Bureau that he was at home, intact, the Bureau said no,
you're in trouble. You see, the FBI expects an agent to be reachable.
If you're not where they can find you, you're supposed to call in every
two hours. Bill had been out of touch for nine and a half hours during
which period the Bureau had mistakenly supposed he could be contacted at home. That was a big point against him. Then there was the
potential embarrassment. What if a police car had stopped and questioned Bill while he was asleep? What if he had been arrested? Mr.
Hoover sent down the worst memo: Serious reexamination of Special
Agent Harvey's occupational readiness is advisable in the light of
wife's deputation that Special Agent Harvey has been morose and
despondent for considerable periods.

"Bill dared to carry the fight right back upstairs. These are the
exact words he wrote to the FBI inquiry: 'My worry is the natural
worry that would come to anyone who has dealt as intimately with the
Communist problem as I have since 1945.' The aide from Mr.
Hoover's office who was conducting the investigation actually sent a
memo up to Mr. Hoover saying that Bill had always been given a
rating of Excellent, and no administrative action should be taken. Mr.
Hoover just told the aide to write another memo. This one said:
'Special Agent William K. Harvey is to be transferred to Indianapolis
on general assignment.' "

"Cruel," I said.

"It broke Bill's heart. If the Agency hadn't been there to ask him
to come over, I think he might have been truly despondent."

At this moment, Mr. Harvey returned with Sam, got in the car,
and we started out again. I clicked off the sneaky.

12

BILL HARVEY FELL ASLEEP ON THE NÜRNBERG–MUNICH AUTOBAHN,
and was so heavy-eyed in the dawn that C.G. insisted on checking in
at a hotel, rather than meeting General Gehlen for early breakfast. In
the elevator, Chief grimaced. "Let's grab thirty minutes of shut-eye
and a shower."

The thirty minutes became one hundred and thirty minutes, then an hour more. Not until noon did Harvey and I get to Gehlen's office.

The General did not look a good deal like my recollection of Dr. Schneider. The absence of the white wig showed a high forehead, and his mustache was gone. He looked no more than fifty years old. His lips were well chiseled, as were his long nose, his nostrils, his small chin. His thin hair was combed straight back. Only his ears remained as large as I remembered, and continued to give him much resemblance to a bat. But I had no time to wonder why General Gehlen had chosen to be in disguise at the canal house. He pointed at me with a quick finger, and said, "Delighted to meet again." I noticed that his pale blue eyes were strikingly different. The left was aloof; the right eye belonged to a fanatic. I had not noticed that much before.

"Gentlemen," said Gehlen, "first things first. Is your young man approved for relevant levels of clearance?"

"You invited him, didn't you?" said Harvey.

"To dinner, perhaps, to reciprocate for a fine dinner, yes, but not to dine out on what I say here."

"He stays," said Harvey. I did not know if Chief's loyalty was to me, or to the sneaky.

"So be it," said Gehlen. "He will remain unless you decide it is unwise, or I deem our colloquy concluded."

"Yes," said Harvey, "we take it step by step."

"Have a smoke," said Gehlen.

He took out a pack of Camels, extracted three cigarettes, and laid them on the desk in front of Harvey. "Dear Bill," he asked, "which one of these coffin nails might distinguish itself to you?"

Harvey examined the offering. "Can't tell without the lab," he said.

"Why don't you," suggested Gehlen, "light the one on the left? Two full puffs. Then, put it out."

"It's your toy. You take it through the hurdles."

"Well, if you are not in the frame of mind to pick up on a sporting chance, I must." The General lit his prize, took the puffs, put it out, and handed the long stub over.

Harvey stripped the cigarette paper carefully. On the inside was a message. Chief read it, nodded casually, as if not much impressed, and handed it over to me.

A short, neatly printed communication was visible:

base chief berlin to pullach
to discuss security of catheter

"Good guess," said Harvey, "but that is not why I am here."

"All the same, are we able to discuss CATHETER?" He looked at me.

Harvey waved a hand in my direction. "Hubbard is cleared."

"Then sooner or later you will tell me the motive for this visit?"

"Affirmative."

"Let me now hear what I am doing so unhappily."

"Kidding is kidding," said Harvey, "but I want you to get your ass off my pillow."

Gehlen giggled suddenly. It was a high-pitched giggle which leaped like a trapeze artist from grip to flying grip. "I will remember that. I must remember that. English is the treasure, a—what do you phrase it?—the treasure *trove* of rude and grossly vulgar remarks that are—isn't it so?—*bissig.*"

"Biting," I said.

"Ah, you speak German?" said the General. "You are one of those rare birds among your countrymen familiar just *ein bisschen* with our foreign tongue."

"Don't count on it," said Harvey.

"I will not. I will put myself in your hands by limping along in my lame English. May I hope it is not also halt and blind."

"It's practically perfect," said Harvey. "Let's go to background."

"Yes. Educate me, then I will educate you."

"We may even be in the same place."

"Zwei Herzen und ein Schlag," said General Gehlen.

"Two hearts and one beat," I said hesitatingly after a look from Harvey.

"Can we agree," said Harvey, "on your losses in East Germany these last six months?"

"I think your young man's valiant efforts in German are charming, but I am not prepared to discuss material relevant to BND while he is among us."

"What," asked Harvey, "do you think we talk about in Berlin?"

I could not remember Chief Harvey discussing the BND with me, but Gehlen shrugged, as if that must be an undeniable if disagreeable fact. "All right," he said, "we have had our losses. May I remind you? Before I and my Org entered the picture, 90 percent of all American intelligence concerning the Soviets proved false."

"Your statistic goes back to 1947. We're in 1956. In the last year, your Eastern networks have been devastated."

"Such ravages are more apparent," said Gehlen, "than actual. The situation in Berlin tends to misguide one's estimate. Admittedly, Berlin shows interpenetration between BND and SSD. I would have to warn you myself if you did not warn me. The mixture of information and disinformation could approach the chaotic unless"—he held up one fine finger—"unless one possesses my foundation in the tradition of interpretation."

"You know how to read what you get and I don't?"

"No, sir. I am saying that Berlin is a study in the use and abuse of counterespionage. It is an evil city when there are more double agents than agents. Double espionage is equal in difficulty, I always say, to *Kubismus*. Which planes push? Which ones pull?"

"Cubism," I said.

"Yes," said Harvey, "I got it." He had a fit of coughing. "It is not," he said thickly, "your handling of double agents that bothers me. We have a little saying in my office: If it calls for an expert to handle one double agent, Gehlen will take on three and triple them."

"Triple them. Yes. Yes. I like that. You are a demon with your compliments, Mr. Harvey." Again I heard that odd intake of breath, somewhere between moaning and crooning, that Dr. Schneider had exhibited once over a chessboard.

"It is not your abilities we question," said Harvey, "it is the goddamn situation. You now have a large number of BND operatives in West Germany who have no instruments to play in the East. A large orchestra with no sheet music. So your boys are getting into mischief."

"Whatever are you saying?" asked Gehlen.

"I'm calling it as I see it. In Poland, you've taken a whipping from the KGB; in Czechoslovakia, you have bogged down; and now the SSD has rolled you up in East Germany."

Gehlen held up a hand. "Not true. Simply not true. You are drenched in gross misapprehensions. That is precisely because you listen with one ear, not two. Take away your CATHETER, and you are deaf, blind, and dumb. Since you do not have reliable Intelligence of your own in Germany, you contracted with the English to construct CATHETER. *With the English,* Mr. Harvey! The English, who are so feeble a presence these days that they cannot even slap Mr. Philby on the wrist."

"Let's leave the British out of this."

"How can you? British Intelligence is a sieve. MI6 might just as well be based in Moscow. It would be more convenient for everyone. As for MI5, well, I will sit down with you on one of these days when we are absolutely alone and fill you in on their real masters. MI5 is not so healthy as they pretend."

"Are *you*? Am *I*?"

"You may be the worst. With your CATHETER! To depend entirely upon intelligence received from such an outrageously overextended venture. To live with a paucity of corroboration from other sources! It is like going into an enemy hospital, lying down on their bed, and hoping that the intravenous they pump into you is glucose, not strychnine."

"I'm the one who's studying the input," answered Harvey, "and my professional reputation is committed to the validity of this product. I testify to the primacy of the conversations we tap into. A gold mine of stuff, Gehlen. You'd love to see it. You'd wallow in it."

"I should, indeed, have the opportunity. I am the only man alive on our side who has the accumulation of experience to interpret what is there. My skin starts to crawl when I think of the insights you are obliged to miss because you do not possess the background, nor the backup personnel, nor the German patience to put your hindquarters into a chair and sit there for a year if that is what it takes to come up with the well-balanced answers. All the same, I can think myself into the nature of this operation. Boxes and cartons of transcripts from your CATHETER always accumulating because CATHETER never stops spewing and spitting out tapes. Rooms full of dejected people over in your Hosiery Mill, yes, your room T-32 in Washington, all those poor people trying to make sense of it. And from that, you pick what you please, and choose to . . . to sneer, no, to . . . to . . . ." and he barked at me, *"anschwärzen.* Translate, please."

"I don't know," I said. I was in some panic. "Pinch nipple?" I asked.

"Yes," said Gehlen, *"denigrate* us. Denigrate us with your very much biased selection of useful-for-you *trinkets* out of a mountain of ore. We at the BND are not in the dire straits you paint us. I have agents of a caliber," said Gehlen, "that no one can match. At the Soviet Union desk—"

"You mean III-f?" asked Harvey.

"I mean right in our III-f, I have one superior soul. At counterespionage, he is outstanding."

"The fellow you call Fiffi?"

"Yes. You know what you know, and I know what I know, so you have heard about Fiffi. You might give your eyeteeth to have Fiffi. He produces for us what others cannot. Here, Harvey, you are the great American in Berlin, you know every secret of the city, but one. You cannot tell me anything dazzling about KGB Headquarters in Karlshorst, can you? There they are, the *sanctum sanctorum* of the KGB for all of Eastern Europe, right across the line in East Berlin, not twelve kilometers away from you, yet what can you tell me that I cannot learn from an air photograph?"

General Gehlen walked over to what looked like a very large rolled-up movie screen on the wall. From his pocket, he took a key, inserted it with ceremonial precision into a lock on the case enclosing the screen, and pulled down a carefully drawn plan in many colors about eight feet wide by six feet high. "Karlshorst," said Gehlen, "from soup to nuts. My bird Fiffi has acquired his information of this place feather by feather, straw by straw. He updates it. He adds to details. I can, at present, point out for you by name each parking space on their lot for each KGB officer. Here," he said, moving his finger with a quiver of pride and much sense of ownership, to another area, "is the lavatory used by General Dimitrov, and this"—he now walked his fingers over the plan—"is the conference room of the East German Ministry of State Security."

"We," replied Harvey, "obtain transcripts of telephone calls going from that room to Moscow. But, proceed! Tell me about the chairs they put their Red asses on," said Harvey.

"We, by way of Fiffi and his informants, can give a comprehensive weekly report on the state of SSD and KGB intelligence operations, while you are still packing up mountains of undigested slag and shipping them over in cargo planes to the Hosiery Mill. The rapier, not the avalanche, let me remind you, is the appropriate instrument of Intelligence."

"I believe your Fiffi is the best thing," said Harvey, "since Phineas T. Barnum."

"I believe I understand the reference. It is insulting. Every item in Fiffi's map of KGB headquarters that we have been able to corroborate is exact."

"Of course it is," said Harvey. "It's too exact. The KGB is handing it to Fiffi. I can't believe this. You Krauts go crazy over shit-holes. Just because you know where General Dimitrov drops his load in the morning, you think you're holding the crown jewels." He pretended to ponder this. "And your other big act," said Harvey. His face was getting a good deal of color now. "Washington! Let's get into that. You've been sending beaucoup material to Washington from your high source, as you term him, in the Central Committee of the Socialist United Party. I don't believe you command that kind of guy in the highest ranks of the East German Communists."

"Dear Mr. Harvey, since you do not have ingress to my files, you certainly cannot demonstrate how my output is fiction."

"Your large assumption, buddy. I might just have a songbird in the BND. Maybe I know what kind of all-out bluff you're running."

"You have a source in the BND? It is a comedy how many sources we can put into focus concerning your show at Berlin Base."

"Yes," said Harvey, "I'm sure you know which one of our juniors has just gotten a dose from a German fräulein, provided said junior has been idiot enough to go to a private doctor. But my key people are clean. My office is sanitized. You do not have the inner picture."

"I ask you to invite your friend Mr. Hubbard to leave us alone for a moment."

"No, we take it as it comes," said Harvey. "I've already discussed this with my aide, and it's shocking. I know you've been telling Washington that CATHETER can be penetrated."

"Of course it can," said Gehlen. "Of course it can. CATHETER is so unstable that even hoi polloi of the lowest sort, the riffraff and trash of the agent pool in Berlin can pick up items on CATHETER. One day, at one of our minor desks in Berlin, who walks in from the *street* but one of the lowest Berlin riffraff, a piece of total abomination. He knows something about something, he announces to us, and he wants to sell it. My man at the desk in Berlin knew nothing about CATHETER that morning, but by evening, once he had finished debriefing your piece of filth, he knew too much. My man came running to me in Pullach by the night plane. I had to emphasize the solemnity of the classification for him. He is reliable, my man, he will not talk about CATHETER, but what are we to do with your bottom-level agent? He has a history to terrify a psychiatrist."

"Let me see if we are talking about the same fellow," said Harvey. "The father of this so-called riffraff was a pornographic photographer who worked for Nazi officials in Berlin?"

"Continue as you will."

"And the photographer ran into a little trouble?"

"Say what you mean."

"In 1939, he was put into a mental hospital for murdering several of the young women he had photographed."

"Yes, he is the father of the agent in question."

"The agent is young?"

"Yes."

"Too young to fight in the war?"

"Yes."

"But not too young to be a Communist, an anarchist, a student revolutionary, a possible SSD agent, a homosexual, a cellar-bar pervert, and now he is committed to you and to me."

"To you. We wouldn't touch him."

"I'll trade with you. We call him Wolfgang. Cryptonym WILD-BOAR. What do you call him? Now that he's walked into your office?"

"Actually, his name is Waenker Lüdke and the name he gave you, Wolfgang, is too close, in its consonants, to his real name, how otherwise? Agents have no sense."

"And the cryptonym?"

"I am already familiar with the cryptonym WILDBOAR that your office bestowed on him. So I do not feel obliged to exchange on this item. You cannot expect me to give something for nothing?"

"You didn't complain in time," said Harvey. "A bargain is a bargain."

"So, you have to possess our cryptonym? For part of your stamp collection? Here—RAKETENWERFER. You like it?"

"Rocket-launcher," I translated.

"You give your word as a German officer and gentleman that you are telling the truth?" asked Harvey.

Gehlen stood up and clicked his heels. "You honor my sense of honor," he said.

"Horseshit," said Harvey. "I happen to know that you flew over to Washington with this tale about Wolfgang. You wanted the Na-

tional Security Council to decide that CATHETER had been penetrated. You tried to scourge my backside. I happen, however, to know
the real story. This so-called riffraff, this Wolfgang, happens to be one
of your best Berlin agents. You had the consummate gall to steer him
onto one of our people working in CATHETER."

"You dare not advance this scenario. It will not hold."

"You, General Gehlen, being one of the eighteen Intelligence
officers, American, English, and German, privy to the conception of
CATHETER . . ."

"That was originally. By now, it's one hundred and eighteen, two
hundred and eighteen."

"Keep to my point. You, General Gehlen, were in a position to
put one of your best penetration agents onto one of my CATHETER
technicians."

"How would I know who are your technicians? Have you no
security at all?"

"General, now that the BND has messed up in East Germany,
your Berlin officers have so little to occupy them that they keep an
eye on every last one of my Berlin people. Child's play for you to
point your pervert of an agent at my sorry little faggot of a technician, get the two of them photographed in the act, then try to
squeeze my sick little fuck-up of a fellow into telling just enough
about CATHETER so that your top agent, my WILDBOAR alias
your RAKETENWERFER, can go into your General Agency and
fool some deskman there, thereby giving you credibility enough to
run screaming to Washington with the tainted scenario you just
tried to palm off on me."

"Diabolical slander!" shouted Gehlen.

"How dare you mislead the Joint Chiefs and the National Security Council about my operation?" Harvey bellowed.

"I must warn you," said Gehlen. "I do not have a high tolerance
for being screamed at. Not in the presence of junior assistants."

"Let me lower my voice," said Harvey. "It seems to me that the
nitty-gritty right here—"

"Nitty-gritty?" asked Gehlen.

"Die Essenz," I said.

"The essence," said Harvey, "of the matter is that my American
technician may be a pervert, but he was also enough of an honorable
American to confess to us that Wolfgang was trying to mulct the secret
out of him. So, Wolfgang didn't get information. Not unless you told

him. Here, therefore, are the alternatives. Either you lied to Washington in the first place, and CATHETER is secure. Or you primed Wolfgang with the essence. If that is so, I will bring you up on charges with your own Chancellory."

"My dear *sir*," said General Gehlen, coming again to his feet, "you are free to get up and give your chair a break! I can assure you. It needs it." With that, he pointed to the door.

It was the end of the meeting. Back in our limousine, Harvey spoke only once. "Mission accomplished," he said. "Gehlen is scared."

13

SAM WAS LEFT TO DRIVE BACK WITH THE VEHICLE. WE RETURNED TO Berlin on an Air Force plane and Bill Harvey was as silent as if curfew had been imposed. C.G. sat next to him and held his hand. So deep was his reverie that he soon began to utter fragments of ideas into the open air. "Yeah . . . won't work . . . tricky payoff . . . don't add up . . . fry Wolfgang's nuts . . ." That was the limit of the sounds that came out of him for the first half hour after takeoff. Then he spoke at last to me. "Get that tape off your back."

I nodded. In the rear of the cabin, I removed the apparatus, and returned to them. So soon as I handed over the tape recorder, however, Harvey raised his protruding bloodshot eyes. "Kid, how many tapes did I give you?"

"Two, sir."

"Where's the other one?"

"In my travel bag."

"Get it."

"Mr. Harvey, it's in the car with Sam." The bag might be, but the tape of C.G.'s voice describing Mr. Hoover's relations with Mr. Harvey was in my pocket.

His telepathic powers must have been going their ruminative round, for he growled, "There isn't anything recorded on the backup reel, is there? No incidental remarks?"

"No, sir."

"Just a good clean empty tape?"

"Has to be."

"Let's see what you have here." He turned on the beginning of the interview, and ran the fast-forward to Gehlen's last speech. The recording, however, was muffled and offered odd doublings of resonance. Sometimes it sounded like the creak of a rocking chair.

"At the Farm, they didn't teach you to sit still when you're wearing a sneaky?"

"Well, sir, they didn't."

"What I hear best is the twitches in the crack of your ass."

"Do you want me to do a transcript?"

"Is there a typewriter in your apartment?"

"Yessir."

"I'll drop you off there."

"Wouldn't it be easier at the office?"

"Yes," he said, "but I'm dropping you at your apartment." He commenced a careful study of me after this remark.

"Hubbard," he said, "do yourself a favor."

"Yessir?"

"Don't leave your apartment."

I looked at C.G. She merely nodded. None of us spoke for the rest of the flight. Nor did he say good-bye when his car left me at the door.

Three hours later he telephoned. "Done the transcript?" he asked.

"Halfway through."

"Can you read the voices?"

"Eighty-five percent."

"Try to do better."

"Yessir."

"Sam phoned in from Bad Hersfeld. Trip report is routine. No BND is following him."

"Yessir."

"I told Sam to inventory your traveling bag."

"Of course, sir."

"He found no tape."

I was silent.

"Provide an explanation."

"Sir, I have none. I must have lost it."

"Stay in your apartment. I'm coming over."

"Yessir."

As soon as he hung up, I sat down. A fiery twinge passed through the canal of my urethra, sharp as a needle from hell. I had been taking oral penicillin in so much quantity that any unpleasant thought was sufficient to make me retch. I was in a pit of gloom, exactly one of those deep and dripping caverns that the dark shadows of Berlin streets seem to propose as one's final lot. My apartment worsened this mood. I had never spent any time in the place. With the exception of Dix Butler, my other roommates and I were almost wholly dissociated, since we were invariably off at work, away at play, or asleep in our separate bedrooms. I knew the scents of their shaving soap in the bathroom better than their voices. After three hours, however, of reconstructing my way through Harvey's interchanges with Gehlen, I could no longer keep to my seat. I began to explore the apartment and learned more about my roommates in twenty minutes than in two months. Since I have not stopped to describe them previously, I will not elaborate on them now except to say that there was a unique combination of neatness and slovenliness present in each of them. One fellow, a code clerk, Eliot Zeeler, punctilious in appearance, had a wholly slovenly room with stale underclothes mixed up with stale sheets and blankets in a tangle with shoes; another had all of his mess—dried orange peels, sweatshirts, newspapers, unopened mail, black-ringed coffee cups, laundry cartons, beer bottles, whiskey bot- tles, wine bottles, an old toaster, a discarded golf bag, and a ripped bolster—all carefully piled into a pyramid in one corner of his room—a social light was this fellow, Roger Turner, well turned out for every party and function that the social resources of the State Department, the Department of Defense, and the Company could offer in West Berlin. I used to pass him coming or going in his dinner jacket. His bed, however, was made, his windows were spotless (which meant he went over the panes himself), and his room was immaculate except for that pyramid of detritus. By contrast, Dix Butler's room was as formally kept as a midshipman's quarters. I said to myself, "I'm going to write Kittredge a letter about all of this," but thinking of her brought me back to Harlot, and thus to Harvey, and my own present and intimate mess. No wonder I was studying the order and disorder of my roommates—I must be looking for a few guidelines to my own. Never did the dilapidated and once prosperous dimensions of these large rooms with their heavy doors, massive lintels, overhanging window-moldings, and high ceilings bother me more. The death of ponderous, middle-class Prussian dreams per- meated the odor of these color-deadened carpets, these stuffed chairs with broken arms, the long bier of the living-room sofa with its claw feet, one missing, replaced by a brick. "Couldn't any of us have contemplated the commonweal long enough to put up a painting or a poster?" I asked myself.

Harvey appeared. He had a neat knock. Two quick raps on the door, a pause, two quick raps. He came in with a look for each of the rooms much like a police dog sniffing through a new abode, then sat down on the broken couch, and took a Colt revolver out of his left shoulder holster. He rubbed his armpit. "It's the wrong holster," he said. "The regular one for this piece is over at a Kraut shoemaker. Being resewn."

"They say you own more handguns than anyone in the Company," I offered.

"They can go kiss my royal petunia," he said. He lifted the Colt from where he had set it beside him on the couch, broke it open, revolved the cylinder, took out the bullets, looked at each one, put each one back, closed the breech, pulled back the hammer far enough to turn the cylinder one round over, then eased the hammer back. If his thumb had slipped, the gun would have gone off. This ceremony succeeded in lifting me right out of my depression and into his adrenaline. "Do you want a drink?" I asked.

He belched for reply. "Let's see the Gehlen transcript." He took a flask from his breast pocket, nipped it, offered me none, and put it back in his jacket. With a pen that wrote in red ink, he corrected the errors I had made. "For conversation like this," he said, "I have total recall."

"It's a faculty," I offered.

"You did a decent job."

"I'm glad."

"All the same, you are marooned in dogshit."

"Chief, I really don't understand. Does this have to do with SM/ONION?"

"Your nifty little scenario does not seem to be holding up. My MI5 man in London thinks Crane was offered a carrot by MI6 and started chewing on it." He belched again and took another nip from his flask. "You dumb stupid son of a bitch," he said, "how did you get into all this?"

"Chief, bring me back on course. I can't follow."

"You are insulting my intelligence. That's worse than outright disloyalty. Have a little respect."

"I do. I have a lot."

"Certain games cannot be tried on me. Know what you need for this profession?"

"No, sir."

"An understanding of light and shadow. When the light shifts, the shadow had better conform. I kept shifting the lights on Gehlen and the shadow didn't move properly. Almost, but not right."

"Will you explain?"

"I'm going to. You work for the wrong people. You have potential. You should have hooked up with Uncle Bill right here. Like Dix has. I've needed a good inside man for years. It could have been you. Now, it can't. Don't you see, Hubbard, how obvious it was to me that somebody collateral to the immediate picture had to have told Gehlen to let you stay in the room? Gehlen made moves to get you out, but they weren't real. The shadow didn't conform to the light. Do you believe Gehlen would allow that much talk about the BND in front of a Company Junior? Do you think an old fox like Gehlen couldn't spot a sneaky on a beginner like you? Buddy, if I had really needed a transcript, I would have put the sneaky on me and hid it in a way that would never be picked up. I put it on you to see if he'd choose to flush it. He didn't."

"You're not suggesting that I am linked in any way with Gehlen?"

"You are somewhere in the floor plan."

"Why would he ask for me to be brought down to Pullach if he were working with me?"

"Double gambit, that's all. Hubbard, there's a time to talk. It's getting close for you."

"I'm bewildered," I said. "I think games are going on, and I don't even know which piece I am. I have nothing to tell."

"I'll give you something to digest. You are under surveillance. You dare not leave this apartment. You have my permission to go quietly crazy here. Drink all you want. Get the DTs, and then come to me. In the interim, offer up a little prayer. Every night. Hope and pray that CATHETER stays secure. Because if it blows, people are going to be up on charges all over the place, and there is no way you won't be one of the candidates. You could end with your keister in a military can."

He stood up, returned his Colt to the holster that chafed, and left me alone. I tried to compose myself by going to work on a transcript of C.G.'s tape.

It took a couple of hours, and I had barely finished before the first of my roommates arrived from work. Then, for the next couple of hours, they were coming and going. Roger Turner was engaged to an American girl who worked for the overseas division of General Motors in Berlin, and he was excited. Her parents, in Europe on a visit, were meeting him tonight. Dressed in a pinstripe gray flannel for this occasion, he was taking them to a cocktail party at the Danish Embassy; Eliot Zeeler, out to improve his colloquial German, was on his way to the UFA Pavilion on the Kufu to see *Around the World in Eighty Days*, which had just won an Academy Award, and was being presented, Eliot assured me, with German subtitles, thereby offering an enjoyable means of improving one's colloquial competence. Did I wish to accompany him? I did not—I didn't tell him that I couldn't. My other roommate, Miles Gambetti, whom I rarely saw, phoned in to ask if there were any messages. He had described himself on the one occasion we talked as a "glorified bookkeeper," but Dix upgraded that. "He's the accountant who watch-dogs our Berlin proprietaries. The KGB would take a crack at Miles if they knew what he did."

"Why?"

"Because once you pick up on how the money is allotted, you can draw a good picture. KGB can name our banks here, and our airline, the religious groups we fund, the magazines, the newspapers, the cultural foundations, probably even the journalists we pipe into, and they have a window on the labor union officials we own. But how much do we allot to each? That shows the real intent. Hell, if I was KGB, I would kidnap Miles."

I was thinking of this conversation now that the night was on me and I was alone in the apartment. Indeed, in curious fashion, I clung to Dix's remark, and pondered the work and functions of Miles Gambetti (who had a most neutral presence, neither handsome nor ugly, neither tall nor short) because I now needed some sense of the size of all our activities, not only in Berlin but in Frankfurt and Bonn, in Munich, in all the Army bases where we had dummy working slots, all the American consulates in Germany, all the corporations where we might have a man or two, I needed some sense of my work as small and in its place, not large, not damned, not doomed. So I prayed that Chief's powers of exaggeration equaled his bulk and I was but a passing mote in his eye. Alone in the apartment, I felt as alone as I had ever been.

Dix dropped by to change his clothes. He was off for the evening.

He invited me along. This time I explained that I was restricted to quarters. He whistled. He looked sympathetic, so sympathetic in fact that I began to distrust him. He was Harvey's man, I reminded myself. I, who had always been able to calculate my loyalties and the loyalty of the members of my family as closely as a table of organization (so that it never mattered if you liked a particular cousin or not—depending on the preordained relation you would call upon, or pay out, whatever sum of loyalty was involved) now felt as unattached as a bubble in a bowl of soup.

I also knew that loyalty was of small concern to Dix. Tomorrow he might turn me in, but tonight he could feel compassion.

"You had to fuck up big," he said, "to buy a house arrest."

"Can you keep it to yourself?"

"How not?" He repeated this with pleasure. "How not?" That had to be a new phrase. Picked up from a drunken Englishman, no doubt. A month ago, he had traded quips with a Russian tank colonel at the Balhaus Resi who spoke only enough English to keep saying "Of course! Vy not?" Butler had loved that. You could ask him anything for the next two days. "Will we win the Cold War?" "Should we have Irish whiskey with our coffee?"—dependably, he would reply, "Of course! Vy not?" So I knew now that I would hear "How not?" for the next week—if there was a next week. I might be coming to the end of all such weeks as this. I might be out of a job—I saw my father's eyes. I might be in jail—I saw my mother's picture hat on visiting day. I was like a man who has been told by his doctor that the disease is, all odds carefully reviewed, incurable. This verdict keeps returning in quantum packets. One plays solitaire, one chats, one listens to music—then, the dire news washes back like haze over one's mood.

I clung to the five minutes Dix Butler would be in the apartment.

"Well, what is up?" he insisted.

"I've thought it over. I can't tell you. I'll fill you in when it's over."

"All right," he said, "I'll wait. But I am wondering." He looked ready to leave. "Anything I can do for you? Want me to bring Ingrid over?"

"No," I said.

He grinned.

"If you run into Wolfgang," I said, "talk him into coming here."

"Dubious."

"Will you try?"

"Since you ask, yes." I had the feeling he would not try.

"One more thing," I said. I felt as if someone who had lived alone in this large apartment for years had died here, and it had been a long and lingering death. No one had been at peace in these rooms since. "Yes, one more thing," I said. "You mentioned that you would let me see Rosen's letters."

"Why do you want them now?"

I shrugged. "For diversion."

"Yes," he said, "that's right. All right." But I could see he was reluctant. He went to his room, closed the door, came out, locked the door, and handed me a thick envelope. "Read it tonight," he said, "and when you're done, slip it back under the sill."

"I'll read in this room," I said, "and if anybody unfamiliar knocks, anyone official, that is, I'll put the letter under your door before I go to answer."

"Approved," he said.

14

Dear Dix,

Well, here I am on hotshot duty in TSS, and there you are, honcho number one to the big man in Berlin. Congratulations. The old training group PQ 31 is doing all right for itself, even if PQ has to stand for *peculiar*—which is what I can say about my work now. Dix, procedure for this letter and any other I send you, is BAP (which in case you forgot is Burn After Perusal). I don't know if work at TSS deserves to be as hush-hush as is presented to us here, but it is certainly a special place. Only geniuses need apply—how did they ever miss you? (Before you get too pissed off, recognize that I mean it.) The overseer for all us Mensa types is Hugh Montague, the old OSS legend, and he's an odd one, remote as Mt. Everest, confident as God. I can't imagine what would happen if you ever tangled with him. Anyway, TSS is but part of his *demesne,* which I deliver as a gift to your love of big words. (*Demesne* is the etymological origin of domain, that is, the lands belonging to the Lord *for which he pays no rent.*) Montague, so far as I can see, pays no rent. He reports only to Dulles. Over at Top Sanctum Sanctorum (true meaning of TSS), we tend to be savage in our opinions of everybody, but on Montague, we agree. Unlike many in the Company, he is no dedicated brown-noser.

Which reminds me. Are you the guy, confess! Are you the guy who wrote on the latrine wall at the Farm, "Rosen is the anagram for Noser, as in Brown-Noser. Keep your nares clean, Arnie." That one ticked me off, I admit it. I'm sure it was you, you see, because of the use of "nares." Dix, you are one cruel son of a bitch. I know how much I value our friendship because I choose to forgive you. I would not forgive anyone else. But I want you to recognize that the allegation is unfair. Because, whatever I am, abrasive, unfeeling of the sore spots of others, too pushy (New York Jew with a lot to do—I know!), but whatever I am, whatever my faults, I am not a brown-noser. In fact, I defeat myself by being rude to superiors. We're alike that way. And I do not forgive most people who bitch me. I like to think they live to regret it.

Anyway, I don't want to be boring on this. I recognize your ambition. I even believe that some day, we two outriders, very much on the flank, having not been born with a silver espionage spoon in our mouth like Harry, may own two big pieces of the Agency. Equal to Montague and Harvey when our time comes.

Montague fascinates me. I've only seen him a few times, but his wife is an absolute beauty, and they whisper around here that she's the only true genius the Company has got, in fact, they say she's made Freud twice as complicated as he used to be, although of course that's hard to believe. One of the Company ills I'm beginning to observe is too much self-exaggeration of our own worth. We're not in a position to measure ourselves, after all. In any case, nobody can say to a certainty what Hugh Montague does. His working moniker—I don't believe it's a cover name or cryptonym, or any one of the variants for cable use—but they do call him Harlot. I guess it's because he's involved in so many things. A true demesne. No rent, no bureaucratic accountability. He's got his own piece of Counter-Intelligence which drives the Soviet Russia Division crazy, and then, he has other people spotted all over the Company. His enemies in TSS say he's trying to be a Company within the Company. Dix, you have to spend time in Washington to learn the ropes. You see, in theory, the Company, bureaucratically speaking, is all posted territory, but Dulles is soft on old OSS heroes and friends, and besides, he doesn't really like bureaucracy. So he creates independent movers and shakers. Knights-Errant, he calls them. They are empowered to cut across categories.

Harlot is most definitely a Knight-Errant. They say he is looked upon as the spook's spook in the Company. The inner poop that we get over at TSS (where we're supposed to *know*!) is that Dulles speaks of him as "Our Noble Phantom." Dix, I have to hand it to you. I used to laugh in the beginning at the way you were gung ho about certain words, but I'm beginning to see the light. Where I went to school, everyone knew the words, so my education may have left me a little too complacent about the real powers of vocabulary. I'm beginning to think *le mot juste* is the Archimedean lever that moves the world. At least, this is true for the Company, I swear.

Back to TSS. I find an unholy desire to tell you about the worst fiasco we ever had, which is why this letter has to be Ultra-BAP. It could fry my *kishkes* if read by the wrong eyes. Do not bother about the meaning of *kishkes*. That is argot from Yiddish and will advance nothing you're interested in. I mention it only because the nominal head of TSS is named Gottlieb, and *kishkes* is the only Jewish word I ever heard him use. Of course, they assigned me to him—I guess they figure we have something in common. Well, not all that much. Some Jews are deep in tradition like my family, which is half religious-orthodox, half socialist—typically Jewish, ha, ha—but some Jews go in the other direction. They become mirrors of their culture. (Like me!) Like Disraeli, the British Prime Minister under Queen Victoria, born of Jewish parents, but they say he had the best upper-class English accent of anyone in the British Isles.

Well, Gottlieb is like that except he's cosmic in scope, interested in everything. Odd! He lives on a farm outside of Washington and gets up every morning to milk his goats. The farmhouse itself used to be a slave cabin, but Gottlieb is a Sunday carpenter, so it's big enough now to house his family. Mrs. Gottlieb, incidentally, spent her childhood in India. That may be the explanation for the goats! She's the daughter of Presbyterian missionaries. Gottlieb also raises Christmas trees. And he has a clubfoot, but loves all the same to square dance. He's only a chemist with a degree from City College, but he's nonetheless a genius. Which is why in summary he sounds like nothing but pieces and parts. I must say, he messed up. Of course, only a genius can when in concert with another genius like Hugh Montague. It actually happened three years ago, but it's still the worst-kept secret at TSS. You can't go out with a colleague for a drink and get a little intimate without being told The Story. I find it interesting. There's some principle of reverse-morale here. Montague is so elevated that

I think The Story makes him human for us. Of course he only failed in a judgment call. He put his bet on Gottlieb, and Sidney did the damage.

Here's the *gen*. (Old OSS word for poop.) Three years ago the big rumor at TSS was that the Sovs had synthesized some magic drug. They could not only control the behavior of their agents, but could fix a spy's memory to self-destruct upon capture. They also had schizophrenia-inducing chemicals to free their agents from all moral concerns. Isn't this what Communism is all about anyway! The magic drug is in the ideology! Anyway, Gottlieb had come upon a physical substance that turns a few corners in schizophrenia. It is called lysergic acid diethylamide, LSD for short, and TSS people harbor the hope that it will become our wonder drug, since present techniques of debriefing enemy agents are too slow. Allen Dulles wants a chemical spigot to turn a defector on and off. Kind of a truth cocktail. LSD inspires one to tell the truth.

Now, it's hard to be sure, Dix, because I only acquired this at several removes, but Gottlieb seems to have had a honey of a theory, worked out in collaboration with Mrs. Montague and her theories. It is built on the premise that the psychic wall which schizophrenia builds to close off communication between opposite parts of the personality is composed of an immense number of lies, and the truth is encysted behind it. Any drug that can induce schizophrenia might also, if used on a start-stop-start-stop basis, induce enough of a vibration in the lies of that schizophrenic wall to shake it and, conceivably, crack it. More normal people, in contrast, only choose the lies that will keep their ego intact. By the Gottlieb-Gardiner theory, a defector's wall, whether psychotic or normal, can be shattered by the use of LSD. First, however, Gottlieb had to test the compatibility of LSD to his purpose. He and a few colleagues tried it on one another, but they were aware of the experiment. Unwitting LSD recipients were what was needed.

So, one night at a small cocktail party a TSS researcher managed to slip a dose of LSD into a pony of Cointreau that a contract scientist was drinking. The victim was not witting of the experiment. Now, I don't know his name—that fact is sealed, but let's call him what he is—VICTIM.

As it turned out, he did not react well. VICTIM returned to his home in a state of agitation. A very disciplined man, he fought the effects of the LSD. No symptoms of overt derangement presented themselves. The only manifestation was that he could not sleep. Then he began to tell his wife that he had made terrible mistakes. Only he could not specify what they were. After a couple of days, he was so agitated that Gottlieb sent him to New York to see one of our psychiatrists. Gottlieb's own deputy stayed with VICTIM in a New York hotel room. VICTIM, however, got worse and worse. Finally, right in front of his keeper, he took a running dive through a closed window and crashed ten stories to his death. They gave his widow and children a government pension, and Gottlieb got away with a slap on the wrist. Montague sent a memo to Dulles: Formal punishment would tend to interfere with "that most necessary spirit of initiative and outright enthusiasm so prerequisite to this work." Dulles did send a personal letter to Gottlieb scolding him for poor judgment, but no copy of this letter—at least so goes the gen—ever landed in Gottlieb's file. Sidney is in fine shape at TSS these days.

I had a strong reaction to the letter. I could read no further. The fear that I was being used by Harlot in careless fashion had just been confirmed. VICTIM kept falling in my mind.

I had to reach a secure phone. Harvey had told me I was now being watched, but that was not certified, and Butler on several occasions had been caustic about the weakness of our surveillance personnel. It might be worth a chance. I put on my coat and went out the door. Immediately, I let myself back in. I had not only forgotten to slide Rosen's letter under Butler's door, but had neglected to put away C.G.'s transcript and tape. These tasks accomplished, I went out again, with considerably less confidence in my clarity of mind.

A cab came by as I reached the curb, and I jumped in. We had not gone a tenth of a mile before I realized that this taxi could have been waiting on the street expressly for me. So I paid him off, darted up an alley, turned in the middle to see if I was being followed, and leaped in my heart as a cat jumped off a backyard fence.

Nothing stirred, however, and so far as I could see by the light that came into the alley from the back windows of tenements on either side, nothing was in sight. So I walked back to where I had entered the alley, and the cab I had paid off was still waiting. I strolled past to catch the driver's eye and he gave me a casual Berlin turn of his hand.

I leaned into his window, however, and said, *"Zwei Herzen und ein Schlag!"* At which he started his motor and drove away quickly.

This comedy proved felicitous to my mood. I no longer felt I was being followed and stepped along briskly for half a mile, occasionally doubling back on my steps. Then I took a cab directly to the Department of Defense, signed and made my way along the hall to the secure phone.

At the canal house, Kittredge answered. "Harry, is it you?" she asked hesitantly, and added, "Do I sound as odd?" Her voice was fluted by the scrambler.

"Well, how *are* you?" I asked. My leg was beginning to quiver at the risk of expressing more. "Oh, God," I told myself, "I'm hopelessly in love." Even a cruel distortion of her voice gave me pleasure.

"It's forever since you've been away," she said. "I miss you outrageously."

"So do I."

"I can't hear you," she replied. "You sound underwater. Am I pressing some wrong button?"

"Haven't you used this kind of phone before?"

"No, it's Hugh's. I wouldn't dare go near. I thought it was him calling. He's in London, you see. Left yesterday."

"Can you help me to reach him?"

"Harry, I'm amazed he even told me which continent he's on."

"So you don't know if he's coming to Berlin?"

"He will. He asked if I had any sweet word to pass on to you. 'Give him *mille baisers*,' I told Hugh."

She began to laugh. I decided she couldn't possibly have said that.

"When Hugh calls," I limited myself to saying, "tell him that we have to talk. It's urgent."

"Don't be surprised," Kittredge said, "if he drops in on you first. But, Harry . . ."

"Yes."

"When you see him, don't complain. He hates complaints."

"Well," I said, "I won't." Speaking to her, my troubles did not seem as near.

"I have wonderful news," she said, "which I'll impart to you on a better occasion."

"Give me a hint."

"Well, before too long, I'm going on leave of absence."

"To do what?"

"Oh, Harry," she said, "just think of me as being in Hong Kong."

Was she going undercover? Into Asia? I had instant visions of

Kittredge in some opium den with Russian and British and Chinese operators.

"Will I see you?"

"Tell Hugh to take you back with him."

"He can't do that. I would have to get clearance from Harvey."

"Hugh does not look at obstacles in the way others do," she said.

At this point, the Scrambler-Descrambler must have started to spark, for a great deal of static came over the line. We said good-bye in a series of staccato echoes. "Good-bye, can you hear me? Good-bye."

As I came out of the main door of the Department of Defense, I could see two men in dull gray overcoats standing about one hundred feet apart on the other side of the street. I took a sharp left and walked at a good pace to the corner. There I wheeled around abruptly. They had not moved. I turned the corner and peeked back. They still had not moved.

I walked down the block, then retraced my steps to peer around the corner again. The two men were gone. I started to walk at random but now with the most overpowering certainty that I was not without a tail. I must have been in the hands of experts, however, for I saw nothing. If I had a sixth sense it was certainly not located between my ears.

A cab was going by and I took it. On the way home I thought of looking for Wolfgang. I had no idea what I would do when I found him, nor did I have much sense of whether he would prove an aid to my fortunes, to Bill Harvey's or, for that matter, to General Gehlen's. I wanted to see him, however—if only to initiate an action. The desire came over me as powerfully as hunger for a cigarette on the day you are giving them up. Of course, I did not know where to locate Wolfgang. I could never find the alley of the cellar bar nor even, probably, its neighborhood. The place had been a distance off the Kufu, and good luck to all the miles of alleys and bomb-scarred housing off the Kufu. I gave up the idea with all the pain of relinquishing a true vocation—I felt not unlike a saint who has failed to climb the mountain chosen for his revelation.

I also contained a feeling, however, dull as lead, but indubitably weighty, that I should hurry home. The actual sight of my street, however, increased anxiety, for on the block, a respectful distance from my doorway, were the same two men who had been waiting outside the Department of Defense. Of course, there was nothing to do about them but go up to my apartment.

Five minutes later, the phone rang.

"Glad you're in," said Harlot. "You didn't seem to be half an hour ago."

"I was in the loo. Can't hear the phone from there."

"Well, I'll send a car. The driver is called Harry. Harry will pick up Harry. In twenty minutes."

"I'm not supposed to leave the premises," I said.

"In that case," said Harlot, "I authorize you to go downstairs. Be prompt." He hung up.

15

I WAITED THROUGH AN ODD TWENTY MINUTES, ALL TOO AWARE OF how the films one had seen could, on occasion, command as large a part of one's brain as family and upbringing. I expected the two men on the street to knock at any moment on my door. I waited for Bill Harvey to arrive. I could also visualize Dix Butler coming into the living room accompanied by Wolfgang. Ingrid now entered the movie of my mind with the clear announcement that she had quit her husband for me. I listened with whole attention to the oaths of a drunk in the street below, but nothing ensued. Just the hoot of a lout. Time went by. When the twenty minutes were almost gone, I took C.G.'s transcript and went downstairs.

Harlot drove up in a Mercedes. "Get in," he said. "I'm Harry." He moved for only a few feet before stopping beside one of the men in the surveillance team. "It's all right," he told them. "Go home now. I'll call you as soon as I need you."

Then we accelerated down the street. "I'm debating whether we can talk at my hotel," he said. "It's reasonably safe and they don't exactly know who I am, although it never pays to underestimate anyone in Berlin, as I'm sure you've discovered by now."

We drove in silence for a time. "Yes, let's go there," Harlot decided. "We can drink in the Lounge. There's no way the management would ever put up with the installation of any bugs. The woodwork is too precious. In the bedrooms, yes, but never the Lounge, not at the Hotel Am Zoo. It's an old place," said Harlot, "and nicely reconstructed. The *portier* is an exceptional fellow, I can tell you. Why, the last time I was here, there were no places available on commercial planes flying out of Berlin. And, for reasons of no concern to you, I did not wish to use the Air Force. Not that week. So I asked the *portier* to see what he could do. Two hours later, I came by his desk and he was beaming. 'Dr. Taylor,' he tells me, 'I managed to get you the very last seat out of Berlin, Lufthansa, this afternoon. In Hamburg you will connect with Scandinavian Airlines directly to Washington.' He was so obviously pleased that I had to ask him how he did it. 'Oh,' he said, 'I told the ticket office that you, Dr. Taylor, are *the* famous American poet, and it is absolutely essential that you be able to attend the Gisenius concert in Hamburg this evening! The rest is easy. Scandinavian Airlines has boodles of seats for America. You will be able to stretch out.' Yes," said Harlot, "that sort of skill is disappearing all over the place."

"And Dr. Taylor was your cover name?"

"Obviously." He seemed annoyed that I had not enjoyed his story more. "What impresses you about the choice of Dr. Taylor?"

"*Schneider* is the word for tailor. Are you that close to Gehlen?"

Harlot looked to be at a rare loss. "Do you know," he said, "it could have been unwitting."

I made no reply. I was not sure of anything I felt. "Well," he added, "Gehlen is awful, and I really can't bear that slippery sort of complacency you find in ex-Nazis who've gotten away with it. They carry such a subtle strain of self-pity. But all the same, Harry, I work with Gehlen closely. He's good at his job, and you have to respect that. The task is Sisyphean in its difficulties."

"I'm not sure he's all that good anymore," I said. "In my opinion, he is no longer a match for Harvey."

"Oh, dear, you will always be loyal to whomever you work for. It's that Cal Hubbard strain. Pure bulldog. Except you're mistaken. I happen to have gone over the transcript Gehlen sent me, and I can promise you, given what each man had to lose and gain, Gehlen came off well. Harvey was an impetuous fool to tip his hand on Wolfgang."

"I still don't understand how you can put up with Gehlen."

"Oh, anyone else with such a life would show no redeeming qualities. I choose to breathe on the ember of humanity I see in that little German."

We had come to the hotel. He left the car for the doorman, and steered me directly to the Lounge. "I had," I said as soon as we sat down, "a talk with Mrs. Harvey. It's here in this transcript. I think it's what you want." He pocketed the papers and the tape without looking at them. That annoyed me. I may have been reluctant to do the job, but I wanted to be praised on how well I had brought it off. "She's loyal to her husband," I said. "So I don't know that you'll find whatever it is you're looking for."

He smiled—was it condescendingly?—and brought forth the pages he had just put away, reading them with an occasional tap of his finger. "No," he said on finishing, "it's perfect. It confirms everything. One more arrow in the quiver. Thank you, Harry. Good work."

I had the feeling, however, that if I had not nudged his attention back to the transcript, he would not have looked at it for quite a while. "Is it of real use to you?" I persisted.

"Well," he said, "I've had to move without it. In the event, what with a few things speeding up, I have had to proceed on the assumption that C.G. would say just about what she did say. So, we're all right. Now, let's have our drink—two slivovitz," he said to the waiter coming up. It obviously did not occur to him that I had no love for the drink he ordered.

"I want to get you ready for the next step," he said on the waiter's departure.

"How much trouble am I in?"

"None," he stated.

"For certain?"

"Ninety-five percent." He nodded. "Tomorrow morning Bill Harvey and I have an appointment."

"Will I be there?"

"Most certainly not. But it will go the way I expect it to go, and in the late afternoon, you and I are booked to take the Air Force shuttle to Frankfurt and connect there with Pan American overnight for Washington. You'll be one of my assistants until we decide what you should do next. Congratulations. I cast you into the pit and you've survived."

"Have I?"

"Oh, yes. You don't know how opposed was your father to the idea of sending you to Berlin. But I told him you'd come out all right, and better prepared. Of course, you mightn't have gotten through it without me, but then you wouldn't have been parboiled if I had not been the chef."

"I don't know that I'm altogether out of it yet." My gonorrhea gave a mocking twinge. As I sipped my drink, I remembered that liquor was supposed to be antipathetic to penicillin. To hell with that. There was unexpected warmth in the slivovitz.

"I'll get you a room at the Am Zoo for tonight," said Harlot. "Do you have a lot of things at your apartment to take home with you?"

"Only the clothes I brought. There hasn't been time to buy anything."

"Go by your place tomorrow after I've seen Harvey, and do the packing then. After all, if Harvey finds out tonight that you've left the premises, he could send a couple of baboons to pick you up."

"Yes," I said. I was feeling anesthetized by the liqueur. I had thought I was full of a good many feelings for Bill and C. G. Harvey, but now they did not seem to exist. I didn't know the beginning of what I was doing, nor would I now know the end. Intelligence work did not seem to be theater so much as the negation of theater. Chekhov once said that an audience who saw a hunting gun above the mantel in the first act expected it to be fired by the last act. No such hope for me.

"Why are you opposed to CATHETER?" I asked.

He looked around. CATHETER was still a dubious subject for conversation in a public room.

"There's a movement now in climbing," he said, "that I abominate. A team tackles a straight wall that offers no holds. But they take along a hand-drill and screw a bolt into the rock. Then they cinch themselves up and drill a hole for the next bolt. It takes weeks to do something major, but any farm boy who can bear the drudgery now becomes an important climber. There's your CATHETER," he whispered.

"I must say that your friend General Gehlen did not like what CATHETER was able to tell us. Especially what it had to disclose about the weaknesses of the East German railway system." Now I was whispering.

"The state of East German railroad yards is not what Communism is about," said Harlot in reply.

"But isn't it our priority in Europe to know when the Soviets might attack?"

"That was a pressing question five or six years ago. The Red onslaught, however, is no longer all that military. Nonetheless, we keep pushing for an enormous defense buildup. Because, Harry, once we decide that the Soviet is militarily incapable of large military attacks, the American people will go soft on Communism. There's a puppy dog in the average American. Lick your boots, lick your face. Left to themselves, they'd just as soon be friends with the Russians. So we don't encourage news about all-out slovenliness in the Russian military machine."

"Bill Harvey said virtually the same thing to me."

"Yes, Bill's interests are contradictory. There's no one more anti-Communist than Harvey, but on the other hand, he has to keep speaking up for CATHETER even when it tells us what we don't wish to hear."

"I'm confused," I said. "Didn't you once say that our real duty is to become the mind of America?"

"Well, Harry, not a mind that merely verifies what is true and not true. The aim is to develop teleological mind. Mind that dwells above the facts; mind that leads us to larger purposes. Harry, the world is going through exceptional convulsions. The twentieth century is fearfully apocalyptic. Historical institutions that took centuries to develop are melting into lava. Those 1917 Bolsheviks were the first intimation. Then came the Nazis. God, boy, they were a true exhalation from Hell. The top of the mountain blew off. Now the lava is starting to move. You don't think lava needs good railroad systems, do you? Lava is entropy. It reduces all systems. Communism is the entropy of Christ, the degeneration of higher spiritual forms into lower ones. To oppose it, we must, therefore, create a fiction—that the Soviets are a mighty military machine who will overpower us unless we are more powerful. The truth is that they will overpower us, if the passion to resist them is not regenerated, by will if necessary, every year, every minute."

"But how do you know you are right?"

He shrugged. "One lives by one's intimations."

"And where do you get them?"

"On the rock, fellow, high up on the rock. Well above the plain." He drained his slivovitz. "Let us get some sleep. We're traveling tomorrow."

As he said good-bye in the elevator, he added, "It's a very early breakfast for Harvey and me. Sleep until I call."

I did. My faith in his ability was large enough to let me. And if I was confused as I put my head to the pillow, well, confusion, when profound, is also an aid to slumber. I did not stir until the phone rang. It was noon. A long sleep had come to me with the reprieve.

"Are you awake?" said Harlot's voice.

"Yes."

"Pack. I'll pick you up at your apartment in exactly an hour. The hotel bill is paid." Then, he added, "You are going to learn a few things in the next year."

My education commenced not a minute after I returned to the apartment. Dix Butler was alone and pacing about in a fearfully bad mood. "What's happened to Harvey?" he asked. "I've got to see him, and he won't even pick up the phone."

"I don't know a thing," I said, "except that I'm going home free and clean."

"Give my respects to your father," he said.

I nodded. There was no need to explain that on this day one might also take into account my godfather. "You," I replied, "seem somewhat upset."

"Well," he announced, and this was all the preamble he offered, "Wolfgang is dead."

I thought my voice was coming forth, but it wasn't. I asked, "Violent end?" I did manage to say that.

"He was beaten to death."

Silence came down on both of us. I worked at packing. Several minutes later, I stepped out of my bedroom to ask, "Who do you think did it?"

"Some old lover."

I went back to my valise.

"Or," said Butler, "them."

"Who?"

"BND."

"Yes," I said.

"Or," said Butler, "us."

"No."

"Sure," said Butler, "it was Harvey's order, and this arm. I did it."

"I'll send you my new address in Washington," I told him.

"Or," said Butler, "it was the SSD. In matters like this, you call upon Vladimir Ilyich Lenin. He said, 'Whom? Whom does this bene-fit?'"

"I don't know whom," I said. "I don't even know what was happening."

"Isn't that the God's truth?" replied Dix Butler.

16

ON THE FLIGHT ACROSS THE ATLANTIC, HARLOT WAS IN A SPLENDID mood. "I must say," he told me in the confidential tone of a dean passing on a rich whisper at commencement, "it proved to be quite a meeting with your friend BOZO."

By the twinkle in his eye, however, I had the uneasy intimation I would not be satisfied by how much he would impart. A merry light in Harlot's eye often ended as a mote in mine.

"Well," he said, "never forget—Bill Harvey began as an FBI man, and they do tend to be paranoid about their personal safety. How could they not? J. Edgar Hoover is always offering the prime example." Harlot dropped his voice even more for the next. "I've heard that Hoover won't allow his driver to take a turn to the left if he can also get there by making three right turns around the block. Whenever I used to ponder Bill Harvey's odd behavior with those pistols, I would usually decide J. Edgar Buddha had infected him. One day, however, not too many months ago, not long before we arranged for you, dear boy, to go to Berlin, I had an intuition: What if those damn pistols were not just Bill Harvey's passages of paranoia? Suppose they were, in fact, a real response to some true danger? What if he had managed to get into something bad?" Harlot extended his forefinger. "Give me a vigorous hypothesis every time. Without one, there's nothing to do but drown in facts.

"So I looked into Harvey's file. Right there, in his 201, is a full account of how he was obliged to resign from the FBI. You know the story. You recorded all that stuff from C.G.'s own lips. But I can see by the way you nod your head that you recall it all. So do I. Every detail that C.G. imparted to you proved to be precisely the same as the version in his 201 file. I anticipated that would be the case when I put you on to C.G. in the first place. Consider what it means. Her version of events, as related in 1956, coincided perfectly with his account in 1947 when he first came to the Agency. It's as if an overlay had been traced over the original version. He obviously spoon-fed the 201 version to his new bride when they got together, and I suspect he reinforced it by repeating the same story to her from time to time. There's the clue. One of the few rules you can count on in our work is that a story will conform in every detail to its earlier version only if the initial account has been artfully fabricated and carefully repeated."

"That's all very well," I said, "but when you arrived in Berlin, you couldn't know whether I had had the opportunity to speak to C.G."

"I was coming over," said Harlot, "ready or not. Your situation was obviously falling apart. Besides, there was all that friction between Harvey and Pullach. Gehlen was playing an awfully fancy game. So, I had to take the trip even if I had no more in hand than my preconceptions. So C.G.'s transcript proved to be wonderfully fortifying. A talisman. I kept it in my breast pocket all through breakfast with Bill. It gave me further conviction that I knew the man I was dealing with.

"Harvey and I had our meeting, by the way, in the Lounge of the Am Zoo. He knew I wouldn't meet him on Harvey home turf. And my hotel would normally have been seen in the same light. But he must have calculated that with all his assets, he could slip a sneaky into the Lounge. After my little talk with you, however, I spoke to the hotel management and arranged for my two surveillance men to spend all of last night in the Lounge. While they could not do any wiring for me, at least no one of Harvey's people was going to slip anything down the flue. We met next morning, therefore, with no recording devices available to either of us other than what paltry instruments we could bring in on our own person."

"How could you ever tape Harvey?" I asked. "He must have known you were wired."

"I had a sneaky on me I did not expect him to locate. A KGB toy the Russians have been testing in Poland. You install it in the hollowed-out heel of your shoe. Battery, microphone, the works. But we're ahead of ourselves. Point is that breakfast—Campari and croissants for Bill, one soft-boiled egg for me—didn't tarry too long on the amenities. We soon moved over to the opening insults. 'Hey, buddy,' he tells me, 'I cut my teeth on dark-alley operations in Hell's Kitchen while you Oh-So-Socials were eating crumpets with English buggers! Ho, ho, ho!' Tells me he's a three-martini man at lunch, 'a double, a double, and a double, ho, ho, ho!' I ask him which gun he's laying on the table. He says, 'It's not the gun, it's the hollow-nose bullets. I'll change my gun,' he informs me, 'before I'll change my shirt.' "

At this point, Harlot took a few pages of transcript from his breast pocket, peeled off the first two, and held them up. "Well," he said, "it's there now. Typed it myself soon as he left. Always get your tapes on paper as quickly as you can. It clarifies what happened. As I look at this little text, I keep thinking of Bill's buttercup mouth, so much at odds with the vile spew he spits. Oh, was he primed to go! He thought he had me." With that, he handed over the first two pages. "Figure out the *dramatis personae* for yourself," he said.

SON-IN-LAW: Now that we've bicycled around the mulberry bush, tell me, why breakfast?

GHOUL: I thought it was time to see who was holding the cards.

SON-IN-LAW: That's good. You're talking about cards and I'm ready to talk about egg on your vest.

GHOUL: Don't believe I'm the one who's dribbled.

SON-IN-LAW: You are covered with protégé juices. Your protégé is, to be precise, in one fuck of a lot of trouble. You see, I know who SM/ONION is by now. Protégé confessed. Aren't you ashamed of yourself?

GHOUL: When I decipher what you are mumbling about, I will subject myself to your moral examination.

SON-IN-LAW: Well, I send this in the open: I'm ready to bring charges on you and General Bat-Ears. For endangering CATHETER. Would it interest you to know I have proof? At this moment, a certain piss-bar pervert named Wolfgang is in custody. He is being debriefed. He has told us a lot.

GHOUL: Nobody has confessed. Nothing to confess to. This Wolfgang person is not in your custody. I received a call at 6:00 A.M. from the south of Germany. The so-called piss-bar pervert is dead.

(Long silence.)

SON-IN-LAW: Maybe a lot of people are going to be nailed to a lot of masts.

GHOUL: No, friend. That's jawboning. Even if you and I were to go head to head with the hand you are holding and the hand you think I am holding, you could do no better than bring both of us down. Nothing could be proved. Both parties irretrievably tarnished. So let's talk instead about the cards I actually am holding. They're stronger than you think. You could not squeak through if you were fluttered.

I had come to the bottom of the second page of the transcript. "Where," I asked, "is the rest?"

Harlot sighed. I must say the sound was as resonant as a low full note on a woodwind. "I recognize," he said, "the extent of your curiosity, but I cannot let you see any more. You will have to wait on the rest of the transcript."

"Wait?"

"Yes."

"For how long?"

"Oh," said Harlot, "years."

"Yessir."

"You may appreciate it more in time to come. It's rich enough." He looked about the plane and yawned fiercely. This seemed transition sufficient for him. "By the way," he said, "I settled the bill at the Am Zoo. Your share, breaking down the Deutschmarks, comes to thirty-eight dollars and eighty-two cents."

I started to write a check. The sum was a third of my weekly salary. "Doesn't the Company cover things like this?" I asked.

"For me, yes. I'm traveling. But Clerical will contest your Am Zoo chit. After all, you have a stipend for your lodging."

Of course, he could have put it on his account. I remembered a night when Kittredge and I were doing dishes at the canal house with a bar of laundry soap. "Hugh," she murmured to me, "may have the leanest wallet in the Company."

"Yessir. Thirty-eight seventy-two," I said.

"Actually, it's thirty-eight eighty-two," he said, and with no transition, added, "Do you mind if I elaborate on a point I was attempting to make last night?"

"No," I said, "I'd welcome it." If I had been hoping to hear something more about Harvey, I received instead a sermon on the subtleties of evil in the realm of Communism. All the while I was obliged to listen, my balked curiosity remained as painful as a venereal twinge.

"I would remind you," said Harlot, "that the true force of the Russians has little to do with military strength. We are vulnerable to them in another way. Burgess, Philby, and Maclean proved it. Can you conceive how badly it sat in me that Bill Harvey was right about that gang and I was wrong? Yet I had to recognize that Bill perceived something I missed, and in time it became one abominable thesis: The better your family, the more closely you must be examined as a security risk. For the Russians are able to get their licks in on whatever is left of the Christian in many a rich swine. It goes so deep—this simple idea that nobody on earth should have too much wealth. That's exactly what's satanic about Communism. It trades on the noblest vein in Christianity. It works the great guilt in us. At the core, we Americans are even worse than the English. We're drenched in guilt. We're rich boys, after all, with no background, and we're playing around the world with the hearts of the poor. That's tricky. Especially if you have been brought up to believe that the finest love you will ever come near goes back to the sentiments of Christ washing the feet of those same poor people."

"How would you feel," I asked, "if I said these things? Wouldn't you wonder which side I was working for?" My thwarted curiosity still lay like lead on my stomach.

"If I thought I was on the wrong side," he answered, "I would feel obliged to defect. I do not wish ever to work for evil. It is evil to recognize the good, and continue to work against it. But, make no mistake," he told me, "the sides are clear. Lava is lava, and spirit is spirit. The Reds, not us, are the evil ones, and so they are clever enough to imply that they are in the true tradition of Christ. They are the ones who work at kissing the feet of the poor. Absolute pop-pycock. But the Third World buys it. That's because the Russians know how to merchandise one crucial commodity: Ideology. Our spiritual offering is finer, but their marketing of ideas proves superior. Here, those of us who are serious tend to approach God alone, each of us, one by one, but the Soviets are able to perform the conversion en masse. That is because they deliver the commonweal over to man, not God. A disaster. God, not man, has to be the judge. I will always believe that. I also believe that even at my worst, I am still working, always working, as a soldier of God."

We were silent. But I could take no comfort sitting beside him in silence. "Ever read Kierkegaard?" I asked. I wanted so much to drill one small hole into the steel plate of Hugh Montague's certainty.

"Of course."

"What I get from him," I said, "is modesty. We cannot know the moral value of our actions. We may think ourselves saintly at the exact moment we're toiling for the Devil. Conversely, we can feel unholy and yet be serving God."

"Oh, don't you know. All that is subtended by faith," said Hugh. "The simple subtends the complex. If not for my faith, I could wield a damned good Kierkegaardian dialectic. Why not say that the U.S.S.R., because it preaches atheism, is in no position to corrupt religion? So, unbeknownst to itself, it is the true bulwark of God. Religious conviction in a Communist environment has to be luminous in its beauty. After all, you have had to acquire it at such personal cost. Russia, therefore, has the social climate to create martyrs and saints, whereas we spawn evangelists. Harry, give in to Kierkegaard's dialectic just once and you're in a lot of trouble. It's worrisome. The possibility that we will all be terminated in a nuclear opera does make our average citizen go all out for pleasure. The truth is that the West builds pleasure palaces faster than churches. A secret desire begins to grow: Maybe there will be no judgment! Should the world blow up, God's faculties will also be atomized. Such may be the unconscious belief. So, the quality of work deteriorates. Everywhere, work deteriorates. Eventually, that has to hurt us much more than it will hurt the Russians. Lava has no need of quality." He sighed again—a long meditative note on the instrument of his voice, and was silent, then cracked his knuckles. "In any event," he said with a smile, "it is wise to celebrate a victory by reviewing morose thoughts. That keeps the devils away." He reached over and thumped my knee. "I'm nervous," he added, "because I feel twice blessed. That, dear boy, is asking for it. You see, quite beyond my good morning with Harvey, there's another matter. I'm your godfather, am I not?"

"Yessir."

"Been a good one?"

"Superior."

"Well, now, return the favor."

"Hugh?"

"Yes. In about seven months, Kittredge and I are going to have a child. I want you to be the godfather."

The plane flew on.

"That's splendid news," I said, "and a great honor."

"You are Kittredge's choice fully as much if not more than you are mine."

"I can't tell you how I feel."

I was numb. I felt nothing. I wondered if I was going to die before I found out what happened with Bill Harvey. Indeed, it would take more than eight years before I would get to know the contents of the full transcript.

PART THREE

WASHINGTON

1

THIRTEEN DAYS AFTER I CAME BACK TO THE UNITED STATES, A RUSsian patrol located our tap on the Altglienecke-to-Moscow cable. If I had still been in Berlin, reverberations from the loss of the tunnel would have been all around me; in Washington, the event was only a far-off rumble. I had returned to a series of changes in my daily life.

The first was in relation to Kittredge. As putative godfather, I was now all but a member of the family. At times, I felt like a first cousin of no particularly healthy sort—which is to say that we felt awfully healthy with each other. Pregnant, she was more of a flirt than ever. On greeting and on farewell, she would kiss me with moist lips. I hardly knew how to measure such affection. Collegiate lore at Yale had hardly been as authoritative as the sexual wisdom of St. Matthew's. There, boys who had gone in for the heaviest petting over summer vacation would come back in the fall to instruct those of us less fortunate: When a girl's lips are wet, and stick to yours just a little, why, fellow, a full-fledged sexual attraction is brewing.

It was brewing. Kittredge, nearly always a happy sight to my eyes, had never appeared more beautiful than in these first months of pregnancy. Her fine features were now enriched by the livelier colors of her character. I could feel the woman within—by which blank check of a phrase I try to pass over the more intimate grasp I now had of what it might mean to go to bed with Kittredge. My night with Ingrid had given some necessary dollop of gross sophistication—I knew that Kittredge was not only this ineffable array of the loveliest manners and graces, but had a body that could shape itself to mine and (here was the gross wisdom) this body might even offer up its secret odor; I assumed that would prove superior to Ingrid's stingy, catlike purchase on the cosmos.

Yes, I was in love, if love is the happy condition of feeling one's hours remarkably well spent even when one does no more than sit in company with the beloved and her husband and listen to a record player while it offers such musical events as Leopold Stokowski conducting the New York Philharmonic through *Boris Godunov*. It was Harlot's contention that Moussorgsky gave infallible insights into the turmoil of late czarist Russia.

Kittredge's taste these days inclined more to *My Fair Lady*. Word had come to Washington that this was the ticket for the season on Broadway, and pregnant Kittredge was now uncommonly interested in hot tickets. To counter Moussorgsky, she gave us Lerner and Loewe. We listened to "I Could Have Danced All Night" until Montague finally asked, "Does a pregnancy circumscribe you all that much?"

"Hugh, stow it," said Kittredge, and the predictable two red spots came to her white cheeks.

"Darling," he said, "you never seemed to care about dancing until now."

And I, traitor to their hearth, was happy that I understood one side of her better than he, and hoped she knew it.

All the same, he was certainly taking close care of my career. I had not been back half a week before he arranged to get me into Intensive Spanish. I was being moved onto the Argentina-Uruguay Desk in the Western Hemisphere Division as my preparation for transfer to the station in Montevideo.

"Why Uruguay?" I asked.

"Because it's small, and you will learn a lot."

Since Montevideo had to be thousands of miles away, it also occurred to me that he might want his godson somewhat separated from his wife after the baby was born.

"You need a place to learn your trade," he told me. "Uruguay is fine for that. You'll come to know the diplomatic community, meet a few Russians, run a few agents, get a feel for the nuts and bolts. I'm looking down the line to years ahead when you'll be working more closely with me. But first you have to pick up the grammar—all the everyday housekeeping that goes into Station work and some of the dos and don'ts in espionage proper."

I confess that if I had heard *espionage* and *counterespionage* used more than a hundred times in the last year, I still did not know that I had mastered the distinction. "Can I train with you now," I asked, "while I'm at the Uruguay Desk?"

"Yes," he said, "but you'll have to wait. I won't be starting up the Thursdays until we get back from the Keep this summer."

"That's two months away."

"Time spent at the Argentina-Uruguay Desk will be invaluable."

Perhaps it was. I did not think so at the time. I was too busy absorbing whole fat loose-leaf books of geographical, political, economic, cultural, and trade union material. Soon enough, I learned that Uruguay was a small coconut-shaped nation on the Atlantic coast, and considerably further to the south than I had expected, for it was lodged between Brazil and Argentina. Uruguay was temperate in climate—hurrah!—void of jungle—fine with me!—the Switzerland of South America—ugh!—a semisocialist welfare state—paugh!—a land of pampas and cattle with only one large city, Montevideo; the entire country, somewhat under four million people, lived on the export of beef and hides, mutton and wool.

Most of my labor at the Argentina-Uruguay Desk went into coding and decoding cables. It was relevant work for it introduced me to operations I would soon be handling myself. For the rest, I slaved away at Intensive Spanish, suffered the heat of Washington through June and July, waited for Harlot and Kittredge's three weeks at the Keep to be over and his mysterious *Thursdays* to commence, and amused myself in the interim by copious speculations about the appearance of the officers and agents at the Montevideo Station. Since our cable traffic used AV/ as the digraph for Uruguay, we did not have to put up with such broken-backed orthographic presences as SM/ONION or KU/CLOAKROOM; now we could employ AV/ALANCHE, AV/ANTGARDE, AV/ARICE, AV/ENGE, AV/IATOR, AV/OIDANCE, AV/OWAL, AV/OIRDUPOIS, AV/UNCULAR, and, my favorite, AV/EMARIA. You never knew. AV/ANTGARDE could be a bellhop, and AV/EMARIA a chauffeur in a foreign embassy. I could, of course, given my desk accreditation, have checked their cryptonyms against the 201 file we kept in one corner of the large office room that constituted our Argentina-Uruguay Desk in Cockroach Alley, but there was no need to know, and I felt too new to push it. Older desk officers were introducing me to complex tasks grudgingly, as if they might lose a piece of their substance. I was content to wait. It was calm work after Berlin, and I had small interest. The summer in D.C. was hot. The Thursdays were what I waited for.

They were certainly talked about. Over lunch in the cafeteria one hot day, two senior officers, friends of Cal, offered me disparate evaluations: "Much ado about nothing," said one. "He's so brilliant it's unholy," said the other. "Why, you don't know how fortunate you are to be selected."

The class, now in its third year, had been commenced as a seminar on Thursday afternoons for some of Harlot's staff plus young officers who had been recommended for a few of his projects. Those were Low Thursdays, but once a month, on what soon came to be called the High Thursdays, important guests showed up by invitation, as did visiting professionals whose Company labors had brought them back to D.C. from various lairs abroad.

On all occasions, we would meet around the conference table in Hugh Montague's outer office, a large room on the second floor of the yellow brick villa that Allen Dulles used for his headquarters. Situated on E Street, well away from the Reflecting Pool and Cockroach Alley, it was an elegant building larger than most of the foreign embassies in Washington. Harlot was one of the few high-ranking officers to work in such proximity to Dulles, and so an added zest was brought to the occasion by the importance of our surroundings. Indeed, Allen Dulles would keep popping in and out, a beeper in his breast pocket prodding him back to his own office, and once, I remember, he made a point of letting us know that he had just gotten off the phone with President Eisenhower.

The lectures on High Thursday were, of course, the most exceptional. Harlot's voice became even more commodious then, and he could not have been more unabashed in his use of rich syntax. How much one learned directly, however, is not easy to measure. He gave no assignments. He might recommend a book from time to time, but never pursued our diligence, no, it was more a matter of sowing the seeds. A few might sprout. Since the Director himself was not only our peripatetic guest but had obviously given his imprimatur, and would often nod at the sheer wonderful glory of the subject—"Ah," one could almost hear Mr. Dulles say, "this wonderfully shrewd and metaphysical and monumental world of Intelligence itself!"—it took no vast acumen on my part to recognize that come a High Thursday, Harlot would teach our group from the top down. His preference was to stimulate his equals: On such occasions, the rest of us could scramble how we might. Low days were of more use to us. Then, the course served, as Harlot once remarked, "to rev up the Mormons." There were five of them, Ph.D.s from state universities in the Midwest, and they were always taking notes, always in crew cut, white shirt with short sleeves, pens in the breast pocket, dark thin ties, eyeglasses. They looked like engineers, and I recognized after a time that they were the galley slaves over in Montague's counterespionage shop at TSS, marooned in prodigiously demanding tasks of cryptography, file-searching, estimate-vetting, etc. To me it reeked of the Bunker, although obviously more purposeful, more lifelong—you could see it in their faces: They were signed up for a career of the highest level of clerking. I was, I admit, snobby, but then, as the son of a Bold Easterner, and thus, by titular descent, a Junior Bold Easterner, Ivy League out of Andover, Exeter, Groton, Middlesex, or Saints Paul, Mark, or Matthew, how could I not begin to feel well installed while listening to Hugh Montague? At full throttle on a High Thursday, he could employ rhetoric that was equal to high adventure. Since memory, for all its vicissitudes, can also be immaculate, I am tempted to swear that, word for word, this has to be close to the way he offered it.

"An understanding of counterespionage presents difficulties to which we must return again and again," he would remark, "but it helps for us to recognize that our discipline is exercised in the alley between two theaters—those separate playhouses of paranoia and cynicism. Gentlemen, select one rule of conduct from the beginning: Too much attendance at either theater is imprudent. One must keep shifting one's seat. For what, after all, are our working materials? Facts. We live in the mystery of facts. Obligatorily, we become expert observers on the permeability, malleability, and solubility of so-called hard facts. We discover that we have been assigned to live in fields of distortion. We are required to imbibe concealed facts, revealed facts, suspicious facts, serendipitous facts."

Rosen had the temerity on this particular High Thursday to interrupt Harlot long enough to ask, "Sir, I know the meaning of the word, but not its application here. What are serendipitous facts?"

"Rosen," said Harlot, "let us search for the answer." Harlot paused. I was all too aware of the way he played with the name. There had been just a hint of mournful woe in the long *o* of Rosen. "Rosen," he said, "assume that you are on a tour of duty in Singapore and a scrumptious blonde, a veritable *bagatelle,* happens to knock on your hotel room door at 2:00 A.M., and she is—let us say it is 90-percent verifiable—*not* employed by the KGB, but chooses to knock because she likes you. That, Arnold, is a serendipitous fact."

Guffaws popped forth. Rosen managed to smile, indeed, I felt his gleam of happiness at arousing the wit of the master. "I thrive on derision," said his manner.

Harlot resumed. "Gentlemen," he declared, "in the more advanced regions of our work, sound judgment is paramount. Is the apparently unsuccessful operation that we are trying to analyze no more than an error by our opponents, a bureaucratic fumble, a gaffe, or, to the contrary, do we have before us an aria with carefully chosen dissonances?" He paused. He glared at us. Just as a great actor can give the same soliloquy to beggars or kings—it does not matter—he was here to expatiate on a theme. "Yes," he said, "some of you, on such occasions, will be in an unholy rush toward the Theater of Paranoia; others will leave their name at the Cinema of Cynicism. My esteemed Director"—he nodded in the general direction of Mr. Dulles—"has sometimes assured me that I hold forth at times too long over at Paranoia House."

Dulles beamed. "Oh, Montague, you can tell as many stories on me as I can on you. Let's assume there's nothing wrong with suspicion. It tends to keep the mind alive."

Harlot nodded. Harlot said: "The man with talent for counterespionage, the true *artist*,"—now using the word with as much nesting of his voice as an old Russian lady saying *Pushkin*—"draws on his paranoia to perceive the beauties of his opponent's scenario. He looks for ways to attach facts properly to other facts so that they are no longer separated objects. He tries to find the picture that no one else has glimpsed. All the same, he never fails to heed the warnings of cynicism.

"For cynicism has its own virtues. It is analogous to the oil that wells up from every crushed seed, every damn plan that went wrong." Sitting near Allen Dulles on this day, I heard him grunt in pleasure. It was a small but enjoyable sound. "Hear, hear," he said softly, and I heard him. "Do not," continued Harlot, "attempt to comprehend the KGB, therefore, until you recognize that they have some of the most flexible and some of the most rigid minds in intelligence work, and their people clash with each other, even as some of ours have been known to do. We must always feel the play of forces in our opponent's scheme. It teaches us to beware of divinations that are too comprehensive, too satisfying. Cynicism teaches you to distrust the pleasure you may feel when previously scattered facts come into a nice pattern. If that happens just a little too quickly, you may have come upon your first hint that you are dealing with a precalculated narrative. In a word, disinformation."

Advanced were the High Thursdays, awfully advanced for the Lows. I would ponder some of his conclusions for many a year. If Montague's method of discourse on such days threw the more inexperienced of us over such high hurdles as the Theater of Paranoia and the Cinema of Cynicism, he could on any Low Thursday return us to the threading of a rusty nut to a dirt-grimed bolt. Indeed, the first day of the first Low had us working for two hours to construct a scenario on the basis of a torn receipt, a bent key, a stub of pencil, a book of matches, and a dried flower pressed into a cheap unmarked envelope. These items, he told us, happened to be the pocket litter left by an agent under suspicion who had decamped in unholy haste from a furnished room. For two hours we fingered these objects, brooded upon them, and offered our theories. I forget mine. It was no better than the others. Only Rosen was to distinguish himself that day. Once all the others had finished their expositions, Arnie continued to look unhappy. "In my opinion," he said, "too many pieces are missing."

"This is the sum of your contribution?" asked Harlot.

"Yessir. Given the paucity of facts, no viable scenario is available."

"Rosen," Harlot told us, "is on the nose. These objects were selected arbitrarily. A correct solution does not exist."

Explanation: The exercise was to alert us to the risk of autointoxication when formulating scenarios. Deductive passions could be loosed all too easily by a dried flower, a cheap envelope, a stub of pencil, the bent key, the torn receipt for $11.08. Our first lesson had been designed to make us aware (in retrospect) of any subtle discomfort we had ignored in the course of working up our explanation. "Respect that subtle hollow," Harlot told us. "When a scenario feels absolutely right, it is usually right, but if your story feels almost right, yet just a little empty, well, then, it's all wrong." The next Low, he told us, would be devoted to espionage itself. Espionage, plain and simple, as opposed to counterespionage.

2

BACK AT THE FARM, THERE HAD BEEN A COURSE CALLED *AGENT RE-cruitment;* it gave no clear picture of the reality. Montague moved us quickly from conventional formulations to the marrow. "Espionage," he told us, "is the selection and development of agents. That can be comprehended by two words: disinterested seduction."

Taking his pause, he added: "If you see me as an advocate of unbridled carnality, you are in the wrong room. We are speaking of *disinterested* seduction. That is not, if you reflect on it, physical. It is psychological. Manipulation lies at the heart of such seduction.

"In our Judeo–Christian culture, therefore, difficulties arise. Manipulation is Machiavellian, we say, and are content to let the name judge the matter. Yet if a good man working for his beliefs is not ready to imperil his conscience, then the battlefield will belong to those who manipulate history for base ends. This is not an inquiry into morality, so I pursue the matter no further than to say that a visceral detestation of manipulation is guaranteed to produce an incapacity to find agents and run them. Even for those of us who accept the necessity, it may prove difficult. There are case officers who have spent their working lives in foreign capitals but cannot point to a single on-site agent they managed to recruit. Such failure tends to produce the kind of unhappiness you see on the face of a dedicated hunter who dependably fails to bag his deer. Of course, the odds in certain countries are very much against us."

I do not think any of us were too bothered by the idea of manipulation at this point. To the contrary—we wondered: Would we be able to do the job? We sat there in a mixture of anticipation and worry.

"At this point," said Harlot, "you may be thinking: So incredible a purpose, so difficult an achievement! How do I begin? Rest somewhat assured. The Agency knows better than to depend on your first instinctive efforts. Recruitment is usually the product of the time and care that is spent in studying each prospective client or target. If, for example, the condition of steel production in a certain country interests us, then a cleaning woman who has access to the wastebaskets of a high official in machine-tool production can, for the moment, serve us better than a high functionary in Agriculture. There is logic to this work, and to a degree, one can instruct you in it."

Everyone nodded profoundly, as if we had come to the same conclusion.

"Today, we will place ourselves in a specific milieu," Harlot said. "Let us suppose we are stationed in Prague, yet can only speak a minimal Czech. How is one to cook the omelette when the pan has no handle? Well, gentlemen, we have a support system. In the labyrinth, we are never alone. It is not expected that you, personally, will try to handle Czech agents who speak nothing but their own tongue. Obviously, there has to be an intermediary whom we can employ, a working native. This fellow is called a principal. The principal agent is the Czech who will solicit his countrymen for you. You will merely guide his work."

"Sir, are you saying that we don't really get out in the field?" asked one of the Junior Bold Easterners.

"In the satellite countries, you won't get out," answered Harlot.

"Then why are we studying recruitment?" he asked.

"To be able to think like a principal. Today, in fact, working in company, we will try to perceive ourselves as one such principal. All of you will now convert into one imaginary Czechoslovakian, an official in the Prague government who has already been recruited by the Agency. Now he—by which, of course, we now mean I, our surrogate principal—is trying to bring in a few more Czechs from nearby government offices. Manipulation commences. The first clue to effective manipulation happens to be the cardinal law of salesmanship. Would any of you be familiar with that precept?"

Rosen's hand shot up. "The customer," he said, "doesn't buy the product until he accepts the salesman."

"How do you know that?"

Rosen shrugged. "My father used to own a store."

"Perfect," said Harlot. "I, as the principal, am there to inspire the putative agent—my client—with one idea. It is that I am good for his needs. If my client is a lonely person with a pent-up desire to talk, what should be my calculated response, therefore?"

"Be there to listen," said several of us at once.

"But what if I am dealing with a lonely man who dwells in isolation out of personal choice?"

"Well, just sit beside him," said one of the Mormons, "enjoy the quiet."

"Clear enough," said Harlot. "In doubt, always treat lonely people as if they are rich and old and very much your relative. Look to provide them with the little creature comfort that will fatten your share of the will. On the other hand, should the client prove to be a social climber who gnashes his teeth at the mention of every good party he was not invited to, then sympathy won't get you much. Action is needed. You have to bring this person to a gala gathering." Harlot snapped his fingers. "Next problem. The client has just confessed to you a secret or two about his sexual needs. What would you do about that?"

Savage, a former football player from Princeton, said, "Satisfy them."

"Never! Not in the beginning."

We were at a loss. Discussion circulated aimlessly until Harlot cut it off. "Confess to similar sexual needs," he said. "Of course, this assumes our client is not a homosexual." We laughed uneasily. "All right," said Harlot, "I will provide an easier example: Suppose the client is ready to be unfaithful to his wife. Not an uncommon possibility in Czechoslovakia. Well, you, good principal, do not try to provide him with a mistress. Do not complicate the relationship by adding so dramatic and unstable an element as a mistress. Instead . . . well, what does one do? Rosen?"

"I'm temporarily at a loss."

"Savage?"

"Ditto."

"Hubbard?"

It seemed to me that the answer had already been provided. "Perhaps you should confess to the same longing yourself?"

"Yes. Hubbard listens to what I say. Confess to similar sexual needs."

"But we still don't know," said Rosen, "what to do if the client's desires are frankly and actively homosexual."

We went around the room again. It was my day in class. This time I had a small inspiration. "I think you should show sympathy, not identity," I said.

"Keep on," said Harlot.

"I suppose you could say that while not a homosexual yourself, you do have a younger brother who is, so you understand the need."

"Well," said Harlot, "we now have an approach. Let us apply it to other vices. Suppose the client happens to gamble?"

The most effective response, we agreed, would be to tell him that one's father also gambled.

We moved on. What if the client wanted to get his oldest son accepted at a prestigious university? The principal might then have to call on influential friends. Some preparations took years.

"One has, however," said Harlot, "to keep a firm grasp on the intrinsic problem. An exceptional friendship is being forged. One is acting as generously as a guardian angel. That can arouse suspicion in the client. He has to be aware, after all, that his job deals with government secrets. Your official might be as suspicious as a rich girl with a plain face who is being rushed by an enthusiastic suitor. Depend on it. Espionage has its parallels to matchmaking. Ministers sitting on large secrets are the most difficult to woo. One more reason to focus on the easier target—the petty official. Even in such modest purlieus, however, you, as the guardian angel, have to be ready to dissolve the client's distrust as it forms. It is reasonable to assume that the client, in some part of himself, knows what you are up to, but is amenable to your game. Now is the time to talk him into taking the first step—that same first step which will lead him into becoming an espionage agent. The success of this transition—term it the *pass*— depends on one procedure so well established that it is a rule of thumb. Do any of you have a contribution?"

We were silent.

"I guess one has got to move slow," said a Mormon.

"No," said another Mormon, who had done missionary work in the Philippines, "fast or slow, make it seem natural."

"You're on track," said Harlot. "The rule is to reduce the drama."

"Is this always true?" asked Rosen.

"None of what I tell you is true," replied Harlot. "At this point, you are being provided with scenarios to substitute for your lack of experience. Out in the field, count on it, your agents are going to act in unforeseen patterns."

"I know that," said Rosen. "It's just I have this idea that the pass, as you call it, can make matters more dramatic."

"Only in counterespionage," said Harlot. "In time, we will take a look at that arcane subject. For now, however, keep the transition modest, uneventful, dull. Reduce the drama. Request something minor. Your purpose, at this point, is not to net information, but to relax your client's conscience. A salesman, as Mr. Rosen's father can no doubt tell us, wants to keep a potential buyer from wondering whether he really needs the product. What procedure is analogous to our circumstances, Hubbard?"

"Do not let the client recognize how much he's getting into."

"Good. You, the principal, are there to allay anxiety. Warm the soup slowly. 'Look, friend,' you might complain to your budding little agent, 'when I want to speak to someone in your office, the number is not available. I cannot pick up the phone and call them—I have to send a letter. No wonder our socialist economy creeps along. If you could let me borrow your department's telephone registry for one night, it would make my work so much easier.' Well, how can the client refuse after all you've done for him? It is, after all, a modest request. The intraoffice phone book is thin. One can slip it into the torn lining of one's overcoat. So the client brings it out to you, and you get it copied immediately, and return it early the next morning before work. Now what do you do?"

We were silent.

"You let a week go by. If any anxiety was aroused in the client's tender breast, it should have settled. Now, ask for a bit more. Can your friend let you have a look at X report? You happen to know that this X report is sitting on one of the desks in his bureau. Nothing weighty, just something your boss would be pleased to see. It could advance your boss's interests to have such information available to him.

"An unhappy sigh from the client," said Harlot, "but he agrees. The report is carried out in his briefcase that night, and is returned to him in the morning.

"The major shift, however, is yet to come. In order for the client to develop into a reliable agent willing to work in place for years, what now is necessary?"

Rosen had his hand up. So did the Mormons. Soon, everyone around the table but myself had raised his hand. I was the only one not to realize that the next step would lead our new agent into taking money for his services.

"It is easier," said Harlot, "than you would suppose. Just as many a woman prefers to receive kisses *and* gifts, rather than kisses solo, so your just-hatched agent won't mind being paid for his sins. A little corruption warms the chill. Remember, however, that hypocrisy is indispensable here. Keep to the model of the young lady. Offer presents before you get around to money. Avoid any hint of the crass.

Pay off, for instance, some old nagging debt of the client. Just one more favor.

"Sooner than you would believe, our novice agent is ready for a more orderly arrangement. If he senses that he is entering into a deeper stage of the illicit, money can relieve some of his anxiety. For criminals, this is always true, and an agent is, at the least, a white-collar criminal. In our case, he has just emerged from an orderly but hitherto unsatisfactory middle-class life. Money becomes awfully attractive when one is perched on the edge. Strike your bargain then. You, as the principal, can bring in an offer from your boss. In return for regular removal of selected official documents, a weekly stipend can be arranged."

Harlot nodded. "An interesting period commences. Our novice's secret work now provides him with excitement. If he is middle-aged, you could say he is having a fling. If young, he might actually be stimulated by discovery of this potentiality for deceit in himself."

Here, Harlot looked around our conference table. Did I have the impression that his eyes rested just a little longer on mine? His gaze moved on. "I cannot repeat often enough," he said, "the importance of this regular cash stipend. It must, however, not be so large as to show up in a bank account, or a new home. Yet it has to be enough to quiet anxiety. Again, we rely on a rule of thumb. A good measure is to peg the supplements at not less than one-third and not more than one-half of the agent's weekly salary. Regularity of payment serves the same purpose here as dependable meetings with a lady-love. Hysteria, always ready to flare up, is abated to some degree by predictable performance on your side. Questions?"

One of the Mormons put up his hand. "Can you afford to let the agent become witting of who he is working for?"

"Never. If you are able to manage it, don't let him know it is the Company. Especially in an Eastern satellite. His anxiety would be excessive. If, for example, he is a Czech Communist, let him acquire the notion that he is working for the Russians. Or if, like a few Slovaks I know, he is an Anglophile, you might slip across the idea that MI6 is funding all this. If he likes to see himself as a spiritual descendant of Frederick the Great, nominate the BND. Question?"

"What if the new agent doesn't want to take money?" I asked. "What if he hates Communism so much he wants to fight against it? Aren't we abusing his idealism?"

"In the rare case, yes," said Harlot. "But an idealistic agent can burn out quickly, and turn on you. So, the financial connection is, if anything, even more desirable with idealists."

"Isn't the real purpose of the money," Rosen now asked, "to keep the agent intimidated? He has to sign a receipt, doesn't he?"

"Absolutely."

"Well, then we've handcuffed him to the job. There's evidence against him."

"The KGB uses such tactics. We prefer not to," said Harlot. "Of course, there will be times when a signed receipt does *underline* the situation. I would argue, however, that the true purpose of the stipend is to give a sense of participation, even if the agent does not know exactly who we are. When you are living at the end of a network, nothing is more crucial than to feel you are not wholly alone. I repeat: Money confirms—here is our paradox—money confirms the virtue of the vice.

"Let us count our gains," Harlot said. "As principal, you have done your favors, avoided traps, made the pass, put the client on regular stipend, and concealed the source. A perfect performance to this point. Only one major step remains. What might that be?"

"Well, you have to train him," said one of the Junior Bold Easterners, "you know, weapons, illegal entry, one-time pads, all the stuff that's got to be learned."

"No," said Harlot, "training is kept to a minimum. He is not an intelligence officer, but an agent. Use him as you have found him. He will be asked to take out official papers from his office. He will be taught to photograph documents that cannot be removed. He must never be pushed, however, unless we are desperate to obtain relatively inaccessible material. That is dangerous use of an asset. A good agent ends up not unlike a good hardworking animal on a farm. We teach it not to gallop, but to pull its load. We regulate its diet. The end we seek is an industrious performer who will help us to harvest dependable product on a regular basis year after year. That is a valuable commodity never to be risked for too little, and never to be asked for too much. Underline this in your thoughts: The *stability* of espionage work is the element that generates good results. As far as possible, crises are to be avoided. Therefore, gentlemen, ask yourselves: What is the last step to be taken in the relationship between the principal and the agent?"

I do not know how the next answer came to me. Either I had

developed some small ability to read Harlot's thoughts, or was growing familiar with his intellectual style, but I spoke out quickly, wanting
credit for the answer. "Withdrawal," I said. "The principal withdraws
from a close relation with the agent."

"How," he asked, "do you know that?"

"I can't say," I said. "It just feels right."

"Hubbard, who would have thought it? You are exhibiting the
instincts of an intelligence officer." The class laughed, and I flushed,
but I knew why he had done this. I had been sufficiently indiscreet
once to confess to Rosen that Hugh Montague was my godfather;
now the class knew it, and Harlot must have picked that up. "Well,"
he said, "instincts are indispensable in our occupation, but I will spell
it out for those of you who are not as endowed as Hubbard. Some of
us have spent a few years here brooding professionally, you might say,
on how to keep an agent in quiet working balance. We have come
to conclude that sooner or later, the principal must separate himself
from his agent. Look upon it as analogous to the shift from early
parental warmth to the increasing discipline that a child has to accept
as it grows older."

"Does this have anything to do with the agent's sense of his new
identity?" asked Rosen.

"Excellent. Identity is no more than how we perceive ourselves.
To become an agent, therefore, is equal to assuming a new identity.
But, note: With each change of identity, we are born again, which is
to say that we have to take another voyage through childhood. So
now the principal will reward the agent only for disciplined behavior.
Of course, the agent, if he has been developed properly, should be in
less need of an emotional bond than of good advice. He no longer
requires a one-sided friendship nearly so much as he can use someone
with the skill and authority to steer him through hazards. Given the
danger, he wishes to believe that so long as he does exactly as he is
told, his new life is safe and moderately prosperous. Of course, he
must learn to take precise instructions. Certain precautions may seem
onerous, but spontaneity is forbidden. In effect, the agent has a contract, and the free insurance that goes with it. After all, in the event
of serious trouble, the principal is ready to pluck the agent and his
family out of the country.

"All right, then. Their new roles established, the principal can
complete his withdrawal from the agent. They still meet, but less
often. After a few years, agent and principal may not even see each

other. The agent, furnished with a dead drop, leaves his papers and picks up his instructions. On those rare occasions when it is crucial for the agent to talk to the principal, a meeting is arranged in a safe house, but since this is time-consuming in a hostile land, they usually stay apart. The principal is out breaking ground with new clients.

"This, gentlemen," said Harlot, "is espionage—a middle-class activity that depends on stability, money, large doses of hypocrisy on both sides, insurance plans, grievances, underlying loyalty, constant inclinations toward treachery, and an immersion in white-collar work. See you next week. Before too long, we will come to more damnable stuff—counterespionage. That is where we say farewell to white-collar mentality." He waved at us and walked from the room.

3

THAT NIGHT, ROSEN AND I WENT TO HARVEY'S RESTAURANT. IF going out to dinner together after the Thursdays was now a habit, it came from no growing affection. I had arrived, however, at the glum conclusion that Rosen was at least as smart as myself, and knew a lot more of what was going on in the Company. He had not only managed to strike up an acquaintance with a variety of experts and many a desk, but had kept up a correspondence with everyone he knew in the field. One of Rosen's heroes, paradoxically, was Ernest Hemingway (paradoxically, I say, since what kind of welcome would Arnie have gotten if Hemingway did not even cotton to Robert Cohn?). No matter, Rosen knew Papa's sayings, and believed that an intelligence officer, like a novelist, should have a friend in every occupation: research scientist, bartender, football coach, accountant, farmer, waiter, doctor, so forth. Ergo, Rosen worked his tables in the Company cafeteria, and never seemed to worry about the size of the greeting. Half of what I knew about Agency secrets, hushed-up fiascoes, or internal power struggles among our leaders came from him, and I noticed that Hugh Montague was not above inviting Arnie to dinner once a month. "It's like examining the contents of a vacuum cleaner," Harlot once complained. "There's an abundance of lint, but you can't ignore the chance that you'll find a cuff link."

A cruel estimate, but for me, Rosen's tidbits were undeniably interesting. He could, for example, fill me in on Berlin. Dix Butler had been writing back to him, and I heard a lot about Bill Harvey, who apparently did not even get three hours of sleep these days. That was the word from Dix. Contemplating the red flock wallpaper in Harvey's Restaurant, I was taken with the serendipity of the occasion. One was dining in an establishment founded a century ago by a man with the same last name; now, at the other end of the restaurant I saw that J. Edgar Hoover was in the act of being seated with Clyde Tolson. I had even been able to observe that the Director of the Bureau proceeded to his table with the heavy grace of an ocean liner. Having heard from C.G.'s lips of the simple inhumanity of Mr. Hoover, I could contrast his massive sense of self-importance with the kindly, limping, gout-ridden gait of Allen Dulles.

Rosen whispered to me, "Did you know that Hoover and Tolson are lovers?"

I misunderstood him. "You mean they have a roving eye for women?"

"No! They are *lovers*. With each other."

I was shocked. After Berlin, this was upsetting stuff. "That's a little too horrendous to contemplate," I told him.

Whereupon Rosen went back to Harvey. Did I want to hear more? I did.

"One joke making the rounds," said Rosen, "is that Wild Bill keeps getting teased about his adopted daughter. His friends tell him she ought to be given a medical examination. The KGB could have planted a subcutaneous sneaky before they deposited the baby on the doorstep. Harvey becomes tight as a tick. The possibility eats at him. It's implausible, but Harvey's under a lot of strain these days."

"You heard this from Dix?"

"How not?"

"Is he faring well?"

"Says to tell you Berlin is glum now that the tunnel is gone."

At the next High Thursday, Harlot would also speak of CATHE-TER. His guests that day were the most impressive single gathering we were to have at any of the seminars. In addition to Mr. Dulles, Frank Wisner was there, and Desmond FitzGerald, Tracy Barnes, Lawrence Houston, Richard Bissell, Dick Helms, Miles Copeland, and there were four or five unfamiliar faces who I could see were Agency moguls. The set of their shoulders, so quietly supporting one or another unholy weight, spoke of elevated rank. Rosen whispered that this lofty gang would all be moving off afterward to a dinner Allen Dulles was giving at his home for Harlot.

This was one time when I knew as much as he did. In the morning, there had been an unexpected visitor at the Argentina-Uruguay Desk. The future Chief of Station for Montevideo stopped by for a chat. Transferred from Tokyo in July, he had come into the office one morning when I was out on an errand, had introduced himself around, and promptly disappeared.

"You won't see him again till Christmas," said Crosby, my section chief. As with other long-emplaced deskmen, nine-tenths of his knowledge was on the dark side. So I heard a good deal about my new COS before I met him. His name was Hunt, E. Howard Hunt, and he was putting in his Washington time paying calls on Director Dulles, General Cabell, Frank Wisner, Tracy Barnes.

"Maybe he has to," I said, "as new Chief of Station."

"That's right," said Crosby. "Chief of Station, and he hasn't even hit forty. Probably wants to be DCI some day."

I liked Hunt when I met him. Of medium height, with a good trim build and well-groomed presence, he looked semimilitary. His long pointed nose had an indentation just above the tip that suggested a good deal of purpose in his trigger finger. He certainly came right to the point.

"I'm glad to meet you, Hubbard," he said. "We've got a lot of house to keep in the upcoming tour. In fact, I'm on the wicket right now trying to talk a few of our Company tycoons into letting us beef up the Station. They all cry, 'Hide the wampum. Howard Hunt is raiding us again!' But it's the truth, Hubbard. In Intelligence, the secret way to spell *effective* is M-O-N-E-Y."

"Yessir."

He looked at his watch with a gesture that had as many fine moves as a well-timed salute. "Now, fellow," he said, "we're going to get to know each other well, but for the nonce, I'm asking for a boon."

"Yours."

"Good. Get me an invitation to Hugh Montague's thing this afternoon."

"Yessir." I wasn't sure I could fulfill his request. When he saw the hesitation in my response, he added, "If you come up short, I can always go over the top. It's no stretch to say that Director Dulles and Dickie Helms are friends of mine, and I know they'll be there."

"Well, that is the sure way to do it," I confessed.

"Yes," he said, "but I'd rather owe this favor to you than to Mr. Dulles."

"I understand," I said.

"Get me into the dinner as well," he added.

When he was gone, I called Harlot's secretary, Margaret Pugh.

"I don't know if we want to invite Mr. Hunt," she said. "He's trying to breed up."

"Could you see it as a favor to me?"

"I know." She sighed. The sound told me much. She was sixty years old and professionally stingy. I had, however, whenever we spoke to one another, done my best to improve her day, and she did keep accounts.

"I'm in the mood to hear a good joke," she said. "Tell me one."

Crosby had furnished a two-liner that morning, but I wasn't certain it could qualify as good. "Why won't Baptists," I asked her, "make love standing up?"

"Why won't they?"

"Because people might think they were dancing."

"Oh, you are wicked," she said. "Oh, dear, oh, dear." But she sounded merry. "I'm going to do it," she decided. "I am going to enable Howard Hunt to mingle with his betters. When Hugh looks at the guest list—which he pretends not to—I will tell him that it was all my fault, and that I did it to start you nicely in South America. Harry, don't confess that it originated with you. Not under any circumstances. Hugh does not believe I can be suborned. I'm serious," she said, as if she could perceive me smiling—which I was—"you have to hold the line."

"I swear."

"He has no humor about his friends getting through to me."

"I swear."

"Oh, you don't know," she said, "how much I'd like to charge you for this."

4

"LAST WEEK," SAID HARLOT, "WE TOOK A TOUR THROUGH ESPIONAGE. In that field, the basic building block is fact. Today, I look to enter the more complex world of counterespionage which is built on lies. Or, should we say, on inspirations? The actors in this kind of venture tend to be adventurers, aristocrats, and psychopaths. Yet, these personnel compose but half of the team. Their less visible counterpart is made up of a support system ready to devote ceaseless attention to detail. Scoundrels and scholars, we see, are in collaboration. The difficulties cannot be underestimated. Just as an honest man feels safe until he lies (since his habits for consorting with untruth are few), so is a liar secure until he is so unwise as to be honest. One cannot trap a total liar. He can say, for example, that he and a young lady were at the opera Tuesday night sitting in box 14, and when you tell him that is impossible since box 14 happens to belong to a good friend of yours who was definitely present on Tuesday night sitting alone there, *as he always does,* why, then, your liar will look you straight in the eye, and tell you he never said he was in box 14 on Tuesday night, it was box 40, and say it with such authority that you believe him. The liar has as simple a life as the honest man."

I was struck with the resonance of the mirth that came forth from the nabobs. They laughed as if good humor on this subject was part of some private preserve.

"Counterespionage, of course, does not permit the luxury of unbridled prevarication. On the contrary, we tell the truth almost all of the time, but tell it under the umbrella of a great lie: We pretend that the agent bringing our Company secrets over to our opponent is in their employ when, in fact, he is one of ours. That is unobstructed counterespionage. It is encountered, however, more frequently in theory than in practice. We and the KGB have both gotten so good that it has become difficult to lie successfully to each other. Should a Polish defector approach us with the desire to be spirited over to America—well, as a good many of us know, we tell him to earn his transatlantic wings by remaining at his ministry in Warsaw as our agent for a couple of years. Let us say he accepts our bargain. The moment he does, we are obliged to distrust him. Has he been dangled before us? We test him. We ask him to get information that should be out of his reach. If he is bona fide, he should have to come back and confess failure. Lo and behold, he produces the information. We know the stuff is accurate because we have gathered such intelligence already from other sources. So we test him further. Again he passes our tests, which is to say, he is too successful, and flunks. Do we drop him? No. So long as we can believe that the KGB assumes they have gulled us, we have an instrument. We can send the Russians off in the wrong direction by requesting precisely those documents that will confirm their erroneous conclusions about our needs. Of course, it is a delicate misrepresentation. We cannot violate too much of what they know about us already, or they will become witting to our use of their agent.

"Do I hear a sigh? The complexity of this is nothing compared to the mires of a real situation. There are so many games available that the only limit upon counterespionage is the extent of our human resources. It requires a host of intelligence people to examine the value to us of each real secret we send over to the other side as a sacrifice to the greater good of moving the enemy's determinations into the wrong direction. So many trained people become engaged in examining the seaworthiness of these calculated lies that counterespionage operations, unless they involve the highest stakes, tend to grind down. The wicked odor that comes up from such activities is neither sulphur nor brimstone—merely our overworked circuits smoking away."

To my consternation, the Chief of Station Designate for Uruguay chose to speak up at this point. "If I may say a word," he said.

"Please do," replied Harlot.

"I'm Howard Hunt, just recently back from a stint as covert ops officer in North Asia, working out of Tokyo, next assignment, COS, Montevideo, and if you'll bear with this interruption, sir, . . ."

"Feel free," said Harlot, "even the children speak out here."

"Good," said Hunt. "I believe I'm expressing the point of view of some of us when I say—with all due respect—that it's never been that way out where I've been, not in my fraction of the total endeavor, anyway."

"Mr. Hunt," said Harlot, "I'm certain it has not been that way out where you are, but believe me, it is very much that way where I am."

Hunt, to my surprise, was not put away by the remark. "Sir," he said, "this is terrific stuff. I'm sure you fellows use it with finesse every day. And who knows, some of the younger people here may get up to your level eventually. I respect it. But, speaking frankly, it's no great help to me." I was surprised at the hum of assent that came up behind him. The guests, many invited by Mr. Dulles, made up a much more divided audience than I would have expected; Hunt, encouraged by these covert sounds of support, now added, "I work with a lot of foreign individuals. Some I can trust, some I don't, things go right, they go wrong. We learn to seize the going situation. There's no time for fine adjustments." The murmur of assent came up again.

"You are speaking of dirty tricks," said Harlot.

"That's one expression for it."

"No harm," said Harlot. "Sometimes capers are essential. Much of what I teach here, after all, is going to get turned on its head out there because—boom!—the explosion does or does not take place. You are in the lap of the gods." At the look on Hunt's face, Harlot nodded. "Would you like a projection of what I am saying?"

"Please," said Hunt.

"Yes," agreed a few of the guests.

"In that case," said Harlot, "it may be worth our time to take a look at operations on the ground level. Allow me to postulate some poor Arab conspirator who is in his home that morning cleaning his handgun in the hope he will terminate an Arab leader a little later that day. This assassin is teamed up with a co-conspirator, equally poor, who happens to be out at the moment looking to steal a car for the job. The second fellow, like most thieves, is impulsive. Scouting for a suitable jalopy, he happens to pass an Arab-American hamburger stand. There, behind the counter, stands a dusky but beautiful young girl. She has been blessed with a pair of divine melons under her blouse. He thinks he will come to less in the scheme of things if he does not spend some time studying those melons at first hand. So he natters away with the hamburger girl. When he finally gets around to pilfering the car and returns to base, he is late. Our assassins, therefore, are not at the proper street corner at the precise hour when the Arab leader is supposed to drive by. They do not know their good fortune. This Arab leader has his own intelligence people, and they have infiltrated the little outfit to which these terrorists belong. If the gunmen had arrived at the right time, they would have been shot down in ambush and never have had a look at the leader. Another route had been chosen for him. Yet, now, the same Arab chieftain's car, quite by chance, happens to stop for a red light where our two conspirators, still driving about in full panic and acrimony over their failure, have just come to a stop in their stolen jalopy. The gunman, seeing his target, hops out of the car, shoots, *voilà!*—a successful assassination. Who but the Lord can unravel the threads of logic in such coincidence? I suspect, however, that there is a moral. Dirty operations, when too precisely planned, tend to go wrong. That is because we are all imperfect and, at worst, serve as the secret agents of chaos."

"Mr. Montague, at the risk of tooting my own horn," said Hunt, "I'd like to say that I played a considerable part in our highly successful operation against Jacobo Arbenz in Guatemala. I would remind you that with no more than a handful of people we succeeded in toppling a left-wing dictatorship. I would not describe our accomplishment as chaos. It was beautifully planned."

"While I am not up," said Harlot, "on Guatemala, I have heard enough to believe we pulled it off by dint of a little luck and a good deal of moxie. I'm sure you put in your fair share of that. Gentlemen, I repeat: Give me a successful coup and I will point you to its father, a misconceived scheme."

There was a stir.

"That's Bolshy, Hugh," said Dulles. "It's wholly cynical."

"You go too far," said one of the notables whom I did not know.

"Get off it, Montague," uttered another.

"Hugh, give us, dammit, give us something less fanciful than these woeful Arabs," said Dulles. He was ensconced in a large leather armchair, his foot in a carpet slipper upon a padded stool. His walking stick stood in a ceramic umbrella stand by his side. He looked testy. I could see another facet of our Director's personality. On occasions like this, he looked not unready to thrash the air with his cane. "No, you fool," he might shout, "not the port! Can't you see I've got the *gout!*"

"A concrete example," said Harlot, "may cause more unhappiness."

"It's not unhappiness that's bothering some of the good people here," said Dulles, "but an absence of the particular."

"Very well," said Harlot, "let's look at the Berlin tunnel. There's a major operation."

"Yes, give your views on that," said Richard Helms. "Agree or disagree, it has to be of considerable value for the rest of us."

There was a formal round of applause as if Helms, by his choice of words, had lifted the carriage of discourse out of the ditch and up on the road again.

"In that case, let us return for a brief spell to fundamentals," said

Harlot. He had managed not to appear too uncomfortable during the altercation, but now that the situation was his to control once more, the full timbre of his voice returned. "Taken from an historical perspective, the gathering of information used to precede operations: The intelligence obtained would direct the venture. These days, however, large operations are initiated in order to acquire intelligence. This is a reversal of the original order, and can prove highly disruptive. Last winter, when the Berlin tunnel was still in operation, hundreds of translators labored over the prodigious output of telephone and cable traffic between East Berlin and Moscow. The effort was analogous to extracting a gram of radium from a mountain of uranium." There were sounds of acknowledgment from his audience.

"Now, suddenly, our gigantic operation collapses. We don't know how. One fine day this past April, Soviet military vehicles converge on the working tip of the tunnel in East Berlin, and in short order are shoveling their way down to the precise place where we have tapped into their cable. The Russians are going out of their way to make the point that they have been tipped off. They know our next two questions have to be: 'By whom?' and 'When?' Frightful questions when one does not know the answers. The careful disciplines of espionage, counterespionage, and counterintelligence have all been buried under the sheer earth-moving vigor of CATHETER. Still, we must pick a route through the wreckage. For *whom,* we do have choices. Given the size of the operation, security had to be stretched thin; someone in the KGB, or the SSD, could have obtained information from one of our technicians. Counterintelligence explores this possibility in the hope that more damaging suppositions will not have to be faced. For the next stage down in our choices is abominable. Is it a mole in MI6? In the BND? Or, someone among us? If these paths have to be pursued, the analysts will be on it for years and are likely to collect half-founded suspicions concerning hitherto reliable officers. *Whom,* therefore, is a nightmare.

"*When* is even worse. *When* poses this dire question: For how long have the Russians known about the existence of the tunnel before they decided to *discover* it? If they only knew for a week, or a month, no great harm has been done—any attempt to feed us tainted information via their tapped phone lines had to be put together hastily. If we knew this was so, then we could afford to ignore the input of the last week, or the last month. The tunnel, however, took more than a year to build. After which, it was in operation for eleven months and eleven days. If the Russians had this considerable period of lead time, they would certainly have had the opportunity to create an immense work of disinformation. That is precisely the Soviet genius. We are posed, therefore, with an outright dilemma. While our Russian emigrés labor away in translation mills at a job that will take at least another two years merely to process the back material on hand, we still do not know whether such intelligence is to be trusted. If we could at least calculate the likely date on which disinformation was introduced, we might be able to interpret what the Russians wish us to believe. Instead, we are obliged to stare at open entrails and make divinations."

"Come now, Hugh," said Dulles, "once again, it is not so bad as that."

"Well, sir, it is from my point of view."

"Oh, dear," said Dulles. "Do you know, I prefer to look on the bright side. We have been given a bonanza in the newspapers and in the magazines. *Time* magazine termed it 'The Wonderful Tunnel.' Some headline writer over at the *Washington Post* classified it as 'The Tunnel of Love.' "

Some of the invited began to laugh. Dulles joined in with a hearty "Ho, ho, ho." In the pause, he dug into his vest pocket for a clipping. "Let me offer an item," he said, "out of the *New York Herald Tribune*. I quoted from it to the President just this morning. *'A venture of extraordinary audacity. If it was dug by American intelligence forces—and that is the general assumption' "*—our Director waited to pick up his full complement of hearty, happy roars of laughter—" *'this tunnel is a striking example of a capacity for daring undertakings. Seldom has an intelligence operation executed a more skillful and difficult operation.' "* He put the clipping away to the sounds of "Hear, hear."

"What," asked Dulles, "is the balance sheet of the tunnel? Tremendous information, formidable headaches. Our business, the business of suspicion, goes on as usual. Nonetheless, we have won an overwhelming victory with the German people, West and East. We're fighting for the hearts of Europe, Hugh, and the fact of the matter is that everybody over there in East Germany is tickled with our tunnel, even the Russian bear, *malgré lui*. Why, my God, half of East Berlin is going over to Altglienicke for a visit. The Soviets have had to put up a snack bar right on the site."

An ambiguous response now rose from the nabobs, curious in the unevenness of its volume. Not all of them found Dulles' riposte

equally amusing, but others couldn't stop laughing. Those of us who
came to seminar every Thursday hardly dared to smile. Indeed, some
of us, myself most certainly included, were bewildered by the intensity
of the disrespect. I could feel a passion in the room to run the flag up
the pole. We had scored in East Germany!

Montague waited for the laughter to cease. "Allen," he said, "in
the face of such victories as you describe, those of us who work in
counterespionage feel properly subservient to good propaganda."

"Now, Hugh; now, Hugh; you know me better than that," said
Dulles, and gave an avuncular wave of his hand.

Harlot resumed his lecture, but I, for one, was more ready to
study the division of feeling in the room. The most hostile of the
officers had jobs in the Agency that you could deduce from their faces.
More intelligent than the instructors we had had at the Farm, they,
like Hunt, still shared that no-nonsense paramilitary glint of the eye
which was so often a substitute, even an effective substitute, for
intelligence itself. I began to wonder at their presence on this High
Thursday. Why had Dulles invited them to Harlot's dinner later
tonight? Would they come as friends, or to study Hugh Montague,
their future foe?

A few days later, I had the small but firm pleasure of discovering
that I was not off by much. "It got a bit political," Harlot said. "Your
new Chief of Station is, I fear, one of *them*. You must not become
infected by him with cheap patriotism. It's as bad as cheap Christianity, and it is running like a virus through the Company."

"Yessir," I said, "you are going to have, I fear, one hard time."

"Bet on me."

"Was," I asked, "Mr. Dulles the least bit on your side about the
tunnel? I didn't receive that impression."

"Well, Allen does like good public relations. He'll even decorate
Harvey before he's done. But, in fact, he is awfully worried about the
tunnel. What if one of us did hand CATHETER over to the Russians?"

"A mole?"

"Hell, no. Somebody responsible. Done for good high patriotic
reasons."

"Are you serious?"

"Can you come near to what I'm thinking?" he replied.

"Oh," I said, "I think I remember that conversation. The tunnel was letting us know that the Russians were weaker than we expected."

"Yes, exactly. Go on."

"But once the tunnel is blown, all such intelligence is tainted. It can't be relied on for military policy. Certainly doesn't allow us to slow things down. We have to keep arming just as we have been doing."

"You are learning how to think," he said.

Thoughts like this, however, kept one on a wicked edge. "Doesn't such a premise implicate you?" I asked. "At least from Mr. Dulles' point of view?"

It was the closest he ever came to looking at me with love. "Oh, I like you, boy, I'm really getting to like you. Allen, yes, Allen is worried stiff. He is indebted to me up to his armpit, but now he has to fear that I'm the one who made what is, from his point of view, a dreadful end run."

"And did you?"

The gleam came back. I had the feeling that no man would ever see such exaltation in his eye unless he had climbed with him to the top of Annapurna. "Dear Harry, I didn't," he said, "but, I confess, it was tempting. We had gone so far down the wrong path with that tunnel."

"Well, what was holding you back?"

"As I once told you: In faith, the simple subtends the complex. Patriotism—pure, noble patriotism—means dedication to one's vows. Patriotism has to remain superior to one's will." He nodded. "I am a loyal soldier. So I resist temptation. All the same, Allen can never trust me completely. Which is proper. Of course, he was worried. That was why I chose to talk about Berlin in front of so inauspicious an audience. If I was the author of the end run, why would I advertise the drear results?" He made a face, as if reflecting on the cost of the mockery visited on him. "I must say," he added, "I was startled at how self-important these operations people are becoming. One has to tip one's hat to your future Chief of Station. He knows enough to parade himself as a bang-and-boomer. However, I looked up his record. He's more a propagandist than a paramilitary. Getting to be Chief of Station is a plum for him. Although, give him credit, he does mix his bullshit with pluck."

We sipped our drinks, we smoked our Churchills. Kittredge,

sitting directly in back of him, had been looking intently at me all through this talk, and now began to make faces behind Hugh's back. I did not know how she could bear to do it to her fine features, but she succeeded in flaring her nose and twisting her mouth until she looked like one of those demons who hover behind our closed eyes as we part the curtains of sleep. Pregnancy was no small force of disruption in her.

"Yes," I said to Harlot, "you were good in what you said on counterespionage."

"Well," he smiled, "wait till we get to Dzerzhinsky."

5

THAT EVENING, AFTER DINNER, WE WENT TO A NIGHTCLUB. IT WAS AT Kittredge's suggestion, and much against Hugh's inclination, but she was insistent. Pregnant, she was insistent. There was an entertainer named Lenny Bruce performing at a new bar and coffeehouse called Mary Jane's, and she wanted to see him.

Montague said, "Bar *and* coffeehouse? One or the other ought to be enough."

"Hugh, I don't care what it's called. I want to go."

An old roommate at college had described this comedian in a letter as "devastating." Kittredge was curious. "She never said *devastating* once in four years at Radcliffe."

"Why do I know this evening will not work?" asked Hugh.

The lighting was harsh, the sound system had squalls, and a small black-painted dais served for a stage at Mary Jane's. The drinks were expensive, and we sat on folding chairs. I remember Montague complaining at the expenditure of a dollar fifty for Scotch and soda against the two-dollar minimum. "Outrageous," he declared in no small voice.

Since we had come in before the second show, there was opportunity to look about. While most of the couples in the room appeared to be office workers in D.C., I estimated that none of them could be employed at the Agency. No, as if I were a personnel officer, I could see they would not do. They were—I thought of a new word making the rounds—*permissive*. There was some sly secret they seemed to share.

The lights went down. Against a black backdrop, a spotlight focused on a microphone and stand. Out strolled a slim young man with short curly hair, dungarees, and a dungaree jacket. If not for protruding eyes and a wan face, he might have been pleasant in appearance. The applause was fevered.

"Good evening," he said. "That's a nice hand. Thank you. I appreciate it. Am I getting all this because my first show was good? Yes, I guess the first one tonight did take off. Yes. A few of you seem to have stayed for the second, haven't you? Yes, you, over there," he said, pointing to a man in the audience, "you were here for the first show and so was your girl." They both nodded vehemently. "And you, too," he said, pointing to another couple, "and you. Yes, there are quite a few people back." He stopped. He seemed low in energy, and surprisingly sad for an entertainer. His voice was mild and color- less. "Yes," he said, "that first show was terrific. In fact, if I say so myself, it was so good that I came." He stood looking out at us with his wan face.

A gasp of delight, half full of pure public terror, came forth from the audience. The most incredible sound issued unexpectedly from Kittredge. She could have been a horse who had just seen another horse trot by with a dead man in the saddle.

"Yes," said Lenny Bruce, "I came, and now I feel out of it. Ah, fellows, I have to get it up for the second time."

I had never heard laughter like this in a nightclub. It was as if the plumbing in the building were breaking up. Laughs slithered out of people like snakes, tore out of them, barked forth, wheezed forth, screamed out. "Yeek," yelled a woman.

"Yes," said Lenny Bruce, "I got to face it. It's no real fun to get it up for the second time. I'll let you girls in on a secret. Men don't always want that second helping. Yes, I can see some of you fellows nodding your heads. Honest people. You agree. It's tough, isn't it? I mean, let's face facts, getting it up again is the *ego* bit."

There was pandemonium. It was followed by applause. I had found my own fever. He was talking in public to strangers about matters that I knew little enough about but still, on my night with Ingrid, had there not been some hint from her for more? The fire and ice of that Berlin hotel room came back to me, and the dread I felt of staying any longer in that rented chamber. Now I did not know if I wished to remain in this club. Where could it all end? Kittredge's eyes, reflecting the spotlight, glowed; Harlot's expression seemed set in stone. And Lenny Bruce had emerged from his fatigue. He seemed to be offering full proof of the proposition that he who gives life to an audience receives life back. "Yes," he said, as if everyone present were either a close friend or a dear adviser, "that second time is for your rep. You women, watch your guy next time he finds some reason not to go for the second shot, oh, he'll lie—he'll say anything—'Honey,' he'll tell you, 'I can't, because of the atabrine.' 'The atabrine?' you'll ask. 'Yes,' he'll tell you, 'they gave us atabrine in the South Pacific to hold off malaria but the Army never told us. It discolors the semen. That shows up when you do it the second time. Yellow! Yellow semen. It looks like pus!' A guy will tell any lie to excuse himself for not producing it that second time. Anything to keep his wife from getting wise to him. Believe me, isn't that what it's all about? Lying to your wife? Isn't that what all the bullshitters mean when they talk about marriage as a sacrament? We know better. Marriage is the advanced course in lying your ass off, right?"

Harlot reached into his pocket to pay the bill, and Kittredge put a hand on his arm. Their eyes locked. "I will not make a spectacle of us," she whispered, "by leaving."

"Maybe we're on to a working principle, fellows," Lenny Bruce went on. "Never tell your wife the truth. Because biologically it has been proven. Women's ears are not constructed to hear the truth. They will slaughter you if you tell it like it is. So, lie your ass off. No matter the circumstances. Suppose you've gone to bed with a new girl in your own house in your own double bed because your wife is away for the day, and you are giving this girl one hell of a *shtup*. Whew!— can you believe it?—in walks your wife . . ."

"What is that word, *shtup*?" whispered Kittredge.

"Yiddish," said Harlot.

"Oh," said Kittredge.

"There you are, lathered up, banging away, zoom, you're trapped! In your wife's own bed. What do you do?" He took a full pause. "Why," he said, "you deny it."

He paused again for the laughter. "Yes," he said, "deny it. Tell your wife any cockamamie story. Tell her you just got home, and here was this naked girl in *our* bed, honey. There she was, honey, shivering with acute malaria. Believe me, she was turning blue with cold. She was dying. The only way to save a life in such circumstances is to warm her naked body with my body. That's the only way, honey, to bring a human being back from fatal chill. Yes, tell her anything. Because in marriage you have to lie your ass off."

"Do you know," said Harlot in a clear voice that obviously did not care how far it might carry, "I understand for the first time what Joe McCarthy was afraid of."

"Hush," said Kittredge, but one small splotch on each cheek had appeared, and I did not know if she was angered more by Harlot or the comedian.

"Of course," said Lenny Bruce, "you can make the case that we were taught to lie by the apostles. They agreed to sell the story that Jesus gave them the wafer and the wine. 'Hey,' they said, 'we ate His flesh. We drank His blood. So, be a good Christian, will you?'" Lenny Bruce whistled. "Hey, hey! That had to be a pretty heavy line back then. You don't think everybody was jumping up to buy it, do you? Why, the first guy who heard it must have said, 'Give me a shovel—I got to dig my way out of this. I mean, what the fuck are they saying, "Drink my blood, eat my flesh." Come on, man. I'm no cannibal!'"

The audience laughed, although uneasily. It was happening too fast, and Bruce's voice was harsh. Two women got up and left the room. A man followed in their wake.

"Sir," said Lenny Bruce, "when you come back from the men's room, don't forget to tip the *shvartzer*. So he'll know you're not a tight-fisted prick!"

The door slammed. "Jerk-off artist," said Bruce. The man walked out of the club to the sound of laughter behind him.

"You know, I think a lot about this sacrament business. The wafer and the wine. They go together like ham and eggs. I start to wonder. Would it work with substitutions? Like give me a piece of that pie, man, I need a little more taste with the *flesh*. Or, keep that coffee hot, I can't drink wine, I'm in A.A., dig?" He shook his head. "Now that we're on the subject, let's get to the Big Lie. 'What! You never *shtupped* a guy? Come on, Mary, not even one stud? Not one leaky drop got in? It was a what-do-you-call-it? A *what*? An *immaculate* conception?' Well, knock off, Mary. I'm not blind and dumb. I don't buy stories that stupid."

Kittredge stood up. She took a step toward the stage but Hugh gave a nod to me, and we managed to escort her outside. "Come back, lady," cried Lenny, "or you'll miss the circumcision."

Hugh turned and said, "Contemptible!" We walked out. Kittredge was weeping. Then she was laughing. For the first time, I was truly aware of the size of her belly.

"I hate you, Hugh," she said. "I was going to smack his filthy mouth."

We drove back to the canal house in silence. Once inside, Kittredge sat down in a chair and placed her hands on her stomach. The spots of red remained on her cheeks.

"Are you all right?" asked Hugh.

"I've never felt such anger. I hope it didn't pass through to the child."

"No telling," said Hugh.

"Why didn't you let me hit him?" she asked.

"I didn't want it to end up in the newspapers."

"I couldn't care less."

"Once you saw what they did with it, you would have cared." She was silent.

"Newspapermen," said Hugh, "are swine. I think I saw a few of them in the place paying homage to your comic genius."

"How do you know they were press?" Kittredge asked.

"Some people offer that look. I tell you, there's an abominable culture breeding away in God knows what sort of filthy dish. And Mr. Lenny Bruce is their little microbe."

"You should have let me at him."

"Kittredge," said Montague, "I am trying to hold the world together, not help to pull it apart."

"Do you know," said Kittredge, "I thought if I could beat that dreadful man with my handbag, I would knock something back into place. I haven't felt so awful since that damned ghost this summer."

"What?" I asked. "What ghost? At the Keep?"

"Yes, there," she said. "Something. I know he wanted to bother my baby."

"Harry, have you ever heard of a history of *visitants* on the island?" Hugh now asked.

"Well, there used to be talk about a kind of phantom, an old pirate named Augustus Farr, but we used to laugh about that. My cousin Colton Shaler Hubbard's father, Hadlock, told us that the creature went *dormant* about a hundred years ago."

I had intended this to have its humor, but Kittredge said, "Augustus Farr," and seemed to be holding off some near-involuntary tremor. "That's just the name to fit my awful night."

I was thinking of Dr. Gardiner and his bloody Elizabethan stumps. That had probably been sufficient to stir some poor shade.

"I don't care if this gets the baby stinko," said Kittredge, "I'm going to have a drink. I need to banish Mr. Bruce."

6

TEN DAYS LATER, I WENT TO URUGUAY ON A PAN AMERICAN DOUG-las Super-6, a four-motor propeller job that left New York a half hour before noon, reached Caracas by evening, and Rio de Janeiro in the morning. I didn't touch down at Montevideo until mid-afternoon. Flying through the night, I spent my nocturnal hours brooding once again upon themes imparted by Harlot. I was beginning to believe that long trips in the dark were the medium best suited for reviewing his precepts.

My final Thursday had been a Low, but Montague chose that day to give us his treasured lecture on Feliks Edmundovitch Dzerzhinsky. Toward the end, he said a few things that kept my mind close to the subject for a long time afterward. Let me offer, then, something of the last Thursday I was to enjoy with Harlot for a number of years.

In repayment, perhaps, for his acerbity on the last High Thursday, Mr. Dulles broke precedent by making the opening remarks himself. "What you will hear today," he told us, "is tricky stuff, but invaluable. From Marx on down, Marxists do not give much credit to the individual as a vital factor in the making of history. Nonetheless, the *amusing* aspect of their Marxism, if you permit me to apply the word to so overbearing and unpleasant a philosophy, is that Communists are always wrong at the critical moment. When we have to listen to an awfully vain tenor who can never hit his high note, we do grow fond of him after a time. His very inability finally offers the dependable pleasure. So it is with Marx and the Communists. The infallible Karl was wrong in his prediction that revolution would come first to the most advanced industrial nations, and was proved wrong again when the contradictions of capitalism did not prove fatal. Marx failed to see that business enterprise has to be considered in the light of its noun— *enterprise! Business* is merely the qualifier. That is because *free* enterprise puts the entrepreneur into a position of peril. He not only gambles with his economic substance but, more importantly, with his moral worth. Given the temptations of greed, a capitalist has to take his chances on Heaven or Hell! That is a lot of enterprise! Marx, contemptuous of the Judeo-Christian ethic, was insensitive to the importance of the individual conscience. His real desire was to get the individual out of history and substitute impersonal forces. It required the evil genius of Lenin, the most determined Communistic human being we encounter in this century, to prove Marx wrong, since there would have been no Bolshevik Revolution in 1917 without the individual named Lenin.

"Soon after, he was followed by another evil artist. In the middle of a large square in Moscow stands a statue of Feliks Edmundovitch Dzerzhinsky. There he perches on his thin legs right in front of the Lubyanka. The square is named after him. How fitting! Founder of the Cheka, Feliks Dzerzhinsky is also the intellectual godfather of the KGB. Those skills in intelligence for which the Soviets are renowned take their inspiration from him, I concur with Hugh Montague. Dzerzhinsky is not only the first genius of our profession, but, like Lenin, is there to remind us that the most powerful element for change in history is still one great and inspired man, be he good or evil. My dear colleague Montague, who is as clever as could be, is going to talk today about this man, this genius of our profession. I was here for the same lecture last year, and can tell you, I enjoyed it so much, I'm back again. Hugh, it's yours."

"Thank you," said Harlot. He paused to draw us in. "Dzerzhinsky's life covers a gamut of experience. The son of a Polish nobleman, he became, in the period before the Revolution, a leading Bolshevik. In consequence, he spent eleven years in Siberian mines as a political prisoner of the czar, and emerged with a tubercular cough. He spoke in a whisper. He assumed he would not have long to live. For this reason, perhaps, he was without fear, and during the chaos of 1917 and 1918, Lenin chose him to create an internal security force, the Cheka. In the Civil War that followed the Bolshevik Revolution, Dzerzhinsky unleashed the first Soviet terror. On principle, the Cheka would shoot ten innocent people before they would allow one guilty man to escape.

"Such feats belong to the abattoir. Dzerzhinsky's true vocation, counterespionage, evolved only after the Reds won the Civil War. By 1921, the Soviet government was trying to govern a fearfully backward, war-ravaged, crippled, half-shattered nation. Tumultuous disorder was Lenin's inheritance from victory. To govern at all, the Reds had to employ many former czarist officials. They happened to be the only people with enough experience to man the administrative desks. This meant that White Russian emigrés had no difficulty in placing their spies throughout the Red ministries. Indeed, it was not even feasible for Dzerzhinsky to pluck them out. The machinery of government would have come to a standstill. So they stayed in place—ex-czarist officials pretending to be Red, but remaining White within. *Rediski*—the word for radishes—became the term to describe these noble folk dedicated to bringing back the Czar. There they sat in the same offices, *rediski* and Chekisti, side by side, wastebasket to waste-basket. What to do? The British and the French are financing the most dangerous of the *rediski*.

"Dzerzhinsky now conceives of an incalculably elevated plan. On a given night, he seizes Alexander Yakovlev, one of the highest leaders of this monarchist circle, a charismatic, cultivated, sophisticated Russian aristocrat. Yakovlev is—at least as *rediski* go—a liberal, a Constitutional Democrat. Feliks not only arrests him quietly, but talks to him in great secret. Following one night of intense conversation, Yakovlev agrees to work for Dzerzhinsky." Harlot held up his hand.

"We do not know the intimate details of what happened on that all-consuming occasion. We have only the bits of information that Soviet historians would later release to the world. According to their Soviet version (which, I must say, has its own internal logic), Dzerzhinsky appealed to Yakovlev's patriotism. Since a number of Yakovlev's fellow conspirators were admittedly fanatic, and were looking to bring off a right-wing coup d'état, the ensuing bloodbath could prove even more catastrophic than the Civil War. Russia, itself, would be the victim. Might it not be more prudent to look for a peaceful coup d'état? That could result in a benevolent constitutional monarchy. 'Let us work together,' said Dzerzhinsky, 'to overthrow Communism. Our common aim will be to save good *rediski* and eliminate bad ones. The cadres that you trust, Yakovlev, will be promoted. You can develop your own directorate within the present government to be ready to take over.'

"Of course," said Harlot, "Dzerzhinsky made it clear that Yakovlev would have critical tasks to perform. He would, for example, have to convince the British Secret Service that they must reduce the scope of their sabotage. For if they didn't, the more punitive forces in the Cheka whom Dzerzhinsky was trying to restrain, would gain power and grind up all *rediski* without discrimination.

"Yakovlev may well have asked: 'How do I convince the British of this? What do I say to the emigré groups? They are exceptionally suspicious.'

"This, I assume," said Harlot, "was Dzerzhinsky's answer: 'You have one formidable advantage. You, Yakovlev, can present yourself as a man who has penetrated the Cheka.'

" 'Yes, and how do I prove this?'

" 'Why,' says Dzerzhinsky, 'you will prove it by furnishing the British with accurate intelligence of the highest order. It will prove accurate, because I, Dzerzhinsky, will prepare it.'

"Counterespionage, in its modern form, was born," said Harlot.

"These two fellows struck a pact. Yakovlev built an intelligence organization out of those *rediski* in whom he had confidence. Indeed, he called it the Trust. Within a year, this Trust had gained the collaboration of the Allies, and most of the emigré groups. Foreign agents were brought into the Soviet under the auspices of the Trust, did their work, and left. Naturally, Yakovlev encountered skeptics in Western Europe, but the size of his operation was awesome. British officials were taken on secret tours of the Soviet Union. Underground religious services were arranged for the more distinguished emigrés. (Needless to say, the Orthodox priests who conducted the Mass were members of the Cheka.) For the next five years, working under the cover of Yakovlev's Trust, the Cheka was able to control every serious move made by their enemies. Emigré agents entered Russia and embarked on operations subtly designed by Dzerzhinsky not to be effective. It is probably the largest neutralization of an enemy brought off in the history of counterespionage."

There was an interruption from Rosen. "I'm confused," he said. "As of last week, it was my understanding that large operations are sloppy affairs that depend for success on fortuitous circumstances. Yet here you speak in praiseworthy terms of a very large operation. Is it because this one happened to work?"

"By half, my answer is yes," said Harlot. "It happened to work. So we respect it. But recognize the difference. This operation was built on a profound deception which was then orchestrated by its creator. While the possibility for error and treachery was enormous, and any number of defections of minor personnel must have occurred over the years, such was Dzerzhinsky's genius for detail that all such betrayals were overcome by intricate countermoves. The beauty of this operation puts a critical focus upon others less brilliantly conceived, less elegantly continued."

"Yessir."

"For our purposes, however, I would put emphasis on the first night of conversation. What was agreed upon between Dzerzhinsky and Yakovlev? From that, we know, all else came forth. Did Yakovlev take up the offer with a view to eventual escape, or did he seriously wish to become Prime Minister of Russia? Did he actually believe Dzerzhinsky was on his side? How did his emotions shift in the years of collaboration? Obviously, Yakovlev's character had to change. For that matter, so did Dzerzhinsky's.

"It is fair to ask: How much of a double game was Dzerzhinsky playing with himself? What if Bolshevism should, indeed, fail? Was Dzerzhinsky looking to his own survival? Such motives may have been larger than Soviet history would lead us to believe. Go back to the primal night. Both men met, and an active, not a disinterested, seduction ensued. When a man seduces a woman, he may gain her not only by strength, but through his weakness as well. That can even be seen as the commencement of love—honest interest in the other's strength and the other's need. When seduction is inspired, however, by the demands of power, each person will lie to the other. Sometimes, they lie to themselves. These lies often develop structures as aesthetically rich as the finest filigree of truth. After a time, how could Yakovlev and Dzerzhinsky know when they were dealing with a truth or a lie? The relationship had grown too deep. They had had to travel beyond their last clear principles. They could no longer know when they were true to themselves. The self, indeed, was in migration. That is the point to this analysis.

"Over the years, some of you may enter into a comparable relationship with an agent. You may show talent. You may play for high stakes. What is crucial—and I insist on this—is that you understand how much that relationship will become a commitment to the whole manipulation of the other person. In consequence, you will have to relinquish much of your own most-guarded privacy. That will involve considerable tunneling into the spiritual foundations of both houses. A flood in the other fellow's cellar might produce unexpected leaks in yours. Ultimate qualities of dedication must be called upon, therefore, or you will sink into a filthy and imponderable morass."

At this point, Allen Dulles brought the jovial and manipulative halves of his own enterprising spirit together long enough to give one hearty clap of his palms, and say, "Wonderfully put."

Harlot went on a while longer, but that was the end for me. I meditated upon a future life in counterespionage as I traveled toward the city of Montevideo in the land of Uruguay, where I would perform the simpler chores of espionage. Two and a half years would pass in learning my craft.

7

THE NIGHT BEFORE I BOARDED THAT PLANE FOR SOUTH AMERICA, Kittredge and Hugh invited me to a farewell meal at the canal house. After dinner, Montague went off to work in his study, while Kittredge and I, on finishing the dishes, climbed to a small sitting room she kept for herself on the second floor. As a mark of my advancement to godfather, I was now invited occasionally upstairs. Once, indeed, when it was late at night and we had talked for hours, they even asked me to stay over, which invitation I finally accepted, but I certainly had the oddest sleep. Small and not quite locatable noises went on until dawn.

If only in my imagination, animals seemed to neigh. In the early morning I was suddenly awake and convinced of the presence of something exceptional. It was then I realized that it was Hugh and Kittredge making love, and no matter how the sounds were muffled by two small rooms between, I could not help but hear them.

I may have been thinking of that early morning while Kittredge and I talked in her upstairs parlor. Since our night at the club, she had been in what I can only term a jagged depression, gloomy but with odd flashes of wit. Rosen had subsequently informed me that Mary Jane was one more term for marijuana, and I had even brought this etymological tidbit to dinner in the naïve hope it would prove amusing. I soon gave up. Kittredge seemed on the edge—I cannot call it hysteria—of some sort of merriment altogether removed from what we talked about. I was glad when dinner concluded and Kittredge and I were installed upstairs. Now that I was actually leaving in a couple of days, I was beginning to feel uneasy. I wanted to speak of such feelings, but she cut me off.

"I can't help you. I'm not a psychoanalyst, you know," she said.

"I am a characterological theoretician. There are about eight of us in the world."

"I wasn't," I said, "looking for free medical service."

She hardly responded. "Do you think the other seven are as ignorant of human nature as I am?"

"What are you telling me?"

"I don't know a damn thing about people. I come up with theories that other people say are wonderful, but I don't know that I am getting anywhere in my work. And I am so naïve. I loathe that Lenny Bruce, I do. I also envy him."

"You envy him?"

"I work hard to keep faith in the sacraments. Our marriage would crack if I couldn't keep to such beliefs with Hugh. And there was this Bruce person, this comedian. So sure of himself. Not even knowing what he mocked. Like a six-week-old puppy that will do it all over the house if you let him loose. But such freedom. So easy."

"I don't know," I said. "He's alone. No other public entertainer dares to talk that way."

"Oh, Harry, why did I ever bring Hugh to that terrible place?"

"Yes. What *were* you up to?"

"Do you know how much anger is in Hugh?"

"And in you? Isn't it possible you are well-suited for each other?"

"No," she said. "Hugh could kill. He could go off his clock. He won't, but the tension is always there."

"He has fabulous control," I said.

"He needs it. His mother, Imogene. Know anything about her?"

I shook my head.

"Well, she used to be as pretty as Clare Boothe Luce. I must say, she's kind of grand for Denver, Colorado, but that woman is a witch. I believe she's evil. Hugh is all but convinced, you know, that she did murder his father. How would you like to grow up with a little thought like that in your coffee mug every morning?"

"Yes, but he has come a long way since then."

"All the same, Hugh can't take in too much human stuff at once."

"Can you?"

"Well, I always thought I could until the other night. That Mary Jane place! I wanted so much for Hugh to obtain a bit of insight into what the rest of America might be like, and then it was awful—I discovered I'm just like Hugh. Narrow as a needle."

"I don't know about your mate," I said, "but you're not narrow. You're wonderful."

"Harry, you have the kindest heart. It's because you're part Jewish, I think. They say the Jews are kindhearted. Is that true?"

"Well, I'm only one-eighth. I hardly qualify."

"It's homeopathic. One touch of the tar, baby." She looked at me with her head at an angle. "Harry, do you know, I feel naked in front of you?"

"What?"

"I've never talked about myself this much before. I try to hide how simple I am. It's easy with Hugh. His mind is on his work. But you know my little secret now. I want to succeed at my job. And I'm too innocent and too ignorant. Do you know I also envy you for going off to Montevideo?"

"It's only espionage there. Hugh says that's no better than nuts and bolts."

"Foo on Hugh. There! I've wanted to say that since I married him. Poo, foo, on Hugh! I envy you, I tell you. *Espionage!*" she said in a breathy, throaty voice. Only after a moment did I realize that she was doing a parody of someone like Marilyn Monroe.

"Hugh does insist that the real game is counterespionage," I said.

"Yes, wonderful Feliks Edmundovitch Dzerzhinsky. Do you know, I'm bored with Hugh."

Bored with Hugh? Now I knew what they meant by time standing still. It did not. It slowed down, and took a turn, and the colors in the room began to alter.

"No," she said, "I adore him. I'm mad about him. Hugh throws one maniac of a good time in bed." The look in her eye suggested that she had saddled up a centaur and was riding him. "It's just that he won't do sixty-nine."

At the look of consternation on my face, she began to laugh. "Hugh is awful," she said. "He says that sixty-nine is nothing but counterespionage for amateurs."

"What?" I had to say again.

"Oh, you know. You're-in-my-brain-I'm-in-yours." I had no time even to be properly startled by this before she added, "Harry, have you ever done *soixante-neuf?*"

"Well, frankly, no. I don't know if I want to think about it."

"I hear it's heavenly."

"You do?"

"One of my married friends told me so."

"Who is it?"

"Oh, Harry, you're as naïve as me. Don't look so stricken. I haven't gone mad. I've just decided to talk like Lenny Bruce. Don't worry, dear godfather of our child, Hugh and I are very much married."

"Good," I said. "I don't think you're nearly so naïve as you claim."

"You may not be the one to judge," she said. "Now, Harry, do me a favor. Write long letters from Uruguay. Really long ones. Tell me all about your work." She bent forward to whisper: "The things I'm not supposed to know. I'm so ignorant of the basic day-to-day stuff. I need this kind of knowledge for my own work."

"You're asking me to break the law," I answered.

"Yes," she said, "but we won't get caught, and it's very simple."

She reached into her blouse for a piece of paper. "I wrote out all the instructions. This is a perfectly safe way of sending letters back and forth. It's all done with the State Department pouch. Absolutely airtight." She nodded at what must have been the look in my eye. "Yes," she said, "I suppose I am asking you to break the law. But not really, darling," and Kittredge gave one of her kisses, a fell, wet, kissing cousin of a full kiss. "Write the longest letters you can," she said. "Put enough in to get us hanged." She gave the oddest laugh, as if nothing in all the world could be as sensuous as conspiracy itself.

I didn't look at her note until I was on the plane. It was but a few lines long:

Just address your pouch envelope to Polly Galen Smith, Route AR-105-MC. Once the pouch reaches Washington, your letters will be delivered to a post office box in Georgetown that Polly still holds but has passed over to me, key and all, since she has obtained an additional box for her own use. Hence, she won't ever know who is writing to me.

Besitos,
Kittredge

PART FOUR

MONTEVIDEO

1956–1959

1

Montevideo
Sunday, October 14, 1956

Dear Kittredge,

I haven't been out of this city since I arrived. From the little
I've been told at the Embassy, our work is often heavy enough to call
for sixty- and seventy-hour weeks. The consequence is that Montevideo, with its one million people, half the population of Uruguay, is
all I'm likely to get a look at for a while.

My hotel, the Victoria Plaza, a brand-new red-brick edifice,
all of sixteen stories high, looks, I fear, like a cardboard carton on end.
"That's where the action is," E. Howard Hunt advised me before I
left, and I assumed that my future Chief of Station would know, and
yes, there is action of a sort—businessmen of various nationalities in
the hotel bar looking to make deals. Since I can barely afford the
room, I've spent my time walking about. You see, on Thursday when
I arrived, my superiors, all two of them, were absent on Company
business, and Porringer, the man who met me at the airport, told me
to look around until Monday and get the feel of the city, because I
wouldn't have a chance later. He was too jammed right then, he
added, to install me properly.

Wonderful. I have the feeling this is the last weekend I am
going to have free until Christmas. My cohorts in our small wing of
the Embassy up on the second floor have the look of Hugh's Mormons. Hellishly overworked individuals.

Well, it's also hell to be alone in a country. I've been so tired
from walking all day that I fall asleep right after dinner—no nightlife
to report as yet—then up again in the morning to stroll around again.
Would you believe it? I find Montevideo half beguiling. That is an
achievement since, to the casual eye, it's nothing remarkable. For that

matter, most of Uruguay looks to be of modest interest. It can boast of no Andes; indeed, it hardly has hills, and there's nothing of the great Amazonian jungle. Just rolling plains and cattle. Montevideo itself is a seaport on the estuary of the River Plata where it enters the Atlantic, and a lot of silt from the riverbottom separating Uruguay and Argentina colors the water a clay-gray brown, not in the least reminiscent of the blue Atlantic we know in Maine. Nor does the port amount to much. It looks like Mobile, Alabama, or Hoboken, New Jersey; all industrial harbors look the same, I guess. Access to the docks is mostly interdicted, so you can't wander down to where they unload. Anyway, the port seems dingy. Winches scream in the distance.

The main street, called the Avenue of the 18th of July, is full of bustle, and has a predictable plethora of stores—nothing special about the main street. An occasional plaza sports a bronze general on a horse.

All right, I know you're ready to comment—what is unique about Montevideo? And I answer: Nothing, until you learn how to look.

At this point, I put aside what I had written. It was not a lively enough letter to satisfy my lady.

> Montevideo
> October 14, 1956

Dear Kittredge,

You wouldn't know you were in South America, at least not by my preconceived idea of this continent. There's no heavy foliage and very few Indians. Apparently, they all died off from infectious diseases brought in by the first Europeans. So, on the street you see a Mediterranean population—Spanish, with an underwriting of Italian. Earthy, serious-looking people. The older architecture, Spanish baroque and Spanish colonial, is not inspiring unless you develop an eye for little surprises. This land has a spirit I could not locate until it came to me: I feel as if I'm living in an ink drawing of Italy in the eighteenth century. I suppose I am thinking of the sort of prints you find in old English travel books—a lonely hiker rests on a knoll, and contemplates an empty landscape. All is in repose. The ruins have crumbled gently and live in peace with the edifices that still stand. Time is a presence high in the sky, hardly moving. Eternity has come to rest at noon.

For example: the Legislative Palace. During the week, all governing takes place here. It is as large as a railroad station and looks like a cross between Versailles and the Parthenon, yet in front of this huge wedding cake, at the debouchment of the grand and empty Avenue of the Libertador General Lavelleja, stands one policeman dressed in the hat and cape of a Paris cop. One bicyclist rides by. It is Sunday, but even so! On a side street off this edifice, a small plump man in a blue workingman's smock is entertaining kids with an incredible foot-and-forehead species of juggling with a soccer ball. It seems medieval. On the next street a beggar sits on a box, his swollen foot stretched out before him.

Now, of course, there's all sorts of bustle in parts of town. The stores have names like Lola and Marbella—merely to sell clothing! Hordes of materialistic-looking shoppers are out on Saturday. Carcasses hang everywhere in the butcher shops, and bloody as hell. In fact, they eat so much meat in this land (238 lbs. a year per capita!) that you can smell barbecue grease on every street corner. It gets into everything you eat, fish, chicken, eggs, all those great galloping beef on the pampas. Yet this smell of the griddle is not the element I find unique. It's the back streets. Montevideo is spreading out all the time, and the old parts don't get rebuilt, merely repaired in a fashion. Most of the natives here are not living in history as we know it. When I left Washington, everybody was concerned with Hungary and Suez and the presidential campaign; now I feel far away from the world's troubles. In Montevideo, all the public clocks seemed to have stopped. It is always 9:00 and 2:30 and 5:21 in different parts of town. Not much on the scale of world history is ever going to happen, evidently, in Uruguay. The trick, I expect, is to know how to live for the sake of living.

For example: the cars. They love automobiles here. You see old vehicles of every make and twenty-year vintage. They keep patching and repainting them. I think the owners can't afford enough paint to do the entire job at once, so they start with a half-pint and cover the worst rust spot first with whatever pigment is available, usually about enough to slap up half of one door. Then a month later, another patch of rust pops out. If they can't find the old paint can, they put on another hue. After a while, the cars clatter by like Joseph's coat of many colors. What verve! I must say they prance like prize bulls at a fair.

In many neighborhoods, however, the streets are peacefully spooky. The other end of the world may be rushing along, but not on some poor block of shabby houses where the only vehicle in sight is an old olive-drab Chevy sporting bright yellow and orange splotches. Such silence prevails that I feel as if I'm in a wood. A boy in the near distance is wearing a yellow sweater, same hue as the bright yellow someone splashed on the old olive-drab car. Another old car, on another old street, is jacked up by the front end, its hood lifted so high that it looks like a duck quacking. It has been repainted a brilliant off-blue. Above it, on a battered old balcony, laundry is drying. I promise you, Kittredge, one of the shirts is the same off-blue as the car.

I think when a land is sheltered from the storms of history, smaller phenomena take on prominence. In a Maine meadow protected from winds, wildflowers pop up in the oddest places as if their only purpose is to delight the eye. Here, down the length of one low, commonplace, nineteenth-century building, I see an ongoing palette of stone and stucco: brown and gray-brown, aquamarine, olive-gray, and tangerine. Then lavender. Three foundation stones in rose. Just as the cars reflect the sediments left in old paint cans, so, under the sooty pervasive city-color is this other subtler display. I begin to suspect that these people keep an inner eye on their street, and if a unique patch of moss-green has been put on a sign, then there, at the far end of the block, someone chooses to paint a doorway in the same hue of green. Time and dirt and damp and peeling plaster work their inter-washings into the view. Old doors fade until you cannot determine whether the original was blue or green or some mysterious gray reflecting light from the spring foliage. October, remember, is like April here in the Southern Hemisphere.

In the Old City, on a street that runs down to the water's edge, the gray claylike beach is deserted. At the bottom of this vista is an empty plaza with a lone column standing against the sea. Can they have selected the spot to prove that De Chirico knows how to paint? So often in these lonely landscapes, one sees a solitary figure dressed in mourning.

The old city, and the medium old city, and the city they have put up in the last fifty years are all, as I say, quietly crumbling. What dreams must have gone into the construction of all these baroque whirls and turns and whorls and fenestrations. On the commercial streets are bay fronts and wrought-iron balconies, round windows, oval windows, ogival, and Gothic and art-nouveau windows, and roof balustrades with broken pediments. Iron gates lean in various stages of disrepair, old doors are bereft of pieces of their molding, and laundry hangs in the apertures of grand windows.

Kittredge, forgive me for going on at such length after being here only a few days, but, do you know, I never had an opportunity to enjoy Berlin, or even look at it. I know you were expecting a little more substance, but a good rule to follow in these matters is to make certain that one's means of sending a letter actually do work.

Yours devotedly,
Herrick

I didn't receive a reply for two weeks. Then came a short note. "Dispense with the excelsior. Send the dry goods. K."

2

I WAS HURT. I DID NOT REPLY. AS I FORESAW, THE NEXT COUPLE OF weeks went by with a great deal of work at the Embassy, and the only change in my personal life during this period was to transport myself and my two suitcases from the Victoria Plaza Hotel to the Cervantes, a considerably cheaper hostelry, situated next door to a fleabag. In the early hours of the morning, sounds came up from the gutter of bottles breaking.

Then came a second note from Kittredge.

November 13, 1956

Dear Harry—forgive all. Some days I feel like Catherine of Russia. Poor Hugh. Poor Herrick. It's all the fault of the impatient child I bear. An imperious spirit will dwell among us before long. In the interim, know that on rereading, I thought your dance of the half-pint paint cans was fun. Will you buy me one of those gaily painted autos for Christmas? We miss you terribly, Hugh without knowing it, I more than making up for both of us. A dear spirit is among the missing. Do write me a nice letter full of shtuff. Detail the daily dreary if you will.

Your number one.

Kittredge

P.S. The routing for mail works perfectly at this end. I assume it's ditto at yours.

November 16, 1956

Dear Catherine of all Russia,

How I prefer the kiss to the knout! Since you ask for my working day, I'll give it. We're an unhappy station. That is because we are waiting for E. Howard Hunt to arrive. The present Chief of Station, Minot Mayhew, is an old Foreign Service officer who had loads of seniority and so was able to sign on in 1947 with the Agency at the level of Chief of Station. He has been at that level ever since, doing stints in Bolivia and Paraguay. Now Mayhew is waiting to retire, and does *nothing*. No social functions. Not much Agency work. He comes in at nine with the rest of us, and by ten is usually over at his stockbroker's. Everyone agrees, however, that he is nifty at one aspect of his job: He keeps up decent relations with the Ambassador. I've heard horror tales, as I'm sure you have, of how strained relations can get at an Embassy when the Ambassador looks upon the Chief of Station with a jaundiced eye. Here, however, due to Mayhew, we're left at peace in our portion of the second-story wing. The Ambassador, Jefferson Patterson, understands Spanish, but can only speak with a stammer, so Mayhew, whose cover title is First Secretary, fields some of the Ambassador's work with Uruguayan officials. Mayhew has also been instrumental in bringing over, via diplomatic pouch, soccer equipment for a Catholic team in Montevideo. Other than that, his rating is close to zero. Our real direction comes from the Deputy Chief of Station, an ex–World War II Marine Lieutenant with a bull neck named Augustus "Gus" Sonderstrom. Augustus must have been a very tough guy once, but has now gone, not to seed, but to beer belly. He tends to give his all to golf, and it's not as silly as it sounds. At the country club, he brings along our Operations Officer or Communications Officer to play in foursomes with various local government and business types. That establishes a climate for favors. The

Russians, despite an injection of new KGB types called "joy-boys" (who wear London suits instead of Russian burlap bags), are not yet competitive in golf and tennis. So, Gus Sonderstrom's social contacts with Uruguayan golfer-officials often lets us hold some good cards. On the other hand, we need all the help we can get. The President of the Uruguayan government, Luis Batlle, represents the Colorado Party, which has won every election here for the last hundred years. Socialist-oriented, the Colorados spend and spend. Uruguay is a true welfare state—which may be why it's so peaceful and crumbling. This Luis Batlle is anti-American and at the moment is working out cattle and hide deals with the U.S.S.R.

I was thrust into all this on my second day of real work in the Embassy, which, by the way, is a splendid white mansion. Vaguely antebellum, it has a veranda fronted by two-story white wooden columns, and is situated on nothing less than the Avenida Lord Ponsonby, next to a park so beautifully laid-out that it could only have been designed by a Parisian landscape artist, circa 1900. In this part of Montevideo, rest assured, nothing crumbles. Our Embassy is as spotless as Navy whites, and Sonderstrom in our first interview wants to know about my tennis game. Seems we need one more good player for the country club intrigues. Did I bring a racket, Gus wants to know.

Well, so soon as my father heard of my assignment to Uruguay, he sent a stiff warning by way of one of his rare letters to me: I was told to avoid the golf and tennis circuit! The idea, according to Cal, is that younger officers who put in their time in this manner must have control of their technique. If you're courting a foreign diplomat, let His Specialness take the set, whereas if you're teamed with your Chief in doubles against a State Department pair, then don't, for God's sake, let the Agency down. "You, son," Cal wrote to me, "haven't, in my opinion, that kind of concealed mastery. I like your fast serve when it goes in—it's got *heart!*—ditto the overhead, but your backhand can't speak back to any opponent who knows how to insult it. So stay away from tennis—you'll drop too many points in other places." Recognizing the wisdom of this, I told Sonderstrom that I didn't even know how to find the handle on a racket. When he brought up golf, I said, "Sir, the one time I got out on a golf course, I shot a five, first hole."

"Fantastic," he said.

"Yessir, and a thirteen and a fifteen on the next two. By then,

I had lost all my golf balls." Actually, I'm better than that, but I wasn't about to tell him.

"What sports are you good at?" asked Sonderstrom.

I said boxing and rock climbing appealed to me. That took care of it. Gus grunted and said there weren't too many rocks in Uruguay and any boxing I did had better not be in bars. I could see he was going to squeeze a little more golf and tennis out of the officers available to him at present, and leave me to carry their excess load in desk work. On the other hand, now that I was, in his eyes, a boxer, he wasn't going to be snide about it. He's really out of shape.

One result, I expect, of being laggard on golf and tennis is that I've caught an all-night chore from one of the Operations Officers. (Yes, he plays tennis!) Maybe it's just the job they pass on to the newest arrival. The irony is that it's the task I enjoy the most because it has a whiff, at least, of cloak-and-dagger, although don't get misled. It's only for one night a week, and couldn't be more untypical of how I spend the rest of my working time.

Called AV/ALANCHE, it's a modest operation involving seven teenagers from a local gang of more or less decent right-wing Catholic youths. They are in the work for the ideological satisfaction and the excitement, and, certainly, the money. We pay each of them the equivalent of ten bucks a night. Their task is to go out under cover of darkness once a week to deface Communist posters, and paint our—that is, *their*—Catholic party slogans over the Red ones. Some-times, we put up new posters where our old ones have been defaced by Communist gangs. I confess I like the action, and I like the kids, although I will confess that I have been out there on the street with AV/ALANCHE just once and then only by dint of convincing Sond-erstrom that it might be my duty to pick up some feel for the op. Actually, active participation is considered too chancy for the Agency since our seven kids in AV/ALANCHE run occasionally into a roving bunch from the MRO, who are very tough fellows indeed, ultraleft-ists who believe in armed insurrection. Not only do street fights break out, but there are arrests. If I were picked up on such an occasion by the police, it could be in the hands of the wrong arm. It seems the *flics* of Montevideo come in political flavors, left or right. Depends on the precinct. (We're in South America, after all.) Sonderstrom al-lowed me to set up my credentials with these kids by going out this once with them, but afterward he forbade it. "I didn't sleep till you got back," Gus told me next day. I had returned at 5:00 A.M. and called him at his home, per instructions, leaving him vastly relieved that I had no fracas to report. All the same, the tension is there. Think of it! Scuttling around the streets in an old truck, working by flashlight as occasional stragglers and drunks pass at two in the morning. Are they lookouts for the Reds? We were defacing PCU posters (Partido Comunista de Uruguay), and that meant going on sorties into working-class neighborhoods. At two in the morning, those barrios are as silent as cemeteries. It brings back that time in adolescence when adrenaline throbs in your limbs like your first taste of booze.

Now, however, on an average Tuesday run with my gang, I position myself a half mile away in one of our radio cars, then keep in contact with AV/ALANCHE-1 through his walkie-talkie. He actually prefers this arrangement. A tough, wiry kid with the greatest head of thick powerful black curls, AV/ALANCHE-1 reassures me that they're better off if I am free on the perimeter to take off and get them bail or hospitalization if things should go wrong.

Sonderstrom, however, tells me to drive by afterward and make certain they did the job. I obey him, but am unhappy about it. These kids are taking risks while I'm secure in my radio car; yet I, in effect, must proceed to distrust them. All the same, Sonderstrom, who usually looks like he's smelling a bad cheese, is not all wrong. Occasionally they complete no more than half a job before they get nervous and decamp. Then, unhappily, they neglect to tell me. I make note of that, but still pay them. If it gets worse, I'll confront AV/ALANCHE-1.

For the rest, however, my daily work is not all that enthralling. In the beginning, the Agency must have been afraid there would not be enough tasks to keep us occupied, since our work can often be a bit intangible, and the country seems huge. (All countries, even modest ones like Uruguay, are huge when you are only a handful of people in an office.) So, a method was developed to make certain that there is always a great deal to do.

Sample day:

I come in at nine, have my coffee, and start reading the local papers. Given my Spanish, that could take two hours, but I push it through in thirty minutes. Slowly over the weeks, the nuances of the political situation become clearer to me. Of course, I also discuss the political personalities and local events with my other two Operations Officers, and the Communications Officer, plus our Station Administrative Assistant, who is Mayhew's secretary. Kittredge, that's the sum of our people in the Station office! Outside the Embassy, we can also boast of two skilled operators on contract—details to be furnished later.

As my office cohorts go over the daily news together, I pick up what I can from the Senior Operations Officer, Sherman Porringer, who is the most knowledgeable about Uruguayan politics. All that stuff in training that failed to interest me—labor unions, local party maneuvering, etc.—is now the meat of daily discussion.

After local news analysis, we peruse all the overnight cable traffic, our own first, followed by a thorough look at our associates' intake since we never know when we will have to fill in. If, for example, my fellow Operations Officer, Jay Gatsby (do you believe the name?—he's one of the most colorless people I've ever met!), is out on a golf foursome with Sonderstrom and, lo and behold, Gatsby's number-one agent, AV/IDITY, calls in, I obviously have to know a bit about Gatsby's projects.

All right, incoming cables digested, we compose our outgoing messages, which we also circulate round-robin so that all are witting of what is being sent out. Along with phone, and an unexpected turn or two, lunch is on us soon enough. In the afternoon, I put in considerable time studying the travel movements of Uruguayan officials, many of whom are Communist sympathizers who visit Paraguay, Brazil, or Argentina for meetings with party colleagues there. We also find a surprising number of trade missions to the East European countries and the U.S.S.R. Our agent AV/OUCH, in Uruguayan Customs at Carrasco Airport, keeps an eye on such movements. Our files build. But time! It all consumes time. Having dinner one evening with AV/OUCH (who is a seedy little family man pleased to get a fancy meal), I talked him into recruiting an agent I am going to call AV/OUCH-2. It got me thinking of Hugh's Thursdays. I'm afraid the Station doesn't have any major agents in serious government work as yet, but it certainly isn't difficult to pick up the petty ones. It's just money. AV/OUCH-2 will be eager to exploit his post in Passport Control to take note of those Uruguayans who are returning with visa stamps from target countries.

Of course, after we locate these local Communists, there does remain the question of what to do about it. Mayhew's lack of initiative hurts. I'd like to try turning a few of these Uruguayan Communists into double agents, but Sonderstrom tells me to wait until E. Howard Hunt arrives.

Let us say it is 3:30 P.M. in our office by now. Be certain, we are now going through the dossiers of the foreigners who will attend our Embassy function tonight. We have to be ready to warn the Ambassador of any dubious Embassy Row guests.

Finally, by way of AV/ERAGE, our Uruguayan journalist (who works the society beat), we keep track of who is being invited to other embassy affairs. It can be worth something to know that a Uruguayan official, secretly a PCU member, is on the guest list at the British Embassy. Is he being wooed by the English, or taking them for a ride? If the latter, do we send warnings?

By sundown, one or two of us may have an agent to meet at a safe house or a café. (I'm not up much on that, yet. Alas!) Then, evening work commences. Since I'm not putting in hours at golf or tennis, and do have a dinner jacket and tails, it's incumbent on me to be present at American and foreign embassy functions. That's droll. In Berlin, I never went to one cocktail party. Here, I'm out every night. My tails, incidentally, bring out the sardonic in Sherman Porringer: He declares that I am a State Department man using the Company for cover. One mighty wit is Porringer. Sherman Oatmeal, my private name for this good fellow, is another owl-eyed Ph.D. from Oklahoma, blue-jowled even with two shaves a day, another quintessentially dank example of our heroic Agency propensity for bottomless work. He is also Sonderstrom's old reliable. Porringer has the largest caseload, the unhappiest wife, the most comprehensive sense of Uruguayan politics, and—I have to admit—is kind of creative compared to the rest of us at initiating new operations. He is, however, desperately jealous of my ability to give a competent performance at parties and dances. Oatsie goes to his number of such affairs, but cuts the wrong kind of figure. Essentially unathletic, he has compensated by serious stints of weight-lifting (keeps his own barbells at home), and, in consequence, is overdeveloped on top, somewhat concrete-posted on bottom. He takes a lady onto the dance floor and steps about in spiritual pain. Being one of these wholly disciplined Ph.D. mentalities who need only to define their will and they will follow it, he is used to telling each limb what to do. Choppy seas for the partner.

Meanwhile, I cavort a little with his wife, Sally. She's a narrow-minded twit, I fear, hates Uruguay, won't learn Spanish, inveighs not too attractively on the stupidity of the servants here, but she does know how to dance. We have fun at that. I must say, it's a pity she isn't more of a dedicated Agency wife. If she wanted to, she could charm a few foreign diplomats, and that, after all, is what we're supposed to do. Sonderstrom, who goes dutifully to these functions (even took tango lessons) steered me aside before the first one: "Get your focus, Hubbard. When we and the Russians show up at the same function, all eyes follow what goes on between us," he adds.

"Should I fraternize, then?"

"With caution." He went on to lay out the hazards and potentialities: While you are not to cut loose and make friends, *feelers* can commence. "Just don't make a date for lunch without prior authorization."

You can guess how Sally Porringer might fit into this. Indeed, I've encouraged her to dance with one or two of these Red devils, but she shook her head. "Sherman said that if he ever saw me flirting with a Communist, he'd put my left tit in a wringer."

"Well," I said, "tell him to have a talk with Sonderstrom. There are many roads to Rome."

"What does that add up to, Buster?" she asked. "I'm a married woman with two children. End of case." Right after that, for the first time, her belly touched mine in our dance, and just as gently as one hand being laid on another in the dark of a movie theater. Kittredge, do women play with two decks? Why do I know that Sally Porringer is dying to flirt with the Russians? I've even got the fellow picked out. There is one recent arrival, their Under Secretary, Boris Masarov, who has a very attractive wife, Zenia—the most beautiful Russian woman I suppose I've seen. Very feminine (if a touch plump) with raven hair and the largest black eyes. In turn, Zenia has an undeniable eye for the men. Exchanging glances with her is like missing a step going downstairs. What a jolt! Boris, by the way, seems the most sympatico of the Russian legation, a good-sized bear of a Russian, albeit a touch scholarly in mien, clean-shaven young face with a mane of pepper-and-salt hair and a sad, wise, agreeable expression, as if you could really talk to him. The others, for the most part, are brutes, or London-suited joy-boys.

Do you know, there's so much to tell and so little time. It's now 2:00 A.M., I'll try to pick up this letter tomorrow night. I realize, thinking over what I've written, that my life couldn't be more different than it was in Berlin. There I knew what it was to be prematurely old. Now I feel young, but ready to take charge of a few things. Hugh was right. Here is the place to develop.

I will not mail this letter until I finish it tomorrow night. I can't get over the shock I'm telling you so many proscribed things. I feel as if I'm shattering sword and vow—some such semi-occult romantic malaise. And all for the higher vow of my lady's hand. Damn it, Kittredge, are you a Soviet agent to have so entrapped me?

H.

P.S. Actually, I feel no undue anxiety on committing all this to the mails. Your pouch routine impresses me as secure.

3

November 17, 1956
(after midnight)

Dear Kittredge,

Trying to convey the feel of these Uruguayan spy grounds seems equal, at times, to tracing a vine through a thicket. How, for example, can I delineate AV/OIRDUPOIS? He is Gordon "Gordy" Morewood, one of our two contract Operations Officers, an old hand who worked for the British in Hong Kong during the thirties and has since put in contract stints with us in Vienna, Yugoslavia, Singapore, Mexico City, Ghana—God, you'd think the man would be fascinating—always out there by himself, never working inside a Station, just taking on jobs like a private detective and being paid for them. Well, Gordy is a huge disappointment when you meet him. He's a small, dour Scotchman about sixty with a gimp leg (arthritis, I believe, not gunshot) and a splenetic disposition. A sour bad ad for old spies. All he seems to care about is his *per diem* which he inflates unconscionably. This man eats well off his expense accounts, and Minot Mayhew refuses to have anything to do with him. That costs us a good deal of telephone time. Gordy is always on the line asking for the Chief of Station, and we have to stall him out and take the abuse. He's capable of saying (and he has the most nasty thin voice), "Look, dear young *novice,* you are altogether incapable of hiding the fact that Mayhew is skulking around the Embassy right now and must be reached by me. I cannot speak to you. You are too low on the pole."

As I write this, he sounds interesting, but he isn't. The voice comes forth in a distracted whine. He always wants more money, and by pestering us thoroughly, knows he will obtain a decent fraction of the new and extra amount. He is certainly adept at using his cover to jack up his expenses, and fields an honest-to-God import-export business in the center of town. It's the perfect setup for Morewood, who imports just about enough gourmet items for the Embassy commissary to make any close accounting of his finances impossible. Our Administrative Officer, Nancy Waterston, a sweet, plain, bright, hardworking spinster, absolutely devoted to Minot Mayhew—for no better reason than that he happens to be her boss—is also devoted to Sonderstrom because he runs the Station, and to the rest of us because we're doing our patriotic job. Needless to say, she loves the Company more than church or kin. You can imagine how neat she is, and how fussy. Gordon Morewood will drive her, we fear, into nervous exhaustion. She pores over his accounts, but he has managed to weave a web that entangles every one of her good accounting principles. I have seen Nancy Waterston close to tears after a session with Gordy on the phone. He is always moving on to new projects, new bills, new receipts, new out-of-pocket expenses. There is no way she can keep up with his divagations from accepted bookkeeping practice. Once, she was desperate enough to importune Mayhew to authorize the dispatch of a top-flight auditor to Montevideo, but Mayhew, with all his detestation of Gordy, nonetheless wouldn't put her request on the wire, which makes me suspect that Gordy is somebody's darling back in Foggy Bottom. Over separate beers with Sonderstrom, Porringer, Gatsby, and the Commo Officer, Barry Kearns, I've heard that Gordy's position is sacrosanct. We cannot say good-bye to him.

Moreover, we can't afford to. He's very good at his job. We would not, for instance, have a mobile surveillance team (AV/EMARIA-1, and 2, 3, 4), consisting of four off-duty taxi drivers, without Gordy. He trained those fellows himself (at a 100-percent override for us, we reckon, on the hours of instruction), but at least we have them in place and they do bring results. Left to ourselves, what with our paperwork and our fifty-fifty Spanish (50 percent of what we say and hear is comprehended), how could there be the time, wherewithal, and savvy to train mobile surveillants? We'd have to bring in a team from Mexico City or D.C., speak of expense.

So, yes, the fact is that we can't afford to say good-bye to Morewood. He's the only consummate professional among us, and when a real problem comes up, we have to call on him.

This time it involved an operation that we characterize as *cumbersome*. We were looking to get a Uruguayan official who has become a Russian agent arrested by the Uruguayan police. Not at all automatic.

But let me take it in order. Over a month ago, just before I arrived, we received an alert from Western Hemisphere Division that gave us reason to be interested in a gentleman named Plutarco Roballo Gómez. A year ago, the FBI reported that Gómez, serving then in New York on the Uruguayan Delegation to the UN, was playing footsie with the Soviets. Now that Gómez is back in Uruguay, and is well placed in his Foreign Ministry job, we decided to call on Gordy to find out a little more about him.

Gordy has learned that Gómez gambles nightly at the casino in Carrasco, and always needs money. On Tuesday nights, however, he does go to visit his mother at her home near Parque José Batlle y Ordóñez, which is the large park adjacent to our Embassy.

We ordered in our mobile surveillance team. AV/ EMARIA-1, 2, 3, and 4 took turns trailing Gómez's car. On the last trip to his mother's house, Gómez drove into the park, got out of his vehicle, and went for a walk. The paths being sparsely lit, Gordy was able to trail Gómez discreetly on foot, but gave up such pursuit when his target disappeared into a clump of bushes. A few minutes later, Gómez emerged, and crossed to a nearby path where he righted a park bench that had been tipped over, obviously a signal that he had serviced his dead drop. After which, Gómez left the park and drove home. On the following Tuesday, just after dark, we staked out the area around these bushes. Porringer, Sonderstrom, and Morewood had a considerable wait, but at ten in the evening, a man Sonderstrom recognized as an attaché at the Russian Embassy came sauntering along, inserted an envelope into the hollow cleft of a tree, and, strolling by the same park bench, stopped just long enough to knock it over. Gómez appeared in the next quarter of an hour, took the envelope from the dead drop, righted the park bench, and went back to his car.

Much of the following week was spent in discussion of what to do. Cable traffic mounted. There was considerable discussion about whether to keep using Morewood. He had charged us a good deal already on these matters, and besides, Sonderstrom has his pride. So, instead of enjoying a Friday afternoon foursome with the Chief of Police and his assistant, Gus just took them to lunch. Over coffee, Sonderstrom introduced the defalcations of Plutarco Roballo Gómez. The Chief of Police, Capablanca (yes, same name as the old Cuban chess champion), was even angrier than his deputy, Peones, and offered to spit in the milk of Gómez's mother. Plans were made to catch Gómez in the act, then arrest him. Sonderstrom came back to the Station in an excellent mood. Not Porringer. Before long, he and Sonderstrom were going at it. Their voices carried through a closed door. Soon, the door flew open and Sonderstrom waved in Gatsby and Barry Kearns and myself to monitor the debate. I would guess he wanted reinforcements.

Porringer argued that Gómez was one of President Luis Batlle's hand-picked protégés, and so the Chief of Police wouldn't make the arrest.

Sonderstrom agreed this was a bothersome element in the equation. "Still, you learn something about a man while playing golf. Capablanca hates missing a shot he should be able to make. I see our Chief of Police as a professional."

"My instinct," replies Porringer, "tells me to go slow."

"I don't know that we can," says Sonderstrom. "Capablanca is laying in the first steps right now. We can't make him look like a fool to his own people."

"That's right," said Gatsby. "Latins are as high on saving face as Orientals."

"I agree," said Kearns.

"In South America," Porringer said, "the *jefe* can always change his mind. It just means his money is coming from a new direction."

"Who," asked Sonderstrom, "is in favor of going for the arrest?"

Kearns' hand went up, and Gatsby's, and Sonderstrom's, of course. I was ready to follow suit, but some instinct held me back. Kittredge, it was the oddest sentiment. I had the feeling Porringer was right. To my amazement, I voted with him. I am linked with Oatsie.

Well, we had an answer. On the next Tuesday, I couldn't join my associates on stakeout in the park because that is the night for AV/ALANCHE, but I certainly heard about it afterward. Sonderstrom, Porringer, Gatsby, and Kearns spent a couple of hours in the appropriate bushes with a squad of Uruguayan police. The Russian attaché came sauntering in about the same time as on the previous occasion, which is *poor* tradecraft. (The local KGB obviously feel far enough away from Moscow to be pretty casual about security.) In any event, he went immediately to the dead drop, primed it, tipped over the bench, and left. By radio came the word that Gómez had parked his car, was approaching on foot. He was actually within twenty yards of the tree when a police car, top light revolving, sirens screaming at the moon, came tearing down a park road toward the stakeout. Gómez, of course, took off instantly. With a great blast of tire dust and screech, the patrol car stopped right by the tree. Out stepped Capablanca. "Oh," exclaimed our law and order worthy, striking his forehead with a mighty sledgehammer of a hand, "I cannot accept this. The radio told me that our man was already apprehended."

In the general confusion, Porringer managed to slip over to the dead drop and withdraw the envelope. Next day, Sonderstrom presented it at the Central Police Station. The note listed each document that Gómez was supposed to photograph in the following week. Sonderstrom stated that this ought to be enough to commence a full-scale investigation.

No, sir, we cannot, Capablanca told him. It is now obvious that some unknown foreign power was indeed spying on the Uruguayan government, but, then, nations always spied on host nations. One needed more than evidence such as this to proceed. Owing to the unfortunate lapse in communications on Tuesday night, for which he, Salvador Capablanca, would take full responsibility, he could see no way to move against Plutarco Roballo Gómez. He would, however, keep an eye on him. I can hear Gordy Morewood cackling away!

It is now 3:30 A.M. and I am tired. I'll sign off, and wait for your next letter. Do write soon.

Besitos,
Herrick

4

THREE DAYS LATER, AN OPEN COMMERCIAL CABLE CAME FROM HARLOT.

NOV. 20, 1956

CHRISTOPHER, EIGHT POUNDS ONE OUNCE, BORN AT WALTER REED ARMY HOSPITAL AT 8:01 A.M. MOTHER FINE, SENDS LOVE, FATHER TRANSMITS FOND REGARDS.

MONTAGUE

NOV. 21, 1956
    SPLENDID NEWS. GODFATHER BEWITCHED.

                                                        HARRY

   I raided my checking account and ordered four dozen long-stemmed red roses to be sent to Walter Reed by way of the Agency Commissary in Washington. Then I went home early from work, stretched out on my mattress (which reeked of insect repellent), and stayed in bed at the Hotel Cervantes from six in the evening to six in the morning feeling as if I had been stomped on by a platoon of Marines.

   Indeed, I did not write to Kittredge until a letter came from her about a month after the birth of Christopher. I no longer knew—if I ever did!—what she wanted from my letters, and I did not recognize the calm, hardworking young man who stepped forth in my handwriting. He had rattled on about his work as if he knew it inside out when, indeed, he only pretended to. Was that how I wished to be seen? The birth of Christopher mocked such vanity.

                                             December 20, 1956
Harry dearest,
        My child is a month old today and I, who was raised by my father to believe that iambic pentameter is the only suitable meter for the passions of murder and love, have decided to throw over his dictates, and become a devotee of the one-step. Thirty days old, Christopher weighs eight pounds, five ounces. Is fed every four hours. Is as beautiful as the heavens. Like a fixated witch, I stare at this blue-eyed creature with his minuscule hams of hands, pink and succulent. Watch! They seek his mouth. I examine his incomparable alabaster skin. My ears dwell on his gurgle of innocence. But I know better. All these corny palimpsests of infantitude hide from us the fact that infants look bitter, mean as rue, and eighty years old in the first minute they're born, and are covered with enough welts and streamers of blood to have been in a car crash. Of course, that face soon disappears, not to be seen again for eighty years. At present, Christopher shines like an angel cherub. I am the only one to remember where he came from—that "shuddery penetralia of caves."
        Does the phrase toll a bell? The only time I attended a High Montague Thursday, Hugh was talking about the *ineffable* interrela-

tions of counterespionage. Leave it to my doughty warrior, he actually said, "Our studies move into penetralia. We search for that innermost sanctum, 'the shuddery penetralia of caves'—for which inimitable phrase, gentlemen, I am indebted to a Mr. Spencer Brown who is so quoted in the OED."

At that moment, Harry, I didn't know if my mustachioed Beau Brummel was the acme of audacity or asininity. I did think it was crass to oblige all you young crew-cuts to listen to such smelly stuff. I didn't go back to the Thursdays. I am becoming more and more like my mother, especially these days. I look at Christopher and am transported to bliss, then, as quickly, am dropped right back into the darkness of our human roots—damn shuddery penetralia. Harry, I can't tell you how much your generous letters have meant. Station work, for all its mediocre sleazy contacts and its tedium and frustration, still seems more sensible than all those highly slanted endeavors with which Hugh keeps himself and his helpmate, me, busy. So, don't stop writing. I love the details. Some of your items nourish me through the worst of the p.p.d.'s. Yes, p.p.d.'s. You, male lummox, probably don't know that I am speaking of *postpartum depression*. You can't conceive of how ill equipped a new mother is at shaping up for the daily grind until you go through these doldrums. Even when I lift my baby out of the crib, and this warm little tenderness of spirit is in my arms, I bawl. For I begin to realize the cost and the beauty of motherhood. Everything within me is being rebuilt on new terms, and who knows how stern and exacting these terms will prove? Hugh comes in from some twelve-hour flap at Technical Services, sees me in the teary mopes, claps his hands, says, "Dammit, Kittredge, Christopher is thirty days old. That's long enough to put up with one leaky faucet of a woman."

Well, I want to kill him. It's simple again. I bless Hugh in my divided heart because anger does lift you up for a while, but, oh, Hugh is such a large part of the p.p.d.'s. As are you. I read your letters, all there, everything given to me, and think, "Why can't I dwell among these idiot station men with their sacred procedures?" So I start to miss you. Keep writing. I do enjoy your epistolary gifts. Your detailed sendings bring light and shadow to the dreamlike two-dimensionality on which my feeble work is projected. *Besitos, estúpido*. Yours, for more Spic-talk.

Hadley K. Gardiner Montague (Mrs.)

P.S. The roses were aces, bearcat, corkeroo! *Mille baisers*. You are the dearest gnat's whistle.

5

Jan. 3, 1957

Lovely mother,

I can't keep from studying the snapshots you enclose. Christopher's cherubic sense of himself pushes right through the silver iodide. I must say he looks a good deal like Winston Churchill, and that delights me. Not every day does one become surrogate godfather to Old Winnie!

I also thank you for my Christmas present. It's summer here now, but the gloves will be most useful come July. I'm glad the roses got to Walter Reed. Did the brooch arrive, however, at the Stable? Don't tell me I was extravagant. Perhaps I was, but so soon as I looked into the antique shop window, I had to buy it for you. The ornament spoke to me of heavy old Uruguayan gentility, and yet, I don't know why, it reminded me of some inaccessible part of you. Can you possibly comprehend what I mean? In any event, don't count me extravagant. In truth, I wasn't. My mother, to my amazement, had just sent me a voluptuous check—it even felt plump and lustful in my bone-dry wallet. (Since I sympathize with your passion-to-know, I will not torture you needlessly.) Five hundred smackers! Sent along with a one-line note—"It's Christmas, so do it up properly, darling." She didn't even bother to sign. Her stationery is her signature. I must say I feel uncharacteristically full of love for her. Just as one grows to resign oneself one more time to her basic stinginess of sentiment, lo, she knows what you are thinking, and comes across with a flashing stroke. Someday I will write a Charles Lamb–like essay on The Multitudinous Vagaries of the Bitch.

Well, I certainly must be full of gelignite and lyddite, peter and soup, to speak of my mother in such fashion. (Actually, I can't resist listing these explosives. I hear them all the time.) We Station hands certainly don't use the stuff very often (once a decade?), but we do know how to throw the cordite and nitro jargon around. *Bang juice* is the latest favorite. Obscene enough to do the job. We naturally passed through a host of Christmas parties these last two weeks, each of the married couples (which involves Mayhew, Sonderstrom, Porringer, Gatsby, Kearns) plus Nancy Waterston and myself as singles, giving an evening at their homes. I, still ensconced in my all-but-fleabag hotel, reciprocated by inviting four couples and Nancy Waterston (Mayhew doesn't show up at any party but his own) to dine, all ten of us, in the grand and overpriced dining room of the Victoria Plaza. In the course of after-dinner drinks, we all got off for some silly reason on bang juice. Kept passing the term around, looking for new connotations—which came down, predictably, to the old connotation. But we had a merry time formulating such bang juice toasts as: "Blessings and bang juice to Augustus Sonderstrom, our own Gus, banging his big woods and juiced-up irons, and may all the bang juice be wiped off his hard-hitting putter," yes, it got as elaborate and stupid as that. From Porringer, of course.

Anyway, I had one insight into Sally and Sherman late that evening. At the end of dinner, about the time we were all thickening up—you can't call it sobering up—they happened to be alone for a moment at one end of the table, and she was looking sour, and he was full of bilious, much-compacted anger. (I know he had to be upset that his elaborate golf-and-bang-juice toast did not go over.) So the Porringers sat there like a warning to all who might contemplate marriage, old before their time. It's awfully sad, because she has a perky little face. Maybe she was a cheerleader in high school, for certainly she has a nice body.

At any rate, I began to notice what the Porringers were doing with their napkins. It told the tale. Sherman had squeezed his piece of linen and released it, squeezed it and released it (with his thighs, I assume) until now, laid on the table, it looked like a piled-up thundercloud. Hers, to the contrary, appeared to have undergone a regimen of successive flattenings from the palm of her hand. Still, the cloth kept rising. Her poor trapped heart?

I think the Porringers are both from the Southwest, college sweethearts perhaps, I seem to recollect that he went to Oklahoma State. The point to this, I expect, is that each of them touches me in the oddest way. Ever since I voted with him against Sonderstrom, his relations toward me have been a study. Stop-and-go. Brusque; friendly. Highly critical of my work, followed by a clap on the back. Superciliously superior, then helpful. I, in turn, don't know if I like him any better. I mention this because he did pass on a plum of a job to me. Right in front of Sonderstrom, he said, "Rick can field this one better than Gatsby, and you and I just don't have the time."

Do you know, I realize that all of this letter has been a preamble to a serious decision. Everything I've disclosed up to now can be seen as venial, but if I fill you in on the new job, and am discovered, I'm in the soup. As are you. So, let us wait a couple of days. I'll write again before the week is out. It's 3:00 A.M. once more. Apologies for this abrupt ending. I have to think this out for myself. It's of too much consequence to rush into.

Love,
Harry

I was not telling the truth about Sally Porringer. We had begun an affair, and it was already into its second week on the night I invited my good Agency associates to dinner. So, the sadness I felt on watching Mrs. Porringer flatten her napkin was more complex than simple sorrow, and not without a tinge of fear. I lived among trained observers, after all, and the affair, if ever discovered, would look dreadful. Having helped me to get an important assignment, Sherman Porringer had been given a set of horns for Christmas.

Nonetheless, I fell asleep with no difficulty. Encountering the cold center of myself was not unreassuring. It suggested that I might be well equipped for the more difficult tasks I would face. I certainly felt cold enough to recognize that a very small part of me, which was nonetheless quintessential, would never forgive Kittredge for having another man's child.

Jan. 5, 1957

Dearest Number One,

I've weighed out the contingencies. As you may have supposed, I am going to tell all. Our operation is called AV/OCADO, and if it works as well as we hope, there's a good deal of entrée. I suppose you could say it's in fulfillment of one of our two major objectives. Ideally, according to the Missions Directive, the Priority is to effect a penetration into the Soviet Embassy, and next Priority is to get into the higher ranks of the PCU. (That last, if you recall, is the Uruguayan Communist Party.)

Well, this second objective is well along. Thanks to Porringer, it's become my baby. I'm inheriting a Priority Task, and I am going to take you into it, for I may need advice farther down the line. I can tell you—I don't want any repetition of that embarrassing Berlin period when I was on the secure phone every other day with our mutual friend. This time I am going to bring the job off on my own.

Let me provide the filler. Did I mention that we have two contract agents? Besides Gordy Morewood, there is Roger Clarkson. He's also done good work for us, and his cover is excellent. He not only works for the most prestigious public relations firm in Montevideo (which handles the accounts for most of the U.S. corporations here), but has put in a lot of time with the local Anglo-American drama group. You would think that is not a particularly fertile place to pick up our kind of information, but it certainly is where the winds of gossip blow. Many upper-class Uruguayans gravitate to the Montevideo Players on the pretext that they wish to improve their English, whereas, actually, the Players has become a classy arena for the great South American upper-middle-class sport—infidelity. Roger Clarkson has served as our facsimile of a KGB joy-boy. He's tall, good-looking, straight nose, blond hair, Princeton—a splendid example of what we're advertising to the rest of the world. In the course of his activities, he's picked up a lot of what is going on at the Legislative Palace. No great haul, but indispensable bits to corroborate or refute the information we receive from our heavier sources—the usual Uruguayan legislators, journalists, businessmen, etc.

Some months ago, Roger came in with a big one. Eusebio "Chevi" Fuertes popped up at the drama group. Chevi is almost as good looking as Valentino, Roger assured us, at least if you are ready to discount a somewhat chewed-up Latin street face. Fuertes, who comes out of Uruguayan working-class stock, went to the University of the Republic here, then married up into a middle-class family of local lawyers and doctors, part of the Montevideo radical establishment.

At present, Fuertes is a member in good standing of the PCU, ditto his wife. He is, however, no stable hardworking Communist, but, on the contrary, is somewhat taken with himself, and is pulled in many directions. For example, he quit his university studies some years ago, and with no money went off to New York. (Only agreed to marry his wife after he came back a year later.) She is apparently a wholehearted party-liner who has already risen high in the local ranks. Everyone, including her husband, expects her to become one of the PCU's national leaders in ten years. She's a lawyer, polemicist, functionary, and her family has, as I say, an old radical tradition.

Chevi, by contrast, pretends to be a loyal member but secretly can't bear whole aspects of the Party, the discipline, the self-sacrifice, and the patience required to obtain power. The year he spent in New

York seems to have affected him eccentrically. He returned to Uruguay admiring America and hating it, but cocky from the experience. It seems among other stints as dishwasher and short-order cook and waiter, he was also some kind of unwilling consort—"never a pimp," he assures Roger—to a Harlem whore.

All this has been learned by Clarkson and passed on to us. It seems he and Fuertes get along famously. They have even double-dated a couple of the ladies in the Montevideo Players. To use a phrase I've recently learned—they *run* together. Roger, who remains agreeably modest concerning his cachet with the local actresses, explained that *studs* (speaking of new words!) often *run* in parallel. So, Clarkson and Fuertes are fascinated with each other.

I confess to equal fascination. I'm learning how much you can pick up about a man by studying reports. Clarkson, who keeps a tidy ship, has been feeding detailed memos to the Station after each evening spent with Fuertes, and I, having been assigned to take over when he leaves for America (which is just a couple of weeks away), read everything Roger turns in as if it were "Gerontion" or *Remembrance of Things Past*. Clarkson's no stylist—he's not, dear God, supposed to be!—but the material, considering my oncoming relation to it, certainly proves stimulating. Fuertes, very clever and very suspicious, is always on the alert against manipulation. He has startling insights into Clarkson, then spasms of rage against American imperialism which alternate with gouts of vitriol against Uruguayan Communists. He most respectfully declares his love for his powerful wife, but soon allows that he resents and detests her. He loves Clarkson yet hints he'll leave a knife in him someday should Clarkson ever betray him, that is, prove to be a CIA agent. This is Fuertes' declared suspicion of our Roger. In a bar, on their last meeting after rehearsal (the Montevideo Players are now doing Paul Osborn's *The Vinegar Tree*), Chevi not only accused Clarkson of working for the Agency but stated that he must be in the CIA since it was well known that 50 percent of the Agency's contract people were employed by American public relations firms.

All this while, Chevi, despite such outbursts, has been drawing closer to Roger. Chevi's real desire, he now announces, is to talk over his problems—as between men. Those problems, he declares, are acute in the region of emotion. (Don't you enjoy the formal turn Latins bring to English?) His hatred of the Communist Party in Uruguay is *una enormidad*, he confesses. Of course, on other days, it is the

Soviet Union that gets berated. They have betrayed the world revolution. Next night, he goes back to blaming the lust for power of the
Uruguayan leaders, and the stupidity of the rank and file. They are not
revolutionary, but bourgeois, he declares. Communism in South
America has degenerated into a hobby of the intelligentsia, a virulent
fever of the decaying middle classes. The villains of every revolution,
from Robespierre to the present, have revealed their attachment to
the middle-class umbilicus. There are times, Roger allows, when he
can't keep up with Fuertes.

Should Clarkson try, however, to put in a good word for the
U.S., Chevi bombards him with polemical abuse. Capitalism feeds on
the excrement of progress. The people of the United States are dispossessed of their souls. Capitalists are pigs. Pigs in limousines. He says at
the end of one of these sessions, "Since I know you work for the
Central Intelligence Agency of the United States of America, and are
aware that my wife and I are members of the Partido Comunista de
Uruguay, and that I am unhappy in such a role, why do you offer no
proposition?"

"Because I'm goddamned if I can trust you!"

Roger is not only bold enough to make that reply, but is
forthcoming enough—or is it scrupulously responsible enough?—to
include it in his *Summary of Jan. 2 Meeting with AV/OCADO.* (Needless to say, Sonderstrom does not leave that little speech uncensored
on its way to Argentina-Uruguay Desk, God, they would have
thrown the book at Clarkson.)

Roger was accoutered with a sneaky that night. Of course, his
recording was garbled a bit, but Clarkson, like a good soldier, filled in
some of the blanks. He claims to have respectable ability at recalling
conversation, and calls the result "*fortified* transcription." For certain,
he has produced a document that I think enough of to reproduce for
you.

AV/OCADO: You do not comprehend me. You are too insulated.
    That is how Americans fulfill their soul-destroying functions.
AV/UNCULAR: Why don't you just cut the crap?
AV/OCADO: *Sí, Señor,* I am full of crap. But how may I cut it? You
    desire to make an offer to me, yet you dare not.
AV/UNCULAR: Have a heart, friend. How am I to begin? You don't
    trust yourself.
AV/OCADO: That is no less than the truth. I am a man who lives

in an anguish that is self-perpetuated. I am lacking in *pundo-nor*. Do you comprehend *pundonor*?

AV/UNCULAR: You are never lacking in *pundonor*. You, *amigo*, have death-guts.

AV/OCADO: I thank you for the sentiment. You speak like a friend. But I cannot trust the authority of your sentiments because in the *cono del sur*, a man must live for his *pundonor*. He must be prepared for mortal confrontation. Yes, every day of his life. Do you know? It is a comedy. Uruguayans live to be eighty. Whether or not we face our death-guts, we live to be eighty. We are *cómico*, my friend. (Long pause.) You do not comprehend me. What can be the value of a friend if he is not the generous spirit of comprehension? You, however, are a North American. You are looking for an edge. A grip on me. Go fuck yourself.

AV/UNCULAR: Hey, let's have another drink. It'll make you more mellow.

AV/OCADO: For people such as you, I must spell it out.

AV/UNCULAR: Have it your way.

AV/OCADO: Spell it out, or spit it out. These are the established modes of communication for Americans, *verdad*?

AV/UNCULAR: We're no good.

AV/OCADO: Now I know it. You *are* CIA. It is in the logic of your responses. I utter scathing insults upon you and your country, and you, a proud and virile North American, do not challenge me to step outside this bar.

AV/UNCULAR: Would you challenge me if I insulted Uruguay?

AV/OCADO: There would be no alternative.

Kittredge, this is the clearest part of the conversation. Over the next ten minutes, it became too garbled for Clarkson to restore. Then, he must have shifted his seat, because their exchanges now came through again loud and strong. Here is more of the *fortified* transcription.

AV/OCADO: I have always stationed myself on the barricades of independent thought. I do not have a group mind, my friend, nor predesigned sentiments due to lack of inner subjectivity. So, at present, I am drenched in the poisons of humiliation.

AV/UNCULAR: Explain it to me. I want to listen.

AV/OCADO: I am a lawyer who serves clients who are too poor to pay their bills. I am a husband who attracts less respect in public than his wife. I may be more intelligent than my spouse, but my ideas veer too far to the right, then too far to the left. That is because I lack sufficient foundation to hold them in place.

AV/UNCULAR: What do you require, then?

AV/OCADO: A salary large enough to give ballast to the discord in myself. I need commercial focus. I am like all the other shits. I want money.

Sonderstrom, Porringer, and myself, after meeting with Roger, are obviously of two minds about whether to take on the two opposed spirits of Eusebio "Chevi" Fuertes. He hates his wife and the PCU enough to work for us—on that we all agree. But will he gear into the job? Will he begin to make something of himself in the Party and take on PCU tasks so diligently that he becomes a high Party functionary? I argue that to achieve equality with his wife would be a real and powerful motivation for him. In that case, what a probe we would have. The breadth of this possibility pushes us into taking him on, but, oh, the tremors. Sonderstrom, who has experience, after all, in these matters, says Chevi is selling himself so hard he could be a dangle. Roger, however, disbelieves that Fuertes is a gift of the KGB. "He's not a good enough actor to orchestrate all that confusion," says Roger. "Over at the Montevideo Players, we see him as a ham."

What aggravates the problem, of course, is Roger's pending return to the States. As of two months ago, his contract was already concluded. Given the potential importance of AV/OCADO, he has delayed his departure twice, but now Roger has given the Station final notice. He is getting married to his childhood sweetheart—one plain Jane by her photographs—and plans to work for her father. This does not make much sense, given the importance of what he's doing for us here—why can't the bride come down to Uruguay? Then we are treated to the subtext: The childhood sweetheart is going to inherit a fortune. She may be plain-looking, but has enough temper for an ugly duchess. Roger does not dare to keep her waiting. Her father, you see, is an advertising tycoon with a hell of a job for Roger. In a week, Clarkson is definitely departing.

It's not the best of situations to insert me at this point, but where's the choice? Roger is not going to kiss Miss Moneybags good-bye.

Sonderstrom, for all his faults, is, I'm beginning to recognize, not the worst den mother. He knows how to put a reasonable face on things. "Your situation could turn out satisfactorily," Gus says to me at the end of the meeting. "With a new case officer in place, AV/OCADO might shape up more quickly. A stranger can be effective in situations like this. AV/OCADO obviously likes to torture his friends."

Succinct enough, but I'm the one in the passenger seat next week.

This time I won't tell you how late it is. Will just sign off. My new cryptonym, specially crafted for the new job, is—I must say they save the tasty ones for me—AV/AILABLE.

Humbly yours,
Available Hubbard

P.S. Did you ever get the brooch?

6

Jan. 18, 1957

Harry, dear,

It's my turn to make a confession. I kept wanting to acknowledge the brooch, but couldn't. You see, I've lost it.

There was the most unsettling premonition when I opened your little package—so small, so carefully wrapped, obviously your Christmas gift—and beheld that breast pin. I knew it had belonged once to some particularly nasty old family who suffered some horrid disaster.

I've always had psychic powers there was no sense talking about. They proved no use to me, and usually came at the oddest times and for the most inconsequential reasons. I even wondered why I possessed this one milligram of magic so altogether unconnected to the other hundred and twenty pounds of me. Since Christopher has been born, however, it's come to focus. It's a gift, a power of maternity, if you will. I developed an exceptional sense of what to have in our house for Christopher, and what should not be there. Dear Herrick, when I opened your package, I wondered if you had gone in for the cruelest kind of joke. It was as if I started to bite into a scrumptious éclair and a roach came swimming up out of the cream. I almost shrieked. That brooch was loathsome. I could not understand how you and I, so close in so many ways, could be so far apart on this one matter. I didn't even want to keep your gift in the house. Yet, given my feelings, I couldn't pass it on to a friend, and it's dangerous, my instincts tell me, to throw away any object you consider *evil*. (Measure my true regard for you by the honesty of these remarks!) I decided finally to sell it. Filthy lucre can, at least, demagnetize the aura of awful things—after all, isn't that what they invented money for? I thought I might wash that cash through another transaction or two, and get it back to you. Such was my plan. Instead, I discovered this morning that the brooch is gone. It has disappeared from the box I kept in a corner of the bookshelf. I can't believe the nurse or the cleaning woman stole it. I'm in a state as I write this, and now hear the baby crying. I'll have to continue in a while.

Two hours later

Well, he had colic. Full diaper. I submit that baby-doo doth smell as if the little creatures discovered corruption all by themselves—that much to back up Original Sin. Then, I had a salary negotiation with the nurse, who feels she's underpaid and wishes to rewrite our original understanding. After which, I had to go shopping for formula plus three medallions of beef to show up in the Montagues' Wellington tonight (two for Hugh), and shallots, and *chanterelles*—how he adores them! When I came home, I decided to clean Hugh's study. (Which I hadn't been near for a week.) First thing I saw was the brooch, hanging from a little metal knob on one of the cubbyhole drawers of his desk. I had never mentioned your gift to him, and now Hugh had appropriated it. He must have thought it was something I picked up in a flea market.

Harry, it's odd. The moment I saw your gift among his papers, I knew it was all right. Hugh is so girded about with his own talismans that I believe he can, without having any idea at all of what he is doing, make wise decisions when it comes to handling these indefinables. Your petite Uruguayan monster is absolutely stripped of its powers so long as it is attached to his desk—oh, never believe this, you can't, but just as I wrote these last words, I had one of those precious little fantasies it's tempting to call a vision. In part, I saw the history of the brooch. The founder of the family who owned it was either a hanging judge or an executioner—some form of expediter of the bloodier social tasks.

Well, even as I wrote this, I stood up, crossed to his study, looked again at fearsome Miss Bijou, and realized it has now become a part of the world that communicates with me. Ninety-nine and $^{99}/_{100}$ percent of such a world is composed of people, hurrah, but there is a tree here and there, and a bird I recollect from my childhood, as well as a pug my father gave me in adolescence. That dog was an absolute spirit; now, this bloody breast pin. Harry, the brooch just told me that you had better watch your step with your highly disturbed Latin Communist. This Fuertes. Do be careful. He could wreck your career.

And do forgive the gloves. Your Christmas, I keep reminding myself, is as hot as July.

Love,
Kittredge

I had bought the brooch on the morning after I began my affair with Sally Porringer. Since I was, at the time of purchase, full of anticipation of a vigorous sexual future, and feeling some guilt toward Kittredge, I picked out the ornament by its price, and had the inner gall to pretend it had been bought on a deep impulse. Had I taken on one more of the mortal debts and curses?

Jan. 22, 1957

Dearest Kittredge,

I am now set up with AV/OCADO, and for the present it's going a little better than one could have hoped. Sonderstrom was right. The changing of the guard has sobered up our Latin friend. Indeed, the transition went off well. We met in a safe house that the Station is maintaining in a brand-new apartment building on the Rambla above Playa de Los Pocitos. There are a good many similar such high apartment buildings now going up and when they're finished, I'm sure the Rambla will look like one more bare, bleak version of Lake Shore Drive in Chicago; already you can feel that developer's aura. In the safe-house flat, taking it in from our picture window on the twelfth floor, the cars below seem as small as dog-track rabbits whipping by the wide clay-colored beach and the greenish-brown sea. Half the adolescents of Montevideo seem to be sporting on that beach. Bikinis galore. Even from this distance, big Spanish hips on the girls. Once again, the 238 pounds of beef and pork per capita shows in this registry of buttocks.

Our safe house is uncomfortably bare. We're paying whatever our substantial rent must come to, yet have purchased nothing in the way of furniture but for the bed and bureau in the sleeping alcove, and the folding couch-bed, plastic dining table, one armchair, one lamp, and a few bridge chairs set about the living room. Plus one discarded Embassy no-color-left rug. I don't understand safe-house economics. If we're anteing up for a luxury apartment, why not make it appealing? (Perhaps this mean agenda has something to do with keeping the agent's stipend low.)

In any event, I don't know how to describe Chevi Fuertes. In advance, I studied photographs of him, and know more of his formal biography than I do, say, of Sonderstrom's, but I'm still not prepared for his presence. He is so alive that you want to shelter him. My first thought was: Kittredge would adore him. He's dark, of course, and thin, with a hawklike nose and a full share of the stygian Spanish gloom that always makes me think of the body pits of undertakers—there! I've just vented my hitherto unconscious dose of resentment at being stationed here. All the same, Chevi takes you by surprise with his smile. The face picks up lights, and a tender if wicked youth peers out at you from the mask of the gloomy man.

Roger Clarkson, having made a point of introducing me brusquely, even perfunctorily, as Peter, proceeds to business. He tells Chevi that an emergency was calling him back to the United States and I would be the replacement. We would no longer meet at the Montevideo Players, but at this safe house.

Chevi said to Roger, "I do not believe your story."

Roger waved his hand ambiguously as if to blend all that was false with all that was true. "Peter is here," he said, pointing to me. "This is the fact."

"I," said Chevi, "do not believe you are returning to the United States."

"But I am."

"No," said Chevi, "you are going to Europe to work with Hungarian refugees whom your people will send back to Budapest for works of sabotage."

"I cannot go affirmative on that," Roger replied. His powers of improvisation are obviously in fine shape. "But you ought to know, Chevi, that they could never put me onto those Hungarians. I can't manage Magyar diphthongs." He gave Chevi a wink. It carried the day. Fuertes obviously needed to believe that his acumen was on the mark. Roger took care of that with the wink. Yes, it said, you happen to be right, but I can't tell you. Aloud, he said, "Why don't we deal with the here and now of the transfer?"

After that, Fuertes listened soberly and answered the detailed questions of our debriefing with long answers. I won't bore you, Kittredge, with the product of these several hours. It was technical, procedural, and relatively smooth. Even as Fuertes gave us the Table of Organization of the PCU and the names of the leaders and section heads, my initial compassion for him began to deepen. He was so obviously divided. Perhaps 51 percent of the man had decided to go with us, but the other 49 percent is still attached to a network of old friendships closely woven into his childhood, adolescence, and university days, his Party work and his marriage, even his old neighborhood.

It was, we all knew, preparatory. One of the tips Sonderstrom had passed along to Roger and myself was to interview Chevi at length about his childhood and young manhood. "It will," said Gus, "initiate a positive bond. He'll feel important. People aren't used to other people taking them that seriously."

Do you know, Kittredge, once again Sonderstrom was right. As Chevi spoke into our tape recorder, I could feel resignation settle in over his gloom. It was as if he had embarked on a boat and was watching the shore of the past recede from the rail. When we were done and the cash payment had taken place, which I, not Roger, disbursed per Sonderstrom's instructions—Chevi is getting fifty dollars a week—I noticed that he literally winced as the money touched his palm. (Do you know—I was perspiring from the effort of counting it out in front of him. It is humiliating to be obliged to humiliate a fellow human being.) I must say paper money had never felt so dirty.

Clarkson then did something subtle and proper. While Chevi had to be aware that we would discuss him in detail so soon as we were alone with each other, still, Roger had the courtesy to leave first. He gave an *abrazo* to Chevi, said, "I'll send a postcard from the Balkans," and walked out the door.

My brand-new agent and I must now have looked like freshmen who will be rooming together for the year to come. We were standing an uncomfortable yard apart.

"I am going to make my first request to you, Peter," he said.

"Whatever it is, I will do it," I replied. I figured the request would not be unpalatable.

"I wish you to ignore every conception Roger has implanted in you about the lineaments of my character. I would prefer that you come to know me by yourself."

"I comprehend," I said.

"I would hope you do." We shook hands on that.

Well, that was a couple of weeks ago. Since then I've seen him twice. We make progress slowly. Chevi may have told me that it would not prove laborious to get to know him, but no one at the Station or back at the Groogs (which has become our exasperated name for our Washington overseers at the Argentina-Uruguay Desk) is ready to buy such an avowal. The Groogs are making us check out everything, from Chevi's legal probity to his hemorrhoids. For fact. Sonderstrom has Gatsby and me looking up police, medical, and school records. We discover that Eusebio Fuertes was an honor student, but was also arrested, when seventeen, for riding around with friends in a stolen car—sentence suspended.

The heavy work, however, begins with cross-referencing of the take. We check out everything he tells us about the PCU against the knowledge we already have about their personnel. While our local files bear no comparison to the Snake Pit, still, files have a tendency to become files. Nothing is more demoralizing than to creep one's fingers over hundreds of folders trying to chase down a confirmatory fact that comes to seem less and less essential as the lost hour slips by. Well, I won't make you suffer with me.

There is also infernal cable traffic with the Groogs. They're terrified that Soviet Russia Division, with all its maniacally suspicious people, will come charging down the hall if we decide that AV/OCADO is a KGB dangle. So, without quite admitting it to ourselves, we're looking to decide he's not, and what he tells us does fit our fact list. At least so far. Of course, we haven't asked him yet to bring back something we can really use, and when I propose that we do, I'm shot down at once. Until we are confident he is not a dangle, we don't dare to show what we are looking for, since that could feed the KGB.

Besides, Sonderstrom informs me, it is still too dangerous. Chevi is not yet ready, and we must not imperil our agent needlessly. I'm becoming impressed with Gus. Big, bald, red-faced ex-Marine, yet his underlying passion is to be virtuous. It makes me think about Americans. You know, the French, they say, have a passion for financial security, and the English, according to my father, care only about manners. You can be a swine and get away with it if your manners are either good, or, better, interesting. But in America, we have to be virtuous, don't we? Even the pimps and the drug dealers have their code, I hear. Roger certainly felt virtuous, going off to marry his moneybags princess. Didn't want the poor ugly girl to die of a broken heart. So, Sonderstrom. He worries about doing his job with decency. Even to throwing a golf game properly. Maybe it's late, and I'm sipping too much *fundador*, but suddenly I love Americans.

I can't say that I always do at the office. The inquiries on AV/OCADO keep coming from the Groogs. It seems Fuertes is the agent-of-the-month, worldwide—I joke—but he is large enough to excite unholy interest back at Headquarters, and I am the one who talks to AV/OCADO, I know what he looks like. I am the *point*! (Of course, I tell myself, this is nothing to how they're debriefing Roger right now in Washington.) Anyway, we move forward like an elephant on clogs. I don't think you need worry yet about any quick perils to my career. What with the Groogs and Upper Whambo (Western Hemisphere Division) and Soviet Russia Division, also known as the Sourballs, nobody will allow me to get into trouble.

I will tell you something that may amuse. Maybe not. The cable presence most feared here, although not one inquiry has come from it, is an odd desk under the mysterious umbrella of your own TSS. It is called GHOUL. That office, or eminence, or whatever it is, reports only to Mr. Dulles. I hear via Porringer that even the Soviet Russia Division is leary of GHOUL. Should this mysterious desk ever suspect that AV/OCADO is a KGB dangle, our lives down here will become unmitigated cable hell. I'm told we'll be on the Encoder-Decoder twelve hours a day answering questionnaires.

Of course, I presume to know who GHOUL is.

I left the matter there. I hardly knew what I was up to, but, then, I was feeling wicked. I wanted to tell Kittredge about Sally Porringer and knew I couldn't, yet, all the same, I decided to try. Recognizing that I might change my mind in the middle of composition, I took up this theme on a new page.

7

Intermission for coffee and *fundador*
2:00 A.M.

Kittredge,

Brand new subject. Please save judgments until you've read all. What I have to tell will not, I pray, affect our friendship. You see, I am now embarked on what may yet prove an ongoing affair. While in Washington you were always trying to find some attractive young lady for me, the woman I'm now meeting *on the sly*—this slippery cliché certainly has the feel of it!—is, I fear, not suitable. In fact, she is married, has two children, and is the spouse, worse luck, of one of my colleagues.

All right, I know you'll ask how it began, and who she is, and I'll reply that she is Sally Porringer, the wife of Oatsie.

Let me give the facts. It began one evening about a week before Christmas after a party at Minot Mayhew's house. Our Chief of Station, having received word that E. Howard Hunt is finally coming to replace him toward the end of January, threw a farewell party for himself in the form of a Christmas gathering. He invited the Station folk and wives, plus a number of his State Department cronies, plus an even larger number of relatively—I thought—undistinguished Uruguayan businessmen and their wives, and I must say it proved nothing remarkable, what with all the other Christmas parties going on.

For that matter, Christmas down here is curiously discordant. That sense of a rose-chill to winter twilight, sweet as fine sorbet, is missed in the heat of summer. One is angry and compassionate in bursts. I mention this because Mayhew's party in his well-appointed house, filled with career mementos and hacienda-type furniture (armchairs with steer's horns), and paid for, no doubt, with his stock-market profits, did improve once he sat down to the piano. "Every man I know," my father told me once, "has an unexpected skill." Mayhew's is to sing and play. He led us through all the expected. We did "Deck the Halls," and "Hark! The Herald Angels Sing," "Noel, Noel," "Jingle Bells," "Silent Night," of course, and then somewhere in "O Come, All Ye Faithful," there was Sally Porringer next to me, her arm around my waist, and swaying in rhythm as we and thirty other people sang along with Mayhew.

I'm no great vocalist, you know. There are all too many inhibiting influences ravaging my impulse to utter golden notes, but I have a little bass in me, and so I get along. Sally, however, elucidated something better from my voice. I don't know if it was due to the fact that I had never before swayed rhythmically while singing, but I heard my voice coming forth, thank you, and this freedom to sing and feel the beauty—not of the words, so much, but all the nuances and timbre of an ice-cold rose-sweet time of year—was going through me again. I felt as if it was really Christmas, even in Uruguay. I had the epiphany I always wait for as December descends into its climactic week, that feeling so hard to live without through most of the year—the conviction (I whisper it) that He may really be near.

Well, I was transported just enough to be fond suddenly of all my cohorts and their wives, and I thought of all the sweet solemn calls of country, duty, rich endeavor, and one's dearest friends. Most of all, I thought of you, because I can often feel that Christmas is near to me again by recollecting your beauty—there, I've said it—and then, even as I'm singing out, "O come, let us adore Him," I look down and see Sally Porringer's face and she smiles back with a warmth and energy that is part of my own sudden good voice, and I liked her for the first time.

After the carols, we sat on the sofa for a while, and I asked her a question about herself. She gave me a considerable amount of her life story in return. Her father was a rodeo rider, but drank too much and left her mother, who remarried a nice grain-and-feed man. Sally and Sherman knew each other in high school (Stillwater, Oklahoma), went on to Oklahoma State in the same class, but never saw much of each other the first three years. He was a grind, getting all kinds of academic honors, and she was on the cheerleaders' team. (I was right about that!) I took a second look at her then. She's pretty enough, if in no striking way, small turned-up nose, freckles, pale green eyes, sandy hair, a slightly harried housewife in her present cast, but I could see how it must have been ten or twelve years ago. She was probably healthy and vivacious then, and was having, as she now indicated, some kind of all-out affair with one of the football players. I expect he ditched her, since in senior year Sherman and she found each other and were married after graduation.

I knew I was now expected to reply in kind, but I didn't feel like raiding my own meager cupboard. So I sat there, and smiled, knowing I had to come up with something. Will you believe it? I went on and on about discovering Skeat at Yale, and I expect she did her best to keep from falling asleep in disappointment. A minute later, just as we were about to move away from one another, Sherman came up. He was Duty Officer tonight at the Embassy. That meant he had to take his car to work and was leaving now. She wanted to stay on. I, being equipped for the evening with a Chevrolet two-door from the Embassy motor pool, offered to drop her off on my way back to the Cervantes. I hardly wanted to, I would just as soon have departed right behind Porringer—I did not like the idea of those paranoid eyes staring at me through the malign screen of his thick spectacles, but she looked so sad at having to leave that I stayed.

A little later, I danced with her. Minot Mayhew was now playing all kinds of what I call Charleston rags, although I know the term is not accurate for dances like the Shag and the Lindy and the Lambeth Walk. I didn't know how to do them, but she did, and we had fun. When he played a couple of slow foxtrots from the thirties— "Deep Purple" and "Stardust" are the ones I remember—she danced just a little too intimately, I thought. It was the sort of semiflirtatious stuff that's acceptable, I suppose, if the husband is still in the room. Which he wasn't. Then, Barry Kearns, our Commo Officer, cut in—to my relief. When I sat down, however, I was irked because she seemed to be enjoying herself just as much with Barry.

Sally was right there with me, however, on the turn of the party tide, and we left together. On the drive back to Montevideo from Carrasco, I searched for subjects to discuss, but we were silent. I was feeling the same kind of tension I used to have years ago at the Keep playing kissing games with the neighbors' girls; there was that awful silence as you marched out of the room with a girl. I remember that I always felt then as if I were passing through the woods during a thaw and every sound of melting water had the composure of a far-seeing purpose.

So soon as I parked in front of her house, she said, "Drive around the block."

I did. The Porringers were living in a small stucco house on one of the medium-income, medium-horizon, only-slightly-crumbling streets in an anonymous area back of the Legislative Palace. Even in summer, the streets are relatively deserted, and the block behind her house was distinguished by several empty lots. We parked, and she waited, and I did nothing. Then she reached around to lock the doors and close the windows. I still did nothing. I think my heart was beating loud enough for her to hear it. I did not really want to make love to her, and I did not want to cuckold Sherman Porringer, although there was, I admit, some dirty little rise somewhere down there. Then she said,

"May I ask you a personal question?"

"Yes," I said.

"Are you a queer?"

"No," I said.

"Then why won't you kiss me?"

"I don't know."

"Prove to me you're not a queer."

"Why do you think I am?"

"You talk so upper-class. Sherman says you're a prep-school kid."

I plunged. She went off like a firecracker. I confess to you, Kittredge, I didn't know that women could be so passionate.

This last sentence betrayed what I had known from the beginning—I was not going to go to conclusion. The carnal details were not to be put into a letter. So I sat back in my chair, looked out my hotel room window at the grim building across the street from me, and recalled how her lips had kissed mine as if our mouths were in combat. Her hands, free of any conceivable embarrassment, hooked onto the buttons of my fly. Her breasts, which she soon freed of her brassiere, were in my mouth whenever she had need to lift her head to breathe, and then, to my horror, as if a long string of underground ammunition dumps in the sexual field of my fantasies were all to be detonated at once, she twisted, quick as a cat, bent down, and wrapped her mouth around the prow of my phallus (which seemed to me at that moment not only larger than I could ever remember, but worthy of the word phallus) and proceeded to take into her mouth the six, eight, nine, eleven jackhammer thrusts of the battering ram she had made of me. Then, in the midst of the extreme ejaculations of such ammo dumps blowing up, she added insult to injury and stuck her finger without a by-your-leave up my anus. I had obviously had one good Oklahoma cow-poke of a fuck, and we hadn't even had sexual intercourse yet.

That was remedied in surprisingly little time. I decided Lenny Bruce knew less than he imparted on the inner logic of the second time. Only one far-off part of me could possibly be working for the ego bit. The rest was hell-bent on enjoying all I could, as much as I could, as fast as I could, and yet, how I was repelled! It seemed manifestly unfair to raid the treasury of sex. In the middle of all my elation, exuberance, sexual wrath, and jubilee, in the midst of all my sense of something awfully strong in each of us smacked totally up against one another, there was the long, faint, elevated horror that Kittredge—for whom I had saved myself; Ingrid did not count!—was forever removed from my first taste of all-out frenzy and lust. I had always assumed this kind of heat could only arrive at the end of the deepest sort of love affair, and with momentum as gravely joyous as the mount toward elation in a majestic orchestra embarked on a mighty symphony. Sex with Sally was a football mêlée with bites and bruises and chocolate squashed in your crotch.

By my third ejaculation, I was weary of her. The car windows were clouded, our clothes were a wadded-up joke, and I hardly knew if I was a stud or a rape victim. Drawing away from her, I managed to induce us to get our clothes together, Sally half-unwillingly. Her kisses—how cruel is the after-shade of desire!—had begun to seem leechlike. I wanted to get home.

I could not leave her at her door, however, like a package delivered by someone else. "I'll call you soon," I said, and felt all the powers of extortion being worked on me.

"Oh, you better," she said. "That was groovy."

Groovy! I had been offered the key to my country. I was now a charter member of that great, unknown middle land of America that I was prepared to defend. And felt a great relief as I drove off because so far as I knew, no pedestrian had passed our automobile on that lonely street. The risk of what we had undertaken was just becoming real to me.

Well, I had seen her since, of course. Once at her home while the children were out with a babysitter—a dreadful clammy occasion when we fornicated in fear that Sherman in full deployment of his paranoid powers would pop home, and we had certainly done better in the Cervantes despite carnal heats on a mattress that smelled of disinfectant. Finally, I dared all the gods of precaution and took her to the safe house above Pocitos Beach, where we coupled in a chair by the twelfth-story window looking down on the passing traffic and the clay-colored waves.

No, I decided, it would have been hopeless to write about any of this to Kittredge, and I put aside the pages I had written about Sally. Because I could not ignore the part of myself, however, that pleaded for some kind of confession, I conceived of a tale to close the gap.

Intermission for coffee and *fundador*
2:00 A.M.

Kittredge,

Brand new subject. What I have to tell will not, I hope, affect us grievously, since our relation is dearer to me than any loyalty or pleasure I could find on the banks of the Rio Plata. You must believe that. I hope you will not be shocked if I confess that after many weeks of the most intense suffering from sexual abstention, I have at last felt bound to go to one of the better brothels here, and after a week or two of the inevitable winnowing out of choices, concerning which I will regale you someday, I have now settled on one Uruguayan girl in the Casa de Tres Árboles, and have what yet may prove to be an arrangement with her.

It makes sense to me. While you will always be the nearest embodiment I can know of the ineluctable quest, so do I also understand that you and Hugh will be together forever, as indeed you should be. There is no one I know closer to greatness than Hugh. Forgive such sententiousness, but I just want to say that I love you and Hugh together as much as I adore you separately, which, mathematically, is like trying to equate finite numbers with infinite sums—I come to full stop: All I wish to say is we must be truthful with one another as best we can, and I just had to have a woman. I know there's no conventional reason to ask your forgiveness, but I do. And I feel innocent, I confess. I hope you won't think that the next observation is facetious or in any way impinges on your work, but I have found that Alpha and Omega are indispensable as tools of understanding for the sexual relationship. Sex with love, or sex versus love, can be handled so naturally by your terminology. I even presume to say that at present my Alpha and Omega are most asymmetrically involved. Very little, or maybe no Omega is present in the act—a good, fine part of me cannot bear the woman, the prostitute, I have chosen. My Alpha, however, if Alpha is, as I assume, full of clay and low mundane grabby impulses, well, obviously, my Alpha is not wholly unengaged.

I went on with the letter, spinning careful false tales of the mood of the brothel and finally signed off, not knowing whether I felt vicious or wise in using my original if now unsent letter about Sally as a guide to the false tale, but I knew myself well enough to feel a certain contentment at my guile even as I was falling asleep. It occurred to me with the last of my drowsing spirits that I might not be as unlike my mother as I had once supposed.

8

The Stable
Jan. 26

Dear Harry,

I was awfully annoyed by your last letter. It isn't the brothel. Of course, you have to explore some of the good and bad experiences these women have to offer. I confess that I did go into a silent tantrum of sheer envy at the way you men are free to explore your sexual curiosity and alter yourselves in the process. I hope not for the worse. Yet what is freedom ultimately but the right to take serious chances with one's soul? I do believe that somewhere in sexual excess—at least for good people, brave people—there is absolution. Am I babbling? Do I sound like that smelly old libertine, Rasputin? What a swath he would have cut with some of the Washington ladies I know!

At any rate, I'm still annoyed with you. First, for shipping off dubious pieces of jewelry whose history you are insensitive to, and now for coming in like an overfed bull to trample over my terminology. It left me grateful for the first time in moons that my theories, for all effective purposes, are sealed in TSS and I am no household name. Because I do not dare to think of how the nuances of Alpha and

Omega would be crunched by the magazine public when even you expose a gross misconception of what it's all about.

I will lecture you, then, one more time. I promise not to go on too long. The key principle in Alpha and Omega is that they are not to be seen as the equivalent of containers for the psyche, the one to the left collecting whores and business routines and baseball games and drunken evenings, while the other broods on philosophy and reads your mail. That's the pitfall for everyone. They start to see it that way. As two carry-all bags. Put part of your experience into one, other part into the other.

Nothing to do with it. I am saying: Multiply by two the complexities of human personality. Postulate two complete and different persons in each of us. Each of these characters is more or less equally well developed. Trickier to grasp is that each is as complex and wholly elaborated as what we usually think of as a complete personality. So, Alpha and Omega can not only be neurotic, but possess the power to form vastly different neuroses. (That dire situation is, of course, reserved for terribly sick people.)

All right, I next postulate that one of them, Omega, originated in the ovum and so knows more about the mysteries—conception, birth, death, night, the moon, eternity, karma, ghosts, divinities, myths, magic, our primitive past, so on. The other, Alpha, creature of the forward-swimming energies of sperm, ambitious, blind to all but its own purpose, tends, of course, to be more oriented toward enterprise, technology, grinding the corn, repairing the mill, building the bridges between money and power, *und so weiter.*

Given these highly delineated and separate personalities of Alpha and Omega, we should be able, if we possess the skills—which, alas, we do not at present—to separate them out from the murky confusion with which we pretend to analyze individuals. In psychology, we try to understand patients by the aid of schemata that are equal to plumbing systems (Freud), or blunder about on the assumption there is only one psyche and it is oceanic (Jung). Harry, I am beginning to think that the world is filled with geniuses, but only a few survive. The rest perish in the desperation of having to repeat themselves. (Since I am certainly no genius, perhaps I will endure.) But I certainly must repeat, over and over, that Alpha and Omega are individual people. Each Alpha, each Omega, is different from all others. One Omega can be artistic, night-dwelling, a seer; another Omega can be Omega only in name, even as you can find a Sicilian,

I suppose, with blue eyes, a cheerful manner, and blond hair. Ditto for Alpha. Sometimes Alpha and Omega borrow or steal each other's properties. They are, after all, wed together like the corporeal lobes of the brain. They can influence each other, or spend their lives in all-out strife for power over the other. The model is marriage. Or, if you prefer, the Republicans and the Democrats. Or the Czarists and the Bolsheviks—is that why the Russians tear themselves apart, and get drunk all the time? Your Chevi Fuertes is a superb example of Alpha and Omega in constant tug of war. You say it yourself when you remark that he is 51 percent with us and 49 percent against, and functioning in great depression. All right, sir, fundamental concepts in place, let us take up your whorehouse capers. "Very little or maybe no Omega is in the act," you write squiffily, as if you were a parson trying not to sniff his fingers after touching a dog turd. Then you are crass enough to go on about Alpha and his grabbies. God, you are a farce. Forgive me if I'm rude, but I'm also becoming aware of how irascible is the territorial imperative in me. So, don't make weak gropes at my terminology. The point about sex is that both Alpha and Omega enter the act and digest the separate experiences they receive. Indeed, they digest them as individually as two people at a play for an evening can sit side by side and come away with separate critical reactions. And somewhat different memories of what they saw. When you say, therefore, that Omega was not in the act, you reveal merely that in sexual matters, Alpha is ruling your ship with an iron hand. Alpha does not listen to any of Omega's variant interpretation of the experience. This is analogous to fascism. Your smug acceptance of a full half of sexual indifference in yourself is a way of stating that you, unbeknownst to yourself, are a sexual fascist. There, it's true, and I'm glad I said it.

Do you find me vengeful? I'm a mother now. Each time Christopher begins to scream in the middle of the night, and this has happened on several inexplicable occasions since your brooch popped up in the mail, I have been ready to curse you, and once almost did, but then didn't—curses are a serious matter with me.

An hour later—I've just fed Christopher

Now I'm fond of you again. I just gave Christopher the best of both my temperamental jugs, and he seemed to like it. We drew closer and closer and by the end were spanning little universes. His fingers kept tapping my breast like a fat man rubbing his own belly after a good meal. This never happened before.

Suddenly I realized I'm in debt to you. I was sweet with the baby because my nasties had been liberated by writing a letter bound to wound you in all your soft places. Well, as Hugh might say: It's time you toughened up.

I will reveal that I've been keeping a plum for you in absolute velvet wrappings. You won't believe how fortunate you are. Hugh and I decided a couple of weeks ago to find out a little more about your Chief of Station Designate, so we invited Howard Hunt, and his wife, Dorothy, to dinner. Oh, Lord and sweet peas, do I have stuff to tell you. Now, you must wait for the next letter. My husband's key is in the lock.

After midnight

Hugh, for once, is asleep ahead of me, and I want to present you with your plum.

Not instantly, however. You do need the background. You see, Howard and Dorothy were invited to dinner as part of the Montague Plan. Hugh never does anything without a reason. While this is certainly not one of his charms, I confess I'm amazed at how often he can get me to carry on like a loyal subaltern, considering how spoiled I was when we commenced our marriage. I do end up working away for his notions, grand or silly. In this case, concerning the Hunts, Hugh, while not about to admit it, did resent the now-legendary High Thursday when his peers came so close to pulling off their palace revolt. I've never talked to you about this, but there is an unspoken War of Succession going on as to who, eventually, will replace Allen. The old boy's gout is getting more frequent in its attacks.

The next question obviously is who will replace him? Is it to be a bang-juice paramilitary and propaganda specialist, a Wisner? Or Dick Bissell? Or, says Hugh to me, do we try to remember what we're all about, and continue to gather *intelligence*? Since we're not really supposed to fight those small nasty wars the Joint Chiefs are always looking to pass on to us, Hugh keeps tugging on that side of Allen which is responsive to espionage and counterespionage. Hugh feels the Russians are preparing deceptions on a grand scale, and the Berlin tunnel, for example, may have been stage-managed by a KGB mole in MI6 from the beginning. Of course, I don't know when my poor ice-climbing goat is going to find time to mine that Berlin mountain of files. He has so many urgent tasks. My father used to be a prodigious worker, but Hugh does put him to bed.

Yet, with all this work load, and me coming to term with Christopher last fall, why, no matter, "Let's have some candidates over to dinner," he said to me soon after the near-fiasco of the High Thursday.

In consequence, a group of worthies has been arriving in twos and fours for dinners twice weekly ever since you've been gone. Hugh's passion is to find someone in the line of succession who will be reasonably sympathetic to his purposes, and by now he has been able to take a look at just about all of the leading possibilities for the next Director. Poor Hugh. Having gotten everywhere by his excellence, he's now telling himself that he should play politics. He may be right. Once Allen goes, the Succession becomes all important to our Montague. Hugh's present role is perfect for his talents. Only a romantic like Allen Dulles could ever have set Hugh up in the role that Allen, if younger, would have chosen for himself. You spoke half-facetiously about GHOUL. Oh, dear boy, GHOUL! I've told Hugh a hundred times to change it to GATES or MANSIONS or MEWS, but no, his grottos call for GHOUL. Well, GHOUL is top-drawer. Am I drunk? I'm sipping a fair lot of sherry as I pen away on this. Hundred-year-old sherry makes me love the very wood of the table I'm writing on. So there we have Hugh and Allen with GHOUL— both boys got their wish. A *sanctum sanctorum* for two. GHOUL's outer office, however, contains scores of super-equipped specialty people with super-secret files all working for Hugh, one nonattributable step removed from Allen. They are ferreting out little trouble spots all over our Company universe, and Allen's successor must prove able to comprehend the value of GHOUL. So, Hugh invites people over to size them up, and his present but glum choice is Dickie Helms. Helms will never come down with two feet on one side of a dividing line until he's located all the shoes on either side. On the other hand, Helms will be inclined, thinks Hugh, to support the continued existence of GHOUL.

Well, by the time we used up every likely in-town GS-18, Hugh had developed a taste for the game and we started inviting some second-rank people to cast new light on the top-drawer faces. That was when I decided to put all this up for some use by my team. "Let's have Howard Hunt," I said.

"Do you mean E. Howard Hunt?" Hugh asked. "How will

we address him? As E? E Howard? How Eee?" This is Hugh's private humor. That is why you never see public signs of it. He's about as funny as a hee-haw cowboy. Don't forget—Hugh, along with all else, could ride a mustang before his legs were long enough to reach the pedals on his kiddie bike. Just a Colorado cowboy.

I talked Hugh into inviting How Eee. Pointed out to my beau that Hunt was in on the Guatemala move. Hugh thinks that may yet prove to be the most catastrophic American victory of all. Smash an oxymoron, and you will encounter the Light! Yes, darling, *catastrophic victory*. Hugh feels it has pointed us in the wrong direction for decades to come. He wouldn't speak to Allen for weeks after the Agency, via Hunt and some of his pals, got Arbenz pushed out. So I had to talk Hugh into studying Mr. E. Howard Hunt, and wife.

Darling, I can't go on. I'm not being a bitch. I *will* finish tomorrow. Don't know why I got into the sherry. Yes, I do know. I'm revealing too much, and feel unfaithful to Hugh. But I do want secret letters from you and must pay the price. On that note, I excuse myself. Christopher is stirring.

K.

9

January 28th, 1957

Harry Dear,

I didn't mail yesterday's letter until I could reread it. It's not as bad as I feared. Indiscreet, but didn't we agree to be just that?

Now, to the occasion. E. Howard Hunt. It's clear after the first five minutes that Hugh and I have invited to dinner a very ambitious man. Afterward, we agreed that if there's anything in the world Mr. Hunt wants in years to come, it is to be DCI. This desire is, I hope, more pathetic than frightening.

"No hard feelings, I hope," is the first bloody thing Hunt said as he came through the door.

"Dear boy," replied Hugh, though he can't be more than five years older, "no hard feelings about *what*?"

"The ruckus. I'm afraid I opened a birdbath for you on a certain Thursday."

"Howard," said Mrs. Hunt, "Hugh Montague may have

thought of other matters since." She did it nicely. She's *tough*. Dark—I found out she's one-eighth Sioux—and determined. I wouldn't be surprised if she's the engine behind Howard's ambition.

Hugh could have left it there, but he's a pertinacious dog. Self-imposed civility is as agreeable to him as dysentery. "Why, Mrs. Hunt," he said, "Howard is right. I haven't stopped brooding. I assumed it was all part of a clockwork plot, and they wound Howard up."

Can you conceive of this conversation opening our evening? But Howard is *breezy*. "No sir," he replied, "I did it on my own. You are looking at an honest-to-God *espontáneo*. That's my vice."

"Have a drink," said Hugh, "we'll measure vices."

I was debating whether to booze a little—would the relaxation sweeten my milk more than the liquor would sour it? Afloat in such primary questions of motherhood, I hate the first twenty minutes of any of these evenings. But Hunt is a talker. By the time we sat down to dinner, I could see that this was his event-of-the-week. Harry, I have to tell you that in no way am I a snob except for the endless amusement of it. It *is* fun to observe a climber trying out new steps on the slippery slope. Nothing makes such people more nervous than to be observed, and of course, I'm not all that encouraging from my catbird seat. I offer an assortment of blank smiles.

Soon enough, he makes the mistake of bragging about his family background, which is, in the main, New York State. Although I grew up in Cambridge, my father happens to be good old stock from Oneonta, N.Y., and that, while nothing to make you hold on to your hat, is still leagues above Hamburg, the particular suburb of Buffalo where the heraldic seat of the Hunts, bless all, was located. Now, Howard does have a few credentials. You may be certain he trots them out. His ancestor, Captain James Hunt, served in the Revolutionary War, and Hunt's Point in the Bronx is named after him. "That's so sweet," I say. Tomorrow I expect he will look up my pedigree and discover Maisie and the ancient relatives on the Mayflower.

Mr. Hunt goes on, and of course, the closer we listen, the more he swings on his own noose. It's a cruel business. He was kind of pleased with his family facts until they hit the light of our cold hearth. His father and mother, for instance, sang in the Cornell Glee Club.

"Oh," I say, "terrific. Your father must have loved Cornell."

"He did. One of the tragedies of his life is that I chose to go to Brown. He was the sort of man, however, never to express his disappointment."

"Good fellow," said Hugh.

"Yes. Dad, I warrant, is no fool. Said to me once, 'I'm on to your work, Howard. I didn't become a Thirty-second Degree Mason for too little, did I?' "

"How odd," said Hugh, "My father was also a Shriner."

"Let's drink to that happy coincidence," said Howard.

"Why not?" said Hugh, "why not?" But I winced. Hugh never talks about his father. It brings back the fatal night. Of course, Hugh can ride right over such rocks without suffering visible scratches on the hull. "Yes," he said, "my father was a secretive man"—a sip of his wine—"and my mother." Second sip.

This warmed Howard. He knew he had been tendered some small favor by the master. I believe Hunt is not without psychic gifts. His next remark was certainly aware of sudden mortality as an appropriate topic. He began to talk about a plane crash. Last summer, the Hunts, scheduled to return to Washington from Tokyo, lost their sleeping bunks on the overnight passage due to a booking error. Since, as Howard put it, "I am not one to subject my family to inferior accommodations when the government has already coughed up *the stimulus* for proper treatment, I chose to postpone our departure inasmuch as a later flight did have bunks available. Lo, the discerning finger of Kismet!" concluded Howard in the mildest voice, as if to discount any outsize claim to magical selection. "Do you know, the first plane went down in the Pacific? All passengers lost."

I think there was a hint of special pride in the way he told the story, as if Providence peered through the smog of mankind long enough to spare E. Howard Hunt and family. After all, they do have large roles to play.

There it is. He isn't so much outrageously ambitious as filled with the idea that he's anointed. Be certain, therefore, in all your dealings with your new boss, not to lose sight of this belief he has in himself. If he weren't half attractive, the man would be intolerable. Too confident for too little.

Item: The Hunts occupied a house in Tokyo designed by Frank Lloyd Wright. Not bad for a Chief of Covert Operations in North Asia. (Howard's highly titled job, so far as I could make out, consisted of propaganda, public relations, and leaving stink-bombs at

Communist meetings.) Hunt, by the way, calls them Who-Me's.

"Who-Me's?" I ask.

"Yes," says Howard. "If they ask, 'Did you leave that odor?' you answer, 'Who? Me?' " He then laughs at his own explanation, with an involuntary whinny, a snaffling sort of sly, skinny laugh. (I think he considers it the appropriate response to genteel humor about the anus.) I naturally am more interested in being given some idea of what it was like to live in a Frank Lloyd Wright house, but he doesn't respond directly to such questioning. His pleasure comes from the name: *Frank Lloyd Wright*. Goes on to describe the moon gate, the courtyard, the garden with granite shrines, and the deep lily pond. "It was, of course, lovely," said Howard, "but upon due consideration, and the assurance by the Japanese gardener that the lilies would eventually grow back, we pulled them out and converted the pond to a swimming pool that could serve the children."

"Didn't you hesitate," I asked Dorothy, "over the lilies?"

"Well, I did," she said.

"I didn't," he said. "Not as soon as I knew it was feasible. Not for a moment. Children's needs precede aesthetic considerations."

As you can see, he's a bit of a menace. When he speaks of his daughter Lisa, for instance, it is all too often by her full name. Obviously likes the euphony of Lisa Tiffany Hunt. "Her birth," he tells us, "is inscribed in the Civil Register of Mexico City, where she was born while I was establishing the first OPC station in that region for Frank Wisner. As a result, Lisa is on the Consular List of Americans born abroad, and belongs thereby to a special and insufficiently recognized natural club of birth."

Just as I've come to the conclusion that this is pretty heavy going—Consular List, my suffering little toe!—why, he crosses me up by adding in a faintly spiteful voice, "Of course, some Americans in foreign settings are just out for the oofah."

"Oofah?" I ask.

"Jack and stack. Stickum." When I am still blank, he translates, "The simoleons, the shekels." I remember that he's already spoken of money as "the stimulus." I expect he has an astonishing number of synonyms for good old filthy lucre. It seems he's not only anointed, but wistfully greedy, and all too keenly aware of the economic sacrifice we make in working for the Agency. He just can't figure out how he'll ever be oofy, and opulent.

All the same, I may be laughing at Howard Hunt a little too

much. He can be as stuffy as turkey stuffing, but he's sly for all that. He's going to love having you on board. He even told Hugh that a friend of his at Brown had gone to St. Matthew's and was on the soccer team Hugh used to coach.

"I remember him," said Hugh. "Tried hard. Slow feet."

Living with a man in holy matrimony is analogous to taking a course in human mechanics. Hugh, I have discovered, has gears in his voice box. They tell me when he is ready to take over the conversation. "I hear you did a nice job of preparation in Guatemala," he now said.

"It killed me," answered Hunt, "to be taken out before the real op began, but the powers that be insisted my job had been accomplished and I was now needed in Japan."

"Well, the powers did lend you that Frank Lloyd Wright house for consolation," said Hugh.

"Hardly compensatory," said Hunt. "It's nettling to hear, far away in Tokyo, that your former assistant was actually invited over to the White House and congratulated by President Eisenhower for his fine work. Most of that fine work was mine."

"I heard from my more elevated sources"—Hugh's reliably effective reference to Allen—"that the President was effusive. 'To take that country with just a few hundred men! All that sleight-of-hand!'"

"I'm glad you can understand how I feel," said Hunt.

"Well, before we quaff the cup of eternal friendship," said Hugh, "let us put it to the test. What would you say if I remark that your famous operation was, in my opinion, a gross error. American interests would have been better served if we had allowed Arbenz to build up a little Communist state in Guatemala." For all his desire to play politics, Hugh is not capable of it.

"What you're saying," said Hunt, "seems awfully liberal to me."

"Say behind my back that I wish to bugger little boys, but do not suggest that I am liberal. I loathe the faintest emanation of Communism. It is a cancer in full metastasis on the body of the Western world."

"Hear, hear," said Hunt. "My sentiments are being most elegantly expressed. Aren't they, Dorothy?"

"Of course," she said.

"But, sir, if it is a cancer, why not operate on it? Whenever and wherever you can."

"Because each cancer is a study in its own anomaly," said Hugh, "and world Communism is a *weak* cancer. You see, Howard, it got into metastasis before it asked itself whether it was ready. It doesn't have the inner wherewithal to fight those cancer wars on every front. Guatemala was, potentially, a desperately expensive proposition for the Soviets. They would have had to invest in that country, supply it, and probably end up feeding it. Their economic system is altogether unsuited for such a job. A huge inefficiency would have been sent to succor a dwarf inefficiency. Why, we could have cost the Russians a pretty penny. And if they had been so foolish as to invest real force, we could have pulled off your surgical incision then. That would have exposed them to serious mockery around the world."

"Wouldn't it also increase the danger of a nuclear war?" asked Dorothy.

"Nuclear scenarios must never be linked to small-scale foreign operations. Nuclear war will come, if it ever does, from another factor altogether."

"Would you name it?" Dorothy asked.

"Despair. World despair. Nuclear war is mutual suicide. A husband and wife make a pact to kill themselves only when they believe they do not have the right to continue to exist. They are spoiling too much. Whereas, in the real world, no two countries are as vain as the U.S.S.R. and the U.S.A. Neither of us can believe for a moment that we could spoil anything. But if I decide that I am wonderful, and it's the other fellow who is the mess, I guarantee you, Mrs. Hunt, I will not embrace him in a deadly grip and jump off the fatal bridge. I will try to get rid of the beast by other means."

"By starving the Russians out?" she asked.

"Exactly. Exhaust their wherewithal. Entice them into places that use up Soviet energies to little avail. Just think of a million Red Army soldiers in Mexico. What chance would they have against us in a land war?"

"I wouldn't want the numbers to get that high in our back-yard," said Hunt.

"They never would," said Hugh. "The Russians are not

that stupid. Would we try to put a million soldiers into Eastern Europe? We certainly didn't make the move in Hungary, did we? Yet we can afford a serious war far better than the Soviets. I repeat. We should have left Guatemala alone. They would have built up a third-rate Communist state that would soon have been looking to us for aid."

"I can't agree, sir," said Hunt. "I believe we must shoot varmints between the eyes before they grow up to raid our crops. I hate Communist rats wherever I find them."

Harry, he was seized, as he said this, with the most peculiar intensity. His voice was as husky as a boy getting ready to kiss a girl, and if he felt close to murder, and I would say he did, it was as a virtuous, if not wholly manageable, emotion.

I saw it then. Do you know, Harry, I fear our lovely country has become a religion. Joe McCarthy only dipped his finger into the bowl of the new holy water. It's not the cross but the flag that is going to stir all those larger feelings people can't live without.

In any event, Hugh had heard enough by now to decide that Hunt could not be bent to any of his uses. So my husband diverted the conversation over to real estate values in Georgetown, about which Howard and Dorothy, as one might expect, knew a lot.

I keep thinking of you working with this odd, semi-inspired man as your future boss. I think Hunt is going to love you. Snobs on the slope always will. Before the evening was done, he let us know that Dorothy was not only one-eighth Oglala Sioux, but descended from the John Quincy Adams family on mother's side, and the Benjamin Harrison family on the father's end. (He made another point of saying, "*President* Benjamin Harrison"—I suppose this august name does not register for all.) "There," he might just as well have declaimed, "is our little tit to your fat tat, Miss Mayflower." Yes, Howard Hunt keeps his kickers for the end. Be sure to tell me all about him.

Yours,
Kittredge

10

HUNT ARRIVED IN MONTEVIDEO IN ADVANCE OF KITTREDGE'S LETTER, and I had formed my own impression by then.

Jan. 29, 1957

Dearest Kittredge,

Well, our new Chief of Station disembarked yesterday with his family: wife, two daughters, son, maid, and Cadillac from the SS *Rio Tunuyan*. Mayhew leaves in a week—which can't be too soon for any of us, including Mayhew. Long live the new Chief! God, Hunt and his wife, Dorothea, came in like F. Scott Fitzgerald and Zelda. Twenty-two pieces of luggage, all monogrammed with an E.H.H., no less. Plus untold furniture and cartons. All this related to us by Gatsby (speak of serendipity), who was deputied to go with Mayhew to the pier and take him through Customs. (We would all have gone but Agency policy is, of course, not to call all that much attention to new arrivals.)

The Hunt entourage, staying at present in a suite at the Victoria Plaza, are already looking for an appropriate home in Montevideo's best suburb, Carrasco, ten miles out of town. Great changes are going to take place in the Station. We know that. Hunt appears quiet and affable, but stimulates a room by entering it. He is obviously, and with total happiness, full of himself. It's his first stint as COS.

Can't write any more at this point. Will finish tomorrow.

Harry

By the next day, however, her letter was in my hand, and I decided to wait on mine. We were considerably apart on Hunt, and I did not wish to receive another lecture. Station work, after all, had become more interesting from the day Hunt came in.

Even before Mayhew had departed (and that did not take the usual month, but was accomplished in seven working days), we had already learned that our new COS was going to be active among us. Indeed, he gave a full address to the troops, all six of us, counting Nancy Waterston, on the day after he landed, and we listened with rising hope as we sat in a semicircle around him in the office.

"Ever since I came back to Washington from Tokyo," said Hunt, "I've been studying this Station, and I can warrant that there will be changes. Before we get, however, down to analysis and rectification, I want you to know the Agency credentials of the man you will be working for. This is my first full Chief of Station slot, but I feel highly qualified and will lay out why. On graduation from Brown University in June 1940, I chose to enlist in the U.S. Naval Reserve, V-7 program, and after a speeded-up program at Annapolis, went out as a midshipman in February 1941, ten months before Pearl Harbor, on the destroyer *Mayo*. At sea, I suffered a combat-related injury climbing an ice-coated turret ladder during a general quarters alarm in the North Atlantic in early December 1941, and the injury was serious enough to give me an honorable medical discharge. Since I can see by your faces that you are ready for more intelligence, I will state that the injury was groin-related, but had no permanent effects. Praise the Lord, I can still pass the ammunition."

We laughed. Even Nancy Waterston. It might have been a small joke to others, but it was a large one to us. We already knew more about Hunt than we had ever learned about Mayhew.

"While recuperating, I wrote a novel, *East of Farewell*, which was accepted by Alfred A. Knopf, Publishers. Soon after, *Life* magazine named me their South Pacific war correspondent to replace John Hersey in such places as Bougainville and Guadalcanal. Back in New York in 1943, I enlisted in OCS, was commissioned, and not too long after, went into OSS training. Assigned to China, I flew over the Hump, and found myself in Kunming when the war ended. A stint of screenwriting in Hollywood soon followed, and from there I went to work on Averell Harriman's staff in Paris for the Marshall Plan, and before long was recruited by Frank Wisner to join the Office of Policy Coordination. Have any of you heard of a brilliant fellow named William F. Buckley, Jr., who's now chief editor of a magazine he founded himself, *The National Review*?"

We nodded.

"Good. It's worth being familiar with that magazine. Buckley was my assistant in Mexico, and damn good. Might be with us still if the magazine world had not called to him. After Mexico, I was posted in Washington as Chief of Covert Operations, Southeast Europe Division. That meant Desk at Headquarters and related trips to Athens, Frankfurt, Rome, and Cairo. Then, I was transferred to the Propa-

ganda and Political Action Staff for the Guatemala op, where with
three hundred men and—I will say it myself—a brilliant psychological
and radio communications campaign, we succeeded in getting the
Arbenz government to decamp. Moses designed the march into Israel,
but he never got there. I, speaking as a poor man's Moses, also did not
enjoy, at first hand, the fruits of my design. I was already en route to
Tokyo to handle Covert Operations in North Asia Command, where
I did my best to confound, confuse, dismay, and dishearten every
effort of the Chinese Communists to spread their propaganda
throughout Japan and South Korea.

   "That brings us to the present. In Washington, at the Argentina-
Uruguay Desk, I could not help but be aware that there's a feeling this
Station is not a mainstream activity. Well, let me pass one bit of
advice. There are no small jobs in our life. South America, in my
opinion, is the land of musical chairs. You never know which leader
is going to lose his seat next. Any Station in South America can
become a center of high Agency focus. We are going to bring initiative, therefore, to the Uruguay Station of a like that has not been seen
here. By the time we're done, the going remark back at Headquarters
will be, 'Yessir, Uruguay is the tail that wags the South American
dog.' "

   We gathered around him afterward and pumped his hand. I
recognized that I was happy. My desire to work was alive again.

                                                   March 5, 1957
Herrick,
     Six weeks have gone by since my last letter. Are you now the
rage of Montevideo, or just the King of the Brothels?
     Please advise.

                                                   Kittredge

                                                   March 27, 1957
Dear Harry,
     I detest owing money or favors to anyone. I loathe it even
more when people I care about are in debt to me. Silence is the
commencement of debt.

                                                   Kittredge Montague

April 5, 1957

Dear Kittredge,

Yes, yes, no and no, yes, no, and yes. You may pick any of the above answers to your questions. Yes, I am the king of the brothels, no, I am not; yes, Mr. Howard Hunt is mad about me, no, he is not; yes, I miss you, no, I don't; I'm too busy to think.

Take this as an apology and trust me. I will write a long letter in the next ten days.

Your own H.H.

P.S. I just realized that Howard Hunt, but for his beloved E, is also H.H., and God, are we different. Hugh, Harvey, Hunt, and Herrick Hubbard. I've always thought H was the most peculiar letter in English, and cite for evidence that the Cockneys never came to agreement with it, and they're a practical people. H is the silent presence in "ghost" and the capital proprietor of Heaven and Hell. It is half-silent as in half, and changes error to horror.

P.P.S. As you see, I'm as mad as you are.

I dispatched the letter before second thoughts could commence. Then I went back to my hotel room and tried to sleep, but the sheets reeked of Sally, formaldehyde, and me. She always left behind a strong odor of herself, half carnal and half grudged out of existence by her deodorants, which didn't always take care of the job.

I hardly knew what to do about Sally. We were more intimate than our affection for each other. And my derelictions of duty were increasing. If Porringer was working triple-time under Hunt, I took time out from my own double-time to arrange a meeting with Chevi Fuertes which I knew would not take place. I had not notified him. Instead, I saw Sally. A week later, I did as much again. Professionally speaking, it was easy to conceal. Agents often missed meetings. Like horses, they bolted at the sight of a leaf blowing by. I had to file bogus reports, but they were routine, and bought two hours each time with Sally in my bedroom at the Cervantes. I, waiting for her, would have my clothes off, and my bathrobe on; she, knocking on the door with a tap followed by two taps, would be out of her shoes and off with her skirt even as we embraced in the first of her powerful kisses. "Glue sandwiches" I would have labeled them if not in the mood, but I was usually in the mood, and, naked in a streak, we grappled toward the bed, stealing handfuls of each other's flesh en route before diving down into the song of the bedsprings, her mouth engorging my cock. There are a hundred words, I suppose, for a penis, but cock is the one that goes with fellatio, and her open marriage with lust, abandonment, and sheer all-out hunger for Hubbard's Yankee prong gave that fellow a mind of his own, a hound off his leash, a brute pillaging the temple of her mouth, except who could call it a temple?—she had confessed to me in one of our postcopulatory conversations that from high school on, she had had a natural appetite, or was it thirst, for this outpost of the forbidden, and, God, it was out of control by the time she came to me.

I, in my turn, was developing tastes and inclinations I did not know I had. Before long, she was presenting her navel and pubic hair toward me, and I, facing the contradictory choices of domination or equality, found my own head reaching to explore her sandy, almost weedlike bush. I am cruel enough to mention how wild and scraggly it looked because that came to mean little. It was the avid mouth behind the hair that leaped out to a part of me that did not know it existed until I was licking and tonguing away with my own abandon which I had never known could belong to my critical lips until they opened into the sheer need I knew to jump across the gap from one bare-ass universe to the next. The only way I ever felt close to Sally Porringer was when her mouth was on my cock and my face was plastered into the canyon between her legs. Who could know what things we had to tell each other at such times? It was not love we exchanged, I expect, but all the old bruises and pinched-off desires— how much there was of that! Lust, I was deciding, had to be all the vast excitement of releasing the tons of mediocrity in oneself. (Then, afterward, when alone in my bed, I would wonder if new mediocrity had been ingested just as much as the old had been purged.) I was discovering that I had the gusto of a high school athlete and the chill estimates of a man so noble in perception of each unhappy nuance as T. S. Eliot.

Say this for the act. When we rose dripping from the sweet and sour mire of feeding on each other, my copulation came pounding happily out of me. To fuck fast was to throw one's heart into the breach and pound enough blood to the head to banish Thomas Stearns of the Eliot family. One gunned the motors of one's soul and the sugar of one's scrotum—what a joy to discover that Hubbards also secreted scrotum sugar—up, up, over the hill, and into the unchartable empyrean beyond. That vision seemed to disappear almost as soon as it afforded its glimpse. I would be happy for a while to know I was a man and that she wanted me and I gave her pleasure. Soon enough she would be stirring once more. She was not insatiable, but near enough. By the third time, I would be thinking again of Lenny Bruce, and the worst of all this passion was not its successive blunting, but the knowledge that when we were done, we would not know how to talk. We were about as essentially happy with each other in this situation as two strangers who attempt to make conversation on a train.

Whatever the shortcomings, two days later, I would want her again. It was hardly an environment in which to write to Kittredge, but some jobs have to be done.

April 10, 1957

Dearest Kittredge,

Your delineation of Howard Hunt was of no uncertain help to me, even if I plead guilty to being the clod who did not acknowledge this earlier. But, Lord, angel, I have been busy. You have had a glimpse of the social side of EH2 (which is what we call Mr. E. Howard H. on occasions when he is not around) but we have been living with the professional end of the man, and he is a martinet for work. That is, the work he inspires us to perform. He takes a lot of time off to play golf, and hunt and fish. We, in turn, have to end up suspending judgment, because his outside recreation is invariably with important Uruguayans. Having taken over Minot Mayhew's role, he stands in as nominal First Secretary of the Embassy at all those diplomatic functions, which, if you remember, Mayhew used to pass on to Sonderstrom, Porringer, and myself. So, that's one change. Howard and Dorothy (who handles social credits and debits like a chief auditor, and manages the Embassy party life with skill comparable to any admiral steering the fleet) have already taken over an astonishingly large part of Montevideo society. We worked and scraped under Mayhew (via Sonderstrom) to eke out a few useful relationships, but Hunt puts all this to shame. He is off every weekend at some large *estancia* in the pampas hunting for *perdiz* and working his American charm on very rich landowners. As a small corollary of this, he's thrown out the old intriguing AV/AILABLE and AV/IARY style of cryptonymming (if you'll forgive my coining one more awful word) and has announced that any term we desire can now follow AV. His saddlebags, for example, come in as AV/HACENDADO. It's a great switch for us traditionalists down here, but, do you know, he's right. There aren't that many AV words left, and according to Hunt, we're going to need plenty for the operations he plans to set up.

Needless to say, most of the new ops are still in the planning stage, but I mock him not. He laid out his credentials first day in the office. Normally one would get tired of listening to a man talk about his deeds, but Hunt left me feeling wistful for my own lack of an exciting life. While I know he can't have done as much as Cal or Hugh, by God, he has had adventures and served in interesting places. All the envy I felt as an adolescent that I missed the OSS has come back. Hunt made me realize how young I am, and how much life experience you need to be a proper Chief of Station. So I ate up what he had to tell us. Kittredge, if you want to comprehend our scene here, forbear quick criticism. Men are more impressed by an action-filled life than women.

On the second week after taking over, Howard made another speech to the effect that there was a power elite in Uruguay whom he had to cultivate: "There may be times when you will think I came down here on good Company money to hunt and fish up a storm for myself. Nothing is farther from the truth. I want you to trust me, so I'll be frank. Yes, I do take pleasure in hunting and fishing. But, get it straight, men. These influential Uruguayans are also rod and gun folk. They like a man who can ride and shoot with them. A man who can bring in a fighting fish on sporting line. Hell, I may even go up to the Argentine Andes to ski with them come this July. But know what I'm up to. Envy is poison in a Station, so fix on this fact: A Station Chief is always working. In the midst of any social gathering, no matter how prestigious, I will be pursuing Company business. End of sermon, gentlemen. Gather round. I have a small assignment for you." Whereupon, he handed out copies of the same communication to all of us. It read:

NGECL	RBNEL	XYEDE	LYNYE	SYRPJ
NJLVS	BFYED	BXNBF	DOLPN	UDBUS
BULZE	YSGGD	NPZVD	MORYE	ILPLU

Kittredge, that's not even half—there are thirty-six of these five-letter groups—but I promise you, I'm tired of copying it. He wouldn't give us a one-time pad, said it was a clear one-for-specific-one, and we could work it out on the periodicity of the letters. "The text deserves it," he said. "Lose an hour this afternoon, and learn again what we're all about."

Well, you know, we were rusty. A clear one-for-one is not hard to decode, but it takes time. Porringer and Kearns were the driving force, and I put in my share. Sonderstrom sat in the corner and looked like he was going to have a stroke. I have never seen Gus' face so red. He's all thumbs on deciphering—even hates to use the Encoder-Decoder—and, of course, we did not have the use of one for this. Our COS had given us back-to-school homework.

Here was the readout:

IFTHE	UNITE	DSTAT	ESIST	OSURV
IVELO	NGSTA	NDING	AMERI	CANCO
NCEPT	SOFFA	IRPLA	YMUST	BEREC

And here again, enough is enough. When we were done, Porringer insisted on reading aloud: *"If the United States is to survive, long-standing American concepts of fair play must be reconsidered. We must develop effective espionage and counterespionage services and must learn to subvert, sabotage, and destroy our enemies by more clever, more sophisticated, and more effective methods than those used against us."*

"My Aunt Mary," said Sonderstrom, "he had us decoding the Doolittle Report."

Kittredge, can you imagine? Who among us is not familiar with such holy text, but Howard had us picking up the peas with a knife. Next morning, on the wall above each of our desks, Nancy Waterston, following his order, had tacked an eight-by-ten piece of white cardboard to the wall of each of our cubicles with the five-letter groups, all thirty-six, neatly typed. Presumably, we are to do our work for the rest of our two or three years here with the Doolittle Report staring at us in that Simple-Simon code. I didn't know whether Hunt was a genius in the making, or a third-rate malefactor. The Doolittle Report! We had fun over beer that evening. "I promise to subvert, sabotage, and destroy our enemies," one of us would begin, "by more clever, more sophisticated, and more effective methods," the second would take up, "than those used against us," would solemnly conclude the third. After which, Porringer, Kearns, and myself would solemnly recite, "Why ell are why ell—eks dee eff dee en—be why ee are why," which is how the letters in the last three five-letter groups do sound. Barbarically collegiate, I know, but we were having fun. I even liked Porringer. He is an incisive type. He told me, "Sonderstrom is looking to get relocated."

"How do you know?"

"I know."

That was over two months ago—oh, Kittredge, I see now how long it's been!—and I can only tell you that Porringer was absolutely right. Four weeks after Hunt came down to us from the Great White North, Sonderstrom managed to get himself transferred to Angola. It was tough on his wife, a fat Irish lady who hates hot climates and loves to sit on stuffed sofas—the wicker of cool African furniture is going to leave a checkerboard on her bland buttocks, I fear—but Angola was the only place that could use a Deputy COS immediately, and Sonderstrom has, he tells us, a real shot to move up to COS at the same Station after a year. Poor Sonderstrom. I'm not sure he has a real shot. He speaks no Angolese—whatever it's called. And once he thought he would replace Mayhew. I've come to recognize how tough the Company can be, which is, of course, as it should be. In any event, I'm now not so much impressed by Porringer's acumen as depressed by my lack of same. Of course Sonderstrom would look to move. Hunt has taken over all his functions, golf and social work, plus all the things Gus didn't and couldn't do, such as cultivating very rich ranch owners in the pampas. Moreover, it was clear by the end of Hunt's first month that he had struck up a tighter, tougher relationship with Salvador Capablanca (the untrustworthy Chief of Police of the Gómez adventure, remember?) than Sonderstrom ever did. According to Porringer, Hunt seized the nettle. Took the Police Chief out to lunch, as any First Secretary of the American Embassy might (remember—this is Hunt's cover title), but right after coffee, in answer to Capablanca's condescending, "Mr. Secretary, now tell me, sir, how can one be of service for you?" Hunt replied, "Easy, Salvador, just tap a couple of embassy lines for me. Soviet, Polish, East German, Czech. That should be enough for starters."

Porringer says Capablanca lost his poise.

"Oh, then . . ." he said, "oh, then . . . you are . . ."

"Yes, I'm CIA," said Hunt. "You don't think I really look like one of those flapdoodles in the State Department, do you?"

Flapdoodle was apparently one great choice of a word. Capablanca laughed as much as if he were having lunch with Bob Hope. (Incidentally, that's what Hunt's ski-jump nose reminds me of—Bob Hope!) But Porringer says Capablanca only laughed so much because he was frightened. Our CIA reputation casts a long shadow. Even the Chief of Police down here thinks we're capable of disposing of people by a snap of our fingers. (Just as well they don't know how relatively law-abiding we are.) In any case, Hunt was playing on such fear. Next thing he said was: "Señor Capablanca, as you well know, such taps can be put in mit or mitout."

"Mit or mitout? Would you explain, Señor Hunt?"

"Mit or mitout your help."

"Oh, I see." Capablanca laughed again.

"But if we do it together, the take can be shared."

"I would have to tell President Batlle."

"*Cómo no*," said Howard, and they shook hands over that.

On the drive back, Hunt listened carefully to Porringer. Oatsie's read was that Batlle would be too anti-American to cooperate, but too spineless to get in the way of our taps. However, the Deputy Chief of Police, Peones, who was also at the lunch, was ready to be recruited. Porringer told Hunt that he had been working on Peones for nine months. (Why does it always take nine months to make an agent? Another one of our Station jokes.) Hunt shook Porringer's hand solemnly. "That will be one A-OK coup," he said. In fact, Kittredge, it now is. Peones has been in the fold since February. Brownie points for Porringer.

After this lunch, Sonderstrom hastened his departure. He and Hunt were civil to one another, but they were not in tune. Now the Sonderstroms are gone and Porringer is, at present, Acting Deputy COS, and expects to take real title. His scrupulosity on detail and inside political savvy will back-stop Howard nicely.

Incidentally, I spent an interesting evening at Porringer's home just a couple of weeks ago. His wife is a serious bridge player, and in the States was working on her National Tournament Rating. Marooned here, she has joined a bridge club in Montevideo, which forces her to learn basic Spanish—"*Yo declaro tres corazones!*" The Porringers brought in a member of Sally's local group for my date, a dolorous, much-wrinkled duenna of seventy or seventy-five who spoke passable English, and played real hot cards. I do an acceptable college rubber, and Porringer is slightly better, but that was the size of the evening. I pass, you notice, quickly over the meal. Sally is, alas, no cook, and we had pot roast that tasted like boiled beef in dishwater, sort of reminiscent of the old St. Matthew's grub. Later, during bridge, the kids would stir once in a while in their all-American bedroom, bunk-bed small and stuffed with half-broken toys, as I discovered when sitting it out as dummy and thereby being the one free to walk the youngest back to her bed after she woke up for the usual nocturnal and fluvial reasons. Why do I tell you all this? It's just that our American domesticity is so strange to me that I look upon it as Martian. (Confession: I envisaged Christopher's bedroom in a few years. Please: no broken toys.)

The banality of the Porringer evening was relieved by one astonishing insight into Sherman. His house looks as you would expect—gray drapes, and blonde-wood furniture, formica dining table and chairs, unpainted stack shelves jammed with books and papers—exactly the way a Midwestern graduate student's apartment figures to shape up. Even a rug made of straw squares sewn together. And frayed. They brought all their furniture with them from Washington because it's shipped at Company expense. (That gave me a sense of all our modest U.S. families deployed around the globe.) At any rate, in the midst of this predictable household is one glass case with eight hand-painted eggs within. They're remarkably well done. A vista of tree and pond wraps around the shell in one. Another is a gothic castle with moonlight shimmering through a purple forest; they all are separate and exceptional—painted by someone who can use those fine brushes with one or two hairs. Then I learn they are in the glass case because, Sally tells us, Sherman has carefully sucked out the egg by way of a tiny hole he drilled. Once that is accomplished, he paints the fragile surface. Enjoys the risk of it. You can lose all you've put in with one careless move. "Would you like to see these gorgeous things up close?" asks Sally.

Well, prepare yourself for the horror. Even as Sherman is passing the first of his eggs to me, said object falls between our fingers to shatter on the floor. I feel as if a baby bird has just croaked. Kittredge, there are clumsy accidents, and there are what I would call third-force accidents. This was in the latter category. The eggshell left his hand and I swear it took its own willful flip into space.

Well, I apologized till I felt as if I were chewing aspirin, and he kept shrugging it off. A bull rage was stirring so deep in him that it will just bury another piece of his much suppressed soul. I'm sure

five, if not ten, hours of immaculate work were lost, and nothing to
do about it. He said at the end of a long time for me, but short enough,
I suppose, for him to get his sentiments in harness again—"Well, don't
feel too bad. It's my least favorite egg. I always take it out first if
strangers are going to handle the stuff." Given the circumstances, I
must admit Porringer was being gracious. His blue-black shaven
cheeks looked as funereal as the occasion.

It's late, and I can't possibly send a letter off which ends on
a note like this. So will hold, and write more tomorrow, and mail you
that.

Your indentured servant,
H2

11

April 11, 1957

I can't imagine why I told the awful egg story, except I do know. Even
as I write this to you, the reason comes home. It was the sound of the
egg as it struck their tile floor. Being just an empty shell, it made the
softest, saddest little sound on breaking. I can't get that out of my
head. Once on a High Thursday, Hugh told us of an ancient Egyptian
saying that the difference between the truth and a lie weighs no more
than a feather.

Enough! The exciting news is that we now have an Observation Post right next to the Russian Embassy, and this is as major-
league as we have been able to get. Once again, credit is due to
Porringer, since the OP comes to us by way of Peones, yet the action
derives from Howard's efforts to wake us up. I have not described
Peones, but you would hate him. He's heavy, very vain, half Spanish,
half Italian, and built to endure. Medium height, with massive shoulders and legs. Large black mustache. Frankly, he's swarthy. Gives off
an animal odor that he covers with scent. Peones knows all the
brothels in Montevideo and scouts them for new talent the way an
assistant college coach will go out to high school football games to
look for recruitments. Well, Porringer, I've learned, is something of
a brothelmaniac himself. Much more than I ever was, so quiet all
contumely. I've settled down. I'm frankly working too hard. But
Porringer and Peones became friends by running together from

brothel to brothel. It's not the most discreet way to develop an agent, but in this case was a dependable means of stoking a relationship. And please don't say *poor Sally Porringer*. I'm sure Sherman has his reasons.

About three months ago, Oatsie made the pass on Peones. Here is the background: Peones not only hates Capablanca, but systematically had been deluding him about Sonderstrom and Porringer. Kept insisting they were bona fide State Department. Conceive of his embarrassment (and Oatsie's) when Howard popped out with the direct admission to Capablanca that the lunch was under the auspices of the Intelligence Agency from the Colossus of the North. Peones was mad as hell after that lunch, but Porringer showed his skills. "Face it, Pedro," he told him—Peones' full name is, yes, Pedro Peones—"we've been working on you for months and you never join us. I tried to hold my Chief back but he's impatient. He wants to know straight out—how much is joining us worth to you?"

"We have a saying," said Peones. "Money buys everything but integrity."

"We say: Every man has his price."

"Mine is concealed. It is sequestered."

"Where might it be sequestered?"

"Why, I tell you, Sherman, it is a little secret, but I tell you: It is sequestered in my *cojones*."

Kittredge, I did not believe this conversation when Porringer recounted it. Pedro Peones' price was located in his no doubt massive testicles. There was, it seems, a girl in the brothels of Montevideo who was so beautiful and so talented that she had gone to Havana a couple of years ago to make her fortune. Now, she had become a legend from the Caribbean to South America. Her name—the working name, that is—comes to no less than Libertad La Lengua (which in loose translation does not signify Freedom of Speech nearly so much as "Ah, Freedom—your tongue!").

Libertad, it appears, has been corresponding lately with Peones. She is the love of his life. If the Central Intelligence Agency would bring her back from Havana to Montevideo—of her own free will, of course—he is ready to serve. Much of Uruguay, via Peones, would be at our disposal: selected government officials, individual dossiers, the telephone company, Embassy Row, and police informers in left organizations. Peones finishes by saying in English, "My country is yours."

Porringer carried the offer back to the Station. Peones' promises are vast, but can he be trusted to deliver? Once the girl is here, what if he fails to come through? Moreover, can we afford it? If she is doing all that well in Havana, her shift of venue may prove expensive. No, Peones promises, the cost will not be prohibitive. The girl sincerely desires to return to him. It is a true love affair, he tells Porringer.

Moreover, says Pedro, we will have to bear no more than the transportation costs. Once she is here, he will establish her in one of several fine properties he already commands. She will be Super-Deluxe. La Montevideana.

So a good deal of cable traffic has gone into these projected costs. It may not be as fearful, economically speaking, as we anticipated. (Two thousand dollars will get the girl here, bag and baggage, first class, bonus included.) Moreover, EH2 knows his way around the appropriate fields in Foggy Bottom. I soon learn that where one COS will get empty pockets on the return cable, another, like Howard, will come up with the kale. You're right. Hunt does talk about money all the time, and has more synonyms for checks and cash than anyone I ever met. "Does Libertad have any idea how many stick-em-ups it will take to transport her butt down here?" is one of his remarks. "Lettuce," he calls the stuff, and "frogskins," "cartwheels" (for silver dollars, I find out), and "farthings." "Bawbees," "tanners," "balboas," "bolivars." It's fun when he gets going.

To my surprise, the biggest impediment is Havana Station. Howard suspects that Caribbean Desk has been using Libertad for specific assignments, but he knows how to pull a few strings on the I-J-K-L harp, and the impasse is adjudicated. We get her. We only wonder a little why did Havana try to throw all that sand into the gears.

Anyway, Pedro is so happy that we now have a new term around the Station for extreme emotional states: it is *Delirium Peones*. In successive fits of generosity—since the girl has not as yet arrived—Pedro has already installed a tap on the phone lines of his detested superior, Salvador Capablanca. Our listening post immediately gives us the confirmation we need—Luis Batlle, President of Uruguay, is even more pro-Soviet than anticipated. Capablanca is completely his boy. We divined that already, but confirmation is to divination as a good meal to an empty belly.

Then comes the super-coup. After the confirmation cable that Libertad was definitively en route, Peones made a short speech to

Porringer. "Sherman," he said, "I am a man who lives by my values. The highest value a man can possess is to be a *caballero*. You will soon see what a *caballero* you have found in me."

Do you know, he was as good as his word? He had a prize prepared. Over a year ago he had obtained a lease on a villa situated next to the Russian Embassy on Bulevar España. These last twelve months, Peones chose to make no money on the rents—merely took in enough to pay his expenses from a family who, in return for the low rental, had agreed to move out on a week's notice. His instinct was certainly acute enough to know that we would give much to be able to put some of our own people into such a building, but he took no steps until he knew that we trusted him enough to bring his Libertad back to Montevideo.

If Sonderstrom were still here, he would be dubious of this prize, and Hugh would approach it as a tainted sweetmeat. Even Gatsby and Kearns spoke up. What if the villa next to the Russian Embassy is already wired by the KGB, and Peones has suckered us in?

Hunt cuts through such arguments. "We'll only use the house as a lookout post on the Soviet garden until a few security people are flown down to check it out. Why, even if the Russians have bugged the villa, they are not going to hear anything of value."

No, we decide, not if we put the right people in. They must be people who know nothing of our business yet will be patient enough to sit for hours behind the window curtains, always ready to turn on our Bolex H-16 movie camera should someone enter or leave the Embassy. While it is getting late for outdoor parties, the weather here in April is warmer than Washington in October, so there figure to be a few gatherings in the garden underneath our side windows before cold weather sets in. Obviously, we have to find the proper tenants pronto. But, where do we get them? We don't want to rely on Peones for this.

Hunt decides to collar Gordy Morewood, and soon we have a father and mother installed in the villa with their thirty-year-old daughter. They're vintage Jewish refugees from the Nazis and came to Montevideo in 1935 or thereabouts. Their name is Bosqueverde, which is changed from the original German, I assume. Grunewald may have been the original. Never altered Hyman to Jaime, however. So it's Hyman Bosqueverde, and his wife is Rosa. Daughter is Greta. They call her Gretel. They are a timid, very retiring couple with a shy, plain daughter, but very close to one another. If the daughter sneezes, the mother shivers. I know all this because Howard has made me their Support Officer.

You see, none of us dare speak to the Bosqueverdes in English (a pity since their English is not bad), but it would be a total giveaway if the KGB had miked the villa. The solution, therefore, was to use me. While my German is not great, I believe I can get away with laying a heavy Spanish accent over it. We hope the assumption will be—if, that is, the KGB is listening—that I'm some Spanish friend of the Bosqueverdes trying to improve his accent.

At any rate, my duties here are simple and small. In return for living in the villa rent-free, the Bosqueverdes are obliged to keep someone near the movie camera and tripod from six in the morning until dark. Since the daughter works as a librarian, I assume she puts in less time than the parents. I visit every third or fourth night to bring over new film and carry back exposed reels. We get the take developed in a safe lab, and I then put in my hours with a movie projector and screen studying the arrivals and departures from the front gate of the Soviet Embassy, ready to attach a new number to each new face. Then the film is pouched up to Cockroach Alley, where Soviet Russia Division has the capacity to recognize faces and attach dossiers to them. As we receive their findings, life becomes more interesting. One of the faces, for example, belonged to a high-level KGB man. He came to the Embassy a couple of times, left again on each occasion after a half-hour visit, and then flew back to Paris, which we were able to determine via AV/OUCH-2 in Passport Control. Of course, we don't know why he made his visit, but SR Division has one more straw for their giant nest.

The garden parties are another matter. Two have been photographed so far, and I run the reels with as much absorption as if I am sitting on the bank of a lake at evening and can't stop studying the light on the water. It's a curious image to use because the Bosqueverdes are not skillful photographers, and the result is close to bad home movies with a telephoto lens thrown in. The pans are abrupt enough to make you feel as if a wrestler is throwing you half across the ring. Still, I study the footage over and over for clues to Soviet Embassy personnel relationships, and can't begin to tell you how absorbing that is. I feel as if I'm watching a film by Roberto Rossellini. I'm tempted to relate more, but would rather wait until the next garden party, which is scheduled for this Saturday. Personnel from the

American Embassy have actually been invited, and while the Ambassador won't go, Hunt may fill in for him as First Secretary, and I could be brought along as Assistant to the First Secretary. How surrealistically splendid it will be if I am present at the party talking to Russians, knowing all the while that I will be able to study them later at leisure. Howard is weighing the pros and cons. He is afraid that if they are indeed tapping the villa they may recognize my voice. I'll give you his conclusion next week.

For now, let me describe our tenants. They live, as I say, rent-free, and Hyman ekes out his income by giving Hebrew lessons to a few young Jewish pupils who are getting ready for their Bar-Mitzvah. Apparently there is a substantial Jewish community in Montevideo. I am absolutely fascinated by these Bosqueverdes. They are the first Jewish family I have ever visited, and everything they do is of interest to me. Almost always when I go over at night, they are drinking tea in glasses, and often are eating some kind of light supper. Sometimes it's cold herring in sour cream with onions, and the smell, while not disagreeable, does permeate the room. They always offer me food and I always refuse it (since my instructions are to get into no long conversations with them and certainly no verbal transactions about reels and equipment. They know enough to hand over the product silently.)

Sometimes one of Hyman Bosqueverde's students will be studying with the old man in an alcove removed from the camera, and I listen to the mutual recital of Hebrew as if all the words are magical. The man and the boy both wear skullcaps, and that seems equally arcane to me. Think of it! They are getting ready for a Bar-Mitzvah in the midst of all this. As I go out, the old lady buttonholes me near the foyer and whispers directly into my ear in a strong German-Jewish accent, "Please, you should take the best care of Mr. Morewood. He works so hard for you."

"*Ja*," I say, "*sí, ja*," and I smile and leave with the exposed reels rattling in my paper bag. (Which also has a loaf of bread sticking out of it.) And I am back on the street and sauntering along for three blocks to my pool car, taking a couple of leisurely stops en route to see if perchance I'm being followed. So far—*nichts!* Good enough. I have the feeling that the villa is not tapped. The Sovietskys simply don't feel the need to keep up to anything like their standards in Berlin.

On the drive to my hotel I keep thinking about the Jews. They are only one-eighth of me but I have this peculiar whole response to them.

Time for bed. Give my love to my godson, and to you and yours.

Harry

12

April 14, 1957

Dearest Kittredge,

The garden party is tomorrow and Hunt has decided that I'm the one to go with him. No doubt about it, he's bold, and I'm pleased. I know the terrain, I've done the chores, and now I'm entitled to the reward. Of course, I'll have to be three times as cautious in future when dropping in on the Bosqueverdes, or else turn the visits over to Kearns or Gatsby (who are, incidentally, jealous of Hunt's growing fondness for me—you were certainly right about that) but, on balance, I'm pleased. To sip cocktails behind the enemy's garden walls—how many can speak of such an experience?

As a result, work hung heavy today, and I left early, and now find an urge to write to you again. There are so many sides to my job that I feel as if I'm only giving you the most partial glimpses. From the day he came in, for instance, Hunt was fascinated by my work with AV/ALANCHE. Before long, he was giving me slogans to pass on to the gang. Howard wants to see in letters five feet high such declarations as MARXISMO ES ODIOSO, or—a real blockbuster—MARXISMO ES MIERDA.

"Howard," I tell him, "I don't believe those kids will want to put *mierda* up. They may be slum children, but they're straitlaced about such stuff."

"Scatology," says Howard, "has a hell of an impact in poor countries. Let me tell you what the Chinese did to the Japs during the war." And he provided a long tale about the OSS giving stink-bomb spray dispensers to Chinese kids who would sneak up on Japanese officers taking a stroll and loose the littlest squirt on their pants. Five minutes later, the officer smelled as if he had been bathing in dung. "What a loss of face for the Japs," said EH2.

"Yes," I say, "that's quite a story." He senses my resistance and lets it go for the time being.

All the same, he is rash. He is trying to get me to accelerate Chevi Fuertes' efforts, and I resist. Chevi is coming along nicely with me. For my devoted readers back in the Groogs, I have developed a fairly detailed picture of the top PCU personnel, and which PCU factions have clout with which unions, etc. Porringer, who has kept on the labor scene these last two years, claims my stuff is good but hardly new—I'd hate to think this is repayment for the broken egg. In any event, Howard now wants me to push Chevi to install a couple of sneakies into the inner office of the PCU. That's no huge job. One has only to replace the present old-fashioned electrical wall outlets (which look like white porcelain doorknobs) with new outlets, built to look exactly the same but containing a miniature microphone and transmitter within. Gatsby has managed to rent a listening post in an office building near enough to PCU headquarters to pick up these limited-range transmissions. So Hunt says the job is in place and all we're waiting for is Chevi to bring his screwdriver.

The trouble is that the office is well guarded. Chevi draws guard duty once a week in the inner office. He and a fellow Communist camp out there for the night. Since the PCU is certainly paranoid about security, neither man is supposed to leave the other alone. They don't even go down the hall to the bathroom. A bucket is left for them. This rule, however, is there to be broken. Once a night, Chevi's companion will pay a ten-minute visit to the loo. That can be counted on. In these ten minutes, Chevi could substitute our porcelain outlet for the other. But if it goes wrong, I don't want to think of what would happen to Fuertes. I'm not certain they'd hurt him physically, but, at the least, he's ruined among his own people forever. (In a sense, he is already, to himself.) Of course, I also have to consider whether I'm being too protective of my agent. That is as bad as being too reckless. In any event, the pressure is on to push Fuertes, and I believe I will. Hunt wants us to get moving in every direction. For instance, Gatsby, under Sherman's tutelage, has taken over Porringer's relations with a centrist labor union that has been keeping us informed on several left-wing unions. Hunt wants more. "We're here to war on the Reds," he says, "not to monitor their social progress." So Gatsby has been pushed into using stink-bombs. A couple of left-wing meetings have been broken up lately by right-wing students whom Gatsby (with an assist from Gordy Morewood) recruited over the last three months. Hunt insists there's double mileage in the use of Who-Me's. "It makes the recipient feel infantile. Helpless infants live in the midst of such smells. So, it deprives these labor leaders of some of their ability to take themselves seriously. That's a vital blow to a labor leader."

Gatsby, whom I don't believe I've described to you, is sandy-haired, scrub-featured, freckled, and, in a word, not very describable. He was never exactly noticeable, not even with a mustache that happened to be dark enough to contrast with his light hair. But Hunt convinced him to shave it off. Now he is truly inconspicuous.

Last note on stink-bombs. AV/ALANCHE-1 through 7 have been armed with pellets. Hunt claims these Who-Me's will beef up morale for my kids. To my surprise, it does. Last time AV/ALANCHE 1–7 went out, they actually got into a pitched battle with a left-wing gang they had been wary of before, but the pellets apparently did the job. On their next sally, they intend to paint MARXISMO ES MIERDA on a warehouse wall near the center of town.

The *next sally* reminds me that the Porringers are also going to the Soviet garden party. I feel like Anthony Trollope. Will Herrick Hubbard convince Mrs. Porringer to dance with the Russians?

Your own Harry

April 15, 1957

Kittredge,

I wish I hadn't dispatched that letter yesterday. Now you are expecting news I can't offer. The Russians called off their garden party. The excuse is that their *residentura*, Samoilov, is ill with flu. It's nonsense. We know better. A quick check with the Bosqueverdes confirmed that Samoilov has been in and out of the Embassy several times this morning.

Whom, you may ask, do we dare to send to the Bosqueverdes' door in broad daylight? It's an ingenious piece of work—another nice touch from the unpopular Mr. Morewood. Gordy calls on a twelve-year-old nephew of the Bosqueverdes whenever he wants Hyman to come out to a pay phone. Since the boy lives near the villa, he merely saunters over in his skullcap to pay, ostensibly, a visit to his Hebrew teacher. Of such *pointillisme* is the complete spy's palette. I wish one could like Gordy more—there is so much to learn from him.

By such means, Hyman Bosqueverde did relay to us the news that Samoilov was walking about and healthy. Why the party was canceled we cannot answer yet. We notified the Groogs, who took it up with Soviet Russia Division. Their analysis is that Khrushchev's friendly gestures of late toward the West are intended to slow down the nuclear buildup in NATO. The invitation to us here in Montevideo was one of the far-flung expressions of such a gambit. Something, however, went wrong overnight, and they pulled back the olive branch. A worldwide checkout on Soviet Embassy parties reveals that the Montevideo bash, plus a party in Johannesburg to which our Embassy people were also invited, seem to have been the only two canceled.

Our best readout after a three-way cable interchange is that the Russians were indicating that a minor, not a major, chill is taking place. As evidence, the entire party was called off, which is far better, on balance, than merely disinviting the American Embassy. God, what a way to waste a day. I'm at raw ends. And Barry Kearns is in a worse state. He had to spend the entire morning and afternoon on the Encoder-Decoder with Soviet Russia Division. When Kearns makes even the smallest error in routing, which is not hard to do, the Sourballs become awfully nasty. (Merely to reach them, however, calls for invoking an entry code that changes with the hour.) Kearns forgot that Washington, of late on Daylight Savings Time, is no longer sixty minutes behind us—well, contemplate the return vituperations. Kearns' error cost the Sourballs some ninety minutes in the Great Bin of Lost Messages until they located his cable. Here is part of their reply:

| NEXTT | IMESH | OWYOU | RCERT | IFICA |
| TEOFI | DIOCY | | | |

I'll spare you the rest of that billet-doux. The SR Division has to be composed of thick-spectacled creatures with half-bald heads, woodpecker noses, and wholly splenetic dispositions.

Poor Kearns. I haven't described him to you, but he's our misfit. Six-four, he weighs much too much, maybe one of the heaviest people in the Agency, lardlike, even soft. I don't know how he played golf for Sonderstrom, although I hear he had some ability to drive a long ball and was a finicky but reasonably dependable putter. His golf bag, however, is gathering dust. Under Hunt's baleful supervision,

Kearns' inadequacies are beginning to show up. He panics, and can easily blow a communications procedure. Kearns also has a heavy hand when trying to joke with the Groogs. There's a cable protocol, I could even call it a cable *panache*, that he lacks. Whereas, Hunt has it. This is what Howard sent last week to the Argentina-Uruguay Desk: NOBODY TOLD ME BUT I BELIEVE TODAY TO BE THE TENTH ANNIVERSARY OF OUR URUGUAY STATION. GIFTS AND CONGRATULATIONS WILL BE GRATEFULLY RECEIVED. DO NOT REMIT CASH.

I can see how such humor won't translate over to you, but given our oft-strained relations with the Groogs, it was a funny cable. They sent back the following reply: WOULD YOU CONSIDER THIRTY THOUSAND AMERICAN PENNIES TO ACCOMPANY THE USUAL FELICITATIONS FOR A JOB PRETERNATURALLY (AS ALWAYS) HALF-BAKED TO A PERFECT TURN.

Well, I'm feeling psychic across six thousand miles. I sense your Furies stirring. Kittredge, do try to forgive the disappointment this letter must be.

Harry

April 19, 1957

Harry,

I believe that I am a case officer manqué. I know that when I expect information and don't receive it, I have to hold on to a temper so terrible that I am convinced my Gardiner forebears own a touch of Druid's blood. Your last letter, to put it kindly, reads like drool from Fathead Lane. What do I care about your third-rate Chief of Station and his Napoleonic urinations into the pee-pot of Uruguay? His cables are equal to his mentality. Your appreciation of such mediocrity inspires me with horror.

As I write this, I am sitting at Harlot's desk looking at your brooch. Note that this is the first time I have ever called Hugh by the name for which he is famous. I wonder what Christopher's proud cryptonym is yet to be? STRUMPET? TOMBSTONE?

The baby is crying. Again. Again. It is because I called him TOMBSTONE. His life is part of my future death.

Brooch
Your brooch

April 20, 1957

Dear Harry,

Forget yesterday's letter if you can. I mailed it immediately upon completion, and that is all I remember. Whatever was in it cannot possibly be more than half true. I suffer attacks like migraine, except my head does not hurt. It's just that I undergo temporary amnesia.

Have you given up your brothel girl or are you deep in the slop-pits with her?

I fear the worst.

I really do not wish to correspond with you anymore.

This is an order.

Cease all communications with me.

Hadley Kittredge Gardiner Montague

If I had sworn that I would not use the secure phone to reach Harlot, the oath had to be broken. Our Station's secure phone was kept, however, in a locked closet in Howard Hunt's office. He was not sympathetic to my request.

"Howard," I told him, "I must have use of it."

"Could you provide the reason?"

"Personal."

Howard sat behind his desk and shrugged. "In that case, why don't you find a pay phone on the other side of town?"

"This is Company business. The man I want to reach won't speak unless the line is secure."

"Hugh Montague. Is he the gentleman?"

"Yessir."

Howard put his elbows on the desk and looked at me from the tent of his upraised and slanted fingers. "Harry, I think you ought to know," he said, "that Harlot is a legend in the Agency for six good reasons and eight bad ones. One of the bad ones is that you can't have a decent conversation with the guy unless you're using a secure phone."

"I accept the fact that Hugh Montague is a man full of quirks. But this happens to be a family matter of first importance."

Howard showed his temper. "The secure phone is placed in my

hands as Chief of Station. You are asking me to abuse this serious privilege."

"For God's sake, I was able to use a secure phone all the time I was in Berlin. It happened to be located right at the end of a corridor in the Department of Defense. Anyone could use it."

"Berlin," said Howard, "is an orgy. A goddamned out-of-control orgy."

"Yessir."

"I can't allow you to use my secure phone for a private matter. That's cutting a hole in the membrane."

"Yessir. But I do have to talk over a family matter."

"I thought we passed that stop."

"Howard, I am godfather to the Montagues' child, Christopher. Upsetting news came to me this morning by way of a letter."

"Isn't Hugh Montague your godfather?"

"Yessir." But I could not hold back the question. "How did you know?"

He touched his thumb with his forefinger several times to indicate a duck quacking. "I had lunch back in Washington with Arnie Rosen."

"Rosey," I said, "is better than an old-fashioned telephone operator."

To my surprise, Hunt laughed. "Here!" He reached into a vest pocket and withdrew a small key. "Help yourself. Maybe I know what it is to be worried about a kid."

"Thank you, Howard."

"And when you're done, not today, but soon, I have a couple of things to talk to you about. Don't ask who, but a couple of people warned me off of one Harry Hubbard. Told me you fucked up in Berlin."

"Maybe I did."

"Well, everybody messes up under Bill Harvey. The real bad word, if you want to hear it, is that you're locked in with the wrong rabbi."

I made no reply. I was damn angry by now and trying to be as calm as stone.

"We can," said Hunt, picking it up, "talk about it over drinks or dinner." He looked at his watch. "Hey, I'm late for one big lunch. This office is going to be yours. Leave it as you found it." He laughed to subdue the edge of his last remark, and was gone.

Using a secure phone proved difficult in Montevideo. I had to pass through relays of operators from Buenos Aires to Mexico City to Washington. It took a half hour to learn that Harlot was not in his office, nor at home, but another call to Location Inquiry-Secure directed me to WILD GARLIC, the cognomen given to Harlot's phone at the Keep. An hour had been spent in Howard Hunt's closet to reach a man I dreaded speaking to.

"Are you calling about Kittredge?" Harlot said for greeting. Once again came the impression of hearing a voice from the other end of a long tube.

"Yes," I said, "just what I am calling about."

"How the hell did you get to Howard's phone? Have to give away a piece of yourself?"

"Probably."

"Doubtless too much."

"Hugh, is Kittredge with you at the Keep?"

"She's all right. Under some sedation, but fine."

I could not see how someone who was under sedation was fine, but he must have heard what I did not say, for he added, "I'm with her. She's not alone."

"Yessir."

He was silent for the longest time, and when he spoke, it was as if he had made a whole decision to tell me more.

"Harry, she didn't go out of her head, you know. It was overload."

"I've been worried," I said.

He snorted. "Worried? I've been grinding a few teeth. Do you know? She was still trying to nurse the baby, and keep up at work, and with it all, most unfortunately, experimenting with a substance. At such times, of course, she would not nurse the baby. Not when the substance was in her."

I could hardly believe what he had said. "The what?"

"Kittredge would never test others before jumping in the pool herself. But her timing was ill advised."

"Is she all right?" I asked.

"I told you. She is mending. She is under sedation. A good doctor-friend of mine is supervising her recovery. Friend of Allen's."

"Did she go to the hospital?"

"Of course not. A psychotic episode in your 201 is about as desirable as joining the Communist Party in your youth."

I could feel his desire to talk. In what a state must he be!

"Hugh, forgive this question, but are you certain she shouldn't be seeing a very good psychiatrist?"

"I know the lot," said Montague. "We run them in and out of TSS in relays. I comprehend Kittredge far better than ever they could. They are not qualified to deal with her fine mind. She is all right, I tell you. In another week, she will be herself. Of course, she must not work for a time, and in future has to forswear any ingestion of substances whatever. It's her ambition, don't you see? The only part of the girl that is not balanced. They don't recognize the stature of her work sufficiently. That's enough to drive a sane mind wild."

"May I speak to Kittredge?"

"She is sleeping. I would not wake her."

"May I call back?"

There was a full pause. I waited, but he did not reply.

"Is Christopher with you?" I asked.

"Naturally."

"And a nurse?"

"A good Maine woman who comes in by the day. I get up with Christopher if he wakes at night." He was silent after that.

I wanted to ask about his office. Who was covering? Kittredge had once spoken of two assistants who were absolutely dependable. They would be guarding the doors at GHOUL. I had a small but inescapable panic that my time on the phone was running out. I would be alone in Uruguay so soon as he hung up.

"May I call later?" I asked again.

His telephone silence, teeming with static, seemed equal to the babble of a myriad of infinitesimal creatures.

"Harry, look into yourself," said Harlot. "You've been a son of a bitch. I want your correspondence with Kittredge to cease."

My first reaction was to wonder whether he had read the letters, or merely knew of their existence.

"Dear God, Hugh," I said at last, "I think that ought to be Kittredge's decision."

"Harry, the birth of a baby is as incapacitating to an ambitious, talented woman as the hole left by a spear. She needs to mend. So cease this correspondence. That is my wish and it is hers."

"I'm going to ask for a leave."

"You may get it, but I won't permit you to see her."

"Hugh, don't cut me off. I'm six thousand miles away."

"Well, you're going to discover the stuff of which you are made. My uneasiest sentiment, now that we are perforce joined by truth for a moment or two, is that you, Harry, are not tough enough. Not for the life work you have chosen. Prove me wrong. Plunge into your job. Take a sabbatical from us until we come around."

With that, he hung up.

13

SINCE IT WAS NEAR MY HOTEL, I HAD THE HABIT OF STOPPING BY THE Central Post Office each morning on the way to work. Sally Porringer would leave letters for me there. Her notes, as one could anticipate, were functional—"Oh, Harry, I miss you so much, I'm just aching for you. Let's figure out something for Saturday," is a fair sample.

It was nice, however, that someone was aching for me. In the month after the last letter from Kittredge, I made love to Sally in a cold fury. It was unfair, but I held Sally responsible for the loss, and copulated in hate, which may have had the obverse effect of melting some icy moraine in her, for she kept telling me I was wonderful. Sexual vanity with its iron-tipped fingers kept clawing me forward, therefore, into more performance, even as I kept asking myself why I couldn't act like other Americans and just find women and forget them. Porringer, for example, was always ready to regale Gatsby and me about his nights in Montevideo brothels. If Sherman, with a wife, two children, and all of the duties of a Deputy COS, could still disport "like the happiest hog on the hind tit," as he put it himself—somber, blue-cheeked, paranoid Porringer—why could I not enjoy it? The irony is that I was even beginning to feel a bit of loyalty to Sally. The paradox of sex is that it always negotiates some kind of contract with love—no matter what, love and sex will never be entirely without relations. If I had added to my clandestine jamborees with Sally all the anger I felt at exercising my brains right out of my head with the wrong girl, and so felt more and more separated from the only woman I could adore like a goddess—strong words, but I was suffering my loss—all this anger had to live nonetheless with my sexual greed. Loss had left me a displaced person in the land of love.

So love slipped over, if only by a little, into my feelings, and I did not despise Sally quite so much, and had compassion for the awful loneliness of her life in a land where the only people who understood her at all were maniacal old lady bridge players, a young, grim, and much detached lover, and a husband who understood her so well he did not comprehend her at all. "Does he think it makes me feel good," she complained once, "for him to announce to company, 'Oh, Sally's a good old girl,' as if I was his 4-H Blue Ribbon in the prize sow contest? I hate Sherman sometimes. He's so needful and inconsiderate," and she began to weep. I, holding her, felt the first beginnings of compassion move out from me and into her. I still looked upon her with a great measure of contempt, but there were limits to how long I could keep my best feelings—that inner chalice of tender compassion—reserved entirely for Kittredge Gardiner Montague when I ached within from every bruise she had bestowed.

Besides, it was too painful to think of her. Was she mad? There was not a night when I did not curse myself for failing to get leave to go back to America. Yet it was hopeless. Harlot was never less than his word. Besides, he could be right. It might be one's duty to suck up the slack.

Nonetheless, I still felt treacherous toward Kittredge whenever Sally and I put in our raunchy hours. Sex with Sally grew more appealing despite myself. I would lie in her arms afterward wondering if Kittredge were on the mend, or had I, across six thousand miles, just sent another thundering blow to the head?

Suck up the slack, yes. I felt like a strip miner through all of May and June. The mild winter of Montevideo might as well have been spent in an Eastern coal pit. I was alone in Uruguay with no letters to write. So I took on work as Harlot had advised. I saw Chevi Fuertes twice a week, and AV/ALANCHE once, AV/OUCH-1 and 2 at Travel Control and Passport Control were on my route, and AV/ERAGE, the homosexual journalist on the society beat, was also given to me now that Gatsby had been put onto Porringer's old trade union contacts. And there were always the Bosqueverdes (who spent their winter photographing the passage of live souls in and out of the Soviet Embassy gate). They were mine. And Howard Hunt gave me Gordy Morewood as well, and I had to deal with his unrelenting demands for cash. On certain mornings, every face was an irritant. Sometimes when Porringer and Kearns and Gatsby were all together in our big office room with its four desks, I knew again how faceless were everyday faces. And how intimate! Every misgrown nostril hair!

Hunt became my friend during that Uruguayan winter, which

was the summer of 1957 in North America. Two months after I spoke across six thousand miles to Harlot up at the Keep in Maine, I was wending my way out to Carrasco twice a week for dinner with Dorothy and Howard. If the high regard I used to hold for Harlot was now buried like provisions kept for one's return from a long journey, the habit of such respect, its shadow, so to speak, became transferred to Hunt. While he had a nasty temper, and was as easy to dislike at one moment as to like at the next, he was still my leader. I was discovering all over again that our capacity for love, when all else fails, attaches easily to such formal investments as flag and office.

In the midst of all this, on an average cold morning, following my habit of stopping at the Central Post Office on the way to work, I pulled my hand out of the box one day with a letter from Kittredge. She had written to me directly rather than by way of the pouch.

> The Stable
> June 30, 1957

Dear Harry,

      Got this address from your mother. I believe open mail will be all right. This is really to tell you that I am now all right. In fact, in a limited sense, I'm thriving. To my modest sorrow, the baby is off my breast and onto formula, but, on balance, it works. We have a daily nurse-housekeeper, and I am back on the job, indeed, no one over at the shop knows I was ill. Hugh managed that with great dispatch. Allen may be witting but certainly no one else. Hugh just brazened it through with a Kittredge-and-I-haven't-had-a-vacation-since-marriage sort of stance that only he could get away with. Of course, he did work at the Keep, and damn hard while I was sorting out the little mad things for myself. Don't repeat this, but the real trouble was not you, nor the brooch, nor the baby, nor Hugh, all of whom I was beginning to see as encircling fiends, but, in fact, was due to the most injudicious experimenting with a fabulous if horribly tricky drug for altering consciousness called LSD. Certain of our people have been trying it the last five or six years with the most fascinating *but* inconclusive results, and I was vain enough to decide to experiment on myself and try to trace LSD's impact on Alpha and Omega. Needless to say, Alpha and Omega got into a frightful hoedown.

      So, this letter is apology to you. I recollect just enough of my deep dive to be certain it was unforgivable. I've wanted to tell you for some time but didn't quite dare to use our old set-up on the pouch. He's forbidden me to write to you and he's correct up to a point. I think I was indulging a species of double life. Chaste, but nonetheless double. I vowed to Hugh I would not correspond with you again unless I told him first. Of course, I crossed my fingers as I said it, so the vow is discounted by this letter. Anyway, as you see, I wanted to take the chance.

It is really to tell you, as I have already said, that I am all right. In truth, I love Hugh now more than ever. He was fabulous to me up in Maine, strong but so concerned. I realized how much he loves me and the baby, and I hadn't really known that before. Hadn't truly taken it in. The spring of his love must come from a source one thousand feet deep. I think without him I might have sunk into much more loss of time and frantic mindlessness.

This is also to tell you that I miss you and your letters. I'm patient. I will wait another three or four months to prove to Hugh that relapses are not in my makeup, not at all. I'm back, but still I want to demonstrate it to him, and by fall—your spring—I am going to tell him that I wish to write to you again, and if he doesn't permit it—well, we'll see. Be patient.

Think of me as your cousin, your kissing cousin, with whom you cannot have congress. Whoopee! *Hélas*. I will always love you on a most special note, but it feels warm and comfy right now, I confess, to think of you as far-off.

Amitiés,
Kittredge

P.S. Hugh never saw any of your letters. I confessed to him that we had been corresponding, but only as college sweethearts who were not about to do anything about it. That much he could tolerate because he had seen the evidence when you would visit. So, my confession confirmed his acumen. I did not dare to tell him how candid we were about other matters. That he would never comprehend and never forgive.

I lied again when I told him that the letters were destroyed by me on the night I took the LSD. Even in the midst of my madness, you see, I knew enough to lie.

14

EVEN WHEN WE WERE ONLY THREE FOR DINNER, OUR SETTING WAS formal. At their long, handsome table, Howard always sat at one end and Dorothy at the other. If he and she were absolute snobs, I was learning nonetheless that to be accepted by such people is not unlike receiving an award; one is bathed in balmy waters. Since Howard's visit to the Stable still smarted, all the more appealing was I, not only for the Hubbard ancestors, but as someone to steal from the Montagues. Howard did not yet comprehend the impossibility of certain social desires. I believe one reason I liked him was that I often felt more than equal to him.

Back at the office, I paid, of course, for these attentions. One of my tasks was to bring the day's reports out to Hunt's house in the evening whenever he had spent the afternoon hobnobbing with Uruguayans at the Jockey Club. I had not been doing it for long, however, before Porringer and crew arrived at the intuition that this was not merely a chore, but that I was a steady guest for dinner. On nights when I was out working as a case officer, Gatsby or Kearns or even Oatsie himself would take the twelve-mile drive along the Rambla out to Carrasco Beach where the Hunts lived in a white stucco villa with red roof-tiles just two sweepingly curved streets away from the sea, but my colleagues were not often asked to remain for the evening meal. Kindness to social inferiors was not one of Dorothy's virtues. Indeed, I winced at the thought of Sally in her clutches. Nor was the thought of Kearns at table any happier. He had the tiniest wife and they looked bizarre when together. Disproportion was enough to dilate Dorothy's nostrils. If Jay Gatsby had graduated from The Citadel and his wife, Theodora, come out of some good Southern ladies' emporium of education called Atkins Emory (or some equivalent concatenation of consonants), that may have been enough to elicit a second invitation from the Hunts, but no more.

The worst afternoon I spent with Sally was the day preceding Howard and Dorothy's arrival at the Porringers' for a payback dinner. Sally's most formidable asset, the ability to say farewell to her mind for thirty wholly concupiscent minutes, was subverted. I made love to a woman with a rigid body and a mind teeming with social fear. Hunt might throw himself into MARXISMO ES MIERDA and ship cartons of pelleted Who-Me's up to the front without a backward look, but he

could not enjoy a repast with people who did not know how to serve
the damn thing. And Dorothy was worse. To the stern blood standards of her one-eighth of Oglala Sioux and the Harrison ancestors
could be added Mrs. Hunt's relinquished title. Dorothy had been
married to the Marquis de Goutière, and had kept house with him in
Chandernagore, which happened to be, Howard could tell you, "the
family seat of the de Goutières. It's near Calcutta."

I never knew if the de Goutières were Franco-Hindu or Indo-
French, and if I heard the sound of "Marquesa" from time to time,
I barely knew how to spell it. But allow Dorothy her due—she was
aristocratic. With dark hair, large dark eyes, a large and aquiline nose,
and lips that could curve into many a nuance of displeasure, she was
curiously attractive, and rarely lacking in inner sentiments of self-
worth.

Whatever were the virtues and shortfalls at the home of the
Hunts, I paid for their hospitality by absorbing a concomitant chill
from my brother operators at the office. No matter. I accepted the
transaction. I was learning a good deal about Hunt's view of the
Station. While dinners in Carrasco adhered to Dorothy's edict that no
outright business could be transacted at table, the half hour before
dinner invariably installed me in Howard's study, and there I was used
as a sounding board. An audible meditation, minutes in length, on the
defects of Gatsby and Kearns would issue from the thriving hive of his
thoughts. I rarely had to reply as Hunt conducted me through each
loose drum skin in our Station. I knew it was only a way of warming
me up for a new job. Porringer was liaison to each of the Uruguayan
journalists and editors we paid to plant our pieces in the Montevideo
press. Last week, however, Porringer had spent more time writing for
the Montevideo periodicals than reading them. "Khrushchev,
Butcher of the Ukraine," went the theme.

So I saw my new task shaping up. While Porringer's contacts with
journalists were as sacrosanct to him as an Oklahoma dirt farmer's
forty acres, I would now be given a heavy share of the writing and
editing. Hunt's litany of imperfect execution of projects by Gatsby and
Kearns was, I knew, the mirror image of their complaints to him that
I was not taking on my proper load. The oldest game at every Station,
I had begun to learn, was to slough dull tasks onto the new man at the
next desk, and Hunt, who could hardly be unaware of what it must
cost to be his favorite, must have decided to unload more of the
shopwork on me. When I agreed, therefore, to put my hand in on the

material Porringer sent over to his three best journalists, AV/ARICE, AV/ENGE, and AV/IATOR, Hunt had obtained his purpose, and could feel expansive.

"Harry, when all is said and done," he told me now, "propaganda is half of what we do. Sometimes I think it's the better half." He opened his desk drawer and shut it as if to take a spot check on whether the Sovs had left a sneaky there recently. "Hate to tell you," he said with his hand to the side of his mouth as if to hold off all alien ears, "just how many newspapers back home also take plants from us. Journalists are easier to buy than horses!"

The maid knocked on the door of the study. It was time for dinner. End of business and commencement of history. Dorothy, who was considerably less talkative than Howard, was always ready to accept his monologues at table, and converted them, I expect, into periods of meditation for herself. After all, she had heard the tales.

I, however, had not, and thought he told them well. Let one suffice for the many.

"Back in Tokyo about two years ago . . ."

"More like a year and a half ago," commented Dorothy.

"You're keeper of the clock," said Howard. "All right, eighteen months ago, the Chinese Communists had the effrontery to announce that they were going to open their first trade fair in Japan. Show off their advanced machine-tool equipment. This set up a hell of a ripple. We knew better, but still! What if they were actually competitive? American interests had a lot of ducats in the pot, so we certainly didn't want the Japanese people looking to China. Well, I managed to slip into their preview and the ChiCom stuff was pathetic. Poor copies of our machine tools. The few good products were hand-crafted. Obviously, they were going to make no dent in the bacon-and-beans department, no, sir, no Almighty Dollars would have to be spent competing with them. All the same, I decided to bomb their exposition."

"Did you employ Who-Me's?" I asked.

"Not at all. This job called for finesse. So I authored a nifty op. Hundreds of thousands of leaflets floated down on Tokyo one night from a plane. 'Come to the Chinese Trade Fair,' said the invitation. 'Free Admission, Free Beer, Free Rice, Free Sashimi.' "

Hunt began to laugh. "Harry, the ChiComs were inundated with Tokyo citizens waving these leaflets. They had to close their doors. They didn't have any free anything. Terrible press. Had to slink their Chinese butts out of town.

"Speak of Brownie points," said Howard. "I think one reason I'm sitting in a COS seat right now was the success of that coup. Of course, I might also have to thank Dorothy." He lifted his glass to her. "Friend," he said, "when you look at your hostess, what do you see?"

"A beautiful lady," I interjected.

"More than that," said Hunt, "I also glimpse the female persona at its most elusive. Ask yourself, Harry, would Dorothy make a spy?"

"None better," I replied.

"You are on course." He sipped his wine. "I'm going to let out one I ought not to. While in Tokyo, she managed to cop the Argentine code books."

"I'm impressed," I said to Dorothy.

"Well, Howard had to bring it up, but I will say it was no great feat. I was working, after all, for the Argentine Ambassador."

"Her Spanish is impeccable," said Howard. "She was his speech-writer."

"Part-time," said Dorothy.

"Part-time just managed to be enough," said Howard, "for Dorothy to pick up the code books during the midday siesta. We had a little team around the corner who photographed her take faster than you can skin a rabbit, and Dorothy got them back before the first *siestero* returned. That was worth a private salute from the North Asia Command. Darling, you are the real article," said Howard. "Why, if we hadn't met in Paris, I would probably have encountered you in Hong Kong on some enchanted evening."

"And what would I have been doing there?" asked Dorothy.

"Running a large espionage mill. Contract players at every price. All nations welcome."

Dorothy said: "Pass the wine before you drink it all."

"Another bottle," said Howard.

We got very drunk that night. Long after Dorothy had gone to bed, Howard kept talking to me. I had never had an older brother, but Hunt was beginning to present some notion of one.

Back in the paneled wood study after dinner, he took out a bottle of Courvoisier, and we honed our after-dinner sentiments. Hunt's study must have had fifty photographs on the wall, silver-framed shots of himself and Dorothy in their separate childhoods, then together in Paris; pictures of their children; pictures of Howard playing the saxophone in a college band; Ensign Howard Hunt, USNR; Correspondent Hunt at Guadalcanal; Hunt at the typewriter for one of his

novels; Hunt in a Chinese dugout with a sniper's gun; Hunt on a ski
lift in Austria; Hunt with a brace of pheasants in Mexico; Hunt at the
beach in Acapulco; Hunt in Hollywood; Hunt with antelope horns in
Wyoming; Hunt with ram's horns in I don't know where—he grew
tired of the tour by the time we got to Greece. He gave a wave of
dismissal to himself at the Acropolis, settled in one big leather chair,
and, obviously provident, was able to offer me its mate.

The more we drank, the more confidential he became. In a little
while, he began to call me Hub. I could see a long career for Hub and
quickly offered an explanation (which had no truth) that one of my
twin brothers had such a nickname.

"Back to Harry," he said equably. "Good name, Harry."

"Thank you."

"What do you see for yourself, Harry, down the road?"

"Down the road?"

"Thirty years from now. Do you see a Director's chair, or is it
fur-lined slippers on Retirement Lane?"

"I like this work. I learn something every day. I just want to get
awfully good at it."

"No attacks of conscience?"

"A few, perhaps, but I'm in need of seasoning."

"Good," said Howard and opened his desk drawer. "What I show
you next is in whole confidence."

"Yessir."

"These are personnel evaluations."

"I see."

"We can skip Gatsby and Kearns. I can't send back anything very
good about them."

I couldn't either, so I was silent.

"Porringer gets his B-minus. You do better."

He must have had some second thoughts because he closed his
drawer without removing any papers. "I give Sherman good marks for
hard work and agent-recruitment initiative, but I have to pigeonhole
him. He's Deputy COS level. Can go no higher until he learns to run
a happy Station. That, I am afraid, is going to stick to him, but my job
is to evaluate without tilt."

"I can see the difficulty."

"You present more of a problem. Bill Harvey is a vindictive son
of a bitch, we can all agree, but something unique came out of him.
He labeled you *untrustworthy*—which is a slash to the jugular. Then he

withdrew it a week later. *'On reconsideration,'* he wrote, *'this man is unorthodox but talented and trustworthy.'* When you come up for promotion, the examiner could begin to wonder what caused Harvey's 180-degree change of heart. That does you no great good."

"Yessir." I paused. "Wow," I heard myself say.

"You need a firm, unequivocal *yes* from me."

"I would think so."

"I believe you're going to get it. I see something in you that a lot of good young officers don't have, good as they are. You anticipate. I am going to say that while still inexperienced, you show potential for high echelon. 'Worth keeping an eye on,' is the plus I intend to put in for you."

"Thank you, Howard."

"It is because you have ambition."

Did I? Knowledge versus power had never seemed a painful choice for me. I preferred the first. Did he see something I did not perceive in myself? I do not know if it was the Courvoisier or Hunt's large assessment of my qualities, but I knew the warmth of flattery in all my limbs. As for Harvey's evaluation, I would brood on that tomorrow.

"The key thing, Hub—sorry! *Harry!*—is not to kid oneself. We all want to become Director of Central Intelligence. To me, that means more than being President. Do you feel that way?"

I could hardly answer in the negative. I nodded.

"Hell, I do. I recognize the odds. Howard Hunt has got one shot in twenty, maybe one in fifty—Dorothy says I have the unfortunate habit of being a little too easy on myself. Call it one in a hundred. That particular *one* is a live nerve. It runs from the top of my head to the tip of my toes. Another ten or fifteen years and I might be in real contention for an empyrean slot. So might you be in twenty or twenty-five years."

"I'm beginning to see what good brandy is all about."

"Ha, ha. Say that again, Harry." He fit his words to his actions by taking a sip from the snifter. He had a nifty way of clicking his ring finger against the glass. "Fine. We comprehend the meaning of the endgame. Here's to high purpose." He raised his glass.

"To high purpose."

"Let me line up one more crucial target for your sights. One of these days you are going to get married."

"It's to be expected."

"A good CIA wife has to be a work of art. About the time they

assigned me to Guatemala, Dorothy was well along in her third
pregnancy. I had to leave her behind in Washington during a most
difficult period. So, obviously, there are pros and cons. Career-wise,
being single can prove a plus for the short term. You can pick up and
move anywhere. But over the long haul, it's an Agency minus to be
without a wife. Objectively speaking, the best wife for a Company
man is a rich girl, wholly presentable on the social side, who is
self-sufficient enough to survive without you for months at a time.

"Let's put it this way. So long as you stay unmarried, take advantage of it. Look for every change of Division they offer you. Broaden
your field. Then, when you have the right girl, and I'm talking about
a masterpiece like Dorothy, get married. You can't make COS without that. A Station Chief is his own kind of Ambassador. We're the
embodiment of what foreigners expect of Americans." He pointed a
long finger up from the brandy snifter at a forty-five-degree angle.
"You see, I have a thesis. We Americans abroad are engaged in
Envy-Control. We've shown the globe a way to live that's clean and
prosperous, so they hate us all over the world. Everything we do,
therefore, has to keep an eye on Envy-Control. They may hate us, but
be sure to leave them feeling impotent in that envy. That's where your
woman makes a difference."

All the while he spoke, I was thinking that that was not what I was
in it for. It could have been the brandy, but I did not think I wanted
to be DCI, no, I was here for the double life. In the double life lay
all my hope for sanity, and I nodded wisely as if the brandy and I were
vintage friends.

15

I DID NOT HEAR AGAIN FROM KITTREDGE UNTIL THE WEATHER HAD
turned warm and my second Christmas in Uruguay was approaching.

Dec. 12, 1957

Harry, dear Harry,

I want to hear from you, and to write to you of all that's
happened to me. So much has shifted within.

Of course, I am breaking a promise. (I refuse to call it a vow,
since Hugh extorted it from me. To give one's word when at one's

weakest is not to give the heartfelt word.) On the dubious logic of this, I decided not to tell Hugh that I am going to correspond with you again. He would not agree, and my life with him would, as a result, grow intolerable. I will not submit to his force; he would never accept my rebellion. Our marriage, which has moved equably, and in all honesty, happily, on the foundation of his prodigious care of me when I needed it most, could be thrown into the doldrums again.

   I have obviously learned much. One lives with what works, but the spirit looks for what needs to be added. By this logic, I need your letters. In consequence, the royal itch to deceive Hugh has sprung up in me once more and I'm going to tell you considerably more about myself than you may expect, in fact, I'll soon overwhelm you with a long one.

Guess Who

P.S. It's safe to try the pouch again. New address, however. Still Polly Galen Smith, but new Route, AT–658–NF

   I returned a two-line letter: "Just to say that your Christmas present arrived intact. I await words and music."

Jan. 5, 1958

Dear Harry,

   Christopher might delight you now. What a splendid little fellow your godson has become. Of course, he is also in that frightful stage other mothers have warned me about—he walks, but does not talk! I cannot tell you how fearful a situation this creates, and it could last for many hysterical months to come. The only way to protect the furnishings is to keep Christopher out on the street in his stroller, or penned upstairs. Once he gets into our parlor, he comports himself like a drunken hellion, staggering about, arms out, trying to overturn all our carefully acquired goodies. God, I love him. Each time I shriek, *"No!"* as he is about to knock over my hand-wrought Elfe or the beautiful Pimm, he offers a resolute manly little grin with just a hint of the glint in Hugh's evil eye. Lord, I am awful when I come face to face with my impeccable love of property. Flesh and blood go to the block before antique value.

   I find as I write that I am preparing you for a considerable confession. I don't know that you've been made aware of the real landscape of my mental abdication all those many months ago. Yes, it was due to LSD, and the brooch, and Hugh, and you, all that I have already admitted to, but there were some unmanageable fantasies as well. And serious and most concrete difficulties. The real cause I have never really talked to you about. It was my work in TSS.

I now relate to you that whenever I think of the corpus of offices and corridors composing Technical Services Staff over in our wing of Cockroach Alley, I tend to think of Allen Dulles wrinkling his nose as he walks down our smelly corridors. In my dreams and daydreams he has a tail and a cloven hoof, simple as that. You do know that he was born with a clubfoot? The Dulles family had him operated on quicker than crackers, so he has only had to limp the least little bit through life except when gout strikes his Satanic appetites. Of course, given Allen's tropisms, he did marry a young lady named *Clover*. (Just change the *r* to an *n*.) Harry, forgive this string of sitting ducks, but there are times when I hate Hugh and I hate Allen for they inhabit me, which, I suspect, is what being a good boss is all about.

Well, don't fret—I'm now over on the meditative side of these unruly emotions, and only tell you this to indicate the previous intensity of my feelings. You see, I've felt badly divided at times on the justifiability of the work we do at TSS. So much of it is sheer mind-control. That comes down to manipulating the souls of other people. Yet, here is my Harlot all for mind-control so long as it's the people he approves of who are doing it. Yes, the great war for the human future—Christians versus Reds! And weren't those Russian materialists brilliant to choose all the blood and fire of red as their emblematic color? Brilliant, I say, for it brought a necessary sense of the elemental to fill their materialistic void. Am I wandering? The one concept I've lived with ever since meeting Hugh is that Communists strive twenty-four hours a day to find ways to coerce the soul of humankind, and so we must labor our own twenty-four to confound them. TSS is the temple where we not only search for secret germs but hypnotic manipulations, abracadabra drugs and psychological methods to take over the enemy before they control us. Hugh, indeed, gave me a stiff lecture before we married. It was to the effect (and this is his favorite thesis on the source of vital human energy) that only when the best and worst in oneself is equally attached to the same mission, can one operate with full strength. In an exceptional moment of candor, he said to me, "I am attached to rock climbing because I have to conquer my fear of great falls—that is the good motive—but I also revel in it because I can dominate and humiliate others, and that happens to be an equally deep-rooted part of me." Harry, I was stirred by his candor. I knew that deep under my glowing college-girl exterior were Shakespearean closets of blood, gore, and other unmentionables. I also knew that Hugh was a man who could steer a cool route through such an underworld in me.

Well, my husband-to-be did have his thesis well in hand. He said we were blessed in our work at the Agency because the best and the worst in ourselves could work together on a noble venture. We were to thwart, dominate, and finally conquer the KGB, even as they, expressing by their lights the good and bad in themselves, were engaged, "tragic fellows" (Hugh's words), in an ignoble venture.

So, on I went to TSS with Allen's blessing and Hugh's strong arm around my waist. I was prepared to dive into the dark depths, but, of course, as soon as I finished training, they wrapped me in cotton. Technical Services Staff, as you can guess, is as highly compartmentalized as any place you're going to work in the Agency. Even now, after five years in TSS's recessive folds, I still can't decide such basic things as whether we go in for wet jobs, or, leaving assassination quite to the side, whether we indulge in even worse deeds, such as honest-to-god termination experiments. If one were to believe the more sinister gossip, it's true. Of course, such rumors do come to me in the large from Arnie Rosen, and I'm not sure he's always to be trusted. (He loves wild stories too much!)

Well, the time is come to let you in on a subconfession. About a year and a half ago, Arnold began to work for me, and soon became my number-one assistant. He's brilliant, and he's *bad*. You have to understand *bad* as an old Radcliffe foible. When we used to say that of a male friend, it meant he was homosexual. Arnold—and you are absolutely not to repeat this—is very much in hiding about his predilections. While he says that he's eschewed all sex since he's come into the Company, I don't believe him. All the same, he swears to it. I suppose he must. Apparently, he was a bit of a queen in high school. Hard to imagine. There he must have been, funny-looking, wearing eyeglasses, school valedictorian, all summa grades, of course, but had an addiction to "debasement," as he puts it. He says it like a black man, not one word but two, "dee basement." He is, when you get to know him (and he drops that awful lapdog admiration which he used to put on for Hugh), a wicked and incredibly funny gossip.

When I asked him how he managed to get through the wings of the flutter bird in the entrance tests, he said, "Darling, we people know how to pass a lie-detector. That's part of our lore."

"Well, how *do* you?" I asked.

"I can't possibly tell. It would offend your proprieties."

"I have none," I said.

"Kittredge, you are the most innocent and locked-up person I know."

"Tell me," I said.

"Darling, we eat a lot of beans."

"Beans?" I didn't get it. Not at all.

"Once you know when the test will be given, the rest is merely a small bout of discomfort. In anticipation, you eat a good plateful of beans."

I slapped his hand. "Arnie, you're a psychopathic liar."

"I am not. The idea is be able to think of nothing but your bowels while you are being fluttered. Your mind couldn't care less whether or not it is telling a lie when the prime drama is to control your sphincter. I can tell you that the test administrator got awfully annoyed with me. 'You're one of those,' he said. 'General tension in all responses. It's hopeless.' 'I'm so sorry, sir,' I told him. 'It must be something I ate.' "

Harry, he's a bit of a demon. If I'd never thought of Alpha and Omega before, Arnie Rosen's existence would have suggested it. He has two totally different personalities—the one I expect that you are familiar with, and this considerably different one for me. I think Hugh had him attached to my court so I'd have at least one wise fellow around. He certainly indulges my outsized curiosity about some of the very strange people one does pass in the corridor. Rosen is full of whispers as to what might be going on. "Kittredge, feel the aura coming off that closed door! It's Dracula's Lair!"

I accept that. I believe it. But, then I wonder if I am hypersensitive to the occult. (One full summer and a half ago, you may recall that I encountered the ghost of Augustus Farr up at the Keep, and to my over-fevered recollection, he limped just like Allen on a bad day. Ho, ho, ho.)

Well, I want to bring you back a few years more than that. To the time when I was wrapped in cotton. Allen Dulles had taken to my Radcliffe senior thesis on Alpha and Omega so completely that he funded me right from the start. On the completion of my Farm training—do you remember that that was the spring we met?—I was set up with a bona fide group of five graduate students in psychology at Cornell who did not even know they were being paid by the Agency. Another bit of nifty cover. I used to fly up to my seminar in Ithaca every two weeks to see how research was progressing.

By every visible measure, I was doing nothing dirty. I was merely developing my chosen work. I may have been a little in love with Allen during those first couple of years. If not for Hugh, I could actually have contemplated going to bed with the man. Allen was *dear*. I certainly loved him enough to want to develop something of exceptional use for him. So I dashed off in the wrong direction. Instead of pursuing Alpha and Omega a little further into the labyrinth of myself, and serving as my own laboratory which—all proportions kept—is what grand old Master Plumber Freud did, that is, spent many years analyzing himself before giving us ego and id, I absconded from my floods and raging furnaces, and went searching too quickly for overt tests the Agency could use to spot a potential agent.

I worked for the last five years, therefore, trying to elaborate a test profile that could be used to detect potential treachery. The final form, as of eight months ago, shows up as twenty test sheets with twenty-five items to check off on each page, and at certain levels we were as good at predicting mental disorders as a Szondi test or a Rorschach.

Extracting a reliable Alpha-Omega profile, however, is back-breaking. We learned to our horror that Long Tom (our in-house term for the five hundred pairings) has to be taken a minimum of five times in order to pick up the style of transition from Alpha to Omega. While certain kinds of bureaucrats keep the two personae wholly separate for years, actors and psychopaths can go back and forth twenty times a day. For such people, the test has to be repeated, therefore, at different hours of the day. Dawn and midnight, so to speak. Drunk and sober. We did end with a pretty foolproof set of vectors to spot a putative agent, or even better, a putative double agent, but administering Long Tom was more difficult than raising orchids.

Harry, for the last five years, I have carried this burden of woe, doubt, misery, and burgeoning frustration. And every year, across the corridor, so to speak—actually, he works out of town—another psychologist named Gittinger, who came to us from his work at the State Hospital in Norman, Oklahoma, has been running rings

around my tests merely by adapting the good old Wechsler Intelligence test to what he calls the Wechsler-Bellevue G. It works. Gittinger, who's a stocky Santa Claus type with a pepper-and-salt goatee,
can use his battery of tests (which require only one session) to spot
defectors and putatives better, I fear, than I can.

Rosen, by the time we came to trust each other, began to
warn me of the turn in affairs: The Wechsler-Gittinger was prospering
at TSS, and I was not.

"What are they really saying?" I asked him at last.

"Well, there is some talk that your work may be only a lot of
talk."

That hurt. Then I had to deal with the news that Gittinger
had been allocated some scrumptious funding through one of our
more elegant foundation covers. He can now play with the Human
Ecology Fund. Whereas my seminar at Cornell has not been renewed.

This has been my introduction to the down slope. Harry, life
has always treated me as a darling, and for much too long. If my
mother merely adored me whenever she came around to noticing my
existence, my father more than made up for it. Ever been fêted by a
rip-roaring Shakespearean? We never did get into formal incest, Dad
and I, but I knew what it was to feel a powerful man's love at the age
of three. It never faltered. Just grew more and more possessive. How
Daddy hated Hugh. I think that's the first storm of passion I ever
encountered out of books. Up to then, our princess trod only on
carpet. Radcliffe was a coronation. I was either adored all over again,
or envied, or both, and didn't even notice. My brain was so fertile that
I could have gone off to a desert island and been deliriously happy
with myself. The only pains I knew were the ferocious congestions
attendant on new ideas. Lord, they were forever streaming into my
thoughts. And as Hugh's wife, *figure-toi*! I was twenty-three years old,
yet grizzled veterans of the intelligence wars were lining up to charm
me. Darling, was ever a brilliant fool more spoiled?

Now, at TSS, after five years, I was on the down slope, and
Gittinger was growing greater by the week and month. Yet it proved
impossible to dislike the man. He's a wise, subtle, jolly Oklahoman
who, as Arnie says, uses his twang like a guitar string. Gittinger has the
power to dispense happy laughter. Sometimes he shows off for us.
Give him a Wechsler-Bellevue G test-profile of a man or woman he
has never met and he will return an interpretation that is about as
complete as a personage out of Proust. Truly formidable. Gittinger is

the only one in the profession who can get such a splendid readout off a mere Wechsler-Bellevue G, but then he works twenty-four hours a day, and has the ability to correlate everything that comes his way, agents, taps, sneakies, verbal interviews, photos (for body language), and handwriting analysis. He charms all of us, because he is, or pretends to be, a modest man. Always downgrades his own work. "Another fellow could do as well with Tarot cards." So he charms all the competitors he's outstripping. (Although it did hurt when Rosen told me that everyone now referred to Gittinger as "our resident genius.") Harry, there was a time when they spoke that way of me. So I knew the pains of a toppled monarch. Yet G. always flatters me. "Your Alpha and Omega will take us yet into the true caves. I just make charts of the surface."

That's all very well, but I've lost out wholly. Gittinger is already working in the field with case officers and agents (wherever a Chief of Station will allow this) and I have become one of his adjuncts. *The Gardiner Annex to Gittinger*, you could call it.

Harry, hear the worst. Shortly before my LSD episode, I had been cut down to one assistant, Rosen, and put onto collation studies with our graphology department. Instead of showing our handwriting experts how to look for Alpha and Omega, the graphologists were now giving ratings to my work.

About this time, Arnold had a long talk with me. It was a preface, I knew, to telling me that he was going to apply for a transfer over to Gittinger's track. "Loyalty is a virtue," he said at last, "but I want to get out of *dee basement*." Suddenly, it was no longer so funny. I saw it through his eyes. To be Jewish in the Agency doesn't call for an automatic welcome, but then to be locked up as well in his little secret. However, he did seem miserable at his own ambition. He also warned me that the time had come for Hugh to intervene.

"Kittredge, you have real enemies in TSS."

"You'd better name a few, or I won't listen to this."

"I can't point to the real estate. It could be some of Hugh's enemies."

"You mean I can't even create antagonists of my own?" God, we were having coffee in the K-shed cafeteria at three in the afternoon, and Rosen was sitting across from me with tears in his eyes. I felt like screaming. "I think I've created a few enemies of my own," I said.

"Maybe you did."

"I was too cocky when I began."

"Yes," he said, "probably."

"And I did show a little too much disdain for some of my colleagues."

"Oh, you know you did." He was virtually crooning.

"I was uncooperative with my overseers. Especially when they wanted to change my terminology."

"Yes."

"But all that was in the beginning. Lately, my worst crime has been to obtain a few extra perks for my best research assistant."

This was meant to stun him precisely between the eyes. It only brought out his anger. I think he was looking to find that anger. "Kittredge, let's go back to your office," he said. "I've got some yelling to do myself."

Whereupon, once we made the long, endlessly long, silent walk back down Cockroach Alley, he did unload a bit. "The fact, Kittredge, is that there's a fundamental flaw in the test. Putative agents make prodigiously good liars. They're not going to reveal themselves just because Mrs. Gardiner Montague has devised a few word games."

"How dare you," I said. "We've loaded the thing with traps."

"Kittredge, I love you," he said, "but whom have you trapped? I just don't think the damn thing works. And I will not spend my life supporting an enterprise that can't stand up."

"Apart from all these tests, don't you believe in Alpha and Omega?"

"I believe in them, dear one. As metaphor."

Well, we were through, and we knew it.

"Arnold, before you leave, tell me the real worst. What are they saying? Metaphor is not the word they are employing."

"You don't want to hear."

"I believe you owe me that much."

"All right." I realized suddenly that he was not a silly man nor a weak man, nor even a witty scamp. Under all, was the person who will yet come out of some further resolution of his impossible A and O, the future gentleman was there before me, a most steady and resolute fellow. We will hear from Arnold Rosen yet. "Kittredge," he said, "the common notion here at TSS is that Alpha and Omega do not really exist. Alpha is merely a new way to describe consciousness, and Omega is a surrogate concept for the unconscious."

"They still can't get it through their heads. How often must I say that Alpha and Omega each possesses its own unconscious. And superego and ego."

"Everyone knows that, Kittredge. But when we try to apply it, we keep being brought back to consciousness and the unconscious all over again, and Alpha is the first and Omega the second. Let me say that such people are not the worst of your detractors."

"Tell me, as I have asked you more than once, what the worst are saying."

"I don't care to."

"As a species of final contribution."

"Very well." He looked into the whorls of his fingertips. "Kittredge, the cognoscenti have decided that your concept of Alpha and Omega is a whole-cloth projection of what can only be your latent schizophrenia. I am sorry."

He got up, he extended his hand, and, do you know, I took it. We shook hands limply. I think we were mourning the end of our work together. Despite all. Since then, I've only seen him in the cafeteria and the corridor. I miss his wit, I will testify to that.

Now, Harry, I couldn't keep this last blow to myself. I told it all to Hugh and he set up a meeting with Dulles and Helms. Hugh probably thought I should pull my own potatoes out of the fire, but I wouldn't go. I could hardly be present to plead my own case if I were being accused of schizophrenia. Well, Dulles told Hugh that he did not for a moment believe my thesis was a projection of my own schizophrenia. What a shocking notion. No, for them, Kittredge's theory remained, as always, profound. "I would even," said Dulles, "call it sacrosanct."

Helms then spoke: Kittredge, in his opinion, was to be seen as a most innovative inventor. Such creative originality often suffered in unfair fashion. "The trouble," he said, "is that we have a psychological reality to deal with. The rank and file in TSS do tend to see Alpha and Omega as some kind of sound-and-light show."

"*Paranoid* sound-and-light show?" asked Hugh.

"Look," said Helms, "we can bat these words back and forth until the courts are too dark to play upon. The crucial difficulty is that it's one thing to support an underground circus like TSS, but it is absolutely *verboten* to let word get around that it is a freak show. Kittredge has had five years and an absence of conclusive results. We've got to find another *boulot* for her."

Boulot. Old argot for *job*, kiddo. Harry, I've never seen Hugh quite as upset as when he related this conversation to me. Do you know, it was on the day your brooch arrived. That may explain a few things. I plunged right off into the LSD. Anything to come up with a new grasp on the testing process. I took terrible travels on that little trip. My vision led me down a long purple road to phosphorescent pools of moonlight where pigs were wading, and worse. I was a young man disporting in a brothel.

These days, I put in four sessions a week on graphology, a fascinating business after all. And I still pursue a few thoughts on the development of Alpha and Omega. Oh, I'll be back, I promise I'll be back.

Now you can see, however, why I want to hear about your life again. And in detail. I sense all over again that I do not know enough about the details of my own life. I certainly never knew how many fellow workers, often strangers, were determining my fate. Your letters give me some understanding there.

Harry, write again. I am truly fascinated with how you spend your days. It seems so long since I've held one of your full letters in my hand. What has happened to AV/OCADO and his tormented soul? And what of your Russian garden parties and dear Hyman Bosqueverde and his wife who whispers nice things about Gordy Morewood? Yes, give me all the rest, your Gatsby with his yellow hair and the dark-brown mustache that Howard Hunt made him remove? You see, I do remember, and want to know more.

You can even write to me about your upwardly mobile COS. I realize now why I disliked Mr. Hunt. He was that worldly principle I was secretly unequipped to deal with. But no longer will I indulge such prejudices. If one would have new ideas, one must find a way to renew oneself. So tell me all about him too. My curiosity deepens, my strictures become flexible. My love for you will always grow apace, dear long absent man.

                                                                Kittredge

16

THE LETTER WAS WRITTEN IN HER SMALL GOTHIC SCRIPT. BY THE TIME
I was done, longing had thrown another noose around my wish to
escape from love.

Jan. 11, 1958

Dearest Kittredge,

I will not try to tell you how near your letter brought you to
me. How deep, how damnable, and how unfair it must all have felt.
I see now why my letters, with their small details, have been agreeable
to you. Let me try to divert you, then. Here at this Station on a busy
day, when two or three things are coming to a boil (or coming apart),
one feels in the midst of a Rube Goldberg machine. Right now, on
Saturday afternoon, it is quiet—a rare occasion!—a quiet Saturday
afternoon in the midst of our January summer. Everyone I know is at
one or another of our clay beaches and coffee-colored sea. It's hot, and
I sit in my shorts, still in the same cheap hotel room, believe it or
not—I'm one of their three oldest residents by now. Kittredge, I pride
myself at how little I need of material things. On the other hand, I
virtually percolate with pleasure in enumerating Station activities. I
feel as if that is my store, and I'm taking proud inventory.

Here is a good portion of the news. The Bosqueverdes have
two awful Washington people from the Soviet Russia Division virtually bivouacked in their quarters. On Tuesday nights, in another part
of town, AV/ALANCHE is fighting pitched battles against the left
student youth group, MRO. AV/ALANCHE are the sign painters, do
you recollect? And there's still Peones and Libertad, and Chevi Fuertes
to bring you up on, plus the Russians, which is to say, our one Russian
couple. I am now on good visiting terms with Masarov and his wife.
Yes, the greatest single change is that I am, under the most stringent
precautions you can imagine, permitted, even encouraged, to cultivate a relationship with Masarov. It has turned the pockets of my inner
life inside out.

Before commencing, however, I must tell you, Kittredge,
how much I adore you. I am absolutely confounded that anyone in
our line of work can doubt for one moment the existence of Alpha

and Omega. Well, a good writing teacher I know at Yale said never to use qualifiers like absolutely unless one was hopelessly in love. Absolutely not.

To my good friend Boris Gennadyevitch Masarov and his gypsy wife, Zenia, then. (She told me once that she was one-nineteenth gypsy.)

"One-nineteenth?" I asked her.

"You are brutal as Russian with fascination for facts, figures, numbers," she responded.

"One-nineteenth?" I inquired again.

"Are good-looking young man. Why ask silly question?"

Having set down this exchange, I see that I have failed to present her quality. She is not shallow. She carries herself as if nothing has transpired in Russia of any moment since Dostoyevsky was saved from the firing squad by the czar's reprieve. I suppose I am saying that she elicits a chord in one's historical appreciation. I now know how an aristocratic woman of the provinces might appear to us in the middle of the nineteenth century. The best of Russian literature comes alive for me when I am around Zenia. So many of Turgenev's dissatisfied women come to mind, and Chekhov's incomparable glimpses of the Russian provinces. Zenia is all of them for me, and more. Yet, she is also a woman who has lived under the horrors of Stalin. Kittredge, you can feel the depredations of Soviet history through the sense one receives of her much-battered soul. While she looks over forty, the Russians show their age in ways we do not. Do you know, I believe they take a certain grim satisfaction in wearing their souls on the wrinkled surface of their face. We Americans would, of course, go squeak before we'd ever let anyone have the satisfaction of thinking he was looking into our spiritual depths, but that may be exactly what the Russians have to offer. "I have passed through cataclysmic days, and permitted state horrors to be visited on friends, but I have never lied to my soul." That is what her face says to me. (She has the most extraordinary deep dark eyes—operative definition of "Otchi Chorniya.") Yet she has to have been around frightful events. She is KGB, after all. Or at least her husband is. Then she tells me that she is thirty-three. Yes, history has cut its lines into Russian faces.

Well, here I am, rushing new people on to you without the courtesy of a little development, but then this friendship with the

Masarovs is the most interesting relation I have at present with anyone in Uruguay, even if it has been put together like an arranged marriage with brokers on both sides.

It began because here in Montevideo we are sometimes a working part of the State Department. "Our cover folds us into the crust" has become one of Hunt's sayings. Of course, he doesn't exactly hate the idea of pretending to be First Secretary to the American Ambassador. As you may recall, that worthy, Jefferson Patterson, Eisenhower's appointee, is a genteel man with a hopeless stammer in English and it gets worse when he attempts Spanish. So, Patterson continues to avoid functions. His deputy, the Counselor, is all right, but his wife, a lush, has been known to take off her shoes at Embassy dances and embark on impromptu high kicks—"*Grands jetés*," she announces. Needless to say, they took her off the circuit. Which leaves the field open to the Hunts, and, on occasion, the Porringers, and myself.

Combine this with the State Department's estimate that Khrushchev's constant appeals lately for armament reductions, while clearly not to be trusted, must be met, nonetheless, with compensatory American moves. We-cannot-lose-another-contest-for-world-opinion is the present State Department stance. Word has even come to us from Western Hemisphere Division: Carefully monitored fraternizing with the Soviets is a viable option. Theoretically, we're always prepared to get friendly with any Soviet who throws us a side glance, but as a practical matter, whenever small conversations commence around the canapé tables, we comport ourselves as if we are offering Christmas politesse to lepers. You don't put a career on the line by fraternizing for too little.

Well, the directive has come in. And we have certainly heated up the GOGOL outpost (which is how we refer to the Bosqueverdes) now that the Russian garden parties are going again. The Sourballs thought enough of this opportunity to send down two of their operators. Nearly all of Soviet Russia Div's people are anti–Soviet Russians, or Poles, or Finns, intensely fluent in Russian. They do make an odd breed. Paranoid and insular to an extraordinary degree, they give off about as much warmth as a barnacle. Yet they sport what could be Irish names if not for the odd spelling. Monikers like Heulihaen (pronounced Hoolihan) and Flarrety (pronounced Flaherty). Heulihaen and Flarrety have been installed on separate eight-hour stints at GOGOL outpost for the last month, and have been photographing the very hell out of the lawn parties in the Soviet Embassy garden.

Hunt calls them our Finnish Micks. Left to themselves, the Finnish Micks would pass over to us about as much information as you could get from a Mickey Finn, but Hunt knows how to play the web back at Cockroach Alley. Result: The Finnish Micks grudgingly provide us with bits of poop and scam.

The largest discovery (accomplished by way of filming the Russians and their guests in the garden, then studying these home movies around the clock) is that a bit of infidelity is going on behind Soviet Embassy walls. There seems a likely connection between the new Soviet KGB chief, the *Resident,* named Varkhov, Georgi Varkhov, who looks exactly as he should, built like a tank, shaved head like a bullet, and—are you wholly prepared?—our own soulful Zenia.

Now, I was apprised of this item after I became friendly, all proportions kept, with the Masarovs. I still think Zenia is soulful, although her taste for Varkhov, if true, puts me off. The Finnish Micks, however, seem pretty certain of their ground. The working logic for such conclusions, as I piece it out, comes to this: In social life, we are always surrounded by hints of infidelity at every party. We see smiles, whispers, glances—all that movie-business sign language. Yet our perceptions are transitory. Hints of behavior are everywhere, but we usually cannot confirm what we have seen. On film, however, if we expend the patience to reexamine each move of our actors, the indeterminate can crystallize into the concrete. By such methods are we provided with a 75-percent certainty that Zenia Masarov and Georgi Varkhov are having a liaison, and Boris Gennadyevitch Masarov is aware of the situation.

I hate to terminate at just this place but an urgent phone call involving my work has just come in. Since I have to go by the Embassy, I will post this letter and do my best to carry it up to date tomorrow. Hopefully, I can send a full account then. Forgive such a brusque ending.

Love,
Herrick

17

THE URGENT PHONE CALL DID NOT INVOLVE MY WORK BUT WAS FROM Sally. She had to be with me. She had just been to the doctor; she was pregnant.

Lately, I had been attempting to see her less often, but the results had been inconclusive. Now she was pregnant. My poor Sally was honest, or honest enough when pushed to the truth (since I did push her), to admit she had also had intercourse with Sherman in this period. She did not know whose child it was. Although she would swear it was mine.

I felt close to nausea. Soon, I recognized that she felt worse. She would not have an abortion, she told me. She would proceed to have the child—"And," she said, "let's hope he doesn't look too much like you." If it was a boy, she was certain it would be mine. Her logic seemed unassailable to her. "I want him to look a little like you," she said.

We sat on the edge of my bed, grasping each other in the way of beggars who hope to draw warmth out of the gnawing hole within themselves. For the first time, we neither took off our clothes nor made love with them on. Even as I pressed her to have an abortion, I knew she would refuse, and found a demon within my inmost worm. The thought that I would be having a child closeted in the home of Sherman Porringer did appeal to a very small part of me. I understood suddenly that evil did not have to be all-consuming, it need touch no more than one rare nerve. I did my best to tell myself that it might be Sherman's child after all. Then I decided that it did not matter. Sherman, devoted habitué of every good (and low) brothel in Montevideo, deserved whatever he got. It also occurred to me that he could have syphilis (in which case, so could I), although, loyal hog to modern medicine, Porringer was always consuming each new antibiotic that came into the Embassy pharmacy. He was a walking myocinizine of a penisulfamilimide.

Sally departed to the tune of mutual agreements to discuss these matters further. I even thought of the child to come. That finally gave me one fine pang. Some part of me might soon be trapped beneath Porringer's roof. I consoled myself with the thought that Sally would be a passionate and loving mother, albeit a loud one with a register of shrieks for the spills and slops of childhood.

I had certainly lost my Saturday. That night I did go to the Embassy, laid my letter into the box for the State Department pouch, and went home to write again.

January 11, 1958

Dear Kittredge,

It's midnight just about. Work has come, work has gone—a crisis with Fuertes proved not critical. I'll fill you in before too long on our Uruguay ace, but prefer first to expatiate on my new KGB cronies.

Of course, I can still hear one instructor at the Farm saying, "Expatiate!" That dependable Agency exhortation! The-space-you-ate, Hubbard, bring-forth-the-space-you-ate—as if memory were a mighty maw. Hark to these wings of metaphor! The truth is that I feel giddy writing to you again. Can it be the altitude? In case I haven't told you, after Luxembourg, Uruguay is the flattest country in the world. At sea level, too. Do you know I've had four drinks with an avocado.

I apologize. I feel just a little too much vertigo to go on. I'll sleep and pick this up tomorrow.

Sunday morning

It's now January 12th, and I will not tear up last night's final *pensées*. I believe, despite the evidence above, that my wits show their own curious gait when I'm drunk.

To the Masarovs. Some time ago, Varkhov, the Resident at the Russian Embassy, invited us to a large party. After cable exchanges with the Groogs and the Sourballs, we accepted. Hunt led the State Department delegation, and Porringer and I took up our cover as First Assistant and Second Assistant to the First Secretary to the Ambassador—shades of Gilbert and Sullivan! Hunt, looking over our team, decided that I needed a date.

"How about Libertad La Lengua?" I said to that.

"How about Nancy Waterston," he replied.

I'm sure it's been so long since I mentioned our Administrative Officer that I must refresh your memory. I believe I described Nancy once as sweet, bright, and hardworking but undeniably plain and very much a spinster. She used to be devoted to Mayhew, and Hunt now gets ditto loyalty. In the beginning, I took her out a couple of times when Mrs. Sonderstrom or Mrs. Porringer or Mrs. Gatsby or Mrs. Kearns couldn't find an unattached single girl for me. Nancy has to be ten years older than myself, and I would guess that she has never been to bed with a man.

Well, if it had been the Swiss Embassy, or even the Embajada de Gran Bretaña, I would have accepted the chore, but I felt curiously diminished to enter the Soviet lair with Nancy on my arm.

Hunt would have none of these niceties. "Do you know the meaning of 'The Colonel requests'?" he asked.

"Howard, Nancy won't enjoy herself."

"She will."

He laughed a lot at that in the sky-high skinny whinny you so detest. He has a long middle finger, and for the life of me, Kittredge (and I hope my candor will not put you off), I had an image of Howard inserting that finger into the poor chaste fold of Miss Waterston. It was the oddest flash to come into the conversation. I saw the finger probing back and forth—a series of wholly authoritative strokes. The mind takes us where it will, won't it?

"You look a little glassy-eyed," said Hunt.

"What is your motive?" I asked about as coldly as I dared.

"It's a ploy, Harry. The King Brothers won't know what to make of you and Nancy."

"They'll see right through it."

"Well, kid, they might not. Because I want you to introduce Nancy as your fiancée."

"Have you asked her?"

"She's amenable. It'll be fun for her."

"Howard," I said, "tell me the real motive. It will go down easier."

"The Sovs are always running a dupe-show on us. I've seen one of their joy-boys with three different Russian tomatoes at three different foreign embassy functions. Each time, the same fellow has the gall to introduce the *lady*"—he held both hands far apart and dipped quotation marks with bent fingers—"as his wife. The time has come to show them a little of our dipsy doodle."

Well, Kittredge, it ended up being quite an evening. We arrived at the Russian Embassy on a Saturday in late afternoon and the light was kind to the soft yellow tones of their stone manse. Like much of Montevideo architecture, it is a hodgepodge of Italian Renaissance, French Baroque, Transylvanian Gothic, Oak Park, Illinois, circa

1912, and plain old Russian samovar, a big sprawling villa with massive doors and turrets and ingrown balconies that look like ingrown toenails, dwarf windows and magnum windows, forbidding outer gates, black-spiked fence with painted gold tips on the spearheads. "Bluebeard's castle," I whispered to Nancy as we entered the outer gate and were steered by a wholly uncompromising young Russian marine to the garden. I had an unruly impulse to look up at the Bosqueverdes' window where the Bolex H-16 is posted, and give a clenched fist of a Communist salute to the Finnish Micks.

Well, I've never described an embassy party on the theory that you're familiar enough with them in Washington, so why be offered details of our lesser spread? Still, the Russians do it up. They had invited about every foreign gang in town—Norway, Greece, Japan, Portugal, Costa Rica, name it, even the Orden Soberana de Malta, the Reino de Bélgica, and the República Socialista de Checoslovaquia. By the time the international tide was in, there may have been one hundred and fifty people on that lawn drawn from as many as forty embassies and consulates. A Soviet offering of hospitality to the world: one ton of black caviar, endless supplies of vodka, plus the usual array of appetizers, most of which struck the eye like a bead of acid-green pigment on a mound of cadmium orange. They also serve red wine and white wine from the Caucasus—some of the worst stuff ever corked—and all the foreign embassy types did their best to practice English on me. There is something so prodigiously fraudulent about the congealed friendliness of these embassy types. Such anxiety in the air. Everyone stirs with the restlessness of birds.

All this was exacerbated by the presence of Americans in the Russian garden. How I wish you could have been here. Your beauty would have polarized the greensward. As it was, I anticipated in advance just how it was going to show in the films. From above, each American and each Russian was the center of a cluster of foreign embassy types. Caught by a telephoto lens, pieces of information seem equal to particles of food. Tongues dart out to snatch each morsel.

Afternoon opened onto twilight, and another mood settled in. Everyone got a little wild (by which I mean no more than a shade over into the indiscreet). Hunt tells me that movie people call this time of day the magic hour since the natural light is soft and wonderful, but the scene has to be captured on film in thirty minutes. (If I ever have to face a firing squad, I hope it's in a garden at twilight—what a thought!) I kept picturing the frustrations of Heulihaen and Flarrety as they bore down on us with their lens and (it better be) ultra-high-speed film. Of course, the more we all acted up at the party, the less light there was to satisfy our Finns.

Pretty soon, those minor and major embassies who happen on this day to have no particular business to initiate begin to leave, and the lawn opens for dramatic action. Now you can pick up what is happening across the garden. Hunt is talking to Varkhov, who in turn is paying court to Dorothy. Before long, Zenia takes a stroll from the Foreign Office to the KGB, which is to say leaves two of Great Britain's officials to join her Resident, and she and Varkhov now laugh loudly at Hunt's jokes. In another corner of the garden, a joy-boy (from Irkutsk, no doubt) is flirting with Sally Porringer, who no longer seems afraid that Sherman will put her tit in a wringer, and I, giddy from caviar after a year of eating meat twice a day, and not impervious to the vodka, move in on Boris Masarov, keeping Nancy at my side. "I want you to meet my fiancée," I say in the best good humor, as if the idea were mine all along.

Kittredge, I must tell you. Given my schooling, I am only now learning what wonderful and mysterious beings women are. I confess it. Nancy Waterston, whose face on a good day would give competition to a parson's daughter, narrow, pinched, and all her features pulled by duty, her small bust unable to protrude beyond the forward hunch of her shoulders, now looked as attractive as if sparklers had been set off on her wedding cake. When a plain woman looks dazzling for an instant, one's breath stands still; the universe is full of surprise. (Which is equal to saying, I suppose, that the universe is meaningful.)

Masarov reacted formally. "I congratulate you," he said. "I lift glass to toast vital spirit of future marriage."

"Mr. Masarov, that is a distinguished toast," said Nancy in her good Midwestern accent so cram-packed with honest step-by-step sentiment. But then she gave a little laugh as such honesty came face to face with her present role. "Maybe you will attend our wedding," she said.

"It will be when?" he asked, and I could not help but notice that he was looking down the length of the lawn to where Zenia and Varkhov were still talking to Hunt and Dorothy. The anguish on Masarov's face (which I cannot say I would have perceived had not the Zenia-Varkhov liaison been advertised to me as a 75-percent likelihood) now seemed analogous to the wound of a tired animal who pauses, blood dripping, before gathering itself to climb one more hill. He downed his drink in a shot and stopped a Uruguayan waiter who was carrying an ice-cold bottle of vodka on a tray.

"We don't know the date yet," said Nancy, "because I believe in long engagements." Was she drunk, I wondered, or merely intoxicated by newfound talents? "That's an old family institution," she told him. "My father and mother went together seven years before their wedding bells spoke up long enough to say, 'Enough of this. Please ring us. We're rusty.'"

"Yes," he said, "may I ask? What does your father do?"

"He's a circus acrobat," said Nancy, and giggled again. Her eyes were dancing behind her eyeglasses. I realized, as if I were cleansing the inside of myself with the nicest pomade of compassion and sweet sorrow, that this must be the liveliest evening she had had in Uruguay. "No," she said, "our country was founded on the idea that you cannot tell a lie. My father is retired, but he used to be a corporate executive in insurance in Akron, Ohio."

Masarov looked relieved, as if a piece of intelligence had just checked out. "My country was not founded," he said in reply. "More likely, was shot out of a cannon."

Be certain, I underlined that last remark for referral to Hunt. Masarov held up his glass. "Toast to future nuptials."

"I like being toasted," said Nancy.

"First, however, learn to drink our vodka. Americans are always telling me is hard to keep up with Russian banquets. Because they do not know secret."

"Oh, give me the secret," she said.

At just this juncture, Varkhov, who was making a tour of his remaining guests, joined us, and jumped in so quickly on Masarov's speech that I realized both men were equally well used to informing all and sundry how to imbibe Russian spirits. Varkhov's syntax in English, however, was what an instructor at the Farm once called *Russky Tarzan*. Articles, pronouns, and the verb *to be* withered away. Primeval grunts were substituted.

"Not sipping," he said. "Never sipping. Gulp vodka. Only"—Varkhov held up one Russian commissar of a flat, heavy palm—"offer toast. First! Deepest toast. Appraisal of relationship. From heart. Offered from heart, drink vodka in gulp." Which he did, and whistled for the waiter to come back. "Fill glasses. Not worry. Small glasses."

We filled glasses. "After vodka," he said, "eat caviar. Better, eat *zakushki*. Appetizer."

"Yes," said Nancy, as if she were well used to obeying orders.

"Then, darling lady never drunk."

"Ho, ho, ho," said I.

"Cynic," said Varkhov.

He held up his glass again. "Toast," he said. "To evening, to future of peace, to lovely lady, to American with mission," and he winked at me. We were all drunk, yessiree baby.

Outside on the Bulevar España you could hear the traffic going to and fro between the city to our right and Pocitos Beach, with its high-rise apartment houses, down to the left. I thought of the safe house where Chevi and I meet. From side streets, the tangential whoops of adolescents ricocheted through the evening air. Quite as abruptly as he had joined us, Varkhov bowed and left for another group.

"Do you play chess?" Masarov asked me.

"Yes," I said, "not all that well."

"But not so badly?"

"I can play," I said.

"Good. You must be very good. I will invite you to my home. It is nearby. And you, Miss Waterston."

"Name the date, I'll bring the cake," she said.

"An old American expression?" he asked. Was I reading too much into him, or was it said with something like longing? He not only spoke reasonably good English but seemed to take pleasure in it.

"No," she answered, "it's as hometown and hicky as you can get."

"Hometown and hicky," he repeated. "Hicky is . . . pustule, pimple?"

"Just about," said Nancy.

Kittredge, this was the hot core of the evening. The string was thrown across the abyss and now the cord and rope will follow. Indeed, it has. I will tell you in my next letter about the evening with the Masarovs.

> My love to you, to Hugh, and to Christopher,
> Harry the Betrothed

In my letter, I had jumped conveniently over the rest of the evening. Nancy was drunk and said she had eaten too many appetizers, so I took her home. Home proved to be three rooms on the second floor of a modest villa on the Calle Doctor Geraldo Ramón not three blocks from the Embassy. "I think freedom consists of being able to walk to work in the morning," she told me in most certain, if inebriated, terms. She certainly had a second voice installed behind the first. I made the mistake of kissing her.

She kissed back as if we were indeed betrothed and getting married tomorrow. I was discovering that the mouth of a virgin spinster was not like others. Her lips pressed against mine, a family seal upon wax. Her teeth offered the faint odor of dentifrice, mouthwash, and tooth inlay, but her breath was a furnace, and back of that was some baleful neutral zone inspired by her stomach. I had an awful set of impulses I could never have been able to confess to Kittredge. I knew that Nancy Waterston could be mine forever if I chose, and the centrality of such power stirred something awfully cold in me. The image I had had of Hunt's finger stroking her vagina with precise professional strokes became the image of my finger. I had been using him as a cover story for my own impulses. It was then I kissed her a second time on the cheek, assured her that it had been a remarkable evening and perhaps we would visit the Masarovs together, and made my exit much impressed with the ability of one kiss to conduct me right up to the edge of a possible marriage.

On the way home, I had time to recollect that Sally (not at all witting of Hunt's improvised matchmaking) had had time to pass me on the lawn, and say, in a husky, shaky whisper which did not promise to be kept down for long, "Cheap son of a bitch, you could at least have some taste."

My immediate concern, however, was that the Finnish Micks might be photographing her lips. Quickly, I said: "A ploy. Hunt's idea. Don't zoom, Sally," and raised my glass in the salute you give to Company wives in whom you have no interest larger than minimal courtesy.

Only now, driving home, did it occur to me that the Russians may also have had a camera trained on the garden. They would have seen my face. What would my words communicate to them? *"A ploy. Hunt's idea. Don't zoom."* I might have given away much too much. On the other hand, it could prove rich in interpretation for Soviet eyes and send them off into far-flung scenarios.

One of Harlot's thoughts now came back to me. Evil, he had once informed me, was to know what was good, and do one's best to tamper with it. Whereas wickedness was merely one's readiness to raise the stakes when one did not know what one was doing. By that measure, I was wicked. It also occurred to me for a moment that everything we were doing in Uruguay might by that logic be equally wicked, but then I recognized that I did not care. Let no one say that the innocent are always good. I drove on to bed.

18

January 27, 1958

Dearest Kittredge,

I was hoping for a letter, but perhaps you are waiting to hear more about the Masarovs. In any event, I feel like writing. You see, I'm obliged to report these days on each step taken with Boris and Zenia. Then the Groogs and Sourballs masticate my cables down to the molecules.

As one example of the present work mode, the Groogs and Sours decide in concert with Hunt (for he refuses to be bypassed on any decision, minor or major) that Nancy should not accompany me to the Masarov home. Their reasoning is that a continuing presentation of Miss Waterston and myself as prospective bride and groom might put our histrionic abilities to too great a test—Nancy's, anyway, Hunt allows. I suspect that Hunt messed up in the first place by putting an Administrative Officer like Nancy into such a slot.

At any rate, Miss Waterston was sufficiently disappointed to show chagrin. "Oh, fudge," she said, "oh, fudge and yee-God crackers," so help me, Kittredge, is what she said. Then, with a sigh and a formal, professional smile—Lord, she is professional—she went back to auditing one more of Gordy Morewood's Byzantine accounts. Poor Nancy—she is so weathered by disappointment.

Meanwhile, I get ready to visit the Masarovs. I call, and, via Hunt's specific instructions, make the date for Nancy and myself. The idea is to keep Zenia at home with Boris. If she knows Nancy is not accompanying me, she may absent herself, and Howard is trying to forestall that. It's deemed more rewarding to get a take on husband and wife together. If the Masarovs are near to a breakup, there may be indications which of the two could be more likely to defect. On the off chance that they present themselves as a strong, well-knit couple, maybe they'll fly the coop together. Such is our advance reasoning.

The day arrives. I trot over for tea and make my apologies about Nancy's indisposition. They seem disappointed. I cannot help thinking that Hunt was right. If Zenia had been told in advance, she might not have been there.

Given the limited supply of desirable real estate in Montevideo, my friendly Russian couple is living in a high-rise apartment house just two blocks further down the Rambla from the similar high-rise in which is located our safe house. The Masarovs are on the tenth floor, and also have a view through their picture window of Pocitos Beach and the sea. There, all resemblances end. They have truly furnished their place. I do not know if it is to my taste, but their belongings do fill the living room. There are heavy velvet drapes looped around the picture window, several fat armchairs and a plump sofa with lace antimacassars, a small oriental carpet on top of a large one, two samovars—one in brass, the other in silver—a number of standing lamps with beaded shades, a large piece of mahogany furniture with open glass cases for the display of their plates and dishes, small casts of heavy nineteenth-century sculpture on every table, a bronze maiden, for example, with a filmy bronze gown clinging to her half-exposed breasts, then Apollo, standing on the ball of one foot, and gold-framed prints of paintings wherever there is space: Cezanne, Gauguin, Van Gogh, plus a couple of Russian painters I do not recognize who portray czars flanked by Russian Orthodox high priests, and nobles dressed half like pirates—must be boyars. In the corner of one painting, a defeated boyar is bleeding to death from a wound in his neck. The agony on his mouth is expressive. Quite a picture to look at every day.

There are also oriental carpets put up as wall hangings, and I count four chess sets, two of which look to be of value. One of the boards is made of inlaid wood.

I can't help contrasting this old-fashioned, middle-class opulence with Sherman Porringer's child-scuffed, dog-chewed, blonde-wood furniture and bookshelves on bricks. The Masarovs, possessing not all that much space (now that they've filled it), have converted the hallway that ties their three and a half rooms together into a long, very narrow library. It is a squeeze for two people to walk side by side, yet both walls are lined with dark-stained oak bookcases. Later I get to look at Boris' collection of tomes, and will tell you that he reads

French, German, English, Spanish, Italian, and several Soviet languages whose names I would not know how to spell. That is a lot for
him to have learned, but, then, he says he is thirty-seven. While this
conflicts with the Sourball dossier, which pegs him at thirty-two, I
must say it adds up. He speaks of the Second World War, where he
rose to the rank of captain, and countless framed photographs on a
collection of end tables are certainly there to verify his military career.
I do take mental note of the shoulder-board epaulets in these photographs so the Sours can check it out. Of course, I am not able to swear
these are World War II snapshots, but they do have the feel of those
times, and on one photograph you can witness for background an
incredibly littered city of rubble and jagged artifacts. "Berlin," he told
me, "in the last days. That is why we are smiling."

"Yes, you must have been happy the war was coming to an
end."

He shrugged. Suddenly, he was gloomy. "Half happy," he
replied gnomically, but then, as if it were not congenial to speak in
such fashion to a guest, he added, "There is always question. Does one
deserve life? Better men have perished."

"Still, you laugh in photograph," remarked Zenia.

"I am happy," he said, contradicting himself.

"We were meeting two days before," said Zenia. "Brishka
and myself. First time."

"You, too, happened to be in Berlin?" I asked.

"Entertain troops."

"Zenia is a poet," said Masarov.

"Was," said Zenia.

"She has not written a poem in two years."

"Oh," I said.

"Close to goofy," said Zenia. *"Moi."*

"Well," I said. (Kittredge, I swear, we have to be as bad as the
English when it comes to receiving sudden confession.) "Well, it must
be difficult to sit in these well-furnished rooms when one's pen is
dry." (To myself, I sounded like the Earl of Phumpherdom.)

The Russians have one virtue, however. They are so abrupt
that no deadening remark can keep a half-life of more than three
seconds. "Well-furnished?" asked Zenia. "Aggregate. Is but aggregate."

I heard "aggravate" at first, so was, of course, confused, until her next speech brought clarification. "His family, my family. Aggregate of Moscow apartment—his father; Leningrad apartment—my mother. Remnants of families now complete."

"None of it yours?"

"All mine. All belongs to Boris. *Aussi*. Also."

"Yes," I said, "and your government shipped it over here for you?"

"Of course," she said, "why not?"

"But your apartment in Moscow must be empty."

She shrugged. "People in it."

We sat down at this point before the second-best chess set and Boris handed me the white pawn. "You are my guest," he said.

Kittredge, you know I am not at all in Hugh's class as a player, but I'm not bad—once I won a low-level tournament of *patzers,* as modest players are referred to, and in a simultaneous exhibition with a ranked master who was taking on twenty Yale students at twenty boards, I happened to be one of three who came away with a draw. The other seventeen all lost. All the same, I am, when it comes to real levels of chess, essentially talentless.

I could sense, however, as soon as we commenced, that the game meant much to him. As if a first whiff of the great international contest for the soul of man had finally entered our mood, I was aware of his tension, and then, reciprocally, of mine. "When in doubt, open with a king's pawn," I said cheerfully to him, and did just that. He nodded curtly, but then was rude enough for the first time—since his manners, as I hope I've indicated, are the best of that whole Russian gang on Bulevar España—to sit in his chair and study me openly for a minute. He did not look at the board, rather at my face, my posture, my uncertain smile, my—in short—my emanations. He made me feel as if I were back in the gym at St. Matthew's, and was going to wrestle with the determined-looking fellow at the other end of the mat in just twenty seconds.

"I think," he said at last, "Sicilian Defense is appropriate reply," and he advanced a queen's bishop's pawn to the fourth rank. Kittredge, I remember clearly that you spoke once of giving chess up at the age of twelve because you could think of nothing else. I would not wish to stir any half-buried cerebration, but I have to tell you this much: The black reply that always puts my king's-pawn opening into trouble is the Sicilian Defense. It seems to take a different turn every time, and I never get to play my game. I'm white, but I'm reacting all the while to what black is up to. It was uncanny of Boris to look me over so carefully, then pick the Sicilian.

Well, that's all you need to know. By the sixth move I was uncomfortable, by the eighth I was beginning to glimpse future defeat, and by the tenth move he had gotten up from his chair in impatience at how long it was taking me—we employed no clock—and came back with a book, and was impolite enough, or superior enough, or maybe it is elegant enough, to sit there reading while I cogitated over my next move. Then, as soon as I had come to a decision, he would look up, pull his upper teeth over his lower lip with the gentlest sound of tasteful appreciation, reach forward, make his move, which always took immediate account of whatever small positional scheme I was hoping to advance, and then without a by-your-leave, go back to his book, which happened to be—do you believe this?—the Modern Library Giant of *Moby-Dick*. He was, incidentally, well into it.

Masarov took a knight on the fourteenth move, and I gave up on the fifteenth. He had all the position by then and his rooks were ready to go. I never succeeded in castling. He kept me too busy.

Now Zenia brings out the tea. There is, in the wake left by the game, nothing to talk about. I comment that she does not use the samovars, but a teapot. "English tea," she replies. I ask for her patronymic. "My father's name—Arkady. I am Zenia Arkadyova."

"The sounds are beautiful," I say. "Zenia Arkadyova."

We make a little game of getting the accent right. "Many sounds in Russian," she tells me, "woods, earth, small animals in forest, rivers. English different. Derives from roads, hills, beaches. Surf of sea."

The largest generalizations are always begging to be adopted by me, but this is too basic.

"I'm sure you are right," I say.

She stares at me. It is disconcerting. She seems to be searching for some person in hiding just behind myself. "May I look at your library?" I ask Boris.

He pulls himself out of the deep depression in which he has sat since the end of the game. He passes with a wave of his hand over the three quarters of his books that are in Cyrillic, and brings me to his American section. In English, text is all of Hemingway and most of Faulkner. Also Mary McCarthy, Tennessee Williams, Arthur

Miller, William Inge, Sidney Howard, Elmer Rice, all of O'Neill, Clifford Odets, and T. S. Eliot—*The Cocktail Party.*

"Do you have ambitions to be a playwright?" I asked.

He grunted. "A playwright?" he replied. "I would not know how to talk to actors."

"Nonsense," said Zenia.

He shrugged. "Hemingway I like," he said. " 'Tis the essence of pre–World War Two America, would you agree?" (" 'Tis!") We had taken another step along the bookcase and were passing the works of Henry James. "Much studied by Lenin and Dzerzhinsky," said Masarov, tapping the binding of *The Golden Bowl.*

"Is that really true?" I asked. I was overcome by such news.

"No," said Zenia. "Brishka makes jokes."

"Not at all. *Golden Bowl.* Perfect symbol for capitalism. Of course Dzerzhinsky would read such work."

"Boris, ridiculous. Is insult to our guest."

He shrugged. "I apologize," he said, and looked me in the eye. "Who do you like? Tolstoy or Dostoyevsky?"

"Dostoyevsky," I said.

"Good. Dostoyevsky writes semi-atrocious Russian, but is, in fact, my preference. So we have possibility for friendship."

"First, I must improve my chess."

"Cannot be done," he said. His candor caught me by surprise, and I began to laugh. He soon joined me. He's got this heavy body and prematurely graying hair, much-lined face, one tough guy, but there's an odd youth lurking in the corners of his expression, as if he hasn't figured everything out yet.

"*Zakuski,*" said Zenia. "Have *zakuski* with more tea. Or vodka."

I declined. She protested. Despite an atrocious accent, her voice is deep and suggestive. At public functions, she seems like a mysterious and sensuous woman, exotic, occult, as removed from both of us as an oracle; this afternoon, she is middle-aged, fussy, maternal, the mistress of a small and very bourgeois establishment. I am finding it hard to piece together any sense of these two people as KGB, whether together or apart. Yet he has gone out of his way to mention Dzerzhinsky—that is obliged to be some sort of signal.

We sit down and chat about cultural matters American. He is interested in Jack Kerouac and William Burroughs, in Thelonius

Monk, in Sonny Rollins, whom I have never heard of. He has a record of Sonny Rollins and plays it for me and beams when I say that I have never heard a better tenor saxophone.

Abruptly, he opens a new direction. "Zenia was telling untruth," he says.

"Zenia Arkadyova was lying?" I ask.

He smiles at my use of the patronymic. "She has, actually, written one poem in last two years."

"No, is awful. Do not show," says Zenia.

"In English," says Masarov. "This year, in Russian tongue, Zenia cannot express herself. Not this year. Is total block. So, in your language, she has essayed . . . attempted . . ."

"*Zakuski*. Little poem. Appetizer," says Zenia. She is wholly flushed now, and her ample bosom is, I could swear, surging. "Nugatory," she says. "Trivial." (Sounds like tree-vee-*owl*.)

"Let him read it," says Brishka.

They argue in Russian. She yields. She goes to the bedroom and comes back with a sheet of cheap notebook paper. On it, in a somewhat unwieldy hand, she has put this head: "Vertigo Is Joy."

You can believe that after encountering such a title, I picked up her offering with no happiness, but . . . let me write it out for you. Lord knows, I've not only got a copy, but can recite it by heart after the workout it got from the Sourballs.

> VERTIGO IS JOY
> Our bird passed away in my hand,
>   its feathers a shroud.
> I knew the moment.
> Its last heartbeat
> spoke to my palm.
> Comrade, said bird,
> do not wait in line
> to mourn for me.
> I fall into depths
> that are great heights.

"Better if in Russian," said Zenia, "but cannot find *les mots justes*. Not for Russian. Words speak from English. Boris gives correct grammar? Correct punctuation? Is correct?"

"Yes," I said.

"Is good? Good poem?"

"I think so."

"Zenia is recognized in Russia," said Boris, "although perhaps not recognized enough."

"Is good for printing in America?" asked Zenia.

"Probably," I said. "Let me take it. I have two friends who edit literary magazines."

"Yes," she said, "yours," and folded it into my hand, and looked at me with embarrassing intimacy considering that we were standing there in front of her husband. "Print with pseudonym for me," she said.

"No," said Boris. "Present as work of a Soviet poet."

"Madness," she muttered.

"I think you might change the title," I said. "It's a little too direct for English."

She would not change her title. She loved the sound. "Am adamant for *vertigo*," she said. In her pronunciation, it rhymes with tuxedo. Ver-*tee*-go.

I left after some discussion of when we would visit again. Masarov proposed a picnic with Nancy and me. I agreed. But, by the time that day arrived, Nancy was not on board, and Zenia had decamped for the day. Boris and I went on the picnic together.

I am beginning to rush, however, and would rather wait for a day or two and finish this off with another letter.

Yours,
Harry

19

February 16, 1958

Dear Kittredge,

It was my intent to get back to you a couple of weeks ago. The Sourballs, however, have been taking me through session after session, and I come back to my hotel room each night hoping to empty my head long enough to find sleep. In addition, I am concerned by your lack of response. Sometimes I even wonder whether my letters pile up unread. Ah, well, if you are interrogated often enough by the Sourballs, there is no drear scenario that will not raise its paranoid head.

You may recollect how modest was my meeting with the Masarovs. Well, the Soviet Russia Division did not think so. After I sent off a lengthy cable to Washington concerning my little get-together with the new Soviet friends, I received by return cable a questionnaire about as long as my last letter to you. Answering it kept me busy for a day and a half. Then, a man flew down to us, care of Soviet Russia Division, to interrogate me personally. By accent and appearance, he has to be another Finnish Mick. He calls himself Omaley. (Pronounced like "homily" without the *h*.) He is not too tall, and very thin, and has horns, yes, horns of hair on an otherwise near-bald head. He also has a profusion of what I am tempted to call reverse whiskers. His chest thatch is apparently so thick that it grows out of his shirt and half up his neck. It gives him a ruff above his collar. He looks like a malnourished wild boar. You can imagine how well Howard Hunt takes to Hjalmar Omaley.

Well, Hjalmar Omaley doesn't care one goddamn what anyone thinks of him. He lives to do his work. Around the second day of living in his implacably chill company, I recognize that he reminds me of the exterminator who used to come to my mother's Park Avenue apartment on those cheerful mornings when cook discovered cockroaches in the oven and was ready to quit because maid was not washing the grill. I don't want to throw your stomach into the next meal, but Omaley looks like a liquidator ready to leave nothing of our enemy but the last of its bodily seepage. Communists are vermin, Soviet Communists are rabid vermin, KGB Communists are rabid *occult* vermin, and I had been in contact with the latter.

Now, I exaggerate. Except, I don't. I was queried on what I could remember of the Masarovs' war photographs until I began to feel profoundly guilty that I could not remember more, indeed, I began to wonder at my lack of motivation in memorizing relatively so little. Hjalmar, who must have simmered in sperm-soups of suspicion before being received by the clear-eyed ovum in his mother's womb, led me through endless rephrasings of each question. I had made the large mistake in my first cable of describing Boris and Zenia as "reasonably agreeable." I had intended to give an objective appraisal, but it stirred frightful concerns in the counterintelligence gang at Soviet Russia Division. I can tell you that I was interrogated on every aspect of the meeting. Could I remember the exact sequence of moves in the chess game? I did my best to replay the game to their satisfaction but could not connect the opening to our final position. This infuriated Hjalmar Omaley. Apparently, Masarov is so good at chess (at least by their original dossier on him—which, I would remind you, places him at age thirty-two, not thirty-seven) that they wanted to see whether he was carrying me in the game; that might indicate whether his motive was to charm me. No, I told them over and over, he was not carrying me—it was embarrassing to have to resign by the fifteenth move.

Next, we catalogued the furniture. The Sourballs are looking into their sources to see if more can be learned about Masarov's father's Moscow apartment and Zenia's mother's Leningrad apartment. After which, they proceeded to interrogate me about the American novels and plays in his bookcase. How new were the volumes? How well thumbed? The question is how close he is to what he presents himself as being—a Russian official with specialties on American cultural affairs.

Then we went to the poem. I had been wired with a sneaky which possessed only an hour's capacity, so the tape was finished before we came to the poem. I was asked, therefore, to reconstruct all dialogue not recorded. In what ways did the couple react to my suggestion that the poem was printable in America? Am I certain that Zenia muttered the word *madness*?

I won't bore you with how long they spent on "I fall into depths that are great heights." (It is, of course, being interpreted as the Masarov offer to defect.)

On the second day, I said to Omaley, "Do you always pursue details this intensively after Agency meetings with Russians?"

He smiled as if only an idiot like myself could ask such a question. I felt as if I were in the dentist's chair.

On the third day, Howard Hunt took me to El Águila, his favorite restaurant, for lunch. The Sourballs were in an uproar, he confided, over the discrepancy in Boris' dossier. Since my report that he was thirty-seven gummed up their Soviet Personnel Record file, they were damned upset. The question now is whether our present Boris is the original, or a new body? "Next question," said Hunt. "Does Boris want to defect, or does he wish to entrap you?"

"For practical purposes, he has," I said. "I can't get any of my other work done."

"This will pass," he answered. "Your bad mark in Berlin may put a little extra heat on you now, but just keep to the positive side of the equation. Get Boris to defect and you will hold all the bouquets." He nodded. "But, buddy, you've got to be more observant next time."

"It doesn't add up," I said. "If Boris wants to come over to us, why would he entertain me and put himself at risk?"

"Given Zenia's affair with Varkhov, Boris' judgment might be off." Hunt now tasted the first glass of wine from the bottle just opened for him, and made a face. *"Joven,"* he said to the waiter, *"esta botella es sin vergüenza. Por favor, trae un otro con un corcho correcto.*

"Bottom line," he said to me. "The situation does not add up. Why fraternize with you? What can you give them, Harry Hubbard? Maybe they believe you can offer them something."

"Way beyond me, Howard," I said, but at this moment, I had an image of Chevi Fuertes' face. Could the Russians be witting of AV/OCADO?

"Back to basics," said Howard. "What do we know for certain? It is that Boris, whether Masarov One or Masarov Two, is KGB. As the Montevideo *residentura,* he is definitely Number Two man under Varkhov."

"Definitely?"

"Heulihaen and Flarrety have studied their films comprehensively enough to establish an authoritative pecking order. They can document precisely whose ass is exposed to whose beak. Varkhov has precedence over the Soviet Ambassador and his minions. And Masarov is Number Two. Meanwhile, Number One is banging the boobies off the wife of his own Number Two, while Number Two seeks to fraternize with you."

"I'm dreading the picnic," I said. "It's not the picnic. It's the three days with Omaley that are going to follow."

"Get a couple of real pieces of Masarov meat, and I will grind Hjalmar's testes into powder. But do your best to avoid inconclusive results."

Thus armed, Kittredge, thus armed. Yesterday, Zenia phoned to ask if Nancy was coming. When I said that she was still indisposed, Zenia gave a grunt that sounded much like Boris. Zenia will not be with us either.

Then, today, Sunday morning—it is now late Sunday evening as I write to you—Boris and I drove out to the country. He took along his fishing gear, and little else since Zenia had neglected to pack a hamper. I felt wrung out and distracted; so, I suspected, was Boris. We hardly talked. After half an hour on the road, he reached over to his glove compartment and handed me a flask of Scotch, which was, under the circumstances, agreeable. On the *laissez-passer* of the booze, we uttered a word or two.

"Do you like the countryside?" he asked.

"Not much."

Kittredge, this was only my second trip out of Montevideo. In almost a year and a half! I can't believe the fact even as I write this; I am such an underground animal! At Yale, I never left New Haven. Here, all my world is contained within the Embassy, the safe house, Hunt's villa in Carrasco, and my cheap hotel room. I think it is because everything I do means so much to me that I simply don't notice from month to month how circumscribed are my movements. I saw more of the city in my first three days than in all the time since.

Of course, outside Montevideo, there is not much to look at. Along the sea are third-rate resorts trying to rise to the second level. Stucco debris stirs dust in half-finished villas by the side of the road. Inland are no more than gently rolling grassy plains, occasionally fenced in with cattle, but, over the whole, monotonous.

Masarov speaks out of a silence. *"Cuando el Creador llegó al Uruguay, ha perdido la mitad de Su interés en la Creación."* We laugh. His Spanish is not as good as his English, but I laugh heartily—partly at the Russian accent in Spanish. It's true. God did lose half His interest in creating the world after He came to Uruguay.

"Yet I like this country," he says. "Conducive to inner calm."

I am not feeling much of that. The highway has dwindled into a narrow two-lane road, much broken and humped and oil-stained by the weight and effluvia of truck commerce, and when we pull over to have lunch at a café *cum* gas station, it is for the omnipresent hamburgers, the local *cerveza,* and the smell of rendered beef fat and onions—what Porringer has called "the whorehouse-full-of-traffic smell."

Yet, Masarov is known in this café. We are apparently near his fishing hole, and he must have stopped here often. I am wondering if these poor roads, flat country, and functional little roadhouse do not remind him of his native country, and, as if we are curiously tuned to one another, he now says on the first sip of beer, "Uruguay is like small corner of Russia. Nondescript. To my liking."

"Why?"

"When nature grows awesome, man turns small." He lifts his mug. "Homage to the Swiss!"

"Whereas here, you feel larger than nature?"

"On good days." He looks at me carefully. "You know Uruguayans?"

"Not many." I am thinking, however, of Chevi.

"Me neither." He sighs and lifts his beer. "To Uruguayans."

"Why not?"

We click glasses. We eat in silence. It occurs to me that Boris may be under as much tension as myself. I remember Hunt's injunction: Avoid inconclusive results.

"Boris," I say. "What are we up to?"

"That will develop."

I feel as if I am back in the chess game. Does he long for a book to read while waiting for each of my cautious moves?

"Let me put it," he says. "I know who you are, and you know who I am."

Now I have to turn on the sneaky. The switch is in my pants pocket, but the shift of position entailed to get my left hand over (for it is the left hand that has been holding the hamburger) cannot possibly appear as clumsy to him as it feels to me.

"Yes," I say, now that I have pressed the recording button, "you claim to know who I am, and that I know who you are."

He will not keep from smiling at this obvious move. "Of such nature," he replies.

"What does that promise?" I ask.

"Extended discourse. Is a possibility?"

"Only if we trust each other."

"Half-trust," he says, "sufficient for such discussion."

"Why choose me?"

He shrugs. "You are here."

"Yes."

"Seem cautious," he says.

"Apparently I am."

He drinks a good portion of his beer at a gulp. "I have more to lose," he says, "than you."

"Well, that," I say, "depends on what you want."

"Nothing," he says.

"Do you want to come over to us?" I ask.

"Are you mad, or clumsy?" he replies in a gentle voice.

Kittredge, I am thinking of how bad this is going to look on the typed transcript. It will not convey the lack of personal offense in his voice. It will, to the contrary, project me as maladroit.

"No, Boris," I say, "I am neither mad nor clumsy. You approach me. Your overtures are friendly. You suggest that we have much to talk about. What can I suppose that to be but an indication of your desire to come nearer to us?"

"Or demonstration," he says, "of absolute ignorance of your people about mine."

"Are you prepared to tell me why we are here?"

"Could disappoint you."

"May I be the judge?"

He said nothing, and we sat side by side at our table looking out to the open end of the café, which had no front window but only an awning that flapped with a sound as sharp as a pistol shot each time a truck went by.

"Let's approach this again," I said. "What do you really want?"

"Political intelligence." He smiled, however, as if to deny the remark.

"I may be more ready to receive than to give."

"Could not be otherwise," he said. He gave a weary sigh. "KGB," he said, "stands for Komitet Gosudarstvennoi Bezopasnosti. Committee for State Security."

"I know all that," I said. "Even a Foreign Service Officer in the State Department knows that much."

He looked amused that I would still insist on maintaining cover. "Many Directorates in KGB," he said.

"I know that as well."

"Will speak of First Directorate, and Second. First is for Soviet officers abroad; Second for home security. Respectively, CIA, FBI."

"Yes," I said.

"Our FBI, Second Directorate, has fine reputation in America. Is seen as effective. But, by many of us, is considered stupid. Wish to hear joke?"

"Yes," I said, "I would."

"Of course," he said. "Why not?"

Now, we both laughed. It was droll. We both knew that my sneaky was on, and everything said would generate analysis. We quaffed our beer. Down the hatch. He clapped his hands and *el patrón* came forward with two more mugs, and a bottle of vodka. It occurred to me that this café could conceivably be a Russian outpost with microphones in the woodwork and a camera in the ceiling cranking away.

Or—Masarov merely came here often enough for the owner to stock a few bottles of vodka.

Yes, Kittredge, droll. Masarov, with a glass in his hand was not unlike other sturdy souls who live for a booze-up—he mellowed quickly.

"Two men," he said, "from Second Directorate are in car following boy and girl in other car through multitudes of Moscow streets, then zip out to highway. The boy and girl have been with foreigners they should not visit, but are children of very high officials, so not frightened. Say to each other, 'We get rid of these yeggs, yes?' " He stopped. "Yeggs?"

"Perfect use of the word."

"Dumb cops. Yeggs. Yes?"

"Perfect."

"So boy and girl pull their car over to side of road. Behind them, other car also stops hundred meters back. Our brave boy gets out. Lifts car hood to indicate motor trouble. What do yeggs do?"

"Tell me," I said.

"Get out of car," Boris said solemnly, "and lift *their* hood. Copycats, yes?"

"Yes," I said, "stupid."

"Our Second Directorate," he said, "has undue complement of stupid people."

"Why do you tell me this?"

"Because your CIA should distinguish between First and Second Directorate. Your CIA sees all KGB as brutes."

"Oh, that's not true," I said. "We spend weeks analyzing what Dzerzhinsky learned from *The Golden Bowl*."

Now he starts to roar. He laughs with a great bellow and smacks me on the back. Boris is one hell of a strong man.

"I like you," he says.

"Vertigo is joy," I reply.

We both laugh again. We are practically hugging one another. When the mirth ceases, he is suddenly and powerfully serious.

"Yes," he says, "in First Directorate, we go abroad. By our work, are obliged to study other nations. Become aware, sometimes painfully, of deficiencies in Soviet system. Within limitations of bureaucratic tact, we give accurate picture to home base. We try to help rectify our great Soviet dream. Yes. Even when answers are ugly and show it is our fault. The leaders of the First Directorate know more of everything wrong in the Soviet Union than anyone in your country."

"That's not the impression we get."

"Of course not. For you, KGB is equal to killers."

"It's a little more sophisticated than that."

"No! Low level! You speak of us as killers. We are professionals. Name one CIA officer who loses one little finger because of us."

"It's the hired help who get it," I said. I was thinking suddenly of Berlin.

"Yes," said Boris, "hired help get hell. True for you, true for us."

I was silent. "When do we go fishing?" I said at last.

"Fuck fishing," he said. "Let's drink."

We did. After a while I began to feel as if he had been waiting all his life to have a dialogue with one American. I was getting to know him so well that it was almost carnal, by which I mean that like most Russians he spoke with his face in mine (I suppose it is due to their small, crowded apartments) and so I came to know his exterior intimately—the places where his razor had missed some stubble, the spike-hairs in his nose, the breath of hamburgers, Turkish tobacco, onions, vodka, beer, and just enough caries to be, I swear, half-agreeable, as if a touch of rot in the mouth keeps a man honest. Hugh once imparted to me that unforgettable line of Engels—quantity changes quality—well, a touch of bad breath is altogether different from the odor of a badly corrupted mouth. I offer this aside because I lived for so long at a café table with Brishka, as he soon insisted I call him—Brishka and Harry, for sure—that the lunch drank itself down into the late afternoon, and the sun glared out of the west into the corner of our eyes as it dipped below the awning open to the road, and once in a while, a car went by or a drunk wandered in or out.

Masarov must have gone on for an hour about Nikita Khrushchev. Nobody in America could understand the Soviet Union, said Brishka, unless they came to comprehend the Premier. He was a

great man. "Great in relation to present situation of Soviet Union."
And he recited a litany to me. *Countless killed,* was the phrase. Countless Russians had been killed in the First World War, countless were
also killed in the Civil War initiated, he would remind me, by Americans, British, and French, countless killed by Stalin in collectivization
of the farms, and countless-countless Soviet soldiers and citizens killed
by Hitler, countless-countless killed again by Stalin after the war. The
Soviet Union had been battered more than "a wife," he said, "who
is beaten every day by an ugly husband. For forty years! If it were
American wife, she would hate such husband. But Russian wife
knows better. Underneath everything in such marriage is man's desire
for improvement."

"I'm lost," I said. "Who is the Russian wife, and who is the
husband?"

"Oh," he said, "obvious. Russian wife is Russia. Husband is
the Party. Some days, one must recognize that Russian wife is at fault.
She may deserve her beating. Looks at ground. Won't move forward.
Husband may be drunk, but looks at sky." He stopped here and
slapped himself across the cheek with a blow hard enough to rattle the
crockery in the kitchen (if it were listening). "Drunk," he said, and
ordered black coffee.

Now his syntax improved. "What I said before is *kvatch.*"

"*Kvatch?*"

"Of no value. Too general. The relation of Communist Party
to people not easy to explain. Soviet children grow up with belief that
one becomes a better person by sheer force of will. *The* will to be good
and unselfish. We try to destroy interest in enriching ourselves personally. Very hard to do. In my childhood, I would feel ashamed of
greedy desires. Weight upon the leader of such a people has to be
immense. All trying to be better than they are. Stalin—I am ashamed
to confess this—lost inner balance. Then Khrushchev, one of the
brave, replaced Stalin. I love Khrushchev."

"Why?" I asked.

He shrugged. "Because he was bad man. And gets better."

"Bad? He was the Butcher of the Ukraine."

"Oh, *they* teach you. *They* give you good course for the
winter, Harry. But, *they* forget spring."

"Who is they?"

"Your teachers. Miss huge point. Take question from Russian point of view. We see cruel people magnetized by power."

"Isn't this a little beyond Marx?"

"Ultra-Marxist," said Brishka. "Comes from Russian people. Not Marx. We expect cruel leaders. Our question is how can leaders transcend origins? Become better men. Stalin was great, but Stalin would not transcend. Turned worse. Evil deeds drive him crazy. Khrushchev *is the* opposite." He slapped himself again as if English were about to misprint itself on his tongue, and he had to jar his brain into line with his mouth. His English might be relatively polished, but underneath, Russky Tarzan lurked. As Boris got drunk, I could feel a cruder mode of expression come nearer and nearer to asserting itself. Of course, he would never say "Khrushchev opposite," but you could feel the words he was ready to leave out. "Khrushchev *is the* opposite."

"Yes," he said, "contemplate Khrushchev. *He is* not wholly popular. Many Russian detractors. Some say *he is* too emotional." Kittredge, you get the idea, I hope. Only this trace of deformation showed. "Yes," he said, "almost all agree Khrushchev is *nyet kulturny*. You comprehend *nyet kulturny*?"

"I speak no Russian."

"Stick to your story." He laughed at this. Like Zenia, he has two persons in him, and they are not accommodated to each other. He had been drunk, and heavy in his sentiments; now, the irony of the chess master leaped out again. "Stick to your story," he said once more, as if he had a clear dossier on me. (Probably he did, and doubtless it was as inaccurate as ours on him.)

"Does *nyet kulturny* mean not cultured?"

"Of course. Crystal clear. Not cultured. Gross. That is worst thing you can say of a Russian"—yes, his better English was still with him. "Hordes of my people lived for centuries in huts. Nobody need to wipe his shoes. Floors were dirt. Animals slept with family. *Nyet kulturny*. Crude. Void of high culture. So, Khrushchev embarrasses many. Will ruin him yet."

"But he's a great man, you say?"

"Believe me. Gross, brutal, minion of Stalin. Yet, grows in stature. Immeasurable bravery to repudiate Stalin. You should try explaining to your people. In Moscow now, many high party leaders say to Khrushchev, 'U.S. has four times more nuclear capacity. We are obliged to catch up.' Khrushchev says, 'If U.S. attacks, we answer.

Both nations *are* destroyed. So, will be no war. Our Soviet need is to develop *our* economy.' Khrushchev resists huge military pressure. Khrushchev a good man."

"On our side, we find that a little harder to believe. We think you are responsible for your past, and you don't shake it so quickly."

He nodded. "That is because you represent corporate capitalism. Linear. Unilinear people in corporation." He took a large swallow of his black coffee, which was thick as filtered mud, and nodded. "Yes," he said, "Americans never understand how Communist Party works. See us as living under total relation to ideology. Grave error. Only corporate capitalism lives in total relation to ideology. We, who you call slave people, more individual."

"I believe you really think that."

"Of course. No two Russians alike. All Americans, to me, are same breed."

"In no way could this be a misapprehension on your part?"

He touched my elbow in amelioration. "Speak of corporate capitalist Americans. Managers. Executive class. They believe American ideology. We believe, but only by half."

"By half?"

"By half, Harry, you bet." Again, his heavy hand clapped me on the back.

"And the other half?"

"Our secret half. We brood."

"Over what?"

"Our soul. I taste *my* soul. American people speak of free-floating anxiety, yes? Lack of identity, yes? But Russian says: I am losing my soul. Americans used to be like Russians. In nineteenth century. When were individual entrepreneurs. Then, still *the* baroque spirit. In your hearts. In American architecture. Individual people, eccentric. Now, Americans are corporate capitalists. Brainwashed."

There was a glint in his eye at the expression on my face. "Khrushchev does not want to lose his soul," Masarov said, "so, works hard to improve *the* world."

"You tell me all this with a straight face?" I confess I was getting angry at his consummate gall.

"Straight face."

"Tell me about your prison camps."

His good mood vanished. "The Russian Bear," he said, "lives with dinosaur's tail. Tail crawls with infestations. From *the* past. Eventually, eat *the* tail. *We* will absorb horrendous history. But, as of now, immense convulsions. Tragedies. Horrors. Still."

I could hardly believe he had said this much. He was scowling at his coffee as if it had been a mistake to leave his old comrade-in-arms, vodka, for this new acquaintance. Then he gave a great sigh as if to clean his breath of old memories. "Do you know about *beri-ozhka*?" he asked. "Birch trees."

"Yes. You are all said to love them."

"Yes." He nodded. "Zenia wrote beautiful poem in Russian about *beriozhka*. Translated into English by me. With liberties, however. Zenia would not recognize it. She would leave me." He looked as if he were about to cry, but instead took out a piece of paper and read aloud to me.

> To THE BIRCHES
> *pale sentinels*
> *silent arrows*
> *light and moonlight*
> *our silver sun*

"Uruguay is not like Russia," he said. "Are no birches here."

Then he tore off the unmarked bottom half of the sheet on which the poem was written, scribbled a note upon it for me, and passed it over. The wording, Kittredge, (and you will soon see why) is offered to you from memory.

> *Caution. Just as one of ours may be, in secret, yours, so one of yours may be ours. Do not trust the people in your Soviet Russia Division. Such remarks can hang me. Silence. Caution. Speak only to your most trusted own.*

I had time to read it carefully before he whipped back the note and held it in his hands. I do not know if I was inhabiting his mind at that point, but I did envision him setting this half sheet of paper on fire in the ashtray, which, I swear to you, he proceeded to do just then, as if I had either willed him to do it, or had read his mind before he expressed it.

Kittredge, that was indeed the curious tone on which we left the café and took the drive back to Montevideo in the late summer dusk of February. It is late now, and I am weary, but we are, at last, caught up.

Devotedly,
Harry

20

IT WAS UNDERSTOOD THAT I WOULD CALL HOWARD SO SOON AS I CAME back from the picnic, but I found myself in a peculiar and rebellious state. I did not wish to be debriefed into the late hours of Sunday night. Instead, I chose to write to Kittredge. It was as if my best hope of understanding what had taken place between Masarov and myself would be obtained by setting it down for her. I knew that once my formal report was perused by Hjalmar Omaley, converted to cable traffic, and subjected to the Soviet Russia Division's questionnaires, the experience would be altered, and I felt some need, no matter how unprofessional, to keep it intact.

I was in a dilemma, however. *"Do not trust the people in your Soviet Russia Division,"* was a dangerous remark to bring back. Since I now had no evidence of Boris' note other than my personal description of it, I was bound to be seen as the untrustworthy bearer of a wholly disturbing communication. Maybe the KGB had designed the afternoon to get me to return with a message that would disrupt our Soviet Russia Division. In that case, it might be prudent not to mention the note.

Of course, there was the real possibility that a movie camera had been installed behind a peephole in the café to record the moment when Boris passed his written message over to me and I read it and he then incinerated it in the ashtray, both of us watching solemnly. In such a case, if I did not report the incident to Hunt and Omaley, and there was indeed a KGB mole at Soviet Russia Division in position to see my report on the picnic, then I would be prey to blackmail if I made no mention of Masarov's message.

I decided to state in my report, therefore, that the note had been passed to me; I would, however, leave out the reference to the Soviet Russia Division. If the intent of the KGB was to increase our suspicion of our own people, then I would be thwarting their purpose. The remaining contents of the note would prove vague. I decided to accept the risk.

Why? As if someone had poked a rude finger into my stomach, the question hit with force. Why, indeed? Why not tell the truth? If it disrupted the Soviet Russia Division, well, they had suffered, no doubt, in such fashion before. Yet I knew I would not change my mind. Not only was living in close quarters with Al Omaley much like cohabiting with a contagious disease, but I did not feel ready to face his meticulous paranoia. I, the messenger, had to be tainted by the message.

All the same, my private motive remained inaccessible to me. Some stubborn depth of instinct was speaking.

It was now ten o'clock on Sunday night, and one could put off calling Howard Hunt no longer. I went down to the street and found a pay phone. On the Avenue of the 18th of July, the night was as quiet as a midnight Tuesday in Green Bay, Wisconsin.

"Where in hell have you been?" was his opening remark.

"Getting drunk with our friend."

"Until now?"

"A confession, Howard. I got back to the hotel at seven, started to call just to say that I was back and would ring again from downstairs in ten minutes, but, so help me, I fell asleep with the phone in my hand."

"Oh, no."

"Did you ever match vodka for vodka with the Russians?"

"Yes. And successfully. Don't you know enough to drink olive oil before you start?"

"Well, maybe I do now."

"All right. One question. Was it conclusive?"

"Not wholly affirmative on that."

"Shit."

"A fair amount of stuff, all the same."

"Enough to begin an all-night session right now?"

"I doubt it."

"Then, I will let it keep till tomorrow. But you get over to the Embassy now. Nancy is waiting to type up the tape."

"Well, yes."

"Hang around to help her with garbled transmission."

"Of course."

"I know this is open wire, boy, but give a clue. What was our friend up to?"

"Wiser minds than mine will determine that."

"Any chance of your buddy riding down the river?"

"Twenty-percent possibility."

"Twenty-percent," repeated Hunt. I could picture his study at Carrasco; I could all but hear his long fingers tapping on the desk. "That's a bit of a disappointment," he said.

"All the same," I told him, "there are a few new flowers in the nosegay."

"We'll be busy tomorrow," said Hunt. "Get some sleep."

"I intend to—after the next three hours with Nancy."

"That's all right, Harry. You were snoring it off while I was pacing my study worrying over what to say at your grave."

My relations with Nancy during the hours it took to transcribe the tape proved as formal as the muted aftereffect of our single kiss, a sad void for her, I was certain, but by two in the morning, the transcript was done, and so was my accompanying report. I went back to the hotel, while Nancy, loyal to the code of all the unsung soldiers, was still sending our text on the encoding machine. Our five-letter groups would be deciphered by communications people in Washington before the dawn.

Hjalmar Omaley, whether alerted by Hunt, or paranoically instinctive, came by some twenty minutes in advance of my departure, a precise timing that enabled him to read my report and go through the transcript just as Nancy was finishing the last page. He had the oddest style of perusal. Reminiscent of the way General Gehlen used to mutter over the chessboard, he all but crooned into the contents. "Holy hooligans, Hjalmar, holy hooligans," he kept saying as he read, but whether this was praise for the operation or astonished disapproval, I had no idea. Just as I was leaving, Nancy, quick as a bird darting into the eaves (for I was not supposed to see it), flashed one tender smile at Hjalmar. It seemed to me then that I would be wiser to worry over the empty space in my own heart rather than the void in others.

By the middle of Monday morning, Howard was in a state of great excitement. The Sourballs had succeeded in closing the discrepancy on Masarov's age. Their Soviet Personnel Record dossier was now in order. While Hunt would not, or could not, provide me with more detail than to say, "Masarov is not thirty-two but thirty-nine, not, as he claims, thirty-seven. Get set for this: He is higher echelon than we thought. Considerably above Varkhov in rank."

"I thought the Finnish Micks had concluded Boris was Number Two KGB here."

"They did, but the Sovs must have been sending contrived signals. It's a kangaroo pouch."

While I had never heard the expression before, the metaphor obviously spoke of an operation where the number-one man is concealed.

"What of Zenia and Varkhov?" I asked.

"In for reappraisal. One thing is nailed down, though. Our Masarov here in Uruguay is one of the leading KGB experts on America."

"Why, then, is he in these parts?"

"That may be the focal enigma, may it not?" said Howard.

If my visit to the home of Boris and Zenia had taken me through heavy cross-examination, the picnic subjected me to an eighteen-hour day with Hjalmar, followed by two more eighteen-hour days responding to questionnaires from Washington. More than once I came close to confessing what I now called (in the last redoubts of the privacy of my mind) "The Abominable Omission," for the questionnaires certainly kept returning to the contents of Boris' note. What certainty could I submit that the message, as recollected by me, was complete: 60 percent? 70 percent? 80 percent? 90 percent? 95 percent? 100 percent? I made the mistake of answering 80 percent. As if they were psychically attuned to the topography of culpability, the Sourballs follow-up question stated: *In your reconstruction, the note has three full statements plus three one-word exhortations. If recall is 80% complete, what is the possibility that a fourth sentence is missing?*

To which I replied: *Zero possibility.*

Repeat query: 50%? 40%? 30%? 20%? 10%? 5%? 0%?

Zero possibility.

Boris note lacks concerted impact. How do you account for that?

I was sitting at a typewriter console hooked up to our Encoder-Decoder. An encrypted question would come in from Washington, go through the decoder, activate the keys of my typewriter, and come out in deciphered, five-letter groups on my typewriter page, which I could read, by now, as quickly as plain text. BORIS NOTEL ACKSC ONCER TEDIM PACT didn't cost me one-tenth of a second more. Then, so soon as I typed out a reply to the comment, my five-letter groups would begin their trip back through the same typewriter and Encoder-

Decoder to the Sourballs in Cockroach Alley. I would sit and wait for my typewriter to commence clacking again. After hours of such back and forth, I began to feel as if I were playing chess with an opponent in another room. Over my shoulder, Hjalmar Omaley read the questions and my answers.

On this last comment, *Boris note lacks concerted impact,* I turned to him.

"What is that supposed to mean?"

He had an irritating smile. His teeth would gleam in concert with the gleam that came off his eyeglasses. "It means," said Hjalmar, "precisely what it says."

This annoyed me sufficiently to type for my reply exactly what I had said to him. WHATD OESTH ISMEA N

PRECI SELYW HATIT SAYS came back.

"All right, we have a problem," I said. "I can't comment if I don't know what I'm replying to."

At Yale, I had always detested the superior sort of graduate student who looked like Hjalmar Omaley. Their heads were invariably held at odd angles. They listened with a half-smile. They appeared to be sniffing the inferior odor of your turds as compared to the integrated concert of their own. They would answer inquiries with questions or with such throwaways as *precisely what it says.* When, however, they finally took account of the subject, they left you in no doubt of their credentials. "We have under consideration," said Hjalmar, "a high-echelon member of the KGB, expert in American studies, who dallies with a minor case officer in a country with small to negligible geopolitical impact. Said KGB officer then proceeds to incriminate himself to said minor case officer by dint of extreme remarks, allusions, and unorthodox comparisons of his country and party to a sordid husband and wife. He abuses Marxist tenets. All such product would guarantee, at the least, his recall, and imprisonment if we were to forward transcript obtained to the KGB and they were to believe it. Do you follow me now?"

"Yes."

"Good. Since he is, however, heading up the KGB cadres here, his own transcript, if he has one, need not be of concern to him. He has obviously been given sanction. There are elements in the KGB who do have sanction to speak freely and, on occasion, act freely. Such post-Neanderthals can be seen as the equivalent of seventeenth-century Jesuits. Are you still capable of following me?"

"Yes."

"Good. We now encounter the specific implausibility of the entire situation. To summarize what I have just said: A major KGB operative who, so far as we can see, has no intention of defecting, nonetheless engages in major conversational indiscretions with the opposition. If there is an entelechy in his process—and there must be entelechy, or else, why commence?—he succeeds in presenting a note which is destroyed almost immediately after it is delivered. That is a dubious business, since the message has no incisive content. It names no person, attacks specifically none of our departments, and in sum, is too general to be disruptive. He has given you a shovel without a handle. What explanation do you offer?"

I was about to reply, but he said, "Wait," and turned on a tape recorder placed next to the Encoder-Decoder. "Speak your piece into that."

The position of the microphone placed my back to Omaley, and I could feel his malign presence leaning in full psychic drapery upon my shoulders.

"Repeat your question," I said.

"What explanation do you offer of your meeting?"

"I think we are dealing with a man rather than a scenario."

"Expatiate."

"I'm not as certain as all of you that Masarov has a clear message to pass on. If he is the number-one man, and his wife is indeed in love with Varkhov, who now, it seems, is his assistant, I believe that could prove disorienting to his behavior."

"Masarov is ruthless, skillful, and highly capable of discharging ultimate functions. It is difficult to believe that his marital troubles, if bona fide, would prove unsettling. In 1941, at the age of twenty-two, as a young officer in the NKVD, he was present in the Katyn Forest during the Soviet massacre of the Polish officers. He is a man, therefore, who has shot others in the back of the head." Standing behind me, Hjalmar did tap me lightly on the head.

Could I place Boris into this new portrait? My stomach was reacting. "Katyn Forest helps to explain his appraisal of Khrushchev," I said.

"To employ Masarov's own terminology—*kvatch*. An attempt to beguile you, misdirect you, have you, in short, follow the wrong shell in his game."

"If you know all of it, why do you keep questioning me?"

" 'Boris note lacks concerted impact.' Try replying to that on the E-D."

I turned to my typewriter and sent the following into the Encoder-Decoder.

ICANN OTDOA NYTHI NGTOR ESOLV ETHIS IMPAS SEIWI LLALT ERMYE STIMA TEOFP ROBAB ILITY OFREC OLLEC TIONO FTHEN OTEFR OM80% TO95%

There was a long pause. Omaley sat there shaking his head slowly from side to side like a metronome oscillating alone in a vault. It was late at night and we were the only two people left in our wing of the Embassy.

FINAL, asked the E-D.

FINAL, I typed back.

This time the pause was short. DOYOU AGREE TOTAK INGAL IEDET ECTOR TEST

Omaley looked happy for the first time in three days.

INPRI NCIPL EYESP ROVID EDJUR ISDIC TIONA LHEGE MONIE SDONO TOVER RIDET HEPRI NCIPL E

"In principle, yes," read Hjalmar over my shoulder, and very much aloud, "provided jurisdictional hegemonies do not override the principle." He laughed. "What would you suppose are the probabilities that your Chief of Station will enable you to avoid the flutter box? Fifty percent? Forty percent?"

There was a high-pitched note so hateful in his voice that I came very close to hitting him. I was still smarting from the tap on the back of my head.

21

"PREPOSTEROUS," SAID HOWARD NEXT MORNING, "OUTRAGEOUS. YOU have been doing your best to stay afloat with a KGB heavyweight, and they want to flutter you because they are not happy with the results? You are absolutely right. This is jurisdictional. I'm not letting any paranoid peacocks drive a truck right through the middle of my Station."

"I'm ready to take the test if it comes to it," I said.

"Glad you said that, but I'm here to protect my people fully as much as I am ready to expose them to appropriate risk-taking." He paused. "I want all the tarps tied down on this one, however. Are you really 95-percent sure of your accuracy about this note? That's what ticked them off, you know. You can't get cheeky with their evaluation process. It's like defiling the Torah or the Koran." He looked most carefully at me. "Between us, cozy as thieves, what is your real estimate?"

"Ninety percent."

"Okay. I have to buy that. But why is Masarov's message so anemic? The name of the game is to maim someone's name."

"Howard, I put it in my report. I have a theory that no one gives credence to: Just a couple of weeks ago, on February 2, the Russians asked for a summit meeting. I think Masarov wanted me to bear the same message that the Russians are sending in a thousand different ways all over the world. 'Give the summit a try, Khrushchev is okay.' Part of their personal propaganda approach."

"All right. Those lines of possibility do stand out in the transcript. But why confuse matters? Boris is an old pro. He knows the cardinal differences between a clandestine note and a political pitch—which, by the way, I don't trust for one minute, those Sovietskys don't want peace ever, just a breathing space to find a new way to screw us." He paused. "But, all right. Boris gives his sermon. We can all cry for the Soviet Union. Countless-countless killed. Yes, and how about the five thousand Polish officers Masarov helped to shoot in the back of the head, and the other ten thousand Polish officers that remain missing? Stalin knew what he was doing. He was killing the cadres of a possible future independent Poland, yeah, those Sovs want peace—I'll believe that when pimps stop taking their cut." He tapped his desk as if it were a podium.

"You ought to be in politics, Howard," I said.

"I could have been in many things. It kills me to look at the properties you could develop out in Carrasco. We pay a stiff price, Harry, for giving our allegiance to the Company. A CIA man makes a whole financial sacrifice for life. But that's another matter. Let's keep the target in our sights. Explain to me one more time your understanding of Masarov's note."

"Howard, I think Boris was drunk and full of misery, half ready to defect and knows he won't—unless he does—he's a Russian, after all, he's half crazy, he loves his wife, he's sinking in guilt, he has a lot on his conscience, he wants to save his soul, and if you add it all up, he must be very self-destructive. He loves Dostoyevsky. I think he wanted to hang himself with that meaningless note, but then he changed his mind and burned it."

"So you buy his speech at face value?"

"I think I do. Why else write a meaningless note?"

"God, you're young."

"I guess I am."

Actually, I was amazed at the felicity with which I was able to lie. How much of my mother was in me after all. For the first time I understood her pleasure in little creations. Lies were also a species of spiritual currency.

"Well, I'm going to bat for you," said Howard.

"I appreciate that."

"Kid, do you have any idea how expensive this could prove for yours truly?"

"I think a lot of people up and down the line will respect you for taking a tough stand," I said.

"Yes. How much won in respect, and how much lost to future deep-dyed, unalloyed enmity. Yes. Tell me, Harry, why are you reluctant to take the test?"

"I'll take it, Howard. I'm ready to. I'm innocent. It's just that they get you feeling so goddamn guilty once they put those electrodes on."

"Say that again. I remember my indignation when they asked me if I were homosexual. Years ago. I controlled myself long enough to say no—when in doubt, observe the proprieties—but, I tell you, fellow, if any man was ever crazy enough to try to put his pecker in my mouth, and I don't care if that man is a buck nigger, six feet six inches tall, I would bite his masterpiece off at the root. So, yes, I can hook on to your feelings. I hate lie detectors too. We'll stop those bastards right where they live. This is, after all, my Station."

I caught a whiff of his breath. He had had a few belts, and that was certainly not his habit for the morning. It was possible that he was more agitated than me.

Howard left soon after to keep a date for lunch with one of his Uruguayan friends. "I'm going to hold the line," he said.

As if to show his trust in me, he quit his office while I was still in it. That was not customary. He usually locked his door. Now, he merely left it ajar so that from her desk just outside, Nancy Waterston could certainly check on whether I was looking into any of his drawers. Just then, the secure phone in the locked closet began to ring.

"Nancy," I said, "do you hear that?"

She did after a moment.

"I think," I told her, "we had better answer it. Do you have a key?"

She did. She made a point of unlocking the closet door herself. By the time she lifted the receiver, there had been twelve rings. "Yes," she said, "He's here. Who wishes to speak to him?" A pause. "Oh, it's classified. Oh, I'm afraid I don't know the protocol on classified secure phone referrals." Meanwhile, she was stabbing her finger directly into the air between us. "For you," her finger was saying.

"I'll take it," I said.

"I don't know," she said, covering the mouthpiece, "who is asking for you."

"Never fear. It's more routine than you'd expect."

"I don't know," she repeated, "who is asking for you."

"Nancy, I could, if necessary, tell you what this is all about, but I won't. You are interfering with a priority."

"All right," she said, then added as she handed me the phone, "it's a woman."

"Hello," I said into the mouthpiece.

"Is that other person standing at your elbow?" said Kittredge in my ear.

"More or less."

"Banish her."

"It'll take some doing."

"All the same!"

"Nancy," I said, "this is a secure phone. I'd like privacy. That is the designated purpose of these phones."

"Only intended for use," said Nancy, "by the Chief of Station."

"In his absence, I have entitlement. This involves something co-developed by Howard and me."

Nancy receded, but grudgingly, like a tide not yet ready to accept its summons back from high water. She left Howard's door still ajar. I, in turn, did not feel ready to close the closet. Under these exceptional circumstances, Nancy might feel emboldened to listen at the keyhole. So, through two half-opened doors, we managed to keep an eye on each other even as I spoke in the lowest tones.

"Are we clear?" asked Kittredge.

"Yes."

"Harry, I love your letters. I know I haven't been responding lately, but I love them. Particularly the last one. It's invaluable."

"Are you all right?"

"Couldn't be better. It's all turned around now. I'm in splendid shape."

Her voice, however, was coming to me out of the long reverberations of the secure phone. All I could determine about her state of being was that she was speaking quickly.

"Yes," she said, "I want your permission on a small but precise fabrication."

"You've got it," I said. Given the proportions of the Abominable Omission, why deny anything small and precise?

"I'm not ready to inform Hugh we're corresponding, because that would upset him much too much, but I do ask for your permission to tell him that you were sufficiently concerned by what took place on your Soviet picnic to place a call to the Stable's secure phone. He was out, I'll say, and so you told me all. Then you and he can get together tonight on this same lovely red phone."

"The first thing wrong with your proposal," I said, "is that your call right now has already ticked off a nasty response. Unless I can come up with a feasible explanation, I'll never be able to get a second call out tonight on my lovely red phone, which, incidentally, dear lady, is housed in a stifling closet—"

"Don't talk so much," she said, "there's an off-putting echo."

"The second difficulty," I said, "is that I don't believe you. I think you've told Hugh already."

"I have," she said.

"About my last letter?"

"No, never the letter. About Masarov's crazy note. Your letter arrived yesterday, yes, yesterday, Wednesday, and I made up the story of your phone call, said it was at 4:00 P.M., and Hugh was sufficiently exercised—"

"Speak more slowly. Did you say exercised?"

"Exercised, not ex-or-cised. Hugh tapped into his source over at Soviet Russia Division, and, yes, the Sourballs are agog. Darling boy, you must have tampered with the message. Hugh gave me the wording. It's not what you put in the letter to me. They must be trying to sweat the last gamma globulin—"

"Slower, please."

"Not getting their last bit of fat, are they?"

"No." Pause. "What does Hugh think of what I did?"

"Thinks your natural instinct has a touch of the divine tar."

"Divine tar?"

"Harry, that's Hugh's accolade. The stuff God filched back from the Devil. Divine tar."

"Well, Kittredge, you've left me impressed with myself."

Suddenly, however, all amusement was gone. "Oh, Harry, it just occurred to me. When you speak to Hugh, do get *our* little story straight. When you phoned me yesterday, you did impart the missing contents to me."

"Yes, I'll keep the new chronology in place," I said.

"I think you're wonderful. However, that's not what's at issue. How are you and my spouse going to speak if you can't get a secure phone?"

"I guess," I said, "that Hugh should ring me at eleven o'clock tonight," and I gave the number of a street phone near my hotel that I sometimes used to call Chevi Fuertes.

"Is it virgin?" she asked.

"Hell, no."

"You must select another pay phone you've never used before. Then phone us at home around eleven tonight on any pay phone. Hugh will pick up. Don't speak to him by name. Just give the color code for the selected phone and hang up. Of course, you had better skew the color code."

"By how many digits?"

"Choose a number."

"Four . . ."

"I just picked two. Make it three then," Kittredge said.

"Three."

"Skewed by three."

"Shouldn't it be a continuing skew?"

"Agreed."

"By the way, only six digits on phones here, not seven," I said. "And I will call at eleven o'clock. If I can't make it, then by midnight."

"Agreed," she said.

"By the way, they want to put me in the flutter box."

"Hugh will probably get you out of that."

"How?"

"Harry, be content."

She hung up before I could say good-bye.

It was a long afternoon and made more nervous by thoughts of the skew. My recall of the color code for phone numbers was still absolute—on that I could feel well trained. Zero was white; 1, yellow; 2, green; 3, blue; 4, purple; 5, red; 6, orange; 7, brown; 8, gray; 9, black. A full skew turned zero into 9, 1 to 8, 2 to 7, so forth. A skew of three changed 3 to 9, 4 to 8, 5 to 7, 6 to 6, 7 to 5, so forth. But continuing skew was a misery. The first digit in the telephone number was skewed by three, the next by three more, or six, the third by nine, the fourth by three again, the fifth by six again, the sixth by nine once more. One didn't dare do it in one's mind but reached for pencil and pad. The virtue of the continuing skew, however, was that anyone tapping in on the first conversation who happened to be familiar with the color code would still, if he did not know the continuing skew, need time to break down the number. By then, presumably, the pay phone would have been used and never employed again.

Hunt returned from lunch and locked his door. I surmised he was on the phone to Washington. Then he called in Hjalmar Omaley, who looked expressionless when he came out. It took no great acumen to recognize that the demand by SR Division for a lie-detector test was not going to be decided by Hunt, but back in Cockroach Alley. The Encoder-Decoder was certainly silent.

Porringer went home at five, ditto Gatsby. Nancy Waterston quit at six, which was as early as she had left in several weeks. Hjalmar soon followed; I had the idea he and Nancy would meet for dinner tonight.

Hunt stopped at my desk as he was leaving. "What was that secure phone call about? More illness in the family?"

"Yessir."

He lost his temper. Mean storm warnings passed across his face. "I don't want you using the red box again."

"I won't."

He slammed out of the office. I understood his fury. He was not going to circle the encampment with our wagons after all.

Alone in the office, I felt gainfully employed for the first time since Sunday afternoon. My regular meeting with Chevi Fuertes was scheduled for Friday at the safe house, and I had to go over his file. Then my accounts with AV/ALANCHE, sadly screwed up. I had not been out with them in two weeks and they were in a state of disarray from a couple of bloody street fights. My undone account books concerned not only AV/OCADO and AV/ALANCHE, but AV/OUCH-1, AV/OUCH-2, and AV/ERAGE, all on my desk to be brought up to date for Nancy Waterston. As I sat alone in the office, I could even feel AV/ERAGE, my homosexual society journalist, sulking—I had not met him this week for a drink. Yet the thought of all these unaccomplished tasks was curiously soothing as if I could wrap them about myself like a poultice against the raw adrenaline of the last three days.

That evening, after choosing the critical phone for my serious conversation with Harlot, I ate alone in a trucker's café in the Old City, an uneasy but pleasurable anticipation suffusing itself into my broiled meats and wine as if I were getting ready to meet Sally on a good night for me. I obtained from the waiter a fistful of change, and my pants pocket, on leaving the restaurant, lolled concupiscently against my thigh.

By ten-thirty, I had chosen the phone booth for the first call, and at ten of eleven, I called the international operator, gave her the number of the Stable in Georgetown, and deposited my coins. When I heard Harlot's voice, I said, "In front of a yellow wall is a white table with a purple lamp. A man in a brown jacket, yellow pants, and red shoes is standing. There is no chair."

"Repeat in brief," said Harlot's voice.

"Yellow, white, purple, brown, yellow, red." That would convert to 10–47–15.

"Twelve to fifteen minutes," said Harlot and hung up.

Ten–47–15 was but the immediate conversion. Calculated for a continuing skew of three, it would come out to 15–45–45.

I had chosen to receive the second telephone call in a nearby bar of reasonable decorum. It had two phones in private booths and thereby offered less likelihood that some stranger would be kept waiting if our conversation should take a while. Indeed, I was in the booth five minutes in advance with the phone up to my ear and my other hand on the hang-up lever so that the apparatus would be able to ring.

In the fourteenth minute, it did.

"Well," said Harlot, "back to the old rigamarole. I dislike pay phones quite as much as you do."

"This one has been interesting," I said.

"Time-consuming." He paused. "Here is the hygiene. If necessary, for purposes of clarity, names are permissible. Should we, for any reason, disconnect, hold your place and I will call again. If you don't hear in five minutes, wait until midnight. I'll call then."

"Make it eleven-forty," I said. "This place shuts down at midnight. I've asked."

"Good fellow. Now, purpose of my call. Verification. There is no doubt in your mind that your drinking pal named the Soviet Russia Division?"

"Zero doubt," I said.

"Why did you not report it?"

"My drinking partner had obviously set me up to do so. I thought I'd spike his game."

"Presumptuous of you."

"I can only say that my deepest instinct told me to follow such a course," I said. "I had a hunch you would want me to follow such a course."

"This is amazing," said Harlot. "Do you know, if you had consulted me, I would have told you to do just what you did. The real object of the Russian's billet-doux was not SR Division, but closer to home."

"My God," I said.

"Yes. GHOUL. I think there is a furry little creature loose in the Soviet Russia Division. They, in turn, agree that the Agency is suffering a penetration, but place the mole in GHOUL. Dear boy, you were instinctively bright. Since you and I, for better or worse, are seen by now as umbilically attached, even Allen would have had to give some credence to SR's claim that the mole is in my cellar, if you had, that is, reported correctly. I expect Masarov chose you precisely for that reason. No question, you see—they're after me. The Russkys do appreciate my value more than the Agency. And I appreciate your new drinking pal even more than the KGB does. He's a hell of a fellow. Stay away from him. Competitively speaking, he's nearly as competent as myself."

"Good Lord," I said.

"You wouldn't care to trade wits with me yet, would you?"

"No, sir. Not yet."

"Ho. Good for you. Not yet. Well, by the same logic, stay away from your new friend."

"If I will be permitted to."

"You will." Pause. "Now, about the lie detector test. You won't have to take it."

"May I query you further?"

"Lord, no. You've got all you need. This call is costing a lot, and I can hardly put it on my expense account."

"Well, good-bye, then."

"Yes. Remember that I'm pleased with you." He hung up.

22

February 22, 1958

Dearest Harry,

There will be no flutter test. If my husband is Byzantine on matters so minor as a dinner party, I assure you that he is Bach's harpsichordist when it comes to tweaking Company strings. So, to pull you out of the clutches of Soviet Russia Division, Hugh chose the Right Gobsloptious Baron of your Western Hemisphere Division, J. C. King. J.C. is not the sort of fellow to welcome Soviet Russia Division's poachers onto his preserve. You are saved. Isn't it a fact that my husband can take care of everyone's career but his wife's?

Actually, Hugh and I have been getting along far better than ever, and since my illness he has been sharing a good deal more of his work with me. You don't know what a great step that is for him. Hugh, for all emotional purposes, was scourged in childhood when his mother killed his father. Since he cannot know whether the death was accidental or purposeful, his Alpha and Omega, built, of necessity, on rival propositions, are like two hill kingdoms facing each other across an abyss. Conceive, then, how difficult it is for him to trust me with any details of his work. (Which, collaterally, is why it would be a disaster for him to know that we are corresponding.) You may ask how I can encourage our letters, then, and I say that Hugh and I belong to a typical bond-and-bombs marriage, which is to say, we are half-wed. Alpha-Hugh and Alpha-Kitt are as joined as our sacraments, but his Omega cannot allow him to put faith in any woman, and my Omega, eager to be free and alone and full of taste for life, is obliged to suffer in the iron parameters of our marriage.

After my illness we did talk about such matters for the first time. I was able to point out that some of our sense of mutual oppression might be relieved by allowing me to live with a few of his adventures, if only in spirit.

"They are not adventures," he told me. "They are webs, and quite as sticky as spiderwebs."

All the same, Hugh proved to be man enough, and husband enough to enter my horrors last summer. When he finally came to understand, despite all his cautions and incalculable filigree of paranoia, that by closing me out of his professional life he was helping to unbalance my mind, he began to reveal to me a bit here and there about the pieces on his playing board. So I may know more now about your situation than you. I wish to give you a warning. The KGB, according to Hugh, has taken great strides in these last few years since Stalin's death. The all-out reign of terror is over, and they have begun to get fearfully skillful again. You might try worrying about them in serious respectful fashion. Hugh's estimate of the Masarov picnic is as follows: The KGB has succeeded in placing a mole in the Soviet Russia Division. The best way to protect said mole is to insinuate a notion into the upper reaches of the Agency that the fellow is to be found in GHOUL. By Hugh's estimate, the KGB set up the picnic in order to hand you a note that would point directly to Soviet Russia Division. This was done on the firm premise that Allen Dulles would then conclude the furry creature was to be located anywhere but in SR Div. Since you were the recipient of the note, but could not produce it, inasmuch as Boris had taken it back, a shadow would fall on GHOUL. The antipathy between GHOUL and SR Division is, after all, no secret. So we would have one more bad mark against Hugh. A provocation set up by the KGB in Uruguay would have been manipulated to great effect by the mole in SR Div back at Headquarters.

The purpose of the picnic, therefore, was not merely to injure GHOUL, but to crimp Hugh's influence in the Agency. That would be a disaster. Hugh is not the man to make such a claim aloud, but I know he feels the KGB are going to be able to penetrate to the very top of the Agency if he is not there to stop them. And it won't take all that many years.

Harry, I know you hate the idea of backing off from Masarov, so I'm going to offer the sum of my modest wisdom. I believe that people like you and me go into intelligence work in the first place because to a much greater degree than we realize, we've been intellectually seduced. And often by nothing more impressive than good spy novels and movies. We want, secretly, to act as protagonists in such ventures. Then we go to work for the Company, and discover that, whatever we are, we are never protagonists. We pop into the spy novel at chapter six, but rarely find out what was going on in chapter five, let alone earlier times. Just as seldom are we privy to what happens in the rest of the book. I offered this once to Hugh, and he said, "If you must feel sorry for yourself, read a book on the calculus of partial derivatives. That will give you paradigmatic solace, darling." The key to our lives, Harry, is in the drear word *patience*. We are incompetent without it.

As a test of your patience, I now inform you that I have news, but it is not for this letter. To whet your appetite to a slather, I will only say that I have changed my slot in TSS. I am now behind one of the doors that Arnie Rosen used to call "Dracula's Lair." Yes, I am being trained for what we might as well term *heavier* work. I've decided it's time to stop being a nice Radcliffe girl and step onto the dance floor with the barbarian in me who, breathing in great secret, does get somewhat short of wind over Lavinia's stumps.

You had better tell me what you are up to, or you simply won't get the next letter.

Love,
Kittredge

23

March 10, 1958

Dear Kittredge,

I have let two weeks go by since receiving your extraordinary letter of February 22, but you gave me such a jolt with talk of Dracula's Lair. I hope you know what you are getting into—whatever it is. I confess to being consumed with curiosity, and am exercised that you tell me no more. Yet, given the long hiatus last year in our letters, I feel, paradoxically, a pressure to bring you up to date on my affairs. I am going through my own kind of heavy moral duty.

I suppose I am thinking of my work with Chevi Fuertes. With the exception of a vacation in Buenos Aires that he took with his wife at Christmas, I have seen him at least once a week for the last fourteen months. The Groogs have developed a great taste for Chevi's output, and they monitor my reports carefully. He is far and away our most significant penetration into the Communist Party of Uruguay, and a measure of his importance can be seen in how my war with the Sourballs was brought to its formal close. A cable came from the Right *Gobsloptious* Baron—where did you ever get that word? (Was it at the age of eleven playing jacks on Brattle Street, your pigtails flying? Gobsloptious—my God!) J. C. King sent the following to Hunt: COMMENDATION CONFIRMED RE AV/AILABLE'S DEVELOPMENT OF AV/ OCADO.

Hugh's virtuosity is unparalleled. The Commendation did the job. Soviet Russia Division was obliged to recognize that a flutter test at this point would poke a very rude finger into the grand eye of J. C. King. So they withdrew. Hunt, concomitantly, has been cordial as hell ever since, and promises to take me along on a visit to an *estancia* one of these weekends. To certify this intention, he is teaching me to play polo on a practice field out in Carrasco. Do you know, human perversity being a bottomless pit, I like him more for liking me more!

In fact, I'm a little taken with myself. King's praise may have been stimulated by Hugh, but the language did enable me to reflect back on these fourteen months, and yes, I think I have brought in enough good work on Chevi to, yes, rate the Commendation.

You may then inquire why I have written so little about my top agent. I suppose I have kept away because the job consists of adding up small pieces of information gleaned from Chevi's tasks at the PCU (Partido Comunista de Uruguay), and I did not wish to bore you.

All the same, in these fourteen months, Chevi has moved up the rungs of that organization. His wife may be the leading woman in the Uruguayan Party, but Chevi has become her effective equal. He may even be ranked, overall, in the top twenty of Uruguayan Communists, and could one day become titular head of the whole shebang. Already, we have access to the thinking of the leadership.

Of course, the reason he has risen so quickly is that the Station made it possible. You may recall that nearly a year ago we had Chevi plant a transmitter in the PCU's inner office. It was a five-minute job consisting of no more than the replacement of a porcelain wall outlet with our bugged duplicate—an enterprise calling for no more than a screwdriver. Still, it was squeaky work and had to be done under *combat conditions,* that is, in the ten minutes that Chevi's associate was down the hall using the john.

At the time, we debated whether it was worth endangering AV/OCADO, but decided that the prospective take balanced out nicely with the relative security of the caper. Chevi showed neither emotion nor enthusiasm. He merely insisted that his weekly stipend be raised from fifty dollars to sixty. (We settled for a bonus of fifty bucks and a five dollar a week raise.) Then he brought the chore off without incident, and we have been receiving the product ever since, although the transmission is often garbled. Since Chevi, however, does not know how spotty our equipment has proved, he assumes we get it all and that motivates him to be scrupulous in what he tells us about the deliberations of upper-echelon PCU.

Moreover, the dispatch with which he carried off the wall-outlet job helped to convince us that he had turned a corner. This often happens with agents. Their early hysteria is replaced by effective calm. In consequence, Hunt decided to advance his career in the Partido Comunista de Uruguay. Marvelous, isn't it? Easier to get Eusebio Fuertes promoted than myself.

Kittredge, this exercise in *applied intelligence* isn't altogether pretty. We don't go in for wet jobs—at least, not down here, although I won't speak for Dracula's Lair, whew!—but our route did get dirty enough to stop in Pedro Peones' office. Reunited with Libertad La Lengua, Pedro was cordially inclined to entrap a couple of PCU officials for us. They were stationed higher than Chevi and very much in his way. So, a kilo package of heroin happened to be found in the car trunk of the selected PCU official (the drug on loan from Peones' narcotics squad). The other Communist was arrested for driving under the influence and then being so rash as to attack the pursuing officers. (After being splashed down with a bottle of liquor, he was then smashed repeatedly, I fear, in the face. That was to show evidence of the battle he *started* with Peones' cops.) While the PCU knew their people were being framed, there was little they could do about it. The first accused was held without bail for allegedly dealing in a large quantity of drugs, and the second was beaten badly enough to be severely demoralized. Replacements had to be found for their jobs.

Now, these victims (if it is any consolation to them) happened to be chosen with considerable care. You might even say the operation was *designed* by Sherman Porringer. I am beginning to see some relation between Oatsie's carefully painted eggshells and the delicacy he brought to this project. Hunt provided the go-ahead—"See what you can do about getting Chevi promoted"—but Porringer put it all into place. Elegant selection of target was what Sherman was hunting for. As he saw it, the key mistake would be to knock out the man directly above Chevi. We had to allow that the PCU would be bright enough to assume Pedro Peones was doing our muscle work, and so their suspicion was bound to fall on the man who was in line to fill the gap. All right, then, reasoned Porringer, look not only for a good man to knock out, but get one whose immediate inferior is not well respected, thereby disposing of two obstacles for the price of one. This double disruption, even though located several rungs up the ladder, would have to benefit Fuertes before too long.

On the drug bust, Peones' victim was a PCU leader of unassailable integrity, but his assistant had a gambling problem, and so was brought to trial by his Party peers on an accusation of collaboration with Peones. Before it was over, the man resigned his office.

Some months later, the second arrest produced comparable results. Chevi had advanced four rungs through our efforts.

Crucial to Porringer's design was that we maintained immaculate hygiene in relation to Peones. Pedro was never given a reason for either arrest, and we even discussed with him attacks on several other Communist officials including Fuertes. Our assumption was that Peones' police office had already been penetrated by the PCU. The best way to obtain Chevi a clean bill from his own Communists, therefore, would be to add his name to Peones' list of intended PCU victims. Indeed, Chevi was soon warned by the Party hierarchy that Peones was looking to entrap him.

Fuertes began to talk, therefore, of the threat to his safety. "I would hate," he told me, "to be beaten up by Peones' *duros* for being a Communist when, in fact, I am a betrayer of Communists. The punishment would fit too closely to the crime."

"You possess a sense of irony."

"I would hope it is loyalty, not irony, that I will discover in you. Can you tell Peones to stay off this body?" He tapped his chest.

"We only have limited influence with the man," I said.

"*Verdad?* That is not what I hear."

"We have tried to set up a relationship, but have had no success."

"Unbelievable. Who can pay Peones more than you?"

"For whatever reason, Peones pursues his own course."

"You are saying, then, that you will not protect me from police goons?"

"I think we can exercise some influence." When he laughed

at this, I added, "We are more law-abiding than you would ever believe."

More recently, Chevi has become suspicious of his rapid Party advancement. A few months ago he said to me, "It is one thing to betray my coworkers, but another to shoot them in the back."

Still, Chevi has changed considerably. I think. For one thing, he is now high enough on the slope to sniff the air of the summit, and that has been tonic to his ambition. For another, his identity has altered.

Kittredge, either his Alpha or Omega has taken over from the other. He has put on more than thirty pounds, and has grown a prodigious handlebar mustache which, in company with the plump pouches beneath his eyes, has given him a jolly piratical South American look. He makes you think of an overweight gaucho riding a skinny horse. With Roger Clarkson, he was always on the run for women; now, he is a glutton for food. AV/OCADO is taking on the shape of his name. The largest disagreement we face these days is where to meet. He hates the safe house. May heaven help me if I forget to stock the icebox! He wants *tapas* and beer, steak and bourbon, and—speak of peculiarities—raw onions with good Scotch! Plus desserts. *Dulces*. Even the sound calls to mind a stream of half-frozen delights sweetening the parched canyon of the throat. He talks while eating. His pieces of intelligence come forth best as food passes in the opposite direction. He punctuates tidbits of information by sucking in small jets of air to clean the spaces between his teeth. At times he acts as gross as Peones. And he keeps coming back to one theme: that we meet more often in restaurants. I have increasing difficulty in refusing him. For one thing, the denizens of our high-rise apartment house muster an astonishing number of rich widows and well-to-do retired tarts, and they study everyone who comes up to their floor. Each time the elevator stops, doors open a crack all up and down the hall. Eyes peek at one voraciously. These ladies must have expected a comfortable old age where they could pull back wooden shutters and set their accumulated bosoms on a worm-eaten second-story windowsill while they observed life in the common street below. Instead, they are now marooned on the twelfth floor and can only keep an eye on who goes in and out of each apartment. Needless to say, Fuertes is also aware of this, and claims it is dangerous. The word could be out among the neighbors that our apartment is kept by *El Coloso del Norte,* and, besides, he might be recognized. He has lived almost all of his life in Montevideo.

I take up the problem with Hunt and he is furious. "Tell the son of a bitch to shove his reports in a dead drop. We'll pick them up with a cut-out."

"Howard," I protest gently, "we'll lose a lot if I can't talk to him." I pause. "What about moving to a more secluded safe house?"

"All safe houses present problems. His real bitch is the *ambiente*. That goddamn furniture! I can't get requisitions for decent stuff. Economies in the wrong place. I hate tacky government mentalities. A posh safe house is a good investment if you can only convince the powers that be." He stopped. "Wigs," said Howard. "Tell him to put on a different disguise each time."

"Won't work," I said, "with his mustache."

"Just tell the cocksucker to shape up. Treat him like a servant. That's the only language agents really respect."

Exiting from this interview, it occurs to me that I may now have put in more hours in the field than Howard. In any event, I certainly know better than to follow his advice. As a practical matter, never treat an agent like Chevi any worse than a younger brother. And most of the time I cater to him. Part of that derives, I know, from my incomplete ability, as Hugh would put it, to toughen up. Damn it, I feel for my agent. Chevi does manage to penetrate into all those close places in oneself where you chart the rise and fall of your ego. (Query: We've never talked about Alpha Ego and Omega Ego and their inner relations. That's a whole study, I know.) Chevi, I suspect, is treating me like a younger brother all the while I am trying to treat him like one. As one example of how he attempts to keep me in place, he loves to speak of his two years in New York when he lived with that Negress in Harlem. She turned tricks, and was on drugs, and encouraged him to be her pimp. After a time, he changes his story and confesses that he actually took on the job. He tells me hair-raising tales about knife fights with other pimps. I don't know how much of it is true—I suspect he is exaggerating—indeed, I would guess he avoided knife fights, but I just can't swear to any of this. He does have a few facial scars. Be assured, however, his tales serve their purpose: I feel inferior to his sophistication. On the other hand, we are always in one or another spiritual contest to see who will end up brother superior.

Lately, I've been having my troubles in this direction. Howard's concept of emblazoning MARXISMO ES MIERDA in six-foot letters on every available town wall has escalated into a small war. If Marxists have their own kind of religious feelings, then connecting Marxism and shit to each other certainly awakens something explosive. The toughest leftist street gangs in Montevideo come from the dock area, and their leaders are high cadre in the MRO, an ultra-left group. Such boys are tough. In fact, they proved so rugged that our kids in AV/ALANCHE were getting chewed up by the street fights. It was no fun, I tell you, to sit in my car a half mile away, and hear nothing but a brief *"Emboscada!"*—ambushed!—over my walkie-talkie, then, fifteen minutes later, see the team come straggling back with an unholy number of bloody heads—four out of seven one night. Then, worse: one boy in the hospital, soon another. Howard called on Peones to beef up our troops with off-duty cops handsomely paid from the Special Budget. Well, AV/ALANCHE won a few fights, only to see the MRO come back with reinforcements of their own. These nocturnal encounters have grown into medieval battles.

In the last year, a small operation of seven kids who did their wall painting once a week, and fell into a skirmish perhaps one night a month, has grown into a series of massive encounters with thirty or forty people on either side using rocks, clubs, knives, shields, helmets, and one bow and arrow, yes, such items were actually found on the street after the last ruckus we won, and finally, a boy on our side was killed about a month ago. Shot dead through the eye. Peones ran a dragnet through two working-class neighborhoods, Capurro and La Teja, searching for the gun and the gunman, and informed Hunt that the killer was taken care of without a trial (which we are now free to believe or disbelieve), but, as you can see, the character of the event is significantly altered. Peones keeps two police cars waiting in the wings to charge in should the battle go poorly. AV/EMARIA, with their infrared camera, were actually used on one occasion to patrol up and down the surrounding streets photographing any and all youths approaching the scene, an absurdly over-weighted venture (speak of expense!) which Hunt did call to a halt once he saw that the results, apart from the labors of identification, were technically inadequate. (You couldn't discern the faces on the film, let alone identify them.) I could have told him as much.

At any rate, the MRO is now on the offensive. YANQUI A FUERA! is getting painted on many walls, and in good Catholic neighborhoods, too. The MRO people seem to have a better sense of where to strike than we do. Hunt decides that one of Peones' cops must be secretly aiding the MRO, and wants Chevi to furnish us with detailed information on the MRO cadres so we can get more a line on this.

Fuertes refuses the request outright. He is a serious agent doing serious work, he says, and we are asking him to inform on street youths. "My pride is that I betray those who are situated above me, not beneath me."

"*Ayúdame, compañero,*" I exclaim.

"I am not your *compañero*. I am your agent. And insufficiently paid."

"Do you think you will get a raise by refusing us?"

"That is a matter of no significance. You will, in either case, continue to treat me like a puppet, and I will attempt to exert whatever autonomy is left to me."

"Why don't we cut through the crap and get to the bone," I tell him.

"Quintessentially American. Get to the bone."

"Will you fulfill our request?"

"I betray big people. Stupid, stuffed-shirt bureaucratic Communists who have sold out their own people for the power they can now exercise at a desk. They are upper filth, and I associate myself with them every day, and become an upper bureaucrat like them. But, I do not delude myself. I have betrayed my people and my roots. I am a viper. Nonetheless, I am not so degraded that I wish to poison those who are smaller than myself. The MRO street boys who come out from La Teja to fight at night are nearer to me than you can ever be. I grew up in La Teja. I was cadre myself in the MRO during university days. But, now, as an entrenched bureaucrat in the PCU, I no longer have the contacts you need. You see, the MRO does not trust the PCU. They view it as too established and too penetrated."

Well, at least I have a plausible report to bring back to Hunt. I am writing it in my mind as I listen: *Profound internecine mistrust between MRO and PCU. Cannot determine Left police sources without penetrating MRO.*

That will use up a month of debate between Station and Groogs. By then, Hunt may be on to something else, or—and now I have an inspiration. The key to working with Chevi is to save mutual face.

"All right," I say, "you will not do it, and I will not threaten you. I accept your version; PCU and MRO lack umbilical connection."

"Put that in the bank," says Chevi. He bends toward me and whispers, "They hate each other." He giggles.

"All right," I say, "point made. Now, I want you to help me. My people are going to need a penetration into the highest places in the MRO." I point upward with my finger to emphasize that I am in tune with the AV/OCADO ethic of punching up, always up. "I want you to provide me with a list of possible high personnel for penetration."

This is the kind of bargain that can be struck.

"I will need two weeks," he says.

"No, I want it for our meeting next week." I am thinking that I will get together with Gordy Morewood and go over the names Chevi brings in. Gordy may even know how to make the approach. All this will take months, but my rapidly aging young backside will be covered. Oh, Kittredge, this was the moment when I knew I was a Company man.

"Next week," Chevi agrees.

With that, he stepped into the hall, raised his hand in greeting, I suppose, to the retired tarts peeking out at him, and, waddling just a trifle in obedience to his increasing avoirdupois, made his way to the elevators.

That son of a bitch. I can assure you, he probably had the names already. By the next week, he came forth with a short list of three figures in the MRO, and Gordy Morewood was on the stick. In turn, by the following week, Fuertes had asked for a raise. And will probably get it.

Yes, Masarov has been only one element in these busy days. Write to me. I need it.

Love,
Harry

24

March 15, 1958

Beloved Man,

I am so glad you seem to have accepted my sermon on patience, since I cannot tell you any more at this point about Dracula's Lair. I have taken too many vows of silence concerning the matter and am just not able to find the sanction in myself to fill you in. Yet, I am still dying to send you letters. When is devotion ever so alive as in wholly private correspondence? Which we have, dear friend.

You took your courage delicately in hand and asked me about Alpha-Ego and Omega-Ego. I must have frightened you in the past for stepping on my preserves! How decent it is of you to live with my theories when everyone else has decided they are last year's intellectual fashion.

Well, it is interesting that you fix on this aspect of my work. Do you know that is where I began? The first crude questionnaires I laid out to try to locate the separate properties of Alpha and Omega did focus on their separate egos. I had an insight at the time, you see: The best approach would be by way of memory tests.

It was an interesting concept. Memory, after all, is often sinister. Nothing within ourselves betrays us quite so much as memory, and ego, I came to decide, was the *overseer* of memory. It does not matter what we may retain at deeper levels; the ego controls the surface and so will distort a recollection if that is necessary to maintaining the ego's view of things.

Well, contemplate the hurdles to be faced with two egos, one for Alpha, one for Omega. No wonder people could not bear my theories. Yet, one characteristic was soon clear to me. Because Alpha and Omega maintain separate banks of recollection, memory was not going to be at all identical in them. Their respective egos have too many separate needs, and, given enough need, memory becomes no more than a servant of the ego—which, I expect, is exactly why the memoirs of successful men are usually so awful.

The easiest route, I concluded, to uncovering the distinctive properties of Alpha and Omega would be, then, to study the respective development of their egos. I would offer each subject some material to memorize, then question him on retention. I expected to discover patterns of recollection coupled with the most surprising lack of recollection, and I did, but I also found that my test did not work with certain kinds of strong and ruthless people engaged in high-level work. They consistently broke the pattern. They had what I came to call *ultra-ego*. They could remember a hideous deed perfectly, and with no large signs of disturbance.

Consider, for example, the indescribably powerful psychic force that enabled monsters like Hitler and Stalin to live with the millions of deaths they left in their wake. At a more modest level, but not vastly more comprehensible, are those responsible for the deaths of thousands. It occurs to me not all too comfortably that Hugh can aspire to that category. Taken by intimate measure, Hugh's ultra-ego is curiously intoxicating to me, and feeds, I suspect, the impulse now driving this girl to become one of Dracula's ladies—an outrageous exaggeration, and yet not altogether. You see, I have never lost completely my presentiment that the transactions of the spirit underworld are very much connected to us here. In this vein, a man named Noel Field is most relevant to my fears. Do you know that I have days when I cannot think of Allen Dulles without invoking Noel Field's image, for he has been incarcerated in Soviet prisons for years and Allen put him there back in 1950. Very much with the help of Hugh.

Believe it, my dear husband did confide in me about this exploit. Allen, I learned, was made to look a hell of a fool by Noel Field back in Zurich during World War II. For some reason, Allen trusted Field enough to add his personal recommendation to the names of a number of Europeans proposed by Field for important jobs with the Allied armies. Many of them turned out to be Communists, and Noel, who had more or less known that, never informed Allen of their political bent. (Like many another Quaker, Noel Field did go in, I fear, for the most overweening permissiveness in dealing with Communists.) Well, Allen paid for that mistake in a number of ways, and never forgave Noel. But it took Hugh, in company with Frank Wisner, to come up with an idea how to pay this enterprising Quaker back. In 1949, we managed to get the word out to a few high Soviets that Noel Field was CIA. Pure disinformation. Hugh handled that part and, you may be certain, left no American signature on it. I expect Dulles, Wisner, and Montague assumed that just as soon as Field took his next Red Cross or CARE trip over to Warsaw he would be imprisoned as a spy and some of his close Communist cronies might have to suffer a bit along with him. It went, however, a lot further than that. Stalin was hopelessly insane by then. Field was thrown incommunicado into a Warsaw jail cell, and before the affair was over just about every Communist with whom he had had dealings, plus their numerous circles of cohorts, were either shot, tortured, or imprisoned for confessing to deeds they had not committed. Some put the number of Party victims at a thousand dead; some at five thousand. When I inquired of Hugh, he shrugged and said, "Stalin gave us another Katyn Forest massacre."

Well, I never knew whether to be proud of my husband's skills in this matter or aghast, and, of course, the Agency now engages in *levitations* that can be seen as amusing or scandalous, depending on one's point of view. Over these last years, we have certainly financed a number of liberal but resolutely anti-Communist organizations who set up a programmatic hue and cry to free the American martyr, Noel Field, from Soviet-Polish oppression.

Later, Harry, during that awful time when I passed through the loneliness of living with my own career failure, I began to think about all those Polish Communists who were falsely executed as traitors. Here was one more example of an evil masterpiece committed by us in the name, and, I believe, ultimately, in the cause, of good, but, oh, the anguish of the victims. I began to wonder if we had not touched some vulnerable edge of the cosmos. I hope this is not so, but I do fear it. I think of the frightful way Herr Adolf massacred millions of people in clean places. They walked into the gas chambers believing they were going to bathe their dirty, tired bodies. Get ready for hot showers, they were told. Then the fatal vents were opened. As I was going under in my own Easter madness, I used to feel as if I could hear those victims screaming in rage, and I began to brood on the possibility that when a death is monstrously unfair, it can send out a curse upon human existence from which we do not necessarily recover in full. Not altogether. Some days when the smog in Washington is inhumanly bilious I wonder if we are not breathing some baleful message from the beyond. You can see how disturbed I am still. Which of course leads me to brood on your dealings with your agent, Chevi Fuertes. What about his life? How responsible are you for what is happening to him? And to the people around him.

Well, I've gotten into awfully solemn stuff, have I not? Let us say I am feeling nervous about my upcoming venture, which may prove no picnic either.

Would you divert me? I know it seems like a small request, but if Howard has indeed gotten around to taking you to one of those *estancias,* would you write to me about that little event? I like the social comedies you get into, and am certain any description of Howard Hunt cavorting with rich Uruguayans will be milk and honey for me—certainly much better than my paranoid fantasies that you are off on brothel expeditions.

Really! We all have to lie so much that a straightforward account is balm to the soul.

Love to you, dear man,
Kittredge

25

I DID NOT KNOW IF I WISHED TO HEAR ANY MORE ABOUT LIES. KIT-tredge's letter disturbed me, and I began to wonder whether some manifestations of ultra-ego were not often present in more minor matters. After all, I, who still saw myself as an honest man, had been lying concertedly to Hugh Montague, Kittredge, Howard Hunt, Chevi Fuertes, Sherman Porringer, and, worst of all, to Sally. For I had made the mistake, all those months ago, of hinting that love along some future tree-lined street was not wholly impossible. Of course, I was hardly in possession of any large funds of ultra-ego, since in her case, I certainly had to pay the price. My lie exploded on the day she saw a headless ghost gallop across my face in the instant I learned she was pregnant. After which, it did not matter what I tried to say; I was confirming what she knew already.

Our abandoned carnal relations began to rear up in my memory like a burned-out building. Sally made a point, when meeting at embassy parties, to be concertedly nasty. Such parties were now the sum of what I had for social life in Montevideo. On those even more frequent nights when I was alone in my hotel room, it would occur to me all too bitterly that I could not even boast of a bar I frequented regularly. We were not encouraged to—CIA men were always poten-tial targets for kidnapping and torture, or, at least, so went the premise. On those occasions when night work or an Embassy function did not have me occupied in the evening, I did not always know what to do with myself—people who work sixty hours a week usually don't. And now there were no late-night options for chancy play with Sally. Before her pregnancy, there had been evenings when Sherman, kept late at the office, would thereby free Sally and me to meet in my hotel. Now, at parties, she would choose a corner to rake me over with a quick speech or two. "Harry," she would say, "Sherman's become a hellion in bed."

"They say marriages go through stages."

"What could you know about marriage?" Sally would reply, and with a bright smile for the rest of the room, as if she were recounting the saga of a three no-trump, doubled and redoubled, she would add, "I bet you are a faggot. Deep down!"

Deep down was where she had just wounded me. I had enjoyed her protestations that no other man ever made love to her so well. Now I had a momentary struggle to keep the tears out of my eyes. Manifest injustice always affected me in such manner.

"You've never looked more attractive," I said, and stepped away.

I saw her soon after at the next Russian Embassy party. As evening came to the garden, we were left again with our natural colleagues, the Soviets. In a reprise of our earlier evening, Hunt and Porringer and Kearns and Gatsby and their wives, and Nancy Waterston and myself, were still around at the end, and on this occasion Hunt obtained a long-held wish. Poking one stiff finger into Varkhov's chest, he said, "Georgey boy, I hear you are going to charm our socks off and take us on a tour of your Embassy."

"Soxoff?" said Georgi, "I do not think I know him." But I was able to pick up the smallest flick of a look he sent in Boris' direction, followed by a slow opening of Masarov's eyes to indicate assent, for Varkhov now said, "Yes, into the Embassy, of course, why not? Everybody," and we trooped in to take a tour of the rooms permitted, which were four in number and grand enough to suggest a museum. The gold and white furniture in these reception chambers seemed suitable for a lady-in-waiting to Louis XIV or Catherine the Great. That turned out to be not a bad guess, for Varkhov now murmured to Hunt, "Furniture from excess at Hermitage in Leningrad."

"Boy, I hear that's one splendiferous pile," said Howard.

"Formidable presentation of czarist-era wealth," replied Varkhov.

We wandered about in these four medium-grand rooms with their high ceilings, extrusive gilt-painted moldings, solemnly profound old carpets, parquet floors, rococo chairs with faded champagne seats, and all the many portraits of Lenin, Stalin—still prominent was Stalin!—Khrushchev, Bulganin, Peter the Great, and hunting scenes. I found myself looking into Lenin's eyes and they kept looking back at me until I recognized that I was drunk on vodka.

More vodka followed. Toast upon toast: To summit meetings! To friendship between nations! To peace on earth! Hoorah, we yelled. After all, there had been so many years of supporting the weight of one another. Tonight, on a river of vodka, we had solved a myriad of problems that would be there again tomorrow, but for tonight, hurrah, we were in the Russian Embassy.

Hunt kept teasing Varkhov. "Georgey, these rooms are for the tourists. Give us the real trip. Let's see the dishes in the sink."

"Oh, cannot. No dishes in sink. Soviet sink clean."

"You just bet your Uncle Ezra on that," said Howard, and Dorothy explained, "It's a figure of speech," since Varkhov was already inquiring, "Uncle Ezra? Is cousin of Uncle Sam?"

Hunt finally got his way. We were taken on a tour through a few of the back offices, which had heavy Russian-made office furniture, but were otherwise not all that distinguishable from ours. As we went along, Masarov had a moment when he was standing nearby long enough to send a wink my way, a quick acknowledgment, I could only suppose, of the grief he had bestowed with his picnic note. As if we had been engaged in a practice sufficiently embarrassing on that Sunday afternoon never to make reference to it again, Boris had proffered no more invitations, and Zenia treated me like a stranger once more, which is to say she revealed again her abstract but nearly overwhelming sexual side, exactly what I had not been favored with in her home where she had been naught but maternal. In public, her sexuality was always saying: "You, a man, cannot begin to comprehend how magical, wondrous, and occult is the labyrinth of my power," but, it was, as I say, an abstract sexuality. You could have been approaching a large city at night from so great a distance that you had to be content with a view of the sky glow.

Now, Masarov gave his wink, and that was all, and we continued to straggle along with glasses in our hands through office rooms, becoming sufficiently separated from one another to leave me, for perhaps thirty seconds, alone in one of their cubicles with Sally Porringer, who was by now just pregnant enough to be looking prettier than ever, and Sally, with what had to be an accurate sense of the time it would take for the next person to reach our small quarters, proceeded to sit down, rock back in her chair, raise her knees and spread her thighs. She was wearing no panties, and my eyes, in consequence, were able to feast on the lost lands below. Then, with timing as precise as a dancing master, she put down her skirt and lowered her legs just as Sherman came along with Dorothy Hunt, but in that suspended interval, while showing herself to me, there had been time enough for Sally to whisper, "It's crazy being in these people's rooms," and I could have leaped across to her. The impulse to spring was so powerful that I was racked for days. I actually telephoned her. In fact, I made a fool of myself. She had touched some fatal spot between the navel and the groin. For the first time, I was tortured at not being able to have her, and Sally, in turn, kept assuring me through the receiver, "I won't bother to see you. Sherman is surprising merry hell out of me *todas las noches.*"

"Sally, I just might be eating my heart out," I told her.

"Well, keep eating," she said, and laughed merrily. What a stomper her rodeo dad must have been.

26

I HAD NEVER HAD SUCH NEED OF SEX BEFORE. ONE NIGHT, I ENDED UP going with—who else could it be?—Sherman Porringer to his favorite brothel, an eighty-year-old emporium in the Old City full of chandeliers and walnut-paneled walls. "Been remiss with the señoritas lately," he confided to me, "but that's because old Sally eats nothing but chili peppers these days."

Some supernatural weeks ensued. Supernatural was the word. Loose at last in Montevideo's brothels, enjoying such forays more than I expected, I found myself fulfilling whole panels of Kittredge's imagination, and often became as fond of the whore I took for a night as I had ever been of Sally. In the relief of knowing that it was sex I loved, Sally, poor girl—for I was now as mean in my memory of her as she to me—began to be remembered, poor Sally, as a randy mustang who would be honored best for introducing me to my true and natural estate, which was to love women at large. Kittredge might once have scorned my descriptions of Alpha and Omega at sex and in love, but my old thesis certainly seemed to fit the new life. Alpha sported with prostitutes, and Omega became the keeper of the dream, yes, Omega might still be in love with the exceptional Mrs. Montague, but that made me no sexual fascist, merely the wise proprietor of a home for two strikingly different individuals, the romantic lover who needed no more than a letter to keep love warm, and the sportsman who could hunt as intently as his father for female flesh.

Of course, flesh was not hard to find in the brothels of Montevideo. I knew the beginner's joy of unlimited game. There was a month or two when it was just so simple as that. Engraved on my retina, and imprinted on my loins, was the emblem of Sally's bare ass on a Soviet chair, and this conjunction of the superpowers was there to offer its libidinous funds.

Porringer was my guide for the first night, and gave a running commentary on all the girls, "That squatty dark one is better than she looks, has a twat will like to jerk you off, it's got a grip," at which the short squatty one gave me a broad grin showing two gold teeth, and of another, "Has the prettiest pussy you will ever see but she only takes it up the dirt track"—a lithe, slim, and sullen girl whose buttocks were her most salient feature—"although, goddamnit," said Porringer, "why not?"—and poked me with his elbow as a tall beauty with the falsest color of purple-red hair came down the stairs. "This one's got nothing to offer but her mouth, can't touch her down below, she's diseased, but the mouth is worth the rest, and penicillin will keep you blessed," whereupon he began to guffaw and slugged his beer. He was a ranch hand in a brothel. His family had been out there in Oklahoma before the 1889 land-grab—as I was to learn on this night in the Arboleda de Mujeres, what a Female Grove!—and I even had an insight into Sally and Oatsie's roots, generation unto generation living on those long, mean plains where the hound of austerity rode in with the dust (or so I conceived it, knowing nothing of Oklahoma but the little I knew), yet, as I saw it, simple human greed had been so deprived of satisfaction out in those lands that it worked itself all the way back to the last human nerve, the one that leads to our soul. Greed, after generations of being denied, had erupted into the hog, Porringer, and the sow, Sally, yes, I was not kind about the wounds I had taken, but my sentiments would hardly bother Sherman. He saw himself, good yeoman legionnaire of the American empire, as owning the females in the countries through which he traveled, good finger-licking food for his omnivorous cock. Or was I, all regional differences to the side, close to describing myself as well?

Even as I was buying my hour from one girl that night, and a second woman for a second hour, and feeling freer with these strangers than in all my twenty-five years of Park Avenue, Knickerbocker Grays, Matty Saints, punch bowl at Mory's, et cetera, et cetera, maybe the taproot where my greed was stored was pouring out at last into the American Century, and I too was out there copulating for the flag. Greed having transmuted itself into a more noble emotion, I felt a glow of inner power, as if I were finally attached to the great wheeling scheme of things.

During this spell of nightlife, I went to mansions that must once have been as grand as the Russian Embassy, and to sheds on the edge of shack towns where the streets were unpaved and the loose tin roofs offered percussive effects when the wind blew. I visited parlors with bedrooms in high-rise apartment houses out near Pocitos Beach, and once, coming home from Hunt's villa in Carrasco, I found a well-appointed brothel in the shadow of the famous Carrasco Casino and Hotel where the girls looked as lovely to me as Hollywood starlets, even if the one I chose (because her nipples pointed most astonishingly toward the stars) offered but an austere Spanish sense of reciprocity and approached no earthquake force with me.

Another night in a cellar whorehouse on a medium-poor street where the oak tables were bumpy with the welts of initials carved across the grain of other initials, I ended up with a short, fat, merry girl whose black eyes gleamed with expert mischief. She was delighted she had caught herself an American and proceeded to explore with her tongue every crevice I had counted as my own and a few I did not even know were there, until even Omega was stirred out of his Kittredge-loving quarters, and I felt as if I were coming all over town and knew afterward as I held that merry little fatso in my arms how men could end up married to girls with but a single skill.

I loved the decor of the brothels. They could be clean or dirty, lavish or bare, bars or sitting rooms, but the lights were invariably soft, and the jukeboxes, which were almost always an extravaganza of colored bulbs and cascades of neon tubing, looked like little frontier towns unto themselves. You could gamble with your money, your heart, your ego, and your health. In the months that followed, I would come down with gonorrhea twice and syphilis once, but Montevideo was not Berlin, and you could trust any doctor on any street to treat you without a report. In Berlin every adventure had seemed to bear a likely cost, payment virtually in advance—here, in a part of the world where silt-filled tides lapped quietly on the shore, infection was the concomitant of a good tour.

Needless to say, this exploration night after night was only possible because a part of me was now more in love with Kittredge than ever. Since I no longer deceived her with one hard-as-clay little American cheerleader, but rather surrounded her with a full chorus of her own sex—even if they were, for the most part, poor and South American—I felt no shame. On the contrary, I was full of interest, for I was proceeding on the assumption that women who looked alike would make love in similar fashion—and it may be as good a hypothesis as any other. I could even tell myself that this quickly acquired loss of innocence would be excellent for my future work in the Agency. Knowledge of people was part of the power, after all, to do one's job.

If I did have an initial period on going into brothels alone with my courage racing as fast as my heart, full of fear that I, as a CIA officer, was open to kidnapping, ambush, torture, or entrapment, such anxiety was soon replaced by the recognition that vice and violence were commercially antipathetic—nowhere in the world was a bad drunk more unpopular than in a Montevidean brothel. If I had also learned the low trick of tipping the bouncer, that merely certified I was knowledgeable and American. The true peril, as I soon discovered, was not peril but loneliness, corrosive visits to loneliness. Soon enough, it began to arrive in the middle of a drunken spree. There was one such night in a cheap whorehouse called El Cielo de Húsar near the docks, and this Hussar's Heaven was a dilapidated and very old house of the early nineteenth century which must once have kept horses in the living room, and so reminded me of the Stable in Georgetown. Here, however, were gaps in the molding and rat portals in the walls; the swaybacked beds had dirty blankets at the foot; the whores were morose. If I was there on that night, it was because my mood was no better, and I made love to my girl in a surprisingly perfunctory performance considering how seriously I took the act by dint of paying for it (penurious were the Hubbard habits concerning the hard and the crisp). Usually I tried to choose women who brought a modicum of art or ceremony to this possible desecration of eternal sacraments—you could take the boy out of the chapel, I said to myself, but you could not take St. Matthew's out of the boy, I was as alone as all that, drink notwithstanding. On the same afternoon, I had actually been curdled enough in my judgment to wonder whether Sally Porringer and I could, all hazards recognized, be able to live as man, woman, and new child, no, that was smashed on the thought of my child's head dented by the last phallic acts of the previous husband, Porringer, just so morbid had my thoughts become, and were still with me that night in the Hussar's Heaven, while banging away on a piece of flesh. I decided that depravity had you in its grip when flesh felt equal to rubber in your mitts. Trying to force the semi-demoralized troops of my loins up one more drunken hill, I could hear from the bedrooms on either side of me the long professional wail of two whores as they came in unison with their clients, or pretended to, their voices crying out into the chill of the South American night—the whore on my left screaming, *"Hijo, hijo, hijo,"* while the one to my right kept grunting, *"Ya, ya, ya."* It was then I knew how it felt to be the loneliest man in the world. Laboring up the bare knoll of pleasure reserved for me on this night, I dressed quickly, and went downstairs for a drink at the bar, which I did not finish—I was obviously coming to the end of my youth when drinks I had paid for would not be finished—and left El Cielo de Húsar to walk to the garage where I had taken the precaution to leave my car.

On the way, I met Chevi Fuertes. It was not a coincidence, but a miracle. So I felt. The sight of his wide and smiling mustache was a providential omen. I was no longer at the end of the first long street of my life, but merely in the middle of a bad evening which had just taken an upward turn. We went off to the next bar to have a drink together and when that, after fifteen minutes, activated the dregs of my professionalism enough to sober me at the thought of being seen together in public, we decided to get into my car and take a drive out to Pocitos Beach to visit a dear friend of his, Miss Libertad La Lengua, who would not be working tonight, Thursday night, he said. I think I should have paid more attention to the way he said *Miss* Libertad La Lengua.

27

April 10, 1958—Late at night
Dearest Kittredge,

It's weeks since I sent a letter, but I feel in no rush to apologize. After all, you keep me on the outside of Dracula's Lair. I do have, however, something I want to narrate. You see, I have met Libertad La Lengua. The legendary Libertad.

Let me offer context. I was due to see Chevi Fuertes last Thursday evening, a miserable rainy night one week ago, and feeling so lonely for you I swear I could smell some of those mules who died

in your parlor one hundred years ago. How far away Georgetown
seemed. One feels at the bottom of the world in Uruguay, or, at least,
such were my cheerful thoughts around the time Chevi Fuertes had
the unforgivable audacity to call my hotel room. Of course, he put a
handkerchief over his pay-phone mouthpiece, so I will admit I didn't
recognize his voice. He's a scamp. He chose to talk in a lisp as if we
were planning a homosexual romp. (God, what if the KGB had a tap?
Think of all those fey agents who would be thrown at me in months
to come. Hubbard, the jewel of the Andes!)

Well, it was a joke. Chevi merely wanted a ride out to the safe
house in Pocitos Beach. Too long a trip by bus. Could I accommodate
him? Kittredge, if I ever train case officers, I'll tell them to learn game
fishing first. You pull in until the moment when you must give slack.
This was such a moment. I picked him up at a bar, and out we drove
to the safe house.

It purported to be a routine meeting. Of late, if you recollect,
he has, in his own grudging way, been filling us in on the MRO but
complains that he is being used as a finger man. Each name he
provided of an MRO leader (four in all) was now in a hospital. "I am
incommensurably stupid," Chevi told me. "There is no possibility
that Peones and his goon squads are not working for you."

When I said, "Peones has his own sources of information,"
Chevi began to laugh.

"I could tell you about Peones," he said. "I know him well.
I grew up with him."

"Yes?"

"In Montevideo everybody grows up with everybody. Peones is an outrageous bully. And a dangerous man."

"Yes?"

"At the highest level, he is a fool."

"Why do you say that?"

"I am going to tell you because I choose to. If I did not so
choose, torture would not make me reveal what I know."

"I agree."

"Por fortuna!" But he was pleased that I took him seriously.
"Pedro Peones," he went on, "is insanely in love with a prostitute
who is a friend of mine. He loves her so much that if it came to it,
he would betray all of you."

"Could it ever come to that?"

"Who is to say? On the face of it, not likely. The woman,

Miss Libertad La Lengua, is a primitive capitalist. The accumulation of capital is all that concerns her. Why should she want Peones to betray any of you?"

"Businessmen can always fall out."

"Muy jocoso."

"Jocoso?"

"Very jocular," said Chevi. "She would urge him to betray your people only if it were worth her while. If the Russians, for instance, were to make her an offer she could not refuse, she would induce Peones to work with them."

"She must be impressive."

"Incalculably so. Once you meet her, you will appreciate what I mean. Her powers are unique."

"Yes, but when am I to meet her?"

"Tonight. At her house." He sat himself down beside the safe-house phone and said, "Peones always visits this lady on Thursday night. Early. He goes to early Mass in the morning, spends the late afternoon with his family, and by evening, cannot wait to be with her for a little while. She receives him at home. Then he leaves. She waits for my call. Shall I use this phone?"

"Do we need to?"

"No. She is expecting me."

"And who will you say that I am?"

"An American friend who works for the State Department."

"You will tell her that you, a Communist, associate with Americans in the State Department?"

"She has no interest in politics."

"Chevi, it is impossible for me to go."

He began to laugh. "I have not told her anything. I will merely say you are an American with lots of money and could soon be parted from it."

"And if I wanted to buy her services?"

"They are not services. They are offerings."

"Are you in love with her?"

"Yes."

"But you would not mind if I purchased her services?"

"She is a courtesan. That is the reality. I accept it."

"Well, if she is a courtesan, I can't afford her."

"I would think not."

Kittredge, we actually speak to each other in this fashion. By the book, one is not supposed to be this friendly, but it is where we have evolved. Actually, he knows and I know that while I may go to a brothel once in a while—do not sneer at this simple need—I would never dare to get into the kind of precipitous financial transaction a woman of this sort could induce. Moreover, it's potentially compromising. We have something of a file on her, courtesy of Western Hemisphere Division, enough to know that in Havana she had links to both sides, Batista and the Castro underground. Yet this piebald set of allegiances is what decides me to accompany my agent on a visit. Hunt tends to be positive. He likes to go with a promising action. I can always tell Howard I went along to check her out. If she has any leftist sympathies that are still active, we need to know more about that. Contemplate the twists or kinks she could put into Peones' mind if she is half as powerful as advertised.

So we went over. She lived in another high-rise building a little beyond the apartment house where Boris and Zenia dwell. I am bewildered by the impulse that drives so many people who can afford something better to choose these blank high-rise habitations that look out over a placid, dun-colored sea—but do not quarrel with the high-rise impulse. It gets you up to the tenth floor, at least. Hers is the sixteenth floor, and a penthouse, no less.

On the way over, Chevi is in a most unusual mood, full of sudden impulses, nasty vapors. He has, for instance, insisted on our crossing of the Rambla against all the high-speed traffic, a dubious endeavor by daylight and downright dangerous at night, yet, he still feels righteous enough after all those self-induced perils to turn around and shriek at a driver who has certainly passed too close: *"Con más distinguidos sentimientos!"* sticking his middle finger into the heavens to accompany this wail of malediction. I wonder if he thinks it is effective curse-work? Then he insists we take off our foot gear, and we scuffle along the beach, cuffs rolled up, toting our shoes, path lit by the moon, and the well-domiciled surf rolling in on thin luminescent ripples of foam. I wonder why he is taking this detour until I realize he is going to describe sexual relations between Libertad La Lengua and Pedro Peones. For that, no ordinary setting will do.

"She said once," Chevi now tells me, " 'No woman can know men so well as myself. I approach my visitor as an enigma in logic, a labyrinth. Each man has a lock to which only I can locate the key.' "

"Chevi," I protest, "Libertad cannot possibly talk that way."

"Well, in fact, she does. One reason is that I have taught her much. I have introduced her to the work of Borges. Do you read Borges?"

"No."

"You must never read him. In five pages, in any of his five pages, he will summarize for you the meaninglessness of the next ten years of your life. Your life, particularly."

I was sufficiently put out to reply, "Enjoy the absurdity of your life, and I will manage with mine." He roared with laughter. He had tweaked the short hairs of the Colossus of the North.

Well, I still did not believe Libertad spoke of locks and labyrinths. "Borges or no," I told him, "one human being cannot calculate another so closely."

"She can," said Chevi.

"How does she make love to you?"

"That is sacrosanct."

"So you choose not to prove your case."

"I will tell you how she makes love to Pedro Peones."

"Yes, how?"

He roared again. He kicked gobs of damp wet clay with his bare feet. He then proceeded to tell me in detail!

Kittredge, it's shocking stuff, and I'd rather not offer it in his words, which made a point of testing my knowledge not only of Montevidean slum talk, but expressions he'd picked up in Harlem as well, argot like *pervy* and *soft pete*, *brand* and *porthole*, *ass-teriors*, *bummy*, and *the latter*, believe it or not. The Spanish was at least more functional. *Vagón de cola*, which I think is *caboose*, *seno de pantalones*, an awful image which pretty directly suggests the *breasts of the trousers*, and one absolute pit, *tubo de salida de gases*, which I'm sure you can translate, but, if not, *exhaust pipe* will do. Chevi delivered his description with an ongoing oscillation of giggles and sniggers that shattered my normal sense of his dignity. He was so full of sneaky guilt and glee. I expect it was his Catholic background regurgitating on him, plus all that Latin sense of scorn. God, are these Uruguayans fixed on flesh, and, of course, all flesh leads to the capitol of flesh, the buttocks. I know now where Latins think the Devil hides himself, yes.

Apparently, Pedro lays himself down on Libertad's bed, his cheeks exposed. Libertad, dressed in what Chevi describes as "elegant leather," proceeds to spank him. Pedro Peones, big as a walrus, laying out there on the bed, belly down over two thick pillows so that his backside looks, as Chevi describes it, *"como dos melones gigantescos,"* and she whips him lightly, stopping only when the pain produces a touch of froth at the corner of his lips. Then she proceeds to bite him, a precise little business which leaves the exposed area scalloped by neatly placed scimitars of teeth markings, after which, just as Pedro is singing away in some melange of sobs, pain, guilt, and pleasure, she croons, "Oh, Pedro, *mi peón, mi pene pequeño* (little penis, no less), *mi perdiz* (my partridge), *mi perfidia* (my perfidy), *mi pergamino* (my piece of parchment), *mi perla* (pearl), *mi permanganato* (yes, pomegranate!), *mi perniciosa pedazo de pechuga* (my nasty little bit of tit), *mi pelado culo* (my bald backside), *mi pepino persa* (my Persian cucumber), *mi perseguidor* (my pursuer), *mi pérsico* (my peach), *mi pezuña* (my cloven-footed beast), *mi pétalo* (petal), *mi peonia* (peony), *mi pedúnculo* (my flower stem), *mi peste* (my plague), *mi petardo* (my fraud), *mi picarote* (my impostor), and with that, having herbified his ears with her alliterations, nipped his cheeks with her teeth, and flicked him with a whip, she bends over, murmurs *"Vaya con Dios, ya, ya, ya,"* and delivers, yes, Kittredge, one lingering kiss *sub cauda*, at which point, Peones, according to my informant, gives back in turn one great oath, *"Madre del Dios"* and wets the pillows with his *"emisiones las mas cataratas"*—Fuertes' final flourish upon the proceedings.

It has been, I fear, all too absorbing a description, and when he is done, I refuse to believe it. Yes, he tells me, these were Libertad's precise words to Pedro Peones as related by her, on one's oath as a man, a lover, and a perfidious agent—he does speak in this manner when carried away by a tale, and then adds, "This is your true portrait of the police bully, the master goon Peones, this is his pleasure. This is the tender if hidden face of our sadist."

"And you are still in love with Libertad after such practices as these?"

"She informs me of her acts. That is her avowal of love. Of course, you cannot comprehend. In your country, your religious devotions, such as they are, have been voided of the profound human transaction of confession."

Do you know, sometimes I believe Chevi became an American agent so that he would not lose an opportunity to keep us up on his low opinion of American merits, mores, and morals.

Well, I will withhold my description of Libertad no longer. We ascend in the elevator, ring the bell to her door, and there she is. I know only that I am in the presence of a creature. She is extraordinary. If the gleam of a candle's flame is pale blond, then she is more blond than fire. I see a halo of platinum hair on a heart-shaped dimpled face, her eyes deep and mysterious blue look at me out of fields of dark eye-shadow, and her mouth—ah, that crimson mouth is just a little too plump and too strong—I am staring at an angel with a heart like a honeycomb, full of sugar and greed. Such is my first impression. Jean Harlow is before me. My second is that she walks like no woman I have ever seen. "Hello," she says in English in a deep and husky voice, "please come in," and with that, turns from the door and leads us through her living room out to the penthouse patio, where we stand by the balustrade and look down sixteen stories to the sea. She has done this quickly, as if she did not wish me to view her face for long in the light. Perhaps she is older than I expected, perhaps ten years older than Marilyn Monroe, if at least twenty years younger than Mae West, but what a way of walking!—it need give precedence to neither lady. Her calves are exquisite, her thighs leonine. Time takes its own breath when she deigns to move. I speak of Harlow and Monroe and Mae West—she is of their party, that sexual party as sure in its essence as cash is green. Cash says, "I am money, first, last, and always; I am more tangible than all of you who are staring at me." So Libertad is an avatar of sex. I feel as if I am in the presence of a goddess, and I comprehend for the first time what it must be like to meet a movie star.

Except, I must tell the truth. It is not agreeable but exorbitant to find her so unbelievably attractive. For the first time since meeting you at the Keep, I have been wholly overtaken.

Mind you, all she said was "Please come in." Now, on the balcony, she reaches into a silver purse that matches her silver lamé gown. (This cannot be the outfit she wears with her whips—no, she must have changed for us.) She can hardly withdraw her cigarette from her purse, however, before Chevi is on her with his lighter. He gives fire. She draws it in. The passage is as continuous as a devotion—I think of an Episcopalian chaplain at St. Matthew's who used to make the sign of the cross with so great a concentration upon the agony of the Lord (at least such was the chaplain's expression) that you could feel the selfsame agony in your chest when his outstretched arm drew the horizontal; now, I am overcome at the solemnity of a cigarette lighter brought to a tip of tobacco; I have never been in the company of a woman so profoundly feminine. I feel as if I have an image at last of the high priestesses of antiquity, and so Chevi's description of her goings-on with Peones appears distorted to me now by the comic violence implicit in such narration. Those were Devil's sacraments Peones was receiving. I feel as if I am on the edge of betraying myself forever, I know not how. I study her smallest move. The arts of all the attractive women she has ever encountered seem to have been absorbed in her person. She must be wholly an Omega. Where are the nicks and welts of a rough-hewn daily world? For that matter, I cannot take my eyes off her breasts. By the light that reaches to the patio, they seem large and wonderfully well shaped, and mysterious in their cleavage, which is just as deep as her voice.

Soon enough I am obliged to realize that she is aware of my occupation; it is apparent she ordered Chevi to bring me.

"Do you like your work?" she asks me. There is a softening of the long *i* in *like*. She has a trace of Southern accent. "Your English is good," I reply.

"I learned my English from an American," she says.

"A wealthy Texan," adds Chevi, "in Havana. He was her protector."

"My protector," she repeats, as if the man will live forever with such cachet.

"A friend of the American Ambassador to Cuba," says Chevi.

"One of *yours*," says Libertad to me.

"I cannot conceive of any of my countrymen failing to be your protector," I say, but the remark goes dead. I wonder if her English consists of no more than thirty-eight useful phrases.

"One of *yours*," repeats Libertad.

"Perhaps she is saying that she would like to meet another," adds Chevi.

"Mr. E. Howard Hunt," she says.

"Oh," I say, not without confusion, "he is, at the present moment, very much married." I confess that the thought of bringing about such an introduction has a sudden but curious appeal to me.

She shrugs her shoulder, a low gesture accompanied by a turn of the lip, as if to say, "What can that matter?" and she turns back to the living room. It is quite a chamber. She has furnished it in gussied-up copies of Queen Anne, Louis Quatorze, Duncan Phyfe, and Spanish Colonial. Gold leaf has been added to all the wood moldings. Whore cushions of satin are everywhere, and our feet stand on a wildly expensive, brightly hued rug whose only virtuosity can be found in the number of colors—God, what strength is in vulgarity!

Her living room looks like a love nest in a furniture store window. Even the ashtrays are as large as fruit bowls.

She is still fixed on E. Howard Hunt. Is Mr. Hunt not an intimate of Benito Nardone?

"You are speaking of the politician," I ask, "who is leader of the Ruralistas?"

Chevi makes a sound of disgust. "You know very well that he is now running for President of Uruguay."

"Yes, I do know that," I admit.

Libertad gives a large smile. Her presence still seems a promise of payment. I am beginning to recognize that a courtesan, like an important athlete, is a single-minded force concentrated solely on its objective: She wants to meet E. Howard Hunt who will introduce her to Benito Nardone. Of course.

I reply, knowingly, "Nardone makes many noises now, but has no chance. The Colorados have been winning this election for the last hundred years."

"This year," says Libertad, "the Blanco-Ruralistas will win. Nardone will win. Your Howard Hunt will introduce me to him."

Her singularity of purpose is insulting to me. I have to recognize that she sees me as nothing more than one step in a connected series. Of course, her femininity still contains me in its cloud, but I wonder if I am not dealing with a force that is personal in touch, intimate in shift of voice, but, like the wind, there for everyone.

We are close to an impasse. I ask why she doesn't obtain her introduction through Peones, but then the answer is so obvious that she merely smiles. Nardone will respect her more if the meeting is brought about by our Chief of Station. So I merely nod ambiguously and stand up to take my departure. To my surprise, Chevi leaves with me. They embrace like old friends, and he pats her most respectfully and tenderly on the behind, then kisses her hand with a sweep of his mustaches. She, in turn, leaves a kiss on the corner of my mouth, at which my cheek becomes as alive as if it had been touched by a bird's feather. Then I recollect where her mouth has been this evening; my face burns like balefire.

"You will introduce me to Mr. E. Howard Hunt," she says.

"I will see what I can do," I am weak enough to reply.

In the elevator going down, I am already furious at Chevi. I contain myself and do not speak until we reach the street, but then I become the one who insists on crossing the Rambla against high-speed traffic. Even after we are across and safe on the sand, I am still laboring to control my temper.

"How could you have put me in so compromising a position?" I say at last. "You are not my friend."

"I," he says, "am devoted to your interests. I merely wanted you to look upon one of the few rare artifacts my country has produced, a work emblematic of Uruguayan genius—a great whore."

"Shut up," I say. "You are wholly untrustworthy."

This anger, to my surprise, leaves him meek. I am wondering if I should have shown such a side of myself months ago. The trouble is that my temper is not a tool in dependable employ. "How could you be so self-centered, so stupid, so careless," I cry out. "You should be cut off!"

"You are attracting attention," he says, and points to two lovers sprawled on a beach blanket over a hundred yards away. Are they looking up? "Let us go back to the safe house. I will try to explain."

"Just remember that you are not indispensable. You are obliged to explain."

He does. We sit there in the safe house. After her living room, these grim government furnishings support me like a good starched shirt. I realize suddenly that my threats of unemployment have put no small fear into Chevi. We are now paying him one hundred dollars a week, which, with expense chits, often comes to one hundred and twenty, or more, and he could hardly afford to give this up. That, however, is but half of his motivation—the other half is obviously connected to Libertad. "It is true," he says, after I slash through his disclaimers as if I am chopping brush, "it is true. I was attempting to make you of use to me, and, I agree, that is a breach. The fundamental relationship dictates that I must be of use to you. One should not violate the fundamental relationship."

"Why did you?"

"Because she requested the meeting."

"Then you have a similar relationship with her?"

"That is true. Fundamental relations came into collision."

He commenced to tell me a story. He had known Libertad for more than half his life. They had gone to school together in La Teja. In his first year at the university they had been lovers. She had adored him. Then he left for New York. By the time he came back, she was a prostitute. Yet on his visits to her, he would never have to pay money. Still, it was awful. Then she decided to become a great prostitute and went to Havana. When she returned, she was no longer in love with him. She merely liked him. He was entrapped. "I despise her," he said, "but I lack the power to deny her whims in relation to me. She has become *una mujer sin alma*."

I know why he chose to say those words in Spanish. They are not so hopelessly banal as "a soulless woman."

Kittredge, I may be developing the instincts one needs for this work. Chevi finished his tale of woe, put his head on our good cheap safe-house shellac-orange maple dining table, and began to weep. I said, "Why don't you stop lying? We are aware of where Libertad comes from. It is not La Teja." I was only pretending to be in possession of such a fact but, then, there was something askew in his story. It was full of that South American pathos which invariably depends on lovers who have known each other from childhood.

"Well," he said, "there are many levels to the truth."

Kittredge, it is very late, and I am going to end right here. I did not learn the truth that night, indeed it took a good bit more, but I promise you that the facts, when I acquired them, were not ordinary. Be patient. I will tell you more in a day or two. I suppose I may as well confess to my annoyance that you chose not to tell me about Dracula's Lair.

Cheerfully yours,
Harry

28

ONE MORE LIE. THE LETTER HAD NOT BEEN CUT SHORT BY A DESIRE TO chastise Kittredge. I simply did not know how to continue. After all, I had begun with the fabrication that Chevi had phoned me, and ever since, had been attempting to balance my account, a common practice in putting Agency reports together. If, for some reason, you could not send the truth back to Washington—if, for instance, you hired Gordy Morewood to do a specific job after the Groogs had instructed you to let him cool his heels, why, then, you gave Gordy another name, and paid him out of a new file. *Double-entry* reporting—an art! Rare was the field man who did not practice it on occasion.

Now Kittredge had been placed on double-entry. I had suppressed a critical passage between Libertad and myself. Wholly at her behest, I expect, Chevi had closeted himself in her gold and marble bathroom for a good twenty minutes during our visit, and in that time Libertad conferred on me one of her royal gifts—fellatio. We had not been alone for a minute before her fingers walked over the buttons on my fly. I will not give the details—suffice it to say that she exhibited such sensitivity to one's shifting states of tumescence that we did not get to the offering until Chevi had splashed enough water in bowl and washbasin to indicate he would soon be back with us—instead, she took me up and down a steeplechase of long and languorous hoops and loops. I might have discharged with sensations extraordinary enough to be hers forever but some residual Hubbard stubbornness, refusing to hand over the drawbridge to a stranger, was there like a mailed warder and slammed a gate in my soul; I came, to my surprise, painfully. Alpha, taken in whole, must have gone clear over the hurdle; Omega shattered darkly below. My loins ached when I was done and I buttoned myself quickly, whereupon she made a point of licking her plump lips as if seed were cream, gave a squeeze of her hand to mine, and kissed Chevi with considerable passion when he came back to the room. I was not about to pass all this on to Kittredge. Yet I hardly wished to mislead her by too much. That would once again violate the spirit of our correspondence. So I had given a fulsome description of Libertad's attractions, as if to communicate by that route the depth of the magnetic field her mouth and lips had put upon the nether parts. At its best, I had felt, I confess, like a superbly prepared canvas upon which a truly notable artist was laying the most purposeful strokes. To make up for any real loss in my account of—yes, I now knew the meaning—of such *exquisite* pleasure, I had exaggerated the initial impact of meeting. In truth, I did not feel in the presence of a goddess until her mouth led me to study the turns of expression on her face. All that beauty! All that hard implacable will to rule the world! I had seen hints of such on many another whore's face as she gave herself to fellatio, but never with such singularity of mission. As I would realize over the next few days, my iron-bound determination not to introduce her to Hunt was springing a few leaks.

April 15, 1958

Dearest Kittredge,

Libertad must have powers. For months Howard has been promising to take me along to an *estancia,* but eleven days ago, on

Friday morning, directly after my encounter with Señorita La Lengua on Thursday night, he informed me that we would be off on Saturday to the *estancia* of Don Jaime Saavedra Carbajal. I can now describe such a weekend for you. It did have a few moments, and I believe I'll tell it as it passes: Travel belongs to the present tense, might you agree?

All right, then! We take off on schedule, Saturday morning, with Dorothy in the backseat and myself riding shotgun, Howard driving his Cadillac as if it were a Jaguar, seat erect and far back, arms extended and hands in leather driving gloves holding opposite sides of the wheel. We motor north over a variety of inland roads, some in crying need of revampment, but a fast drive all the same of one hundred and fifty miles through South American towns usually sleeping beside a river, usually dusty, and rarely disturbed by any sound larger than our even-breathing Cadillac motor. On either side of us, the pampas begin to seem a veritable outer space of grass. Dorothy, napping in the rear, snores ever so faintly, no more sound to it than one fly meandering in a summer pantry, but Hunt's nostril quivers at this small public delinquency, and I think of Libertad. Perhaps there is enough of a crack in his marriage, I try to tell myself, to justify the introduction.

I can see why Dorothy sleeps. The land is flat. One can cover five miles before topping the low ridge that originally appeared to be but a half mile off; to divert myself, I keep estimating such distance while listening to Hunt expatiate. He is full of Fidel Castro these days. Western Hemisphere Division is receiving analyses to the effect that Castro may yet overthrow Batista, and Hunt is grumbling over the State Department's general lack of concern. "There's a Castro lieutenant called Guevara, Che Guevara, whom we gave safe passage to out of Guatemala along with Arbenz. That boy is more of a lefty than Lefty O'Doul."

I am counting the miles to the horizon. By mid-afternoon we arrive at the gate to the *estancia,* which announces itself by means of two mournful stone columns, each twenty feet high and twenty feet apart, there to honor, I suppose, the pitted dirt road that takes us a long slow way to the hacienda. A thirty-six-hour party is commencing. Don Jaime, the wealthiest landowner in Paysandú province, is a powerful, sturdy man with a ram's horn mustache who exudes hospitality while his wife, cold and gracious, soon steers me into paying court to the young Uruguayan ladies present, much as if I were a nineteenth-century artillery officer at a tea party. Any romance with these protected señoritas would take three years of Sundays, however. Even the wives would cost you a year! Still, I flirt assiduously with the female folk of local ranchowners, local *hidalgos,* and local grain, feed, and mill owners as we all (that is, the men) get drunk. I'm surprised at the low level of the guests, which is to say that the money seems to have accumulated faster than the old family manners I had been expecting, but still there are gardens around the house, and agreeable half-wild copses of woods with paths, vineyards, arbors—it's easy to take our drinking into the evening. They imbibe prodigiously out here in the pampas, wine and Uruguayan cognac, rum, and—touch of class—Scotch. Don Jaime Saavedra Carbajal's house is low and sprawling, with cowhide for chair covering, and steers' horns for arms and backs. Of course, there's also dark Victorian stuff, long English hunting tables, mournful stuffed sofas, mahogany cabinets, and atrociously second-rate family portraits. The carpets are old orientals topped with Brazilian jaguar skins, antique rifles are mounted above the fireplaces, the windows are small with many panes, and the ceilings are low. Yet the house is kind of imposing. I can't say how. It does sit ten miles back of its own gate, and you pass thousands of cattle in the endless meadows on the way from the gate to here, not to mention guest houses, gardens, sheds, and barns.

The male company spends a good part of Saturday evening talking about horses, and Sunday morning we all go out for a pickup polo game in a surprisingly well-groomed, close-cropped meadow with goalposts. I have all I can do to get out alive. The competition, while spotty—one or two real polo players, in addition to several fine horsemen of whom Hunt, I have to tell you, is one—are filled out by a string of substitutes like myself who are brought in and removed more quickly than the polo ponies. Howard, if you recall, had given me some elementary instruction on the polo field in Carrasco, but under game pressure I am in trouble. I can get mallet to ball with my forehand, but am just about hopeless for backhands. Hunt takes me aside to whisper, "Don't try to hit anything on your left. Just go stirrup to stirrup with the other fellow's mount and ride him out of the play."

I follow his advice and discover that if not always successful, at least I'm beginning to have fun. This is the most rough exercise I've taken on in more than a year, and I love it. I can feel my father's combative blood (which, for me, may be what happiness is all about). The moment I'm maneuvered off the ball, I gallop gung-ho all over

the place trying to find the man who cut me off. These epiphanies of
martial lust, horse to horse, man to man, come to their climax when
I'm chucked from my steed pretty abruptly and land on my back, all
the wind knocked out, a most curious sensation of choking passively
as chargers veer overhead, their hooves going by like sledgehammers.
God, even in my breathless state I saw the eyes of the horse who came
closest to running me over. He, too, had a divided heart, half in panic
that he would hurt himself, half in a fury to charge right through my
supine feast of torso.

Well, I had to take the next two chukkers off, but when I
returned to the game (which involved getting my will in hand), the
wives and daughters and older *hidalgos* on the sidelines, and the players
and the substitutes, all applauded, and Hunt came up to put his arm
around my shoulder. Suddenly, I am in love with myself, with risk,
with all the revelations of pain. I ache all over and feel virtuous, but
it is obviously the high point of my day.

On Sunday night, however, after the barbecue, is the event
of the weekend. Benito Nardone arrives. Possessed of a high forehead,
a pronounced widow's peak, long nose, and sensuous lips, plus dark,
V-shaped eyebrows and large, somewhat haunted dark eyes, Nardone
was not at all what I expected. At worst, he looked like the classiest
gangster on a movie lot. Am I thinking of George Raft?

Nardone makes his speech in the library as the men gather
around brandy and cigars. Atmosphere is solemn—black leather tomes
in near-black wooden bookcases. I decide that Nardone, son of the
people, his father an Italian longshoreman from the docks of Montevideo, appeals to this group precisely because he is not one of them—
he has no money, no family to back him, no title: By their lights, he
should be a terrorist or a Communist, but he quit his youthful ties to
that left-wing world and has become the leader of the right wing. As
he swings into the core of his fund-raising speech, I can see the ball
of money rolling downhill with more and more pesos adhering to it,
for he knows how to talk to the center of fear and wrath in all these
hidalgos and *hacendados*: They love to hear what they want to hear—I
am beginning to think that politics is built exclusively on the comforts
of such cant. "In these times," says Nardone, "a workingman no
longer thinks of passing on to his family more than was given to him.
On the contrary, the Uruguayan workingman's most searching inner
question today is whether to retire with partial security at the age of
thirty-seven, or with full economic protection when he is fifty.

Señores, we do not wish to be, nor can we be, the Switzerland or the Sweden of South America. We cannot continue to support a welfare state that encourages such inanition."

They applaud him, and applaud a good deal more when he offers as contrast to the lazy, corrupt life of Montevidean officeholders, the hardworking, honorable, virtuous industry of the herders and simple farm people in the pampas, all true Ruralistas. Of course, I have been hearing all year from Colorados in the capital that the farm workers are exploited unconscionably by the landed gentry. This political side of the evening puts me, therefore, in a depression. I am obliged to realize once again how essentially ignorant I am about these matters, and even ask myself why I joined the Company and gave myself to it all these years—more than three years now—when I'm not really interested in politics, and in fact have exactly what I need in the way of understanding: For all our faults, the U.S. is still, I believe, the natural model of government for other countries.

Nardone may have picked up a whiff of my thoughts since he ended by offering "a salute to that great nation of the north founded and maintained by individual initiative." He was applauded for this too, of course, but not, I think, so much out of love for the U.S.A. as in recognition of his good manners toward Don Jaime Carbajal's foreign guests. Nardone, pointing to Hunt, then added, "This most distinguished representative of our friends to the north has often graced my understanding with his thoughts. My friend and fellow horseman, Señor Howard Hunt."

"Hola," cries that crowd.

After which follow billiards, snooker, and bed. I could have taken the opportunity to talk to Nardone or to Hunt about Libertad, but hesitated—indeed, I have been on edge all weekend with this. Curiosity intrigues me to help her; caution forbids it. Now, in the morning, we return to the city.

On the drive back, I am down on myself and decide that I have been living a most secluded life in Uruguay, but that is the way I want it. With the exception of the polo game, I did not really enjoy the *estancia*. The pampas on a daily basis would bore me. Oh, there were quiet vistas where a stream curved around a grove of white-leaved cottonwoods, and the sun gave a pale gold light to the tall grass, but I am also thinking of some of the villages we passed on the way back, shanty poor with tin roofs that banged like loose shutters in every strong breeze. There is a prevailing wind out in these pampas called *la bruja* (the witch), and it would drive me loco if I had to live out here.

Kittredge, I hope this letter proves satisfying to you. In the pampas, listening to *la bruja*, I wondered what your situation could be and whether you were in peril, trouble, difficulty, or merely suffering like me from some small dislocation of the soul.

Cheers, love,
Harry

P.S. Dorothy slept again on the way back, and this time I did bring up the subject of Libertad. When I mentioned that I had met her, Hunt's curiosity was aroused.

"How did that happen?"

I improvised a reasonably good tale to the effect that I had been introduced to her at El Águila by AV/ERAGE, our society journalist.

"I warn you," I said, "she is looking for an introduction to Benito Nardone."

"That is one request she can file in the department of idle dreams," he answered on the spot, but, a little later, he tapped me on the arm. "On reconsideration," he said, "I like the idea of looking her over. She may have some input to offer on Fidel Castro. How he disports *in camera,* so to speak."

We decided to make it lunch, Tuesday, in a small restaurant of Hunt's choosing, far out on the Bulevar Italia. Kittredge, I knew how the place was going to look before I saw it—sufficiently nondescript to ensure that no one Hunt was acquainted with socially would ever be there. In any event, we set it up for the next day, Tuesday, just a week ago. I've decided to be the last of the big spenders and will get off another magnum of a letter to you tomorrow night.

29

April 16, 1958

Dearest Kittredge,

Lunch began with a most unexpected turn that I should have anticipated. Libertad did not, as had been arranged in advance with Chevi, come alone; to the contrary, she walked into the restaurant accompanied by no less a personage than Señor Fuertes himself.

While Hunt has never met Station's starring agent, AV/
OCADO (since, thankfully, there has never been a crisis pressing
enough to justify bringing them together), I can promise you that I
went through a bad moment. Even though Hunt seemed to accept
Libertad's description of her escort—"My friend and translator, Dr.
Enrique Saavedra-Morales"—I had to keep issuing injunctions to
myself: *"Stop seething. Stop seething. Cool down!"*

All the while, Libertad glowed. Hunt may even have melted
a drop in the face of such incandescence. "Señorita," he said in his best
Spanish, "I admire your language and choose to speak in it more than
is wise for me," whereupon she laughed encouragingly. "Perhaps my
command, such as it is," he went on, "will dispose of the need for a
translator, although I welcome your friend, Dr. Saavedra. I would
ask," he said, turning to Chevi, "whether you are related to Don
Jaime Saavedra Carbajal?"

"A distant relation," said Chevi. "I do not know whether he
would acknowledge this poor branch of the family."

I could have been in a heavily loaded airplane which now, at
the very end of the runway, has just managed to take off.

We ordered. It was precisely the sort of low-priced middle-
class restaurant I had foreseen. The menu was limited, the linen, while
not quite yellow, had certainly said farewell to white, the tables were
occupied by no more than a few local businessmen at one end and two
middle-aged ladies of modest income at the other, and the waiter
looked to be mired in debt and old lottery tickets—yes, Hunt had
chosen an eating place that would be oblivious to the unorthodoxy of
our meeting, or any other.

On the way over he had said, "Does Libertad know my
name?"

"No question of that."

"And my function?"

"I would say so."

"Then I will have to inform Peones of the meeting."

"Must you? I don't think she will say a word to him."

"No, she won't, will she? Nothing to gain from that."

"No, sir."

He clicked his tongue once. "Well, we won't allow this one
to become a folly," he said.

Under the circumstances, you can predict how much room
he offered Libertad to trot out her better tricks. Obviously, the first

item on her agenda was to excite the gallantry of Mr. E. Howard
Hunt, but the lady's charms kept rubbing against the given: Glamour,
when unattached to social prominence, has rapidly diminishing impact on Howard.

After his first speech, therefore, he came down to business
quickly. We were hardly into our martinis (which Howard insisted on
mixing himself at the table—thank God!) before Miss Paradise was
being interrogated.

"What can you tell me of Fidel Castro? Did you meet him in
Cuba?" Howard asked.

It was too soon. Chevi allowed his eyes to encounter mine for
the first time since we had sat down; his expression was as miserable
as my inner sentiments.

"Yes," said Libertad. "Fidel Castro is now in the hills."

"Yes," said Hunt, "I know that."

"In the Sierra Madre of the Oriente," she said.

"Exactly," said Hunt. "But how did you meet him?"

I was embarrassed. Interrogation might not necessarily be one
of Howard's skills, yet he could certainly do better than this. There
was no preface and certainly no encouragement. Not even the promise of a look did he allow to pass between Libertad and himself.

All the same, she tried to be forthcoming. She was prepared
to pay cash. "Fidel Castro," she said, "had a romance with my dearest
friend in Havana. Of course, now that he is up in the mountains, my
close friend does not see him as often."

"But she does see him?"

"On occasion he slips into Havana. It is then they make their
visits."

"What else does he do in Havana?"

"I am informed that he raises money and speaks to groups."

"Did you attend any such meetings?"

"Only once, but for the purpose of being able to tell my grand
friend, Fulgencio Batista, exactly what was being stated. Señor Castro
spoke like an angry revolutionary and said, 'Fulgencio is supported by
the Yankees.' "

"You heard him say that?"

She nodded profoundly.

"Do you know Señor Castro well in any other manner?"

"During my sojourn in Cuba," she said, "I lived with but one

man, even as now I live only with your friend whose name I do not
need to speak."

"No need," agreed Hunt.

"I am loyal to the man I admire. A matter of principle."

"Commendable," said Hunt.

"So, señor, I have no intimate knowledge of Fidel Castro.
But my girlfriend," Libertad now said in English, *"told me plenty."*

"All right," said Hunt, "Let's move on to the *nitty-gritty.*"

Libertad gave a smile of comprehensive wisdom. "He is like
other men," she stated.

"Could you enlarge on that?"

"He is young and strong. A little shy. He talks politics to the
women."

"Does this come directly from your girlfriend," asked Hunt,
"or is it general gossip?"

"Nitty-gritty," said Libertad. "He is like other Cuban men.
He is selfish. It is all over once he is done. He is normal."

Hunt did not look impressed that for his pains he had obtained no more than the knowledge that Fidel Castro was normal.

"How often," he asked, "does Castro come to Havana?"

"Perhaps once a month," said Libertad. She sighed as if to
suggest that she had said enough, and Chevi now spoke. "Would you
say that you are dissatisfied with the information my dear friend
Señorita La Lengua has provided?"

"I would be satisfied with any response from a lady as charming as your companion," Hunt replied, "yet, by the light of my
sources, Fidel Castro has not come down out of the hills in the last two
years."

"Since Libertad La Lengua says he has been in Havana," said
Chevi, "I would be prepared, señor, to go beyond your sources."

"Oh," said Hunt, "I will certainly honor the lady's opinion.
We will make further inquiries."

Chevi said, "A wise course."

Silence. Libertad entered the void. "I have heard," she said,
"that your friend Benito Nardone is a lonely man."

"He seems busy enough to me," said Hunt, and laid his hands
on the tablecloth, fingers extended like rays, as though to ward her off.

She, in turn, placed her hands on Hunt's fingers, a move I
would not have chosen. "I want you," said Libertad, "to tell Benito

that he is the most attractive man I have ever seen. I speak not merely for Uruguay but of all countries I have visited."

Hunt extricated his fingers. "My dear," he said, "I could bring him fifty such messages from ladies virtually as attractive as yourself, but I don't. That is not the basis of our relationship."

Her eyes were lambent. "You would not do this for me?"

"You must," said Hunt, "be content with the wonderful strong fellow you have."

The pause went on long enough to arouse the miserable intimation that Hunt was going to get up and leave—his temper had been taken too lightly. Chevi inserted himself again. "Allow me," he murmured, "to speak of myself."

Hunt nodded.

"I am a poor professor of classics," said Chevi, "a man who must content himself with his powers of observation, for he occupies no greater place in the arena."

Kittredge, I could not believe Chevi's audacity. Bad enough to call himself Saavedra since Hunt, if curious, could check with Don Jaime concerning the less august branches of the family, but to be a professor of classics as well! If I recollected correctly, Howard, back at Brown, had taken several courses in Greek and Latin civilization. I can't pretend I was the least bit easy about our new direction.

"Observing you, señor," said Chevi, "I applaud your incisive spirit. You are a man who advances matters. So, this poor professor of Greek is ready, despite the gulf between your situation in life and his own, to buy you and your friend a drink."

"I accept," said Hunt, "provided I keep mixing the martinis."

"Yes," said Chevi. "You will mix the martinis, we will drink them, and I pay for this round."

In English, Hunt said: "It will all come out in the wash."

"Ha, ha," said Chevi. "A searching expression. I speak as an admirer of the American, not the English, tongue. It is rough-hewn, American, but an appropriate language. It is there to serve the soldier-gladiators of a new empire. But then, you are much like the Romans."

"With all the advantage," said Hunt, "of being closer to the moral concerns of the Greeks."

"Ha, ha. A wonderfully incisive point," said Chevi.

I was struck with his powers as an actor. Roger Clarkson, Chevi's first case officer, used to describe him as a ham, but Roger may not have been along on any improvisation like this. Chevi now inhabited poor Dr. Saavedra. "Sir," he said, "I wish you to take no offense at these remarks, but I have been obliged to observe the peremptory fashion in which you dismissed the interest, admittedly ambitious, that Miss La Lengua exhibited in relation to Benito Nardone. I must remark that in my modest opinion you are grievously mistaken." Libertad nodded profoundly. "Benito Nardone," continued Chevi, "is a man of the people who has been obliged, by the dictates of his political career, to leave old friends behind. If he succeeds to become President of Uruguay, he will then be in need of restoring credibility with the populace. This need can be satisfied uniquely by Libertad La Lengua. She is a woman of the people who has become a lady, even as he has become a gentleman—"

Hunt cut him off. "Do you know, I think this is a nonviable analogy." Later, Hunt would say to me, "All Benito needs is a whore who still reeks of her police chief," but Chevi, nothing if not modestly telepathic, overtook him in turn. "I would submit, señor," he said, "that you are feeling some natural concern about the possible wrath of this lady's present protector, but I assure you, the personage in question would have to feel honored to lose the love of his life to the future savior of Uruguay."

"Yes," said Libertad, "Pedro would accept the loss."

"My dear," said Hunt, "I would not wish to discourage anyone."

Libertad said: "Many an Argentinian did not believe at first in Juan Perón and his Evita. Yet much of history was changed by that great lady."

"I could not agree more," said Hunt, "and I am certain that through your many sources you will yet meet Benito and you will charm him personally as you have charmed many an important guy before. Perhaps there will be a day when your dreams come through. I, however, cannot give a direct hand since that would be inappropriate to my role as a guest in your country." He had finished mixing the martinis, and now he handed her another, and smiled. "Let me offer a salute to your beauty."

"To her beauty," said Chevi, swallowing most of his second martini at one gulp.

"And a toast," said Hunt, "to a splendid fellow, Pedro Peones, strong, wise, highly motivated."

"Twenty-three skiddoo," said Libertad.

We laughed hard enough to break the pall for about as long

as we could laugh. The food arrived and it was not good. A rubbery fish fried in a somewhat rancid oil was served with a rice that clumped together in gobbets. The repast would make small inroad on the martinis.

Chevi was, by now, in a mood I could recognize. Back at the safe house, I would have been preparing for a temper tantrum. "Of all things upon earth that bleed and grow," said Chevi in English, "an herb most bruised is woman."

"What?" said Hunt.

"It is from Euripides," said Chevi, "from Professor Gilbert Murray's translation of *Medea*."

"First-rate," said Hunt.

Chevi held up his glass. "I applaud your martinis."

"Bottoms up," said Hunt, and drained his glass. I had never seen him drink as much at lunch. It must have taken a few of his resources, after all, to be adequately indifferent to Libertad.

The lady had hardly given up. She sent a look to me, and I felt spineless enough, Kittredge, to nod solemnly as though I were in her service. Then, her toe found my ankle and gave it a nudge.

Chevi merely offered a smile. "Do you recognize," he asked, "how much respect I have for Americans? I value their great power and their confidence."

"You have expressed an opinion," said Hunt, "with which I am wholly in agreement."

"That is why I regret so clearly," said Chevi, "that one cannot have profound conversations with your countrymen. There is an impermeability to their insularity."

"Talk is cheap, we say," said Hunt.

"On the contrary," Chevi replied, "I prefer to quote from my beloved Greeks: 'Forge your tongue on an anvil of truth, and what flies up, though it be but a spark, shall have weight.' "

"Sophocles?" asked Hunt.

"No, sir."

"Pindar?"

"Of course."

"Now I am mindful," said Hunt, "of one of the more pithy remarks of Thucydides. It has just come back to me. In paraphrase, of course."

"Paraphrase is acceptable, señor. Thucydides, after all, is not a poet," replied Chevi.

"There are three deadly foes of empire," said Hunt. "One is pity, the second is the spirit of fair dealing, and—in answer to your desire to get me heated up enough to beat my gums—the third foe of empire is the enjoyment of discussion." He held up a hand. "Now, my country is unique. It does accept the yoke of empire that history has laid upon it, but we make every effort to break out of Thucydides' three iron rules of tyranny. We try to be compassionate. We attempt under grievous circumstances to be fair, and, for the last, I admit that I am just bibulous enough to like a good discussion."

I don't believe he was drunk so much as autointoxicated. Both of them were. It was as if they were ready to love each other, or fall off a cliff while grappling together, but the air between having been washed by two double martinis, they had lost all interest in Libertad or me.

I must say that I, in turn, was just drunk enough to be obliged to restrain my impulse to say proudly: "Howard, this is our number-one agent, AV/OCADO." Never again do I dare dry gin on slippery footing.

"Empires," said Chevi, "must, however, establish an equable relationship between gods and men. For it is the nature of both to rule wherever they can."

"Agreed," said Hunt. "Self-evident."

"Of course, if there is but one God, He will certainly condemn you for overweening pride."

"*Hubris,*" said Hunt. "I don't see my country as suffering from that. Never forget," he told Chevi, "that we are in the American Century because we are obliged to be. A good nation of great yeomen has taken up the yoke, sir, in the war against Communism, the war of Christianity against materialism."

"No, sir," said Chevi. "Communism is merely your excuse. You have an empire to lose, but you do not know who you will lose it to."

"Sir," said Hunt, "are you suggesting that we are hated in unexpected quarters?"

"Yes."

"Well, that used to be the burden of power for the English. Now, it is ours. I will tell you, Dr. Saavedra," said Hunt with all the dignity implicit in great alcoholic clarity, "we wouldn't want friendship coming to us for too little."

Libertad yawned.

"Bored?" asked Hunt.

"No," said Libertad. "We must go up to my penthouse and drink *beaucoup* toasts to each other."

"In truth," said Chevi, I do not know that I would wish to live in your empire. Sometimes I view it as a community of bees who cling to the leader in an ecstasy of enthusiasm and patriotism."

"Are we still with the Greeks?" asked Hunt.

"One cannot know where Thucydides ends and I begin. I am only Dr. Saavedra, after all," said Chevi.

"Doctor," said Hunt, "your last remarks concerning my country are rubbish."

"With your permission. I am Saavedra–Morales, a loyal Greek to your Roman, an epigone of the new empire, an acolyte of Batista and Nardone. Politically speaking, I am with you. That is because I have but one life and, upon consideration, you and yours are to my advantage. But when we have departed into the long shadow of history, your side, which is now my side, will not win. It will lose. Can you tell me why?"

"I cannot conceive why. You tell me I do not even know whom we are fighting."

"You don't. You and your people will never understand us. We are deeper than yourselves. We know the turning of the tide. When that unique revolutionary, Fidel Castro, first landed in Cuba in 1956, he lost all but twelve of his men. He was ambushed by the troops of Batista. Hunted by day, hunted by night, Castro and his people stayed with poor peasants. By the fifth night, Fidel said, 'The days of the dictatorship are numbered.' He knew. He could see by the humanity on the faces of the peasants who sheltered him that Cuba was ready for a profound change. You, sir, will never understand us."

"But you say you are with me," said Hunt. "If you are with me, who the hell is *us*?"

"You may scorn my use of pronouns, but I live in the midst of them. *Us* are the dark people. Yes, Commander, the dark ones. Latins, Muslims, Africans, Orientals. That is *us*. You will never understand *us*. You do not comprehend that we are in need of honor. We wish to lift ourselves above shame. You see, sir, there are times when persons like myself feel as if we have sunk so low that we cannot recover our honor. If I strive to perform some act that is good or brave, I discover even when I succeed that all I can receive in my heart for such a worthy act is a temporary remission from the pervasive presence of shame. My honor has been lost forever."

Hunt nodded wisely. It would take a larger wave than the embodiment of Dr. Saavedra to wash him away. "It is not our American civilization," he said, "that excites your misery, but your own sin, fellow. As above, so below." He handed a martini to Chevi and filled his own glass with the last of his mix in the pitcher. "Let's get to the facts," said Hunt. "You sit here and drink my liquor and make a big powwow speech about the dark ones. Well, how do you know, pal? Darkness of complexion may reflect something dark and self-destructive in the soul. The divine intuition may be trying to inform us of something. Ever hear of the sons of Ham?"

"Yessir, it is racial superiority that one always comes back to," said Chevi.

"No, sir," said Hunt, "it is character. I would like to tell a story."

Chevi waved his hand languidly. The exigency of gin had descended finally upon him.

"You talk—I listen," he said.

"Aren't fading, are you, pal?" asked Hunt.

"Trot it out," said Chevi.

"This concerns my father," said Hunt, "so I think we can slack off on the tension here."

"I sue for your pardon, señor."

"I accept. I thank you. I can say that my father has been an honorable man," said Hunt. "A lawyer. In later life, a judge. A good father. He taught his son to fish and to box, how to ride a horse, how to shoot. Once, when I was ten, we were driving on a back road through the Everglades in Florida."

"Yes," said Libertad, "near to Miami."

"We came across a large rattlesnake sunning itself on the edge of a ditch. My father stopped our vehicle and told me to retrieve my brand-new repeating .22 rifle, purchased the day before for my birthday, out of the car trunk. I discovered, however, that it was too heavy for me to hold, aim, and fire. Before I could panic, my father took the gun, laid the sights on the rattlesnake's head, and encouraged me to pull the trigger. That snakeskin is still on my wall." He nodded. "And I still remember the bond of trust and affection I felt for my father as a ten-year-old boy."

Kittredge, I was pretty drunk myself by now but not so washed out that I couldn't remember that Hunt had used a longer

version of this same speech—for, God, it's a speech!—a couple of
nights ago at the *estancia* after Nardone asked him to say a few words
to the assembled group. Now, Libertad and our good Dr. Saavedra
were on the receiving line. I thought it was kind of crass for Hunt to
repeat himself so soon in front of me, but he did pass along a wink.
I must say his eyes were illumined by the gin; dammit, he was a
luminous figure.

"Yes," said Hunt, "my father was a brave man. His law
partner in Florida once absconded to Havana with a sum of several
thousand dollars. My father merely transferred his Browning automatic from his desk drawer to his pocket, bought a ticket on the Pan
American plane leaving that very night for Havana, made a tour of the
bars, and found his partner in Sloppy Joe's, a notable emporium.
Whereupon he walked up to the fellow, put out his hand for the cash,
and was returned all of the essential that had not yet been lost to
women, drink, and the crap tables. A compassionate man, my father.
He did not prosecute his former associate. He would even share a
drink with him in later years."

"Fenomenal," said Libertad.

"All right," said Hunt. "Today, in Carrasco, two streets from
my house, lives Colonel Jacobo Arbenz, who has recently returned
from the Iron Curtain country of Czechoslovakia. I speak of him
because I helped to overthrow him and his Communist-sympathizing
government in Guatemala four years ago."

"Qué golpe, maestro," breathed Libertad.

"Now Colonel Arbenz and I nod to each other at the golf
club. These are curious and would-be liberal times, but I will never
agree that that gentleman with his Communist sympathies can be my
true neighbor. I always think of his father. Colonel Arbenz's father,
you see, committed suicide. He filled his mouth with water, raised a
pistol to his lips, and pulled the trigger. This mode of self-destruction
guarantees the most prodigious disarray of after-effect." (I translate,
Kittredge, from Hunt's Spanish—*el desarreglo prodigioso después del
hecho*—a linguistic display!) I must say Howard could not keep a grin
off his face, but then Libertad actually made a low noise in her throat.

"Señores, señorita, I relate this fact not to take pleasure in
Colonel Arbenz's family misfortunes, but to point out that the differences between our fathers is kin to the difference between the separate
philosophies of freedom and authoritarianism.

"So I say to you, Dr. Saavedra, that I reject your notion that my country would ever wish to deprive you and the various peoples and nations you claim to represent of anything remotely resembling that inviolable human essence, honor itself. No, sir. My father, you see, brought me to the Greeks, and thereby, in college, to the study of the classics. He even obliged me to memorize one great statement by Aristotle. Yessir, Aristotle told me that there is a life out there higher than humanity: Men can only find it by discovering that particular something in themselves which is divine. Are any of you feeling sober enough to keep up with this? I quote: 'Do not listen to those who exhort you to keep to modest human thoughts. No. Live, instead, according to the highest thing in you. For small though it may be in power and worth, it is high above the rest!' "

Chevi roused himself for one last charge. "No, sir, it is we, not you, who subscribe to the wisdom of Aristotle, for he is a Greek, that is to say, a human from the dark side suffused with reason and light."

Hunt went for his watch with that, called for the bill, added it carefully, put in his quarter of the share while I laid down mine, waited for me to sprinkle some small change for our half of the tip, saluted Chevi, kissed Libertad on the hand, said, "You have a good, firm hand, my dear," and walked out with me, but not so quickly that I could avoid a last look from Libertad. She showed no suggestion that she would ever care to hear from me again.

We stopped at a café to drink three cups of espresso each, followed by two tablets of Sen-Sen, but I will not pretend much work was done by either of us after we returned to the Embassy. By five, I managed to phone Chevi at his law office, woke him up, and told him to meet me at the *law library*, which, by our understanding, is nothing less than the safe house we keep in the high-rise above the Rambla. I can promise you that a few disclosures are to follow, so I will continue with another letter tomorrow.

Yours, as ever,
Harry

30

April 17, 1958

Dearest Kittredge,

The encounter with Chevi at the safe house went on for hours, but I will spare you the early portion, which consisted of my belaboring him not only verbally but actually coming close at times to hitting him physically. He is absolutely maddening. He tried to excuse himself for coming along with Libertad on the ground that he was there to protect me. "It would," he kept saying, "have been a disaster for Hunt to commence anything with her," and he nodded vigorously. "I will yet explain. She is not what she seems to be." Then he would say nothing for a while.

Yes, I could have killed him. I would have if I had not been too miserably hung over and too quickly sobered up, and it was all of an hour before I could feel enough human interest to ask Chevi where he had picked up his Greek erudition. It turned out that he had spent a few hours stuffing himself with quotations. "A whim," he said, "I did not wish to arrive empty-handed."

"But how did you know he would not speak to you in Greek? He studied it in college."

"He is a janissary. Janissaries retain no culture."

"You are mad."

"It was worth the chance."

I was angry again. "Do not tell yourself that you are out of trouble," I said.

"I recognize that I am not."

"You are going to relinquish Libertad."

"Oh," he said, "that is not truly necessary."

"It is completely necessary. Your fundamental relationship is with the Agency."

"Yes. You are my first and only."

"Let's be done with all this," I shouted. "You will give the lady up."

"May we discuss it tomorrow?"

"Hell, no," I shouted. "If you do not observe the absolute letter of this ruling, your termination is inescapable." I nodded profoundly. "Toward those who betray us, our justice is unstinting."

Actually, to terminate the relationship means I'll be bombed by the Groogs. Why? they will ask. All the same, Chevi does not see through me. The use of such a word as *unstinting* certainly strikes fear into a compromised heart.

"I will see her no more," he states suddenly. "I give her up as of this moment." I have no idea if he is telling the truth. It is as sudden as if a wall had collapsed. "I am going to tell you the truth and then you will see that I have indeed protected you."

I am thinking that we could turn him over to Pedro Peones. I am startled by how large my heart can feel when it is ice-cold. For the size of the fury I'm containing, I might as well have a boulder in my chest. Something in his lies disturbs me profoundly.

"You cannot begin to give her up," I say, "until you tell the truth about her."

He looks into my eyes. Our staring contest goes on for many moments and each of us takes turns at growing stronger than the other, or, should I say, less of a liar—I do not know. Finally, he says, "You do not know the truth, or you would never have asked for this meeting today."

"Until you tell me, I cannot compare your knowledge with mine."

He smiles at this evasion, but wanly. He is even more exhausted than myself. "I will tell you," he says, "because the objective reality is now clear. I must denude myself of her."

"Denude?"

"Desnudar . . . privar . . ." He finds it. "Divest myself of her. Indeed, I should not have supported her request to meet Hunt. When all is said, she is too impossible a whore."

Now he wraps his arms mournfully around me in a full *abrazo*, as if we are brothers embracing at a wake, and says, "Libertad is not a woman, but the female transformation of what was once *un hermafrodito*." He sighs so audibly that I receive all of his breath and the dead smell of onerous responsibilities carried too long. Since I have shown little response—I think he is speaking in metaphors—he adds, "true and profound change. *Metamorfosis quirúrgica.*"

"Surgical transformation?" I ask.

"Sí."

"Where?"

"In Sweden."

"Have you . . . ?" I want to ask if there is a passage. Stupid questions jostle for position in my brain. "You have a good firm hand, my dear," I can remember Hunt saying.

"She can assume the fundamental position," Chevi says mournfully. "But only in the dark. She plays a deception with her fingers. She oils them. She performs some magic with her knuckles. She bragged to me once that she had seventy men in Las Vegas in thirty days, and not one was aware that he had not in fact entered her. That it was only *un juego de manos.*"

"A sleight of hand?"

"Yes. *Prestidigitación.*"

"Her breasts?"

"Hermaphrodites have breasts. In addition, she takes hormones."

"All right. I've heard enough," I said. In fact, I had been continuing the conversation because I knew that the moment I ceased asking questions, I would have to believe all that he said, and then I might be ill.

My emotions were so exceptionally crossed at this point that, Kittredge, I swear I could feel the simultaneous existence of Alpha and Omega, yes, Alpha, our own manly case officer out in the world of operations and paperwork had to wonder: Was he, himself, a homosexual? That stands out, doesn't it? To be so attracted to a transvestite, or whatever else you could call it—a transsexual? I writhe in the bonds of embarrassment as I write this.

Yet, another part of me knows that Libertad, no matter how low and sordid she may be, is nonetheless an evocation of the female spirit. Somewhere out there between *he* and *she,* Libertad has managed to absorb the quintessence of femininity! She is not a woman, but she has become a creature replete with beauty. She is all the beautiful women put together! By Omega's generosity of view, I could tell myself that I was not homosexual, but devoted to beauty, the beauty of women. Can you conceive of feeling such opposed emotions at once? Yes, of course you can, you are the only one who could.

Poor Chevi. Libertad is an agent in the world of women, and he is an agent in the world of men. So he can assuage his loneliness— for who could be lonelier than Chevi?—by being close to her. I was now forbidding that.

I returned his *abrazo,* full of feeling for him, and we had a drink while he showed me the pictures of his wife and son that he carried in his wallet. Both are sturdy, both are dark, his wife a woman of olive eyes and raven hair. The gloom of the gargantuan tasks that lie upon the Communist world are fully in her expression. She has monumental breasts, a woman who would run weighty operations—whether in a factory, a family, or a Party cell. At least, such were Harry Hubbard's concealed editorial sentiments. Chevi sighed again while looking at her—she was all he was going to have for a while. I felt a shiver in my soul. For both of us.

No doubt you will find a surfeit of bathos in this. I do myself. Be certain I was content to drive him home without further ado, but it all returned with a headache so soon as I had reached my hotel. The question was how much to divulge to Hunt next day at the office.

Let me break for dinner. A little *churrasco*, sausage, and black pudding will build me up for the last mile.

Later

The next day, Wednesday, did not go quite as expected. I was prepared for a horrendous session with Howard, which, if he considered AV/OCADO compromised, could bring on a thirty-six-hour stint with the Groogs on the Encoder-Decoder, but he was not at the office. Mid-morning, he called in to tell Nancy Waterston that he was going to accompany Nardone on a campaign swing for the next twenty-four hours.

"As for the rest of us," Porringer muttered, "we just keep to the usual dumb and daily."

Sherman was an unlikely ally, but, then, the virtue of a hangover may be that it freshens old clichés. Any port in a storm! Porringer, whatever his flaws, is not stupid.

We went out to one of those sprawling ubiquitous sidewalk cafés. Dusty metal chairs, coffee-sticky eating surfaces, ads for aperitifs on the awnings, ill-dressed housewives eating gritty ice cream, adolescents playing hooky from their lycée. I think the only place in the world where outdoor cafés really make sense is in Paris, but ours, alas, is not in Paris, but Montevideo, although it is named Café Trouville, no less, and must have forty or fifty dingy little round white metal tables sitting on the sidewalk of the Bulevar General Artigas. That, as you would expect, is an artery of traffic. Such conduits in South America get named after generals. Avenida de General Aorta, Bulevar de General Carótida, Avenida del Almirante Cloaca. If these misrepresentations are needlessly cruel to Montevideo, a city which has never done me any harm, it is because on mornings such as this, a second-rate seaport can certainly serve as the representative cloaca of our filthy world. Or is this describing my awful mood?

After the first twenty minutes (which consisted of listening to Porringer vent his gripes about Hunt), I got down to business. What does he, Porringer, know about Libertad?

"There's very little I don't know about *her*," he states, and actually pats his stomach. "So, you open."

Yes, he has all the hincty nasalities of a successful graduate student who is sitting on more bibliographical references than you can ever muster.

I decide to take a chance and prime his pump. That will probably get him to pool his information. It is always difficult for Porringer to hold back on command of a subject.

I tell him, therefore, what Chevi told me about the sex change.

"Yes," he said, "I was debating whether to warn you about Chevi."

"Why didn't you?"

He shifted his seat. "He's your agent. I don't leave my farts in every lark's nest."

I was thinking he must have been waiting for AV/OCADO to blow up in my face.

As if he had read my mind, he added, "I didn't want to get the Station in a stir about Libertad. Nor do you."

"Can you tell me what you know about her?"

He nodded to himself as if Judge Porringer, having taken an agreeable recess, might be deciding in favor of the supplicant. "Well," he said, "I didn't like this business from the get-go. Peones could have any whore in Montevideo—I mean, he is more dedicated to rank pussy than I am. So what was he looking for in Cuba? It had to be a freak. It had to be. I sent inquiries up to Havana about the lady, and all I got back was cover-up. I checked it out, therefore, with a well-positioned friend in Western Div, but Libertad was back here with Peones before my pal could dispatch the primary material. I did learn that her Havana protector was a big Texas crony of the American Ambassador down there, and that was why we couldn't squeeze any juice out of Havana Station. A little later, I discovered—just a little too late—that Libertad was one more drag-queen hermaphrodite who had gone to Sweden to get her fire-hose turned inside out."

"Inside out?"

"You mean you are not witting to Swedish chirurgery?"

"Can't say that I am."

"Live and learn. A Swedish sawbones won't just chop off your dick and testicles and hold out his hand for payment. These Olafs think they are virtuosos. They remove the inside meat, but save the outer skin of the sac and penis for the humanitarian reason that both swatches of epidermis are loaded with erogenous nerve endings. Then the surgical team cuts a new hole—which, I fear, leads nowhere—and lines it with all this premium tissue. Give me a Social Democrat every time, especially if he's Swedish."

He was like a water buffalo. Impossible to get him moving; once under way, no reason to stop. "I had," he said, "a few questions of my own. Here we were with Hunt. A Station Chief whose idea of covert action is to own the local cops. Howard is in love with Peones, and Peones is in love with La Lengua. And I am in possession of information that is going to be about as popular as syphilis on a petri dish. But you know me. I still want more. So I ask around in the local bagnios, and, kid you not, brother, they are ready to tell all. In her pre-Havana days, Libertad used to be named Roderigo. Roderigo Durazno, no less. A specialty act. Full penis and testes which he couldn't use for much, and full set of breasts. Kind of a centerpiece for orgies. You know." He put down his cup and grimaced. "This coffee is awfully sour." He waved to the waiter, pointed to his empty espresso, and said, "Roderigo wanted a sea change. Saved his pesos. Went to Sweden. After the operation, *she* went to Las Vegas to try out the new hole." (Kittredge, I can't help it. This is how he speaks. Think of him as a technician in Carnal Engineering.) "Well, Hubbard, her plumbing didn't function like the Swedish scientists had predicated. The new hole was too delicate to take the guff. Maybe some wires got crossed. And her back hole, which in days of yore in Montevideo had been the old reliable, was now, because of its proximity to the operation, not employable for anything but the evacuative function—which is what God intended in the first place until all us dirt farmers came along. So the good old days of taking it up the ass were done. How does she manage now? The whorehouse madams with whom she still pals around tell me she's got a trick with her hands can fool any man. I find that hard to believe, but there you are. She nailed her Texan in Las Vegas, he took her to Havana, and she kept it secret from him for many a month. He thought he had himself a dynamite blonde who loved to fuck in the dark. I don't care how much money a man makes, he can still be the stupidest asshole alive, wouldn't you say? How about a sandwich and a drink? This talk has made me hungry."

So we lunched at Café Trouville on *tapas* and *cerveza* and watched the traffic grind along. "Any time," he said, "that a hooker can fool a john by simulating a vagina with a little oil and five good fingers, you can count on it—she will brag. And other whores will brag on her. It must have traveled from Cape Horn to the Caribbean. Havana Station picked it up. Wonderful news for them. They had to tell the American Ambassador that his Texas crony was living with a surgical bombshell scandal. After they all came up for air, the Texan prepared to divest himself. In consequence, Libertad wrote a love letter to Pedro Peones, who used to know her as Roderigo Durazno. Now, when he saw nude photographs of her as a blonde, he went insane. Too bad I only found this out too late. Needless to say, Libertad makes me nervous. Any man born half a woman who gives his nuts and dick to the fishes is not likely to say to the KGB, 'Go away, you are not a good Christian.'" He nodded. "That's my take."

I now asked the question I had been afraid to ask. "Does Howard know about Libertad?"

"You better get to understand Howard *and* the Agency. They're both old ladies. Grand old ladies."

"I'm not sure I follow you."

"Ever been in a room with a grand old lady when somebody toots? To tell the truth, I never have, but they say the grand old lady doesn't miss a stitch. The fart, señor, he do not exist."

"Come on, Porringer, Howard's no fool."

"I did not suggest he was dumb—I was saying he knows when to breathe. So long as Peones is the fullback who will always get us the three yards we need, Howard will choose not to be witting." Porringer burped. "Looks like we're coming around to you again, *joven*. Concerning AV/OCADO, I would say that I am worried, but not frantic. Analyze the options. I would assume Chevi is still reliable. Could you say there is any possibility that he is a double agent?"

"It doesn't add up," I said. "Why would the PCU wreck its own ranks just to build a double agent who does not lead us, but merely feeds us?"

"He led you to Libertad."

"True."

"All the same, I kind of agree. It doesn't add out. All that finesse to set up a double agent in Montevideo? Not worth it. I think we have to take first things first." He reflected, and then he repeated somberly, "First things first."

Kittredge, I've noticed the odd remarks that people do repeat on occasion. I wonder if it's not the double, if separate, assent of Alpha and Omega, a way of saying, yes, all of me is behind this, first Alpha, now Omega, both parties accounted for. "Yes," Porringer decided, "let's keep the lid on. You and me can live with this. We don't want to get Howard upset. He'll have to call in people from Western Division to look it over. On the other hand, if and when AV/OCADO blows up, you will catch most of it. Well, you certainly get it now if you tell, and, if you wait, it may not blow. Chevi, meanwhile, has to keep away from Libertad. He will, once you make it triple crystal clear that if he don't, his ass is in Peones' iron hands."

We shook our iron hands on that, and quit Café Trouville. I would fill you in on what has happened since, but it has all been quiet. Nothing new has occurred. Kittredge, we're caught up to date.

Let me conclude, then, with one odd remark of Sherman Porringer's. On the way back to the office, he said, "Satisfy one mystery for me?"

"Sure."

"Why doesn't my wife have a single decent word to say about you?"

"She told me once that she didn't like my accent."

"Oh, that could bear improvement, but I still don't get it. You may be nothing remarkable, but I guess you're half-ass okay with me. Even if you can't hold an eggshell."

Can a noble society be founded on the judgment of one's peers?

Love to you, dear Kittredge,
Herrick

31

April 30, 1958

Harry, dear Harry,

Bizarre as your days have been, they seem normal next to my chores. I know I am being outrageously secretive, but I still can't tell you anything. I'm girded about with vows of absolute silence concerning The Project and hesitate to disturb any webs. I don't believe I'm thinking of Agency retribution. It's more a question of roiling the gods.

Angel man, I have this uneasy fear I may never be able to tell you. Then, on other days, I think I'm going to burst if I don't pass it on. You must, however, not stop sending your letters. I love them. I particularly enjoy the way you describe certain situations as if we are sitting side by side. I know my correspondence has been one-sided lately, and it's going to get worse, I fear, because soon I won't be able to pick anything up at my letter-box—I will be far away from Washington.

Love, dear man,
Kittredge

P.S. More I think of it, more I come to the conclusion that you must only write to me on the first of each month, although keep being as generous with your pages, please. I've arranged with Polly to pick up your letters at the Georgetown post-office box so long as I'm away. There is, incidentally, no need to be concerned about her discretion for I've guaranteed, artfully, I believe, that she remain ignorant about thee and me. Since she has to see the name you put on the return address, don't use your own dear moniker. Put Frederick Ainsley Gardiner on the envelope instead. You see, I've gulled her with a tale. Otherwise, she'd suspect I was having an affair with you, and would feel bound to gossip about it. To forestall that, I've already confessed to her that Frederick Ainsley Gardiner is my secret half brother, natural son from a hole-in-the-wall affair my father had eighteen years ago. Dear young Freddy is now living in Uruguay, where Daddy supports the old morganatic wife and his unseen but beloved bastard and allows them to use his last name. It's an awful thing to do to dear Daddy (although I suspect he's created such fantasies for himself often enough) but in any event, this is the sort of story Polly will believe. You met her at dinner once with her husband. He's State Department—remember him?—very tall and solemn as an owl, but sterling family stuff (if only he weren't so dull!). She's my old college roommate and, for a Radcliffe girl, absolutely ditsy about sex. Has affairs with conspiratorial panache, but does get loose-mouthed when she is impressed with the name of her lover. (Is that a common human failing? queries your innocent Kittredge who has only Montague's half-bald scalp on her belt!) Polly is having loads of hanky-panky now with Jack Kennedy, who, all the papers say, is going to make a serious run for the Democratic nomination in 1960. I can't believe it, not Jack Kennedy! From what I hear, that beau hasn't done a day's work in the Senate since he's been there, but one can't blame him—he's such a boon to the ladies. Polly does go on about her oh-so-clandestine *rendezvous* with Jack. She's obviously not trustworthy at keeping her own secrets whole, but if she does blab about Frederick Ainsley, it'll lack interest. Who here in these ordinative D.C. swamps would care about my father's supposed pecadillos?

Anyway, dear Freddy A., I adore you, and we will have better days. Just remember to send your letter once a month. Start on June 1. Don't even know where I'll be on May 1.

Love again,
K.

P.P.S. To repeat: I won't write anything for a while. Trust me.

I might have been trying like never before to charm her with my letters, but now she was not going to write at all, and I was rationed to once a month. To avoid a plunge into the pits of depression, I spent my night hours in the office catching up with a myriad of Station tasks. Work became my diversion. For want of another, work became my best friend, and indeed there was an interesting couple of weeks revolving around our old nemesis in the Uruguayan Foreign Ministry, the enterprising Plutarco Roballo Gómez, saved from arrest almost a year and a half ago by the clamor of Police Chief Capablanca's sirens in the park. Gómez remained a high official in the Foreign Ministry, and no doubt, was still smuggling Uruguayan files over to the Russian Embassy. Although Hunt only arrived after the old operation was botched, he nonetheless did not let a week go by without reminding us of Plutarco Roballo Gómez, still free out there, still feathering nests for the Reds. Hunt's vein of venom about Communists was as immaculately personal as if he were speaking of his mother-in-law. I, no matter how much I wished to feel somewhat more combative, looked upon the Russians and ourselves, at least in Uruguay, as rival portfolios of stocks, but Hunt was as immediate in his reactions as one of those long-nosed basketball coaches whose team is doing poorly on the floor. In compensation, when a good operation got going, Howard gave off that special warmth only the sour-faced can bestow with a smile.

He started to smile about the time Gatsby got lucky. If intelligence officers tended to measure their respective importance at the Station by the penetrative powers of their agents, in much the manner that a serious hostess will calculate the desirability of her guests, I had, while running AV/OCADO, been holding the social honors, and Porringer and Hunt could certainly lay claim to cultivating Peones, a prize heavyweight. Until now, however, Gatsby had been relatively unproductive, for he had only developed two medium-rank agents; the rest of his contacts were what Gordy Morewood called "rubbish collectors."

Now, one of Gatsby's middling sources, AV/LEADPIPE, a gold smuggler who operated through a border crossing between Uruguay and Brazil, informed Gatsby that he was on close terms with an official in the Foreign Ministry who could obtain Uruguayan passports. Did the Station wish to buy a few? We did. Acquiring foreign passports was always a standing Station objective. Yes, Hunt told Gatsby, buy five, and get LEADPIPE to give you the name of the official putting them up for sale. The name came back and it was Plutarco Roballo Gómez. Our office came alive.

LEADPIPE's car was enriched with a bug. In the next meeting, following Gatsby's instructions, LEADPIPE asked Gómez to repeat the serial number of each passport.

"Uriarte, you are young, successful, and enterprising," said Gómez. "Why do you take up our time with these clerical procedures?"

"Tarco," said LEADPIPE, "it is so much more agreeable if you aid me. My mind reverses numbers when I have to do it alone."

"You are mentally unstable," said Gómez.

"Inclined to madness," muttered Uriarte.

They bargained over the price. It was all there on the tape recorder. Hunt mailed a duplicate of this wholly incriminating tape to the editor of *El Diario de Montevideo* together with a package that included the five numbered passports; *El Diario* had a front-page story, and Gómez had to resign his post. Word spread through local government circles that the fall of Plutarco Roballo Gómez was due entirely to the efforts of the CIA.

"Secrecy," Hunt told us, "sometimes has to take a backseat to propaganda. Because of Gómez, we used to be the laughingstock of

Montevideo. Now the locals perceive us as dangerous to our enemies, devoted to our principles, and just too damn tricky to keep up with. Let's maintain that image."

My good luck came next. Over at the Russian Embassy, we learned by way of GOGOL that Varkhov had been acting untypically. Five times in three days he had left the Embassy for an hour, only to return with an annoyed expression. I decided to look into this. At the nearby grocery where many of the Soviet Embassy personnel purchased their food, we had a *rubbish collector*, no less than the son of the shopkeeper. He had, at the urging of his father, been studying Russian for several years. When Hyman Bosqueverde informed me that the father could no longer afford the lessons, I had arranged to pay for the boy's instruction out of petty cash. The opportunity to have somebody in place to chat with the Soviets was too good to pass up. I even gave the boy a cryptonym since Hunt was all for carrying a full complement of saddlebags. It could only make us look more impressive back at Headquarters. The grocery store clerk became AV/GROUNDHOG. It became one more of the Station jokes. GROUNDHOG was sixteen years old.

On the heels of Varkhov's new activities, however, I met GROUNDHOG at a café to give him specific instructions. While his Russian probably had a long way to go, I told him to do his best to get Varkhov's chauffeur (who was always purchasing Pepsi-Cola at the grocery store) into some kind of conversation about his boss's traveling habits of late. The chauffeur brought the subject up himself. Did the boy know of any deluxe apartments for rent in the area? Varkhov's mysterious trips out of the Embassy were explained. He had been going to see real estate agents.

Hunt loved this piece of news. He checked out his lists, and handed me a sheet of paper with twenty names. "These are wealthy individuals, sympathetic to us, who might have just the kind of place Varkhov is looking for. We can probably work with one of the realtors Varkhov has gone to already, get him together with a landlord on this list."

On discussion, we decided to pass it over to Gordy Morewood. He knew every realtor in Montevideo.

Gordy, as usual, gave good results. We selected a charming ground-floor apartment in a small villa on Calle Feliciano Rodríguez, owned by an old gentleman named Don Bosco Teótimo Bland-enques. Varkhov was introduced to him by Gordy's real estate man, and Varkhov, a fierce negotiator, ended up paying considerably less rent than his share of the villa was worth. Don Bosco knew, of course, that we would make up the difference, and add a dividend.

We also had to obtain Señor Blandenques' permission to install a few sneakies. No ordinary installation would do; Hunt wanted "a high-efficiency audio op."

Don Bosco did not mind the risk, he informed us. He had no fear of Varkhov should the Soviet discover his cooperation with us. "I would invite him to a duel," said Don Bosco. "I have not engaged in such a confrontation for twenty-eight years, but that is only because I have faced each minute of each day of all the days in these last twenty-eight years with the knowledge that I have taken an oath to demand satisfaction from any person who presumes to speak improperly to me. This vow, señores, provides me with equanimity." Teótimo Blandenques' sentiments were certainly fortified by the curve of his sweeping white mustache. "My difficulty," added Don Bosco soon after, "is, however, with the technical equipment. You would have to drill many holes. I do not believe in sullying venerable walls."

Don Bosco's villa had been subdivided into two apartments twenty years ago, and that must have sullied a few venerable walls, but Don Bosco's eyes suggested that it was not advisable to throw such facts into the pot. Instead, we waited, and over cocktails, noble Don Bosco gave way to Blandenques, the *rentier*. Howard obtained permission to put in the equipment. We would have to pay an overcharge of 30 percent, and make reparations afterward to all walls, woodwork, stone foundations, or molding disturbed by the audio installation.

"The old thief," said Howard, "will probably ask Gordy Morewood to represent him on the reparations committee."

I was frightfully depressed that night. While there was nothing to keep me from writing to Kittredge whenever I wanted, then hoarding my pages until June 1, I realized that a letter which could not be sent off so soon as it was completed did not seem to serve quite as much purpose. Besides, I was missing Kittredge physically. On successive nights, I awakened from the midst of a dream in which I was making love to her. That had not happened before, and I was shocked at the carnality we expressed. It was more than worthy of a brothel. I began to wonder if I was being fueled by some rich mixture of anxiety in relation to Libertad, Peones, and Chevi. All was quiet there, and I could hope that nothing would stir from that quarter, but it did amount to one more large uncertainty to carry through days of work and nights of uneasy sleep.

32

June 1, 1958

Dear Kittredge,

I wish I could say a multitude of events have whisked me right up to June 1, but that, I fear, is hardly so. You are the witch-goddess who keeps our Station humming *so long as I send letters to you.* When I cease, it all seems to stop.

Of course, a few things did pass our way this month. Vice President Nixon stopped in Montevideo on his South American junket, and Hunt took him on a tour through our Embassy quarters, savaging Station cover pretty completely, I expect, by offering outrageous thumbnail sketches of each of us to Mr. Nixon and Mrs. Nixon as, viz, "This is Sherman Porringer, who can tell you anything you might want to know, Mr. Vice President, about Uruguayan labor unions and how we aid them in getting rid of their leftists."

Porringer, bless him, was so embarrassed that he hee-hawed like an Oklahoma mule.

"Good democratic spirit in some of these unions?" asked Nixon.

"I wouldn't say no to that," said Porringer. Thrice weekly we had to listen to his harangue on local labor leaders: "Stupid sons of bitches, Uruguayan meatballs." Now Hunt tells him right in front of Vice President Nixon, "Well, if you wouldn't say no to that, would you say yes?"

"There's some real democratic spirit around," Porringer manages to mutter.

Hunt now chooses to deliver his piece in front of all of us rather than take Mr. and Mrs. Nixon back to his office. I don't know if it's nervousness, bravura, or the calculation that he might as well impress us too, but, in any event, as Chief of Station, he's entitled to his two-minute aria before returning our guests to the Ambassador. "Mr. Vice President," says Hunt, "I am going to presume on this occasion to restore for you a wholly minor incident in your busy life, but I do recollect an evening when my wife, Dorothy, and I, repairing to Harvey's Restaurant for a bit of after-theater supper, had the great good luck to be seated near to you and Mrs. Nixon. May I say that on impulse, I walked over to your table and introduced myself. You were kind enough to invite Dorothy and me to join you."

"Howard Hunt, I can recall that occasion very well," said the Vice President.

Kittredge, to me, it did not look as if he did. Nixon has a deep voice that makes you think of some valuable driller's-bit packed in oil; the lubrication slides him through many an embarrassing episode. A politician's life has to be filled with half-recollections, wouldn't you think? So many people. At any rate, his voice may have come out as smarmy as a British radio announcer stating, "And now Her Majesty is passing the expectant throng," but his eyes sent one quick signal to wife, Pat, and she, lean as whipcord, said, "Yes, Dick, it was on that night four years ago when you addressed the Society of Former FBI Agents."

"Indeed," said Dick, "a sterling group, SFFA, and not so slow on the draw when it came to the question period."

"Ho, ho," said Hunt.

"The Hiss case came up," said Pat Nixon.

"I remember," said the Vice President, "that you, Howard, congratulated me on what you called 'my indefatigable pursuit' of Alger Hiss, and I had to thank you. In those days, there was still, concerning that matter, a lot of *división de opiniones*, if I'm employing acceptable Spanish."

"You certainly are," said Hunt. He looked in danger of bouncing on his toes, he was thus excited. "I remember," he said, "it turned out to be a particularly pleasant half-hour discussion of the foreign and domestic scene. Your memory is superb, sir."

"A most pleasurable meeting," concluded Nixon, and shifted his weight, a signal doubtless to Hunt, who now steered him down the hall to the Ambassador's office. I wish you could have seen the Vice President, Kittredge. Nixon's an ordinary man in appearance, yet he's not. He must be as completely the instrument of his own will as Hugh Montague. Can you conceive of two people, however, who are more unalike?

Hunt now comes back to say to us, "Gang, you have just met the next President of the United States."

I wonder if Howard is considering a resignation from the Agency in order to work for Nixon in 1960. He's growing dissatisfied these days, and the cause is our new Ambassador, a nicely tailored specimen named Robert Woodward whom Hunt was complaining about before Woodward even reached the Embassy. "Another eminent nonentity," was Howard's initial description. "The man's ambassadorial credentials consist of a stint in Costa Rica."

Woodward, however, proved no nugatory presence. He ties into a State Department bloc who are flat-out opposed to the Agency, and one of his first questions to Hunt was, "What mischief are you fomenting down here?"

"I," Howard informed us, "replied to him, 'My mandate does not extend to overthrowing a friendly government, sir.' "

Woodward then gave a lecture which Howard will be dining out on for years. " 'Mr. Hunt, please recognize,' " goes Howard's imitation, " 'that this country of Uruguay, while small in size, is the finest democracy extant in South America. There are few nations which can lay claim to being as well run, as clean of corruption, and so much of a model to less fortunate small nations. Uruguay is the Switzerland of South America.' " Howard repeats all this for Gatsby and Kearns, Porringer, Waterston, and myself, then repeats, "*clean of corruption!* Why, these welfare-state crooks in the Legislative Assembly can purchase a new foreign car every year *free of duty*. What is that worth when they sell it? Ten thousand extra frogskins?"

He's right, of course. Uruguay is corrupt. The liberals steal and so does the right. Don Jaime Saavedra Carbajal, for example, is not above herding thousands of his cattle over the Jaguar River into Brazil as a means of saving untold customs duty. In a word, smuggling. The border police certainly have to be bought off. Howard doesn't disapprove, however. It reminds him, he says, of how the first great Texas fortunes were built. I don't see how this alters the judgment, but then, it's not the day to argue with Howard. The real problem is that Station no longer has its way with State. While we never mingled all that much with their personnel, we could always cater to our vanity by trotting over to any of the offices in the Embassy; the boys there, whether thirty years old or sixty, were properly resentful of the warm welcome we receive from the State Department ladies.

Now we've become the greaser gang. State Department personnel are beginning to act hollow and overfriendly, as if they are our social superiors but don't want us to know it because greasers do wreck property. Two weeks ago Hunt was notified that Woodward and his new deputy will attend all the foreign embassy functions; Hunt can, in effect, take a well-deserved rest in the evening and enjoy his family. Needless to say, this removes us from the foreign embassy circuit, a blessing—I'll be able to read a book—but social ostracism does have its bite even if you don't mind what you are being cut out of. Hunt is, of course, inwardly livid.

Final note. There is, actually, more going on than I admit to. Over the last month we've managed to set up a love nest for Zenia Masarov and Georgi Varkhov, an operation that—how could it be otherwise?—involved numerous steps. Apart from managing to bait the trap, technicians had to fly down from Washington to install the audio and test the bugs, the best of which is emplaced in no less of a salient than one of the posts of a four-poster bed.

I have to admit that we at the Station may be showing a certain prurient anticipation. In ten days, we'll see if it works. I could let you know earlier, but will accept your strictures for what they are. July 1 will have to prove soon enough.

Yours,
Harry

33

July 1, 1958

Dear Kittredge,

Zenia and Georgi turned out to be having a passionate affair. I'm amazed at how much I am feeling for Brishka, and, believe me, she now speaks of him often. One is almost inclined to say, "Poor Varkhov!" for he has to hear constantly about the husband whose wife he is presumably despoiling—Zenia is voluble concerning her sense of shame. Naturally, Porringer will make a point of saying, "No woman ever got injured by a good fuck," a bracing piece of information, and wouldn't it be nice if it were true?

Meanwhile, I have been given the monitor's role in AV/ RATHOLE, which is the unbemused name Hunt has bestowed on our eavesdropping operation. I don't know if I'm dealing with a comedy or a monstrosity. Can humans be held accountable for what they say in the midst of the act?

The mechanics often prove droll. While the audio promises

to be the best yet devised for this kind of tap, and we are able to receive conversations from the living room, the kitchen, the dining room, and the bedroom, there are gaps when Zenia or Georgi rattles a plate, or, worse, the bedsprings take over. The Finnish Micks go over after every visit to pick up the tapes from a bedroom we've rented on the floor above, and come back to their desk in our office to spend hours translating. Then, I try to put it into better English without losing any hard intelligence. Since the Sourballs also receive the raw Russian transcripts a day later in Washington and can decide for themselves what is truly of value, I begin to wonder if I am needed. I take this thought to Hunt who assures me that my little unhappiness is but a cavil. "Just keep up your output," he tells me. I have a hunch he is sending copies of my stuff to a couple of his *primes* in Western Division.

The worst of it is that the boil-down is minimal. Varkhov goes to his love-nest to forget about his office, and Zenia meets him because she is "captive of exotic alien obsession." We hear a great deal about that. Varkhov comes through in the tapes as even cruder human stuff than anticipated—apparently, he is descended from a long line of serfs, and his father rose to be a railroad engineer, that is, a locomotive driver, while he, Georgi, distinguished himself as a young if all but uneducated platoon Commissar, survived Stalingrad, and was some sort of hit man or executioner for the GRU during the Red Army's advance to Berlin. He's a butcher boy according to Zenia's wrought description—he deals in "flesh, bones, and now you deal with me." She speaks mournfully and often about her inability to be in control of herself. "I read books concerning collapse of virtue in women, but books do not warn sufficiently. Not Flaubert. Not even Tolstoy. Chekhov maybe. A little. Not enough. Dostoyevsky, the worst. No good for understanding sufferings of spoiled women mired in worship of devil's flesh."

"Who is a devil?" Georgi protests. "I am one man under impossible circumstances. I worship your husband for his wisdom."

"Not so much as you worship center of me, my pussy hair. Liking what your nose finds? Brishka adores such. You no. Too scared. Strong man scared. Center of sin in pussy hair."

I'm sorry, Kittredge, but after the Finnish Micks do their literal translation, I am hard put to get it back into enough English to give an idea of what Zenia and Georgi sound like. That last in raw translation came to me as "turpitude in crotch hairs, stinking crotch hairs." Don't look to Russians for the delicate touch.

She upbraids Varkhov for quite a time as *"nyet kulturny."* I am generally familiar with the expression via Masarov, but Gohogon, another of the Finnish Micks, assures me that this is a forceful insult among Russians—either you are a cultured person, or you are without culture. Zenia Arkadyova feels degraded exactly because she is full of passion for this *nyet kulturny,* Varkhov. "I had five aunts, all ladies, all dead. Would faint with one look at you."

His replies to such remarks usually have to be inserted in the transcript as: VARKHOV: . . . (grunts).

I become sufficiently curious to get Gohogon to let me listen to the raw tape. Another element reveals itself. Zenia's words may be brutal, but her voice is soft, melodious, welcoming. His responding grunt is one of pure happiness, something like a hippo snorting in muck. *Khorosho,* he replies, which comes out much like a grunt itself when uttered in a hoarse voice. "Horror-show," is the nearest aural equivalent. In fact, *khorosho* means okay, pure and simple okay.

"I disgrace my family," says Zenia.

"Khorosho."

"You are a dog."

"Khorosho."

"You are a pig."

"Khorosho."

"Specimen of greed."

"Khorosho, khorosho."

I begin to think of Peones. Is there a principle here? Do brutes look to be whipped? Is there a scale of inner justice?

"Tell me more," he says. "Am here to listen."

"Are unworthy."

"Okay."

"Unworthy of my husband."

"Understood."

"You revolt me."

"I don't," said Varkhov.

"No, you don't. Come here. I need you."

Groans, heavy breathing, bedsprings. Maniacal cries at the end. (Yes, I do listen to the raw tape.) You cannot always tell which voice is which. "Fuck me, fuck me out of my heart. You are my liberty, my shit," cries Zenia Arkadyova, yes, it is her voice, and even on the tape I can feel her reaching from the hole in the center of herself to that place in the universe where perhaps there is something other than a hole. I don't know whether to be moved or appalled. Listening to the tape, I can feel the sweet nausea of her desire and wonder if I have pinched some unnatural nerve in myself.

Hunt visits my desk from time to time with exhortations to extract the nitty-gritty. "Restrict it to the gamy stuff. I want to spear Boris in the pits. None of that fraudulent muck about 'how wonderful my husband is.' Hell, Harry, human perversity being what it is, a man can forgive a wife who keeps talking about him while she's with the other guy. So, just look for the give-it-to-me-you-goddamn-great-fucker stuff. The good passages. We'll squash the heart right out of Brishka, that poor, misunderstood KGB mass-murdering bastard."

So I commence editing. A fearsome product results. Another example, be it said, of the validity of K. Gardiner Montague's thesis on A and O. If I allowed myself, I'd be in a whirl of disturbed feelings about what I'm doing, but Alpha has taken over, Alpha appears to thrive on the excitement of bringing off a good job with obdurate, even repellent, material. Not that this is entirely repellent. Kittredge, in honesty, I am not unmoved by the depth of Zenia's voice. Can you imagine me ever admitting this to anyone but you? Yet our good Reverend Hubbard has to confess that even Varkhov's grunts, listened to long enough, do strike human chords: tenderness in the midst of animal greed, sorrow in the heart of all his harsh curses. He comes—all right, I will tell all—shouting, "Whore, mother-of-pigs, filth I fuck," incredible, awful stuff which evokes an aria of responsive ecstasies from her. If I allowed myself, I could feel diminished by the power of their carnality. But I have my Alpha, good, determined work-soldier, and he runs the operation. It even becomes tedious piecing through the transcripts for "good passages." With the aid of Gohogon, I find the equivalent bits on the tape and splice them. Then I listen as if it were music. Of course, the cuts don't always work. Whereupon I have to play the raw tapes and try to find other moments of Russian sound that could bridge the transition. Since I don't know the language, my choices often make no great sense word for word, but miss by miss and bit by bit, I do patch together a workable, even overwhelming, actualization on edited tape of what Hunt was looking for. If he's been complaining every day at how long it takes, he is generous enough, old clam-lipped Howard, to express his praise finally at my good job. And I am pleased. Deep inside of Omega, hopelessly incarcerated, a subparticle of my soul is mourning for

Brishka, but Alpha has carried the day. Indeed, the week. I feel like a sound editor and/or radio director. I have created an interesting vocal work. I swear, before the power of a tough job well done, moral qualms have no more force than blades of grass before a lawnmower. Or, so it seems while working.

Now, of course, the question arises of what to do with the finished product. Hunt, predictably, is all for blasting Boris Masarov out of his socks. Send him the tape, and then no matter what happens we can count on a sizable profit. At the least, if he decides to swallow it, he and Varkhov will have to work together. More likely, Masarov will attempt to have Varkhov sent back to Moscow, or will apply for return himself. That will be time-consuming for the Soviet team.

Of course, there is always the larger possibility that Varkhov can be blackmailed into working for us. Ditto Masarov. Could this tape so demoralize him about the value of his present life that he would consider defection?

Hunt argues sensibly that Boris is likely to look upon us as even more of an enemy than before. Hjalmar Omaley, who has flown in from Soviet Russia Division again, is, of course, all on the side of working for a defection. The Sourballs are geared for that. Arguments go on between Omaley and Hunt that must reflect the scene at Headquarters between Western Hemisphere Division *cum* Groogs on one side, Soviet Russia Division on the other. I won't consume pages of this letter by listing any more of the debates, scenarios, lacunae, and, via Omaley, paranoid accusations. Hjalmar is seeing Nancy Waterston every night, and Hunt no longer knows whether to trust her. *Un tour de drôle.*

In the middle of all this, arrives the following cable. Decoded, it reads:

TO: AV/HACENDADO
FROM: KU/GHOUL-1
CONGRATULATIONS ON RATHOLE. SPLENDID DEMOPO. FELI-
CITATIONS.

Demopo, Kittredge, stands for *Demolition Options,* that is, wreaking havoc on your opposition.

Hunt was in heaven. "This is the first recognition from your guy since he invited me to dinner two years ago." He hawked his throat. "On second thought, Harry, you know how to read the man. What *is* Harlot up to? Does he want to come in on this?"

"He would never approach you directly if he wanted to take it over," I venture. It's amazing, Kittredge, how one becomes an expert. I, who have never understood Hugh for one moment, am now explaining him to others.

"Well, what is he saying?" asked Hunt.

"He's offering genuine felicitations, I believe. After all, it is a nice operation."

"Hell and soda water if it isn't," Hunt exclaims. He can't quite trust me when it comes to Hugh Montague, but on the other hand, I am saying what he wants to hear. So he *tends* to believe me. Then shakes his head. "There's got to be more to this cable."

"Why," I asked, "don't you give him a ring?"

He sighed. I think he was a little reluctant. "This one calls for the red phone," he said at last.

I left Howard's office. In fifteen minutes, I was summoned back. He was in a glow. "Montague's not all that bad when he chooses to be forthcoming. Wants to speak to you now. Wants to congratulate you, too."

When I got on the secure phone, however, count on it, Howard was still hovering in his office. So I did not dare to close the door. Your own dear mate greeted me by saying in that oft-familiar tunnel voice, "Declare loudly how glad you are that I like it."

"Yessir," I said, "I'm awfully glad that you like it."

"All right," said Hugh, "enough of that. The cable was merely preamble to get you on the secure phone. I'm not keening in on RATHOLE. Its promise is small. Masarov and Varkhov are made of the hard stuff. They will never defect. In any event, it's not my playground. I'm calling with a query for you. How would you like to be transferred to Israel?"

"You don't mean it? Isn't that a plum?"

"Take it more slowly. It's very much Angleton's show over there. As my representative, you'd be working uphill. However, I do hold a couple of slots. Not every last soul in the Mossad is enamored of Mother. A couple of top-shelf Israelis are more inclined to work with me."

"I guess I had better think about this."

"You had better. On the positive side, the Mossad are the diamonds in the intelligence game."

"Yessir."

"You will come out a master, or broken."

"Broken?"

"Crushed." He paused. When I did not reply, he went on. "No question. It's Angleton's fief. You will be the enemy as far as *Jesus* is concerned." He pronounced Jesus as *Hey-sooz*, James *Jesus* Angleton.

"Why are you proposing I go, then?" Unfortunately, I had to whisper this for fear Howard would hear me.

"Because you may survive. *Jesus* does not hold all the cards. I've marked a few for myself."

"Can I think about it?"

"Do. You're at a fork. Brood."

"How do we pick this up again?"

"Call Rosen. He's now my slave Friday. Telephone him at TSS-Tertiary on one of your open lines. Chat away. Harmless buddy-buddy stuff. If you've decided that Israel is go, you need merely remark, 'How I miss Maine now that I'm in Montevideo.' I'll take care of the rest."

"And if one decides in the negative?"

"Then, boy, don't use the code. Rosen will have nothing to report to me."

"Yessir."

"Two days to determine your mind." He hung up before I could ask about you, Kittredge. Not that he would have told me.

I will not try to describe the next forty-eight hours. I felt exalted; I dwelt in terror. Angleton's reputation is easily as fearsome as your husband's, but then it is to Hugh's and Angleton's honor that Agency people speak of them as legends without ever quite knowing what they do.

I was able to learn two things about myself in the next two days. Dear Married Lady: I entered the abyss of my cowardice and smelled the noxious fumes therein; I climbed the highest peaks of my hitherto unglimpsed high ambition. I even thought of the moment I got back into the polo game. I ended by telephoning Arnie Rosen at TSS on an open Station phone, resolved to speak of my longing for Maine.

So soon as I approached that, however, he cut me off. "Forget all about a vacation," he said. "Your request for leave is canceled."

"What?"

"Yes."

"Why?"

"Oh, oh, oh," he said.

"I can't bear this," I told him. "Give me some notion."

"It's your mother. Your mother prevents your trip to Maine."

"My mother? Jessica?"

"Yes."

"She can't."

"Well, she's the reason, although she's not the executor of the decision."

"Who is the executor?"

"Let's say it's your father." A pause. "Yes. Paradigmatically speaking." Another pause. "And your host sends deep regrets at being unable to send the plane fare."

I thought I could glimpse a picture, then wondered if I could. "Arnie, hit me once more." We could have been trading favors for futures.

He was so good at this game. "Well," he said, and he did say *well* as if he were opening a door, "I, for one, would never be allowed to go to those woods."

"Why not?"

"They're too anti-Semitic in Maine."

That offered enough. There was reason to feel the answer was going to make its way to me.

"Yes, and how is Kittredge?" I asked. "Have you and she made up?"

"Well, I'd love to, but she is far away."

"How far away?"

"Think of Australia and you'll be wrong. Ditto Poland. I wish I could tell you where." He hung up.

A box of Churchills arrived via embassy pouch two days later. Inside was a card in Harlot's immaculately small handwriting: "Your errant godfather." I had solved the question by then. Even as Hugh is Harlot to some, so Angleton is Mother to many. But he is not *my* mother, Jessica Silverfield Hubbard. Rosen, doubtless, was reminding me that I was one-eighth Jewish. As for my father? *Paradigmatically speaking!* That had to refer to Company policy. Of course. The Company would not send a Jewish case officer to Israel. Conflict of interest. I had no idea if this originated as an Agency determination, or came by request of the Mossad, or had been agreed upon by both. In any event, Kittredge, your own peerless Harlot had forgotten that a little part of me was Jewish until Personnel, bless them, probably reminded him. For a few days, Kittredge, I must say it was curious to think of myself as Hebraic.

On the other hand, even though I have been up to my neck with RATHOLE, I now have difficulty believing that I am wholly in Uruguay. I must confess to you that I have a private teleology. I still believe I was born for a purpose and will strive to reach a certain end, even if I can neither see the end nor name it. Forty-eight hours in the scenario-factory of my mind had been spent coming to the conclusion that I must accept a dubious, and conceivably career-smashing, job because I was fated to go to Israel. Then, abruptly, I discovered I wasn't destined at all. Knocked out on a technicality. It has left me awfully detached about RATHOLE. And don't you know, Kittredge, that may be just as well. RATHOLE seems in danger of decomposing even as we deal with it.

The Sourballs, you see, won the battle. Their decision prevailed: We have to try to get a defector out of this, and the consensus settled on Varkhov. Masarov, the old hand, it was agreed, would simply prove too difficult, too outraged. So Station discussed approaches to Georgi. Porringer is for tailing Varkhov's chauffeured car with one of the cabs from AV/EMARIA. Sooner or later, Varkhov will stop at a café for lunch, and then Omaley and Gohogon, bulked up by Porringer or myself, can be summoned by radio via AV/EMARIA to move in on Varkhov, hand him the tape and a phone number, and tell him to play it *for himself alone*. We-can-all-be-friends will serve as the theme of this pageant. Hjalmar, however, hates such an outright approach, and SR Division is behind him. Meetings, they argue, must be kept to a minimum. We could, of course, just mail it to Varkhov directly at the Russian Embassy, but how would we know he received it?

I suggest we use one of our villa keys to leave the tape in Varkhov's love nest. If the locks have been changed by him, we can hire a locksmith. Disadvantage: The locksmith could attract the notice of the neighbors. If that happens, the operation is blown.

Of course, once we leave a tape, the love nest goes into terminal, anyway. I propose that we send AV/ALANCHE-1 (leader of the sign-painters and a most trustworthy kid) over with our keys. We can do this at a time when we know, via GOGOL, that Varkhov's car is parked on the street back at the Russian Embassy. AV/ALANCHE-1 need merely try the lock. Whether the keys work or not, he must depart immediately. At least we will know then whether we can open the door.

First rate. My idea is implemented on a Friday afternoon, and we learn that the lock has not been changed. After the weekend, then, we will make our move. We've discovered by now that no matter how many times a week our villa on Calle Feliciano Rodríguez is used by Varkhov, he always has a tryst on his Monday break for lunch (because, as we learn from the tape, he has spent the weekend with his wife and is heartily sick of her!). We decide, therefore, to leave the spool with a tape recorder sitting next to it right on the table in his entrance foyer. An accompanying note will suggest a place and time of meeting. All he has to do for assent is to substitute a blank piece of paper, also provided, in place of the note. All stated in immaculate Russian, thanks to Hjalmar. There is a concept behind this. The *House of Love on Feliciano Rodríguez Street* (as we now with a curious mixture of superiority and embarrassment term the theater of operations for this sticky caper) is always approached and entered by Georgi a half hour before Zenia. To prevent his chauffeur from getting a glimpse of her, the limousine is always dispatched right back to the Embassy. Then Zenia arrives by cab and stops a block away. Walks to the door. Georgi, given his advance half hour, is out of his clothes and hungry as a Russian bear. But she delays him. Sometimes, she makes him put his clothes on again. "We must start as equals," she tells him. Fascinating, but the point is that we do have a predictable half hour at the commencement when he is alone.

Come Monday morning, therefore, our Company gift is deposited on the foyer table, and Gatsby, who is the least likely to be familiar on sight to either of our Russians, is waiting in a surveillance cab half a block away. Fifteen minutes later, Georgi, right on time, enters the House of Love. Ten minutes later he comes out. He is perspiring visibly. He starts to pace the street. These perambulations become progressively longer to and fro until they take him right past Gatsby, who is still sitting in the parked taxi. Oh, my God, Georgi recognizes Jay. He stops on the sidewalk, salutes him, sticks his thumb to his nose, waggles his fingers, raises a mallet-like fist, smashes it down on the hood of the taxi hard enough to bestow a sizable dent in the metal, and then, seeing Zenia, strides off to meet her, whereupon they enter the house again. Gatsby, in a perfect perspiration of his own, waits in the taxi and has to haggle with his driver over what it will cost to repair the damaged hood. A half hour later, Zenia, distraught, leaves with Georgi, and they hail a cab. When Gatsby attempts to follow at the book-approved distance, Georgi, at a red light, has his own vehicle back itself up a full hundred yards, all the way to Gatsby's car, gets out, leaves a second dent on the other side of the hood, and jumps back into his cab. Realizing, I think, that discretion is somewhat pointless by now, Varkhov even drops Zenia on the Rambla one building away from her high-rise, and returns to the Embassy where he pays off the driver and shakes his fist at Jay Gatsby even as the latter drives off.

There's always the chance Varkhov will notify the police that his apartment was entered, but that will take time. So soon as Jay calls in, I'm sent over quickly with Gohogon to see what has been done to Don Bosco's property. It's a nightmare. First of all, Georgi has broken off his key in the front door so we can't get in. Fortunately, there's a rear entrance he has overlooked in his rage, and we also have the key to that. He has done a job. The four-poster bed is smashed, the tape recorder is smashed, the tape, unspooled, is in and out of the toilet bowl and all over the bathroom floor like a slither-pit of tape-worms, the living-room furniture has hordes of stuffing ripped out, a couple of the walls show dented plaster (from those mallet-like fists)—no need to go on. I feel the fires of the Russian heart burning through the icy Russian winter. I jest, but then I don't. It gives me a glimpse of the terror Europeans hold of the barbaric passions waiting out in the East for them.

Naturally, all hope for a defection is now lost. Hunt, backed by Western Hemisphere Division and the Groogs, is arguing that a defection was never in the cards, and the alternative is to use our demopos. "Speed is of the essential," he cables to Washington and in return is given the go-ahead. There is very little to lose. Duplicate tapes are mailed to Masarov at the Embassy, and delivered to the doorman in his high-rise apartment. At a party given by the Swedish Embassy, a third duplicate is left in Masarov's overcoat pocket. Given Ambassador Woodward's injunction that State Department presence at embassy functions be *unsullied*, none of us have been invited, but Porringer does know the Uruguayan hatcheck girl employed by the Swedes well enough to induce her, by way of half a week's wages, to plant the tape. All of this is at a desperately low level of tradecraft, but, of course, it no longer matters. Saturation is the only way we can be certain Boris receives the goods. No note, of course, is sent. No need for that now. Let Masarov and Varkhov battle it out.

We sit back and wait. Days go by. No apparent results. The Russians then notify us of a reception for Yevgeny Yevtushenko, a young and apparently outspoken new Russian poet. Enclosed is the information that Yevtushenko gives readings in Moscow and Leningrad to stadium crowds of as many as twenty thousand people. While not a singer, his popularity is comparable to the American Elvis Presley's. All personnel at the American Embassy, states the invitation, are specifically invited. So Woodward feels obliged to bring along Hunt, Porringer, Kearns, Gatsby, Hubbard, and Waterston in addition to his own stodgy crew. Since it's the heart of winter now, the party is given inside and is formal enough to remind you of czarist receptions.

Varkhov and Masarov head up the receiving line. Zenia and Mrs. Varkhov, a fat lady, are between them. They are all a tad nervous, but then, so are we. Varkhov makes a point of clicking his heels when Jay Gatsby goes by with wife, Theodora. I could swear that Masarov winks at me, or was it an involuntary twitch? Zenia, flushed, and looking most vulnerable, as if she is about to weep or to laugh, but can provide no warning, even for herself, of which it will be, is nonetheless looking more beautiful than I have ever seen her. Forgive the crudity of this next thought but it did occur to me that shame bestows a rich light on a woman's flesh. Exposed, she is also, despite herself, oddly triumphant. Wherever you are, Kittredge, do not become too furious at this.

At the height of the evening, Yevtushenko is asked to read from his work. Easily as tall as me, he is not bad-looking. Has the sinewy build of a ski instructor. Loudly, he reads his poetry like a young baritone doing a full-voiced *récitatif*. His Russian seems to be full of onomatopoetic effects. It's hammy acting, but Zenia's eyes gleam like gems. "New spirit of Russian people," she confides to me, as if I were not one of the agents of her attempted downfall. Later, the Belgian Ambassador was to whisper to Hunt that Zenia and Yevtushenko are having an affair.

I wonder. Yevgeny Yevtushenko is quite a fellow. Speaks a harsh English, but practices it assiduously. Draws me aside and wants to know how far I can swim.

"Oh, two miles, anyway," I tell him.

"Can swim ten. In ice-cold water." His eyes are wild and blue and stare at you with peremptory force, as if he can bend you to his will inasmuch as his will is pure and only wants your friendship.

I have no idea whether he's up to something. "Are interested in wedding customs?" he asks of me.

I shrug.

"Siberian wedding custom fascinating," he says. "Siberian groom pisses glass until full of urine. Bride drinks urine. Barbaric, yes?"

"Sounds a bit *nyet kulturny*."

My use of Russian does not reach him. "Barbaric, yes, but wisdom, yes. Yes, also! Because! What is marriage for poor people? Babies, wet diapers, ca-ca. Stinks. Small stinks. Good wife must live with such. Hence, Siberian custom. Good beginning for marriage."

"It's unfair," I said. "The bridegroom doesn't drink the piss."

"Agree. I agree. Unfair to women. You show sense of justice for era of tomorrow. Let me shake your hand. I salute you."

He shook my hand, his eyes stared wildly into mine. I had no idea if he was a talented poet, Zenia's new lover, a KGB joy-boy, or, first of all, entirely mad. I did not even know how much he knew of what we had been up to. But he made me feel cheap, that son of a bitch—I don't even know how.

Kittredge, I miss you so much I could cry in my beer, at least, if I were the demonstrative sort, like Yevgeny Yevtushenko.

Love,
Harry

34

A FEW WEEKS AFTER I SENT MY LAST MONTHLY LETTER TO KITTREDGE on July 1, an envelope bearing a postmark from Arlington, Virginia, arrived at my hotel addressed directly to me. It contained no message, only a key wrapped in a tissue. The next day another letter, with a Georgetown postmark, contained a letterhead from a bank in Arlington on which was written the number of a safety deposit box. A third envelope brought a receipt for the first payment on the box, plus a notice that it was to be maintained by quarterly payments. A few days later, the pouch finally brought me a full letter from Kittredge with, as always, the name of Polly Galen Smith substituted for her own on the return address.

July 26, 1958

Beloved Harry,

I am back in Georgetown and will be heading up to Maine in a few days. Now that you have received your key and box number, let me inform you that when you return to Washington and open your Arlington box, you will find about thirty strips of 35mm negative in an envelope, and each strip contains ten to twelve exposures. Your letters to me are on that microfilm. I propose you take my letters through the same photographic process, then deposit them in a Montevideo box until you are stateside where you can lay them to rest with the Arlington cache. In the interim, of course, you must keep paying the stipend on the rent for the P.O. box. It will be worth it. Someday, when you and I are old, the letters might be worth publishing. The impersonal parts, that is.

Harry, you have no idea how close your correspondence came to being destroyed. In the closet of the little bedroom where you used to sleep over on occasion, there is a rough baseboard molding that I was able to pry off and re-nail without any great show. Behind that board was a suitable space, and over the last year and a half whenever your mail collected, I would get out my hammer. Of course, for short periods, it was simpler to interleaf your more recent communications between the pages of some book or magazine that Hugh would never pick up. *The ABC of Crochet*. Such stuff. Of course, about the time last month's copy of *Vogue* was looking a bit pregnant, I would make sure I had recovered every one of your pages, and then would pop the trusty baseboard loose, squirrel away your letters, and nail back the board.

Hugh, however, has antennae that reach into God knows which cubbyholes, so he's given my heart a start now and again. Once he even picked up the very copy of *Mademoiselle* which held your latest letter, rolled it into a cylinder, and began rapping his thigh with this improvised phallic instrument until, to my relief, he dropped the magazine to the floor without opening it, and pulled out a rock-climbing newsletter from the magazine rack. Some squeak. I thought I was in a suspense film. Another time he spent a weekend with a hammer going over boards in the house. Thank heaven for my own tendrils. I had touched up the paint on my battered baseboard nails just the week before. I couldn't decide whether I anticipated him, or he was reacting to microscopically subtle shifts in the house. It's frightening to live with a man who has the sensory apparatus of a cat. It's also thrilling, and certainly helps to make up for the wretched, if most manly (ugh!), smell of Hugh's breath after Courvoisier and Churchills. Smoking a cigar is the most intimate insult a man can offer to a woman. If you ever have a wife and want to lose her, just puff away in her antique bed on one of those giant tobacco-turds. How transparent are people's vices.

I digress, but then I'm highly distractable these days. It's only two weeks since I've come home, and in another ten days, we return to the Keep, where I intend to stay all summer, with or without Hugh. I need the Maine air more than my mate at this point, because, God, Christopher has gone into an awful slump while I was gone. He kept waking up out of frightful nightmares, in response, I think, to what his mother was going through thousands of miles away, and now my little boy looks awfully pale and sort of seedy, like a worried ten-year-old rather than his year and a half. His mother feels as if she has aged commensurately. The work I was doing taught me one terrible lesson: *Things can go wrong!* So the act of hiding your letters in Hugh's domain no longer gave me wicked pleasure. The possible consequences were too large to take on any longer. As a result of my experience on the Project, I have passed from believing for the most part in good outcomes to expecting the worst. And the worst, I have discovered, lays waste to all that is good in oneself. How innocent I have kept myself to discover this only now! But I have, and your letters, your beloved letters, offered the naughtiest warmth all this time, and enabled my marriage to breathe. Carnally considered, I have always had an unholy high passion for Hugh—I don't know any other men, but there can hardly be another so phallic. (He's like the knobs and pistons of the Almighty Engine itself.) All to the good for a piece of frozen New England steel like me, but then there are also his deadening cigars, and his glacial powers of concentration on anything but me (until I happen to come around to his attention again). There, in the middle were your letters, a tender leavening agent. I could betray Hugh just a little and thereby feel loyal to him.

A devil's game. I believe in matrimony, you know. I do think sacraments are taken between God and oneself, and are just as binding as legal contracts are supposed to be in all of the corporate, judicial, industrial world. Such contracts can be broken, but not too many or society's ills reach critical mass. By analogy, I think if too many sacraments are violated, God communicates less with us. So, marriage to me is a holy vow.

I was ready, therefore, to say I love you and good-bye, dear man, but then, how could I leave you wholly frustrated by the constraints of my vow not to talk about what happened to me during the Project. I have the oddest sentiment that I must tell you something equally secret, equally important to me, or I will violate our own unspoken pledge. That covenant weighs on me as much as my vow. I do manage to travel in the heaviest circuits, don't I, but then I am very much like my father—greedy for absolute knowledge on the one hand, and somewhat timid about the world on the other. My father solved his dilemma by stuffing all of Shakespeare into his commodious brain and thereafter subsisting on the massive snobbery of his scholarly holdings. At its worst, it was, I fear, a somewhat turdlike existence— forgive me, Father!—but then my Daddy Professor may have been a catalyst drawing down ugly forces onto others. Did I ever confide in you about the ghost of the Keep, Augustus Farr? I've been visited by him, and—this I have never told anyone—the first time was on that Easter night so long ago, when Daddy read to us from *Titus Andronicus*:

> *Whilst Lavinia 'tween her stumps doth hold*
> *The basin that receives your guilty blood.*

Do you recall? Inwardly, I was transfixed. I clearly pictured my own wrists as stumps holding a basin in which was the head of my beloved Hugh. You, for some reason, hovered in the background. It made me wonder if you were the executioner, and this was the oddest way to picture you since I certainly thought you were the most attractive young man I had ever met, just as pretty as Montgomery Clift, and so solemn, so shy, so intensely filled with purpose. Best of all, you were not yet formed. It is your salvation that you had no idea how nifty you were to women in those days or you would have gone hog-belly-up, as I fear you have in the year and a half you've sported away in your Uruguay brothels. But, then, I am close to attacking you again, which is a danger sign I have come to recognize. I think it is because I have an implicit dread of what I am going to tell you next. On that long-ago Easter night, I had a fearful experience. Augustus Farr, or his incubus, or whatever creature it may have been, visited me in my bed at the Keep, and submitted me to horrors. I felt like a dark and dirty midwife to Shakespeare's bloody foils and foul deeds. I was in the filthiest transport of carnality, and little beasts of the underworld inhabited my mouth. Do you recall how earlier that afternoon I had spoken so prettily of how Hugh and I had our Italian Solution? That night, Augustus Farr became my sexual guide into those dark and stinking depths where beauty also dwells, and I realized what Hugh and I were actually doing with one another while I was still ostensibly a virgin. Later, on my wedding night that same summer at the Keep, Hugh, formally and most bloodily, did at last deflower me, and I had the connubial good fortune to come into union together with him, spasm for leap, leap for spasm, and he vaulted like a goat from height to height, and knew how to fall, a most extraordinary experience, yes, I may now be hurting you, dear Harry, but I do pay cash, and when confessing, will confess all, yes, there, in the last long illimitable leap, was Augustus Farr, ensconced, limb and breath, with Hugh and me. My greed must have called him forth—my greed that went as deep as my father's buried mountains of lust and lore. I had never known that good and evil in oneself could speak to each other with such force and by such a dance.

For a long time I felt that Augustus Farr did not try to come near again, not after that wedding night, but I think he may have succeeded in putting his signature upon my marriage. Of course, marriage occupies so many strata in oneself that it may be over-dramatic to speak of a malign imprint upon an entire relationship. On the other hand, a clove of garlic in a wedding cake is nothing to ignore!

Farr, however, did not appear again until the sixth month of my pregnancy, during Hugh's and my vacation in '56 at the Keep, but then he certainly showed up on an August night as we were having *sexual congress*. Call it that because Hugh was more than a little backed-up before my large belly. Polly Galen Smith once told me that she was making love right up to the day before her baby was born—just so madly does she adore sex!—but this was hardly true for Hugh and me. We were having sexual congress. On that particular night of which I speak, however, I felt as if I were the plumpest concubine in a seraglio, and wholly depraved. I remember wishing that someone could watch Hugh and me.

Such subterranean stirrings must have communicated them-selves to my dear partner, because now there was nothing collegial any

longer—Hugh and I were mad for one another all over again, and I
felt the baby stirring and very much a part of us. Then, suddenly, we
were a good deal more than that. An evil presence—call it what you
will—was also with us. In the full silence of the night, I could feel the
libidinous resonance that evil knows how to deliver. I find it not at
all easy to relate even now, but I had rosy-hued (that is, fiery) visions
of human degradation and heard cries of pleasure reverberating in the
fetid pits below. Augustus Farr was as near to me then as my husband
and my unborn child, there partaking of our Saturnalian rites. I felt
that if I did not stop at that instant my child-to-be was going to be
taken away in some fiendish exchange. I remember thinking, "It's just
a thought," for I was fearfully excited and wanted to go on, and Hugh,
I remember, took us through the plunge with a loud and inhuman cry.
Then I began to weep for I knew that Augustus Farr had been there
with us. I did not wish to believe it, and can hardly write this now—
my hand trembles—but he had stolen—well, I won't write down my
dear child's name. He walks at an odd pace these days, and sometimes
I think there's a devil's hitch to his gait. He does have a very slight
in-turn of the right foot, and Allen is his other godfather. We actually
celebrated the idea of two godfathers, one for Alpha, one for Omega.
Christopher can choose between you when he grows up. As of this
writing, you are the only godfather who is aware that there is another.
Please don't feel insulted. You are certainly equal in my mind to
Allen.

Well, I won't say any more about Farr on this occasion. I can
only remark that I have not lost my presentiment that the transactions
of the spirit underworld are very much connected to us here, and since
then I have felt, irrationally or not, that Christopher's safety depends
on my fidelity to Hugh. This loyalty, I have come to conclude, is
weakened by your letters. They are making me fall in love with you.

Now, from the moment I saw you in my parents' parlor at the
Keep, a part of me knew that you and I could go through life together,
wonderfully comfortable and intimate with one another. I've always
loved you, you see, but it never used to count for more than a
collateral enrichment to my devotion for Hugh.

During the last couple of years, however, your letters have
stolen a place in my heart. I have come to dislike you, hate you, feel
horrible jealousy, and worst of all, been tormented by a cunning little
sense of anticipation which speaks of sexual concupiscence. To put it
plain, and I detest this piece of vernacular because it is so accurate and

allows no illusions, I have had the hots for you, yes, the foul, yearning, roller-coaster hots of all the gut-bemired sentiments, exactly what used to belong entirely to Hugh. Now it was being stimulated by you as well. Alpha and Omega had shifted in their agreement, and I knew what it was to be carnally in love with two men at once. Bad enough if it is Alpha for one and Omega for the other—that is a common human condition. It may even be half natural (if also the Devil's greatest hole-card) that all of us find it easy to be in love with one person by way of Omega, and another through Alpha. But I feel as if you have gotten into both. My poor Alpha and Omega both are damned, for they are each half in love with you, and that succeeds in confusing my balance.

Harry, do you have any conception of how monumental is Hugh's importance to me? The part of myself that is not free of worldly desire has to respect all the strengths and powers he can and does endow me with. I could never bear living in any role inferior to the higher powers of society. (My father, who is exactly like me, turned into an insufferably pompous pedant about the time he realized that he rang no loud bell in the grand and vaulted halls.) I may be worse. And then my mother's buried ambition might be even greater. How, otherwise, did she get so dotty?

So, I took on the Project. I can tell you that it dealt with the manipulation and control of other humans, and the means employed soon became solemn and sticky. It was full of explosive potential for TSS if it were ever to come out publicly. Indeed, Hugh and Allen were so afraid of something going wrong that they decided to try it out in a controlled environment, governmentally speaking. Do you know where? In Paraguay. I was probably less than a thousand miles away from Montevideo. I dreamt of you every night, and lusted for you in an empty bed, horrified that my womb, yes, *womb*, could permit such disloyalty to Hugh. How I hated you for rooting away in the spoor of every low brothel. I know you did that. And once or twice, I almost bought a plane ticket to drop in on you for a weekend. That's how bad it got one dip below the navel. Hugh came to visit and thought he had a wild woman on his hands.

Anyway, as you learned by way of Chevi and Libertad and Varkhov and Zenia, yes, what a nasty little vein of crotch-turpitude (yes, I like that) is loose in us. I have discovered how harsh is my secret nature. One person, one of our subjects, was destroyed in Paraguay, and I, while not the initiator, was the monitor of the accompanying experiments, and I did not feel quite as sick over it as the occasion called for me to be. We live in a great moral truss-work, after all. To fight the Opponent, we will dare evil ourselves, and I feel as if I have. Only I did not come back with a compensating good. Our experiment failed. Have I endangered my soul?

The answer shows in curious fashion. I feel, as I say, ten years older and bleak as hell within. As soon as I came back to Georgetown I decided, therefore, on certain measures. Since I had taken on a bold gamble, and it resulted in negative and messy results, the patina of failure was close to inhabiting my career permanently.

I made, in consequence, two decisions. I saw Allen Dulles and asked for detached duty. I am going to try to write my postponed major opus on Alpha and Omega. He gave me, somewhat to his relief, I think, his private blessing, and I am off to Maine, where I will work all year, and conceivably for years to come. *Whatever it takes*—which is the expression we used in Paraguay for getting the ugly deed done.

That was the first decision. For the second, I decided to cease living with you in my mind. I mean, by this, that we stop corresponding. Then, much as I wished to keep your letters, I decided it was too dangerous. If Hugh ever discovered them, it would smash my life. (Since I have been instrumental in smashing at least one South American's life, I felt vulnerable to the frightful costs.) Besides, I was getting addicted to your letters. The only answer was cold turkey. I would put your correspondence in an office shredder.

When it came to it, however, I could not, no, not destroy your offering completely. So I used my office equipment (at which I'm now a practiced soul) and microfilmed this record of Harry Hubbard's mind, and heart, and nose, such as it is, for Uruguay and for me, and deposited the package in your new box. I've also just shredded the whole heavy pack, nearly a carton full of your last twenty months and more of writing to me on your dime-store stationery. And felt so dizzy and out of sorts afterward that I did something never done before and went into a bar alone after work, sat down at a cocktail table trembling at such exposure of myself in a public place (still a Radcliffe girl!), and downed two bourbons neat before I stood up, surprised that no one had accosted me, went home, and explained away the whiskey breath by confessing it had been one hell of a day. Christopher cried when I started to kiss him.

There it is. I am serious to the death over this, Harry. We are not to communicate with each other, and I will refuse to see you

when your tour is over and you come back to Washington. Pray for
me to do good work in Maine. How long our separation intends to
go on is beyond my intuition. I sense it will be years. Perhaps forever.
I would not give you up if I did not love you. Please believe me. I
must cling to my sacrament. Under it all, I believe that God still bleeds
when we break our vows.

I love you,
Good-bye, dear man

35

IT WAS THE LAST LETTER I RECEIVED FROM HER IN URUGUAY. FOR MANY
months, I would open my eyes with the uneasiness of those bereaved
who awaken in the morning without being able to tell themselves at
first what is wrong. They know only that someone is gone. Then
memory presents itself like a hangman at the door.

She had spoken of loving me. That made it worse. I could not
have mourned her more if she had been my bride. A pall descended
over work. My correspondence with Kittredge had allowed this far-
off Station to seem part of the ongoing history of the world. Now it
was merely a far-off Station. Deprived of my audience, I felt as if I
were perceiving less. No longer did each small event take its place in
an ongoing scenario. In desperation, I commenced a diary, but it, too,
became matter-of-fact, and I gave it up.

Attempting to rise out of such torpor, I used my accumulated
leave to visit Buenos Aires and Rio. I walked for miles through lively
cities, and drank in elegant cocktail lounges and at high, stand-up
plank tables in steamy smoking drinking holes. I traveled like a ghost
without fights or encounters. I visited famous brothels. I was for the
first time aware of the distaste for men that one could find on the
mouths of whores. When I came back to Montevideo, I went up the
coast to Punta del Este and tried to gamble, but found myself too
parsimonious. Bored, I could not even say for certain that I was bored.
I even had a last night with Sally.

Sherman Porringer and Barry Kearns, having finished their tour
in Uruguay, were going back to Washington for reassignment. There
were good-bye parties. At one of the last, four days before departure,

Sally Porringer said to me, "I want to visit you."

"In years to come?"

"Tomorrow evening at seven."

She had had her baby, a boy whose resemblance to Sherman was thankfully complete. "Yes," she said, "bygones are bygones and I want to see you. For Auld Lang Syne." She had power over a cliché. So we had a last wall-banger on the bed of my little room. She was still angry, and lay stiffly beside me before we began, but her practical nature won out. She was not a bridge player for too little. Never pass on a playable hand.

In the middle, I discovered myself listening to the sounds we made, and realized that I was comparing them (and somewhat critically) to the climactic duets of Zenia Masarov and Georgi Varkhov. I even entertained the hypothesis that the Soviets were taping Sally and me. That did stimulate my inner life for a day or two. Could the Russians process the tape in time to get it to Sherman before his departure? Would Porringer and I throw a stitch across the wound and stand together in public for a last farewell? We owed that much to Masarov and Varkhov, who kept demonstrating their ability to work together (since neither had gone back to Moscow).

After Porringer and Kearns were gone, replacements came in (who deferred to me as a knowledgeable veteran). Then Howard Hunt had a bereavement. One night when he and Dorothy were at a country-club dance in Carrasco, the Embassy watch officer telephoned to say that Howard's father had died. Hunt left in the morning for Hamburg, New York, and was a somber fellow on his return. I began to like him more genuinely. He had his grief and I was living with my sorrow. It was agreeable to sit in each other's company. Either one of us could serve as poultice to amputated sentiments in the other. I came to understand Howard a little better. Early one morning when I had driven over to Carrasco to deliver a couple of economic research papers on South America that I assumed he would pass on to Benito Nardone, he took me out for a walk while breakfast was being prepared. Across the street from his villa was a Catholic lycée. Hunt's two daughters, dressed in white blouses and wide black floppy bow ties, accompanied by the Hunt's Argentine governess, were entering the school door. He waved, and said to me, "You have to love a woman to convert to Catholicism for her." The corners of his mouth turned sour. "My father," he said, "was still getting used to the idea of his son as a Catholic." Howard shrugged. "There is a heap of intense feeling back there in America. Somewhat anti-Roman, wouldn't you say?"

"I suppose."

"Do you believe it reaches into our domain? Concerning, that is, decisions on placement?"

"Well, I would hope not," I replied.

He sighed. He was having his troubles with Ambassador Woodward. I never did learn whether Howard's money derived from royalties on his early novels and subsequent wise investments, or had come in from Dorothy's side of the marriage. There was no question, however. He did live better than the average Chief of Station, and Ambassador Woodward was now envoying such criticism through the State Department and over to the Agency. Hunt learned that his scale of living was being attacked as too opulent for a man supposed to be no more than First Secretary at the Embassy.

Last year, I might have filled more than one letter to Kittredge with the unexpected turns of such an office game. Inhabiting a depression, however, was, I discovered, not unlike camping out on the marble floor of a bank. Sharp sounds damped into murmurs, echoes told you more than clear speech, and you always felt cold. While I was party to Hunt's side of the trouble, and even wanted Station to triumph over State, that was about all the team spirit I could muster.

At this point, J. C. King, Chief of Western Hemisphere Division, came down on a visit, and closeted himself with Hunt. One could not labor in the vineyards of Western Hemisphere Division (which extended from Mexico to Argentina) without picking up a few stories about J. C. King. I already knew, by way of Porringer, that the Colonel had lost an eye on Utah Beach, won the Congressional Medal of Honor, and amassed a fortune after the war. It was Porringer's tale to tell: "King decided that the people of Brazil would go for condoms. 'There's no demand for contraceptives in Brazil,' everybody told him, 'it's a Catholic country.' Well, King was just stubborn enough to go against the smart money and he built the first condom factory south of the Amazon. Put down his own savings, borrowed more, and who could believe it? Condoms took off in Rio de Janeiro like jet planes. King," said Porringer, "is now one of the wealthiest men in the Agency, and has a slew of plantations on the Panaga River in Paraguay."

I would never have divined all this without the briefing. The

Colonel was tall, showed a pronounced limp, wore an eye-patch, and was so soft-spoken that he seemed almost hollow. There could be no explanation for him without Alpha and Omega.

I expect that Colonel King's wealth did Hunt no harm. Ambassador Woodward had put such phrases on the record as "flamboyant preening, unsuitable for government servants."

"You must have had to put up a strong defense," I told Hunt afterward.

"I didn't defend myself," said Howard. "I attacked. I told Colonel King how effective I had been in getting Nardone in. Why, at the victory party on election night, I was the only American official to be invited from the Embassy. Woodward had even predicted that Nardone could not win. The only way he ever did get to meet Benito before the inauguration was to ask this humble servant to arrange the introduction. Mr. Woodward cannot forgive me for that favor. You may be certain I got my story across to J. C. King. 'Woodward can go to blazes,' he said before he left. He didn't even admonish me to lower the profile. In fact, the Colonel says he has an interesting prospect for me."

Soon after, Hunt was called to Washington. On return, he invited me once more to Carrasco for dinner, and in the study, over brandy— no longer did I smoke cigars—he told me of the new order of business. "Just when you think your luck is down, it takes a turn. I've been invited to participate in a major move. This one will be a lot larger than Guatemala."

"Castro? Cuba?"

He pointed his index finger at me to show I was on target. "We're going in for a jumbo move. Cuban exiles to win back their land. Hellaciously covert." The light in his brandy snifter seemed to be radiating from his face. "I'm to help stage it. Before we're done, we will stock more groceries than the Agency has ever put up on the shelf. Yet, all sequestered. Fabulously sequestered. Ideally, there won't be one overt piece of evidence to show U.S. involvement." He ran his finger around the rim of the glass long enough to induce a clear note. "Would you care to come aboard as one of my assistants?"

"I can't think of anything I would like more," I said. I meant it. Under twenty wrappings of apathy, I felt a first stirring of anticipation. Part of my depression might well be due to not knowing where to go after Uruguay. No longer could I see myself in one of Harlot's mills. To live in Washington, and avoid Kittredge? No. I said to Hunt, "I would very much like to work with you." Yes, the fires of the vow gave promise of blazing in me again.

"Let me state from the outset," said Hunt, "nothing is going to be off-limits on this one."

I must have shown some lack of clear focus, for he brought his head forward and mouthed the next few words. "It might get wet out there."

I nodded silently. "All the way?" I murmured.

He took his time before pointing a finger to the ceiling.

36

MY WORK CAME ALIVE. THERE WAS MUCH TO TURN OVER TO THE NEW officers. A year ago, I would have found it difficult to say good-bye to AV/ALANCHE-1 through 7, but my street gang was larger now, and half of it was composed of Peones' cops. Indeed, he virtually ran it from his office. An important man was Peones now that Nardone was leader of Uruguay.

Nostalgia, all the same, proved able to grow in the thinnest soil. It actually moved me that I would no longer oversee AV/OUCH-1 and AV/OUCH-2 in their task of checking off the travelers who went through Passport Control, nor did I have to lose an evening now and then appeasing AV/ERAGE, our society journalist, when he had been ignored for too long. AV/EMARIA-1, 2, 3, and 4 would not be there to call when I was in need of a surveillance cab, and poor GOGOL was about to be shut down. The take at the Russian Embassy was now deemed too small to warrant expenses. The Bosqueverdes would be looking for smaller quarters. Nor could Gordy Morewood phone my desk on Monday morning to haggle over accounts. My replacement would deal with AV/OIRDUPOIS now.

I also had a few sentimental farewells to offer the Montevideo brothels. I was fond of several girls; to my surprise, they were fond of me. Show business, I told myself. But then it occurred to me that prostitutes and clients were not unlike actors in a play. For the little while that they lived together, it did not have to be wholly unreal.

There was AV/OCADO to deal with. The after-effect of Libertad had been to give me an overdose of case officer's caution. I had done no more for many months than bring out my weekly list of questions to the safe house and wine him and dine him there. I had even learned how to cook. The days when we argued over whether it was safe to meet in restaurants were done.

Chevi's work did go on. I cannot say whether it became less important, or only seemed so in the slog of my long depression, but I began to wonder at the value of all the detailed answers we received about projects undertaken in the Partido Comunista de Uruguay. Was it worth the effort? I hardly knew if I cared. It used to irritate me that Fuertes, who was heavier by the week until he was in every danger of growing obese, was also becoming more timorous about his safety. He swore that he did not see Libertad any longer, yet on each visit he seemed to worry a little more about the volume of Peones' rage should our Police Chief ever discover the facts. "You do not know the man," Chevi insisted. "He is a fascist. Much like Nardone. His cruelty develops in proportion to his power. Why else be a fascist?"

"We will not let him hurt you," I said.

"Then you admit that you control Peones?"

"No."

"In that case, I have much reason to be afraid," he said.

I did not know how to reply. Chevi provided the answer.

"You do control him," he said. "That is why you believe you can protect me. It would be better to draw a circle around my name and inform Peones he is not to enter such an area."

"It would be equivalent to telling his office that you are connected to us. Members of the PCU, even if you have not been able to locate them, have certainly penetrated his office."

"You do not need to tell him why you wish to protect me," said Fuertes. "The police are used to providing dispensation in the midst of ambiguity."

"Chevi, I can no longer follow what the hell you are talking about. I think there is something else."

"There is," he said. "The solemn fact is that Libertad called me last week to issue a warning. She said Peones had heard recently that she was seen in public with me. Many months ago. But he is insanely jealous. It could have been the lunch with your Chief of Station."

"Oh, no," I said.

"She said Peones had been prepared to work me over, but that she commanded him to give up such ideas. She told him that we had always been chaste. If he touched me, she would never see him again. It was a passionate speech delivered with voluminous depths of feeling. She could not love me more, she declared, if I were her brother. That does not mean Comandante Peones believed her. But we are people who respect the authority of passion whether it is directed toward carnality or loyalty. Pedro understood. He would suffer the price if he doubted her speech."

"Then you have nothing to fear." I could not even begin to estimate the damage as yet.

"I have everything to be afraid of. He has no need to strike at me directly. His people will do that."

"Won't he have to face Libertad?"

"No. He will disavow the policeman who injures me. He may even punish the man. I assure you, such histories are easily blurred. Libertad will not give up the advantages she obtains from Peones if his guilt is imprecise."

"Imprecise? Only Peones could be the instigator."

"Not necessarily. Torture is becoming more of a practice. Nardone hates Communists. He hates them even more than J. Edgar Hoover. Many wounds of self-esteem have been laid on Nardone by the Communists. So he has an intellectual position that is equal to a sadistic faith. Nardone believes that the left is a cancer which can only be extirpated through torture. The martyrdom of Anarchists and Communists is upon us."

"By whose authority? By which laws? Tell me of such situations. I don't believe it."

"A policeman can always arrest you. For crossing the street in the wrong place. But now, once you are arrested, it is a different drama. There is no left wing inside the police station to protect you. Three people high in my Party ranks have been cruelly treated in the last month. Crippled, no, but neither will they feel like fucking their women for a year."

"Verdad?"

He began to laugh. Was it because my answer had been sufficiently shocked to come forth in Spanish?

"I exaggerate," he said.

"Do you, or don't you?"

He shrugged. "I am now afraid of torture."

We agreed upon the following: If he had any advance warning of arrest, he would make a call to me. If he could not speak himself, his message would contain the word RAINFALL.

Two weeks before I was scheduled to leave Uruguay, a man

telephoned the office late one afternoon to say he was calling for RAINFALL. He would not identify himself, although he stated that Señor Fuertes had been arrested in the last hour and was now being held at Central Police Headquarters. Only a cop on the scene would be privy to such facts. It was equivalent to saying that Fuertes had bribed the man to call me and thereby had blown his cover.

I was furious. I was more of a case officer than I had supposed. I did not feel concern for Chevi so much as outrage at his panic. Was he squeaking for too little? "Dammit to hell," I shouted as I hung up the phone.

There was no way not to recognize, however, that Chevi's situation was serious. I had a large moment of anxiety but decided to take the calculated risk and ask Hunt to accompany me. Howard would probably not bother to wait until Chevi was released.

Hunt was, however, predictably upset. "Of all the goddamn fiascoes. Our best agent's cover splattered all over Montevideo. His usefulness to us is over."

"I know, but it's happened."

"It's personally embarrassing. Archie Norcross is coming in Monday to take over from me. Instead of handing the man a nicely run Station, I've got to help him wipe up this broken egg."

"I'm sorry."

"We should have alerted Peones on the need to protect AV/OCADO."

"Howard, we couldn't. Chevi's cover would have been jeopardized."

"Well, I'll call Pedro now. One phone call can do it."

Would it? I had another bad moment. Peones, however, was out of Uruguay. There was a policeman's convention in Buenos Aires.

Howard looked at his watch. "I'm due for a dinner at the country club. We can take care of this in the morning."

"You don't want to wait for morning. A lot of damage can be done to a man's body in a night."

"You think it will really make a difference if I go down with you to the jail?"

"Howard, I'll be seen as a minor official in the State Department. But they will know who you are. It will work. You can leave as soon as they get the message."

He threw up his hands. "I'll call Dorothy. What the hell. I lose an hour at most. Tonight is only one more round in the farewell festivities." He pulverized his cigarette. "That dumb dodo, Chevi Fuertes. Calling us in." He sighed. "Well, we can at least set an example of how well we take care of our agents."

Police Headquarters was in the Municipal Court Building, an eight-story edifice put up around the turn of the century for new and expanding commercial ventures. Now the shades of failed enterprise lingered in the lobby. The law and the police had taken over.

We did not even go by the jail. It was in the rear of the lower floors, and I suggested that we go searching instead for Peones' assistant. His office, we discovered, was six flights up, and the elevator was not functioning.

The stairs were wide and double-banked between each landing. I had time to contemplate the gloom. What capital disappointments had collected in these vaulted silences, what dank smells lingered on the courthouse stairs. Wherever they had failed to reach the cuspidor, cigar butts lay like swollen beetles on a field of old linoleum.

We were so intent upon conserving our breath so as not to fall short-wind of the other that we actually walked on past the sixth floor to the seventh and were turning down the main corridor before we realized that something was wrong. The entire floor was empty. Office doors stood open to rooms void of furniture. The evening light entered through soot-coated, unwashed, ten-foot windows. It was as if we had missed a bend in our life. I had time to wonder if death was like this, a dirty, unoccupied hall with no one to receive you.

"Can you believe it?" asked Hunt. "We've gone too far."

Just then, damped by steel, beams of timber, and thick plaster, came cries from the floor above. They were much reduced in volume but sounded nonetheless like the unsprung whimper that comes from a dog run over by a car. The sense of loss reverberates to the horizon. Neither Hunt nor I could speak. It was as if we were in someone else's home, and incredible groans of intestinal strain were coming through a bathroom door.

"I must say it," whispered Howard, "those sounds do go all the way in, don't they?"

Afterward, once we reached the sixth floor and found Peones' assistant and introduced ourselves, Hunt's name inspired the Deputy to come to his feet and offer a salute. Our work went quickly. It was fortunate we had come when we did, the Deputy assured us; no investigative activities had yet commenced. Señor Eusebio Fuertes would be released in our custody.

"No, in his," said Howard, pointing to me. "I'm late for an engagement."

I waited, in fact, more than an hour for the release, and when I saw Chevi, he was silent and we did not speak until we reached the street. Then he did not cease speaking for the next four hours, by which time I had had to promise him vast tracts on the moon. He offered a delineation of his condition: He was in peril and besieged on both sides—at the mercy of Peones; at the mercy of the PCU. They would be inclined toward revenge. "I am a dead man," he said.

"The PCU would not murder you, would they?" I was, I confess, commencing a report in my mind on "Termination Policies of the PCU."

"They," he said, "would merely expel me from the Party. Then it would be up to the Tupamaros. Extremists in the PCU would speak to the Tupamaros. That can be equal to elimination. There is only one solution. You must get me out of Uruguay."

I spoke of Rio de Janeiro and Buenos Aires. Too dangerous were both, decided Chevi. I offered him the rest of South America, Central America, Mexico. He shook his head.

"Then where?" I asked.

"Miami." He would leave his wife and family. They were too Communist. He would go to Miami alone. We must obtain him work in a decent place. A bank, for example. A man who spoke Spanish, but was not Cuban, could be most useful in dealing with Cubans, who were all notoriously unreliable concerning money.

"I shall never be able to get you terms as good as that."

"You will. The alternative is too horrible to contemplate. To protect myself, I would have to seek the Montevideo newspapers. Such publicity would be more horrendous for me than for you, but I learned one thing in this jail—I do not wish to die. To underwrite my safety, I would be ready to dive into the hell-hole of public exposure."

In twenty-four hours, we obtained false papers, passport, and a visa to America. He went to work in a Miami bank. One of our proprietaries. I would not have bet on it that night, not after eight consecutive hours on the Encoder-Decoder with the Groogs (for that provided me with ample reason to be sick of him), but there would come a time in Miami when Chevi and I would work together again.

THE BAY OF PIGS

May 1960–April 1961

M I A M I

AFTER HOWARD HUNT DEPARTED, I REMAINED IN URUGUAY FOR SEV-
eral weeks and did not return to America until the beginning of May.
Owed several weeks of vacation, I went up to Maine, expecting to
pass through Mount Desert and drop in on Kittredge at Doane.

I never found the courage. If she rebuffed me, what would be left
for fantasy? The romantic imagination, I was discovering, is practical
about its survival.

I went further north, instead, to Baxter State Park and hiked up
Mount Katahdin. It was a dubious venture in May. The black flies
proved near to intolerable, and I was not free of them until I reached
the winds that blow across the high, open ridge that leads to the
summit.

That ridge is called the Knife Edge. To walk it is no great feat, but
still, it is a mile long, and plunges a thousand feet on either side. While
the route is never less than several feet wide, the ice in May has not
melted altogether from the Knife Edge, and later, descending the
north slope, one is left in deep shadow at three in the afternoon. I
slogged through gullies filled with snow and began to feel as if I were
not only alone on the mountain, but a solitary citizen of the United
States. It came upon me like a revelation that the state of my ignorance
on such large and general matters as politics could be deemed appall-
ing. Was I an anomaly in the Agency? Berlin had passed me by, and
in Uruguay I had become active in a country whose politics remained
strange to me.

Now I was ready to go to work on Cuba. It was incumbent to do
research. I went back to New York, found an inexpensive hotel off
Times Square, and spent a week in the Reading Room of the New
York Public Library trying to bone up on our Caribbean neighbor. I
read a history or two, but retained little—I fell asleep over the texts.

I was prepared to overthrow Castro but did not wish to acquire any history of his theater. I contented myself with studying back issues of *Time*, on no better ground, I fear, than that Kittredge had once informed me that Mr. Dulles, when he wished to float a point of view favored by the Agency, often used the magazine. Besides, Henry Luce had come to dinner at the Stable.

Castro's first year as leader, however, remained hard to follow. There were so many quarrels in Cuba. Blocs of ministers seemed always to be resigning in protest over newly promulgated laws. Before long, another item took my eye. Senator John F. Kennedy of Massachusetts made the announcement on January 31, 1960, that he was going to seek the presidency. He looked young to me. He was not twelve years older than myself, and I certainly felt singularly young. Two weeks of leave had almost done me in. On the other hand, every saucy girl I saw on the streets of New York looked ravishing.

I ended by inviting my mother to lunch. I had not known if I would see her; my implacable absence of feeling for her sat like a gasket on my diaphragm. I could not forgive her for I hardly knew what. Still, she was ill. Before I left Montevideo, a letter came from her which mentioned in passing that she had had an operation, a quiet statement of fact, no more, after which she offered news of relatives on her side of the family I had not seen in years, then followed that up with open hints. "I have a good deal of money now, and so little idea of what to do about it—of course, a few foundations do offer flirtations." It took no acumen to recognize that she was saying, "Damn you, pay attention or I will give the caboodle away."

If I knew nothing about politics, I cared in those years even less about money. Out of pride itself, I felt indifferent to such a threat.

There was, however, a last page in the letter with a very large P.S. Her writing hand itself had extorted what her will was not ready to admit—"Oh, Harry, I really have been ill lately," she burst forth. "Don't flinch, son, but I've had a hysterectomy. It's all gone. I don't want to talk about that ever again."

All up the warm forested spring flanks of Katahdin with the thousand nips and stings of the no-see-ums, down the out-of-season freeze of late afternoon, through the hours of drowsing at library tables, one guilty imperative kept working away beneath my lack of feeling for my mother. I realized that I was anchored to a pang of love. Now it kept dragging on me to call. I finally invited her to lunch at the Colony. She wanted Twenty-One instead, that male redoubt! Was it to take possession of my father?

Her hysterectomy, I saw on greeting her, was already—full capital loss—marked on her skin. She looked shocking to me. Not yet fifty, defeat—the pale shade of defeat—sagged into the lines of her face. I knew, even as she came toward me in the anteroom off the entrance of Twenty-One, that she had indeed lost all that she said was gone. With it had foundered the game of love at which she had been adept for thirty years, and all the empty pockets of the heart given up to such games.

Of course, I did not think too long in such directions. She was my mother. Indeed, I was struggling with contradictory feelings. While I hugged her on greeting and felt to my surprise some true sense of protection for the small, leathery, middle-aged woman she had become since I had last seen her at the Plaza three years ago, I did not trust such tenderness. All too often, the whores of Montevideo had brought out in me a perverse sense of their poignancy, and I had embraced them with equal concern. As I held her now, she gripped me back so fiercely that I soon felt confusion and was no longer near her at all.

Over lunch she brought up my father. She knew much more about his life at this moment than I did. "His marriage is in trouble," she assured me.

"Is that a fact or a supposition?"

"He's in Washington—yes, he's back—and very much on top of some venture, or whatever you term those things, and he's alone."

"How do you know? I don't even know."

"New York has scores of sources. He is in Washington, I tell you, and she has chosen to remain in Japan. Mary, that big white dutiful blob. She's not the sort to camp out in a foreign country unless she's got herself a lover."

"Oh, Mother, she could never take her eyes off Cal."

"A woman like that has got one big move in her. I'll bet she's fallen in love with a small, respectable Japanese gentleman who's very rich."

"I don't believe any of this."

"Well, they're separated. You'll find out soon enough, I expect."

"I wish he'd gotten in touch with me," I blurted out, "now that he's back."

"Oh, he will. Whenever he gets around to it, that is." She broke a breadstick and waved the little piece she kept for herself, as if she were now going to let me in on a secret. "When you see your father," she said, "I want you to tell him that I said hello. And if you can, suggest to him, Herrick, that my eyes sparkled as I spoke." She gave an uncharacteristic cackle, as if visualizing a pot that would soon be on the fire. "No," she said, "maybe you'd better not say that much," only to murmur, "Well, perhaps you may. Use your judgment, Rickey-mine"—I had not heard that little name in years—"You have gotten even better-looking," she added, and was less good-looking herself as she said it. The operation weighed on her like a social humiliation she simply could not lift from herself. "Rickey, you are beginning to remind me of the young Gary Cooper, whom I once had the pleasure of inviting to lunch."

I could feel only one small twinge of tenderness, but at least it was pure. After our farewells were taken, I had a drink by myself in a midtown bar, savoring the emptiness of the off hour, and pondered the nature of love, yes, weren't most of us who were in love no more than half in love? Could Alpha and Omega ever come to agreement? Harboring kind thoughts for my mother made another part of me feel colder than ever. How could one forgive Jessica for commencing to lose her looks?

That night, all too depressed, I realized that I had given up my identity as a case officer in Montevideo, and now had nothing to replace it. One matures within an identity. One regresses without it. I picked up the phone and called Howard Hunt in Miami. He said, "If you want to cut your vacation by a few days, I sure as hell could use you. I have a few wonders, and one or two horrors, to relate."

2

HOWARD LOOKED LEAN, KEEN, AND VERY MUCH IN HIS ELEMENT. SINCE the night was warm, we ate at a little open-air restaurant on SW 8th Street, which thoroughfare, he quickly informed me, was called *Calle Ocho* by the Cuban exile community. Our restaurant, sporting an awning, four tables, and a charred barbeque grill, had only a plump little Cuban woman for cook, and a large fat husband to serve, but the menu of blackened beef, hot peppers, plantains, beans and rice was considerably tastier than Uruguayan grub.

Hunt had just been on assignment to Cuba to get a quick feel for the land. He had picked up his operational alias, drawn his travel advance, and connected with a flight to Havana, where he had checked into the Hotel Vedado. "After which," said Hunt, "I took deliberate survey of my most cheerless room, and having determined to my satisfaction that there were no sneakies in the mattress, and no bugs on the telephone, I embarked on a tour of the Cuban capital. *Barbudos* everywhere, Harry. God, I hate those bastards with their sweaty skin and those dirty beards. Their filthy fatigues! They all carry Czechoslovakian burp guns, and God, they show off—that variety of cheap macho pride when a bully has a new toy. Harry, you can *smell* the mentality of these cheap murderous hoods in the way they throw those weapons over their shoulders. Any angle they choose. It makes you wonder if they know enough to put the damned safety on.

"And the women. Cacophonous as a tribe of she-goats. Ugly manifestations come out of women when you put them in uniform. A surprising number of old girls are in the *milicia* now, and they throng the streets, with no better purpose than to assault your ears with their cadence: '*Uno, dos, tres, cuatro, viva Fidel Castro Ruz!*' Humorless, those ladies. Lousy cadence."

"Sounds awful."

He took a solemn measure of his beer. "It was even worse than I knew it was going to be. Half of Havana is trying to skip. Lines of people at our Embassy trying to get visas to the U.S. They want to get away from all the louts and vulgarians who have floated to the top.

"I went to visit Sloppy Joe's," he said. "I do, whenever in Havana. It used to be a lighthearted pilgrimage. After all, my father made his dramatic entrance there thirty years ago to get back that money his partner had absconded with. So, I've always seen Sloppy Joe's as a brawling, warm-spirited place where you might encounter Hemingway at one end of the bar, although, truth to tell, old Ernie doesn't show up much anymore. I also popped into the Floridita, but no luck there either. Both are desolate. Sullen bartenders, Harry, dead air. The only place still going is the bordello above the Mercedes-Benz showroom. That much for Castro's pompous pronouncements about national purity. Why, there are more prostitutes and pimps on the street now than ever in Batista's time. Old Fulgencio could at least police Havana. But now the whores come out like cockroaches in the hope that some tourist will toss them a morsel of business."

"Did you provide any?" I was tempted to ask, and then to my surprise, voiced just that remark. In Uruguay, I might not have dared, but tonight I felt as if a new era was beginning for Howard and me.

Hunt smiled. "You're not supposed to ask such questions of a happily married fellow," he said, "but I will suggest that if anyone ever inquires why you think you're qualified to be in espionage, the only proper response is to look them in the eye, and say, 'Any man who has ever cheated on his wife and gotten away with it, is qualified.' "

We chortled together. I don't know if it was the fleshy odor of cooking oil coming off that little barbeque griddle, or the divided message of the tropical sky above our awning, sullen and accommodating at once, but I could sense the nearness of Havana. Already, on my first night in Miami, watching Cuban exiles pad up and down Calle Ocho, I felt an edge of sinister exhilaration. Rum and the intoxication of dark deeds lay ahead.

"Every night," said Hunt, "outside my hotel window at the Vedado, I could hear *barbudos* cackling to each other on the street. All the sounds you associate with street gangs. The worst elements of the Havana slums. Only now they swarm around in police cars. I could hear them popping into buildings, *bang bang* on the door if it didn't open quickly enough—conceive of the reverberations—those massive old wooden doors in those great old Havana walls. God, it stirs the phantoms of the Caribbean. Then these *barbudos* come out with some poor wretch, and every mother's son of them has unslung his burp gun just to intimidate the crowd before they drive off, siren going, flasher going. It's sad. Havana nights used to awaken sensuous suggestions in a fellow. Something in the very sultriness of the nights. Those beautiful stone arcades on the Malecon. But now, it's all revolutionary justice. You can't walk on a Havana street without hearing loudspeakers inflicting hours of unwanted propaganda on the unwilling ears of the masses. People are dispirited."

"Did you speak to many Cubans while you were there?"

"My assignment called for me to look up a few people on some classified lists. They all have the same sad story. Worked with Castro, fought with him, and now they'd like to gut the hell out of him."

He looked around our restaurant as if to make certain we were wholly alone, a formal gesture, no more. It was 11:00 P.M., and we were the only customers left. The cook had closed her griddle; her husband, the waiter, was asleep.

"As soon as I came back to the States," said Hunt, "I made the following recommendation to Quarters Eye: Assassinate Fidel Castro before or coincident with any invasion. Let this be a task for Cuban patriots."

I heard myself whistle. "Quite a recommendation."

"Well, back in Uruguay I wasn't just vocalizing about going for the head. The problem is to get rid of Castro in such a way that we cannot be blamed. That, I would say, is tricky."

"How did Quarters Eye respond to your suggestion?"

"I would say it is very much in the hopper." Hunt gave off a ground wave of implacable piety. "In fact," he said, "my suggestion is being considered right now by your father."

"My father?" I asked all too simply.

"Hasn't anyone told you how important your father is to all this?"

"Well, I suppose not."

"I applaud your father's sense of security."

I didn't. It was one thing not to hear from Cal for a year at a time, but it was humiliating to learn in this fashion that he was part of the operational hierarchy for Cuba. I did not know if I was sadly dented, or crushed.

"How well do you get along with Cal?" I now asked Hunt.

"We're old familiars. I worked for him in Guatemala."

"I never knew." Why couldn't I keep family pains to myself? "Cal gave me to believe he was always in the Far East."

"Well, he was," said Hunt, "except for the Guatemala op which he did for Richard Bissell. I must say, Harry, our security is like one of those English maze gardens. Intimates can pass within a few feet of each other, and never know that a dear friend is just on the other side of the hedge. Your father has to be one of our aces at keeping security."

I was passing through a bitter thought: The only reason Cal didn't tell me anything about himself was that I never won his attention long enough to receive a confidence. "Yes," said Hunt, "I always assumed we didn't talk about your father because you were trying to impress me with how good you were at security."

"Down the hatch," I said and swallowed more beer.

I was appalled, and I was overstimulated. My relation to everyone else in the Cuban project, including most certainly Howard Hunt, was now turned on its head. I had been supposing that Hunt had chosen me to come along with him because I had proven to be a first-rate young officer in Uruguay. That composed at least half of my affection for him. Now I had to face the likelihood that he saw me as a grip up the greasy pole of advancement.

On the other hand, I did feel a reflexive surge of family pride. Whom had they chosen, after all, for such a difficult and dangerous project but my father? I felt ready to get drunk on dark rum, and, in corollary, felt much impressed (and surprised) by the weight of the readiness for murder that sat in me. Much closer to the heart than I had expected. Yes, I was all for rum, dark deeds and the intoxication of the Caribbean.

3

HUNT HAD SPOKEN OF A MOTEL OUT ON CALLE OCHO WHERE A FEW notorious Cuban exiles used to hide out after their attempts to assassinate President Prio and President Batista had failed. Since the motel's name was the Royal Palms, I expected a modern hostelry with four or more stories and picture windows in aluminum casements. Instead, I found a damp tropical patio surrounded by an equally small motor court, low in rent, one story high, and painted dark green to hide water stains on the stucco. A couple of moldy palm trees showed infestations of insects around their scabrous base. I was no lover, I discovered, of stunted palms, fallen fronds, and rotting shrubs. Indeed, the courtyard was so cramped that you had to park your car around the corner. Although each of the rooms off the patio was in perpetual shadow, the motel caught my reluctant rent money; I seemed to have a tropism for dank living quarters. A corner of myself seemed to insist on the lower depths. I used to go to sleep at night thinking of all those frustrated Cuban gunmen who had perspired on the same mattress as myself.

Living in the kind of place Raymond Chandler might have chosen for Marlowe to visit long enough to knock on one sleazy door, I did not learn as much as I expected. Single men were occupying some of the rooms and whole families squatted in others, all Cuban; the management consisted of an old lady, blind in her right eye from glaucoma, and her dark and gloomy son. He was missing almost all of one arm but nonetheless proved dexterous with a broom, tucking the end of the handle into his armpit. At night, accompanying the sounds of many a quarrel, I would hear a good deal of Cuban music issuing out of portable radios, and the din would have been sufficient to keep me from sleeping if I had not learned from reading a few books that the Afro-Cuban blood of the drummers was speaking directly to the gods—to the African gods and all their attached and saintly Catholic ghosts. In the ears of the gods, therefore, would I fall asleep as my neighbors turned up their radios. The air smelled of garlic and cooking oil.

I slept easily. I was happily tired. My early work in Miami harbored an astounding parade of faces and locations. If I was still, by gross description, an office worker, I now spent half of many a day driving my government-issue Chevrolet Impala at high speeds over the endless, welcoming boulevards and causeways of Miami and Miami Beach, not to speak of field trips out to the Everglades and the Keys. We were seeding an operation in Southern Florida that would extend from north of Fort Lauderdale two hundred miles down to Key West, and from Dade County across Big Cypress Swamp to Tampa and the Gulf. Since we also had to be able to disavow the operation, we needed safe houses that could never be recognized as such, and many of them, in consequence, were loaned to us by wealthy Americans or Cubans living part of the year in Miami. Later in my career, I would learn that the Company was not above keeping castles on the Rhine, chateaux in the Loire, and temples in Kyoto, but those were exceptions: The best security, by standard rule, was inconspicuous safe houses, austere and functional.

In Florida, that law was broken many times over. If I saw my fill of cheap hotel rooms and seedy apartments, I also met with Cubans in houses flanked by large lawns and swimming pools. Outside the picture window, cinched to the dock, was the launch that belonged to the residence. In this empty house, the half dozen Cubans who had been brought together for a meeting were temporarily fumigating any aura of excessive wealth with an around-the-clock smoke-out of cigars.

Do I speak of such meetings abstractly? Be assured—I was not without my private awe at the unpredictability of our Cuban friends. Some were as mustachioed as pirates, others as bald as well-seasoned politicians, but one of my tasks was to chauffeur them out to whichever posh safe house had been chosen by Hunt in Key Biscayne, Coconut Grove, or Coral Gables for the political meet. Later, I would bring them back to rooms almost as mean as my own and would wonder at the logic of transporting them to an elegant if temporary milieu.

Hunt continued to be my guide on such matters. "If we were to keep them in top-drawer accommodations, their arrogance would be unholy in a week. You have to get a grasp on Cuban mentality," he said. "They are not like Mexicans, and they are certainly not comparable to Uruguayans. They are not in the least bit like us. If an American gets depressed enough to think of committing suicide, well, he just might, but if a Cuban thinks of packing it in, he tells his friends, has a party, gets drunk, and kills someone else. They're even treacherous about their own suicide. I attribute it to the tropics. The jungle excites hysteria. A beautiful jungle trail allows you to step on a scorpion. A caterpillar can drop on you from a leaf tree overhead and sting you half-unconscious. Cubans act macho in order to keep down that hysteria. Our task is to punch into all their emotional lack of balance, and I'll tell you, boy, it can be done. That's exactly what we did to Arbenz in Guatemala."

He had told me the story in Montevideo, but I was to hear it again. "Harry, we had only three hundred men, three patched-up planes, and"—he held up a finger—"one radio transmitter working out of the Honduras side of the border, but we kept sending out messages to imaginary troops using a code so simple that we knew Arbenz and his people would be able to crack it. Before long, we had them reacting to our fake messages. We'd mention military units loyal to Arbenz, and talk in code about how they were plotting to defect. Within a week, Arbenz was keeping his battalions locked up in their barracks. He thought they'd march straight over to us. We kept increasing the size of our army, too. 'Can't dispatch two thousand men right now, but will manage twelve hundred today. Tomorrow we can send you the rest.' It was all calculated to sow maximum hysteria in the other side. Arbenz quit Guatemala before the three hundred men we did have could even march into Guatemala City, and all the commies broke for the hills. One of our most masterful jobs.

"Now, we are going to hit Castro with so many reports of multiple landings that he won't know which tip of Cuba we're aiming at."

"May I serve as devil's advocate?"

"That's one reason you're here."

"Castro," I said, "knows all about Guatemala by now. Che Guevara was one of the people working in Arbenz's government."

"Yes," said Hunt, "but Guevara is only one voice among many. Our built-in advantage is that Cubans are without equal in the energy they devote to rumor-mongering. That little vice is going to be used by us. Right now, right here in Miami, with more than a hundred thousand of them already defected from Castro, we are going to flood their rumor mill with misleading information which will end up on Fidel's desk. Since we are positioned in the very center of that hive of rumors, we can push Castro in any direction."

"Can't we be as easily misled by the disinformation Castro sends back?"

Hunt shrugged. "Call it a battle of disinformation. I'll take our people over his. We are less hysterical, after all."

Hunt had been a novelist, I kept reminding myself, before he became a Company man. I could sense a romantic fellow who might be even more of a wild goose than me. Since he could also be as close as a straight-edge at keeping to the Company book, he kept me aware of the separate manifestations of Alpha and Omega, and that was an insight I could do without. Alpha and Omega inundated me with thoughts of Kittredge. A little later that day, forced off the road by a caterwaul of rain, I sat on the shoulder, motor turned off, my head on the wheel, and—to my horror—came close to weeping. Just so suddenly had I been overcome by whole longing for her. It was often like that. In the turn of a mood I would be desolate at the whole absence of Kittredge's presence. I suffered abominably from the frustration of not being able to write to her, and kept writing letters in my mind. Tonight, before I went to sleep, I might compose another. But for now, the rain having ended, I started my car and sped down the highway again along interstates pale as ivory in the sun. I even had the luck to see a white egret standing on one leg in a dark swamp to the side of the road.

4

THAT NIGHT, I ACTUALLY WENT SO FAR AS TO WRITE OUT A LETTER BY hand. The act involved a most curious suspension of disbelief, for I knew I would not mail it.

Miami
June 15, 1960

Dear Kittredge,

How can I explain what I'm doing these days? I have so many small jobs and so little precedent to guide me. At worst, I am a flunky to Howard Hunt and pursue his whims; at best, I am Roberto Charles, aide-de-camp to the legendary Eduardo, who is Political Action Officer for the oncoming Cuba op and is commuting many a day between Miami, New York, and Washington while I am left to protect our cover story, which is that Eduardo is an important steel executive fighting Communism in the Caribbean and has been asked to do this work by people with the *highest political connections*. Of course, this hardly deceives our Cubans, but it does fire them up. They want the Company to be in on this.

All the same, Howard can be guilty of awfully capricious impulses. For instance, he wanted me to use Robert Jordan as a cover name. "Some of the Cubans," I told him, "may have read *For Whom the Bell Tolls*."

"Never," said Hunt, "not our guys."

We settled on Robert Charles. Pocket litter, credit cards, and a banking account followed quickly. Our Miami office has all the capability needed to deliver such stuff, so I now have certificational backing as Robert Charles. *El joven Roberto,* the Cubans are starting to call me, I fear.

As for work habitat, we keep our desks at Zenith Radio Technology and Electronics, Inc., in Coral Gables just south of the South Campus of Miami University. After being so long in Montevideo, I cannot tell you how odd it feels not to pick up my occupational cover from the American Embassy. But now I'm a sales representative for Zenith, our capacious operations headquarters—Zenith! From the exterior, it looks like what it used to be, a long, low office building with adjoining sheds for light manufacturing. Inside, however, it's been converted entirely for our use. We can even justify the wire fence and high security level at the gates since we, of Zenith, are working on government contracts.

Inside the building, more than a hundred of us have been installed already. By the ratio of desk space to square feet, we've even out-crowded I-J-K-L, although our air conditioning, at least, works —it damn well better; we're in Miami! And we have even hung up bogus production charts and award plaques in the lobby.

Behind such front, we are enclaved up to the nose; I couldn't begin to know what most of the other personnel are up to, but then the majority of my activities take place away from the office. I spend a lot of my time with Eduardo's Cuban exiles, and two days a week are spent receiving new Cubans for our project. Every exile in Miami seems to know by now that training bases are being set up in Central America, so Tuesday morning finds me at one of our storefronts downtown, while on Friday I drive up to Opa-Locka; in both places, I monitor interviews with recently arrived and long-term Cuban exiles who want to join the strike force. My Cuban assistant conducts the conversation in such rapid Spanish that usually I must ask what took place. It's absurd. The secret—absolutely no secret—is that the Agency is behind all of this. Despite our fiction that the expenses are being underwritten by individual wealthy citizens of the generous-hearted U.S.A., an eight-year-old could spot the Company hand. I suspect the prevailing wisdom up at Quarters Eye is that after Castro falls to the exile movement, the Russians will scream that we master-minded it, and we will ask them to prove it.

At any rate, each time a story breaks in the *Miami Herald* about more Russian presence in Castro country, we are besieged. What these Cubans are signing up for, of course, is left very much open. They do not know if they will become part of an invasion army, or will be dropped back in Cuba to become guerrillas in the hills. I am on the lookout for candidates who can serve in either capacity. I not only sit in on the interviews, but study the questionnaires and make the first cut. In addition to rejecting the men whose stories don't add up, we do tend to trust Cubans who come from Catholic Action student groups more than solitary Cubans who just walk in. Indeed, the first of my tasks is to check out the applicant's local references; nearly all of our volunteers must be able to show traceable roots in their local communities, and we have a genealogical computer at Zenith to check them out. It's not a job of any great strain. Any fellow

who passes through me and our computer still gets fluttered before
being dispatched to Fort Myers for early training.

I do, however, study the faces that pass. So many are both
dignified and corrupt—a most unlikely mixture of attributes. I confess
that there is some personal quality I cannot define about dark skin,
some compound of pride and license. These Cubans are so different
from myself, so alert to their honor, yet ready to indulge themselves
in personal peccadillos that would leave me morally congested. I have
also noticed that they are as proud of their names as a vain beauty is
of her face. While there is an occasional José López or Luis Gómez,
a Juan Martínez and a Rico Santos, such commonplace monikers are
overwhelmed by our truly orchidacean samples: Cosmé Mujal; Lucilo
Torriente; Armengol Escalante; Homoboro Hevía-Balmeseda; In-
nocente Conchoso; Angel Fejardo-Mendiéta; Germán Galíndez-Mi-
goya; Eufemio Pons; Aurelio Cobían-Roig.

Well, my dear, you get the idea. Many look like Quixote; a
few like Panza. There are lawyers with starched collars and mustaches
twirled to points at the tip. Some are so dandified they could step out
of Proust, young, dangerous *señoritos,* others so menacing, so full of
gangsterismo, that a state trooper would impound their jalopy on sight.
They all come through—young students still pocked with acne, pale
and petrified by the honest if terrifying choice they have made to
endanger their lives, and there are old parties, fat in the gut, looking
nonetheless to recover something of their youth. Physical weaklings
pass before me bright with fever, cowards pushed forward by the scorn
of peers. Three or four drunks usually show up, and one or two
professional soldiers who remained with Batista to the very end and
therefore cannot be selected. In they march—enthusiastic and/or paranoid, some brave, some timid, but all christened with a flourish:
Sandalio Auribal Santisteban and Aracelio Portela-Almagro, Alejo
Augusto Meruelos, Reinaldo Balan. Fireworks must have gone up in
all the middle-class skies above their cribs.

Naturally, my work takes a few practical factors into account.
I've been obliged to give some study to the five political parties that
Hunt and I work with—the Christian Democratic Movement
(MDC), the AAA, the Monti-Cristi, Rescat, and the Revolutionary
Recovery Movement (MRR).

Are you disinclined to know the differences? Leave it that
these groups, in varying degree, see themselves either as liberal capital-

ists or social democrats. Like Castro, they also hate Batista. Ergo, our cover story, to the degree that it is believed, only succeeds in arousing the suspicion that Hunt and his *wealthy Americans* are trying to put Batista back in power. Unholy accusations do fly. I can hardly believe Cuban displays of temperament. These, after all, are supposed to be leaders! They head up the five exile groups—the Frente Revolucionario Democrático—which is the *Front,* that Washington chose as a somewhat left-of-center coalition selected precisely not to alienate all that large part of Latin America that leans to the Marxist side of the street. On the other hand, they are also considered close enough to the center to keep Eisenhower, Nixon, and Company from becoming too miserable. As I must repeat, politics is not my strong suit, nor is it, I would assume, very much yours, but I've come to realize that a lot of our foreign policy is built these days on trying to undo the old Joe McCarthy image. We have to convince the rest of the world that we are more progressive than the Russians. This puts us in a paradoxical situation down here: Hunt is, if anything, more conservative than Richard Nixon, and wouldn't mind replacing our guys with a right-wing group more congenial to him. Yet this is the team he has been given to work with, and to the degree they do well, his Agency standing will prosper.

No routine task. I am perpetually amazed at how small a country we are dealing with. Cuba may be eight hundred miles long, but everyone here seems to have lived in the same quarter of Havana. These men have not only been associated with each other for years, but claim to have known Castro personally. It is not impossible, then, that one or more of them could be his agent. Even if they are trustworthy, they get along about as well as a highly charged Latin family, full of murderous dissension. Our five Frente leaders have been at serious political odds with one another over the last thirty years, thereby leaving Hunt in the unenviable position of striving to move them forward as a team while keeping them apart.

Such are our elevated cohorts. One is a former President of the Cuban Senate (before Batista abolished it); another was Foreign Minister under President Carlos Prio Socarras; a third used to be President of the Bank for Industrial Development, yet they do not impress me as being all that distinguished. Indeed, it is sometimes hard to believe they held such serious positions in government.

At this point, I considered signing off. Since I would never mail this letter, I was feeling as sad as a man dancing alone on an empty floor.

Kittredge, just now I tried to go to bed, but it proved impossible. I think I have to confess the loneliness of my present condition. I am living in motel poverty and it is absurd—what I spend here for rent could provide me with a small furnished apartment in a modest outlying neighborhood, yet I resist such a choice even as I have resisted every small invitation from colleagues at Zenith. I have no social life, and that is my fault. I just do not care to make the solemn effort to be agreeable. In Uruguay, it was easier. One's social life used to be all too comfortably folded into the round of Embassy parties. Here, however, with Agency personnel coming into Miami from every Station on the globe, and not an embassy in sight, we are more like a boomtown. With one notable exception. Everyone comes to Zenith in the morning, then scatters out at night to whatever Florida housing matches one's paycheck. So I have two choices—I can hobnob with married couples, or get drunk every night with bachelor officers like myself. I want neither. The married couples, will, of course, have the wife's girlfriend waiting for me, and/or the children's plastic bicycle upended in the front yard; the bachelor officers give me pause. All too many down here are reminiscent of the paramilitaries at the Farm—drinking with them could prove more of a task than any work I might encounter in the day.

Of course, there is always Howard Hunt. He and Dorothy did become a large part of my evening life in Uruguay. But now, Dorothy remains in Montevideo until the children's school term is over, and Hunt commutes between Washington and Miami. I see him about once a week for dinner, and he invariably gives me another lecture on marriage. He no longer seems quite as central to my life. Under this hot Florida sky with its oleander and bougainvillea nights, its redolence of passion flowers on residential streets, I feel as if I am waiting for—it may be the most hopeless word of them all, Kittredge, but it does apply—I am waiting for romance, that good American wine distilled, I know, from the essence of many a cheap thrill out of many a movie forgotten.

Here I did stop writing, and went to sleep. In the morning, I awoke with the bleak recognition that it was not possible to safeguard a letter like this in my motor court and so I had to stop at my safe deposit box to cache this unmailed item there.

At Zenith, later in the day, as if the labor of writing my letter had produced its own small work of magic, I received an open call from Harlot. He wanted to talk to me. Could I find some excuse to run up to Washington? I could, I said. Howard had been talking about sending me up.

"When earliest?"

"Tomorrow."

"See you for lunch. One o'clock. Harvey's Restaurant." The phone clicked in my ear.

5

"I'M SURPRISED," SAID HUGH MONTAGUE, "THAT HOWARD HUNT permitted you to visit Washington in his stead. He so looks forward to popping in."

"Well, my mission doesn't appeal to him," I answered. "I'm here to scrounge up some welfare for the Frente. It takes time, and you don't get much in the way of results."

" 'Guns, not butter,' I can hear our people say. How much do you need?"

"Ten thousand might be good for Frente morale. It'll enable our leaders to take care of a few of their needy."

"Piss on Frente morale. I merely look forward to confounding Howard with your fund-raising abilities. If he keeps sending you up to get more, you and I can restore our somewhat rusted links."

He had been just this affable through drinks and the entree. We did not speak of Kittredge, nor of son Christopher, but otherwise it was as if we had been seeing each other often.

"Yes," he said, "I'll get you the money."

I did not have to ask how. It was accepted rumor that Allen Dulles put away pots of funds in the nooks and floorboards of every branch, division, and directorate. Harlot, I was certain, kept the maps.

"It's nice to visit a man who only has to make one phone call,"

I remarked, but the air went dead on my flattery.

"Why did you sign up for this Cuban business?" he asked.

"I believe in it," I answered. My voice, unhappily, was dogged in my ears. "It could be a most direct way of fighting Communism."

He snorted. "Our purpose is to undermine Communism, not to martyr it. We don't have to *fight* them. I'm aghast. Have you learned nothing from me?"

"I learned a lot." I halted. "I learned a lot," I said, "and then I didn't have any contact with the instructor."

You could always count on the cold benefit of being able to look directly into his eyes. They were devoid of incidental affection. "Well," he said, "you are a tricky case. I don't want to waste you, and don't know how to use you. That, in sum, is why I've let you dangle." He hawked his throat. "All hope, however," said Harlot, "is not dead. Lately, I've had a thought or two in your direction."

On the flight to Washington, I had had ample time to recognize how much it had cost to stay out of touch with him for so long. "Well," I answered, "I won't say I am not ready to listen."

"Oh, no, not yet," he said, pushing away dessert to light a Churchill. After a first puff, he reached again into his breast pocket to offer me one—were his brand of Churchills the best Havanas ever made? Puffing on his gift, I understood Cuba better—perfumed fecalities had been blended with honor and iron will—yes, alchemy lurked in the nicotine.

"Oh, no, not yet," he repeated. "I don't want to let go of Cuba just yet. Do you have any idea of what a comedy is cooking?"

"Well, I hope not."

"Prepare for a farce. Cuba is going to be our penance for Guatemala. It can't be helped. Likeable Ike has not read Martin Buber."

"Neither have I."

"Read him. Buber's *Tales of the Hasidim*. Perfect. Enables you to dazzle visitors from the Mossad. Those beady Israeli eyes go moist when I quote Martin Buber, their fellow Jew."

"May I ask how Buber is relevant to Cuba?"

"He's relevant. There's a nicely balanced tale he tells of this poor, infertile, married woman who is so obsessed with having a child that she travels across half of the Ukraine on foot in order to meet a traveling rabbi. In the late eighteenth century, these gentlemen called Hasids were not unlike our evangelists and used to make tours through the Russian hinterland. Accompanied by a horde of followers, a Hasidic rabbi would wend his way from ghetto town to ghetto town, accompanied invariably by a brilliantly handsome and seductive wife. The Jewish women, unlike our more pagan Christian cheerleaders, were always drawn to the power of intellect, which, in this near-medieval situation, centered, you may be certain, on the rabbi. In our tale, the sad, barren Jewish housewife has to travel endless versts across primitive country beset by every sort of riffraff, but she does reach her goal, whereupon, our peripatetic eminence blesses her. 'Go home to your husband,' he says, 'and you will have a child.' She returns safely, conceives, and nine months later, delivers a bouncing babe. Naturally, another woman in her village, desirous of the same result, decides in the following year to make the same trip. This time the rabbi says, 'Alas, I can do nothing for you, my dear. You have heard the story.' Moral: We won't take Cuba in the same manner we rolled up those Guatemalan Communists."

"I said as much to Hunt."

"Pity you don't tend to your words." He sniffed at his cigar smoke as if somewhere in the center of the cloud was a line between judgments good and bad. "I can understand why Eisenhower is off his feed. That business last month when Gary Powers was shot down in his U-2. Likeable Ike caught with his hand in the cookie jar. Khrushchev cussing him out for all the world to hear. And then the Negro sit-ins. That must have deranged him a bit. He keeps talking about Cuba as *the black hole of Calcutta*," said Hugh Montague, sipping his brandy.

I had often noted that a trip to a restaurant with Harlot had to obey its signal forms. The check was carefully calculated out for our separate shares; coffee and Hennessey always concluded the repast; and he never seemed to care how long lunch took. I asked Kittredge about that once, and she laughed sadly and said, "Lunches are his hobby. Afterward, Hugh works on such days until midnight." By the manner in which he now turned the end of his cigar in an ashtray, his fingers dancing lightly on the shaft, I could see that lunch at Harvey's would go on for a while. Once again, we had become the last table on our part of the floor.

"What do you think of this place?" Hugh asked me.

"Adequate."

"It's J. Edgar Buddha's favorite joint, so one wouldn't expect better, but then, I've decided lately to keep switching my midday *endroit*. Makes it more difficult for others to keep up with your conversation. And I do have a sensitive matter to discuss."

He was coming at last to the point of our meeting. As I had observed from attending a few poetry readings at Yale, good voices do not offer the best stuff first.

"I want," he said, "to get right to the point. What would you think of resigning from the CIA?"

"Oh, no." I had a whole unhappy recall of the time he told me not to do any more rock climbing.

"Don't cross before you see the road. I'm going to propose a venture so secret that if I have misjudged your reliability, you will know too much. So put aside all your notions of how we keep the secrets. It's not by the aid of all those fenced-in kraals and coops. Forget them. They leak. But, here and there, is a coffer where we do hold some real stuff. From our inception, Allen, in close conjunction with a few of us, has kept one operation sacrosanct. We have a few officers who never did get to put their name on a 201 file. No payment, no paper. *Most Special Fellows.* Allen's term. I want you to become a Most Special Fellow." He did tap his glass lightly while whispering these last remarks to me.

"For instance," he went on in that whisper, "if our Harry Hubbard were to resign now from the Agency, one could underwrite a quick twelve-month course with highly respectable pay by a prestigious Wall Street brokerage house, followed by assignment as a customer's man to some very good clients. Most Special Fellow would then, under the guidance of more practiced hands, manage certain selected fortunes until he had learned the business for himself. That would enable him to enjoy the career of a rising stockbroker for the rest of his life. An agent in place. Over a long career, Most Special Fellows are used sparingly. I promise you, however, that one can serve to extraordinary purpose on those special occasions when the work is needed. You might be out there stirring huge cauldrons of international finance while blessed with a cover nigh impenetrable."

I did not trust this presentation. I was thinking it was a hell of a way to be told you ought to resign. He must have picked up my sentiment, for he added: "If you wish a little Muzak to accompany the proposition, I will add that we only make this offer to young men we deem extraordinarily talented when"—he held up a forefinger—"they are not concomitantly gifted with those bureaucratic instincts so requisite to doing a proper job within the formal structure. Allen needs a few of our best people out there, ready to lend a covert shoulder to the wheel. Do you have the courtesy to feel honored by the seriousness of this offer?"

"I would be," I said slowly, "but do you know, I enjoy the daily routine of the Company. I don't believe I would be as devoted to bonds and margins. I'd rather take my chances here."

"You might not do all that well. Your temperament is to work alone rather than on a team."

"I don't really care how high I climb. I don't think ambition is my guiding principle."

"What, then, do you look for among us?"

I thought for a moment. "Some extraordinary job that I alone might be able to bring off," I was surprised to hear myself say.

"You feel ready for the exceptional?"

I nodded. Whether I did or did not, I nodded. He was, as always, impenetrable, but I began to suspect that he had known I would not want to become a stockbroker. Perhaps he had merely been marinating me in a throwaway scenario so that my powers of rejection would be softened.

The next proposal came soon enough. "I've got another of these *ex officio* jobs for you," he said, "and this one, I hope, you won't turn down. You will, of course, have to take it on in addition to all of Hunt's precious stuff."

"I assume it's to report only to you."

"Depend on that. You will keep no official records." Holding his cigar in the three-finger bridge one forms around a pool cue, he tapped his middle finger lightly on the cloth, so lightly as not to dislodge the ash. "You understand, of course, that Allen does keep me around to serve as a floating spirit of investigation, and that does get one in and out of some places in the Company."

"Hugh," I ventured, "everyone knows you have a pipeline into everything."

"The legend may be mightier than the few pipes laid," he said, and his fingers kept tapping the cigar until the ash looked ready to go, whereupon he twirled it to his plate. "Of course, I have GHOUL." That was worth a pause. "And GHOUL does keep up with the FBI. I sometimes have a good idea of what J. Edgar Buddha is tucking away into his more private recesses."

I had an odd reaction. It seemed excessive. The hair stirred on the back of my neck. I felt as if we were two priests alone at a refectory table and he was showing me the key to the sacred closet where our relics were stored. I did not know if his confidence was sacrilegious, but I was powerfully and somewhat agreeably disturbed. He had touched my inclination to get into things others did not know.

"I will," said Harlot, "furnish more information as soon as you accomplish the first element in your task."

"I know I'm ready," I said.

"You will have to strike up acquaintance with a certain young lady whose activities are, by now, surrounded with FBI taps. Given the candor with which she talks into her telephone, it is obvious she does not know that she is sitting well within the shadow cast by Buddha's huge posterior. One might think of her as a damsel in distress, except one can't. She's too enterprisingly promiscuous."

"A call girl?"

"Oh, no. Just an airline stewardess. But she's managed to get herself wrapped into liaisons with a couple of prominent gentlemen who don't add up when taken together."

"Is either one of these men American?"

"Both, I assure you."

"Both? May I ask why the Agency is involved?"

"It's not. Except for GHOUL. Let us say that GHOUL is interested because Buddha is interested. We may yet have to consider Buddha as much of a threat to this nation as Joseph Stalin ever dreamed of being in the old days."

"You're not suggesting that Hoover is a Soviet agent?"

"Heavens no. Just one hell of an agent for himself. I suspect he would like to control the country altogether."

I was recalling an evening at the Stable when Harlot had given me his sense of our duty: It was to become the mind of America.

"I see I will have to take a great deal on faith," I said.

"For now. Once you get to know this airline stewardess, however, I will offer you entry to the material. I have the Bureau tapes on the girl, and what a tale they tell. They're yours, I promise, once you meet the mermaid, and *hook* her." In case I was not appreciative of the verb, he added, "The deeper, the better."

"What does she look like?"

"You'll feel no great pain." He reached into his breast pocket and brought out a color snapshot taken probably from a moving car. The features were a bit blurred. All I could discern was a good-looking girl with a nice figure and black hair. "I don't know that I would want to depend on an identification from this picture," I told him.

"It's close enough. You'll meet her, you see, on your plane back to Miami. She's working the First Class section of the 4:50 P.M. flight on Eastern this afternoon, and I'll bump your return ticket up, and find a way to bill the extra disbursement."

"She's based in Miami?"

"There's the beauty of it."

"And if I get to know her well?"

"You will be as amazed by our country as I am."

"Whatever do you mean?"

"Well, we're all stuffed with these incredible radio and TV romances. Trashy novels. Not *us,* but, you know, *them!* Our fellow Americans. All that love glut and plot pollution. But when it comes to the real stuff, our Lord is more of a commercial novelist than the novelists. This is one hell of a story. It even surprises me."

He was to tell me more before we broke lunch at 3:30 P.M. The young lady's name was Modene Murphy, her nickname was "Mo," her father was half-Irish, half-German, and her mother of French and Dutch descent. She was twenty-three years old and her parents had a little money.

"How was it made?"

"Oh," said Harlot, "the father is a skilled machinist who patented some kind of valve for motorcycle intakes just after the war, sold the patent, and retired." Modene, he went on, had grown up in a rich suburb of Grand Rapids where her family was, if not respected, accepted at least for their money. "She's some sort of minor debutante," said Harlot, "the Midwestern sort. Of course, there's neither enough money nor enough of anything else for them to have any idea of how far away they really are from everything. I suspect being a stewardess gives her some sense of social balance, although I am really at a small loss to explain her choice of occupation."

"What makes you think I'll get along with Modene Murphy?"

"I've no idea you will. But your father, remember, used to be good at this sort of thing in OSS days. Perhaps a spark will trot across the gap. Yes," he said, "and one more bit of news. One would like to keep it simple, but I'm afraid we have to give you another name. We won't be able to backstop it either, since you are definitely not getting into our records on this, but I can obtain some rudimentary pocket litter for you, and, yes, even a credit card. You'll need that to squire the lady around."

"Let me keep Harry for a first name," I said. "I'd like to react naturally to her."

"Yes," he said. "Harry. What's your mother's maiden name?—Silverfield. Is that considered Jewish?"

"No," I said.

"Well, let's make it Field, in any event. Harry Field. Should be easy to incorporate."

I did not know whether I felt promoted or down-graded now that I had three names.

6

IT'S HARD TO SAY THAT I WOULD HAVE BROUGHT OFF THE FIRST LEG OF my mission if not for a curious piece of luck. In the Eastern waiting area, just before boarding my plane, I encountered Sparker Boone, an old classmate from St. Matthew's. One of our lesser lights, he had always been built like a pear armed with buck teeth. He had now added a premature bald spot to the back of his thin, sandy hair. Of course, I had no wish to go down to Miami with Bradley "Sparker" Boone when I was hoping to present myself as Harry Field, but on boarding the plane, I could find no way to avoid his invitation to sit with him since First Class was half-empty. I had to content myself with obtaining the aisle seat.

He told me soon enough that he had become a photographer for *Life* magazine, and was on his way to Miami to photograph some of the leading Cuban exiles. Before I could digest how worrisome, from an Agency point of view, this news might be (since *Life*—Kittredge had also assured me—was considered by us to be somewhat less dependable than *Time*), he added, "I hear you're in the CIA."

"God, no," I said. "What gave you that idea?"

"The grapevine. St. Matt's."

"Someone is playing fast and loose with my name," I told him. "Why, I'm a sales rep for an electronics company." I was about to present the evidence when I recollected that Robert Charles happened to be the name embossed on my business card. My only excuse for such near-carelessness is that I was prodigiously distracted. To my small panic, both stewardesses in the First Class section fit Harlot's description: They had dark hair, and were attractive. I did not feel ready to settle into a conversation until I made certain which girl was Modene Murphy.

The answer, however, soon declared itself. One stewardess was carefully groomed and well featured; the other was striking enough to be a movie star. As she went up and down the aisle checking seat belts and overhead compartments, she looked much pleased with herself, and tended to passengers' needs with a subtle contempt, as if there was something second-rate about having needs to begin with. She did not seem to belong to her job so much as to be an actress in a role. The worst of it was that I thought her looks were marvelous. Her hair was as dark as Kittredge's, and her eyes were a brilliant, insolent green, ready to suggest that she would compete with you over everything from an early-morning run down a powder trail to the first knock in gin rummy; she had a figure described immediately by Sparker as "a body I would kill for"—Sparker with his wife and bald spot and two daughters, their snapshots already presented to me, yes, Sparker, with his house in Darien, still ready to kill for possession of Modene Murphy, yes, I had the right girl. The nameplate pinned to her breast, which I glimpsed when she stopped to tell me to strap my safety belt, was confirmation.

I started to take off my jacket. "Could you hang this up, miss?" I asked.

"Put it on your lap for now," she said, "we're about to take off," and without a glance to see what kind of man might be attached to the voice, moved to her bucket seat.

Once we were in the air, I had to ring for her. She picked up my jacket, and was gone. It was Sparker who gained her interest. With a knowing grin, as if the procedure had been successfully tested before, he reached to the floor, set his camera bag on his lap, and proceeded to load film, first into a Leica, then a Hasselblad. She was back before he was done. "Can I ask you?" she said. "Who do you work for?"

"*Life,*" said Sparker.

"I knew it," she said. She called to the other stewardess. "What did I say, Nedda, when this one"—pointing to Sparker—"came on the plane?"

"You said, 'He's a photographer for *Life* or *Look*.' "

"How could you tell?" asked Sparker.

"I can always tell."

"What would you have said was my occupation?" I asked.

"I didn't give it consideration," she answered.

She was leaning over me to get her face closer to *Life* photographer Boone. "How long are you going to be in Miami?" she inquired of him.

"About a week."

"I want to ask you some questions. I don't like the way my pictures come out."

"I can help you on that," he said.

"You seem very serious about photography," I added.

She looked at me for the first time, but presented no more answer than the smallest turn of her lip.

"Where," she asked Sparker, "are you going to stay in Miami?"

"At the Saxony," he said, "in Miami Beach."

She made a face. "The Saxony," she said.

"You know all these hotels well?" he asked.

"Of course."

When she came back, she handed him a slip. "You can get me at that number. Or, I may call you at the Saxony."

"Whew!" he said so soon as she moved down the aisle again. I watched her talking with animation to a businessman in a silk suit whose manicured nails gleamed from three seats away. It took no more than that to put me in depression. I had been keyed on this meeting ever since Harlot announced it at lunch. With all I had done and not done in my life, I had certainly never picked up a girl before. The iron hand of St. Matt's was still upon me. I felt helpless before this Modene Murphy. By comparison to myself, she seemed incredibly sophisticated and abysmally ignorant—hardly a fit.

"Sparker, let me have the girl's number," I said.

"Oh, I can't do that," he told me.

Back at St. Matt's, he had been easy to bully. Memories returned of chastening him in a headlock. Now, meeting ostensibly as equal adults, he would try to prove stubborn.

"I've got to have it," I said.

"Why?"

"I feel as if I've met someone who will mean a great deal to me."

"Yes," he said under my stare, "I can let you have her phone number. I can tell. She is not the girl for me." His breath was sour as he spoke to my ear. "She looks awfully expensive."

"Do you believe one has to pay her?"

He shook his head. "No, but these stewardesses demand a very good time if they give you a date. I can't feel comfortable spending that kind of money when my wife and children can use it."

"That makes a strong case," I said.

"Yes," he said, "but what will you do for me?"

"Oh," I said, "you might try naming it."

"I want a contact with a good Cuban hooker. I hear they are unforgettable in bed."

That offered an image of Sparker Boone stroking his bone on the recollection through the sere and golden years.

"What makes you think I can take care of that?" I asked.

"You're CIA. You have that sort of knowledge at your finger-tips."

It was not altogether untrue. I could ask one or two of the exile leaders. They would have, at the least, a friend in the business of brothels.

"Well, I will take care of it," I said. "You have my word. But you have to do something else for me."

"What? You're getting the better of the bargain as it is."

"Not at all," I said. "You have to watch out for Cuban hookers. The worst can be venal and ill-spirited." I was improvising. "The ground has to be prepared. I will take pains to have you introduced to your Cuban date as the friend of a very influential man. That will make a big difference."

"All right," he said, "I go along with that. But what is this 'something else' you want me to do for you?"

"Speak positively about me to Modene Murphy. You obviously have her attention."

He frowned. He had his own kind of authority after all. "You are not an easy sell," he said.

"Why? Why not?"

"Because she has made up her mind about you."

"Yes. And what has she determined?"

"That you have no money."

I felt reduced again by the thought of Modene Murphy.

"Sparker," I told him, "you'll find the way when you talk to her."

He pondered this just long enough to suggest that he might also remember the headlock I used to put on him. "I think I have a handle," he said.

"Yes?"

"I'll tell her"—he held up his palm—"that while you won't admit it, you're CIA."

"This is the damn stupidest thing I ever heard of," I burst out. "Why would that interest her?" But I knew the answer.

"If it's not money," he opined, "then it has to be adventure. I know her prototype. *Life* has the same cathexis as CIA for women like that."

It was coming in on me again that my plane ticket was in the name of Harry Field. I would have to be introduced to her by that name.

My stomach was upset. Bad enough for Sparker to be convinced I was an Agency man; now, I would be demonstrating it. The Agency rule of thumb, I reminded myself, was to hold out. Hold out at all costs.

"Boone," I said, "I have to let you in on something. I am in electronics but I don't work in Miami. My shop is in Fairfax, Virginia. I'm going down to Miami to see a married woman whose husband is very jealous."

"Weighty stuff."

"Very. My lady-friend warned me not to use my real name. Her husband works for an airline so he has access to passenger lists. She says he could not be held accountable if he found out I had come down to Miami. So I booked myself in as Harry Field. Harry Field," I repeated.

"Why in tarnation do you want the stewardess's phone number if you have a woman in Miami already?" He actually had to reach into the side flap of his safari jacket and take out the piece of paper to read her name. "Why this Modene Murphy?" he concluded.

"Because I'm struck by her. I can warrant that it never happened to me in this manner before."

He shook his head. "What name should I give her?"

When I told him, he savored the moment by having me spell it. "H-A-R-R-Y F-I-E-L-D," I heard myself saying.

The flight had entered on a bumpy course. For the next hour, no one could quit his seat. By the time we came into clear night sky, the trip was into its last half hour. He went up then to the galley, and I could see him talking to Modene Murphy. They laughed together a few times, and once she looked at me. Then he came back to his seat for the descent.

"Mission wholly accomplished," he said.

"What did you tell her?"

"You don't want to hear. You'll only deny it." He smiled in such a way as to tell me that if he was going to do a job, he certainly did it well. "I gave her to understand," he said at last, "that Harry Field is the best in the field given his kind of occupation."

"Did she believe it?"

"The moment you even hint at secret work the suspension of disbelief is total."

He was right. After we landed, she came up with my jacket and handed it to me wordlessly. Her eyes were shining. In that instant, I learned the true force of a cliché—my heart leaped tangibly in my chest.

"May I call you?" I asked at the door to the plane.

"You don't know my number," she whispered.

"I'll find a way," I said, and walked off quickly.

Sparker was waiting in the exit lounge. He had an invoice to collect. "What is the name of that Cuban girl you are going to introduce me to?"

Not until I offered my vow that I would leave a message for him tomorrow at the Saxony would he surrender Modene's address to me. She was staying at the Fontainebleau.

"Someone," he assured me before we separated, "has to be picking up her bill."

I took a moment to look again at him. I might be a poor excuse for a salesman of electronic products, but he was certainly out of focus as a photographer for Life. So soon as we separated in the terminal, I bought a copy of the magazine and turned to the masthead. He was not listed under the photographers but among the photo editors. He was half a fraud. That cheered me. Modene Murphy did not have so formidable an eye after all.

I was employing just this thought to underwrite my confidence when I called her room at the Fontainebleau next morning. She was as sweet, however, as when she had said good-bye to me at the airplane door. "I'm glad you called," she said. "I really want to talk to you. I need some kind of wise man to confide in." Then she laughed. "You know, an expert." She had a gutty little laugh that proved agreeable, as if something unpolished in her was very much there to develop.

She had been out late last night, she explained, and would be shopping all day. She had another date for tonight, but "I have a window from five to six-thirty, and can fit you in there."

We chose a cocktail lounge at the Fontainebleau. Before I was to see her, however, I had to suffer a small panic in mid-afternoon when a lunch meeting with the Frente at a safe house gave every sign of going on into the night. I would miss my date with Modene.

We were enmeshed in a dispute over money. The more I looked at my watch, the more I grew to dislike the man who went on the longest. He was the former leader of the Cuban Senate, Faustino "Toto" Barbaro, and for this luncheon Barbaro had worked up a proposed Frente budget of $745,000 a month for "elementary needs." Our accountants, Hunt replied, were ready to allocate $115,000 a month.

The meeting became a shouting match. "Inform your *wealthy Americans* that we see through their various subterfuges," Toto Barbaro bellowed. "We do not require handouts. We have the capacity to drive our own historical vehicle. I would remind you, Señor Eduardo, that we overthrew Batista with no assistance from you. So, give us the money for arms. We will do the rest."

"For God's sake, Toto," said Hunt, "you know our Neutrality Act puts every restriction in the way."

"You are playing with banal legalisms. I wielded the gavel in a Senate chamber filled with lawyers, *Cuban* lawyers. When it was to our advantage, we used the legal mode to paralyze the issue, but when, Señor Eduardo, we were ready to move, we excised those same restrictions. You are mocking us."

"You talk to him," said Hunt in a rage, and left the room. Howard knew when to use his temper. Frente bills were coming due, and the only American who had the power to negotiate was gone. In the face of much sullenness, the offer of $115,000 was accepted *pro tem*, and I was able to close the meeting. I was even able, by way of Barbaro, to pick up the name of a young Cuban widow who, he promised, would not prove too cruel for my old classmate, Sparker. It was another lesson in politics—by means of this favor Barbaro entrapped me into a date for dinner later that week. Politics, I was discovering, was the fastest way to mortgage the future. All the same, I had a drink with Modene coming right up and was on the causeway into Miami Beach before a quarter to five and could leave my car with the valet at the Fontainebleau on the mark of the hour.

DRINKING WITH MY AIRLINE STEWARDESS IN THE MAI TAI LOUNGE, I
would look away when our eyes met. I hardly knew how to talk. Sally
Porringer provided the only near model to Modene, and with Sally
there had rarely been problems with conversation—one pushed buttons to evoke themes: how much she loved her children; how much
she disliked her husband; how much she had loved her first love, the
football player; how much she loved me; how worthless I was; how
irresponsible; how close was suicide. Sally had her share of open
wounds and uncauterized anger.

Modene Murphy, however, if one could believe her, was ready
to enjoy everything. She liked the beach because it was so clean.
"They take care of it." She liked the pool at the Fontainebleau
because "the barman makes the best Planter's Punches in Miami
Beach," and the Mai Tai Lounge "because I love to get drunk here."
She even approved of Eastern Airlines because "I have it absolutely
under my thumb. You suffer," she informed me, "through your first
few years on an airline because they can move you about at their
merest whim, but now I have it under control. I not only choose my
routes, but the days I work."

"How did you get all that leverage?"

"Let's talk about you," she said.

"I'm not interesting," I told her. "Or, at least, electronics is not
interesting. Not if you're selling it as I am. It's just wires."

What compounded my discomfort was that I had a tape recorder
going in the attaché case accompanying me today (newest of the toys
to come down to Zenith from Quarters Eye) and so I would be
obliged to listen to my own remarks later.

"You may be an expert," she said, "but it is not in electronics."

"What kind of expert am I, then?"

"You are able to find out things about people that they don't want
you to know."

"Well, that's true. You're right. I'm a private detective."

"I like you," she said. Then she laughed. "I approve of your style.
It's so controlled."

"Controlled? Why, I twitch every time I look at you."

She slapped my hand lightly.

"In fact," I said, "I'm mad about you." I stammered slightly as I said this and realized it was the only way to make such a remark. I sounded sincere to myself. "That is," I said, "I have known women before who meant a great deal to me, and there is one woman I have been in love with for many years, but she's married."

"I know what you're saying," Modene told me wisely.

"But I have never experienced the . . . the impact I felt the first time I looked at you."

"Oh, you are trying to woo me. Beware! The first time I saw you was in First Class with your head down. All I could notice is that you don't take very good care of your scalp."

"What?"

"Dandruff," she told me solemnly, and burst into laughter at the look on my face. "Maybe it was only lint," she said, "but you certainly don't have a woman looking after you."

"The way Sparker's wife takes care of him?"

"Who?"

"Bradley Boone, the *Life* man."

"Oh, him. I have no interest in him."

"Why did you offer the impression that you did?"

"Because I want someone to teach me photography."

"Is that why you gave off that very large suggestion of liking him?"

"I just go after what I want and *ensnare* it." She gave vent to her gutty earthy little laugh as if she couldn't believe how outrageous she was.

"I think you're terrific," I told her. "You gave me such a turn-around. I never felt that before. Not even with the woman I love." I looked at her eyes and took a large swallow of my drink. I had already decided I was not going to pass the raw transcript on this over to Harlot.

"I want to kiss you," she said.

She did. It was a small embrace, but her lips were soft and I certainly didn't get to the bottom of them. "You're earthy," she said as she withdrew.

"That's good, I hope."

"Well, I seem to attract earthy people."

My lips were feeling the tactile echo of her lips, and my breath was resonant. *Earthy?* Well, that was news! "Who are some others you would characterize in such fashion?"

She wagged a finger at me. "Kiss and tell."

"I don't mind."

"I do. My life is private to me. I cater to my privacy."

"Don't any of your friends know anything about you?"

"Let's talk of something else," she told me. "I know why I want to see you, but why do you want to see me?"

"Because one look at you and—I have to confess—a force came over me. I never felt that before. It's the truth."

What was the truth, I wondered? I had been lying for so long to so many people that I was beginning to feel mendacious relations with myself. Was I a monster or merely in a muddle? "What I guess," I said to her, "is that you feel this kind of impact when you meet someone who's absolutely equal to yourself."

She looked dubious. Was she thinking of the condition of my scalp?

"Yes," she said, and gave me a very careful second kiss as if assaying samples for ore content.

"Can we go somewhere?" I asked.

"No. It's ten after six and I have to leave in twenty minutes." She sighed. "I can't go to bed with you, anyway."

"Why not?"

"Because I've reached my quota." She touched my hand. "I believe in serious affairs. So at any given time I only allow myself two. One for stability; one for romance."

"And now you are fully booked?"

"I have a wonderful man who takes care of me in Washington. I see him when I'm there. He protects me."

"You don't look as if you need protection."

"Protection is the wrong word. He . . . takes care of my needs on the job. He's an executive at Eastern. So he makes certain I get the flight schedules I want."

Her executive sounded somewhat smaller than the giants Harlot had been promising.

"Do you love him?"

"I wouldn't say that. But he's a good man, and he's absolutely dependable. I can count on him trying to make me happy."

"You don't talk like any girl I've ever known."

"Well, I would like to think I'm a bit unique."

"You are. You certainly are."

She tapped the bar with one very long fingernail. "Right here, however, Miami Beach, is my port of choice."

"You have the longest fingernails," I said. "How do you keep from breaking them on the job?"

"Constant attention," she said. "Even then I've been known to rip one occasionally. It's painful and it's expensive. I spend half my pay getting nail splints."

"I would think this hotel is expensive."

"Oh, no. It's summertime. I get a rate here."

"Isn't it far from the airport?"

"I don't care to stay with the other girls and the pilots. I'd rather spend the time traveling in the hotel van."

"So you don't like being with your crew?"

"No," she said, "there's no point to it unless you want to marry a pilot, and they are unbelievably stingy. If three stewardesses and the pilot and the copilot share a dollar-and-eighty-cent taxi ride with tip, depend on it, the pilot will ask each of the girls to contribute thirty-six cents."

"Yes," I said, "that's small beer."

"I still haven't told you what I want you to do for me."

"No, you haven't."

"Do you like Frank Sinatra?" she asked.

"Never met him."

"I mean, do you like his singing?"

"Overrated," I replied.

"You don't know what you're talking about."

"You oughtn't to ask a question if you have no respect for the answer."

She nodded, as if to indicate that she was certainly familiar with my variety of reply. "I know Frank," she said.

"You do?"

"I dated him for a while."

"How did you ever meet him?"

"On a flight."

"And he took your number?"

"We exchanged numbers. I wouldn't reveal something so private to me as my phone unless a celebrity was ready to offer his first."

"What if his proved to be a false number?"

"That would be the end of him."

"It seems to me that you got to know Sinatra well."

"I don't see how that is any of your business. But maybe I'll tell you someday."

We were now on our third drink. Six-thirty was certainly approaching. I was studying the pastel curls and whorls of the Mai Tai Lounge which suggested the French curves of a draftsman's template. Through a plate-glass window, I could look out on an enormous pool, amoeboid in shape. Along one arm of that man-made lagoon was a man-made cave and there another bar had been installed where swimmers could sit in their bathing suits. Down the near distance, on the other side of a pedestrian walk, past a wide beach whose packed sand looked to have received fully as much treatment from rolling equipment as a tennis court, were the waves of a lukewarm sea.

I did not know how to pursue the subject of Frank Sinatra. Was he one of the two prominent gentlemen who did not add up when taken together?

"What is it that you want to find out about Sinatra?" I asked.

"That's not the point of our conversation," she replied. "I have no interest in Frank at this time."

"Although he was once your port of choice."

"You have a nasty streak," she said. "And that's just as well. Because what you may discover if we see each other again is that I might prove your equal."

"Nothing could be more nasty than not seeing me again. So, I will tell you. I am sorry."

"Let me make it clear. I do have a port of choice here in Miami. As you put it. Only, he's up in Palm Beach when he's in town. And I am in love with him." She pondered this as solemnly as if she were indeed observing her heart, and said, "Yes, I love him when I am with him."

"All right," I said.

"But I am not often with him. He is a very busy man. In fact, he's incredibly busy right now."

"Well, what can I find out for you?"

"Nothing. In fact, you will never know who this man is."

I swallowed the last of my drink. It was 6:28 and I decided to take one firm St. Matthew's resolve that I would be up and on my way at the hair-crack exactitude of 6:30 P.M. "Then I guess there is nothing to do for you after all."

"You have to stay a minute," she said.

"I don't know if I can."

"Of course you can." It occurred to me that she wasn't altogether unlike my mother. Did imperious women pass on hints to one another along filaments of nocturnal silk? "In fact, this man is so seldom to be seen these days that I'm contemplating a change. There is another man paying a great deal of attention to me."

I took a leap. "Is he a friend of Sinatra's?"

"Yes." She looked at me. "You are good at your work, aren't you?"

I was beginning to wonder if maybe I might be. "Yes," I said, "but I can't do a thing for you unless you tell me his name."

"Well, I can give you his name but it won't be the right one. At least, I'm pretty sure it's not."

"Might be a start."

"I know it's not his real name. Sam Flood. He calls himself that, but I never came across anybody in the newspapers with that name, and he is a man whom others respect so much that he has to be *prominent*."

"How are you certain that he counts for as much as you think?"

"Because Sinatra doesn't respect anyone personally when they're around him, but he respects Sam Flood."

"I'll see you tomorrow night," I said, "same time here. By then I'll know who Sam Flood is."

"I can't meet you. I'm supposed to work the 6:00 P.M. flight tomorrow evening," she told me.

"Why don't you get your executive in Washington to hold you over one more night? I thought you controlled such things."

She took a new measure of me. "All right," she said. "If you can leave a message before 2:00 P.M. tomorrow that you have the real identity of Sam Flood, I will take care of switching my flight day."

We shook hands. I wanted to kiss her again but a glint in her eye suggested that I should not.

8

SINCE I HAD TO SEND A CODED REPORT TO QUARTERS EYE ON HUNT'S lunch with the Frente, it was necessary to go back to Zenith. Once there, it required no more than a hike down the hall to start a search for Mr. Flood.

Back in Washington, at the I-J-K-L, was a large computer called PRECEPTOR available to any Zenith computer linked to Quarters

Eye. PRECEPTOR was reputed to have fifty million names in its data banks. I was not surprised, therefore, when sixteen listings for Sam Flood came back on the printout. Fifteen, however, did not seem notably eligible: a major in the Air Force stationed in Japan, a plumber in Lancashire, England, a Royal Mountie in Edmonton, a black marketeer in Beirut also known as Aqmar Aqbal—why go on? The entry of interest was *Flood, Sam, resides in Chicago and Miami—see WINNOW.*

WINNOW was a computer on a higher level than PRECEPTOR and required a code entry number for ingress. Such information was locked away in Hunt's safe. Since I did not care to wait until morning, I decided to call Rosen. He was bound to be in possession of forty or fifty code entries he was not supposed to hold.

To my agreeable surprise, Rosen was not only in, but entertaining company. I did not have to satisfy him, therefore, on my need to know. He was obliged to get back to his guests.

"I do hate giving out an entry without some sense of your purpose," he nonetheless complained.

"Hunt wants the background on a Cuban exile who we think has a criminal record."

"Oh, well, see!" said Rosen. "You do well to confide in me. WINNOW will just send you on into VILLAINS. You probably need both call groups. Hold it. Here it is. Respectively, the punch-in code is XCG-15, and XCG-17A as in capital A, not sub-a."

"Thank you, Arnie."

"Let's talk when I'm not so busy," he said, "feeding drinks to friends and guzzlers."

Rosen certainly had a sense of where the bodies might be kept. WINNOW did send me on to VILLAINS and there I located Mr. Flood. The printout offered the following agglutination of information:

SAM FLOOD (one of numerous aliases) for MOMO SALVATORE GIANGONO, born in Chicago May 24, 1908. Better known as SAM GIANCANA.

Over 70 arrests for crimes since 1925. Has been booked for assault and battery, assault to kill, bombing suspect, burglary suspect, gambling, larceny, murder.

G.'s staff now estimated at 1,000 "soldiers" in Chicago. G. also maintains ruling position over such

loosely associated small-fry personnel as burglars, collectors, crooked cops, extortioners, friendly judges, friendly politicians, friendly union leaders and businessmen, gamblers, hijackers, hit men (assassins), loan sharks, narcotics peddlers, policy runners, etc., estimated at 50,000 total.

Annual estimated gross in Cook County—2 billion dollars.

NOTE: Above is unverified Chicago and/or Miami police data.

FBI evaluation: Giancana is verified solitary boss of the Chicago syndicate with interests extending from Miami, Havana (now defunct), Cleveland, Hot Springs, Kansas City, Las Vegas, Los Angeles, to Hawaii.

Giancana is one of three largest criminal figures in America (FBI estimate).

I went to sleep bemused. Join the Agency and discover the subterranean palaces of the world! I awoke, however, at four in the morning with one livid phrase in my head: *Giancana is an avatar of evil!* The words drilled through me with the shrill of a tin whistle. What was I getting into? I thought of my first rock face more than ten years ago. Indeed, I had the same thought: One did not have to do this!

When day came, I could pick up the phone and confess failure to Modene Murphy. She would take her 6:00 P.M. flight and see me no more. Then I could report a negative outcome to Harlot and be done with him as well. To keep on, however, as proposed—to hook the mermaid!—might be equal to catastrophe. It was obvious that Modene liked to talk. What I had most enjoyed about her just a few hours ago—that she was indiscreet, and so enabled me to get on with my job —did not delight me now. If we were to have an affair, and she told Sam Flood, well, which one of his fifty thousand hoodlums or one thousand soldiers would break my legs? Honest fear, jumping now like a raw tooth, called for a drink. I tried to estimate the risk. Coldly viewed, how much might it amount to? I could hear Harlot's contempt: "Dear boy, don't snivel. You are not a member of Mr. Giancana's mob and he will not dismember you. Recollect—you belong to the campground of the Great White Folk; Sam, willy-nilly, was born into the fold of the dirty plug-uglies. They feel honored when we choose to mix our meat with theirs."

With a second drink, I actually fell asleep. When I awoke at seven, it was another day, another state of expectations, and myself, another man. If my nerves were still awash, I could feel anticipation as well. Call it high funk. I thought again of rock climbing, and those days with Harlot when I awakened each morning to the knowledge that I was very much alive (because, after all, it could be my last day on earth). I was remembering how this sense of oneself as endangered and valuable was not the worst emotion to feel.

I also awoke with a great longing for Modene. By solipsistic measure, I now had one monument of a hard-on. Love for Kittredge, no matter how grand, could not subsist forever, I now decided, on letters rarely written and never sent. All the same, I felt conspicuously unfaithful to one-half of myself.

9

"I KNEW IT," MODENE SAID, "YES, I CERTAINLY KNEW IT. SAM HAD TO be out of the ordinary."

She was reading my summary of the printout from VILLAINS for the third time. "Oh, it seems to add up," she said, "but it doesn't." "Why not?"

"Because I feel safe with Sam."

I debated for a minute whether to introduce her to the paradoxical potentialities of Alpha and Omega, but then it occurred to me that I might like Fidel Castro if I met him, and there were those who said that Stalin and Hitler had been known to charm a few. Who could keep a true monster from presenting a wholly agreeable Alpha?

"You know," she said, "Sam is an absolute gentleman."

"One wouldn't expect that, would one, after reading this?"

"Well, of course, I had the advantage of not knowing who he was. So I could study him for himself. He is very cautious with women."

"Do you believe he is afraid of them?"

"Oh, no. No, no. He *knows* women. He knows them so well that he's cautious. You ought to see him when he takes me shopping. He knows exactly what I want and how large a present I will allow him to buy me. For instance, it's now understood between us that I won't accept any gift that comes to more than five hundred dollars."

"Why draw the line there?"

"Because the gift is still modest enough so that I owe him nothing. After all, I am giving him nothing."

"Is that because you are otherwise engaged with your other two dates?"

"Are you condescending to me?"

"No," I said, "I'm actually furious."

"Yes," she said, "there you are, sipping a Pimm's Cup, looking just as cool as that ridiculous piece of cucumber they put in it, and you are pretending to be furious."

She was wearing green shoes and a green silk dress as green as her eyes. That was the only visible change from the day before. We were at the same cocktail table in the same near-empty lounge by the same plate-glass window looking out on the pool and pancake beach and it was 6:00 P.M. again. A long brutal summer afternoon in Miami might be descending toward evening outside, but we were ensconced in the timeless comfort of drinking our way into twilight, and four in the morning of last night was far away. I leaned forward and kissed her. I do not know if it was my reward for punctual delivery, or whether she might even have been waiting for twenty-four hours to kiss me again, but I felt in some small peril. It might not be impossible to fall in love with Modene Murphy. The superficial precision with which she spoke was only a garment one could strip from her; beneath, unprotected, must be desire, as warm and sweet, as hot and out of hand as perhaps it was supposed to be. I knew now what she meant by earthy.

"That's enough," she said, "that's enough of that," and pulled herself back a critical couple of inches. I did not know whether to be more impressed with her or myself. I had never had such an effect on a girl, no, not even Sally. My only question was where to take her—would she possibly allow us to go to her room?

She wouldn't. She sat there beside me, and told me I had to respect her rule. Did I have a pen, she asked. I did. She drew a small circle on a napkin, then divided it with a vertical diameter. "This is the way I lead my life," she said. "I have one man in each half of the circle, and that has to be sufficient."

"Why?"

"Because outside this circle is chaos."

"How do you know?"

"I don't know how I know, but it's clear to me. Do you think

I could actually go around kissing everyone the way I just kissed you?"

"I hope not. May I kiss you again?"

"Not here. People are still looking at us."

Three middle-aged tourist couples sat at three separate tables considerably removed from one another. It was summer in Miami Beach. Poor Fontainebleau. "If you won't," I said, "give up your man in Washington, then why don't you relinquish the one in Palm Beach?"

"I wish I could tell you who he is. You would understand."

"How did you meet him?"

She was obviously proud of herself. It was evident she wished to tell me, but she shook her head.

"I don't believe in your circle," I said.

"Well, I haven't lived this way all my life. For two years the only man was Walter."

"Walter from Washington?"

"Please don't talk about him that way. He's been kind to me."

"But he's married."

"It doesn't matter. He loved me and I don't love him, so it's fair. And I didn't want anyone else. I was a virgin when I met him." She gave her gutty little laugh again, as if the most honest part of her must come forth from time to time. "Well, of course, I soon started to have another fellow now and again, but the second half of the circle did stay vacant much of the time. That's when you should have come along."

"Kiss me once more."

"Stay away."

"Next thing, Sinatra walked into your picture."

"How do you know?"

"Perhaps I feel close to you."

"You are up to something," she said. "You may want me but you're up to something."

"Tell me about Sinatra," I said.

"I can't right now, and I won't. I will say that he ruined it."

"Will you ever tell me about that?"

"I don't think I can. I have determined that one's life should never extend beyond the full rule of the circle."

I was thinking: I am falling in love with another woman who likes nothing better than to talk about herself in her own self-created jargon.

"Why don't you give up Walter," I said, "and let me enter the circle?"

"He has seniority," she said.

"Then take a furlough from the guy in Palm Beach. You never see him."

"How would you feel if he came back," she said, "and I said good-bye to you?"

"I might try to keep the new status quo."

Her laugh came forth as if she liked me enormously, but I was, no matter how you looked at it, ridiculous.

"What is the first name of our fellow from Palm Beach?" I asked. "I can't keep calling him Palm Beach."

"I'll tell because it won't do you any good. It's Jack."

"Walter and Jack."

"Yes."

"Not Sam and Jack?"

"Definitely not."

"Nor Frank and Jack?"

"Negative."

"But you did meet Jack through Sinatra?"

"Oh, my God," she said, "you've guessed right again. You must be terrific in your profession."

I did not say it aloud: I had so little to choose from, that Sinatra had become the only option.

"Now, you have to go," she said.

"No, I don't. I'm free this evening."

"Well, I have a date once again. With Sam," she said.

"Break it."

"I can't. When I make a date with someone, it's a contract. Ironbound and lockjaw. That's me." She threw a kiss wordlessly from three good feet away, but in the pursing of her lips and their release, a zephyr of tenderness floated over. "I go out tomorrow at 8:00 A.M.," she said, "and won't be back for more than a week."

"More than a week!"

"I'll see you," she said, "when I return from Los Angeles."

"Unless Jack is with you."

"He won't be. I know that much."

"Why," I asked, "are you going to L.A.?"

"Because," she said, "Jack invited me. I arranged to get the time off from work."

I went back to Zenith again. PRECEPTOR, when queried, came in with a five-page printout on SINATRA, FRANK. Under *friends and acquaintances*, was a considerable list with but one Jack, *Jack Entratter, Sands Hotel,* and the note: *might be member of The Clan.* After this, came an entry: *for The Clan, see WINNOW.*

I did not have to go on to VILLAINS. There in WINNOW, under *The Clan,* were: *Joey Bishop, Sammy Cahn, Sy Devore, Eddie Fisher, Sen. John Fitzgerald Kennedy, Pat Lawford, Peter Lawford, Dean Martin, Mike Romanoff, Elizabeth Taylor, Jimmy Van Heusen.*

I sent an unsigned telegram to Harlot in Georgetown. SINCE OUR FRIENDS TURN OUT TO BE JUAN FIESTA KILLARNEY AND SONNY GARGAN-TUA ISN'T IT TIME TO DELIVER YOUR GOODS TO THE FIELD?

I did not believe that Jack from Palm Beach could possibly be equal to John Fitzgerald Kennedy, ready in Los Angeles to be nomi-nated for President at the Democratic Convention, and yet Ockham's Razor was always there to remind me that the simplest explanation ready to explain all the facts was bound to be the correct explanation. I did not have too many facts, but all the ones in hand fit Jack Kennedy. I had no difficulty in sleeping, for I did not try. Harlot called the motel at six in the morning and the proprietor, blind in one eye, did not look much better in the other when I answered the knock on the door that summoned me to the motel office phone.

"Try not sending open telegrams," was how Harlot began. "Suc-cess has left you manic."

He was not slow to the point. I was to come to Washington immediately.

10

TWO CUBAN EXILES, REPORTING TO ME ON THE UNDECLARED ACTIVI-ties of their political groups, had to be serviced this same day in morning and afternoon appointments at two safe houses twenty miles apart. Not able to reach the second agent in advance, I could only tell Harlot that he would have to wait for my late afternoon departure. On arrival, I took a cab from National Airport to his house in George-town, and in the antique dining room we ate hamburgers and de-frosted french fries, a detail I recall because he put them in the pan himself. It was the cook's night off and Harlot commented that as a boy in Colorado he had rarely eaten anything else for supper, which was one of the very few items about his childhood he ever imparted to me.

"Whom did you eat with?" I asked.

He shrugged. "I ate alone."

He got up from the table, led me to his office, opened a double-width attaché case to show a three-inch stack of files, then locked the case and handed me the key. "This is all yours for now," he said, "and you are to keep these papers in your safe at Zenith."

"Yessir."

"I don't want you leaving any of this out on your desk during the day, nor keeping one scrap of paper in your motel." In the course of our low-amenities dinner, he had inquired about security arrangements at Zenith and the shape of my living conditions at the Royal Palms.

"Well," he said now, "how would you characterize the situation?"

"Incredible."

"Kennedy's role is clear enough to me. If elected, he will be our first priapic President since Grover Cleveland. But just what is going on with the other one, Gargantua, as you thought to put it in that *circus* telegram?"

"I was heedless."

"You were intoxicated with yourself. In our work, that's equal to catching typhus."

"Who could comprehend my meaning but you?" I asked.

"J. Edgar Buddha, for one. You simply don't have the expertise to send open telegrams."

"Yessir."

"Go in for one more gaffe of this dimension, and you won't work for me again."

"Yessir."

He cleared his throat as if to declare a new venue. "Now for the hygiene. The project will be referred to as HEEDLESS. Giancana will be called RAPUNZEL. Kennedy—IOTA. Let Sinatra be STONE-HENGE. The girl ought to have a man's name. How about BLUE-BEARD?"

I nodded; unhappily, I nodded.

"Her old high school friend, Wilma Raye, with whom—you will

discover—she talks all the time, can be AURAL. With an A-U, not an O—A-U-R-A-L.

"Yessir."

"I haven't had the time to go through four bloody inches of transcript. I've merely skimmed the stuff. You are to digest all the provenance in this attaché case and summarize it for me. Leave out nothing essential. It's FBI product, but the transcription, while electronically refined, is still garbled. Par for the Bureau. So clean it up for me. I want the essentials. When transcriptions are too diffuse, summarize the take. Extract from the mess some purchase on the comings and goings of this enterprising Bluebeard."

He looked at me carefully. "Will you be able to bed the wench?"

"Fifty-fifty." The answer popped out of me. "I have to wonder if I'm qualified."

"I'm sure that's what all the Soviet joy-boys say before the KGB sends them out. I say: Become her confidant. Of course, you must try not to leave your voice on FBI tapes. Take her to a different hotel room each time."

"That's expensive."

He looked gloomy indeed.

"Will you authorize me to use safe houses?" I asked. "I can think of several in Miami that are not bad."

"Oh, Lord, we're stepping on the Torah now, aren't we?" He pondered the possible hazards. "Let's commence with hotel rooms," he said. "If expenses get out of hand, we'll reconsider the safe-house option."

"Yessir." I paused. "Assuming I reach the exalted place, we do have to look at other difficulties."

"Trot them forth."

"What with the FBI tapping her phone at the Fontainebleau, they are bound to hear her mention Harry Field sooner or later when she talks to friends. She may even suspect that Field is an Agency man. That's no wild supposition in Miami. The FBI could get a fix on me."

He nodded. "Is there any way to get the girl not to talk about you?"

"Perhaps I can convince her that RAPUNZEL will break my legs if she doesn't protect me."

"Well, that might stanch the drear and open wound of verbosity."

He winked. "Do you know, if not for my duties to the Agency, I might have been just as talkative as she is."

"You?" I said. "Like her?"

"In our work, the impulse to divulge a secret is comparable to strong sexual desire in priests." He clapped me on the back with considerable amusement, as if once again I could have no idea whether he was winching away on my leg. "Old sport," he said, "there's a midnight plane to Miami. Let's get you back."

He drove me to the airport, a rare courtesy from Harlot. On the way, I picked up nerve sufficiently to ask about Kittredge and Christopher.

"I see them once a month," he said slowly, as if weighing his trust in me. "We have fond reunions in Maine. But, yes, Harry, it is lonely. Of course, it has to be. She is working on a book."

"Is it going well?"

"The portion Kittredge showed me is remarkable, in my opinion. Wonderful on narcissism. She has a new theory I've not come across before, and Alpha and Omega work out very well in it. Narcissists, by her measure, are people whose most powerful human relations all take place within themselves. It's brilliant, and I hope others see it so. She needs the recognition, does our girl." He stared straight ahead, his hands on the wheel. "Kittredge is also a remarkably good mother to Christopher. The little boy is splendid. I miss him in ways I can't even begin to describe to myself."

We pulled up to the airline entrance and he shook my hand. "Let's have some fun with this. Our work is cruel until we learn how much fun can be found in it."

I slept on the plane. I was tired enough to sleep again when I reached Miami, but I went off first to my office, put the contents of the attaché case in my safe, and then caught another couple of hours on top of my desk which, as a bed, was one foot, unhappily, too short. I dreamt that RAPUNZEL had fifty thousand trolls tying my legs with spider's thread.

11

HARLOT AND I WERE COMMUNICATING WITHIN THE CONTINENTAL United States, and so I could send long cables into a special code box at GHOUL with as much confidence as if I were employing a secure phone. One's working life, in consequence, was not overly beset with security procedures. My emotional life, however, took one fell whack. How could I wish to refer to Modene as BLUEBEARD? Harlot's insistence on these ugly-headed cryptonyms struck me as punishment for the open telegram. Of course, Hugh's great-grandfather on his mother's side had been a mule skinner whose animals were legendary for being able to start up on a steep hill under a heavy load: Mean genes doubtless persevered best—employing Harlot's cryptonyms made me feel like one of those mules. It was not all that easy to delve into Modene's past relations with Sinatra, Kennedy, and Giancana, but I also had to suffer from the transmogrification of her name to BLUEBEARD. That was, yes, a whack on my emotional life. A woman out of my measure—how could I judge whether she was a palace cat or an over-passionate angel?—was now to be charted like a migratory bird with a research number banded to her leg. All good and great jobs sooner or later prove cruel, I kept telling myself.

SERIAL: J/38,741,651
ROUTING: LINE/GHOUL—SPECIAL SHUNT
TO: GHOUL-A
FROM: FIELD   10:00 A.M. JULY 10, 1960
SUBJECT: HEEDLESS
            Since security in these communications is not at issue, and the real names are employed in the FBI transcripts, I wonder if we can dispense with the cryptonyms? BLUEBEARD et al., is seriously off-putting.
            Await your immediate instructions.

                                                                    FIELD

    They came in an hour, and on *low-privilege circuit*, a way of reminding me that SPECIAL SHUNT was at Harlot's terminal, and I did not have the means to decipher a special code. He also signed it GAINS-

BOROUGH, a substitute for GHOUL. Any word beginning with a G that also contained at least two of the four remaining letters, H, O, U, and L could suffice. (GUINEVERE, for instance, would not do— it had only a U to go with the G, but GASHOUSE, with H, O, and U, certainly would.)

SERIAL: J/38,742,308
ROUTING: LINE/ZENITH—OPEN
TO: ROBERT CHARLES
FROM: GAINSBOROUGH   11:03 A.M. JULY 10, 1960
SUBJECT: SECURE PHONE
          Call me immediately.

                                        GAINSBOROUGH

It took an hour to get through. "I'm inclined to indulge you," Harlot began. "It does, however, set a dreadful precedent. Real names, you see, distort our judgment. Especially for big game. Sediment has already collected, you see, in our evaluation from old newspaper stories. Whereas an ill-fitting cryptonym can stimulate insights. Wrenches one's mind-set out of context."

"Yessir." I felt as if I were back in a Low Thursday. Sitting in the airless plywood booth that housed our secure phone, a first drop of perspiration made its virgin run down my back.

"I can see your side of it, however," he went on. "This is out of the ordinary course of things. The prime question is whether the material is ultrasensitive or farcical. So, write your report with cryptonyms, or without. Shift back and forth when the impulse takes you. We do want to find out who is doing what to whom, don't we?"

"I appreciate your flexibility," I said.

"Good. Now, you be equally open."

"Yessir."

He hesitated, as if looking for some way to offer a verb its cryptonym. "Would you say, Harry, that the girl might prove out choice in the hay?"

I took my time to answer. "Hugh," I said at last, "on the basis of the evidence so far, I would expect the hay to be a most positive factor in her relations."

"Good fellow. Go to work," he said, and hung up.

SERIAL: J/38,749,448
ROUTING: LINE/GHOUL—SPECIAL SHUNT
TO: GHOUL-A
FROM: FIELD   8:47 P.M. JULY 10, 1960
SUBJECT: HEEDLESS

The key question is BLUEBEARD's veracity. She seems artless. She speaks easily of matters others might keep secret. Yet one soon discovers that she is not without gifts for mendacity. For example, my first understanding of her personal situation was that her personal life had been maintained in two halves, each complete, one with a man in Palm Beach she would not name (IOTA) and the other with an airline executive called Walter.

This considerable misperception, provided by her, lasted until I learned through her telephone conversations early this year on Jan. 3 and Jan. 5, 1960, with AURAL that Walter had been asked to walk the plank shortly after STONEHENGE entered BLUEBEARD's life. While BLUEBEARD certainly enjoyed the perks Walter's executive position brought to her flight job, STONEHENGE must have made it clear that with his wide range of contacts, a felicitous work schedule could be continued mit or mitout her married boyfriend. Exit Walter. If this sounds cold-blooded, I expect it is.

BLUEBEARD's continuing relationship with Walter was, however, maintained with me as a fiction. Perhaps it has workaday use for such everyday suitors as FIELD. The only firm conclusion, however, is that she can lie with authority.

Now, to our chronology. I am going to speak of the period from December 10, 1959, to January 10, 1960, as High Stonehenge. Modene met Sinatra while working the flight from Washington to Miami on December 10 and, given her ability to attract attention, we can take it as in the course of things that Sinatra would invite her to be his guest for the following weekend in Las Vegas.

In her numerous phone calls to AURAL during this period, she provides a portrait of the STONEHENGE milieu. Sinatra had reserved a suite for her at the Sands Hotel, and when she demurred at the cost, making the point that she could not afford it herself, nor equally could she permit his generosity, he laughed and said, "Honey, you're with me. The hotel will eat the tab."

Las Vegas, December 17–19, 1959. Sinatra keeps a large bungalow at the Sands in an enclave of other similar bungalows reserved for the Clan, and has been known to spend day and night drinking on the patio adjoining the pool that is used exclusively by himself and the Clan. (Present membership is Joey Bishop, Sammy Cahn, Sammy Davis, Jr., Eddie Fisher, Peter Lawford, Dean Martin.) As Modene describes it to Willie Raye (AURAL), the Clan impresses her as well named.

During the transcript of a telephone conversation with Willie, Modene says, "That first day around the pool was as awful as the first day in a new school. They talk in a special code. Somebody says 'Ring-a-ding,' and everybody starts to laugh. That is, everybody knew when to laugh but me."

From: *Transcript Dec. 21, 1959*:

WILLIE: I'd have packed my bags and left.

MODENE: I nearly did. If not for Frank, I would have.

WILLIE: Did he save the day?

MODENE: Well, not at first. I have to tell you. It was a shock seeing him in Vegas. He was all gotten out in his favorite colors. Orange and black. He has no taste whatsoever. He keeps bird-of-paradise flowers in his suite. In case you don't know, they're orange and black.

WILLIE: It couldn't have been that bad.

MODENE: Well, it wasn't. But only because they kept playing his songs around the pool.

WILLIE: Did it work?

MODENE: Well, we did get together.

At this point of working on my report to Harlot, somewhere after ten o'clock of an air-conditioned evening in the recirculated nicotine air of empty Zenith offices, I confess that I stopped typing for a moment and ground my teeth just once. If these details were likely to prove as fascinating to Hugh Montague as the first accounts of life on Uranus, I was denigrating some elusive filament of feeling in myself. This girl-woman, vain as a male lion and able to travel in the company of royal gorillas and a bona fide presidential candidate, had nonetheless responded in some degree to me. I was ready to believe that if we ever went to bed, we might each find a way out of the labyrinths of the past. Wasn't every improbable love affair a jailbreak? I sat with my fingers poised over my typewriter and wondered if this factual rundown of the behavior of Modene would injure something in the nature of the escape.

From: *Transcript Dec. 21, 1959* (cont'd.):

WILLIE: Is Frank as good as they say?
MODENE: He might be.
WILLIE: He doesn't look that well built.
MODENE: Frank doesn't have to be.
WILLIE: I guess he knows how to get a mood going?
MODENE: He's considerate. He knows the importance of details. Under his shell is a gentle and sensual man. He doesn't even ask for something back. He's the active one.
WILLIE: Who would ever believe it?
MODENE: Unselfish.
WILLIE: You're describing a paragon.

Ten days later, Modene spends the New Year's weekend at Sinatra's house in Palm Springs. Similar conversations ensue with Willie—"I love him when he makes love. He is so full of finesse." During the day, while Modene sits in the living room, Frank rehearses new songs with a pianist. Sinatra will walk around the room, repeat a few bars, and squeeze her arm or shoulder whenever he passes. Hours go by. "Frank," Modene explains to Willie, "is on stage so much, that he loves to stay home when he's not. It's restful."

WILLIE: It sounds like bliss.
MODENE: I love Palm Springs.
WILLIE: How is his house furnished?
MODENE: Oriental in motif.
WILLIE: That little Italian guy must think he's the Devil.
MODENE: He knows how to get power. (Jan. 4, 1960)

When they meet again, however, in Palm Springs on January 17, an episode occurs. Excerpt from transcript of January 20:

MODENE: It's over.
WILLIE: You aren't serious?

MODENE: I will never allow myself to be that positive about a man again.

WILLIE: What happened?

MODENE: He destroyed it.

WILLIE: How?

MODENE: I won't talk about it.

WILLIE: That's awfully cruel of you. To excite my curiosity and then frustrate it.

MODENE: He wanted me to enter a situation that I could not enter. Not with him. Not under any circumstances.

WILLIE: I see you're going to stick little pins in me and poke them around.

MODENE: He tried to introduce another girl into our bed.

WILLIE: What?

MODENE: I'd had a little too much champagne, and I went to sleep early. When I woke up, there was a tall black girl in the same king-size bed with us. She was practicing you-know-what on him. He waved for me to join them.

WILLIE: What did you do?

MODENE: It's so picayune. I began to cry.

WILLIE: Well, of course.

MODENE: I don't like to cry. When I do, I can't stop. I just went into the bathroom and cried for half an hour, and when I came out, the girl was gone, and Frank was wholly apologetic. I told him it was a little late in the day for regrets. I was overplaying my hand, but I didn't care. My vanity has never been so injured. He finally shrugged and said, "You're great, you're even kind of scintillating, but, honey, let's face it, you could be too square for me." "Frank," I told him right back, "I am not going to be the one to apologize."

WILLIE: You did have a particularly strong reaction.

MODENE: Well, it wasn't prudish. Believe me, I've never done anything like that, although I suppose I could.

WILLIE: *Modene!*

MODENE: If I didn't love a man but did enjoy him on the earthy side, and didn't think anyone was going to get hurt, well, I might join a threesome, or I might not.

WILLIE: Couldn't you say that to Frank?

MODENE: I did. I slept in the guest bedroom that night and I locked the door. But in the morning, I did explain my point of view. He said, "Well, where's the fire, then? You're not solid square." "You missed the entire point," I told him. "Which is?" he asked. "Frank," I said, "I adored the tenderness you offered. But I made the mistake of thinking that such intimacy was for me. Last night I realized that you feel kindred emotions for all women. They are part of your music. It just broke my heart when I realized it wouldn't be me alone."

WILLIE: Modene, I've always said you have no fear of the bottom line, good or bad.

MODENE: Well, he did react. He held me at a little distance and put his hands on my forearms and said, "In two weeks, I am going to kill myself when I realize that you were the one for me." I started laughing. I had to. He was such a funny little guy at the moment. Almost a jerk. But he was acting that way on purpose, trying to sidle his way back into my affections. I said, "Oh, Frank, let's remain friends." Do you know what happened then?

WILLIE: Of course not.

MODENE: An expression came into his face of a sort I had not seen before. I have seen him get angry and ugly toward a couple of his hangers-on, and he can be death to strangers who butt into his mood in public, but I never saw him look calculating before. He said, "All right, we'll be friends. You will have a valuable friend in me," and I felt as if I'd been shifted as neatly as you please from one part of his brain to the other.

WILLIE: Sounds sinister.

MODENE: Well, I'm exaggerating. But it certainly was one of those click-click moments. (Jan. 20, 1960)

It may be significant that she is soon introduced to IOTA. It is now 1:00 A.M., so I will send out what I have here, and resume tomorrow afternoon, which I have succeeded in reserving for this work.

FIELD

12

SERIAL: J/38,759,483
ROUTING: LINE/GHOUL—SPECIAL SHUNT
TO: GHOUL-A
FROM: FIELD   3:11 P.M. JULY 11, 1960
SUBJECT: HEEDLESS

Two weeks later, on Feb. 5, 1960, STONEHENGE called BLUEBEARD in Miami. Would she come out to Palm Springs? "The star man is going to pop in," stated the singer, a reference to IOTA.

"What if your friend doesn't show up?" Modene asks.

"You can take the next flight home."

Modene describes it to AURAL as a typical Palm Springs weekend for Sinatra. Celebrities, friends, and business associates fly in from Los Angeles, Las Vegas, and La Jolla, but Modene finds herself put up by Sinatra at the Desert Door (which she considers second-rate), and spends the first twenty-four hours in Palm Springs taking taxis out to Sinatra's home, then going back to the Desert Door again. IOTA has not made an appearance, and she is ready to return to Miami. "Aren't I good enough for you?" jeers Sinatra, and assures her that she is mistaken—Jack Kennedy is definitely coming. (In recounting this to AURAL, Modene confesses to a Friday-night bout of paranoia; she suspects that should Senator Kennedy arrive, Sinatra will exercise a species of revenge by not introducing her.)

Kennedy, however, shows up next day with his entourage, and takes a suite at Modene's hotel. "I had everything wrong," she remarks. "I thought the Ingleside Inn was where you were supposed to go, but now I discovered that Frank had put me up at the most exclusive place in town, although if you weren't in on that little fact, you could hardly distinguish the Desert Door from a dude ranch."

The above is taken from the FBI transcript of her phone call to AURAL on Feb. 17, 1960, a few days after the weekend.

> WILLIE: Is Jack incredibly handsome?
> MODENE: I think he could have been a movie star.
> WILLIE: What was he wearing?
> MODENE: Gray flannels and a dark blue sport jacket. He looked very well groomed. His appearance, actually, is fabulous. His

teeth are as white as teeth can ever be, and he has a suntan which sets off his eyes. They're crinkly Irish eyes with an intimate twinkle as if both of you know something that nobody else does.

WILLIE: You had that much of a reaction just shaking hands?

MODENE: Well, it was all I had for a while. Two of his sisters were in the group, and a whole flock of men and women I didn't know, and they were all unbelievably adept at knowing how to steer you away from the inner circle. I wasn't going to take a bony elbow in my boobs just to get a little nearer to this man —I drifted away. Do you know, ten minutes later, he found me in the lobby and made a lunch date for the next day. He even apologized for not being able to see me that night. Political fund-raiser, he explained.

WILLIE: Frank didn't invite you to that?

MODENE: They use a phrase out here to describe people who contribute a lot of money—heavy hitters. Only heavy hitters are invited, I suppose. Although I do blame Frank. He has a way of bringing you up, dropping you back, and then beckoning to you to come forward again. Willie, it is much easier to be Frank's romantic interest than his friend.

WILLIE: It sounds like a bad evening for you.

MODENE: A couple of the Senator's political assistants tried to invite me to dinner, but I ate alone in my room. That was, to say the least, somewhat below my expectations. If it hadn't been for the lunch date he promised, I would have left in the morning.

WILLIE: But you did get to be alone with him next day?

MODENE: Yes. He suggested we have lunch on my patio, not his, so that we wouldn't be interrupted.

WILLIE: Wasn't he afraid of gossip?

MODENE: There are so many women after him that gossip wouldn't know where to start.

WILLIE: What did you talk about? I would have been paralyzed.

MODENE: As we were sitting down, just the two of us, I can't say I felt in command of the situation. But he is, in my opinion, a superb politician. He actually got me to believe that he was genuinely interested in what I had to say. He has the gift of making you feel that the two of you are equal. When he asks questions, he listens carefully to the answers. He wants to know all about you. I found out afterward that except for his time in the Navy, he's lived a very privileged life, and I would guess he's looking for a little more of the common touch. To make up for the gap, I suppose, in his knowledge of ordinary people. He was fascinated with the fact that I was a cheerleader in high school. Also with the fact that I am an only child. He comes from such a large family. And, of course, he supposed I was Catholic, although I explained that it was only on my father's side and that was long lapsed, and we weren't a church-going family. "How do you feel about voting for a Catholic?" Jack asked. I was going to tell him that it made no difference to me, but I knew he wanted more of an answer, so I said I was thinking of one person who swore he would never vote for a Catholic because he hated the Church so, having once been Catholic himself. Well, the Senator kept after me—who was this person?—would I describe him? Finally, I admitted it was my father. "Is he Republican?" "Lately, maybe," I told him, "but he used to be a union man and a Democrat." A sigh came out of Kennedy, a sad little sound, as if the election might be getting lost right around there, what with all the bitter lapsed Catholics who might come out to vote against him, but then he smiled and said, "Well, I wonder how large a number we have to multiply your father by."

WILLIE: I never would have told him the truth.

MODENE: On the contrary, it broke the concealed layer of ice, if you know what I mean. I felt it would be dumb to give dull answers to him because then his interest would move on. Willie, he is almost like a woman in that one way. I felt that my mind was just as important to him as my looks. When he asked what I thought about voting for a man as young as himself, I said that would certainly be an obstacle with voters who had their minds made up in advance, but since most of them were Republicans anyway, it might not matter. His youth would be an asset, I told him, if he could get the voters to realize all the advantages of having a young man in office. The president is part of everybody's family, I told him. Eisenhower, for instance, is everybody's uncle. He really is Uncle Ike. "Well, then," said Senator Kennedy, "where do I fit in? Am I to see myself as the nephew?" "Oh, no," I said, "you have to be the attractive young man who is marrying into the family. If they feel you're going to fit in, they'll accept you, but it's even better if they think the family itself is going to be more fun once you're a part of it."

WILLIE: You said all that to him? You amaze me. I didn't know you ever thought about these things.

MODENE: I never did. He brings it out in you. I feel awfully bright around him. I could have fallen for him just for that alone. We certainly kept talking.

WILLIE: I would have quit while I was ahead.

MODENE: Not me. He asked what I thought of Nixon, and, as you are well aware, all I know is what I see on television. But Jack encourages you to respond to your instinct when you're with him, so I said, "I think Vice President Nixon is your biggest advantage. Deep down, people don't like him." "Why?" he asked. "Because," I said, "he looks hungry. People don't like someone who's always hungry. It gets them uneasy." "Well, why?" he repeated. "Because," I said, "hungry people make us wonder if there is any real peace anywhere." "If you're right about Nixon, that is certainly good news," he said, "provided I win," and when we both laughed, he said, "I've enjoyed this lunch enormously. I wish I could spend the rest of the afternoon with you, but I'm on a plane in an hour. However, I want very much to see you again. I meet a lot of people and you're rare, you know. You belong to yourself alone."

WILLIE: I would call that a consummate compliment.

MODENE: I was ready to shine his shoes. He took my phone number and said he would be happy to give me his except that it would have no useful meaning right now since he slept in a different town every night. It was going to remain that way for months to come. He'd call me very soon, he said. (Feb. 17, 1960)

IOTA proves to be a man of his word. From February 16 to March 3, 1960, we have transcripts of eight phone calls to BLUE-BEARD. On Feb. 25, in Denver, he proposes meeting on the night of March 3 at the Waldorf-Astoria. She agrees, and the transcripts of calls from Madison, Chicago, Wheeling, and Baltimore (Feb. 26, 28, Mar. 1, Mar. 2) show increasing anticipation.

Given the demands on your time, I offer here only two excerpts—one from Charleston, West Virginia, on February 20, and the other from Baltimore on March 2, the night before they meet at the Waldorf.

BLUEBEARD: Your roses arrived. You couldn't have known that long-stem red roses are just about my favorite flower.

IOTA: Do they sit well in your vase?

BLUEBEARD: They are lavish.

IOTA: Well, I'm glad something works. Today, in West Virginia, Hubert caught us unprepared. Said we were on a campaign spending spree. We had no quick answer for that. West Virginia is a very poor state.

BLUEBEARD: It must be a madhouse at your end.

IOTA: You can't imagine how I look forward to our calls. All day long I know I have a treat waiting. When you are not in, I'm frankly disappointed. (Feb. 20, 1960)

The telephone conversation, March 2, from Baltimore.

IOTA: You promise to be there tomorrow?

BLUEBEARD: I will. I have a confirmed reservation. I will be waiting for your knock on the door.

IOTA: Please don't disappoint me.

BLUEBEARD: You don't know me if you think I would. (March 2, 1960)

On the third of March, their affair is begun. We would learn more if the bug placed in their room by Buddha's technicians had functioned properly, but I expect the job was done under unfavorable conditions. (Private security at the Waldorf Towers is reputed to be excellent.) The transcripts are so garbled that one has to depend on BLUEBEARD's description of the event to AURAL on March 6.

WILLIE: Why won't you admit you slept with him?

MODENE: Of course I did. That's not the issue.

WILLIE: Was it memorable?

MODENE: Let me be.

WILLIE: Are you in love?

MODENE: Probably.

WILLIE: Is he?

MODENE: Aren't men always in love with women for a little while, while they are making love?

WILLIE: I wish I could say that.

MODENE: There is no sense in talking about it. You and I have a different frame of reference.

(silence)

WILLIE: What's wrong?

MODENE: I just don't know. I'm afraid of getting hurt. He sees a thousand people a day.

WILLIE: Well, so do you on a day you're working. Hundreds of people, anyway.

MODENE: But I think only of him.

WILLIE: Is he better in bed than Frank?

MODENE: I don't want to get into that. (March 6)

They quibble for several pages of transcript before the lady is forthcoming.

MODENE: I guess I have two gears: One is always ready to go; the other is a burned-out clutch. Either I get my makeup on fast and it's right, or, curtains—I just keep putting it on again. And I kept thinking I should change my dress. By the time he knocked on the door, I was worn out. I really didn't want to see him. It felt like a ghost story. The girl is madly in love, but does the man exist?

WILLIE: He's pretty real to me.

MODENE: Do try to understand. He was the voice in my ear. For three weeks, I rocked myself to sleep hearing his voice. And every morning, there would be eighteen long-stem red roses. I pricked my finger once while arranging them, and that little thorn hurt me as much as if he had said something cruel without warning. Now we were alone, and I felt too shy to kiss. Then we did, and my lipstick got all over his mouth, and his lips felt like sandpaper. We didn't know how to talk. We were like third cousins who've just been told to get married. And he didn't seem as attractive as in Palm Springs. His face was puffy. "I look terrible, don't I?" he said to me. "Terrible is too strong a word," was the best I could answer. "When you campaign," he said, "you shake hands with so many people you don't really like, and you eat so many meals standing up, and you hear your own voice saying the same thing so many times, that after a while, the part of you that is most alive has gone into hiding down in your gut. That's why politicians have that funny look on their face when campaigning. They're always afraid they are going to break wind.

WILLIE: Break wind? What does that mean?

MODENE: If you don't know, I can't tell you. I would have to use a word I simply won't use.

WILLIE: I get it. *Smelly*. What a crazy president he's going to make.

MODENE: That's what I said. I started laughing. "You're an unbelievable kind of leader," I told him, "because you don't take yourself too seriously." He answered, "The trick is to keep that way." Suddenly I felt comfortable with him again. He is a lot like me.

WILLIE: A lot like you? Modene! You take yourself so seriously.

MODENE: I don't. Not completely. There are layers and layers to me. And to him as well. I believe he is still trying to get to know himself in just the way I am always trying to discover who I am. That's why you have to keep trying for more. Do you know, it was a relief after we finally got to bed.

WILLIE: Who is better, Jack or Frank?

MODENE: You should have been a newspaper reporter. Jack tells me they have one button you can always push. Curiosity. Just get their curiosity up, says Jack, and you can torture them for hours. You are not going to get the answer.

WILLIE: Well, I know who you think is better.

MODENE: I'm not going to ask. (March 6, 1960)

A remark to AURAL (March 9, 1960) speaks of loneliness physical in its intensity—"Now that he's not here, it's as if my insides have been taken away from me." Whole happiness and whole desolation seem to be her relation to IOTA.

STONEHENGE, if I may offer an evaluation, is another matter. STONEHENGE's attentiveness to her needs—the plethora of oral gifts it is suggested he provides—must affect her like a drug, an addiction. Should I pursue? Await your comment.

FIELD

13

Await your comment. Harlot's answer to that query would come back in the morning, but by then I was under the yoke of a massive hangover. The night before, after sending the cable to GHOUL—SPECIAL, I had taken Toto Barbaro out for his long-promised dinner and had made the mistake of matching drinks with him. Now my only consolation was that the drinks had cost me nothing. Howard, to my surprise, proved amenable about putting that dinner on the expense account.

"I'm glad you caught the watch on Barbaro, not me," he even conceded. "Wine him, dine him, pump him for what you can pick up, but promise nothing."

I was weary at the beginning of dinner. I had slept on my desk two nights in a row.

Toto was waiting for me at the restaurant he had chosen. It was Spanish, medieval in décor, dark, and about as expensive as expected. El Rincon de Cervantes was its name, and that was almost squeezed out of my memory by the force of the *abrazo* Barbaro tendered as I came up to the table. He was a powerful man. I began to perceive how a good deal of communication could be put into one hug, for he stood up often that night to embrace Cubans who came by. I took such interruptions as a respite. After many a *golpe* of Cuban rum, and singular varieties of eel and squidlike *tapas,* Barbaro always came back to the budget.

What a weighty presence! He had a large round head, bald but for a collar of cropped gray hair that ran from ear to ear at the back of his neck. Since his head sat bluntly on his shoulders, he would have appeared wholly porcine if not for the scholarly edge of his steel-rimmed eyeglasses. Due to his bulk, he wore black turtleneck shirts, and if he had added a turned-around white collar, he could have been taken for a heavyset priest—no merry fellow to spend time with. Cuban humor seemed for a time as dark as Cuban rum. Over and over, we went back to the budget. After a while, I realized that he did not argue to convince me, but to pound me down. My meat tenderized, I might be less ready to oppose him on something else tomorrow. "Your Eduardo is not generous," he would tell me.

"The decision is made high up," I would reply. "You are only embarrassing Eduardo."

"That is a small discomfort for him, and a large one for me. You offer one hundred and fifteen thousand dollars a month! That is an insult. Our need for money is serious. Can you conceive of how many poor Cubans are among us in Miami? Some are too old to learn a new language, and poorly suited for the excessive speed of life here."

"I brought you ten thousand dollars from Washington."

"Divided by five, it came to two thousand for each of the Frente leaders. It is not even to be dignified by your word—*pittance*."

"Suppose," I said, "that we were to give you the seven hundred and forty-five thousand dollars a month that you request. You are a man of goodwill. You would have to choose between good boats or giving more bread to your poor, and I believe you would choose the bread. Then your military actions would fail to produce results. Your soldiers would be underequipped. So, the man who approved your sum would suffer the consequences. A promising career might come to a quick end. Who in Washington is ready to take such a chance on his career?"

He reached forward to tap two fingers on my chest. "Since you are young, Chico, I will not repeat your lack of discretion to others. But you have just revealed your so-called wealthy Americans to be, in fact, the CIA officers they are."

"I was not speaking properly."

"Speak in any manner you wish, but do not try to convince me that your money-man isn't CIA. I can smell you CIAs."

"I am not one."

"You, Chico? No, not at all. And I am not a Cuban, but a cockroach." He ran his fingers across the table like a centipede in full gallop and roared with laughter at the vehemence of his own humor.

"A rose by any other name can smell as sweet," I offered, and that set him laughing again. When he went back to the budget, it was with less animosity. "Your wealthy American"—*El americano opulento de usted,* were his actual words—"has much to learn about the Cuban people. Without liberty, we degenerate. We become all the bad things you think we are. Under the heel of a master, we react with the viciousness of a slave. We are corrupt, inefficient, untrustworthy, and stupid. No human being is worse than an unhappy Cuban. Put us, however, in command of our own fate and no nation in a military struggle is more resourceful, brave, loyal, and inspired. Our history is to make successful revolutions with only a few hundred people. That is because we are the spirit of true democracy. As José Martí once said,

'*Liberty . . . the essence of life. Whatever is done without it, is imperfect.*' "

"Hear, hear," I said. How the rum was turning in me.

"To your American democracy," he replied, held up his drink, and swallowed it. I did the same.

"Yes," said Toto, "your American democracy may try to comprehend our Cuban democracy, but it cannot. For yours is based on equal votes. But ours is to be found in the intensity of our feelings. When one man has more desire to change history than another man, his vote should count for more. That is how we vote in Cuba. By our feelings. Give me the money, and you will have Cuban democracy. Your money, our blood."

"It's a wonderful premise," I said. "In my country we take such ideas and debate them in high school."

"You are young enough," said Toto, "to be my son. Yet because you work for the wealthy American, you jeer at me. I, however, still need your money to buy guns, so I will try to provide you with a better comprehension of my country. Cuba is a land with one crop. Some say two crops and speak of our tobacco but, in fact, we survive by raising sugar. That is all we can raise to our advantage. Since the world market for sugar fluctuates, our fate has always been out of our control. Our sugar has sold in this century for as little as a penny a pound and for as much as twenty cents. Economically speaking, we are a roulette wheel." He sighed. He laid his heavy hand on my forearm. "We are the tail that is wagged by the economic fluctuations of other people's history. We have, therefore, an abnormal desire to make our own history. Such is the nature of gamblers. We trust our emotions."

The occasion was improving for me. I do not know if it was because of the drinks, but I could follow his Spanish, and he was growing eloquent on the differences in our politics. "The price of failure for an American legislator," he now assured me, "is personal humiliation. Your people measure their value by their ego. When an American loses in politics, he must suffer, therefore, a hole in the ego. But in Cuba, to lose in politics can be equal to losing your life. Assassination is for us, you see, one of the basic forms of rejection. An interesting difference."

"I agree."

"Fidel is a good fellow when you meet him, do you understand?" he said.

"I hear."

"He is the leader of Cuba for a simple reason. *Cojones.* You cannot find a man with more balls."

"Why do you hate him, then?"

"I do not hate him. I disavow him. When I was a student during the early 1930s, I used to support Ramón Grau San Martín. That was of value to Ramón. I was considered the toughest guy in my class, and at the University of Havana we did not measure each other's worth by intelligence. We measured it by our *cojones.* We were the toughest students in the world. You could not be a respected student at the University of Havana if you did not carry a gun. I was number one in my class; my ambition was to eliminate our very corrupt and tainted President then, a man named Machado. I would have succeeded, but our political leader, Ramón Grau San Martín, did not have the *cojones.* When he told me that he would not support us in such a venture, I smashed his desk with my bare hands. Roberto, I lifted it up and hurled it down so hard that it broke apart. I was respected in my day.

"Now, Fidel, in his time, was equally well regarded," said Toto. "I recall that he entered an impromptu contest with other student leaders one day in the late 1940s. A dare. You had to ride your bicycle into a stone wall. At top speed. None of the other leaders could do it. At the last moment, they would turn to the side. Fidel pumped at total velocity into the wall. Then his friends transported him to the clinic. He emerged one hour later with a bandage around his head, a broken nose, and a full speech in his mouth."

"Why do you disavow him?"

"He is irresponsible. He should have been a bandit. Like your ruffian of the West, Billy the Kid. He has the will never to turn back. The greater the danger, the happier his smile. Even though Communism is not temperamentally congenial to him, he responds to it because Communism says: The will of the people is embodied in the will of the leader. That is the only role large enough for Fidel's will. So he puts up with the Communists. In consequence, he is absolutely the worst kind of ruler for Cuba."

"Who would be the best?"

"Oh, Chico, I would say it must be a wise man, a democrat, with a judicious respect for the eternal Cuban balance. Such equilibrium in my country is to be found between compassion and corruption."

"Toto, you do fit the bill."

"I do not take offense. An understanding of reasonable forms of corruption is precisely what Fidel lacks. And Guevara is worse. They do not comprehend the fluvial nature of corruption."

"Fluvial?"

"Like a river. Riverine! Hear me! I oppose greedy plundering. Excessive greed should not be rewarded. But sympathetic corruption —that is another matter. Responsible positions must be responsive to gifts. A modest stream helps to flush away the filth even as it elucidates the seductions of light. Fidel is a man who cannot comprehend the value of corruption. He is too dark in his heart. His errors of judgment are immense. I could name members of your American rackets." He stopped.

"Mobsters?"

"Yes. Men of your rackets. Very large figures. They do not forgive Castro for taking away their casinos. A monumental error. Fidel has inflamed these persons. You do not cut such men off from their rich source of income unless you are willing to kill them."

We had been eating and drinking for more than two hours, and his face was red, his breathing noticeable. Each time he puffed on his cigar, I would be given a sense of the great smoke-mutilated bellows of his lungs. Speak of the fluvial, his breath had its own streambed to traverse. His inhalations rattled on my ear.

Still he spoke. The waiters stood at the back of the room. It was late, but Barbaro called them forth for another *golpe*. I felt myself growing more uneasy than the situation seemed to warrant.

"We Cubans like to declare that the evening waters of Havana Harbor reveal at twilight every color of a peacock's tail. You cannot believe the sight until you see the variegations. Here, in your Biscayne Bay, there are hints of such tropical splendor, but your water looks to the east. So it does not reveal the magic of our Cuban universe. So many colors. Such a disclosure of heavenly and infernal lights. In Havana, we see a reflection on the harbor sea of all our emotional hues. We become aware of what is noble in our existence and what is besmirched; we see the resplendent, the luminous, the sordid, the treacherous. We peer into the very colors of odium. In Havana, at twilight, we see each one of the elemental transitions." He stood up abruptly and said, "I am in over my head," and when I looked at him in some surprise, for whatever speech I had next anticipated was hardly this, he reached for his pillbox, opened it, did not find what he was looking for among a dozen pills in half as many colors as the evening waters of Havana, and then made a circle of his hand and arm to indicate that the meal was over, the evening was gone, and I must put money on the plate for the waiter. "Out of here," he said.

Close to lurching in his gait, yet more peremptory than ever, he took my arm as though guiding me rather than hanging on to my torso for support. We left the restaurant at a controlled gait and proceeded to my car which, given the hour, was alone in the lot.

"Take me to my motel."

He lived in a motor court not far from mine. I drove with every expectation that he would collapse. When I stopped at a light, he waved me through.

"You are having a heart attack," I said.

"*Sí.*"

"Let's go to a hospital."

"Too far." He coughed. "My medicine is sufficient."

Before we reached his room, he was as wet as a hard-worked horse. There was one moment during the ride when he must have thought he was going to die, for, as if I were his brother, he cried out, "Aiiiigh, *hermano!*" and banged his forehead against my shoulder.

Inside his room, he collapsed on the bed, held up his thumb and forefinger to show me the size of the bottle—it certainly was small—and said, *"Nitroglicerina."*

The greatest fear I had at that moment was that I would open the cabinet and not be able to find his bottle, but before I could suffer such anxiety, I saw his medicine. The nitroglycerine label was on one of the seven prescription bottles before me in different hues and sizes. Standing side by side on a small glass shelf, they looked not unlike chess pieces on the back row.

I did not believe what next ensued. He put two small white pills beneath his tongue, excused himself, shut the door to the bathroom, and after a bout of vomiting and other water-closet engagements, came out sufficiently recovered to break open a bottle of *añejo* and insist on another *golpe*. He took his first drink with still another nitroglycerine pill.

"One of these days, I will die of a heart attack," he told me, "and it will come in payment for my gluttony. Such gluttony, Chico, has been my obvious substitute for the *prodigious greed*"—actually he said, *voracidad prodigiosa*—"that I was too honorable to indulge when President of the Senate."

"Olé," I said, and raised my glass.

"One of these days," he repeated, "I am going to die of a heart attack. When I do, you will ask for an autopsy."

"Why?"

"To see whether I was poisoned."

I tried to smile politely. I was feeling the old Hubbard family-imperative: Never respond quickly to an extravagant declaration. "Well," I answered, "could you be somewhat more specific?"

"I will die of a heart attack," he stated once more. "An autopsy can determine whether or not it was chemically initiated."

I sighed. Under the circumstances, it may have been a strange sound to make, but I was not about to take on myself a vow I might not wish to keep. "Only the police," I told him, "or your relatives, Toto, can ask for such an autopsy. I do not fit either category."

"At this moment, you are physically nearer to me than my own son. And you are certainly more elevated than the police. You are able, in fact, to instruct them what to do."

"I cannot even fix a traffic ticket."

"Chico, you need never admit to me that you are CIA, but please do not feel the obligation to keep protesting. I will embarrass you no more than I must. One matter, however, is crucial. A word needs to be sent upstairs." He uncurled one finger in an upward direction. "To our father," he said, and for one moment I thought he was referring to the Father of us all, but then he added with a droll twist to his lips, "Our father who is *your* father."

"You do not even know him," I said.

"I know of his position. It is crucial that your father and I speak to each other."

I could at last perceive Faustino Barbaro's excellent reasons for seeking my company. While I could not say that I liked Toto all that much, I felt, all the same, betrayed.

"I won't attempt to get in touch with my father until I know more."

"This concerns his welfare."

"You are able to protect my father's welfare?"

"Two men have approached me. Bad guys. They claim they are working for him."

"Who are *they*?"

An emanation came off him about as agreeable as lard congealing in a pan. I could feel his fear. "*They* are dispossessed," he said at last.

"Poor people? Cubans?"

"No. Americans. Rich Americans." He looked unhappy. "Think! It is not abstruse."

"Castro expropriated their casinos?" I asked.

By one-quarter of an inch did he nod.

"Let me put this conversation in perspective," I said. "The group I represent has contacts with many kinds of people. I do not see elements of the unusual in what you are telling me."

"That," he said, "is because you are not looking at a conclusion that will anticipate the ultimate. *El último,* Chico."

At this moment, my sense of alarm grew as large as if an emergency vehicle with an outrageous siren had just come around the corner. It occurred to me that Faustino Barbaro's room could certainly be bugged. This conversation might be a provocation.

"I will certify to you," I said, "that in no manner could my father ever be associated with such a project, and so it is folly to speak about it further."

I do not know what was betraying my statement, for it came out in a clear voice, surprisingly authentic to my ears, but Barbaro sat back in his chair, pointed a languid finger at one of the lamps as if to say, "Who knows where *they* have installed their little things?" and gave me the benefit of a slow and impudent wink. "In that case, Chico," he said, "perhaps you will not call Papa after all," looking all the while content as if he knew that no matter what, I must.

I slept that night. Five minutes after I reached the Royal Palms, drink in combination with the events of the evening took me out like a blow from a jackhammer.

14

I WOKE UP WITH A FULL SENSE OF WOE AND WAS STILL HANGING IN THE weight of my hangover when Harlot's reply to yesterday's communication came into Zenith on low-privilege circuit at 10:32 A.M. It was just as well, I decided, that I was there, hangover or not, to receive it.

SERIAL: J/38,761,709
ROUTING: LINE/ZENITH—OPEN
TO: ROBERT CHARLES
FROM: GALILEO   10:29 A.M. JULY 12, 1960
SUBJECT: BABYLON BAZAAR

      May I say that your Babylonians are as strange to me as
Kwakiutl Islanders. Addiction to a plethora of oral gifts? I have always
subsumed the oral under the verbal. In my experience, responsible
people allow but one deviation from the progenitorial compass, to
wit, the age-old practice of bugger-up. There, commemorative
power can be gained at the expense of temporary pollution. (Old
agricultural equation.) Obviously, your Babylonians inhabit other
tierra. I always thought an oral gift was a strawberry sundae. Keep up
this otherwise splendid collaboration. Let all hang high on the hayride.
When crinkly-eyes enters big white mansion, will they deck the halls
with bales of hay for Miss Hayride?

                                                            GALILEO

      I sat at my desk for a half hour. I hesitated to move. To the livid
landscape of my brain was now added the irremovable image of
Kittredge on her knees, Gardiner moon up before the priapic com-
memorations of Hugh Montague. I did not know whether to be in
a rage, full of concern for Hugh's mental condition, or obliged to
recognize I had just been handed my leader's conception of a joke.
      I still had a full day's work ahead of me to be followed by the
nightly stint on HEEDLESS. I decided to ignore Harlot's message.
One would have to live with the possibility that he was now teetering
on some far-off balance board, yes, Hugh Montague, my guide to
fortitude, spirit, Christ, grace, dedication, and master of the rare art of
Intelligence, was also a priapic wahoo!
      Besides, I was full of my own fury. The sexual lavishness of
Modene's life! My past seemed so paltry. What had I to muster but
Montevidean whores, plus one sordid affair with Sally Porringer?
Modene's description of Sinatra—"gentle, active, earthy"—cut into
me like a stiletto. There was one question I did not care to ask myself.
Could I make a better lover? The answer had to be: Not likely! Not
with the Hubbard synapses!
      I made a visual study of my surroundings for the next few minutes.
It was a mode of procedure I often employed for restoring concentration. If I have not described any office I have worked in through these
years, there has been little need. The walls are always white, off-white,
yellow, tan, or pale green. The furniture is metal and gunboat-gray.
The desk chairs are white, brown, gray, or black, offer pads for your
seat, and can swivel from desk blotter to typewriter stand. The visitor's

chair is plastic: yellow, red, orange, or black. The floor, when not covered in gray linoleum, offers green or brown carpeting. The choice of photographs is unofficially limited. If I had a good snapshot of Modene, I would not have kept it on my desk. It would have stood out more than a bottle of ketchup. I did have a map of southern Florida on one wall, a map of Cuba on the other, and on the partition between was a calendar with twelve photographs of Maine harbors. I had a dark green wastebasket, an oak end table with an ashtray, a mirror near the door, a metal bookcase with four shelves, and a small cast-iron safe. In addition to fluorescent lighting plugged into a rack overhead, I had a desk lamp. I had had offices like this in every place I worked for the Agency, and I was yet to have an office of my own where the walls reached the ceiling. On my floor at Zenith, in a large loft-sized space, were eighty such stalls.

Sometimes I would decide that the purpose of such installations was to keep the mind working when the brain was ready to come apart. My gray, partitioned walls looked back at me like a pale blackboard on which all the writings had been many times erased. I took up my work again. Not until evening did I return an answer to Montague.

SERIAL: J/38, 762, 554
ROUTING: LINE/GHOUL—SPECIAL SHUNT
TO: GHOUL-A
FROM: FIELD   11:41 P.M. JULY 12, 1960
SUBJECT: HEEDLESS

Aware of your reactions, I will try to be more succinct.

On March 4, 5, 8, 11, and 14, there are phone calls, IOTA to BLUEBEARD, from Concord, New Hampshire; Harrisburg, Pennsylvania; Indianapolis; and Detroit. Long-stem roses, eighteen to a bouquet, are delivered every day. The conversations address themselves warmly to their next meeting.

On March 17, however, comes a shift in tone. A phone call, IOTA–BLUEBEARD, is received at the Willard Hotel in Washington. Transcription is, I fear, seriously garbled.

IOTA: Has Frank called you?
BLUEBEARD: Not recently.
IOTA: I tried to get you in Miami Beach last night.

BLUEBEARD: What a pity. I happened to be out.

IOTA: I hope it was with a good friend.

BLUEBEARD: Oh, just a stewardess I work with.

IOTA: (garbled)

BLUEBEARD: (garbled)

IOTA: (garbled)

BLUEBEARD: (garbled)

IOTA: Yes, of course. Why wouldn't you want to go to the opening of Frank's show at the Fontainebleau?

BLUEBEARD: I *have* been looking forward to it.

IOTA: How long will Frank be in Miami?

BLUEBEARD: Ten days.

IOTA: What a good opportunity to see him.

BLUEBEARD: (garbled)

IOTA: I want to plan a date for us at the Waldorf on the 26th. Will you arrange your flight schedule around that?

BLUEBEARD: Of course. But . . .

IOTA: Yes?

BLUEBEARD: The date seems so far away.

IOTA: (garbled)

> The rest is garbled. (Mar. 17, 1960)

From March 18 to March 31, while Sinatra is playing an engagement at the Fontainebleau, BLUEBEARD makes four round-trip flights between Miami and Washington. When off-duty, she stays at the Fontainebleau. During this period, there are no transcripts of calls from the candidate, but we do learn from BLUEBEARD–AURAL Mar. 31, that STONEHENGE, soon after BLUEBEARD arrived, sent a man called The Exterminator over to her room to unscrew her phone and reassemble it. Queried about this by BLUE-BEARD, STONEHENGE replies: "I'm getting cautious in my old age." We can assume a Buddhist phone tap was found and removed. This may account for the absence of BLUEBEARD–IOTA transcripts during the March 18–31 period.

Nonetheless, we do have two calls (March 21 and March 31) from BLUEBEARD to AURAL. The likelihood is that a separate phone tap was put in by the Buddhists at AURAL's home in Char-levoix, Michigan. Part of the conversation of March 21 is worth quoting at length.

MODENE: I never know in advance whether Frank will be Dr. Jekyll or Mr. Hyde, but when he chooses to be nice, the stars, Willie, do fall on Alabama. I have to tell you that living front and center does appeal to me after all these weeks of hole and corner with Jack. I adore Jack, but Frank, on stage, is another kind of human altogether. It's close to overpowering. For the dinner show, I sat at a table with some of his friends, and all eyes were on him.

WILLIE: Who was at the table?

MODENE: Oh, Dean Martin and Desi Arnaz are the ones you'd know. But who cares? All eyes were on Frank. He snaps his fingers to establish the beat and pandemonium takes over. Every wife in the audience was ready to run away with him. And during the love songs, it's the husbands who start to cry.

WILLIE: What did he sing?

MODENE: I can't name it all. "Love Letters in the Sand," "Maria," "How Deep Is the Ocean," "Just in Time." It couldn't have been better. He ended with "He's Got the Whole World in His Hands."

WILLIE: Have you started up with Frank again?

MODENE: Miss All-Knowing, you happen to be wrong. He's mad about Juliet Prowse. She's with him all the time.

WILLIE: That might not keep him from trying to say hello to both of you at once. (Mar. 21)

At this point, Modene hangs up without warning. There is another transcript dated one minute later, of Willie calling the Fontainebleau. The desk clerk tells her that Miss Murphy, by request, is receiving no outside calls.

That is all we have until there ensues a long conversation with Willie on March 31, initiated by Modene. Much of this, in my opinion, is worth inclusion.

WILLIE: Where is the candidate these days?

MODENE: Away. Campaigning.

WILLIE: You didn't see him in New York?

MODENE: No.

WILLIE: I thought you were going to see him on March 26th?

MODENE: Well, I didn't.

WILLIE: Did he break the date?

MODENE: I missed the plane.

WILLIE: You what?

MODENE: I missed the plane.

WILLIE: What did he say?

MODENE: He asked why, and all I told him was, "I miss flights. I have to make so many at work that when I'm on my own, I *miss* flights."

WILLIE: That must have been the end of you and Jack.

MODENE: Not at all. Jack and I spoke the day after, and we're going to meet in Washington on April 8th, after the primary in Wisconsin on April 5th.

WILLIE: Then he wasn't upset?

MODENE: He was cool about it. But I believe he thinks, just like you, that I started up with Frank again. Sometimes I wonder if the only reason he took up with me in the first place is because he wanted to see if he could take a girl away from Frank.

WILLIE: On what will you swear that you didn't go back to Frank again?

MODENE: You can't uncover a fact if it is not there to be found.

(silence)

WILLIE: What were you wearing at the Fontainebleau's farewell party for Frank?

MODENE: I chose a turquoise blue for my gown, and shoes to match.

WILLIE: Oh, my God, with your black hair! It had to be stunning. I can see your green eyes setting off that turquoise blue.

MODENE: It took some thought.

WILLIE: I'm so envious. Did you meet anyone new at the party?

MODENE: Frank introduced me to a man named Sam Flood who seemed unbelievably sure of himself. Everybody at his table was in total deference to him. I enjoyed the table. The men around him all looked like they belonged in a musical comedy.

WILLIE: Were they that handsome?

MODENE: No. I mean a *Guys and Dolls* sort of musical. One of them must have been six-feet-six and over three hundred pounds. And another was meaner-looking than a jockey. The rest came in about five sizes. But the moment this man Sam

Flood sat me next to him, the others didn't even dare to look up from their plates. Then the Clan made a point of coming up to the table. They all had to say hello to this man, Sam Flood. He sat like a king. Sometimes he didn't even bother to acknowledge the person. Sammy Davis, Jr., walked over with a big smile and Sam Flood waved the back of his hand in dismissal. Sammy just fled. "Don't you know who that is?" I asked Mr. Flood. "I know," he said, "who *that* is. *That* is the two of spades. Forget him."

WILLIE: What does this Sam Flood look like?

MODENE: Average size. Almost ugly. But kind of attractive. He's well dressed and has a good suntan. He looks manly, although in a quiet way. Maybe he's president of General Motors.

WILLIE: Ha, ha.

MODENE: When Frank walks into a room, everybody jumps. But Sam is like the pope. I will say that something very heavy comes off him. He's both attractive and repellent at the same time.

WILLIE: Fascinating.

MODENE: Exactly.

WILLIE: Did he make a date with you?

MODENE: He tried to, and I explained that I couldn't because my job had me flying to Washington at eleven in the morning. He said, "I'll have you switched to a better flight." I said that I wanted to go as slated. I didn't tell him how furious everyone at Eastern is by now with my sweetheart schedule.

WILLIE: How did he take the rebuff?

MODENE: He said, "I've been brushed before, but never with such nifty strokes." Then he started laughing at his own joke. I swear, Willie, this Sam Flood is one gentleman who likes himself.

WILLIE: That was all you saw of him?

MODENE: That, I fear, is only the beginning. When I got back to Miami two days later, there were twelve dozen yellow roses in my room, six dozen for the day of my arrival, and six dozen for the day before.

WILLIE: Don't yellow roses signify jealousy?

MODENE: If they do, he's making a very large point. There have been six dozen yellow roses every day since.

WILLIE: Do you think Frank told him about Jack?
MODENE: Isn't that the question? (Mar. 31, 1960)

Yours,
FIELD

I went back to the Royal Palms after work. It was close to midnight, and if I was over the worst of my hangover, I began nonetheless to brood over Giancana and his yellow roses. Sleep became hallucinatory. The large old air conditioner would start up like a hippo lumbering to its feet, only to settle down again with a grunt. The heat came back. In sweats and chills, I drowsed, and awoke in the morning with a sense of dread, for I now had the conviction that I ought to call my father.

15

PART OF THE PROBLEM WAS HOW TO REACH HIM. I KNEW NEITHER HIS call numbers nor his cryptonym. Still, he had to be working directly under Richard Bissell. There would not be more than two or three officers at such a level in Quarters Eye. When I came into Zenith later that morning, I consulted our table of organization and found SPINE, GUITAR, and HALIFAX on the appropriate plateau.

One was not supposed to select a cryptonym on the basis of its agreeability to oneself, but my father was bound to ignore such a rule. At the age of seventeen, he had won a sailing race for junior skippers that ran from Bar Harbor to Halifax (in Nova Scotia), and that was near enough for me.

Using the closed-circuit telephone to Quarters Eye, I had only to dial the three digits belonging to HALIFAX, and my father's secretary, Eleanor, answered. I recognized her voice at once. She was a woman I had met on a few occasions, a trim and somewhat grim young spinster who had grown middle-aged in his service and wore her hair in a bun. Stationed with him everywhere—which is to say, Vienna, the Near East, the Far East, and, for all I knew, Honduras during the Guatemala operation—she had acquired her own office renown. It was rumored, Kittredge had once told me, that Eleanor was Cal's mistress.

I paid more attention to Eleanor, therefore, the next time I saw her. She was not conspicuously friendly. Her lips were preternaturally tight, and her eyes were ablaze. She kept the secrets. Indeed, it occurred to me so soon as I heard her voice on the line today that I did not know whether Eleanor was her first name or a Company sobriquet.

"*Eleanor,*" I said, "this is Robert Charles down at HAW-THORNE. If you'll check it out against the Quarters Eye Manifest, I think you'll agree that I can be allowed phone ingress to HALI-FAX."

"We can dispense with the Manifest," she answered. "I know who you are, Robert Charles."

"That saves a stitch."

"Dear boy, do you expect this girl to run down the hall every time a new voice chimes in from Zenith? It's easier to memorize the lot of you."

What a second wife, I was thinking.

"Well," I said, "is target in?"

"Is the route *open, confide,* or *seek*? You have to specify, Robert," she was happy to remind me.

"*Seek.*" That would be the secure phone.

"He'll call you back in an hour," she declared, and hung up.

While I waited at my desk, there were memos to catch up on. Since I had begun work on the transcripts for Harlot, my desk at Zenith had become a bottleneck in memo flow. As many as fifty memos collected on occasion. While half of such notes could be filed or thrown away, not every memo could wait. Coming back to my desk after a day away at the recruiting stations, I never knew whether to get ready for amusement or woe. I was, therefore, leafing through the accumulation when the pool secretary buzzed. I was wanted on the secure phone.

The booth at Zenith was a sweatbox. *Seek* would not function until you closed the door, and then the air-conditioning was cut off. You could perspire in geometrical progression to the time elapsed on the call. I heard "Robert Charles," uttered originally, I am certain, in a loud, hearty voice, but thanks to the scrambler-descrambler it entered my ear like the hollow of a tomb. "Are you the character Eleanor claims you are?"

"Definitely on duty, sir."

"Ha, ha. Did you think I didn't know where you were?"

"I was considering just that possibility."

"Eduardo filled me in. Son, you won't necessarily believe this, but I was planning to chew some bread with you next time down. Hell, we could even break a cup."

"I look forward to that."

"Okay, what are we about?"

I knew him well enough to get to the point in three seconds. "The word here," I said, "is that you're planning to squench a certain big guy." *Squench* happened to be our old summer word for running over a Maine jackrabbit. "My source," I added, "is in the Frente."

"Boy, this is a secure phone. Will you damn well tell me which one of those windbags you are listening to?"

"Faustino Barbaro."

"I've heard of the gentleman. One fat politician."

"Yessir."

"What did he tell you?"

"That he wants to talk to you."

"Many people do, including my own son. But they don't always get around to explaining what they're up to."

It was no more comfortable than it had ever been to arouse my father's wrath. I could see his blue eyes blazing. All the same, I was not going to bypass the message.

"Barbaro has connections with the mob," I said, "and claims a couple of them are saying that you assigned them the job of eliminating Fidel Castro."

"No truth to it," he replied instantly. There was a pause and then he said, "How long have you been living with this foul rumor?"

"For two nights. As you can see, I didn't give it so much credence that I rushed to the phone."

"Well, you ought to know. It's not my style, nor is it Mr. Dulles', nor Mr. Bissell's, to go in for a rotten load of clams."

"Wouldn't seem so, would it?"

"Who are those guys Barbaro named?"

"He refused to tell me—insisted he must speak to you."

"Damn it, I may have to follow up." He coughed. I expect he was about to hang up, but realized I was still his son. "Are you nicely sited on your job?" he asked.

"Yessir."

"Working hard?"

"I know how to work."

"I've heard that. Hunt put in some good reports on you during the Montevideo stretch. Except for that KGB provocation some joker tried to leave on your watch. Hunt may have waffled a bit there."

"Howard Hunt is not perfect."

"Ha, ha. I'll see you a little sooner than you think," he said, and hung up.

16

SERIAL: J/38,767,859
ROUTING: LINE/GHOUL—SPECIAL SHUNT
TO: GHOUL-A
FROM: FIELD   10:54 A.M. JULY 13, 1960
SUBJECT: HEEDLESS

On April 12, a bonanza. In a protracted conversation, BLUE-BEARD tells AURAL about a meeting in Washington with IOTA on April 8, an ensuing visit to RAPUNZEL in Chicago on April 9 and 10, her return to Miami on April 11 *in company with RAPUNZEL,* and another rendezvous between BLUEBEARD and IOTA at the Fontainebleau on the same day. While BLUEBEARD does not speak of a direct encounter between IOTA and RAPUNZEL, it could certainly have taken place without her knowledge: RAPUNZEL, indeed, checked in at the Fontainebleau on April 11.

Here, at the risk of provoking your patience, I have included much of what you may consider extraneous detail, but I confess to being fascinated by it. *Transcript of April 12:*

MODENE: Jack had just won the primary in Wisconsin, so I expected him to be in a good mood, but he was in a very serious frame of mind when I came to his house.

WILLIE: He invited you to his home? Oh, my God, the chances that man takes. Where was his wife?

MODENE: Well, she's up in Cape Cod, so he was alone in Washington. I did get the feeling that I am not the first woman to be invited over for a small dinner.

WILLIE: What is the house like?

MODENE: It's in Georgetown, on N Street—3307 N Street.

WILLIE: I know Georgetown, but I can't visualize that block.

MODENE: Tall and narrow houses that run a long way back. But, I was surprised at how small the rooms were.

WILLIE: Wasn't it lavishly furnished?

MODENE: Well, the couches and chairs are plumped-up and extra-soft. For my taste, over-furnished. It's not his style, I would say, but hers. There were certainly enough photographs around to give me the impression that she is a tense lady. She looks very tense to me. I think she needs all this super-comfort before she can begin to relax.

WILLIE: What kind of antiques does she have?

MODENE: Period pieces. French. Small and elegant. Must have cost a fortune. I guess she likes spending her father-in-law's money.

WILLIE: Wouldn't you?

MODENE: I haven't thought about it.

WILLIE: And what did you eat?

MODENE: Let me tell you, that was a large disappointment. Jackie Kennedy may know all there is to know about high French cuisine, but when she's not there, her husband goes Irish. Meat and potatoes.

WILLIE: Too bad.

MODENE: I didn't care. I wasn't in a mood to eat. We were three to dinner. There was a big gloomy fellow named Bill, a political troubleshooter, I suppose, and he and Jack spent the meal analyzing the prospects in West Virginia. The population is 95 percent Protestant, and Bill kept repeating, "Humphrey has succeeded in convincing those people that you are rich and he is poor like them." "All right," said Jack, "what's your prescription?" "Old-fashioned trench warfare. Go at 'em, Jack. Call in your favors." Jack started to laugh. I could see that he didn't think too much of this fellow. "Bill," he said, "I know that much already," and in the way he said it, Willie, I could tell. He is one tough fellow.

WILLIE: You're lucky to know a man like that.

MODENE: After Bill left, Jack and I had a nice slow drink, and he told me how much he had missed me. Let no one say that man does not know how to talk to a woman. He had an interesting story about a black tribe in Africa who believe that everything has a spirit, even a dress, for instance. He said to me that when a beautiful woman puts on a beautiful dress, it isn't that she looks more beautiful because of the gown, but because the *kuntu,* the spirit, of the gown happens to be in harmony with the *kuntu* of the woman. So the effect is magnified because the spirits cooperate with each other. Few women have that kind of rapport with their clothing, he said, but I did.

WILLIE: You're right. Jack Kennedy knows how to talk to a girl.

MODENE: Then he took me on a tour of the house. At dinner, I had only seen two servants, but however many there are, they were all off in their quarters, and just the two of us wandered through a lot of rooms and ended up in the master bedroom, and there we sat on one of the twin beds, and continued to talk.

WILLIE: The master bedroom! I don't believe this fellow. I'd kill my husband if he ever did that to me.

MODENE: Well, I certainly felt two ways about it. I told myself he must be very unhappy with his wife. And I have to tell the truth—this night was just what I needed for my morale. So I may have felt a little guilty, but I was certainly ready. It all happened quietly as if he had been pouring some wonderful intangible potion into me and now I was a full vessel. I won't apologize for it. That is how I felt. And it was wonderful making love to him. It took away a lot of doubts. He's just there, and so appreciative. I wanted to do a lot for him. He's not as active as Frank, but it didn't matter. If I was afraid of anything, it was of how much I could fall in love.

WILLIE: Beware.

MODENE: Yes, beware. He said to me when we were done, "You don't know how much you bring to me. Making love to you, I know that I can walk away from a defeat." "Stop talking like that," I told him, "it's alien to your way of thinking." "No," he said, "if I don't get the nomination, I'm going to abduct you to some private island in a great blue sea. Just you and me and the sun and the moon. We'll live as if we were born naked, and I promise you, we will remain that way." "Hold your horses," I said. "You are trying to deprive me of my *kuntu.* I will sacrifice everything to you but my wardrobe." Willie, we laughed until I thought we wouldn't stop.

WILLIE: Did you sleep over?

MODENE: Oh, no. I couldn't have faced the morning. He's mar-

ried, after all. I knew I had to fight the very idea of falling in
love.

WILLIE: I've never heard you get this carried away about a man
before.

MODENE: Well, after all, Willie, why not?

WILLIE: When did you see him again?

MODENE: April 11th. At the Fontainebleau. He went all over the
country in the two days between. West Virginia, Arizona, I
don't even remember where.

WILLIE: Did Jack know about your trip to Chicago?

MODENE: I told him.

WILLIE: You told him about Sam Flood?

MODENE: Jack can think what he wishes. If he can't believe that
I am trustworthy, well, then let him suffer.

WILLIE: I don't believe you. (April 12, 1960)

I interrupt the transcript at this point. The question, indeed,
is whether to believe BLUEBEARD. The objective situation does
run cross-grain to the tale she tells. We know that her meeting with
RAPUNZEL was arranged in advance, and that the situation in West
Virginia calls for strong measures. Is RAPUNZEL being asked to put
his shoulder to the wheel?

QUERY: DO YOU HAVE COLLATERAL INFORMA-
TION ON THIS POINT?

FIELD

SERIAL: J/38,770,201
ROUTING: LINE/ZENITH—OPEN
TO: ROBERT CHARLES
FROM: GALLSTONE   10:57 A.M. JULY 14, 1960
SUBJECT: CHICAGO
          Illegal gambling very heavy in the fief of the 95 percenters.
Local sheriffs are much in liege to lieutenants of Robert Apthorpe
Ponsell. Local sheriffs asking, however, for feed bags to move the
horses. Large supply of oats reputed to be available. Source: Jebbies.
GALLSTONE

The *95 percenters* was an obvious reference to West Virginia, but
Jebbies took a while to interpret. I had always thought of Jebbies as

Jesuits. Then I tried J.E.B. which brought me to J. Edgar Buddha. I was back with the FBI. Robert Apthorpe Ponsell had to be RAPUN-ZEL.

SERIAL: J/38,771,405
ROUTING: LINE/GHOUL—SPECIAL SHUNT
TO: GHOUL-A
FROM: FIELD   12:32 A.M. JULY 15, 1960
SUBJECT: HEEDLESS
      Continuing transcript of April 12:

WILLIE: Are you trying to tell me that you were in this man Flood's company for forty-eight hours and he didn't make one single pass?

MODENE: He took me around everywhere. To meetings with his people, to restaurants. Everywhere. Since he had me on his arm, everyone supposed I was his girl. That was enough for him.

WILLIE: But how did you hold him off?

MODENE: I told him I was in love with Jack Kennedy and that I am a one-man woman. He said that was okay with him. He has a singer, a blonde. She's famous, he said. "Her name would knock you on your ear." Then he added that he was faithful to her. I tried to get her name but he wouldn't give it.

WILLIE: How could he conduct business meetings in front of you?

MODENE: He and his friends talk in Sicilian, I suppose it is, and it must be a special dialect because when I said I was going to study Italian so I could follow what they were saying, I thought he would never stop laughing. "Honey," he told me, "you could go to school for twenty years and you wouldn't learn word one of my language. You've got to be born into it." That got me mad. Sam can get me madder from a standing start than anyone I ever met. I said to him, "Don't be so cocksure. I can learn anything."

WILLIE: You're naïve. This man is a gangster.

MODENE: Well, don't you suppose I've figured that out for myself?

WILLIE: Do you have any idea of what you're getting into?

MODENE: You'd have to be blind not to. Some of the people

around him have shoulders as wide as a trailer truck, and broken noses that spread all over their face. And names! Scroonj, Two-toes, Wheels, Gears, Mustard, Maroons, Tony Tits, Brunzo. They seem so surprised when you remember their name. How can you forget them?

WILLIE: All you did in Chicago was go around with him?

MODENE: All over. So many nightclubs. He is so powerful. We went into a restaurant and it was completely crowded. So a couple of waiters just lifted up a table with all the half-eaten food and plates on it for six people and carried that table into some vestibule. Those six people had to get up and move out there. Then they brought in a new table with only two place settings for Sam and me. He didn't even nod. He could lift one finger and the restaurant would be closed down. You know it. I felt terrible for the people who were told to move.

WILLIE: Did you really?

MODENE: I didn't really. I love being the center of attention and Sam will give a woman that. The truth is, I felt like Frank Sinatra. Everyone in the restaurant was watching the way I brought my fork to my mouth, and I do like that. I'm happy to twirl a fork when people are watching.

WILLIE: You should have been a model.

MODENE: I could have been a model.

WILLIE: You still claim that you're in no danger of having an affair with Sam?

MODENE: Put it this way. If I ever drank way beyond my limit, I might make that kind of mistake with him, but I did count my drinks. And Sam was a gentleman. We did a lot of talking, however, about the Kennedys. He hates Jack's father. He says, "Joe made more money in the liquor business than I did. You could take lessons from him on how to screw a friend. In fact, he screwed me," and Sam started laughing in his crazy way again. After which he wiped his lips carefully and said, "Jack might be the good guy in that family. He's not afraid to talk to the real people. But Nixon! Too hard to trust. Tricky Dick is in nose-deep with the starched fronts. The richees. Tycoons like Howard Hughes and the oil people. Those richees like to pretend guys like me don't exist. So, I might do business with Jack before doing business with Nixon. Only I might not. That brother of his, Bobby, wanted to make a fool of me in public. Maybe Bobby don't know the old Italian saying, 'Revenge is a dish.' When I know you better, I'll tell you the last part of that one." And he laughed again. I said, "It looks like you might have a problem." "Me?" he asked. "I don't have any problem that I don't have an interesting solution to," and he began to laugh all over again.

QUERY: HOW DID BOBBY KENNEDY TRY TO MAKE A FOOL OF SAM FLOOD? SECOND QUERY: WHAT IS THE LAST PART OF REVENGE IS A DISH?

MODENE: Sam and I flew back to Miami early Monday morning, and Sam insisted on taking me around and shopping until evening when Jack would be coming by the Fontainebleau. Let me tell you. Sam knows how to shop. He can tell diamonds from paste at fifty feet.

WILLIE: Well, so can I. Even if I have no diamonds. (April 12, 1960—to be continued)

Will terminate for tonight and finish by tomorrow night. If possible, please respond a.s.a.p. to the queries.

FIELD

17

SERIAL: J/38,776,214
ROUTING: LINE/ZENITH—OPEN
TO: ROBERT CHARLES
FROM: GARRULOUS   11:37 P.M. JULY 15, 1960
SUBJECT: DISHES

Answer to first query: From Select Committee on Improper Activities in the Field of Labor Management, Sen. McClellan, Chairman, 86th Congress, 1st Session, June 9, 1959, lines18,672–18,681:

MR. KENNEDY: Would you tell us? If you have opposition from anybody, do you dispose of them by having them stuffed in a trunk? Is that what you do, Mr. Giancana?

MR. GIANCANA: I decline to answer because I honestly believe any answer might tend to incriminate me.

MR. KENNEDY: Would you tell us anything about any of your operations, or will you just giggle every time I ask you a question?

MR. GIANCANA: I decline to answer because I honestly believe my answer might tend to incriminate me.

MR. KENNEDY: I thought only little girls giggled, Mr. Giancana.

Answer to second query: OSS working undercover in Italy, 1943, did encounter the following piece of Sicilian wisdom: "Revenge is a dish that people of taste eat cold."

GARRULOUS

SERIAL: J/38,780,459
ROUTING: LINE/GHOUL—SPECIAL SHUNT
TO: GHOUL-A
FROM: FIELD   11:44 P.M. JULY 15, 1960
SUBJECT: HEEDLESS

Thank you for prompt response on queries. Continuation of transcript AURAL–BLUEBEARD, April 12:

MODENE: Actually, I could have kept shopping with Sam instead of rushing back to the Fontainebleau, because it was the longest wait for Jack. When he finally did arrive, I thought he might be on medication. His face was puffed and swollen. He smiled and said, "It's happened. My feet are starting to hurt." "It's all right," I told him, "you still look good to me." But when we kissed, I realized he was in no mood to make love.

WILLIE: That must have set you back.

MODENE: I felt close to him. What a compliment! To keep our date even when he's entirely wrung out. We just had sandwiches and wine. And he started talking again about the desert island.

WILLIE: I wonder if he and his wife will stay together if he doesn't become President.

MODENE: Well, as you can imagine, I've given a little thought to the subject.

WILLIE: Are you building up any expectations?

MODENE: I can only say I never felt closer to Jack. It was evening and we sat in silence. Then he had to go. He told me that it might be our last meeting for a while, since all his effort would be going into West Virginia now, and even if he wins that, there'll be nonstop days and nights of preparation for the convention in July. He seemed to get sad at the thought of how long we'd be apart, and we sat in the room and held hands, and he said, "I don't suppose there has been any time in my life that could have been less propitious for you and me than these madhouse months, but if it's really there for us, we will bear up. We will bear up, won't we?" he said, and I had to do all I could not to cry.

WILLIE: I feel like crying.

MODENE: The trouble is that I don't know what kind of life to go back to. After you've been around people like Frank and Jack, who are you going to date for an encore?

WILLIE: I predict that Sam will take up a large role in the near future.

MODENE: Oh, no. While we were shopping, he told me the name of his girlfriend. It's Phyllis McGuire of the McGuire Sisters. He is off in Las Vegas right now seeing her. I'm all alone by the telephone. (April 12, 1960)

There are occasional calls to AURAL in the next two months, and references to long-distance conversations with IOTA and RAPUNZEL. It is evident, however, that such communications are becoming infrequent. After the West Virginia primary, however, IOTA did phone her. BLUEBEARD's subsequent conversation with AURAL (May 11) may be worth inserting.

MODENE: Well, he called me the same night. I could hear his political people celebrating in the background. He told me that he didn't think he could be stopped now, and was going to hold a vision—he used exactly that word, *vision*—of our reunion in Los Angeles after he won the convention. And he invited me to come out for the week of the convention.

AURAL: Are you appropriately thrilled?

BLUEBEARD: I was very happy he said that. And I feel at peace now. I know I can wait these next two months. I'm feeling awfully sure of myself again. (May 11, 1960)

18

IN THE SECOND WEEK OF JULY 1960, I DISCOVERED THAT I WAS NOT inhabiting the summer so much as I was living in the previous spring, for in my mind, I was following Modene through her travels between Miami, Chicago, and Washington; indeed, I only became fully aware of how removed I was from my own life when I walked into the officers' lounge at Zenith one July evening and there on the television set was John Fitzgerald Kennedy speaking to a press conference at the Democratic Convention. I watched with all the shock of passing through an occult experience. It was as if I had been reading a book and one of the characters had just stepped into my life.

It was then I recognized that the fact that Modene was now at the convention in Los Angeles had not held as much reality for me as the account of her earlier activities I had been sending out each night to Hugh Montague.

Hearing Jack Kennedy's reedy voice on TV, however, put me through transformations. Time, I discovered, was no unimpeded river, but a medium of valves and locks that had to be negotiated before one could reenter the third week of July. It took a day before I began to call the Fontainebleau every few hours to see if Modene had returned. When she finally came back to her room on the evening of the ninth day, her phone was ringing as she came through the door. I am certain she took it as an omen and must have concluded that I was gifted with remarkable powers, for she immediately burst into tears.

Shortly after my arrival, forty minutes later, our affair commenced. The mermaid was hooked—a singular dislocation of metaphor! If the barb had been set, it was in me. I had never gone to bed with a girl so beautiful as Modene. If there had been nights I was not likely to forget in the brothels of Montevideo, they also revealed the trap in commercial pleasure; as my body encountered new sensations, so did the rest of me tear off in moral panic: To go so far, when one cared so little! With Modene, however, it took no more than a night to fall in love. If half of me loved her more than the other half, all of me was moving, nonetheless, in the same direction. I did not know if I would ever have enough of Miss Modene Murphy, and this passion was even larger than my anxiety that I was breaking the first commandment handed over by Harlot. If a sneaky had been planted in her room while she was away, then I was engraving my voice onto the tapes of the FBI. Even in the middle of our first embrace, I kept telling myself that they would at least remain ignorant of the name of Harry Field. For on my race over to the hotel after receiving her call, I had prepared a piece of paper on which was written: *"Call me Tom, or call me Dick, but Harry never."* Of course, we embraced as the door clicked shut behind me, and stopped for breath and kissed again, and then she was crying when we finished, so I did not get to hand the note over for the first five minutes, and by then, since she was no longer weeping, but laughing as well, she took in the message and laughed some more. "Why?" she whispered.

"Your room has ears," I whispered back.

She nodded. She shivered. A wanton look came over her face. In the midst of loose mascara and smeared lipstick, she was lovely. Her beauty depended on arrogance, and that had just returned. If her room was bugged, she was, at least, a center of attention.

"Tom," she said clearly, "let's fuck."

I would know her better before I would know how seldom she used the word.

On that night, the more Modene and I learned about each other, the more there was to learn. I was not accustomed to being all this insatiable, but then, I had never made love before to the mistress of the man who might yet be President of the United States, nor to the girl who had had an affair with the most popular singer in America, nor to the woman who might be the lover of a brute overlord in crime: All that, and I had not fainted on the doorstep—a monster of resolve was on the prowl in me. I could not have enough of her.

When it was all over and we came down at last to a little sleep in each other's embrace, she whispered to me on awakening at two in the morning, "I'm hungry, Tom, I'm hungry."

In an all-night diner in the southern end of Miami Beach, down in the twenty-four-hour sprawl on Collins Avenue of all-night movie houses and all-night stripper bars, of motels that rented by the hour while their names hissed in their neon signs, we ate sandwiches, drank coffee, and tried to talk. I felt as if I were on a boat, and dead-sweet drunk. I had never been so relaxed in my life. It was only by a last inward tide of duty that I could introduce her to the idea that we needed a private code. She took to it immediately. The urge to conspire lived as brightly as a genie in her. We decided to meet in the bars of hotels near the Fontainebleau, but the name of each hotel would stand for another—if I spoke to her of the Beau Rivage, I would mean the Eden Roc; the Eden Roc would be the Deauville, and mention of the Deauville was a signal to go to the Roney Plaza. An 8:00 P.M. date would be for six in the evening. I worked out the transpositions in duplicate and handed her one of two pieces of paper.

"Am I in danger?" she asked.

"Not yet."

"Not yet?"

I did not know if I wished to come back to any world at all. "Mr. Flood worries me," I said at last.

"Sam would not touch my fingernail," she said fondly.

"In that case," I said, "he might touch mine." I regretted the remark instantly.

"You know," she said, "I feel wonderful. My father was a motorcycle racer, and I think his blood is in me tonight. I feel high."

A black pimp at the other end of the diner was trying to catch her eye and in the absence of such contact was leaving his evil cloud on me.

I felt as if I had come into the place I had been expecting to enter all my life.

19

IT WOULD TAKE TWO WEEKS BEFORE I FOUND OUT WHY SHE HAD BEEN so distraught on her return. Now that we were lovers, Modene told me less about herself than in our two short meetings for drinks. We could talk about her childhood and mine, about singers and bands, movies and a book or two—she did think *The Great Gatsby* was overrated ("The author doesn't know *anything* about gangsters") and *Gone with the Wind* was a classic, "although it took the movie to convince me of that."

I hardly cared. If we were married, her taste might be a hurdle of the first order, but then it occurred to me that I had never asked myself how much I admired *The Great Gatsby*. One was not supposed to wonder about that. Not at Yale. It was like asking yourself whether you were moved by St. Francis of Assisi.

We agreed, at any rate, on *The Catcher in the Rye*—"Heaven," said Modene, "although not a *great* classic," and that was enough to do with books. We ate and drank well. She knew every good restaurant in southern Florida. Whenever I had a day off, and there was more time now that HEEDLESS was up to date, we would (despite her long fingernails) go waterskiing or scuba diving in the Keys and spend Saturday night in the bars of Key West. It was amazing I did not get into fights. At bottom, I felt so green in the role of squire to an incredibly lovely girl that I would be on battle-alert whenever anyone looked at her. Hardly confident of my mastery of martial arts—the stint at the Farm had obviously not been enough—I was covertly measuring every conceivable opponent until I came to learn that one seldom got into a fight before one's woman provoked one. Modene forestalled such possibilities. I did not know exactly how she managed, but processing ten thousand or more people a year on an airplane may have had something to do with it. She was pleasant to strange men but not accommodating, and made it clear that I was her date for the evening and she was with me. So, I survived. I prospered. I may even have looked a little more formidable than I felt. I was, in any event, ready to die before I would ever yell, "You can have her, you can have her," and knew I would wonder forever if Dix Butler had been telling the truth.

We also drove to Tampa, and to Flamingo in the Everglades. If we would spend a day together as preparation for our night, part of the joy was to be together in a car. She loved convertibles. Soon, I was renting them. I had a principal I could never touch until I was forty which consisted of bonds issued by the City of Bangor in 1922. It had been passed on to me by my paternal grandfather, and I could use the interest, although by family protocol, I was not supposed to. Who knew why our family did what it did? I, at any rate, good Hubbard, always predeposited such interest. Now parsimony would screech at me through each pole vault into the heaven of Modene Murphy. I was beginning to suffer so much from the gap between my richest and stingiest impulses that *Tom* Field began to dip into Harry Hubbard's accumulating interest to splurge on splendid meals and a rented white convertible.

How Tom and Mo loved to drive! Our weather was hot, rainy season was on, and I came to appreciate a South Florida sky. That sky could rest weightless upon you for a splendid morning, its bowl empty and blue over the Everglades like the great empyrean of the American West, but if Florida lands were flat, flat as water level, the sky had its own mountainous topography. Torrents of rain could approach as quickly as sunlit ravines fall into the unforgiving shadow of their cliffs. The changing shape of a cloud was, therefore, never to be ignored or you would not get the top up in time. Some cumulus sailed into one's attention off the spinnaker bellows of a tropical gust; other puffs curled on themselves like hooks prepared to gouge the fabric of the sky. Under a black ceiling of atmospheric wrath, storm clouds massed above one another in ranges and ridge lines that the land below could never offer, and insects were whipped by one's car stream into dark expectorations against the windshield, their small, exploded deaths still pitting the glass after gouts of rain.

How water could fall in southern Florida! One moment I might be close to doubling the speed limit, my highway no more than a long white arrow launched against the horizon; then, clouds would appear like hooded strangers. Ten minutes later, curtains of downpour would force me to the shoulder. A celestial rage, as intimate but almighty as a parent's wrath, would beat upon the metal skin of the car. When the rain ceased, I would drive through southern Florida with her head upon my arm.

We never talked about what had happened in Los Angeles. She did not refer any longer to Jack or to Sam. They seemed to have disappeared, and, given the size of her wound, I was not about to approach such questions. Sorrow and silence were her sensuous companions. I, well used by now to mourning for Kittredge, could ride beside Modene without speaking for an hour at a time. I lived with the lover's optimism that silence brought us nearer. It was not until I began to suspect that her thoughts could wander while making love, that I came to realize how much of the beloved candidate remained with us. Sometimes, in the middle of the act, I could sense her mind going far away from me, and I would feel the subtle sense of pall that comes over a party when it has just passed its peak.

About this time, a letter came in from my father by way of the Quarters Eye pouch. It is characteristic of him that with the variety of means open for communication within the continental United States —prearranged pay phone to pay phone, Encoder-Decoder, special shunt code line, secure phone, standard Agency phone, and a number of other modes too technical to enumerate—my father employed an old OSS means. He wrote a letter, sealed it in an envelope, girded it about with three-quarter-inch strapping tape (half as strong as steel), stuck it in the daily pouch to wherever it was going, and was done with it. While it might have taken two experts half a week to steam loose such a chastity belt and restore the envelope, there were more brutal methods of interception. The letter called attention to itself and could simply be stolen. Not once in his career, my father would boast, had he ever lost a communication by this means of sending it—no, he would correct himself, once he did; the plane carrying the pouch went down—therefore, he was damned if he was about to give up dispatching his messages without the feel of his hand on a pen sending out his own words directly.

I read:

Dear Son,

I'm going to be in Miami on Sunday, and this abbreviated communication is to say that I would like to spend it with you. Since I don't want to get off on a wrong note, let me issue in advance the unhappy news that wife Mary and I, one year short of our silver wedding anniversary, are now, after six months of separation, entering the process of getting a divorce. The twins, I fear, have lined up on her side. I have assured Roque and Toby that the schism is, under the circumstances, comparatively friendly, but they seem bitter. She is their mother, when all is said.

We need not dwell on this news during my day in Miami. Just wanted to alert you. Let's kick up our heels and get to know one another again.

Fondly,
Cal

I had been looking forward to a day with Modene, and under the changed circumstances, even thought of introducing her to my father except (1) I was afraid he would steal her, and (2) I was pleased that he was going to give me this much private time—it seemed unique in our annals that he would spend that many hours with me.

Then Modene solved my problem by deciding to work that Sunday, and I was able to greet him alone when he came off the plane. He was looking gray under his tan, and spoke little for the first hour. It was only ten in the morning and he wanted to go directly to the beach. "I need a run," he said, "to get the office cramps out of my gut." I nodded glumly. "We do what you want to do," I said, and knew he was going to push me into a race. He always did. Ever since

I had turned fourteen, he had engaged me in serious runs every time
we were together, and every time I lost; I sometimes thought the
greatest event in my father's life had taken place long before he was
in the OSS or the Agency: It was that slot bestowed on him by the
Associated Press as left halfback on the Second All-American Team of
1929. Of course, he never forgave himself for not making First All-
American, but then, that was my father.

I had made friends with the pool guard at the Fontainebleau, and
so I took Cal there and we used an empty cabana to change—I had
had the foresight to bring extra trunks along—and then we went out
on the beach for our run.

I was blessing Modene. If, among her charming contradictions,
she maintained her long, silver fingernails at every cost to herself, there
was also the lady who was competitive at sports. If I could introduce
her to sailing and show her all sorts of improvements to her tennis
game, she learned quickly, and high-board diving and speed swimming were proficiencies she could impose on me. When there was
time, we would, at her insistence, run together on the beach. Short
on sleep and always in the act of eliminating a little too much booze
from my ducts, nonetheless I was more or less ready for a set of jousts
with my fifty-three-year-old father, and he, I was both relieved and
saddened to see, had the hint of an extra inch around his waist.

"We won't go all out," he said, "just jog for a while."

So we set off to the north on the unending sand of Miami Beach,
wide and packed and much too hot already. To our left, on the side
of the land, were the monoliths of the big hotels, white, shining,
monumental, monotonous. The sky began to revolve just a little
under the heat, and a narrow band of protest soon tightened around
my skull at the inhumanities I was visiting upon the civil society of my
body; on we jogged, side by side, for a mile, his breath coming
unashamed and heavy, his sweat lining the curves of his powerful hairy
chest, and I stayed even with him, determined that on this day,
fortified by the unseen presence of Modene, I was going to beat him
at last.

We turned around after a mile and a half, both of us tired and
panting, both of us going along stride for stride, but now we no longer
spoke. He did not ask me any longer how the tarpon and sailfish were
taking to the hook on the sport-fishing cruises, he did not mention the
seven-hundred-and-eighty-pound tuna he had caught on the first day
out of Key West on a fishing vacation eight years ago, no, now he was

silent, and I was silent, and the level sand began to feel like the longest uphill grade I had ever climbed while the sky overhead began to seem as unstable as a dance floor to a drunk. I knew we would run until one of us fell, or we finished up back at the Fontainebleau, and since I wouldn't quit, and he wouldn't, we kept running on that level, side by side, up the endless grade of sand itself, and neither of us dared to break into the lead for fear there was no reserve to call upon—one might gain three steps on the other and collapse. Then, as we came into the last few hundred yards, the long curve of the Fontainebleau three hotels away, then two, then one, we spurted, which is to say we each churned in the sand and ran one modest increment faster, and all the world was in danger of turning black before I won by five yards and touched the railing of the boardwalk at the point where we had begun.

It took fifteen minutes of walking up and down the beach before we were ready for a swim, and when we came out of the water, the race still unspoken between us, my father began to spar with me. It was open-hand and allegedly not serious, but he was an awful man to spar with. He was clumsy, he was unorthodox, he was fast for a heavyweight of his age, and he could not really scale down his punches. I had learned enough at the Farm to be quick enough to avoid most of what he threw at me, although his jab when he caught you with an open slap did rattle one's teeth, and when I made the mistake of replying with a slap-jab of my own, he began to throw rights. He was just slow enough, and enough of an old-fashioned boxer, to give clear warning each time, but that alert was crucial because his body could still coordinate itself into the full heft of the punch, and each of the rights I slipped, or ducked, went by like a freight train. I had to content myself with throwing medium-stiff replies into his solar plexus until—and this was much to my happy surprise—he held up his hands at last and hugged the life out of me. "Kid, you've learned how to box, I love you," he said, and if he looked very pale under the tan, he was, with half of himself at least, honestly happy.

We finished by arm wrestling on one of the picnic tables at the boardwalk. This was *pro forma*. He always won with the right hand. No one in our family, or in the circle of our acquaintances, or for that matter in the Agency—at least by legend—had ever beaten him. I used to wonder what would happen if he and Dix Butler got together.

Now he disposed of me with the right hand and the left. We did it again, and he beat me without pain in the right, and took a little longer on the left. By the third time, I gained a draw with my left arm, and we were both content.

"I'm proud of you," he said.

So, close to heat prostration, regurgitation, and stroke, we went for another easy swim, dressed, got back into my Company car—I did not dare to show him the white convertible I had leased on the interest of the Bangor bonds—and down we went to the Keys, going as far as Islamorada before our stomachs came back to us sufficiently to feel hungry. At a fish-house joint whose deck gave separate views of the Gulf and the Atlantic, we got down to stone crabs and beer, and I was able to realize that all of the four hours spent until now were as much a personnel recruitment test as an inquiry into the capacities of his oldest and, until this day, third-best-loved son. We just kept looking at each other, and smiling at each other, cuffing each other on the shoulder open-handed, and quaffing beer, digging with our two-tined forks into crabmeat about to be lathered with mayonnaise. God, we loved each other. "This damned Agency has done as much for you as I ever did," he said.

"No, sir," I said, "my father Cal Hubbard is not a fathead," and the memory of the day I broke my leg skiing came over both of us at once. And we beamed at one another like explorers who have crossed a continent together and now share a view of a hitherto unglimpsed sea.

"Rick, I need an assistant down here," he said, "and I expect you're the guy. I was hoping you would be, and now I believe that you are."

"I believe that too," I said. I was thinking of Modene. I had never loved her more. I knew more about her than anyone else in the Agency, and I did not know anything about the lady other than that I adored her, and she had given me some kind of strength I had never quite felt before. "Give me a tough job," I said, "and I'll be there with you."

"This one is tough enough," he answered. "First of all, it is absolute hush-hush. So let's start with that. I like everything about you, but for one element."

"Name it."

"Your friendship with Hugh Montague."

I cannot pretend that I was not surprised, but all I said was, "I don't know if we're all that friendly these days."

"Why was he having lunch with you at Harvey's Restaurant, then?"

"I needed his help on exile welfare." I went into explanations. My father's eyes were hard on me all the way in much the way they had kept up with my movements as we boxed. I do not know if he was wholly satisfied when I finished, and I was rueful that our splendid beginning for this day had now been bent to this degree, and was doubly rueful at the collateral intelligence provided by simple Washington gossip: I knew my father well enough to understand that he wanted a vow from me. "Anything you say," I told him now, "will not be repeated or in any way hinted at by me to Hugh Montague."

He held out his hand and shook mine with the grip he used to get at the marrow in your finger-bones. "All right," he said. "I'll brief you on Hugh. He's a great man, but at present, he worries the hell out of me. I can't prove it, but Allen may be feeling the same way. Bissell, of course, just can't abide Hugh Montague. They're a built-in cock-fight. The trouble is that Hugh knows too much about everything going on. God, he's sitting on every crossroads in the Company. It's Allen's fault. Right from the start, Allen wanted one of us free and clear of all the others to keep an eye on everything, and report directly to Allen. That way Allen would have a hedge against our own bureaucracy running things without him. In consequence, Hugh has security overrides that allow him to pipe into what-all. His fief has become a goddamn spiderweb, an empire within the empire. And he is unalterably opposed to the Cuba op."

"Well, I am for the Cuba op."

"You damn well better be."

I was debating whether to inform my father about the work I was doing for Hugh, and decided I would not. A new instinct, immediately and incredibly alert, was telling me to work with Hugh and Cal, work with them both—each in his own enclave. It might be the first time in my life I could lay claim to a driver's seat. If I was appalled by the extradimensionality I was taking on for myself, I was also growing enamored—I confess this—with what might be the ultimate possibilities of myself. No, I had not fainted on the doorstep.

"In fact," said Cal, "I'm so opposed to Hugh's attitude at this point that when Allen asked me to take on a most special task, I told him that I would on the proviso that Hugh Montague not be given one whiff of it. Allen promised to go along with that."

I nodded.

"The line of communication," Cal said, "goes from Allen to Bissell to me. Now it's going down to you. I do have a case officer working New York and Washington, but now I need one in Miami. I will add you to the team. Circumscribed, wouldn't you say?"

"Yessir."

He squinted at a fishing boat bucking a chop in the channel between two far-off Keys. "Rick, I must admit that I am feeling very respectful of this operation. I haven't been off my feed as much since I was fourteen and knew I was going to start my first varsity football game at St. Matthew's, the youngest student ever to make the first team varsity there, I'll remind you. So, yes, if I wake up in the middle of the night, just between us, I'll tell you—yes, I do gulp air. Because the core of the Cuban op—and I can give it to you in one sentence —is that Allen has now decided that Fidel Castro is definitely to be eliminated."

Had he forgotten my secure telephone call to him? "That's common gossip around here," I said.

"Yes," said Cal, "you're dealing with Cubans. Any possibility, no matter how macabre or extravagant or sensational, is everyday gossip to them. But no Cuban believes deep down that he can knock Castro's hat off. We can, however. We can do just that, and we will."

"What about Toto Barbaro?"

"For now, ignore Barbaro. He has enough of a nose to want to get near to me. Follow no leads with him, therefore. Think of him as doubled. He probably is."

"Yessir." I paused. "Is there a timetable?"

"Castro is to be gotten out of the way by early November."

"Before the election?"

He looked at me. "Exactly."

"Can I ask how high up this goes?"

He shook his head. "Son, it's a lifework to understand this Company. You never stop learning how the gears fit. But there's one sense you must develop. We all gossip a little more than we should, and we are not above trying things out verbally to hear how they fall on someone's ear. Only, there are certain inquiries not to make. Real security depends on a key, one simple key. Unless you are told where a project was initiated, don't go looking for the source. You don't want to know. Because when you get down to it, we cannot trust ourselves. So I don't want to be informed whether this started with President Eisenhower, or Richard Milhous Nixon, or Allen himself.

It's come down with enough force for me to think Allen cannot be the initiator, and I would warrant it is not Bissell. He prefers to take a clear order and work out the filigree. All right, you say, if they are talking of November, it must be Nixon. He's Action Officer for Cuba, after all, and he's bound to win the election if Castro is off the board by then and we have Cubans fighting in the hills. Still, we don't ask. Because it could be Eisenhower. When Patrice Lumumba came to Washington last month, the State Department treated him like Mr. Africa. They talked Ike into putting Lumumba up at Blair House— hoping to impress him with the fact that he was squatting in the shadow of the White House—but Mr. Lumumba is a revolutionary, and he didn't feel all that impressed. He and his people smoked marijuana constantly, and left their butts smudged all over the State Department seal in the ashtrays. Then Lumumba had the consummate moxie to ask the State Department if they would provide him with a white prostitute, preferably blond. He wanted a little feminine company at Blair House. Well, Eisenhower is reported to have said, 'Castro and Lumumba have to be right out of the Black Hole of Calcutta. Can't someone do something about these people?' "

My father now shrugged. "That may have been all it took to kick off our Castro op, Nixon taking his cue off that remark, but all I have received from Allen is the go-ahead to talk to Bissell. And all I got from the latter worthy was that a decision had been made to work with underworld figures who have lost their casinos in Havana. Top hoods with an investment in Cuba would be likely candidates for such a job. No one outside our ranks would suspect that they were the trigger men for more than their own good and sufficient reasons. 'All right,' says Bissell, 'fill in the blanks.' 'Wouldn't care to send us a clue on how to start?' I ask. 'Up to you,' says Bissell, 'you know a good many people.' Indeed I do, but are any in category? I had a ridiculous couple of days, Rick. I've been in the Far East so long that I can find you a Hong Kong mechanic adept at pulling out toenails a millimeter at a time, but the sad truth is that I have a paucity of skilled low-life contacts in the U.S. I didn't know where to start. When it came down to it, I didn't know the right Americans. I even thought—and I'll disinherit you if you repeat this to anyone—that I might call on my old friend Lillian Hellman. She had an affair years ago with Frank Costello of which she is still very proud, and I thought maybe she would give me an introduction to the old tiger gangster boss. Lucky for me, I looked into it first. Costello is pretty much out of it these days. Along about then, I was called in by Bissell and handed the plumbing. I am to work with Bob Maheu, he tells me. Well, that's another matter. You're going to meet Maheu in Miami, I expect. Used to be FBI, now he's Howard Hughes' man. Has also done work for us. I teamed up with Bob Maheu years ago in the Far East and he's one incredible fellow." My father spent a moment contemplating his palms. "That's about the size of it. Hierarchically, I've got all the responsibility; operationally, I sit on the sidelines and wait for Maheu to report to me. It's not a situation I instinctively enjoy. And as for where it all started, well, Howard Hughes comes to mind as quickly as Nixon. But I can't pretend that I'm happy. Hell, let's get the bill and drive back."

When we were on the road to Miami, he did expatiate a bit. "There are going to be a few meetings soon," he said. "I may or may not attend them. Maheu has his down and dirty contacts but I, of course, have to maintain some hygiene."

"Where is the role for me?" I asked.

"Harry, I can't promise in advance whether this job will occupy you for an hour, a week, or whether it will consume you. I honestly don't feel as if I have my own hands on it yet."

"I've never seen you so pinch-mouthed about things," I said. It was a large remark for me to make, but his gloom brought it forth.

"It's hellish breaking up with Mary," said my father.

We drove in silence for a while.

"It's all my fault," said Cal. "Mary had learned to live with my infidelities, but she couldn't bring herself to forgive me after I took the maid into our bed in Tokyo one fine afternoon when I thought Mary would be out shopping until evening."

"Christ Almighty," I said. "Why did you ever do that?"

He sighed. "I guess sex without risk can get to be an uncomfortably intimate transaction. Besides, every Hubbard is one part mad. Know what I'm proudest of? On New Year's Eve, just fourteen years ago, 1946, first New Year's Eve of the peace, just before I turned forty, I had sexual intercourse standing up with a girl I'd met that night at a party at the Knickerbocker Club." He paused, with enough pent-up confidence to extract my compensatory "Yes? What is so special about that?"

"We were doing it at four in the morning on the uptown end of the Park Avenue island that runs from 62nd to 63rd Street with about two thousand windows looking down on us, and I felt as strong as I have ever felt. A police car came along, and this Irishman stopped and stuck his head out the window and said, 'What the hell do you think you are doing?' and I answered, 'Fornicating, officer. We're fornicating till the cows come home, and a Happy New Year to you.' "

"What did he do?"

"Just gave one disgusted look—pure New York cop!—and drove on." My father began to laugh with the sheer enjoyment this memory would never cease to radiate from his past into his future, and when he stopped, the road still went up from the Keys, and I could feel him brooding again about the rupture of his marriage. When he spoke, however, it was of something else.

"You know, son," he said, "I happen to feel equal to what they're asking on this job. Once in the OSS, I was obliged to do away with a partisan who had betrayed us. I ended up having to kill him with my bare hands. A gunshot would have been too loud. I never told anyone until today." He looked at me. "Today is the day. Maybe I've lost a wife and gained a son."

"Maybe you have." I didn't trust myself to say more.

"What I mean by I never told anyone is that I never spoke before of the sense of realization you can get killing another human, I mean, that intimately. I didn't know if I was a good man or an evil man for a long time after. But, finally, I realized it didn't matter—I was just a hellion. So it isn't what we've got to do that gives me pause, it's that I don't have my hands on it. Not yet."

20

ON THE SAME NIGHT, AFTER MY FATHER FLEW BACK TO WASHINGTON, I had a late date with Modene. She was returning to Miami on an evening flight, and we were going to a safe house. She did not like hotels. "Miami Beach is a very small world to its residents, and I am highly noticeable among them," she had told me.

After that, I chose a small but elegant place on Key Biscayne that had been leased to Zenith by a wealthy Cuban who would be in Europe for the summer. I was ready to gamble that it would present no problem for a few meetings. I used to pick her up at the airport in my white convertible and wheel us over Biscayne Bay along Ricken-backer Causeway to the villa off North Mashta Drive. We would spend our nights in the master bedroom, and waken in the morning to a view of royal palms, white habitations, mangrove shore, and pleasure boats in Hurricane Harbor.

I was, of course, balancing a set of lies between Harlot and the safe-house desk at Zenith, but the risk seemed small. Hunt was the only intelligence officer in South Florida who had the right to ask me what I was using the safe house for, and while he would be routinely notified of the fact each time I signed a chit for safe-house use (and Hunt was the man to know a good address by its name—North Mashta Drive would certainly alert his attention), still, I was protected by our procedural restraints. The villa, for purposes of signing out, was merely listed as Property 30G. If I was using it a good deal, Hunt, if curious, would still have to look up its address and owner by way of a classified in-house manual; why bother? Given our hordes of Cubans, we were using safe houses all the time. So, I had little to fear. Once, in a dream, I did awaken long enough to see Hunt's ski jump of a nose peering around the master bedroom door to take in the sight of Modene and myself in carnal clutch, but that was a dream. I was impressed by how little distress I carried compared to what I would have gone through if it had been my first year in the Agency. Perhaps I was beginning to live with Harlot's dictum that in our profession we learn to get along with unstable foundations.

So I could feel pride in my illicit use of La Villa Nevisca. The stucco walls were as white as any edifice on the South Florida shore, and its name in English, House of the Light Snowfall, proved worth repeating to Modene who exhibited such naïve pleasure in the translation that I began to wonder how long it had taken her father to get accustomed to his money. Sometimes, when her precise way of speaking—the product of years of elocution lessons—began to pall on me, I confess that I began to see all Midwesterners as simple. In defense of such large prejudice, I must say that whenever a building was possessed of charm, or a touch of history, she was too impressed. She liked windows with odd shapes, wood filigree porches, pastel-colored edifices in general, and romantic names—La Villa Nevisca was perfect! She was even impressed with replicas of Southern mansions in Key Biscayne. (It became important to me, therefore, not to compare her in any way to Kittredge.) All the same, I could not keep from envisioning Modene's childhood on well-to-do Grand Rapids streets and concluded that her contempt for my low station in life—"I guess you're the poorest man I ever dated"—was more than equalled by her bottomless awe of my attainments: Yale, and a profession I could not talk to her about. I did not even try to tell her about St. Matthew's.

I am being unfair. She knew what she knew, and her self-confidence was absolute on certain matters. She loved to dance, for instance. After a couple of evenings in a nightclub, however, we more or less gave it up. I was adequate on the floor, and she could have been a professional. If she showed me variants of the samba and the merengue, the cha-cha and the Madison, if she could go into a triple lindy off a double lindy, it was only to demonstrate her skill: She had no desire to raise my abilities through collaboration—it would make her feel *silly*, she explained. The aristocratic reflex of an artist was in her rejection: One does not wish to dull one's talent. In preference, forswear the art.

On the other hand, I came to recognize that my accent fascinated her. She declared that she could listen to it all night with as much pleasure as if Cary Grant were speaking. I came to recognize that Cary Grant was her point of reference for people whose minds were occupied with niceties, and I understood then why she would not teach me how to dance, no, no more than I would spend a part of my life teaching her to speak. She spoke well enough. If it could pall at times on my ear, well, she had other virtues.

Once she said to me (and I heard echoes of Sally Porringer), "You're such a snob."

"Do you know," I said, "so is your dear friend Jack Kennedy." Then I could not resist the cruelty—"Wherever he is."

"He's trying to win an election," she answered, "so how could he have time for me? Of course, he doesn't."

"Not even for a phone call." My jealousy was scalding my heart as directly as boiling soup on a tender lap.

"He's not a snob," she said. "He has an intense interest in everyone around him. Unlike you, he's the best listener I ever met."

I was not. She would start to speak and my mind would wander over to her carnal virtues. I never saw her but in a cloud of sexual intent. I did not have to listen to her—she was so much more than what she was saying. Soon, we could go to bed, and then I would find her brilliant again, and delicate, deep and fierce, yes, dear, greedy, generous, warm, and her heart would be ready to melt in sorrow and joy, all this for me on any night when we could transcend each and every annoying impasse of the evening and get to bed. Then I did not have to worry whether I knew how to dance.

Libido may be inner conviction, but libido rampant is megalomania. My mind would tell me that I was the greatest lover she had ever had; somewhat later, libido, by three parts out of four consumed, I became again the man who did not know how to dance. Sinatra knew how. So did Jack. They knew.

"You're mad," she would say to me. "Jack Kennedy has a bad back. He got it in the war. We never danced at all. It didn't matter. I wanted to listen to him when he talked and I loved to talk while he listened."

"And Frank? Frank doesn't dance?"

"It's his profession."

"Dancing?"

"No, but he understands it."

"And I don't?"

"Come here." Lying in bed, she would kiss me, and we would commence again. I would scourge the fourth part of my libido. Next morning, I would be in a towering depression. It would seem to me that I was nothing but a pit stop in the middle of a race. Kennedy would be back; Sinatra might always return, and Giancana was waiting. How crude were my emotions now that they were exposed to myself!

I do not know how well I was prepared, therefore, when a communication came in from Harlot on August 1.

SERIAL: J/38,854,256
ROUTING: LINE/ZENITH—OPEN
TO: ROBERT CHARLES
FROM: GLADIOLUS   10:05 A.M. AUGUST 1, 1960
SUBJECT: BABYLONIAN PARTOUSE
         Call me on SEEK.

                                                    GLADIOLUS

His conversation was brisk: "Harry, I had one hell of a time collaring this transcript. It's BLUEBEARD–AURAL on July 16th of convention week in Los Angeles. Buddha has kept it not only in Special File, but Select Entry. Still, I plucked it forth. Pressure points pay off."

"How soon," I asked, "can you get it over to me?"

"Will you be at Zenith four o'clock today?"

"I can be."

"Expect my man at your desk on the dot."

"Yessir."

"Are you mermaid-witting yet?"

"No, sir," I lied, "but on the way."

"If it takes too long, it will accomplish less when you get there."

"Sir?"

"Yes?"

"*Partouse*. It's Parisian slang, isn't it?"

"You'll see soon enough."

At 4:00 P.M., a man I recognized as one of the two baboons who had been in Berlin with Harlot four years ago, came into my office, gave a short nod, handed over an envelope, and left without requesting my signature.

"July 17, 1960. AIRTEL TO DIRECTOR FROM FAC SPOONOVER, subject SELECT, recorded July 16, 7:32 A.M. to 7:48 A.M. Pacific Time."

MODENE: Willie. Please listen. It just blew up with Jack.

WILLIE: It just blew up? It's nine-thirty in the morning here. So it must be seven-thirty your time. What's happened? Not one phone call all week.

MODENE: What I mean is it blew up last night at three in the morning, and I haven't slept since. I'm waiting to get on a plane. I'm at the airport. I didn't sleep.

WILLIE: What did he do?

MODENE: I can't tell you yet. Please! I've got to be orderly about it.

WILLIE: You really are upset.

MODENE: He put me up at the Beverly Hilton all week and said I was his guest, but I felt awfully tucked away. I never knew if I was going to be alone with room service or he would call me out late at night.

WILLIE: Did you go to the convention?

MODENE: Yes. He had me in a box. Only, I think it was the number-four box. There was the Kennedy family in the first one, and more family and friends in another, and then there was a third where I saw a good many important-looking people in the box next to mine, but my box was odd. Some of Frank's friends were installed there, whereas Frank was in

the Kennedy family box. My box was second-rate people, I
don't know how to describe them. Boston politicians maybe,
gold teeth practically, although not that crass. And one or two
women I most certainly did not like the look of. Very expensive hair-jobs, like, "Do not ask who I am. I am the mystery
woman."

WILLIE: But you did see him?

MODENE: Of course, nearly every night.

WILLIE: How many nights did he miss?

MODENE: Well, three out of seven. I used to wonder if he was with
one of the women in my box.

WILLIE: He must have been feeling equal to dynamite.

MODENE: One night he was so tired I just held him. A wonderful
glow came off him. So deeply tired, so happy. One night, he
was wonderful. Full of energy. His back, which usually bothers him, was feeling absolutely relaxed. Jack Kennedy is one
man who should have the right to go around with a healthy
back, because it's just right for him.

WILLIE: He probably had a shot of painkiller. I've heard that
rumored.

MODENE: It was a consummate night and I had nothing I wanted
to keep in reserve for myself. But then I didn't see him for the
next couple of nights. Then, the day they chose Lyndon
Johnson for Vice President, Jack was very tired and I just held
him, but last night . . . (pause) Willie, I don't want to turn the
faucet that opens the waterworks.

WILLIE: If you can't cry around me, you are in double-duty
trouble.

MODENE: I am in a public place. At a pay phone. Oh, damn, it's
the operator.

OPERATOR: Will you deposit seventy-five cents for the next three
minutes?

WILLIE: Transfer the call to my number, Operator. It's Char-
levoix, Michigan. C-H-A-R-L-E-V-O-I-X, Michigan, 629-
9269.

MODENE: On the last night, the parties went on forever. Toward
the end, Jack took a group to a friend's suite at the Beverly
Hilton and he whispered to me to stay, so I hovered around
the edges, and that is an embarrassing position. I stayed as long
as I could in the bathroom fixing my hair, until it was down

to a few of his top political workers and himself and me, then I drifted into the bedroom, and he came in and sighed, and said, "At last, they are all gone," and I went into the bathroom again to undress. When I came out, he was in bed, and I couldn't believe it—there was also another woman, one of the ones I had seen in the convention box. She was just about out of her clothes.

WILLIE: My God, is he taking lessons from Frank?

MODENE: I went right back into the bathroom and dressed and by the time I came out, the other woman was gone. I couldn't stop shaking. "How did you ever find the time to manage all this?" I asked. I was awfully close to screaming. I couldn't bear it that he was so calm. He said, "It did take a bit of juggling," and I came very near to slapping him. He must have seen the look in my eye because he said he hadn't done it to offend me, he just thought this part of life was an enhancement. "An enhancement," I said. "Yes," he said, "it's an enhancement for those who can appreciate it." Then he told me that he once loved a French woman very much who delighted in such arrangements, even had a name for it —la partouse. P-A-R-T-O-U-S-E. If you were ready for it, there was no harm done, he said, although obviously, as he could see by my reaction, he had certainly made an egregious error.

WILLIE: Egregious!

MODENE: Yes. I said, "Jack, how could you? You have everything," and he said, "It's all over so soon, and we do so little with our lives." Can you believe that? He's such an Irishman. Once they get their mind fixed, you need a pickax to break into the concrete. He started to fondle me, and I said, "Let go, or I am going to scream." And I left him there. I went to my room and drank Jack Daniel's until dawn. I didn't answer the phone.

WILLIE: Oh, Modene.

MODENE: I'm not even drunk now. I am cold sober. There is too much adrenaline in me. He had the gall to have eighteen red roses sent up to my room with a bellhop. Just before I checked out. It had a note: "Please forgive the stupidest thing I've ever done!" Well, I want to tell you, I spent well over

a hundred dollars and ordered six dozen yellow roses to be
delivered to him right away, and signed, Modene. He'll get
the message.

WILLIE: Does he know about Sam's yellow roses?

MODENE: Of course he does. I made a point of telling him. I liked
to tease him about that.

WILLIE: It sounds to me like you're cooking up a welcoming party
for Sam.

MODENE: No, not Sam! Not now! I have to see what kind of
mood I'm in when I get back to Miami.

WILLIE: We're going to have some crazy time if this guy gets
elected president.

MODENE: Willie, I'm hanging up. I don't want to start crying.

I had an odd reaction. I asked myself whether I would ever try to
bring another woman into bed with Modene, and knew I would not,
but that was only for fear of losing her. If she ever brought a woman
to our bed, well, that I might like very much. There were times,
especially lately, when—St. Matthew's be damned—I thought we
were here on earth to feel as many extraordinary sensations as we
could; perhaps we were supposed to bring such information back to
the great Debriefers in the sky.

Soon enough, however, I began to recognize how much real
anger I was holding. It seemed to me it was all Sinatra's fault, and I
could understand my father's propensity for terminating life with
one's bare hands. What a pity that Sinatra would not come through
the door of my cubicle at Zenith at this instant—my rage was in my
fingers and as palpable as a ball of clay. I muttered to myself, "Modene,
how could you have done this to us?" as if she was as responsible for
her past as for her present with me.

Yet, time, soon enough, picked up: We pretended Jack Kennedy
did not exist. It was almost a viable proposition. I did not know
whether she saw me as a dressing station in the great hospital of love's
wounded, and I was the pallet on which she could recover, or
whether she loved me magically, which is to say, had been struck by
love on the night she returned to Miami, and I was her man. She kept
speaking of how good-looking I was until I began to peruse my face
in the mirror with the critical self-interest of a speculator going over
the daily listing of his stocks each morning.

All the while, I was trapped in work and fearful of the day when the baboon would show up at the desk with new transcripts from Harlot and I would learn that she was seeing Jack Kennedy again.

21

ABOUT THE MIDDLE OF AUGUST, HUNT MADE A MOVE HE HAD BEEN preparing for some time, and our Frente leaders transferred their headquarters to Mexico. It was considered by Quarters Eye a necessary piece of camouflage for the oncoming operation, and Hunt welcomed it. His children, having finished their school term in Montevideo, were soon coming back to America with Dorothy, and I think he had been facing the difficulty of locating good lodging in Miami where costs were prohibitive. Now he and Dorothy might find a villa in Mexico City. Besides, he could feel once again, as he had in Montevideo, that he could run his own show.

Back at Zenith, left in charge of the Political Action Section, I actually moved up to a larger office with a window. If it looked out across a crabgrass lawn to our wire fence, our guardhouse, and our gate, and there was no more to see across the road than a spread of low, flat-topped modern buildings belonging to the University of Miami, and so, *qua* window, was but a mean gain, still, I had taken my first step on the rung of hierarchical ascension.

Otherwise, the new job was no boon. I now had to watch over Hunt's unfinished business in addition to my own. This included public relations concerning the Cubans who were arriving daily in every kind of boat. Given the ties we had developed to individual reporters on the Miami newspapers, we now could count on a feature story every few weeks about exiles who had just floated over from Havana on rafts newsworthy for the crudity of their construction. Some consisted of no more than a platform of two-by-eight planks lashed to oil drums welded together, and the thought of this journey across one hundred and eighty miles of open water from the port of Havana to Miami was awesome, and so diverted attention from the less exceptional fact that the great majority of our exiles were still coming in on airlines from Mexico and Santo Domingo. Then, late one moonless night, while out on the patio of La Nevisca, I watched a powerboat tow a full load of people and two rafts out to sea, the sight barely visible by starlight, and next morning, lo, the rafts had floated in again, the press was called, and one of the people I had personally registered two weeks ago at Opa-Locka, a particularly engaging curly headed young Cuban, would grin at me the following day from the front page of the second section as if he had just arrived. I was learning that in publicity it was obscene not to lie. Of course, I felt no great moral stirrings—I just wished that Hunt had briefed me better. The virtue of military operations, I was deciding, was in the whole simplicity of the decision to win.

Meanwhile, Hunt stayed in touch by cable and phone. From across the Gulf of Mexico, he still attempted to control the work handed over to me. I was now nominally in charge of his sector of agent recruitment, but many of our activities bore few dependable returns. It was easy to find agents who would take our pay, but how many in our pool of gossip-mongers, student idealists, petty criminals, unsuccessful pimps, marginal businessmen, new Cuban shopkeepers, boatmen of all varieties, exiles waiting to be shipped out for training, ex-soldiers from the Cuban army, and Cuban-Americans from the U.S. Army, plus a superstructure, if you could call it that, of Cuban journalists, lawyers, respectable businessmen, and career revolutionaries could give us accurate information? "Our agents," as Hunt pointed out, "tell us what they think we want to hear."

Meanwhile, in August, hurricanes were building in the Caribbean, Calle Ocho was springing Spanish signs in neon, new arrivals were sleeping on our recruiting-house porch in downtown Miami, and Quarters Eye circulated a handbook among Zenith personnel listing the hundred and more exile organizations in the Miami area, a work of redundancy, since we had made the same compilation at Zenith. I was also sitting in on committee meetings with other case officers trying to work up an operative procedure that would shape the exiles into self-policing groups who might weed out the Castro agents in the exile community. FBI reports, which we also circulated at Zenith, put the number of such DGI men at two hundred. It was an in-house joke. Three months ago, the number had been the same. There was every expectation that three months from now the FBI would still be speaking of two hundred DGI agents running amok in Miami.

Then, early in September, another envelope banded about with strapping tape came in the Quarters Eye pouch.

It began:

I'm enclosing a letter from Bob Maheu. If you can't bury it in a safe place, destroy it. I have a copy.

Dear Mr. Halifax,

This is to inform you that I have met with a well-recommended top banana of the Mafia who calls himself Johnny Ralston. Since he has his own expropriated investments to recoup, he is, to say the least, well motivated.

Naturally, I went into this lunch as a representative of some wealthy figures who are willing to pay for an authoritative stroke to the tune of $150,000. Well, the Ralston gentleman can be acerbic. He threw back the name of Meyer Lansky. "Meyer has a price out," he said, "of one million dollars for the same job."

"Yes," I assured him, "but once you are successful, you have to collect it. Do you care to be the man who has to ask Meyer Lansky for that amount of money?"

Since I taped the conversation, let me give you the rest directly.

R: How can I trust your people to be good for one-fifty?
M: We will put it in escrow.
R: Why are you in this?
M: Because of my sense of serious obligation to this country. I have been told that you have similar feelings of patriotism.
R: I will lay it on the line: I feel so patriotic I would like to obtain my citizenship. Fuck your hundred-fifty thousand bucks—I want those citizenship papers. I am tired of being pulled in by immigration officials.
M: Your citizenship can be arranged.
R: Yes, and I have been doublecrossed before.
M: There is no way such an arrangement can be promised in advance. After the event, you would have every leverage for obtaining your desired result.

At this point in the lunch with Ralston, there is a malfunction in the recording that goes on for a few minutes. Probably I pressed too severely against the back cushions, a regrettable hitch to be avoided next time.

While I cannot recall in detail what transpired over this gap, I can assure you that I did my best to convince him he could depend on "my people" to get what he wanted.

Son, let me cut in here. Never trust Maheu altogether. He's enough of an old hand to know how to flex his butt while wearing a sneaky. I suspect he excised some of the tape. I would presume it covers his admission to Ralston that the "wealthy figure" he's representing is the Agency. Obviously, it is to Maheu's advantage to let Ralston in on such a matter because the Company is better situated than private individuals to obtain his citizenship. (Although, God knows, we could have trouble there with Immigration.) In any event, once Maheu returns to the tape, Ralston is considerably more amenable and agrees in principle to come aboard. He does, however, tell Maheu that he wants to meet "the guy who talks to you. I want to shake hands with the real stuff."

This enclosure is merely to keep you advised. If any observations are stimulated, pass them along. I do wonder what Ralston's real name might be.

HALIFAX

The next morning, I received a coded memo from Harlot sent over a medium-security circuit.

Buddhists report that one Johnny Roselli, a close associate to RAPUNZEL, met with Robert Maheu for lunch at the Brown Derby in Beverly Hills. Unfortunately, no reliable sources were available. That most curious meeting leaves us therefore in Ponder Gardens.

GREENHOUSE

"Reliable sources" were tape recordings. Obviously, the FBI had been able to do no more than take note of the luncheon. Hugh, however, had given me a leg up on my father. Once again, I walked down the hall, obtained access to VILLAINS, and punched into it for Johnny Roselli. A good deal came back.

JOHNNY ROSELLI aka Johnny Ralston, aka Rocco Racuso, aka Al Benedetto, aka Filippo Sacco. Born in Italy (Esteria) in 1905, immigrated to the US in 1911, grew up in Boston, is reputed at age 12 to have assisted a relative in burning down a house to obtain the insurance.

First arrest, 1921: narcotics peddling.

In 1925, Filippo Sacco becomes Johnny Roselli. Works with Al Capone on liquor shipments.

Reported expert at extortion, gambling, labor racketeering, Roselli becomes a West Coast cohort of Willy Bioff and George Brown of the International Alliance of Theatrical Stage Employees and Motion Picture Machine Operators. Early in World War II, Roselli became close friends with Harry Cohn, head of Columbia Pictures. Lent money by Cohn at no interest to buy into Tijuana Race Track, Roselli, in gratitude, purchased matched twin star rubies set in matching rings for Cohn and himself. Both men still reputed to wear such rings.

When Sammy Davis, Jr., was conducting a "torrid" love affair with Kim Novak, Roselli, as a favor to Cohn, is reputed to have convinced the Negro singer to forgo any further favors. Novak was Cohn's number-one blonde star at Columbia during this period. It is reported that Sammy Davis, Jr., blind in one eye, was told by Roselli: "Cool off on the blonde, or you lose the other eye." Davis complied.

In 1943, Roselli served 3 years, 8 months of ten year prison term for extorting reported two millions plus from the film industry. On release, became the Top Coordinator for Las Vegas and Southern California rackets. His appointment was overseen by Sam Giancana, reputedly head of Mafia's Grand Council.

Roselli is now known as Don Giovanni of the Mafia. Ambassadorial in appearance. Is called the Silver Fox. Reputed to be a loner. Has family but never visits them. Has, however, put his younger sisters through college.

Physical description: Slim. Medium height.

Well-chiselled features. Silver-gray hair. Reported credo: "Never threaten me. I have nothing to lose."

I sent this printout to my father by SPECIAL SHUNT/HALI-FAX, and added a note that I had looked up RALSTON in VIL-LAINS and found nothing, but happened to come across ROSELLI AKA RALSTON, a fortuitous accident, I added, since there were thousands of entries under R.

Next day a call came in from Cal on open phone. "Get thee to a nunnery at 4:00 P.M.," was all he said, and it meant, "Call my private line from an outside phone at 1:00 P.M." When I reached him during my lunch break, he was as garrulous as if he'd just had three cups of coffee. "Thank you," he said. "I went right over to K Building to bring Bissell up to date on the meeting between Maheu and Roselli. Thank you. I didn't feel like telling Bissell that Maheu was meeting someone whose name I could not offer. Well, Rick, right there in Bissell's office was Allen Dulles, and, of course, he couldn't resist looking at what I'd brought over on Johnny R. I could see that Allen was reading the printout upside down. For that matter, Bissell kept the paper well out on his desk so as not to obstruct Allen's view." My father began to chuckle. "Have you practiced reading upside down lately?"

"Not daily," I said.

My father laughed louder. "Son, in OSS days we used to believe that was the only ability you needed other than a little moxie."

"Yessir."

"Allen has made it clear he's to be kept one watertight compartment away from all of this, but, just the same, he couldn't resist comment. 'Well,' he said, 'these are fishy waters, aren't they, Cal?' 'Damned fishy waters, sir,' I said. He smiled. 'Cal, I'm just going to make one remark: Use your judgment. Use your judgment, Cal, because it's always kept you out of the very worst trouble, hasn't it?' 'No, sir,' I said, and we both laughed, because we both knew that if anything goes wrong, the tar is on my fingers. All the same, this one appeals to me. It's lopsided, but it's fancy, isn't it?" he said, and added, "I wonder if you can find out where the lunch took place. Maheu was staying at the Beverly Hills Hotel, so it could have been the Polo Lounge."

"I'll do some research," I told him.

SERIAL: J/38,961,601
ROUTING: LINE/QUARTERS EYE—OPEN
TO: HALIFAX
FROM: ROBERT CHARLES   10:46 A.M. SEPT. 6, 1960
SUBJECT: RESTAURANTS

      I presume to take up Company time and encoders sufficiently to bring you up to date on Los Angeles restaurants you might like. I'd pick the Brown Derby. I hear via the Yale grapevine—an old class-mate, of all things, is working for Harry Cohn—that that's where the cognoscenti go.

ROBERT CHARLES

    On the next morning, another letter bound in strapping tape was in the pouch for me:

Sept. 7, 1960

Son:

      Your restaurant guide is most useful. It helps to bring a transcript to life.

      Now, I confess that I did not fill you in on all the details of Maheu's first meeting with Roselli. Such reserve is *pro forma* since you had no real need to know, but, considering your good work lately, it makes me happier to bring you up to date. Roselli has a friend named Sam Gold whom he needs to take into the project. So he claims. Gold has deep contacts in our target country. Next question is whether Sam Gold happens to be Meyer Lansky or Sam Giancana. I've had a talk with the case officer I've assigned to work on this in Washington and New York, an ex-FBI worthy I believe you know. Says he had you in training, one dour but most capable gent named Raymond Burns, Bullseye Burns. According to Ray, these Mafia boys have the predict-able habit of holding on to their first names while using a false last name with the same initial, viz—Johnny Ralston for Johnny Roselli. Sam Gold puts us on track for Sam Giancana. Maheu, however, warns me not to assume Lansky is out of the game—Sam Gold could also be the redoubtable Meyer. Whoever he is, Gold is ready to come in. I assume that the mobster who recaptures the gambling casinos will then have a clear and dominating position in the Syndicate.

      For the interim, a meeting has been set up at the Plaza Hotel

in New York on September 14 involving Maheu, Roselli, and Bullseye Burns. Since Roselli insists on meeting a "top-drawer associate,"
it is up to Bullseye to rise to the occasion.

> Keep the Hubbard fortunes prospering, son. Yours, and love,
>
> Dad

On the next day, another message came from Cal:

> Sept. 8, 1960
>
> Son:
>
> I enclose a copy of Maheu's report on the Plaza meeting at
> Trader Vic's:
>
>> Dear Mr. Halifax,
>>
>> The restaurant din made for low-level accuracy in our
>> recordings. Neither Mr. Burns' take, nor mine, has proven satis-
>> factory. I am, thankfully, a longtime hand at keeping mental
>> notes when there are obstacles to viable recording. So I offer my
>> recollections of the proceedings, and place reliability at 90 per-
>> cent for substantive matters, and 60 percent, at least, on precise
>> word-to-word reconstruction. On the other hand, given the
>> noise, our Bureau *friends* could not possibly have tapped in.
>>
>> Ralston sized up Case Officer Burns quickly, and was
>> rude. Ralston said: "Take no offense personally, fellow, but I can
>> see you are on the kiss-ass level. That is inadequate for this
>> operation. Pass the word to your boss: Do not try to fuck me
>> over."
>>
>> I must say that the language came as a shock since Ral-
>> ston, in appearance, is as silky and well gotten up as George Raft.
>>
>> Burns had to spend time assuring Ralston that the next
>> meeting would be on a "higher level" and was a good soldier
>> about it, but from old days in the Bureau together, I know his
>> temper. Raymond Burns has a virulent hatred of hoodlums high
>> and low. I do not wish to denigrate old "Bullseye" since I am
>> aware of his bulldog tenacity and other sterling virtues, but for
>> liaison with Ralston, we cannot anticipate any hope of future
>> compatibility.
>>
>> Burns, however, had the massive discipline to be silent,

and I kept pursuing the main subject. In response to my inquiry, Ralston finally stated that our next meeting would take place in Miami Beach at the Fontainebleau, September 25.

We proceeded to modes and methods. Ralston said, "You don't want a fire-hose for the job. This can't be St. Valentine's Day."

My understanding from our initial meeting is that you want the signature of the operation to suggest the Mafia. Five hoods with machine guns would offer a clear message to the world that gangland did the job.

These fellows, however, want none of that. I think we have to forgo the most useful option. The question may then arise whether we still want to work with these particular elements. While I, of course, make no recommendation, Ralston also said, "We have all the contacts needed to get to El Supremo."

"What method do you propose?" I answered.

"Pills," said Ralston. "Powder it into his chow. He'll be sick for three days before he gets sick enough to call for a priest." We ended by agreeing the pills would be passed on to Ralston on September 25, at which time it might be advisable for you to meet him.

Sincerely,
R.M.

A note from Cal followed this memo:

I'm naturally concerned. We'll have to make haste to be ready by the 25th. The order, via suitable intermediaries, has been placed with the Office of Medical Services, who will probably have to use some of the more exotic labs in TSS. There is no possibility that Hugh won't sniff out some of this. The question is: How much?

HALIFAX

22

By THE MIDDLE OF SEPTEMBER, I HAD SUBLET AN APARTMENT, AND Modene and I entered our first crisis.

It began with a change in her schedule. Due to a temporary shortage of stewardesses in the Southwest, her base, she informed me, was to be shifted to Dallas for a few days, and she would have to absent herself from Miami for four nights in a row.

If I sensed she was lying, I kept such bad news away from myself. She would call me at my new lodgings every evening with detailed accounts of the day's trip: Once she telephoned from New York; on the following night from Dallas; once she went to Memphis and back to Dallas on the same day. She underwrote these trips with tales of passengers who had been particularly good or horrendous.

By the fourth day, I could believe her no longer, and checked her story. Given the number of exiles who flew on Company business to New York, Washington, New Orleans, Mexico City, and points south, not to speak of the alert that was always on in Miami for Castro agents coming into southern Florida, we had a number of Agency contacts at the airport. It took our pool secretary no more than fifteen minutes and two phone calls to bring me the information that Eastern Airlines stewardess M. Murphy had been on four-day leave and would be returning to town this evening, September 14.

Jealousy lives for the facts. Meeting Modene in downtown Miami, I felt purposeful. It was late, and we went at once to my new apartment in Coconut Grove on the second floor of a small made-over Spanish Colonial house, and I made love to her before we had done any talking, a military matter; if our bridges were blown, it was crucial to get new pontoons across. So I knew what it was to be desperate with love. I fucked in hate. There, in my own modern, furnished apartment which I could desperately not afford, I was desperately in love with half of me, and that half could find but half of Modene. Speak of being drawn and quartered by love, I remember looking with hatred at her long fingernails. They had ruined pieces and parts of many evenings for us, those fingernails lacquered, even elegant on the upside, patched and splinted beneath. The fingernails belonged to her vision of an exotic (if still unrealized) dragon lady who shared very little of her existence with that other girl who lost her temper when she could not beat me at tennis, poor Alpha-girl with her handicap. Alphie had to wear gloves to protect her nails, and what with adhesive tape and putty fillets on the fingertips for underpinning, paid for it at a rate of about two lost games a set, and still ripped her nails. She wept over that, more, I suspected, than she would ever cry for me, furious tears at the wasted hours and contradictory purposes of those mandarin nails, but how well she could use them at night by the light of a candle in a restaurant, how perfect was the poise of her cigarette in its holder, yes, her spiritual roots, I decided, were as far from one another as the orchid and the weed.

On this night when she came home, I did not speak of what I knew. If I was not incapable of killing her, all the same, I never could. Was that what it meant to be desperately in love? She made no effort to explain why after four days and nights of the hardest dislocations of her former flight schedule, she had no time off, but, to the contrary, would be out again tomorrow on a Miami-to-Washington-and-back-to-Miami in the same day, only to be booked like that for the next two days as well (an unheard of gymkhana—seven working days in a row!), no, she must have known I was bright enough to calculate that she had been on some species of vacation, yet I learned no more until a week later when a BLUEBEARD–AURAL transcript was delivered to me at Zenith by GHOUL's resident baboon. Modene had spent the four days in Chicago with Sam Giancana. Polishing the transcript, I could see that Willie's curiosity was at least equal to mine. Had Modene slept with Giancana?

No, Modene insisted, she had not gone to bed with Sam. She had come to like him. "Frankly, Willie, he is all too human."

"Do you feel sorry for him?"

"No. He is too strong for that. But there is sorrow in his life."

"Such as?"

"Stop cross-examining me."

Their exchanges became repetitive. I compressed their conversation to manageable length and offered Harlot a portrait of Giancana.

WILLIE: Did he take you to his home?

MODENE: Absolutely.

WILLIE: Is it a palatial mansion?

MODENE: No, but it's elegant on the outside and very well built. Like a fort. Lots of careful stonework. And it's way out in Oak Park.

WILLIE: North of Chicago?

MODENE: Yes. Oak Park. I impressed Sam when I said to him, "This is the small town where Ernest Hemingway grew up." "Who is this guy Hemingway," asked Sam, "one of your boyfriends?" and of course I said, "Wouldn't you like to know." And Sam said, "You think I'm an ignoramus, don't you? Well, we got newspapers out here. I see this man's name, Hemingway; Hemingway and me, we're the two most famous people in Oak Park," and he started to laugh. He always laughs the loudest at his own jokes. I guess he's been living alone with himself for a long time.

WILLIE: The house. What's the story on the house?

MODENE: Will you wait? Inside, it's nothing fabulous. Small rooms, heavy Italian furniture. Down in the basement there's one room without windows that is his office. It has a long table for meetings, I guess. But he also keeps a breakfront cabinet down there with some amazing glass pieces. He is a collector. You see another side of him altogether when he reaches in and takes out a piece. His finger movements are so delicate. Willie, if I were ever going to have sex with Sam, this is exactly what would initiate such impulses.

WILLIE: So one thing did lead to another?

MODENE: Stop.

WILLIE: Why won't you tell me?

MODENE: Nothing to tell.

WILLIE: What did you do at night?

MODENE: He loves piano bars. The smokier, the better. He calls for a number and then he sings along with the pianist. Only, Sam keeps changing the words. You know: "Why won't you take all of me? Me and you and all of me. Just put out the lights and go to sleep." The poor pianist. Sam has a voice like a broken foghorn. I couldn't believe it—I was having fun.

WILLIE: Did he get serious?

MODENE: Yes. He told me about his mother's death. I found that heartbreaking. She saved his life, you know. When he was about five and growing up in the Italian slums of Chicago, she heard a car come whipping around the corner, and there was Sam playing in the gutter. His mother leaped out to get her child back on the sidewalk and so she got hit by the car. She died. I felt so sorry for Sam. Then he told me about his wife. She was very delicate. She was born with a weak heart, and her family, although an immigrant Italian family, must have been a cut or two above his because all her folks looked down on him. And then, to top it off, he had been in jail for car theft. When he came out, he and his wife were so poor that they lived in a cold-water flat and sat around the stove and held their two little girls and toasted orange peels for candy. And one of the little girls had a weak heart too. It was all kind of touching. You see, before she knew Sam, his wife had a fiancé but he died early. So, she was always mourning the dead fiancé. It took a long time for Sam to feel like the true husband.

WILLIE: That's so clever of him.

MODENE: Why?

WILLIE: He's letting you know that he can put up with the idea of Jack Kennedy.

MODENE: He keeps calling me Miss Classy.

WILLIE: I wonder if he's afraid to go near you. Because of Frank Sinatra. What if he doesn't stack up by comparison?

MODENE: Willie, you are so inaccurate. In the first place, Sam knows I would never tell Frank. And in the second, Sam would be a different kind of lover. Much more emotional.

WILLIE: I am sorry, but Sam sounds lugubrious to me.

MODENE: Well, he's not. He can make you laugh till you don't stop. He told me a story about Bobby Kennedy, when Bobby was getting ready a couple of years ago to have Sam called up before the McClellan Committee. Do you remember the McClellan Committee?

WILLIE: Yes. They investigated crime.

MODENE: Well, Sam made a point of getting himself decked out like the cheapest kind of gangster, you know, suit and shirt all black, with a silver tie, and the moment he came into Kennedy's office, he knelt and fingered the wall-to-wall carpet and said, "This would be great for a crap game." Just then a lawyer came into the room and Sam grabbed him, patted his back and thighs and yelled out, "Don't get near Mr. Kennedy. If Bobby gets killed, they'll all blame me."

WILLIE: I guess it is kind of funny.

MODENE: Absolutely. I needed a break in the mood.

WILLIE: Pardon me for asking, but what's wrong with Tom?

MODENE: Nothing. I don't want to talk about Tom.

WILLIE: Will you tell him you saw Sam?

MODENE: Certainly not.

WILLIE: Are you sure you won't? You said the more jealous Tom became, the better he was as a lover.

MODENE: This topic is, as of now, exhausted.

On open circuit next day came a message from GLAUCOMA inviting me to use the secure phone.

"Those girls, Harry," were Harlot's first words, "do go all over the place, but it proves useful. I've had a little research done, and now can assure myself that Mr. Giancana is one hell of a liar. He was never saved by his mother. It was his stepmother who was killed in the car accident, but she was saving Sam's little stepbrother, Charles. Giancana's real mother had died years before on a somewhat less heroic note. Infection of the uterus."

"Yes, he is a liar." In fact, I could not believe the intimacy of his lies. A man who was ready to break your legs should not have to lie about his mother.

"Moreover," said Harlot, "Giancana did not go through any shenanigans in Bobby Kennedy's office. One of my people checked with a former McClellan staff member, and it develops that a gentleman named Joey Gallo was the comedian on that occasion. Sam merely appropriated the story."

"Yes, a total thief."

"Now, who is this Tom that little Miss Bluebeard refers to? Have Tom and Harry formed a fratry known as Field?"

"Yessir. It was my way of telling you."

"You are telling me that you have hooked the mermaid?"

"It happened most recently."

"Why is there no material resulting from this?"

"Because our lady is not at all forthcoming, sir, and I don't wish to rouse her suspicions."

"Well, get started, boy. Giancana may be using her as a courier to Kennedy. Be a good Tom and try to find out if the girl is carrying any messages."

"I'll try," I said.

"Do better than that."

"I'll try," I said. "It's going to take time and luck."

"Plus a cold tit," he said, and hung up.

23

HOW WAS I TO TELL HARLOT ANYTHING ABOUT THE AFFAIR? MODENE had never been able to come with a man before. So she told me, and I believed her. Could I not? How she could come! I do not know what amalgam of her alcoholic father and her socially ambitious mother contributed to the whole, but now I knew why women filled me with awe. If certain ladies, Sally Porringer, most notably, could remind you of a sledgehammer assaulting a wall, Modene came from her fingers and her toes, her thighs and her heart, and I was ready to swear that the earth and the ocean combined at such moments in my beautiful, athletic, and fingernail-tortured girl. I would feel her body pass through me, real as my own existence. So I made my peace with her lies. About the time I despaired of ever being able to cozen, elicit, trick, bully, or otherwise stimulate a confession out of Modene, she, perversely, offered me one. It was the first of several to follow, and reminded me of our first meeting.

"Do you remember Walter?" she asked me one day.

"Yes."

"I feel like telling you about Walter."

I had enough sense not to say: "I'd rather you tell me about Jack." Instead, I nodded. We were in bed, and cozy; we could speak of small horrors as though they were on the other side of a window.

"Do you still see Walter?" I asked.

I looked forward to enjoying her reply that she did not, but instead she said, "Yes, I see him sometimes."

"Now?"

She nodded. She could not speak. I wondered if it was from fear she would burst into laughter at the expression on my face.

"Since I last saw Jack," she said at last, "since the convention, I have seen Walter again."

"But why?" I did not make the next remark, and then I had to. "I'm not enough for you?"

"You are." She only paused for a moment. "Except that there must always be two men in my life," she said. She seemed pleased with this fact, as if she had invented a fail-safe for any and all emotional disaster.

"Then you have been seeing Walter all the time you've been with me?"

"No, just a few times. Just so I could feel there was someone else in my life. It allows me to enjoy you more."

"I don't know if I can bear this," I said.

"Well, I couldn't see Jack. He did something I didn't like. Would you be happier if I had been with Jack instead?"

"Yes," I said, and knew at that instant why jealousy is so perverse an emotion—it enriches our wits—"yes," I said, "I would rather you had seen Jack."

"You are lying," she said.

"No," I said. "At least I could compare myself to someone worthwhile."

"Well, maybe we can do something about that," she said. "Are you inviting me to start up again?"

"You couldn't. I don't know why you broke with him, but your pride is hurt. I know that much."

"Oh, I could never approach him," she said, "unless I was asked to. Unless there was some kind of external reason."

"There are no external reasons," I told her, "in matters such as this."

"Well, there are. Suppose a good friend asked you for a big favor. Would you oblige?"

"You are being awfully abstract," I said.

"Suppose this good friend wanted you to pass a message to someone you weren't talking to anymore."

"The recipient would still believe you were looking for an excuse to approach."

"Yes," she said, "that is true unless he happened to be in touch with the other person in the first place." She yawned sweetly. "Can we make love?" she asked.

Her confessions, for this night at least, were at an end.

I sent a message to GHOUL—SPECIAL SHUNT next morning. It read:

RAPUNZEL and IOTA maintain some contact through BLUEBEARD. Will try to discover the content of such communications. Foresee implicit obstacles.

FIELD

Harlot's reply:

    If it takes weeks, well, you've gotten me used to walking around in the same old clothes.

GLOCKENSPIEL

24

SUNDAY, THE TWENTY-FIFTH OF SEPTEMBER, MY FATHER CAME TO Miami on the earliest plane out of Washington, and in considerable anticipation, I accompanied him to a meeting with Robert Maheu at the Fontainebleau. I say anticipation because Maheu had become a legend in the Agency. Given our compartmentalization, that was no routine achievement. An ex-FBI man who now maintained his own detective agency with Howard Hughes for a flagship client, Maheu could lay claim to more than a few professional feats. I had often heard of a monumental job he pulled off in 1954 for Richard Nixon, who was then, in the interests of an American oil group, looking to complete a multi-million-dollar coup at the expense of Aristotle Onassis.

It is possible Maheu was even more renowned among us for the pornographic movie he was reputed to have made on black-and-white film with two assistants, a man and wife from his office serving as actors to represent, respectively, Marshal Tito of Yugoslavia and a large-bosomed blond mistress. Excessively grainy, streaked with light, the movie was filmed by choice under abysmal conditions and a few stills were extracted from the result. No one could later declare to a certainty whether the pornographic lover was or was not Josip Broz Tito when the product was circulated among carefully selected circles in Europe as a means of discrediting the Marshal.

On meeting, Robert Maheu looked to be the most elegant private detective in the nation. He was wearing a pin-striped suit with a vest, his Windsor knot was immaculate, and I would have taken him for a continental banker with a particularly expensive mistress.

"I'll be going down the hall in a little while to have a chat with our new friends," Maheu remarked, "and the news I've received from them is that Santos Trafficante will be present with Sam and Johnny today."

"Good Lord," said Cal, "Trafficante from Tampa?"

"Sam has brought him in. Says we can't do it without him. Of the three, Santos does maintain the largest resources in Cuba."

My father nodded. "What are the chances," he asked, "of taping your meeting?"

"Mr. Halifax, a few weeks ago, I might have been able to. But now, after several get-togethers, I've become one of the boys. I tell you this not as a question of where my loyalties are—they are, of course, with us—but rather as a practical matter. It simply won't work. Giancana and Roselli are feelers. They test your biceps, they run their hand down your back. In effect, you can't shake hands without getting frisked."

"Is an attaché case," asked Cal, "too obvious?"

"They clam up," said Maheu, "at the sight of one. I have to go in clean. But, as you know, I've trained my memory. I can save the high points for you."

Perhaps he did. When he returned to my father's room two hours later, it was to tell us that Giancana was stoked up.

" 'Robert,' he said to me, 'I have used a couple of names in my day. Cassro is one of them. Sam Cassro. I used Cassro before I ever heard of Castro.' Roselli actually whistled. 'You must be destined for this,' he said. Giancana answered, 'I have had the same thought myself. Destiny. Robert,' he said to me, 'I hate Castro. I hate that syphilitic, murdering bastard. I am ready to do it, Robert.'

" 'Good,' I said.

" 'I am ready, except for one practical matter.' Then he paused," remarked Maheu, "and gave me a very sly look. 'Maybe,' Sam said, 'the job is not necessary. I have heard it from the inside: The guy with the beard is syphilitic. He will not live six months.'

"Trafficante cut in at this point," said Maheu. "It was the first time that he spoke, but I will underline my observation that even Giancana listens to him. 'Castro,' Trafficante said, 'has 360-degree vision. With all due respect to Sam, I do not think Fidel Castro is all that ridden with syphilis, since his brain seems to be working very well these days.'

"Giancana was not ready to reply to that. So, he changed the subject. He picked up this Sunday's *Parade,* which happened to have an old mug shot of him, and said, 'Can you believe how fucking ugly they make me look?' Roselli jumped right on this, of course. 'A conspiracy,' he says, 'to tell the truth.' Giancana goes, 'Ha-ha.' Then he stands up and pokes Roselli in the chest with a finger. 'The fact of the matter,' says Sam, 'is that they got a fellow on these magazines, a worm they keep in one of the closets who comes out and crawls over fifty fucking photographs they got of me, and when he finds the *worst,* the worm pisses on it. Then these other newspaper creeps come in and sniff his piss—here's the photograph we want, they say, sniff, sniff, and they print it. Always the worst photograph,' says Sam."

"You have total recall," said Cal.

"Just about," said Maheu. "I like this side of meeting with the boys. They are funny. Trafficante pops into the conversation to say, 'Think of the impact you make on people, Sam, when they finally meet a good-looking fellow like you.' "

"This is entertaining, I must admit," said Cal, "but what was substantive?"

"Very little. These fellows sidle up to a proposition. They keep their business vague."

"We have a target date for late October. At the latest, early November."

"Comprehended. The little shipment we discussed has been handed over to them. They assure me they are going ahead. They refuse, however, to divulge specific plans. There was some talk about a young lady who is the girlfriend of a gunrunner named Frank Fiorini who has been active in the Cuban exile movement. Apparently, she had an affair with Castro a year ago, and now this Fiorini is trying to convince her to go back to Havana, pop into Fidel's bed, and drop a powder into his water glass. As backup, they are relying on a restaurant where Castro eats often, and the headwaiter is sympathetic to us. Nothing, however, has been nailed down to my satisfaction. We have no choice but to depend on people who can be as reliable or unreliable as they choose to be. I will not pretend this is a sound operation."

"When do I get a look at your buddies?" asked Cal.

Arrangements were made for him to drop into the Boom Boom Room tomorrow near midnight. Richard Nixon and John Fitzgerald Kennedy would have had their first debate by that hour, and Maheu would be eating with Giancana.

"Fine," said Cal. "I have a host of errands in Miami tomorrow." What they were, however, he did not impart to me.

Late on Monday night, so late that it was early Tuesday morning and Modene and I were sleeping in our new king-sized bed, I received a call from my father. "I'm wondering about the hygiene at the Fontainebleau," he said, "inasmuch as I am calling you from my room."

"If you haven't brought your own bug-killer, assume the infection approaches plague levels."

"Oh, we can cope," said Cal. But I could sense how drunk he was. "It's easier than getting up to go to a pay phone."

"Couldn't we have breakfast tomorrow?"

"I'm gone with the dawn, old buck." He coughed his heavy cough. "I'll pouch you a line."

It was just as well he did. When I removed the strapping tape, it read:

Son—

I was introduced to His Nibs as a sportsman acquaintance of Bob Maheu's. "Sportsman, huh," asked G., "what do you go out looking for?" "Big game," I told him.

"Like Hemingway," he said.

"Yes," I said.

(Have to tell you—we were scorching the air with our mutual adrenaline.)

"Mr. Halifax is an old friend of Ernest Hemingway's," said Bob.

Giancana, I must say, took that one up. "I'd like to meet your friend," he said. "Hemingway and me got things in common. I know the burg where he grew up."

"Yes," I said, "Oak Park."

He stuck out his hand as if now he could trust me. "Oak Park," he said, "you got it."

I asked his opinion of the debate. "A richee versus a guy who's sucking up to the richees. Take your choice, Mr. Halifax."

Bob said, "Mr. Gold is for Jack Kennedy."

"On points," said Giancana, "I score it. More mileage with the richee."

After I said goodnight to them, I was up for a while in the other end of the hotel, their Poodle Lounge, dreadful name for a place to get drunk in—I expect the ladies' room is called Tinkle Time. At any rate, Maheu came by for a nightcap and told me Giancana is obsessed with the way Castro spoke for four hours today at the UN, same day—get it!—as our presidential debate. Giancana said to Maheu, and I quote Robert's masterful Rules of Recall, "How are you going to kill a guy who can talk for four fucking hours? If," said Giancana, "you stick a shotgun up his ass and pull the trigger, he won't even fart."

Son, that had me laughing like a banshee. If you remember, I called you up. For five minutes it must have seemed awfully important to me to get that arcane piece of hoodlum savvy over to you. How drunk, oh Lord, how drunk. The bones won't take it much longer.

It's hard to explain, but I rather like this Giancana. He gives me the confidence (on the most casual level of conviction, of course) that he knows as much about his business as I about mine. Let's hope I'm right. I do wish security didn't keep me from getting a little closer to him.

Yours,
Cal

In Post Scriptum:

As you've gathered by now, I am something of a hands-off executive. I cannot tell you how many times a day I send up blessings to Tracy Barnes and Dick Bissell for catching the brunt of administrative chores at Quarters Eye. Even so, I expend sixty minutes each morning reading cables-in, and another thirty for cables-out, every blessed working morning, and double on Monday. I think it is for this reason that I write letters, and preferably late at night, when my demons and old ghosts argue with me. I tell you this in case you have similar troubles. A good letter organizes the mind. So, if the mood comes on you, give me the rundown which, given our larger preoccupations, neither of us got around to last weekend, concerning your daily Zenith stint now that Howard Hunt is in Mexico. Even more, give me some idea of what Howard is really up to out there. The verdict at Quarters Eye is that Hunt is too ambitious, and so never sends the bad news until he is absolutely obliged to.

Incidentally, use the pouch. Address it: EYES ONLY, HALI-FAX. Bind it with the right tape, needless to say.

Dad

I did not try to gauge whether I had a conflict of loyalties. It was enough that my father wanted some intelligence from me.

25

Sept. 28, 1960

From: Charles to Halifax:

Since Hunt left Miami on August 15, he has been making a thoroughgoing attempt to establish the Frente in Mexico City, but is having trouble. The facts, as I receive them from Howard by cable or phone, may be old news to you. But I will proceed on the assumption that I offer a few new items.

The core of the problem is Win Scott. I know Mr. Scott is one of our most esteemed Station Chiefs, but my guess is Howard was off to a built-in bad start once he brought an operation into Mexico City that was not directly under Scott's jurisdiction. In addition, the Mexican government—again my assessment comes from Howard—is over-impressed with Castro's potential to stir up the revolutionary sentiments of the populace, so they are offering small welcome to Cuban exile movements. Howard has lost whole working days getting Frente officials through Mexican customs. Moreover, the Mexican authorities keep harassing the newspaper office of *Mambí,* the Frente's weekly sheet here. *Mambí* has been prey to daily persecutions via fire laws, foreign labor restrictions, trash removal fines—the usual.

In the meantime, Howard, who certainly likes his perks, has had to put up with a rent he terms "wholly excessive" for a small furnished house in Lomas de Chapultepec. The cover story he imparts to old social friends is that he has resigned from the Foreign Service because of disagreements with the leftist drift of our policies in Latin America and is now hard at work on a novel. In the course of picking up these bygone relationships, Howard has also managed to recruit an American businessman with old Agency ties to rent a couple of safe houses for us where Howard can meet with the Frente. Under no circumstances, however, are the Cubans allowed to learn where Don Eduardo lives. The separate lives of Don Eduardo and E. Howard Hunt are not permitted to encounter each other. This generates a considerable amount of daily travel. Howard made certain the safe houses were on the other side of the city.

Needless to remark, paranoia has not lessened in the Frente. Distrust of the U.S. abounds. The leaders may be in Mexico at our request, but the body of their movement remains in southern Florida; hence, they claim our concealed motive is to elevate them into figureheads for world opinion, even as we remove them further from the real and future leaders who command the invasion force. Working against this premise, Howard has had his hands full at more than one ugly meeting. For a further complication, Barbaro is not there now. He went back to Miami a month ago on an errand, and the others can talk about little else but Faustino's failure to return. Hunt has been importuning me to get on Toto's tail.

Barbaro, when I do see him, swears that he will go back to Mexico as soon as he can get his affairs in order, but is strangely wistful about it. I think he would really like to, but is trapped. Howard is convinced that Barbaro is engaged in a criminal caper involving considerable money. Howard says we need a Miami-based agent to get the goods on Toto, and I have been chasing through stacks of three-by-fives. Sad to relate, the most promising of the candidates, if I can recruit him, is not even a Cuban but a former Uruguayan Communist who used to work for me in Montevideo. I was instrumental in having him flown out to Miami one step ahead of the local cops and his former Party associates. His name is Eusebio "Chevi" Fuertes and he now works in a Miami bank that launders some of our money for the exiles. Barbaro, incidentally, uses the same bank, which fact brought me to consider bringing Fuertes into this.

I must tell you that I hesitate to employ him. I had a reunion with Chevi last night and it gave me pause. He is all but pro-Castro, so if I did not know him well, I would not go near him. In Montevideo, however, he acted in much the same manner, forever deriding the possibility that America, being capitalist, could ever have a decent motive. Yet, no agent was more valuable to us in Uruguay. When it came down to it, he hated the Communists even more than he hated us. Of course, if you have some agent you would prefer, well, so would I.

Incidentally, Fuertes has already provided me with one extraordinary piece of local news. It seems everyone in the Frente, Barbaro most of all, is terrified of a wealthy Cuban millionaire named Mario García Kohly who is a devout Batistiano, considers Castro equal to Satan, and sees the Frente leaders as concealed agents for Castro, and therefore prime subjects for assassination. Kohly has ties with a former Cuban senator named Rolando Masferrer who maintains an army of thugs and killers from the Batista days; they are holed up in a place called No Name Key which Kohly owns. Via Fuertes, I hear that some of our Agency people (certainly unknown to me) have been trying to put together a private invasion army for Kohly, and provide him with boats. If successful, it would be a disaster, I think, since such an adventure would produce a civil war. (Of course, I may be seeing too small a part of the picture.) Fuertes, whose instinct for gossip impresses me as salient, adds that the *deepest* rumors in the exile community assert that Kohly's support comes from the White House. Not the top, but awfully close to it.

I must say that with Hunt gone, I have been so busy that I did not expect this letter to prove as enjoyable as it did. I persist in hoping that some of my stuff has *stance* for you.

One looks forward to your next visit.

Your health,
Harry

26

Sept. 29, 1960

Dear Dad:

It appears that I do enjoy writing to you, since here is another letter on top of yesterday's, and I am keeping my lady friend—about whom I will tell you one of these days—waiting. She is not a lady to cool her heels.

I want, however, to say more about my meeting with Fuertes. I need your reaction to his trustworthiness.

First, a word about Chevi's appearance. When recruited three years ago in Montevideo he was an exceptionally handsome fellow, slim, rather muscular, and a knockout with the ladies. Becoming an agent altered him drastically. He ballooned in weight, grew an extra-long, down-raked handlebar mustache (semicomic), and was otherwise a slob.

Here in Miami, he is still much overweight but has become a dude. Wears tropical three-piece suits in off-pastels. Panama hats. He smokes Havanas with Habanero aplomb, and looks more Cuban than the Cubans.

While I will make no claims to Bob Maheu's powers of recall, I believe that what I will offer you here is substantively accurate (90 percent). I did take notes as Fuertes spoke.

I must say that it is disconcerting how much he knows about

us and what we're up to. He is a born coffeehouse type and frequents all the Cuban restaurants, from Versalles on down to the lowest hangouts on Calle Ocho. He not only sweeps in gossip, but, a born intelligence man, evaluates it. On the day I invited him over to a safe house, he knew, for example, that September 19 was the date we set for completion of the Guatemala training camp, and the site is called TRAX and will train an exile brigade of 400 men.

    With no difficulty, he lays out the sociological components of TRAX. Ninety percent of Brigade trainees, he tells me, are students and professionals of middle-class background. Ten percent are workers, peasants, and fishermen. (That is certainly correct—I've been at the recruiting stations.) He can even specify trainee garb and weapons, to wit, combat fatigues with black baseball caps, and grease guns. All correct, Chevi. Where do you get it? But we know. To Cubans, revolution is a family matter, and everyone talks to everyone in the family.

    Chevi did surprise me with his next statement. "I calculate," he told me, "that on the day of the invasion there will be no more than 1,500 men."

    I smiled back at him. I didn't have a clue myself. I decided, however, to play devil's advocate, and said, "It's impossible. That number of men could not take Cuba."

    "They could," Fuertes told me, "if Castro is truly detested by the masses. After all, Batista was hated, and Castro required less than a thousand *barbudos*. Of course, now the realities are different."

    He proceeded to give me a lecture. When Castro was still in the hills, there was but one doctor for every two thousand people. "There's an old Cuban saying," he informed me: "Only the cattle are vaccinated." Then came a somewhat leftist presentation. (I believe his statistics, but distrust something in the liturgical aspect. Still, his figures did startle me.) Under Batista, 4 percent of the Cuban peasantry ate meat regularly; 2 percent ate eggs; 3 percent, bread; 11 percent, milk. No green vegetables. Rice and beans everywhere. Half of the homes on the island were without toilets of any kind. Yet, in Havana, there were traffic jams and TV sets. To be a Habanero was to believe that Cuba was an advanced Latin American country. "Havana, not Cuba," he remarked, "is the spiritual center of your exiles. They are all middle class."

    "You sound like a man who is for Castro," I said to him.

    "No," said Fuertes, "as always, my heart is divided." I must warn you that he is not without a Latin penchant for metaphysical bluster. "The man who spends his life engaged in a contest between his right hand and his left hand is always choking within," he said solemnly.

"Why are you not for Castro?" I asked.

"Because he destroyed the liberties. A man like me, placed in Havana, would be dead or in the underground."

"Then, why are you not against him?"

Right here he began an interesting, if long-winded, disquisition on the nature of revolution and capitalism which is guaranteed to irritate the hell out of you.

Capitalism, says Fuertes, is essentially psychopathic. It lives for the moment. It can plan far ahead only at the expense of its own vitality, and all larger questions of morality are delegated to patriotism, religion, or psychoanalysis. "That is why I am a capitalist," he says. "Because I am a psychopath. Because I am greedy. Because I want instant consumer satisfaction. If I have spiritual problems, I either go to my priest and obtain absolution, or I pay an analyst to convince me over the years that my greed is my identity and I have rejoined the human race. I may feel bad about my selfishness, but I will get over it. Capitalism is a profound solution to the problem of how to maintain a developed society. It recognizes the will-to-power in all of us."

As you must have gathered by now, he is in a state of beatitude when he can sit in a chair, drink an *añejo,* and pontificate. So he posed a dichotomy I had never thought about before—the fell difference between the dumb and the stupid. "It is a profound difference," he said. "The dumb are weak mentally, and that is sad, but final. The stupid, however, have made a decision to be stupid. They exercise a willful negative intelligence. Their need-to-power is gratified most easily by obstructing the desires of others. Under Communism, where the present is presumably sacrificed for the future, the stupid stop up all the industrial pores. Slovenliness and inefficiency are their secret pleasures. Under capitalism, however, a greedy but stupid man is faced with a painful choice. So long as he remains stupid, he cannot satisfy his greed. Often, therefore, he is obliged to open his mind to be large enough to find some way to thrive. So, men who would be obstructive under Communism become instead, under capitalism, successful pricks and rich shits."

Not resting for a moment there, Fuertes next said, "On the other hand, the Communist cadres are indispensable to Castro. Without them, his revolution would be wholly disorganized. With them, he has a bureaucracy capable to some degree of running the country."

"Then you are not saying that Communism is bad for Cuba?"

How hard it is to bring him to focus. "No," he says, "I am not certain. I paid a visit six months ago. The women impressed me. You should see how they look in their red blouses and black skirts when they march and sing in unison. Communism is solidarity for them."

I must say that I was thinking at this moment of Howard's description of the same ladies. If I recollect, Howard called them "as cacaphonous as a tribe of she-goats."

"Indeed," said Chevi, "these women are profoundly moving to me. They have a sense of their own existence that they never had before. Castro has a visceral sense of how to provide theater for the masses, magnificent, grandiose, political theater. Why, when Batista fled Cuba at the end of 1958, Castro did not rush to Havana. He started from the Sierra Maestra, and stopped in each major city on the route to make a four-hour speech. Overhead would be a large black helicopter. It was a sensational choice. The angel of death above, and equal to the liberation. Death was a fundamental part of his revolution. Of course, the women understood. The Spanish mentality perceives us as here on earth to bleed and to die—that is the given. If there happen to be more doctors, more education, more decency in the economic details, well, what a trinity—blood, death, and progress —a revolutionary program for Latins."

"Why," I ask him, "isn't that equally obtainable with the exiles? They are far to the left of Batista, but they are also for freedom as well." (I must say—having been around the Frente—that I sounded a little undercooked to myself.)

"Yes," said Fuertes, "but can any radical improvement be accomplished in a poor nation's economy without a reign of terror? Castro answers in the negative. The only human motive more powerful than greed, he suggests, is terror. If the exiles take back Cuba, the corrupt who are among them—most numerous, I promise you—will form a network of greed. They will triumph over the idealists."

"So you are back with Castro?"

"I am with neither, I am with both. I am for myself."

We discussed pay. He wants a great deal, $300 a week. Plus bonuses. I believe he is worth it. Fuertes obviously likes to inhabit two worlds at once, but I think I can manage him if he is inclined to work a double game.

Please advise.

Harry

My father's answer came the next day. The envelope read: EYES ONLY ROBERT CHARLES.

Communication of Sept. 29 received:

Your Uruguayan sounds like a sophisticated Communist to me, and a complete double-dealer. He is so corrupt, however, that the money may keep him in line. I will approve if you obey certain basic procedures:

1) No more political discussions with him. He could be probing your attitudes and passing them on.

2) Keep to limited objectives always. I will send you specific assignments. Do not stray. He will give you the kitchen sink when all you want is one washer. Get him down to the washer. I will, of course, test his take by whatever corroborative opportunities are available to me.

3) Never get to like the guy too much. I don't care if you did save his life.

4) Absolute case-officer protocol. *Never* connect him to anyone in Zenith or Quarters Eye without advising me in advance.

5) The first objective to use him on is the fat Cuban you took to dinner. Call the fat Cuban RETREAD.

6) Let's choose BONANZA as the saddlebag for your windbag friend.

HALIFAX

27

BEFORE I COULD HAVE ANOTHER CONVERSATION WITH CHEVI, HOWard Hunt flew back abruptly to Washington, and obtained permission from Quarters Eye to return the Frente to Miami. Since it was Cal who authorized the move, I assumed my letter had contributed to the decision, although as I later learned, one of the safe houses in Mexico had been discovered by the Mexican police, and given the general situation our other safe house would probably prove useless.

So, Howard brought the gang back to Miami. He was gloomy. He could receive no kudos on his record, and Dorothy was hardly pleased at the disruption this had caused in the lives of their children. Schools would have to be changed once more. Besides, Howard would have to use his living quarters in Miami for working situations. To protect Don Eduardo's cover, was he to ask his daughters to take on other last names as well? It was hopeless. The Hunts had to suffer a temporary separation. Dorothy rented a house in the environs of Washington and Howard kept his apartment in Miami. Of course, they now needed new fictions to explain to relatives in America why they were living apart.

His woes did not sweeten his temperament. If I had been under any impression that I was covering his absence with efficiency, he soon set that vanity packing: My record-keeping was exposed for what it was, passable, and when it came to the laundering of exile funds, Howard was not pleased with the number of transactions I had assigned to couriers (in the hope, as I tried to explain, that payment by hand rather than by check would cut the trail). The problem, of course, was that there were few available couriers we could trust with large sums. It usually came down to me, and I had enjoyed wearing money belts with sums as large as a hundred thousand dollars in them. Indeed, part of the pleasure revealed itself one night when I managed to have the money belt on, even as I was undressing for Modene. The knowledge that her slightly mysterious lover was carrying wads of cash managed to ignite new afterburners in Modene and in me—yes, I liked being a courier.

Hunt would have none of that. It was irresponsibly dangerous. Let word get out, and one could get robbed or killed. There were ways to transfer funds by written order that could still confuse the record. For that, he had a more experienced intermediary, a fellow named Bernard Barker. He would introduce me to him.

I had made other mistakes as well. The lesser members of the Frente with whom I had been dealing in Howard's absence had begun to work out some military plans. They went into considerable development of detail and in the course of that, I had looked at many a map of Cuba, all eight hundred miles of the island, and began to enjoy various problems in logistics and strategy. Hunt, however, explained to me that military discussions with the Frente had to be seen as a harmless exercise, entertaining to one's sense of irony. "I recognize," said Hunt, "that it is tragic for some of these Cubans to remain innocent of their tactical impotence, and I am going to have no pleasure in explaining this condition to them when the time comes, but, Harry, face up—the key factor we confront is the DGI agents sent in by Castro. They are bound to pick up Frente plans and pass them back to Havana. So keep tipping your input toward disinformation. This operation is too important to leave it to Cuban generals."

"I know you're right," I said, "but it does get to me."

"Ethics, Harry, has to be subservient to the mosaic."

I was thinking of the boatmen. A portion of my labor had gone into calling various boatyards from Maryland down to Key West and across the Gulf from Galveston to Tampa; we were in the business of buying used powercraft. Each night, boats were going out with Cuban exiles, some to plant explosives, others to infiltrate a few people back into Cuba where they could link up with underground organizations. A boatman might be getting killed right now as we spoke. I sighed. It was hard to know whether history was a chart you could study, or a tide.

One morning not long after Hunt's return, I received a call from Dix Butler. He was coming to Miami for a short visit. Could we have dinner?

My first thought on hearing his voice was that Modene must not meet Dix. Love, I decided, was all too determined to explore one's courage or the lack of it. I actually moved a supper date with Modene over to a later date in order to keep her away from Dix.

Butler, however, came off the airplane in a flat mood, and did not get around in any hurry to explaining his mission in Miami. In fact, we did not leave the airport. We drank in the nearest lounge.

"How long here?" I asked.

"Two days. I'm looking a couple of people over."

"Can I ask who you are working for?"

"Negative."

We drank for a while. We barely talked. Neither of us brought up Berlin. We were acting like men between whom nothing much had ever taken place. All the same, his flat mood menaced the air.

Out of a silence, I asked, "Are you still with Bill Harvey?"

"I might be." He took a full pause. "I might not."

"What is Bill up to?"

"Count on it," he said. "Whatever it is, it is crazy enough for King William."

We laughed—somewhat experimentally.

"I assume," I said, "that he's now in Washington."

"Decent assumption."

"Are you working for him?"

"Is your name Arnie Rosen?"

I had forgotten how powerful was Butler's jab.

"In fact," said Dix, "that's how I found you. Through Arnie Rosen. Ask *him* what I'm doing. *He* probably knows."

"I assume you are working for Bill Harvey."

"I might say no. My work is peripatetic."

He was wearing an expensive gold watch and a tropical silk suit that must have cost five hundred dollars.

"Can you tell me where you've been the last three years?"

"Laos."

"The Golden Triangle?"

"It's the mark of an asshole to keep asking questions," said Dix.

"If," I said, "you told me what you are here for, I might be able to help you."

"You can't," he said. "I'm looking for a couple of Cubans who can handle weapons, steer a boat, live off the jungle, fear nothing, manage their rum, and thrive in filth. Got any recruits?"

"You'll find them."

"Let's wipe this conversation." He literally passed his hand over his face before he said more equably, "I have a couple of appointments to get to."

"Good," I said.

He stuck out his hand. I shook it. He did not try to destroy my metacarpals. He contented himself with staring into my eyes. I suspected he had been drinking since morning. "We're all in it together, right?"

"Yes," I said.

"Do you respect Castro?" he asked.

"I think I do."

"I hate the son of a bitch," he said.

"Why?"

"He is a year younger than me, and he has done more than I have done so far."

I thought of making a joke, but he was too serious. "Look," he said, "at any given moment, there are something like twenty superior people on earth. Castro is one of them. I am another. God, or whoever it is—it could be a fucking committee for all I care—has put us twenty down here on earth."

"Why?" I asked. "To torture you?"

He laughed at that. He was merry for a moment the way a lion would be merry if the wind blew in one good unexpected whiff of carrion. "You," he said, "are making decent efforts not to be stupid."

Well, indeed, I was glad I had not brought Modene.

"Still," he said, "you have it backwards. We are put on this earth to entertain the gods. By our contests. I respect Fidel Castro, but I am not overawed by him. I have a prayer: Put Fidel and me in the jungle together, and I am the one who will come out alive."

After that, he was silent. Then, he was morose. When I finished my drink, he barely nodded as I left the table.

I called Rosen from the nearest pay phone, and woke him up. It was his night to catch an early sleep, but he did not grumble; in fact, he was quick to ask, "Did the big fellow look you up?"

"Certainly did. And certainly has a number of things he doesn't care to talk about."

"Yes," said Rosen.

When he said no more, I waited before I asked: "Could you fill me in?"

"I could," said Rosen, "but why should I? Our relations, Harry, are becoming a one-way street."

I was more drunk than I realized. I almost made a long speech to Rosen. It would have said that in our work, the little piece one held of the whole was such an intense and crystalline piece of information that it created a tension, even a thirst in oneself to be filled in on, yes, the *collateral* data, so, of course, we all gossiped and wanted to know more. If we laughed at Arnie, it was envy, yes, Rosen, I said in my mind, it's a form of respect, when all is said, that we call you to find out, but all I managed to mutter after what must have been a not wholly ineffective silence was, "I suppose, Arnie, if you don't tell me, I won't sleep as well."

"So instead you woke me up." This made him laugh, even gave him a good one, as if it suited his notion, after all, of our relations, and he said, "The big guy had to leave Berlin under a cloud."

"Because of Iron-Ass Bill?"

"No. Because of an Inspector General. Iron-Ass actually saved him. Got him transferred to Laos."

"And that's all."

"That's all I know."

"No, it isn't."

"How can you presume to make that remark?"

"Because I know as much as you. I know he was in Laos."

Rosen found this funny as well. "God, are you drunk," he said.

"Yes, I had bourbon for bourbon with the butler."

"Oh, you don't want to do that. Butlers are notoriously ramrod, if you know what I mean."

"What I mean is, what is the big guy doing now?"

"I won't tell you. Not under these auspices. I will only say—so that you don't feel obliged to suck your thumb through the night—that he is associated once more with William the King, and it's so hush-hush that it's vanguard, supersecret, a fence, let us say, around the fence. Please do not ask me any more."

"I won't, because you don't have that much to offer."

"You are absolutely right."

"Tell me then about the Inspector General who came to Berlin."

I could feel his relief. This news was, after all, less sensitive. "Well the big guy had an ex-Nazi agent whom he no longer trusted, so he strung the fellow up and put turpentine on his genitals. Said it was to get a little closer to the truth." Rosen began to laugh. "I know, it's painful, but I have to laugh because the big guy said, 'I made the Kraut hop. Think of all the *Juden,* Rosen, that this Nazi once kept hopping.' And it was true, according to Dix—oh, hell, I'll use his name. My phone is safe. I make certain it is. And you're at a good pay phone, right? Dix says he, personally, always kept a double standard. That meant less mercy to ex-Nazi agents who had gotten naughty than run-of-the-mill agents who had gone bad. Only, Dix made one mistake. These ex-Nazis have a network. The turpentine victim complained to an influential friend in the BND. Bad luck for Dix. We had an Inspector General in Berlin that week who has a permanent burn on one side of his face. Naturally, the IG had sympathy for another burn victim. Dix was in the worst trouble of his life until Bill Harvey used his weight to get our big guy transferred to Laos." Rosen sneezed. "You've done it again. I've told you all."

"My blessings," I said.

Later that night when I filled Modene in on a few modest things about Dix, and confessed that I had not wanted her to meet him, she was pleased. "You have nothing to fear from a man like that," she said. "I could never be attracted to him."

"Care to tell me why?"

"If he is the way you say he is, he is fixed in his mold of life, and I could not change him. I can't be too attracted to a man I cannot change."

I was about to say, "Can you change Jack Kennedy or Sam Giancana?" but I held back. Instead, I said, "Do you believe that you can alter me?"

"Oh," she said, "it's just difficult enough to be interesting."

28

AS THE PRELUDE TO A COUPLE OF BAD WEEKS FOR MY FATHER AND FOR me, Nikita Khrushchev took off his shoe one afternoon at the United Nations and began to hammer on his desk with it. That same date, October 12, Robert Maheu received word in the morning that the pills to poison Fidel Castro had reached their final destination in Havana. I had an odd reaction. I began to wonder whether some mute sensor in the Premier's brain was telepathic and Khrushchev had stirred into anger without quite knowing why. If such speculation came under the head of what my father called "freestyle thinking—costs nothing, accomplishes nothing," I could still hear the echo of that shoe. In my ear, it tolled like a bell announcing the end of Castro's life; in advance, I mourned him and concluded that Castro had betrayed something grand in himself. Such contemplation of one's enemies produces rich melancholy.

Of course, he was not exactly dead, not yet, and my work continued, and my nights with Modene. I never slept during those weeks without expecting a phone to awaken me with an announcement of Castro's demise, but the phone never rang.

At the end of the third week in October, a letter, via pouch, came from my father. It was not Hunt's habit to pass by my cubicle first thing in the morning, but the old Chief-of-Station instinct may have been working. Hunt, in fact, was sitting in my chair, the letter held between two fingers as I came in. Standing up, he passed it over to me wordlessly. The heading read: ROBERT CHARLES EYES ONLY.

"May I ask whom this is from?"

It was within his prerogative to ask. Technically speaking, anything that passed under my eyes belonged to his eyes as well. I might run a small and secret operation, but I was not supposed to keep it secret from him, not on demand.

"Oh, well, it's Cal's," I said. "He likes to correspond in this fashion. Uses it for personal correspondence."

"Is that really so, Robert?" He called me Robert whenever we were at Zenith. I called him Ed. Howard deemed it necessary.

"It's true, Ed."

"Well, it's also unheard of. I could bring your father up on charges."

"What are you saying? Come on!"

"I wouldn't, of course. But a Senior Officer has to set an example."

"I won't pass that remark on to him."

"No, of course not. It's something for me to bring up with the man if I feel so inclined."

"I wouldn't bring it up at all."

Hunt looked furious at my impertinence, and then he shrugged. "One more rogue elephant on my watch."

"Nothing to worry about," I said. "It *is* personal correspondence."

When he was gone, I read the letter. Many another important message has become no more than a line of summary in my memory, but I recall all of this letter. It is burned into my brain by the livid attention I gave to it; I could not help but shudder at the thought of Howard reading it.

Oct. 25, 1960

Start BONANZA on RETREAD. No need for personal contact yet. Just have him dig into RETREAD's accounts. If, as I expect, they are spread over several banks, BONANZA may have to contact a few friends in rival institutions. This is not an uncommon practice among young bankers, I can tell you. (They never know where they'll be looking for work next.)

That, son, will constitute the good news. Now, prepare yourself for a shocker. But first, let me describe the messenger. Richard Bissell, one's immediate boss these days, is an impressive figure of a man. Not for physicality, mind you. He is a big man, but I could bounce him off a wall. It is his mentality. He is at home in fine and contemplative halls of mentality. You are familiar with the Cathedral of St. John the Divine on 110th Street and Amsterdam Avenue in New York? Of course you are. St. John's is a wondrous center for meditating upon the monumentality of thought itself. And to me, Dickie Bissell is the embodiment of that spirit. I want you to picture him. He is six feet six at least, imposing in height even for you or me, and, for fact, when you are sitting down with him, he still seems somewhat overhead. At a desk he will listen to person after person most attentively while he bends paperclips slowly and thoroughly in his long white fingers. Otherwise, he gives you all his attention, his head towering above his pale long hands—Rick, I have to tell you they are as white as good breeding itself, an odd remark to make, except that when I was a boy, that's how I saw good breeding—pale, long hands. Bissell keeps toying with paperclips as if they are tactics and operations, little endeavors down on the plain, so to speak, *particularities*, and he, great massive white man, hovers above, great white massive brain power embodied in white, puffy establishment body— Lord, he is the archetypal dean of Harvard, huge, gentle, wholly removed from all the goddamned dirt of operations. His features are delicate. Son, he's almost beautiful in the chiseled perfection of his chin, his lips, his nostrils, and the shaping of his eyes behind his horn-rimmed glasses.

Well, isn't the above just as pretty a piece of writing as I've ever sent your way? Did I tell you that for a year after World War II, I thought of trying to become a writer, then gave up? All that rich personal material from OSS, but I didn't want to make a fool of myself. Besides, writing gets you looking at your wife out of the corner of your eye. About the time Mary would remark, "It's getting to be picnic-weather time again," I would be ready to add, "she said," so I decided to put my art into my letters, ha, ha.

At any rate, here I am resolutely straying from the point. I have reason: Bissell, whom I obviously could revere (if only he didn't have a bit of potbelly, but a thunderously good boss all the same), called me over from Quarters Eye to K Building this morning and handed me a memorandum from J. Edgar Hoover to Richard Bissell.

During recent conversations with several friends, Giancana stated that Fidel Castro was to be done away with very shortly. When doubt was expressed regarding this statement, Giancana reportedly assured those present that Castro's assassination would occur in November. Moreover, he allegedly indicated that he had already met with the assassin-to-be on three occasions. Giancana claimed that everything has been perfected for the killing of Castro, and that the "assassin" had arranged with a girl not further described to drop a "pill" in some food or drink of Castro's.

Bissell looked at me and said, "All right, Cal, how did Mr. Hoover obtain such information?"

Son, if you ever get in one of these situations—sooner or later, we all do—start by enumerating all personnel in the know. It gives you time to think. It also separates out the likely possibilities. I started by naming the Director, which produced a baleful look from Bissell. "The Director," he said, "is not associated with this. Begin with me."

I didn't argue. After Bissell, I came next. We could trust ourselves. Then Sheffield Edwards. Ditto. It was Bullseye Burns' turn. He had been an FBI man but could probably be vouched for. Besides, he had not been at the Fontainebleau.

"Your son," said Bissell, "is touchy ground for us. But I will accept your evaluation. Can you vouch for him altogether?"

"Yessir," I said. "One hundred percent. That is one good young man." (I did not tell him that the family vice is hyperbole.)

Which left Maheu and our three Italians.

"I see no reason for Maheu to play a double game with us," said Bissell. "It might sweeten future associations for him over at the Bureau, but look at how much he loses here if the job doesn't come off."

"I couldn't agree more," I said.

"Is Roselli sincere in desiring citizenship?"

"Maheu swears to that."

Which left Giancana and Trafficante. We agreed that I needed a sit-down with Maheu to go over their bona fides.

The key to the problem is, how much has Hoover really picked up? Bissell's thesis is that so long as the FBI does not know of our relation to Giancana, Hoover's memo cannot hurt us. Yet why is Buddha sharing his information with the Agency? Does he have more, or does he wish us to believe he has more?

When Maheu came up to Washington, I learned that Giancana has a girlfriend named Phyllis McGuire. She's one of the McGuire Sisters, who sing on TV for Arthur Godfrey. There was some sort of gutter splash a year and more ago when Julius LaRosa and Dorothy McGuire were getting a little too open about their hanky-panky, at least for Godfrey's taste—that monumental hypocrite! Godfrey couldn't live without fast and fancy sex is what I happen to know, but won't let his minions enjoy same. Remember? He said Julius LaRosa was lacking in humility. If this country ever goes under, it will be for needless, egregious hypocrisy. At any rate, the McGuire Sisters are lively girls apparently. Phyllis owed, I was told, a marker in the neighborhood of $100,000 at the gaming tables of the Desert Inn; Giancana was gallant enough to tear it up for her. What a nice way for a romance to begin! Our Giancana, Maheu now assures me, is close to insanely jealous of Phyllis McGuire. It seems the lady has a soft spot for one Dan Rowan of the comic team of Rowan and Martin—can you keep up with these people? Maheu's first hypothesis is that Giancana told Phyllis about the Castro project in order to impress her; then Phyllis, in her turn, told Rowan. Somewhere in all those links, the FBI has a taping, and it could be on McGuire.

Now to Maheu's backup thesis: Giancana is deliberately shooting his mouth off to any number of cronies. Reason: He wishes to sabotage the operation. Motive? Maheu shrugs. Giancana might be advertising his ties to the Agency in order to get the Department of Justice off his back. He is certainly not to be trusted.

Next comes Maheu's read on Trafficante: For years, Santos was the mob's number-one man for gambling operations in Havana, and still has the best networks there. After the revolution Castro kept him in jail with a suite of rooms, a TV set, visitors, special food. It sounds like one hell of a protracted negotiation. Trafficante's claim is that he promised the moon to Castro, but has not delivered since he got back to Tampa. So, he is anxious to eliminate the big Cuban before the compliment is returned. All the same, I suspect that Castro is doing business with Trafficante, and Toto Barbaro is in on it. Just an intuition here, but I have come to trust such instincts.

Let us get to your role. I have, as you may have noticed, more than filled your need to know. Do take exceptional care of this letter. Indeed, give it to the shredder if you do not have an *endroit*. Or get one. They're worth the expenditure. For years, I confess to you, I've had a safe deposit box in a remote little bank up north. Another in

Boston. One in Washington, of course. Think on these lines. If you can preserve my letters, do so. Some decade, long after I'm gone, Agency barriers may come down, and you might want to do a memoir of your old man. Assuming he's worth the portrait. If so, these letters will help to flesh it out. For today, and this week, however, I believe you do have real need to know all this, since I will be less easy to reach. My next ten days have to be spent on direct military matters. I can tell you that working with Joint Chiefs staff is about as agreeable as transferring from Yale to Indiana State.

In my absence, stay close to Maheu. He and I came separately to the same conclusion: We need a tap on Phyllis McGuire's phone in Las Vegas. It will enable us to know whether she is witting. Maheu suggested the Agency do the job, but I cannot chance any of our people being implicated should something go wrong, so I told Maheu that the ball, like it or not, was in his court. After all, what kind of private detective is he?

Later

Ay, caramba! Maheu called to tell me Giancana is going to quit unless we lay in a tap on Rowan. Sammy is obsessed with McGuire's possible infidelity. He must find out. Why not put the tap on McGuire, you may ask, but my assumption is that our guy doesn't want his calls to Phyllis monitored. Rowan, therefore, it must be. Maheu next proceeded to entertain me with an imitation of Giancana expressing his sentiments: "If this tap comes in with the goods, I will cut Rowan's balls off and glue them to his chin. I will give him a fucking goatee to go with his mustache." "Is it," asks Maheu, "Rowan or Martin who has the mustache?" "Who gives a fuck?" answers Giancana. "I'll cut off his nose and shove it up his ass."

I'm left with the cold assessment that this is a risky caper. You will find, I think, that the larger one's stake on a job, the more a surrealistic element is likely to pop in. Here we are waiting on tiptoe, day after day, for news that the big tree has fallen in Cuba. Yet, in the midst of such unholy anxiety, up pops the little Eyetalian demon and swears to become a veritable Abaddon—O ye angels of the bottomless pits! I *hate* everything about this Giancana business. My disaster warning system (which used to advise me from a half mile off that an irate husband was on his way back to the very connubial bed I was in the act of despoiling) now tells me to beware of this one. Rick, stay on top of it! Maheu is only intermittently forthcoming, so don't hesitate to ask tough questions. Get him to review his safety factors before we give the go-ahead on the job. Fill me in directly by pouch.

Yours from sleepless Halifax

Oct. 28, 1960

Great Caliph Halifax—

I don't know if Maheu is a bad man or a fine man. I have seen a good deal of him in the last couple of days, but he is simply beyond my reach. A ponderous yet velvet dimension resides out there. One knows when one is outmatched.

I limit myself, therefore, to focusing each new question on the gap left by Maheu's answer to the previous one. We make progress, but I am sure he sees me as some sort of pill to be taken on the hour.

Nonetheless, I have learned this much: Trafficante and Giancana are certainly devoting time to the Havana op. Sammy, of course, has a good deal of other business here in Miami, as does Traff in Tampa, so it isn't as if they labor full time in our interest. Still, our agent has arrived in Havana with the medicine. Much depends on whether this former girlfriend can become Fidel's sweetheart again. Her American-based boyfriend, Frank Fiorini (who fought with Castro in the Sierra Maestra and is now associated with some very hard-core hoodlum Cuban exiles in Miami), has passed on to Maheu the information that El Caudillo sleeps heavily after making love, snores, and in the past was not wholly satisfactory to the girl's olfactory senses. (At least so she has told Fiorini.) It seems Castro's cigar breath is offensive.

God, we hang on these details as if they were the relics of a saint!

I give the above to bring you up to date on our off-shore venture. Now, for Vegas. I have imparted your concerns to Maheu and he assures me that the job will be relatively safe. For one thing, we will *not* tap the telephone. A spike-mike, no larger than an eight-penny nail, inserted in the baseboard near the phone will record whatever the target says on the phone, and in addition we will hear any conversation that takes place in the room. In addition, we are not breaking the federal and Nevada statutes that forbid wiretaps. No law exists against eavesdropping from an adjoining room, even if it is by way of a spike-mike.

Perfect, I tell him, but what if the man doing the installation is caught?

Maheu gave me an interesting rundown on the precautions to be taken. For one thing, the operator will occupy a suite in the same hotel. He will remove the lock to the door between his living room and bedroom, and bring it to a selected locksmith in Vegas who can then fashion a master key for all the guest rooms in the hotel. Now our operator can knock on the target's door, and if there is no answer, open it. He will have an assistant standing by to whom he will hand over the master key. The assistant will spill a few drops of whiskey on the operator's suit, and take off down the hall while our operator enters target's room and proceeds to make the installation, after which he sets the door button on lock and leaves. If for any reason target should happen to enter the room while the operator is there, the cover story will go as follows: Our operator is drunk (indeed he reeks of booze), he doesn't know how he got into the room, the door must have been open, he displays his own room key, and wanders out. If it is a house detective who interrupts him, the routine will be similar except that a hundred-dollar bill is likely to change hands.

"What happens," I asked Maheu, "if security comes in suddenly and there is our man on the floor with all his tools out?"

"That is a contingency which a skilled operator would not allow to evolve," said Maheu. "His tools are small and carried in loops on the inside of his vest. The drill is no thicker than your finger, and the screwdrivers have flat handles. It's a jeweler's kit, you could say. Only one tool is kept out at a time."

"What about sawdust?"

"Carefully gathered up as soon as it is created, then disposed of via the toilet fixtures."

"Couldn't the operator be on his knees," I ask, "using a drill on the baseboard just at the moment security comes in?"

"Not at all. The door to target's room will be on the chain. No one, therefore, would be able to enter without a chain-cutter. Our operator will have time to pick up his tool, stow it on his person, go to the door, unhook the chain, and commence impersonating a drunk."

"But," I persist, "if there is a body search, the tools will be discovered."

"Yes, but a body search is not the most likely of contingencies."

"Still, it could happen."

"There are no final guarantees."

"What would eventuate if there is discovery?"

"Well, there can be no legal charge against the operator for the spike-mike. The case comes down to breaking and entering. Since neither the lock nor the door is broken, a good Vegas lawyer ought to be able to get it thrown out of court. Of course, the operator has to stand fast. We'll get a good fellow."

Maheu is planning to use the DuBois Detective Agency in Miami. The operator will be a man named Arthur Balletti. Neither DuBois nor Balletti is to know any more than that they have been hired by Maheu, and he has provided them with the target's room number.

Maheu's precautions do impress me. Given our need to keep abreast of who is telling what to whom, I would vote for a go-ahead. Under the circumstances, reasonably safe.

                                                    ROBERT CHARLES

29

ON THE NIGHT OF OCTOBER 31, I AWOKE IN THE EARLY HOURS WITH a feeling that it was imperative to check for messages at Zenith. Since the sleep had been heavy, I thought at first I was in my own apartment, and it took the view of moonlight on Biscayne Bay as seen through the picture window of the master bedroom to remind me that Modene and I were not only at La Nevisca and ensconced in the king-size bed, but sleeping heavily from the effects of several sticks of marijuana.

We had started to smoke earlier this night after her flight-mate told her, "It is great for sex," and gave her half an ounce. Our evening turned paranoid. Modene confessed that Sam Giancana made her nervous. "If he wanted to spy on us, he has the people to do it. He could locate your apartment in no time. Even this place."

"Are you sleeping with him?" I remember asking.

"I told you that I am not. But we are friends, and he does want to sleep with me."

"What do you tell him?"

"That I am in love with Jack."

"Which is true."

"It is half-true. Just as it may be half-true that I am in love with you."

"But you don't tell Sam about me."

"I tell him that I sleep only with Jack."

"And do you? Are you back with him?"

"You know the answer to that," she said.

"It is yes."

"Yes."

I felt as if I were bleeding within. Yet, the professional requirement was on me: Ignore pain, pursue inquiry. So I said: "Maybe Sam and Jack are in contact with one another."

"They may be."

"Through you?"

"I resent your asking. I know who you work for."

"Whatever are you talking about?"

"You are a special agent for the FBI. Your friend, the *Life* photographer, told me."

Good Sparker Boone. "It's not true," I said. "I happen to work for the Treasury Department. Bureau of Narcotics." When she did not answer, I nodded. "I'm a narco."

"Why don't you arrest me? Because I am going to turn you in." She took another puff on our stick of marijuana and handed it back to me. Soon enough, we began to make love.

Images of Modene in bed with a would-be President crowded in upon images of vichyssoise and hamburgers in the dining room on N Street. The theater opened in my mind with all the solemnity of a curtain rising on a heavily furnished stage. Yes, there was Modene in the middle of an antique bed performing various kinds of whoopee. Lucky candidate. Large hydraulic pressures in my groin were abstractly reminiscent of lust. Sex on marijuana was bizarre. Large and occult was its arena. Beautiful were the curves of the belly and breast, and eloquent was the harmonium of universal sex; its laws came into my senses with one sniff of her dark-haired pussy, no more at other times than a demure whiff of urine, mortal fish, a hint of earth—now I explored caverns, and our bodies began to obey a master rhythm that came from as far away as the drumbeat of an unseen army, one rhythm, wondrous, yet impersonal. I could have welcomed Jack Kennedy into bed with us at that moment. What the hell, we were all equals in the great eye of the universe; the thought took me over the hill; I was rocked about in the engines of orgasm, and felt sensations as strange as lives one would not know how to inhabit: I saw Fidel Castro sleeping with the blond mistress of Frank Fiorini on a Havana bed one hundred and eighty miles away. A cigar was in the mouth of El Caudillo as he snored. Then I forgot them all, and rolled down the hill, and slept in the tomb of the drug marijuana, and awoke —was it an hour, was it more?—with weights upon my thoughts as heavy as the air of the Everglades in summer. Sleep was possessed of entrails; I had to tear myself loose from them. There was that imperative in my brain: I had to call the night officer at Zenith.

When I did, there was a message: Contact HALIFAX at Rock Falls.

Still in a half-sleep, code words came to the surface more sluggishly than pond fish in a swamp—Rock Falls meant . . . Rock Falls meant *Call my office as soon as possible.* Adrenaline was pressing against torpor—bronze glow across a leaden sky. I did not care at this moment if I ever saw marijuana again.

There was a pay phone on the road to the Rickenbacker Causeway. I could drive there to make the call. I would have to assume that if Modene awakened, she would not panic at finding herself alone in a safe house with no means of transportation, no, not at all. She could, yes, by all means, *ring for a cab.* My brain made large leaps to solve little problems.

By the time I reached Cal at Quarters Eye, it was 3:14 A.M. "Give me your number," he said. "I'll call you back in eight to ten minutes." His voice offered no more than a modicum of recognition.

Just outside my phone booth, the mosquitoes were demented. I felt the synthetic nature of Key Biscayne soil; beneath one's feet were shells and ground coral, channel mud, shoulder asphalt. Inside the telephone booth, sizable bugs darted from glass door to glass wall on a high electronic hum. Then the call came through.

"Listen," said Cal. "In Vegas, this afternoon, Maheu's operator, Balletti, went into the target's room, set to work on the telephone, and then got so hungry that he couldn't finish the job. He decided to go down to the coffee shop. During the interim, he left behind a few tools, a couple of phone taps, and a half dozen wires stripped and ready for splicing."

I could feel my stomach yawing, a physical event I had not experienced so keenly since childhood.

"A head chambermaid happened to come by," said Cal, "to

check the room. She saw the evidence on the floor. She called the house detective. He was waiting in the room when Mr. Balletti came back from lunch and opened the door with his master key. Mr. Balletti did not reek of whiskey."

"Oh, no," I said.

"Do believe it," said Cal. "When they arrived at the police station, Balletti called Maheu at his Miami office. In order for the police to make the phone connection, Balletti was obliged to give them Maheu's number."

"Oh, no," I said again.

"Well, yes," said Cal. "Wiretapping is a federal offense. For some godforsaken reason, Balletti had not tried to put in a spike-mike, no, he was in the act of tapping the telephone. A federal offense. In a few days we will have the FBI on Maheu's ass, and he will proceed to support that weight for as long as he can take it, and will then proceed, I expect, to tell the Bureau that he was doing a special for us."

"Have you spoken to Maheu?"

"I have been on the phone for hours with everyone. Bullseye Burns, believe it if you will, has been in my face. Representing the Office of Security. I discovered this afternoon that our overall project actually began with the Office of Security. They hired Maheu, and then, to cover their bald, incompetent asses, Sheffield Edwards talked to Dulles, Bissell, or whoever-it-was, to get me in on liaison. Unfortunately, it was never quite made clear to me that this was not entirely my show."

"Could that be in your favor now?" I made the mistake of saying.

"Not at all. The Office of Security is claiming that I proceeded without Bullseye Burns or Sheffield Edwards. The fact of the matter is that I did, and that I have been had." He came to a halt and started to cough. Phlegm volutes overlapped in his bronchia.

"Now," he said, having delivered one quantum of the misused past to a handkerchief, "we still have to have a real talk with Maheu. Believe me, I have been occupied with Sheffield Edwards and his stalwart henchman, Bullseye Burns, who had the temerity to suggest that I shunted him aside in order to give his job to a tyro named Robert Charles."

"I am a tyro," I said. "I advised you to go along on Maheu's plan."

"Yes, you were a bit of a fathead. But I was a horse's ass. Maheu has Howard Hughes to deal with daily. He is busy. I know that. He is no longer a private detective; he is a confidence man. He does public relations. How dare he give you such a splendid summary of how to do the job and then choose people who fulfill none of his precepts?"

"Did you tell him so?"

"At white heat," Cal growled. "Until I realized that I need him to hold the line. So I backed off just a little. Now, you go over and quiz Maheu quietly. Go over right now. To his office. He is expecting you. Has been for the last three hours. Where the hell were you tonight? Don't you ever pick up your telephone?"

"I was out."

"Doing what?"

"Fucking."

"Well, at least one of us isn't being fucked."

Yes, he had come a long way from St. Matthew's. "Do you want my report in the morning?" I asked.

"Hell, yes. Make certain it is in the early flight pouch."

HALIFAX EYES ONLY

November 1, 1960, 5:54 A.M.

Maheu and I shared coffee from 4:00 A.M. to about 5:30, at which time I came back to Zenith to begin this report. Needless to say, I took copious notes, and can give you an accurate summary and reliable quotes.

Let me say that even if I was taken in once by Maheu's confidence, I would testify that he seems genuinely upset. We spoke in his private office which, as you might expect, is lavish, carpeted, and honored with an antique sideboard. He took the lights down a little, then opened the blinds for the hints of dawn on Biscayne Bay. We have impressive black clouds this morning. It fits the mood.

Maheu stated that his previous rundown on how to perform the operation described the way he would have done it. He finds himself guilty for neglecting to check out Balletti's procedure in more detail.

Here is what, in Maheu's belief, did occur. For whatever reason, perhaps to save a few extra dollars, Balletti did not hire a backup man in Vegas. It is possible, says Maheu, that Balletti never had any intention of installing a spike-mike. They are difficult to adjust, and may not have been available on short notice. Balletti, however, says Maheu, claims to have misunderstood him. Maheu does not believe that for a moment.

Now, as to the master key. Balletti did not, in the absence of an assistant, bother to hide it in the hotel hallway, but put it back in his pocket. An unforgivable exhibition of carelessness. Moreover, he did not carry a flask, nor purchase a small bottle. Fastidiousness, or the desire to save on cleaning bills may have been "the withholding factor."

Finally—the descent to the coffee shop "for sustenance." Maheu assured me that that is not at all inexplicable. Breaking into a stranger's abode kicks off, he says, deep-seated psychological mechanisms. Thieves often defecate on living room carpets, or on the counterpane of the master bed. Some get hungry. It is a primitive reaction. The hotel was quiet, and Balletti did not believe there was one chance in a thousand that a chambermaid would check up. "I do not approve, however, of his odds," said Maheu.

When I asked why Balletti made the mistake of phoning him, Maheu shrugged. "I can offer no explanation other than that he lost his head."

This is Maheu's official explanation. There can be, of course, another track. For some time, Maheu resisted my questions. I had, finally, to suggest that I was following leads you had suggested. "You are asking," Maheu said at last, "were we set up by Giancana?"

"The question does exist," I told him.

"We are now in the realm of uninformed hypothesis," said Maheu.

"Let us speculate."

"It is possible," he said, "but what would be Sam's motive?"

What was tacitly agreed upon is that our project with "the boys" has to be placed on hold. As Maheu avowed, it is in the Agency's interest that nothing happen to Castro right now. Since the FBI is well aware of Giancana's interest in assassinating the Cuban leader, they might connect that to the Vegas hotel room and Maheu. No new ventures, therefore.

I confess that I enjoyed talking to Maheu. At the end, almost incidentally, he said in passing, "Do tell Mr. Halifax that I, too, have people who are angry at me." Again he raised one eyebrow. It must be Hughes or Nixon of whom he speaks. That is why I do not think there is any likelihood that we were set up by Maheu himself. Hughes, by all accounts, is very much a Nixon man.

Yours in time for the pouch,
Robert Charles

30

ON NOVEMBER 2, A CABLE ARRIVED FROM CAL ON ZENITH/OPEN. It read: THANK YOU FOR A GOOD CLEAR ASSESSMENT.

That was the last communication from my father for a period, and it was just as well. My work for Hunt was increasing by the day. Rumors had swept Miami that there would be an invasion of Cuba in advance of the election on November 8, and a fever undulated in from Havana. The traffic in agents had never been higher. In a memo sent to my father at Quarters Eye, Howard wrote, "Zenith is bogged down with a small army of amateur spies who assume that espionage needs no more for technique than a little nepotism they can call on in Cuba. Of course, once we dispatch them back to the homeland, they seem to contact no one but friends and relatives. It should not take a classical education to realize that not every friend is, in troubled times, a true friend. Nor does the history of *el Mar Caribe* allow one to forget that Latin families in these tropical climes do manifest loyalty and treachery in equally balanced Shakespearean proportions."

Hunt was pleased enough with this memo to show it to me. I gave him literary praise without too much of an undue tug on my taste. After all, he was right. We were losing a lot of our young spies. Local networks in provincial Cuban towns were being rolled up every week and the agents who were successful in reporting to us were in conformity with Hunt's oft-repeated axiom that a spy, left to himself, will tell you what he believes you want to hear. I was obliged to put a grade of credibility on reports going up to Quarters Eye; 10 and 20 percent became the marks I issued most often. I was dealing with such statements as "Camaguey is ready to revolt," "Havana is seething," "Guantánamo Bay has become a shrine for Cubans," "Castro is in deep depression," "the militia is ready to revolt." Little of it was specific; nearly all was operatic.

I had to deal, however, with a couple of gung-ho paramilitaries at Quarters Eye, unknown to me except as VIKING and CUTTER. They were always dissatisfied with my evaluations. "How do you know you're not crimping the intake?" they would ask by phone. I could only assure them that at Zenith we were panning tons of sludge, and anything that looked remotely like gold went north.

While Howard never encountered a day without trouble among the Frente, his difficulties were intensifying. Manuel Artime was now training with the Brigade, and that sent a signal. Artime was a devout Catholic and perhaps the most conservative of the five leaders. The rumor at Zenith was that the Agency planned to make him the next President of Cuba. In reaction, the older leaders of the Frente were demanding to be sent to TRAX as well. Meanwhile, Toto Barbaro kept screaming, "Just give us twenty million dollars. Repayable after victory. We will get our own boats to Havana."

"How," asked Howard, "do you plan to get those boats past our Coast Guard? Be patient," he would add, "trust the clout of my backers. Former Ambassador to Cuba William Pawley and other wealthy businessmen like Howard Hughes and H. G. Hunt are very close to the next President of the United States."

"What if Nixon does not win?" one of the Frente members might ask.

"I can only hope that our situation will remain the same under Kennedy," Howard would reply.

A few days before the election, Barbaro asked me out for a drink. "You must tell your father," he said, "that the entire Frente leadership, all five of us, are endangered."

"By whom?"

Barbaro would never answer a serious question too quickly for fear one might not appreciate the cost to him of an honest response. "There is good reason," he said after sipping on his *añejo,* "to be afraid of Mario García Kohly."

"You have spoken of him before."

"In Kohly you can find a Cuban millionaire who is truly of the extreme right wing. He even thinks that Artime is a soldier of Satan. As soon as the Frente lands in Cuba and declares itself the provisional government, Kohly is ready to assassinate each and every one of us five leaders. He has independent funds, and he will use Rolando Masferrer's men from No Name Key."

"This is nonsense," I said. "Your safety will be defended by the Brigade."

"The Brigade." He made a face. "Members of Kohly's army have infiltrated the Brigade. I tell you, we leaders will be executed a few days after the landing. You cannot conceive of the danger. For many years, Kohly's father was Cuban Ambassador to Spain. Kohly is a follower of General Franco. Now we have heard that Nixon will give support to Kohly." He laid a hand on my arm. "You will tell your father?" he asked.

I nodded. I knew I would not. The story was too wild. I gave it a grade of 20 percent. I knew, however, that I would speak to Hunt about it.

Hunt was furious. "A rumor like this can demoralize the Frente. You had better talk to Bernie Barker. He knows Faustino Barbaro inside out. He'll tell you that if Barbaro is afraid of being assassinated, it is because he damn well ought to be."

"Can I talk to Barker?" I asked. "I want to get to the bottom of Barbaro's story."

"I would just as soon," said Howard, "dig out a latrine."

It was agreed that on election night Hunt, Barker, and I would watch the returns together. A divorcée who lived next door to Howard on Poinciana Avenue in Coconut Grove was going to have a party.

"Can you bring a girl?" asked Howard. He poked me with a finger. "Or don't you know any?"

"Oh, yes," I told him, "I have a girlfriend."

"Well, good for you," said Howard.

"Ed, do me a favor," I answered. "My girl is kind of friendly with the Kennedy family. I would appreciate it if you didn't noise your opinion of Jack too loudly."

"Well," said Howard, "that is a piece of news. I promise, under the circumstances, Roberto, to muffle my more strident feelings."

31

ACTUALLY, I WAS GLAD TO TAKE MODENE TO A PARTY. SHE HAD NO real friends in Miami; I had none; we often met late at night when her return plane was an evening flight, and we certainly made love too often. Sometimes, on mornings after we had smoked marijuana, we looked at each other with the flat, eternal distaste of lovers who have become roommates.

We tried to go out to dance. I suffered again. Sometimes, after asking my permission, she would accept an invitation from a stranger, go forth to the floor, and leave me hoping that her partner was without skill. Once we double-dated at Joe's Stone Crabs with another airline stewardess and her boyfriend, a pilot who had a mind like a meticulously plowed field: "What kind of job do you do, Tom?" "Electronics." "That's great." My warning bell went off. I might have to talk about the instrument panel on his plane. "Electronics are great," I told him, "but kind of boring. I'm really more interested in the election."

So, Modene and I stayed at home. That is to say, I signed us out to La Nevisca, and we had congress in the master bed. I tried to exorcise John Fitzgerald Kennedy out of her flesh and must have driven him into her mind. It came over me on election night that Modene's composure was not to be taken for granted this evening.

Nor mine. I hardly knew whether I wanted Kennedy to win. She might look upon me then as his understudy. And if he lost, well, I could remember talk of desert islands large enough for two. This election was going to bring me no romantic gain.

All the same, if Jack won, then I, by the intermediary of her body, would still have touched immortality. The ferocity of this squalid satisfaction was white as a blowtorch in my compromised heart. On to the party!

Our hostess, named Regina Nelson, proved no advertisement for divorce. Once blond, now a redhead, she had grown wrinkled from old marital bitterness and daily exposure to the sun.

"I knew a Charles family once in South Carolina," said Regina. "Any relation to you, Bobby?"

"Sorry. No family in South Carolina."

"Your girlfriend calls you Tom. But sometimes she says Harry."

"Robert Thomas Harry Charles," I said.

"Your girlfriend is gorgeous."

"Thank you, Regina."

"If she's ever too beautiful for you, give me a ring."

I hated her house. It had the kind of pastel furniture, cream colored rugs, and bamboo wallpaper that would never need a bookcase. There were mirrors in ornate gold frames but no pictures were hanging. The standing lamps stood as tall as the guards at Buckingham

Palace, and the bar took up one end wall. A dark silver-dusted mirror gave backing to the bottles on the shelves. We were in Coconut Grove, and the land where the house now sat had once been a swamp.

"Is Ed your boss?" Regina asked.

"Yes."

"Do you know, when he first moved in next door I thought he was a homo."

"Ed doesn't look like one," I said.

"You'd be surprised," said Regina, "what comes out in the wash."

"Does he act queer?"

"Well, he's very fussy about the way he keeps his house. He is always coming over to borrow furniture polish or detergent, but maybe that's because he wants to get to know me better."

I realized that I not only desired to get drunk tonight, but would succeed. Beyond Regina, past an arched doorway, was the television den, a buff-colored leather pit. Modene sat alone by the TV, bourbon in hand, and studied the tube.

Regina said, "Cubans keep visiting Ed's house. At night. I have heard that Cubans are AC/DC."

"It's more like they exhibit deep feeling for each other," I told her.

"Poor Ed. I can tell by looking at him. I just might start to take care of that poor lost soul."

No response needed. "I don't mind inviting Ed to my party," she said, "or him inviting people like you and your girl to drink my booze, hell and hello, everybody's here to do that, aren't they? 'Just spend the green, Reggie-girl,' I tell myself, but I don't know half my guests. People's tongues look kind of long when they're lapping up your liquor and you don't even know them."

"I'm going to fill my glass," I said.

I didn't know anyone at the party either. There must have been fifty people in her living room, and they looked like realtors to me, and lifeguards, and beach girls, and insurance salesmen, and divorcées —I realized suddenly that I had been living in Florida for months and knew no one in the state who was independent of the Agency. A retired businessman, a golfer with a sixteen handicap, now began to talk to me about his putting game, and as I drank I measured in my mind the length of the Hubbard tongue dipping into Regina's booze.

Modene was still by herself. The arched bow of her back and

shoulders formed a guardrail around the TV set.

"How is it going?" I asked.

"It looks like he still is winning, but it's not as sure anymore," she said.

A still photograph of Jackie Kennedy appeared on the screen. "The candidate's wife," said the TV set, "is expecting a baby. If elected, President and Mrs. Kennedy will have the first baby born in the White House." The still photograph gave way to a picture of Kennedy Headquarters in New York.

"Is he doing well in the Midwest?" I asked.

"Shush," said Modene.

I felt a blast of rage worthy of my father. She had not even turned to look at me.

In a corner of the living room standing together were Hunt, Hunt's assistant, Bernard Barker, and Manuel Artime. I did not wish to visit with them, yet I did not want to talk to anyone else.

"We were speaking," said Hunt as I came up, "of a well-substantiated rumor that the Soviets are going to give Castro some MIGs. Delivery date next summer."

"In that case," I said, "we have to get to Havana first."

The two Cubans nodded profoundly.

The gabble of the party was not unlike a jungle canopy beneath whose shelter we could speak. That gave its own pleasure. It felt better to talk shop here than in the cafeteria at Zenith.

"Will Castro be able to find enough Cuban pilots to make those jet fighters operational?" asked Artime. "He has not much of an Air Force."

"Right now," said Hunt, "Cuban pilots in Czechoslovakia are receiving advanced training on those same MIGs."

"Son of a bitch," said Barker.

Hunt turned to me: "How is the election going? Kennedy still ahead?"

"Nixon seems to be catching up."

"I hope so," said Hunt. "If Kennedy wins, it will be hard to identify the enemy."

"Don Eduardo," said Artime, "certainly you are not suggesting that any American president would desert us? Why, Kennedy even said to Nixon in their debate that the Eisenhower administration had not done enough about Cuba."

"Yes," said Hunt, "I saw that exercise in gall. Think of what it must have cost Nixon. There at the podium, right on live television, Dick Nixon, the Action Officer for Cuba, has to bite his tongue all the while that Kennedy is pretending to be the man who is going to do something."

"All the same," said Artime, "Castro should have been dead by now."

"I thought he might be," said Hunt.

"I could kill Castro myself," said Artime. "I could kill him with a bullet, a knife, a club, a few grains of powder in a glass." His voice grated on me. Artime was singularly handsome, a well-built man with broad shoulders and a fine mustache, but his voice rasped on my ears. It was the voice of a man who had pushed himself to every limit, and now would push more. Fuertes had not been charitable about Artime. "I do not like him," Chevi had said. "He arouses his audiences by reading bad sentimental verse of his own composition. He sets his people amok with emotion. He looks like a prizefighter, yet he is fraudulent."

"That is a strong word."

"He was frail as a boy. I have heard that when he was a young adolescent, all the other students would pat him on the ass. In some manner, he grew out of that."

"I would say he transcended it," I told Fuertes.

"Yes, but there was a price. His voice tells you what such transcendence must have cost."

"Castro will not live," Artime said now. "If he is alive this month, he will be dead next. And if he is not dead next month, then next year. Such evil will not survive."

"I drink to that," said Barker.

We sipped our drinks.

At the other end of the living room, a carpet had been rolled back, and a few people were trying out a new kind of dance. I could hear the words on the record: "Let's do the Twist." I found it bizarre. One young vacuous blonde with a beautiful sun-ripened body kept insisting in a loud voice that they play the song again. I hated all of it. I thought it was strange in the extreme that the dancers did not hold each other but stood apart and rotated their hips like people alone in a room leering into a mirror. Maybe I was more drunk than I recognized, but I felt as if I were defending a country I no longer understood.

"Look at the wiggle on that blonde," said Hunt with a sad, lopsided, half-superior sneer.

"Yes," I said, "you can whistle while she works." I did not like myself particularly for this remark, but Barker laughed so vigorously that I wondered if I had thrown it out for him. He was a small blockhouse of a man, sturdy, square in build, turning bald, and his lips were humorless. He had been a cop in Batista's security forces. "Don Eduardo," I said, "believes you can tell me some interesting things about Toto Barbaro."

"He is a piece of shit," said Barker.

"What kind of *mierda*?" I asked.

That produced another laugh. When it concluded, Barker said, "He works for a gangster in Tampa."

"Can the gangster be Santos Trafficante?"

"You are the one who said that, not I," said Barker, and gave a sign to Hunt that he was ready to leave.

"You and Bernie," said Hunt equably, "will have other opportunities to talk." Artime also left, and Hunt and I went to the bar for another drink. "Your girl strikes me as most attractive," said Hunt, "albeit somewhat shy."

"No," I told him, "she's really a frightful snob. She wants nothing to do with any of these people."

"Yes," said Hunt, "it's not my idea of a party, either."

"What's the real story on Barbaro?"

"I'll fill you in on what I know if Bernie Barker remains no more forthcoming."

Modene turned off the television set and came toward us. "Let's leave," she said. "They can't tell any longer who's ahead, and it's going to take hours to learn."

I could sense a turn in Hunt's mood. "On that premise," he said, "I think I'll stay and have another drink for Richard Nixon."

"I could have guessed," said Modene. "You don't look like a man who would vote for Jack Kennedy."

"Oh," said Hunt, "I have nothing against him. In fact, I met Jack Kennedy years ago at a debutante's party in Boston."

"What was he like then?" asked Modene.

"Well, I can hardly tell you," said Hunt. "For one thing, he must have had a little too much to imbibe because at the end of the evening he was in a corner chair and sound asleep. I will confess I did not

discern at that moment, in those highly relaxed lineaments, any suggestion of a presidential candidate."

"I hope I can remember how you put it," said Modene, "because
I want to tell the story to Jack," and she inclined her head to Hunt,
led me past our good hostess, Regina, and into the night.

"My God," I said, "you *are* a snob."

"Of course," she said. "I wouldn't have anything to do with
people like that if they lived in Grand Rapids."

32

OUR EVENING WAS NOT NEARING CONCLUSION, HOWEVER. "THAT MAN
who spoke to me at the end is your boss?" she asked.

"We work together."

"He doesn't look much like an FBI man."

"He isn't."

"You are. That's why you are with me. To learn all about Sam
Giancana."

"You're upset," I said, "because the election is up in the air."

"Of course I am upset. And I am drunk. But that doesn't change
it. You do want to know an awful lot about Giancana."

"I couldn't care less. All I really desire at this moment is to smoke
some marijuana."

"No," she said, "not while the election is in doubt. To make love
right now would be equal to desecrating a grave."

"I think you are serious," I said.

She nodded.

"I'm going to sleep," I said.

"No," she said, "you are going to stay up and watch it with me."

"Well," I said, "if we don't make love, I am still going to smoke
marijuana. That is the way I want to watch the returns."

"We must have an understanding," she said. "I will take some
too, but only for the purpose of watching the returns with you."

"That will work," I said, "if you don't get horny."

"I am not about to," she said. "But I will tell you this much about
Sam Giancana. The only reason I didn't go to bed with him is because
of a private feeling."

"Would you describe your private feeling?"

"I felt that if I indulged myself with Sam, I might lose the election for Jack."

"Do you expect me to believe that?"

"When things count, people must keep their promises. I told Jack that I wouldn't sleep with Sam."

"Is Giancana that attractive to you?"

"Of course he is. He is a superior person."

We went to my apartment that night and smoked marijuana. By one in the morning, the TV analysts were saying that the final result would depend on Texas, Pennsylvania, Michigan, and Illinois. "At present, however," said the television voice, "Illinois looks to be the swing state."

Modene nodded profoundly. "Sam said he would bring it in for Kennedy."

"I thought Mayor Daley was going to take care of that."

"Mayor Daley will take care of some parts of Chicago and Sam will bring in the other areas. The Negroes and the Italians and the Latins and a lot of the Polish wards take orders from Sam's people. He has the leverage on the West Side."

"Sam told you all this?"

"Of course not. He wouldn't talk to me about things like that."

"Then how do you know?"

"Walter explained it to me. Walter used to work in Eastern's office in Chicago. The airline people have to know all of that kind of stuff in order to get along with the local unions."

"Do you still see Walter?"

Modene said, "Not since I started seeing Jack again."

"It doesn't matter," I said. "I know that you get more from me than he could ever give you."

"What makes you certain?"

"Why else would you spend time with me?"

"Because I am trying to discover if I have the temperament for marriage, and you might be suitable should I ever decide to come down to earth."

"Do you want to get married?" I asked.

"To you?" she asked.

"Why not?"

"If you are not the poorest man I know, you are certainly the stingiest."

We began to laugh. When we were done, I asked, "Do you really want Jack to win?"

"Of course. Do you think I want to look at myself as the mistress of the also-ran?"

"Is it better to be courtesan to the king?"

"That is absurd. I do not see myself as a courtesan."

I remember feeling a peculiar glee. "I guess you really indulge the hope that he will divorce his wife and marry you. You do see yourself as First Lady?"

"Stop being nasty."

"It could come down to that. First Lady or courtesan."

"I do not look ahead."

"You can't. His wife is pregnant, and tomorrow, he and she will be on television."

"I never realized before how cruel you are."

"That is because you force me to look at the back of your neck while you are waiting for another man to come onto TV. He is not even in the room."

The voice coming to us from the television set now said, "It looks as if Texas may be swinging toward Kennedy. Perhaps the choice of Lyndon Johnson as running mate will yet pay off."

"You can see how wise he was," said Modene, "to pick that awful man, Johnson."

"I don't care. I'm angry at having to look at the back of your neck. I want to take a little more marijuana and fuck."

"I feel a little demented," she said, "and you are causing it."

"That's the marijuana speaking."

"No. It is because history is being made tonight, and I want to feel a part of it. Yet, I can't."

"Neither of us," I said, "is any part of it at all."

"I am. I certainly am—if you would stop badgering me."

"Come on," I said, "do you know how many girlfriends Jack Kennedy has?"

"I don't care."

"One in every port."

"How do you know?"

"I know." There had been FBI lists coming in from Harlot lately.

"Why don't you tell me how you know?"

"Maybe," I said, "I have seen a few reports."

"Am I on them?" She began to laugh at the expression on my

face, and I realized that whatever in her was most loyal to John Fitzgerald Kennedy was therefore most furious at him, and so she could enjoy the idea that she was now a center of attention to strangers who were observing her activities in reports. It occurred to me that she never minded undressing with the shades up.

"Do you mind," she said, "if I talk about Sam? He is a very funny man."

"I would not have thought of him as funny."

"Oh, he is. He is so foul-mouthed when he chooses to be. But in a humorous way."

"What do you mean?"

"Give me another toke." She puffed on my stick of marijuana. "He loves to talk about sex. Like you, he wants to know what Jack is like."

"Do you tell him?"

"I lie. I pretend that Jack is similar to you, and can be very attentive."

"Although he isn't?"

"Of course not. He's too hard-working. He's too tired. He needs a woman who can devote herself to him."

"In which way?"

"Well, you know *which* way."

I now felt the pang of knowing exactly.

"What does Sam say?" I asked.

She turned her eyes from the television set long enough to look at me. Her expression had never been more remorseless nor more attractive. "Sam says, 'Honey, if I ever put my mouth on your yum-yum, you will, guaranteed, be fucking hooked forever.' "

"Chop me down," I said, "Sam says that?"

"Yes," she said.

"Are you tempted?"

"Sam is a man who would want every last bit of me. That is appealing."

"Don't I want every last bit of you?"

"Yes," she said, "you do. And you certainly try to get it. But, after all, in your case, why not?" She began to laugh from the depths of a heart which, at this moment, did not sound free of rancor.

It was long past two in the morning when the announcer stated: "No concession has yet come from Nixon. Illinois, however, is now considered to be definitely in Kennedy's total, and that, added to the victory in Texas, plus reports that Pennsylvania and Michigan look definite for the Democrats, enables us to go off the air with a firm expectation that the election has been won by John Fitzgerald Kennedy."

Modene gave a whoop and turned off the set. "I know," she said at last, "what he is going to say in the morning."

"What will he say?"

" 'Now my wife and I prepare for a new administration and a new baby.' "

"How do you know?" I asked.

"Maybe he rehearsed it with me. He's a devil."

"Well, so are we all."

She gave me one passionate long pent-up kiss, and with that, we made love, and I wanted every last bit of her. After all, in my case, why not?

33

November 25, 1960

Son,

I've been holding off on writing, but then things have been quiet here at Quarters Eye since the election. In effect, we are waiting to see where we are.

Found myself in low spirits over Thanksgiving. Kept thinking of Mary, my old sweet whale of a wife, and now she's lost to me. She is thinking of getting married to a little Japanese businessman who is probably sitting on more wealth than the state of Kansas, and here am I, old blow-spout of the other half of this beached-whale duo, feeling egregiously elegiacal. Clark Gable died last week, and I discovered to my surprise that I had always felt a large identification with the man.

Now, comprehend it. I really don't know anything about Clark Gable, and even felt envious of him last summer. There he was, making a flick with Marilyn Monroe, lucky dog. Son, if they ever held an election in this country for the woman you would most want to bed up with for a night, how could that young lady fail to win? So, yes, I envied him. Now he's dead. Maybe she kept his old heart running up and down too many hills. And I find that I'm mourning him although I don't know bird-all about the fellow. All the same, actors fascinate me. Their work is in some sense near to our work, and yet they are not like us at all. While my contact with actors has been limited, I have found them disappointing. They are without our core of motivation. Lacking such point of reference, an actor can't keep trying to be someone other than himself without having to pay for it. Such, at least, is my concept of it. All the same, I did love this guy Gable. It's hard to tell you cynical younger dogs about the kind of identification we older fellows have with movie stars of his ilk. Sometimes, back in the Second World War, I would talk to him in my head. Particularly after I'd pulled off something good. "Would you have done as well, Clark?" I'd ask. Who knows where these conversations originate? They're silly enough, in any case.

I suspect that part of my meandering frame of mind is still due to the Las Vegas fiasco on Oct. 31. I've been taking flak from it. Three questions hang over me these days. One: Was it an act of Providence? Two: Did Giancana throw sand into the gears? Or three: Is the FBI now witting? We don't have the answers, but I am certainly paying for all three suppositions. *First*: Providence. My confreres are now concluding that Cal Hubbard may carry an undue share of bad luck. *Secundum*: Terrible judgment on Cal's part to pick a hoodlum like G. I'm inclined to agree even if I did no more than inherit Maheu who did the picking. But then, we amputate the "yets" and "buts" in our kind of work. Just take the blame. It's faster and neater.

Now, *Three*, worst of all. What if the FBI has been tracking this one from the beginning? The last contingency has frozen all activity.

Result is, I have been receiving an undeniable chill from Allen's office, Bissell's office, and Barnes' bailiwick. We all recognize that if worse comes to worst, I'll have to carry the slop pail. We must partition Allen off from this. That's fine by me, and a reasonable exercise of duty, but it puts a pall on your best feelings when the chill comes in advance.

It's not so bad that I can't handle it, but, Rick, if there is such a thing as male menopause, I could converse with medical authorities about it. I feel a sense of doom, and it is infecting my natural optimism for exciting projects.

Well, let me introduce you to more interesting matters. Despite my nearness to Outer Purdah, the stories still get back to the old boy. Allen Dulles and our President-Elect John F. Kennedy had a powwow down in Palm Beach on the 17th of November. I'll bet you picked up not a single reverberation from your slot sixty miles away in Miami, but we heard about it up here. Allen didn't come back with a won game. As I get the story, Kennedy expressed a few doubts about the oncoming Cuban push and wanted to discuss demobilizing the Brigade. Allen responded with his Dutch uncle mode: "Are you, Mr. President-Elect, truly prepared to tell this fine group of young Cuban men that they must disband against their will? Why, all they ask, at every risk to their lives, is to have the opportunity to restore the democratic government of their country."

Kennedy obviously has salt. He didn't flap. Took in all that Allen could deliver and then came back with the following: Said he was prepared, in principle, to move ahead, but had to emphasize how very crucial it was that no United States involvement show. Overtly aggressive moves against Cuba could stimulate the Sovs to carry out a few threats.

Let me add this, Kennedy says: If our involvement in Cuba does show its face, we will, of course, be obliged to win.

Couldn't agree more, replies Allen.

Well, Mr. Dulles, says Kennedy, if we want to win all that much, why begin with the Brigade? If a sizable military operation is what is really called for, why even bother with the CIA in the first place?

He had Allen painted into a corner on that one. He could come away with no more than a highly qualified go-ahead. No *visible* American involvement. In any event, the invasion has been put off for a few months. By the time Kennedy gets his inauguration out of the way and has an administration functioning, we'll be in early spring of 1961.

During this interim, the Brigade is likely to get restless. I call it a toss-up. If their discipline doesn't hold up, they will self-destruct in Guatemala. Interesting times lie ahead.

Yours,
No-Bucks Halifax

34

SERIAL: J/39,354,824
ROUTE: LINE/GHOUL—SPECIAL SHUNT
TO: GHOUL-A
FROM: FIELD   10:11 A.M. DEC. 20, 1960
SUBJECT: HEEDLESS

    Regret to inform you that FIELD has lost all access to BLUE-
BEARD. Catalytic factor: Buddhist interlopers.

    Can report that on December 19, BLUEBEARD returned
alone to the Fontainebleau after shopping with RAPUNZEL. In the
lobby were two men wearing felt hats. A minute after she went up to
her room, the front desk was on the phone. A Mr. Mack and a Mr.
Rouse wished to see her. They were FBI, stated the front desk. She
did not have to open her door, said the clerk, but it might save time.
Otherwise, they would come back.

    She agreed to meet with Mack and Rouse. They soon in-
formed her that they were inquiring into her relation to RAPUN-
ZEL. She claims to have told them nothing. Later, to FIELD, she
described this interview as "wholly disagreeable." Unfortunately, her
suspicions of FIELD are now inflamed. She has accused him of being
"in cahoots" with Mack and Rouse. She declares that she will not see
him any longer.

    These events took place yesterday evening. In FIELD's opin-
ion, the relationship is concluded. There is no room left for a cover
story.

    If the new situation holds constant over the next month, will
you require a Final Report?

                                          FIELD

    Harlot would hardly be satisfied with this description, but then his
displeasure at the loss of BLUEBEARD was going to be larger than
his pique at the lack of detail.

    I could have provided him with more. In the hour I spent with
Modene, every speech of Mack and Rouse was repeated. When she
called me at Zenith not long after they left, she had been calm, so calm
indeed that I could feel her hysteria stirring. "I've had visitors," she
said, "and you probably know them. Can you come over before I get
too drunk?"

So soon as I arrived, she began to describe the encounter.

Mack spoke first. He was tall and heavy.

"You are Modene Murphy?"

"Yes."

"You are on friendly terms with Sam Giancana?"

"Who is he?"

"He is also known as Sam Gold."

"Don't know him."

"How about Sam Flood?"

When she paused, he repeated, "How about Sam Flood?"

"I know him."

"He is the same man as Sam Giancana."

"All right. What of it?"

"Would you be interested to know how Sam Giancana makes his living?"

"I have no idea."

"He is one of the ten most wanted criminals in America."

"Why don't you pick him up?"

"We will," said the FBI man named Rouse. He was of medium height, slim, and had sharp teeth. "We will as soon as we are ready. For now, we can use your help."

"I know nothing that could help you," said Modene.

She saw a sneer on Mack's face. "Do you," he asked, "accept gifts from Sam?"

"If they are appropriate, and not too expensive."

"Are you aware that he has a Las Vegas tootsie?" asked Rouse.

"What is a tootsie?"

"A tootsie is a girl," said Mack, "who takes money for favors. Did Mr. Giancana ever slip you any green?"

"What?"

"Money. He hand you money?"

"Are you calling me a tootsie?"

"Does he kick in for your hotel bill?"

"Are you ready to leave?"

"Just nod your head," said Rouse. "Have you met Johnny Roselli, no? Santos Trafficante, no? Tony Accardo, also known as Big Tuna, no? Have you met individuals named Cheety, Wheels, Bazooka, Tony Tits?"

"I can't recall. I meet many people."

"Never came across Tony Tits?" asked Rouse. "He's a man."

"I don't care what he is. I'm asking you to leave."

"How do you support yourself?" asked Mack.

"I'm an airline hostess."

Mack consulted a piece of paper, "Your rent here is $800 a month?"

"Yes."

"But Mr. Giancana never kicks in?"

"I've asked you to leave twice."

"There seem to be a lot of wrapped packages in this room right now. Are they presents?"

"Christmas gifts."

"From Giancana?"

"A few."

"Mind telling me what they are?"

"Do you mind minding your own business?"

"It becomes my business," said Mack, "once you are receiving money or its equivalent in gifts from Giancana, a criminal source."

"Why," asked Rouse, "would someone like yourself, of self-supporting income, according to your claim, associate herself with a gutter hoodlum?"

"I'm going to call the desk and ask the house detective to throw you out."

Mack smiled. Rouse smiled.

"I'm going to ask them to tell you to get out of my room. It is not your hotel."

"We are going," said Mack, "but guarantee you, Miss Murphy, we will come back. In the meantime, ask yourself what additional information you might have to offer us."

"Yes," said Rouse, "you will see us." He smiled. "Keep your nose clean, Modene."

She called Giancana the moment that they left.

"Watch out," said Sam, as soon as she began to explain, "your phone could be hot."

"Can you come over?" she asked.

"That would be no good thing for you."

"Sam, what should I have said?"

"You said the right thing. They were fishing, that's all. For dead stinking fish. They can't take a shit without sucking their toes. They would lick their own ass if they could reach it. That's in case you're listening to me, you bastards."

"Sam."

"Sweetheart, if these cocksuckers show up again, tell them I'll supply front-row tickets for J. Edgar Hoover and Clyde Tolson getting it on in Macy's store window. Big changes coming, you scumbags! Modene, you are a queen, and as innocent as the fucking snow."

With that, he signed off. She said Sam was not only talking to the FBI fully as much as he was talking to her, but she had never heard him in such a state of excitement.

When she finished her story, she said to me, "Are you one of them?"

"One of who?"

"Mack and Rouse."

"I can't believe you said that."

"You are in cahoots. I know it. Something has always been wrong between you and me."

"If you believe that, why do you tell me what they said?"

"Because what they said is knocking around inside me."

"I believe you."

"Besides, they report to you anyway." She began to laugh. "I know for a fact," she said. "You are FBI."

"What would it take to convince you that I am not?"

"Then, who are you really working for?"

"Why don't you use your imagination?" I said. "Or is that in short supply?"

It was a fatal remark.

"Get out of here," she said.

"I think I will."

"I knew it couldn't go on," she said, "but I didn't know it was this close to the end."

"Well, you've found a way."

"I think I have."

"You have."

To my surprise, I was as angry as Modene.

"Don't try to call me," she said.

"I won't be likely to."

"God, I dislike your person," she said. "You are such a dull cock."

Shutting the door behind me, I felt an odd calm. I had no idea whether I would see her again in a day, a year, or never, but at the moment, it did not matter. I had just been treated to what Kittredge used to describe as "the changing of the guard." If there was a parliament in the psyche, the party in power had just been voted out. I did not think Modene and I would come together soon. "Dull cock," she had called me. Her father must have been one ungodly wheel at riding other racers off the track.

35

I SUFFERED IN THE NEXT WEEK. OF COURSE. IF SOME LARGE PART OF ME no longer wanted to put up with periodic cuckoldry, nor the firm limitations of her mind, so did longing for Modene return at the most unpredictable times. I could no longer walk into a restaurant with that beautiful girl on my arm.

Still, there was a clear line of demarcation. I had no real desire to hear from her. I was even weary of the pride of having her, since it fed my absence of dedication to anything else. It seemed important again to give myself to the job. History was going to be made in the next few months. To wind up any doubts on the matter, a communication from Harlot arrived two weeks after my cable to him.

SERIAL: J/39,268,469
ROUTE: LINE/ZENITH—OPEN
TO: ROBERT CHARLES
FROM: GLOUCESTER   10:23 A.M. JAN. 3, 1961
SUBJECT: EFFICACY

It appears that girls talk to girlfriends more freely than to boyfriends. See you anon.

GLOUCESTER

It was his way of saying that there was no need to send me any more of the BLUEBEARD–AURAL transcripts.

Before the middle of January, another long letter arrived from my father. I had to admire his ability to find cures for despondency.

January 12, 1961

Son:

Beware of melancholy, an old Hubbard trait. It hit me very badly yesterday to read that Dashiell Hammett died on January 10. I felt abominable. The radio was playing this dreadful new song, "Let's Do the Twist," just as I opened the paper to receive such news. I put in a call of condolence immediately to Lillian Hellman and that's the first time we've spoken in ten years, although I believe she was glad to hear from me. I don't know if I ever told you, but Lillian is also an old friend. I will admit we are one strange link-up, but in the days when I would drink with Hammett, Lillian got wind that I was in hush-hush. That didn't bother her a bit. I'm not one to kiss and tell, but Miss Hellman couldn't keep her hands off this then-younger presentation of meat and bones. Some of the Casanovas I've known used to call it a clue to the hunt: Look for a good Christian every time. Well, I'll pass on to you, son, the local recipe from your dad's battle-scarred experience: Make it a strong-minded Jewish girl with power-ful leftist inclinations. Can't beat those ladies for types like me.

I tell these out-of-school tales only to indicate the nature of my friendship with Hammett. He knew about my affair with Lillian. I think he even approved of it. He was the damnedest Communist I ever met. The fact of the matter was that Lillian still adored Hammett, but he had drunk himself out of any kind of connubial relations a long time ago. So, if it had to be other men, and it had to be, because Lillian was a woman of imperious appetite (used to call her Catherine the Great to her face, which she loved), Dash didn't mind entering the process of selection. He was all for our affair. I never fooled myself, however. It was Dashiell Hammett she loved. He always seemed immortal. Not like a god so much as a dry, silvery angel, a piece of driftwood there on the beach for eternity. It's hard to believe he's gone.

I not only had regard for him as a writer but as a man. He never tried to pump me for literary material. I believe he respected the caul in which we work. It was as if just by the osmosis of drinking together he could pick up enough about the complexities of our work-code that if he wanted to I'm sure he could have popped me into a book. One classy gent, and he's gone.

As you know from my last letter, I've been subjected to The Chill. I think it must have been at its worst around December 18. It certainly ruined Christmas. But we were all under a cloud anyway.

December 18 was the day Dulles and his prize dodo, Deputy Director General Cabell, brought Barnes and Bissell and myself together with our top project officers for a look at our Cuban situation now that we're under Kennedy management. Allen wanted a review of all that was wrong as well as right in order to get out in front of criticism.

A lot of disheartening reports ensued. We have had all too many networks rolled up. And our air drops have been off. We are using former Air Cubana commercial pilots, and these guys can't do pinpoint navigation. They've been sitting on a superhighway of radar between Miami and Havana so long that they've lost directional finesse. Invariably, they miss the mark. In fact the drop that worked most accurately was a fiasco engineered by His High Asshole General Cabell.

It seems we were flying some arms over to a group, and Cabell wanted to know how much of the cargo space was filled. One-tenth capacity happened to be the answer. "That's wasteful," said Cabell. "Don't send a plane over nine-tenths empty! Get some rice and beans on the craft. Our Cuban team down there can probably use it."

Well, it happened to be a precise drop in a specific place. The receiving party was too small to handle a full load.

"I do not want to hear that," said Cabell. "Put some forward lean into this mission."

David Phillips, one of our Latin American hands, said to Cabell, "General, I've spent four of the past six years in Cuba. Rice and beans is the national dish. I can assure you, there's no shortage."

Cabell answered: "Ever hear of an Appropriations Committee? I'm not going up to the Hill to explain to some congressman why we sent over a plane nine-tenths empty. Load up the rice and beans."

That was one night, son, when our plane did hit the target. The radio message was so frantic that it came back in English: YOU SON OF BITCH. WE NEARLY KILLED BY RICE BAGS. YOU CRAZY?

We all made sure that Allen Dulles received a copy. He is stuck with Cabell as his Number Two because the man is a Four-Star Air Force General, and that keeps the Pentagon less unhappy about us. Of course, the General is now renowned in good circles as "Old Rice and Beans Cabell."

Care for any more bad news? Maritime ops are proving equally dismal. Castro's coast guard is showing a high percentage of kills. The DGI seems to know a good many of our landing sites in

Cuba in advance. I've been trying to get us to outfit a mother ship that could work just outside the 3-mile limit from Cuban waters. We could equip it with advanced radar. The smaller boats carried on its davits need only be dispatched when the nearby coast, monitored by radar, proves to be clear. The problem is to get such a large craft in readiness quickly.

Now, for first-rate news! The main invasion—and this I pass on to you as a blood confidence—has been confirmed for Trinidad. That small city is on the southern shore between Cienfuegos and Sancti Spíritus. Perfect location. There are mountains nearby to hole up in should things go badly, yet two provincial capitals are close enough to capture in the first couple of days, provided the push goes right. Best of all, Cuba is narrow at that point, seventy miles wide, no more. We could cut the country in half pretty quickly.

Here's another bit of blood gossip not to be repeated. We've buried a function in the woodwork. It's called ZR/RIFLE and is a capacity that I wish we had developed in advance of all our Maheu projects. Bissell has asked Helms to get it started, and Helms promptly consulted your godfather. Who does Sir Hugh propose to oversee the new capacity, but Bill Harvey? Amazing—taking into account their old enmity.

I end here for the nonce. I'm having a night out tonight which I do look forward to, but will pick up this communication tomorrow.

Friday, the Thirteenth
That was one good night, last night, fellow. Allen had the wit —God, I love that man when he's at his best—to invite all the new Kennedy muckamucks to an evening with a number of us at the Alibi Club. He wanted to put the top new Washington folk into a more gung-ho frame of mind for the Cuban op, and I believe we brought it off. I must say, the Alibi Club was the perfect place for this, just as fusty inside as, let's say, the Somerset Club in Boston. The old menus on the wall set the note, "Turtle Soup, 25 cents," and the martinis are good. It relaxed the young new Kennedy breed, and a few of them are pretty young, I must tell you, and awfully bright, and fitted up with an all-around alert system as to where the next cue is coming from. Bright young top-of-the-Law-Review gents, but instinctive as well. On the other hand, they are certainly in way over their heads. With all due respect to your mother's ancient blood, they do remind

me a bit of Phi Beta Kappas (Jewish) at a coming-out party. There was also a contingent of Kennedy's Irish Mafia, just as suspicious as FBI monks, and tough, flinty, ready to strong-arm an issue. However, they are also just ignorant enough to be in over their heads. So the get-together was a good idea. Bissell made a hell of a speech in his gold-plated archbishop's style. Presented himself as paleface of all the palefaces. Took one of his long fingers, poked himself in the chest, and said, "Take a good look at me. I'm the man who eats the sharks in this outfit." That had its impact. A distinguished churchman was talking dirty. It was our way of saying, "Just give us an assignment, brothers, and we will ram it home. We are not afraid of responsibility. We take on high risk. If you want to move mountains, call on us." You could see all the Kennedy people imbibing Bissell's qualifications, Groton, Yale, Ph.D. in economics, and ready to eat sharks. Why, he's even taught at MIT.

I must say, we did feed them good stories. How to steal a country with three hundred men à la Guatemala. Cloak-and-dagger has to be the second-oldest profession, Allen told them. And in the course of it, lots of first-rate toasts were exchanged. Then Allen called on me. Damn, the glint in his spectacles was adjuring me in no uncertain terms to recount my now hoary exploits with the secretaries. Back in 1947, in case you never heard, I captured scads of poop on what Truman's Cabinet people were planning because I got to know (in the Biblical sense) a few of the top office girls. Last night, I rounded it off by saying, "Of course, we don't do these things anymore." The Kennedy people loved it. I think the note Allen wished to strike was that we were absolutely the right organization for a roistering jack-in-the-sack like our own President-Elect.

I wasn't going to let myself, however, get stuck in the Department of Legends as one more over-the-hill stunt man, so I went off on a reasonably witty presentation to the effect that we can look forward, White House and CIA, to great times together since we possess in common a liking for the work of Ian Fleming. Let's give a toast to good old Ian Fleming, I said, holding the flagon high. Someone actually did mutter, "His work is such crap!"—I can hear you speaking in that young voice—but I came back with, "Ian Fleming, a stylist for our time." And a few of us on the Agency side, which I suppose comes down to Dulles, Bissell, Montague, Barnes, Helms, and myself, were thinking of those rather Ian Fleming–like toys that have come out of Technical Services, such as the depilatory to take off

Fidelito's beard back in 1959 when he visited the UN. At an effectiveness level, it was all pure Dartmouth yahoo crap, but a few of us
in the room knew that I was pretending to more, so it was permissible
to laugh like hell. We got the idea across. They now understood that
we were monkeys with as many tricks in our cage as they had in theirs.
We communicated the notion that if you want a quick answer to a
knotty problem, CIA is the place to go. Not, repeat, *not* the State
Department.

Dean Rusk got a longer and longer face as the evening wore
on. I think he was the first to sense what a splendid theatrical grasp
Allen has on how-to-make-new-friends in transitional times. Rusk
looks constipated. Probably loses half an hour every morning on the
evacuation detail.

In any case, I am now on the move again. At least within.
Which is what morale is all about.

Your good father,
Big-Bucks Halifax

P.S. Despite all this self-congratulation, I won't neglect to mention
RETREAD. He worries me. BONANZA ought to be able to follow
the money trail RETREAD has to be leaving in his Miami banks if
he is as crooked as I expect he is.

36

IN MONTEVIDEO, AFTER KITTREDGE DISCONTINUED OUR CORRESPON-
dence, I used to see a good deal more of Hunt, and now, bereft of
Modene, I began once more to have dinner with him a couple of
nights a week. History was repeating itself. Howard's mood was not
far from mine. Dorothy was in Washington, and the news received
each night by telephone was often of her mother who was hospitalized
with an inoperable cancer. In addition, his social life, so important to
him, was hardly thriving. He might keep up with Palm Beach parties
in the society columns, but he was driving through no gates these days
in white dinner jacket; the royal palms and poinciana trees on the great
estates, the tiled fountains, stone urns, and balustrades of the Palm
Beach palaces were remote; he walked no paths between jasmine and
bougainvillea, and danced with panache on no marble floor. Nor did

he spend his afternoons at Hialeah watching pink flamingos cross a green lawn, no, Howard was in Miami to work, and the scent of oleander and azalea did not reach the cubicles of Zenith. Howard was at that place in his career where success could raise him to the level of a Senior Officer, and failure might put a stop to his ambition.

He certainly pushed himself. If his own politics were, as he put it, "to the right of Richard Nixon," he swallowed the polemical contumely of dealing with Cubans whose social views were to the left of him. When asked for his own ideological position by Barbaro or Aranjo, he would reply, "I'm here to oil the gears."

He served. If Manuel Artime was the only member of the Frente with whom Hunt could feel some philosophical kinship, Howard worked nonetheless to hold the Frente together. Watching him operate, I came to understand that politics was not ideology, but property. The Frente was in Hunt's portfolio and that, as I was soon to discover, was of determining significance. I was soon to discover that Howard had not only learned to bear up with Toto Barbaro, but was ready to protect him. Be it said, I had not needed my father's prod to keep Chevi Fuertes working on Barbaro's bank accounts, and he was producing results. Chevi had succeeded in tracking large movements of money through Barbaro's separate checking accounts, and Cal's instinct was confirmed—the trail of deposits and withdrawals began to point to the Miami lottery whose winning number was pegged on the circulation figures of the Cuban peso. One rumor prevalent in the exile community was that these figures were rigged by Havana so that Trafficante could be given the winning numbers in advance, and a portion of his profits even went to paying off the operations of the DGI in Florida. If this rumor was valid, then Trafficante was not only the Agency's most important asset in the proposed assassination of Fidel Castro, but might be Castro's most important agent in America, and Toto, in his turn, could be serving as Trafficante's paymaster to the DGI in Miami. The more he kept screaming for money to liberate Cuba, the more he was working for Castro.

Armed by what seemed better than half a case, I spoke to Cal via secure phone. He promptly returned me to Hunt. "I could come in from above," said Cal, "but I won't. Not this shot. Howard has been holding an impossible situation together, and I won't smash into it. Bring your findings to him."

Hunt, to my surprise, showed little response. He would, he said, peruse the summaries of cash flow in Barbaro's accounts. When I did not hear any more after a few days and I pressed him, he was noncommittal. "I don't know that we have enough to hang the guy," he said at last.

"Does Bernie Barker agree with you? He said Toto was a shit."

"There's a measurable distinction between a shit and a double agent."

Fuertes was not surprised at Hunt's lack of reaction. "The next act is commencing," was his conclusion. "To avoid any imputation that the exiles who replace Castro are related to Batista, your new President Kennedy is going to insist that new leftist groups be taken in. It is a comedy. Barbaro, a wholly corrupt politician, once represented some species of left-wing camouflage for your Frente. But now that Kennedy is bringing in serious figures like Manuel Ray who is far to the left of Barbaro, Toto has become the new center. You do not remove the center of a coalition. Without Barbaro, do you think Manuel Artime would be able to speak to Manuel Ray? No, Toto is crucial. He can hold hands with Manuel of the left and carry messages to Manuel of the right."

"But what if Barbaro is working for Castro?" I asked.

"Toto," said Fuertes, "would not know how to function if he did not have a finger in every hole. Of course, his fingers are filthy, but Toto sees nothing but visions." Fuertes looked at me then with something close to intense dislike, and added, "It is a common feeling in our work."

I considered writing an anonymous letter to Mario García Kohly exposing Barbaro as a Castro agent. I soon heard, however, via Fuertes again, that Trafficante, ringmaster of every intrigue, was also in close contact with Kohly. How, then, could Kohly and Masferrer decide whether to eliminate Toto or do business with him? Profiteers, murderers, patriots, turncoats, informers, drug dealers, and double agents all swam in the same soup, and I became depressed once more over my competence to deal with such people.

Now came word from TRAX that there was open dissension in the Brigade. Pepe San Román, the commander, had graduated from Cuba's military academy while the country was under Batista, and then served with distinction in the United States Army. That, probably, was why Quarters Eye had selected him. Men who had carried arms for Batista were, however, hardly going to be trusted by men who had fought with Castro in the Sierra Maestra, and neither group was congenial to the younger troops. Given these factions, there had been a strike in the Brigade; training had ceased; Pepe San Román had resigned. He could not lead men into battle, he said, who did not trust him. He was, however, reinstated by the American officer who was on liaison to the Brigade. The striking troops now threatened to mutiny. Before training could recommence, sixty men were dismissed. The other malcontents would only agree to go back to duty if Faustino Barbaro were allowed to visit the camp. I was beginning to see why my father did not rush to get rid of Toto.

The long-standing request of the Frente to be given a trip to TRAX was finally accepted, therefore, by Quarters Eye. Artime would fly over with Barbaro, Hunt would accompany them, and I was dispatched as well, "on orders," said Hunt, "issued by HALIFAX."

"Well," I said to Howard, "a little ability and a lot of nepotism do go a long way."

I think he liked the remark. I was frankly excited. Nepotism be damned. This was the first serious excursion I had gone on for the Agency, and it came at a good time, for it underlined the virtues of living without a woman. If I had still been seeing Modene, my false explanations would have elicited her distrust. Now I did not have to suffer being in a place where I would not be able to phone her. I could pack a bag, buy mosquito repellent, pick up a pair of jungle boots, and be off.

37

GUATEMALA
TRAX, FEB 17, 1961

HALIFAX EYES ONLY

Tomorrow, at dawn, the mail plane goes out from Retalhuleu, twenty-five kilometers from here, and the pouch, one is assured, will reach Quarters Eye within forty-eight hours. I, however, feel one whole planet removed from the States. TRAX (which, somewhat more affectionately, is called Vaquero by the Cubans) has been bulldozed out of the jungle and rests on volcanic soil, making up one hell of a dark gumbo in the ever-present rain. The Cuban swamps cannot prove more uncomfortable. I will not go on any more about the jungle surrounding us in these mountains except to say that it is not New England in the fall.

We left Opa-Locka on a C-46 cargo carrier. A black flight. I know you've been on more than a few, but it was my first experience of taking off without wing lights or, more important, runway lights, and at the risk of imposing on your patience, I will state that I felt as if I were in the belly of the whale. The plane was chock-full of supplies, and Hunt, Artime, Barbaro, and myself, wrapped in blankets against the high-altitude cold of our large compartment void of heat, had to sleep on top of cartons and between heavy gear. Coffee and sandwiches, courtesy of the pilot and copilot, were fed back from time to time.

Even in the dead of night, Barbaro was ready to harangue us. I have seen the man in various stages of anxiety, but never more intense than over the last few days. Sometimes I think that sustained argument, like those nitroglycerine pills he takes, is but one more form of release for his constricted arteries. All night, he kept exclaiming that the troubles at TRAX had ensued because of the previous lack of an invitation for him to visit Guatemala, and now it was his mission to rid TRAX of its Batisteros.

While it was certainly not agreeable to listen to Toto saw away on his obsessions—"Give me the money and I will conquer Cuba"—Hunt's gifts as a horseman showed up well. He just rode the old nag out, occasionally interjecting enough argument to enable Barbaro to assume he possessed our attention. I tried to sleep, but I was furious. It took the sum of my respect for you and Hunt not to shout, "You old fraud. You pimp for Trafficante."

We came into Guatemala City with the dawn, and after breakfast, transferred our stuff onto an Aero Commander, the President of Guatemala's own private plane, indeed.

I saw the country then. We flew astonishingly close to the jungle as we crossed between great extinct, ash-haunted cones of huge volcanoes. Your travel guide will submit that he never saw foliage so quintessentially emerald as in the unholy green light that came up from the jungle below, and the landing on a mean slash of dirt strip carved into the flank of a mountain would have been a stunt man's delight. We sashayed to a stop ten feet from the jungle wall. I had no fear. I am Cal Hubbard's son.

This place is so remote that I do not know how any word ever gets out. On the Jeep ride up to Vaquero, several thousand feet of climb were involved, and we hair-pinned it over many a mud track no wider in many places than the vehicle, and had the leisure to peer over vertical drops all the abject distance down to the airstrip. One begins to think of an honorable, if highly covert, Agency funeral.

As I learned over the next couple of days, you must build a camp before you train anyone, and the first members of the Brigade and their cadre had worked as carpenters and road builders, drained swamps, poured cement, and put up an electric plant while chopping down untold new acres. Naturally, the flora and fauna reacted with outrage. There were hosts of poisonous snakes uncovered, and scorpions galore. No one in the field dared to go to sleep without turning their sleeping bags inside out. Ticks were large enough to be mistaken for acorns. When Cubans complain of the onslaught of insect life, you know that you are visiting hell on stilts.

Fortunately, our accommodations are in the main house of the coffee plantation which serves as base for TRAX and is relatively civilized. We sleep in a tin-roofed, gabled structure with a porch around all four sides. My cot has mosquito netting, and through the windows are to be seen the bountiful acres of our host, Roberto Alejo. His coffee shrubs—I do not know whether to call them small trees or bushes—stand out in close checkerboard formation over cleared hills and dales. On our other side is level terrain offering a parade ground, barracks, mess halls, and a flagpole carrying the white star of the Cuban flag on a red, white, and blue field.

Be certain that as soon as we had washed and come back to the living room, Toto began to denounce Pepe San Román and Tony Oliva for their leadership of the Brigade. They immediately quit the room. They are obviously not men to be trifled with. I, like you, I presume, have a set of mixed feelings about military people, but these two gentlemen prove impressive. San Román is slim, lithe, mean-faced, and absolutely consecrated. No excess weight. I think it would never occur to him that he would not die for the cause if that was required. Humorless and full of Cuban honor—which seems to come in even larger sizes than they fit you for in Spain. Oliva, who is a Negro, fought for Castro, then parted company with him. Struck me as more complex than San Román, but equally dedicated, and if anything, tougher. A lot to take in, you may say, in one quick look, but I assure you, we were all of us sufficiently fired up to decide a good deal about each other over a handshake. In any event, the abrupt departure of San Román and Oliva kicked off a quarrel between Hunt and our American commandant here, one Colonel Frank, a beefed-up bull of a Marine Corps officer who won his medals at Iwo Jima and looks capable of lifting the rear end of a Jeep out of the mud. He may, however, be fatally remiss in the top drawer. Recently, he sent twelve Brigade "malcontents" up a tropical river in canoes to a wholly inaccessible place called a "reindoctrination camp," and seems oblivious of the trouble that has caused to the other Brigade members' national pride. They naturally wish to discipline their own people rather than have Americans do it for them. Colonel Frank then took Howard and me off to the side and proceeded to berate us. "What were you meat-heads thinking of when you brought Barbaro here? If you don't get the son of a bitch out of TRAX, my Brigade will blow up."

Howard held his ground. It wasn't automatic. Howard would be no physical match for Colonel Frank, and say what you will, that is always a factor.

"I'll handle Toto Barbaro," said Howard (in what under the circumstances, was a viable voice), "if you quiet down San Román and Oliva."

Well, they got into one hell of a staring contest before Frank said, "Take care of your end," and stomped off.

Later in the day, Barbaro did remain civil when he spoke to the troops, but he also said that it would be neither honest nor responsible to pretend that he had not come with a most serious message: The Frente was the future government of Cuba, no matter what others (he made a point of staring at Artime) might have told those assembled soldiers. So the Brigade should not take any major decision without referring it first to the Frente.

The men were at parade rest—I counted over six hundred. Perhaps a third cheered for Barbaro, a third issued Cuban cat-calls (which run the gamut from mouth blats to simulations of parrots, roosters, and wild beasts). Most disquieting in terms of morale was a middle group who stood more or less mute but looked not at all pleased.

I got an inkling then of what Hunt can be capable of. Standing next to me, looking pale as icy resolve itself, he said, "I vow to silence that son of a bitch."

Afterward, at the main house, San Román issued an ultimatum. If Barbaro did not support him openly in front of the troops, he would resign.

"Toto," said Howard, "come with me to my room. I have a few things I wish to speak to you about."

What ensued has been called "The Miracle of La Helvetia." When they came down, Howard was still pale and certainly resolute; Barbaro seemed half-broken. He spoke to all of us, San Román, Oliva, Alejos, Artime, Colonel Frank, Howard, and myself long enough to say that he was now convinced he must make a good and careful study of conditions here at Vaquero before determining his own political certainties. This afternoon and tomorrow morning he would study maneuvers in the field.

There seemed a curious finality to his remarks, as if he had already decided on what he was going to say tomorrow to the troops. Howard hinted to us that he had told Toto to be ready to be flown back to Miami on the next plane as a mental case if he did not cooperate, but such a story hardly holds up. The Frente would have been torn apart by such a move. Deny it if you will, but I believe I now know why neither you nor Howard would react to my findings on Trafficante's rigged lottery and Barbaro's connection to it. There's no sense in playing your trump card until the game is there to be won! I feel as if I have learned something invaluable.

The rest of the afternoon proved interesting. We were able to watch the troops' impressive competence in small arms fire, heavy and light machine guns, and the mortar and artillery range. I couldn't stop looking at Barbaro. He was exhibiting peculiar merriment. For instance, he was full of manic excitement when invited to fire the 50mm machine guns, and couldn't stop laughing after his gun jammed. He kept hefting all the equipment to see how heavy it was, tried on one man's helmet, slung a rifle, threw a couple of defused grenades for practice, and then a live one on the range, only to complain happily that he had thrown out his arm. I realized after a while that he was acting like a man who is enjoying his retirement. All the while, Howard kept nodding his approval and taking photographs of the leaders, the troops, the terrain, accompanied by the Hunt pipe and a most photographer-like smile.

Next morning, the Brigade was addressed by Artime and Barbaro. Artime has a cosmically poetic style that can prove downright embarrassing to our northern ear. He treats each large sentimental notion as if it were his dancing partner. "It is the will of the heavens that we are gathered here, far from home. . . . It is God's desire that we sweat and live in fear, and overcome such fear, and thrive in brotherhood until we bring the flag of our Brigade back to Cuba, back to Havana, back to a land where Cubans may love each other again."

Verbs like *vencer, triunfar,* and *imperar* predominate. "We will win, we will triumph, we will prevail. We cannot fail in this war against the steel-tipped hearts of the Communists, but even if we are all massacred on the beachhead"—at which point an astounding sound came up from the Brigade, full of fiber at the thought of losing their young lives, yet an ecstatic cry, as if there had been some glimpse of heaven in the fall to the ground—"even if all of us are lost, none of us are lost. For the Americans are behind us, and they are a proud nation and will never accept defeat, and they will be there after us in wave after wave."

Wave after wave of impassioned applause washed back to him. Artime is the most curious leader. He is the spirit of charisma when he speaks; when he is done, he is just like one more guy with nice manners. Two personalities, for sure, and the younger one is very young, and not nearly so sure of himself. It comes out when he is forced to offer up a piece of prime bullshit as when introducing Barbaro in flattering terms, "a man without whom Cuban history would not be the same over the last twenty years." Before Toto had said a word, the troops must have sensed that some kind of fix was in, for they catcalled as much as they applauded, and the moment Barbaro began to tell them of the high opinion he was taking back to Miami of the Brigade, an opinion, he declared, that would enable the exile community of Miami to feel proud of their heroes, Toto was met by a mixture of applause and derision. Now it was as if all the men who had been for him yesterday were against him, whereas all of San Román and Tony Oliva's supporters overrode the booing with ovations.

Toto ended with a paean to discipline, to sacrifice, to the expectation of triumph: "Legend awaits the heroic actions of this Brigade." Do you know, I felt wistful. Oratory is such a rich comfort if you can just let yourself get into it. We will certainly leave TRAX tomorrow under a general impression, now shared by San Román, Artime, Alejos, and even Colonel Frank, that our trip has been a success.

I think it was. For me it was. On this, our last night, I visited the barracks and had the opportunity to talk, to listen, and to come away with the impression that these men are emotionally ready to give their lives. I would say they even have religious dedication to their ideals. I can hardly communicate the kind of intensity that comes over conversation as they speak of their willingness to give, as they put it, *"todos"*—yes, all things. I was not unmoved. I hope this has given some picture of the situation at TRAX.

ROBERT CHARLES

The message I really wished to send would have been more extravagant. On the last night, closeted with the Cubans I had recruited, I was quietly overcome by their readiness to die. Sitting among them, I felt a sense of holy, even chilly exaltation, as if one could hear in these mountains and valleys, a muted refrain of cymbals clashing and voices singing, and felt close to Cal, because I knew, although I could hardly say how, that these were the sounds heard by men dedicated to war. That night, falling asleep to the sound of jungle downpour, I wondered whether the Crusaders and the conquistadors of Cortez had also heard that faint, beautiful, and sinister echo. Were the Australians going up over the trenches at Gallipoli aware of such music, and the Red Army marching into battle against the Whites? Did the Whites hear the same siren on the rock as they battled with the Reds? Certainly my father had heard these strains parachuting down into a strange land.

It was then I realized that if I had been a member of the Brigade, I would have been ready to enter any purgatory with them. I understood their hatred of Castro. To hate Castro offered exaltation that could not otherwise be approached, and I felt much moved by what was awaiting our Brigade. The enormity of attacking Cuba with so small a force weighed upon me; I wanted to be able to hate Castro with sufficient intensity to make their mission more possible.

38

I HAD NOT FELT TOO MUCH PAIN IMMEDIATELY AFTER LOSING MODENE, but then some wounds are anesthetized by the shock of the laceration. Returning from Guatemala was more difficult. I soon called the Fontainebleau. I was determined not to speak to her, but at least I could learn whether she was still in Miami. The desk clerk told me that her base had been moved to Washington. Would I like a forwarding address? I would not. It cost me something to say that, as if we were separating all over again.

New difficulties with the Frente awaited Howard and myself. The proposed linking-up of the Frente with Manuel Ray's forces was dividing ranks. Half of the exiles in Miami appeared to believe that Ray was an agent for Castro.

On the other hand, Manuel Ray was laying claim to the largest underground network in Havana, and, in addition, Presidents Betancourt of Venezuela and Muñoz-Marín of Puerto Rico were well-disposed toward him. It was reported that they had serious influence with Kennedy's administration.

I felt for Hunt. He worked so hard. He had done his best to advance the political agenda of Cubans whose political programs he could hardly endure. Now there was every intimation he would soon be forced to accept a Cuban he considered cousin to a Bolshevik. "Just look at Ray's policies," he would complain. "Keep Castro's nationalization of banks and public utilities; keep socialized medicine; don't restore any confiscated properties. Maintain close relations with the Communist bloc. Why, Manuel Ray is Castroism without Castro."

Next day, Howard was called up to Washington. He came back to Miami with the news that Dr. José Miro Cardona—by choice of Quarters Eye—was going to head up the Frente. Cardona had been President of Cuba for the first few weeks of Castro's triumphal arrival in Havana, but soon resigned and went to Argentina. Recently, the CIA brought him to Miami. He was, Hunt told me, a prestigious figure. He would be able to unify the Frente far better than Toto Barbaro.

"Just one thing wrong," said Hunt. "Until now, whenever Quarters Eye has asked Ray to join the Frente, Ray was arrogant enough to tell them that it would make more sense for the Frente to join *him*. Now that Dr. Miro Cardona is coming on board, however, I think Ray will sign up."

"Where does that leave you?"

"I haven't decided."

By the second week in March, Hunt was summoned once more to Washington, where Bissell informed him that Manuel Ray was indeed joining their ranks.

Hunt replied: "This is tantamount to liquidating the Frente."

My father, who had been asked to attend this meeting, now said to Hunt, "Couldn't you force your guys to accept Ray?"

"Yes," said Hunt. "I could force them, but I'd rather not be asked to try."

"Why not?"

Hunt provided a full answer to the question. Later, Cal said that he could not remember the reply. "Hunt was just being a royal pain in the ass," Cal said. "I have no use for Manuel Ray, but it was obvious that Howard had to get on the train or get off. Instead, he was arguing."

Telling it to me, Hunt repeated his speech. I knew why my father had not listened. The remarks were too well rehearsed for Cal's taste. "We," Hunt said, "have trampled heavily on the pride of men who, in their own country, were distinguished, highly respected citizens. Over a period of time, these men of the Frente have come to realize that in Miami they are not much more than puppets. Despite that, they go on doing what I ask because they know there's no other way their country can be rescued. They have become just about entirely dependent on us. I can't face them, however, with a proposal to make Manuel Ray their equal. Rather than compromise on the issue, I prefer to withdraw."

"What was the reaction in Bissell's office?" I asked Hunt.

"A prolonged silence. I took in the message. I said, therefore, that I'd like to come back to Washington. I could work with Phillips on our radio broadcasts for the invasion. I can assure you, they were relieved to have me come up with such a proposal."

"It must have been a long plane ride back to Miami," I said.

"Time enough," he said, "to change one's thinking about more than a few things."

I invited Howard to dinner, but he was going out with Bernard Barker to tour a few Cuban hangouts and say some farewells. Tomorrow, he would be on his way to Quarters Eye. On the drive home to my empty apartment that night, I decided that Howard Hunt had lost more than his job. I did not pretend to understand the Agency, but I thought he had probably come to the upper limit of his career. No job was supposed to be too onerous to take on.

All the same, next morning over breakfast, I accepted Hunt's invitation to work with him at Quarters Eye. If I remained at Zenith, I, too, might have no future. Whoever succeeded Howard would hardly be partial to his former assistant. Whereas, at Quarters Eye, as propaganda officers, we would, Hunt calculated, still be flown to the beachhead with the Frente. A spill of adrenaline as pure as the fear of jumping from a quarry wall into ice-cold water confirmed my decision. I would fight against the steel-tipped hearts of the Communists after all.

So, the move was put into the paper mill, and a week later, my orders were cut. I sublet my apartment in Miami, and got ready, upon his sudden if unexpected offer, to bunk with Cal in Washington.

Just before I went up to Quarters Eye, the Frente was reorganized into the Cuban Revolutionary Council. Dr. José Miro Cardona became President, and Manuel Ray's group was proposed for membership. In a meeting at the Miami Skyway Motel, a couple of Agency officers I had never seen before, large men calling themselves Will and Jim, dressed in three-piece gray flannel suits, declared to a near-riotous group of exiles that if the proposed change did not take place, no further aid was forthcoming. The executive wisdom of the Agency had just been demonstrated. When it came to promulgating stern measures, send out a couple of strangers.

39

MY FATHER WAS LIVING IN MEAN QUARTERS. A DECOMMISSIONED SAFE house had become available through the Agency rental office, and he picked it up for low rental. I believe it was his pleasure to save money in this manner in order to have more bounty available for food and drink. To celebrate my arrival, he took me to Sans Souci.

We had a splendid meal on Saturday evening, and the restaurant was so full, and the mood so powerfully festive, that we talked freely. Given the din, no recording mechanism yet developed could have picked up our conversation, and I, after a week of closing down Hunt's desk and living as liaison to the ice-cold executive team of Will and Jim, was as merry as a man on the first day of vacation.

"It may interest you to know," Cal offered, "just what happened to the last batch of pills."

"The ones given to the girl?" I asked.

He nodded. He began to laugh.

"Well, what did happen?" I asked.

"It appears," said Cal, "that the girl put the pill in the bottom of her cold cream jar in order to take it through Cuban customs. A couple of nights later, lying there beside a soundly snoring Fidel

Castro, she got up to dig out the little pellet and drop it in a glass of water on the end table within reach of the Caudillo's hand. The pill was missing, however. Either it had melted in the cold cream, or Castro's security had found it."

"Are you saying that they were witting to her?"

"The girl thinks so. Castro had been, it seems, a masterful lover that night—which was considerably out of character for the kind of buckeroo he usually is—at least, according to the girl. On this particular evening, however, he was Superman. This, apparently, kicked off her suspicions. She says he is a man who would take pleasure in knowing a mistress was trying to kill him provided, of course, she could not succeed. In fact, he might be sufficiently amused by it to be generous afterward. She is now back in Miami and tells her boyfriend, Fiorini, that Castro says no one will ever be able to kill him because the highest practitioners of *santería* gird his person day and night with all varieties of sorcerer's protection. 'For a Marxist, I am curiously partial to magic,' Castro actually said to her."

"Did you get all this from Maheu?"

"Hell, no," said Cal. "The bare outlines Maheu provided made me curious enough to interview the girl myself."

"And what did she look like?"

"Ravishing, but frightfully nervous. She is just sufficiently paranoid to believe that the DGI could have a hit man out looking for her."

"And what is her boyfriend like? This Fiorini?"

"Adventurer. Heavily suntanned. He'd look happy with a bloody shark's head on his deck."

"Isn't he linked with Masferrer?"

"I expect you're right."

And Masferrer, I told myself, was linked with Mario García Kohly, who was ready to kill the Executive Committee of the Frente —or would it be now the Cuban Revolutionary Committee?—when they landed on the beachhead in Cuba. I must have been growing paranoid at the length of these link-ups, for I asked, "Did the girl have fabulous dark hair?"

"Yes," said my father, "and green eyes. A nice combination."

"Do you have a picture of her?"

"Regretfully, no. Not with me tonight." He took a sip of his Grommes and Ulrich bourbon, a bottle of which, he confided to me, Sans Souci always kept on hand for him. "By the way," he said next,

"I've been researching into some of that *santería* stuff. You won't believe the potions those *mayomberos* cook up. I obtained a recipe for confounding any and all dark purposes of your enemies: You boil the head of an executed murderer together with seven scorpion tails from midnight to two in the morning. You add a little blood from the *mayombero*'s arm, shred a cigar butt, dissolve a drop of quicksilver, put in lots of pepper to season the cadaver meat, fold in ground herbs, tree bark, ginger, garlic, cinnamon, ten live ants and twenty live worms, offer several carefully selected incantations, add one dried lizard, one squashed centipede, a quart of rum, two dead bats buried last night and dug up tonight, three dead frogs, ditto, a small log of wood teeming with termites, and the bones of a black dog. Last of all—crucial to the soup—one quart of Florida water. I call that *cooking*." He roared with happiness. "I suppose gathering all that stuff is no more life-consuming than tradecraft." His face went blank for a moment in the midst of his laughter, an indication to me, as always, that he was debating whether to tell more.

"We're but a couple of weeks away from the beachhead," he now said in so low a voice that I was just about reading his lips. Without pause, he said, "Let's get you some Hennessey for the coffee," and signaled to the waiter. "Now that you're working down the hall," he went on, "I want you to have a better conception of what went on last month. Needless to say, treat it like homeopathic medicine. One drop at a time fed to others when necessary."

"Yessir."

"Trinidad was the place to land," he said, as soon as the waiter who brought my brandy had stepped away, "but Dean Rusk put the weight of the State Department into blocking that option. I don't trust Rusk's goodwill. When he was head of the Rockefeller Foundation, Allen asked for a look at the diaries of Rusk's top people on their return from visits to international figures. Didn't Rusk just refuse! Couldn't *imperil,* he said, the *integrity* of the Rockefeller Foundation. Whereupon, Allen went ahead and managed to read their mail anyway. Through an operation—it may interest you to know—that Hugh set up. I don't know how it happened, but Rusk found out. Now Rusk does not trust Allen. You can bet he doesn't! All we keep hearing from Rusk, therefore, is that the President does not want the Cuban affair to jeopardize larger U.S. interests. Goddamnit, Harry, there's nothing larger right now than Cuba. Cuba is the hot spot and we're mucking it up. Trinidad was the town to hit. Good landing beaches, and all the rest. But Rusk had to put the kibosh on it. Too much *noise*, he said. What if women and children get killed? So we lost to State. Trinidad was out. The new landing place is located back of the devil's asshole. An area called Bahía de Cochinos. Bay of Pigs. Cherish the name."

"Does it have any virtues?"

"It's inaccessible as hell. We will establish a beachhead with no pain. How we are going to deploy from that perimeter, however, is another matter. The beachhead is surrounded by swamp. It will be hard for Castro to get at us, but just as hard for us to get out. Of course, there won't be *noise*. Just us Cubans and the fish. Compliments of Dean Rusk."

"Could he be passing on negative signals from Kennedy?"

"No question," said Cal. "Kennedy's inclination is to *mañana* the invasion. We had a date in March, now it's been moved into April. In fact, I don't believe we would have any date at all without Allen. He keeps pressing on the President as hard as he dares. Informs him that the Soviets are supplying Castro at such a rate that by May, it will be too late. Keeps telling Kennedy that the Joint Chiefs have rated the Brigade as the best-trained force in Latin America. 'Mr. President,' says Allen, 'if the Brigade is never employed, you are going to have a disposal problem. Think of this incredibly motivated force rattling around in southern Florida with nothing to do.'

" 'Well,' replies Kennedy, 'the invasion must appear Cuban. Since all the world is bound to know we're behind it, the bandages must be clean.'

" 'Nothing will show,' says Dulles. Then he says to the President, 'I feel more confident about this Caribbean job than I ever did about Guatemala.' "

"I can't wait," I said.

"You'll be in it," said my father. "You are going to the beachhead with Howard Hunt."

"Definite?"

"Definite."

That fine leap of fear, almost as sensuous as the stirring of sex, went from my heart to my lungs, to my liver, to all of the capital cities of my soul. A large phrase, but then the brandy was ready to declare what everything was all about.

"Take my advice," said Cal. "Keep a diary over the next few weeks. I never did during the war, and God, I miss it now."

"Maybe I will."

"Security is always a problem, but you can insert your pages in the mail slot in my safe. No one goes near my safe."

I was silent. I was trying to mask an amalgam of small panic and pride that my father thought enough of me to suggest a journal.

On our way out of Sans Souci, Cal said, "I forgot to tell you that while I was in Miami to interview Fiorini's lady, I happened to take in the third Patterson-Johansson fight."

"You didn't tell me you were in town."

"I've been in Miami a number of times without telling you," he said so clearly that I had no desire to pursue it.

"How was the fight?"

"A good club fight, no more. And they are supposed to be champions! I mention the evening only because I happened to run into Sammy Giancana again, and he was in a splendiferous mood. Had the most attractive girl on his arm. A true stunner. The sort you have to be ready to kill for. Most marvelous combination of black hair and green eyes."

"Did you get her name?"

"Something like McMurphy or maybe it was Mo Murphy. The name hardly suited her."

"Is she the same girl who was with Castro?"

"Certainly not. What gave you that idea?"

"You described Fiorini's girl as having black hair and green eyes."

"I didn't." Now he was distressed. "Did I misspeak, or did you mishear? Fiorini's girl is a blonde with green eyes."

"Then I believe you misspoke."

"How peculiar." He punched my bicep hard enough to let me share his pain. "Maybe a *mayombero* is doing a job on me," he said.

"Never."

"Before *your* brains go, keep a journal."

"Yessir."

"Bequeath it to someone from the start. It will focus your entries."

40

April 1961

In the event of my demise, these journal pages are to be delivered *by hand* to Kittredge Gardiner Montague, TSS, Detached Duty. My father, Boardman Kimble Hubbard, will serve as my executor and vet these entries for security should he deem it necessary. I do not wish to embarrass Mrs. Montague or my executor.

Let this first entry serve, therefore, as a cover page. Subsequent entries will be placed in envelopes and transmitted to safekeeping as per mode agreed upon.

Quarters Eye, April 4, 1961

This page marks the first sealed entry.

After some deliberation, I have decided to keep a journal. The invasion of Cuba is to take place on April 17, and that is precisely two weeks from today. So soon as a perimeter is secured, I expect to be flown to the beachhead with the exile leaders of the Cuban Revolutionary Council. It occurs to me that I may be describing the last two weeks of my life.

April 5, 1961

I would like to apologize here, Kittredge, for my mode of transmission. You may ask why I simply didn't pass it on to you care of Hugh. Please do communicate to him that no man with the possible exception of my father has had more influence on my life. Hugh possesses the most powerful and decisive mind I have ever encountered, and it is precisely for this reason that I do not wish him to be an intermediary between you and me. If, for his own good and sufficient reasons, he were to judge that you should not see these pages, he would destroy them. For that matter, even the thought that he might read this journal would inhibit the writing of it. After all, I have been hopelessly in love with you from the day we met at the Keep, eight years ago this summer. If I die in battle, extinguished by some errant shell that missed a more military mark, I will go out cherishing my love because it provides me with the moral wherewithal to face my death and fight for a cause that—considering the fell complexities of Alpha and Omega—is a cause I would say I believe in. Our fight against Communism does offer dignity and sanction to the lonely quarters of one's soul. I suppose that I am in the proper occupation, therefore, and I do love you. Since I revere Hugh, yet am here admitting to unfocused designs on the security of his home, I now see myself as his Shade.

Enough. I have said what did not, perhaps, need to be said. For the rest, let me keep this journal lively enough to satisfy some of your omnivorous curiosity on how things work.

April 6, 1961

Given the irregular nature of our much-enclaved Agency, it occurs to me that perhaps you do not know where Quarters Eye is located.

We are a good stone's throw away from the I-J-K-L, and have our own World War II shacks on Ohio Drive, a former Wave barracks that actually faces the Potomac. Needless to say, we require special ID and maintain our own communications center which neatly bypasses the rest of the Agency. It worked for Guatemala, goes the theory, and will again.

Well, we may have moved our distance from the Reflecting Pool, but the drains continue to clog in the Washington swamplands, the old barracks floor creaks, and the poor ventilation reminds us of the old problem; shower as we do, and raid the exchequer for deodorants as we must, nonetheless we discover all over again that we are not odorless beasts. I mention this as the intimate cruelty that is put upon our work. Never have so many good people devoted to personal cleanliness and dedicated labor had to suffer such an awareness of close quarters. This may be the penance we were not prepared to pay. Every time I come back to work in Washington I am reminded of it. One term for our local bastion is Stale Quarters.

At any rate, there's not much to picture. Two floors of a large barracks. Upstairs is the Newsroom—Hunt's and my bailiwick. Desks, posters, propaganda displays in various stages of development. Always the ubiquitous cubicles. One studio at the north end for draftsmen. We are comparatively good on light compared to the first floor where the War Room is located (and requires still another ID card—took forty-eight hours to clear me, even if Cal has an office adjoining). The War Room, of course, is where one wants to be. Enough communications systems and cable-snakes to compete with a film set; large maps and charts covered with acetate overlays, still virgin, for the most part, of grease pencils. One has entered a sanctum. I am reminded of a surgical theater. There is the same kind of palpable hush before the first incision.

April 7, 1961

Howard's immediate boss in Quarters Eye is called Knight. In Uruguay, Howard used to speak of earlier days in Guatemala when Knight was working for him, so I happen to be in on the fact that the fellow's real name is David Phillips. This sets up an embarrassment. One must pretend not to be aware. What compounds the irony is that it doesn't really matter. It wouldn't wreck a thing at Quarters Eye if we knew him as Dave Phillips. In Miami, cover may be another matter, but the general feeling up here is that we're laying on a little too much hygiene. Hence, this journal will call him David Phillips. It's how I think of him, and it is a perfect name for what he is, a tall man, reasonably built, a Texan with a pleasant face, not too strong, not too weak, and reasonably manly. He looks intelligent, yet not overly cultivated. Central Casting would take him for a CIA man, and, at the moment, he rules the propaganda roost here. Around 1958, he cut his CIA ties and opened a public relations office in Havana on the sound expectation Batista would lose. He anticipated that all the old publicity firms would then be *persona non grata* under Castro. What he didn't count on, he now admits, is that Castro would move to the left so quickly that the Communist Party would not allow anyone but themselves to take care of publicity. Naturally, the Company also had Phillips doing a bit of contract work in Havana, so when he pulled up stakes and left for America, Tracy Barnes signed him on again, and with a promotion. Phillips is now a career man on the express elevator. While he and Howard get along ostensibly well, I would guess they relate like in-laws.

Phillips has been pleasant enough to me, and I like him, although not that much. Perhaps it's his air of corporate geniality. He could have worked the front office for General Motors, IBM, Boeing, General Foods, Time, Life, name it. I expect that he's as ambitious as Howard.

Moreover, he has a social vice that puts me off. Phillips is always telling stories. They are funny enough provided you put in a little work behind your laugh. While chuckling away at his tales, I feel not unlike a pastry tube being squeezed for a bit more whipped cream. One sample is sufficient: "I knew," he begins in practiced fashion, "an American newsman in Beirut who once had the following experience on the road to Damascus. He was driving a Volkswagen when the young soldier on guard at the Syrian border proceeded to stop him. Why? On the charge that he was smuggling an automobile engine across in his rear trunk. To cut down on corruption, the Syrian government had plucked their loyal guards right off the farm, and this new lad in uniform had never before seen a vehicle with a rear-mounted motor. My friend, however, being an old hand, shrugged, turned around, drove one hundred yards down the road to the Lebanese guard post, and then backed up to Syrian customs again.

"The guard went to the rear (which two minutes ago had been the front of the car), opened it, discovered it to be empty, and said, 'You may enter my country.' So my friend got his story by driving into Syria ass-backwards."

Do you know, Kittredge, how many anecdotes at just this level of exaggeration are forever being swapped back and forth around here? I realize that I've always avoided Agency men like Phillips where I could. Their brand of humor reminds me of the one drink before dinner that is taken by people who do not like alcohol but are following doctor's orders.

At any rate, we have a troika. Phillips tells his jokes, Howard whinnies, I chuck-chuck-chuckle, and our laughter, once it has lasted respectably long enough, stops like a slow-moving car with good brakes. I swear, there are more damn ways to lose your soul.

April 9, 1961

A report has come to the War Room regarding the cargo vessels we leased. They are to serve as troop transports and have arrived at Puerto de Cabezas in Nicaragua. By way of HALIFAX, I learn that they are gangrenous old tubs with rusty cranes and winches and are bound to cause a slowdown in loading supplies. Our people on the spot did not have a favorable reaction. "It gave me a cold feeling," reported one of them to Cal.

Let us hope this is not symbolic of the venture. I alternate between fever and chill. While the Brigade was most impressive in February, their numbers have since doubled. In consequence, half the troops have to be seriously undertrained. The Fifth and Sixth Battalions were created just a few days ago out of recruits who signed up in the last couple of weeks, and one can worry about the collective makeup of our personnel, since it is indubitably a middle-class army and has only fifty Negroes in the ranks. Which could prove a problem.

More than half the population of Cuba is black. In addition, the Directorate of Intelligence tells us that only 25 percent of the Cuban population is opposed to Castro. Somehow, that causes less concern. It seems our pride here at Operations is to pay no attention to what comes over the transom from the Directorate of Intelligence.

All the same, I keep being bothered by that statistic; can only 25 percent of the Cuban population be opposed to Castro? If it is true, why won't the man permit an open vote? I must say that I keep swinging back and forth in confidence. Chills when I think of Castro's army. We estimate it at thirty thousand trained soldiers, and his militia could come to ten times that. Of course, our assumption is that the militia will fall away from him at a great rate. *All wars in Cuba have been won by the smaller force.* In other words, Cuba is a magical system. So I experience what I would term *good fevers* at the thought of the outcome. Combat, according to Cal, is the largest magic show of them all and always takes place "on that damned old darkling plain," fraught with coincidence and intervention. Yes, I worry over the Brigade.

April 10, 1961

A report has just been forwarded to me from Zenith. My number-one Miami agent, the same Chevi Fuertes I worked with in Uruguay, keeps warning me about two gentlemen named Mario García Kohly and Rolando Masferrer. There is serious talk in Miami that their ultra-right-wing group is planning to assassinate the Cuban Revolutionary Council en masse, just so soon as that political body is flown into Cuba. To me it sounds more like a threat than an execution, but the element to give pause is that if I were Castro, Kohly's underground in Cuba would be precisely the people I would not wish to arrest until they had fulfilled their mission against the Cuban Revolutionary Council. This is to assume that Kohly, like the others, has been penetrated by Castro.

When I go with this concern to Cal, he shakes his head at me. "Do you ever read the newspapers?" he asks.

It is right there for me in the first section of the *Washington Post.* Rolando Masferrer was indicted today by a Federal Grand Jury in Miami for conspiring to send a military expedition to Cuba. That is a violation of neutrality laws.

"Well," I say, "we don't always mess up, do we?"

"Not always," says Cal.

later, April 10, 1961

Hunt, Phillips, and myself, at work in a conference room on the second floor, must sound like we are programming a computer to print poetry on demand. Come D-Day, our Swan Island shortwave transmitter is going to bombard Havana and the provinces of Cuba with enough transmissions to paralyze whatever section of the DGI is assigned to intercepting our messages to the underground. The transmissions, while nonsense, will have the ring of tradecraft. It is a neat concept. Our people in Cuba will ignore messages they do not understand on the assumption those words are being beamed to other groups. But the DGI will feel obliged to deal with each and every transmission. In preparation, as good conscientious wordsmiths, we fine-tune our output. "The jackal is loose in the sugarcane," for example. We argue whether jackals are indigenous to Cuba, and whether they have a tropism for sugarcane. We do not want to send any message that will reveal an ignorance of Cuban natural history. We could certainly use one sophisticated Habanero right at our side. Instead, we call on the Caribbean Desk in the Directorate of Intelligence. Since they are excluded from the operation, we request no more than a rundown on flora and fauna and agricultural techniques in the eastern and western halves of Cuba. Then we'll know if we can employ, "The owl hoots at midnight," "The bobcat moves over the ridge," "The swamps are draining," "The papaya fields show smoke." Or, best of all, "Wait for the eye of the Antilles."

April 11, 1961

The cherry blossoms came out today on the Potomac. A faint reflection of that natural bounty is in our collective mood today at Quarters Eye, or do I make a case out of a few errant smiles?

The Cuban Revolutionary Council, hereinafter known as the CRC, has by means of one or another subterfuge been brought up to New York to meet with their overlord, Frank Bender, a bald, cigar-smoking East European who speaks no Spanish. He has gotten them into one small meeting room at the Commodore long enough to announce that the invasion is very much in the works, and that if they wish to be flown to the beachhead, they now agree to be sequestered in a hotel suite in New York for the next few days— security forbids any closer information. They will be able to make no phone calls. If any one of them does not wish to agree to this, he is free to leave and free to miss the invasion. Bender, an old hand at East

European ironies, also gets across the notion that any CRC leader who did not wish to join such an agreement might find himself a security risk and be sequestered alone. Naturally they all agree to go into the communal lock-up. Hunt claims that these elaborate steps are necessary because of Manuel Ray, but I can think of Toto Barbaro, and am just as happy that none of them can now send out a message. It does occur to me that we must have used at least twenty people from Zenith to set up the various pretexts that brought these six highly individual Cuban gentlemen to New York. Well, we are good at that, and so should we be.

Bender, who is now cloistered with this crew of esteemed prisoners, informs Hunt that they are importuning him already for advance news. "If we are to be captives," they say, "can we at least have the compensation of acquiring some privileged knowledge?"

In the meantime, to steer CRC publicity, Knight has hired a Madison Avenue public relations firm named Lem Jones Associates. Actually, he has rehired them. Lem Jones has already done work for the Frente. I can see by the expression on Phillips' face that I am in for one of his stories.

"I would say," commences Phillips, "that Lem Jones earned his Frente money last September. Castro was slated to speak at the UN that month, and Lem and I decided to confront him with a couple of busloads of Cuban women. 'Mothers from Miami.' It was to be 'a Caravan of Sorrow' and would climax with a prayer session at St. Patrick's Cathedral.

"En route, however, from Miami, our chartered Greyhound buses were seriously slowed. We had carefully selected four pregnant women, and now we discovered that they had to pee every ten miles. We came in late at Washington, D.C., and missed a press conference. Ditto, Philadelphia. The Caravan of Sorrow entered New York one full day late, but we did get news shots of the ladies praying in St. Patrick's. It made the papers and the wire services. I would say Lem Jones has earned his reemployment."

April 12, 1961

The tempo of real action is commencing. One can feel it in the War Room.

I learn today that the loading of the supply ships at Puerto de Cabezas progressed even more slowly than anticipated. The winches kept fouling, and a huge hatch cover on one of the ships had rusted in place. Hours of effort were expended in prying it loose. The Brigade troops, however, full of high morale, threw themselves into manhandling the cargo. My imagination is sufficiently vivid to hear winches screaming and hoists wheezing from one end of the harbor to the other. So soon as they are loaded, off they go to anchor a few hundred yards away, their share of the Brigade already on board. Word comes back that the troops are sleeping in hammocks below deck and on tarpaulins over the hatch cover. The officers, still living in pup tents on shore, will celebrate a Mass tonight after receiving their full orientation on the invasion plan. Only then will they learn where they are going to land in Cuba.

Our people in Puerto de Cabezas also reported that Luís Somoza, President of Nicaragua, adjured the Brigade to: "Bring me a couple of hairs from Castro's beard." Our observer added: "Since Somoza is a plump and powdered dictator with pancake makeup, I'm afraid his expectation of hearty applause had to put up with a few snickers as well. One rugged Cuban yelled back, 'The beard above or the beard below?' "

It is also being bruited about at Quarters Eye that our rented freighters from the García Line are so old they will lend absolute authenticity to our claim that the invasion is financed by Cubans and run by Cubans. No self-respecting American would ever go near such tubs. Phillips comments: "Keeping this operation authentically Cuban may have been carried a little too far."

                                                                    still April 12
I keep alternating between two systems of perception. One part of me fastens on every report from TRAX and Puerto de Cabezas. The other reminds me that the fate of the Brigade may yet be linked to my own. In a week or less, I will join them on the beachhead. That does not yet feel real. As a result, my anxiety lives in my body like a mild grippe and sensitizes each movement of my limbs.

Now, it occurs to me that if I am on the beachhead, I can be captured, and if they conclude, as they will, that I am CIA, they could torture me. I could talk. (Could I? I do not possess the answer.) I realize that I may know too much. This produces a childish reaction —I am furious at everyone in the Agency who has told me too much. "It will be your fault, not mine," I actually say to myself, and am appalled. The truth is that I have no basis in experience by which to measure these new ventures. So I am as wild in my thoughts as a man alone at a party to whom no one speaks.

still April 12

The large news today at Quarters Eye has been Kennedy's statement at a packed press conference this morning. "Under no conditions," he declares, "will there be an intervention in Cuba by the United States Armed Forces."

Naturally, these words are striking enough to be put up in type on the Newsroom billboard and downstairs in the War Room. Hunt is beaming. "A superb effort," he concludes, "in misdirection." We know the aircraft carrier *Essex* is waiting in Puerto Rico to rendezvous at the Bay of Pigs.

Down in the War Room, however, Cal is much less pleased: "If Kennedy means what he says, we can get out the black drapes."

Cal is obviously counting on a full military follow-up by the U.S. That suggests Bissell and Dulles are of the same persuasion. The assumption has to be that Kennedy will never accept defeat. Arguments rotate around this. Does our President mean that he will not intervene under any circumstances, or is it a masterstroke, as Hunt hopes?

In the War Room, I am more aware than ever of how prodigiously large is our map of the Bay of Pigs. I see it as a species of technological magic to pose against the bloody, twisted chicken necks in the *mayombero*'s soup.

later—April 12

Another piece of news takes over the rest of the day. A Soviet spaceman named Yuri Gagarin orbited the earth in a spaceship. That is to say—the language is new—he has circumnavigated the planet in a space capsule. At Quarters Eye, most of our people are glum. It is a frightful shock. How can the Russians have won the race into space? On the other hand, my father takes hope. "It couldn't have happened at a better time," he says. "This could get Kennedy's Irish up."

No one says Bay of Pigs around here. We speak of Red Beach, Blue Beach, and Green Beach. Shades of Normandy? Tarawa? Iwo Jima?

April 13, 1961

I missed an interesting remark made yesterday by Jack Kennedy at his press conference. "The indictment of Mr. Masferrer of Florida, on the grounds that he was plotting an invasion of Cuba in order to establish a Batista-like regime should indicate the feelings of this country toward those who wish to establish that kind of administration inside Cuba."

April 14, 1961

Today, D minus 3, the Brigade is under sail. Our troops are crowded into five old tubs; our operation is called Zapata. Tomorrow, D minus 2, eight exile B-26s will take off from a Nicaraguan base near Puerto de Cabezas and launch an air strike against three Cuban airfields. We aim not only to knock out Castro's air force, but to prove to the world that the operation was performed by Cuban defectors flying Cuban planes purchased by Cubans. The prevailing opinion at Quarters Eye is that a large air attack on D-Day itself would have too American a signature. Hunt and I are agitated by the choice, however. Bombing these airfields on D minus 2 is going to give Castro time to roll up our networks. It is likely, then, that there will be no serious underground in Cuba on invasion day. Late at night, when we argue in our living room, Cal will not admit to this logic, but I have an intimation for the first time of how calculating Allen Dulles must be. While he is taking off to Puerto Rico tomorrow to fulfill a speaking engagement he agreed to make months ago—which hopefully will confuse the DGI into thinking the invasion is not that near—I decide that only Mr. Dulles could have made the cold estimate that if our networks in Cuba were now, on balance, so infiltrated as to be of as much use to Castro as to us, then let him arrest all those tens of thousands of Cubans in a massive roundup. Most likely he will be imprisoning a great many of his own double agents as well. This could produce extremely bad morale for his intelligence forces further down the line. As for our underground morale—well, that appears to be expendable.

Hunt and Phillips are also worrying about the millions of leaflets that will *not* be distributed during the D minus 2 air strike. All payload on the B-26s has now been given over to bombs for knocking out Castro's planes. Later, if there are more air strikes (no one seems certain how many have been authorized, and Phillips is beginning to pound the desk because he cannot find out), we may be permitted to drop some paper, but any thought of a Guatemala-like coup seems to have been put on the back burner. To mollify us, we are assured that the supply ships will carry the leaflets. "Once we have a beachhead and an airstrip, your input will come in very handy."

"Too late," Phillips tries to explain. Since he may be the most impressive physical specimen in Quarters Eye, as much an Agency man as a cadet at Sandhurst is a Sandhurst cadet, it is odd to see him so frustrated that his mouth and face crinkle like a five-year-old refusing tears. "They can't get it straight," he says. "We're the fore-play. Are we going to introduce foreplay after fornication?"

April 14, later entry
On pressure from the State Department, someone above us, possibly Bissell, has decided that in the air raid tomorrow, an extra decoy plane can fly directly from Nicaragua to Miami. It will purport to be a Cuban B-26 who defected from Castro's air force, bombed the Havana airfields, and then flew over to us.

Hunt foresees all manner of things going wrong with this caper, and gets on the Encoder-Decoder to Happy Valley which is our code name for the airport in Puerto de Cabezas. He proceeds to explain what is essential in the way of preparation. The plane must look as if it took a bit of a drubbing in combat over the Cuban air space. Camouflage artists can put bullet holes and burn marks in appropriate places. Hunt's comment: "This one gives me the col-lywobbles. Get one detail wrong and it can all come undone."

Knowing that the air raid will strike at dawn, most of the Quarters Eye personnel are staying over tonight. We rest on army cots with surprisingly nonstandardized mattresses—either bone-hard or flaccid—drink coffee, and idle out the hours. I suppose all situations that require one to wait for news from outside are prison-like. One is suffering sensory cut-off, which is, I suppose, what prison is all about.

8:00 A.M., April 15, 1961
The room stank of cigarette smoke through the night, and the stale, near-sickly odor of too many men sleeping with too much tension. Shortly after dawn, however, the cable traffic concerning our three strikes commenced. A wing of three B-26s called "Linda" has for its target San Antonio de los Baños, a big and crucial military

airfield thirty miles southwest of Havana. "Puma," another flight of three B-26s, will hit Camp Libertad just outside Havana, and "Gorilla," the third wing, two B-26s, is to strike the other end of the island, Santiago de Cuba Airport in Oriente Province.

Now the reports come in all at once. All three airfields have been simultaneously bombed and strafed. Havana is erupting into hysterical broadcasts, and our Cuban pilots are reporting to us that Castro's air force has been wiped out on the ground.

How our sleeping dormitory is transformed! At 6:30 A.M. windows fly open, and we are cheering. There is a whoop of a rush to get clothes on and go down to the War Room. More euphoria there. Officers are hugging each other. Bissell is receiving congratulations. "Nothing official," I hear him say, "we still have to wait for official confirmation from our U-2 photographs," but he is beaming. I hear other officers murmuring, "It's over. Havana might as well be in our hands."

Meanwhile, the lone B-26 that flew from Happy Valley to Florida landed at Miami International Airport, and the pilot was immediately led away by Immigration and his plane impounded. We listen to American news reports that the Miami pilot was wearing a T-shirt, a baseball cap, and dark glasses, and looked remarkably cool smoking a cigarette. His airplane had certainly been chewed up. One engine was dead, and the fuselage showed many bullet holes.

A statement comes out of New York from Miro Cardona. "The Cuban Revolutionary Council has been in contact with and has encouraged these brave pilots." We have a ten-inch black-and-white TV set in the War Room, and I watch Cardona as he speaks to reporters. He looks tired. He removes his dark glasses and says to the press, "Gentlemen, look into revolutionary eyes that have known little sleep of late."

"Are the raids a prelude to invasion?" asks a reporter.

Cardona smiles. He spreads his hands like an umpire calling "Safe." Cardona says: "No invasion, sir."

Barbaro, however, seated next to him, says, "Spectacular things have begun to happen." Barbaro looks hysterical to me.

an hour later

Bizarre events as well. At Key West, an unforeseen emergency landing had to be made by one of our bona fide exile bombers when it developed engine trouble after participating in the strike at

Camp Libertad. When real events conform to fictional scenarios, no one is prepared. The local high school in Key West was getting ready to celebrate Olympics Day at Boca Chica Naval Air Station. They were there with all the trimmings: track events, parents, marching bands, cheerleaders. All canceled. Olympics Day was called off by the Navy.

Then another B-26 from the San Antonio de los Baños strike had to land at Grand Cayman Island when one of its fuel tanks failed to feed. Since Grand Cayman flies a British flag, returning the pilot and plane to Happy Valley will not be automatic. As Cal remarks, "You can't trust the British on things like this. They can get formal at the goddamnedest times."

The director of Immigration and Naturalization appears on the TV news from Miami. He refuses to give the names of the two pilots who have landed in the U.S. Their families in Cuba must be protected. A reporter asks: "Wouldn't Castro's air force generals know the names of their own pilots?"

"I cannot help you," says the director. "These pilots have requested that their names be kept secret."

Hunt shakes his head. "I can hear the bilge sloshing in the hold."

He is right. All through the day, reporters in Miami and New York keep posing new questions. I begin to see that they are another kind of force in our field of forces, and have a homing instinct for every hole in the tissue of a tale. One reporter actually managed to get close enough to the plane that came down in Miami to notice that the muzzles on the machine guns of the B-26 were still taped. While that is done routinely to keep dust and detritus out of the breech, it also means the guns were not fired. That question hangs in the news reports. All through the Newsroom and the War Room, I can hear men muttering, "These son of a bitch reporters—whose side are they on?" I can hear myself saying it. The questions are getting worse, and no answers are coming back. The radio and TV announcers are underlining "No comment" with more of a resonant pause each time.

In the UN, Raul Roa, the Ambassador from Cuba, has a run-in with Adlai Stevenson. I catch reports of that on radio all afternoon. Stevenson is saying: "These pilots defected from Castro's tyranny. No United States personnel participated. These two planes, to the best of our knowledge, were Castro's own air force planes, and, according to the pilots, took off from Castro's own air force fields. I have a picture of one of these planes. The markings of Castro's air force are clearly visible."

I feel merry and woeful all at once. It gives me an odd and unexpected sense of importance that so famous a personage as Adlai Stevenson is ready to lie for the Agency. It is as if he, too, is part of that transcendental wickedness that partakes of goodness because its aim is to gain the rightful day. Nonetheless, I am depressed as well. Stevenson seems such a consummate liar. His voice is absolutely sincere.

"I don't know that he's witting," says Hunt.

Raul Roa certainly is: "This air raid at dawn is the prelude to a large-scale invasion attempt, supported and financed by the United States. These mercenaries have been trained by experts of the Pentagon and the Central Intelligence Agency."

At a White House press briefing, Pierre Salinger, the Press Secretary, denies any knowledge of the bombing.

later

Toward evening, I stop by my father's office to share a cup of hot coffee. He is not in a good mood. Word has just come in of the first casualty. On the *Atlántico*, one of the rented freighters, there had been .50-caliber machine-gun practice, and the mountings tore loose from the (no doubt rusted) deck plates. A spew of bullets lashed the deck. One man dead, two wounded. A burial ceremony at sea. Full uniform, prayers, and the body goes into the sea at sunset.

Cal Hubbard sees needless death as a bad omen; he is also worried about Adlai Stevenson. "I don't think Adlai knows those two planes were ours. Tracy Barnes gave him the orientation, and Tracy can be vague if he chooses to be. There will be hell to pay when Stevenson finds out. God, he might talk Kennedy into scrubbing the invasion." Cal immediately adds, "That won't happen," as if the force of his will can become as much of a factor as the untrustworthy air absorbing his words.

evening

Tonight, after dark, Hunt is paid a visit by Dorothy. He slips out of Quarters Eye and they sit in their car and talk. He has not told her that we are leaving for the beachhead in less than seventy-two hours. He has not even packed a bag. He will probably join the Cuban Revolutionary Council shortly after they are flown down to Opa-

Locka, and there he will pick up some chinos and army boots. Ditto for me. I picture Howard and Dorothy in their car, talking of her mother's recent death, the children's school—their domestic agenda. We are heading into tropical country but again I feel a chill. It is not quite real to me that I am going to war. Nonetheless, my death is vivid to me. I can picture my dead body. Since this journal is for Kittredge, I presume to ask: Does Omega tease Alpha with images of that death it is more willing to meet than its uncooperative partner?

Sunday morning

Few of us slept well on our cots last night. Even though the invasion is not scheduled until early tomorrow morning, men kept getting up and going down to the War Room. Over coffee and doughnuts, Phillips regales us with a story. One of the secretaries, taking her turn on a cot for a little rest last night, was panicked to awaken to the sight of a strange man sleeping in the bunk next to her. He was very big and very pale, and she had never seen him before. Was he an interloper? No, Phillips said, he was Richard Bissell, our leader, catching forty winks.

About 9:00 A.M., with half of Quarters Eye absent for an hour or two to see their families and/or go to church, disturbing news rises from the War Room: The aerial photographs, after close scrutiny, reveal that the strike on the Cuban airports yesterday was less success-ful than first reported. Not all of Castro's planes were destroyed. Apparently, our Brigade pilots had seen what they wished to see. By the War Room's count, two-thirds of the Castro force is destroyed or out of commission, but there still remain three or four T-33 jet trainers, the same number of Sea Fury fighters, and two B-26 bomb-ers. A cleanup mission is needed, therefore, to finish the job. Our air operations officer was ordering such a move when General Cabell, now Acting Director in Mr. Dulles' absence, came back to the War Room from a Sunday morning of golf.

I was out of hearing, but soon learned that Cabell refused to approve this second strike without calling Secretary of State Rusk first, and Rusk, in turn, asked him to come over to the State Department. Richard Bissell, visibly upset, departed with Cabell.

Two hours later, our second air strike is still being held up. The mood at Quarters Eye has shifted again. As Cal explains to me in passing, the main body of troops are scheduled to land around 2:00 A.M. Monday morning, and the supply ships have to be unloaded before dawn; otherwise, they could be mangled by the remains of Castro's air force. It is possible to finish the task before morning light, says Cal, but only if everything goes well. That's a good deal to ask of an untried invasion force coming in by dark on old ships to an unfamiliar shore.

two hours later

We are still waiting. It is late afternoon. We are getting worried. The lead story in the Sunday *New York Times* by Tad Szulc has done all too good a job of chasing after "puzzling circumstances." The questions are getting worse. Why, for instance, are the pilots' names still being withheld? Then there is the question of the B-26 nose. Castro's planes have transparent Plexiglas turrets—the Miami B-26 showed a solid nose.

Hunt outlines the real trouble. Our fake story has to hold until the landing is accomplished. Once we have an airfield operating in the Bay of Pigs, our little fiction about the defecting pilots can be buried by immediate and real events. In the meantime, however, the State Department may have lost its stomach for more air attacks. All we know is that the meeting between Rusk, Bissell, and Cabell continues, and queries from Happy Valley concerning the delayed air strike continue to pile up. The mood is reminiscent of a waiting room.

I am busy, however, preparing messages with Hunt and Phillips. They will be broadcast many times this night to Cuba from our clandestine radio station on Swan Island and, hopefully, will prove most confusing. "Alert! Alert!" we send out. "Look well at the rainbow. The fish will rise very soon. Chico is in the house. Visit him. The sky is blue. Place notice in the tree. The tree is green and brown. The letters arrived well. The letters are white. The fish will not take much time to rise. The fish is red." Too late I pick up from our language expert at the Directorate of Intelligence that "fish" is one more word in Cuba for phallus. Oh, well, "the phallus is rising, the phallus is red."

Next comes in a Reuters teletype from Havana describing a funeral procession thirty blocks long that moves slowly through the streets of the capital behind the bodies of those who were killed in the air strike yesterday. The bodies had lain in state at Havana University through the night; now the cortège advances to Colón Cemetery where Castro is waiting to speak.

An hour later, Reuters provides excerpts of Castro's speech.

"If the attack on Pearl Harbor is considered by the American people as a criminal, treacherous, cowardly act, then our people have a right to consider this act twice as criminal and a thousand times as cowardly. The Yankees are trying to deceive the world, but the whole world knows the attack was made with Yankee planes piloted by mercenaries paid by the United States Central Intelligence Agency."

I show the teletype to Cal. He nods. "I've heard," he says, "that Stevenson is in an absolute rage. He's found out our B-26s were not true defectors, and threatens to resign. So I don't believe they'll give us another strike. The political factors are going to ride right over the military considerations."

He is right. Bissell comes back at dusk, haggard, grim, composed. The invasion is on, he tells us, but the air strike is off. If the ships are not unloaded by dawn, they will have to withdraw, and go out to sea until the second night, when they can come back to finish their unloading.

I am struck by the reaction. The unhappy news is, at least, equal to the good news, yet the fifty or more of us assembled to hear Bissell start to cheer. *The invasion is on.* We are committed. The President is committed. That is the essential. The game is on. I believe we cheer in relief at no longer having to steel ourselves against rejection of the entire project.

I see that we are not without resemblance to a chorus, and feel as if I understand Greek drama at last. We are not merely a group of individuals commenting on the actions of the gods, but have become our own human field of force, and will seek, through the intensity of our concentration, to bend destiny toward our desires. Before long, we have begun to brood on the need to bring the supply ships and unloading craft closer to the beachhead. I would not be surprised if many of us, in our minds, are oiling the gears of the donkey engines on those rusty old freighters.

later

There is a lull in the evening, and I am closeted in the john again, adding to these notes. Soon the local legend will have it that Hubbard doesn't keep a tight sphincter. If my absences every few hours are noted, and my hope is that in the general intensity and confusion they are not, all good and well. If, on the other hand, I get to be known as Shit-House Harry, that will establish the cost of this journal. I wish, by now, that I had not started. If they taught us one principle at the Farm over and over, it was to take no unnecessary notes. Even as I write, I feel constrained. I am careful not to speak in any too great detail about our War Room personnel and their specific tasks, I try to describe no more than historical moments and, of course, the divagations of my own mood, but I still have to marvel at the basic impropriety of my father's makeup. He encouraged me to do this journal, knowing full well that such activities are, at best, professionally inappropriate. I marvel at myself. I obey him. How great is my need to get a little nearer to him.

All the same, these hours of writing, these meditations on whether or not I am preparing myself for the incalculable pressures of a beachhead headquarters and a conceivable visit to eternity, would be close to intolerable without this journal. And the risk is small. Every time I write a few pages, they are enclosed in an envelope and dropped in the mail slot in Cal's safe. I assume he collects them every few days for deposit in one of his secure boxes. In fact, as if it would compound the trespass, we do not talk about it.

Hunt has just informed me of the latest update on our itinerary. If by dawn the supplies are landed and the beachhead is secure, then we will be on our way to Miami to join the exile leaders. In another twenty-four hours, or less, we will be on the beachhead. Indeed, in the early hours of this morning, the CRC left New York for Opa-Locka. So soon as they debarked from their plane, they were immediately installed—I will not say incarcerated—in one of the barracks on the old air base. Naturally, they are in a half-boiled state; half-simmering, half-boiled over. I have never been able to come to terms with the all too readily available hysteria of the Cuban temperament, but I can appreciate their feelings in this situation. After all, they are on the outskirts of Miami, not ten miles away from their wives and families, yet they cannot get out. Being politicians, they would love to join the festivities. What we hear from every side is that the Cubans in southern Florida have taken off on a nonstop fiesta ever since the air attack Saturday. The recruiting offices have long lines. Everyone in Miami now wants a chance to join the battle against Castro. At Opa-Locka, however, the exile leaders are suspended between high elation at the commencement of war activities, and the quintessential Cuban gloom that comes from regarding their immured impotence in the face of events.

I find an ax-hewn poetic justice in the fact that Frank Bender is the Agency man shut up with them at this point. Bender, from the little I saw of him when he would fly down occasionally to Miami, never got along well with Hunt or the Frente. An East European street man with tradecraft forged and annealed in the espionage mills of Vienna and Berlin, Bender has one principle from which he works backward—results. He is bald, wears eyeglasses, chews cigars, is abrasive as a corncob, and for months, whenever Hunt was speaking to him on a nearby phone, I would wait for the crash of the receiver when Howard's end of the phone came slamming down. Now, however, they are almost friendly. Bender, after putting up for three days with six Cubans in a hotel suite, and contained with them now in a barracks, is suffering from enough claustrophobia to metamorphose Howard's voice into a friendly sound. Sometimes, Bender even talks to me. "Give me some news, boychick," he says. "Something to divert these guys. They're ready to eat the rug."

"Tell them," I answer, "that Castro said the American news services purvey fantasy. 'Even Hollywood,' and I quote him, 'would not try to film such a story.' "

"Ha, ha, the son of a bitch is right," says Bender.

Howard yells over to me, "Tell Frank to inform them that things are going according to plan."

"They hate the plan," says Bender. "They want to be in the action."

"Tell him," yells Hunt, "that I sent his regards to his wife."

"Bring down a box of cigars," says Bender. "I'm running low."

Two hours later, he calls again. Barbaro wishes to speak to me. "I have three words for you to pass on to your father," he says. "These three words are Mario García Kohly. Kohly, Kohly, Kohly. Ask your father if Kohly is under observation as fully as we are."

"Kohly can do nothing now," I say. "Masferrer has been arrested."

"There are many Masferrers, and only one Kohly. He is a bomb, and we will all be exterminated in the blast," says Barbaro.

A little later, Cal, on being asked, remarks that Kohly is merely a single cannon among 184 pieces of loose ordnance below decks. (This is the number of separate refugee groups in Miami.)

late Sunday night, close to midnight
We are trying to catch a few hours of sleep before the landing begins. The prepared text of the Cuban Revolutionary Council

Communiqué Number 1, carefully crafted by Hunt and Phillips, is now complete. In a few minutes we will phone it in to Lem Jones, and he will mimeo it, get into a taxi, and start distribution to the news services. They should have it by 2:00 A.M.

> THE CUBAN REVOLUTIONARY COUNCIL WISHES TO AN-
> NOUNCE THE PRINCIPAL BATTLE OF THE CUBAN REVOLUTION
> AGAINST CASTRO WILL BE FOUGHT IN THE NEXT FEW HOURS.
> THIS TREMENDOUS ARMY OF INVINCIBLE SUPERPATRIOTS HAS
> NOW RECEIVED ITS INSTRUCTIONS TO STRIKE THE VITAL BLOW
> FOR THE LIBERATION OF THEIR BELOVED COUNTRY. OUR PARTI-
> SANS IN EVERY TOWN AND VILLAGE IN CUBA WILL RECEIVE, IN
> A MANNER KNOWN ONLY TO THEM, THE MESSAGE WHICH WILL
> SPARK A TREMENDOUS WAVE OF INTERNAL CONFLICT AGAINST
> THE TYRANT. OUR INFORMATION FROM CUBA INDICATES THAT
> MUCH OF THE MILITIA IN THE COUNTRYSIDE HAS ALREADY
> DEFECTED.

I have had no time to think, but I have to wonder if we have any partisans left. This afternoon there were reports from Reuters of Castro's response to the Saturday air raid. Huge roundups of Cubans are taking place in Havana and Santiago. I am beginning to wonder all over again at the wisdom of our first air raid. I suppose we were afraid that Castro's reconnaissance planes might spot the approach of the Brigade's rusty freighters if we waited too long and so Fidel would have time to disperse his air force, but how much has been lost by not striking everywhere at once? Well, I will not question my military superiors.

12:30 A.M., April 17, 1961

I am back in the loo, writing away. The paratroop contingent of the Brigade, 176 men strong, took off a while ago from Happy Valley after a steak dinner. Their breakfast will be an apple. Now they are due to land in a couple of hours to set up roadblocks. For days I have been looking at a wall-sized map in the War Room of an area forty miles high and eighty miles wide, and it occupies the inner panorama of my mind. Perhaps I should describe the projected beach-head. Once action starts, there will not be time.

Our landing will occupy an L-shaped line of coast. The Bay of Pigs is a narrow body of water running from north to south for twenty miles down to the shore of the Caribbean, which is on an east-west axis. One part of our force (two battalions) will sail up the Bay of Pigs to the head of this body of water and debark at Playa Larga (Red Beach). Our main force will come in at Girón on the Caribbean shore some ten miles around the bend. Playa Larga and Girón are thus thirty miles apart on a good road newly built by Castro. Further to the east, another twenty miles along the Caribbean coast, is Green Beach. There, a third force will come in later. Within twenty-four to forty-eight hours, it is expected that our forces will link up and we will have fifty miles of shore protected by the Bay of Pigs and the Caribbean to one's rear, and the great swamp of Zapata three miles to the fore. Miles ahead of our main body, the paratroopers will be sitting astride the three roads that traverse the swamp.

I think of the paratroopers flying from Nicaragua to Cuba. The droning of C-46 motors mixes in my mind with muttered outcries from the dreams of men asleep on cots beside me even as I stir and get up and walk to a stall in the men's room to pen this entry.

6:15 A.M., April 17, 1961

Much has happened in the last six hours.

The invasion force succeeded in getting ashore at Playa Larga and Girón by 2:30 in the morning, but little else followed by plan. We are receiving messages from the area through roundabout means—the command post at Girón radios back to the Brigade's command ship, the *Blagar,* and thence to an American destroyer twenty miles offshore which relays the same communication to the Pentagon and to us in the War Room. It is hard to determine how much is fact, how much is false report, but after confirmations and refutations, this much I now know. The landing beaches were not sloping sandy aprons as expected, but jagged coral pocked with underwater rocks. In the dark, it took longer than expected to set out luminescent buoys on the sea lanes of approach. Most of the supply launches assigned to the troops could not reach the shore because they grounded on the coral; the men, holding rifles overhead, had to walk in through chest-deep water. Much equipment was soaked, including many radios. Their temporary (we hope) loss of function accounts for the slowness of our communications with the Brigade.

There was also an unforeseen hurdle. A small detachment of Castro militia were on shore, and a few firefights took place before the locals surrendered or decamped. Several microwave radio transmitters were still warm when our Cubans captured the equipment. So Castro will be heard from earlier than expected. Cal, passing me in the corridor, said, "He will try to mop up the operation before there is enough of a beachhead for us to be able to justify flying in the provisional government."

All the news arriving now becomes a function, therefore, of that race to build up the beachhead. The paratroops are in varying degrees of peril. On the eastern front, out toward San Blas to the north, the roadblocks are well armed and supplied. Some of the citizens of San Blas are even carrying supplies and volunteering as nurses. On the western front, however, at the roadblock north of Playa Larga, the paratroopers' supplies landed in the swamp (once again, we trained the troops better than the pilots) and the men have had to fall back to the beach.

So, at Playa Larga, Tony Oliva, the Commander of the Second Battalion on the western front, has been engaged in combat ever since he landed. It has been mess, horror, and some success. Both landings, Playa Larga and Girón, were supposed to be unopposed, both met fire from small detachments of militia stationed near the beach. Both Brigade battalions prevailed and are now dug in, but hours have been lost. The cheap, second-hand landing craft that we chose to camouflage the operation seem to have functioned badly. What radio traffic we receive from the combat area offers repetitive messages of outboard motors failing, boats wallowing through delays in the dark, and time-consuming imbroglios with the coral reefs. From something Cal said a couple of days ago, I believe the Agency was warned by Naval Intelligence that the Girón coast could present many such obstacles, but we chose to ignore those briefings. Once we lost Trinidad as a landing site, the Agency must have decided that we could afford no more such shifts or there would be no plan to execute. We are obviously on a do-what-it-takes program. Is there trouble landing?—get the stuff ashore any way you can. That is why the supplies are now coming in too slowly. It looks like no tanks will get onto the beach before daylight when the supply ships must move away from shore.

I have to cease this entry. I can hear commotion in the hall.

11:30 A.M.

It is five hours since the last entry, and much has taken a turn for the worse. The remains of Castro's air force appeared over Girón at 6:30 this morning, just six planes, and one was shot down, but we, in turn, lost one supply ship, and another is now foundering in shallow water three hundred yards offshore.

Some frightful facts appear. The *Houston* did succeed in getting all of the Second Battalion off at Playa Larga by dawn, but the Fifth Battalion, full of green recruits, was still on board when the *Houston* took a direct rocket from one of Castro's planes. Since the ship was also carrying ammunition and gasoline, it was a miracle that none of the inflammables were struck. The vessel did suffer a serious hole below the waterline, however, and headed for shore where it grounded less than a quarter mile out and began to sink like a dying bull (or so I see it), oil and bilge seeping out of its wounds, even as the Fifth Battalion jumped into the sea and swam to shore. They were strafed from the air. Reports put their deaths between twenty and forty, and other casualties are as yet uncounted. Tony Oliva, Commander of the Second Battalion at Playa Larga, needs those Fifth Battalion troops to back his advance, but they are at present ten miles south and presumably regrouping.

Just a few minutes later came a larger disaster. Another of Castro's planes hit the *Río Escondido* with another rocket, and that boat suffered a large explosion and sank. The survivors are still uncounted (although many were rescued by the *Blagar* which steamed up to help), but the real damage, as we have been learning over the last couple of hours, is that the *Río Escondido* carried most of the necessities for the first ten days of fighting—ammo, food, medical supplies, fuel —nearly all of it.

Now we are receiving reports that the Brigade has succeeded in unloading only 10 percent of its ammunition, *probably enough for today,* but the supply ships have fled out to sea and will not be able to come in again until tonight. The Third Battalion, which was supposed to land at Green Beach, twenty miles to the east, had to be diverted instead to the base at Girón. It is now set up on the right flank, just two miles to the east of town. If Playa Larga on the western front does not hold, and Oliva's Second Battalion has to retreat all those thirty miles back to Girón, the beachhead will be only a few miles wide. In such a worst-case scenario, it is crucial that supplies get in.

That leads to the next problem. The freighters were told to rendezvous with the U.S.S. *Essex* in order to be protected from further air raids, but the ships' captains are not responding to radio instructions. Their merchant crews, while Cuban, obviously do not have the same high motivation as the Brigade. Result: The *Blagar*, the *Caribe*, the *Atlántico*, and the *Barbara J.* are scattered all over the Caribbean.

The only good news is that we have a small airfield in the environs of Girón, and it is in decent condition. One drop of sweat goes right down my spine when I tell myself that that is the airfield where I will be landing. Hunt, however, comes by to say that our flight down to Florida to join up with the Cuban Revolutionary Council has been delayed by the bad news. In the interim the CRC has dealt out its portfolios. Cardona is, of course, the President, and Manuel Artime (at present with the Brigade) is called "Delegate in the Invading Army," but Toto Barbaro, a genius at checks and balances, is Secretary of Defense. Manuel Ray has received Chief of Sabotage and Internal Affairs, just the post he would seek if Hunt's suspicions of him as a Communist are accurate.

Hysteria, nonetheless, reigns at Opa-Locka. One of the Ministers (Barbaro, I suspect) has sworn to kill himself unless he is released. He keeps telling Bender that he must speak to Allen Dulles. Bender has been on the telephone to Dick Bissell adjuring him to send a couple of impressive Kennedy people down to Opa-Locka to calm these putative statesmen's nerves. Arthur M. Schlesinger, Jr., and Adolf Berle are mentioned.

Work at Quarters Eye has come to a standstill for many of us. Occasionally a cable comes to the War Room and its contents activate a few people into intense activity for a period—we are all eager to do *something*—but for the most part, we are like idle gears waiting to be engaged. The B-26s stationed in Nicaragua are constantly in the air, but the three-and-a-half-hour flight from Happy Valley to Girón and the equally long flight back consumes so much fuel that they can put in no more than fifteen minutes over the beachhead. Carrying 3,000 pounds of bombs and eight rockets and eight .50-caliber machine guns plus fuel, these bombers manage to lift 40,000 pounds into the air. Which happens to be 4,000 pounds of overload. And all this is achieved by not carrying a tail gunner inasmuch as the weight of his machine gun, ammo boxes, firing rig, etc., would come close to an additional thousand pounds, and that is enough weight to consume the fifteen extra minutes of gasoline made available for air time over the battlefield. How vulnerable these B-26s, bereft of a tail gunner, must be, however, to Castro's remaining fighter planes.

One unreflective fellow here—how happy I am that I am not speaking of myself!—asked why the B-26s weren't kept on the local airfield. Answer: They would be destroyed by Castro's planes.

3:00 P.M., April 17, 1961

Tempers are drawing fine. David Phillips, who obviously prides himself on his urbanity, is beginning to get downright testy. We are in an outright cauldron of indecision about what kind of CRC bulletins to release to Lem Jones Associates. Are we to acknowledge any difficulties in the operation?

We come up with the following: THE CUBAN REVOLUTIONARY COUNCIL WISHES TO ANNOUNCE THAT ACTION TODAY WAS LARGELY OF A SUPPLY AND SUPPORT EFFORT TO FORCES WHICH HAVE BEEN MOBILIZED AND TRAINED INSIDE CUBA OVER THE PAST SEVERAL MONTHS.

We added a "quote" from an unnamed statesman: "I PREDICT THAT BEFORE DAWN THE ISLAND OF CUBA WILL RISE UP EN MASSE IN A COORDINATED WAVE OF SABOTAGE AND REBELLION. . . . MUCH OF THE MILITIA IN THE COUNTRYSIDE HAS ALREADY DEFECTED."

Actually, the Brigade had so far captured a hundred militia, of whom half subsequently defected to us. We extrapolated the future of Cuba from that ratio.

Dean Rusk was somewhat more cautious. A transcript of his morning press conference is now passing around the Newsroom. It is incredible how many cigarettes are being smoked, how many ashtrays not emptied, how many mimeographed papers of every description end up on the floor. We Agency hands are normally the neatest people in America, but the tension of these last few days has extorted a species of excretion from our nerves. A gray excretion, be it said. All is gray —the news itself, the cigarette ash, the smoke, the detritus on the floor, the gray footprints on the fallen paper. Yes, we exude information as fast as we receive it.

Q: There is a very puzzling case of this pilot who landed in Miami after saying he had defected from the Cuban Air Force. Castro has challenged us to produce him. Why do we not allow the press to see this man? Is the Immigration Service making policy for the State Department?

RUSK: I think this is a question which started as one on the Immigration Service and became one on Cuba. I would not wish to answer that question this morning.

Q: If the rebels succeed in establishing a solid foothold in Cuba, would we be prepared to consider or to grant diplomatic recognition?

RUSK: That is a question for the future into which I can't go this morning.

Q: Mr. Secretary, I will get off Cuba.

RUSK: Thank you. (laughter)

Others, however, are not obliging the matter so quickly. Crowds, rocks, and smashed windows at the U.S. Information Agency in Bogota; tear gas employed in Caracas against an unruly demonstration. *Izvestia* reports "alarming news." I skim statements by foreign ministers in London, Paris, Rome, Bonn, Warsaw, Prague, Budapest, Peking, New Delhi, Kinshasa. More mimeos for the floor. Outside on Ohio Drive one can see the Monday-afternoon traffic going by. Motor launch passengers pass on the Potomac. At this moment, we might be the most important office in Washington, yet we are relatively idle. I feel hollow, exalted, twisted by caffeine, angry, and full of a most peculiar, even an alienated sentiment—I am a participant in history as it is being made, but only as a spear carrier playing his own small anxious part in the opera.

I cannot rid myself of a small sense of outrage as I read early editions of the evening newspapers. They are not *responsible*! The rumors printed in small type leap out at me like headlines:

CUBAN NAVY IN REVOLT

INVADERS HIT BEACHES IN FOUR OF CUBA'S SIX PROVINCES

RAUL CASTRO CAPTURED

THOUSANDS OF POLITICAL PRISONERS FREED

CASTRO READY TO FLEE CUBA

Outrageous rumors daring to appear virtually as facts. I feel righteous that I am in Intelligence. At least we lie with some finesse. Then I think of our bulletins for the Cuban Revolutionary Council. That is not Intelligence. I hate Hunt for a moment, as if he is responsible for traducing me into propaganda. I realize that my nerves are living in two places at once. I had thought I would be in Opa-Locka by now and on the beachhead tomorrow; I am still in a consortium of stale armpits. Is anything so stale as exhausted deodorant? The gray excreta of our nerves spews onto the trays and the floor.

3:30 A.M., April 18, 1961

Battles at Playa Larga and San Blas go on through the night. Castro's troops reached the front at 3:00 P.M., twelve hours ago, and heavy action ensued. Reports seem to confirm that his men were mangled in the first attacks. Now the Brigade is under heavy artillery and tank fire and is answering with its own tanks, 4.2-inch mortars, and white phosphorus shells. The claim is that massive casualties are being inflicted. I cannot sleep. The battle sounds epic.

3:44 A.M., April 18, 1961

Unable to sleep, I listen to Radio Swan. An hour later, a transcript comes in of their broadcast to the Cuban underground. It may be worth entering in this journal. What the hell; Hunt, Phillips, and I worked on it hoping to inspire fear in all the Fidelistas who might be listening.

"Now is the precise moment for you to take up strategic positions that control roads and railroads. Take prisoners or shoot those who refuse to obey your orders! Comrades of the Navy, . . . secure your post in the Navy of Free Cuba. Comrades of the Air Force, listen closely! All planes must stay on the ground. See that no Fidelist plane takes off. Destroy its radios; destroy its tail; break its instruments; puncture its fuel tanks! Freedom and honor await those who join us. Death will overtake the traitors who do not!"

6:31 A.M., April 18, 1961

More from Radio Swan:

"People of Havana, attention, people of Havana. Help the brave soldiers of the liberation army. . . . Today at 7:45 A.M., when we give the signal on this station, all the lights in your house should be turned on; all electrical appliances should be connected. Increase the load on the generators of the electric company! But do not worry, people of Havana, the liberation forces will recover the electrical plants and they can be placed in operation rapidly."

7:00 A.M., April 18, 1961

The Brigade won the battle at Playa Larga, yet lost the ground. By all our reports, Castro's casualties were high. His troops were obliged to attack along a road surrounded by swamp on either side. It sounds like an operation where one wounded human inches forward behind another, dead flesh a shield for bleeding flesh.

As I write the above sentence, I recognize that my senses are not wholly under control. I see myself in the wounded man pushing the dead man. I feel the dirty, intimate stickiness of blood.

Castro's troops could not break through. In turn, Oliva's Second Battalion has run out of ammunition. The Fifth Battalion, dragged ashore from the stove-in *Houston,* are without weapons. They never did join up with Second Battalion. A retreat has been ordered from Playa Larga to Girón. The fifty-mile-long beachhead is falling backward into a five-mile perimeter.

The worst news is that no new supplies came in last night from the sea. I must have gotten up four times during the night to read the cable traffic from Girón. It is confounding. The crews of the *Caribe* and the *Atlántico* must have been berserk with panic. The first ship is now 218 miles south of the Bay of Pigs and shows no sign of returning for supply operations. The *Atlántico,* a mere 110 miles south, is asking to be off-loaded into LCUs *fifty miles from shore.*

It seems the explosion of the *Río Escondido* was the local equivalent of an atom bomb going off. Huge mushroom of smoke. An end of the world boom heard thirty miles away. While much of the crew was rescued by the *Blagar,* that same demoralized crew is now paralyzing all action. While the Brigade lost most of its ammunition and communications when the *Escondido* went down, the *Blagar* has enough supplies to keep our Cubans fighting for another two days. If it can get them in. But the *Blagar* is crawling back to Girón. It will not reach the shore by dawn, and that means it will not be able to unload again today. The survivors of the *Escondido* have so infected the *Blagar* that its crew now threatens to stop the ship's motors unless they are given American destroyer escort to shore. Since this is in negotiation (with the White House, I assume) they do permit the ship to return *slowly.*

I try not to sit in judgment. If I had been blown into the water, perhaps I could no longer control my will. The root of the problem with these mutinous crews goes right back, Phillips explains, to the way we obtained the boats. The García Line who rented them to us (offices in Havana, New York, and Houston) was not only a bona fide shipping firm but indeed the largest in Cuba. The owners' decision to defect from Castro was doubtless not passed on to the crew who thought they were signing on for routine voyages.

later

The situation has become so acutely intolerable for Pepe San Román that he took off in one of his battered launches to scour the seas, looking to find a supply ship. Of course, from six miles out, which is as far as the launch, given its asthmatic motor, dared to go, he could do nothing but transmit code-name cries by radio: DOLORES, THIS IS BEACH, NEED YOU. AM TRYING TO FIND YOU. DOLORES, PLEASE ANSWER BEACH.

I couldn't help observing that the text was as desperate as the notices in a personals classified.

By dawn it seems evident that we will not be able to supply the beachhead until tonight. In compensation, President Kennedy did agree during the night to allow six of the B-26s in Nicaragua to try a strike against the remaining planes in Castro's air force.

We are, however, cursed. This morning, black, low-lying tropical clouds cover Havana's airfields.

Of course, the fact that this flight was authorized after the same mission was vetoed on Sunday has put everyone in an ugly mood. "Irish Hamlet" may be the one epithet applied to Kennedy that is not too vicious to memorialize, and Cabell has hardly been seen on these premises since he paid that catastrophic visit on Sunday morning in golfing clothes. There is also some resentment of Bissell. The story, as it is coming out (and I have heard two virtually congruent versions from Cal and from David Phillips) is that when Bissell and Cabell went to Rusk's office in the State Department on Sunday afternoon to argue for the need to reinstate the bombing raid, Rusk, obviously more concerned with our compromised situation at the UN, proceeded to call President Kennedy at Glen Ora. Over the telephone, he did give a fair presentation of Cabell and Bissell's arguments on the need for a second air strike, but then told the President that he did not agree. Whereupon Kennedy said he would go along with Rusk, who now relayed this message to our officers, and pointed to the phone. Did they wish to speak to the President? They did not. Three days later, you can still hear the muttering at Quarters Eye. Of Cabell it was to be expected, but why had Bissell been silent?

I asked my father. He put a quick end to that subject. "Dickie was afraid," said Cal, "that if he pushed too hard on the absolute necessity of a second air strike, Kennedy might reply, 'If it hangs on that thin a thread, call it off.'" Cal gave me one wild look. "Every now and then in a man's life," he said, "one can have a little trouble with an erection. What's the advised procedure? Get it in, boy, even if it's only the tip. Then, pray to God for reinforcements. Please, God, just let an elephant step on my ass."

How my father, son of the greatest headmaster St. Matthew's ever had, developed his sexual view of the universe is to me, after eight years of living with the idea, the best single proof of the existence of Alpha and Omega.

3:00 P.M., April 18, 1961

Roberto Alejos' brother, Carlos, the Guatemalan Ambassador, has just made a speech to the UN in answer to Cuba's charges. As I watch on TV, Carlos Alejos says, most forcefully, that the troops who landed in Cuba, were not trained in Guatemala. His country, he solemnly states, is not about to allow its territory to be used for aggressive acts against fellow American republics.

I am overcome. In part, I must admit, it is with admiration. Large lies do have their own excitement. I much prefer a major mistruth in the name of a real purpose than all that pandering to Mothers of Miami and Caravans of Sorrow.

4:00 P.M., April 18, 1961

The front is relatively quiet this afternoon. Castro's forces, a little more respectful after their mauling last night, are moving cautiously down the road from Playa Larga to Girón. At San Blas, on the eastern front, where equally heavy fighting took place yesterday, there has been some realignment of our troops. The Third Battalion, which went ashore with Pepe San Román at Girón and has seen no action so far, is moving over to the eastern front to relieve the paratroopers at San Blas. The Fourth Battalion, dispatched to Playa Larga yesterday in lieu of the half-drowned Fifth Battalion, has now been pulled back to cross over to the eastern flank. The Sixth Battalion, playing musical chairs with the Fourth, has shifted to the western end. It occurs to me that I have not accounted for the First Battalion. Then I realize they are the paratroopers. Yes, they are back taking a well-earned rest in Girón for a few hours. I think of beer bottles in cantinas, and men diving under tables when Castro's planes come over. I have no idea if the image has any validity.

At TRAX, Pepe San Román impressed me as lean and lithe, with a small, pinched, totally consecrated face, utterly humorless. Whole determination to win. It was obvious he was altogether capable of sending men out to die since he had no doubt of his own ability to do so. Now he is at the edge of his temper.

> BLAGAR: This is Task Force Commander. How are you, Pepe?
> PEPE: Son of a bitch. Where have you been, you son of a bitch? You have abandoned us.
> BLAGAR: I know you have your problems. I've had mine.
> GRAY: (an Agency man on the *Blagar*): Pepe, we will never abandon you. If things are very rough there, we will go in and evacuate you.
> PEPE: I will not be evacuated. We will fight to the end here.
> GRAY: What do you need?
> PEPE: Weapons, bullets, communications, medicine, food.
> GRAY: We will get you all these things tonight.
> PEPE: That's what you said yesterday and you did not come.

5:02 P.M., Tuesday, April 18, 1961

Cal tells me, via his State Department leads, that Khrushchev sent a strong note to Kennedy. He has part of the text and shows it to me.

> Written at an hour of anxiety fraught with danger to world peace: It is not a secret to anyone that the armed bands which invaded Cuba have been trained, equipped, and armed in the United States of America. There should be no misunderstanding of our position: We shall render the Cuban people and their government all necessary assistance in beating back the armed attack on Cuba. Sincerely interested in a relaxation of international tension, we shall, if others aggravate it, reply in full measure.

Kennedy's answer is available to us. He is going to say that in case of outside intervention, the U.S. will feel obliged to honor immediately its hemispherical treaty obligations.

The fish is red!

8:00 P.M., April 18, 1961

A message from the *Blagar*: PROCEEDING BLUE BEACH WITH 3 LCUS. IF LOW JET COVER NOT FURNISHED AT FIRST LIGHT BELIEVE WE WILL LOSE ALL SHIPS. REQUEST IMMEDIATE REPLY.

12:30 A.M., April 19, 1961

The *Blagar* waits for an answer even as we have been waiting all night. It has taken this long for Bissell, General Lemnitzer of the Joint Chiefs of Staff, Admiral Burke, Dean Rusk, and Robert McNamara to get a meeting underway with the President. Very much in the way was a formal reception at the White House tonight. The President and First Lady have to greet his Cabinet, members of Congress, and guests.

No sooner has the President left the party for the meeting, however, than one of my father's contacts, a Congressman present at the White House reception, reaches Cal to tell him about it. I have always known that my father is, by half, a gregarious man, but I had never realized until the last two weeks of bunking with him how many tips, leads, sources, feeds, ties, and links he has to Congress and Departments of the Government. Where Hugh Montague is devious and full of pressure points he can tap, my father treats it all as a social matter. He is full of friendly curiosity, or so, at least, he presents himself, and given his personal force, which always leaves you feeling as if you're setting more weight on one foot than the other (for he is certainly capable of tilting you), people do come forward with answers to his inquiries. Tonight, from the mouth of this minor Congressman, who is delighted to be able to get through to a senior officer in CIA, Cal has learned the following: The President, immaculate in white tie and tails, and Jackie Kennedy on his arm in a pink evening gown, came down the main stairs to the ballroom at 10:15 P.M. while the Marine band in dress red uniforms played nothing less than "Mr. Wonderful." The President and the First Lady had a dance looking "elegant as champagne," then mixed with the guests until close to midnight, whereupon apologies were made, and the President left the party, went to his office, and now is closeted with the high officials who are going to help him to decide the fate of the Brigade. Cal informs me that Bissell has some daring and wholehearted goals to shoot for at this point. My guess is that Bissell has been in contact with Allen Dulles in Puerto Rico. According to Cal, Admiral Burke and General Lemnitzer in company with Bissell will ask Kennedy for the following: (1) Complete air support from the U.S. Navy carrier *Essex*, now twenty miles off the coast of Girón; and (2) Bite the bullet! Put ashore the 1500-man Marine battalion stationed on the *Essex*. In short, the tip is in; reinforce it. Bissell and Company will argue that this is the only way for the U.S. to save face.

I can't get over the picture I hold of the President coming down the main stairway of the White House with his wife (who in my mind now looks more and more like you, Kittredge). It might as well be a film by George Cukor, or Rouben Mamoulian. High intrigue *cum* white tie and tails. Of course, I haven't really slept in two and a half nights. My mind leaps like a fly with one wing.

2:30 A.M., April 19, 1961

About a quarter of an hour ago, Bissell came back to Quarters Eye. Needless to say, we all gathered about him. He looked tired to me, but spoke as if much has been gained. The President, he said, had authorized six jet fighters from the *Essex* to provide air cover over the beach from 6:30 A.M. to 7:30 A.M. They would be there to protect the B-26s from Castro's fighters. While our jet fighters were under orders not to be the first to fire, they were now authorized to reply. With such protection, the Brigade's B-26s ought to be able to cause serious damage to Castro's troops and tanks at the battlefront. During that hour, the *Barbara J.*, the *Blagar*, and the LCUs can also unload their supplies at Girón.

I, knowing how much military aid was asked for, and how little has been granted, am surprised at the enthusiasm with which the news is received. Perhaps it is no more than the power to be electrified by some kind of positive response when fatigue and despair have hollowed one out, but you can feel the difference. Even Cal is not without enthusiasm. "We asked for a lot, and didn't get it, but those were bargaining chips. When Admiral Burke spoke of sending in the Marines, Kennedy had to offer something."

"Is it enough?"

"Well, Kennedy can't pretend he's a virgin anymore."

3:30 A.M., April 19, 1961

I walk around with a knot of anxiety as large as an apple in the long road of my esophagus. It is all very well to send B-26s in under an umbrella of American jet fighters, but what Kennedy may not know, and Bissell did not necessarily tell him, is that nine of the sixteen B-26s with which we began, are down; most of the remaining bombers are battered. Since Sunday night, the pilots have been up in the air almost constantly. What with seven hours for each round trip and at least two trips a day, they are exhausted. In fact, some of them, not believing in our promise to give jet support, now refuse to take off. Someone, obviously without authorization, must have promised jet support yesterday that did not materialize.

Cal has also informed me that two of the four planes going out on this mission are actually being flown by Americans, two to each plane. Four Americans, contract pilots, any one of whom, if he parachutes out and is captured, can sink us internationally. Moreover, one of the Cuban pilots on this mission has served notice that he will not take his B-26 past Grand Cayman Island, 175 miles south of Girón, unless he is met by fighter cover.

Well, he will not be met. Fighter cover doesn't begin to show until they are much nearer the *Essex*. In any event, it's academic. That same pilot has just radioed in that his right engine is gone and he has to turn back. We are down to three planes. I try to conceive of how difficult it must be to fly dangerous missions once you have lost the belief that your side can win. Your brave actions must begin to seem suicidal. Valhalla is for victorious warriors.

I am by now in that state of mental disarray where simple computations have to be made over and over again. If the planes are to arrive at 6:30 over the beach, then they must leave at 3:10 A.M. our time, or 2:10 A.M. Nicaraguan time.

Since Bissell only returned at 2:45 A.M., I am trying to calculate how the B-26s can possibly get to the beachhead on time. Then I realize (while imbibing all the spiritual ecstacy of an epiphany opening its gates) that even if Bissell did not leave the White House before 2:30 A.M., the decision to accompany the B-26s with *Essex* jet fighters had to have been reached earlier. The order probably went out at 1:45 A.M. So, of course, the planes had time to take off.

A simple calculation, but I am perspiring, and feel beatific from the ardors of the calculation. If three nights of three hours of sleep has done this to me, how well will I function under combat? I do not want to lose respect for myself, but I feel drawn too fine. By the look of everyone around me, I am not certain they are faring better. It is my hope that real combat delivers energies that staff work leaches out.

6:30 A.M., April 19, 1961

All of us are ill. The three B-26s, flying in prearranged radio silence, appeared promptly over the beaches of Girón at 5:30 A.M., *our* time. Since the support from the *Essex* was not due till 6:30, the

Navy jets were still being brought up to the carrier deck about the time Castro's T-33 trainer jets came along to shoot down two of the three B-26s. The survivor, seriously crippled, managed to get away, and, at last report, is skittering back to Nicaragua on one engine while staying a hundred feet above the water. Naturally, none of our supply boats were approaching the shore at 5:30, and no ammunition has been landed. The *Essex* jets, which were only empowered to protect the B-26s from attack 6:30 A.M. to 7:30 A.M., will not even take off now.

Everyone is trying to determine how the error was made, but a wall of obfuscation has come up over this point.

I have a theory. Assuming other minds have been stretched into skews of calculation comparable to mine, someone in Quarters Eye must have sent a message for the B-26s to be over the beach at 5:30 *their* time, and something happened to the possessive to make it come out in Puerto de Cabezas as *their time in Cuba*, or 4:30 A.M. Nicaraguan time. Consequently, the planes took off at 1:10 A.M. Nicaraguan time, or 2:10 A.M. our time, and what with radio silence, no one knew.

This is my explanation. I have heard five others. The most convincing is that Bissell and Admiral Burke never checked with each other, so separate orders were transmitted to Happy Valley and to the carrier fleet. Cal whispers that the Navy is always on Greenwich Mean Time and we are sometimes on Standard Time. Oh, God! I can feel in me—I must admit it—a vein of pure nastiness. It is taking a lively, private pleasure in all these massive military mentalities failing to anticipate the one crucial trouble spot. The pleasure whips through me as fast as a squirrel crossing an open yard, then shame at myself wells up with more volume than I expected; behind it flows the woe of all that is being lost, and I am relieved to know that I am human, loyal to the team, and not a monster after all.

7:30 A.M., April 19, 1961

On the western front, a few miles to the west of Girón, Castro's forces are attacking. Also on the San Blas road. Troops pressing from the east. To the south is the Caribbean.

10:30 A.M., April 19, 1961

This journal may no longer be necessary. The messages sent to the *Blagar* by Pepe San Román tell most of it.

6:12 A.M. Enemy on trucks coming from Red Beach are right now 3 km from Blue Beach. Pepe.

8:15 A.M. Situation critical. Need urgently air support. Pepe.

9:25 A.M. Two thousand militia attacking Blue Beach from east and west. Need close air support immediately. Pepe.

On it goes. Obviously, no one explained to Pepe San Román that the jet support was only for the B-26s. In their absence, nothing.

1:30 P.M., April 19, 1961

More messages. "Out of ammo." "Enemy closing in."

3:30 P.M., April 19, 1961

They are still holding. I don't know what last negotiations have taken place between Quarters Eye, the Joint Chiefs, and the White House, but the Commander-in-Chief, Atlantic, that is, CINC-LANT, has been instructed to bring off an evacuation. In force, if necessary. A copy manages to make its way among us. (Two days ago, such breach of security would have been unheard of—I am beginning to understand why old OSS men are the way they are. Security is for cold wars, but combat calls for mutual participation.) I hardly feel as if I am in the CIA any more.

CINCLANT was told: HAVE DESTROYERS TAKE BRIGADE PER-SONNEL OFF BEACH TO LIMIT CAPTURE. DESTROYERS AUTHORIZED RE-TURN FIRE IF FIRED UPON DURING THIS HUMANITARIAN MISSION.

Two destroyers will lead the *Blagar,* the *Barbara J.*, the *Atlán-tico*, and the LCUs in to shore. The only trouble is that after the aborted attempt this morning, the supply ships dispersed again and are now about fifty miles out to sea.

At this moment, I am put to work on the last communiqué, Number Six, to be issued by Lem Jones Associates. I am given the guidelines by Hunt and Phillips who, I realize, are even more emo-tionally decomposed than myself. Decomposed? Or is there a brush-fire burning within? I feel as if we are all in danger of being overrun by incoherence. I am happy to have a task to perform. I feel like a fire fighter.

4:20 P.M., April 19, 1961

BULLETIN #6, CRC, CARE OF LEM JONES ASSOCIATES. TO BE RELEASED UPON NOTICE TONIGHT:

886 N O R M A N   M A I L E R

The Revolutionary Council wishes to make prompt and emphatic statement in the face of recent astonishing public announcements from uninformed sources. The recent landings in Cuba have been constantly, although inaccurately, described as an invasion. It was, in fact, a landing of supplies and support for our patriots who have been fighting in Cuba for months and was numbered in the hundreds, not the thousands. The action taken allowed the major portion of our landing party to reach the Escambray Mountains.

I had difficulties writing the paragraph. Three times I misspelled "uninformed" as "uniformed." Mental fatigue takes on its images. I am in a dungeon, and a woman with an enormous vagina is waiting outside my door. I know she is enormous because her mighty thighs are spread and Hunt and Phillips are stroking her with a giant feather. Her greed to be stroked is insatiable. She has no interest where the feather went one minute ago. She wants to know: Where is it now?

I begin to laugh. We are the gnomes who seek to please the great American public. To my horror, I am suddenly close to throwing up. Then I realize why. From the stalls around me comes the odor of vomit. My nostrils are so acute that I can not only smell Scotch and vodka, but am convinced that the metallic odor of each pocket flask is in the spew, and so is the pharmacological smell of Dexedrine. We've been spinning along on the stuff for days. I have an intimation that this is how one feels when a marriage is breaking up.

When I come out of the loo, I am assigned to write a few vagaries to take the place of the radio broadcasts we had prepared to send into Cuba after early victories. I compose it now: "The fish are brightly spotted. Javier is carrying his hoe. The whale will spout on the full of the moon. The grass is waving. The seed is dispersed."

There will be no argument over these choices.

5:00 P.M., April 19, 1961

I read a last message. It came via the *Blagar* at 4:30 P.M. I HAVE NOTHING TO FIGHT WITH. AM TAKING TO THE WOODS. I CANNOT WAIT FOR YOU. PEPE.

5:30 P.M., April 19, 1961

This was followed by a transcript of a conversation which concluded at 4:40 P.M.:

GRAY: Hold on. We're coming. We're coming with everything.
PEPE: How long?
GRAY: Three to four hours.
PEPE: You won't be here on time. Farewell, friends. I am breaking
     this radio right now.

It is believed that Pepe San Román, Artime, and their staff are
heading into the Zapata swamps. Thirty or forty of them may succeed
in making their way into the Escambray Mountains. Like Castro
before them, they can build a mighty guerrilla movement. Or so, I
suspect, goes the thinking of Artime and San Román.

6:00 P.M., April 19, 1961
Men are starting to leave Quarters Eye. Others remain. Most
are not needed any longer. Nonetheless, they remain, as I do. Perhaps
we have some elusive quality in common. I begin to think we must
all be the sort of people who stay up till three in the morning listening
to repetitive news broadcasts about a catastrophe, hoping to hear one
new detail.

Indeed, one new detail does arrive. This Wednesday morning, the exile leaders threatened to smash their way out of their
barracks. Bender succeeded in convincing them that the bad publicity
would be a media bloodbath. Everyone will lose dignity. To keep
them placated, Arthur Schlesinger, Jr., and Adolf Berle flew down this
morning. Now, word comes back that the Council is in the air, and
will land soon in Washington where they will be taken to see President Kennedy. Several of the exile leaders (Cardona, Barbaro, and
Maceo) have sons fighting in the Brigade. Others have brothers or
nephews. All are now dead or captured. In this swamp of desolation,
I feel something positive for Kennedy. It is a decent act, I decide, to
meet them at this time.

Dick Bissell comes up to the newsroom, and tells us that the
exile leaders are now in a safe house near Washington, D.C. "Will
you," asks Bissell of Hunt, "escort them to the White House?"

"I can't face them," says Howard. "They trusted me and I
can't face them."

Frank Bender will accompany them instead. I think of wildly
corrupt and wholly compromised Toto Barbaro engaged in small talk
with the President. What does it matter?

Phillips slips a word into my ear. "I don't think it was the

Cubans that Howard can't face, but the President. I would bet Howard wishes Kennedy six feet under and I don't know if I disagree with him."

The last teletype I read before leaving Quarters Eye was a wire service pickup of a story in the *Miami News*. "Rebel invaders claimed today to have driven fifty miles and scored their first big victory in the battle to topple Fidel Castro."

Well, at 9 P.M., Bulletin #6 will go out from Lem Jones Associates to confirm that nonexistent fact.

I send out last instructions to Happy Valley. Tomorrow, one of the remaining B-26s is to take our undistributed leaflets hundreds of miles out to sea, and dump them.

So ends this journal which I tried to present in a nondramatic style appropriate to the posthumous tone. Now that I am instead alive, I will transfer all of these pages from Cal's safe deposit box to mine.

41

ALLEN DULLES CAME BACK FROM PUERTO RICO EARLY THURSDAY morning with a terrible case of gout. To my father, who had gone out to meet him at Andrews Air Force Base, he said, "This is the worst day of my life."

On that same morning three exile leaders were flying back from Washington to their families in Miami, and I was on board to expedite any problems they might encounter. While it had been deemed discourteous to send our Cubans back alone, none of my superiors wanted the job, so I volunteered one moment before it would have been assigned to me.

It proved a quiet voyage. As heavy as pallbearers, we sat in our Air Force seats, and, on arrival, so soon as I had arranged for transportation, we shook hands gravely to say farewell. It was obvious they had seen enough of the Agency.

Since I was done with this task before noon and could take another Air Force plane back to Washington in the evening, I decided to drive downtown, park the car, and walk about in the April warmth. Crossing NE 2nd Street, I felt an impulse to enter Gesu Catholic Church, a noble armory all of 180 feet wide and not much less than

300 feet in length, a Miami edifice to be certain, offering pink and green walls and golden-yellow chapels. I had gone there several times over the last ten months to service a dead drop in one of the missal books in the fifth pew of the thirty-second row off the southern aisle.

So, yes, I knew Gesu Catholic Church on NE 2nd Street. I had also dropped in there on my own after bouts of love with Modene, and I do not know why, but the church was balm, I found, for sexual depletions of the spirit. I even used to wonder, if in no serious way (since I understood that I was not the least bit inclined), whether one more High Episcopalian might not be tempted just a little to become a Catholic. As an expression of that random impulse, I had even on one occasion asked Modene to meet me in the back of Gesu at the votive candles, a choice that I suspect irritated her. She had not been inside a Catholic church for over a year, and then it had been for another stewardess's wedding.

Today Gesu was not empty. The last Mass had taken place well over an hour ago, and the next was not due till five in the afternoon, yet the pews were not empty, and everywhere were women praying. I did not want to look at their faces, for many of them were weeping as well. My ears, keened to the private silence I could always hear within the larger solemnity of a church, became aware at last, in the slow befuddled manner of a drunk who has wandered right up to the edge of the sea, that today there was no silence. Lamentations never ceased. Into them poured, as from many smaller vessels, murmurings of sorrow from the throats of separate men and women, mothers and fathers, brothers and sisters of the lost Brigade, and the dimensions of the loss came over me then with such power that for this one rare time in my life, I had a vision of the suffering of Christ and thought, yes, such suffering was real, and this is how the mourners must have felt as they waited in the shadow of the cross and heard His agony, and feared that some tenderness of spirit was vanishing from the world forever.

That much I felt, and knew the vision was a self-deception. Under my pain was rage. I did not feel tender or loving, but full of the most terrible anger at I knew not what—was it the President, his advisers, the Agency itself? I had the rage of a man who has just lost his arm to the gears of a machine and does not know whether to blame the engine or the finger in some upstairs office which flicked the switch to turn it all on. So I sat alone in church, a stranger to my own lamentations, and knew that the end of the Bay of Pigs would never end for me since I had no real grief to build a tomb for my lost hopes. I was condemned instead to the black, obsessive rings of one oppressive question: Whose fault was it?

At that moment I saw Modene on the other side of the church. She was sitting by herself at the end of a pew with a black lace handkerchief on her head, and she had knelt in prayer.

I saw it as a sign. A sense of happiness as quick as the light on a blade of grass when the wind turns it to the sun came to me, and I stood up and walked to the back of the church and over to her aisle and up to her pew and sat down beside her. When she turned around, I knew that I would see the same light come into her green eyes that I had seen in the long thin palm of the grass blade, and she would whisper, "Oh, Harry."

When the woman turned, however, to look at me, it was not Modene. I was staring at a young Cuban woman who styled her hair in the same manner—that was all.

I had not permitted myself to steal near to any feeling of what I had lost, but now it was there. I had lost Modene. *"Disculpame,"* I blurted out and stood up and left the church, only to stop at the first pay phone and call the Fontainebleau. The desk clerk did not react to her name, but merely rang her room. When she answered, I discovered that my voice was near to mutinous. The words almost did not come out.

"God, I love you," I said.

"Oh, Harry."

"Can I come over?"

"All right," she said, "maybe you had better come over."

Her room, when I arrived, proved small enough to suggest she was certainly paying for it herself, and we made love on the carpet on the other side of the door, and from there made our way to bed, and I may have been as happy making love as I had ever been, for when we were done and holding one another, I heard myself say, "Will you marry me?"

It was an amazing remark. I had had no intention of making it, and thought it was desperately wrong so soon as I said it, for she would hate the life of an Agency wife, and, good Lord, she could not even cook, and I had no money unless I broke into the safe of my tightly closed principal and accruing interest—yes, all practical considerations came rushing into my thoughts like travelers arriving too late to catch the train—and were swept away in the big steam and blast of the departure—yes, I wanted to marry her, we would find a way to live together, we were extraordinarily different and wildly connected, we were the very species of cohabitation out of which geniuses are born, and I said again, "Modene, marry me. We'll be happy. I promise you."

To my surprise, she did not throw her arms around me and burst into celebratory tears, but broke out weeping instead with sorrow that came out of so deep a place in herself that she could have been the vehicle for all the grief collected in Gesu Catholic Church on NE 2nd Street.

"Oh, darling," she said, "I can't," and left me waiting for her next words long enough to recognize the true horror that sits like a phantom at the root of every lover's wings. It was coming in on me that the higher I had flown, the more I had been traveling alone, so high on my long-hoarded love that the profound sweet calm in which she received me could have been—now, and much too late, I knew—the whole numb body of grief itself.

"Oh, Harry," she said, "I tried. I wanted to get near to you again, but I can't. I just feel so sorry for Jack."

LIFTING THE WINDOWSHADE, *I looked out on the courtyard. The sky, leaden in hue, seemed closer to twilight than dawn. My watch, corrected to Moscow time, said six o'clock. I had read through the night and it was morning. Or had I read through the night and the day? No chambermaid had knocked on the door. Did I not hear her?*

Had I slept? I felt no hunger. I must have read and slept, read and slept, sitting in my chair, the converted flashlight in my hand, the filmstrip pushed forward frame by frame upon a white wall. Had I read every page? I did not know that I had to. It is possible I had drowsed, read again, and passed through many a frame without seeing a word. Whether I had read or merely advanced each strip of film, the events had entered my mind. I was not dissimilar to a blind man who is led by a guide down a path he knows well enough to take by himself.

As I looked into the courtyard, the sky was darkening. I had been living in the early years of my professional life for close to twenty hours. Yes, for twenty hours, not eight, I had been at it and nothing untoward had stirred. Was it possible that I had found the sanctuary of a magic circle? The anxiety of my last weeks in New York, that urgent and unendurable anxiety, was quiescent. Perhaps I would read and sleep through this night. In the morning I could return to the coffee shop of the Metropole and have some breakfast. They were bound to serve some sugared and soured species of fruit drink, and there would be black bread, and one sausage looking like a finger that had spent a month in water. There would be coffee that tasted like coffee grounds. Accursed country of whole incapacities! Yes, I would eat my breakfast tomorrow morning and come back here to read about Mongoose, and our further attempts to assassinate Fidel Castro. Just so far had I advanced in my memoir before that catastrophic night in Maine that overtook my writing and my life, and left me to spend a year in New York

*writing about no more than that night. Memories wheeled about me like
matter from an eruption in space. Such memories would return to me again
so soon as I had no more to read.*

*I was grateful then for each envelope of microfilm still unprojected. For
another day at least, I would not have to leave my room. Even as I had
found a burrow in the Bronx, I could hole up here. Indeed, the feeble
daylight that made its way down the airshaft reminded me of the gloom of
the other airshaft in the apartment building on the Grand Concourse.*

*Yes, I was alone, and I was in Moscow, and I was all right so long
as I kept to the narrative. It would move, frame by frame, on the old white
plaster wall of this old hulk of a hotel. Leading Bolsheviks had once
gathered here in the early years of the Russian Revolution. Now I had three
slices of bread saved from dinner nearly twenty-four hours ago, and a full
night before me in which to sleep and to read in my small room with its high
ceiling deep inside the wings and corridors of the Hotel Metropole.*

PART SIX

MONGOOSE

1961–1963

MIAMI
WASHINGTON
PARIS

1

ON THAT MORNING FOLLOWING THE BAY OF PIGS, WHEN ALLEN
Dulles returned from Puerto Rico with a case of gout, my father was
to describe him as looking as if he had died.

I do not know whether Cal's remark shaped my view, but in the
months and years that followed, I always thought of Mr. Dulles as a
man who, by some inner measure, was dead, even if it would take
seven more years before he passed away, and that event was going to
provide a notably unhappy Christmas week for those who were still
close to him. I remember that on the evening he took ill I was in
Saigon. It was Christmas Eve of 1968 and I was writing a letter to
Kittredge who would send me details of his demise in the return mail,
and I would hear more of it in the late spring of 1969 at lunch with
her in a crab-and-beer hutch of a roadhouse on the Virginia Tidewater. Our affair had by then begun, that affair which was yet to uproot
our lives and send tragedy plummeting upon us.

That, however, lay ahead. In the spring of 1969, Christopher was
still alive and Harlot most certainly had the full use of his legs. He
might be a cuckold, but, not at all witting of that, he remained a
priapic prodigy, more ramrod than the lover who had, to a degree,
replaced him—that younger lover whose ability to woo Kittredge
originated in the felicities of his mouth and lips, offering "delights so
rare one knows the rapture of a feather's fall," a phrase Kittredge
uttered once in passing, and I never dared to ask if it came from a
poem I ought to have recognized; but then, I hardly cared—the words
were accurate. We adored each other. No two friends could ever have
been more dear. Our lovemaking was as close as the little turns of our
talk, curving in and out of our mood like the fine and artful ridges of
a well-formed ear.

That afternoon in a roadhouse shack, cracking our crab claws with lobster pincers on an unpainted trestle table, she told me again of Allen Dulles' final and much-delayed death, and "the way it came was as bizarre as his birth." I had all but forgotten that he was born with a clubfoot, his toes curled into the same black warp as Lord Byron, but she reminded me that his father, the Reverend Allen Macy Dulles, Presbyterian, who had been so liberally advanced in the early 1890s as to preside at the remarriage in full church ceremony of a divorcée, could not, nonetheless, endure the sight of his son's deformity. Did it speak of caverns of damnation? He had the infant operated upon before baptism would expose him to the gaze of the Foster and Dulles relatives. "Once Hugh told me about Allen's foot, I have never been able to see him otherwise," Kittredge remarked. "No other man stood so securely with one foot in the full glory of the sun while the other was stuck in the mucky dark."

Dulles began to die his last and corporeal death on the evening of the large party he and his wife, Clover, gave on Christmas Eve of 1968, and if the best of Langley's seventh floor was present, the Montagues, the Helmses, the Angletons, the Tracy Barneses, the Lawrence Houstons, the Jim Hunts, as well as old friends from the State Department and a few chosen foreign dignitaries, it was a tribute, finally, to Dulles' old reputation that a full seven years after his retirement his guests could find the generosity to come out on the last night of what had been a week, after all, of pre-Christmas drinking, but they were paying him the honor of confirming that Allen Dulles might be off the board, yet his chair had never been filled; they would commemorate him one more time even if he was old, bent, and kept his gouty foot in a carpet slipper. Yes, remarked Kittredge, they had all popped over to salute him, but he did not make an appearance. Only his wife, Clover, was present to receive the guests and lead them over to the drink and the reliably good food—fluttery, once beautiful Clover, slender and as unfit for combat as a violet—"ditsy Clover, never quite there," Kittredge would say and then remark that Clover was as vague as the desire for vengeance when there is no real desire, only the marks of old matrimonial rancor. Allen had made love to half the women he knew in Washington, and Clover had even done her best to make friends with some of her husband's more serious mistresses; yet through such bouts and rounds, Clover had exacted only the smallest, most systematic revenge, although it must have jabbed like a spear in Allen's gouty foot: Clover spent money with the full license of a financial illiterate. The Dulleses were invariably in debt or nibbling on their principal. Each affair produced one more ballroom gown; one too many affairs, and the living room would be redone. They had been married for close to fifty years and she loved him, but she detested him. "Very long marriages develop divinely opposed strata of Alpha and Omega," Kittredge could not resist adding.

Now, at the party, guests began to notice that Allen had still not come down. Kittredge was perhaps the first to detect his absence. There had not been a meeting, after all, in the eighteen years since Allen first encountered her that he had not flirted like the Devil discovering his own true angel; Kittredge, in turn, loved the hearty promise of all that had never been embarked upon; they loved each other in the wholly enclosed way that will allow love, on occasion, to be perfect. They could count, instantly and dependably, on an improvement in their mood when they encountered each other.

So, Kittredge was the one to notice. Allen was most certainly not to be seen at his own party, and she told Hugh, and insisted, since Clover remained vague about his absence, that Hugh take a reconnaissance of the upper floor of the house. There was Allen in his bed, unconscious, the color of a wax effigy, and in a deep sweat.

Hugh came down to convince Clover that her husband was frightfully ill. "No," said Clover, "it's just flu and spells. He gets these things."

"On the contrary," said Hugh. "He has to go to a hospital at once."

Hugh called an ambulance while Kittredge whispered a few words to hasten the drink-up and departure of the guests, and the ambulance came, but Clover almost did not go along, and then rushed out in such a hurry that she forgot to take her coat. Allen proved to be very ill, and Clover was obliged to leave him at the hospital, coming home by herself at midnight. Chilled by the return trip in a poorly heated cab, she ran hot water for a bath, but was feeling so cold that she got into bed while waiting for a full tub, and fell asleep, thereby waking on Christmas morning to discover that the overflow had taken down the sculpted moldings of all the ceilings on the downstairs floor, and her furniture was buried in a blizzard of wet plaster. It would not be known for certain until the next day that the Hartford Insurance Company did not, under the circumstances, consider itself liable for the damage.

"I don't care," said Clover, "what it costs to fix it. I just don't want my husband to find out."

He did not, said Kittredge. He had died in the hospital.

That may have been his end, but since I had thought of him as near to dead for many years, I pondered his slow extinction. Had his soul died years before his heart and liver and lungs? I hoped not. He had enjoyed so much. Espionage had been his life, and infidelity as well; he had loved them both. Why not? The spy, like the illicit lover, must be capable of existing in two places at once. Even as an actor's role cannot offer its reality until it is played, so does a lie enter existence by being lived.

If this is a poor epitaph for Allen, let me say that I mourned him devoutly and most enjoyably through all of my illicit lunch with Kittredge in the spring of 1969. But let me stop at this point for I am already eight years ahead of myself.

2

ON TUESDAY, APRIL 18, 1961, THE SECOND DAY OF THE BAY OF PIGS, Robert Maheu had seen fit to inform the FBI that the arrest of the wiretapper Balletti in Las Vegas last October 31 had indeed involved the CIA, and that he, Maheu, had been told by Boardman Hubbard to refer all FBI inquiries on this matter to him.

Well, of course, my father had promised Maheu that if all went wrong, there would be rescue. Obviously, Maheu had decided— "prematurely," remarked my father—that it had gone wrong. Now the FBI wanted to talk to Cal Hubbard.

My father knew what was to be done. He would inform the Bureau by letter that the CIA would object to Maheu's prosecution since that was bound to reveal sensitive information regarding the invasion of Cuba. It was also decided that such a letter would be even more effective if Boardman Hubbard was not available for interviews. "Overnight," Allen Dulles said, "I grew too old to protect you."

Telling it to me, my father said, "I didn't reply, 'I'm the one who's there to protect you,' but what the hell, it was exactly what I was doing."

It was agreed that Cal would take up a post in the Far East once more. "Japan," said Cal when asked what he wanted, and added to me, "I'll pry Mary loose from that little Jap she's looking to marry. *Banzai!*"

So, changes commenced. I, who did not know at that moment whether I wished to go back to Miami, stay in Washington, or become assigned to a far-off station, inherited my father's apartment, and, in acknowledgment, I expect, of Cal's present services to the Director, I was assigned to Mr. Dulles' office as one of his assistants. I would help to oversee the move from the I-J-K-L to the new mega-complex in Langley now being completed fifteen miles out on the Virginia side.

It was nepotism. I only objected within, and then by half. If I knew that I could never respect my own career until I brought off something impressive for the Agency on my own, free of father and godfather, I was ready all the same to remain in Washington. I wanted to see Kittredge. I had the hope she would not continue to keep herself apart.

My job took me through the late spring, summer, and fall. Alan Shepard, our answer to Yuri Gagarin, became the first American in space, and on that same date, May 25, a number of Freedom Riders in Mississippi were attacked, beaten, and arrested. On June 4, Kennedy and Khrushchev had a summit meeting in Vienna, and there were other rumors that Khrushchev had been derisive about the Bay of Pigs. By late in July, sharp increases in military spending were being called for in Congress.

I cannot begin to describe how separated I felt from these events. I list them in the order they occurred; it offers the character of my reaction. Events went by like signposts. I was discovering that one's wounds need not be visible nor personal, and I was mending from the Bay of Pigs. I was not too unhappy to be busy with the endlessly detailed but essentially modest scenario of moving Mr. Dulles' office over from Foggy Bottom to Langley. The hot working days went by in a Company car. The Virginia forest was burgeoning by the Potomac, and the shade trees of a Southern summer offered their presence.

One approached the citadel of Langley by taking a turn off the highway at a small sign saying no more than BPR (for Bureau of Public Roads), and the approach drive was on a narrow two-lane that went a half mile to the guardhouse, which gave no more than a glimpse of a red-and-white-checked water tower. Beyond was Leviathan itself. To me, it looked not unlike a huge, maladroitly designed passenger liner. Langley was, if encountered less metaphorically, merely a mammoth building seven stories high with a continuous band of windows running all the way around the second floor and the seventh floor; this may have given the illusion of upper- and lower-class decks. Fields and trees and immense swatches of asphalt parking space surrounded the area; we were on 125 acres; we had cost $46 million. It was whispered—for the architect was never allowed to know exactly—that more than 10,000 people were going to be using it before long. Sometimes, when my car would be trapped on the George Washington Memorial Parkway behind an endless file of green shuttle buses carrying people from the I-J-K-L to Langley, I would swear that total was too small. The Mausoleum, for that also became its name, was in fulfillment of Allen Dulles' dream that all of the CIA might operate someday in one edifice, to the vastly improved efficiency of us all—it was a common criticism that Allen Dulles was a remarkably inefficient man. He was, at the least, possessed by too many ideas and liked to pursue them all, as was visible to anyone who encountered the clutter on his desk; such men dream of efficiency.

We were given it. There were those who said that from inside, the Mausoleum looked like a set of corporate halls and offices, forever debouching into more halls. There were intimate lobbies and wings that reminded one of a bank, or of a hospital. We had a great white marble lobby by the entrance with our seal embedded in the floor, and on the wall to the right was a bas-relief in profile of Allen Dulles, and a wall of stars on the other side honored all those who had died for us in the line of duty. High on the wall was an inscription from the Gospel According to John, eighth chapter, second verse: "Ye shall know the truth and the truth shall make you free." The truth, I told myself on one of the worst moments of the summer, was that in order to be free, we had put up a building that made you feel as if you were working in a fascist state. Immediately, I regretted the extreme metaphor of such a remark, but there was enough unhappy evidence to keep the thought lurking. Once the monumental task of bringing over our records, division by division, branch by branch, Desk by Desk, was accomplished, it was no longer feasible to get around in the place. You had to muster different badges to get by different guards. On the first floor, where the corridors were wide, the Agency housed its service functions—infirmary, travel office, credit union, the cafeterias for different ranks, and the vaults for records management; we had another wide corridor for all the clubs in CIA—photo club, art club, hiking club, chess club; we had shops; we were a foretoken of all the small-town shopping centers that were yet to come with their closed-in, all-weather malls.

Upstairs, our corridors went on forever, and as we moved into offices through summer and fall, problems arose with air-conditioning. If one of the unspoken reasons for leaving the I-J-K-L was the smell of drains in the Washington lowlands, now, unhappily, despite advanced designs carefully installed, the offices still stank. Our thermostats did not work, and we perspired. That is, the thermostats did work, but since the heat was now adjustable for every room, people were always turning the temperature up and down until the system overloaded. Administration then turned off the individual thermostats and we were air-conditioned as a gross whole, which in practice meant that some offices became too hot and some too cold. Before long, many of the younger officers, retaining the skills acquired in *Locks and Picks*, found ways to take the little padlocks off the levers. After all, we were people with a taste for manipulation and control. So we put our heat levels back on individual choice, and the system as a whole broke down again. The contractor was finally sued for faulty installation, but the case went nowhere; the Agency was not ready to supply the data necessary to make its brief for fear of revealing collateral matters.

Before long, we had rising waves of security procedure, and some rose to high tide and never went down again. In every corridor were armed guards. At night, it was impressive to see them stalking the halls. For years there were none of us who did not lock every last piece of paper in our safes, and put whatever needless notes were left into the paper-shredder, but if one was in a hurry to get out after work, we deposited trash and empty milk cartons in our private safe to be disposed of in the morning. Reprimands for leaving any kind of paper behind were too serious.

I do not know what else it accomplished, but it gave gravity to our labors. Each piece of paper that one handled took on a density more palpable than ordinary paper until sometimes in the outside world, reading a magazine or merely handling a piece of stationery for an ordinary letter, one would be struck with its ineffable lightness, and so much so that years later on reading Kundera's *The Unbearable Lightness of Being*, I thought immediately of the difference between papers that were secret and full of their own weight, and the lightness of free paper that you could throw away without any concern larger than that you might not be totally tidy. Certainly there were enough official notices to dispose of. Each day, through all those months of July, August, September, and October of 1961, bulletins came into every office to describe progress on the new building.

One hot day in August, an all-office memo on particularly stiff beige bond paper was distributed to every cubicle at Langley:

NEW BUILDING, TOILET FACILITIES

While adequate for the transition period, toilet arrangements, after full personnel-investment of the New Building is completed, may prove inadequate. To anticipate the contingency that distressed individuals could form up in long lavatory queues, a time-consuming and stressful procedure, this directive is now issued to sanction personnel afflicted by inadequate queue lead-time to exercise free and fair use of the shrubbery contiguous to the circumference of the main building.

WARNING

Despite the concerted efforts of Agency gardeners, said shrubbery has not yet been wholly checked-out for poisons oak, sumac, and ivy, which flora have been known to initiate exacerbated tinglings in mucous-bearing enclaves. A picture is therefore attached to this bulletin of the most prevalent of these plants, the *Rhus vernix,* commonly termed poison sumac, a.k.a. poison dogwood. Full view and profile appended should accelerate process of recognition thereby avoiding itchy implosions of said mucous target zones which, once aroused, can prove counterproductive to those research projects requiring sedentary work postures for sustained periods.

Old Rice and Beans Cabell, soon to leave the Agency, may have been giving vent to the hurricane of foul spirits left in him by recollections of Quarters Eye, for he pushed Security to find the authors of the prank.

Our culprits turned out to be two Junior Officers in Training, former members of the Harvard Lampoon, who had joined the Agency together, trained together at the Farm, and were now to be discharged side by side.

On the top and seventh floor, Mr. Dulles' office had become as deluxe as government standards would permit. It was paneled in walnut, thickly carpeted, and the nonstop sequence of picture-glass windows gave us a vista of the hills rolling out from our CIA estate. Mists rose from the Potomac. Early in the morning one could watch that mist come in off the river.

Mr. Dulles' secretary, a formidably dear old lady, instituted a tradition of feeding the birds who visited the seventh-floor patio. Before long, the three baboons guarding the Director's office were assigned by her to clean out the feeders each morning. Other daily rituals commenced. The Director, who had worked for years to raise Langley, seemed to know, as we installed the last details of his office, that he would not inhabit his seat for long.

I suspect he was not all that happy with the realization of his dream. He did not really move over from E Street until his new office was wholly completed, and even then, by the end of summer it was evident that he would invest his new quarters in not much more than ceremonial fashion.

Occasionally I would be invited to ride along in his limousine and he would speak cordially of my father, and express his pleasure that Cal and Mary were together again, a piece of news I had barely received myself in a postcard, but for the most part, the Director was like a man in mourning. If he could rise sufficiently to be cheerful for a minute or two, he rode for the most part in a silence close to stupor.

On September 28th, he accompanied John McCone to the Naval War College at Newport, and there President Kennedy announced at the graduation ceremony that Mr. McCone would be the new Director of the Agency. Howard Hunt, who had been working busily in Mr. Dulles' old E Street office on the official history of the Bay of Pigs, happened—lucky Howard!—to be along with Mr. Dulles on the drive back to Boston after the ceremonies at Newport. It came as no surprise to me that they traveled without conversation, Mr. Dulles' gouty foot up on a stool and pillow. Finally the Director did remark, "I am tired of living *sub cauda*," upon which he fixed Hunt with a look, and added, "Hunt, you are the Latinist. How would you translate *sub cauda*?" "Well, sir," said Hunt, "not to be rude, but I believe it means more than its literal translation. I should say a good English substitute might be 'under the cat's tail.'" "Yes, excellent," said Dulles, "but it's the cat's bum, you know, that I'm referring to," and then, as if he were all alone in the car, he said to no one in particular, not to Hunt, the chauffeur, nor even to himself, but to the gods, I would wager, of admissions waiting on the next stage, "The President said to me in private that if he had been the leader of a European power, he would have had to resign, but in America, since he can't do that, it must be me. That's all very well, but don't you think Robert Kennedy might have been asked to step down as well?"

Toward the end of October, shortly before John McCone was installed as the new Director, Mr. Dulles did make the full move to Langley and hobbled around like a wounded buffalo for a couple of weeks. I had a feeling that he hated the place, and wrote a letter to my father in which I said as much. Cal responded in surprisingly strong language.

Oct. 10, '61

Yes, son, I took the tour of Langley before I left and couldn't agree with you more. I sometimes wonder if, under it all, Allen has no comprehension of how important is architecture for making the man. I fear for us at Langley. The I-J-K-L was certainly dreadful, but one could get fond of all those falling-down shacks and barracks. Allen lost sight of the prime point—charm has to be preserved. I-J-K-L may have been full of old pull-chains and quirky corridors and hideouts and secret closets from which you could exit into an adjacent hall, but that creaking old mess was, at least, ours. Langley is going to be memos and meetings. Technical collection is going to get more and more of the budget, and working with good agents will become a lost craft. Farewell to chamber music. Hello, Muzak!

How could Allen have done this to us? The poor man knows so much and finally didn't know better.

Now we have McCone. Bechtel, Inc. A compact man. Short. Light hair. Blue eyes that you will find to be as cold as ice. He wears steel-rimmed eyeglasses. I would suspect his heavier product does not come out in turds, but slices.

It had been a reasonable letter until now, but I had learned that when my father made references to excrement, we were going to move from urbanity to maniacality.

As you gathered from my postcard, Mary and I are together again. It's not love, I suppose, so much as the deep inroads of habit. After twenty-five years, giving up a wife is as bad as cutting out drink and cigarettes. In fact, it can hardly be done. I'm very fond of the girl, as you know—she's my big white whale. I went back to Japan to push that little Japanese businessman right out of her life, but do you know, it's horrendous, she won't admit it, although I can divine as much, but there was some kind of unholy letch between them. It becomes obsessive for me on occasion, that damned little Japanese bugger all over her front and back with his kamikaze war cries, the little son of a bitch. I get hateful to Mary when I think of it.

This is one hell of a thing to pass on to one's son, but you, Rick, are the only soul who may have the decency not to laugh at me for too little. I am worried about keeping full control of my temper. I had a hell of a shock a couple of months ago when Hemingway committed suicide. God Almighty, I beat him once in arm wrestling at the Stork Club, on a night in 1949, and I feel, therefore, one part in a thousand responsible, for he saw the light in my eyes and I saw the misery in his. Sherman Billingsley nearly eighty-sixed me for lèse-majesté.

In any event, Ernest's death is the worst thing. Suicide with a shotgun in the mouth! I'd like to think it wasn't really a suicide. He probably had cancer, and you know the cure for that. No doctor would dare to admit it, but I know. It's to dare your death, night after night. Look at the evidence. There was Hemingway, singing songs all evening and cheerful with his wife Mary. Then, blasto! Goes alone to a room and blows his brains out? No. He had to have been playing with it for nights. Exploring all the no-man's-land between life and death, the places where the dread fog gathers. I propose that that brave man went in every night, put the barrel of the shotgun in his mouth, reached down for the trigger, and pulled it ever so gently into no-man's-land. If he went too far with the squeeze, he would be dead; otherwise, he might gain a little life. A species of cancer cure. The doctors can go flog themselves as far as I'm concerned, but that is what Ernie was doing, daring death, and he probably got away with it for many a night. Then, on July 2, he dared to pull that trigger a little too far. He couldn't do anything physical anymore, not really, not ski, not box, might have had his pecker down below the horizontal, but, by God, he could still dare death. That is my hope. My secret fear is that he just crapped out and blew it all up. Son, I've been dogged-down by these deaths. Clark Gable, Gary Cooper, Dash Hammett, now Hem. It's taking its effect. It makes me hate that son of a bitch Jack Kennedy even more. I don't want to be too damn bigoted, but the fact is you can't trust Catholics—there could have been some esoteric Vatican tie-up between Kennedy and Castro. There, I've said it. Castro had a religious boyhood, did you know that? Research him in

SOURCES, cross-check him in VILLAINS. He and Kennedy in cahoots would explain why Fidel is always holding an ace to our king.

I know I rave, but the wrath builds up. Until I screw that little Jap right out of my thoughts, I am simply not getting the benefit of being back with Mary. Do you understand it? I never missed her very much. I missed the habits, the dull habits most of all. I missed playing double solitaire with her—that, somehow, was able to anchor all the mischief I was enjoying outside. Now, I have to wonder what there is worth protecting.

Rick, I'm probably going to pick up my pen tomorrow and apologize for this letter. You may as well know, son, we Hubbards have a vein of mixed bile and madness. *Even the Headmaster.* He used to whip the stuffings out of me—didn't I for good cause deserve it!— but as you ought to know, we Hubbards do our best to keep it under cover. For good cause. The output, once expressed, is too god-awful.

Miss you, good roommate.

Dad

I was beginning to fear that I now understood why my father, years ago, had been so eager to have my head operated on.

3

I HAD A FEW PROBLEMS OF MY OWN. THE FIRST WAS TO DECIDE ON THE next step in my career. Every time I considered cutting loose from father and godfather, recollections came back of early days in the Snake Pit. There were hours when I did not feel ready to get anywhere on my own.

In any event, the question persisted: What was I to do next? Before he left for Japan, my father had indicated that some kind of operation was going to continue against Castro, but did I wish to go back to a Miami that would be bereft of Modene?

I could apply, of course, for Paris, Rome, Vienna, or London Station. They might, however, be too prestigious; I could end up as a flunky at such posts. Besides, my preference did not have to be honored. I could also find myself in Iceland or Palma de Mallorca.

Whether I was well regarded in the Agency or not had to be, of course, the salient question, and the answer was not automatic. Despite all his obvious abilities, Porringer must have finally irritated Howard a little too much, because, last I heard, Porringer had chosen to apply clear across the Branches, the Divisions, and even the Directorate of Plans, and was now buried in the Directorate of Intelligence. It was what happened, in effect, if you had to apply to Personnel for assignments.

In the circumstances, I decided to seek Howard out. My father's eminence was, after all, under a cloud, and Harlot had been noncommunicative. I did not know what kind of job Howard might be able to offer, but who else was there? I did not wish to go to David Phillips, and Richard Bissell was not only in disfavor, but too high for me to make a call upon his time. If I had been wise in these matters, I might have approached Richard Helms. The word (as I could have learned by calling Arnie Rosen) was that Helms would be DDP once Bissell walked the plank. Helms, after all, had stayed clear of the Bay of Pigs.

Well, I was not witting. I did not understand that Richard Helms might right now be selecting his cadres of young officers for that powerful future. Rosen would have known, Rosen would have been ready for Helms if willing to engage the risk that Harlot might be permanently offended.

These were, however, subtleties beyond my modest instincts for advancement. I had to content myself with inviting Howard Hunt to a drink after work.

His immediate tasks for Dulles now completed, Howard was out at the Domestic Operations Division on Pennsylvania Avenue performing "interesting initiatives" for Tracy Barnes. When I responded that this sounded "unclarified," he said, "Let me put it that the Domestic Operations Division was established only after a considerable internecine struggle."

"Can you tell a fellow more?"

He could. The DOD was ready to take on projects that "are unwanted elsewhere in the CIA. I am the Chief of Covert Action in the DOD."

"I don't know if I'm getting much picture of the working day."

"Small-fry stuff. Support for books and publishers we think are in need of a helping hand."

When I was silent, he added, "Milovan Djilas' *The New Class,* for instance, put out by Praeger."

"It sounds easy," I said.

"It is. I have time these days for family, for friends, and for a second career. You see, I've been approached by Victor Weybright who, in case you don't know, is the editor in chief of the New American Library. He wishes me to write an American counterpart to the James Bond novels that New American Library already publishes. I took up the idea with Helms and he agrees this might not be disadvantageous in the vein of public relations. I'm starting what I will call the Peter Ward series. Under a nom de plume, of course. David St. John."

"A good name."

"It's taken from David and St. John Hunt. My sons."

"Of course." I swallowed my drink. "That is all you do down at DOD?"

"For now."

Were we to order two more drinks? I would be paying, and I wanted value. "One is tempted to ask what you are waiting for."

"I can only repeat," said Howard, "that we take on the projects unwanted elsewhere in the CIA."

We left on that. It was only when I woke up in the middle of the night that it became absolutely clear to me that Hunt had passed on no more than his cover story. The Domestic Operations Division, if I was to take my guess, must be engaged in special activities concerning Cuba.

Two days later, a telegram came to my apartment. It said: SIGN UP ON NO STRANGE SHIPS. GLOBETROTTER.

It occurred to me that Howard had spoken to Tracy Barnes, who, in turn, must have discussed my merits with Montague. I hardly knew whether to be pleased or wary that not all interest had been lost in Herrick Hubbard.

If I have been giving a portrait of the kind of low ruminations my mind, when unhappy, is capable of producing, I will say that the inanitions of my mood, which had lasted through all of this despondent spring and summer, were relieved at a stroke—I am tempted to call it a *coup*—by one phone call, make it two.

The morning after receiving the telegram from GLOBETROTTER, my phone rang just as I was on my way to Langley, and the voice of a woman, mechanically muffled by several thicknesses of handkerchief, spoke into my ear. I could not be certain I knew her, not instantly; the voice was as blurred as a record turning too slowly. Besides, the conversation was finished before my ear was ready.

"Call me in twelve minutes at the following number: 623-9257. Please repeat."

"623-9257." I could not believe it, but I saw an orange wall in front of which was a green table bearing a blue lamp. A man with a black jacket, green pants, and red shoes was sitting in a brown chair. "623-9257," I said again.

"It is now 7:51. You will call me at 8:03. You will employ Bell hygiene."

"Message received," I said. "8:03. Bell hygiene."

"Ciao." The phone clicked.

I could not believe it. In training, it had been one's dream to be ready, always ready, for such a moment.

I began to laugh. The woman could be no one other than Kittredge. I had not felt as merry since the bulletin on the uses of Langley shrubbery had crossed my desk.

There was a bank of pay phones two blocks from the apartment, and at two minutes and fifty seconds past eight, I put in my dime. The voice that responded no longer came to me through a handkerchief.

"Harry?"

"Yes."

"It's Kittredge."

To my small horror, I could say no more than, "Yes."

"Harry, have you ever heard of a girl named Modene Murphy?"

"Why do you ask?" But now my larynx was hardly loyal to me.

"Oh, Harry, you're FIELD, aren't you?"

"I choose not to answer that."

"I knew it all the time. Harry, like it or not, Hugh has chosen me as *your* replacement. I'm up on *your* reports."

"All of them?"

"All, and more. You don't know the ensuings."

Well, if it had been something like a year and a half since we had been in any kind of communication, this was a hell of a way to start up.

"Kittredge, can I see you?" I asked.

"Not yet."

"Why not?"

"Because I don't want to meet you behind Hugh's back, and I certainly don't want to have to look at the two of you *en famille* at dinner."

"How is Christopher?"

"Divine. I would perish for that child."

"I would like to see him. I am, after all, his godfather."

She sighed. "Do you have a post office box?"

"Well, yes, I do."

"Give me the number," she said, and as soon as I did, she added, "I think we're back in business again. I'm going to send you a long letter."

"How soon?"

"By tomorrow it should go out. It's written in my mind already."

"And how do I reach you?"

It developed that Kittredge had a post office box as well.

"You sound wonderful," I said.

"Patience," she said, and hung up.

4

October 20, 1961

Dearest Harry,

While I cannot know how much has happened to you in the last year, the denouement of Pigs must have taken its toll. A good part of you so identifies with your work that each Agency mishap must come as a personal loss.

Of course, I am thinking of the old model Herrick Hubbard, circa 1959, and we have been out of touch. For that matter, I do not want you to picture me as I was after that awful morass in Paraguay.

I've changed. So much as one can change profoundly in a couple of years, I would say that I am not at all the same. Do you know that with the exception of a monthly visit from Hugh, and four stints a week of cleaning and Christopher-watching from a good Maine housekeeper, I was alone at the Keep, worked on my book alone, and took care of my son for over a year?

Living all-but-alone in Maine through a winter, is equal, I think, to being suspended in a diving bell. You do scrape bottom on the underwater ledges, but you're awfully strong when you come up. I was. I had a curious year. I developed a momentous psychological theory. (Momentous for me. Might be modestly useful for others.) I don't want to describe it to you in too much detail at this point, but can say that two of the most unresolvable problems in psychoanalysis today are narcissism and psychopathy. No one knows how to treat such conditions. The Freudians are comparable on these matters to fourteenth-century cartographers who left vast empty spaces on their maps of the world.

Well, Alpha and Omega, if one accepts the premise, does offer a good grip on the matter. I don't feel enthusiastic enough at this moment to give you a once-over-quickly on the theory, so, will only indicate that trying to develop a book out of the above wore down my literary spirit, such as it is. Day after day, for a year, I struggled at it, and discovered that I was out beyond my powers. I have simply not had enough personal life to illumine my thesis with the thousand everyday examples it demands. I wanted to come forth with a magnum opus full of intellectual charisma, but had to recognize once again —I am simply one more bright girl too soon married, too soon motherized, my backside on the bank and one toe in the career-river. You don't shape history with that posture.

Now about this time (which brings us close to a year ago), Hugh began to importune me to come back to Washington. Up till then, it had been a contest between his will and mine. We were both suffering acutely but not confessing to one bleat of discomfort. Finally he said, "I want a marriage. I have spent my life trying to escape the inevitable. I don't want to end up in a monk's cell."

I was awfully moved. You know he adored his mother and in fact even slept in the same bed with her until he was ten years old. I suspect it was a way she had of keeping his father at arm's length. Then, the *disaster* occurred. Hugh, at the age of eleven, not only had a dead father but was obliged to live with the dire possibility of a murderous mother. He drew very much away from her and spent his adolescence as a solitary. His rock climbing started then. Can you conceive of it? This private and very young adolescent off on solo hikes in the Rockies, climbing freestyle before there was a word for it. One must be in awe at the depth of the desperation that he actually managed to get under control through this drastic cure of taking great risks. Suddenly, after all our years of marriage, my husband was awfully real to me, and I was prodigiously moved.

By half. My Alpha was molten. My Omega rock-hard. I amazed myself. I understood for the first time how hard I am down at Omega-core. I wrote to him that I would return only if we could shift the basis of our marriage. I would not go back to the isolation of being kept just about completely out of his work. He may not have understood in the past, but one reason I always became so feverish-minded at the Stable was that too great a need had grown up in me to find excitement and satisfaction in social relations—those vetting dinners, for instance, where we looked for a replacement for Allen. What foolishness! That could not be enough.

What did I want, then? It was to share his work. In fact, his *secrets*. He couldn't agree to that, he tried to explain—I was asking him to rupture his *vow*. Your vow be damned, I told him. Our marriage is a sacrament. That is a deeper vow.

He agreed finally to let me in. I came back not only to Washington, but to his work. Not even to most of it, of course, but he would empower me (his term!) to collaborate with him on one or two of his projects. (Which he calls *pieces*.) I discovered Hugh's skill at negotiation—I ended, you may be certain, with less than I could have obtained. No matter. What I have gained is fascinating enough. I am now his junior partner, and it is sweet to sup on a couple of the secrets. I believe he even enjoys revealing the top-drawer manifestations of his mind. Domestic tranquillity threatens to lap at our feet.

Not too seriously, however. We're still combatants. This last November, for example, we had a horrendous row. I had not even been back in Washington for more than a month when my old friend Polly Galen Smith was at the doorstep. Now, I know you remember her as our epistolary cut-out between Washington and Montevideo, but I can't remember how much else I told you about Polly. Her husband, Wallace Rideout Smith, is no longer at State but has transferred over to the Agency and is now one of our muckamucks at the other end of things—Administration. And a duller man never walked a Company corridor. Did I write to you about them once before? Polly, as I believe I've told you, has been deliriously unfaithful to Rideout Smith for years—not in quantity, but she does take abyss-jumper risks. I think it's just as simple as that she enjoys men the way all of you men are supposed to enjoy us.

At any rate, Polly and I get along famously because we are so different. She came to me again about a month before the presidential inauguration to ask "one hell of a favor." Would I let her use the Stable for an hour early Wednesday afternoon while Hugh was away working and I might be shopping? She had a friend who lived two blocks to one side of me in Georgetown, and there was Polly three blocks on the other side. Her friend was the busiest man in Christendom right now, but they had "absolute grabs" for each other. Well, who was he? State secret, she answered. Impossible, I said, there's Christopher to think of, and the maid. Not so, she said. Christopher is still in nursery school at 2:00 P.M., and the maid has Wednesdays off. She had *cased* my situation.

I won't say yes until you let me in on who the man could be, I told her.

Can't be done, she said. In that case, I responded, you and your buddy-buddy will just have to find a motel.

Oh, God, no, Kittredge. Well, why not? Too prominent, the man is too prominent, she kept saying. At last I dragged forth the name. Her beau was none other than her old senatorial pal of two years ago, now our presidential jock-elect, Jack Kennedy. The reason they needed a place just so convenient as mine involved the concerns of the Secret Service. Told in advance, they will remain a discreet half block away. Moreover, Jack can duck out of his house on N Street between meetings, then slip back without raising a stir about sizable gaps in his schedule.

I had one instant of revelation: snobbery, property, propinquity, and good old *droit de seigneur* revealed their trusslike interrelations in me. Harry, I had to say yes. I wanted the President-Elect of the United States infusing my rooms with his carnal presence. I think I became aware at that moment what a slut I could have been with another kind of upbringing.

How I envied Polly. Envy is mean! I found myself insisting on a particular payment. I wasn't going to have Jack Kennedy investing my linens with his spoor when I hadn't even met the man.

Polly protested as if I'd broken a bottle of stink, but she had to give in. So commenced their Wednesdays. They were going to love Wednesdays at the Stable, she said, even if the whole thing was going to take up no more than thirty minutes—an item I was to discover when we arranged how the encounter would take place. I was to pretend to come home unexpectedly, but *on the minute*. "If you're two minutes late, he'll be gone, and if you're five minutes early, you will walk in on the finishing touches." Polly, you can see, is to the point, and that, I comprehended, is exactly why they got together in the first place. I have not met a man who is more to the point than Jack Kennedy, unless it is his brother Bobby. (Of course, their father, I hear, leaves them both in his wake.)

At any rate, I saw him. Even as I turned my key and came through the door to my own parlor, my heart fluttered twice—once for history and once for the person. He is awfully attractive and I think it is because he is not out of measure. I was talking to a man to whom I felt equal, which I must say is bottomlessly agreeable. And he's so direct and sure of himself that it comes off as a natural quality rather than arrogance. He is nice. And so amoral. And so unflappable. Polly was trying to keep from guffawing, which was forgivable—two of her best friends, after all, were meeting, and he—whether or not she had told him—seemed not at all surprised by my supposedly unexpected entrance. (Perhaps she did tell him in advance and he had worked it out with the Secret Service. Indeed, on reflection, they had to have done just that.)

"Do you know," he said for greeting, "you and my wife have a slight resemblance to each other. It's uncanny."

I thought of Jacqueline Kennedy's father, Black Jack Bouvier. Then I had to compare him to my father and I said, "Oh, dear, next to your wife I'm dry-as-dust," and felt shabby suddenly, a most unexpected feeling for me, but it is all genes, isn't it? Folio dust was coming out of my pores by way of my father's pores. Or so I felt! "Dry as dust," I repeated when he just kept smiling, considerably more comfortable in my parlor than I was.

"Oh," he said, "we will see about that," and offered a glint of a very good smile.

"Ho, ho, curfew," said Polly Smith, and Jack gave a small salute and was out the door, leaving Polly behind. "Till next Wednesday," he said.

Polly stayed for tea, and I began to feel disloyal to Hugh. I was so avid to hear about Jack.

By the time Hugh came home, I was in a confessional mode. I said nothing before we went to sleep, and nothing again on the next night, but, I was beginning to feel those unruly intimations of dread that I call "the dark wobbles." I can't suppose you don't remember. They were touched off in me once by that awful brooch you sent from Montevideo. Well, it was coming on again, and I knew I had to tell Hugh. He couldn't have taken it worse. "I feel sullied by it," he said. Then he said, and you don't know how much this is out of character for him, "I couldn't feel worse if that fellow Jack Kennedy had buggered me!" Can you conceive of Hugh speaking like that?

"It was Polly, not I," I said to him, "who was in the receiving position."

"That will be the last time she receives in our house," he answered.

"No," I said. "I can't do that to her."

"It pollutes everything here, including the child. Can you make no distinction between the relatively sacred and the wholly profane?"

Well, I was going to strike my colors. He was right, after all, and I knew it; I have also learned, however, that Hugh has no respect for you if he wins too quickly, so I thought I'd hold out till the Tuesday before the next Wednesday and let him think he'd won a major match.

Talk of presidential timing. I'm beginning to see how Jack got where he is. I did not say a word to Polly but on Monday an invitation was delivered by hand. Could Mr. and Mrs. Montague come to dinner on N Street Tuesday night?

I must say that Hugh went through a major stomach upset. I have never known him to throw up in such manner before. And I realized what it was about. He was dying to go to N Street. He wanted to be familiar with Jack Kennedy, oh, how he wanted that. If for nothing else, then for the Agency. But be damned if he was going to have his home tom-catted up. Yet, if Polly were cut off before Wednesday, wouldn't dinner be rescinded for Tuesday? Of course, we could go and then cut the lovers off. No! You didn't do things like that to the President-Elect!

All this is speculation, mind you; Hugh was vomiting so audibly that I would have held his head if I dared, but then he emerged from the loo long enough to say, "It's clear to me. You call Polly now, or I will."

I had to love him even if I couldn't bear the thought of giving up dinner with Jack, but who can deny characterological integrity when it is on that scale? I called Polly. I was able to say no more than, "Hugh's on to the game."

"Oops," she said, "are sirens ringing?"

"No. But cancel your venue for Wednesdays."

Do you know, the dinner invitation was not rescinded, and Hugh, to my surprise, had a hell of a time, and I got along with Jackie Kennedy satisfactorily. Under all that false innocence, she's awfully sensitive to what's wrong in people and she knew there was something just a little off in me vis-à-vis her husband. Still, we got on. She knows

a good bit about eighteenth-century Piedmont and Charleston cabi-
network, and had a special little slave tale to tell. It seems one of the
greatest furniture makers in Charleston—Charles Egmont—was a former slave whose liberty was given to him by his owner, Charles
Cawdill, who set black Charles up in his own shop and they split the
profits. She tells such tales with great intimacy, as if with some maid-
enly pain she is offering you one of her jewels. But, oh, Harry, that's
a complex and troubled woman!

Meanwhile, Hugh and Jack were certainly getting along. At
one point, Jack confessed to Hugh that it was a pleasure to meet "the
mythological Montague." "Mythological?" says Hugh, his mouth all
twisted up as if he's being asked to kiss a turkey's tucker.

"Let's say the apocryphal Montague," says Jack.

"I'm only a minor factotum in the Department of Agriculture."

"Come off it. I've heard about you for years."

Well, I could see them cooking up some special understanding. Hugh was brilliant once he got going on Soviet skills at disinformation. To my horror, he started to give the President-Elect and his
wife a lecture; to my large pride, he brought it off.

Now, since the inauguration, we get invited back from time
to time to the White House. To the more intimate White House
dinners, mind you. At the last soirée, Jack chose, while dancing with
me, to ask about Polly.

"She pines for you," I said.

"Tell her I'll call one of these days. It's not out of my mind."

"You are awful," I said.

He got that glint in his eye. "Do you know, for a beautiful
woman, your dancing is a hint stiff."

I wanted to cream him with my evening bag. Alas, I didn't
dare. He's not that splendid a dancer himself, but oh so schooled. Like
a rider with a cultivated seat who doesn't really take to horses.

All the same, we get along. I think he's wary enough of Hugh
not to entertain notions about me, but we do have the next best thing
—promise.

Later

I don't want to exaggerate. We're invited to sup with them
at their House perhaps not more than once a month. And on one
occasion, they came to the Stable. Relationships, however, do

deepen. Between Jack, that is, and myself. Jacqueline Kennedy and I are on a plateau—awfully equal stuff passes back and forth between us, and I respect her because she does not wield rank over me any more than is implicit in the rich-mouse country-mouse syndrome, but, then, that is the price you pay for such entrée. Meanwhile, Hugh and Jack are off in a corner. You know Hugh—at his best when one on one. And Jack, no matter how furious over the Bay of Pigs, is fascinated with cloak-and-dagger and smart enough to know that Hugh is the *saucier* in that kitchen. And, of course, as laid out above, Jack is chummy with me.

I never realized how much this was disconcerting Hugh until one day this summer, toward the end of July, he suddenly put the BLUEBEARD dossier in front of me. "Here's another side to one of your friends," he said. I think he expected me to be put off by the contents, but I wasn't; I know Jack's nature: Promiscuity is the price he pays to open the gates to his other skills. Jack Kennedy is like a child that way. Must have his daily reward, and it's in the forbidden jam. Good for him, I say, so long as I'm not part of the private preserve. If he can do a little more good than harm, God will doubtless forgive him for all the girls whose hearts he jiggled and juggled. I'm sure he sees it that way.

But I did lose a bit of respect for Hugh. He should not have handed me the file. In truth, I wouldn't forgive him if it were not for Ty Cobb's death on July 17.

Hugh once remarked that your father broods over the obituary columns instead of enjoying them, but Ty Cobb is a signal figure in the Montague arcana. After all, Ty Cobb's mother killed his father in much the same way that the Montague family tragedy enacted itself. So, when Cobb died (of prostate cancer, by the way—poor man—once so fleet on the base paths!), Hugh took a tumble, and finally handed over the BLUEBEARD file.

As you may expect, I was riveted to it. Of course, I kept wondering whether anyone but you could be Harry Field. (Hugh wouldn't relinquish that morsel.) And yesterday, receiving verification, I confess that I went through a turn.

Well, I not only have digested your reports, but some later BLUEBEARD transcripts you have not seen, and I'm worried, as is Hugh. He's been doing his subtle best to get our young President to recognize what an incubus is J. Edgar Buddha on any administration, especially this one, but in the interim, I don't believe Jack comprehends how many pressure points are being handed over to Hoover. That man could end with a total choke on the Kennedy windpipe. Modene is so fabulously indiscreet. I am not going, as you did, to memorialize her meanderings with her friend, Willie, which I find misleading since under the guise of telling nothing, she tells her friend (and J. Edgar) all, even if it takes too long to find out! I am going to summarize what I have learned and save you the time you did not save me.

In brief, Modene suffered the lacerations of the abandoned during Jack and Jacqueline's visit to Paris at the end of May. Do you recollect? Our First Lady was a sensational success in Paris. Jack even said, "My real mission in Paris is to escort Jacqueline Kennedy." God, how all that must have been etched into your poor girl's brain. And, of course, our ogrish Sam G. couldn't resist twitting her on the raw nerve. "Are you jealous, Modene?" he kept asking. "Not at all," she kept replying. In recounting it to her stalwart Willie (whom, I must say, I picture as post-deb, blond, and seriously overweight—did you ever obtain a description?) Modene does, however, burst into tears. It comes out that earlier in May, before the trip to Paris, Jack had Modene in bed at the White House. Can you imagine? After a surprisingly dreadful lunch of cold soup and ketchup on the hamburgers—Irish!—Jack took Modene from the family dining room on the second floor to a bedroom, same floor, with a commodious bed. There, they consummated their reunion. She is madly in love again. Or so she will tell Willie that night.

This transcript does happen to be worth offering for flavor.

WILLIE: Wait a minute. The guards just allowed you to walk into the White House?

MODENE: Of course not. I had to go through the gate, and then there was a short, well-built little man named Dave Powers who came down to meet me. He had a twinkle in his eye, permanently, I think. Looked like a troll. The President, he said, was having a swim and would be by soon. Dave Powers kept saying, *"the President"* with a high hush in his voice as if asking you to kneel in church. Of course, he left as soon as Jack came in to lunch. By then Dave Powers had gotten it across to me that he's the fellow who wakes Jack up every morning and tucks him in at night. He certainly makes you feel you are in the White House.

WILLIE: It's not a very sexy place, is it?

MODENE: I would say it is like the inside of a Quaker church, only heavier. Sacred trust sort of feeling. I never wanted a bourbon so much. It was early Saturday afternoon, the place was deserted, and I kept having the feeling I would never get to see Jack. After Powers took me upstairs to the family quarters, though, it was less uncomfortable—I was familiar with all that N Street furniture they had moved over to the second floor.

After lunch, they journey to the bedroom. Following the preliminaries, Jack receives her on his back. Which French king was it who used to greet his mistresses in that manner? Louis XIV, perhaps, given that pampered look. In any event, as Modene explains it, Jack's "lumbar condition" has grown worse. "Cares of office." She is happy to serve the master, but a nugget of discontent remains. "I don't mind which position is chosen. Different positions bring out different sides of me. Only I prefer to get to them on my own."

Mind you, all this while, through a window near the double bed, she can see the Washington Monument.

Dear man, I have to wonder what your reactions must have been while reading the earlier transcripts. I hope I understand you well enough to assume that such perusal spurred you on to greater heights with Modene—or was it faster flats? We do want to shine in the eyes of the Immortal Race Steward.

Oh, Harry, is all this due to the teasing I was never able to give to that younger brother I never had?

I return to the essential. Despite Jackie's triumphs in Paris, Jack does get in touch with Modene again early in June, and all through the summer, on fearfully hot, deserted, dog-day Saturday afternoons in Washington, he keeps bringing her to the same double bed. They used to say of Joe Kennedy that the longer you were in a business deal with the man, the more he took from it, and the less you brought home. Something of that lament creeps into her conversations with Willie. All the same, she finds justifications for Jack. "He is so tired. He does have many concerns to deal with."

It is a most peculiar period for our BLUEBEARD. She is based now in Los Angeles. She is actually sharing an apartment in Brentwood with four other stewardesses. Hardly the Modene you knew! From this base, however, she keeps waiting for the next summons to Washington. Meanwhile the Brentwood apartment is a focus for parties. Actors, marriageable young corporate types, a couple of professional athletes, one or two fringe film executives, and a prodigious amount of drinking. I'm not familiar with evenings of this variety, but gather there's a great deal of dancing and a fair amount of marijuana. Then she's always ready to fly to Chicago or Miami to spend a weekend with RAPUNZEL. Yet—her steadfast claim—there is "no sexual link." I won't bore you with Willie's doubts about this.

What speaks loudly is dissipation. Modene keeps gaining weight, and is drinking so much that she actually goes "as a tourist" to an AA meeting, but is "appalled by the gloom." She is also taking stimulants and depressants. Her hangovers are described as "calamities." A tennis game outside her window sounds "like an antiaircraft barrage." She keeps referring to "a crazy drunken summer." When working, she suffers "as never before." She calls Jack frequently. Apparently, he has given her a special number to reach one of his secretaries. According to Modene's account, Jack does call back when not immediately available. And she has offered hints that last summer she did carry a manila envelope from IOTA to RAPUNZEL. All the same, Jack keeps teasing her. "Don't," says Jack, "let it get too personal with Sammy. He's not a fellow to trust with the collection plate."

Hugh, in one surprising moment of candor, said to me, "I suspect this has to do with Castro. Under it all, your Jack has an IRA mentality. Trust that Mick instinct. He wants to get even. Get even and you can enjoy your old age."

I find the most curious feelings in me. I've always thought of myself as ruefully patriotic, that is, I love America, but it's like having a mate whose gaffes keep you exclaiming, "Oh, my God. He's done it again." I am outraged, however, that this man Castro, who is probably more qualified to be captain of a pirate ship than a head of state is now gloating over us. It does bother me. And I know it rests like a thorn in the Kennedy heart. With his love of intrigue, it might not be unlike Jack to pick such an outré back channel as Sammy G.

Toward the end of August, our girl is invited once again to lunch on Saturday in the small second-story dining room. This time, however, Dave Powers is invited to eat with them.

MODENE: At the end of the meal, Jack said to me, "Modene, I am picking up a few tales out of school." "Tales?" I asked. For the first time since I knew him, I didn't like his tone. Not at all. He said, "Did you ever say to anyone that I tried to get you to accept another girl to go right in there with us?"

WILLIE: He spoke in such manner right in front of Dave Powers?

MODENE: I think he wanted a henchman there for the record.

WILLIE: Maybe you were being recorded?

MODENE: Don't say that. It's offensive enough already. I certainly had the feeling that he was doing it for Dave Powers' benefit. As if to announce: "Well, here is this unlikely tale, but were you, Modene, malicious enough to go around spreading it?"

WILLIE: You must have been furious.

MODENE: I don't make a habit of swearing, but instinct told me to get downright coarse. So I said: "If you ever tried something so low as hoping to put another girl into the sack with you and me, I sure as hell would be the last one to run around with that story. It's an insult to me."

WILLIE: You did tell him off.

MODENE: He had transgressed the line of privacy.

WILLIE: I appreciate what you are saying.

MODENE: Yes.

WILLIE: Except you did tell it to me.

MODENE: I did? . . . Yes, I did, didn't I? But you don't count.

WILLIE: Did you tell anyone beside me?

MODENE: I may have told Tom. I can't remember. Do you know, I really can't remember. Do you suppose pot and alcohol if taken with sleeping pills might injure a person's memory?

WILLIE: Yes.

MODENE: Well, I do remember telling Sam.

WILLIE: Oh, no.

MODENE: I couldn't stew in it alone.

WILLIE: What happened after you told him off?

MODENE: I kept on the high road. I asked him how he dared to discuss something that personal in front of a third party? Jack must have made some signal then, because Powers left the room. Then Jack tried to make amends. Kept kissing me on the cheek and saying, "I'm awfully sorry. But a story did get back to me." I told him if he didn't like tales out of school, maybe he ought to comport himself in another manner. And then very suddenly I said, "Let's break it off." I couldn't believe I had said it. He tried to get me to stay. I think, after all this, he still wanted to get me in bed. Men are single-minded, aren't they? I finally had to say, "You are insensitive. I want to leave."

WILLIE: You just took off?

MODENE: Oh, no. He wouldn't permit that. Dave Powers had to take me on a tour of the White House.

WILLIE: I'm sure they wanted to check on whether you were under control. All they needed was some mad beauty running out of the White House and ripping off her clothes on Pennsylvania Avenue.

MODENE: You are particularly humorous today.

WILLIE: Sorry.

MODENE: The tour was painful. Dave Powers had done it so many times before that I wanted to scream. I felt as if I were working an all-seats-occupied flight. Dave must have taken forty-five minutes guiding me through the Green Room and the Red Room and the Oval Room and the East Room.

WILLIE: Do you remember any of it?

MODENE: Don't I just? "Elegance is the fruit of rationality."

WILLIE: What?

MODENE: "Elegance is the fruit of rationality." That was in the East Room. Dave Powers kept talking about the noble proportions of the East Room. When we got to the Oval Room, he had to say, "It's traditionally employed for White House weddings." Then he began to describe all the shades of blue that the Oval Room has seen. Originally, under President Monroe, it was crimson and gold, but Van Buren changed it to royal blue, then President Grant made it violet-blue, and Chester Arthur's wife altered it to robin's-egg blue. Mrs. Harrison picked out a cerulean blue.

WILLIE: There is nothing wrong with your memory.

MODENE: Thank you. Mrs. Harrison's cerulean blue was a figured wallpaper.

WILLIE: Thank you.

MODENE: And then Teddy Roosevelt made it steel blue. Harry Truman altered it back to royal blue.

WILLIE: Amazing.

MODENE: I was sick. I wanted to get out of there.

I can feel for Modene. Men don't understand how much importance women attribute to composure when they are feeling nothing but emotional debris. The moment Modene does get back to her hotel, she packs her bags and catches a flight to Chicago.

It is here, I must tell you, that she begins her affair with Sam. However, I don't feel ready to write to you about that today. I would feel more secure if you would answer this letter first.

Yours provisionally,
Eiskaltblütig

P.S. Can you believe it? That is one of Hugh's nicknames for me. I, who am as unformed and overheated within as Lava Inchoate.

5

Oct. 22, 1961

Dear Ice-cold Lava,

If we are to correspond, I would like to leave Modene out of it. Can we discuss other matters? I am, for instance—believe it if you will—ready for your theory on narcissism. Why don't you give me some idea of that? I expect your formulations can apply to a few people one knows. Yes, and what you may have to say on psychopathy.

As for myself, I am in a strange place. My career is in irons. No tradewinds blow. Hints, however, of a new wind. A bird streaking across my inner sky turns abruptly to fly back in the direction from which it came. Or, at least, that is what I glimpsed while my eyes were closed. Then, an hour ago, a phone call from your husband. I am to have dinner with him at Harvey's Restaurant on Saturday, October 28, at 7:00 P.M. General Edward Lansdale, he states, will accompany us. A job for me is to be part of the evening's agenda, promises your good man Hugh. Then he hangs up.

Do you know what lies behind all this?

Your Harry

October 26, 1961

Dear Harry,

Let me answer your questions later. First off, I think I will take on your curiosity about narcissism and psychopathy. It leads, you see, to a point I want to make about you and, even more, about me. So, herewith, in extreme summary, my thesis on narcissism—a pot of notions!

To begin, cleanse your mind of the common impression that a narcissist is a person in love with himself. That diverts us entirely from the real point. The crux of the matter is that *you can detest yourself intimately and still be a narcissist*. The key to narcissism: *One is one's own mate*. Where relatively normal people are able to express a good share of their love and hate toward others, the narcissist is worn out by these emotions, for Alpha and Omega engage in endless trench warfare within. The self is seeking for an armistice with itself that almost never comes.

This fundamental inability to have relations with others is revealed most clearly in a love affair. No matter how close and loving two narcissists may appear to be, it is merely a reflection of their *decision* to be in love. Underneath lies spiritual depletion.

Yet, the paradox, Harry, is that no love can prove so intense on occasion, and so full of anguish and torture, as the love of two narcissists. So much depends on it. For if they can succeed in coming close to the other person, they can begin to live in a world outside themselves. It is like taking the leap from onanism to honest copulation.

About psychopathy, I speak less confidently. It is kin to narcissism, yet critically different. While other people are never as real to the psychopath as the inner strife between his Alpha and Omega, the trench warfare of narcissism is now replaced by slashing combat within. Both Alpha and Omega keep raiding each other, looking to gain immediate power. Tension, not detachment, is the prevailing condition. Indeed, this tension is so great that the psychopath can make love and/or attack others physically while feeling no responsibility for the act. After all, a psychopath lives in the dread of not being able to find any action that will decrease his or her tension; whatever offers relief, therefore, carries its own justification. The fastest relief for a psychopath is the sensation of lift-off provided by a sudden shift of psychic authority from Alpha to Omega. That is why psychopaths can be charming one instant, barbaric the next.

Needless to say, the reality is never so simple as my schematics. In life, the psychopath and the narcissist are, in fact, each trying to become more like the other. The narcissist wants to be able to get out of detachment, to act out; the psychopath looks for detachment.

It is better to perceive the two as poles in a spectrum of displaced personality that extends across the gamut from the most hermetic narcissism to the most uncontrollable, brutal psychopathy. As a small example, your Modene began, I suspect, as an absolute narcissist—her parents must have doted on her so totally that she was left contemplating nothing but herself. Now, via the ministrations of Sammy G., she is on the road to becoming a bit of a psychopath.

I don't want you to think of me as being naught but judgmental. What I say of Modene can apply in some degree to myself as well. I, too, am an only child, and no one could have begun as more of a narcissist than myself. (How, after all, could I have conceived of Alpha and Omega if I had not lived with them from early childhood?) So I do not judge Modene—I am well aware that narcissists are drawn toward the psychopathic.

Curiously, yet logically, there is one vice, therefore, that tempts both narcissist and psychopath. It is treachery. The psychopath cannot help himself; in raw state, his treachery is not under his control. (Which is what we mean when we speak of psychopathic liars.) Since the psychopath oscillates between Alpha and Omega more rapidly than most humans, Omega or Alpha feel entitled to violate whatever promise the other made in the previous hour. The narcissist, more congested, tends to explore the nuances of betrayal rather than to exercise it. Always present, however, is that balked desire to break out. Treachery is the means to such acceleration.

So, I come closer to my intimate passion. It is to betray Hugh. Not carnally. My sexual vow is the armature of my sanity. How I know this, I cannot say, but I keep my sexual vows. Yet the urge to betray him is profound. I sublimate such instincts by writing to you. I form a bond with you. An enclave of two. It frees me for other purposes.

You see, I have real intimations of what I desire. The great ship of this nation is not rudderless, but the compass is skewed. I cannot tell you what a shock the Bay of Pigs has been for those of us in the Agency who merely looked on. If we do not know how to steer a course through history, then who can? We are supposed to serve the President, but most of our Presidents have had an inner light so dim that we have been obliged to take the lead ourselves.

Now we have a President who is alive, who can recognize error, is human, vain, wise, willing to learn, and with a keen nose for the balance between prudence and risk. *It is crucial that he be well informed.* He deserves that. He leans—with one-hundredth part of himself, or do I exaggerate?—upon the Montagues. Nonetheless, that one part in one hundred is very much alive. I believe he is as ready to listen to me as to Hugh.

So I discover that what I learn from Hugh is not enough. I want more. You may speak of this as egregious vanity, but I wish in some most determined part of myself to become my own intelligence center.

It is madness, you will say. Too inchoate for Little Miss Lava.

No, I tell you, not so. Half of everyone in the bloody Agency has the same passion and keeps it in the same closet. Few of us dare to admit to it. I do. I want to know what is going on. I want to influence the steering of the ship. Despite my warps and flaws, I feel as capable of fine judgment as my husband, and he is wiser than anyone I know in the Agency or anyone else in this holy swampland, Washington, D.C.

What, you may ask, can you contribute to our surround of two? Plenty, buddy. I have taken care of that, you see. You were right. Your career was indeed in the doldrums. Hunt failed to come through for you after the Zenith stint. On your performance, he described you as "sporadic in work habits and often distracted." Perhaps the fault comes down to the time you spent with Modene in bed. You were on the good ship to nowhere.

All the same, I said to Hugh the other day, "You've got to do something for Harry." He answered, "I don't know that I want to. He bollixed up BLUEBEARD." It was the first time he admitted that you were Harry Field.

I pointed out to Hugh that you had gone reasonably far. Others in such a squalid op might not have attained anything at all, not even the lady's lips.

"He didn't use his position to advantage. He could have gotten so much more. On the other hand, if he was that much in love, then he was singularly lacking in the integrity to tell me to stuff it." So went Hugh's judgment.

Do you know, I think he is secretly fond of you. Hugh approves of almost no one's work, but you are his godson and he does not forget that. We discussed suitable jobs until he came up with what I think is the right one for you. It is to serve as liaison between Bill Harvey and General Edward Lansdale in the new Cuban op that is now shaping up. I don't have to underline how super-octane this

promises to be. I can tell you in confidence that it is called Operation
Mongoose in honor of that ferocious ferret from India renowned for
its skill in killing rats and poisonous snakes. MO/NGOOSE, you see.
MO refers to the Far East, and most conveniently is a Pentagon
digraph rather than one of ours. Helms chose it. He thinks it will
confuse the nosy among us. The curious in the Agency will assume
it's something we and the Pentagon are up to in Asia.

    Actually, Mongoose is overseen by Special Group, Aug-
mented, General Maxwell Taylor as Chairman, standing in for Bobby
Kennedy. (If you think Jack is agitated about Cuba, I can assure you
that Bobby is virulent on the subject, intimately virulent. So there's
lots of push to get a great deal done. The idea is to overthrow Castro
by any variety of means.)

    General Lansdale has now been put in charge of Mongoose
and, directly under him, representing the Agency contribution (which
promises to be nine-tenths of Mongoose), is your old pal Bill Harvey.

    Hugh and I discussed it carefully. This is an out-of-category
job. It could prove prestigious or nugatory, and that, Harry, is not
entirely up to you. You could be in the lap of the gods. Career
advancement so often depends on recognizable career slots—this
many years spent at minor Desk A, then abroad to minor Station A
(read: Uruguay), then larger Desk, larger Station, und so weiter. You,
dear boy, are a little out of category and will probably remain so.
Liaison, however, will keep you close to some active people. Lansdale,
for example. He is, by all reports, a consummate maverick and has had
an army career that is not at all typical. He never went to West Point,
nor served in the regular army, merely a reserve commission in
ROTC. All through the thirties, he worked in advertising and public
relations, and during the war for OSS. (Propaganda, I expect.) After
VJ Day, he wangled an assignment to the Philippines as a Major in the
Reserve, and began to distinguish himself. I'm sure you must know
something of his now legendary career. He was immortalized by
Graham Greene (invidiously) in The Quiet American and made much
of by Lederer and Burdick in The Ugly American. Fact is, he turned the
Philippines inside out and proved most instrumental in defeating the
Communist Hukbalahap. Next, he just about managed Ramon Mag-
saysay's successful bid for the presidency. Recently, has been very
close to Diem in Vietnam. The man has credentials. Maverick, but
inspired.

    The immediate problem was how to sell you to Lansdale.

Hugh knows him barely—in fact, Hugh plans to get to know him better at dinner tomorrow night. It was Cal did the deal. I prevailed on Hugh to call Cal in spite of their recent chill over Pigs, and your father, who knows Lansdale and has worked well with him in the Far East, certainly came through. Right on the phone from Japan, he gave the following quote to us which is, indeed, the same recommendation he gave to Lansdale, nothing less than, "Harry's a good young man and getting better all the time. I'm fortunate in being able to call him my son." Then he added to Hugh, "Don't tell your godson. It'll swell his head."

Hugh wasn't about to. I do. For your morale. Which, Harry, you are going to need. The reason Hugh chose Harvey's Restaurant for your dinner is that you are not only going to be liaison between Lansdale and Harvey, but between Hugh and Harvey. If that doesn't make you enough of a conjunction, you will also keep nourishing me every step of the way. Just as I am going to keep on feeding you. I know that I am now indulging the worst hubris, but I do believe we are two of the purest spirits in the Agency. Even when it comes to treachery, the CIA still needs purity of intent.

Aren't I mad? Listen, love, I know that after Berlin, the thought of working for Harvey can hardly appeal to you, but this I will say: Hugh has some absolute grip on Wild Bill. You need fear nothing there. I'm working on Hugh to find out what it is, but can promise that it's powerful.

I do hope you will keep up your end of things now by giving me a full account of the dinner tomorrow night.

Love, conspiratorial love,
Kittredge

6

Sunday night, Oct. 29

Dear Kittredge,

Last night Lansdale spent a small but definite portion of dinner instructing me in how circumspect I must become. "You will be handling material that originates in the National Security Council," he said, underlining the gravity of the source. Hugh then fixed me with one of those looks that pin you to your own guilt. I, of course, nodded to both of them.

You are right. I feel an absolute exhilaration at linking up with you. And I will adhere to my part of the bargain (save for an occasional betrayal for prophylactic purposes).

To business. It was an odd evening. I could see it had pretty much been decided in advance that my job was in place. Lansdale, given his declared affection for my father, was hardly about to join us for dinner in order to declare at the end of the meal, "Sorry, young man, you won't do." I will confess I enjoyed myself.

Part of the interest for me was in how Hugh and Ed Lansdale sized each other up. I suppose Hugh's GS rating has to be about as high as Brigadier General, which is Lansdale's rank, so they met in that manner as equals. Though Lansdale has been in OSS, and was CIA, I gather, in Vietnam, he is not at all an Agency man. Not in manner. Indeed, as you warned me, he is *sui generis*.

In any event, your husband and Lansdale looked to get some measure of each other by comparing war stories. Hugh only told one and I wondered at that until I recognized that he was comporting himself as a judge. Let Lansdale be the one to show his wares. For that matter, it was only after Lansdale had narrated four or five good tales that Hugh decided it was time for one of his, and then entertained us with a hilarious if minor episode concerning the Nasser government. It seems Hugh was in Cairo trying to convince Nasser to accept some Agency program, but he couldn't even obtain an audience with the great man. Hugh, therefore, typed out a detailed memo laying out his project, stamped it TOP SECRET, and left it on the top of his chifferobe. He knew it would be photographed by the security people the moment he stepped out of the hotel. "Next day, Nasser called me in to discuss the matter."

Kittredge, do you know, I recollect a dinner guest at the Stable, one tricky gentleman named Miles Copeland, telling the same anecdote. This gave me an insight on Hugh. Since war stories, I am sure he would argue, are an inferior form of discourse, use any one that serves your purpose, and don't look back. You can even make them up. I think he did not want to blow Lansdale out of the water with any of his real stuff.

The General is another matter. He delivers each one of his presentations with all the sincerity of an inspired salesman. He's an odd, tall man, who does not, but for his crew cut, look in the least like an Army general. In his fifties, he is mild, pleasant, soft-spoken, and not bad-looking—a long, straight nose, good dimpled chin, full mustache—but he has hollow eyes. I don't know quite what I wish to say here. They are not weak eyes, but they do not have any light in them. It's as if he is inviting you to enter some private hollow. I suppose I wish to say that he is the next thing to a hypnotist and seems to suck you right into the center of his concentration. Yet he is full of contradictions. He has to be sophisticated, but it doesn't show. He even seems innocent. When it came my turn to produce a war story, I told the tale of Libertad La Lengua and that produced some very high-pitched giggles from Lansdale.

I would guess that sexual matters are strange to him. He presents himself as sweet, idealistic, and possessed of a puckish sense of humor. Once, on a military tour of the Ryukyu Islands in 1946, surrounded by local children, he instructed them to shout at the Americans who would be following, "My papa is Major Lansdale. Major Lansdale!"

That story was the opening gun. Next, he showed a more curious side of himself. "I had once," he said, "early on, to deal with a Luzon official who was a truly corrupt fellow, and when the showdown came, he locked himself in his room and brandished a pistol at the window. I had to establish myself with the local folk, so I called out, 'Sir, take a shot at me. It will be a pleasure to cut you down.' Do you know? He surrendered.

"Afterward, one of my people asked if I was that good a shot. I confessed to him that I did not know anyone who took longer to whip his pistol out of a shoulder holster."

"Weren't you taking a risk with such a confession?" asked Hugh.

"No, sir. My strategy does not depend on gun handling but on psychological warfare. In our battles with the Hukbalahap we used to maneuver our helicopter into position over them, and assail their ears with a bullhorn. One of my best Filipinos would harangue the poor souls below. The guerrillas knew it was a helicopter, but hell, it was also a voice from *above*. Since we had good intelligence, we knew the names of some of the Hukbalahap. They were all out of the local barrios, and our people knew their people. My fellow spoke to them with material such as this: 'We see you hiding down there, Platoon 3. We see you, Commander Miguel, and you as well, José Campos. Yes, we can also see you, Norzagaray Boy, and you, Chichi, and Pedro, and Emilio. Don't try to hide, Carabao Kid, because we see you, and Cuño, and Baby. We have heard all about you. Believe us, we are coming back to kill you tonight. Our soldiers are approaching. So, to our friends among you, we say, "Run." To our private ally who told us all your names, we say, *"Muchas gracias, amigo."* Now, save your-selves. Escape from this platoon.'

"Well," said Lansdale, "after we'd flown off, half of those fellows down there wanted to flee. Of course, the hardcore began to wonder who our friends were, and soon held a kangaroo court. A few platoon members were executed by morning. That bullhorn killed more guerrillas than any mortar.

"We also trained our best scouts in the Philippine Army to work at night. The Communist boast in the Far East has always been that the Americans can drive along the roads by day, but the Commu-nists own the night. To win the war, we had to appropriate the powers of darkness.

"I decided to take advantage of the local demons. Anthropol-ogy is worth as much as firepower. In one area that we were trying to wrest from the Huks, there was intense belief in a hideous vampire called an *asuang*. I decided to employ this demon."

"Fascinating," said Hugh.

"I thought so. We saturated the area with stories that the *asuang* was stirring. Then, on a given night, one of our crack patrols set themselves up near a trail the Huks were known to use. We did not trigger the ambush until the last man passed. To our good fortune, he was a straggler and my people were able to overpower him, then drag him off the trail. Quick as you could say Jack Robinson, one of my boys spiked two holes in his throat. Then the poor victim was held up by his heels until all his blood drained out. After which, we put him back on the trail. We knew that when the Huks returned to look for their missing fellow, they would find a bloodless specimen with two small holes in his throat. Be certain that the news went around the Huk encampments that the *asuang* was on the prowl. Defections, as expected, were numerous. The Filipinos believe, you see, that the *asuang* will only attack those who have enlisted on the wrong side."

"How are you going to apply these intense principles to Cuba?" asked Hugh.

"The real need is to go out in the field and get to know the people you are dealing with. The Bay of Pigs was a classic study in aloofness. Officers sitting at desks reading so-called objective reports. Written by specialists who were as remote from the reality as themselves. You cannot learn the scene at second-hand. Lazy intelligence always calls for more firepower."

"Hear, hear," said Hugh.

"The key is to take Communist precepts and convert them to our use. The harder the Communists attack some weak point in a country's social fabric, the more honest we have to be in strengthening that weak point. It's what I've been trying to get across to Diem and Nhu in Vietnam. Work with the people. Let *them* run the show. Policymakers in the military are too much in love with brute force. The only real defense against Communism is 'of the people, by the people, for the people.' "

Hugh, by now, had lit his first cigar. "Yes," he said, "It's apparent to me, Ed Lansdale. Your heart is in the Far East, not the Caribbean."

"So it is."

"May I ask why you agreed to take on this job?"

"Well, sir, you don't argue with the President of the United States. He did ask me."

"One can't say no at such times," agreed Hugh. "I do, however, foresee a problem."

"I'm here to listen," said Lansdale.

"The problem, as I see it, is that you are placed between Bobby Kennedy and William Harvey. Both, you will soon discover, are eager for results."

"No more than I am," said Lansdale.

"Yes. But your method, as I comprehend it, is to develop rapport with the people. In this case, the Cuban people. Unfortunately, they are not going to be as available to you as the Filipinos, nor the Vietnamese. You will not be stationed among them. You will not be free to mingle with the denizens of Sancti Spíritus, or Matanzas, or Santiago de Cuba, or Cienfuegos, or, for that matter, Havana. You will be restricted to a corps of Miami exiles who have already failed because of their specific vices."

"Which are?"

"Unbridled license. To a Cuban, a valuable secret is a flag to dazzle his friends, or to wave in the face of his enemy."

"We encountered something of the sort in the Philippines."

"You were on the ground there. The first move belonged to you. Your troops could travel faster than your secrets be exposed. Now you need time to build an underground."

"Yes. I want it to be composed of Cubans fighting for *their* principles rather than for ours. I plan to zero in on those exiles who were against Batista and originally for Castro. We will work with them within Cuba, and select our points of attack most carefully, so as not to bring down unholy reprisals on the locals."

"Do you believe you will have that luxury? Two months ago, our redoubtable young Attorney General, Robert F. Kennedy, openly scourged Richard Bissell in the Cabinet Room at the White House. Bissell is a man of some dignity and twice Bobby's size, 'but,' said Bobby to Bissell, 'you are sitting on your ass.' "

"Now Mr. Bissell is on his way out," said Lansdale.

"Certainly is. Dick Helms is in. Smaller, meaner, and much more to the point."

"I don't know if I follow you," said Lansdale.

"You claim anthropology is more useful than firepower. Admire the metaphor, but take warning: There is not much anthropology left to Cuba. The original natives were wiped out three centuries ago. Then came the slave ships. Cuba's culture, you may find, is equal to its economy: uprooted Spaniards and ex-slaves, sugar, rum, coffee, tobacco, rumbas, mambos, tourists, sex shows, and *santería*."

"I," said Lansdale, "might add two words. Sin, and Catholicism. Both—may I underline this?—are highly motivational. When you are short on anthropology, try motivational research."

"I know you are thinking of more than an advertising campaign to rid Cuba of Mr. Castro."

"Yes, sir, I plan to get in a little deeper than that. The Vietnamese have a beautiful axiom. 'No man,' they say, 'can govern a nation without the mandate of heaven.' So, in Cuba, we'll try to take away the mandate."

"Which is?"

"One of Castro's key supports, in my opinion, is the identification he so cleverly cultivates between Jesus Christ and himself. To his advantage is the spelling. *Castro* and *Cristo*. You may notice that the consonants are the same, C, S, T, R. Only the A and the I differ, and they are vowels. It is an advertising principle," said Lansdale, "that consonants repeated in two words produce subliminal link-up."

Kittredge, I took a chance and tested the waters. "In addition," I broke in, "there is Hernando Cortés and Castro. C, S, T, R appear again."

"Yes," said Lansdale, "a good point. Castro/Cristo can also be seen as Castro/Cortés, a great general."

"To the degree that this concept is full of merit, you have taken on more difficulties," said Hugh. "How will motivational research obviate these mystical links?"

"We will find our route," said Lansdale. "It's never the way it looks. For example, the depilatory powder that was discussed for possible use on Castro's beard?"

"Of course," said Hugh.

"I gather that discarded attempt is now a subject of some hilarity in the top echelons of the Agency."

"There's been a grimace or two."

"Too bad I wasn't in on it. I might have convinced a few. It sounds foolish, but I would have looked at the depilatory as a viable option."

"If I may say so," I said, "I don't understand why. Even if the attempt worked, and Castro's weak chin was revealed, wouldn't he have been able to conceal the loss with a false beard and wait until his hair grew back?"

"I can't agree," said Lansdale. "If a beautiful woman loses her locks and has to wear a wig, golly, you can count on it—word will get out. Word always gets out. Secret knowledge carried in whispers from person to person has more power to convince than active denunciations. Besides, a false beard can always come loose by accident. Castro would certainly have been ill at ease in anticipation of such an event."

"Do you know, it's been fascinating to dine with you, General," said Hugh. "I anticipate with interest your task ahead with Bill Harvey. It will go well, doubtless."

"I hope so," said Lansdale.

"If," said Hugh, "he gets too Bolshy, call on me. I won't promise the moon, but I am able, occasionally, to muscle Wild Bill over a millimeter or two."

We all laughed somewhat cautiously, I thought. I didn't know whether to be in awe of General Lansdale or to feel sorry for him.

He surprised me, however, by his next remark, which was in my direction. "As liaison," he said, "you will have to be a translator and a diplomat. Explain to me: What is your friend Hugh Montague trying to tell me?"

I was on the spot, Kittredge. I knew Hugh would not take to being translated. Nonetheless, the job gets first call. "At the risk," I said, "of speaking on my own, I would say that Bill Harvey is only ready to deal with those Cubans he can control completely."

Hugh gave a small nod of approval as if the godson's intelligence might be presenting a few hopeful signs.

Lansdale said, "We will see about that."

It was the moment when I arrived at my first real insight concerning the General. He was not ready to go into detail about what he was going to do in Cuba because he suspected that his principles were never going to be applied here. I think the only reason he took this job is that it is the largest ever offered him. He has, by what I have picked up in the last day or so, been kicking around the edges of big-time military for fifteen years now. He may be a celebrated maverick, but he now wants open respect from his peers and superiors. So he is going to be engaged in what he sneers at most— running an operation from a desk. We will see. I am curious.

To end the evening, Lansdale told a pretty good tale. It seems that at their first meeting, President Kennedy said, "From what they tell me, General, you are America's answer to James Bond."

Lansdale shook his head. "I assure you, I got off that mark as quickly as I could. The last thing in the world to have to live up to. James Bond! I suggested to the President that a closer candidate could be found in the very fellow the CIA has put in charge of Mongoose for field operations, William King Harvey. 'You,' replied the President, 'have me curious now. Could you bring this fellow, Harvey, around to the White House? I would like to meet him.'

"Well," said Lansdale, "two days later, I transported Bill Harvey from his basement at Langley clear over to the White House. While we were sitting in the anteroom to the Oval Office waiting to be called in to the President, I had an intuition. Thank my stars! I turned to Harvey and said, 'You are not carrying a handgun by any chance?' to which he replied, 'Yes. I'm armed,' and proceeded to withdraw a particularly hefty piece of Magnum-*cum*-what-all from a shoulder holster. By Jesus Christ and Castro, I almost dived through the floor. How would the Secret Service react to a strange man waving his howitzer in the White House? 'Please,' I said to Harvey, 'keep your thing hidden.'

"Most quietly, I assure you, I then took a stroll over to the Secret Service desk and informed the young man sitting there that my companion wondered if he could check his firearm while we were closeted with the President. Then, as if that hadn't been a near-enough deal, just as we were about to enter the Oval Office, I suppose Harvey decided that he had better divulge the existence of what he called his 'hole card.' There it was, another gun in another holster belted to the small of his back. He dug under his suit coat, whipped out a .38 Special, and proferred it to a couple of most discom-bobulated Secret Service agents. From there, we actually reached the Oval Office. I had time to whisper, 'Why, for God's sake, all the ordnance?' His reply: 'If you knew as many secrets as I do, you too would carry a gun.'

"Well, once the meeting began, it certainly proved an odd one. Right off, the President started kidding Bill about the sexual exploits of 007, and Harvey muttered something to the effect of being a little overweight these days. 'As you can see,' he said to the President, 'I don't fit the description anymore. I guess I was more like 007 in my salad days. Different-girl-every-night sort of thing.'

" 'Well,' said the President, 'General Lansdale did single you out.'

" 'Yessir,' said Harvey. After our audience was concluded, Bill said to me on the way out, 'I acted like an asshole, but, my God, dammit, it was the President.' "

In a couple of days, Kittredge, I'm due to report. I'll close my desk, take the elevator down, and locate Bill Harvey in his bunker. Presumably, he will provide another desk.

Incidentally, Hugh told me on the way home from dinner that Harvey is considerably depressed these days. The Agency found out recently that the Berlin tunnel was blown even before it was completed. All the while that Harvey thought he had been on top of it, there was a British officer working for the Russians. I don't want to think of what's now going on in the Hosiery Mill. "The damage may be an order of magnitude worse than the Bay of Pigs," said Hugh. "In fact, it's so bad, I expect we will not only sweep it under the carpet, but burn the rug."

Well, I don't know that this letter equips you to run the

Agency and the nation, but it is fun writing again. There's nothing so
good for my soul as a long letter to you.

Devotedly,
Harry

7

THROUGH THE FALL OF 1961 AND THE WINTER OF 1962, CORRESPON-
dence with Kittredge continued. I would write at least twice a week,
and although she did not reply as often, she frequently had more to
say. For that matter, her information was probably more reliable:
Mongoose was a much compartmented operation. While I was prepared to describe its properties, I could never be wholly certain of
distinguishing fact from hearsay. Whispers circulated ceaselessly in
JM/WAVE, and that was inevitable. Before we were done, more
Agency personnel had come down to Miami than were ever assigned
to Pigs. Indeed, our CIA portion of Mongoose, JM/WAVE, became
the largest CIA station in the world.

Given our size, therefore, and the speed with which we had been
put together, rumors abounded, security was weak. That was hardly
surprising. The highest standards of secrecy in CIA were usually
exercised by Agency scholars exploring land grants in Manchuria in
the seventeenth century. They could be depended upon not to
breathe a word of their discoveries. We, however, in Harvey's basement at Langley, or spread out once more over half of southern
Florida with JM/WAVE projects, gossiped unconscionably. How was
Lansdale hatching his eggs for Mongoose? What was coming down
from General Maxwell Taylor, or Bobby Kennedy? What was the real
stance of the White House? Florida brought one close to those questions, whereas at Langley the recognition could not be avoided that
one was merely a part of government instead of an agent of History.

I was quartered in Washington; I was stationed in Miami: It is
hard to say where I lived. I soon suspected that my job had been
manufactured by Lansdale out of no greater need than to keep on
pleasant terms with my father. The duties (or lack of them) revealed
the superficial aspects of the new position. Lansdale did not need me
very often. He had his own cadre, and trusted them.

Before long, I was down in the basement with Harvey. We took the first steps toward crossing an abyss of distrust. All the same, we did our best to get along. Maybe I reminded him of heroic days in Berlin. Indeed, our relations were not all that dissimilar even now. He ruminated aloud, he clammed up, he confided in me, he withdrew. After a while, I began to feel like the young and unfaithful spouse of an older man with settled habits. He could never forgive me for my transgressions, but he did enjoy my company. I even rode with him again in the backseat of his bulletproof Cadillac while he slugged his martinis and I took notes en route to the airport. Before long, he had me jumping down to Miami with him. Since his corpulence could no longer be wedged into an Economy seat, he flew First Class, one of the few Agency officers allowed such a perk, and thereby allowed me the rare luxury of my own First Class seat whenever he needed me along.

Often, I stayed over in southern Florida to oversee a subproject that he had initiated. Each week I was further away from liaison with Lansdale, and the General didn't seem to care. When I would report in, he would usually meet me in the anteroom to his office on his way to a meeting with officials from State, Defense, or Special Group, Augmented, and say in passing, "Are you keeping Harvey happy?"

"Doing my best."

"Keep it up. That's useful work," and he would be gone.

Harvey was not particularly suspicious of my relation to Lansdale. It was Montague's shadow that prevailed. Harvey's assumption was that I had been assigned to him in order to report back to Harlot. In substance, that was true. If Harlot had asked me for information, I would have supplied it, I suppose. I did not really know. I wanted to be my own man. I even confess to feeling injured, at least to some small degree, that Harvey did not trust me more; I was putting in twelve-hour days for him, and work provides its own sense of integrity. The irony is that in my letters to Kittredge I was, objectively speaking, reporting every last matter of interest on Harvey, but then, I did not believe she would pass it on to Harlot. Indeed, how could she account to her husband for such pieces of information?

All the while, I wondered at the force of Montague's grip on Wild Bill and thought often of my last couple of days in Berlin, and the four-page transcript of which Harlot had shown me but the first two pages. Harvey was not certain how much I knew, but he would make his references, and they were not oblique. "I don't care what kind of grip you think that prick has on me, he can go fuck himself." About once a week, Harvey would drop such tantrums in the manner of a black Florida cloud delivering itself of a squall, after which, back to work we would go.

There was enough to do. Lansdale had landed in his job running at full speed. Before a month was out, he had assigned thirty-two planning tasks to the Agency, the Pentagon, State, and whoever else was cooperating on Mongoose. Among the tasks was collection of intelligence; defection of Cuban officials; propaganda operations; sabotage operations; and an invasion scenario for U.S. forces whenever the new Cuban movement would be ready to overthrow the government. Lansdale sent out one memo calling for "a revolution that would break down the police controls of the state. Reliance is to be placed on: (a) professional anti-Castro emigrés, (b) labor leaders, (c) church groups, (d) gangster elements, if necessary, for certain tasks."

The memo concluded with a peroration. "It is our job to put the American genius to work quickly and effectively. The conclusive overthrow of Fidel Castro is possible. No time, money, effort, or manpower is to be spared."

"Who is he kidding?" asked Harvey. "Everybody knows that is Lansdale taking dictation from Bobby Kennedy. Nothing spared! Yes. They give us the language, and we can do the dirty work. Thirty-two tasks!" said Harvey, getting ready for his own peroration. "Somebody ought to tell Lansdale that the labor leaders in Cuba are gangsters, the gangsters buy out the churches, and the priests spend their money on fortune-tellers. You don't look for *a, b, c,* and *d* categories. You look for people who can do the job. I don't care if you bring me a one-eyed Martian with a longshoreman's hook on his cock and the guy drinks cat piss at midnight, I'll take him if he's a stand-up Joe who likes to blow bridges and can obey my orders. This Lansdale, with Bobby Kennedy in back of him, is talking about revolution? He better get it straight. Any Cuban I do not control will have nothing to do with my operation. Leave it to Lansdale, and we'll have a revolution which will bring in a new kind of Communist who wears his insignia on the right tit instead of the left. Screw that noise. I say, fuck Cuba up good. Stuff the worst shit you can find into the economic gears. Wound the cocksuckers. Demoralize them. The only thing I agree on with Lansdale is that we will destabilize Cuba. But, I tell you, that candy General is a goddamn hypocrite. Yesterday, there were Thirty-two Tasks. Today, he gives us a new one. Task Thirty-three: Incapacitate the sugar workers during the harvest. The son of a bitch knows just enough to cover his ass. 'It will require,' he says, '*policy determination* before final approval.' Well, even I, who am no internationalist, thank you, can see what is wrong *internationally*. Listen to his take: 'The chemicals employed are to be guaranteed by priority studies to do no more than sicken Cuban sugar workers *temporarily*'—italics are mine, Hubbard—'and keep said sugar workers away from the fields without permanent ill effects. *Nonlethal* incapacitating chemicals.' Brother, I have heard everything now—can you imagine what we could look like to the rest of the world? Depend on it—Special Group, Augmented, is going to table Task Thirty-three.''

Special Group, Augmented, did. A week later, Harvey read the refined Thirty-two Tasks with a bilious eye. One phrase stated, "Gangster elements might provide the best potential for attacks against Cuban Intelligence officials." Harvey was on the boil. "You are not supposed to put things like this on paper," he said. "Gangster elements! Hubbard, I am aware of the principle that in combat, men die, but this happens to be Murder, Incorporated. Who, presumably, will handle it? Why, our friend Bill Harvey with his Task Force W will do the wet jobs. Bill Harvey can catch it if something goes wrong. I'll say this for Lansdale. He is a complex individual. He doesn't want a poor innocent Cuban killed unless we can show a real purpose behind it. Then he takes a sip of water and asks me to target a couple of hundred Soviet-bloc technicians. Add them to the hit list. I am somewhat underwhelmed by his plans, the cocksucker.''

Harvey dictated a memo to SGA: The emphasis for Mongoose, in his opinion, ought to be placed on acquiring more intelligence. I had learned by now that such memos had nothing to do with Harvey's real intentions, indeed, they could have served as model form letters in our unwritten Book of Agency Etiquette. By now, I could put the book together myself. If you had to perform a task that strayed beyond the limits of our charter, it was crucial to establish a trail of paper that would confuse anyone trying to follow what you had done. The rule of thumb was to commit to writing the opposite of what you were intending. If Harvey was sending out saboteurs to wreck factories, he called, on paper, for the intensification of our intelligence efforts.

Lansdale had been a solitary operator for too long, Harvey decided, so he now had a tendency to put everything in writing. Harvey said: "I knew a whore once up in Alaska. One big fat old Eskimo mama with a cunt as wide and comfortable as the rear seat of a Cadillac. That's Lansdale's mouth—just as big.''

The real problem, I soon concluded, was that Lansdale might have compromised some of his ideas, but he had not given them up. Lansdale wanted real underground organizations; he was searching for autonomous Cubans looking to obtain their own real intelligence. Which, presumably, they would share with us. He did not seem able to recognize that Harvey, when it came down to it, preferred to have no underground rather than one over which you could only exercise sporadic control. Therefore, Harvey was building up cadres with trustworthy exiles that he could use in paramilitary operations. How else could JM/WAVE maintain any kind of security in the open atmosphere of Miami? "The emphasis," said Harvey, "is going to be on the case officer, not the agent. The case officer here is going to be equal in importance to a priest. Our exiles have got to be ready to tell him everything. Read me? Hubbard, you had that job for a couple of years. How feasible would that relationship be for you?"

"Fifty percent probability," I replied.

"Good." He grunted. "I like your answer. You must have been one soft case officer."

"Not as soft as you think," I said back, and he laughed. "Shit, you merely got your toes wet in Uruguay. You were tooling around with the tulips."

Lansdale finally took me into his office one day and asked, "Do you have any input with Bill Harvey?"

"I can get a personal message to him. In fact, I think he would prefer to hear from you that way."

"Not in writing?"

"Not in writing, sir."

He sighed. "I've spent a good part of my life trying to learn to do things the military way. They won't move in the military unless you back them up with clear orders on paper. Harvey, obviously, is accustomed to the opposite."

"Yessir."

"Tell Harvey I said that I would like him to remember I am not the enemy."

"Fuck he isn't," said Harvey on receiving this message.

When next I visited the General, he said, "Harry, I like to know where I stand. I will underline my next remark. *I believe in getting along with people*. If I ask you to pass this on to Bill Harvey, what reply will he give?"

"I can't answer that, General."

"Well, you just have, in fact."

"Yessir."

"I'm going to lay something out for you. So you can still communicate my point of view."

"I will try."

"I certainly hope you will. Because what JM/WAVE is doing now in Cuba amounts to no more than random hit-and-run raids. No overall strategy. No reaching out. I don't know what anyone expects these stunts to accomplish. The other day, a bridge was blown up. 'Why'd you do it?' I asked Harvey. 'What communications were you trying to destroy?' Do you know what he answered? 'You never told us not to blow the bridge.' Hubbard, that's the wrong kind of independence. I want to put an end to all this aimless sabotage. I want to save Cubans from pointless death. I cannot repeat it often enough: Americans who go abroad must possess a real dedication to the highest principles."

He had been speaking with such self-absorption that only at the end did he notice I was taking notes. "Oh, you don't need points of reference," he said. "Just tell him that I have been gentle beyond reason, but that next week will see some changes."

"Yessir."

"If you have an opportunity, pass those same sentiments along to Montague."

I would not. I could predict Harlot's reaction. Cuba was a morass. The actions chosen by Harvey would at least reduce the danger implicit in the Kennedys' enlightened notions of war. Prevention of leaks was worth more than the dubious search for illumined results. Indeed, Kittredge had written as much. "Hugh, you see, is convinced that Castro's intelligence will always be superior to ours. He has the power to kill his traitors; we can merely cut ours off from the weekly paycheck. Our agents are fighting for freedom, yes, but also for future profits in Cuba. Greed does make for corrupt intelligence. Whereas a lot of Castro's people believe they are in a crusade. Besides, Castro knows Cubans better than we do. Castro has KGB methods to guide him. We have politicians to satisfy. So when it comes to Cuba, his DGI will always be superior to our CIA. Conclusion: Cut the losses. Of course, Hugh doesn't talk that way around President Jack, just tries to nudge him a little in the proper direction. I, being a woman, and therefore not wholly responsible, can twit Jack about Cuba. I do. 'Oh,' I say, 'don't you think Castro is holding trumps?' and then I pass on Hugh's analysis as mine. But lightly. Ladies are there to relax the President, not to confound him. I will say for Jack that he does listen carefully. He is not gross in his political passions. I wish I could say the same for Bobby, who is much more emotional. Perhaps in another letter, I will try to describe Bobby for you."

Lansdale's counterattack soon arrived. If he had expressed contempt for military methodology, he knew how to employ it. Daily questionnaires now came to the basement. Soon after we returned them, secondary questionnaires brought follow-up queries. Harvey sent memos to McCone full of complaint:

> We are required to furnish Special Group, Augmented, in nauseating detail such irrelevancies to the purpose of an operation as the gradient of the landing beach and the composition of the sand. We are asked to specify times of landing and departure, which times are often impossible to predict or coordinate. Full listing of ordnance employed is supposed to be attached to each plan even though said battle plan may consist of no more than six Cubans armed to the teeth out in a rubber boat trying to slip by Castro's coast guard. They are doing everything possible to make it impossible for us to accomplish anything. Then they complain that nothing is happening. Can matters be made less restrictive and stultifying?

The questionnaires kept coming. Through January and February of 1962. Once, taking the noonday flight of Eastern Airlines to Miami on what we called "the milk run" (since you could always pick out new Agency men moving down to JM/WAVE with the wife and kids), King Bill turned to me and said, "I've got the troops, and he's sitting next to nothing but a desk. I'll show the son of a bitch what dirty fighting is."

I never knew if Harvey was the author of the next caper, but it was easy enough to suspect him since he seemed to take an artist's pleasure in telling me the tale. At a joint meeting of Mongoose committees, a Colonel named Forsyte from the Defense Department brought forth the idea of Operation Bounty. "Defense doesn't even want to take credit for this concept," Forsyte had said. "We're just stealing one of Ed Lansdale's ideas."

Operation Bounty was a proposition to cover Cuba with handout bills announcing that sums from $5,000 to $100,000 would be paid for the deaths of various high Cuban officials. Castro's life, however, would be given a value of two cents.

Lansdale had come to his feet immediately. "This is awful," he said. "It's wholly counterproductive."

"Why, Ed, are you against this?" McCone had asked. "Isn't it in line with your principles?"

"Hell, no," Lansdale had replied. "This idea will boomerang. You don't deride Castro in ways that are excessively crude. On the contrary, we have to recognize that the Cuban peasant now has better living conditions than before. They are not going to accept such ridicule of Castro."

Later, Harvey would comment: "With those few words, Lansdale lost McCone, half of State, and half of Defense. You don't tell McCone what Castro has accomplished. 'What,' asks McCone now, tight as a tick, 'would you say, General, is then the proper note to strike?' 'Oh,' says Lansdale, 'I would emphasize how the Devil gives you everything but freedom. All the material goods you need, but no, sir, no freedom. We want to get across that we can give them all that they get from Satan, plus freedom in addition.' "

"Jesus on a ham sandwich!" said Harvey. "McCone doesn't want to hear about Satan, Maxwell Turner looks embarrassed, Roger Hilsman from State is choking back his laughter. Maybe there were ten principals around the conference table and thirty flunkies back of them, and you could slice the fog with your hand. Lansdale has no sense of when he's losing a war."

One week later, a story circulated through Task Force W that Lansdale was looking to seed Cuba with the rumor that Castro was the Antichrist, and the Second Coming was near. It was rumored around the Basement that Lansdale had promulgated this scenario at a National Security Council meeting: On a moonless night, an American sub could surface in Havana Bay long enough to fire star shells into the sky. This would be done on a scale sufficient to suggest that Jesus had risen, Jesus was walking toward Havana by way of the water. Rumormongers in Havana could then disseminate the story that Castro had also been out there patrolling the bay with his Coast Guard cutters and had managed to keep Christ offshore. Done properly, this could ignite an enormous reaction. Conceivably, it could topple Castro.

A man from the State Department was supposed to have remarked, "It sounds like *elimination by illumination* to me."

The story kept Lansdale miserable. In a letter from Kittredge, she mentioned in passing: "He called Hugh again last night to complain about the *canard*. Swore it was not true. Claims nothing of the sort was ever said at NSC and that the foul report came out of the woodwork at Task Force W. Lansdale obviously thinks it's Harvey. I wonder if it's Hugh."

8

ON THE IDES OF MARCH, A NOTE CAME FROM KITTREDGE: "BE A DEAR, Harry. You've been telling me a good deal about JM/WAVE, but it's all in bits and pieces. Can you offer an overview? I'm not sure I even know just what JM/WAVE is."

March 23, 1962

Dear Kittredge,

I wasn't sure I could satisfy your request. JM/WAVE is *large*. Last week, however, on receipt of your letter, I saw it all. It was a most unprecedented place for a vision—I was at a meeting of Special Group, Augmented. I can tell you: Officers on my level don't usually get near. Can I take it for granted that you're wholly familiar with Special Group, Augmented, its personnel and protocol? On the chance you're not, let me say that it is not to be confused with either Special Group or Special Group CI (for Counter-Insurgency). In order, Special Group meets in the Executive Office Building at two o'clock every Thursday with such Presidential Advisers as Maxwell Taylor, McGeorge Bundy, Alexis Johnson, and John McCone. They review the new (since last Thursday) military events in the world. When they are done with business, Robert Kennedy comes over from Justice, and Special Group CI takes over. That has to do with Special Forces. That is, the Green Berets. The final meeting of the day, usually in late afternoon, is Special Group, Augmented, and that is devoted wholly to Cuba.

Last week, Bill Harvey had to give a presentation, and brought me along as his back-up. The task can be onerous. You hover over two jumbo-width attaché cases filled with documents Harvey might conceivably have to refer to: I am the man in the chair behind him, poised to keep his continuity fumble-proof. If anyone around the table brings up some matter discussed in the last six months, I have to be ready to provide the relevant document. When you have time to organize the filing partitions yourself, as I did, it is not quite as difficult as it sounds, so the meeting was worth it for me, no matter how charged up I was feeling under the pressure of my task and the formidable heft of the officials present. I confess to feeling the real weight of human gravity when I find myself in the same room with McNamara, McCone, Helms, and Maxwell Taylor, and this formidable sense of sharing the air with heavyweights is always present, no matter how they banter with each other. Their badinage, in fact, is about as friendly as a sharply angled tennis game. All the same, no question, it was worth it. How many times have I passed the bay windows and balconies of the old Executive Office Building and wanted to see it from the inside? Although our conference room is about what you would expect—heavy leather seats with upholstered arms for the principals, an Irish hunt table for the conference, and a set of hunting prints (Potomac steeds, circa 1820)—I felt as if I had passed a milestone in my career.

Harvey's attendance at the meeting took up about forty-five minutes. He was nervous while waiting with me in the secretary's anteroom, nervous as only I can tell (by the new load of gravel just dumped into his voice). God, but the man has two voices; there is the not so little one he reserves for working staff, and the quiet-in-public presentation in Wild Bill's low, deep, all-but-inaudible burble. No one can come up with a longer train of words to transport a simple thought than William King Harvey when he does not wish to be understood too clearly. Today he had been asked to give a report on agent activities for Mongoose and relevant installations around the world. Since I have gone into some detail with you on many of these, I will merely enumerate them now. He began by spending a few minutes on the Frankfurt operation. That, if you recollect, Hugh had his hand in. A large hand. It involved convincing a German industrialist whose code name is SCHILLING (an old friend, apparently, of Reinhard Gehlen's) to ship out-of-round ball bearings to a Cuban machine-tool plant. I remember you wondered at the ethics of that, whereas I was impressed with Hugh's skills in convincing a German, whose company reputation has been built on high-precision bearings, to debase his standards in the name of the-threat-that-is-Cuba. I mean, I don't like it particularly, but have come to the grim conclusion that one long-term way to defeat Castro is to wear him out. Harvey also mentioned the English buses that we were able to doctor up on the Liverpool docks. (Early breakdown in Havana is the prognosis, he announced to the SGA members.) He also expatiated on our credit operation which is using advanced banking techniques to block Cuban credits. Do you remember? We have banking agents in Antwerp, Le Havre, Genoa, and Barcelona. You said you couldn't follow the technical aspects. Well, I just about can. Most Cuban consignments do not get sent out now from Europe and most of South America unless there is payment in advance. "This," he informed the SGA, "is the fruition of an Agency directive sent out by me, with the concurrence of Mr. Helms and Director McCone to every one of our eighty-one Stations abroad. Said directive assigns a minimum of one Agency officer at each Station to focus on Cuban affairs." He pointed at one of my attaché jumbos. "In that file, pursuant to said project, are the 143 separate operations already activated in consonance with our paradigmatic advisements."

I must say Harvey does it with his own kind of skill. He gave fifteen minutes to descriptions of "hardcore work," citing more than a hundred of our commando raids in Cuba, and the progress of a major plan to blow up the enormous Matahambre copper mine works. Then, since this happened to be the one meeting at which Lansdale was not present, Harvey delivered "our implementation of the Lansdale Program."

That consisted of "saturated leaflet drops" on Camaguey, Cienfuegos, Puerto Príncipe, and Matanzas. The leaflets invite the Cuban people to carry matches for impromptu sabotage attempts. Unguarded cane fields, to cite one instance, can be burned. Telephone receivers can be left off their hooks in telephone booths. "Done at peak traffic hours in enough places, communications can be affected."

That all of this was penny-ante, Harvey knew all too well, but he chose to deliver it as, indeed, the Lansdale Program.

After a time, catching my second wind, I began to feel secure enough about the contents of my file case to drift off. Harvey was droning on about our JM/WAVE "maritime capability," which sounds respectably beefed-up because we refer to recreational yachts as "mother ships" and pleasure craft as "gunboats." The naval problems that we had at the Bay of Pigs are going, of necessity, to be repeated now. All our boats and ships are comparable to agents, in that they have to be able to live two lives at once. How simple if we could just use the U.S. Navy, but we can't, not on raids, and so an endless masquerade goes on with our boats being repainted every few weeks, and their registrations switched. A "gunboat" is really no more than a pleasure craft with a couple of .50-caliber machine guns in the bow, but all this flimflam is, believe it if you will, highly necessary, since every one of our craft leaving for Cuba is breaking the Neutrality Act. The FBI, Customs, Immigration, and even Treasury (supposed to be on the lookout for drug smugglers) are getting kinks in their necks from not looking in our direction.

At any rate, I had an epiphany in the midst of these prestigious surroundings. As Harvey talked on, I began to think of one of our bases in Miami, 6312 Riviera Drive, a modest mansion like many another in Coral Gables, stone wall, iron gate, two-story red-tile quasi-Spanish hacienda—a nice, cool, handsome house when all is said—a cupola for philosphers graces the roof. Nothing remarkable about it until you move into the backyard, but that sits on the Coral Gables Waterway, which at this point is hardly more than a canal that leads to Biscayne Bay and, with patience, the Gulf Stream. Kittredge, it is hard to believe. Cubans going out on missions that could leave them dead in the Cuban mangrove swamp come in through the front door like handymen, pick up their ordnance inside, including the black hoods they will wear on the trip so that the Cuban pilot, if captured at some later date, cannot identify them, and as soon as darkness comes, they take off in what looks to be a high-speed, luxury-equipped fishing boat, but, no, it's our concealed gunboat. What a peculiar war. It is hard to conceive of battle when the houses on the waterways from which these boats go forth are pink stucco or canary yellow, cobalt blue or lime green, and their gardens and flowering trees are a riot of magenta and red, while the palms offer that enervated languor I so often feel in the tropics. Has it taken all of the life-force in these scabrous trees merely to stand erect under the heat?

We have obtained such a collection now of safe houses, *naval* bases (6312 Riviera Drive), dumps, and fancy living quarters that I am tempted to describe the extremes. For instance, we keep a hunting camp in the Everglades which amounts to no more than a Quonset hut on a hummock in the swamp with a clearing for a helicopter to bring in VIPs like Lansdale, Harvey, Helms, McCone, your own Montague, Maxwell Taylor, McNamara, or for that matter, the President and his brother. Waloos Glades Hunting Camp it is called,

PRIVATE PROPERTY, NO TRESPASSING, and the place exists solely to set up meetings between people who do not want to be seen in public. If Bobby comes down to Miami, for instance, it is a media event. This way, he can fly into Homestead Air Base, then helicopter over to Waloos Glades for a meeting with some Latin American leader he may not wish all of southern Florida and the DGI to be witting of.

Another installation: An ugly dirt road bearing the lovely name Quail Roost Drive leads through a pinewood to a weather-beaten Florida bungalow up on stilts with a wraparound porch. It is the tradecraft school that focuses on radio transmissions. Others teach guerrilla tactics. I have visited ten such spots. At Elliot Key, for example, the dock itself is hidden in the mangroves. The Boston whaler that gets you in and out, a sixteen-foot job, has to push through mosquito-choked foliage merely to enter the four-foot-wide riverlet that leads upstream one hundred yards to the dock, from which a coral road wide enough for a Jeep transports supplies back through the thicket to a slatternly old house surrounded by jungle. Inside is a barracks dormitory—sixteen cots—a good-sized kitchen, and a shrine. No latrine, just an outhouse. Fresh water comes in by boat and Jeep. Add an equipment shed for arms, fatigues, jugs of mosquito repellent, and a couple of outboard motors, and you have a training camp, wholly isolated, to weld Miami exiles who want action into a force of "strike-brothers," an odd phrase, but the military mind, I am beginning to decide, is not entirely without acumen when it comes to understanding how to motivate a combat man.

At the other extreme of these logistics, nearby to Zenith headquarters (which JM/WAVE now occupies), we keep a large warehouse to supply our raiders with everything from *barbudo*-like false beards, to the latest Cuban army uniforms. Every variety of ordnance that the Soviets and Eastern-bloc countries are now providing to the Cubans—mortars, machine guns, submachine guns, hand-guns, bazookas, flare-guns, what-all, is available in our warehouse. I wish you could watch the play of expression on the face of a true warrior like my not undisturbing friend Dix Butler's when he goes through the fifty-four illustrated pages of our catalogue. You can peer over the lip then into the real cauldron of combat soup.

Now add to this diorama of JM/WAVE all the apartments, hotel suites, motels with cooking facilities, plus the University Inn of the University of Miami (which we've just about appropriated for middle-level transient officers), include the DuPont Plaza in downtown Miami (for the higher grade ratings), and we have a small city within the city for Agency personnel and their families. Do our case officers come to five hundred in number? Six hundred? You don't get to count noses. We are dealing with something like 2,500 Cuban agents, part-time agents, subagents, messenger boys, flunkies, and job-holders who do the cooking in places like Elliot Key. The number grows. We pay them each about $300 a month on average out of a foolproof system of special checks that can be cashed only at a couple of special windows in the First National Bank of Miami's main branch on Biscayne Boulevard.

Given the closeness with which some of us work together, we tend to eat and drink together as well. I won't describe the pubs and joints: The names will furnish their own decor—the Lounge at the Three Ambassadors Hotel; the Stuft Shirt Lounge; the 27 Birds—all I can say is that for the first time since training at the Farm, I go out drinking with my confreres at large, and every night. We go hunting for women less than you might expect. The true phenomenon is the size of the operation we are all engaged in, and deep on my third or fourth bourbon I come to realize why I am ready to work hard for Harvey despite his foul strictures and foul moods. Lansdale has nice ideas, but is, I fear, steering an unfamiliar ship, whereas Harvey has given us a government unto ourselves. Our proprietaries and dummy corporations come to more than fifty by now—detective agencies, gun shops, boat repair outfits, sport fishing fronts—all that you might expect, but we also have a Caribbean Research and Marketing office on nothing less than Okeechobee Road, and our own realty agency to front for our safe houses, our own travel agency to field the monthly outlay on airline travel, our import-export firm to handle the logistics of every kind of supply, our printing shop to take care of a variety of jobs, an employment agency for our exile personnel, not to mention our electronics maintenance shop and our fish and hunt club for weapons training. We haven't even reached the Agency guts located at Zenith. There, our intelligence mill acquires more space every month, and the photo labs process the daily U-2 flight-take over Cuba. The post office in Zenith, large as a ballroom, vets the mail between Miami and Havana, and there is the clippings room where world press reaction on the U.S. and Cuba is collated, and, not least, Sanctum South, where the file cabinets keep gathering reports from thirty or forty branches of the Cuban underground. Harvey, with his mistrust of networks that he has not built himself, calls it the Sanctum Maleficarum.

Perhaps the best way to give you a conception of our power and emplacement here is to note the state and national laws that we are ready to bend, break, violate, and/or ignore. False information is given out routinely on Florida papers of incorporation; tax returns fudge the real sources of investment in our proprietaries; false flight plans are filed daily with the FAA; and we truck weapons and explosives over Florida highways, thereby violating the Munitions Act and the Firearms Act, not to speak of what we do to our old friends Customs, Immigration, Treasury, and the Neutrality Act.

Under Harvey's firm sense of how to deal with newspaper editors, we also control, for practical purposes, most of what gets printed locally concerning Cuba. Our work with the local journalists is often done over drinks and is pleasant enough. Harvey's policy is "never lie to a reporter until you have to." In effect, our publicity department writes the stories. The local Fourth Estate doesn't have to work much, in consequence, and should they choose to resist us, we cut off the pipeline. "Hell, we're no worse than a company town," says Harvey. He likes having the media under his seat.

Such is my purview of JM/WAVE. Yet if I try to explain the mood and morale of the enterprise, I come up short. It is not like anything I have known in the Agency since my early fantasies at the Farm when I thought we'd be engaged in high-risk activity every moment. It's not that we are now, but we do live in the glow of such work. Dix Butler, for instance, was assigned by Harvey as an observer on the day the Green Berets put on a spectacular at Ft. Bragg for Jack Kennedy, and the reports he brought back were luminous with excitement for us, as if the plethora of stunts and physical feats that the Green Berets can pull off is analogous to the boldness of some of our own plans.

The concept of the Green Berets, as I'm sure you know, is to provide special fighting men who can deal with radical guerrilla forces in Third World countries like Laos and Vietnam. Some of the younger mentalities in the Pentagon, plus the President, and Maxwell Taylor, plus, most certainly, Bobby Kennedy, are excited by this training. I will add that in Bobby's book, *The Enemy Within*, there is a telling sentiment: "The great events of our nation's past were forged by men of toughness" and to exemplify it, he offers quick sketches of

Merrill's Marauders and Mosby's Raiders, Francis Marion, the Swamp Fox—in short, our guerrilla heroes. The Green Berets are the natural follow-up to this, and on the day Jack Kennedy visited, he was taken out to McKellar's Lake where an absolute hellzapoppin was put on. Scuba divers swam underwater to fight on shore with waterproofed firearms; skydivers dropped onto the lake beach from free-falls fifteen thousand feet up. Trailing colored smoke, they crisscrossed repeatedly to festoon the sky, only opening their parachutes at the last moment to avoid a fatal splat on impact; judo teams whipped through hand-to-hand battle, and other Green Berets climbed high poles that the Engineers had pile-driven into the lake and then took a great slide down on cables set at steep angles. Caribou and Mohawk helicopters made very low-level passes in front of the Presidential stand, and something like a thousand men who had managed to keep perfectly concealed in the bush on the other side of the lake jumped out with sudden war cries and shot off hand flares—a mock-up of how an infiltration force might assail you. For climax, a man stepped from an airborne helicopter carrying some sort of rocket-pack on his back, and skittered through the air to set down right in front of Jack Kennedy. Then a covey of eight Caribous dropped untold thousands of leaflets over the staging area. Every last one had the President's picture on it.

As I write, I can feel your outrage. It is not that they are doing all that—perhaps it is necessary, you will say—but why, Harry, I can hear you thinking, are you all this excited about it? Well, I am. Dix Butler was even thinking seriously of a transfer to the Green Berets, and I realized that I had joined the Agency on the supposition that my active life would be like that. Perhaps it's due to living with Cal's OSS tales. Life in the Agency is not dull, yet a more adventurous side of myself does feel the need for physical action, and yes, a taste for combat.

Now, you ought to know I am not about to desert Intelligence—never! I feel, on balance, a happy man. I am doing what the greater part of me wants to do. How many can say that? The Green Berets, however, do have a special, even a *clandestine* cachet for a good many Agency officers that colors many an attitude here in JM/WAVE. Dix Butler has his brothers.

For example: the *coyotes*. Dix is liaison to them. I have discovered that there is a grapevine running from Alaska to Miami and all points between. There must be a couple of thousand ex–football players, ex-rodeo riders, ex-stuntmen, bikers, ex-cons, ex-cops, ex-

boxers, unemployed bartenders, itinerant ski bums and surfers, who
have all heard a piece of news about JM/WAVE and/or the craziness
of some of our Cubans; and they come down here for the action. You
would think they would go to the Green Berets but that is too military
for them. They don't want to take all that many orders. All the same,
they would like to hook up with the Agency; they would choose to
become case officers. If I think about it, I do feel sorry for them. "The
first requirement," I would have to tell them, "is to learn how to use
a typewriter." Of course, I just smile when they ask about applying
to the Agency, and say, "Well, contract work right now may be more
in your line," and when they ask how to get that, I reply, "Don't try.
People will come to you."

I hear your question: How do they know that I am associated
with the Agency? Officially, they don't. I keep telling them I am in
electronics to which they nod wisely, but, of course, such conversations only occur when I am out for a night of barhopping with Dix
Butler. He is the jolly friar of this gang and must have good contact
with more than a hundred. He can tell you the athletic record and/or
court file on each one of them, and this, while congenial work for
Dix, is at Harvey's behest. Butler, I have discovered, is once more
doing for Harvey what he did so well in Berlin—he keeps Harvey in
touch with all of the possibilities in the *wider* social environment.

Since we are not using Americans on the raids or infiltrating
(to my knowledge) any Agency men into Cuba itself, there are not too
many contracts for the coyotes. Dix uses them for the occasional
irregular job. Most of their work, however, does not come from the
Agency. Since they tend to band together in various shacks and
boardinghouses around town, a gang of them will often be hired by
one Cuban exile group to lean on another; they become enforcers.
More immediately for us, they hire out as gunmen on proposed
missions to Cuba for certain wealthy Cubans and/or wealthy Texans
who want to put on their own war theatricals. In practice, there is a
hell of a lot of talk, a few hours of casual training, a weekly trip to a
rifle range, many plans drawn and redrawn on the proposed mission,
and then it is invariably scrubbed because passions run down and the
wealthy Cuban loses his nerve. (There is always fear of a DGI reprisal
on family members left in Cuba.) Or else, the coyotes just take the
money and, if they lack respect, fail to show up. And, of course, the
coyotes also deal in marijuana and some of the harder drugs.

For Harvey, they are an excellent source of intelligence on

what the less approved exile groups are up to. A few even qualify for
contract work and find boats for us, or repair them, or run a scuba
diving school for our putative Cuban frogmen.

I have spent evenings with Dix in one or another coyote
abode. We sit on packing crates, or on the floor, or I, as an honored
guest, am given a dangerously flexible old rocking chair, and Dix
holds court while we pass around the bottle of bourbon we've
brought and then drink out of their jug of red wine and toke up.
Bourbon, red wine, and marijuana produce a sledgehammer of a
hangover, but I can't say I don't take to the mixture of off-beat
relaxation and high tension. There is gossip aplenty in these evenings.
One hears about what all the heavy hitters are doing—Fiorini, Masferrer, Kohly, Prio Socarras, the mob. Knowing remarks are made.
"Brickbat has got to be Trafficante's boy," or "Zero-Zero Group is
buying bazookas—they want to pulp one of Fidel's tanks."

"Who is running the purchase?"

"Tiger Turk."

"Tiger Turk is no fire-eater."

"Strictly a wax-nose."

"Well, anybody can get bull-horrors when the feds are on
your case."

"Hell, men," says another, "the feds are right here. They're
getting ready to fuck all of us raff."

This is a reference to Dix and to me. Dix loves it. He takes
a toke, passes it on, speaks while exhaling, "Why don't you little-wigs
stop bitching about John Fate?"

Laughter comes up on this. Of course, the evening is not
entirely without risk. If there are twenty men in the room, Dix could
handle most of them, but there are a few . . . "I might have to extend
myself," he says.

I feel like a weak sister. I assume—I can *only* assume—that I
might have a chance with a third to a half of this crowd, but then you
are dealing with fellows who run from six feet six and three hundred
pounds to a Mexican dwarf named Goliath, nickname Golpe, who is
reputed to be an absolute monster with a knife. (Who could protect
his legs in a knife fight with Golpe?) Dix, however, dares his vengeance every time. He calls him Adobe, much to Golpe's distaste.
Adobe is one more word for Mexican around here.

"Don't say that."

"Well, then, how about *Cuspidor*?"

Uneasy laughter.

It is a curious world. We, at the opposite end of existence in the Agency, are, by contrast, so neat. Yet occasionally, a bona fide cowboy will come out of these coyotes, a contract agent we can count on.

"Gerry H. is pecker, he's paw-paw," is the accolade. Translation: "Nobody has bigger balls."

Most of them are doomed to drink, doomed to blow themselves up. They have female strays whom they call "groupies"—a new word for me. If the woman is a little older and has some personal force, as do some of the bikers' women, they are called "earth mamas." I feel like General Lansdale discovering anthropology.

When you get down to it, not that many nights end in personal warfare or blood (although I have witnessed two in the last month), but there is no such thing as an evening that does not obey the unity of the three themes, drinking, fighting, and (in respect for you) fornication; the only debate is which of the first two might be more important. People come in and out of the shack all night and receive a greeting which, unless there are old friendships or enmities involved, is in direct proportion to whether they have brought more or less wine and booze than they will drink. You have to be *mud* to come empty-handed.

Why am I so taken with this language and these people? Is it because they live their lives with no schedule for tomorrow? Their sense of the present is truly intense. One evening when just a few of us were drinking in a smaller *pad* (another word I like, for God, you do feel a sense of how much humans can act like caged animals), a former stuntman named Ford (who had broken his leg in several places and thereby was out of the one lucrative profession he had found) happened to be fooling around with a newly sharpened bayonet. He kept making knife passes at his best friend, Jim Blood, a.k.a. Oxey, and Oxey, taking a dislike to the implicit threat, punched Ford in the chest whereupon the bayonet flew up into the air and came down on Ford's shoulder. He bled like a just-slaughtered beast on a marble altar. We got towels, newspapers, old shirts—nothing could stop the flow.

"Shit, it's a vein, not an artery," said Ford. "Sew it up."

There was talk of getting a doctor. But a doctor, any doctor, might report it. "Sew it up," said Ford. "It'll be all right."

So, Oxey Blood, just as drunk as Ford, got black thread and

a straight needle, sterilized it with a match, and sewed the wound. It took a while. His fingers were smudged with carbon from the needle, and there were false starts, and once a stitch, half into Ford's deltoid, had to be pulled out again, and all the while I was becoming more and more aware of the stink surrounding the house. We were out in the boondocks twenty miles south of Miami on the edge of a mangrove swamp where the odor of rotting vegetation and dead marine life is strong enough to steer the mind into visions of gangrene. Since the needle had no curve, the stitches had to go straight across for more than an inch, and all you could hear was the grinding of Ford's teeth. He was not going to cry out; between stitches, he drank the last of some oversweet brandy that the rest of us were magnanimous enough to let him have for his own while the job was done. Six stitches. It still oozed blood along a three-inch gash, and will get infected and will scar up like a hump beside a ditch, but the evening was a good one for Ford. He had not cried out. Which we all talked about afterward. In prison, they say you have nothing but the standing achieved by your courage to stand up to other people. Courage may be your only capital, but that buys all the nutrients you need for your ego. I admire the simplicity, and the strength it takes to be that free a man.

Of course, this freedom can prove unrelenting. Dix Butler is suffering from the frustration that he cannot go out on raids with the Cubans he oversees for Harvey. He loves a few of the boatmen. There is one named Rolando (real name Eugenio Martínez) who is a consummate small boat pilot. Rolando, no, let me call him Eugenio, since everyone down here knows him by his real name, is a contract player on a high level, an intelligent, dedicated Cuban who has to be the equivalent of a World War I ace flying many missions. Martínez will take a boat out five or six times a month, and if another trip is needed, there he is, walking through the front door of 6312 Riviera Drive. Now, the standard operating procedure, as worked out in Harvey's basement at Langley, is that the *prácticos*, that is, the boat pilots, are never supposed to see the faces of the Cubans they are bringing in for a landing. The hoods are worn throughout.

Like all projections on paper that involve the exiles, this procedure breaks down. Cuban families are endlessly related. So, in the case of Eugenio Martínez, one of his cousins is often one of his raiders; the two even make jokes about the hood. Dix also knows the cousin, and just before a particularly wild mission, where they were going to set a tire factory ablaze, which could involve a firefight and more than a few casualties, Dix yelled to the cousin as he stepped on board the boat, "Amadeo, bring me back an ear."

"What's it worth to you?"

"A hundred bucks," said Dix.

Amadeo returned with two ears.

Butler pretended to complain, but in fact he came up with $200, whereupon Amadeo took him off to a Cuban restaurant in Key Largo where they spent Dix's money on a feast with two hookers, and accounted for a lot of broken dishes.

I don't know that I should have told you this. Setting the bare facts down on paper can be misleading. I await your answer. I will not say there is no uneasiness in this quarter.

Your reliable correspondent,
Harry

9

March 27, 1962

Dear Lout,

Oh, that mighty circus—JM/WAVE! What is happening to you? Your character, so quick to distinguish nuance, so firm in its integrity, seems to be disappearing. I feel that you want to present yourself as gung-ho, but given the way you write about Dix Butler you seem to be undergoing a high school crush.

Let me remind you of our purpose. With all our abominations and excesses, we are a superior society to the Soviets because there is an ultimate restriction upon our behavior—we believe, most of us Americans, in God's judgment upon us (even if it is the last thing one can ever talk about). I cannot emphasize how crucial such a last inner fear, such a modesty of the soul, is to the well-being of society. Without it, the only thing infinite about human beings becomes their vanity, which is to say, their contempt for nature and society. They generate an inner belief that they know a better way to run the world than God. All the horrors of Communism come out of the vanity that they know that God is only a tool employed by the capitalists. Joseph Stalin's paranoia was the diseased end of such certainty. Ditto Lenin's vanity. Hear me, Harry. I judge myself by the same standard I judge the Communists. Without my belief in God and in judgment, I would be a monster of vanity, and

Hugh would be diabolical. Vanity is the abominable conceit that one could run the world if only one weren't so weak.

Your coyotes—lower-grade psychopaths. You may admire them, but they root around in petty crime like the giddy goats they are, ramrodding it around in the sludge. You must remember. If we are to fight evil with evil (in the belief that under the circumstances it is necessary), we must avoid random wickedness like the plague. I fear for this nation I love so much. I fear for all of us.

Take what I say in the spirit intended. Don't sulk.

Love,
Kittredge

Sulk was not the word. I was pissed off. It occurred to me that Kittredge knew nothing about men. I gave up the thought of explaining to her that the natural condition of men's lives was fear of tests, physical even more than mental tests. Highly developed skills of evasion went into keeping ourselves removed from the center of our cowardice. We took on a profession, and in time, marriage and a family, some of us entered a bureaucracy, and we developed programs for our leisure activities, insulated ourselves in habit. So I could not help it—I admired men who were willing to live day by day with bare-wire fear even if it left them as naked as drunks, incompetent wild men, accident-prone. I understood the choice. It was not one I could ever take on for myself, but I honored them, and if I had a high school crush on Dix, then damn her to hell, and, yes, to hell with her. I did not answer Kittredge.

That gave me time to recollect. On the day I met her, she had just come back from her first go at ice climbing; she was happy. She must have overcome a good bit of bad stuff in herself that morning. I was debating whether to look to send a reply on that basis when a letter arrived at my post office box in Miami. (Since I still visited it every other day, even if it involved rising a quarter of an hour earlier, it is obvious that I was hoping to hear something better from her.)

April 23, 1962

Dear Harry,

You did sulk, didn't you, and perhaps there was cause. There is such cruelty lurking in me. I wonder if you remember that Easter

Sunday afternoon years ago when my father read from *Titus Andronicus*? He would never admit it, but no matter how poor that play, it is one of his secret favorites. I remember he once said: "Shakespeare has the best comprehension of vengeance. He knows. It must not only be dark, but precise. What can be more precise than to cut off a hand at the wrist?"

Daddy's Alpha never got into anything more bloody than an academic skirmish or two, but Daddy's Omega was dark and precise. I think he passed that on to me. I do not know why I take such relish in scourging your manhood. I suspect it has to do with Hugh. I resent how he has preempted this question of being a man until it is now a code unto himself. It gives him whole sanction never to take a backward look. I, who am always peering in all directions, resent Hugh profoundly, and, yes, I know, I take it out on you.

Nonetheless, you have much to learn about the dimensions of manhood. It is the ability to live with responsibility *and* danger that makes a man, and, do you know, I've decided that I admire the Kennedy brothers, Bobby almost as much as Jack, for just that reason. You discover that they are so much more responsible than they ought to be.

Now, I don't want to exaggerate their virtues. They are as silly as most men in many a way, and if one ever had any doubt of it, you need only be given an invitation for a Saturday afternoon at Hickory Hill, as Hugh and I were, to see where misplaced enthusiasm can lead you. Those same Green Berets who so captivated your pen were among the invited, and about twenty of us well-dressed guests were treated to a dozen of those fatuous if strapping young studs jet-popping ten feet above the croquet sward, while others—Tarzanians, I call them—were swinging on ropes from tree to tree. Bobby loved it—I think he suffers from the same set of misplaced affections as you—but then he also loves Hugh. Why? Because Hugh distinguished himself in a touch-football game. How would he not? They don't know that Hugh coached soccer and is still a sinewy concentration of will and gymnastic reflex. I was proud of my bald beau—in fact, he caught the winning touchdown pass. Thank God it was for Bobby's side. So we were in the thick of things at dinner. Afterward came the point of the evening. We were treated to a prestigious lecture.

Since the Kennedys are always trying to break records in all pursuits, Bobby has now decided that Cabinet officials, Presidential

Advisers, and other key White House people ought to establish themselves on the intellectual slope and once a month, therefore, a night
is given over to hearing some distinguished economist or scientist who
is (leave it to the Kennedys) very much in the public eye at the
moment. Sometimes, I think the K's take their cues from *Time* magazine.

Time recently featured the logical positivist philosopher A. J.
Ayer, and so here was Ayer tonight, superb Oxford accent, et al.,
lecturing the Kennedy clan and cohorts on the necessity for *verification*.

Now, Freddie Ayer is a nice enough man personally, or
would be if all of him were merely his Alpha; he is courteous, witty,
decent, all of it. But then there's that arid, sterile, rather ugly Omega
that British philosophers do keep downstairs. The English truly detest
philosophy. Logic is their game. Their minds are happiest when most
resembling their gardens. Culture, to them, seems to consist of lovely
quotes in bloom. Listen to Freddie Ayer talk for an hour on the limits
of philosophy—learn that nothing much is worth retaining in meta-
physics inasmuch as you can't verify most metaphysical propositions.
You come to realize that the logical positivists are trying to cut out all
the Alps and lush forests of the speculative worlds. Perhaps it is to get
us ready for a universe of computers. I may like Freddie Ayer for his
personable qualities, his good manners, especially his pipe, but I do
detest logical positivism. Viscerally. It would consign my speculative
work to the trash bin.

Well, Ayer had his audience. A notable crew full of Rusks and
Galbraiths and Maxwell Taylors and McNamaras. Esteemed ilk. And
of course they were more in agreement with him than not. Logical
positivism, given its ability to euchre the more intangible questions of
ethics out of the game, has to appeal to bureaucrats. So Ayer was
creating his own kind of impressive spell (even if logical positivism
would speak of spells as not worth talking about) when a voice cried
out right into the middle, "Doctor Ayer? Professor Ayer?"

"Yes?"

It was Ethel Kennedy. Now, she is not one of my favorite
folk. She's a study in energy—hordes of children and still active in all
sorts of ways, but she's got an awfully heavy set of mind. It's that
earthy Catholicism which knows all the answers and doesn't think too
much of the questions. "Doctor Ayer," she said, unable to hold herself
in for another moment, "what about God?"

"What do you mean?" he asked.

"Well," she said, "in all you've talked about, there's not one mention of Him."

Ayer was most courteous. That was true, he agreed. In effect, God was outside the purview of logical positivism. This was a philosophy, after all, which concerned itself only with those rational problems whose propositions could be verified.

"Yes," said Ethel, "but where in all of this is God? What do *you* think about God?"

Now, she must have been drinking. She had certainly had a long day as hostess and was now off on a hectoring tone—low stubbornness is the unkind way to put it. "I don't hear anything about God in all that has been said."

"Ethel," came Bobby's voice from the back of the room, *"drop it."*

Professor Ayer went on to the preordained conclusion.

That story has a lot to tell about Bobby. I'm sure his real agreement was with Ethel, but the Kennedy logic is that everybody on the team better get behind a project. The project tonight was to *listen* to A. J. Ayer.

This is a small example of the emphasis placed in Kennedy quarters on loyalty. Jack is blessed. He has a brother devoted full-time to his aims. There is no treachery permitted toward one another in the workings of that family. Which is why, I suspect, they are so successful. I contrast it to the peculiar depth of treachery that existed in my own family, never overt, but I do not think my father or mother ever shared a thought. Alpha marched ostensibly with Alpha and never a voice was raised, but I doubt if there was an hour when the Omega of one was not scheming against the other. In the sacrament of marriage, that is treachery. Some day I will tell you of how they made love. No, I will tell you now. I discovered them one night in Cambridge when I was ten, for their door was open by an inch, and I, often on the edge of sleepwalking in those years, was wandering the halls, so I peered in. Their lovemaking proved another form of treachery. I was not going to, but I *will* tell you now. Maisie was asleep, or most certainly pretending to be, and my father was working his way upon the corpse. I was a junior at Radcliffe before I divined that there might be other ways to make love.

Seen as sweet, attentive, and a dear daughter, I grew up seething at the expanses of frozen waste they had laid into me. Now I specify treachery as the nostrum for the narcissist and the psychopath;

964 N O R M A N   M A I L E R

yes, I suppose that is true. I certainly am intrigued by treachery. A Shakespearean childhood.

The Kennedys, Bobby most of all, are immune. Bobby has absolute loyalty to Jack. There is no question in my mind that he would die for him. Yet they are unalike. Jack, for example, is near to himself. His Alpha and Omega, while at odds about such matters as duty and pleasure, are, I suspect, very much at ease with each other, much like old roommates who know what to expect, and do get along. Bobby has an A and O that inhabit the same room, but neither seems to have the faintest interest in what the other is up to. His Alpha and Omega choose separate associates fully as much as a lover would look for a different kind of companion than would a taskmaster. To see Bobby walking around Hickory Hill with any of his numerous brood is to recognize how much he loves children. He holds their hands with an instinctive delight in the joys of sheltering a child's feelings, and that is a quality few men possess. When he feels compassion for strangers, as I will soon delineate for you, it is comparable to the tenderness he offers to his children. He is very much a lover in that sense, although the love comes forth not as desire but concern. Whereas Jack, under all that calm, is, by contrast, as full of acquisitive desire as a reporter teeming with curiosity about a story he wants to get. Women serve as sources of knowledge for Jack—an express route for coming into contact with the Unknown.

Bobby is a Kennedy and so he, too, is acquisitive. But for results, not people. He takes on new programs as if they were personal conquests. That makes him an overbearing whipmaster to some. I think he lives in the terror that if he does not take on all the important jobs for Jack, everything will bog down. So, at work, from all I hear, he is always in an enormous hurry. His style of cross-examination when trying to find out why something went wrong is nonstop. I probably know better than you of the kind of pressure he puts upon Lansdale and Harvey concerning Mongoose. I can tell you from what Hugh chooses to divulge that being questioned by Bobby Kennedy when he is in a hectoring mood (yes, like Ethel!) is analogous to having adhesive tape removed from every square inch of your body. Unrelenting.

Part of the trouble is that while Bobby wants a great deal from everyone, he cannot always know what to tell others. After all, some of the knowledge he needs cannot be acquired by questioning. In February, he took a trip around the world for Jack, had a stop-off in

Saigon, and announced that American troops are committed to remain in Vietnam until the Vietcong is beaten. That leaves him personally committed to Vietnam, the Green Berets, and all the attendant follow-up. Yet much of April has been taken up with fighting U.S. Steel and Bethlehem on their price rises, and the civil rights problems are with him all the time. Then there is organized crime. He is still trying to get Jimmy Hoffa. He also keeps up a running feud with Lyndon Johnson, whom he despises. J. Edgar Hoover even more. It seems Hoover lets him cool his heels whenever Bobby goes down the hall of the Department of Justice to pay a visit. In return, Bobby has given strict orders to have his Airedale, Binky, exercised in the corridor just outside Buddha's suite of offices. Yes, it's urination and counterurination; Bobby, you see, gives as much to small-sized wars as to large ones, and all the while, Fidel Castro remains paramount in Bobby's emotions, yet does not receive enough real time and attention. On those Thursdays when Bobby sits over for Special Group, Augmented, he is—as Hugh obtains it—just heating up the air to conceal his paucity of knowledge. Bobby's instinct, which can be excellent, is to light the fire beneath any undertaking that is not showing enough progress, then dig into the attendant bureaucracy, convey to those slow-grinding wheels that his own sense of urgency will soon become the most uncomfortable source of heat for them. He can spend a morning saturating some subdepartment of State or Defense or Justice with a set of calls to officials at every level of the hierarchy. Activates the ant's nest from top to bottom. He is awfully good at that. He hates sloth and circular habit. Like many another spark plug, however, he has no patience. He cannot comprehend that because there is a problem, there is not necessarily a solution.

That is why he cannot comprehend Castro, and will not put in the concentration on Mongoose that it needs. Yet he is screaming for results. I would say I understand why Jack and Bobby are so intense on the question. On our second visit to Hickory Hill, I did get into a conversation with Bobby, and he cut me off on Castro. "The man's got to be stopped," he said. "What if he ends up with long-range Russian missiles? Have you thought about that, huh? Have you thought of that? This country could be under the thumb of an irresponsible fellow."

Perhaps the clue is there. They do not begin to understand Castro—that is, they do not know (1) how serious he is, and (2) how flexible. They fear him in the way rich boys are uneasy with poor boys, yes, just like you and your coyotes. Under it all, they obviously admire Castro. Admiration is an intolerable ferment when it resides beneath the skin. So, of course, they have to hate him. If the Kennedys are going to form an admiration society, it will not be for a man who rose to power by fighting through a jungle in which they might have perished, no, when it comes to a fan club, they'll give their plaudits to Robert Frost and Camelot.

Never forget, however, the power of Bobby's compassion. It redeems him. I don't know that he has had a good night's sleep since the Bay of Pigs. He broods over those thousand and more men of the Brigade who sit in Cuban prisons now. For that matter, both Kennedy brothers have shown a superior sense of responsibility. They took on the blame for Pigs when it was not really their fault. I don't know if the greater culpability belongs to the Joint Chiefs of Staff or CIA, but, in fact, when one has to choose between fools, what is there ever to choose? The Joint Chiefs never got around to studying the reality of the problem. Do they sit in a pomade of complacency? I know they never doubted that Castro's air force could not survive a major attack by the exiles' B-26s, nor did they question whether the Brigade would have any real shot of crossing eighty miles of swamp to reach the Escambray Mountains. In turn, Quarters Eye did their best to nudge the Joint Chiefs over to a favorable evaluation of the possibilities; then Quarters Eye used the formal optimism of the Chiefs to convince Jack Kennedy. Of course, the Joint Chiefs never did their homework and all of you managed to lie to yourselves while telling other lies to the Brigade about the military, air, and naval support coming from us. So Jack Kennedy, three months in office, got taken. He was a decent man in response. He accepted the blame. Even Hugh, who is wholly Republican (whenever he can hold his nose long enough to vote), began to respect Jack at that point. And since Pigs, Jack has never stopped feeling responsible. Back in May, when Castro offered to exchange the Brigade prisoners for five hundred bulldozers, Jack induced Milton Eisenhower to form a committee of prestigious Americans who would raise the money. Eleanor Roosevelt, Walter Reuther—immaculate backing. But Goldwater and his Senatorial co-horts killed it. Did you pay attention to that? It was terrible. Goldwa-ter seized the headlines. If we sent tractors to Castro, he said, our prestige "would have to sink even lower." I couldn't believe he would use such a situation to make political capital. God knows what those men are enduring in prison. And Homer Capehart: "If we accept, we will become the laughingstock of the entire world." That pompous ass! And Styles Bridges: "How much more humiliation must be taken from this Communist dictator?" I realized for the first time that no matter what dubious deeds we commit for the Agency from time to time, we are honorable people next to that opportunistic slime. And Nixon! As if honor wouldn't melt in his mouth, he says, "Human lives are not something to be bartered."

In the face of that kind of political abuse, poor Milton Eisenhower quit, and the deal fell through.

Jack has not, however, given up. When the Tractors for Freedom Committee collapsed last June, some exiles started a Cuban Families Committee for the Liberation of the Prisoners of War, and the Kennedys granted them tax-exempt status. The Committee did not get very far, however, through the summer, but recently Castro has been in touch with them and is looking for a deal. As a warrant of his good intentions, he sent back to Miami—as I'm sure you are aware—those sixty crippled prisoners who arrived last week. At Bobby's request (and I was naturally delighted that he thought I would be of value on this) I flew down to Miami to give him a private observer's view of the event. I was more than a little involved, however, with the possibility that you might be there. I was both glad you weren't and also disappointed. (My Alpha and Omega are as far apart as outstretched arms—what *would* it be like to love someone with both halves of oneself?) At any rate, chin up, dear Harry, I soon forgot all about you. There was a crowd of something like fifteen or twenty thousand Cubans jamming the airport, and while Cubans appear to like crowds, I don't. As a privileged witness, however, with last-minute credentials from the Department of Justice, I was able to see from up close how these sixty maimed men, Castro's bait, so to speak, came off the plane, sixty men with year-old wounds, meeting a field of relatives and friends twenty thousand strong, all waving white handkerchiefs. The near relations were, of course, gathered in a nearby chorus of weeping humans. Harry, sixty men came off the plane, all crippled, leg missing on one, arm gone on another, a third was led, eyes shut forever. People were trying to sing the Cuban national anthem, but broke down. How slowly and painfully they came down the ramp. A few knelt to kiss the ground.

As soon as I was back to Washington, Bobby received me in his office and wanted to hear every last detail I could furnish. Just two nights ago, he invited Hugh and myself to meet one of the returnees, a fellow named Enrique Ruiz-Williams (nickname Harry), and he was marvelous, a burly honest fellow, appearing simple in manner until I realized that it was rugged honesty, not naïveté, that one was dealing with. He has one of those deep voices that comes up out of the chest with no impediment as if there is a lot of clear-minded force in the soul and the voice is its natural wind. You realize after a time that the man is exactly what he appears to be. (Which can happen only when Alpha and Omega are in rapport.)

To my pleasure, Harry Ruiz-Williams had had a couple of conversations with Castro, and what I heard intrigued me. During the fighting at the Bay of Pigs, Ruiz-Williams was thrown into the air by an artillery shell and came down with half a hundred pieces of shrapnel in his body and both feet smashed. Bobby later told me that he had a hole in his neck, another wound in his chest, broken ribs and a paralyzed arm.

In such condition, he was, of necessity, left behind in a small house by the sea with other wounded men when San Román and the remains of the Brigade retreated into the swamp. Later that day, Castro arrived with his troops and came to look at the wounded. Williams reached under his pillow for a pistol and tried to fire it. Perhaps he merely made the attempt. He was in a fever and does not remember exactly. He did, however, hear Castro say, "What are you trying to do, kill me?"

Williams answered, "That's what I came here for. We've been trying to do that for three days."

Castro, apparently, was not angry.

"Why wasn't he?" I asked Williams.

"I think," said Williams, "that Fidel Castro saw my answer as a logical response."

Before Williams left Havana with his wounded mates, Castro spoke to him again. "When you get to Miami," he said, "be careful not to talk bad about America because they will get mad. And don't talk bad about me, because I will get mad. Stay in the middle." Irony is obviously in no short supply for Mr. Castro.

In turn, Harry Williams is most impressed by Bobby Kennedy. "When I met him," he told me, "I was expecting to see a very impressive guy, the number-two man in the country. But there I saw this young man with no coat on, sleeves rolled up, his collar open, and his tie down. He looks at you very straight in the eyes. I was able to tell him everything I thought. The United States is responsible, I told him, but the Brigade don't want to play the Communist game."

Since that first meeting, Bobby has been using a good portion of his valuable time to advise Williams. It is typical of Bobby. Politicians expend emotion in about the way successful people invest their money—coldly, and for profit. Jack's honor, therefore, is that he will not express an emotion unless he feels some faint but legitimate glow within; Bobby's honor is to spend emotion lavishly, like a poor man buying gifts for his children. The Brigade has become one of Bobby's orphans. He will not give up on it. He will get them out before it is over.

Devotedly,
Kittredge

10

I HAD BEEN IN MIAMI ON THAT DAY, APRIL 14, 1962, WHEN THE SIXTY wounded members of the Brigade came back to Miami, but I had not been out at International Airport. Harvey had given orders that JM/ WAVE personnel, unless on specific assignment, were not to be present for the occasion. All too many of our Cuban agents might be able to point us out to friends.

If I had known that Kittredge would be there, I would have disobeyed the order, yet, now, reading her letter, I was critical of the tone. I thought she was becoming much too impressed with both of the Kennedy brothers.

One did not have long to brood about it. A note came two days later by way of the pouch.

April 25, 1962
Harry,
        Forgive the shift in method, but wanted to reach you overnight. Sidney Greenstreet, of all people, was over for dinner this evening. Afterward, while doing my best to make conversation with Mrs. Greenstreet, Sidney and Hugh, having settled in the study, got into quite an altercation. You don't often hear my husband raise his voice, but clearly, I heard him say, "You will most certainly take him along, and that's an end of it."

I am reasonably certain you are the person referred to. Keep me informed.

Hadley

That was a name Kittredge took on sometimes when communicating by pouch. And Sidney Greenstreet had to be Bill Harvey. Harlot often referred to Wild Bill as "the fat man."

Kittredge's note gave the alert. I was not surprised when a cable came in for me that morning via LINE/ZENITH—OPEN signed GRANDILOQUENT. It merely said: "Place a call via *seek*." Harlot and I were back to the secure phone.

"I have a job again," were his first words. "Let us promise ourselves it is not too large for you."

"If there are doubts," I answered, "why choose me?"

"Because I've since learned what it was you were working on with Cal. That's good. You never told me. I need someone who can keep his mouth shut. You see," said Harlot, "this looks to be a bit more of the same, although under better management."

"Yessir."

"Rasputin remains the target."

It was a mark of progress that Harlot expected me to grasp what he meant. Rasputin could only be Castro. Who else had ever evaded so many attempts on his life? Of course, there was really no need to use concealment—we were on a secure phone—but Harlot had his penchants.

"The fat man was miserable," he went on, "to learn that I've made you his companion for all this, but then he will grow used to the notion. He had better."

"I have a question. Are you heading this one up?"

"Let's say I'm sharing the bridge with Old Tillers."

"Has McCone given approval?" It was not a proper question to ask, but I sensed that he would reply.

"Don't think of McCone. Heavens, no. He's not equipped."

I didn't have to inquire about Lansdale. Hugh would not invite Lansdale. "What do we call it?" I asked.

"ANCHOVY. A palette of tinted anchovies. Fat man is AN-CHOVY-RED; you are ANCHOVY-GREEN; I am ANCHOVY-BLUE; and Rasputin is ANCHOVY-GRAY. You'll be meeting soon with a gentleman whom Classy Bob used to employ. Johnny Ralston. He will be ANCHOVY-WHITE.''

"And what about"—I did not know how to describe him. Of course, we were secure on *seek*, but given the manners of the moment, I did not want to use his name—"what about Touch-Football?"

"Yes, call him that. Good. Touch-Football. He doesn't really want to know. Just keeps exhorting everyone to bring in *results*, but don't bring his nose into contact with his mind.''

"Yessir."

"You will accompany ANCHOVY-RED everywhere on this venture. Doesn't matter whether he likes it or not."

"Will he call on me every time?"

"He will if he doesn't want any uncomfortable moments with me."

On that, Harlot hung up.

I would not have long to wait. Harvey, I knew, was at Zenith today. My phone soon rang. "Have you had lunch?" he asked.

"Not yet."

"Well, you are going to miss it. Meet me in the car pool."

His Cadillac was waiting, motor running, and I reached the vehicle just enough in advance to open the door for him. He grunted and signaled to me to get in first and slide over. While we rode, he did not speak, and the bad mood that came off the bulk of his presence was as palpable as body odor.

Only when we were on the Rickenbacker Causeway to Miami Beach did he speak. "We are going to see a guy named Ralston. You know who he is?"

"Yes."

"All right. When we get there, keep your mouth shut. I will do the talking. Is that clear?"

"Yessir."

"You are not equipped for this job. As you probably know, you have been handed to me. In my opinion, it is a mistake."

"I'll try to make you change your mind."

He belched. "Just pass me that jug of martinis, will you?"

Along Collins Avenue in Miami Beach, he spoke again. "Not only will you keep your mouth shut, but you will not take your eyes off this greaseball, Johnny Ralston. Keep looking at him as if he's a piece of shit and you will wipe him if he moves. Keep thinking that you are capable of splashing acid in his eyes. Don't speak or he'll know it's nothing but cold piss."

"The picture is clear by now," I said.

"Nothing personal. I just don't think you have the makings for this mode of procedure."

Roselli was living in a brand-new houseboat moored on Indian Creek, across Collins Avenue from the Fontainebleau. Lashed next to it was a spanking new thirty-foot power cruiser with a flying bridge. A slim, well-tanned, sharp-featured man about fifty with elegantly combed silver hair was sitting on the deck of the houseboat, and he stood up when he saw the Cadillac come to a stop. Dressed in a white shirt and white slacks, he was barefoot. "Welcome," he said. I noticed that the houseboat was named *Lazy Girl II*, and the power cruiser moored to it, *Streaks III*.

"Can we move out of the sun?" asked Harvey as he came on board.

"Come inside, Mr. O'Brien."

The living room of the houseboat was more than thirty feet long and was decorated in flesh tones like a suite at the Fontainebleau. Puffed-up furniture full of curves undulated along a wall-to-wall carpet. Sitting at a white baby grand piano, with their backs to the keys, were two girls in pink and orange halters, yellow skirts, and white high-heeled shoes. They were blond and suntanned and had baby faces and full lips. Their near-white lipstick gave off a moon-glow as if to say that they were capable of kissing all of you and might not mind since this was exactly what they were good at.

"Meet Terry and Jo-Ann," said Roselli.

"Girls," said Harvey, speaking precisely between recognition and dismissal.

As if by prior agreement, the girls did not look at me; I did not smile at them. I felt that I was going to be surprisingly good at not saying a word. I was still seething, after all, from my boss's evaluation of me.

Harvey gave a small inclination of his chin in the direction of Terry and Jo-Ann.

"Girls," said Roselli, "go up on deck and get some more tan for yourselves, will you?"

The moment they were gone, Harvey lowered himself distrust-fully to the edge of one of the large round armchairs, and from his attaché case withdrew a small black box. He switched it on and said,

"Let me open our discussion by telling you that I am not here to fart around."

"Totally comprehended," said Roselli.

"If you are wired," said Harvey, "you might as well take it off and get comfortable. If you are operating any installed recording equipment, you are wasting tape. This black box scrambles all reception."

As if in assent, a small unpleasant electronic hum came up from the equipment.

"Now," said Harvey, "I don't care who you dealt with before on this matter, you will at present deal with me and no one else."

"Agreed."

"You agree too quickly. I have a number of questions. If you don't answer them to my satisfaction, I will cut you off the project. If you make noise, I can throw you to the wolves."

"Listen, Mr. O'Brien, do not issue threats. What can you do, kill me? As far as I am concerned, I have visited that place already." He nodded to certify these words and added, "Drinks?"

"Not on duty," said Harvey, "no, thank you. I will repeat: We know why you are in this. You entered the U.S. illegally when you were eight years old and your name was Filippo Sacco. Now you want a citizenship."

"I ought to have one," said Roselli. "I love this country. There are millions of people with citizenship who despise this country, but I, who don't have my passport, love it. I am a patriot."

"There is," said Harvey, "no room to double-cross me, or the people I represent. If you try any tricks, I can have you deported."

"You do not need to talk like a hard-on."

"Would you rather," asked Harvey, "have me say behind your back that I am holding you by the short hairs?"

Roselli laughed. He was all by himself in this merriment but he kept it going for a while.

"I guess, Mr. O'Brien," he said, "you are one total example of a prick."

"Wait until I show you the warts and the welts."

"Have a drink," said Roselli.

"Martini. Scotch over the cubes, spill it out, then lay in the gin."

"And you, sir," said Roselli to me, "what would you like?"

I looked at him and did not reply. It was more difficult than I had expected not to offer small courtesies to people I did not know. Besides, I wanted a drink. Roselli shrugged, got up and went to the bar near the white baby grand piano. Harvey and I sat in silence.

Roselli handed Harvey his martini. He had also mixed a bourbon on the rocks for himself and a Scotch for me which he made a point of setting down on an end table next to my chair, a deft move for Roselli, I decided, since a bit of my attention kept returning to the drink.

"Let's address the positive side of the question," said Roselli. "What if I bring this off? What if the big guy—"

"Rasputin."

"What if he gets hit?"

"In that case," said Harvey, "you get your citizenship approved."

"To success," said Roselli, lifting his drink.

"Now, answer my questions," said Harvey.

"Shoot."

"How did you get into this project in the first place?"

"Classy Bob came to me."

"Why?"

"We know each other."

"What did you do?"

"I went to Sam."

"Why?"

"Because I needed to get to the Saint."

"Why?"

"You know."

"Don't worry about what I know. Answer my questions."

"The Saint is the only man who knows enough Cubans to select the guy who is right for the job."

"What did Sam do?"

"Besides fuck everything up?" asked Roselli.

"Yes."

"He dabbled. He picked a few people. He didn't break a sweat."

"He did, however, get Classy Bob in trouble with the Bureau."

"You are the one who said that."

"You are the one," said Harvey, "who said Sammy fucked everything up."

"I don't know what he did. But I thought we were set to go. Rasputin was supposed to be off the board before the election. Nixon for President. So I ask one question: Did Sam jam the gears?"

"We are referring to October 31 of last year in Las Vegas."

"Yes."

"Sam did it, you say?"

"I," said Roselli, "would rather avoid what I cannot prove."

"Sam," Harvey said, "is bragging that he has worked with some of my associates."

"For a guy with a closed mouth, Sam can open it," said Roselli.

"Why?"

"Vanity."

"Explain that," said Harvey.

"When Sam started out, he was just one more ugly little guy with an ugly little wife. Now, he goes around saying, 'We Italians are the greatest lovers in the world. We can out-do any nigger on his best day. Look at the evidence,' says Sam."

"Who does he say this to?"

"The dummies around him. But word gets out. He brags too much. Vanity. He says, 'Look at the evidence. Two world leaders. Kennedy and Castro.' " Here Roselli stopped. "Forgive me. You mind if I use the names?"

"It's secure," said Harvey, "use them."

"All right," said Roselli, "two guineas like Sammy G. and Frank Fiorini are fucking Kennedy and Castro's broads. Modene may screw Kennedy but she comes back to Sammy, says Sammy, for the real stuff. I would say he has an excessively exaggerated idea of himself. When I first knew Sam G. he used to wear white socks and black shoes, and the white socks was always falling down. That's what a meatball he used to be."

"Thank you," said Harvey, "you are giving me a clear picture."

"Sam is a big man in the States," said Roselli, "Chicago, Miami, Vegas, L.A.—don't mess with him. Cuba, no. He needs the Saint for Cuba."

"And Maheu?"

"His loyalty is to Howard Hughes."

"Is Hughes interested in Havana?"

"Who isn't? Havana will put Las Vegas back in the desert again."

"This collates," said Harvey. "You are not to deal any longer with Bob and Sammy. Consider them untrustworthy and surplus."

"I hear you. I concur."

"Down the hatch," said Harvey. He held out his martini glass for a refill, and after one good gulp, added: "Let's look at the situation with Santos."

"He is the menu," said Roselli.

"Horseshit," said Harvey. "Trafficante works with us, he works with Castro. How are you to trust him?"

"The Saint works with a lot of people. He used to work with Batista. He is close to some of the Batista people today, Masferrer and Kohly. The Saint has friends in Inter-Pen, in MIRR, Alpha 60, DRE, 30th of November, MDC and CFC. I can name a lot of organizations. Around Miami, half the exiles is taking hits on the other half, but the Saint is friends with all. He is friends with Prio Socarras and Carlos Marcello in New Orleans—a very big friendship—and Sergio Arca-cha Smith. With Tony Varona and with Toto Barbaro. With Frank Fiorini. He is friends with Jimmy Hoffa and some of the big oil money in Texas. Why shouldn't he be friends with Castro? Why shouldn't he be friends with you? He will tell Castro what he wants to tell him; he will tell you as much as he feels like telling you. He will do a job for you and do it right, he will do a job for Castro and do it right. His real loyalty—"

"Yes," said Harvey, "the real loyalty?"

"To the holdings in Havana."

"What about Meyer?"

"Santos is also friends with Meyer. He don't worry about Meyer. If Castro goes, Santos will be holding the casinos. That is bigger than being Lansky or Jimmy Hoffa. Santos could become number-one in the mob. That is equal to being the number-two man in America. Right under the President."

"Who taught you to count?" asked Harvey.

"It's a matter of debate. Give me that much."

"If I was Santos," said Harvey, "I would put in with Castro. Castro is there. He can give me the casinos."

"Yes, but then you got to run them for Castro."

"A point," said Harvey.

"Castro will never give the casinos back," said Roselli. "He is keeping them closed. He is a puritan right up the ass. I know Santos. He will come along with us to get Castro."

"Well, I have my hesitations," said Harvey. "There is a little prick with fire coming out of his ears named Bobby Kennedy. He does not cut a deal. Sammy may have helped to bring in Illinois for Jack Kennedy, but the FBI is persecuting Sammy right now. Santos can read that kind of handwriting."

"Santos will take his chances. Once Castro is dead, Santos has a lot of cards to play."

A silence came over both men. "All right," said Harvey, at last, "what are the means?"

"No guns," said Roselli.

"They do the job."

"Yeah," said Roselli, "but the guy who makes the hit would like to live."

"I can get you a high-powered rifle, equipped with a silencer, and accurate at five hundred yards."

Roselli shook his head. "Santos wants pills."

"Pills," said Harvey, "have too many links. Castro has always been tipped off."

"Pills. We need delivery next week."

It was Harvey's turn to shrug. "We will produce the product on date specified."

They spent the next few minutes talking about a shipment of weapons for an exile group that Trafficante wanted to supply.

"I will deliver the ordnance myself," said Harvey.

He stood up, packed away the scrambler, and shook hands with Roselli.

"I'd like you," said Harvey, "to answer another question for me."

"Sure," said Roselli.

"Are you any relation to Sacco of Sacco and Vanzetti?"

"Never heard of the cocksucker," Roselli said.

11

THE CONSCIENTIOUS EFFORT TO LOOK AT ROSELLI AS IF HE WERE something to wipe off the wall, had left me as tired as an artist's model who has been posing in one position for too long. Harvey, who may have been equally tired, did not speak on the ride back, but merely kept filling his glass from the jug of martinis.

As we were getting out of his Cadillac, he said, "When you report to his lordship, tell him to clear Trafficante with Helms. It's rotten meat all the way, and I am not sitting down to this meal alone."

I sent a six-page description to LINE/GHOUL—SPECIAL SHUNT of what had transpired, but all the while that I was writing to Harlot, I found myself debating whether to tell Kittredge as well.

I decided not to. Some material was too privileged. On the other hand, I had to tell her something. I sent, therefore, the following fiction:

April 27, 1962

Dear Kittredge,

The most extraordinary course of action is underway, and I can see why Harvey did not want me as his adjutant, and Hugh thought I was acceptable. You must, however, not indicate to His Nibs that you have even the smallest intuition of what I will tell you, for we are sitting on a good deal—the attempt is going to be made to kidnap Fidel Castro. If successful, we will fly him to Nicaragua un-harmed and let Somoza, who loves publicity, take responsibility. It's the nonaccountability scenario of the Bay of Pigs again, but this time it could work. The Nicaraguans will put Castro on trial. Special laws will be written for the occasion declaring it a major felony for a Latin American statesman to allow Soviet Communism any entrance into this hemisphere. The gamble is that this prodigious theatrical caper will succeed in making Castro look more like an underling than a martyr. And, of course, Cuba will be in disarray.

The dangers are obvious. Our greatest fear is that Castro could get killed in the process, which is why Harvey is now on a talent hunt to recruit only the most special Latin personnel. This also enables me to see why he had so little enthusiasm for taking me on. I am obviously out of my element. On the other hand, given the stakes, Hugh must have wanted someone whom he can trust to report exactly what Harvey is up to.

I will provide more details as our meetings with various extreme exile groups continue. My next letter will, presumably, be longer. Refer to the op, incidentally, as CAVIAR.

Devoted to the facts, ma'am,
Herrick

The mendacity did not bother me. In truth, I felt pleased with my ingenuity. If Castro was assassinated, I could ascribe it to a failed kidnapping; if nothing occurred, well, the job proved too difficult.

On the same day, a letter from Kittredge crossed. I offer an extract from it.

. . . Don't be dismayed if I have been sounding grandiloquent lately. The reason I wish to know so much about what you are doing is not because I am suffering under the weight of so Faustian an ambition as to comprehend the Agency and guide the Brothers K through perils ahead, no, my motive is essentially modest provided we disregard the prodigious announcement I wrapped around it. In truth, I need to know much more about everything if I am ever to be able to write about Alpha and Omega in many walks of life. I get out, of course, and I do meet people, but I know so little of how the real gears work in that hard fearful real world out there.

I was stricken on reading this passage. Kittredge wanted to know how the real gears worked and I was designing surrealistic machinery for her. A line came back to me from a book whose title I could not recall—"For it's exactly when we come closest to another, that we are turned away with a lie, and blunder forward to comprehend ourselves on the misperceptions of the past."

Now I was agitated. I had to remind myself that she could also play games, and some were not particularly attractive. I returned the following note:

April 28, 1962

Kittredge,

It is some months now. What is it you have been waiting to tell me about Modene? Half-loves die best when fully buried.

April 30, 1962

Harry dearest,

I owe ten thousand apologies. I haven't had the time to write the full letter that this subject deserves. Since I have thirty pages of transcript you haven't seen, I am tempted to send it to you in a stout package, but I know that I owe you a summing up and will try to provide it. Allow some time.

In the interim, keep me abreast of CAVIAR. I can't believe your last letter. No wonder the fat man is a legend. And Hugh! How fortunate is society that he did not choose to become a master criminal.

May 1, 1962

This is written in a great hurry, Kittredge.

Three days ago, I flew up to Washington, picked up some knockout drops from TSS that will be used for CAVIAR, and flew back the same day. The following noon, Harvey and I met with an Italian-American representative of the Nicaraguans in the cocktail lounge of the Miami Airport. This Italian who walks among us as one Johnny Ralston was wearing a custom-tailored silk suit with a silver sheen to match his hair, alligator shoes, and a gold watch. Harvey was wearing his usual white shirt and black suit, sweat stains in the armpits from the shoulder holster, and his shirt was blousing up above the belt from the other handgun he packs in the small of his back. I was feeling like an impostor. (I was wearing a tropical shirt.) Harvey had his double martinis, Ralston sipped Stolichnaya on the rocks, and the four capsules I had transported were duly passed from hand to hand.

After drinks we went out to the airport parking lot where Harvey pointed out a van to Ralston. I had been busy since 6:00 A.M. renting that particular U-Haul and helping to fill it with about $5,000 worth of Czech rifles, East German handguns, and various explosives, detonators, radio transmitter-receivers and one fine piece of boat radar from our JM/WAVE warehouse. Harvey merely handed the van keys over to Ralston and we all walked away. Once again I discovered that even the cleanest transfers of this sort do bring out a drop of sweat in the small of the back.

Later that afternoon, hell broke loose of another variety. Bobby Kennedy was down for a couple of hours to look over JM/WAVE, and so Harvey took him on a tour through the halls of Zenith. Needless to say, they are not happy in each other's company. In the Message Center, Kennedy wandered off by himself and started reading the code-outs on a few of the cables. One of them certainly caught his eye, doubtless a piece of information he could whip out at the next gathering of Special Group, Augmented, so he tore it off the roll and started for the door.

Harvey raced after, "Here, you, mister!" he yelled out. "Just hold on. Hold on! Where do you think you are going with that piece of paper?"

Kennedy stopped as if shot. Harvey, catching up, was now able to pay him back for a few of those scalding SGA sessions. "Attorney General," he boomed out—no small voice today!—"do you know how many message indicators and operational codes are salted onto that message? I can't let you out of this room with such a piece of paper," and so speaking, he grasped culprit paper with one hand and opened Bobby's fingers with the others. I can't conceive of what the ultimate repercussions of this will be.

Yours—H.

May 4, 1962

Dearest H.,

About a month ago, Hugh and I were invited to a small supper at the White House, and before we left, Jack took me aside for ten minutes and told me in strict confidence that he had had an extraordinary lunch that day with J. Edgar Hoover. I don't know why I was chosen as confidante—can it be my virtuous face? You and I know, however, what a poor choice Jack made! Secrets sit in me about as comfortably as half-triggered tumors. I wanted to pass the little fact on to Hugh, but, at some pain, didn't.

Now I discover that I want to tell you. It burns in me with an unholy fever. I sense that Hoover was talking to Jack about Sammy G. and Modene. The transcripts you have not yet seen do suggest a purpose for Hoover's visit.

You are aware, of course, that Modene, no matter what kind of blow she received last summer when Jack suggested she might be telling tales out of school, was pleased to be invited again to the White House at the end of August; she certainly sounds happy describing it to Willie. According to Modene, Jack told her that he loved her. I don't know whether to believe it. Polly Galen Smith confided to me that one of Jack's virtues is never to mix sex with love. He told Polly that a woman ought to have an understanding from the outset whether it can or cannot be a question of love. Jack does seem irrationally sweet on Modene, however, and it may be that she satisfies some virtually lost side of him—maybe it is that carefree Omega fellow who might have preferred to be a ski bum, or a Newport deckhand, addicted to sun and sea and splendid vacations, but is serving at present under lock and key to Presidential Alpha, always on the job.

After an Indian summer Saturday or two, Jack and Modene move on, however, to the cold fall. His back begins to bother him again. The unmistakable impression is that they have passed their high mark as lovers. Now, as she expresses it to Willie, "he wants me to be the one who makes love."

"Well, you told me he is a very tired man," says Willie.

"Maybe," says Modene, "he just likes being tired a little too much."

This is the ugliest remark Modene has so far uttered on the subject, but in late November she says, "I dread getting a call from the White House. I love Jack, but I don't enjoy seeing him in that place."

Harry, I know what she is talking about. The White House, for all its patriotic pull, does give off the grave and measured consensus of a courthouse. I think the old manse has lived through too many weighty compromises and suffered the platitudes of a few too many powerful politicians. I exaggerate these negative aspects because Polly Galen Smith, having had her several trysts in the same quarters, tells me that the White House could be affecting Jack. "It certainly seems to be draining his appetite," she said to me once.

All the while, Modene is seeing more of Giancana, although irregularly. He is not wholly dependable. For example, this last October, just two months after they first went to bed, Sam shifted his attentions from Modene back to Phyllis McGuire and traipsed around Europe for a month with the singer. Either Mr. G., like Modene, needs two lovers, or can it be that he was furious at Modene for continuing to see Jack? In any event, as I discovered, their affair had not been wholly consummated. The evidence had seemed clear to me at the time, but I did not read the relevant transcript with Willie on August 16 skillfully enough.

MODENE: Well, I finally said yes to Sam.

WILLIE: I can't believe he was willing to wait all these months.

MODENE: It has been more than a year. And every day there were six dozen yellow roses.

WILLIE: You never got tired of receiving all those roses?

MODENE: I cannot have enough of them.

WILLIE: All right. How was it with Sam?

MODENE: I cannot have enough of him.

WILLIE: You are really telling me?

MODENE: It was virtually complete.

WILLIE: What does that mean, virtually complete?

MODENE: Figure it out for yourself.

As I say, I did not recognize we were being given a description rather than a performance rating. After that sole indication, Modene would not refer to relations with Sammy for quite some time, although Willie was always after her for more. The following is from early November 1961:

WILLIE: Why did he ask you to marry him if he was going to disappear with his singer?
MODENE: He happened to be very unhappy when I told him that my first loyalty is still to Jack.
WILLIE: But you told me that Sam has it over Jack.
MODENE: He is more demonstrative. Sam shares himself with you. He has a lot of gusto. It's as if you are both eating Italian food out of the same plate.
WILLIE: And Jack is a one-way street.
MODENE: Yes, but I am the woman on his street. Sam knows that. He knows there is one thing I share with Jack that I will not get into with Sam.
WILLIE: And what is that?
MODENE: The last thing.

I will protect you from the three pages of transcript that ensue before we learn that "the last thing" is, carnally speaking, the first. Sam has never been allowed to enter Modene. So, three pages later:

WILLIE: I can't believe it.
MODENE: We do everything but.
WILLIE: How can it be so good then?
MODENE: It is earthy. Sometimes I think sex can be more intimate that way.
WILLIE: You're too sophisticated for me.

On Sam's return from Europe, he shows Modene a great many good times in Chicago. At the hangouts, she is treated like a queen. In bed, it remains *everything but*. I will not judge her. Years ago, I remember putting your nose out of joint by confessing that Hugh and I had an Italian Solution. All the same, it irked me that I could not quite grasp Modene.

It is later than I expected. Tomorrow I will write about the second and true seduction of the lady. Bear with me.

Love,
Kittredge

12

THE PROMISED LETTER DID ARRIVE THE NEXT DAY, BUT NO LONGER exists. As soon as I read it, I destroyed it.

I do not regret that altogether. It brought me to recognize how intensely I had been mourning the loss of Modene. I could even feel the loss in my fingers as they fed the last page to the paper-shredder. I was in a fury at Kittredge for sparing no details.

All the same, it is a loss. One of Kittredge's best letters is gone, and my literary task might be simpler now if I had it before me. Much later, sixteen years later, I did, however, obtain, in 1978 (by way of a senator's aide), a copy of the transcript upon which Kittredge based her letter, and it will have to suffice. Let me not make too much of it. A good many years have gone by.

In January of 1962, Modene's parents were in an auto accident. Her father took a turn at high speed, hit a patch of ice, and ended upside down in a ditch. Her mother escaped unscathed, but the father was left in a coma; the only question was whether it would take a few days or several years for him to die.

Modene grieved to a surprising degree. As she confessed to Willie, she had hated her father for years. When drunk, he had treated her mother badly. Nonetheless, she felt herself to be very much like him. At the end of a week-long visit home, she wept in her mother's arms because now she could never come close to her father, and she had always assumed that would sooner or later transpire.

After Modene returned to work, however, she felt recovered, and was surprised at how little her father's condition now seemed to affect her. Then, a week later, on a three-day visit to Chicago, she discovered that she was at the border of a nervous collapse. She could not sleep for fear that her father seemed to have died; he seemed to be visiting her in the dark. Yet, in the morning when she called Grand Rapids, he was still alive—in coma, but alive. (It may be worth noting that Kittredge, in a monograph called *Half-States of Mourning in the*

Dual Persona, was subsequently to suggest that mourning, like love, was rarely experienced in anything like equal proportion by Alpha and Omega. Indeed, in troubled cases, when a territorial war over mourning rights waged within the psyche, the appearance of ghosts became a not uncommon manifestation.)

After the second night of such visitations, Modene felt ravaged. Giancana, in deference to her practice of never spending an entire night with him, came to her hotel room to pick her up for breakfast. Quick to sense the depth of her disturbance, he told her that he would make a few calls and then devote the day to her.

On this occasion, then, he did not take her from bar to clubhouse for his meetings, but had a picnic hamper put together with several bottles of wine, a quart of bourbon, the accompanying ice, and told her in a calm voice that they would have a private and personal wake, and he would help her to bury the ghost of that father who was not yet dead. He had a handle on such things, Giancana stated.

Driving his old sedan, he confided to her that he could get close to her father because he, Sam, could have been a motorcycle racer himself, and to prove the remark, gave her a demonstration as they drove out through the shabby, working-class back streets of West Chicago, whipping corners at high speed to demonstrate how a skid-turn could be taken at the last moment under "conditions impossible for other drivers. I could have been a stunt man," said Giancana. "So could your father." He drove that day out on South Ashland Avenue to a squat, dark church called the Shrine of St. Jude Thaddeus. "This place," Sam said, "is not named for Judas, but Saint Jude. He is the saint for special cases, the hopeless cases, doomed people."

"I am not doomed," she told him.

"Put it this way. He takes care of the stuff that's out of line. My daughter Francine had eyesight so bad she was almost blind, but I brought her here. I'm no churchgoer. All the same, I made a full novena, nine visits, and Francine's eyes got to the point where she can see with contact lenses. They say St. Jude gives intercession for those who are without hope."

"I do not see myself as without hope."

"Of course not. But this is a special case concerning your father."

"How do you expect me to come here nine times?"

"You don't have to. I've done the nine. I carry the intercession."

She knelt and prayed at one of the smaller chapels of St. Jude and was painfully aware of other people who prayed with her. "Crippled people," as she would describe it later to Willie. "Some of them looked insane. There was the oddest mood in the place. I felt my father was very near to me and he was angry. 'You are praying for me to die,' I heard him say in my ear, but I was in a far-off mood, as if I was learning how to live in a cave. St. Jude's is like that. Very much so. I felt as if I was in one of the old Christian caves. Maybe that was because there was not much ornamentation on the walls. It's a poor church."

After they left St. Jude's, he drove out to a cemetery whose name she never noticed, but his wife, Angelina, he told her, rested there. Within the dim but expensively illumined interior of a mausoleum, kept always at seventy degrees, he set out the picnic hamper on the stone floor in front of the stone bench on which they sat. While they ate and drank, he repeated the account he had given her once of life with Angelina. She had been short in height and thin, and ill from birth with a spinal defect. Yet he loved her. Angelina, however, had not really loved him, not for years. "She still lived with the memory of her original fiancé who died young. She was faithful to his memory. I had to win her over," said Sam, "and I succeeded. After she died, she used to come to visit me at night. Believe me. On her invitation, I would visit this mausoleum." As he spoke, they ate and they drank and began to kiss.

At this point, I will use the copy of the transcript.

WILLIE: You began to kiss him in that mausoleum?

MODENE: There was nothing wrong with it. Do you have any conception of how hungry you can be for a live person's mouth when there has been a tragedy in the family?

WILLIE: I can follow you, I guess.

MODENE: Well, you are always asking me what really happened.

WILLIE: I would rather be shocked than frustrated.

MODENE: You will be shocked. Sam is no ordinary man. He understands all the things that I start drinking to stop thinking about. He told me again how the Sicilians understand dead people, and ghosts, and curses, and can find a way through situations where other people would be lost. He told me that Angelina would have to help us if I cooperated with him. He had taken me to this place, to her mausoleum, because we had to show Angelina that we were not afraid of her. For that, we would have to do something we had not done before.

WILLIE: What?

MODENE: We had to fuck.

WILLIE: Did he use the word?

MODENE: Yes. He stopped using it in front of me months ago, but now he said we had to fuck right there in front of her. He said that he had never forced it on me because he was a little afraid of Angelina himself, but now he wanted to do it. He loved me. He was prepared to take a chance on things going wrong for him also.

WILLIE: This sounds awfully sick and crazy to me.

MODENE: Wait until you are invaded by a ghost. Maybe your idea of what is acceptable behavior will go through a change.

WILLIE: You actually agreed to do it with him right there?

MODENE: He took a blanket out of the picnic hamper and spread it on the floor. I lay down and let him put it in me for the first time. Then I stiffened. I would not allow him to finish.

WILLIE: Oh, my God, after all that?

MODENE: I felt her presence. It was as if an old gypsy woman was whispering in my ear. She was saying, "Enough is enough." I thought she was right. It froze me. Sam and I started to argue right on the floor. I was as tight as a clenched fist. "It's all right," I told him, "but we have to finish somewhere else or none of it will work." Do you know, he understood. He got up, he got dressed, he was very flushed, and I have to tell you that he looked sexier than I have ever seen him. He picked up everything, put it in the hamper, and drove me over to his house. I have never been more sexually excited in my life.

WILLIE: You have said as much before.

MODENE: Never like this. I couldn't wait to get to his house. It was spooky in the tomb, but now I felt wild. I hate to say this, but do you know, Sam has an odor to his private parts that reminds me just a little bit of oil and gasoline, and that reinforced my impression that he could do something about my father.

WILLIE: I don't know if I want to follow any more of this.

MODENE: You asked for it, and you can listen to it. When we reached Sam's house, we rushed down to the private office in the basement where he has his serious meetings with the mob, and after he locked the door, we tore off our clothes and made love on the carpet of the floor. I kept thinking of all the

men who walked through there and I am sure that Sam has
made some decisions around that table to kill people—and, I
have to say that had me so excited that I was ready as soon as
he was. Afterward, we just lay there loving each other. Do
you know, when I got back to my hotel that night, there was
a message to call my mother. She told me that my father had
died just that afternoon, and I said, "Mother, I am so happy
for all of us."

One comment in Kittredge's letter I do not forget:

Do you know, Harry, much as I would like to believe that
this is a pure manifestation of Giancana's Omegic powers, I must also
—thanks to living with Hugh—contemplate the possibility that Sam
sent out orders that morning to locate some compliant orderly in her
father's hospital who, for the appropriate *pourboire,* would pull the
plug. Having some idea of how difficult such matters can be to
arrange, I lean, I confess, to the occult explanation, but do feel obliged
to recall us to Hugh's epistemological dilemma: "Do we enter the
Theater of Paranoia or the Cinema of Cynicism?"

13

MY KNOWLEDGE OF J. EDGAR HOOVER'S LUNCH WITH JACK KENNEDY
is based on no more than the fact it took place and Kittredge told me
about it. Nonetheless, I was to think of that curious meal many times
over the years until it took on the incontrovertible confidence we
usually reserve for the validity of a few uncommon memories. What
I am offering, then, is a conceit, yet I am ready to pledge that it could
not have been otherwise.

I do recall one detail that Jack imparted to Kittredge. It is no more
than that Hoover refused an aperitif before lunch, but then one fossil
bone is enough to give us the dimensions of a dinosaur.

"Well, I'll drink to your health, if you won't to mine," said Jack
Kennedy. "Sure you wouldn't care for a Campari? I've heard you are
partial to Campari."

"That is not, I would say, highly accurate," was the reply. "I have been known on rare occasions to say yes to a martini during the midday break, but for today, soda." After a sip from his glass, Hoover proceeded to say, "I am disappointed that Mrs. Kennedy is not joining us for lunch."

"She went up to Hyannisport yesterday with the children."

"Yes, now that you remind me, I heard as much. I suppose her trip to India had to take something out of her."

"It's just you and me," said Kennedy, "per your request."

"At my request, yes it was. Well, I regret not being able to say hello to your beautiful wife. I thought, incidentally, she was most impressive in that tour she provided of the White House for our television audience. In my opinion, she is a notable asset to the White House."

"Certainly is," said Kennedy, and asked, "Do you have time, Mr. Hoover, to watch television?"

"As much as work and engagements permit, which is not frequently, but I do enjoy TV."

"Oh. Tell me. What might be your favorite program?"

"A couple of years ago it was *The $64,000 Question*. I confess to thinking that I might have won no inconsiderable sum if I had ever appeared on such a show in a category suitable to myself."

"I expect you would have done famously."

"We aren't going to have the opportunity, are we? It was so discouraging to me, as one of untold millions of viewers, to find out that the producers were rigging the results. What a sordid example of corruption in supposedly respectable places. I really cannot forgive Charles Van Doren."

"That's interesting," said the President. "Why do you single him out?"

"Because there's no excuse. How can a boy with all his advantages engage in felonious activity? Ethnic people are always claiming that their poverty is their excuse, but what claim can Charles Van Doren make for accepting the winning answers in advance? I lay it at the feet of Ivy League permissiveness." He sipped at his soda. "To happier subjects. I can tell you I was enthralled by John Glenn's three orbits. No doubt the Russians now feel our breath on their back."

"I am glad to hear you see it that way," said Kennedy, "because it sometimes feels like we're a mile behind them in a five-mile race."

"I have no fears. We will catch up."

Into lunch they went.

Over the vegetable and barley soup, the President referred to the one hundred points that Wilt Chamberlain had scored in an NBA game.

"When was that?" asked Hoover.

"About three weeks ago. You must have heard. It is an astonishing feat."

"Well, I did," said Hoover, "hear of it, but do you know, basketball is not a sport to elicit my interest."

"Really?"

"It's boring. Every twenty-four seconds, ten giants leap up in the air for the ball."

"Yes," said Kennedy, "and there is not much to do about it, is there?"

"Well, I don't know what you mean exactly."

"I, for one, am impressed with the way colored athletes seem to be taking over the game," said Kennedy.

"Aren't you leading my conclusion?" asked Hoover. "I did not say they were *Negro* giants going up for the ball."

"For fact, you didn't."

"I am ready to champion the more respectable Negro aims, but, then, you may have touched on the problem. These people seem to show more aptitude for producing great athletes than great leaders."

A Yankee pot roast was served with boiled potatoes and peas. When the waiter, who was black, had left the room, Jack Kennedy said, "I don't know that I would hesitate to name Martin Luther King as a great leader."

"Well, I would," said Hoover. "I would have a ton of hesitation about naming him anything positive."

"You are expressing a strong reaction, Mr. Hoover."

"I never employ strong language until I do, Mr. President. Martin Luther King is the most notorious liar of our time, and I can prove it. If the day should ever come when you may need it, I warrant that I have enough on Martin Luther King to cool off a few of his more outrageous demands."

"Yes," said Kennedy, "and one of these days you are going to let me into those special files, aren't you, Mr. Hoover?"

"Actually," said Hoover, "as it happens, I am here today because of my concern on just such another matter in my files."

"Revolving, in particular, about what, might you say?"

"Well," said Hoover, "it does revolve in some particular around the associations of one of your friends."

"Which one," asked Jack Kennedy, "of my friends?"

"Frank Sinatra, I would say."

"Frank does have a wide range of associations."

"Mr. President, this is not a pumped-up newspaper case of an entertainer shaking hands at various tables in a nightclub. This concerns Sinatra's ongoing ties with Sam Giancana, one of the very top figures in the Mafia. It also concerns a young lady who seems to have shared her favors with both gentlemen, and we have reason to believe, with others as well."

Kennedy was silent.

Hoover was silent.

"Would you like coffee?" asked Kennedy.

"I think I would."

The President rang a bell and the colored waiter brought it in. When he was gone, Kennedy said, "This, then, is the size of it. You are suggesting that my friend Frank Sinatra ought to watch his association with Sam Giancana."

"Yes," said Hoover, "that would take care of most of it. There could be one loose end."

"How loose?"

"I would call it loose. The young lady with promiscuous connections is named Modene Murphy, and she seems to be most friendly with one of the President's secretaries here in the White House."

"How extraordinary. I will have to look into that. I can't imagine how you could pick up anything on our lines."

"We can't. We wouldn't. You may sleep soundly on that. It's just that given Miss Murphy's continuing link with Sam Giancana, we thought it requisite to obtain entrance into her telephone traffic. That was not routine. Mr. Giancana sends his people around regularly to check her equipment. However, we did obtain enough short-term insertion to be able to verify that she is, on occasion, in contact, sometimes for a few days consecutively, with White House circuits."

He sipped his coffee. "I will let the matter rest at your discretion," he said and stood up. "When Mrs. Kennedy comes back from Hyannisport, please give her my regards."

They talked about spring training as they walked to the door. Mr. Hoover was going down to St. Petersburg to catch a few days with

the Yankees, and Jack Kennedy asked him to convey his regards to
Clyde Tolson, who would accompany Mr. Hoover. Mr. Hoover said
he would.

14

A FEW WEEKS LATER, BY WAY OF FBI REPORTS SENT FROM KITTREDGE
to me, I was to learn that on the day following J. Edgar Hoover's
lunch at the White House, my father, still in Tokyo, became the
recipient of a cable from Buddha himself. THE CRIMINAL DIVISION OF
THE DEPARTMENT OF JUSTICE HAS REQUESTED THAT CIA SPECIFICALLY
ADVISE WHETHER IT WOULD OBJECT TO CRIMINAL PROSECUTION
AGAINST THE SUBJECT MAHEU FOR CONSPIRACY TO VIOLATE THE WIRE
TAPPING STATUTE. AN EARLY REPLY WILL BE APPRECIATED.

Then, on April 10, 1962, Hoover sent this memo to Assistant
Attorney General Miller in the Department of Justice:

> Boardman Hubbard has now advised that prosecution of
> Maheu would lead to exposure of most sensitive information
> relating to the abortive Cuban invasion in April 1961. In view of
> this, his Agency objects to the prosecution of Maheu.

Bobby Kennedy then called a meeting on May 7 with Lawrence
Houston, the CIA General Counsel, and Sheffield Edwards, the Director of the CIA's Office of Security. In response to the Attorney
General's pointed questions, they were obliged to admit that Maheu
had offered Giancana $150,000 to kill Castro. At this juncture, as
Sheffield Edwards would recount it to Harlot, Robert Kennedy said
in a low, precise voice, "I trust that if you ever try to do business with
gangsters again, you will let the Attorney General know."

On May 9, there was a meeting between Robert Kennedy and
J. Edgar Hoover after which Hoover penned a memo for his personal
file:

> I expressed great astonishment at such Agency activities in
> view of the bad reputation of Maheu and the horrible judgment
> of using a man of Giancana's background for such a project. The
> Attorney General shared the same views.

From an out-of-channels note written by Hugh Montague to Richard Helms two days later:

> Had a talk with the Sibling. Sibling said he had seen Buddha and would never forgive us for this one. Said the worst was that Buddha insinuates, although not for the record, that it was the Labor Lord who first put Sir Chipmunk up to offering us Rapunzel and his warren of friends. I replied that this, while not verifiable (shades of A. J. Ayer), did have to be mind-boggling, and the remark enabled me to traverse the abominable abyss just long enough to get out of his office. We are having to bury so much under the carpet that I fear the lumps will soon be felt by the common toe.

In the margin are my penciled notes:

the Labor Lord—Hoffa, doubtless
Sir Chipmunk—can only be Maheu

On May 14, five days after Hoover had visited Bobby Kennedy, William Harvey, on instructions from Harlot, called Sheffield Edwards to say that should the Attorney General inquire, he could be informed that no employment of Roselli was being contemplated. Edwards said he would put a memo to that effect in his files.

Now that there was a piece of paper pointing in the wrong direction, Harvey contacted Roselli, who said that the pills had gotten through to Cuba. "Let's use them," said Harvey.

During all of this period, FBI surveillance of Giancana intensified.

MODENE: I feel ready to throw up before we even leave for the airport. I know there will be FBI men waiting for us, and I have learned to recognize them. They stand out like penguins.

WILLIE: You are exaggerating.

MODENE: When a person has one thing on his mind, and only one thing, he stands out in a crowd. From the moment we approach the gate, I can see them. They used to follow us quietly, but now they come up and speak loudly. They want everyone to hear them. "What do you do for a living, Giancana?" they ask. "That's easy," Sam tells them, "I own Chicago. I own Miami. I own Las Vegas." It happened twice in a row as we were getting on a plane. Sam began to think he was in control of it. "They've got no answer, Modene," he told me. "They are working on salary, and that's the end of their story."

WILLIE: Well, I guess he knows something about how to give it right back.

MODENE: Yes, but he doesn't know when to stop. The last time we took a trip together, Sam changed the ending. He said, "I own Chicago, I own Miami, I own Las Vegas. What do you own, empty pockets?"

Well, he happened to make this remark to the one FBI man we can always count on running into in Chicago, a big fellow with a crew cut who scares me. He is always so tense. He obviously wants to lay hands on Sam. The moment Sam spoke the words "empty pockets" this agent's eyes started boiling. I don't know how to express it otherwise. He turned right around and said to all the passengers waiting to get on the plane, "Here is Sam Giancana. Look at him. He is the most notorious cheap hoodlum in the world. He is scum. You are going to be sitting on this plane with the most complete piece of filth you will ever see in your life."

They had never done anything like this to Sam before. "Shut your mouth," he said, "or I'll take you on myself."

I was frozen. Sam is half the agent's size. And the agent got the most frightening look. "Oh, Sam," he said, "throw the first punch. Please throw the first punch." He was almost crying he was saying it so softly.

Sam managed to control himself. He turned his back on the agent and did his best to ignore him, but the big fellow kept saying, "Please, Sammy-boy, take a poke. Take the first poke, you yellow piece of filth." I'm not certain, but I know Sam had to be frightened. He turned as pale under his suntan as if he had a skin beneath the skin. "I can't get on this plane," he said to me. "I can't sit for three hours."

WILLIE: What about your bags?

MODENE: I made the mistake of saying just that to him. "Let's get out of here," he shouted, and we started down the corridor with the FBI men yelling and screaming at us as if they were as crazy as reporters. And the agent kept muttering in a low voice so only we could hear, "Two pounds of shit in a one-pound bag."

WILLIE: I can't believe FBI men would be so crude.

MODENE: It is my experience that they get a little unbalanced around Sam. I think they are very angry that they don't have anything on him they can prove. Sam is too smart for them. Even under these circumstances, he actually got the last word. As we were stepping into a cab, Sam turned to the big agent and said, "You lit a fire tonight that will never go out."

"Is that a threat?" the man asked.

"No," said Sam, quietly and politely. "It is a statement of fact." The agent actually blinked his eyes.

Then the FBI followed our cab all the way to Sam's house, but Sam didn't care. "They can wait outside all night and get bit by mosquitoes." We went downstairs to his office which he says is 100-percent wiretap-proof and he called some of his people and told them to come over.

WILLIE: Wouldn't the FBI spot them walking in?

MODENE: What does it matter? They've seen the same people meet with Sam a hundred times. If they can't hear what is being said, what can they gain?

WILLIE: You have really learned how it works.

MODENE: I am full of love for Sam.

WILLIE: I think you are.

MODENE: I am.

WILLIE: Then you are really over Jack?

MODENE: I am full of love for Sam. He told me that he never confided in a woman in his life, but that I was not like others and he could talk to me.

WILLIE: Tell me. What did he confide?

MODENE: I don't know if I can. I promised Sam I wouldn't use my own line anymore, and now I am breaking the promise. But I just can't stand those pay phones.

WILLIE: I thought your line is swept clean.

MODENE: Even so!

WILLIE: Tell me. I can feel that your line is clean.

MODENE: Sam said he hated Bobby Kennedy. That he has hated him ever since he had to go up before the McClellan Committee back in 1959 when Bobby was their Special Counsel. You know how witnesses say, "I refuse to answer on the

grounds that it might incriminate me"? Well, Sam was worried about that. Apparently, he had such a bad time in school.
He could not learn how to read. He said he still wants to
giggle when he has to read aloud. Bobby Kennedy kept
asking questions like "Did you dispose of the victim by burying him in concrete?" and Sam would try to read aloud from
his card about not incriminating himself, but would giggle.
Bobby then said: "I thought only little girls giggled."

　　　Sam told me he still gets the sweats when he remembers.
It was in spite of Bobby that he worked for Jack. Sam assumed
that Jack would call off the FBI. That would be his revenge
on Bobby. Only it didn't work out.

WILLIE: Is Sam angry with Sinatra?

MODENE: He is furious. Sam thinks I don't know a word of Sicilian
　　but I have a very good ear and I have picked up a little.
　　Whenever his people say *farfalletta*, they are talking about
　　Sinatra.

WILLIE: What do they mean?

MODENE: *Farfalletta* is a butterfly.

WILLIE: How did you find out?

MODENE: Because Sam's people use their hands a lot to express a
　　thought.

WILLIE: Yes, but how did you know that they were talking about
　　Frank?

MODENE: Because they also say Sinatra. Or Frankie. While they
　　are using their hands. This night, it was obvious to me that
　　Sam was telling them how disgusted he is with Sinatra. A
　　couple of them started to talk about squashing the butterfly.
　　They would mash their palms on the table. Sam just gave a
　　diabolical grin. I know that grin. It means he is going to make
　　money where no one else could. When the night was over,
　　Sam said, "I decided to put the skinny guinea to work." (May
　　20, 1962)

From an FBI report, June 10, 1962, Special Agent Rowse:
TO: Office of the Director
RE: Giancana
SUBJECT booked Frank Sinatra, Dean Martin, Sammy
Davis, Jr., Eddie Fisher, and Joey Bishop to do full-week engage-
ments at Villa Venice, a roadhouse in NW outskirts of Chicago,

believed to be owned by SUBJECT. Pursuant to such infusion of talent, SUBJECT also enjoys profits from the now heavy traffic at his all-night gambling shop established in a warehouse two blocks away from Villa Venice. Gambling revenues are returning SUB-JECT estimated $1,500,000 a month for a duration of three months. Information from a reliable witness is that each enter-tainer receives only a fraction of his regular stipend, inasmuch as they were invited to Chicago by Sinatra.

Excerpt from AURAL transcript, June 12, 1962:

WILLIE: Did you read about Jack's birthday party at Madison Square Garden?

MODENE: Of course.

WILLIE: I saw it on television.

MODENE: I wasn't watching.

WILLIE: Marilyn Monroe was fabulous. She sang "Happy Birth-day, Mr. President." Modene, she was sewn into a dress that has to be an engineering feat.

MODENE: Marilyn Monroe is having an affair with Jack.

WILLIE: You know for sure?

MODENE: I can tell.

WILLIE: Are you upset?

MODENE: Why should I be?

WILLIE: Oh, come on, Modene!

MODENE: No. When something ends, it is finished. I don't miss Jack Kennedy. I am angry.

WILLIE: I thought you said it was coming to an end anyway.

MODENE: Well, it was. It was certainly over once J. Edgar Hoover jumped into it. Jack called me the same afternoon and said it was the last phone call either of us could make through the White House switchboard, but then—I will say this for him —he gave me a private line at the White House I could use for emergencies.

WILLIE: Did you try the special number?

MODENE: I wasn't going to. But then the FBI started visiting me at my apartment in Los Angeles. That was embarrassing to my roommates. I mean, they could see that these weren't two boyfriends coming over for a drink.

WILLIE: I would have thought that was the least of your problems. You hardly ever see your roommates.

MODENE: The FBI makes me very nervous. I have attacks of vertigo these days. It is frightful. I hardly do a flight anymore. Sam has got my schedule down to three a month, but when I do work, I get the staggers. Once, I had the dropsies. Three trays in one flight.

WILLIE: Oh, no.

MODENE: I finally decided to use the special line. I asked Jack to call off the FBI, but he wouldn't. He kept telling me that Sam was the person they were after, and I should just laugh into their faces. "I can't," I told him. "They are too much for me." At that point, Jack got openly irritated. "Modene," he said, "you are a grown woman and you are going to have to take care of this on your own." "You mean," I asked, "you and your brother don't have the power to call off the FBI?" "Yes, we do," he said, "but the cost might prove excessive. You just take care of it and leave my mind free for some reasonably important things that are going on, believe it or not." And you know, he said it in just that flat sarcastic Boston accent of his. I cringe at the way he said, "Believe it or not."

15

Tokyo
August 15, 1962

Dear Rick,

It's been too long since I have written to you, but I've held off, waiting for good things to tell. I'm afraid, however, that I am living through one upsetting death after another, and you can throw in a couple of FBI visits to spice the gloom. I must say I am fairly good by now at wearing Special Agents out, and, of course, the Far East version of the Buddha Gang is composed of reasonably civilized fellows, who realize that in the Far East, they are just serving as liaison. So they respect my feelings.

Another of my old friends, however, has become an intruder in the dust. William Faulkner died early last month. While I can't claim the pleasure of having seen much of him lately, I do remember one glorious evening back in 1946 right after the war when Dashiell Hammett and Faulkner and myself were drinking at Twenty-One. Do you know, for two hours Faulkner didn't say a word. I'm not even sure he was listening. Once in a while, we would nudge him, and he would raise his head and say, "The secret, gentlemen, is that I am just a farmer." Well, Dash would rarely give you more than a smile, but even he had to roar over this, as if Faulkner had made the wisest, most humorous remark in the world. I was feeling so sad Bill had died that I made the mistake of telling Mary.

"Oh, Cal, come off it," she said, "you can't claim that you've lost a bosom pal. Why, you haven't even had a letter from the man in fifteen years."

"Yes," I said, "but he was a great writer."

"You know," said Mary in that voice she gets when the question is already decided for her, "he was a great writer, I suppose, but I simply cannot read him. He is one of those people who pack everything up so tightly inside themselves, that, oh, my dear, they do nothing but make strange noises."

Thank God, I don't strike women. I would have laid hands on a man for less than that remark. I am frankly worried about my temper. You see, those words of Mary's went around in my head until I decided she was not really talking about Faulkner but trying to tell me something about her Japanese businessman whom I have sent back to the woodwork, or the bamboo mats, or wherever he is skulking, but to speak of people like Bill Faulkner as all packed up inside and making strange noises when she was obviously thinking of her Japanese mooey-mooey had me sweating my palms.

Maybe it is all these deaths. Too many friends have bought the last look. Do you know that what deranges the mind most in the hours after combat is remembering the expression that comes to men's faces as they die. Often that expression never belonged to them before. So I brood over the demise of people I care about. I confess to wondering what their last expression might have been.

Now it is Marilyn Monroe. Her suicide on August 5, yes, just ten days ago, has preoccupied me. Did you know that Allen Dulles proposed sending me to visit Miss Monroe in Hollywood in 1955? Wanted me to talk her into starting a romance with Sukarno. Allen may have been bewitched by a conversation he had once with Marlene Dietrich. She confided to our Great White Case Officer that she regretted not meeting Hitler in the thirties because she was certain she could have "humanized" him and thereby saved tens of millions of lives. Well, I would have vulcanized Hitler in preference to humanizing him, but Marlene doubtless knows a thing or two I don't. Allen, in any event, put the thought in his special kit bag and was ready to let Sukarno have a little go with Marilyn Monroe. I believe I did mention this to you once in passing. Allen, I hope you realize, was serious, and so, soon enough, was I. What a treat of an assignment! You get something like that once every ten years. I didn't give a damn about Sukarno. It was the thought of meeting Marilyn. I would have had to convince the lady of the patriotic importance of the job, and that might have entailed capturing her heart. I studied her movies, I can tell you. I saw *Gentlemen Prefer Blondes* three times, and once in a while, Allen would say, "I haven't forgotten about you and Miss Monroe."

Well, by the time he got around to it, we were in 1956, and it was too late. Marilyn was not in Hollywood but New York, and was having the love affair of the year with Arthur Miller. What a waste. I always thought I could have been her sweet daddy dynamite. Now she's dead.

The next is upsetting. I am keeping tight rein on my imagination, but I am not in the least certain that she was not murdered. We have a case officer here who is on good terms with Forensics in the Tokyo Police—since the coroner in Los Angeles, Thomas Noguchi, is also Japanese, Forensics was able to obtain a copy for me.

Now, Rick, I am not a ghoul. You know that much about your booze-ridden father—yes, I am drinking at this moment, love to drink while composing a letter to you, oldest son—and I don't feel the need to defend myself. I will tell you that I had to get ahold of that coroner's report. Call it instinct, call it the product of close to twenty years in Intelligence, but I felt a gut-ache about it.

Rick, I have perused it, and it is a time bomb. Coroner's report shows that Marilyn had enough barbiturates in her bloodstream to kill two healthy women, yet *nothing* in her stomach. One tablespoon of a "brown mucoid liquid." That's not nearly enough. You cannot take the forty-plus pills necessary to raise the barbiturate in your blood to such a level and show no more than one tablespoon in the stomach. *She was injected.*

Now, you know she was having an affair with Jack Kennedy. Conceivably with Bobby as well. I cannot rid myself of the suspicion that if she was threatening to blow the whistle on one or both of those boys, they might have come to an executive decision.

Did they pack her in? I hate the very thought of it. The average President of the United States often commits what history will later judge to be serious human error. After all, presidents are loose in the high energy of world events. To kill an individual woman, however. That is anathema. I reject the idea. But it comes back to keep me awake. I hate the Kennedy brothers. Indecisiveness at the Bay of Pigs was one thing, but cutting off a lovely lady's life—no! I try to reason it through. Did they? I am in doubt. I think they could have done it. Am I off on a mental bender? If so, it may be due to the climate of opinion among Agency folk out here. Down in South Vietnam (where Rough and Tough are now serving) they take to Kennedy a little more because of his *afición* for the Green Berets, but not up here in General MacArthur land. Agency people in Tokyo do not see all that wide a distinction between Kennedy and Castro. (Pinko, pinko!) The Bay of Pigs has left an ineradicable bitter taste. So, yes, I'm not alone in walking around with this terrible suspicion. You can hear it all through the North Asia Command. Son, I now have the mental equivalent of a tumor in my head, and it won't come out until I figure this one through. I am looking into Marilyn's demise.

Your own Sherlock Halifax

POST SCRIPTUM: How fares Mongoose?

16

MARILYN MONROE MURDERED! I DECIDED EVERY MAN WAS ENTITLED to one insane thesis. In any event, I was not eager to get back to my father about Mongoose. For months, I had been sending letters to Kittredge whose first line produced some variant of "I know I have not had much to say about our progress lately, but then there has not been a great deal to report." Then, I made as much as I could of our small raids.

Nearly every night, one or more of our boats in Miami or the Keys would slip out to a rendezvous on the Cuban coast; there were weeks when as many as twenty craft took that hazardous round trip. Expanding on my father's concept of mother ships, Harvey had acquired several yachts capable of carrying good-sized launches for the landing parties. We even had two Navy patrol craft, the *Rex* and the *Leda,* serving as our flagships. Each time I encountered them at a dock or in a marina, they had taken on new hues. A once peacock-green deck and aquamarine hull would now be a tawny-pink superstructure with a white hull. Harvey was determined to keep our fleet looking like pleasure craft rather than gunboats; the artillery— 40mm naval cannon, .50-caliber machine guns and recoilless .57-caliber rifles— was kept below, and both flagships carried a knock-down crane on the fantail that could, when assembled, lower and raise our 120-horse-power inboard fiberglass boats for the short, quick run to shore. Harvey registered these men-of-war out of Nicaragua, and had them owned by paper corporations attached by more pieces of paper to ship companies owned by Somoza. The docking fees for the boats were picked up by Oceanic Mangrove, a company that operated out of a desk at Zenith. "I can play the shell game with a 180-foot ship," Harvey liked to say. The salaries of the Cuban crew came out of a canning company in Key West. I kept looking to satisfy Kittredge's passion for details, but letters to her had begun to weigh on my nerves. I kept contemplating the size of the disaster should Harlot discover our correspondence. That would be horrendous unless he chose to divorce her (and I could marry her), but what if some Agency man other than Hugh came across our correspondence? In that case, Kittredge and I could continue writing to one another from maximum security cells. While the danger itself must have appealed to her, I took on the calculated risk of these letters as but one more burden on Harry Hubbard's mule-packing soul and kept pushing myself to tell her more. There was always more.

Harvey, to keep control, had built each network into a separate cluster of cells, and since he liked to keep each cell apart, we ended with custom espionage shops which often performed but one function. We had, for instance, a group of four accountants in the Ministry of Finance in Havana whose labors were elegant: They had succeeded in embezzling enough government funds to finance a good part of our operation in Cuba. I had images of Castro searching his desk for a particular paper in a mountain of office debris and never finding the document he needed because one of his personal secretaries had already passed it on to us. Cuba would rear up in my dreams as a compost heap; I had to wonder how the country could function at all; then I would decide that in its chaos was its strength. Cuba lived with so much disarray that whatever we added merely became part of the heap. It was the only answer to how Castro's DGI could function at all when our intelligence, so closely guarded, could not control most of JM/WAVE's Cubans. Sometimes, after a successful sortie, our exiles, on returning to Miami, would call an unauthorized press conference to boast of their exploits, and would follow that up by taking a processional down SW 8th Street in Little Havana. Adoring Cuban women would lay palm leaves on their path. Harvey, in a rage, would cut off these raiders' salaries, but after a month or so, he would be obliged to take them back. We could hardly let JM/WAVE Cubans hook up with the wilder exiles. Even so, we often lost our best boatmen. After all, we discouraged publicity, they craved it. Good publicity, they told me, was equal to *camburos maduros*. If "ripe bananas" comes out to the literal meaning, "hot pussy" is the working American equivalent.

I would have liked to write to Kittredge about Roselli, who was particularly active all spring and summer, but he kept embarking on ventures that came to nothing. The pills we gave him would reach his final contact and go no further. "Conditions are not appropriate," we would hear. I could be sympathetic to the honest fear endured by any waiter who would have to work each night with the anxiety that Fidel might or might not drop into the restaurant around midnight. Doubtless, such agents ended by flushing the pills away. ANCHOVY a.k.a. CAVIAR was going nowhere.

Sometimes I would write to her about the ongoing war between Lansdale and Harvey, but it, too, was predictable. Harvey had nothing but epithets for Lansdale: "All-American-boy-genius," "peanut head," "Li'l Abner," and "whacko" were standouts. Lansdale, in turn, had his complaints. "It is impossible," he would inform me, "to get anything working with Bill Harvey. If I ask for a full estimate on some serious undertaking, I count myself lucky if I get back a one-sentence memo. If I tell him that I want more, he will answer, 'I don't intend, General, to go into mouth-gagging detail on every last wrinkle of this endeavor.' Once, I reached across the desk, looked Harvey in the eye, and, swear to this, nearly grabbed him—and I am not a physical man. 'Bill Harvey, get one thing straight,' I told him, 'I am not the enemy.' It did no good. No good at all. Care to hear his response? He lifted one of his overstuffed legs, rolled to the side and broke wind right in my presence."

"Broke wind?" I interrupted, as if this were a matter to be confirmed.

"Yes. Farted. An atrocious-smelling production. No Shakespearean villain could have given me a clearer sense of odium. What an awful person Bill Harvey has to be! He reached down to his ankle, unstrapped his sheath knife, and proceeded to clean his nails. He is intolerable."

I nodded from time to time as Lansdale was speaking to indicate that I was indeed listening. I did not reply. I did not know how to say a word without betraying Harvey, or myself, or sounding unsympathetic to Lansdale. I also realized by now that I was not supposed to answer. If I had commenced my work in liaison on the assumption that I was a connective principle, a conjunction, so to speak, I had by now decided that I was but a semicolon, installed to keep the elements in some kind of extended relation, well apart.

17

Wednesday, September 6, 1962

Dear Kittredge,

Were you in Maine for the latter part of August? I took my two weeks through Labor Day, the most I've had since the spring of '60 when I climbed Katahdin in the last of the May snows. This year I made the mistake of spending my time (free room and board) with my mother in Southampton, and almost got married. (Joke, darling, an absolute joke.) In truth, I don't know who was after me most, the single girls to whom my mother had sung my praises, or her younger married friends, but I was ready to throttle the lady responsible for my existence since I do not think there is anyone in Southampton who does not know by now that I am an Agency hand. It was revolting, or would have been if the sexual emoluments had not been so attendant on the knowledge. God, we in the Agency are bum-rated all over the world as evil and sinister manipulators of downtrodden nations, etc., etc., but don't those summer lasses make a beeline for a man just because he is not totally unpresentable and, haven't you heard, is, yes, so bad, a CIA man. I realized in two fast weeks that I did not need to worry about the interest and principal on my own funds anymore. My mother is richer than she will admit and, no matter what, is bound to drop some capital on my head; besides, I have at least ten good years in which to marry one or another medium-bracket heiress. I could have gotten betrothed to some real mazuma in these couple of weeks if I had had any inclinations in such direction, yet discovered to my surprise that I despise most rich people. They—I have, in my innocence, just come to learn—are narcissistic beyond measure. *Me and my money* seems to be the sum of their inner relations. Alpha and Omega, take your pick! Worse! Wealthy narcissists lack that which other narcissists provide, a bit of charm. What an irony! I am defending the West in order to protect the Wall Street–garnered gains of these Southampton splendidos. I may need a refresher course in the evils of Bolshevism mit materialism. *Encore, je blague.*

The truth is that I enjoyed my vacation, am delighted to be back, and am warmed up to tell you about a pitched battle in early August between Harvey and Lansdale that was waged entirely with memos. In fact, I thought about it more than once during vacation, for it was bizarre in its origins, and classic in the outcome.

Picture one more meeting of the Special Group, Augmented. It is a large enough gathering on this occasion to include myself again. Needless to say, some true bureaucratic bottoms are in the room— General Maxwell Taylor, General Lemnitzer, Robert McNamara.

I am once again a flunky outrider. I sit with my two legal attaché cases behind my principal, William King Harvey (who is representing McCone), and the meeting, again bereft of Bobby Kennedy, drones on over Mongoose. The principals, relieved of Bobby's whip-it-up intensity, are only present in formal fashion. (The main passion on this August afternoon is not to fall asleep.) We have been through too many reports concerning progress gained here and progress ongoing there, with not a damn thing to tell us whether the middle or end of Mongoose is anywhere in sight.

Harvey, for example, offers a synopsis of one of our sabotage jobs that worked nicely. Earlier in the month, a Cuban freighter called the SS *Streatham Hill,* en route to the Soviet Union with a cargo of 800,000 bags of Cuban sugar, was obliged to put into San Juan, Puerto Rico, for repairs. Harvey said in his low voice, "I don't know why the Cubans can't keep their engine bearings free of sand," an in-line SGA joke—yet, given the somnolence of the late afternoon, only a few smiles were cracked. During the enforced layover, some of our Puerto Rican contract agents succeeded in impregnating the cargo with a nonpoisonous substance called bitrex, "suitably named," said

Harvey, "because it converts a sweet taste to a bitter one. The Russians will receive 800,000 bags of unusable sugar."

Lansdale made the mistake of asking, "How did our people succeed in infiltrating bitrex into each of those 800,000 bags?"

"The bags are not to be taken literally as the packaging modality," said Harvey most patiently, "but as a unit of quantity. The sugar is carried loose in the hold compartments. Figure on about 10,000 tons of sugar impregnated with bitrex."

Robert McNamara, who had been silent until now, started to speak. It was obvious he had been listening to neither man. McNamara is a most solemn potentate from the ramparts of Defense, but as I receive it, the Washington establishment's verdict—at least as it gets down to me—is that he, of all Cabinet officers, is the most brilliant and purposive. All the bureaucratic virtues surround his name. I suppose that has to be true, but at SGA meetings he is a bore. Maybe he was distracted that day. He was certainly ruminating aloud in bureaucratese, and had succeeded in leading us to the land of border somnolence. I snapped alert in the middle, however. Awash on his lusterless recapitulation of our Mongoose endeavors, I thought I heard him propose the elimination of Fidel Castro! Then, I could hardly decide from what he said next whether he had or hadn't: "While not in the least in favor of projecting this alternative option into Mongoose capability-potential, I can see, nonetheless, a viable skew in the end-result, which, speaking strictly from a theoretical point of view, might present us with a major shift in the regnant Cuban political situation. On the other hand, techniques for subterranean expression of the alternative just cited may be insufficiently developed . . ."

Kittredge, I remember telling myself, "He can't possibly be saying what I think he is," and everyone else, of course, is agog. What did he mean? Is he going on about assassination? No one responded.

The meeting ended on schedule. Everyone left. I was certain that McNamara's speech was not going to reach the minutes. A few days later, however, on August 13, a memo came in from Lansdale summarizing the "emergent directives" at the last discussion in Special Group, Augmented. Lansdale listed: economic sabotage, paramilitary action, intelligence activities, and political activities. To this last, he added, "liquidation of leaders."

Since Lansdale had also sent the memo to SGA people at State, Defense, and the USIA, Harvey was apoplectic. "Just let his memo leak out, and some congressional committee will start delving into who is developing executive-action capability. That's when Bill Harvey will be requested to put his ass in a paper-shredder."

Harvey fired off a memo to Helms: "I have called General Lansdale's office and pointed out the inadvisability and stupidity of putting this kind of comment in writing in such a document."

You may be certain, Kittredge, that Helms passed it on to McCone who queried Lansdale. As I heard it back via Harvey, Lansdale answered, "Well, sir, I had my considerable doubts as to the utility of the suggestion, but I was trying to be comprehensive. In contingency planning, you do want to cover the waterfront."

It sounds exactly like Lansdale. McCone has now told Harvey that McNamara's remarks were inappropriate. "Why, if I ever got myself involved," McCone said, "in something like this, I might end up getting excommunicated." As a recent Catholic convert, he does think of such things.

Ergo, McCone has moved in on Lansdale. The wings are clipped. Instead of proceeding to "Phase Two: the inspiring of revolt," McCone proposes that Lansdale "seek a split between Castro and the old-line Communists. This is sensible action and attainable."

I do not know if Lansdale is aware of how much he has lost.

It is good to be writing to you. Perhaps this year we can share a Christmas punch.

Love,
Harry

18

From a letter to Kittredge on September 12, 1962:

. . . This is news of a dispute I called to Hugh's attention. Since he may not have kept you abreast, I will confide that an ominous event is on the horizon. Last Saturday, September 8, Harvey called me up to Washington. I went with no inner grace, since one of the small punishments King Bill visits on me for serving as Hugh's conduit is to keep me at work over a weekend. Be certain, if he shows up on a Saturday or even a Sunday at his office in Miami or in Washington, I will get called in.

This time, however, the job is important. A photograph from the Directorate of Intelligence has been smuggled over to Task Force W's basement in Langley; that is a high order of contraband. A contest of wills between Operations and Intelligence may soon commence.

Indeed, I am coming to learn that Intelligence is not a well-chosen collection of secret facts, but a designed product; the form is derived from whose will is stamped upon the facts: Harvey says the Soviets are exporting medium-range nuclear missiles to Cuba, and the Directorate of Intelligence is arguing that they are not. Since medium-range missiles can reach from Havana to New York, Washington, or Chicago, these are no small peas we contend over. U-2 overflights do reveal missile launching pads in the area west of Havana, but the Directorate of Intelligence insists that the sites in question can handle no more than ground-to-air antiaircraft missiles. Apparently, there was an understanding reached in Vienna between Kennedy and Khrushchev that Castro can deploy defensive weapons such as SAM missiles, which only have a range of twenty-five miles. This, of course, in no way permits medium-range nuclear-strike powers.

Well, what I call the *Saturday* photograph was slipped over to Harvey on Friday night. It was taken of the Soviet freighter *Omsk* out at sea one hundred miles from Havana. The ship's hatches are covered with their tarpaulins, so all one can determine on superficial reading of the evidence is that this type of freighter may be equipped with very large hatches in order to load lumber, but the Russians are not shipping timber to Fidel, not with all those Cuban forests thick as revolutionary beards, no, something other than gross lots of wood has to be in the hold. One of Harvey's camera experts, after scrutinizing the photograph, determines through the shadow thrown by the hull of the *Omsk* that the ship is riding very high in the water so its hold has to be filled with large objects of low density. "Medium-range missiles," growls Harvey, "fulfill that category."

I have never seen Wild Bill so happy. He already knows that Oatsie Porringer, with whom I worked for years at Montevideo Station, is one of my contacts at the Directorate of Intelligence, so he asks me to rout Oatsie out on this Saturday. Porringer is the only example I can name of a good case officer who has switched over from Operations to Intelligence. Now, according to his own evaluation, he is making a name for himself in "a rat-shit corner of technology." Porringer, it seems, has become our expert in cratology, the science of calculating by its size and shape what a crate or carton is likely to be holding.

Well, Porringer and I don't like each other all that much, and I don't get along with his wife, so I haven't spent one social evening with them since we've both come back to the States, indeed, two quick lunches in the Company cafeteria has been the scope of our *communitas,* and both repasts were unpleasant. Porringer, bitter at the lack of recognition his stint in Uruguay received, is envious of my assignments. I know he thinks I do not deserve them.

So soon as he hears, however, that it is Harvey who wants him to come over, he is wholly cordial to the idea. He has been wanting to meet the legend for many a year, and they get along on this Saturday fairly well. It is unorthodox for Harvey to receive him, but I know my boss by now. His instinct tells him that we are dealing with medium-range missiles, so he is going to need his personal cratologist for the next few weeks. Therefore, he gives an audience to Porringer, and the *Omsk*'s cargo is narrowed down to missiles, plastic toys, toilet paper, wicker furniture, or any of five other lightweight cargoes. Only medium-range intercontinental missiles, however, require hatches as large as the *Omsk* can provide.

Since that Saturday meeting, I have been kept busy through the weekend and now into Monday riding herd on two Junior Officer Trainees who work with me at checking every possible route out of Bahía Parva, a harbor west of Havana where the *Omsk* docked on September 9 and immediately proceeded to unload in the middle of the night. We have been checking every road that is wide enough to transport a missile over a distance of one hundred miles out from Bahía Parva. That is not as impossible a study as you would think; the road, after all, has to be able to accommodate a truck trailer some eighty feet long going through tight corners in the villages and around hairpin turns in the mountains.

Needless to say, most of the thoroughfares out of Bahía Parva sooner or later prove unfeasible, but we do come up with one likely route, and Harvey actually has an agent occupying a house on a street in the town of San Rosario, through which the delivery will presumably pass. Rest assured, radio messages are being delivered to our agent. He has to be one of our more important people in the area since he is already in possession of a burst transmitter.

From letter to Kittredge, September 14, 1962:

. . . It is coming to climax sooner than expected. Our agent in San Rosario radioed back on the night of September 12 that a trailer truck towed a large missile past his house. Says he was able to estimate the length closely because he has already measured the frontage of the villa across from him. The missile is twenty-three meters in length. That has to be a medium-range nuclear torch.

Harvey has instructed our fellow to pack a suitcase. We are going to get this agent out of Cuba.

I will keep you posted. . . .

From Kittredge to me on September 16, 1962:

I pray devoutly that the Fat Man is wrong. A great bag of bile is playing on a fife. All this means to Harvey, should he be correct, is that he is on his way to becoming Chief of the Soviet Russia Division, but I see Christopher in my arms as the great bombs go off. Castro is a monster. How dare he let the Russians feed him missiles? Or, worse, did he ask for them himself?

From Kittredge to me on September 17, 1962:

I've calmed down. I realize one's job has to be followed through, hour by hour, task by task. Do keep me up, please, on exactly what is happening. I would ask Hugh (who is particularly quiet these couple of days) but even though the world may be approaching its end, I do not dare to violate the secret of our correspondence.

From my letter to Kittredge, September 18, 1962:

Sherman Kent of the Board of National Estimate has told McCone that there has been no Soviet installation of missiles.

McCone disagrees. He is banking on Harvey's estimate. Harvey, as you predicted, is in his element. McCone said to Harvey, "You had better be right," and Harvey said he was. Here I come, sings Harvey in the bathroom, Soviet Russia Division, here I come.

From Kittredge's letter to me, September 20, 1962:

Although Sherman Kent is no fool and has good people working for him, Hugh, of course, disagrees with the Board. He rates the personnel over at the Directorate of Intelligence as much too soft. I know he is thinking of the round-shouldered, clammy-palmed, clerical look of so many of their ex-professors. The root of it, Hugh thinks, is that many of them were Stalin-worshippers during the war without quite realizing it, and still see the Soviet Union as a crippled giant needful of peace to bind the wounds. "They don't understand," opines Hugh, "that Marxism is a faith for which people are willing to die. Reason always collapses before the inner readiness of others to give up their lives to a vision. I am ready to die for Christ, and these intoxicated warriors of Communism are willing to die for the mystical bonds of materialism. Irrationality is the only great engine in history."

Harry, I see the Company as one huge Alpha and Omega with the D of I as the more rational component, and Operations, obviously, as the faith. I am, on ninety-nine out of a hundred occasions, happy to live with you and Hugh in the phratry of Operations, but, oh, God, I am praying tonight that Sherman Kent is right and Wild Bill Harvey is wrong.

Incidentally, I ought to tell you what I know about McCone since you might be having close dealings with him soon. He is not, by superficial measure, a nice man. On the day he took over from Allen, he happened to take notice of the Great White Case Officer's *bulletproof* limousine. "Oh, yes," Allen told him, "it's nifty. One can immerse oneself in a paper, and never have to wonder if some *espontáneo* down the road can take a potshot through your window."

Well, that night, just as McCone was leaving in his un-armor-clad Mercedes-Benz limousine, he gave an order. He wanted to depart from Langley on the next evening in his own duplicate bullet-proof limo, whereupon twenty frantic slaveys went to extraordinary lengths through the night to get General Motors to make one ready, and, yes, fly it in on a cargo plane—how fortunate that we have an accordion valise for a budget! They were even soldering the last connections onto the dashboard when McCone came down with his attaché case, strolled over to the new vehicle, got in, and had the chauffeur drive him off without saying thank you to a soul. Duty is its own blessing and needs no reward. I fear people like that. Hugh laughs and says, "When it comes to our real work, McCone can't distinguish between his sphincter and his epiglottis, so he does his best to keep us at arm's length. That is exactly where Helms and I want him."

It's true. McCone does put a moat around himself. He has, for instance, sealed off the door between his Deputy's office and his own. He doesn't want the Deputy able to pop in on him. Marshall Carter has to come through the anteroom like the common folk. Carter, who has his own sense of humor, attached a fake but most lifelike-looking hand to the sealed-off frame of the interoffice entry as if his arm had been cut off at the wrist when the last slam was heard. Of course, McCone is so standoffish that Carter need never fear a surprise visit from his boss.

I tell you this as a form of escape from the heavy concerns you have loosed in me. Perhaps it is a small warning as well. If you have dealings with McCone, do not expect your ego to come out unscathed.

From my letter to Kittredge, September 25, 1962:

. . . Well, I've been on the job through the weekend again. Last Thursday, September 20, our Cuban agent completed his odyssey from San Rosario to Opa-Locka. Kittredge, I can hardly believe it. He is an accountant. That profession seems to breed half the unsung heroes of the Cuban resistance! At any rate, he proved to be a tall, well-built fellow with a large nose, strong black mustache, and a high-pitched nervous laugh. I would have had to dream up Alpha and Omega all by myself to account for Señor Enrique Fogata.

Harvey came down to JM/WAVE for the interrogation (wanted to take a look at our prize before we shipped him over to the D of I), and of course I was there to serve as Wild Bill's personal translator.

Our Spanish-speaking interrogator started off by scourging Fogata (per Harvey's instructions) with the news that many an exile has come over full of tales about missiles in empty fields, empty stadiums, and empty swimming pools. All the stories have been disproved.

Fogata replied, "I know what I see." *(Lo que veo, conozco.)*

"That is just what we are going to find out," the interrogator told him, and presented Enrique with drawings of a great variety of missiles from every major arsenal of the world. All the pictures, however, were the same size. Your only way to choose was by the shape of the profile.

Fogata seemed in no trouble, however. The object he had seen was clearly imprinted on his mind. Without hesitation, he pointed to a Soviet medium-range ballistic missile.

"What length was it?"

"Twenty-three meters."

Enrique was flown up to Washington that evening. It took more than a day before the Directorate of Intelligence would communicate back to Harvey, and then their comment was that they did not buy our agent's story. They are arguing that the object he saw was probably twenty-three feet long, rather than twenty-three meters and he had confused the measure and was still confusing it. (I think they assumed we had told him the correct length.) As I wrote to you over a week ago, intelligence derives from whose will is stamped upon which facts. McCone—thank you for the warning—is going along quietly with Harvey, but there is whole unhappiness between Intelligence and Operations. At present, this is where matters stand.

I don't wish to worry you, but I did have the following conversation with Harvey.

"When the facts come out," he said, "we will have to lay an air strike on Cuba."

"What if the Russians escalate?"

"They won't," said Harvey. "They're only shipping missiles because they think we won't do anything. They're trying to show the world that they can stand on tiptoe right on our window ledge. I say, knock them off."

Kittredge, half the Pentagon feels exactly the way Bill Harvey does.

As for me, I am beginning to wake up in the middle of the night with a great weight on my chest. This may be the first time that I do not wish I was standing in John F. Kennedy's shoes.

19

THE DISPUTE OVER ENRIQUE FOGATA'S POWERS OF PERCEPTION ENDED with a victory for Bill Harvey. On October 14, the walls of the Directorate of Intelligence were breached. Intelligence had to concede to Harvey that the photographs brought back that morning showed excavations for the installation of an intercontinental ballistic site outside a Cuban town named San Cristóbal. Since McCone was taking a belated honeymoon in Italy with his new Catholic wife, and was located in a small Italian village, Harvey had to employ *open-speak* on the phone; his syntax was reminiscent of how we used to translate Latin at St. Matthew's. "Sir," said Harvey, "that which you, and you alone, said would happen, did." McCone remarked that he was coming home forthwith.

There had, of course, been intimations of such crisis already. On October 10, Senator Keating of New York announced the presence of nuclear missiles in Cuba (which made it evident that we had our own leaks in the basement at Langley), and in the confidence that this information was bona fide, the House Republican Caucus spoke of Cuba as "their biggest Republican asset," a reference to the congressional elections in November. Clare Boothe Luce wrote an editorial for the October issue of *Life* equal to a clarion call: "What is now at stake is the question not only of American prestige, but of American survival," and I thought of that delicately boned blond lady whom I had met one night at the Stable after my return to Washington from the Farm, Mrs. Luce a beauty in the style of my own mother (although somewhat more of a beauty since Mrs. Luce seemed to give off a silvery light), and I pondered the exaltation she must feel at having the means to call the world to war.

After October 14, Washington began to remind me of a ship with an unstanchable leak; one could measure the spread of seepage from first light to evening dark. People congregated on the phone all week. To work in the capital was to become aware all over again that Washington was a hierarchy of secrets and one could find one's relation to History by the number of confidants who would give you access to their collection. Rumors rolled across the city in the rhythm of a powerful surf. In the White House, in the Executive Office Building, and at State, office lights were burning all night long. People drove by the White House at one in the morning to look at the office lights. Rosen was on the phone with me five times a day to present his latest find; if I did not wish to verify or deny it, nonetheless I had to. I owed Rosen too many markers to be able to refuse him now that he was calling them in. I had time to think that if we were all obliterated in a nuclear holocaust, Rosen would not want to go out into that atomized empyrean holding onto unpaid debts.

When I went on errands to the Pentagon, the high officers I passed in the corridors had the look of wild moose in the Maine woods. That the approach of war brought on tumescence was verified forever for me. I was walking by men who did not know whether they would be heroes in a week; or dead; or, for that matter, promoted; their collective anxiety was on fire. So many of these officers had spent their lives getting ready for a great moment—it was as if one lived as a vestal virgin who would be allowed to copulate just once, but in a high temple: The act had better be transcendent, or one had chosen the wrong life. This epiphanic vision of my military brethren gave me less acute pleasure after I recognized that it applied to me as well; if we went to war with Cuba, I felt obliged to get into combat too. I wanted to be in battle when the bomb fell. If flesh and psyche were obliterated at one stroke of a nuclear moment, perhaps my soul would not be so scattered if the death were honorable. Could anyone claim that was less than faith?

I was back in Florida by the 21st of October, and next evening President Kennedy announced to the nation that offensive missile bases large enough for intercontinental weapons had been installed in Cuba by Soviet technicians. The Soviet Union had lied to the United States, the President said. Therefore, a naval and air quarantine of Cuba would now be imposed to halt all further shipments of Soviet military equipment. If missiles were launched by Cuba, the U.S. was prepared to retaliate against this "clandestine, reckless, and provocative threat to world peace."

I listened in the company of Dix Butler. The bars were filled in Little Havana and Cuban exiles were dancing in the streets. I was enraged. All of my country might yet be destroyed, everyone I knew maimed or dead, but the exiles were happy because they had a chance to get back to Cuba; I remember thinking that they were an unbelievably selfish and self-centered tribe, still furious at the loss of the wealth they might have been amassing in Cuba, although now they were making money in Miami; middle-class Cubans, I decided, had a prodigiously large sense of the rights due to themselves, and little sense

N O R M A N   M A I L E R

at all of the rights due to others. They would gamble all of my great
nation against Fidel Castro's beard. This set of thoughts blazed their
way through me so quickly that they were soon gone and I was
dancing in the street with Cuban men and women, drunken Hubbard, who usually didn't dance and might have lost a girl because of
that; now he could move to Cuban rhythms—for an hour, the pelvis
of Herrick Hubbard escaped its bonds.

Afterward, Butler and I dived into a bar, had a few drinks, and
made a pledge. "I," he said, "am tired of sending men out. I never
know when they won't come back. Hubbard, in an emergency like
this, we can count on Bill Harvey. He'll let us go out with the
boatmen."

"Yes," I said, "I want to dig my feet into Cuban soil." I was very
drunk.

"Yes," he said, "when the war starts, some of us have to be there
to meet our troops."

We clasped hands on the profound value of this.

In the morning I awoke to great fear. I was bound to a compact
built on booze. A little later, following the raw instincts of a hangover,
I went to my postal box and found a long letter from Kittredge. I read
it standing in the post office at Coconut Grove, and it seemed as if she
were sending it to me from the other side of the world.

October 22, 1962, 11:00 P.M.

Dearest Harry,

These days, which may be the most momentous we will
know, have put a new kind of strain on one's control. To listen to my
friends reacting to news which I, three days closer to the source, know
is now obsolete, has given a glimpse of why people go mad and shout
to the rooftops.

You see, Hugh and I have been installed in a most peculiar
association with the brothers K. I have indicated some of this to you,
but as time goes on, the friendship has taken on more importance,
and, then, I haven't told you all.

Jack became fascinated some months ago with a Soviet official, obviously KGB, about whom you wrote to me while you were
in Uruguay. It is the same Boris Masarov, and he works out of the
Russian Embassy here, although *loosely* attached. Apparently, Khrushchev is wild about whatever special quality it is that Masarov possesses

—perhaps it is the sad, ironic Russian wisdom that Khrushchev apparently lacks. In any event, the Soviet Premier reached down through the ranks to pluck this man up to the very top; Masarov was sent over to America as Khrushchev's personal liaison to the Kennedy brothers. I have noticed that Jack likes playing a couple of possibilities at once. In relation to the Soviets, this means a representative to embody the hard line, and another for the soft; depending on events, the President can move toward a freeze or a thaw in relations. Khrushchev also plays with two hands, but has added another element, a wild card.

Masarov seems to be in Washington to initiate conversations with Bobby—these, presumably, to be passed on to Jack; the talks, apparently, range far and wide. For instance, I know from Hugh that one of Masarov's main functions is to leaven relations between Khrushchev and the brothers K. The Premier, apparently, is a man who likes to converse with his hands on people. He may send you to Siberia next week, but in the interim, let's keep it on a warm and personal level. So, for instance, Bobby and Boris were in close touch during the last Berlin crisis, and it was Masarov who was told by Bobby that the United States would certainly fight if the Soviets didn't remove their tanks from the Brandenburg Gate. Do you know, Masarov passed it on to Khrushchev and within twenty-four hours the tanks were gone. In turn, Masarov tells Bobby that in Khrushchev's opinion, America is still run by Rockefellers, J. P. Morgans, and Wall Street, but he is beginning to see that his old ideas about the Kennedys have to be changed.

So much for the love affair. My husband says not to be carried away by it for one moment; Hugh has been familiar with Masarov's dossier for years and says he is one of the most talented and brilliant KGB men that the Soviets have. That sad and winning charm conceals a faculty considerably more executive.

Perhaps there is a principle agreed upon here by both Khrushchev and the Kennedys: If your brightest people are usually not where they ought to be in the ordered establishment, then pluck them up and use them for special ventures. I think persons so anointed are chosen because they can speak their own mind, or listen incomparably well. I do a little of the first and a great deal of the second.

Concerning my case, Bobby and Jack are not nearly so interested in my powers of counsel, but do like to hear themselves speak candidly (which they cannot do all that often with working subordinates or opponents). I am called on, therefore, to listen. Hugh is called

1018 N O R M A N   M A I L E R

on to speak up. Be assured that we saw a lot of the Kennedys last week.

They were enraged at Khrushchev and they were not feeling too good about Masarov. For months, Boris had been giving Bobby assurances that the Premier would never send nuclear missiles to Cuba. I suppose the operative principle is that you never tell a lie until it will be maximally effective. Of course, Masarov claims that he is as surprised as the Kennedys.

No matter where the lie originates, you can be certain that Jack is, at this moment, as personally ill-disposed toward the Soviets as he has ever been; in such a frame of mind, he is nonetheless obliged to withstand some powerful pressures being applied by the *Executive Committee* of the National Security Council. (Let me tell you that it is one committee I pay attention to!) Everyone in White House circles is using the words *hawk* and *dove* these days, and be assured, some formidable hawks are perched up in Excom. As of October 17, a lot of them were all-out for bombing Cuba immediately. Just obliterate the missile bases! You find among these high-force presences such men as Maxwell Taylor and Dean Acheson, most of the Joint Chiefs, plus McCloy, and Nitze and McCone. Bobby, who has been the leader of the doves, has argued that any surprise bombing would involve killing tens of thousands of civilians. "It's a moral question," he said to me in that wonderful, innocent way of his. For a very tough young man, he is always discovering the wheel. But I know the thought of death does bother him very much these days. Neither Jack nor Bobby has ever spoken word one to me about Marilyn Monroe, but I feel that her suicide shook them somewhat. The death of others seems awfully palpable to Bobby these days. And yet there he is presiding over the Executive Committee of the National Security Council while they argue whether to initiate a blockade (McNamara, Gilpatric, Ball, Stevenson, and Sorensen) or, as the hawks keep insisting, loose that air strike without prior notification of war.

"That," Bobby tells them, "is right along the lines of Pearl Harbor."

He made the mistake of saying as much to Dean Acheson, who was sufficiently incensed then to take a private lunch with Jack last Thursday, October 18. Dean Acheson is proud of the fact that he detests emotional and intuitive responses. He said, "Mr. President, there is no choice. You have to call an air strike. The more comprehensive, the better."

Well, Acheson may be old, but he is still as imperious as

Cardinal Richelieu. He was not Secretary of State for too little during the early years of the Cold War, and the few liberal tendencies he might have retained were badly chewed up by his defense of Alger Hiss. Acheson, but for that old gray mustache, even looks like a hawk. "One can analyze the problem from this or that approach," he tells Jack, "but there is only one effective response. Obliteration of missile capability."

"I am not happy with that," said Jack Kennedy, "and Bobby keeps coming around to remind me that such an air strike smacks completely of Pearl Harbor."

"I cannot believe you said that," Acheson told him. "Bobby's clichés are silly. Pearl Harbor could not be more thoroughly useless as an analogy. It is only a label to hide behind. The duty of the presidency is to analyze intolerable problems, and come up with appropriately clear answers. Moral anguish is worth less in the sight of heaven than skilled and disciplined analysis. Tears can be the subtlest creation of the muddled and the weak." Harry, I promise you, Dean Acheson does talk with just this sort of authority. I would hate to be a small bird in his talons.

Later that afternoon, however, a visit-and-search blockade of Soviet ships approaching Cuba was more or less decided upon by the Executive Committee (McNamara now in the lead) and sent up as a proposal to the President. Next day, Acheson appeared again and said the question had to be reopened; dealing with the Russians was a contest of wills. Since a showdown was going to be inevitable, such confrontations lost their force if too long delayed. A blockade was delay. Secretary Dillon agreed. So did McCone. General Taylor told them that an air strike, to be effective, had to come as quickly as possible. To be gotten ready for Sunday morning, they had to decide it right now, here, on Thursday afternoon. If for Monday, then a decision no later than tomorrow.

If I had been in these councils, I cannot say how I would have reacted. I am a dove, I suppose, but I feel unspeakable anger toward the Soviets. Harry, do you know, listening to Bobby, it came upon me that he is wise. I am beginning to realize he has balance. That same afternoon, in the face of Acheson's scorn, he told Excom that the world would see an air strike as a sneak attack. We had never been that kind of country, he said, not in one hundred and seventy-five years. It was not in our tradition. We certainly needed forceful action to make the Russians realize that we were serious, but we also had to leave them room to maneuver. Assuming they could recognize that they were out of line on Cuba, we ought to allow them a way to pull back. Blockade was the answer.

That speech of Bobby's to the Executive Committee proved convincing on Thursday. By Saturday, however, the question was wide-open to debate again. McNamara argued that an air strike would kill hundreds if not thousands of Russians stationed on the missile bases, and we could not predict Khrushchev's reaction to that event. An air strike, therefore, would lose us control of the situation. An escalation might commence. That could lead to an all-out war. Maxwell Taylor disagreed. This was our last chance, he argued, to destroy the missiles. The Russians, once they no longer possessed such capability in Cuba, would not attempt an escalation; our nuclear powers were superior to theirs. McGeorge Bundy and the Chiefs of Staff supported Taylor.

The President did not give his decision until yesterday, Sunday morning. At that point, he chose the blockade, and began writing the speech he delivered to America tonight. I know he was dreading the political repercussions. The Republicans have been screaming for weeks that there are missiles in Cuba, and he is only now admitting it to the public. So, the loss can be large. Politically speaking, it would have been more advantageous to order the air strike. Then the Republicans would have had to unite behind him.

In any event, we must now wait. It is going to take a few days for the Russian ships to reach the blockade. I am feeling so emotional tonight that I picked Christopher up out of his bed and hugged the sleeping angel so hard that he woke and said, "It's all right, Mommy, everything will be all right."

I have the strongest sense of dread, and miss you, Harry, you are dear to me. Do not do anything insane with people like Dix Butler.

Love,
Kittredge

20

EARLY WEDNESDAY EVENING, OCTOBER 24, I HOISTED MYSELF OFF A barstool in a cantina on SW 8th Street, picked up my tote bag, and went out to the street with Dix Butler to hail a cab. We were on our way to 6312 Riviera Drive. The radios in all the bars on SW 8th Street were reporting in English or Spanish that two Soviet ships had come within fifty miles of the line of quarantine the U.S. Navy had established around the island of Cuba.

There had been no day in my life like the Monday, the Tuesday, and the Wednesday just passed. In Washington, printouts were being circulated among key personnel at the White House, the State Department, the Pentagon, and at Langley to show the route of evacuation to underground shelters in Virginia and in Maryland. At JM/WAVE, maps of southern Florida were distributed to a few of us. As I now learned, we had built a twenty-man fallout shelter two years ago in the swamps of the Everglades, and I thought this an interesting achievement since little enough earth in the Everglades could be found two feet above water. A rumor passing from Langley to JM/WAVE had Bobby Kennedy declare that he was not going to a shelter. "If it comes to evacuation, there will be sixty million Americans killed, and as many Russians. I'll be at Hickory Hill."

When I passed the story on to Dix Butler, he said, "How do you know Bobby doesn't have his own dugout at Hickory Hill?"

That may be taken as a sample of the observations being passed around Zenith. Emotions had gone careening in all directions, as if a stone had been thrown into a flight of birds. It did not seem condign that we should all die so soon. Now when I felt rage it seemed to scald my chest; sorrow was uncomfortably close to weeping; cynicism, on revealing itself, tasted poisonous. It was hard to say who had become more unpopular at JM/WAVE—Fidel Castro, the Cuban exiles, or the brothers K. Bill Harvey was convinced that there would yet be a sellout to Cuba. "If we don't have a shooting war, Khrushchev will piss all over Kennedy in the negotiations."

Given such quick alternations of exhilaration and gloom, the thought that there might be power never yet unleashed in oneself also had time to come forth. Miami, soft as a powderpuff, murderous as a scorpion, lay suspended like Nirvana; no one could, when all was said, resist waiting. Except for Harvey. He chafed like a boil about to burst on its incarcerating collar; it took very little effort by Dix Butler to convince the boss of JM/WAVE that he should allow us to go on a mission. Harvey was all for improvising a few missions in this week of emergency.

He did take me aside long enough, however, to say, "Hubbard, I don't know if I give one toot whether you come back or not, but if you do, and the world continues, I want my ass covered. So you are not to tell Hugh Montague that you are going. Should he contact me concerning you, I will tell him that you took off spontaneously on a job I was restricting to Dix Butler, but that I won't press charges, which I won't—that is, between you and me, I won't—unless you make the mistake of telling the truth to His Lordship. In that case, it will be your word against mine, and you are about to be counterdocumented. Since you want to go out with Butler, write a memo and sign it. You can have it say, 'I, Herrick Hubbard, acknowledge the receipt of memo number 7,418,537 and will obey instructions pursuant to it.' "

"Have I seen 7,418,537?"

"You will now." He read it aloud. "All personnel in Office B, JM/WAVE, are hereby instructed to remain within a ten-mile radius of Base for duration of crisis, and will keep themselves in constant availability."

"Yessir," I said.

"I am putting 7,418,537 out now. It will be on your desk in ten minutes. Send your reply as soon as you receive it."

I did. I felt weightless. It occurred to me that I was absolutely free. For I might be dead in two days. So I could lie once again to Hugh Montague. Wild Bill, after all, was using us to some purpose. We would embark on Eugenio Martínez's boat, La Princesa, with cartons of flares, and bring them into Cuba on rubber dinghies to hand them over to one of Harvey's networks. These flares would then be available for the Cuban underground to light the way at night for an American invasion force.

It is significant to my state of mind that that was all I knew about our mission. Waiting in such passivity, I wondered if the about-to-be-born on the last day of their nine months in the womb do not also feel the high sad sentiment that all they know of existence is about to be lost forever for they are embarking on an endeavor of high risk.

I was obviously swimming in much emotional soup. I remember standing before a full-length mirror in my furnished apartment trying to attach these highly undisciplined sentiments to the stern expression on the presentable, tall young man who looked back at me. I had never felt further away from the image in the mirror. "Is this what goes on with movie stars?" I recall asking myself.

Early Wednesday afternoon, Butler drove us down to one of our proprietaries, a marina on Key Largo, and we loaded a fourteen-foot inflatable black rubber dinghy with 1,500 pounds of cement-brick and sand to simulate the weight of the equipment and men we would be carrying. Then we rode out to the smaller keys, pushing into mangrove swamps while throttling each of our twin outboards down to a purr, then vamped the craft through shallows at low tide, raising the outboards if necessary, scraping bottom. When Butler was satisfied, we went back to the mooring, carted one motor into a shed, and there in an unlit room with the engine mounted to the inside of a half-filled barrel of water, we practiced simple maintenance in the dark, stripping the little beast and reassembling it. Years ago, I had had one long day like this at the Farm, when they drove us to a cove just south of Norfolk, and brought us up to much the same sort of intense half-competence. What I had learned then I had all but forgotten; would I remember tomorrow what I was studying now?

We drove back to Miami in late afternoon, went to a cantina, had three Planter's Punches "in honor," said Butler, "of the plantations we will soon be restoring to their greed-ass shit-bag owners," and drank to that, and to Berlin—a touchy toast was that—"and to Nirvana," said Butler, which managed to startle me since I had been resting on just that word in my mind. Were we all growing telepathic now that the end of the world was near? It seemed a logical proposition. I sighed, and the Planter's Punch carried me back to how beautiful the sea had been this afternoon outside Key Largo, a luminous pale green sea, twice luminous as the shelf dropped off into the iridescence of aquamarine. A myriad of silver minnows escorted our dinghy to the mangrove swamp, threaded the roots beneath the water and were lost to view.

Now we had gone through the door at 6312 Riviera Drive and in a wardrobe closet changed into black high-topped sneakers, black denim pants, a black turtleneck sweater, a black hood with holes for eyes and mouth. It was hot in this anteroom. The polyester suits and tropical shirts of a dozen other men were already suspended from hangers and poles, but I was comprehending why the life of the executioner must be worth its other pains. Dressed all in black, I did not seem to inhabit myself any longer so much as I was an acolyte to the communions who would guard the dominion of death; it was then I comprehended that I had never understood the Agency until this moment; now I knew why I was here. One should not spend one's life in the halls of a great profession without descending at least once to the cellar chambers—a metaphor, but then I was consuming metaphors on this night the way others in the same brew of anxiety might chew on facts; death was but a metaphor for metaphor, even as the square root of minus one was the mandrake root to guide us into that other world where there might be no roots. I kept thinking of the minnows that swam around our dinghy before disappearing into a forest of underwater foliage not two feet deep.

The interior of 6312 Riviera Drive was barely furnished, but then the model for a barren habitat is a safe house. We passed through a living room paneled in dark wood and by an archway into a dining room where four dark Spanish chairs were grouped around a mahogany dinner table, and I thought of the solemnity of middle-class Spanish life; the wives somber, the children solemn, the father guilty beneath the moral weight of a querulous mistress furious at his parsimony even as she wears the black lingerie he has purchased for her, yes, I must be a servant of death when an empty room offered the intimate history of an unhappy family I had never seen. How close had the Russian freighters approached by now to the line of quarantine?

Beyond the dining room was a door to a glassed-in porch that looked upon a patio; at the other end was the wharf. A large white fishing boat, immanent as mausoleum marble, was rising and falling with the small breath of the tide. I had time to think of Giancana's dead wife before I stepped on board. Below were ten men in black hoods sitting on bunks in the galley, and only a few looked up. The air proved close if not yet foul, and the lurch of the ship at its mooring was not agreeable.

We waited. We did not speak beneath our hoods. The inboard motors started up, vibrating their intent through my feet, closer to the purpose than I might be. From above, like the sounds of a surgical team impinging on one's ear through partial anesthetic, I could hear the skipper calling out orders in Spanish. We were casting off. Down in the galley, with no more illumination coming through the portholes than the dock lights of the Miami houses along the canal, our motors sounded as alive as the growl of beasts.

We traveled at low throttle to reduce the wake, and I fell asleep passing through the narrow canals of Coral Gables into Biscayne Bay, and by the time I awakened we were in the open sea and the lights of Miami were far to the stern, their sky-glow as plum-colored as that last rose hue of sunset before evening is committed to night. Off the bow, more than a hundred miles to starboard, fainter than the penumbra of the moon, came a glow from Havana itself. It was a black night but a clear sky, and I had time to think that by tomorrow evening, both cities might be burning, and would we witness the sight from land or sea? "Eugenio is going to take us in between Cárdenas and Matanzas," said Butler. "We'll make Cuba by three in the morning."

I nodded. I was still drowsy. In truth, I was stupefied. It occurred to me that death should not come to one in this thick and clouded state.

"Do you want some rum?" asked Butler.

"I'd rather sleep," I said.

"Man, I'm drum-tight. It'll stay that way until we get back."

"I would have expected no less," I told him, and went below again, thinking no good thoughts about Butler, since he had now given me to understand that sleep before combat was no virtue, but an overindulgence. If Butler's character was not splendid, his adrenaline was nonetheless superb.

In the galley, men were lying down any way they could, two to a narrow bunk, four on the galley table, two on the galley deck, now three as I joined them. The floorboards were damp, but warm enough in any event, and since others had gone up on deck, there was room to stretch out; I slept between the sloshing of the bilge and the battering of the hull against a rolling swell. The fetid odor that rises from men who eat garlic and perspire in black clothes went through the galley; by the shielded light of a blue ten-watt bulb over the sink, I watched Cubans inching up their black hoods with the instinctive movement of a sleeper wishing to breathe more easily; then pulling them down over their face in the reflex of awakening. To what end were these hoods? Was it their families they were looking to protect, or the bonds of magic? On this dark tropical sea where the Gulf Stream met the long roll of the Atlantic, magic was only a minor ally of commerce, but on the southern shore of Cuba, incantations washed in from the Caribbean. I thought of the facsimile of the Matahambre copper mines that we had constructed at full scale in the Everglades. Over the last nine months, exile commandos had trained there for demolitions work. Mock raids had been practiced. In each training raid we had satisfied the scenario, which was to succeed (figuratively) in dynamiting the model, but we had never been able to blow up the real works. In the last attempt on the Matahambre, eight raiders went ashore in the black hours after midnight, and were flushed by a Castro patrol. Six of the commandos made it back to shore long enough to be evacuated. That had been our most ambitious effort on the Mata- hambre, and it, too, had failed ignominiously. They never reached shore.

Now we were being sent out. We had dispensed with detailed preparation. We were to do no more than rendezvous with a few Cubans who would know where to conceal the flares for the techno- logical magic that would follow—a full invasion force, several orders of magnitude more mighty than *santería*. Half asleep, I mused.

Then it occurred to me that I might be entering sleep for the last, or for one of the last times I would ever sleep. The mystery came over me then as never before, and I understood that we live in two states of existence, wakefulness and sleep, exactly those daily manifests pro- vided us for life and for death; we were two histories living in one; at that moment, I wished to write a last letter to Kittredge adjuring her never to give up her theoretical work, for it was profound, yes, profound, and so adjuring her, was waking up—I did not sleep after all—merely lay in the poetic detritus that blows about the marketplace of the mind as one returns from the deep, and I sat up, and felt ready for action even if there were hours to wait. Then, taking a few deep breaths of the foul air of the galley, I pulled down my hood and went on deck.

Butler was up with the skipper on the flying bridge. I knew the man, Eugenio Martínez. I had written about him to Kittredge. He had made more sorties to Cuba than any other boatman in southern Florida; he was a hero with a sad story, of which half of JM/WAVE was by now aware. He wished to bring his parents out of Havana, but Harvey had forbidden it. Even as I came up the ladder, he was approaching the subject.

"Tonight, a guy stops by me and says, 'I have my hood on, so you do not know who I am, but I know you. You are Rolando.'

" 'If you know me so well,' I say to him, 'then you know I am Eugenio Martínez and am only called Rolando.' 'That I know as well,' he answers, 'but we are told to call you Rolando.' 'Of what use is that,' I say, 'when even the DGI knows Rolando is Eugenio?' You see, Mr. Castle . . ."

"You can call me Frank," said Dix.

"All right, Frank, Frank Castle. Frank, I will call you. The argument I hear from Mr. O'Brien, your boss, the corpulent man, is that my parents are well known at their home in Cuba, and it is certain capture for me if I try to reach them. I accept the logic of such matters because I am, by part, Spanish. If you are blessed and cursed with such blood, it becomes your duty to obey the laws of logic. That is a necessity for violent people if they detest chaos."

This speech had been so clearly uttered that I assumed Eugenio Martínez might continue speaking. I was mistaken, however. He could serve a silence. We served with him. His silences supported as much cerebration as speech. Up on the flying bridge, we rolled in the swell—the horizon, like a compass needle, doomed forever to adjust itself. Below was the ongoing message of the inboard motors working for us, working for us. We listened to the silences in the lull between each wind. Martínez had listened for so many nights that the silence may have belonged to him. He had a long triangular face with a long Spanish nose and dark eyes in a full depth of socket that seemed ready to take in all his experience, a way, I suppose, of saying that he had seen a good deal and paid the price. I thought his eyes were haunted —had he seen as many ghosts as corpses?

That is a great deal to perceive at night under a clear but moonless sky, so I will admit that I had drunk with him two nights ago at Butler's suggestion, and, as is obvious, honored him now. Even my father, however, fond of saying, "I wouldn't trust a Cuban as far as I could throw him, although I would be happy to throw him through a plate-glass window," had also said, "Give me a hundred men like Eugenio Martínez and I will take Cuba myself." So I was pleased to be up on the flying bridge and felt as open to hero-worship as on any fevered day at St. Matt's. It would not have surprised me if the sky behind us were to go up in a conflagration of fiery mountains, and the unspeakable white light that propelled the mushroom cloud would sear our eyes. No more would it have surprised me if Havana, down the main a hundred miles to starboard, had flared up like a rocket in a tower of flame. The reality of our situation only came to me through the flexing of my feet in response to the roll of the boat. I could sense that we must be near to Cuba. If I was not yet able to see land, Communist searchlights, full of agitation, were flashing away from twenty miles off like that flutter of heat lightning when the forces above are not yet large enough to drive a bolt through the sky.

I had studied the map and knew where the dinghies were to put in to shore, but the coast was irregular. Mangrove swamps, dignified on the map as offshore keys, sat next to coral reefs. So soon as we had transferred the men, the flares, and our ammunition from *La Princesa* into the dinghies, we would run due south a few miles to find our beach. Let there be, however, one patrol boat to roar out of its concealment in the mangrove keys, and we would have to race off to the nearest inlet too shallow for them to follow.

Now, the closer we came to Cuba, the more we saw of other ships. Freighters and fishing trawlers passed in the distance. A U.S. Naval convoy of eight vessels, its flagship a destroyer, out, doubtless, from Key West, sailed by to some destination in the east—was it the line of quarantine? We were traveling in radio silence. All the same, my interest in the world had diminished. What we were about to do was beginning to seem all that there was to do. For the last hour, our *prácticos* had been busy pumping up the rubber dinghies, checking equipment, breaking out assault rifles from the racks, and stacking cartons of flares on deck. Butler and I sat at the edges of this, ranked somewhere between Agency observers and honored guests. If we were to measure the venture by our usefulness, our presence might be a folly. I knew the physical taste of fear then, and it was nothing remarkable. An upwelling of bile embittered my nose and throat. It occurred to me that keeping control of myself might not be automatic.

Butler spoke at that instant. "You and me are in the same dinghy," he said, his voice agreeably husky.

"Good."

"You'll be my passenger."

I didn't know whether to feel relieved or humiliated.

"These are okay men," he went on.

"You know them?"

"I've trained with a couple. If it goes all right, there is nothing to it. If it goes wrong, you don't need training. It will be a mess. For the Castros more than for us."

"You sound like you are up on this."

"I hit the beach at Girón."

"You what?"

"Unofficially."

"Why didn't you tell me before?"

He shrugged.

I had no idea if he was telling the truth. It seemed to me that he could be. I was angry. I had thought somehow that we were going out as innocents together. I knew that some intolerable condition between us, present at the edge of every mood since our one abominable night in Berlin, might be thereby shriven. But now I saw myself as a sacrificial clown. Yes, it was better to be angry than afraid.

I spent my last thirty minutes on *La Princesa* trying to familiarize myself with the Czech machine pistol handed to me. It had a curved magazine holding thirty 9mm rounds, could be set for semi or full automatic, and could probably, if need arose, be fired from the hip out of a careening dinghy. Not even hours of practice could guarantee such shooting.

The dinghies were put over the side and loaded, waterproof carton by waterproof carton. Next came ourselves, six men in each boat. Eugenio Martínez came to the rail to say good-bye.

"*Suerte,*" he whispered, and we clasped hands. I felt cleansed; I was setting out.

This lofty intuition was maintained for as long as it took to keep one's balance and sit down. The swell was sullen, and we were pitching too much for spiritual illumination. "Straight in, due south," said Martínez at the last. He would meet us at approximately this place on the waters in twenty hours—that is, at eleven tonight—it was now three in the morning—or, if we did not appear, would come back on each following hour through the night.

The dinghy had a compass and a wheel mounted on a plywood dashboard. Butler, steering the boat, was taking us in at ten knots, a speed slow enough for the muffled sound of our twin exhausts to blend with the wind. The chop was in our favor. It would not be easy to detect a black dinghy from any distance when the bob of the wave rose higher than our profile except when we were lifting over a crest. We did not speak. Words could carry more clearly than the throb of a motor. Yet, I could hear another motor, faint as the wash of surf on the shore, and realized it was our companion dinghy moving toward its separate rendezvous. The night air was heavy. We pushed forward slowly, as if ensconced in pillows, the dinghy so closely loaded that our freeboard was not six inches, and we shipped a little water with every rise and fall, and bailed it out with plastic milk jugs cut in half, painted black, attached by a length of rope to a ring in the rubber floor of the dinghy; the sound of bailing added to the quiet advertisement of our passage.

Shore was approaching. A line of phosphorescence washed onto a narrow beach. Were our people waiting for us, or would we be met by Castro's militia? The rubber bottom grated on the sand, and I stood up with the others and stepped over the side of the dinghy into a few inches of water, my muscles as tight as a clenched fist. Without a sound, all six of us pulled the dinghy twenty feet up the beach, enough to reach the shelter of a small sea-bent tree whose leaves bent so low as to paw the ground. In the night silence, a gourd fell. Its impact on landing was as raucous as the cry of an owl. Out of the thicket behind the beach came a swarm of small sounds, crawling, creeping, unstinted, inexhaustible—in that thicket was the mill of generation itself. To the rapt advance of vegetation growing came the sounds of insects eating the vegetation.

"Hubbard," whispered Butler, "I need you."

He had removed the cushion of his driver's seat from the dinghy and it now unfolded into a long black bag. We inserted our heads, turned on a pencil light, and studied his map. "We're off the mark," he whispered. "We can't be off by more than a quarter of a mile, but is it to the east or the west?" I peered at the map. At the place where we were supposed to have put in, a stream flowed down from the woods to divide the beach. Where we had landed was no stream.

"Well," I said, "the current was running west to east."

"I know," he said, "but I could have overcorrected."

As we came in, I had perceived a low knoll some few hundred yards to the west of us. By the topographical lines on our map, the knoll had to be a thousand yards west of the stream.

"Go east," I said.

Under the black enclosing blanket, we spoke with our faces inches apart. I felt a distinct desire to terminate this dialogue. Butler, however, kept studying the map as if to deny my conclusion. "You may be right," he said at last, and we withdrew.

Now the question was whether to send a man east to reconnoiter the beach and, ideally, locate our waiting guerrillas, or push the boat into the surf once more and ride along parallel to the shore. If I had been in command, I might have sent one man east. He would attract less attention and if intercepted the shots would warn us. Butler, however, decided to get back into the water. Our reception party would be expecting a rubber boat, not a man on foot.

"One more item," said Butler. "If there is a firefight, and we are captured, don't get caught with that rifle."

"I know that," I said. Harvey not only had told me as much, but drew a finger across his neck for punctuation. Before we left, he had provided us with a cover story that could prove sufficient. We were here in Cuba as reporters for *Life* magazine, ready to describe a raid; Butler was the photographer, indeed he had a camera with him, and I was the writer. Our *Life* accreditation had been gotten ready for us overnight by a JM/WAVE shop. If we were caught, Wild Bill would contact an editor he knew at *Life*. The magazine would back us up. Such was our cover. Yes, here on the beach, just arrived, two stringers down from New York, Frank Castle and Robert Charles, marginal journalists shipping out on a gamble. It was not particularly reassuring cover, since I had had no time to work up my biography, but it could suffice. Who in the DGI would know a great deal about the inner workings of *Life* magazine?

Even as we dragged the dinghy back into the surf, my mind was developing the scenario. If captured, I would tell the DGI that I had been in Miami for only a week, long enough to meet some coyotes. I would describe the coyotes. That would check out, doubtless, with what the DGI knew. For the next few minutes, as we rode parallel to the shore not two hundred feet out, searching the beach for the mouth of a small stream, I felt as creative as an actor discovering the subtler character embedded in his role. I decided on my boyhood. It had been spent in Ellsworth, Maine. My father was a carpenter; my mother a housewife. I would have graduated from Ellsworth High, which would mark the end of my formal schooling. The DGI would not have a yearbook from Ellsworth High—conceivably the KGB, but not the DGI.

It was just as well that I enjoyed my scenario, for that proved the last fruitful meditation I was to have for a time. Around a slight turn in the beach, we came upon a stream, and Butler rapped my shoulder once in affirmation, and took us in to shore. Once again we landed, once again we dragged the dinghy into the cover of a low tree, and waited, and listened to the sounds of vegetation growing.

Since no trail went up into the bush, only the stream which was no more than a brook, we reconnoitered it far enough to post a *práctico* at the first bend. He was back, however, in twenty minutes. The mosquitoes had proved too fierce. Butler handed the man insect repellent and sent him back.

We waited. The password was *parangón*. The reply was *incompetente*. My hearing grew ready. *Parangón*—paragon. Would it come in a hoarse voice or a whisper? The insects came instead. I took out my repellent and shared it with Butler. He was impatient with waiting. Back went our heads into the black bag to study the map once more. If, for the sake of hypothesis, we had made an error of more than half a mile on the first approach, then the knoll from which I had taken my calculations could have been mistaken for another headland further down the coast. Our faces six inches apart, our breath disturbed by the anxiety that we were losing any authoritative relation to this map, we argued.

I refused to give up my interpretation. We did not remove our heads from the bag until the penultimate moment. For in another ten seconds the missing Cubans came forth from the brook in the company of our *práctico*, and a whispered set of greetings were joined in the darkness of the low trees that bordered the beach. I thought of how much quick happiness was available in war! I had rarely taken to strangers so much as these six Cubans who had joined us at the head of the stream, and in the dark I could not even see their faces.

In the beginning, there was much translation. Our hosts spoke a dialect I could not comprehend. So they were obliged to address themselves to a *práctico* who communicated with me. It took time. Whispered links were lost, and there were problems to discuss. Once the boat was unloaded, were we to drag it up the stream until we found a clearing large enough to hide it, or should we let out the air, stuff it in the thicket, and use the foot pump on our return to blow it up again? When it developed that there was no likely place upstream, we took the second course and bound the deflated rubber skin into an object the size of a large suitcase, then located a hollow for it.

Now we were ready to transport the flares. They came in forty-pound cartons. Since the guides who had come to meet us knew the turns of the stream where the Castro militia could set up an ambush, one of them took the point, another the rear, and all of us, Butler, myself, the four *prácticos*, and the six locals, each shouldered a forty-pound carton. That took care of all but two boxes. When the heaviest man in our welcoming party handed his machete to a friend and put a carton on each of his shoulders, Butler decided to do the same, thereupon giving me his assault rifle. Loaded with one carton and two weapons, I joined the others as we went up the brook in the dark.

We slogged along in water that came to our knees, switched from bank to bank on the rocks, slid in mud, sat down in mud, dropped a carton from time to time. In places, the stream became a pool and we walked in water to our waists. I do not know if we covered a mile, but it felt like five and took considerably more than an hour and much agonized breathing before we reached a dirt road adjacent to the watercourse and found a clearing where the cases could be stacked. A truck, we were promised, would arrive before dawn to transport the flares. The people with us knew no more than how to guide us to the clearing. Now we were told that it would be wise to return to the beach. It was always possible that the militia would drive along this road.

"I'm staying here," said Butler, "until the truck arrives."

One of the Cubans tried to explain the situation. If the militia were to come by and discover the cartons, that would not be good for the local community. On the other hand, it would not necessarily be a disaster since a gang from Matanzas could have been squirreling away their ordnance here. Should we be found, however, a skirmish with the militia had to ensue, and then there could be dead men to account for. It was better if we went back right now.

"Tell this dude," said Butler, "that there is nothing more important than our flares. We are going to wait until the truck arrives."

I never had to translate his remark. Our vehicle came along then. It was not a truck, but an old and very large Lincoln sedan, showing a faded green paint job in the dawn.

We loaded fourteen muddy cartons into the trunk and rear seat of the car, and with no more than a blanket to cover all visible loot, the driver, who looked young enough to be a student, offered one remarkable smile, his teeth as white as his mustache was black, and took off in the direction he had come.

There was now nothing to do but go back downstream. We would have to spend our day in the thicket hoping to find a place where we would not be tormented altogether by insects. Tonight, we would inflate our dinghy and return to *La Princesa*. I could feel Butler's disappointment that no more had happened.

I could understand. There should have been more. It took no more than twenty minutes to return to the beach. I will not dwell on our day. We were in tropical woods and foliage. There was nothing for it but to pick a spot in the brush, drench ourselves in insect repellent, and try to sleep in the miserable condition of starting up each time a sound came from the forest. Out at sea we could hear patrol boats, and above us, in the spiderweb of sky visible through overhanging foliage, jet planes passed. Once in the morning and again

in the afternoon, a helicopter took its airborne promenade along the
beach. Time passed in a misery of insects macho enough to fight
through repellent and make the sting. I discovered that the secret was
not to push against the phlegmatic disposition of time.

At twilight, a fiery apocalypse descended in the west between
green and purple clouds. With evening, the insects grew ferocious.
Butler would wait no longer and had us move the rubber boat out to
a sandbar near the mouth of the stream. Still protected by foliage, we
took turns on the foot pump and in half an hour, it was inflated. We
were loading the last of our rifles, ammunition boxes, and machetes,
when a gunboat, perhaps thirty feet long, motored along, scanning the
beach. If it had been less dark, we might have been detected.

Fifteen minutes later, we put out to sea. It would not take thirty
minutes to reach our rendezvous, but we no longer wanted to stay on
land. It was as if we had to quit the dark earth body of Cuba, too
fecund, too strange. I felt like an insect buried in the thick mat of an
enormous beast, nothing visible of his head, his tail, his limbs.

We rode out, hunched over in a low profile, and I, sitting beside
Butler, my eye on the compass and the tide, muttered small correc-
tions to him from time to time. Although he was never partial to the
suggestions of others on how to adjust any of his skills, since he was
possessive of all of them, he had come to recognize that I knew more
about boats than he did, as well I should with a boyhood of Maine
summers, even if little enough of it had been spent in blubbercraft
stink-pots such as this, but, yes, I knew navigation, and he sensed it,
and we were on the mark, and thirty minutes early. No Martínez, no
sight of *La Princesa*, but at least we were past the coral reefs and the
mangrove keys, and if a patrol boat was going to bear down on us
now, it would not come from the near lee of a dark island.

With Martínez nowhere in sight, we headed further out to sea.
There was the likelihood, or so we had been told in Miami, that the
Cuban coast guard would not respect the three-mile limit if no American gunboats were visible, but we rode higher in the water now, our
weight reduced by 560 pounds of delivered flares. If the twin outboards held up, our dinghy ought to compete with the speed of any
old and much-repaired Cuban craft.

A half hour later, after completing the four turns of a nautical
square, we came back to where I hoped and calculated *La Princesa*
would be. It was another dark night and another clear sky, but far to
the east, clouds were being driven by wind.

Butler began to question my navigation. Could I have taken us through a trapezoid? Could I swear we were in the proper place?

"We are at the coordinates of the rendezvous," I said with all the confidence I could muster (although confidence was a tattered flag within), but I knew we could not steer by committee, so I convinced him to take one more square, this time but a half mile on each leg. At 11:15, *La Princesa* came motoring toward us looking as large as a galleon. Butler shook my hand. "We'll make a team yet," he said, and *La Princesa* idling, we came alongside, unloaded the dinghy, pulled it up after us, and went to the galley for coffee. I wondered if it ever felt better after a good day of rock climbing with Harlot.

It was then Butler asked about the line of quarantine. "It's over. The Russian ships have turned back," Martínez said. He repeated this news to the *prácticos*, and they received it without great happiness. There would be no invasion of Cuba now. Our flares would moulder in whichever dubious place they were stored.

Martínez had a more immediate concern, however. The other boat had missed its rendezvous. Martínez said, "That is why we were late. We waited for the others. Now we go back to look for them again."

It was a long hour. We ground along at half throttle, suffering a whiplike roll in the new wind that came out of the east. Tropical rain followed. I could see by our nearness to the mangrove keys that we were considerably closer to land than the three-mile limit.

Martínez said, "If they were chased from shore, they will be hiding in *these* keys," and he pointed with his pencil light to some mangrove isles on the chart. "I know the *práctico* who is leading the party. He is familiar with these lagoons. In there it is too shallow for the Castros to follow."

"What have you heard from Mr. O'Brien?" asked Butler.

"It was he who told me about the Russians."

"What else did he say?"

"He said: Return to Miami. *Pronto*."

"Why?"

"He said to tell you he was handling all kinds of hell." Martínez shrugged. "That may be true, but how am I to leave men behind?"

Butler nodded. He looked happy. "Hubbard," he said, "you and me have to go out and look for them."

Martínez nodded.

It was foolhardy. We would search through unfamiliar lagoons for

Cubans who might not even be there, but I would make no objection. It was easier to go back into those waters than to live with the knowledge that Butler was my moral superior.

We were ready. On our return, we would rendezvous with Martínez at a point midway between two mangrove keys on our chart. It would be inside the three-mile limit and that could prove hazardous for him, but it was simpler for us. Every hour for the next four hours, he would make a running pass through that area, and if we were not back by then, we were all in trouble, for it would be close to dawn. Now we spent twenty minutes in the galley going over the charts to mark the shallows in each of the keys and reefs we would be exploring.

Out in the dinghy, with no more than Butler and myself for ballast, handling was lively. At twenty knots we planed from wave to wave until the roar of the echoes chased us down to low throttle again, but now we knew the speed of our craft.

The area Martínez had chosen for us to explore contained in three square miles five keys and four coral lagoons. Methodically, shallow by shallow, our twin outboards raised until we drew no more than six inches, we ventured into every pool and bottom we could find in the dark, running aground in sand and mud, backing off, only to run aground again. Our rubber bow, bent by the trap of submerged roots, sprang back when we were free, our bottom scraped on shoals, we could have been blind men feeling our way through a cave. It was curious. The deeper we explored into each shallows, the further away seemed Castro's coast guard. I began to feel as if we were infiltrating our way into an organism. Swarms of insects welcomed us in each lagoon, and we traversed the coral reefs ripple by ripple, my eyes beginning to see a spectrum of differentiations in the dark until I hated to flash the pencil light on the chart, for it deprived me for a little while of such keen sight. I realized that I was feeling something close to affection for Butler. He had forced me into our venture, yet it was worth it. How much it was worth! Entering this wilderness of swamp, wild growth, and water was equal to exploring every cavern of myself where demeaning fear was stored. On we went.

There were few openings in the mangrove keys, and many entrances dwindled into trackless swamps, but we kept the anticipation that in one of these shallow flows we would find our people. So we thought, and at the depth of each small exploration, one of us would cry like a mournful bird, *"Parangón."*

In the third hour, in the lightening air before the last dark hour preceding dawn, we heard a man croak back, *"Incompetente."* So, we found him. A weak voice. He lay with one foot caked in blood on the rubber floor of his ruptured dinghy. He had ripped the boat open on a coral reef, had reached this stream, and tugging the boat behind, had lacerated his foot.

Where were the others?

Dead, he said. Captured. There had been an ambush. They had all been ambushed, and only he and his friend had escaped to the boat.

Where was his friend?

Dead. A patrol boat had chased them. His friend had taken a machine-gun bullet that blew him out of the boat. Right in the middle of the pursuit.

"Bullshit," whispered Butler to me. "He threw the dead man overboard so the dinghy would go faster."

"None of the story works," I said.

It didn't. On the pretense of looking at the blood oozing through his boot, I used the pencil light to study his face. He had a scrawny beard, a straggling mustache, a thin and sallow face—he looked like a man you would not trust: one more failed version of the son of God.

Did it matter now what he had done or failed to do? Unless he had dashed off in the boat while the others were ambushed on land, his real story, whatever cowardice it might protect, was probably true to this degree: The others were gone. He certainly had the look of a man who had lost the men around him.

There was one more question: Was the patrol boat that had chased him into this narrow inlet still circling the key?

We found the answer. We had just emerged from this swamp when a cabin cruiser with a searchlight in its bow came around a low promontory and bore down on us.

How loud was the machine gun! How dazzling its light! Tracers struck the water to the right of us, then to the left, for we were careening side to side. Were we two hundred yards from the patrol boat or was it closer?

I remember that I had no fear of dying. Adrenaline kept prayer at bay. I was enormously excited. I was full of awe. Death was a great temple and we stood at the gate—the light from the muzzle of the machine gun seemed as livid as a high-voltage spark jumping a gap. The sky seemed to jump, or was it our boat? The stars leapt like fireworks. I remember letting loose a prodigious whoop. Butler screamed at our pursuers, *"Fuck your eye-e-e-e-e-s."* He would stand up from time to time to draw a higher angle of fire, then dip into a quick turn. Each time he stood up, the machine gun would fire at his head, and its tracers went into the air. Since those tracers were no longer kicking up water to the left or right of us, the machine gunner lost his aim and Butler would veer off at a wild angle to escape him for a few seconds. Once, we even lost the searchlight as well, and streaked in the dark around the bend of a key and on over a coral reef we had negotiated already and knew we could draft. Before that shallow, the patrol boat had to bear off. In a fury, it sounded its Klaxon. The siren screamed through the dark as loudly as if the invasion of Cuba had commenced after all. Butler was sobbing from laughing so hard. "All cops are the same," he said. "All the world over."

We picked up another channel on the other side of the reef, put our dinghy up to full throttle and plotted a course for rendezvous. A mile to the east, I could see our pursuer searching every lagoon and shore with its light. I punched Butler on the arm. It was inescapable. No one was worse than Butler.

"You son of a bitch, you are fucking pure," I said, which was as much obscenity as I had ever put into a sentence. It all went into the broil. Given the noise of our outboards, he could hardly hear me.

21

October 30, 1962

Dear Kittredge,

Well, we have all gone through such exceptional experiences these last ten days. I am still piecing together the various crises with the Russians, and, of course, I wait to hear what you will add to these matters. I will say that I am impressed once again by your psychic powers. In your last letter to me—it does seem a year ago—you said, "Do not do anything insane with people like Dix Butler."

I did, and have lived not to regret it, and would write to you about our eight-reeler in the swamps but am worn out. Suffice it that after two trips in a rubber dinghy through Cuban territory, we managed to get back to our mother ship, *La Princesa*. I wish to write to you now about its skipper, a remarkable man named Eugenio Martínez.

The return trip, incidentally, was gloomy. We lost five men and Eugenio did not wish to return without looking for them through another day, but a radio message came from Harvey. Martínez was *commanded* to come back. It was an emergency, stated Harvey.

Martínez followed these orders, although they went against every instinct in him. He fell into the most palpable depression. It was a bad loss. Whole networks have been rolled up in Havana, but our sea missions usually get away with lighter casualties. So we drank a lot of rum to fortify ourselves against the chop returning to Miami, and before it was over, Martínez told a gloomy tale I want to pass on to you. It enabled me to recognize why he reacts to depression as if it were his antagonist. Ghost-ridden, his dread is deep at not returning for those lost *prácticos*.

The story he told concerned an old friend named Cubela, Rolando Cubela. By the portrait Martínez gave of him, Cubela was a student leader back in the early fifties when there must have been a dozen such fellows at the University of Havana ready to overthrow Batista. Fidel Castro happens to be the man who emerged from the crucible, but there were others. Cubela was one of them. Rolando Cubela de Cuba. Sounds like a *jefe,* does it not? Martínez went into no details on Cubela's appearance, and I did not dare to interrupt, since Eugenio does speak out of an inner gravity that tends to solemnize one's reactions when around him, but I did receive a powerful impression that Cubela is a man of some physical stature, more than ordinarily handsome, and full of presence (not unlike Castro, what?). For that matter, Cubela, according to Martínez, has now become one of Castro's intimates.

Let me take it in order. Back in 1956, Martínez and Cubela belonged to a student group who believed in calculated assassination of government officials. Under Batista, there was a plenitude of sadistic officers, but the Martínez-Cubela concept was not to attack the worst monsters, because truly bad officials stirred up enormous animosity against the regime. It was Batista's decent officials who had to be done away with—they confused the issue! The target selected, therefore, was the chief of military intelligence, a gentleman named Blanco Rico who was not only opposed to torture, but had a reputation for courtesy to his captives. By vote of their cell, Cubela was selected to pull the trigger. I couldn't, incidentally, quite make out the politics of this group—some sort of anarcho-syndicalism, perhaps, with middle-class roots. Cubela, for instance, was studying medicine —ah, these Cubans! On a night in October 1956, at which time Castro was already in the Sierra Maestra, Cubela managed to encounter Blanco Rico in a Havana nightclub called Montmartre (homage to Toulouse-Lautrec!) and proceeded to put a bullet through his head. "Rico died," said Martínez, "but only after he lived long enough to look Cubela in the eye and smile. That smile has been described to me one hundred times. It was generous. To Cubela, it said: 'My friend, you have made a grave mistake, and I forgive you, even if my ghost will not.'

"At that moment, of course, Cubela did not linger. He ran out into a waiting car, drove away to a place of concealment, and in a week we smuggled him out to Miami. I joined Rolando the following week. Havana was no longer comfortable for our people. With the death of Blanco Rico, the Batista police were running amok.

"One of our group came from a family who had money in Miami. Alemán. He owned the Miami Stadium and a cheap motel. That was where we lived. At his motel. The Royal Palms."

Kittredge, I am afraid I interrupted Martínez here. "The Royal Palms," I said, "is exactly where I stayed when I first came to Miami."

"That, Robert Charles, may be why I tell this story." He swigged his rum. *"Salud."*

We drank. He talked. I will not try any longer to suggest his speech. I find even as I attempt to recapture his tone that I miss a portion of it. And, of course, I find myself improving his English. Let me summarize what he said, and where I do recall an expression that truly belonged to him, I will, of course, offer it to you. It seems that the Royal Palms was housing a good number of revolutionaries at this time, all rent-free, ar.d Cubela and Martínez lived there as roommates. Cubela was considered a hero, but Blanco Rico dominated his dreams. "Blanco Rico keeps smiling," Cubela told Martínez. "It goes so far into me that a cancer is forming in my intestines."

Cubela recovered, however. Rico disappeared from his dreams. So he decided to go back to Cuba and fight for Castro in the Sierra Escambray. Since this was another front, separate from the Sierra Maestra, Castro, pleased to have a man of Cubela's caliber, bestowed on him the rank of *comandante,* the highest rank in Fidel's army. Cubela and his men even entered Havana three days before Castro completed his triumphal march across Cuba, indeed Cubela was in command of the force that occupied the presidential palace.

For months, he drove around Havana in a grand touring sedan. On a drunken night, "not able to distinguish sufficiently between happiness and the lofty emotions of a maniac, he had a smashup. He killed a young girl." That death brought back to him the ghost of Blanco Rico. Before long, Cubela was talking to a psychiatrist, who, in his turn—he worked for another revolutionary group—was trying to convince Cubela that the only way to put Blanco Rico's ghost to rest was to assassinate Fidel Castro. "In Cuba," said Martínez, "even our psychiatrists are *pistoleros*."

Kittredge, I have not wanted to interrupt this story to dwell on the circumstances of the telling, but we did hear it up on the flying bridge of *La Princesa*. The rigging of our platform was creaking on every roll of the ship. Since Martínez had waited out the day in the Gulf Stream hoping Harvey would rescind his order to return and we could make another search for the men who were missing, it was late afternoon and we were getting low on gas before we turned north. The story was heard, therefore, at night. It is not difficult to visualize ghosts in these waters. As I listened, it occurred to me that our famous specter of the Keep, Augustus Farr, did perform his acts of piracy in the Caribbean, and I must say he now felt near to me, but then, I had not really slept in forty-eight hours.

Somewhat abruptly, Martínez concluded his tale. It seems Cubela told Martínez, "Do you know, one day I will kill Fidel Castro."

I shall never comprehend Cubans. Even though Cubela now occupies a high position in the Ministry of Foreign Affairs, and would certainly have nothing to do with his old friend Martínez, "I am," says Eugenio, "convinced that he will in fact terminate Fidel's days on earth."

We returned to Miami to discover that Harvey's days here are numbered. It seems that in this last week, while Russian ships were approaching the line of our blockade, Harvey sent out sixty men to Cuba in different operations right in the teeth of Bobby Kennedy's order to call off all raids.

Well, Harvey is of the old school: They call your bluff and double it. His hatred for the Kennedys—which up to now I have virtually spared you—has magnified so much in the last six months that he is beginning to see them as the root of all evil. I wish I could pretend this is his special aberration, but, in fact, a poisonous bile is circulating through JM/WAVE in reaction to the missile crisis. Our Cubans feel let down, and our own personnel are of the same mind. There is much talk that we were too easy on Castro and Khrushchev. As you may have gathered, there has always been loose talk about assassinating Castro; the Miami Cubans serve up the idea daily. The follow-up joke around here these days, however, is: "When does the elimination take place?" "Of whom, Fidel?" "No," goes the reply, "Jack."

Such sentiments represent a minority of the personnel at JM/WAVE—we, like all other places in the Agency, do keep our midwestern Ph.D.'s with their wives, children, and threewheelers on the lawn, but, in truth, Kittredge, the mood is ugly. A lot of people say they were ready to go to war last week (especially now that they realize they don't have to) but I know the intensity of the root feeling. In my small taste of combat (we had to evade some machine-gun fire) it felt exhilarating at the time. Now, however, I wake up angry many a night and want to fire back. If I feel thus warlike, be assured that others are raging.

In any event, Harvey not only broke Kennedy's no-raid rule, but got caught. When Bobby queried Harvey directly, Wild Bill sent back the following memo: "Have complied with your directive, but three of my teams are beyond recall."

That produced an incredible set-to at the next meeting of Excom. Harvey wrote a memo for his own files after it was over, and even ended up showing it to a few of the selected troops, including myself. He was so agitated that he actually was desirous of my reaction. The memo rambles and is full of the inner disturbance with which it was written, but, considering that Harvey does not come off well, I was able to say that I respected his scrupulous reporting of the exchange with Bobby Kennedy.

KENNEDY: You are dealing with people's lives and you go off on a half-assed operation such as this? Things were as delicate as spun glass out there. On whose authority did you send sixty men into Cuba at a time when the slightest provocation might unleash a nuclear holocaust?

HARVEY: These operations were consequential to military requests made of me for the underwriting of invasion contingencies.

KENNEDY: Are you saying the Pentagon put you up to this?

HARVEY: In the spirit of mutual underpinning of coordinated projects, affirmative.

KENNEDY: Bullshit.

At this point, Bobby polled every military presence in the room. McNamara, Maxwell Taylor, General Lemnitzer, and Curtis LeMay were among those asked whether they were witting of this. All replied: Negative.

KENNEDY: Mr. Harvey, we need a better explanation. I've got two minutes.

HARVEY: With all due respect to the high level of personnel in this room, and in no sense contravening input to which the gentlemen here polled have access, the disposition of military decisions does not in all cases cover the impromptu and counterdelegated, since in-practice directives often contradict antecedent decisions.

KENNEDY: Why don't you try English?

HARVEY: You ordered an immediate halt to all operations against Cuba. I made a clear distinction between operations and agents. I initiated no operations. But I did not wish to have the United States find itself in a shooting war in need of all the intelligence it could get and lacking same. I decided to make one last attempt to send some agents in.

At this point, Harvey's memo to himself states:

On this set of remarks, the Attorney General gathered his papers and left the room. Several others followed. John McCone, also present, departed without taking me aside to offer his customary critique of what I had presented. Later, by virtue of information relayed to me by several concerned high Agency friends and close associates, I have become privy to the knowledge that Director McCone said to Ray Cline, Deputy Director of Intelligence—the quote is as relayed to me—"Harvey has destroyed himself today. His usefulness has ended."

Intercession by Richard Helms and Hugh Montague has delayed activation of this eventuality. I am inclined to interpolate here that Director McCone's present esteemed position as prime detector of the medium-range missile installment in Cuba is due to my diligent efforts to illumine him as to Communist investiture of such nuclear ordnance in our adjacent waters.

Set down in a state of clear recall two hours after the National Security Council Executive Committee meeting on October 26, 1962, held in the Joint Chiefs of Staff War Room.

WKH

This morning, Harvey could rent out his office as a funeral parlor. I feel sorry for him. Doubtless, I am too tolerant to make an ideal Agency man. Contradict me, I implore you.

Devotedly,
Herrick

On rereading this letter, I decided to remove my account of Rolando Cubela. If there were to be any more attempts on Castro, Cubela might be of special use. That night, therefore, I put together a succinct version of his history, spoke of Cubela's present high status in the Cuban government, and sent it not only to Harlot, but to Cal in Tokyo. I notified each of them that the other had received the same communication.

Harlot's answer came first:

Good nose. We are in need of a likely fellow. Buddha, you may be interested to hear, is now dipping his enormous belly into Cal's old swimming hole. I pass on to you for immediate consumption by the paper-shredder the following communication from J. Edgar to Robert K., dated October 29. J. Edgar didn't even wait for the missiles to be put to bed.

An underworld informant of the FBI has stated confidentially to me that he can arrange Castro's assassination. While I would certainly agree with the Attorney General that the CIA's plot with the Mafia has been foolish, I now feel ready, if desired, to offer the good offices of the FBI. The informant was, of course, told that his offer is outside our jurisdiction and no commitments can be made to him. At this time we do not plan to further pursue the matter. Our relationship with this informant, however, has been most carefully guarded and we would feel obligated to handle any re-contact of him concerning the matter if such is desired.—JEH

Say nothing further, therefore, about your find. From now on, refer to him as AM/LASH. GOLIATH.

P.S. Too bad about Harvey. An irreplaceable loss to me.
Repeat: Destroy this communication. OTI.

OTI meant *on the instant*. I did not comply. I put it in my Miami safe deposit box.

Next day, a brief letter came from Cal by Tokyo pouch:

Hugh and I are in accord for once. We will contact AM/LASH. (A damned awkward saddlebag, but then we have a collateral agent called AM/BLOOD. We just do the best we can.)

It may interest you to know that McCone has already told me to get ready to replace Wild Bill, albeit I will receive a reduced and highly discreet version of Task Force W. Believe me, it will soon be renamed. I would feel elated to get back in the trenches again were it not for Bill Harvey. What a tragic lapse. That poor hardworking man.

Your own HALIFAX

22

November 15, 1962

Dear Kittredge,

You complain that you felt an odd "air" to my last letter. It left you "truncated." I would offer a reminder that your promised account of the missile business remains nonexistent. The longer you wait, the more all that is bound to become nothing but history.

I will say that my brief sojourn in Cuba left me with intense animus against Castro. I would expect the worst from Khrushchev no matter how he has mellowed (if turnips, that is, can mellow), but by

Castro I feel betrayed. How could he have jeopardized his country and mine by accepting such an adventure?

The other night I received a little illumination on this matter that I would like to pass on to you. Since our expedition, Butler and I have been getting along fairly well and now eat and drink together a good bit. Much of the old mutual tension—about as easy to live with as the edge of a razor blade—has abated. So I went so far as to attempt a reclamation project. You see, Harvey assigned Chevi Fuertes to him a few months ago, and they don't get along. Fuertes, by my lights, is brilliant, and I'm trying to get Butler to recognize as much, for Chevi will give more of his best when he can thrive on applause. The other night I invited him to join us for dinner at an expensive restaurant in Fort Lauderdale where no Cuban any of us know is likely to pop his head in. I foresaw it as a treat for Chevi to dine out with his old case officer and his new one, but to give an idea of how crude Butler can be, the first thing he said as Chevi joined us was, "Get it straight, you are taking care of your end tonight. We pay enough for you to afford it."

"I will treat you both," replied Chevi, just a bit too grand in style, and so succeeded merely in irritating Butler further. Chevi, by Dix's view of things, was competing, and Dix is so prodigiously competitive that I would wonder at his sanity if I did not understand his rationale. He is monumental enough in his own eyes to be President of the U.S. If he is contemptuous of Kennedy, it is because Jack, by Butler's lights, is a rich pretender. Whereas if Dix ever gets into politics, he will go all the way on his own.

At any rate, it was no good beginning. I wanted to receive Fuertes' analysis of the missile crisis, for he has an insight into Khrushchev's and Castro's motives that we do not get from Agency folk or exiles, but Dix has only one ear at best. It fires him up that Fuertes knows more about Latin America than he does. Butler has his own critical powers, but hates to encounter superior insight on any subject. Chevi, in turn, having to stomach a good deal of hectoring from Butler over the jobs he performs for him, was not at all unhappy to stretch his intellectual wings.

With my aid and Butler's grudged interest, Fuertes managed to give an exposition that I will summarize together with occasional interruptions by Butler.

The key to the entire episode, Fuertes told us, is that, in the

beginning, Castro did not want the missiles. He argued with Khrushchev that they made no military sense. The U.S. would always have
overwhelming superiority. No, said Castro, give us sophisticated instructors and up-to-date ordnance. Let the Americans be obliged to
recognize that a land war could cause them many casualties.

"How do you know all this?" asked Butler.

"You are aware of the nature of my sources."

Fuertes was referring to his Miami contacts in the DGI. Butler, however, shook his head. "There is no way they could keen in
on this stuff authoritatively."

"Culture offers its own authority," said Fuertes. "I have pondered the nature of Castro for years. I comprehend Communist psychology. I have natural powers of synthesis."

"I never met a man with *natural powers of synthesis*," said
Butler, dicing the words, "who was not ready to abuse them."

"Let us say," I interrupted, "that Chevi will offer us a hypothesis."

There were further interruptions of this nature, but the above
is exemplary. Let me give you the notion as it finally emerged.
According to Fuertes, Khrushchev convinced Castro to accept the
missiles, but only by appealing to his honor. "That is the secret to
manipulating Fidel," said Chevi. "Castro likes to perceive himself as
a phenomenally generous person."

Up to this point, Khrushchev suggested, he had been helping
Castro. Now, Fidel could help him. His own Politburo had become
critical of the Soviet Premier's middle course with the United States.
As they saw it, a mockery existed in world balance when the United
States could maintain missiles just across the border from the U.S.S.R.
in Turkey, and the Soviets could offer nothing comparable. So
Khrushchev was looking to make a dramatic shift in the way that the
world perceived the two superpowers. Be assured, dear Fidel, the
United States would never go to war over missiles in Cuba. He,
Khrushchev, knew this. After all, the Soviets had seen the impractical-
ity of a showdown on Turkey. Together, therefore, said Khrushchev,
Fidel and he could steal the imperialists' lightning.

"This is what you learned from your sources?" said Butler.

"It is what they have heard. They are close to people who are
close to Castro."

"I call that gossip."

"No, Mr. Castle," said Fuertes, "it is gossip fortified by close scrutiny. No one is of more interest to Habaneros than Fidel. His passing comments, his private disclosures, his moods, are all open to the surrounding world of his intimates."

"And on the basis of your profound understanding of Fidel Castro and Cuban culture, are you prepared to tell me what you think, *personally*, of Castro's acceptance of the missiles?"

"More than ready," said Fuertes. "In my opinion, morally speaking, Castro had a fall from grace. Castro was correct in the first place; Cuba has no need for missiles."

"You are saying that he acceded," remarked Butler, "merely to return Khrushchev a favor?"

Fuertes had the opening he needed. He now delivered the lecture behind the lecture. What has to be understood, he explained, is the immensity of the glamour attached to the possession of nuclear missiles. There is not a leader in a Third World country who does not covet them. "It is equal to sex with a movie star. When Khrushchev agreed to remove the missiles in return for the United States forswearing any future invasion of Cuba, Castro was not pleased but enraged. He was losing his missiles."

"He had been taken," said Butler. "First Khrushchev lied to Kennedy; then he lied to Fidel. All Khrushchev wants is to get American missiles out of Turkey. We know the White House will give him that. We have a pussy for a President."

"I hear," said Chevi, "democracy in action."

"You bet," said Dix. "Now you tell me. Why do I have the impression you still cotton to Castro?"

"I may work for you, but I do not have to imbibe your prejudices. I like Fidel, yes. He is sympathetic. Yes! He is like all of us in Latin America who would change the given. There is one difference, however. He is more manly."

Within the objective of the evening, Chevi was not being responsible. I broke in long enough to say, "If you admire Fidel, why do you not join him?"

"Because I detest the Soviets. Unlike Fidel, I spent my youth in the Communist Party. I know just what he has gotten himself into. And, may I say, that is the fault of all of you."

Butler slapped his fist on the table loudly enough to turn a few heads in the restaurant. "Haven't you learned, Chevi, how to talk to Americans? You put a drop of oil on a piece of flannel. Then you wipe our ass carefully. I am tired of being told what is wrong with this country."

My mission was now dead in the water. We drank our coffee, paid up, and left in three separate cars. Ten minutes after I reached my apartment, Chevi rang the bell.

"Is it wise for you to be seen here?" I said.

He shrugged.

I poured a brandy and he talked. He was miserable with Butler; he was afraid of him; he kept waiting for Dix to turn on him physically. "It is not a stable environment."

"Why do you provoke it?"

"Because I would lose all respect for myself if I did not. Miami is worse than Uruguay. There, I merely double-crossed people I had grown up with. Some of them deserved it. Here, I am betraying brave men."

"The DGI?"

He nodded. "They are in danger of their lives every day. The exiles tear them apart as fast as they discover them."

"Do you come to visit me so that the DGI will kill you?"

He shrugged again. Now I understood the gesture. It was the saddest he could have made. A piece of paper is blowing down the street; why bestir oneself to pick it up?

I poured him more brandy and he talked for the next two hours. I was tired, but I must say, Kittredge, I was also beginning to wonder if our good double agent Fuertes was not working for the DGI more devotedly than for us. The fact that he had come to my apartment disturbed me. That could mean he was indifferent to his own welfare, or—just as likely—the DGI was well informed about his work with us. I was depressed by the knowledge that it was my duty to pass this suspicion on to Butler.

Still, I listened to Chevi. I had to. He has insight into matters I find puzzling.

Deep in brandy, Chevi's mood improved. He talked a good deal about Cuba. It startled me how close he sounded at one moment to your husband. "What is to be said of a country," remarked Fuertes, "that built its economy on African slavery and sugar? Consider its other products: rum, tobacco, brothels. Sexual specialty acts. *Santería*. When you live in a land where every day you have to ask yourself whether you are as evil as your economic roots, then, of course, you generate superhuman pride as a species of compensation. That is why Fidel is always seeking the all-but-unattainable, the gem concealed in history."

I am afraid I repeated, "The gem concealed in history?"

"There is a vision some of us seek that is beyond the limits of danger."

"I do not follow." (Kittredge, I did.)

"Fidel looks to what is unattainable." Chevi belched delicately over his brandy. It made an odd hissing sound. Perhaps his demon had just broken wind out of the wrong aperture. "Yes, you all try to kill Fidel," he said, "but I am the one who knows how."

"Why would you? You love him."

"I am operatic by nature. Dostoyevskian. I would kill him to come a little closer to the monstrosities in myself. Then I would weep for him. As it is, I laugh at all of you. So many attempts, so many failures."

"What makes you think we are making such attempts?"

"It is common knowledge in the DGI, Robert Charles, or whatever your name is this year." He laughed unpleasantly. "I do not know why you keep trying. I could do better."

"Yes. How would you go about it?"

"I repeat: By appealing to what is best in him."

"That is a principle, not a plan."

"Oh," he said, "you are looking for a procedure. Why don't you find a seashell of exceptional beauty. Fidel likes to scuba dive."

"I understand," I said.

"No, you do not. You would fill such a seashell with explosive plastic and put it on a reef where Fidel goes spear-fishing. You would enlist an accomplice to lead Fidel to the precise place. Then you would expect him to seize it. Close, Chico, but no cigar. His inner warning system—which is absolutely remarkable—would tell him to hesitate. The great rationalist of materialism, Fidel Castro, who kicks a wall, breaks his toe, and smashes a mirror when he hears that the Russians will take away his missiles, is yet so sensitive to American plots that even as he puts forth a hand to pick up an exceptional seashell, he will withdraw that hand. You need more than beauty to capture the fellow."

"I wish you would keep talking," I told him. "You create movies with your mouth." I was getting a little drunk myself. I was also beginning to feel ugly toward Fuertes in a way I could not quite name. He was so corrupt; he was so sure of himself.

"Yes, yes, movies. Excellent! Here is a concept for film. I would not only place the seashell in a coral cave, and use a paid servant of the CIA to lead Fidel to it, but I would have a *mayombero* cast a spell on a manta ray. The creature would fall in love with the seashell and never leave it. There it is, guarding the shell. That is when Castro might lose his awareness that this is a provocation. He would look to kill this dangerous opponent in order to obtain the prize." Fuertes began to laugh. "Yes," he said, "all you have to do is find a *mayombero* in Miami, or a marine animal trainer in Langley."

I let him finish his drink, then showed him the door.

Please write soon and in full. Is something amiss with you?

Devotedly,
Harry

Bemused by Chevi's scenario, I passed it on to Cal. In his answering letter from Tokyo, he wrote:

The manta ray business is wilder than pig squeal, but I must say I now feel a personal interest in pulling every hair out of the big Cuban's beard. How does he dare to live with himself? We will get him yet, thee and me. Soon.

HLFX

23

November 28, 1962

Dearest Harry,

Yes, I've been remiss in offering you any good running account of Jack and Bobby's negotiations with Khrushchev and Dobrynin, and now it's too late. You were right. I feel tedium descend on me at the thought of reconstructing all the fine moves. What does remain alive for me is Jack's unflappability as the Russian freighters approached the line of quarantine. There are moments when great political leaders not only receive the emoluments of the gods, but their terrors. Is this too grandiose? I don't care. I love Jack Kennedy for finding his balance between two horrors, submission or extermination, and maintaining that balance through all the stunts that Khrushchev pulled after the Russian freighters turned around. I will tell you, Harry, that I did not really believe in Jack Kennedy's pristine worth as a President before this happened. I liked him enormously because he had not gone dead inside like most major politicians—but for just that reason, perhaps, I secretly assumed he would not be equal to those monster Soviets who come to power with buckets of blood in the hall. Ditto Bobby. How could two Americans, well brought up, innocent as the well-to-do always are, manage not to panic? What bravery they showed at the core—to stay so long at the edge of the precipice! Even Hugh, who thinks that Khrushchev got out of a losing game with a little more than he should, does respect Jack a bit more. I, in contrast with Hugh, am deeply moved. Two brothers who love each other are worth more in the balance of history than one wily, filthy brute.

I expect you will be disappointed, but I am going to offer no more than a quick tour of the negotiations. Our side, naturally, wanted the missiles out, plus the removal of fifty Ilyushin bombers Khrushchev "sold" to Cuba. We also called for UN teams to be empowered to do ground inspection on the missiles. In return, we would offer our pledge not to invade Cuba, given the understanding that Castro would not try to subvert Latin America. Clear enough on paper, but it did depend on the timing of each proposal. Jack, you see, had to keep steering between his own hawks who wanted to make no deal at all unless we obtained everything on our terms, and doves like Adlai Stevenson who felt that it had been enough for Khrushchev to pull back his freighters. Moreover, Castro was not amenable to anything. He wouldn't give up his Ilyushin bombers; he wouldn't allow inspection of the missile sites; he wouldn't even agree to relinquish the missiles.

Harry, I won't give you any more of it. The key to these matters, I have discovered, is to separate out what is essential. Removal of the Cuban missiles was essential. So, Jack, by not insisting immediately on the recall of the fifty bombers (which are only a small weight in the whole balance), and by accepting Castro's refusal to permit UN teams (since our U-2 overflights dispense with the need for on-the-ground inspection), has been able to maneuver Khrushchev into getting these nuclear projectiles out of Cuba despite all of Castro's tantrums.

Enough. If I had not restricted myself to this quick tour of the problem, I would have had to send a ten-page letter every day for a week. Which is not what is on my mind. I would rather talk to you about Bobby Kennedy. He does occupy my thoughts these days. Since the summer, Bobby has been inviting us out fairly steadily to Hickory Hill. This, even though we are patently not Ethel's favorites. She is a good sort, I'm sure, a hearty soul full of compassion for the wounds she can see in people around her, if a bit brash and judgmental in relation to wounds she is oblivious of, but of course, she is *so* Catholic, and there are all those children. If I were in her place, I would end up as a heavy drinker.

Hugh is invited, I believe, for his tennis game, which is precise, elegant, ruthless. Everyone wants him for a doubles partner (until he deigns to give them a tongue-lashing). I, who used to be a fiend at field hockey during Radcliffe days, have a mean, determined, damn-you-I'll-get-it-back sort of game which cheers no one, but I don't lose that often to the women, and make few friends in the course of winning. Christopher, terribly shy at six, has a hell of a time with all the Kennedy children who overwhelm his reluctance to join any-thing. I'm not happy at how he suffers on our occasional Sundays over there but: "It's his first rite of passage since leaving your prenatal auspices," Hugh remarks. Dependably, he adds: "You've spoiled him rotten."

On balance, Hickory Hill is less fun for your Kittredge than it should be, but since I adore Bobby and he delights in talking to me, we do have some fun. It is all very chaste. Secretly, I think Bobby is dying for an affair, but, my God, where would he go with it? *Time* made him Father of the Year. So he indulges cerebral communion with ladies like me. We even discuss issues on the telephone. He lets you in on that crackerjack mind of his, at once innocent and forth-rightly logical. He is absolutely impressive in his energy. No one, with the possible exception of Hugh, has the beans to oversee as many separate activities. Apart from civil rights and the brouhaha at the University of Mississippi, the missile crisis, and the never-ending hunt for Hoffa and the Mafia, plus routine stuff at Justice, plus the Green Berets, plus your Mongoose (which has to be the least successful venture he ever took up), there is the occasional whopper that over-whelms everything. This last month it was the care and concern he gave to ransoming the Brigade. It proved to be a remarkable perfor-mance. Do you remember when I wrote to you about Harry Ruiz-Williams, that wonderful Cuban with smashed feet who has been working all these months to try to get Americans and Cuban-Americans to put up the millions of dollars needed for ransom? I don't know whether you paid close attention, but at that time a lot of Republicans attacked the Kennedys for daring to consider exchanging tractors with Cuba for the prisoners. Ugly. All those Cubans rotting away in jail, while our politicians were making political capital of the cheapest sort of knee-jerk anti-Communism. Well, now that same Brigade has been in jail more than a year and a half. Bobby tells me that a wealthy Miami exile who used to have a ranch in Cuba went over as a ransom emissary and was shocked by the condition of the men. He told Bobby that cattle who are going to die get an unhealthy look on the back of their necks, and the prisoners now give off exactly that appearance. "I can't put it out of my mind," said Bobby to me. "The back of the neck!" The ex-rancher also said: "If you are going to rescue these men, Mr. Attorney General, this is the time. If you wait, you will be liberating corpses." "You are right," said Bobby, "we put them there, and we are going to get them out by Christmas."

I think only Bobby could have pulled off the operation that followed. Castro wanted $62 million in ransom for something like 1,150 men. Great damage had been done by the attack, was his claim, and thousands of Cuban militia were dead as a result of the battle. Now, a year and a half later, $50,000 a man was not an excessive indemnification. If he could not get 62 million in dollars, then he would take it in goods. If not tractors, then in drugs, medical supplies, and baby food.

Originally, this ransom was to be obtained by the Cuban Families Committee, composed of a group of mothers in Miami and Havana who had sons among the prisoners. At Bobby's recommendation, they selected for their negotiator James Donovan, a canny lawyer who was able to get on with Castro. Donovan, apparently, has a rough, in-close New York style, the finger-to-the-ribs sort of needling. According to Bobby, Donovan, on his first visit to Havana, told Castro that there was no alternative to ransoming the prisoners. "If you want to get rid of them, you have to sell them. That means you have to sell them to me. There's no world market for prisoners."

Castro, apparently, takes to this kind of talk. "Yes," he answered, "but how is the Cuban Families Committee going to raise money? They have been trying for over a year and they still don't see the first million. What they have discovered is what I could have told them in the first place. Wealthy Cubans are the worst rich people in the world. That is why I am here and the wealthy Cubans are in Miami."

"We may not get the money," said Donovan, "but we will get the medical supplies."

Now it was Bobby's turn. He had to convince the drug industry to donate their product. No mean feat. Before he even started, he said to me over the telephone, "I don't know how we're going to do it, Kittredge, but we will." He had the following problem: The drug industry is under investigation for antitrust violations by Congress, by Justice, and by the Federal Trade Commission. Some of these drug moguls may actually have been breaking the law. Naturally, like all semidishonest corporate types, they are stuffed with self-righteousness, self-pity, and no sense of what they have done wrong. They hate the Kennedy administration; in their mind, it is against big business. By patriotic reflex, they hate Castro even more, but the Brigade prisoners they look upon as failures.

Nonetheless, Bobby brought the industry leaders together in Washington and delivered a most moving address. (Which I did hear about from several sources.) He said the Brigade was composed of brave men who, in all the pain of their defeat, had never turned upon America. Was it not our responsibility to rescue these good men, the first to fight Communism in our hemisphere, before they perished in the desperate conditions of Castro's jails?

Well, these big businessmen were moved enough to open negotiations with Bobby. When I asked him if his speech made the difference, he laughed. "With these guys, you feed the belly as well as the heart." So Internal Revenue found a way to allow large tax rebates on the drug donations. Some of the drug companies even ended up with profit from their charitable acts, and, of course, they stamped little American flags on each package in their shipment, not withstanding that a few of them also tried to empty their warehouses of stale and/or obsolescent drugs. One way and another, given his sharp nose, Bobby brought it off. As of this writing, it is still not certain the Brigade will reach Miami before Christmas, but there is no doubt in my mind. There may be last-minute hitches all over the firmament, but Bobby will get those prisoners back. You can look forward to a hectic but happy week down South.

Yours, dear cousin,
Kittredge

On the day before Christmas, the Brigade was flown in from Havana to Miami, and on December 29, President Kennedy addressed them at the Orange Bowl. I managed to be one of the forty thousand people in the audience.

I felt disoriented. Sitting high up on the twenty-yard line, the podium was far away, and Jack Kennedy seemed but a small figure in a cavernous valley, a man speaking to a bank of microphones that looked no larger than the legs of a hermit crab poking out from a snail shell. If I choose so surrealistic an image, it is because the situation was bizarre. I was looking at Modene's ex-lover. He was the one who finally had not wanted her all that much. Since she, somewhat earlier, had not wanted me, I had to wonder if I was the only man in all of the Orange Bowl who had such an unhappy if intimate purchase on the presidency.

I was no better prepared for the crowd. Working these last two months in the subdued offices of Zenith, I was unready for the impact of a stadium full of Cubans in a state of high elation. Ecstasies of ovation for the return of the lost and the damned flowed around the arena. Currents of sorrow commemorated the loss of a land they could never have loved as much when they were there.

I recall the pandemonium. From the onset of the ceremony, when all 1,150 men of the Brigade marched onto the field and took up positions at parade rest in precisely ordered files, the uproar of the fathers, mothers, wives and sons, daughters, nieces, nephews, uncles, aunts, and cousins of the first, second, third, and fourth step removed, gave every promise of contributing to the largest sound one had ever heard in a stadium, and that was doubled by the entrance of the President and Jacqueline Kennedy in an open white Cadillac. A myriad of Cuban and American flags began to wave as the President and his lady dismounted to stand at attention next to Pepe San Román, Manuel Artime, and Tony Oliva and the Cuban national anthem was played, and "The Star-Spangled Banner." Then, the emotion of these gathered families able to sustain any ceremony no matter how protracted, the President moved through the ranks of the Brigade, shaking hands personally with every soldier who caught his eye, and applause lifted, as if we were all at the largest graduation ceremony ever conducted; each of President Kennedy's handshakes was equal to the realization of a family saga.

Pepe San Román spoke first: "We offer ourselves to God and to the free world as warriors in the battle against Communism." Then, he turned to Jack Kennedy and said, "Mr. President, the men of Brigade 2506 deposit their banner with you for your safekeeping."

The local newspapers had spoken of how the Brigade flag had been carried away from the Bay of Pigs in one of the few boats available, and Kennedy unfurled it now to one more operatic ovation, turned to the soldiers, asked them to seat themselves on the grass, and replied, "I want to express my great appreciation to the Brigade. This flag will be returned to you in a free Havana."

I thought a new war had begun. *"Guerra, guerra, guerra,"* they shouted in the exaltation of being confirmed in the high holy sanction of one thought for all. Back to war! For war!

And I, a working agent in the cause of Intelligence, had an insight. They were free for this instant of the ongoing fatigues of my divided soul, which, but a day ago, had been their divided soul. *Guerra!* War was the hour when Alpha and Omega could come together. For some, at any rate.

I had to admire Jack Kennedy in the next moment. It was possible that he would have tasteful instincts in the midst of an avalanche. He asked: "Would Señor Facundo Miranda, who preserved this flag through the last twenty months, come forward so we can meet him?" Señor Miranda and he shook hands, and then Jack Kennedy said, "I wanted to meet you so I would know who to give this flag back to."

The ovation was near to never-ending. In the embrace of those emotions, he gave his speech. "Although Castro and his fellow dictators may rule nations, they do not rule people; they may imprison bodies but they do not imprison spirits; they may destroy the exercise of liberty, but they cannot eliminate the determination to be free."

This patriotic experience was interrupted for me by the sight of Toto Barbaro. He was working his way closer and closer to the podium. He would be there at the end to shake hands.

"I can assure you," said Kennedy, "that it is the strongest wish of the people of this country, as well as the people of this hemisphere, that Cuba shall one day be free again; and this Brigade will march at the head of the free column."

What was happening, I wondered, to the negotiation—so impressive to Kittredge—that Kennedy was working up with Khrushchev? Had the hot blood of the politician overwhelmed the cool arteries of the President? Or was I attending a new declaration of war against Cuba?

In the morning, my father called me from Washington. "I hope," he said, "that we get a transfusion out of all this."

24

January 15, 1963

Dear Kittredge,

This is to announce the reappearance of Howard Hunt. I had not heard from him in fifteen months, but we had dinner a few nights ago. Last seen before this occasion, he was buried in the Domestic Operations Division under Tracy Barnes, either, per his cover, writing spy fiction for New American Library or engaged in more cloak-and-daggered stuff. Wouldn't let on.

I suspect he was chugging along on a parallel track with Bill Harvey, albeit dealing in more ultra-right-wing Cuban types—I can't be certain. He won't tell. I saw him for no more than our one evening which came by way of a call saying that he wanted me to join him for dinner with Manuel Artime. So this letter is to impart what I learned from Artime about the Brigade's experience in Cuban prisons.

It was a good night. Do you know, I entered the Agency for adventure, and by now it feels as if, after a day at a desk, most of my excitement has come from dining out? *My Life in Central Intelligence; or, The Hundred Most Memorable Dinners.*

Well, this was one of them. Howard, still stationed in Washington, has obtained for his exclusive Miami use one of our best safe houses, a jewel of a villa out on Key Biscayne called La Nevisca. I used to engage the place occasionally during the pre-Pigs period, but Howard occupies it now, and demonstrates for me that there are amenities to Agency life. We had a corkeroo of a repast, polished off with Château Yquem, served up—I only learn of their existence at this late date—by two contract Agency caterers, who shop for special occasions, chef it forth in haute cuisine, and serve it themselves.

This was five-star. Howard is obviously back in full self-esteem. For all I know, his key passion is to get to just some place like this every night.

At any rate, I felt like an interloper. If Hunt and Artime do not love each other, they are fabulous actors. I do not know that I have ever seen Howard manifest more warmth toward anyone, and thereby was introduced to the untrammeled hyperbole of real Cuban toasts. The art, I discovered, is to raise one's glass as if addressing a hundred folk.

"I drink to a remarkable man," said Howard, "to a Cuban gentleman whose funds of patriotism are inexhaustible. I drink to a man I esteem so highly that, never knowing whether I would see him again, I chose nonetheless to name him, *in absentia,* the godfather of my son, David."

Artime replied in ringing terms—now I know *ringing terms!* He would defend his godson, if need arose, with his life. Do you know, Kittredge, I never heard a man sound more sincere. Artime, if finely drawn from his twenty months in prison, has gained, all the same, in personal impressiveness. Before, he was charming but a hint boyish, and considerably too emotional for my taste. Now, he is more emotional than ever, but his charisma embodies it. You cannot take your eyes off him. You do not know if you are looking at a killer or a saint. He seems endowed with an inner dedication that no human force can overcome. It is far from wholly attractive. My grandmother, Cal's mother, was equally endowed for church work—I do not exaggerate!—and she died at age eighty of cancer of the bowel. One senses the inflexible beast of ideology in such persons. Nonetheless, after spending an evening with Artime, I wished to fight Castro hand to hand.

Let me give you a full presentation of Artime's response to Howard's toast.

"In prison, there were hours," he said, "when despair was the only emotion we could feel. Yet, in the depths of our imprisonment, we were even ready to welcome despair, for that at least is a powerful emotion, and all feelings, whether noble or petty, are but streams and brooks and rivulets"—*riachuelas* was the word he used—"that flow into the universal medium which is love. It was love to which we wished to return. Love for one's fellow man no matter how evil he might be. I wanted to stand in the light of God so that I could regain my strength to fight another day. I was grateful, therefore, for the power of my despair. It enabled me to rise above apathy.

"Yet, despair is spiritual peril. One must rise out of it or lose oneself forever. So one needs stepping-stones, trails to ascend, rungs to a ladder. When one is lost in the black current of limitless misery, the memory of friends can sometimes be the only bridge that leads one back to the higher emotions. While I was in prison, no American friend appeared before my mind with more of a beautiful presence to lift my tortured spirit than you, Don Eduardo, you, *caballero espléndido*, whom I salute tonight in all the honor of feeling myself blessed by the high moral obligation to be the godfather of your son, David."

On they went. I came to recognize that the first good reason for inviting me is that my Spanish is satisfactory, and two grown men cannot speak to each other in such elevated fashion without having at least one witness for audience.

Artime began to talk about prison. Which I certainly wanted to hear about. Much of what he had to say was, however, contradictory. Where the food proved decent in one jail, it was wretched in another; if Brigade leaders were put away in individual cells for a time, they were soon brought back into prison dormitories; when, for a period, treatment turned courteous, it later became ugly. Conditions in one prison bore little relation to the next. They were moved frequently.

This exposition gave me a sense of the turmoil outside the walls. Right now, in Cuba, theories and events must be colliding, for there appeared to be no consistent intent behind the incarceration.

From what he told us, Artime's first hours of imprisonment were his worst. At the dire end of the Bay of Pigs, seeking to avoid capture, he took off with a few men into a trackless swamp called Zapata. He said he had had some idea of reaching the Sierra Escambray, eighty miles off, where he would initiate a guerrilla movement. Two weeks later, his group was rounded up.

Artime was the most important Brigade leader yet captured by Castro's counterintelligence. Since I must assume you are not all that familiar with his background, let me try a quick summary. I hope it was not Samuel Johnson who said, "None but a talentless wretch attempts a sketch." Artime, educated in Jesuit schools as a psychiatrist, was not yet twenty-eight when he joined Castro in the Sierra Maestra: In the first year after victory, however, feeling himself to be "a democratic infiltrator in a Communist government," he set out to build an underground movement. It did not take long for him to become a fugitive hunted by the police. Clothed in the cassock of a priest, and carrying a pistol inside a hollowed-out missal, Artime walked up the steps of the American Embassy in Havana one morning, and was shortly thereafter smuggled out to Tampa on a Honduran freighter. Doubtless, you first heard of him as a leader in the Frente, then in the Brigade. Artime, however, managed to maintain his underground group in Cuba as well. With such tripartite credentials, be certain he received no ordinary interrogation after capture.

Of course, he was in no ordinary condition. The swamp was arid, and choked in thorn bushes. Fresh water was rare. After fourteen days of thirst, no one could speak. They were not able to move their tongues. "I had always thought," said Artime, "that I was one of the people called upon for the liberation of Cuba. God would use me as His sword. After I was captured, however, I came to believe that God must be more in need of my blood, and I had to be prepared to die if Cuba was ever to be liberated.

"Back at Girón, however, as soon as they studied my diary and recognized who I was, one of the counterintelligence said, 'Artime, you have something to pay for all you have done to us. Do you wish to die like a hero, quickly, and by a bullet? Then cooperate. Declare that the Americans betrayed the Brigade. If you fail to help us, you will go out in misery.'"

When Artime would not sign such a declaration, his captors drove him to Havana, where he was brought into a basement room whose walls were lined with old mattresses. There, his shirt removed, his arms and legs strapped to a chair, a spotlight in his eyes, he was questioned for three days.

Not all the voices were angry. Sometimes a man would tell him that the Revolution was prepared to have compassion for his error; such men were replaced by others with harsh voices. Forced to stare into the spotlight, he never saw any of their faces. The angry voice would say, "Innocent Cubans died for this man's vanity." One interrogator pushed a photograph into his face. He looked at a field of dead men. Corpses from the three-day battle stared back at him.

"I am going to kill you, cocksucker," said the angry voice. Artime felt the barrel of a pistol against his lips. He looked at Hunt and at me. "I was calm. I could not believe it. I said to myself, 'This is how wild horses feel when the bridle goes into their mouth. Yet, this bridle is the exercise of God's will.' Then a man who had a gentle voice said to the man with the angry voice, 'Get yourself out of here. You are making things worse.' 'I won't leave,' said the angry man, 'the Revolution gives me just as much right to be here as it does you.' They kept arguing," said Artime, "until the bad one left. Then the good one said, 'He is in a state of great disturbance because his brother was killed at Girón.' "

"Were you ever close to breaking?" asked Hunt.

"Never," answered Artime. "I did not see how I was going to live, so there was nothing to break." He did nod his head, however. "On the third day, they put me in a cell, and I was visited by a man named Ramiro Valdes, who is Castro's chief of G-2." Valdes seemed concerned with Artime's appearance, particularly the burns received from cigarettes. "Who were your interrogators?" he asked. "We will treat them severely. The Revolution wants revolutionaries, not fanatics. Please describe them to me, Manuel."

"Commander," said Artime, "I never saw their faces. Let us forget about it."

Hunt, in a husky voice, said, "I would have wanted to locate those sons of bitches."

"No," said Artime, "I did not believe Valdes. I knew he wished to establish a good relation with me. Then he would commence conversion. But I was not the proper person for such intentions. My situation as a prisoner was less real to me than my inner psychology. I felt that God was testing Manuel Artime. If I passed His tests, Cuba would become more worthy of liberation."

"Which was the most difficult test?" I asked.

He nodded, as if he liked the question. "Valdes ordered a good dinner to be brought into my cell. There was chicken and rice and black beans. I had forgotten how much I love to eat. No food had ever tasted better, and for a moment I was not ready to die. The beauty that is in life itself received my attention. I began to think of the sweet and simple barnyard life of the chicken who was providing me with this feast. But then, I said to myself, 'No, I am being tested,' and I no longer felt so tenderhearted toward the white meat of the breast. Suddenly I thought, 'I have an immortal soul, and this chicken does not. I am in the devil's hour.' "

A more difficult test came to Artime after he had been a prisoner for a year, had gone to trial, and was awaiting the court's verdict. By then he was accustomed to being alive; so it occurred to him with some force that his refusal to collaborate at the trial was bound to result in a sentence of death for himself.

"At that moment I realized that I would never have a son. To a Cuban, that is a sad thought. When a man feels unfulfilled, he is not ready to meet his end. Therefore, I asked a guard for pencil and paper. I wanted to write out exactly what to say when I was shot. Concentration upon that event might remove the temptation to wish one could stay alive. So, I decided to tell my executioners: 'I forgive you. And I remind you: God exists. His Presence enables me to die while loving you. Long live Christ the King. Long live Cuba Libre.' That took me through the temptation."

Soon after, he was visited by Fidel Castro. By Artime's description, Castro came to the prison at two in the morning six days after the trial and woke up Pepe San Román, who yawned in Castro's face, then stood before him in his underwear.

"What kind of people are you?" asked Castro. "I cannot comprehend. You trust the North Americans. They turn our women into whores and our politicians into gangsters. What would happen if your side had won? The Americans would be here. We would have to live with the hope that if they visit Cuba often enough, we will teach them how to fuck."

"I would rather deal with an American than a Russian," San Román answered.

"I ask you not to waste your life. The Revolution has need of you. We have fought you, so we know how many men in your Brigade have valor."

"Why," asked Pepe San Román, "didn't you say that at the trial? You referred to us as worms. Now you wake me up to tell me that we are brave. Why do you not leave? Enough is enough."

"Enough is enough? My God, man, I wonder if you even want to live."

"We agree on something. I do not want to live. I have been played with by the United States, and now you are playing with me. Kill us, but stop playing."

Castro left. Artime's cell was next. When he saw him in the doorway, Manuel assumed the Maximum Leader was paying this visit in order to execute him. "Do you finally come to see me," asked Artime, "so that you can try to make a fool of me in front of your men?"

"No," said Castro. "The only reason that I did not approach you earlier is I knew you were weak from the swamps. I do not wish you to think that I will make fun of you. In fact, I would ask: How are you now?"

"Very well. Though not as well as you are. You are heavier than you were in the mountains."

Castro smiled. "As yet in our Revolution, not all eat equally. Chico, I am here to ask what you are expecting."

"Death."

"Death? Is this your understanding of the Revolution? To the contrary, we are here to look for the potential in each other. Your side looks to improve the condition of those people who have obtained a good deal already. My side hopes to improve the lot of those who have nothing. My side is more Christian than yours, I would say. What a loss that you are not a Communist."

"What a pity that you are not a democrat."

"Artime, I will demonstrate that you are wrong. You see, we are not going to kill you. Under the circumstances, that is very democratic. We accept the existence of a point of view that wishes to destroy us. Tell me that is not generous. The Revolution is sparing your lives. You may have been sentenced to thirty years in jail, but you will not even have to serve your sentence. Since you are so valuable to the Americans, we are ready to ransom you. In four months, you'll all be gone."

Well, as we know, it took eight.

Toward the end of the evening, Artime shifted the ground of discussion.

"We have yet to commence the true fight," he told Howard and me.

"You can't be ready to go into action this quickly," said Hunt.

"Physically, we still must recover, yes. But we will be ready before long. I feel sorry for any man who believes he will stop us."

"Jack Kennedy can stop you," said Hunt. "He thinks it is obscene not to deal in two directions at once. I will warn you, Manuel, I have heard rumors that the White House is ready to make a deal with Castro."

"The devil," said Artime, "is defined as a man who has his head put on backwards."

Hunt nodded profoundly. "Smiling Jack," he answered.

Hunt has changed, Kittredge. He always had a good deal of anger in him, divided neatly into two parts: half for the Communists, and half for the manner in which his achievements have not been properly recognized. Now, however, his hatred breaks through the skin of what used to be his considerable urbanity. When the crude stuff pops forth, it is strikingly disagreeable. Hunt is not the sort of man who should ever reveal this side of himself.

"Many of us," said Artime, "do not have a clear view on the Kennedys. For example, the brother, Bobby, took me on a ski trip last week. I cannot say I do not like him. When he saw that I do not know how to ski, but was ready to plunge down—you call it the *fall line*—of every slope until I fell, he would laugh and laugh, and then say to me, 'Now I have seen fire on ice.' "

"The Kennedys are adept at charming those they wish to have on their side," said Hunt.

"With all due respect, Don Eduardo, I believe the President's brother is serious about Cuba. He has new plans, he says, and wants me to be a leader in them."

Hunt said: "I would suggest that you develop your own operation. Once you are privately funded and free of the government, I know people who can give you more assistance than if you are directly under Kennedy's nose."

Artime said: "I am not happy with complexity. I heard the President say, 'This flag will be returned some day to a free Havana.' To me, that is an absolute commitment to our cause."

Hunt smiled. Hunt took a sip of his brandy. "I repeat your words: The devil is a man who has his head put on backward."

Artime sighed again. "I cannot pretend that there is no division among my people concerning the subject of the Kennedys."

"I heard that some of you did not want to hand the Brigade flag over to Kennedy?"

"We were divided. That is true. I was uncertain myself," said Artime. "I have to admit that I like the Kennedys better now that Bobby took me skiing."

"Is it true?" asked Hunt. "Was the flag handed over to Jack not the original, but a duplicate?"

Artime looked most unhappy. He threw a glance at me, at which Hunt waved his hand as if to say, "It is all right. He is one of us." That startled me. Hunt is not the kind of enthusiast to put unqualified trust in someone as marginal to his purposes as myself. "Was it a copy?" Hunt persisted.

Artime inclined his head. "We compromised. We made a

duplicate flag. It was the forgery that was given to President Kennedy. I am not happy about such a deception. Some of the strength we put into our flag may now drain out of it."

Hunt looked curiously pleased. Writing this, I think I now understand why. Since he was not told the story in confidence, but with myself present, I believe he now feels more free to divulge this item to others. Kittredge, my sentiments about Jack Kennedy are hardly clear-cut, but Hunt's animus makes me frankly uneasy.

Later that night, I had an extraordinary dream in which Fidel Castro and Manuel Artime entered a debate. Artime said: "You, Castro, do not comprehend the character of faith. I am not here to defend the rich. But I must feel compassion for them since God will not be charitable toward their greed. God saves His special mercy for the poor. In Heaven, all injustice is reversed. You, Fidel, claim to work for the poor, but you commit murders in their name. You seal your revolution with blood. You blind the poor with materialism, and thereby remove their vision of God."

"Chico," answered Castro, "it is obvious that we have opposing points of view. One of us has to be wrong. Let me deal with your proposition, therefore, on such a basis. If I am in error, then any human beings that I have injured in this life will most certainly be well received in heaven.

"If, on the other hand, Artime, no God exists to punish the rich and the unjust in the afterlife, what can you say about all of our poor peasants whom your soldiers slaughtered? You killed them on the road to Girón because of your fear that Communism might succeed in Cuba. In that case, your forces will have wasted not only their lives but ours.

"So, Manuel," said Castro, "choose my way. Then, logically speaking, no matter which one of us is correct, you come out better."

Kittredge, that dream concluded in a most curious fashion. Bill Harvey's voice boomed out suddenly: "You are both in error," he shouted. "There is no justice. There is only The Game." Those last two words kept echoing until I woke up.

Have you had any news concerning Wild Bill? The rumor down here is that he's being shunted—or is it demoted?—over to Italy as Chief of Station.

Ever yours,
Harry

25

February 15, 1962

Dearest Harry,

I am not surprised that you dreamed about Bill Harvey, for much has been going on with his situation. Director McCone, as you know, was prepared to cut him out of the Agency until Dick Helms saved the day. Helms may be the coldest man I know, but he is loyal to his troops, and that, in practice, does serve as a working substitute for compassion. At any rate, he played on many a theme to restrain McCone from firing Harvey outright—spoke of the pleasure to be taken by KGB and DGI if Harvey had to resign, plus discouragement of initiative in Junior Officers. To satisfy McCone's heart as well as his mind, Helms did go on about the inner tensions that hardworking Senior Officers accumulate through a career of ongoing crises and personal financial sacrifice. McCone, who I'm sure is as wealthy as Midas from his years at the Bechtel Corporation, finally softened the sentence to a leave of absence. Dick then told Harvey to go to ground for a month and enjoy the clear understanding that he will be reinstalled into an appropriate slot just as soon as McCone is out of the country. Our new Director of Intelligence does love to take long trips with his brand-new spouse to far-off Stations. There he is received in maharajah-plus fashion. Set up in a suite at the best hotel, he puts in a seven-day week of golf, hears what he wants to hear from the Station hands (now that he can ride on his high missile laurels), and leaves *the little details* to Helms. Talk about Reynard in a chicken coop! Helms is running the Agency (with wonderful assists from Hugh), but so quietly, I'm certain word has not yet reached you and the other juniors. Harvey, per Helms' promise, was back at Langley before Christmas and nicely installed in an obscure corner of the Italian Desk. There he will stay long enough to pick up the rudiments of his new post, which (as soon as McCone departs again for Africa, Asia, or Australia) will be Chief of Station in Rome. It is hardly equal to Chief of Soviet Russia Division, but, under the circumstances, there ought to be no complaint.

Hugh, however, is most upset over Harvey's departure. I am being egregiously indiscreet, but am holding a fierce piece of scoop I must pass on to you. Ever since the missile crisis, I've been attempting to divine why Hugh was so eager to defend Harvey. Wild Bill has always been difficult for Hugh to stomach. The Fat Man persists, for instance, in addressing Hugh at open conference meetings as *Monty*, and that is but a modest clue to how they chafe each other. I don't possess the specifics, I only know that Hugh has some sort of grip on Harvey. In a showdown, Bill *always* gives way. The root factor still remains unknown to me, but I did learn recently that Wild Bill is truly invaluable to my Montague. As part of the pay-as-we-go plan between Hugh and myself, which calls for divulging something new and special to unhappy Kittredge once a season (in much the manner that another kind of woman gets a fur coat on her birthday), Hugh, from time to time, feeds me a royal tidbit. This last was a lollapalooza. Harry, do you know that the man who furnished Hugh with all those exceptional FBI transcripts on Modene & Co. was none other than Bill Harvey? It seems an old and well-placed acquaintance in the Bureau was willing to feed prime stuff to the Fat Man. Who then passed it on exclusively to Hugh. Naturally, the news that Wild Bill is going to Rome put Hugh in a dither, but knowing my husband, I am certain he has already worked out the route for a new underground railway.

Isn't that a stunner? Bill has been feeding Hugh for some years now with the most special FBI product. Harry, take this disclosure seriously. I am just beginning to feel the shock of putting it on paper.

Do you know, I have to ask myself: Why do I betray Hugh? The answer must be: in order not to act in even more treacherous fashion. I feel kin to the convicted killer who gave as answer to the question of why he murdered two nice old ladies who lived next door, "I didn't want to slice up the three little girls who lived on the other side." Don't you agree that a dreadful act is often performed in order not to commit a greater wrong? "My religion forbids suicide," the alcoholic declares, "so I will only drink a quart tonight." All the same, I feel as if my act encourages wrath in places I cannot even name.

All right, now that Harvey is going to Rome—would you believe it?—he kicked up the traces. He had a farewell dinner with Johnny Roselli in a public place, and the Bureau taped it. How do we know? Because the transcript came back immediately to Bill Harvey from his still active Bureau source. The Fat Man was so shaken that he took it to Hugh for advice. How he must have hated that! Hugh told him to have a meeting immediately with his well-placed source. In the next twenty-four hours, therefore, Harvey took a trip down the eastern shore of Maryland to join his FBI man in some out-of-the-way bait-and-rowboat shack, from which they rowed out far enough from shore to assume the confidence that they were not overheard. Out there in one of the coves of the Chesapeake, Harvey convinced his Bureau buddy that this transcript had to be killed. The source finally agreed that he would not release it into the FBI mill, a potentially perilous move for source, but if not done, Bill Harvey's doom would have been on McCone's desk last week. This, of course, assumes J. Edgar would have played the card rather than hold it. But then, who can sleep when Buddha has your card?

Are you curious about the transcript? I'm going to satisfy your itch pronto. The Roselli dinner took place in Miami at a restaurant called Joe's Stone Crabs. The tape, however, happens to be wobbly not only from restaurant clatter and Bill Harvey's damnably low voice, but some electronic glitch in the second half. Critical fragments are not clear. You know Bill so well by now that I am going to ask you to try to reconstruct the few missing comments. Odds are, Hugh says, Harvey and Roselli are merely venting mutual wind, but the *Oberhofmeister* would like a better sense of the whole, and I tell you frankly I'm not up to doing it myself.

Don't send back a treatise. No footnotes to the alternative possibilities. I can do that myself. Rather, provide me with your best clear presentation of what you think was said. I just want to be certain this is drunken blow-off, and not building toward a rogue op. It's fifty-fifty that Harvey has slipped his center.

Helms, nonetheless, is readying him for Rome. "It is no longer a critical Station," says Helms to Hugh. Yes, let us all say damn to Italian sensibilities. Hugh, if reluctantly, will support Harvey, but give me your reconstructed version first.

Love,
Kittredge

March 2, 1963

Dearest Kittredge,

I trimmed the irrelevant stuff, all the ordering of drinks, natterings, drunken trail-offs. I also added brackets around those portions where gaps had to be filled in the transcript. Most of them pile up toward the end. I must say I feel that the greater part of my insertions have to be close to what was said. In fact, I am amazed at how familiar I have become with Wild Bill's syntax.

ROSELLI: Can the Bureau pick us up in this joint?

HARVEY: If they have a long-range sniper-mike, yes.

ROSELLI: How do you know they don't?

HARVEY: Fuck them. I'm drinking and I am relaxing.

ROSELLI: That's when it happens.

HARVEY: In this din, who can record us? You got something to say, say it.

ROSELLI: You are a cop. You could be setting me up.

HARVEY: Want to get your teeth cleaned?

ROSELLI: Hey, I like you. I could love you, Bill O'Brien, if you had an agreeable personality. Only, let us look into it. You are not in shape to clean my teeth.

HARVEY: I could shoot you between the eyes.

ROSELLI: Well, we are all waiting for you to shoot somebody.

HARVEY: I'm biding my time. You know how much I carry in my head?

ROSELLI: No.

HARVEY: Meyer Lansky. I carry as much as Meyer Lansky.

ROSELLI: You don't. Einstein don't have a head equals Meyer.

HARVEY: Shit. I carry half the U.S. government on my brain pan.

ROSELLI: Yeah. The half that Uncle Sam sits on.

HARVEY: You are right for once.

ROSELLI: Thank you.

HARVEY: You got guts.

ROSELLI: I stand up.

HARVEY: You do, huh? Why couldn't you carry out our little assignment?

ROSELLI: If I tell you, you won't believe me.

HARVEY: I'd hate to think [you lost your nerve.]

ROSELLI: You say that to me? Take it back, or [we don't eat a meal] together.

HARVEY: Let's have a little dinner, I say.

ROSELLI: I will have to accept that as your crappy way of taking it back.

HARVEY: How is Sammy G. these days?

ROSELLI: He is fucking what used to be a sweet classy broad named Modene Murphy and he is also running around with Phyllis McGuire who he is asking to marry him.

HARVEY: Is the Murphy broad involved in any other way with Sam?

ROSELLI: She is just quietly going crazy.

HARVEY: That is all you can pan out on Giancana?

ROSELLI: Other than a few details.

HARVEY: Details?

ROSELLI: He is miserable these days.

HARVEY: Miserable?

ROSELLI: Well, the FBI got to Sammy. On the golf course. I got to hand it to them. They are evil motherfuckers. [They put one foursome] ahead of him, and a foursome behind. I'll feed you a secret that is no secret. Sammy G. can't play golf for shit. He takes a couple of heavies along with him who are guaranteed to lose no matter how bad Sam plays. [He never gets on the course with real people.] So Sammy forgets that he is no golfer. But yesterday, the Feds stand around the green waiting for him to putt. And he keeps missing the hole. They fall on the ground laughing. "Hey, Sammy," they say, "we hear the spooks gave you a badge. Show us your little badge. Show us yours, and we'll show you ours. Come on, Momo," they say, "flash your CIA thing. We will salute." He goes crazy. He's going to die of a stroke.

HARVEY: How do you know this took place?

ROSELLI: Just because his heavies are heavies, you think they can't talk?

HARVEY: Are you telling me that even his flunkies don't like the guy?

ROSELLI: He's a spoiler. He is a sick fucking individual. There was a casino man cheating big on Sam in one of the Vegas clubs. An executive who should know better. Okay, that's the death penalty. But Sam said, "Make it an example nobody forgets. Kill the son of a bitch *and* his wife." Which is what they did. Sam is no good. He is what I call treacherous. I say he tipped off the house detective on that bum phone tap business.

HARVEY: You can't prove it.

ROSELLI: Listen, I wanted Nixon to get in. Sam wanted Kennedy. If he had had a brain instead of an ego, he would have gone for Nixon. But, no, Sam wanted to get screwed by the Kennedys.

HARVEY: I always thought you and Sam [were in on the Vegas] stunt together.

ROSELLI: Why would I chop my own dick off? [Do you know

what I] lost that day in Vegas? A U.S. citizenship. Since I'm
nine years old I have never had one morning where my
identity was legit.

HARVEY: I hear violins.

ROSELLI: You are closed off to decent feelings. You look at me as
a hood, so you don't understand. I am a guy who is ready to
die for his patriotism. I am a patriot.

HARVEY: Calm down. [I don't care what] you are. [I might have]
criminal tendencies myself.

ROSELLI: You are crazy. You are incorruptible.

HARVEY: That's right. I never once indulged myself. Not on the
money side. For a reason. Get it straight. I could have been
on your side. I just didn't allow it. Cause if I had, Meyer
Lansky would now be small potatoes. I would be the richest
man in the world.

ROSELLI: It's never too late to get on board.

HARVEY: You are not [large enough] for my idea.

ROSELLI: I like people who swap loose talk for cold piss.

HARVEY: Wait until we get good [and drunk. Then] I'll tell you.

ROSELLI: We are good and drunk.

HARVEY: Cheers.

ROSELLI: What would be your idea? Tell me about the big job,
Uncle Bill.

HARVEY: Vegas. I want to pull off a heist in Vegas.

ROSELLI: You would be dead. Name me one joint in town that is
not impregnable.

HARVEY: Impregnable to two hoods. Three cowboys. Nobody has
ever put their mind to the problem. I don't say: knock off [a
joint. I say:] take the town. Give me the desert every time.
Land [with a small army.] Five planes. They carry three hundred [men. A couple of] tanks. Small artillery.

ROSELLI: You are beautiful. Fucking copper. Insane!

HARVEY: You take the airport. You move a man into the control
tower. Divert all the air traffic to Prescott, to Phoenix. Com-
mandeer the parked cars [you need.] Infiltrate [the town, cut
off the] phone company, the TV, radio. Surround the police
[facilities. Vegas is like] a goddamn artificial heart on a table.
All you need to do is [take possession of the] wires feeding it.

ROSELLI: You have a gorgeous fucking mind. Who is in your
goddamn army?

HARVEY: Cubans. Take any five hundred that are over in Nicaragua right now, train them to get ready to hit Castro, and then on the last day, tell them the mission [is shifted]—you need volunteers for something else. Three hundred volunteers. [You tell them Castro] has taken over the mob. Vegas now pays Castro. [So, we are going to rob] Castro money in Vegas. You can get a Cuban to believe anything provided he can fire a bazooka.

ROSELLI: Fighting cocks. Just pull their tail feathers.

HARVEY: Everything scouted [in advance.] In ninety [minutes, you] scoop up the preponderance of cash [in that town, back to the] airport with the wounded, load up the planes, out to the Pacific, [back to base] in Nicaragua.

ROSELLI: The Air Force would be on your ass fifteen minutes after you set down at the airport.

HARVEY: Do not believe it. The Air Force is the Government, and the Government, [when it is in a state of] confusion, needs twenty-four hours. A thousand asses [have to cover themselves before they] unzip one fly.

ROSELLI: It's good you are an incorruptible.

HARVEY: Isn't it?

ROSELLI: You are a maniac. Where would you get the money to fund the job?

HARVEY: [It takes just one] Carlos Marcello, one Santos Trafficante.

ROSELLI: Ha, ha. What would you do with the loot?

HARVEY: Adopt a prize kid. Groom him to be president.

ROSELLI: Your attic is on fire. I got a lot of good friends in Vegas.

HARVEY: [Tell your friends that the] security they put on each [joint is nothing but a joke.]

ROSELLI: I have told them that much myself. The kind of security [we need is people] who can think like you. Anticipate. Foresee major operations [against the property.] Fucking incorruptibles. West Pointers. [I would sign] up an entire graduating [class.] To protect the serious [amount of money] that is out there any night.

HARVEY: *Arriba.*

ROSELLI: My head is on fire.

HARVEY: Go pay a visit to the Buddhist monk.

ROSELLI: The who monk?

HARVEY: The guy who poured gasoline on himself last week.

ROSELLI: The guy in robes who set himself on fire? The priest? In Asia?

HARVEY: Saigon.

ROSELLI: Right. Made himself a torch. What a party. I still don't have the guy [out of my head.]

HARVEY: Think about it. That's patriotism.

ROSELLI: Flaming shish-ke-bab.

HARVEY: You are one hell of a patriot.

ROSELLI: This is a farewell party. So I try to lighten the occasion. I drink to your new job.

HARVEY: Thank you.

ROSELLI: Where are you going?

HARVEY: Forget it.

ROSELLI: Right. Cloak-and-dagger. Right.

HARVEY: Rome. O'Brien is going to be king of the guineas.

ROSELLI: There is absolutely no need to talk in that manner around me.

HARVEY: I tend to forget you're a guinea.

ROSELLI: Have it your way. I will just keep count.

HARVEY: They are sloughing me off at a second-level slot, buddy.

ROSELLI: Sure. I got it. You go around calling people guineas, but you are holding your asshole in your hands like it was a tin cup. You want to rip off Vegas. Watch out—you'll be a bum. You better do yourself a favor. Learn to talk to Italians before you go over. Don't try to take away their pride.

HARVEY: The world is full of bullshit. Did you know? Bullshit, Rosy. Let's drink.

Kittredge, the rest of the transcript is non-consequential. I hope you like this. I leave interpretations to you.

In a rush,
Harry

P.S. I confess to some upset at Roselli's passing reference to Modene. Have you nothing to send on to me about that?

26

March 8, 1963

Harry dear,

A fine job even if what they were up to comes down to no more than whale-spout. I must say I feared the references to Modene. I knew they would leave you in no happy state but, on the other hand, you are the only one who has listened to both men speak on other occasions.

I will confess I have been thinking about Modene. Several weeks ago, Hugh handed me a new batch of AURAL–BLUE-BEARD transcripts with this comment: "I have the impression these ladies are no longer relevant. However, do take a look."

With Hugh, one doesn't know. He can always be setting a trap. I studied, therefore, close to a hundred pages of chatter between Modene and Willie. Since the calls were made by Modene on a pay phone, count on it, a good deal of conversation consists of no more than listing the annoyances of an outdoor booth. Harry, I will send you the transcripts if you insist, but they won't differ from my summary. I say you would do better to treat yourself to a drink before reading on.

Modene has not been in touch with Jack for many months. As you divined from Roselli's comments, Modene is unhappy. She is drinking heavily. At Sam's suggestion, she quit working for Eastern and now lives in Chicago. Her expenses are covered by Giancana, and she doesn't do much else than wait for him to come back to town. She complains constantly of putting on weight, but in the next breath tells Willie that Sam does not speak any longer of marrying her. She looks for Phyllis McGuire's name in the gossip columns, she fights with Sam. She says to Willie: "How would you like to be Number Two?" "Are you going to leave him?" asks Willie. Modene's answer: "I don't know how." She is pregnant. She and Sam agree she will have an abortion. There are complications. She needs a secondary operation. She believes Sam put the doctors up to botching the job.

The FBI, in turn, has been harassing Modene. There are days when she will not go down to the corner for a half-pint of cream to put in her coffee since she feels they are in wait for her. Why does she think this? Because her doorbell rang that morning, and she did not answer it. In fact, she does not answer her doorbell for anyone she is not expecting. Even her devoted Willie may be growing tired of Modene. They compare weight-gains. As I suspected, Willie is chubby. Of average height, she is now up to 155. Modene, two inches taller, weighs 145. The conversations suggest that yes, just possibly, Modene is taking up too much of Willie's time.

On second thought, I will enclose one transcript of a conversation between Modene and Sam. How Buddha's acolytes managed to obtain this jewel is, of course, a question. We know how carefully Giancana keeps Modene's apartment swept of bugs, but let us assume the exterminator had a hangover that morning, or was sufficiently implicated in one criminal matter or another to be obliged to do a job for the Bureau.

MODENE: Why won't you take me to San Francisco? I feel like going.

GIANCANA: You won't have a good time. It's business.

MODENE: You are seeing Phyllis.

GIANCANA: McGuire is on tour in Europe. She is in Madrid. I'll show you the clipping.

MODENE: Yes, you care so much about her that you cut out clippings and keep them in your pocket.

GIANCANA: I got to. That's the only way you'll believe she is where she is.

MODENE: She is your Number One girl. That's what she is. Do you know what I am?

GIANCANA: Don't get crude.

MODENE: I am cleaned out. An empty bag.

GIANCANA: Don't talk that way.

MODENE: I am a surgical shell.

GIANCANA: Will you keep your voice down?

MODENE: Why don't you take Number Two to San Francisco now that Number One is away?

GIANCANA: I can't, baby.

MODENE: Because you don't want to.

GIANCANA: It is because of your stipulations.

MODENE: What are you talking about?

GIANCANA: The night I took you to Denver. You stipulated the kind of room. No suite. Just one room. I can't spend time in one room. I need space.

MODENE: Well, I must have it arranged so that there is only one room. I cannot rattle around in a suite. I told you. I hear things in the next room. When we are off on a weekend, you go away for hours. So I want to know that I am safe in one room with a double-bolted door.

GIANCANA: How can we go anywhere, Modene? You are not in the right kind of shape. What if the FBI jumps us at the airport?

MODENE: Don't take me.

GIANCANA: Just let me get a suite at the St. Francis, and I will take you along.

MODENE: It has to be a single room.

GIANCANA: I'll get a suite for me, and a single for you. When I go out to see people, you can stay in the single. We'll sleep in the suite.

MODENE: I will not sleep in a suite. During the night, I hear noises in the other room.

GIANCANA: Then stay right here and get drunk.

MODENE: Since you have given me the choice, I prefer to stay here. But I need money for moving expenses.

GIANCANA: Yeah, what town are you moving to?

MODENE: I am remaining in Chicago. But I am moving to a studio apartment with a single room. (November 15, 1962)

Harry, I do not know if you wish to contact Modene, but I have, after some deliberation, enclosed her new address and phone number. It is in the small sealed envelope also enclosed in this manila envelope. I hope you will not call on too small an impulse.

I do miss you. If only we could find a way to see one another without risking all our inner discipline.

K.

27

ONE EVENING IN A MIAMI BAR, I THOUGHT OF HOW MODENE USED TO putty the underside of her long fingernails and bind them in adhesive tape before she would play tennis. Maybe it was the drink, but tears came to my eyes. I might have called her if the telephone number had been in my wallet rather than in its sealed envelope in my locked office desk.

I have said nothing of my private life during this period, but then, nothing is much worth recording. I had dates with a few of the more attractive secretaries who worked at JM/WAVE, and the ladies seemed to be looking for a husband while I was certainly not searching for a wife; soon enough, I would go back to drinking with Zenith confreres. When boozing grew too heavy, I would stop for a day or more and write a long letter to Kittredge.

It was a curious period. The wheels had begun to turn once my father came back from Tokyo, but he was under instructions to reorganize JM/WAVE into a leaner operation. By March we were scaled down—which proved almost as time-consuming as building us up. Transfers wore heavily on my father's conscience; having been sent out on occasion to regions of the globe that he deemed inappropriate for his skills, he would study the 201 of each officer he was now shifting to an undesirable Station, and would review the file a second time if the man was taking his family along. I thought that was more than gracious until I realized that Cal was protecting himself as well, for he did not wish an undue number of appeals to be recorded against his judgment.

The Cuban sorties that we sent out through the first months of 1963 were usually chosen with reference to the budget. Any project that had been on the books long enough to run up a sizable expenditure would receive Cal's sanction more easily than a new op whose curtailment would be inexpensive. Since this practice usually involved saving Bill Harvey's projects at the expense of new ones that Cal had conceived, I also perceived this as more than fair until I realized that, once again, my father had his low motive nicely in gear with the good one. "I can't keep explaining to the Company auditors," said Cal, "that a money-guzzling op I shut down because it showed no results was commenced on Bill Harvey's watch and is not my fault. Those auditors never listen. They're just as lazy as the law allows." My education was advancing.

Our largest problem in this period, however, derived from ongoing negotiations between the White House and the Kremlin. Those powers were overseeing the gradual removal of the missiles, and there were hitches. Bobby Kennedy would prod us to throw in a raid from time to time—nothing severe enough to jar the larger transaction, but if Castro wouldn't honor certain pledges that Khrushchev had made, we, in turn, were not about to forgo attacks on the Cuban coast. It was fine-tuning. The trouble, however, was that the exiles kept tweaking the strings with their own very much unauthorized raids. Alpha 66, Commando 77, Second Front, MIRR, or any one from a number of sleazier outfits (whose names shifted more quickly than we could replace labels on their file jackets) often succeeded in firing a rocket at a Soviet ship or blowing a bridge on some dirt road back of the Cuban shore. That was fine-tuning with a Chinese pitch pipe. The Russians would complain that we were backing such moves, which was exactly what these Miami Cubans wanted the Soviets to believe.

From the Kennedy point of view, it was not the time for this variety of misunderstanding. Senator Keating of New York, now soaring politically on a Republican thermal, was claiming that the Soviets had filled a number of Cuban caves with unregistered missiles. Helms kept sending memos to Cal to furnish more intelligence. Yet it was not possible to verify the claims. We kept getting reports from our agents in Cuba that Castro was storing tanks, munitions, even airplanes in caves. If the cave's mouth had a gate and a guardhouse, as indeed it would, any Cuban peasant relaying such observations to an underground group might be all too quick to mistake a large gas tank for a missile. And if they didn't, the exiles in Miami only passed such news on to Keating after heating up the interpretation.

It was, yes, a delicate balance, and on March 31 the White House announced that it would take "every step necessary to halt the exile raids." Such steps soon engaged the Coast Guard, Immigration, FBI, Customs, and JM/WAVE. Government, I now discovered, was an organism with one outstanding property—it did not look back. The FBI went into many an exile camp in southern Florida and came out with bomb casings and truckloads of dynamite. Local Cubans were indicted. Our financial support to Miro Cardona and the Cuban Revolutionary Committee was terminated, and Cal's raids were closed down completely by the National Security Council. "Politics is weather," was Cal's reaction. "We'll just wait it out." He passed an advisory across his desk to me. "Next time you're down in Florida, worry about this first. Came to me from a gentleman named Sapp. Charlie Sapp. Chief of Police Intelligence in Miami. Considering the nature of his work, Sapp is a singular family name, wouldn't you say?"

We laughed, but the advisory was still on the desk. It read: *Violence hitherto directed at Castro's Cuba may now be turned toward governmental agencies in the United States*.

"I called Mr. Sapp," said Cal. "He kept talking about anti–Castro

extremists. Inflamed tempers. Wild coyotes. Says a new lunatic fringe
has been forming ever since we missed going to war in October.
Right now this handbill is being stuffed into letter boxes in Little
Havana, Coral Gables, and Coconut Grove. I took the wording down
right over the phone." Cal read aloud: "Cuban patriots—face into the
truth. Only one development will make it possible for Cuban patriots
to return to their homeland in triumph. That is an inspired act of God.
Such an act would place a Texan into the White House who is a friend
to all Latin Americans."

"Who does it purport to be from?" I asked.

"No name. It is signed: 'A Texan who resents the Oriental influence that has come to control, to degrade, to pollute, and enslave his
own people.' The rhetoric does suggest John Birch Society."

"Yes," I said, "all we poor enslaved American people."

"Well, you don't need to get college-boy about it," said Cal. "It
doesn't solve anything to feel superior to the John Birch Society."

"What the hell are you talking about?"

I had never presumed to speak like this to him. I had forgotten the
heat of his temper. An oven door might just as well have opened
across the desk.

"All right," I said, "I apologize."

"Accepted." He caught it in midflight like a hound wolfing a
chunk of meat.

But I was not without my own anger. "Do you really believe we
are enslaved?"

He cleared his throat. "We are polluted."

"By whom?"

"That is a complex question, isn't it? But ask yourself whether the
Kennedys have a sense of *a priori* value."

"What if they don't?"

He was still breathing heavily. "At St. Matt's, my father used to
tell us that a man without *a priori* values soon gets into a pact with the
Devil."

"I take it that you believe this."

"Of course I do. Don't you?"

"I would say by half."

"That is a damned unsatisfactory remark," said Cal. "Half devout.
Why *are* you in the Agency?"

He was going too far. "I like the work," I told him.

"Your reply is insufficient. Don't you recognize that in Castro we are dealing with Communism in its most macho form? He appeals right across the board to the three-quarters of the world that is dirt poor. A wholly dangerous man."

I did not answer. I was thinking that only half of Fidel might meet my father's prescription. The other half could yet prove congenial to the half of Kennedy that was, I suspected, inclined to have a dialogue with Fidel Castro. But then, I was another half-man, ready to live with the bearded one and equally ready to abet his instant elimination. No, I could not answer my father.

"Would it surprise you to know," said Cal, "that our dear friend Hugh Montague could have written that John Birch letter?"

"No," I said, "not ever. The style would repel him."

"All the same," said Cal, "he does feel that some form of Satanic embodiment is degrading, polluting, and, yes—I'll say it—*enslaving* the yeoman virtues and values that this country used to possess."

"Does Hugh hate Kennedy that much?"

"He might."

"It is not the impression I get from Kittredge."

"Kittredge may have a good deal to learn about Hugh."

"Yessir."

He was done with the conversation. The light went out of his eyes and his strong features looked as implacable as they must have appeared in those ruthless college days when he was on the way to making Second All-American. "Watch yourself in Florida," he said.

Miami proved quiet over the next couple of weeks, but there was an undeniable sullenness of spirit on Calle Ocho; when we drank at our watering holes, there were jokes about satchel-charges coming through the window. Our situation reminded me of hot summer afternoons in adolescence when the air did not move for hours, and I was certain something would happen that night, even if it never did.

April 10, 1963

Dear Harry,

I am beginning to suspect that Jack Kennedy has such an active Alpha (and equally lively Omega) that he is not only inclined to explore in two opposed directions at once, but prefers to. And, do you know, I suspect the same is true for Castro. I have picked up some special stuff on the man by way of an Agency debriefing of James Donovan, who just returned from Havana after a new set of negotiations.

Donovan's mission was to obtain the release of a considerable number of Americans who are at present in Cuban prisons. When Bobby asked Donovan to take this on, he said, "Jesus Christ, I've done the loaves and the fishes. Now you want me to walk on water."

I think it is precisely this Irish humor that enables Donovan to get along with Castro. Of course, it was a return trip and they were old hands by now at dealing with each other; Castro even took Donovan and his assistant, Nolan, to the Bay of Pigs where lunch was served on a launch, and they devoted a good part of the day to skin-diving and fishing. All the while, they were guarded—I do enjoy this—by a Russian PT boat.

Here is the part of their conversation which I think you will find interesting. Hugh certainly did.

"Last November," said Donovan, "when I ran for Governor of New York State, I got licked. I'm beginning to think I'm more popular down here."

"Truth, you are very popular here," said Castro.

"Why don't you," asked Donovan, "have some free elections? Then, I could run against you. I might get elected."

"That," said Castro, "is exactly why we do not have free elections."

From there, they moved toward the edges of some serious political talk. It seems Bobby is trying to get the State Department to lift travel restrictions on trips to Cuba—*trying,* I say, because Jack has left that matter to be contended over by State and the Attorney General's office—which does annoy Bobby. "It's preposterous," he said, "to prosecute American students because they want to take a look at the Castro revolution. What's wrong with that? If I were twenty-two years old, that is the place I would want to visit." Or that, at least, is what Donovan passed on to Castro.

On hearing those sentiments, Fidel seemed interested. "Can that have any bearing on the future of American policy?" he asked.

"Well," said Donovan, "things might be getting a little more open. We did clamp down on the exile groups. From your point of view, you might call that a positive step. Now, it might be your turn. If you release your American prisoners you will remove one hell of a stumbling block."

"As a purely hypothetical question," said Castro, "how do you believe that diplomatic ties might be resumed?"

"Oh," said Donovan, "in exactly the way porcupines make love."

"I have heard the joke, but I no longer recall the answer. How *do* porcupines make love?"

"Well, Fidel," said Donovan, "porcupines make love very carefully."

Castro was much amused by this, and before the session was over, remarked, "If I could have an ideal government in Cuba, it would not be Soviet-oriented."

"You need to offer a little more than that," said Donovan. "There has to be some understanding that Cuba will keep a hands-off policy in Central and South America."

They proceeded no further, but later in the visit, a doctor named René Vallejo, who is Castro's friend and physician, made a point of taking Donovan aside. "Fidel," he told him, "wants to further the relations of which you both spoke. He thinks a way can be found. We must tell you, however, that certain high Communist officials in the Cuban government are unalterably opposed to this idea."

On their return, during their debriefing, Donovan summed up Castro as "most intelligent, shrewd, and relatively stable." His assistant, Nolan, later reported to Bobby Kennedy that Fidel "was not difficult to deal with. Our impressions do not square with the commonly accepted image. Castro was never irrational, never drunk, never dirty."

"What do you think?" Bobby Kennedy asked Nolan. "Can we do business with that fellow?"

The question was ironic—no more than Bobby's way of indicating that he has just absorbed a piece of information for future reference. Castro, however, seems serious enough about new overtures. On Donovan's suggestion, Lisa Howard of ABC obtained ten hours of interview with Fidel and returned from Cuba wildly in love with the man, I fear. In fact, although she would not admit it, and there was naturally a limit beyond which we could not probe since it was a voluntary debriefing, I suspect she had an affair with him.

If you would ask how I obtain such close knowledge of this kind of matter, take the obvious deduction. I was, yes, at the debriefing. I can tell you parenthetically that Hugh has finally found a way

to increase my Agency stipend, which has been fixed for years. I have
been put on temporary leave from the Agency, and promptly reinstated as a contract agent. The daily rates are excellent and I can work
anywhere from one hundred to two hundred days a year, and make
more than before, and obtain interesting assignments, plus, key to our
present understanding, be more of a help to Hugh. It does work well.
Arnie Rosen was Hugh's liaison for the first debriefing with Donovan, and I, looking over the results, became sufficiently interested to
come aboard during the session with Lisa Howard.

   She is petite, blond, and would be very attractive to men, I
think, if she did not suffer from what I call "media hollow." These TV
interviewers all seem scraped out within—all too superficially pleasant, but livid within. They are not quite like other people. Is it because
they must live with all those electronic machines? Or, is it because
they engage every day in the violation of human reserve? They are so
lacking in animal integrity. I think we can agree that most of us are
rooted in particular animals. It does seem fair to speak of different men
and women as leonine, or ursine, bovine, feline, doelike, elephantine,
simian, birdlike, beasty, so forth. I put it this obviously to underline
what I would next say: If animals could speak, can you imagine how
hideous it would be for the animal kingdom if they had television
shows where sparrows interviewed gorillas, or snakes conversed with
poodles? What a violation of their separate immanence to assume
there was an animal bond between them that permitted instant communication on a variety of subjects with no regard for their private
essence. It would certainly leach the spirit out of them. You wouldn't
be able to distinguish the crocodiles from the gazelles. Awful! Well,
that is what happens, in my opinion, to TV interviewers. Lisa Howard
was bright, peppy, eager to please us at the debriefing, and more than
eager to get her pro-Castro points across. However, she was hollow.
Do you know, the more I decided that she had had an affair with him,
the more I lost respect for this fabulous Fidel. It occurred to me that
he might have low taste of the awful basic variety—you know, "I'm
dark, and you're an American blonde, so wowsy-boom!" That kind
of man never looks for essence, but then, it is the hallmark of vulgarity
to live by image alone. That much less for you, Mr. Castro, I thought.

   All the same, Lisa Howard had some more or less solid political stuff to pass on, and did try to be objective. The simple, small,
useful stuff of what he said and she said was, however, scanted. Too

much of it kept coming to us predigested, no matter how we pushed for details.

She did provide one cutting edge. René Vallejo and the new Foreign Minister, Raul Roa, favor accommodation with the U.S.; Che Guevara and Raul Castro are wholly opposed. I hear Hugh and Cal licking their chops. Castro is obviously in a bind. He ended by saying to Lisa Howard, "President John F. Kennedy will have to make the first move."

Yes, right into the teeth of Nixon and Keating!

I sat back and observed. I am best at that. However, I did press one question. It was most unprofessional since I had not prepared the ground, but then, Rosen and a couple of prominently expert Agency folk were consuming the time, and it just wasn't in my credentials to take over. I only had room, therefore, to ask: "How much, Miss Howard, of Mr. Castro's desire for rapprochement with us is due, you might say, to his personal pique at Khrushchev?"

"Oh," she said, "I don't think any of it. He's much deeper than that."

Her idea of depth and mine do not necessarily coincide, of course. I am dubious that any man who would see poor over-extended Lisa Howard as a blond film star *type* can be above personal and intimate spite.

Khrushchev, that wily old peasant, must have a good sense of Castro, for he has invited C to the U.S.S.R. for an extended visit, perhaps as much as a month. My guess is that Castro will be wined, dined, fed with economic subsidies (to make up for his disastrous sugar harvest), and will come back with refreshed Communist blood in his veins. Indeed, the thigh-touching with Donovan and Howard may have been undertaken to make Khrushchev nervous.

All the same, we are entering a time that will have a new signature, I think.

Devotedly,
Kittredge

28

IF I WAS *FASCINATED* BY FIDEL CASTRO, BY WHICH I SUPPOSE I MEAN attracted and repelled at once, I did not doubt my political feelings. I agreed with Cal. Fidel was dangerous and not to be trusted. Was it for this reason that my father and I, by early May, began to pass through what I can only call a highly controlled maniacality? If the description seems excessive, perhaps it is, but Cal was in full command of Special Affairs Staff (precisely the name to replace Task Force W), his office on the seventh floor at Langley was large, his chair impressive, light was begging to dance in his eye, and there was nothing innovative to do. Since he was also convinced that improved relations with Cuba were on the Kennedy agenda, the romance of the seashell and the manta ray, once wild as pig squeal, began to enter the manly zone of the necessary. If we did not quite believe it would work, we were nonetheless drawn to the possibility. When a piece of intelligence arrived that AM/LASH in late April had gone scuba diving with Castro, my father was convinced. We would give it a go. Since other tasks I was taking care of for him would bring me to Washington for a few weeks, I was there to shepherd the project through the labs at Technical Services.

I never had to wonder about the Hubbard family balance after a few hours at TSS. I knew I was sane. The personnel at TSS had such detectable differences from the rest of the Agency. I would not say that the slide-rule gang were more childlike than the rest of us, but mottoes were strung together out of paper cut-out letters to dangle in festoons from the ceiling: "When It Falls Apart, Don't Scream," is the one I remember. No, there was another: "Blastogenesis Is But One Form of Ingenuity"—whatever that meant. I did find the labs curious. While there was many another quarter in the Agency, particularly the Directorate of Intelligence, where half the men were bald and all wore glasses, here at TSS, people looked happy. Some walked the halls emitting larynx-bursts of opera; others kept their heads ensconced in a report.

I had been assigned a technician called "Doc" who was young, slim, potbellied, half bald, and wore glasses. It was not automatic to separate him from others when he was in a group, but then, he did not expect you to recognize him. His eyes were on the project. We were looking to develop a seashell with a manta ray for escort. I saw true happiness in Doc. "This one will stretch us in a couple of places we haven't even flexed. Off the top, I would say we need input on whether to ship a couple of live specimens up to our tank here, or send some equipment down to Miami." He put out his palm in apology. "I'm just thinking out loud. Forgive me, but the problems are nifty. We'll have to think-tank it before we make a move because this one could put real distortions into the budget. I know we won't have to run an obstacle course getting an okay from upstairs—after all, you come to us from upstairs!—but we ought to cook up some feasibility profiles. And, of course, check out the seashell. Can we pack it with enough soup to give appropriate payoff? Or should we install a mine underneath? But you better get ready for that. Mines can be touchy creatures."

By my next visit, this question was resolved. "They can store enough soup in a whelk spiral," said Doc, "to pop a black hole into space. Total obliteration through ten-foot radius." The manta ray, however, was not free of *kinky-kinks*. Should they try using a live one? "Feasibility there is bound to be below the line," said Doc. "We'd have to drug Mr. Manta, and then he's likely not to react. Our understanding is that good old Ray has to be macho enough to attack and get himself spear-gunned."

"Exactly."

"With your concurrence, we're all for constructing our own synthetic-fiber manta ray prototype. Provisionally, let's refer to that as a *mantoid*. I won't say yet whether such a facsimile can be built to function in off-setting modes."

"That is, first alive, then mortally wounded?"

"Precisely. We will bury a watertight computer on-site with a lead into the facsimile. That way we can certainly program Señor Mantoid to activate his flippers so long as he is in idling mode. We might be able to work up a manta ray body language that will give every appearance of saying, 'Hey there, Mr. Swimmer, please don't come any nearer with your spear-gun. Not if you know what's healthy.' We can program the mantoid for that. But I have to consider your bold swimmer. Once he shoots at our facsimile—are we also to assume he will not miss?"

"Not this guy. He won't miss."

"Super. Just to be sure, we can put in an option. If there is no register of spear-entry, we can inhibit the death dance. Easily achieved within these parameters. But how are we to program Señor Mantoid's behavior after the spear has missed? Should he still be programmed to attack, or does he merely say, 'I've had enough, thank you very much,' and decamp? We can't option up for that without capacitating the computer up two orders of magnitude. Too much! It's vastly better to assume bold swimmer doesn't miss."

"Project such assumption," I said.

"All right, then," said Doc, "we'll try to locate some film on manta ray behavior during the first ten to twenty seconds after spear-gun entry wound. If Film Tracer Desk can't come up with such footage, we just spear-gun a manta ray or two in our Florida tank with collateral cinematography. That should provide us with a carload of film data." He held up one finger for caution. "All the same, should the work-up bring back a negative likelihood factor, we'll have to hand you a no-no. None of us want that, but I have to tell you: Responsibility, around here, is king."

"When will you know?"

"We should be out of parameters in two weeks."

Through the interim, Cal was getting together our material. The link to AM/LASH, a gentleman christened AM/BLOOD, turned out to be a Cuban lawyer, a Communist, nicely in place in Havana; he had known Rolando Cubela since their days at the University. Now, per Cal's instructions, another Cuban (who dropped into Cuba by parachute on a night flight) reached AM/BLOOD for preliminary talks; in turn, AM/BLOOD talked to AM/LASH, who, we now learned, was most unhappy in the Foreign Ministry, and ready to consider the seashell option.

Now Cal had to come to a decision. Did we alert Cubela to the full scope of his mission? It was Agency policy not to sacrifice agents knowingly, but at Cal's level, you could take a shot at ignoring policy. AM/LASH, Cal decided, ought to be told no more than that he was to lure Castro to a specific place on the reef.

On the other hand, it would set a wretched precedent to sacrifice an agent in this manner. It would be doubly wretched if the tale got out. Cal said, "I'm drawn to the odds. That son of a bitch Castro was ready to use missiles on us. Hell, if I knew it would work, I believe I would trade my own life for his."

"Does that answer the question?" I asked.

"Well, what do you say? Do we wit AM/LASH or label the guy expendable?"

"There's no choice," I said. "He can't be such a fool as to lead

Castro to a predesignated spot on a reef and think it's all going to happen thereafter in slow motion."

"Fellow, you are too inexperienced to know," said Cal. "Give an agent too many specifics, and he will panic. The waiter that Roselli's people hand-picked to deliver Castro his poison drink was told too much. A grave error. The waiter's hand was shaking so badly that Castro invited the guy to taste the drink. In fact, that makes me wonder whether AM/LASH is the man for the scuba stunt. He is already asking for guarantees. He told AM/BLOOD that he does not love Castro so much that he wishes to jump into the hereafter with him. That sounds, dammit, like he's going to ask for a sniper's rifle with scope."

"Why don't we wait," I said, "until we find out if TSS can build the manta ray?"

Cal nodded gloomily. "I have an old Hollywood friend who used to be an intimate of Irving Thalberg's—you know, the great producer of the 1930s? Well, Thalberg once said to him, 'Do you have any idea of how wasteful we are? Not one in twenty of our projects ever gets made into a film. Not one in twenty!' Rick, I ask myself, do we do any better here?"

29

IN FACT, THE PARAMETERS DID BRING BACK A NO-NO, BUT BY THEN IT was the third week in May, and other possibilities were stirring. Our officers at the American Embassy in Moscow reported that Castro was reacting favorably to his Soviet hosts, which upset Director McCone. He soon proposed to Bobby Kennedy and the Standing Group of the National Security Council that we "subvert military leaders in Cuba to the point of their being willing to overthrow Castro."

My father, receiving this news from Helms, gave me a wink. He had developed in the last month an odd, ribald wink, as if a girl we were talking about had just walked into the room. If the manta ray was now behind us, the prospect of employing AM/LASH remained alive. Indeed, the wink referred to AM/LASH. Cal and Helms had labored for a month to bring McCone around to his last proposal. "Always look to the language," said Cal. "We've built a foundation for ourselves almost as good as a directive. *'Subvert military leaders to the point where they will be ready to overthrow Castro.'* Well, son, tell me: How do you do that by half? You can subvert a foreign military officer, but you cannot control his every move. If Cubela manages to put a large hole into Fidel Castro's head, we will be able to point to McCone's remark. No one at Standing Group countermanded him. We are functioning, therefore, under the sanction of a general authorization. Always look to the language."

Two weeks later, on June 19, Jack Kennedy sent a memo concerning Cuba over to Special Group: "Nourish a spirit of resistance which could lead to significant defections and other by-products of unrest."

"By-products of unrest," said Cal, "enhances the authorization."

Of Helms, Cal's opinion had never been higher. "Dick has been perfectly choke-proof on this," he told me. "It takes moxie to give the go-ahead for AM/LASH. Helms knows as well as you or I how unstable Mr. Cubela has been in the past, but he also knows that we have to finalize Castro or a lot of Third World leaders are going to get the wrong impression. Why, Helms sees the importance of this sufficiently to put his own future up for grabs. He is bound to be the next DCI after McCone, but he is not playing it safe, not with Cubela. I respect that."

"Yessir."

I do not know whether my own sense of oncoming events affected my perceptions all summer, but I had to wonder whether everyone might be losing some part of their control. I know I squandered the good part of a week obtaining the answer to a simple question. "Where," Cal wanted to know, "is Artime now? I want to locate him in my mind."

Hunt wouldn't tell me. "I can't sacrifice someone else's security," he informed me. I followed up reports that Artime was in New Orleans with Carlos Marcello and Sergio Arcacha Smith; in the U.S. Army at Fort Belvoir; in Guatemala; in Costa Rica, Mexico, Miami, Madrid, Venezuela, and Nicaragua. It proved to be the last. Chevi Fuertes supplied the information. Under Somoza's benevolent sanction, Artime was training an army of several hundred Cubans, and his bills were—or were they not?—being paid by the Agency. That last detail I would have to discover for myself. Cal sent a query to Harlot who returned the following reply: "Look no further than Bill Pawley, Howard Hughes, José Alemán, Luis Somoza, Prio Socarras, Henry Luce, Carlos Marcello, Santos Trafficante, or friends of Richard

Nixon. Take your pick. God leads Artime to the money, and Howard Hunt may be the guiding light. Unlike Manuel Artime, I do not have God inside my heart. Nor Howard's angelic certainties. God inhabits my conscience instead. He asks: Is this worth pursuing? Artime has three hundred men. He will march them up the hill, and then he will march them down again. Whereas thee and me and your boy-wonder ought to have a chin-chin. You see, I have come to share your conviction that something must be done about the Great Unmentionable."

Well, that was news. Harlot had been looking upon Cuba as no more than a mote in the dust of the great Miltonian contest between CIA and KGB. "Yes," said Cal, "one has to wonder why Hugh has come around."

Dinner with him did not materialize until early in August. I had entertained the illusion that Kittredge might be there, but Cal and I arrived to learn that she was in Maine at the Keep. The meal, served by Merlinda, the Montagues' cook, was roast beef and Yorkshire pudding, if I recollect, with a magnum of Haut Brion '55—is it a prank of memory that the year of the wine is recalled?

We were illumined by Glenfiddich before we sat down, and Harlot was in a fine mood, and waxing wicked. Even Helms was dipped. "He'd be perfect if one didn't sense that when alone, he bites his lip." For all my father's newly acquired love of Helms, he roared with delight. I, however, could as easily imagine Harlot saying: "When Cal Hubbard charges through the forest, one does root for the trees." I had to hope that he would never come around to me. Addressing the defects of others, he would show the same far-off gleam of the eye that a dentist often fails to conceal when he has brought his drill up to the cavity and can begin raiding your molar of its rot. Dean Rusk came under scrutiny—"Incapable of going forward if there is a cloud in the sky." Nixon fared worse. "Would have been a prize for the devil but that worthy wearied of gazing upon him." Eisenhower was "a large balloon soaring on inert gas," and Kennedy is "sufficiently skilled in duplicity to make a good Chief of Station."

Rosen would soon be honored by a large share of attention. Tonight, Harlot was lit-up, and had a tale to tell.

"You are aware, of course, of Arnold's half-kept secret?" he asked.

"Yes," I said.

"I don't know how you can live with it," Cal burst out. "Rosen might end up in a police station one morning after a night in the men's room."

"Of course, Rosen is in peril," said Hugh, "but not, for God's sakes, in a men's room. A Turkish bath, perhaps. Or the wrong boy in a hotel room. Nonetheless, I have affection for Arnold. He does live in his own kind of peril and it keeps him observant. We can all use some of that."

As if he had been accused of lacking just such a vital faculty, my father said with some annoyance, "Why bring his name up at all?"

"Because I feel indiscreet. So I will divulge a small operation. Both of you must vow not to pass it on."

"So vowed," said Cal, raising his hand. The gesture was automatic—I could recognize they had engaged in this ritual on more than a few occasions.

"So vowed," said I, joining ranks.

" 'Rosen's Raid' I call it," said Harlot. "He came to me a couple of months ago and asked what I thought of his prospects for advancement. 'Or the lack of them,' I answered. I did not waste his time. 'Rosen, you can go far,' I began, 'but only if you get yourself a wife.' 'Would you,' he asked, 'say the same for Harry Hubbard?' 'Certainly not,' I said, 'he's neither ambitious nor homosexual.' "

When I chose not to react, Harlot went on.

"Well, I won't take up our time with the demoralizingly sad little tale Rosen had to tell. His closet is a dungeon and he is most unhappy with his habit. He would like to break out. He feels what he terms 'subliminal stirrings' he has never felt before toward the other sex. I tell him that it wouldn't be a bad idea to commence a new habit. 'Sex,' I tell him, 'for those who are interested only in the bottom line, is naught but a notably agreeable friction in a familiar channel.' 'Should I start with whores?' he asked, and promptly confessed to a most interesting notion that he might be able to cross the bridge with such a highly promiscuous partner, because then he would be in propinquity with all the men who had gone before him.

" 'Do stay away from whores,' I said. 'Since we are speaking frankly, I will suggest that you may simply be too Jewish to bear their scorn.' 'That's half of what I've always found in sex,' Rosen answered. 'Scorn. I'm used to that.'

" 'Yes,' I said, 'but if you form an attachment to whores, you'll never find the kind of woman who would be suitable not only to you, but—face the real level of the bar—suitable to the Agency as well. At least, if you wish to rise!' 'Well, you could be right,' he said, 'but decent women inspire nothing in me.' 'Nonsense,' I answered, 'there is no greater pleasure than that obtained from a conquered repugnance.' 'You are quoting the Marquis de Sade,' said Rosen. 'Indeed I am,' said I, and we had our laugh. 'Yes,' I told him, knowing that I had turned the argument, 'work up an entirely new set of habits on some virgin slate.' 'Do you mean literally a virgin?' he asked. 'Why not?' I said. 'I believe I do. I can think of someone.' 'Who is it?' he wanted to know, 'have I met her?' 'If so, only casually,' I said, 'she came back from South America to work for me a couple of years ago, only far down the hall from you. She was bright enough, but not right for what one needed. I encouraged her to resign from the Agency, and had her installed at State. Now she works for Rusk.' Rosen lit up at this job description. He is *so* ambitious. 'What is she like personally?' he asked. 'A churchgoer,' I told him, 'plain as a post.' 'Well,' he said, 'that makes it sound like an arranged marriage.' 'So it is,' I told him. 'We're not inclined to waste each other's time, are we? Your coreligionists used to go in for arranged marriages in the *shtetl,* did they not? Your blood must be teeming with such arrangements.' 'Yes,' he answered, 'but the bride was not a churchgoer.' 'Yes, but then, you are not much of a Jew any longer, are you?' I countered. 'No,' he said, 'not much. The emotional bond, however, is desperately deep.' 'How deep?' 'Well, not so deep that I can't take a look.' 'Before you do,' I said, 'I want to say that you're not getting the connection for nothing.' 'No?' 'No,' I said, 'you will not only woo her, but manage to traduce her loyalty from Rusk to you, where, of course, it will bubble on tap for me.' Do you know, I like Rosen. His eyes came right back at me with the sweetest smile. 'Good,' he said, 'at last I'll be able to practice some of those low techniques you imparted on Low Thursdays.' What a rejoinder. I had to laugh. He's alert, is Rosen.

"Since then, it has been in the works. I gave him a few photographs of the lady, and the church she frequents, Old First Presbyterian, near Judiciary Square. Do you know, J. Edgar Buddha's first communion was there? Rosen hopped to it. Sat behind her for one Sunday, across the aisle on another, bumped into her on the way out, exchanged names—she couldn't have been more thrilled: A potential convert from Judaism was as exciting to her as an Italian tenor to an English lady. They agreed to meet at the Friday-night church social. Dinner on the following Tuesday. On the next Friday, he walked her home from the church social and managed to kiss her in the hallway. Naturally, I was acting as his case officer. 'Didn't you feel it was appropriate to push further?' I asked. 'I was not wild about her breath,' he replied. 'Well, you've got to get past the nonessentials,' I told him. Since then, we've been pushing it."

"Is this woman's name Nancy Waterston?" I asked.

"Of course," said Harlot. "In fact, Nancy spoke most pleasantly of an evening she had with you in Montevideo. I almost thought of putting you on the job instead of Rosen."

"Wouldn't it have been more likely to get going with Harry?" asked Cal.

"Up to a point," said Harlot. "But Rosen, I think, will be ready before long to get through the crux. After that, he may have to marry the girl. I think it's exactly what it is going to take. She has her own money, is loyal as a hound to whomever is her boss, and so, contrary to the normal precepts, we have to encourage a massive sexual entanglement. We've had some curious obstacles en route, I must say. For three evenings in a row, Arnold could not bring himself to go past the point of kissing Miss Waterston on the lips. 'Everything rebels,' he said. 'Or are you merely too timid?' I asked. 'Yes, I am frightened,' he agreed. 'Take her to a movie,' I said. 'Put your hand on her shoulder. Then, at a given moment, move it down to her breast.' "

Harlot now looked at us. "One phenomenon never fails to amaze me. It does not matter how sophisticated an agent you are dealing with, sooner or later there will be some undeveloped aspect that will call for elementary instruction. So, with Rosen. I had to lead him through the petting game. 'If you cannot bring yourself to shift your hand,' I told him, 'count to ten slowly, and, of course, silently, and in that time concentrate on the fact that you will have no respect for yourself if you fail to obey the challenge. Then, at the count of ten, plunge.' Rosen took it in, and replied, 'That is a technique Julien Sorel employed in *The Red and the Black*.' 'Certainly is,' I said, 'and Stendhal was a master psychologist.' Do you know, the moment he could picture himself as Julien Sorel, it commenced to work. You turn the lock in every agent with a separate key. Rosen made progress. By now, I can tell you, they are commingled in a heap on her living room floor. No coitus, not yet, but Rosen is getting there. She is consumed with a taste for hours of polymorphous perverse, which is, I suppose, the level of sex most suitable to swamp creatures. Carnality that is all but consummated has become her cup of tea. I believe it is going to work. Rosen now sees her every night, has confessed to his hitherto homosexual bondage, and she is wholly captured. In her mind, they are both virgins. Since he is also Jewish and she has obviously made up her mind to convert him, we have an effective *quid pro quo*. Rosen gives up his religion plus his bachelordom; she gives us top-level tap into State."

"I don't know that you have an equation," said Cal.

"Care to make a side bet?"

"Yes. One of us pays for dinner at Sans Souci within sixty days."

"You're on," said Harlot. "I expect to eat and drink at no expense to myself. *The Red and the Black* has proved most useful, you see. Not unlike Madame de Rênal, Miss Waterston is consumed with passion. At my suggestion, Arnold absented himself for a couple of days and she was absolutely beside herself. I am convinced that before long, he will blossom into honest priapic ventures. After all, she provides him with such a sense of power and purpose."

"Wait till he wakes up to the fact that she is, by your words, 'plain as a post,' " said Cal.

"I regret the characterization," said Hugh. "Arnold now shows me photographs of her in summer dresses. She has blossomed. I tell you, before she will allow herself to lose her Reed Rosen, she will come to understand that his career is of first importance to both of them, and that the Agency is a better guardian of the chalice than State. Leave it to Arnold. He's coming onto the high ground now, and he does know how to maneuver. Another man might have seduced the woman in a week and taken a year to decide what to try next."

"Well, let us root for you to win," said Cal, "even if I have to buy the wine."

"Yes," said Harlot. "After all, knowing what Rusk is up to may yet count for a good deal."

"Well, I might just agree."

"Of course," said Hugh. "Since Cuba is now of interest to me, Rusk can be a factor there. A couple of years ago when everyone, including you, Cal, saw the Caribbean as the main go, I knew it was incidental to the show. Now, after Pigs and Mongoose, it's on the back burner. I, however, am worried stiff. Cuba can be used most adroitly these days by Khrushchev and Mao."

"I don't know about that," said Cal. "Khrushchev and Mao are two gentlemen who, at this moment, seem pretty far apart to me."

"On the contrary," said Hugh, "I see them as actors in a scenario of far-reaching disinformation. I will pose a chronology—ponder it, would you? In May, right in the midst of Castro's visit to Moscow, Peking announced its desire to hold talks with the U.S.S.R. Stated object: Bring to an end all ideological rifts between them. Then, last month, Soviets and Chinese held most secret meetings in Moscow. By their termination on July 21, the attempt at conciliation was an announced failure. The Soviet Union declared its advocacy of "peaceful coexistence with the U.S.," and the People's Republic of China publicly judged that course to be an abject surrender to capitalism. We were witnessing—it was generally agreed upon by Western correspondents and diplomats—nothing less than a full-dress split in the international Communist movement. I say we are being handed a scenario."

"To what end?"

"To divide us. I tell you, they are bringing off a gargantuan production in disinformation. It will yet overshadow Dzerzhinsky's manipulation of the Trust."

"They can never manage to keep it secret," Cal said. "Too many of their people have to get in on it sooner or later."

"Not nearly so many as you expect. What the hell, they are free of public opinion, so they need never worry over the morale of their middle-level cadres. Tell a good Communist to despise Red China on Monday and smile at it on Tuesday—he will be able to function with only a small dislocation of the gut. Even if they can't keep it an absolute secret, it is going to work. World opinion follows the form of things rather than the substance. Already this masterpiece of disinformation is known to a few of us Agency folk. We set out to convince our own leaders. Can we? Dubious. Why, even Helms is of two minds over it. And all the while, the few Communists in the know will be elaborating their scenario. We will be provided with border clashes. We will hear scalding vilifications of each other. Separate spheres of influence will emerge in the Communist world. Of course, we will buy it. Their inner guard will play on us with consummate art."

"How do you fit Cuba into this?" I asked.

"As the lead horse. Castro will make overtures of peace. Russia will not be far behind. Communism will begin to seem human. Some of it, at any rate. Can it be Christian not to make friends with reformed enemies? I tell you, they will end by inhabiting our councils and our economy. Where we can never trust all of Communism, we will certainly put our trust in what we think is the more amiable half of a now-divided entity. We will even think we control the balance of power.

"In consequence," said Harlot, "I have come around to thinking that Castro must go. Before Mao and Khrushchev gave their assent to this elevated form of theater, Cuba was but a folly for the Soviets; now, it could be the prettiest piece on their board."

"Is Castro aware of the scenario?" I asked.

"I would surmise," said Harlot, "that he is too young and too emotional to be taken into the councils of the elders. Only when passion is ready to transmute itself into will can one be trustworthy at the highest level."

His eyes were the embodiment of his own statement. Luminous as the light of still water was the steel-tipped manifest of his eyes.

30

The Keep
August 20, 1963

Dearest Harry,

I am frightfully concerned about Hugh. Have you ever considered whether he is mad? Or whether I am? Poor Christopher. Sometimes when I rebel against the injunction I have put upon us not to meet nor even to talk on the telephone, I wish you could see Christopher. His eyes are so blue, a brilliant blue, as if blue is the best color for fire. Otherwise, my Christopher is a quiet and gentle child of six, vastly in awe of his prodigiously austere father (who still approaches him as if he were a small and polluted creature in a large wet diaper), but my son is also wary, I fear, of his mother. I think he is waiting for me to scream. Perhaps he will not trust me until I do.

Dear Harry, let me commence again. Hugh has entered some tunnel of absolute logic that simply refuses to look at the world as it might be. I know he has communicated his theory of The Great Disinformation Sino-Soviet Swindle to you and Cal, for he wrote to me that he had you both over for dinner the night after I left. He has been delivering himself of this prodigious tirade all summer, and (worse luck!) has called the tune through June and July as to what the Russians and Chinese would do next. All the same, it is obscene, in my opinion, to postulate that one hundred men are manipulating a world of several billion humans. "You are ignoring the variety of possibility that God chose us to have," I said to him, but he cannot be reached by argument. Hugh has been waiting all his life for the shade of Dzerzhinsky to pay him a visit. He obviously feels he is the only mortal in CIA who can appreciate KGB on a transcendental scale.

I keep trying to tell him that Russia and China cannot *pretend* to have a profound schism. Humans are, if nothing else, too perverse to be able to carry out such an orchestrated scheme of such immense and immediate disadvantage to themselves. But I will not deaden your head with the teleological and dialectical models that Hugh elaborates. For the present, it is enough to say that he has been looking to convert any number of critically situated people in the Agency to the new religion and must believe I am one of them, for we have had terrible fights over what he does with his thesis. For example, Hugh was so ill-advised as to use the half hour of private conversation he manages to obtain about once a month with Jack Kennedy in a futile attempt to brief him on the real nature of Sino–Soviet policy. Jack is the last person to hope to convince of such a concept. He has such a shrewd, sardonic sense of human foible and the little traps that spring out of the simplest things. I was watching both men from across the room— the upstairs family parlor, as it happened to be—and I must tell you that Jack was sitting a full foot further away from him at the end than at the beginning.

Did Hugh wake up next morning with a rueful sense of how much he had lost? No! He was in a rage at Jack Kennedy. "That man," he kept saying, "is superficial. It is a horror to recognize how superficial he is."

Two days later, Hugh decided that we must break relations with Jack and Bobby.

"Do that, and I may leave you."

"You, too, are superficial."

It was the worst. We never speak to each other in that manner. It took forty-eight hours, but Hugh apologized, and I admitted that I could not leave him. Of course, the issue was still before us, nothing resolved. Oh, we explored the gap. It was one of the few times in our marriage when we were able to talk about facets of ourselves that were not at all agreeable to reveal. Hugh confessed to feeling like a fraud when with the Kennedys. "I am always pretending to be more amused than I am. For a time, I thought it was my duty. I might grow close enough to have influence. But these Kennedys never know what I am talking about. They come from an intellectual tradition that is comprehensive, humanistic, and six inches deep. At bottom, there is nothing we can agree upon. If they are servants of any power higher than themselves, it is not the God who is near to me."

"They are good men," I told him. "Flawed, and not profound enough for you. But do you recognize how rare it is to have keen and reasonable men with a touch of vision? Not automatic, Hugh."

"I consider it a vice of the soul," he said, "to fail to suffer over one's lack of profundity. Unless one's brain is dumb from birth, superficiality is a choice made by the self-indulgent. It is painful in the extreme to live with questions rather than with answers, but that is the only honorable intellectual course. I cannot bear that chirpy Bobby Kennedy, always building his beaver's nest with a few more facts. He needs to look into the abyss."

I did not say, "As you have." I couldn't. It was true. Hugh has not only to wonder whether his mother is a murderess, but is he responsible for those hundreds—or is it thousands?—of Polish Communists whom Stalin consigned to the pit after Hugh and Allen Dulles played their mean game on Noel Field, yes, Hugh sleeps over the chasm. But I fear that he is mad. He said to me, "I know my theses are true because I verified them last week."

"However did you accomplish that?" I asked.

"By my trip to the Shawangunks. I wasn't at all easy about that. I haven't done any real rock, after all, in quite some time. There was one night before I left when I did not sleep. I had a vision of my end. I almost said good-bye to you. To make it worse, on the morning I arrived at the Gunks, I fell in with a crew of young climbers who were not only good but kept calling me 'Pop.' No jibe goes unremarked when you are among good climbers. It is the surest place for measure I have ever encountered. So I had to surpass them. I did. I embarked on a free climb up a 5.8, no ropes.

"I knew that if I kept my head, odds in my favor were better than even—still, you are never more alone than on a free climb. 'If I can do it,' I said to myself, 'then the Soviet-Chinese deception is confirmed. I will take that as a sign.' "

Harry, I wanted to weep. Are all good men as full of folly? For if they are, we may be doomed to fall into every trap that is set for the brave, bold, and bloody blind. Yet, I don't know. A great deal of me responds to just this inner vision in Hugh.

Well, I did not tell him any of that. I informed him that I had become a swollen, greedy, worldly creature who loved nothing so much as to be invited to dinner at the White House or to an afternoon at Hickory Hill. If he persisted in his threats, I would not be able to accept such invitations for fear that he would insult Bobby or Jack. Before I would risk that, I would not see them. I would also not forgive him. Never. Next morning, I decided to take Christopher up to the Keep.

And here I have been. I am much too angry at Hugh. I could not tell him the real truth about what he is asking me to relinquish. He would not understand that it was life-giving to learn that I was neither a mad genius, nor an overeducated and underexperienced girl, but an attractive woman who had her bit of wit to offer the President and knew he was happy in his heart to talk to her. I believe I had influence on him. I say to myself, "This is hubris," but do you know, Harry, nothing is more painful to relinquish than hubris itself? I am beginning to comprehend that there is more to the Greeks than their acceptance of the dark verdicts of heaven—there is also our human rage, larger, perhaps, if only for an instant, than the determining hands of the gods.

I love you,
Kittredge

POST SCRIPTUM: If I speak of love, can you feel the full force of its opposite? I could as easily have written: I hate you.

K.

31

I DON'T KNOW WHETHER IT WAS THAT PARTING SHOT, BUT I DID NOT reply to her letter for a long time. Loneliness sat in me like an empty wallet. I had many an impulse to open the envelope that contained Modene's telephone number, and once, I came so close to calling her that the urge expired only as my finger touched the dial.

Work took me over. I never gave myself to it more. Indeed, I was finding myself of use to my father. He had a mind that could crack a

lobster claw with the pinch of his concentration when he was moved
to concentrate, but that was not every day. His desk often looked like
an unmade bed, and unpursued matters were as painful to his intermittent capacity for organization as unhappy recollections on a hangover.
I loved him, I discovered, but recognition of such emotion came
through my new passion for taking care of details. I was obliged to
cover no narrow spectrum. There were occasions when I even sent
his laundry out, and I certainly went over his memos to McCone, to
Helms, to Montague, and to the fifty officers still working at JM/
WAVE, I vetted incoming cables, and assigned priorities and route
patterns to traffic initiated by us. I actually began to enjoy the chores
of administration, since Cal's secretary, Eleanor, had been overworked for years and was in her own need of an assistant. To our
surprise, Eleanor and I got along. These days, the contents on my desk
were more real to me than where I lived; indeed, Miami and Washington sometimes presented no more difference to me than my separate office cubicles at Langley and Zenith. I was overcome again with
how partial was my knowledge of all I oversaw. Indeed, the more
small power I acquired and the more I partook of beginnings, middles,
and ends, the less available seemed the trinity of a satisfactory narrative.
I found myself reading spy novels on evenings I spent alone, and they
were satisfying in a manner that was never true of work with all its
partially glimpsed projects, ops, capers, researches, stunts, and scenarios, but then, the spy novels were never true to life. I even had an
extended rumination about the nature of plot. In life, it seemed to me,
plot was always incomplete. No matter!—it was also the focus of half
of one's strivings—for we never strain harder than when we see
ourselves as protagonists in a plot; the other half of one's personal
history is but an accumulation of habit, error, luck, coincidence, and
large helpings of that daily sludge which is the ballast of narrative if
you insist upon perceiving your life as a connected tale. I was grateful,
therefore, to have a summer when I could live with only a few
personal matters, a great many external details, and the knowledge that
my father and I made, when all was said, a respectable team.

    Some aspects of his work, however, he kept from me. I knew he
was building his ties to AM/LASH, but I can hardly say how long it
would have taken to learn any more if we had not had a flap on
September 8 large enough to convince Cal that it was time to bring
me in. That morning, he handed me a clipping from the *Washington
Post* so soon as I came into his office. The story was datelined Havana.

On the night of September 7, Castro had attended a party at the Brazilian Embassy where he made a point of taking aside a reporter for the Associated Press: "Kennedy is the Batista of our time," he declared. "We have discovered terrorist plans to eliminate Cuban leaders. If U.S. leaders assist in such terrorist plans, they will not themselves be safe."

"I would call that," said Cal, "a message for us."

"Can you provide the background?" I asked.

"AM/LASH is now stationed at the Cuban consulate in São Paulo, Brazil. One of our case officers there has been meeting with him."

"I guess that's all I need," I answered. Given the variety of places in Havana one could choose for a chat with the local AP man, Castro had selected the Brazilian Embassy.

"Yes," Cal said, "Counterintelligence is going to camp out this morning in Richard Helms' office."

They did. There were several such meetings in September, but by the end of the month, Cal was able to say, "We're still operative." I looked over a copy of the final memo sent to Counterintelligence by Helms: "If AM/LASH has not been doubled by Castro, and the evidence, as of this point, cannot be termed conclusive, then we are giving up one of the most, if not the most promising Cuban asset in our reach. No one with whom we are on speaking terms in the Caribbean approaches AM/LASH's proximity to the Cuban leader. On balance, the answer declares itself. We will continue with AM/LASH."

I had a reasonably good suspicion of why Helms was supporting my father. By mid-September, we had become aware of a covert peace agenda between the U.S. and Cuba at the United Nations. Harlot still had his line into the Bureau, and so we kept receiving FBI taps on the Cuban Embassy in Washington and the Cuban delegation to the UN. The Bureau also had a tap into Adlai Stevenson's office in the UN building, or thus I supposed, since envelopes from all three sources came into our office every morning from GHOUL. It did occur to me that Ambassador Stevenson's office should have been out of bounds for the FBI, but who would suggest that to Mr. Hoover? In any event, material came in abundance. Given my meditation on the scattered fragments of plot that composed the sad porridge of the Intelligence officer, I was at last in reasonably full reception of a comprehensive chowder.

On September 18, William Attwood, Special Adviser to the American delegation at the UN, sent a confidential memo to Averell Harriman, who was then serving as Undersecretary of State for Political Affairs:

> The policy of isolating Cuba, I would argue, has intensified Castro's desire to initiate trouble and conflict in Latin America and has left us stiffened into the unattractive posture, as world opinion perceives it, of a big country trying to bully a small one.
>
> According to neutral diplomats at the UN there is reason to believe that Castro would go to some length to obtain normalization of relations with us—even though this would not be welcomed by most of his hard-core Communist entourage.
>
> All of this may or may not be true. But it would seem that we have something to gain and nothing to lose by finding out whether in fact Castro does want to talk and what concessions he would be prepared to make. If Castro is interested, I could travel to Cuba as an individual, but would, of course, report to the President before and after the visit.

A few days later we came into possession of the summary that Attwood provided Adlai Stevenson on Harriman's reaction. The proposition, he declared, would put the Kennedys on a course of high risk: "Any of a number of Republicans who obtain even the faintest sniff of this could bring down sheer hell to pay." Nonetheless, Harriman told Attwood that he felt "adventurous," and suggested that Robert Kennedy be approached. Bobby wrote on the margin of Attwood's memo, "Worth pursuing. Get in touch with Mac Bundy." In his turn, Bundy told Attwood that "the President might look favorably upon working Castro out of the Soviet fold." Encouraged by this much favorable reaction, Attwood got in touch with the Cuban Ambassador to the UN, Carlos Lechuga.

Meetings between Helms, Harlot, and Cal soon followed. Their strategy, as it came down to me, was to steer Special Group, by way of Director McCone, into approving new sabotage operations in Cuba. So soon as such authorization was obtained, Cal mounted a quick raid on an oil refinery, and the boats and men were dispatched on the heels of a hurricane that struck the Caribbean on October 6. The raiders never reached their target and two of the sixteen men who landed in Cuba were captured.

Cal did not seem unduly upset. Of course, he had not known the men. Neither did I. Dix Butler, responding to a call from me, had put the operation together in a rush. Whether it was bad luck or he prepared it poorly we could not decide without an inquiry, but the day when personnel were available at JM/WAVE for such investigations was certainly over.

Butler was furious, however. Over the phone from Miami came excoriations of Langley mentality until I could restrain myself no further and said, "All right. My father is responsible. I am responsible. And you? Can you accept any of the fault?"

"No," he said. "You gave me Chevi Fuertes in the first place. I had to employ him as liaison."

"You couldn't have been authorized to use him. Not for a job like this."

"There was no time. Repeat: *no time*. I was *obliged* to use him. I think he tipped off the Cuban coast guard."

"How could he? You didn't tell him where the men were going in, did you?"

"He might have sent out a general alert."

"Where is he now?"

"I don't know. He's hiding from me. He did not show up at his job in the bank."

"Has he disappeared altogether?"

"He phoned me. He said he will come in when I have cooled down. I am going to have a showdown with Fuertes which he will never forget."

"Did you tell him that?"

"I told him that there was nothing to cool down about. It was a time to regroup, not point fingers."

I had no idea of whether to warn Chevi, seduce him into a meeting, or confront Butler with charges. That made for three disagreeable options, and besides I did not know where Chevi was hiding.

On October 13, Castro denounced the raid: "What does the United States do when we Cubans are striving to recover from a hurricane that killed one thousand of our people? They send saboteurs armed with pirate ships and explosives."

We were able, therefore, to count our gains. Fidel Castro was unhappy, and Attwood's labors, in consequence, would suffer. Then a Bureau transcript of a conversation in the Cuban delegation's UN office came from Harlot, and we learned that a secret meeting with Castro was still being proposed: Would it be possible to fly Attwood to a small airport near Havana?

Adlai Stevenson, briefed by Attwood, was concerned. "Too many individuals may be privy by now to the new Cuban agenda," he said. Attwood replied that the only government figures who knew about these contacts with the Cubans were, to the best of his knowledge, the President, the Attorney General, Ambassador Harriman, McGeorge Bundy, Stevenson, and himself.

Since Cal and Harlot had been seeding the groves of Langley with selected extracts from our take, and the FBI was stocked with UN reports to be leaked wherever Hoover saw fit, and JM/WAVE and the Cuban exile leaders were being informed by everyone, it seemed to me that the only principals not in the pipeline by now must have been Secretary of State Rusk and John McCone. There were mornings when Cal's office would receive as many as four or five memos from different suites at Langley calling our attention to Attwood's Cuban overture, and all of the memos were based on rumors Cal and I had surreptitiously disseminated the day before.

Hunt even took me to lunch in the senior-grade cafeteria at Langley to fulminate over what he had heard. "I always knew that Smiling Jack could not be trusted, but this is egregious betrayal. Can your father get word up to Dick Helms?"

"He can only try," I said to Hunt.

"If Cal isn't ready to exercise the direct route, I might take a crack at bearding Helms myself."

"Well, don't use up any favors. Cal can reach him."

"Give my regards to your father. Is he in good spirits?"

"Today? Very."

He was. Yesterday afternoon, October 24, John McCone, flanked by Richard Helms, Hugh Montague, and Boardman Hubbard, had succeeded in convincing Bobby Kennedy and Special Group to authorize thirteen major sabotage operations, one a week on average from November 1963 through January 1964. An electric power plant, an oil refinery, and a sugar mill were among the targets selected. "The timing is satisfactory," Cal declared. "Now things will never settle down. We can burn an ulcer into Castro. That bastard! Daring to play with Soviet missiles! I could immolate myself, kamikaze fashion, Rick, if I knew one hand grenade would take out Fidel, Raul, and Che Guevara in the same flash of light."

He meant it. My father, as he grew older, sprouted small short-comings which gave every promise of growing larger, but if he could move you to wince at his follies, you could hardly laugh at him. He had no fear of dying. Death was one embrace that was brought off best if you took an enemy with you.

That was the larger part of my father, but every lion has his ghost. He was also, I came to discover, as delicate as an old lady to the shades and whispers of enemy intrigue. On October 25, the day after Special Group authorized our thirteen raids, and not twenty minutes after I came back from lunch with Hunt, I found Cal in a thoroughgoing bad mood. Yesterday afternoon, just about the time he was arguing his case at Special Group, President Kennedy, he had learned, was giving a full half hour of interview to an esteemed French journalist named Jean Daniel. The Frenchman, whose interview had been arranged by Attwood, was on his way to Havana, and there were no taps—alas!—into the Oval Office. There was, however, a Bureau report of a conversation at the UN on the night of October 24:

> Attwood informed Ambassador Stevenson that while Jean Daniel stated that he was a professional journalist and would not repeat his conversation with President Kennedy, Daniel found such conversation "highly stimulating" and further stated that it might be "conducive to eliciting productive response from Fidel Castro."

"Yes," said Cal, "you can visualize it. Smiling Jack introduces Jean Daniel to Mrs. Kennedy. After all, our First Lady charmed Paris. You are not going to allow a top-dog French interviewer to go home without meeting her. Then Jack tells Jean that he is not opposed to collectivism, *per se,* just its abuse by the Soviets. Probably says that he can find a way to live with Cuba next door. Jack Kennedy has the ability to make a large difference sound like a family misunderstanding."

"How do you know all this?"

"Spend a season watching the Washington snakes in their mating rites, and it's amazing what you know."

Let no one say my father had no instincts for divination. Fifty days after Jean Daniel met Jack Kennedy, the journalist's account of the meeting appeared.

From *THE NEW REPUBLIC*
DECEMBER 14, 1963

President Kennedy received me at the White House on Thursday, October 24. . . . As we passed through the small room where his secretary was working, we caught a glimpse of Mrs. Kennedy leaving by a French window on her way to a private garden of the White House. The President called her back to introduce me.

It was still Indian summer in Washington. The weather was very warm and both the President and Mrs. Kennedy were very lightly dressed, thus enhancing the impression of youth, charm, and simplicity which was in rather surprising contrast to the solemnity of entering these august chambers. After she left, the President invited me to be seated on the semicircular sofa which was in the middle of his office. He sat in a rocking chair opposite the sofa. The interview was to last from 20 to 25 minutes, and it was interrupted only by a brief telephone call. . . .

My notes are very specific and I shall let President Kennedy speak through them: "I'd like to talk to you about Cuba. . . ." John Kennedy then mustered all his persuasive force. He punctuated each sentence with that brief, mechanical gesture which has become famous.

"I tell you this: I believe there is no country in the world . . . where economic colonization, exploitation, and humiliation were worse than in Cuba, in part owing to my country's policies during the Batista regime. I believe that we created, built, and manufactured the Castro movement out of whole cloth and without realizing it. I believe that the accumulation of these mistakes has jeopardized all of Latin America. This is one of the most important problems in American foreign policy. I can assure you that I have understood the Cubans, I approved of the proclamation which Fidel Castro made in the Sierra Maestra, when he justifiably called for justice and especially yearned to rid Cuba of corruption. I will go even further: to some extent it is as though Batista was the incarnation of a number of sins on the part of the United States. Now we shall have to pay for those sins. In the matter of the Batista regime, I am in agreement with the first Cuban revolutionaries. That is perfectly clear."

After a silence during which he was able to note my surprise and my interest, the President continued: "But it is also clear that the problem has ceased to be a Cuban one and has become international, that is, it has become a Soviet problem. I am the President of the United States and not a sociologist; I am the President of a free nation which has certain responsibilities to the Free World. I know that Castro betrayed the promises made in the Sierra Maestra, and that he has agreed to be a Soviet agent in Latin America. I know that through his fault—either his 'will to independence,' his madness, or Communism—the world was on the verge of a nuclear war in October 1962. The Russians understood this very well, at least after our reaction; but so far as Fidel Castro is concerned, I must say I don't know whether he realizes this, or even if he cares about it." A smile, then: "You can tell me whether he does when you come back. In any case, the nations of Latin America are not going to attain justice and progress that way, I mean through Communist subversion. They won't get there by going from economic oppression to a Marxist dictatorship which Castro himself denounced a few years ago. The United States now has the possibility of doing as much good in Latin America as it has done wrong in the past; I would even say that we alone have the power— on the essential condition that Communism does not take over there."

Mr. Kennedy then rose to indicate the interview was over. . . .

32

AT THE END OF OCTOBER, MY FATHER TOOK A THREE-DAY TRIP TO Paris, but only on his return did I find out that he had met with Rolando Cubela.

Earlier in October, Cubela had informed LYME, his case officer in Brazil, that he was about to be moved to Paris, an assignment he considered more suitable to his position as "second-in-command within the Foreign Division of the Interior Ministry." While this title confirmed our conviction that he had close ties to the DGI, that did not remove the possibility that he was also ready to aim a sniper's rifle at Fidel Castro.

There had been difficulties, however, setting up the rendezvous with Cubela in Paris. He insisted that Bobby Kennedy be present. It was his intention, Cubela announced, to become the next leader of Cuba, and he wanted assurances of political support from the Kennedys.

While there was obviously no possibility of asking Bobby Kennedy to go—my God, it could be a trap!—neither was there any inclination to inform him. One could certainly meet Cubela without Bobby. The real problem at this point was who to send to Paris as a *personal representative* of the Attorney General. Cal volunteered.

Perfect. No one would argue that Cal lacked the bottom to pass himself off as a close friend of the Kennedys.

Next, it was decided that Paris Station was not to be alerted. On the contrary, it would be more effective to fly LYME over from São Paulo to Paris. He could then guide Cubela to whichever nondescript café in the depths of the Twelfth Arrondissement had been chosen by Cal. "I like the Twelfth for this kind of get-together," said Cal. "It has a slew of bistros where you will never run into anyone you've met since birth." Yes, a simple sit-down was preferable to alerting Paris Station that Senior Officer HALIFAX was on his way to see a man who could prove a problem and might be carrying a gun. "Station," said Cal, "would sprinkle so much hygiene on the premises that Cubela would bolt."

My father went over to Paris, then, on October 28 and came back on October 30. At their meeting on October 29, Cubela got drunk in an hour. He would only accept this personal representative of the Attorney General, he told my father, on the full understanding that the President's brother was a very busy man. On their next meeting, however, he would want to receive a handwritten letter from the Attorney General. It must contain Mr. Robert Kennedy's personal promise that a successful completion of the proposed mission would result in the full powers of the U.S. government being brought to bear in support of the presidential candidacy of Rolando Cubela during the first free Cuban election. "On the other hand," added Cubela, "if I do not succeed, you will owe me nothing but my expenses—which can prove considerable."

"What does he look like?" I asked.

"About what you'd expect," said Cal. "He's tall, dark mustache, certainly attractive to women, shows circles under his eyes, is probably partial to cocaine, and would be a whole pain in the ass to hang around with for more than a night."

I felt frustrated. There was not all that much to my father's account. "Did he," I asked, "talk about nothing but his political prospects?"

"Well, we did get into the hardware. On my next trip, he wants

to be handed a few sophisticated tools. He rattled on about our
'technical felicities' until I didn't know whether he was referring to
sneakies or sniper-sticks, so I decided to be blunt: 'Are you speaking
of the assassination-mode capability?' I asked. He went wild. 'Do not
use that word again in my presence,' he cried out at me. By God, we
were virtually alone in the café but still his voice was rising. I had to
put a heavy hand on his shoulder. Which he threw off, although it did
quiet him down enough for him to hiss: '*Elimination* is the word! You
eliminate a problem, that is all!' I suppose I had made a bad move by
being so explicit, but I did want to jar the guy into focus. He was
getting vague and megalomaniacal. A heavy drinker. Of course, not
every successful assassin has to pass a sobriety test. I cite John Wilkes
Booth as the classic example."

"You are not too happy with Rolando Cubela?"

"Miserable. Hugh and Dick Helms do, however, agree with me
—he's all we've got." Cal nodded. "See for yourself. I've decided to
take you along on the next trip."

"I can't say I'm not pleased."

"I didn't want you on the first one. I was feeling kind of spooked.
If something went wrong, I didn't want you in the middle. I like to
be able to measure my share of the fault."

Was he kind enough not to say that others had not wished me to
go? That was but one more question, and we had come to the point
where there would be, I expected, no more answers. My father was
hardly about to admit to me that Cubela, by a preponderance of
evidence, was bound to be a double agent, and Helms and Harlot
might be pursuing this matter precisely to bring to Fidel's attention
that the Agency was not only still set on killing him, but that a *personal
representative* of the Kennedys was going to play a serious role in the
plot. The coldest part of my heart was not without admiration: Castro's distrust of the peace overtures would be greatly increased. Was
I beginning to comprehend how the game worked? I even felt a cool
happiness in being so removed from myself, as if exactly this subtle
distance from one's soul was the acme of elegance. Like Harlot, I
might yet become the instrument of my will.

On their side, the peace offensive was continuing its efforts. An
FBI report informed us that Dr. Vallejo had told Lisa Howard on
October 31 to alert Attwood to stand in readiness for the flight to
Havana in a private plane. Vallejo said it would be sent over by Fidel
himself. There had to be a strong likelihood, however, that Vallejo

was merely pursuing a few of his own unauthorized hopes, for on the same day, October 31, on Cuban television, Castro brought out the two commandos captured in the raid we had dispatched on the heels of the hurricane, three weeks ago. Under the TV lights, these exile Cubans produced the name of their case officer (Dix Butler was immortalized as Frank Castle), and the actual location of 6312 Riviera Drive was announced, plus a description of our JM/WAVE weapons armory. Castro must have anticipated large media reaction in the United States, but the Agency was quick to suggest that the commandos had been brainwashed, and the story received no particular attention. Castro was predictably enraged: "The American press refuses to report these attacks even when confronted with evidence they could easily have substantiated. You can see that in this free press of which they boast, the wire services and the CIA act in unison, elaborating and developing the same lie in order to disguise the truth."

Cal smiled. "Whose ox is being gored?" he asked.

I held on to that. I did not believe that we owed Castro any debt in the way of reasonable treatment—no, not after the missiles—but it did no harm to be able to refresh one's sense of sanction.

Meanwhile, our access to Rusk's office was improving. While Nancy Waterston's level of entry was, at best, restricted, some high-level memos did pass her desk. Her limitations as an agent—we called her EUPHONY—remained more prominent than her virtues, however. She refused to undertake the emotional turmoil of photographing documents. In compensation, she did have a rare faculty for recollecting exactly what she read, and would come home at night to type out long, detailed recapitulations of confidential papers for Rosen. Since her attention had, by our design, not been fixed on Cuba (so as not to alert her to our interests until she proved reliable), all we received through most of October was information on Rusk's reaction to a coup d'état in Honduras, the sale of wheat to the U.S.S.R., and the resignation of Harold Macmillan as Prime Minister, none of which was close to our heart. Harlot called Nancy's submissions "gists."

By the beginning of November, however, her work produced a few results. Secretary Rusk was beginning to react to the Cuban overture, and EUPHONY was busy furnishing Rosen with the gists of memos Rusk had been firing off to some of his people in the State Department: "Diplomatic Caribbean investments of long standing are not to be undercut by maverick negotiations." Et cetera. Before long, by way of EUPHONY, we learned that Attwood had been told that the State Department's enthusiasm for the Cuban overture was, in a word, "constricted." A memo out of Rusk's office on November 7 went as follows:

> Before the United States Government can even contemplate entering into minimal relations with the Cuban government, all political, economic, and military dependency on the Sino–Soviet bloc must cease, together with all subversion in the hemisphere. Castro would have to renounce Marxism–Leninism as an ideology, have all Communists removed from influential positions, be prepared to offer compensation for all properties expropriated since 1959, and return all manufacturing, oil, mining, and distribution industries to private enterprise.

"Sounds like Rusk wouldn't mind a little unconditional surrender," I remarked.

"Well," said Cal, "that may be the best thing about the old stump. He hates unforeseen movement. If he stays in one place long enough, he figures Kennedy will circle back to him."

In Havana, we were keeping Jean Daniel under light surveillance (which was not without its demand on the limited resources of our Cuban assets) but the observers were confident that Daniel had obtained no access to Castro during his weeks in Cuba, and had been obliged to content himself with tours of mines, sugar refineries, and schools for children in the provinces. The Cuban overture looked to be, as Cal put it, "in irons."

All the same, we were taking nothing for granted. The next meeting with AM/LASH was now arranged for November 22, and I began to ride a fine sense of anticipation. On nights that found me in Washington, I would attend Agency language classes to brush up on my conversational French. It was hardly necessary. If all went well, Cal and I would be in Paris for only a day, but I gave myself to it as a solemn undertaking; the rigor of French syntax seemed, under the circumstances, to be not without sacramental overtones for the task that lay ahead. It is interesting that the closer we came to the date, the more I began to see Cubela not as a double agent, but in all the spectral light of an unimpeachable assassin.

33

On November 18, President Kennedy gave a televised speech at a dinner of the Inter-American Press Association of Miami, and Dix Butler and I watched in a bar.

I could not help contrasting this evening to the apocalyptic reception Jack Kennedy had had at the Orange Bowl in December, eleven months ago. Tonight, there was no standing ovation when he concluded, and most of his speech was received in silence. The audience, composed in large part of Miami exiles, were exhibiting their suspicions. When Kennedy referred to Cuba's "small band of conspirators" as a weapon employed "by external powers to subvert the other American republics," and added, "This and this alone divides us—as long as this is true, nothing is possible—without it, everything is possible," no large response came back.

Afterwards, Butler gave his verdict. " 'Get rid of the U.S.S.R.,' " said Dix, " 'and you can have your socialism, Mr. Castro,' is about what he was saying." Dix gave a wide and wicked grin. "I can think of a lot of Cubans in Miami who are going to stick pins tonight in their wax effigy of Jack Kennedy."

"I don't know that many Cubans anymore," I said.

"You never did."

I would have paid up at that point and left, half in outrage at what he said and half in gloom at the truth of it, but he put his arm around my shoulder. "Hey, buddy, cheer up, you and me go boom-boom in a boat. Hey? Nay?"

"You are easier to get along with," I said, "when things are happening too fast to open your mouth."

"I agree. Go where the wild goose goes." He nodded. "Hubbard, these are farewell drinks. I've worked a transfer to Indochina. I am going back to the best hashish in the world." At the moment, he was slugging bourbon on the rocks with a beer chaser. "Say my good-byes," he said, "to Chevi Fuertes."

Well, turns in conversation with Butler never took long to get around the corner. "Where is Chevi?" I asked.

"I don't know."

"Have you seen him?"

"Since last we spoke, yes. As a matter of fact, yes. I have seen him. In fact, I had it out with him." He nodded at the solidity of this fact.

"I had him alone in my motel room, and I accused him of being DGI."

"How did you get him there?"

"That's a tale to tell. No matter. He just likes to hang around in my company, believe it if you will. He was duded up. Light blue suit, yellow shirt, orange tie. You and me would look like candy cocksuckers, Hubbard, but Chevi has an eye for *accommodating* pastels. Looked pretty. For a fat double dealer, he looked pretty. He could open a downtown haberdashery. 'Excuse me,' I said to him, 'seeing you is such a wrench that I've got to go to the loo.' Hubbard, it was true. I had a full-gauge movement."

It was tempting to suggest to Butler that if he ever rose to the higher levels of the Agency, it would be prudent not to get into the periodicity of his bowels, but I resisted the impulse. Just as well. He wanted to talk. He said, "Follow it! When I came out, I sat Chevi down in a chair and began to work him back and forth."

"Back and forth?"

"A head swivel. A good slap to the left, a good one to the right. I had my ring on, so that pulled the cork. He began to bleed all over the yellow shirt and the orange tie. 'You are an idiot and a beast,' he said to me.

" 'No, Chevi,' I told him, 'it is a little worse than that. Tonight you are going to admit that you are DGI.' What a speech he brought forth. The complexities of his work. If I recorded it, I could give lectures at Langley Manor. Chevi had dealings, he admitted. After all, he had done liaison for me into every exile group, MIRR, Alpha 66, Commandos L, DRE, Thirtieth of November, MDC, Interpen, Crusade to Free Cuba, Anti-Communist League of the Caribbean. He didn't stop. He must have figured that so long as he kept talking I wouldn't work him anymore. He listed each and every reason that he is our highest paid agent in Miami, and I said, 'Let's get down to it. You also have dealings with the DGI.' 'You know I do,' he told me, 'you encourage me to.' 'Yes,' I said, 'provided you fulfill my instructions to the letter.' 'Understood,' he said. 'No,' I said, 'not understood. You have cut some very dangerous corners. You give the DGI more than I license you to give them.' He actually nodded. 'I may extend the boundaries,' he said."

"Chevi admitted that?" I asked.

"Of course he did. He was under the gun. 'Yes,' I said, 'how far were those boundaries extended?' 'You have to understand the game,' he said. 'I do,' I said. 'Then you understand,' he said, 'I have given material to the DGI that would increase their trust in me.' 'Yes,' I said, 'we believe you are a double agent working for us. And maybe they believe you are doubling for them.' 'Yes,' he said, 'but they are in error.' 'No,' I said, 'the DGI is not stupid. Maybe you are giving them as much, or maybe a little more than you are giving us.' 'No,' he said. 'No?' I asked. 'At my very worst,' he said, 'I am a neutral market-place.' 'Does this extend,' I asked, 'to letting them know the night that we will run a raid? Is that why two of my people got picked off, and I was named on Havana television?' 'No,' he said, 'I am a neutral marketplace. I give clean information to both parties.' You bet. I saw the key to his action then. 'You,' I said, 'have *your* man in the DGI. You are thick with him, and he is thick with you. You are both going down on each other, aren't you, you faggots?' 'No,' he said. 'Yes,' I said, 'that is bad enough, but why did you give the date of my raid over to the DGI?' 'No,' he said, 'I wouldn't do that.' "

Butler blew out his breath and looked at me. My father once remarked that as they die from the hunter's wound, big game animals go through startling changes of expression. I saw Butler look wicked, woeful, merry, terrified, then pleased with himself over the next twenty seconds. "Hubbard," he went on, "I lifted him out of his chair, manhandled him into the john, held his head over the toilet bowl which—don't shy from this, Hubbard—I had not flushed, no, by anticipation and design, not flushed—I am a calculating case officer —and I said to Chevi, 'Tell me now, or you can taste the truth.' 'No,' he said, 'didn't do it, Dix baby, believe in Chevi.' Now, I wasn't going to force the issue. The threat, I recognize, is invariably greater than the execution—I, too, am witting of Clausewitz—but the force of something that I would call the force of completion came over me, and I shoved his head into that stinking bowl, and rubbed it around there. I was shrieking away: 'Cuba, *sí*! Yeah? Castro, *sí*! Yeah?' "

The bartender came over, "Keep down the Castro talk, can you, gentlemen, there are a couple of Cubans here, my regular customers," but, seeing the look on Butler's face, added, "thank you," and de-camped.

"Next time," said Butler to me, "he better come back with a length of pipe."

I was silent. I was usually silent around Butler. "Did he confess?" I asked at last.

"No," Butler said. "Every time I lifted his head, he kept saying,

'What I keep in me, you will never get.' He was phenomenal! 'What I keep in me, you will never get!' I finally had to throw him into the shower. I actually got in with him. I started to scrub him, and he went berserk. It was like catching a raccoon in a garbage can. I jumped out of the shower. I was laughing. But I wanted to cry. I loved Chevi Fuertes then. I love him now."

"What!"

"Yes. I am shit-face drunk. But he was shit-face then. By externals. Through coercion. I am shit-face from the misery of having done it to him. Because I enjoyed doing it, and I enjoy suffering remorse, and now, Hubbard, I feel a lot of disquiet. Because he has disappeared with his lover in the DGI. For all I know he is in Cuba, and I am on my way to Indochina. A taste for combat is the only gift God ever gave me."

"Let's get out of here," I said.

"Was I right or wrong with Fuertes?"

"You know what I will answer."

"But what if he did betray me?"

"What if you were wrong?"

"Your anger sits up there above your belly button. It's in your mouth," said Butler. "So I don't care how you judge me. Up or down, no matter. I did what I did to Chevi because I decided to. Hubbard, you will never believe this, but I would like to become a calculating case officer like you." He began to laugh. "Believe that, sucker," he said, "and I will export opium to Hong Kong."

I managed to get him home without an episode. That is the only credit I will take for the night. When I returned to my apartment, an envelope had been slid under the door.

the 18th November

Dear Peter (alias Robert Charles),

Can we say I knew you when? One of the first American expressions I learned was "I knew you *when*." Yes, I knew you as a decent fellow in Montevideo, Peter, ignorant, astonishingly ignorant on nearly all world matters were you, Peter, but then no more ignorant than your colleagues in Miami—the ignorami cowboys of the CIA. I have had enough. As you read this, I will be in Cuba where I belong, although said decision has dragged me through a personal pilgrimage of disillusions with myself and the seductions of your world, to which I overadhered. You understand? I used to despise Communists because to them I first belonged and knew they were spiritual hypocrites. I could feel all the honesty dying in me while in their company, which in Uruguay was closer to me than always and forever, and I despised their spiritual hypocrisy. They never did anything with a simple understanding that it was for themselves, no, they didn't enjoy a good meal because they were gluttons and liked being gluttons, no, they ate the good meal because it was *their duty* to keep up morale for the sake of the cause. Bullshit. Avalanches of bullshit. My wife in Uruguay, the worst. Power, propriety, righteousness. I hated her enough to hate all Communists. I kept wishing I was back in Harlem where I lived with a Negress prostitute. She was greedy, she had a straight line to her stomach and to her pussy. If a man talked in a loud voice, she liked him better than a dude with a nice quiet voice. She was simple. She was capitalism. I decided that capitalism was the lesser evil. When you did something, you did it for yourself alone. And it worked. Minus times minus is plus. A world of greedy people makes a good society. Capitalism was surrealism. I liked that.

But now I have had many months of living under the thumb of a white capitalist, Dix Butler, who will be very rich one day for he is the stuff out of which the fortunes are made. What he does is always for himself alone, and I have come to the conclusion that is even worse. In the name of his principle, which is himself—"That which makes me feel good is *the* good." Ernest Hemingway, correct? Subject to that principle, I found my head in a shit bowl. For further information apply to Dix Butler. Excuse me. Frank Castle. Tell Frank Castle the DGI knows his real name. Dix Butler. I gave it to them yesterday. And how do I know it? Because he told it to me when we were making love. Yes, I have had an affair with Dix Butler. Does that amaze you? I, who used to be one of the leading white man studs in Harlem, and totally in Montevideo, have lost the connection to my manhood. Yes, over the last few years, *after working for you, in fact*. But then I did leave Uruguay in a panic with my cock between my legs. Nothing but a treacherous son of a bitch. In Miami, I got so treacherous it was a daily habit. My asshole grew to have more status for my soul than my penis—why? That may be no mysterious matter. Virility is pride. And I was a bag of shit. What is the apple of the eye in a bag of shit? The asshole, señor. I tell you all this, Peter, I mean Robert Charles of the innocenti, because it will shock you. I wish to do that. You are so naïve. Prodigiously naïve, but you try to run the world.

Arrogant, naïve, incompetent, self-righteous. You will judge me adversely for being a homosexual, yet it is you who is more of one than any of us, although you will never admit it to yourself because you never practice! You are a homosexual the way Americans are barbarians although they do not practice openly. They go to church. And you work for your people so that you will not have to scrutinize yourself in the mirror. No, you peek right through your two-way CIA mirror to spy on others.

I go to Cuba full of fear. What if the average Cuban Communists are as stupid as Uruguayan Party members? America is choicer country for shits. Even shits like me. And I worry that Fidel Castro has not matured out of his own wickedness and cannot admit to himself that he was wrong to accept the missiles. But I will find out. I will no longer be able to indulge both sides of my nature. Visualize it therefore as a personal sacrifice. Communism will triumph to the extent that human nature can swim through its own shit. I feel like a pioneer.

Suerte, good fellow. Know that I will always have love for you. Despite all, as the English say.

Adios,
Chevi

I finished reading the letter. Its contents were still boiling in my head when the phone sounded. Was it by some nuance in the ring itself that I knew Señor Eusebio Fuertes was calling?

"Where are you?"

"Across the street. I saw you come in. I was waiting. Have you read my letter?"

"Yes."

"Can I visit?"

"Yes." That was all I could manage. I had begun to shake. Once in Maine, on a rock face to the side of the Precipices, I had had a quivering in my knees that Harlot was quick to describe as "sewing-machine leg." Now my hands were trembling. I knew why Chevi was here.

He looked merry coming through the door as if he had arrived at that freedom from consequence which is indifferent to the verdict. I would now have to make the choice. I could detain him, or give him my sanction to go to Cuba. Each of these options was intolerable.

"Yes," he said, "I have come to say good-bye. All the while I was writing the letter, I did not think I would. I had contempt for you. I did not wish to see you in person. But now I am finished with all that." He looked around. "Do you have an *añejo*?" He gave an evil smile. "A Cuban rum?"

I handed him a bottle with a Puerto Rican label and a glass. My hands, thankfully, were equal to the job.

"Do you know why I have come?" he asked.

"I think so."

"May I add a thought? You have vices, Roberto, and many faults, but I still perceive you, now that I have emitted my resentments, as a decent man. Therefore, I cannot leave without saying good-bye, for that would violate your decency. That would violate mine. I believe an economy of goodwill exists in the universe. An economy which is not inexhaustible."

"No," I said, "you want me to arrest you. Then you can find a little peace. You will feel justifiably bitter. Otherwise, you wish me to give you my blessing. Then you will have all the pleasure of knowing that you were successful at last in getting me to . . ." I did not know how to say it—". . . in getting me to violate the confidence of others."

"Yes," he said, "you are my equal."

"Just get the hell out," I said.

"You cannot arrest me. I see that you cannot."

"Go," I said. "Learn all you can about Cuba. You will come back to us yet, and then you will be worth more."

"You are wrong," he said, "I will become the determined enemy of your country. Because if you let me go, I will understand that you no longer believe in your own service."

Could he be right? I felt an intolerable rage. I may have been as physically powerful at that moment as my father. I certainly had no fear of Chevi other than the fear, true son of Boardman Hubbard, that I might kill him with my bare hands. Yes, I could destroy him, but I could not take him into custody. He was my creation. All the same, I could not rid my mind of a miserable marriage of images—as I looked at his dapper presence in my living room, I still pictured his head in Butler's toilet bowl.

"Just get out," I said. "I am not going to take you in."

He swallowed the rum and stood up. He looked pale. Can I claim it was Christian to wish he was going to Havana with no more than half a heart?

"Salud, caballero," he said.

I was cursing him ten minutes after he was gone. I had all the misery of knowing that I had delivered a new obsession to myself. I was full of dread. When I went up to Washington a few days later, the capital felt as heavy as hurricane weather in Miami, and that is not a small remark; Washington, whatever its vices, has never been renowned for haunted precincts or eerie moods. Yet, I found it so. I had betrayed the Agency. This sentiment grew so powerful that I entered at last into the mathematics of faith. Sin and penance met each other in the equations of my mind. I took a new vow that from this day on, no matter how half-hearted or quartered by anxiety, I would consecrate myself to the assassination of Fidel Castro.

34

ON THE DAY BEFORE WE LEFT FOR PARIS, CAL RECEIVED A SHORTWAVE radio message from one of his agents in Havana. It informed him that on the previous night, November 19, Fidel Castro had paid a visit to Jean Daniel's hotel and spent the next six hours in an interview with the journalist.

While we were to have no sure notion what thoughts were exchanged between the two men until Jean Daniel's two-part article appeared on December 7 and 14 in *The New Republic*, my father was not short of speculation on November 20.

"This meeting took place," said Cal, "because of what Kennedy said in Miami two nights ago—'This and this alone divides us.' That is why Castro saw Daniel."

When I did not reply, Cal added, "Are you as unhappy about all this as I am?"

"Well, the news does give a good deal of purpose to our trip."

"Yes," said Cal, "we won't be gilding the lily, will we?"

Several weeks later, I would read every word Jean Daniel reported Fidel Castro to have said on November 19. By then it was mid-December, and I would find myself on the other side of my vow. I had to wonder then how I would have felt if I had known the contents of Daniel's interview before I left for Paris. Would I have believed what Castro said? If I had, would I have been prepared to tell my father that I could not deal with Cubela in good conscience, and so, if he requested, would resign from the Agency? By December, I no longer knew how I would have felt in November, for every perspective had altered. Thoughts of resignation were by now no more than a dull woe. One does not quit a profession any more quickly than one amputates a limb.

THE NEW REPUBLIC, Dec. 14, 1963
by Jean Daniel

In the "Pearl of the Antilles, rum-perfumed and steeped in triumphant sensuality," as Cuba is described in those American tourist folders still lying about in the hotels of Havana, I spend three closely packed and intensive weeks, but thinking all along that I would never get to meet with Fidel Castro, I talked with farmers, writers and painters, militants and counterrevolutionaries, ministers and ambassadors—but Fidel remained inaccessible. I had been warned: he no longer had any desire to receive journalists, least of all Western newsmen. I had practically given up hope when on the evening of what I thought was to be my departure date, Fidel came to my hotel. He had heard of my interview with the President. We went up to my room at ten in the evening and did not leave until the following morning. Here, I shall recount only that part of the interview which constitutes a reply to John F. Kennedy's remarks.

Fidel listened with devouring and passionate interest: he pulled at his beard, yanked his parachutist's beret down over his eyes, adjusted his maquis tunic, all the while making me the target of a thousand malicious sparks cast by his deep-sunk lively eyes. . . . He had me repeat certain remarks, particularly those in which Kennedy expressed his criticism of the Batista regime, and lastly those in which Kennedy accused Fidel of almost having caused a war fatal to all humanity.

When I stopped talking, I expected an explosion. Instead, I was treated to a lengthy silence, to a calm, composed, often humorous, always thoughtful exposition. I don't know whether Fidel had changed, or whether those cartoons caricaturing him as a ranting madman which appear in the Western press perhaps corresponded to a former reality. I only know that at no time during the two complete days I spent with him (and during which a great deal happened) did Castro abandon his composure and poise. . . .

"I believe Kennedy is sincere," Fidel declared, "I also believe that today the expression of this sincerity could have political significance. I'll explain what I mean. I have not forgotten the Machiavellian tactics and the equivocation, the attempts at invasion, the pressures, the blackmail, the organization of a counterrevolution, the blockade, and above everything, all the retaliatory measures which were imposed before, long before there was the pretext and alibi of Communism. But I feel that he inherited a difficult situation: I don't think a President of the United States is ever really free, and I believe at present Kennedy is feeling the impact of that lack of freedom. I also believe he now understands the extent to which he has been misled, for example, on the Cuban reaction at the time of the attempted Bay of Pigs invasion. I also think he is a realist; he is now registering that it is impossible to simply wave a wand and cause us, and the explosive situation throughout Latin America, to disappear. . . .

"That may be the situation now. But over a year ago, six months before the missiles were installed in Cuba, we had received an accumulation of information warning us that a new invasion of the island was being prepared. . . .

"What was to be done? How could we prevent the invasion? Khrushchev asked us what we wanted. We replied: *Do whatever is needed to convince the United States that any attack on Cuba is the same as an attack on the Soviet Union.* We thought of a proclamation, an alliance, conventional military aid. The Russians explained to us their concern: first, they wanted to save the Cuban Revolution (in other words, their socialist honor in the eyes of the world), and at the same time they wished to avoid a world conflict. They reasoned that if conventional military aid was the extent of their assistance, the United States might not hesitate to instigate an invasion, in which case Russia would retaliate and this would inevitably touch off a world war. . . .

"I am here to tell you that the Russians didn't want and do not today want war. One only need visit them on their home territory, watch them at work, share their economic concerns, admire their intense efforts to raise the workers' standard of living, to understand right away that they are far, very far, from any idea of provocation or domination. However, Soviet Russia was confronted by two alternatives: an absolutely inevitable war if the Cuban Revolution was attacked; or the risk of a war if the United States was refusing to retreat before the missiles. They chose socialist solidarity and the risk of war.

"Under the circumstances, how could we Cubans have refused to share the risks taken to save us? It was, in the final analysis, a question of honor, don't you agree? Don't you believe that honor plays a role in politics? You think we are romantics, don't you? Perhaps we are.

And why not? In any event, we are militants. In a word, then, we agreed to the emplacement of the missiles. And I might add here that for us Cubans, it didn't really make so much difference whether we died by conventional bombing or a hydrogen bomb. Nevertheless, we were not gambling with the peace of the world. The United States was the one to jeopardize the peace of mankind by using the threat of war to stifle revolution. . . ."

The conversation now turned to Kennedy's Alliance for Progress in Latin America. "In a way," Castro said, "it was a good idea, it marked progress of a sort, an effort to adapt to the extraordinarily rapid course of events in Latin America. But Kennedy's good ideas aren't going to yield any results. . . . For years and years, American policy has supported the Latin American oligarchies. Suddenly a President arrives on the scene who tries to give the various Latin American countries the impression that the United States no longer stands behind the dictators. What happens then? The trusts see that their interests are being a little compromised; the Pentagon thinks the strategic bases are in danger; the powerful oligarchies in all the Latin countries alert their American friends; they sabotage the new policy; and, in short, Kennedy has everyone against him."

I asked Fidel where this is all going to end. How will the situation develop? Even if the United States used against you what you call the alibi of Communism, *it still remains that you have chosen Communism*, that your economy and your security depend upon the Soviet Union . . . in a world where peace depends on mutual respect for a tacit division of zones of influence.

"I don't want to discuss our ties with the Soviet Union," Fidel Castro cut me short. "I find this indecent. We have none but feelings of fraternity and profound total gratitude toward the U.S.S.R. The Russians are making extraordinary efforts on our behalf, efforts which sometimes cost them dear. But we have our own policies which are perhaps not always the same (we have proved this!) as those of the U.S.S.R. I refuse to dwell on this point, because asking me to say that I am not a pawn on a Soviet chessboard is something like asking a woman to shout aloud in a public square that she is not a prostitute.

"If the United States sees the problem as you have posed it, then you are right, there is no way out. But who is the loser in the last analysis? They have tried everything against us, everything, absolutely everything, and we are still alive. . . . Are we in danger? We have always lived with danger. To say nothing of the fact you have no idea how many friends one discovers in the world when one is persecuted by the United States. No, truly, for all these reasons, we are not supplicants. We ask nothing.

"I have just talked to you as a Cuban revolutionary. But I should also speak to you as a peace lover, and from this viewpoint, I believe the United States is too important a country not to have an influence in world peace. I cannot help hoping, therefore, that a leader will come to the fore in North America (why not a Kennedy, there are big things in his favor!) who will be willing to brave unpopularity, fight the trusts, tell the truth, and most important, let the various nations act as they see fit. We ask nothing, neither dollars nor assistance, nor diplomats, nor bankers, nor military men, nothing but peace and to be accepted as we are! Why should it be impossible to make the Americans understand that socialism leads, not to hostility toward them, but to coexistence?"

In conclusion, Fidel Castro said to me: "Since you are going to see Kennedy again, be an emissary of peace; despite everything, I want to make myself clear. I don't want anything. I don't expect anything, and as a revolutionary, the present situation does not displease me. But as a man and as a statesman, it is my duty to indicate what the bases for understanding could be. To achieve peace a leader would have to arise in the United States capable of meeting the explosive realities of Latin America halfway; Kennedy could still be this man. He still has the possibility of becoming, in the eyes of history, the greatest President of the United States, the leader who may at last understand that there can be coexistence between socialists and capitalists, even in the Americas. He would then be an even greater president than Lincoln. I know, for example, that for Khrushchev, Kennedy is a man you can talk with. Other leaders have assured me that to attain this goal, we must first await his reelection. Personally, I consider him responsible for everything, but I will say this, he has come to understand many things over the past few months; and in the last analysis, I'm convinced that anyone else would be worse." Then Fidel added with a broad and boyish grin: "If you see him again, tell him that I'm willing to declare Goldwater my friend if it will guarantee Kennedy's reelection."

35

Hôtel Palais Royal
November 22, 1963

Dear Kittredge,

It is such a while since I have written to you. So it feels. I am sitting in my room at the Palais Royal, a fustian small chamber furnished in Art Nouveau—Truman Capote even signed their guest book, "My home away from home!" (Probably does that everywhere.) It is three o'clock on Friday afternoon, and in something less than two hours, Halifax and I will get up and go to meet the *special* person who is the object of our trip. I am alone here sorting out my thoughts and all the while feeling the most passionate desire to talk to you. If, in referring to this project, I speak, for example, of *Halifax*, it is because I wish to send this out posthaste, and a pouch will not be available. My declaration must travel by ordinary mail.

Enough! I want to tell you that I love you and will always love you. If I never forget this for a moment, not in nightmares, or even, if the inadmissible truth be told, in another woman's arms, still I have never been able to bring myself to tell you. But I am in Paris today on an honest-to-god mission, a sense of anticipation in my chest spiced by the smallest hint of dread—my veteran companion Halifax calls this state "the tender butterflies—no better feeling." I can barely wait for the moment when he will knock on my door and we will go out to our rendezvous. Yet I also feel a curious serenity, as if I could remain here writing to you all day. In this hour, Alpha and Omega appear to be much at peace with each other, as if dawn and evening live side by side in me, and so I am able to tell you that I not only love you but will wait for you all my life, and am prepared to live with such a state in a full understanding of the profound loyalties to others that are woven into your life, yes, I will love you with no demand greater than that you forgive me for having placed such a burden on you.

Can this be the awesome if subtle magic of Paris insinuating itself into my confession? Today is overcast, and Paris is the only city I know whose hue in such weather is lilac-gray. The sky and the building stones, the Seine itself, are here to speak of the minor symphonies to be found in a panoply of gray, yet these same minor tones produce the most thoughtful, harmonious, and overpowering emotions. Walking on the Left Bank this morning, I came to recognize that this is the day on which I must tell you how I have loved your beauty and your fierce and passionate heart, yes, from the hour I met you.

I will say no more. Is it calculating to hope that you will have these pages to read whenever you doubt me? I feel in so uncharacteristically wise a state (now that this confession has erupted out of me) that I wish to talk about myriads of absurd little matters. Halifax and I, for instance, had an extraordinary lunch at Tour d'Argent. You cannot go wrong when Halifax is ravenous and in Paris. Rather than bore you with the details of a meal you did not attend, suffice it that we started with *champignons farcis duxelles*, fortified with a bottle of St. Emilion '53—heaven's feather touched the Tour d'Argent. I never knew before how shallots, garlic, butter, and grated nutmeg could illumine a mushroom cap. The wine explored my throat. I had an inkling of the joy I might know if we were ever to break bread in some restaurant we looked upon as belonging secretly to us.

If irony is redemptive, and one would hope it is, then let me promise you that in the midst of this superb food we wandered through topics of conversation that skirted the underwritten solemnity of our mission. I will say this much—we are going into a sit-down with an enemy agent. Of course, it is in a neutral, even friendly, environment, so I must not make too much of it, but this is a legitimate, heavy-duty sit-down. I must say it does produce levity *cum* solemnity.

Halifax can always improve such a mix. His men must have loved him in the OSS. All the way across on Pan Am yesterday he entertained me with vivid anecdotes. He is a bit afraid of airplanes, which reminded me of a theory Dix Butler used to maintain, that strong men are the ones most reluctant to travel by air for fear of their own deviltry, which might find a way to work itself into the motor. On hearing Butler's down-in-flames thesis Halifax entered an amendment: "There's an awful fascination to be found in eliminating one's fellow man," he said. "It does give entrance into a select fraternity. The man we're seeing tomorrow is a fair example of that." Halifax then went on to tell me—and I had heard rumor of this before—of a killing binge in Italy with the partisans. Before it was over, Halifax had slain five Germans in three days, two by rifle, two by his own Luger (taken in booty), and one with his bare hands. "I never did settle down from that," he said. "My life has revolved around it. Do you know, it has provided me with a considerable sense of superior status, a private sense of empowerment, and a great worry on occasion that I am mad."

"Why ever mad?" I asked.

"Because I rather enjoyed those three days. The Headmaster surprised me once by saying that the hardest task the Lord can set on a man is to be the angel of death to the corrupt, the damned, and the evil. Only rare men qualify for that, he assured me. I couldn't believe it. My father, a clergyman, speaking approvingly of human extermination! Of course, along with all else, he had that personal glint in the eye, that oafish strength a good many Yankees can lay claim to. I know I am in possession of it."

Do not be confused, Kittredge, by his use of "oafish." It is not a pejorative as employed by Halifax, no, he is referring to sexual drive. "I am a dyed-in-the-wool Yankee when it comes to sex," he confessed to me. "Harry, I don't believe I ever had an erection I didn't feel I earned and deserved."

"That would crimp my style altogether," I said.

We had a good laugh. Just then a rather attractive stewardess whom Halifax had been ogling from airborne minute one through the flight (thereby eliciting a rising glissando of smiles from her) stopped finally to chat with us. Halifax, naturally, saw it as entirely his doing, but to his chagrin, her interest was in me: "Aren't you a friend of Modene Murphy's?" she asked. When I allowed that the answer was yes, she said, "I used to work at Eastern with her, and Modene talked about you all the time. I recognized you from the snapshot she carried with her. She thought you were neat."

"Oh," I said, "I wish she'd told me."

We agreed that whoever ran into Modene first would convey the regards of the other.

Well, Halifax took in all of that, and then notified me that he had known about Modene, and had always wanted to meet her, although by dint of discreet questioning, I could recognize that all he meant was that he had heard Agency gossip to the effect that I was gadding about with a good-looking airline stewardess, bully for me.

I don't want to try your patience. It is axiomatic that a beautiful woman does not always wish to hear about another, but I address myself to your magnaminity for a purpose. Halifax now made an astonishing confession. He was having what he termed "erectile lapses." I mention it not to give his secret away, but to explain him. I feel as if I begin to comprehend his monumental depressions over

Mary—their last years must have been full of such *lapses*—and, in contrast, his present excitement about this mission. He went over to Paris on a look-see a few weeks ago and came back full of himself from being back in action. "I feel ready," he told me, "to pull down a few stud fees again." I assumed that he had merely resumed relations with his secretary, Eleanor (who adores him), but the old girlfriend now current again is—click your safety belt! I'll bet she didn't tell you— Polly Galen Smith. She does get around with the right people.

So, yes, Halifax was in good spirits. He protects his health by walking into the crucible and out again. While there is no physical danger in our upcoming meeting, at least I don't think so, all sorts of small and large catastrophes could arise concerning security and one's career. A flap at this point would sound like the cranking of a giant pterodactyl's wings. But Halifax steering toward *risk* is in the highest spirits. As if his blood were Mediterranean, he speaks with grave pleasure about murder and death. All the while, we are being fired up by a *filet de boeuf au poivre* and now a Pommard '56. He is engaging his ongoing obsession: It is that Marilyn Monroe was murdered.

As he goes on talking about this through lunch, my mind reels. The turn of conversation is considerably removed from what I had anticipated. We had, of course, already gone over our corollary scenarios concerning which choices to make if things take a wrong course in any way during the meeting. We had gone through that in the office and on the airplane. All the same, I had assumed that lunch would be taken up at least in part with a review of our business, but, no, "We've got it down," he tells me, "let's talk of other things." Off he goes on his thesis. I am repelled at first, because the thought of murder in relation to that lovely, sad, and merry young comedienne will spoil my meal. I think Halifax, however, may understand me better than I comprehend myself. I think he senses instinctively that for loosening up one's large and small reflexes, it can be tonic to contemplate someone else's undertaking even if in this case it is a dire and hideous scheme. Facing one's own grave possibilities, it does no harm to ponder equally weighty concerns in another fold of concealed endeavor.

I am going to try to tell it in his words. After all, I have credentials—I have listened to the good and worthy Halifax on enough occasions to hear his voice in my ear when I write about him, and he was more than articulate on this occasion: "Do you know," he told me, "I was absolutely convinced in the beginning that she was either done in by a word from the Kennedys, or, conceivably, by their direct act. It is not difficult to give an injection if a person trusts you. Either Jack or Bobby could have said to her, 'This is a dynamite mix of vitamins. Works wonders.' The poor girl was ready for anything in pill or needle form."

Kittredge, I believe I had better explain to you that this has been Cal's ongoing preoccupation for fifteen months, and he has not only collected all the limited evidence, most notably the coroner's report, but it is as if, after working in Intelligence all his life, he has made the case of Marilyn Monroe his hobby. He assures me that all the facts in the coroner's report point to murder. To account for the barbiturate level in her blood, she would have had to take at least fifty capsules of Nembutol and chloral hydrate. This would have been bound to leave a large residue in her stomach and small intestine. In the stomach, however, reports the coroner, there is only a teaspoonful of fluid.

Now I am not going to put down any more of these details since I think they would repel you. Besides, he has cited them to me enough times to provide me with the uneasy suspicion that he has a case. What made the talk novel at this lunch is that he has finally changed his conclusion. You see, Halifax has suspected Jack for these last fifteen months—which may give you an idea of how much animosity is loose in the Agency these days toward our President. Once in a while in the middle of the night, I would find myself in the graveyard of vile assumptions long enough to think: "What if he is right?"

Mind you, all the while that Halifax is furnishing these clinical items, he is cutting his filet precisely, one quarter-inch slice at a time, touching it lightly to the *au poivre* gravy, feeding himself English style, fork in his left hand, deft cuts with the knife, expressive lifts with the fork, the minutiae of autopsy procedure being laid out all the while carefully for me. In the guise of a reporter, he had actually done an interview with the coroner by telephone, managing to accomplish this small feat by dragooning one of his cronies on the *Washington Post* to agree to allow him the use of his name.

"Mind you," says Cal, "I had it fixed in my mind *from the first* that it had to be the Kennedys. I wanted it to be them. I would not have minded chopping this administration into the smallest shreds," and at that moment, his face was red enough to suggest that his jaws were working on moose-hide. "I will only remind you that Kennedy dealt CIA a blow at the Bay of Pigs from which we may never recover. We were slathered with shame. No, I will never forgive Jack Kennedy for not knowing his mind. On the other hand, I am an officer in Intelligence, and we do not go off half-cocked. So, I began to face up to the likelihood that the Kennedys would not have had an unmanageable fear of Marilyn Monroe exposing their escapades. My God, Jack reached the presidency with as long a tail of big and little loves strewn behind him as the tin cans tied to a newlywed's flivver. Yet, never a hint in the major newspapers. A man running for high office is sacrosanct: twice so, once he is President. If Marilyn had come forth to the public with her tale, the Kennedys would probably have replied that she was their friend, and a remarkably talented woman, and they could feel unhappy along with the rest of her fans that she had had a nervous breakdown. Ergo, why should the Kennedys risk everything by killing her? One had to face it—one's thesis wasn't walking too well on its own feet.

"Then I learned by way of one of Bill Harvey's less savory contacts who goes back, in fact, to our Maheu days—that Jimmy Hoffa had managed to get a sneaky into Marilyn's bedroom, and a tap on all her phones. Hoffa, apparently, has a fellow named Bernard Spindel who is the preeminent wiretapper in America. A little more skillful, you may believe it, than our Vegas folk.

"That fact brought back my suspicions of the Kennedys. For if there was a wiretap, there was bound to be bedside chatter. It would substantiate the claim that there was carnal congress with the lady. But, again, my reason prevailed over animus and ire. I had to decide that the media would never allow the power of the presidency to be breached by any accusation, no matter how well documented, that would be delivered by a neurotic actress waving a telltale tape furnished by a labor racketeer.

"Then, it came to me. It had to be Jimmy Hoffa who arranged the cold-blooded, calculated extermination of Marilyn Monroe. No one in the universe hated Bobby Kennedy as much as Jimmy Hoffa. Since Marilyn had at least five specialists I can name who were available for prescribing pills, and there must be twenty others I don't know, Hoffa found a way to induce one of these practitioners, doubtless by getting something on the guy, to agree to the deed. Hoffa had a slew of private detectives to return him that kind of information.

"*Voilà!* Hoffa's doctor of choice visited Marilyn and injected

her fatally. Since everyone knew she was unstable, the public would
certainly believe that she had committed suicide. The first headlines
would announce that in screamers. Forty-eight hours later, however,
when the evidence didn't add up, the press would begin to hint at foul
play. By the end of a week, the accumulation of evidence would
clearly suggest that she had been injected, which is to say, murdered."

"You are not supposing that the Kennedys would have been
named in the headlines?"

"No. But keep in mind that a few thousand people in Washington, in L.A., and in New York were already witting to the gossip
that Marilyn had a fling with Jack and Bobby both. Can you conceive
of the whispering after her death? I bet Hoffa figured that half of our
nation would catch up with the idea that not only was she murdered,
but certain people were trying to make it look like suicide. Hoffa
would have succeeded in setting off a whispering campaign pointed
to the Kennedys. Try winning an election with that festering underneath."

"Why then," I asked, "does everyone still think it is a suicide?"

"Because Hoffa miscalculated. He anticipated every detail but
one. Ever since he came into office, Jack has been charming up the
police chief of every major city he visits. He gets them to believe that
once the '64 elections are history, J. Edgar Hoover will be encouraged
to resign. Top cop in each major city begins to think he might be the
next head of the FBI. I think the moment that Los Angeles chief saw
how the evidence on Marilyn was pointing toward murder, he took
some pains to have it declared a suicide. He wasn't going to allow the
Kennedy name to be washed about. What?—lose all chance of
becoming Buddha's replacement? Hoffa certainly underrated the
Kennedys."

Kittredge, it was an incredible lunch. Before it was over, a
man and a woman, two of the tallest, slimmest, most stylish English
people I have ever seen came in. The woman was carrying a white toy
poodle, and on greeting the maître d'hôtel, she handed it over. "Take
care of Bouffant like a good dear, will you, Romain?" she said in that
absolutely unselfconscious English accent that can never be acquired,
not even by marriage. And Romain, a darn superior headwaiter up to
now, set the beastie down on the sacred carpet of the Tour d'Argent
and began to address it in a French variant of baby talk, "Ow, Bouffie,
how are *you*, delightful *dog*!" and then rose to his feet, signaled to a

waiter to watch over the creature (for the next two hours, presumably), and escorted the Viscount and the Viscountess, or whoever they were, to a table by a window over the Seine. Halifax whispered, "Wouldn't you love to get on spanking good terms with her?" No erectile lapses in the air for him right now.

I have written this long letter in all the pleasure of talking to you. In a few minutes, Halifax, whose room is down the hall, will knock on my door and we will go out to meet our man. I wish I could tell you more. Will indeed someday.

I feel blessed. How much I love you. It lifts my soul above horror, adventure, and surprise.

Devotedly,
Harry

36

CUBELA, WEARING A TAN SPORT JACKET AND BROWN PANTS, CAME INTO the Bistro de la Mairie accompanied by a man in a blue yachting jacket, gray flannels, and horn-rimmed glasses—LYME—who nodded to us and walked out. But for three workingmen standing at the bar by the entrance, we had the place to ourselves, all of the dark floor, dark walls, round bar tables, and one disinterested waiter.

Cubela walked toward us like a heavyweight coming into the ring. My father had described him as tall, but he was heavier than I had expected and his mustache was full, powerful, and pessimistic. He would have been a good-looking man if his face had not been puffy from drink.

"Mr. Scott," said Cubela to my father, who promptly replied, "Señor General, this is Mr. Edgar." I nodded.

Cubela sat down with solemn grace. He would have an Armagnac, he decided. We said no more until the waiter brought it, whereupon Cubela took a taste and asked in a heavy Spanish accent, "Il n'y a rien de mieux?" to which our waiter allowed that it was the brand of Armagnac the café served. Cubela nodded in displeasure, and waved him away.

"You have brought the letter?" he asked. Cal nodded. "I would like to see it, Mr. Scott." His English was superior to his French.

The letter was brief, but composed by us with no small care. One of the experts at GHOUL had forged the handwriting on stationery that carried the embossed seal of the Attorney General's office.

November 20, 1963

This is to assure the bearer that in recognition of his successful efforts to bring about a noteworthy and irreversible change in the present government of Cuba, the powers of this office, and all collateral loyalties attendant thereto, will be brought to bear in full support of his high political aims.

Robert F. Kennedy

Cubela read it over, took out a pocket English dictionary, looked up the definition of several words, and frowned. "This letter does not fulfill the understanding arrived at in our last meeting, Mr. Scott."

"I would say it takes care of your specific requests completely, Señor General. You need only contemplate the meaning of 'irreversible change.' "

"Yes," said Cubela, "that addresses half of the fundamental understanding, but where does it say that the older brother of the signatory is well disposed toward me?"

Cal took back the letter and read aloud, " 'The power of this office and *all collateral loyalties attendant thereto* . . .' I think you will find that is a clear reference to the sibling."

"Sibling? Sibling?"

"El hermano," I said.

"It is very abstract. In effect, you ask me to accept your promise on faith."

"Even as we accept your promises," said Cal.

Cubela showed small pleasure in being overtaken. "Whether you trust me or not, you will go back to your home in Washington. For me to trust you, however, means that I must risk my life." He withdrew a magnifying glass from his jacket pocket, and a clipping from a magazine. I could see that it was a printed sample of Robert Kennedy's handwriting.

For several minutes, Cubela compared the script in the letter to the sample in his clipping. "Good," he said at last, and stared carefully at both of us. "I would ask you a question, Mr. Scott. As you know, I once shot a man in a nightclub. In fact, I assassinated him."

"I thought you detest the word."

"I do. And now," he said in Spanish, "I will explain why. It is not because of some fracture of my nervous system that is unable to bear the enunciation of such syllables because that might recall to me the expression on a dying man's face—no, that is what my detractors would claim, but no truth is there. I am a calm man possessed of *pundonor*. I have depth of resolve. I see myself as the future *comandante* of the tragic island that is my nation. For these reasons, I detest the word. The assassin, you see, not only destroys his victim but the part of himself that contains his larger ambitions. Can you ask me to believe that the President of the United States and his brother are ready to help the political career of a man whom they must talk about during the privacy of their own councils as a half-crazy hired thug?"

"In a time of turmoil," said Cal, "your past will matter less than your heroism. It is your heroic actions in the next few months that will bring you to public view."

"Are you saying that your sponsors will accept me in such circumstances?"

"That is exactly what I am saying."

He sighed heavily. "No," he said, "you are saying that at the summit of the mountain, there are no guarantees."

Cal was silent. After a while, he said, "As a man of intelligence, you know that one cannot control political weather absolutely."

"Yes," said Cubela, "I must be prepared to take all chances. Of necessity. Yes, I am prepared," he said, and let out his breath with such a burst that I realized he was ready to perform the assassination today. "Let us concern ourselves with equipment," he said.

"The telescope is ready," stated my father.

"You are speaking, I presume, of the rifle I have described that has a range of accuracy up to five hundred yards, equipped with a Bausch and Lomb telescopic sight of two and one-half times magnification?"

My father, in reflex, tapped on his glass through the length of this speech. Then he reached forward across the table, put his hand on Cubela's arm, and nodded profoundly, although he did not say a word.

"I will accept your concern for precautions," said Cubela. "Forgive me. Now, may I inquire into delivery?"

"Mr. Lyme will service your location."

"I like Mr. Lyme," said Cubela.

"I am pleased to hear that he is likeable," said Cal.

"The telescope will fit into an attaché case?"

"No," said Cal, but added "do you play pool?"

"Billiards."

"The case we will hand over to you looks like the kind that is used to carry a billiard cue. The kind of cue, of course, that comes in two pieces."

"Excellent," said Cubela. "And the other detail?"

"Yes," said Cal. "The piece of sophisticated equipment. The surprise. I have it on my person."

"May I see it?"

Cal removed a ballpoint pen from his tweed jacket and clicked the button. A hypodermic needle sprang forth. He clicked the button a second time and a thread of liquid darted from the needle like a wall lizard's tongue. "It's only water," said Cal, "but this pen has been designed for use with the common reagent . . ." He removed an index card from his pocket and held it up. It read: BLACKLEAF 40.

"Where do I find such as that?" asked Cubela.

"In any chemical supply house. It is a common reagent employed for insects."

"Of all sizes?"

Cal nodded again. "Most effective."

Cubela took the ballpoint pen and pressed the button several times until all the water had been ejected. "It is a toy," he said with some petulance.

"No," answered Cal, "it is a sophisticated instrument. The needle is so fine that one does not feel it entering the skin."

"You are asking me to walk up to the subject and inject him?"

"The needle is so fine that it causes no pain. It attracts no attention whatsoever."

Cubela looked at both of us with contempt. "Your gift is a device for a woman. She sticks her tongue in the man's mouth and puts the needle in his back. I am not about to use such tactics. It is shameful to eliminate one's enemy in that manner. One does not attack a serious Cuban with a hat pin. I would be subject to ridicule. And rightly so."

He stood up. "I will accept the carrying case with the billiard cue from Mr. Lyme. But this I reject." He was about to depart, then stopped. "No," he said, "I will take reception of it after all," and he put it in his breast pocket.

My father surprised me by his next remark. "For yourself?" he asked.

He nodded. "If the large effort fails, I have no wish to live through the immediate consequences."

"*Cómo no,*" said Cal.

Cubela shook his hand, then mine. His hands were cold. "*Salud!*" he said, and walked out.

"We'll get the billiard cue to him in Veradero," said Cal. "He has a little villa on the beach, three hundred yards away from the beach house that the subject—as he calls him—inhabits on vacation. I hate to say it, but I am getting my hopes up for this fellow. He could deliver a present before Christmas." Cal let out his breath. "Do you mind paying the bill? I need to take a walk." He paused. "We should leave separately in any event."

"All right," I said. "I'll follow you back to the hotel."

Through the café window, I could see the lights on the street. The November evening had long passed, and at 7:00 P.M. it was now dark enough for midnight.

I did not know exactly how I felt, but then I was not in a situation where it was automatic to comprehend one's reactions. In truth, I wanted Rolando Cubela to kill Fidel Castro; I hoped that Helms, Harlot, and Cal were not merely sending out a provocation to the DGI. No, I wanted an execution to be there at the end of the road. I did not begin to have the profound hatred for the Maximum Leader that Hunt or Harlot or Harvey or Helms or Allen Dulles, or Richard Bissell, or Richard Nixon, or, for that matter, my father or Bobby Kennedy contained; no, there was a part of me that kept thinking of Castro as Fidel, yet I was looking for the death of Fidel. I would mourn Fidel if we succeeded, mourn him in just the way a hunter is saddened by the vanished immanence of the slain beast. Yes, one fired a bullet into beautiful animals in order to feel nearer to God: To the extent that we were criminal, we could approach the cosmos only by stealing a piece of the Creation—yes, I understood all of this and wanted Cubela to be an effective assassin rather than a ploy of the DGI whom we, in turn, would use in a superior ploy. A successful assassin was worth a hundred provocations.

I sat at my table alone, finishing the cognac I had not touched during the interview. Then I began to notice that the few working-men standing at the bar had gathered around the café radio. It had been playing *bal musette* dance music for the last hour, but now a commentator's voice could be heard. I could not discern what was being said. The tone of voice, however, was urgent.

In another minute, the waiter came up to me. *"Monsieur,"* he said, *"vous-êtes américain?"*

"Mais oui."

He was a tired, weary, gray-faced waiter, well over fifty, and wholly unremarkable in appearance, but his eyes looked at me with profound compassion.

"Monsieur, il y a des mauvaises nouvelles. Des nouvelles étonnants." Now, he put his hand gently on mine. *"Votre President Kennedy a été frappé par un assassin à Dallas, Texas."*

"Is he alive?" I asked, and then repeated, *"Est-il vivant?"*

The waiter said, *"On ne sait rien de plus, monsieur, sauf qu'il y avait une grande bouleversement."*

37

THE NEW REPUBLIC, Dec. 7, 1963
by Jean Daniel

Havana, Nov. 22, 1963

It was about 1:30 in the afternoon, Cuban time. We were having lunch in the living room of the modest summer residence which Fidel Castro owns on magnificent Veradero Beach, 120 kilometers from Havana. The telephone rang, a secretary in guerrilla garb announced that Mr. Dorticos, President of the Cuban Republic, had an urgent communication for the Prime Minister. Fidel picked up the phone and I heard him say: *"Cómo? Un atentado?"* ("What's that? An attempted assassination?") He turned to us to say that Kennedy had just been struck down in Dallas. Then he went back to the telephone and exclaimed in a loud voice, *"Herido? Muy gravemente?"* ("Wounded? Very seriously?")

He came back, sat down, and repeated three times the words: *"Es una mala noticia."* ("This is bad news.") He remained silent a moment, awaiting another call with further news. He remarked while we waited that there was an alarmingly sizable lunatic fringe in American society and that this deed could equally well have been the work of a madman or a terrorist. Perhaps a Vietnamese? Or a member of the Ku Klux Klan? The second call came through: The President of the

United States was still alive. There was hope of saving him. Fidel Castro's immediate reaction was: "If they can, he is already reelected." He pronounced these words with satisfaction.

Now it was nearly two o'clock and we got up from the table and settled ourselves in front of a radio to get the NBC network in Miami. As the news came in, his physician, René Vallejo, would translate it for Fidel: Kennedy wounded in the head; pursuit of the assassin; murder of a policeman; finally the fatal announcement—President Kennedy is dead. Then Fidel stood up and said to me: "Everything is changed. Everything is going to change. . . . All will have to be rethought. I'll tell you one thing: at least Kennedy was an enemy to whom we had become accustomed. This is a serious matter; an extremely serious matter."

After the quarter hour of silence observed by all the American radio stations, we once more tuned in on Miami; the silence had only been broken by a re-broadcasting of the American national anthem. Strange indeed was the impression made on hearing this hymn ring out in the house of Fidel Castro in the midst of a circle of worried faces. "Now," Fidel said, "they will have to find the assassin quickly, but very quickly, otherwise, you watch and see, they will try to put the blame on us for this thing."

38

AT THE PALAIS ROYAL, THE WOMAN ON DUTY AT THE DESK WAS weeping. In my room, the telephone seemed more of a presence than the bed, the window, the door, or myself. I took out a folded slip of paper from a recess of my wallet, and gave the number to the hotel operator, who told me that the overseas line had been *accomblé* for the last half hour, but she would try. Within less than a minute, my phone rang. The call was waiting. The line was no longer *accomblé*.

"Modene," I said, "it's Harry."

"Who is it?"

"Harry Field. Tom!"

"Oh, Tom."

"I'm calling to tell you how sorry I am."

"About Jack?"

"About Jack."

"It's all right, Harry. I had three Valium as soon as I heard the news. Now I feel all right. I had already taken three Valium before that. It may be for the best. Jack was a tired man. I used to feel sorry for him, but I think it is all right now because I am tired too. I understand his need for rest."

"How are you?" I asked as if we must absolutely commence this conversation over again.

"I am fine," she said, "taking into account the limitations of my condition. But I do not know if you want to hear about that."

"I do want to," I said. "I wanted to reach you so soon as I heard the news about Jack."

"Do you know, I was just lying here. I was looking out the window. It is a nice day in Chicago. It is odd for something like this to occur on a sunny day."

I was about to ask how Sam Giancana might be, and hesitated, but then it occurred to me that it would not matter very much what I said considering how much Valium she had taken. "How is Sam these days?" I asked.

"I do not see him anymore. He sends me a check every week, but I do not see him. He became so angry at me that we stopped speaking. I think that was because I kept cutting my hair shorter."

"Why did you do that?"

"I do not know why. Well, yes, I do. A girlfriend of mine named Willie said that long hair absorbs more than its share of nourishment from the physical system. I did not know that I could afford any excessive expenditures of vitality. So I kept cutting my hair. Then I had it shaved off. It seems more simple to wear a wig. It's a blond wig. I think it would look good on me if I were not overweight. I am also having a hysterectomy next week."

"Ah, Modene."

"Do you have tears in your eyes, Harry? I do. I guess that is one for the *Guinness Book of World Records*. To shed tears after swallowing three extra Valium."

"Yes, I have tears in my eyes," I said. It was almost true. With but a little more effort, I would not have had to tell another lie.

"You were very sweet, Harry. I used to believe sometimes that you and I might have a chance, but, of course, there was always Jack. I want you to feel good about that, Harry. You see, we met too late. Jack and I were already star-crossed. Now he's gone. I do not find that a shock. I knew he did not have long to live."

"How did you know, Modene?"

"Because I do not have much time either. It is in my palm, and it is in my charts. It is in my innermost feelings. I always knew that I would age quickly. I suppose I felt that I only had half as much time for it all."

There was a pause. I could think of nothing to say. Therefore, I said, "If my travels take me to Chicago, should I come to visit?"

"No," she said, "I don't want to let you look at me now. It is too late. If it were not too late, I might think of seeing you again, but, Harry, it is too late. I am en route to the end of the road. Where the shadows dwell." She paused. "Do you know," she said, "it has just come over me that Jack is dead. That lovely man. He is dead. It was so fine in character for you to call, Harry, and give your condolences. Otherwise, I would be the only one to know that I am a widow. In a manner of speaking, I am. Do you agree?"

"Yes," I said.

"You are a fine man," she said.

She hung up on those words.

39

THE NEW REPUBLIC, Dec. 7, 1963
BY JEAN DANIEL

Toward three o'clock, Fidel Castro declared that since there was nothing we could do to alter the tragedy, we must try to put our time to good use in spite of it. He wanted to accompany me in person on a visit to a *granja de pueblo* where he had been engaging in some experiments.

We went by car with the radio on. The Dallas police were now hot on the trail of the assassin. He is a Russian spy, says the news commentator. Five minutes later, correction: He is a spy married to a Russian. Fidel said, "There, didn't I tell you? It'll be my turn next." But not yet. The next word was: the assassin is a Marxist deserter. Then the word came through that the assassin was a young man who was a member of the Fair Play for Cuba Committee, that he was an admirer of Fidel Castro. Fidel declared, "If they had had proof, they would have said he was an agent, an accomplice, a hired killer. In saying simply that he is an admirer, this is just to try and make an association in people's minds between the name of Castro and the emotion awakened by the assassination. This is a publicity method, a propaganda device. It's terrible. But you know, I'm sure this will all soon blow over. There are too many competing policies in the United States for any single one to be able to impose itself universally for very long."

We arrived at the *granja de pueblo*, where the farmers welcomed Fidel. At that very moment, a speaker announced over the radio that it was now known that the assassin was a "pro-Castro Marxist." One commentator followed another, their remarks becoming increasingly emotional, increasingly aggressive. Fidel then excused himself: "We shall have to give up the visit to the state farm." We went on toward Matanzas where he could telephone President Dorticos. On the way he had questions: "Who is Lyndon Johnson? What is his reputation? What were his relations with Kennedy? With Khrushchev? What was his position at the time of the attempted invasion of Cuba?" Finally, and most important of all, "What authority does he exercise over the CIA?" Then, abruptly, he looked at his watch, saw that it would be half an hour before we reached Matanzas, and practically on the spot, he dropped off to sleep.

40

August 12, 1964

Dear Harry,

Is this our longest period of not writing? It is curious. For months, I have had no desire to reach you by way of a letter, yet so often I was truly close to picking up the phone. I couldn't, however. After your lovely declaration to me, was I to cry out, "Hello, Harry," as if that impassioned avowal from you did not exist? Yet I could not say, "I feel as you do." For, I don't. I certainly didn't. Your last letter arrived on Monday, the 25th of November, probably about the time that Jack Kennedy's funeral procession was progressing—oh, so slowly!—up Pennsylvania Avenue toward St. Matthew's Cathedral. Your poor letter. I read it while sounding the bottom of the most lugubrious mood I have ever known. That night I was certain Lyndon Johnson would be a disaster, and I expect, sooner or later, he will fulfill this prediction, for he impresses me as the greatest of William

Faulkner's characters—the linchpin of the Snopes family.

No surprise, then, if I felt *lugubrious*. To lose a man one values and have him replaced by a person one despises does give meaning to the sour melancholy of the word. By the next day, I recognized that a condition so dismal was but one more form of protection against real horrors. Your letter became a monstrosity. I thought: What if all these unspeakably horrid speculations about Marilyn Monroe in which you and Cal seemed to revel were also a contribution to Oswald's deed? A clergyman I know once said that American society was held together by God's sanction. All that kept us from bursting into our vastly inchoate parts was the divine blessing. One has to wonder if that is not exactly what we have used up. How many transgressions does it take? I thought of Allen and Hugh and that frightful game they played with Noel Field and the Polish Communists, and then I tried to ponder upon my own small horror in Paraguay, which I still cannot confess to you, nor wholly to myself. I writhed at the dreadful game Hugh wanted you to play with Modene, and the business that brought you and Cal to Paris—I don't even want to contemplate what that might have been. Yes, multiply such deeds, and one has to wonder what kept Jack alive so long—particularly when one adds his own transgressions to the list. So I disliked you for declaring that your devotion to me was absolute and then in effect saying, "Well, that's done. Let's move on!" I had, as you can see, no immediate happy reaction to your letter, but I was suffering that night from my own pauper's share of widow's grief—a pauper's share. For if I had always thought that I liked Jack Kennedy, now I recognized on the night of his funeral day that I had loved him in all my starched and chaste fevers—what an unfeeling fool I had been about my near motives. Of course, innocence is my protection against Daddy's madness entering my skull, and Hugh's maniacal will taking possession of my womb. I blamed Hugh most of all for Jack Kennedy's death—I was close to madness.

Do you know what saved me? It was the thought of Bobby. I fell in love again, but this time with no carnal nestings concealed. I think I came to love Bobby Kennedy out of the depth of his suffering. I have never been in the presence of a man wounded that deeply. They say he said shortly before he went to bed on that dire Friday night in the Lincoln bedroom at the White House, "God, it's so awful. Everything was really beginning to run so well," and then he closed the door. The person who told me this was standing in the hall and heard him break down, heard that little monolith of granite,

Bobby Kennedy, begin to sob. "Why, God?" he cried out.

When Bobby asks, "Why, God?" the question has to hover over a metaphysical divide. He is that serious, after all. I believe he was asking whether there is indeed an answer, or can the universe be absurd? For if an answer existed, he would have to have the courage to descend those terrible steps into the depth of his motive and his brother's motive over all these years. Were they striving for the ideal of a more exceptional America, or were they enjoying the perversities of the game?

You know, for months after that, he went to his office and met with his assistants, tried to conduct business, and was like a dead man. He did not care. He knew that he had lost more than a brother. The private telephone he had once had installed on J. Edgar Hoover's desk so that the Director of the FBI was obliged to pick it up and answer him personally was now moved to Buddha's outer office, where the secretary, Miss Gandy, is adept at saying no to all persons less august than her sacred boss. Bobby was now less august. Lyndon Johnson and Buddha are old friends, and the Attorney General's office has been put out on a siding. The great war against the Mafia that Bobby saw as the fundamental purpose of his job was put out with him. Neither Hoover nor Johnson had any particular wish to take on the Mafia. Hoover never gets into a battle he is not certain of winning, and the American Communists are a much easier foe; Lyndon Johnson is not about to fight all those boys who oil his gears. So the Syndicate flourishes, and Bobby is out. Hoover doesn't even speak to Bobby anymore. Johnson, you see, has given Hoover a special exemption from the law that requires old government bulls to retire at the age of seventy. "The nation cannot afford to lose you," said Johnson to J. Edgar in the Rose Garden before the press and the cameras. Perhaps you saw that moving moment in the history of our republic.

So, yes, the brother was lost and the power was stripped. Jimmy Hoffa remarked to a reporter, "Bobby Kennedy is just another lawyer now." Yes, the ultimate irony is that he is no longer dangerous to his enemies. A secretary-treasurer of one of the Teamster locals sent a letter to Bobby explaining his plan to solicit money to "clean, beautify, and supply with flowers the grave of Lee Harvey Oswald."

Yet, Bobby is not free of guilt. There is always the shade of Marilyn Monroe. And Jack's Modene. And all of the others who have to disturb his Catholic sense of behavior. I do not know what went on with Cal and you and Hugh and Castro but I can guess, and I do not know if Bobby knew what he was activating when he kept pushing on Harvey and Helms. Bobby knows so little about us. One night he began to talk of muffled suspicions and stifled half-certainties, and said to me, "I had my doubts about a few fellows in your Agency, but I don't anymore. I can trust John McCone and I asked him if they had killed my brother, and I asked him in a way that he couldn't lie to me, and he said he had looked into it and they hadn't."

I told that story to Hugh. You know how rarely he laughs aloud. He actually struck his thigh. "Yes," he said, "McCone was just the man to ask."

"What," I asked him, "would you have answered?"

"I would have told Bobby that if the job was done properly, I would not be able to give a correct answer."

It is sad. Bobby wanders about in that deep pain. His blue eyes are now a clouded milky sick-pup color. He strives to conceal the hurt, but his expression continues to say: "I am going to live, but when will the pain cease?"

Do you know Jacqueline Kennedy has dimensions I did not expect. She was reading Edith Hamilton's *The Greek Way*, searching for her own answers, I must suppose, and she made a point of lending Bobby the book. He spent hours, then days last Easter reading and memorizing passages. The one that meant the most was from the *Agamemnon*. Bobby read it to me: "Aeschylus says: *He who learns must suffer. And even in our sleep, pain that cannot forget, falls drop by drop upon the heart, and in our own despair, against our will, comes wisdom to us by the awful grace of God.*"

In every life there is one literary passage meant for each one of us alone. Bobby does not acquire his understanding of new subjects through his intelligence as do you or I or Hugh. We proceed by pushing our intelligence to the cutting edge, hoping to explore the nature of new material; Bobby acquires new knowledge through his compassion. I believe he has greater funds than anyone I ever encountered. (At least within Omega. They say that when he plays touch football now, he knocks old friends down for the fun of it. Alpha, obviously, still can snarl.) But compassion, "that awful sum of pain" (Euripides, my friend), is close to him. He has underlined passage after passage in *The Greek Way*. "Know you are bound to help all who are wronged," he takes from the *Suppliants*. Yes, he will be an expert yet. He also quotes Camus: "Perhaps we cannot prevent this world from being a world in which children are tortured. But we can reduce the number of tortured children." Do you know that the first time he went out after Jack's death it was to a Christmas party at an orphanage —yes, the last live nerve of a politician can never be extirpated—but nonetheless, it had to be painful to go out, my God, you could see it hurt him to walk—there was no part of his body between chest and groin that was not in pain. He entered the playroom of the orphanage where these children were all waiting to see him, and although they had been romping they now went silent. It was such an extraordinary event for them. One little boy, about six years old, a black boy, ran up to him and cried out, "Your brother's dead. Your brother is dead." I think the boy wanted no more than to be recognized as someone who was bright enough to remember what he had been told: A big man was coming over whose brother had died. This was the man.

I was at that orphanage, Harry. You can conceive of the rent in the atmosphere. "Your brother is dead!" We all turned away. Some awful wave of disapproval must have washed out from us all over that little boy, for he began to cry. Do you know, Bobby seized him up and hugged him close as kin, and said, "It's all right. I have another brother."

That was when I fell in love with Bobby Kennedy. Harry, I suspect that I tell you all of this not to avoid facing into the wonderful first page of your letter, but to attempt to explain to you that in the course of feeling love for Bobby, and so opening myself at last to some stirrings of compassion for others, I have come nearer to you. I have a feeling about us. I do not know how it will come about, nor in which year, nor do I even hope for it to happen too quickly—I confess a fear bordering on awe. Knowing our small compass for wisdom or suffering, I fear that our pains, when they arrive, will seem all-sweeping. But this I do confess—I am no longer in love with Hugh. That is to say, I love him; I respect him enormously; and all too many of my physical reflexes, to put it so, have been dragooned. They respond to him. He owns my body more than I wish, or desire. But I do not like him any longer. He has such contempt for the dead Kennedy and the live one; and there I have drawn the line. I cannot feel compassion for his horrible boyhood any longer. I am a wife incarcerated in the jail that holds all unhappy wives—I have half a marriage. I am one with the legion of women who have half a marriage.

So I think that our day will come. You must wait, you must be patient—*we cannot make a single false move*. I would be too afraid for

you, for me, and for Christopher. But I do live with the first page of
your letter, and perhaps time will wait for us. Perhaps there will come
a time that is our time. I never said this before. I say it now. I love you.
I love you with all your faults, and, God, Harry, they are compendi-
ous, you lout.

Kisses,
Kittredge

AFTERWORD

WASHINGTON
ROME

1964–1965

1

PATIENCE WAS TO PROVE AN OPERATIVE WORD. MY AFFAIR WITH KIT-
tredge did not commence for another six years, and then, for several
years we would meet once a week, or sometimes, given the demands
of circumspection, no more than once a month, until the dreadful
hour when Hugh and Christopher took their tragic fall, and we were
wed in the haunted ravine of that event.

All this lay ahead. I was to live for a long time with the shock of
the assassination in my heart and in my bones, and it was even in the
air I breathed at Langley, until time reduced at last my sense of that
momentous catastrophe and it blended into the history and whispers
of the halls, the weight of the fact now no greater than itself—another
impost on the guilt of our lives.

Harlot, however, turned unrelenting in his powers of exaggeration. He knew the seed of consternation that now dwelt in the taproot
of many an Agency dream; he memorialized The Day. He ended with
a monologue I was to hear more than once, if always with different
and most specially chosen associates.

"On that unique Friday afternoon, November 22, 1963," was the
way Harlot usually began, "I can tell you that we all congregated in
the Director's meeting room on the Seventh Floor for a bit of sum-
mitry, all of us, satraps, mandarins, lords paramount, padishahs,
maharajahs, grand moguls, kingfish, the lot.

"And we sat there," said Harlot. "It's the only time in all these
years that I saw so many brilliant, ambitious, resourceful men—just
sitting there. Finally McCone said, 'Who is this Oswald?' And there
was a World Series *silence*. The sort you hear when the visiting team
has scored *eight runs* in the first inning.

"Let us not try to measure the gloom. We could have been bank
directors just informed that a time bomb was ticking away in the vault.

Everybody's safety box has to be emptied. But you don't even know at this point how much you have to hide. I began to think of some of the very worst of our people. Bill Harvey over in Rome. Boardman Hubbard in Paris with AM/LASH. Suppose Fidel produces Cubela? The mind runs amok at such times. Everyone was inhaling everyone else's ghosts. We were waiting for the little details concerning Oswald to commence belaboring our wits. My God, this man Oswald went to Russia after working at Atsugi Air Base in Japan. Isn't that where they tested the U-2? Then this Oswald dares to come back from Russia! Who debriefed him? Which one of us has been into him? Does it even matter? Our common peril may be even more embracing than our individual complicity. Cannot, oh, cannot someone do *something* about Oswald? No one utters the thought aloud. We are too many. We break up our meeting. It has congealed, after all, into silence. We meet all night in twos and threes. Information keeps coming in. Worse and worse. Marina Oswald, the Russian wife— that's how new it all was, we didn't say 'Marina' but 'Marina Oswald, the Russian wife'—has an uncle who is a Lieutenant Colonel in the MVD. Then we hear that George de Mohrenschildt, whom some of us happen to know, a most cultivated contract type, has been Oswald's closest friend in Dallas. My God, George de Mohrenschildt could be earning French money, German money, Cuban money, maybe de Mohrenschildt is earning our money. Who is paying him? Where *did* Oswald hang his hat? None of us goes home for the weekend. We may be enjoying our last hours at Langley. Then comes Sunday afternoon. The news rings around the corridors. Blessed relief. Dead leaves waltz in the garden. A marvelous hoodlum by the gemlike name of Jack Ruby has just killed Oswald. Stocky Jack Ruby can't bear the thought of Jacqueline Kennedy's sufferings at a public trial. We haven't encountered a man so chivalrous since the War of the Roses. The mood on the Seventh Floor is now like the last reel of a film by Lubitsch. We hardly keep back the twinkles. I've always said since: I *like* Jack Ruby. The fellow who paid his debts. The only matter not settled to my absolute satisfaction is whether it was Trafficante or Marcello or Hoffa or Giancana or Roselli who sent the bill.

"In any event, we are home free. There will now be mess enough to smudge the record forever. I remember divining the outcome on that very Sunday night. I asked myself: Who has nothing to fear should the real story come out? That is a list to pursue. The Republicans have to be worried: Their right-wing Texas tycoons could be involved. The liberals must be close to primitive fright. Castro, even if he is innocent, cannot speak for all the elements in DGI. Helms has the Mafia to contemplate, plus rogue elephants, plus our malcontents at JM/WAVE. By definition, one cannot account for an enclave. Yes, CIA might have much to lose. So might the Pentagon. What if we discover that the Soviets were steering Oswald? One can't have a nuclear war just because an Irish *arriviste* got bumped off by the Reds. And what if it is the anti-Castro Cubans in Miami? A damn good likelihood after all. That will bring us back to the Republicans, to Nixon, the lot. No, not quite the lot. A skilled Vietnamese gunman might be avenging his dead ruler, Diem. The Kennedy gang can't afford exposure on that one, can they? Corrosion of the legend might work its way down to the martyr's bier. And then there is the FBI. How can they allow any of these suppositions to be examined? Each one suggests a conspiracy. It is not to Buddha's interest to advertise to the world that the FBI is singularly incompetent at detecting conspiracies they do not hatch themselves. No, none of this is in the interest of supposedly omniscient, wide-bottom Buddha. Oswald, as the sole killer, is, therefore, in everyone's best service—KGB, FBI, CIA, DGI, Kennedys, Johnsons, Nixons, Mafia, Miami Cubans, Castro Cubans, even the Goldwater gang. What if a John Bircher did it? I can feel the furor in the veins of every conspirator who ever talked about killing Jack Kennedy. They can hardly trust themselves not to have done it even when they know they didn't; after all, how can any one of them vouch for all their friends? A broth of disinformation has been on the stove ever since. I knew that we would enter upon a most prestigious investigation that would prove a model of sludge. So, I decided to save myself much untold watching of the pots, and moved right back to serious work where one can make a perceptible dent."

Whether Harlot was actually calling upon his powers of detachment that Sunday night sixty hours after the assassination, or summarizing what he had learned in the months that followed, I, in my turn, was not able to summarize the situation. I was mired in the death. If obsession is a species of mourning for all the fears we bury in unhallowed ground—the unhallowed ground, that is, of our psyche—then I was obsessed. The death of Marilyn Monroe would not leave my mind. If, according to my father, Hoffa could conceive of such a crime in order to leave an unstanchable political wound in both Kennedys, then how many people could I name who might be ready to kill Jack in order to ignite a war against Fidel Castro?

Harlot might have recognized that no pattern can be pulled from such a porridge, but I did not. I lay captive to the velocity of my mind and it raced around the track on many a night. I thought often of Howard Hunt and his deep friendship with Manuel Artime. Hunt had the time, the opportunity—did he have the depth of rage? He might, by way of Artime, have a line into the most violent members of the Brigade. When my mind wore out from asking questions about Hunt, I moved on to brood about Bill Harvey. I went so far as to check on whether he had left Rome on that particular Friday in November. He had not. Then I realized it did not matter. One could run such an operation from Rome. Or could one? And where was Dix Butler? Was he already in Vietnam, or had he stopped over in Dallas? I could not determine that. I also wondered whether Castro, by way of Trafficante, had succeeded in one assassination where we had failed in many. There were hours in those sleepless nights when I could not keep from picturing Oswald and his narrow, tortured, working-class face. Oswald had been down to Mexico City in September. Cal showed me a memo. Headquarters at Langley had cabled Mexico Station for the names of all contacts of the two leading KGB men at the Russian Embassy in Mexico City. Station came back with their response. The taps on the Cuban Embassy and the Russian Embassy produced Oswald's name and Rolando Cubela's. Oswald had even made a phone call from the Cuban Embassy to the Soviet Embassy. In a harsh and highly ungrammatical Russian, the man who called himself Oswald had insisted on speaking to "Comrade Kostikov."

"That's dubious," said Cal. "We know that Oswald spoke Russian well."

"And Cubela?"

"Ah, Cubela. He had talks with Comrade Kostikov. We don't know what about. I expect he has contacts with everyone."

"We've dropped him, of course."

"Heavens, yes." Cal shrugged. "In any event, it's over. The FBI is going to tell us that Oswald acted alone."

Had J. Edgar Hoover done it?

My thoughts did not rest. One day, during the hearings of the Warren Commission, Chief Justice Warren inquired of Allen Dulles, "The FBI and the CIA do employ undercover men who are of terrible character?" And Allen Dulles, in all the bonhomie of a good fellow who can summon up the services of a multitude of street ruffians, replied, "Yes, terribly bad characters."

"That has to be one of Allen's better moments," remarked Hugh Montague.

I was at the point where I was ready to believe that Allen Dulles did it. Or Harlot. Or, in the great net of implication, Cal and I might be guilty as well. Thoughts raced. I had not yet approached my first piece of universal wisdom: There are no answers—there are only questions.

Of course, some questions have to be better than others.

2

September 12, 1964

Dearest Harry,

Wasn't it Fidel Castro who said that a revolution must be sealed in blood? I suppose that the equivalent—if on a personal scale —is in the way a married woman will certify her seriousness toward a lover by an act of treachery *not necessarily carnal* toward her mate. Today I wish to consummate such an act. The contents of this letter are going to offer you some exceptional material about Bill Harvey. This is, indeed, the most privileged stuff Hugh has ever imparted to me, and now that I share it with you, the circle of possession will be limited to Hugh and Harvey, and to you and me—no one else.

Here, then, is one of Hugh's special secrets. Four pages of transcript from a conversation he had with Harvey in Berlin. Since you know William the King in the real way of having worked for him, you will have much, doubtless, to recast in your mind, but I felt only the pride of new possession and the emptiness that can accompany such pride. My inner reaction was lamentable. I thought: A year of nagging, and now, what does it matter? I have learned a hard dark secret about that abysmally driven fellow, Bill Harvey. Yet, in truth, I abuse the gift by dismissing it so. I am more than fascinated.

When I finished the four pages of the transcript (of which there is only one copy, and, I promise you, Hugh took that back from me on the instant I finished reading), I asked him who else had seen these pages, and he then coughed up the startling admission that he had given you a glimpse of the first two sheets more than eight years ago. "Of course," said Hugh, "the first two pages count for little. The poor boy was half-destroyed with frustration."

Well, Harry, I will do my best to restore your ravaged half. Since I do not have the transcript, I will have to summarize what I recall. Right about the top of page three, Hugh mentions to Harvey that he has had a little chat with Bill's first wife, Libby, and much devolved from that. Do you remember all the fuss about the conked-out car in the rain puddle? Remember? Libby called the FBI because her husband had not come home and she was worried. In the story Harvey gave to the Agency in 1947, he chose to resign from the FBI because Buddha was transferring him to Indianapolis as the precise punishment for sleeping all night in a stalled-out car and never phoning in to Bureau. Well, when Hugh spoke with Libby about all this some nine years later, she was still as bitter as only an ex-wife can be. She never called the Bureau, she said. Why would she? Bill was out every night until 3:00 or 4:00 A.M. Hugh checked her story with his own Bureau source who had access to the logs. Indeed, no phone call was made that morning in 1947 by Libby Harvey. Hugh's conclusion: Harvey's story had been a piece of theater designed by Buddha to get King Bill nicely installed in the Agency. Hugh told me that Hoover had managed by various means to slip a dozen of his best men in among us to serve as most special agents, did it neatly in those early days when, as Hugh says, "we were good, sweet, simple, and inno-cent." Of them all, however, Harvey was the best. He had been giving Hoover invaluable Agency material for close to ten years.

At the end of the four-page transcript, you can sense that Harvey is about as reduced as he is going to get. I do remember the following exchange literally.

"You won't believe it," he said to Hugh, "but I really do hate Buddha."

"Yes," Hugh tells him, "J. Edgar Hoover is no good, and you do love us la-de-da assholes, don't you, even if you have been doing your best to deal Buddha our best cards all these years!"

"I have more good friends over here than there," Bill an-swers.

"Well, what good double agent doesn't?" Hugh replies. After which, he absolutely lays it out: "Here is the grim remainder, Bill. I am going to take you at your word: You do like us more than Buddha. So you are going to obtain top input from his special files. I don't care how you do it. And if J. Edgar ever discovers what you are up to, and turns you back to himself, well, triple agents do go under quickly. I will bring on the giant baboons. Is this *claro, hombre?*"

"Claro," he replies.

That is the exchange, Harry, to conclude the transcript. Of course, you can guess my first question to Hugh. "Have you," I asked, "been running Bill ever since?"

"Ever since my trip to Berlin in 1956. Yes. It was a most successful breakfast. Poor Bill. Living with two faces all these years, he has been obliged to drink for both."

As you see, Harry, much food for thought. Treachery gives me the shivers. I have just said farewell to one of my serious married vows. That should keep you for a while, greedy puss.

Your Kittredge

3

FOR A TIME, I WROTE PASSIONATE LETTERS TO KITTREDGE BUT SHE DID not respond. Finally, she referred to the Talmud. "Here, Harry, is wisdom for the small part of you that is Jewish. When the old Babylonian Hebrews did not wish to indulge a powerful temptation, they built a fence around their desire. Since one fence is never strong enough to hold the impulse, they built a fence around the fence. Therefore, I do not see you, and I do not encourage love letters. Tell me, rather, what you are learning."

Reluctantly, I complied. The letter that follows can serve as a sample.

September 12, 1965

Dear Kittredge,

I note that it is a year to the day since you sent me the special information pertaining to William Harvey, and I have not ceased thinking of him since. In fact, I hear about his doings from Cal, who is dreadfully upset at what a mess Harvey is making of Station in Rome. The more Cal thrives as Helms' troubleshooter, the more he has to wonder whether Helms, when he becomes our next Director, will assign Cal to be his Deputy. So the power of the escalator has entered my father's estimates, I fear. Cal is getting as authoritative as he used to be in my boyhood. We clash. I believe he's furious because I won't be his assistant any longer but have chosen to work for Hugh.

But then, it was impossible for my father and me to keep together after Paris. There is no reason for it, but, do you know?—bad conscience lives between us. And Cal has a sense of doom again these days. I do not know if Harvey is the reason, but he is obsessed with him. You see, Helms, most reluctantly, is getting ready to pull Wild Bill back from Rome and send him out to pasture. Who, however, gets the assignment to tell the man he's through? Helms wants Cal to go over and do it. "That will cushion the fall," he tells my father. "One of us ought to be there to guide him down the steps." Cal, however, is having what I am almost tempted to call a failure of nerve. "I can't do it," he has said to me more than once. "I would never forgive Bill Harvey if he came around to tell me that I was through. I would assume the man was gloating, and it might put me into a most untenable state."

"All the same," I said, "if Helms wants you to do it, you can hardly refuse."

"Well, I can ask you to be my surrogate. If I send my son, that shows respect."

"I could end up in close quarters with Bill."

"Rick, I wouldn't drop this plum on you if I didn't believe you could carry it off. An uncomfortable hour or two, yes, but you are my son. When the time comes, you may have to do it. Let us hope he resigns at his own behest."

We left it at that, but I, for the first time in my life, do not trust my father. I think his fear is career-inspired. I think he is afraid Harvey will make some kind of mess that Boardman Hubbard, future DDP, does not wish to be associated with. I hope I am wrong. I keep hoping, yes, that Bill Harvey will resign, or take a turn for the better. The trouble resides, I think, in the way his job came about. The problem, if you recollect, was that Helms had to spirit Harvey out of McCone's sight. Only Rome was open. To tempt the palate, Helms gave Harvey an ambitious bill of fare. "Look," he said, "Rome is now a cream-puff shop. The intelligence we receive is spoon-fed to us by the Italian services. It's a disgrace. We haven't turned one KGB man there in ten years. The situation calls for your talents, Bill. Go in there, be yourself, rough as a cob, subtle as a Medici. You can turn that place upside down."

Helms, according to Cal, was just firing the guy up so that he wouldn't have to see the job as a demotion. But Harvey charged in. Now, while it is true that even our best people in Rome Station were hardly more than skilled adjuncts to State's party circuit, and no real intelligence was being acquired, Harvey did play hell with everybody working there. After all, Rome had become a lovely place for old case officers. One could live at last in the lap of a few amenities. Harvey put them on stake-outs. He kept prodding these suave old hands: "Have you recruited your Russian today?" Of course, no Russians were recruited. For topping on the cake, Harvey violated Roman pride as well. He lobbied hard to get his own Italian in as head of one local intelligence service. When Bill finally managed to place this chosen person, the man was such a figure of ridicule to all his new Italian associates that he turned on Harvey. He actually began to obstruct him. Finally, he informed King Bill that no more American taps were going to be allowed on the phone lines of the Soviet and Eastern European embassies. Bill had stage-managed a disaster. A few episodes like that and Harvey grew famous for being bombed at lunch. He would snore until nudged awake.

Then he had a heart attack. He recovered. He kept drinking. One morning, behind the closed door of his office, a gun went off. No one moved. No one dared to look in. Who could face the mess that William Harvey's walls might offer? One brave secretary finally grew brave enough to push open the door. There was Harvey at his desk, cleaning his gun. It had gone off by accident. Harvey winked.

Kittredge, I think it is getting close. The other day, Cal told me that Helms said, "I would like to take Harvey's fat head and ram it through a wall."

Well, it looks like I am going to be the one to get the job. My chances for coming back alive have to be at least one hundred to one in my favor, but, Lord, that *one* is a live underdog, isn't it?

Love to you and to Christopher,
Harry

4

A HALF YEAR WENT BY BEFORE THE CALL CAME, BUT COME IT DID.

He knew why I was in Rome. He had sent a limousine to meet me at the airport and a man to take me through Customs. When I entered his office that evening, he was dressed, I remember, very much as I was. We were both wearing dark-gray flannel single-breasted suits. We had on white shirts and repp ties. Mine was red and blue; his was green and black. We sat down in his office at 8:00 P.M. with the understanding that we would go out for dinner at 9:00. A quart of bourbon, an ice bucket, and two glasses were on a tray. We drank for the next seven hours and never saw dinner. A second bottle was emptied. It may have been the most intense drinking I have ever done and I flew back to the U.S. with a hangover potent enough to keep me away from hard liquor for the next few months.

At the time, however, the booze went down like water, or, to be accurate, like gasoline. My adrenaline was in full supply. If I was burning the liquor almost as fast as I drank it, I may have been enabled thereby to enter the high-octane nervous system of William Harvey. I certainly came to understand how he could take it down in the quantities he did: William Harvey had not had an hour in his life when he was free, by his own measure, of outside menace.

We began quietly enough. "I know why you're here," he said in his low voice, "and that's all right. You were sent to do another man's job."

"I'm not here because I want to be," I answered, "but I know why I was assigned. It's because I, at least, know what you've achieved, and what you stand for."

"You were always good with the horseshit." He chuckled, an uncommon sound to come out of him. "Back in Berlin, you drew some circles on my ass, SM/ONION."

"I was scared stiff all the way."

"Of course. Everybody who works for Hugh Montague is scared."

"Yessir."

"Now you're here to fire me."

"That's not the word."

"Well, it will become the word because I'm not going to go."

"I believe the decision has been made." I was taking as long a pause as I could with each reply.

"In case you don't know," he said, "you are only a towel boy in a whorehouse."

"I always wondered what I was."

"Ha, ha. Right now, Cal Hubbard is in Washington trying to hold back his royal shits. He told you to call him the minute you're done with me, right? Any hour at all, right?"

"Of course. He's concerned over you."

"Never trump horseshit with bullshit. Cal Hubbard is defecating green. He is afraid that I will take out my handgun and fire a bullet through my eye into the occipital. He'll be blamed for the suicide."

"They want to find the right slot for you. The high-level appropriate slot. My father, more than anyone, feels you were treated most unfairly by John McCone."

Harvey beamed. "Can I see the letter he wrote to John McCone?"

It went on this way for an hour. I absorbed his abuse, his irony, his indifference to dinner. Somewhere in the second hour, he began to talk in longer bursts. "You are here to get me to agree to come back," he said, "and I am here to state that I am ready to return in the first body-bag that can be passed through a pig's asshole. It is harder, Hubbard, to pass through a pig's asshole than through the eye of a needle. So we don't have much to negotiate. On the other hand, let us talk. I want to get to the bottom of why there is a difference of opinion in how I am bringing off this job. You see, I never received any cooperation. I have come to decide I was sent to the wrong place on purpose—to grind Wild Bill right on down to his pension. Fuck all of you. I don't retire. I was not given the cooperation I was promised, and that is why Rome has produced no results. Did you know that Hugh Montague has Italian sources in this town at the overhead level?"—he raised his palm horizontally far above his head —"yay-high agents he put in place and built up years ago, dagos with a Minister's portfolio. Hugh Montague furnishes me no access to them. 'You'll have to get along with the pussies you've got,' is his message—Hugh Montague, for whom I did more than I ever did for anyone else. The man is a study in the monumental thanklessness of senior-level ingratitude. You, Hubbard, have always been his towel boy."

"Have another drink," I said, "it will make you more mellow."

"Fuck you. I am not a party to any cosmic appreciation of the depths to which I have sunk. That is not the readout I provide myself." He reached into his shoulder holster and took out a Magnum. I did not know if it was a Colt or a Smith & Wesson revolver, and I debated whether to ask him but could not see what purpose the question would serve. He sighted it, then broke it open and inspected the cylinder. With his handkerchief, a clean one, he wiped it down.

"People say," said Harvey, 'There he goes again.' " He swung the cylinder back in and pointed the gun thoughtfully at me. "They have come to the conclusion that this is an act, and what they do not recognize is that I feel a real inclination which goes right down into the most honest part of me to pull that trigger and blow somebody's name right out of their body. Give them back to the great compost heap. The only reason I have not squeezed the little bitch up to this date is that there has never been a proper matching-up. When I feel the impulse most keenly, as now, the recipient has not been worthy of entering into history with me. So, I have not squeezed the trigger. If Hugh Montague were here tonight, however, he would be a dead man," and Harvey took aim now, and did pull the trigger on an empty chamber. "If it were your father, I might flip a coin. But you—you are relatively safe." He set the handgun down on the desk. "Sit back," he said. "Let us talk of other matters."

That was the first time he had aimed at me that night, but it would not be the last. We would come back to the gun. The longer it sat on his desk, the more it took on the presence of a third party who chose not to speak.

"I would ask you," he said, "what do you think of Lee Harvey Oswald?"

"I think there may be a few things to find out about him."

"Shit, Hubbard, you call that an answer? Have some bourbon." He poured for us both. "I was asking the question because Oswald's name intrigues me. As you may know, I hate that son of a bitch Bobby Kennedy with an odium that can bring me to my feet, gun in hand, out of a deep sleep. An old Bureau reflex. I could pop Bobby Kennedy where he stands if he were sitting where you are now. And this Lee Harvey Oswald—he hated Bobby too. The brother who is left receives the full hatred of the bullet. So I played with the idea of Oswald, but not as an Agency man—I did not ask myself who was running him, or was he an *espontáneo*, no, I just played with the name, Lee Harvey Oswald, a bizarre moniker. Then it struck. Take off the Oswald, that is not a name I can comprehend, but keep the Lee Harvey. When I was a boy they called me Willie Harvey. Do you think God is trying to tell me something? I began to explore the background on Lee Harvey. Amazing stuff. Do you know his favorite TV show when he was an adolescent? It happened to be: *I Led Three Lives,* which was that Philbrick piece of crap about the FBI. Well, shit, Lee Harvey, so did I, William King Harvey, lead three lives for the FBI. I say there is more than coincidence here. I have pondered it, Hubbard, and I have come to a profound conclusion. There is opposition to entropy. The universe may not necessarily wind down. There is something forming that I would call new embodiment. Entropy and embodiment may be as related as antimatter and matter." He belched reflectively. "Yes," he said, "the forms deteriorate and they all run down to the sea, but other possibilities come together in their wake to seek *embodiment*. Blobs are always looking to articulate themselves into a higher form of blob. There *is* a tropism toward form, Hubbard. It counters decomposition. I tell you this because I felt an invisible bond between Lee Harvey and me, a bond that reinforces my notion of embodiment. A nascent embodiment. It was looking for more form. Is that clear, Hubbard?" He belted another bourbon.

He talked. There was one hour past the middle when he did not stop for all the hour. He spoke of how it felt to know that one had had a purchase on genius and lost it, "had it leached out of me, inch by vicious inch through your godfather, Hugh Montague—by God, there's almost reason to shoot you," and he picked up the gun again.

It happened twice more. On the last occasion, he held the gun in a line with my head for ten minutes. I concentrated on exhaling my breath. I knew that if I could get all the bad air out of me, the good air—or what was left of it—would take care of itself on the way in. Sited in his line of fire, I was returned to one of the last days of the two weeks of rock climbing I had done in that summer half my life ago, in the fortnight I met Harlot, and I remembered how on one of the very last days I stood on a rock ledge six inches wide for almost half an hour, while Harlot, all but trapped, was making delicate essays above to find a way through a particularly unaccommodating over-hang, and all the while I did not believe that I would be able to belay him if he fell. I was anchored to my face of rock, but I did not like the anchor.

In that half hour, I came to know what it was to spend one's existence on a vertical rather than a horizontal plane. I remember that I looked out on all the flat land below and it was as removed from me as the vanished continent of Atlantis. Now, sitting across from Bill Harvey, with his gun pointed in my direction, I came to know what it was like to live on a line, and I did not take it at all for granted that I would be alive when the dawn came up, which was, I knew, the most powerful safeguard I possessed to keep Bill Harvey from com-mitting his finger to the trigger. It was too close to smile.

Toward the sixth hour, Harvey began doing imitations of Fidel Castro. They were hopelessly broad, and no two men could have

looked more unalike, but Harvey may have been searching for em-
bodiments. Or was it the conjunction of the hour, the bourbon, and
our mutual adrenaline? I could sense the moment when he was ready
to allow me to laugh, and I actually could chortle at the vast farce of
William Harvey deeming to present himself as Fidel Castro. " 'I can
forgive you,' " said Harvey, thrusting his FBI nose upward in profile
to his unseen witness in the heavens, " 'you of the United States for
trying to kill me. For I have discovered in the course of your failures
that capitalism is more inept than I supposed.' Has that got the tone,
Hubbard?"

"Keep going."

" 'I am ready to forgive such concentrated if impotent efforts, but
I cannot overlook the way you had your imperialist colleagues ship us
boatloads of tainted motor oils that corroded our engines whereupon
you proceeded to mock the inefficiency of our socialist system.' Have
I got the son of a bitch down pat?"

"Close."

" 'Yes, I can forgive your attempts to assassinate me, but I am
obliged to tell you that the American spirit, from our Cuban point of
view, is bizarre. LSD is sprayed in a broadcasting studio in the hope
I might inhale its effects and begin to sound ridiculous to my people,
plans are made to dust tubercular bacteria into my diving suit, there
is talk of cigars dipped in poison and exploding seashells. Who was the
progenitor of all these ideas? My friends, I discovered the source of
such inspiration. It came from the British literary character James
Bond. I became curious about this agent James Bond who seemed
such a fool, such an impostor of a man of action. I had research done,
therefore, in our excellent University of Havana facilities on the
character of the author of James Bond and discovered that this gentleman, Ian Fleming, is a worn-out asthmatic Lothario with a wheezing
heart and exhausted loins. Of such men are your American legends
concocted,' " concluded Harvey in his embodiment of Fidel Castro,
and bent over double with a terrible coughing attack. When he was
done, he put the gun away.

He would take it forth one more time, but the tide of the night
was moving out. At last he stood up and said, "Let's take a walk. I'll
make up my mind on the walk."

We strolled around the Embassy. Harvey said: "The KGB tails me
all the time. When it comes to petty viciousness, they are as small as
goat turds. Why, I even believe they were the guys who let the air out

of my tires the other day when I parked near the Spanish Steps." He wheezed. "Somebody could take a shot at me right now, I suppose. I am still a target. But that's all right." He wheezed once more. "Okay, Hubbard," he said, "I will go back. But first I want to throw myself one hell of a party. I'll have a fountain—I figured it out—a fountain to spurt champagne, then recover it and jet it out again. To renew the fizz, we will insert a CO_2 cartridge in the plumbing." He beamed. "Tomorrow, I will send out a cable to all Stations worldwide that I am going back to Washington. Let me add the codicil that I will haunt you, and yours, if anyone or anything indicates I am returning in disgrace."

"There won't be any suggestion of that," I said.

"Oh, there better not be." He put his arm on my shoulder. "You hold your liquor, Hubbard. You seem able to keep your seat. Maybe you have your father's moxie."

"Never a chance."

"I wish I had a son," he said. We had come back to the American Embassy and strolled by the sentry at the gate. He took me on a tour of the back wall. "I have one thing to tell you," he added.

"Yessir."

"I am the man who uncovered Philby."

"We are all witting of that."

"But after I uncovered him, I began to wonder if it was the Russians who decided to blow his safety. If so, I told myself, there is only one answer. They were looking to protect something larger. *Someone* larger. Now, the question I pose is *who*? It remains the question. I'll ask you to guess who the big guy is."

He said no more, but one part of my brain was singed forever with the fear that it was Harlot.

Harvey ended these hours of alcoholic festivity by urinating all over a piece of the back wall of the American Embassy in Rome. In the middle, he said, "Hubbard, you will never know how close I feel to Jesus Christ when I take one good piss like this." Then he butted heads with me to say good-bye, a last gift, a headache to take home with the hangover.

MOSCOW, MARCH 1984

THAT SINGULARLY ANTICLIMACTIC PHRASE, "a headache to take home with the hangover," brought me to the last page I had written for Alpha. I had carried the memoir no further. Sitting on my bed in my narrow room off the airshaft on the fourth floor of the old Metropole in Moscow, staring up at an absurdly high ceiling whose proportions gave an echo of the larger space which must once have existed in the reign of the last Czar, I knew only that I had not wanted my manuscript to end, I did not wish to be done. Those two thousand and more frames of manuscript on microfilm had been equal to money in my pocket—a primal safeguard against the rigors of a strange and hostile land. Now my capital had been consumed. I was out of the book, and on my own, off on a mission whose purpose I could not name but for the inner knowledge that I knew it. For if the answer was not alive in some cloaked corner of my mind, then why would I be here?

I thought of Harlot then, and of his incommensurable vanity. An old legend came back to me. In the days of the Reflecting Pool, there had been a night when Harlot entered the office of an assistant who was quartered in the I-J-K-L, and standing there in the dark, looked across the intervening distance between himself and the next building. In a lighted office across the court he saw one of his colleagues kissing a secretary. Harlot promptly dialed that office, and as he watched, the man separated himself from the embrace long enough to pick up his phone.

"Aren't you appalled by yourself?" Harlot asked.

"Who is this?"

"God," said Harlot and hung up.

The last time Hugh Montague had spoken to me about God was the last time I had taken the trip from Langley to his farmhouse on the eyebrow *of the four-lane truck road. He had expatiated that afternoon on the theory of Creationism, his brilliance, one can certify, not at all diminished.*

"Would you say, Harry," he inquired, "that two such words as 'sophisticated fundamentalist' make one oxymoron?"

"Can't see how it wouldn't," I told him.

"Intellectual snobbery," replied Harlot, "is your short suit. You would do better to ponder the meanings that can be extracted from apparent folly."

As so often, a flick into the eye of your ego was the price you paid for obtaining the products of his mind.

"Yes," he said, "Creationists rush to tell us that the world, according to the Bible, was commenced five thousand and some hundreds of years ago. It makes for merriment, don't it? Fundamentalists are such whole fools. Yet I said to myself once, 'What would I do if I were Jehovah about to conceive of this creature, man, who, as soon as I create him, will be hell-bent—given the equal opportunity I have offered Satan—to discover My nature. How can that not become man's passion? I have created him, after all, in My image, so he will wish to discover My nature in order to seize My throne. Would I ever have permitted such a contract in the first place, therefore, if I had not taken the wise precaution to fashion a cover story?' "

"A cover story?" I did not wish to repeat his words, but I did.

"A majestic cover story. Nothing vulgar or small. Absolutely detailed, fabulously complete. Just suppose that in the moment of striking that agreement with Satan, God brought forth the world complete. Five thousand and some hundreds of years ago, we were given an absolutely realized presentation of the world. God created it ex nihilo. Gave it to us complete. Everyone began to live at the same instant of Creation. Yet all were given a highly individual background. All had been put together, of course, from nothingness infused with divine genius. The creation of this imaginary past was God's artwork. All who lived, all men, women, and children of all varying tribes and climates, the eighty-year-old, the forty-five-year-old, the young lovers, and the two-year-old were all created at the same instant that He placed the half-cooked food on the stone-hearth fire. All of it appeared at once, the animals in their habitat just so much as the humans, each creature possessing its separate memory, the plants in command of their necessary instincts, the earth bountiful here and unfulfilled there, some crops even ready to go to harvest. All the

fossil remains were carefully set in the rock. God gave us a world able to present all the material clues that Darwin would need fifty-odd centuries later to conceive of evolution. The geological strata had all been put in place. The solar system was in the heavens. Everything had been set moving at rates of orbit to encourage astronomers to declare five thousand and more years later that the age of the earth was approximately five billion years. I like this notion immensely," said Harlot. "You can say the universe is a splendidly worked-up system of disinformation calculated to make us believe in evolution and so divert us away from God. Yes, that is exactly what I would do if I were the Lord and could not trust My own creation."

What was it Harlot had said once on a Low Thursday? "The aim of these gatherings is to acquaint you with the factology of facts. One has to know whether one is dealing with the essential or the circumferential fact. Historical data, after all, tend to be not particularly factual and subject to revision by later researchers. You must look to start, therefore, with the fact that cannot be smashed into subparticles of fact."

Yes, I had been delivered from the book of documents into the world, and all of Russia lay before me. But I had one fact that was essential, even if it was no more than the hypothesis that, for fact, Harlot was here in Moscow. A man who could conceive of the universe as a distortion fashioned for purposes of self-protection by God was a man to live in monumental double dealings he had created for himself, larger than any agency he served. No, there could be no reply to why I was in Russia unless I believed that Hugh Montague was here and alive, and I had a fair chance to find him. For if here, he would choose to reside in Moscow as a most honored colleague of the KGB, yes. Given his wheelchair, he might even be dwelling within a stone's throw of the statue of Dzerzhinsky. I felt one step closer to the concealed life of my mind. The thought that Harlot might be inhabiting a room but a few hundred yards away from this room enabled me to know at last what Bill Harvey had meant nineteen years ago when he spoke of an embodiment. Harlot, living in the shadow of Dzerzhinsky Square, was my embodiment.

I might never finish the book of Harry Hubbard and his years in Saigon, nor the stretch of service in the White House when one lived through Watergate, no, nor the commencement of my love affair with Kittredge, no, that was as removed as childhood. Unlike God, I had not been able to present all of my creation. I was out of the documents and on my own, and my life was more exposed than it had ever been, for I was taking the longest leap of my life. Could I be ready to find my godfather and ask him, along with everything else I would ask: "Whom? In the immortal words of Vladimir Ilich Lenin, 'Whom? Whom does this all benefit?' "

TO BE CONTINUED

AUTHOR'S NOTE

Over the last seven years, whenever I would mention working on a novel about the CIA, nearly everyone, and I think this is a compliment to the Agency rather than to the author, would say, "I can hardly wait." The next reaction, particularly among people who were not familiar with how a novel gets written day by day, would appear in the following polite form: "Do you know someone in the CIA very well?" which is, I expect, a substitute for saying, "How do you understand enough to write about *them*?"

I would generally answer that, yes, I knew a few people in the organization although, of course, I could not say much more than that. While this was not without its truth, the general assumption that to know a couple of intelligence officers will prepare the solid ground for writing about a good many of them, is as innocent, when you get down to it, as asking a professional football coach whether he has stolen the secrets of the team to be played next week. I assume he would answer, "We don't have to. Professional football is a culture, fellow, and we are steeped in it. Besides, we have enough imagination to write the game plan for the other guys as well."

So, I could have answered that I wrote this book with the part of my mind that has lived in the CIA for forty years. *Harlot's Ghost*, after all, is the product of a veteran imagination that has pondered the ambiguous and fascinating moral presence of the Agency in our national life for the last four decades; I did not have to be in the organization, nor know its officers intimately to feel the confidence that I had come to understand the tone of its inner workings. A Russian Jew of the early nineteenth century who happened to be consumed with interest about the nature of the Orthodox Church would not have had to be on intimate terms with a priest to feel that his comprehension of Russian Orthodoxy was possessed of some accuracy. He would, of course, have required some inner link, some sense that he, as a Jew, if he had been born into Russian Orthodoxy, might have become a monk. In turn, it would not have been all that impossible for me to have spent my life in the CIA provided I had come from a different background and with a different political bent.

I am obviously suggesting that some good novels can stray far from one's immediate life and derive instead from one's cultural experience and one's ongoing imaginative faculty. Over the years, that faculty can build nests of context onto themes that attract it. The imagination may proceed in many a direction at once—the life of the President of the United States and a day in the routine of a homeless man might be covertly occupying separate parts of one's brain at once. Novelists not only live their own lives but develop other characters within themselves who never reveal their particular intelligence to the novelist's conscious mind until, perchance, the day they come into one's working literary preoccupations.

Now, the process, of course, is not always so magical. In the case of a novel like *Harlot's Ghost,* one does a great deal of research. If I have not absorbed one hundred books on the CIA, then I must have come near, and I had the great good fortune that, as I wrote, new works on the subject of Intelligence kept coming out, and some of them were very good. If this had been a book of nonfiction, I would have had footnotes and attributions on many a point, plus an index and bibliography, and indeed I will pay my respects to the volumes that surrounded me these last seven years before this disclaimer is done.

Nonetheless, *Harlot's Ghost* is a work of fiction, and most of its main characters and the majority of its accompanying cast are imaginary. Since they move among real personages, of whom a few are prominent in our history, it may be important to explain how I used the books I studied.

Some nonfiction awakens the imagination. Its personages take on the luster of good fictional characters, that is, they seem as real and complex as men and women we know intimately. The larger share of nonfiction, however, deadens perceptions. Nonetheless, when one is consumed with a subject, even mediocre treatments can, if read with sufficient concentration, enlarge the working imagination, which, once it becomes passionate, and focused, begins to penetrate the obfuscations, cover-ups, evasions, and misapprehensions of all those middling tomes that are so poorly written that the best clue to what really took place is to be found in the evasions of their style. A man who has been coaching football for forty years need only watch a high school running back for a few plays to decide whether potential is there. Ditto for good prize-fight managers watching an amateur throw one left hook. Say as much for novelists who have spent their lives at it. I have done enough indifferent writing over the years, and spent so much time contemplating why it is bad, that by now I can read another author's work and penetrate on occasion to what he is or, even more important, is not really saying. It is similar to that exercise in counterintelligence where one attempts to differentiate the lies from the truths your opponent is offering.

To a degree, it could be said that my comprehension of the CIA comes from books I have reinterpreted for myself quite as much as from works that informed me more directly. The result, and this is all I will claim, is that I have given the reader my sense of what the Agency may have been like from 1955 to 1963, at least as seen through the eyes of a privileged young man who grew up in it. It is a fictional CIA and its only real existence is in my mind, but I would point out that the same is true for men and women who have spent forty years working within the Agency. They have only their part of the CIA to know, even as each of us has our own America, and no two Americas will prove identical. If I have an argument to make, then, on grounds of verisimilitude, I will claim that my imaginative CIA is as real or more real than nearly all of the lived-in ones.

In the course of putting together this attempt, there was many a choice to make on one's approach to formal reality. The earliest and most serious decision was not to provide imaginary names for all the prominent people who entered the work. After all, that rejected approach would have left one with such barbarisms as James Fitzpatrick Fennerly, youngest man ever to be elected President of the United States.

It was obvious, therefore, that one would have to give Jack Kennedy his honest name. It would not damage the novel. He would be as intense and fictional a presence in the novel's life as any imaginary human could ever be; one could only strip him of his fictional magic by putting a false name on him; then the reader's perception becomes no more than, "Oh, yes, President Fennerly is Jack Kennedy—now I will get to learn what made Jack Kennedy tick."

Something of the same was true in lesser measure of E. Howard Hunt and Allen Dulles. Concerning the latter, the problem was not large since he is not a central character here; with Hunt, who is a figure in these pages, the decision was not as immediately found. I debated for a time whether to call him Charley "Stunt" Stevens, and decided that would be the cruelest invasion of his integument, since many a sophisticated reader would soon enough be saying, "It's Howard Hunt," and would next believe—having relaxed into the presence of the false name—that every word I wrote about fictional Hunt was true; whereas, when I name him overtly, readers are free to disagree. They can say, "That is not my idea at all of Howard Hunt."

Looking, then, for inner sanction, I found it in two of Hunt's autobiographical works, *Give Us This Day* and *Undercover*. They established the parameters of his character, and enabled me to write about Howard Hunt within the comprehension gained from his two books. I have, of course, except on those rare occasions where I quote from his printed remarks for a sentence or two, made up his dialogue. My guide was not to go beyond the characterological limits of his own account—I did not give him sly tasks I did not believe he would carry out merely because I wished to enliven my pages.

The real character with whom perhaps the greatest liberties were taken was William Harvey. There is a well-written and most entertaining book called *Wilderness of Mirrors* by David C. Martin, and it is only fair to state that its portrait of Harvey captured my imagination and stimulated it to press beyond the nonfictional restraints of Martin's book. My William Harvey bears relation to the deceased William Harvey and certainly follows his career, oversees him at the Berlin Tunnel, in his marriages, at Mongoose, in his feuds with a real General Lansdale and a real Robert Kennedy, and ends his career in Rome. None of that is made up. Since Martin's book seems to be the source, however, from which derive other descriptions of Harvey in other books, I decided to make my Harvey more imagined (and less close, I expect, to the real man than Howard Hunt).

With Harlot, we move a step further into the unbounded and fictional. James Jesus Angleton, "Mother" in CIA legend, was obviously the original model for Hugh Montague, but since very little was known publicly about Angleton at the time I began this novel, and he was obviously a most complex and convoluted gentleman, I decided to create my own intricate piece of work, the wholly fictional Hugh Montague, and, of course, his equally fictional wife, Kittredge.

Similar in kind is Cal Hubbard. Strains of Tracy Barnes and Desmond FitzGerald can obviously be found, but since I knew very little about either of those gentlemen, it is fair to say that Hubbard, like Montague, is all-but-entirely fictional.

Harry Hubbard, Dix Butler, Arnold Rosen, Chevi Fuertes, Toto Barbaro, the Masarovs, the Porringers, the personnel at the Farm, and nearly all other minor characters in Berlin, Uruguay, and Miami are fictional. Castro, Artime, Barker, San Román, Tony Oliva, Eugenio Martínez, and a number of other Cubans briefly seen are real, as are the U.S. government officials in Special Group, Augmented, and William Attwood and Lisa Howard. The decision to mix real and fictional minor characters came not from the desire to sink into docudrama but to attempt to rise above it. At the cost of repeating the theme of this disclaimer, it is the author's contention that good fiction—if the writer can achieve it—is more real, that is, more nourishing to our sense of reality, than nonfiction, and so I mixed the factual with the fictional in order to prove a point: If the reader's imagination is rewarded with a large and detailed mural of a social organism moving through some real historical events, then the reader's last concern is to be provided every instant with a scorecard of what actually happened and what was made up. My hope is that the imaginary world of *Harlot's Ghost* will bear more relation to the reality of these historical events than the spectrum of facts and often calculated misinformation that still surrounds them. It is a sizable claim, but then I have the advantage of believing that novelists have a unique opportunity—they can create superior histories out of an enhancement of the real, the unverified, and the wholly fictional.

Let me give the most extreme example of this premise as it applied to this work. Judith Campbell Exner wrote a book in company with Ovid Demaris called *My Story,* which gave a detailed and, under the circumstances, tastefully candid portrait of her affairs with Frank Sinatra, Sam Giancana, and Jack Kennedy. It was a decent book and gave off an agreeable air—one tended to believe its facts.

Since the incidents in that work were complementary to my attempt, I decided to make use of her account, although not directly. I did not feel, for example, that I could write about Judith Campbell Exner with more insight than she had exhibited. I felt bound by the precise edges of her account, yet, novelistically, I needed to go further. So I decided to create an imaginary character, Modene Murphy, whom I could comprehend better because she was a reflection of my understanding. She would be a little bit like Judith Campbell, yet considerably different. Her actions would parallel Campbell's in many ways, that is, she would have affairs with Sinatra, Kennedy, and

Giancana, she would be harassed, as was Campbell, by the FBI, and she would find in the end a comparable misery. Her inner life, however, her dialogue, and most of her specific situations would belong to Modene Murphy. So it would not be Judith Campbell I was writing about; all the same, Campbell's experiences would offer the inspiration and the historical sanction to conceive of a similar history.

That treatment is, in effect, the model of reality I used for most of this novel. The events described are either real, or able to respect the proportions of the factual events. I have looked to avoid exaggeration. If I have succeeded, *Harlot's Ghost* will offer an imaginary CIA that will move in parallel orbit to the real one, and will be neither an over- nor underestimation of its real powers.

Let me express my appreciation for the following books. I will list them in alphabetical order, by author, and put an asterisk next to those works for which I feel a considerable debt.

E.C. Ackerman. *Street Man: The CIA Career of Mike Ackerman*. Ackerman and Palumbo, 1976.

*Philip Agee. *Inside the Company: CIA Diary*. Boston: Stonehill, 1975.

———— and Louis Wolf, eds. *Dirty Work: The CIA in Western Europe*. New York: Lyle Stuart, 1978.

Stewart Alsop. *The Center*. New York: Harper and Row, 1968.

Christopher Andrew. *Her Majesty's Secret Service: The Making of the British Intelligence Community*. London: Heinemann, 1985.

Charles Ashman. *The CIA-Mafia Link*. New York: Manor Books, 1975.

William Attwood. *The Reds and the Blacks*. New York: Harper and Row, 1976.

Bradley Earl Ayers. *The War That Never Was*. New York: Bobbs-Merrill, 1976.

James Bamford. *The Puzzle Palace*. New York: Penguin Books, 1983.

John Barron. *KGB*. New York: Reader's Digest Press, 1974.

Louise Bernikow. *Abel*. Seattle: Trident, 1970.

Frei Betto. *Fidel and Religion*. Havana: Publications Office of the Council of State, 1988.

Celina Bledowska and Jonathan Block. *KGB-CIA, Intelligence and Counterintelligence Operations*. New York: Exeter Books, 1987.

William Blum. *The CIA: A Forgotten History*. London: Zed, 1986.

Robert Borosage and John Marks, eds. *The CIA File*. New York: Grossman, 1976.

Benjamin C. Bradlee. *Conversations with Kennedy*. New York: Norton, 1975.

*William Brashler. *The Don: The Life and Death of Sam Giancana*. New York: Harper and Row, 1977.

Vincent and Nan Buranelli. *Spy-Counterspy: An Encyclopedia of Espionage*. New York: McGraw-Hill, 1982.

Michael Burke. *Outrageous Good Fortune*. Boston: Little, Brown, 1984.

David Chavchavadse. *Crowns and Trench Coats: A Russian Prince in the CIA, an Autobiography*. New York: Atlantic International Publications, 1990.

Ray Cline. *Secrets, Spies and Scholars*. Reston, Va.: Acropolis, 1976.

———, et al. *The Central Intelligence Agency: A Photographic History*. New York: Stein and Day, 1986.

William Colby. *Honorable Men*. New York: Simon and Schuster, 1978.

H.H.A. Cooper and Lawrence J. Handlinger. *Making Spies: A Talent-Spotter's Handbook*. Boulder, Colo.: Paladin Press, 1986.

Miles Copeland. *The Game of Nations*. New York: Simon and Schuster, 1969.

★———. *Without Cloak or Dagger*. New York: Simon and Schuster, 1974.

★William R. Corson. *The Armies of Ignorance*. New York: Dial Press, 1977.

———, and Robert Crowley. *The New KGB*. New York: William Morrow, 1986.

———, Susan B. Trento, and Joseph J. Trento. *Widows: Four American Spies, the Wives They Left Behind, and the KGB's Crippling of American Intelligence*. New York: Crown, 1989.

★Cecil B. Currey. *Edward Lansdale, the Unquiet American*. Boston: Houghton Mifflin, 1988.

★Peer de Silva. *Sub Rosa: The CIA and the Uses of Intelligence*. New York: Times Books, 1978.

Frank Donner. *The Age of Surveillance*. New York: Knopf, 1980.

★Allen W. Dulles. *The Craft of Intelligence*. New York: Harper and Row, 1963.

Felix Dzerzhinsky: A Biography. Moscow: Congress Publishers, 1977.

John J. Dziak. *Chekisty*. Lexington, Mass.: Lexington Books, 1988.

Eddie the Wire. *The Complete Guide to Lockpicking*. Port Townsend, Wash.: Loompanics, Unlimited, 1981.

Edward Jay Epstein. *Deception: the Invisible War between the KGB and the CIA*. New York: Simon and Schuster, 1989.

———. *Inquest: The Warren Commission and the Establishment of Truth*. New York: Viking, 1966.

★———. *Legend: The Secret World of Lee Harvey Oswald*. New York: Reader's Digest Press, 1978.

Harold George Eriksen. *How to Find Missing Persons: A Handbook for Investigators*. Port Townsend, Wash.: Loompanics, Unlimited, 1981.

★Judith Exner (with Ovid Demaris). *My Story*. New York: Grove, 1977.

★Christopher Felix. *A Short Course in the Secret War*. New York: Dutton, 1963.

Bernard Fensterwald. *Coincidence or Conspiracy?* New York: Zebra Books, 1977.

Jim Garrison. *On the Trail of the Assassins*. New York: Sheridan Square, 1988.

★Antoinette Giancana and Thomas Renner. *Mafia Princess: Growing Up in Sam Giancana's Family*. New York: William Morrow, 1984.

Anatoly Golitsin. *New Lies for Old: The Communist Strategy of Deception and Disinformation*. New York: Dodd, Mead, 1984.

Sen. Gravel Edition: *The Pentagon Papers*. Boston: Beacon, 1971.

Robert J. Groden and Harrison Edward Livingston. *High Treason, the Assassination of President John F. Kennedy: What Really Happened*. New York: Conservatory Press, 1989.

Trumbull Higgins. *The Perfect Failure: Kennedy, Eisenhower, and the CIA at the Bay of Pigs*. New York: Norton, 1987.

Warren Hinckle and William W. Turner. *The Fish Is Red: The Story of the Secret War Against Castro*. New York: Harper and Row, 1981.

*Heinz Hohne and Hermann Zolling. *The General Was a Spy*. New York: Coward, McCann and Geoghegan, 1972.

John Hollander. *Reflections on Espionage*. New York: Atheneum, 1976.

William Hood. *Mole*. New York: Norton, 1982.

————. *Spy Wednesday*. New York: Norton, 1986.

*Jim Hougan. *Spooks: The Haunting of America—The Private Use of Secret Agents*. New York: William Morrow, 1978.

————. *Secret Agenda: Watergate, Deep Throat, and the CIA*. New York: Random House, 1984.

E. Howard Hunt. *The Berlin Ending*. New York: Putnam, 1973.

*————. *Give Us This Day*. New York: Arlington House, 1973.

*————. *Undercover*. New York: Berkley-Putnam's, 1974.

*Henry Hurt. *Shadrin: The Spy Who Never Came Back*. New York: McGraw-Hill, 1981.

*Haynes Johnson. *The Bay of Pigs*. New York: Norton, 1962.

Lyman B. Kirkpatrick, Jr. *The Real CIA*. New York: Macmillan, 1968.

Philip Knightley. *The Master Spy*. New York: Knopf, 1989.

————. *The Second-Oldest Profession: Spies and Spying in the Twentieth Century*. New York: Penguin Books, 1988.

Richard W. Krousher. *Physical Interrogation Techniques*. Port Townsend, Wash.: Loompanics, Unlimited, 1985.

Jonathan Kwitny. *The Crimes of Patriots: A True Tale of Dope, Dirty Money, and the CIA*. New York: Norton, 1987.

Robert J. Lamphere and Tom Schachtman. *The FBI–KGB War: A Special Agent's Story*. New York: Random House, 1986.

Mark Lane. *Rush to Judgment*. Troy, Mich.: Holt, Rinehart and Winston, 1966.

Aaron Latham. *Orchids for Mother*. Boston: Little, Brown, 1977.

William J. Lederer and Eugene Burdick. *The Ugly American*. New York: Fawcett Crest, 1958.

*Victor Marchetti and John D. Marks. *The CIA and the Cult of Intelligence*. New York: Knopf, 1974.

*David C. Martin. *Wilderness of Mirrors*. New York: Harper and Row, 1980.

J.C. Masterman. *The Double-Cross System in the War of 1939 to 1945*. New Haven: Yale University Press, 1972.

*Patrick J. McGarvey. *CIA: The Myth and the Madness*. New York: Dutton, 1972.

*Ralph W. McGehee. *Deadly Deceits*. New York: Sheridan Square, 1983.

Cord Meyer, Jr. *Facing Reality: From World Federalism to the CIA*. New York: Harper and Row, 1980.

Jan Moen. *John Moe, Double Agent*. Edinburgh: Mainstream Publications, 1986.

William B. Moran. *Covert Surveillance and Electronic Penetration*. Port Townsend, Wash.: Loompanics, Unlimited, 1983.

*Robert D. Morrow. *Betrayal: A Reconstruction of Certain Clandestine Events from the Bay of Pigs to the Assassination of John F. Kennedy*. Chicago: Henry Regnery Co., 1976.

————. *The Senator Must Die: The Murder of Robert F. Kennedy*. Santa Monica, Calif.: Roundtable Publishing, 1988.

*Leonard Mosley. *Dulles: A Biography of Eleanor, Allen and John Foster Dulles and Their Family Network*. New York: Dial Press, 1978.

*Malcolm Muggeridge. *Chronicles of Wasted Time (2): The Infernal Grove*. London: Collins, 1973.

★Carl Oglesby. *The Yankee and Cowboy War*. Kansas City, Mo.: Sheed, Andrews and McMeel, 1976.

★Bruce Page, David Leitch, and Philip Knightly. *The Philby Conspiracy*. Garden City, N.Y.: Doubleday, 1968.

Oleg Penkovsky. *The Penkovsky Papers*. New York: Ballantine, 1965.

Barrie Penrose and Simon Freeman. *Conspiracy of Silence: The Secret Life of Anthony Blunt*. London: Grafton, 1986.

Eleanor Philby. *Kim Philby, the Spy I Married*. New York: Simon and Schuster, 1967.

★Kim Philby. *My Silent War*. New York: Grove Press, 1968.

★David Atlee Phillips. *The Night Watch*. New York: Atheneum, 1977.

————. *Secret Wars Diary: My Adventures in Combat, Espionage Operations, and Covert Action*. Bethesda, Md.: Stone Trail Press, 1980.

Chapman Pincher. *Too Secret Too Long*. New York: St. Martin's, 1984.

————. *Traitors*. New York: St. Martin's Press, 1987.

Richard H. Popkin. *The Second Oswald*. New York: Avon, 1966.

Dusko Popov. *Spy/Counterspy: The Autobiography of Dusko Popov*. New York: Grosset and Dunlap, 1974.

Richard Gid Powers. *Secrecy and Power: The Life of J. Edgar Hoover*. New York: The Free Press, 1987.

★Thomas Powers. *The Man Who Kept the Secrets: Richard Helms and the CIA*. New York: Knopf, 1979.

L. Fletcher Prouty. *The Secret Team*. New York: Prentice Hall, 1973.

John Patrick Quirk, David Atlee Philips, Dr. Ray Cline, and Walter Pforzheimer. *The Central Intelligence Agency: A Photographic History*. Gilbert, Conn.: Foreign Intelligence Press, 1986.

John Ranelagh. *The Agency: The Rise and Decline of the CIA from Wild Bill Donovan to Bill Casey*. New York: Simon and Schuster, 1987.

Burt Rapp. *Shadowing and Surveillance: A Complete Guidebook*. Port Townsend, Wash.: Loompanics, Unlimited, 1986.

Anthony Read and David Fisher. *Colonel Z, The Secret Life of a Master of Spies*. New York: Viking, 1975.

Jeffrey T. Richelson. *The U.S. Intelligence Community*. Cambridge, Mass.: Ballinger, 1985.

Felix I. Rodriguez and John Weisman. *Shadow Warrior: The CIA Hero of a Hundred Unknown Battles*. New York: Simon and Schuster, 1989.

Ron Rosenbaum. "The Shadow of the Mole," in *Harper's*. Oct. 1983.

★Arthur Schlesinger, Jr. *Robert Kennedy and His Times*. New York: Houghton Mifflin, 1978.

Stephen Schlesinger and Stephen Kinzer. *Bitter Fruit: The Untold Story of the American Coup in Guatemala*. Garden City, N.Y.: Doubleday, 1982.

★Senate Committee on Foreign Relations. *Hearing on CIA Foreign and Domestic Activities*. Washington, D.C.: USGPO, 1975.

★Senate Select Committee on Government Operations with Respect to Intelligence Activities. *Alleged Assassination Plots Involving Leaders*. Washington, D.C.: USGPO, 1975.

Arkady N. Shevchenko. *Breaking with Moscow*. New York: Knopf, 1985.

Harris Smith. *OSS*. Berkeley: University of California Press, 1972.

Joseph Burckholder Smith. *Portrait of a Cold Warrior*. New York: Putnam's, 1976.

Frank Snepp. *Decent Interval*. New York: Random House, 1977.

Bernard Spindel. *The Ominous Ear*. New York: Award House, 1968.

*Stewart Steven. *Operation Splinter Factor*. Philadelphia: Lippincott, 1977.

John Stockwell. *In Search of Enemies*. New York: Norton, 1978.

Anthony Summers. *Conspiracy*. New York: McGraw-Hill, 1980.

Viktor Suvorov. *Aquarium: The Career and Defection of a Soviet Military Spy*. London: Hamish Hamilton, 1985.

Tad Szulc. *Compulsive Spy: The Strange Career of E. Howard Hunt*. New York: Viking, 1974.

———. *Fidel, A Critical Portrait*. New York: William Morrow, 1986.

*Hugh Thomas. *Cuba, the Pursuit of Freedom*. London: Eyre, 1971.

Gregory F. Treverton. *Covert Action: The Limits of Intervention in the Post-War World*. New York: Basic Books, 1987.

Hugh Trevor-Roper. *The Philby Affair*. London: William Kimber, 1968.

Andrew Tully. *CIA, the Inside Story*. New York: William Morrow, 1962.

Stansfield Turner. *Secrecy and Democracy: The CIA in Transition*. New York: Houghton Mifflin, 1985.

Ernest Volkman. *Warriors of the Night: Spies, Soldiers and American Intelligence*. New York: William Morrow, 1985.

David Wise. *The American Police State*. New York: Random House, 1976.

David Wise and Thomas B. Ross. *The Espionage Establishment*. New York: Random House, 1967.

*———. *The Invisible Government*. New York: Random House, 1964.

Peter Wright (with Paul Greengrass). *Spycatcher*. New York: Viking, 1987.

Peter Wyden. *Bay of Pigs: The Untold Story*. New York: Simon and Schuster, 1979.

CHARACTERS, ORGANIZATIONS,

CRYPTONYMS, COVER NAMES

(NOTE: Characters who appear in only one episode
and are not referred to again are not listed, but an asterisk precedes
all real historical personages, and all actual cryptonyms;
a dagger precedes the names of those people who were directly
involved in the Watergate break-in.)

*Dean Acheson   Secretary of State under Harry Truman, member of Ex com under
    John F. Kennedy
*Roberto Alejos   owner of the tract of land in Guatemala given to TRAX
*AM/BLOOD   cryptonym for Cuban contact to Rolando Cubela
*AM/LASH   cryptonym for Rolando Cubela
ANCHOVY-BLUE   operational name for Harry Hubbard in ANCHOVY project
ANCHOVY-GRAY   operational name for Fidel Castro
ANCHOVY-RED   operational name for William Harvey
ANCHOVY-WHITE   operational name for Johnny Roselli
*Aureliano Sanchez Aranjo   Frente leader
*Manuel Artime   Frente and Brigade leader
*William Attwood   Special Advisor to the U.S. delegation to the UN
AURAL   code name for Wilma Raye, Modene's friend
AV/AILABLE   cryptonym for Harry Hubbard in Montevideo
AV/ALANCHE 1–7   slogan-painting gang working for CIA in Montevideo
AV/ANTGARDE   cryptonym for agent run by Gordy Morewood
AV/ARICE   cryptonym for journalist working for CIA in Montevideo
AV/EMARIA 1–4   cryptonym for mobile surveillance team in Montevideo
AV/ERAGE   cryptonym for journalist working for CIA in Montevideo
AV/FIREBOMB   cryptonym for Chief of Uruguayan Army Intelligence
AV/GROUNDHOG   cryptonym for grocery-clerk agent in Montevideo
AV/HACENDADO   cryptonym for Howard Hunt in Montevideo
AV/IARY 1–3   cryptonyms for the Bosqueverdes
AV/IATOR   cryptonym for journalist working for CIA in Montevideo
AV/LEADPIPE   cryptonym for Uriarte, an agent run by Jay Gatsby
AV/OCADO   cryptonym for Chevi Fuertes in Montevideo
AV/OIRDUPOIS   cryptonym for Gordy Morewood

*Arthur Balletti   private detective hired by Robert Maheu
Faustino (Toto) Barbaro   Frente leader
*†Bernard Barker   Howard Hunt's assistant in Miami
*Tracy Barnes   CIA officer
*Luis Batlle   President of Uruguay
*Frank Bender   CIA officer
*Richard Bissell   CIA officer
Don Bosco Teótimo Blandenques   owner of Montevideo villa rented to Varkhov

*Capt. Roy E. Blick   officer in the Washington, D.C., police force
BLUEBEARD   code name for Modene Murphy
BONANZA   cryptonym for Chevi Fuertes
Bradley (Sparker) Boone   St. Matthew's classmate of Harry Hubbard
Greta Bosqueverde   CIA agent in Montevideo
Hyman Bosqueverde   CIA agent in Montevideo
Rosa Bosqueverde   CIA agent in Montevideo
BOZO   cryptonym for William Harvey
*McGeorge Bundy   member of Special Group, Augmented
*Guy Burgess   friend and colleague of Kim Philby and an agent for the KGB
Raymond James (Bullseye) Burns   a training officer in CIA; later, in CIA Office of
    Security
Damon Butler   first mate in Augustus Farr's crew
Dix Butler   Harry Hubbard's classmate at the Farm
Gilley Butler   one of Harry Hubbard's neighbors in Maine
Wilbur Butler   Gilley Butler's son

*Gen. Charles Cabell   DDCI and Acting Director during the Bay of Pigs operation
Salvador Capablanca   Montevideo Chief of Police
Don Jaime Saavedra Carbajal   Uruguayan landowner
*José Miro Cardona   head of the Cuban Revolutionary Council
Carey   code name for CIA agent stationed in London
*Justo Carrillo   Frente leader
*Marshall Carter   DDCI under John McCone
Frank Castle   cover name for Dix Butler in Miami
*Raul Castro   Fidel Castro's brother
CATHETER   cryptonym for the Berlin tunnel operation
Robert Charles   cover name for Harry Hubbard in Miami
Chloe   Harry Hubbard's mistress in Maine
Roger Clarkson   CIA contract agent in Montevideo
COLT   cryptonym for William Harvey
*Miles Copeland   CIA officer
Crane   code name for CIA agent stationed in London
Crosby   officer on Argentina-Uruguay Desk
*Rolando Cubela   second-in-command of the Foreign Division of the Interior
    Ministry of the Castro government

*Jean Daniel   French journalist
*DEA   Drug Enforcement Agency
*Marquis de Goutière   Dorothy Hunt's first husband
*DGI   Castro's intelligence service
DN/FRAGMENT   cryptonym for Harry Hubbard in Snake Pit paper trail
*James Donovan   negotiator for Brigade prisoners
*Allen W. Dulles   Director of the CIA
Snowman Dyer   fisherman (d. 1870) on Bartlett's Island, Maine
*Feliks Dzerzhinsky   father of modern Soviet espionage

*Sheffield Edwards   head of CIA Office of Security
Eleanor   Cal Hubbard's secretary
EUPHONY   cryptonym for Nancy Waterston

Augustus Farr   pirate captain who once owned Doane's Island
Harry (Tom) Field   cover name for Harry Hubbard when with Modene Murphy
*†Frank Fiorini   Cuban exile and gunrunner, a.k.a. Frank Sturgis
*Desmond FitzGerald   CIA officer
Flarrety   Soviet Russia Division operative
*Sam Flood   alias of Sam Giancana
FLORENCE   cryptonym for C. G. Harvey
Eusebio (Chevi) Fuertes   member of Uruguayan Communist Party recruited by
    CIA

GALLSTONE   a cryptonym for Hugh Montague
GANTRY   a cryptonym for Hugh Montague
Maisie Minot Gardiner   Kittredge's mother
Rodman Knowles Gardiner   Kittredge's father
Jay Gatsby   CIA officer in Montevideo
Theodora Gatsby   Jay Gatsby's wife
*Reinhard Gehlen   ex-Nazi working for the BND in Germany
GHOUL   a cryptonym for Hugh Montague
*Sam Giancana   Chicago Mafia don
GIBLETS   cryptonym for William Harvey while Chief of Base, West Berlin
*Roswell Gilpatrick   member of Department of Defense and Special Group, Aug-
    mented
*Gittinger   psychologist working in TSS
*Arthur Godfrey   TV host in the fifties
Gogol   nickname for Hyman Bosqueverde
*Sam Gold   alias of Sam Giancana
Plutarco Roballo Gómez   Uruguayan Foreign Ministry official

HALIFAX   cryptonym for Cal Hubbard on Cuban operations
*Dashiell Hammett   American author
*Col. Hank   U.S. Army commandant at TRAX
Harlot   an in-house name for Hugh Montague
*Averell Harriman   Undersecretary of State for Political Affairs under John F.
    Kennedy; formerly Governor of New York
*Clara Grace Follich (C.G.) Harvey   William Harvey's second wife
*Libby Harvey   William Harvey's first wife
*William King Harvey   former FBI man; COB, West Berlin; later head of Mon-
    goose; then COS, Rome
HEEDLESS   cryptonym for operation with Modene Murphy
*Lillian Hellman   American playwright
*Richard Helms   CIA officer, DDCI under McCone; later DCI
Heulihaen   Soviet Russia Division operative
*Lawrence Houston   CIA officer
*Lisa Howard   journalist for ABC-TV
Boardman Kimball (Cal) Hubbard   father of Harry Hubbard
Colton Shaler Hubbard   cousin of Harry Hubbard
Doane Hadlock Hubbard   Hubbard ancestor who built the Keep
Hadley Kittredge Montague (née Gardiner) Hubbard   third cousin of Harry Hub-
    bard; wife of Hugh Montague; later wife of Harry Hubbard
Herrick Hubbard   known as Harry or Rick

Jessica Silverfield Hubbard   mother of Harry Hubbard
Mary Bolland Baird Hubbard   second wife of Cal Hubbard
Roque Baird (Rough) Hubbard   half-brother of Harry Hubbard
Smallidge Kimball Hubbard   grandfather of Harry Hubbard; Headmaster of St. Matthew's
Toby Bolland (Tough) Hubbard   half-brother of Harry Hubbard
Randy Huff   cover name for Dix Butler in Berlin
★Dorothy Hunt   wife of E. Howard Hunt
★†E. Howard Hunt   COS in Montevideo and propaganda officer during the Bay of Pigs operation

IOTA   code name for John F. Kennedy in HEEDLESS
Ingrid   dollar-a-dance girl at Die Hintertür

★JM/WAVE   CIA base in Miami during Mongoose
★U. Alexis Johnson   Deputy Undersecretary of State for Political Affairs, member of Special Group, Augmented

Barry Kearns   Communications Officer in Montevideo
★J. C. King   chief of Western Hemisphere Division
★David Knight   cover name for David Phillips
★Mario García Kohly   pro-Batista Cuban exile leader
KU/CLOAKROOM   cryptonym for Harry Hubbard during his assignment to the Snake Pit
KU/ROPES   one-time cryptonym for Harry Hubbard

Libertad La Lengua   courtesan in Havana and Montevideo
★Gen. Edward Lansdale   director of Mongoose
★Meyer Lansky   leading criminal, based in Miami
★Julius LaRosa   entertainer on Arthur Godfrey's TV show
★Carlos Lechuga   Cuban Ambassador to the UN
★Gen. Lyman Lemnitzer   member of Special Group, Augmented
William Madden Libby   alias on Harry Hubbard's passport in 1984
Mr. and Mrs. Lowenthal   Harry Hubbard's landlords in the Bronx
LYME   cryptonym for Rolando Cubela's case officer in São Paulo

★Sir Donald Maclean   British intelligence agent stationed in the U.S.A., working for the Soviets
★Antonio Maceo   member of Cuban Revolutionary Council
★Robert Maheu   ex-FBI, private detective for Howard Hughes, occasional contract agent for CIA
Minot Mayhew   COS, Montevideo, before arrival of Howard Hunt
Maria   bartender at Die Hintertür
★José Martí   revolutionary and poet during Cuba's struggle for independence from Spain
★†Eugenio Martínez   Cuban exile boat captain
★Rolando Masferrer   pro-Batista Cuban exile
Boris Masarov   Undersecretary of Soviet Embassy in Montevideo
Zenia Masarov   wife of Boris Masarov
Freddie McCann   CIA Junior Officer in Berlin

Martita Bailey (Bunny) McCann   wife of Freddie McCann
*John McCone   DCI replacing Allen Dulles
*Dorothy McGuire   one of the McGuire Sisters, a singing group
*Phyllis McGuire   Dorothy McGuire's sister; Sam Giancana's girlfriend
*Reggie Minnie   boxing instructor at the Farm
*MI5   British domestic intelligence service, comparable to FBI
*MI6   British foreign intelligence service, comparable to CIA
MK/ULTRA-17   a cryptonym for Kittredge Montague at TSS
*Mongoose   operation subsequent to Bay of Pigs to destabilize Cuba by a variety of
    covert means
Hugh Tremont Montague   high-level CIA officer, a.k.a. Harlot
Christopher Montague   son of Hugh and Kittredge Montague
Gordon (Gordy) Morewood   CIA contract agent in Montevideo
*Mossad   Israeli intelligence service
*MRO   ultra-left, sometimes violent Uruguayan political group
Modene (Mo) Murphy   Eastern Airlines stewardess and mistress to John Kennedy,
    Sam Giancana, Frank Sinatra, and Harry Hubbard

*Benito Nardone   Uruguayan politician elected head of government
Regina Nelson   Howard Hunt's neighbor in Miami
*NKVD   Soviet secret police, a precursor of the KGB
*Archie Norcross   COS replacing Hunt in Montevideo
*NSC   National Security Council

O'Brien   code name for William Harvey in dealings with Johnny Roselli
*Tony Oliva   Brigade leader
*Dr. Frank Olson   victim of CIA experiment with LSD
Hjalmar Omaley   Soviet Russia Division operative
*OSS   Office of Special Services, U.S. intelligence service organized during WW II,
    precursor of the CIA
Otis   cover name for a CIA agent stationed in London

Gen. Packer   representative of Joint Chiefs visiting Berlin
*Joe Pecora   alias of Santos Trafficante
Pedro Peones   Deputy Chief of Police in Montevideo
*Kim Philby   British intelligence officer working for the Soviets
*David Phillips   chief propaganda officer at Quarters Eye
Susan Blaylock Pierce   American consulate employee in Berlin
Sally Porringer   wife of Sherman Porringer
Sherman Porringer   CIA officer in Montevideo
Margaret Pugh   secretary to Hugh Montague

*Johnny Ralston   alias of Johnny Roselli
RAPUNZEL   cryptonym for Sam Giancana
*José Ignacio Rasco   Frente leader
RASPUTIN   code name for Fidel Castro
*Wilma (Willie) Raye   Modene Murphy's friend
RETREAD   cryptonym for Toto Barbaro
*Blanco Rico   military intelligence officer in Batista government of Cuba
*Raul Roa   Cuban Ambassador to the UN

*Rolando   cover name for Eugenio Martínez
*Johnny Roselli   California-based Mafia member
Reed Arnold (Arnie) Rosen   classmate of Harry Hubbard at the Farm; later Kittredge Montague's assistant at TSS
*Dan Rowan   entertainer
*Jack Ruby   killer of Lee Harvey Oswald
*Enrique Ruiz-Williams   Brigade fighter released from Cuban prison

*Pepe San Román   Brigade leader
*Charles Sapp   Chief of Police Intelligence in Miami
Peter Sawyer   cover name used by Harry Hubbard in the Bronx
Dr. Schneider   an alias for Reinhard Gehlen
*SGA (Special Group, Augmented)   a committee of high-ranking military, Cabinet, and other government personnel overseeing Mongoose
Charley Sloate   cover name for Harry Hubbard in Berlin
Polly Galen Smith   classmate of Kittredge Montague at Radcliffe
SM/ONION   cryptonym for Harry Hubbard in Snake Pit paper trail
Augustus (Gus) Sonderstrom   Deputy COS in Montevideo
*SSD   East German intelligence service
STONEHENGE   cryptonym for Frank Sinatra

Dr. Taylor   cover name for Hugh Montague in Berlin
*Gen. Maxwell Taylor   member of SGA
*Clyde Tolson   J. Edgar Hoover's assistant and companion
*Santos Trafficante   head of Mafia in Cuba operations during Batista regime and afterward in Southern Florida
*TRAX   Brigade training camp in Guatemala, donated by Roberto Alejos
*TSS (Technical Services Staff)   a division of the CIA specializing in psychoactive drugs, poisons, special weapons, and other exotica
Roger Turner   one of Harry Hubbard's Berlin roommates

Vassily Vakhtanov   Soviet defector
*Dr. René Vallejo   Castro's friend and physician
Georgi Varkhov   KGB chief in Montevideo
VQ/BOZO   Bill Harvey's office in Berlin
VQ/COLT   paved parking area behind Harvey's Berlin home
VQ/GIBLETS-1   Bill Harvey's private office in his Berlin home
VQ/STARTER   cryptonym for Harry Hubbard in Berlin

Nancy Waterston   Administrative Officer in Montevideo; later worked in Secretary of State Dean Rusk's office
WILDBOAR   cryptonym for Wolfgang
*Frank Wisner   CIA officer
Wolfgang   German agent for CIA
*Robert Woodward   U.S. Ambassador to Uruguay

*Miguel Ydígoras Fuentes   President of Guatemala
*Yevgeny Yevtushenko   Soviet poet

Eliot Zeeler   one of Harry Hubbard's Berlin roommates
*ZR/RIFLE   "executive action" (i.e., assassination) operation

PLACES

Avenue of the 18th of July   main boulevard of Montevideo

Bangor   city in Maine
Bartlett's Island   small island off western shore of Mt. Desert
Blue Hill Bay   large bay to west of Mt. Desert Island
Boiler Room   nickname for CIA file chamber prior to computerization

Calle Ocho   SW 8th Street, main street of the Cuban exiles in Miami
Camp Peary   field training center for CIA officers-in-training, also known as the
    Farm
Carrasco   a wealthy suburb of Montevideo
Casa de Tres Árboles (House of the Three Trees)   a Montevideo brothel
Cathedral   a trail on Mt. Katahdin
El Cervantes   the cheap hotel where Harry Hubbard lives in Montevideo
Charlevoix   Lake Michigan resort town
Cockroach Alley   another name for the I-J-K-L Complex
Colony   a Manhattan restaurant

Department Store   CIA slang for the largest brothel in Saigon
Doane   small island off Mt. Desert Island owned first by the Hubbard family, later
    sold to the Gardiners
Document Room   CIA repository of newspapers, journals, and reports awaiting
    filing

The Farm   another name for Camp Peary
Frenchman's Bay   body of water to the east of Mt. Desert Island

Georgetown   a residential district in Washington, D.C.
Girón   main landing site at the Bay of Pigs
Grand Concourse   major avenue in the Bronx
Green Beach   a landing site for the Brigade at the Bay of Pigs
Guantánamo   U.S. Marine base in Cuba

Happy Valley   another name for the Brigade airfield in Guatemala
Harvey's   a Washington, D.C., restaurant
Hickory Hill   Robert Kennedy's estate near Washington
Die Hintertür   Berlin nightclub

I-J-K-L Complex   four long office sheds around the Reflecting Pool in Washington, D.C., containing the greater part of CIA offices prior to the completion of Langley headquarters in 1961

Katahdin   highest mountain in Maine
The Keep   Hubbard summer home on Doane Island, Maine, later sold to the Gardiners
Kinshasa   formerly Léopoldville, capital of the Congo, now Zaire
Ku-damm   short for Kurfürstendamm
Kufu   short for Kurfürstendamm
Kurfürstendamm   major hotel and shopping avenue in West Berlin

La Villa Nevisca (House of the Light Snowfall)   a well-appointed safe house in Miami
Long Doane   main trail on Doane Island

Malecón   boulevard in Havana that runs along the sea
McLean   Virginia town near Langley
Midway Airport   domestic airport in Chicago
Morey's   student bar at Yale
Mt. Desert Island   an island off the coast of Maine, forty miles south of Bangor

Northeast Harbor   town on Mt. Desert Island

Oak Park   suburb of Chicago
Oneonta   town in upstate New York

Palm Springs   desert resort in California
Penobscot River   river in eastern Maine
Playa de Los Pocitos   beach in Montevideo
Playa Larga (Red Beach)   Bay of Pigs battleground
Puerto de Cabezas   seaport where the Brigade's supply ships were loaded with troops and their equipment
Pullach   BND headquarters near Munich
Punta del Este   resort town in Uruguay

Quarters Eye   CIA headquarters in Washington for Bay of Pigs operation

Rambla   boulevard fronting the beach in Montevideo
Retalhuleu   Guatemalan airport used by Brigade
Royal Palms   run-down motel in Miami

San Blas   village near Girón
Sans Souci   a Washington, D.C., restaurant
Schönefeld   airport outside of Berlin
Sheremetyevo   international airport in Moscow
6312 Riviera Drive   house in Miami with private dock for clandestine naval raids on Cuba
Snake Pit   nickname for CIA file chamber prior to computerization
The Stable   Kittredge and Hugh Montague's house in Georgetown

Swan Island   site of clandestine radio transmitter sending coded messages to Cuba
    during the Bay of Pigs
Swivet   CIA office at Tempelhof, West Berlin

La Teja   poor neighborhood in Montevideo
Tempelhof   airport in West Berlin
Thyme Hill   Dix Butler's horse farm in Virginia
Twenty-One   a restaurant in midtown Manhattan

Victoria Plaza Hotel   hotel in Montevideo

Waldorf Towers   apartment-hotel attached to the Waldorf-Astoria

Zenith   CIA headquarters site in Miami

FOREIGN PHRASES

abrazo embrace
accomblé inoperative, overwhelmed
ambiente ambiance
añejo a dry rum
Ay, caramba! Can you believe it!
Ayúdame, compadre. Help me, my friend.

barbudos lit., "bearded ones"; nickname for Castro's soldiers
beaucoup much
Besitos, estúpido Kisses, stupid

caballero gentleman
caballero espléndido distinguished gentleman
café con leche coffee with milk
casa del Coloso house of the Colossus (i.e., the United States)
casa ella in her house, referring to her
cerveza beer
chez les Russes among the Russians
chico kiddo
ciao good-bye
claro of course; agreed
cojones testicles
comandante commander
cómico comical
como dos melones gigantescos like two giant melons
con más distinguidos sentimientos with my most distinguished sentiments
Cómo no? Isn't that so? Right?
coño sur lit., "cone of the south"; i.e., South America from the southern border of
    Brazil to the Straits of Magellan

desnudar to denude, divest
división de opiniones controversy
droit de seigneur feudal right of the first night
Du liebst mich? Do you love me?
Du liebst mich ein Bisschen. You love me a little.
duros tough guys, thugs

eiskaltblütig   ice-cold-blooded, cold-blooded
el caudillo   the leader
el Mar Caribe   the Caribbean
el mundo sintético de Miami   the synthetic world of Miami
el patrón   the owner
Embajada de Gran Bretaña   Embassy of Great Britain
embajaderos   ambassadors
emisiones lo más elegantes   most distinguished emissions
Encore je blague   Again, I joke
en el fondo   at bottom
en famille   in the family
espontáneo   an amateur who jumps over the railing into a bullfight
estancia   ranch

fenomenal   phenomenal
Fidelistas   followers of Castro
Figure-toi!   Conceive of it!
flics   police
fundador   brandy

gangsterismo   gangster style, or way of life
golpe   a shot of liquor; a blow, a punch
granja de pueblo   village farm

Habanero   native of Havana
hacendado   rancher, land-owner
hermano   brother
Hola!   Hey! Hello!
hombre   man

Il n'y a rien de mieux?   Nothing better?
inter alia   among other things

ja   yes
joven   young man
Joven, este botella es sin vergüenza. Por favor, trae un otro con un corcho correcto.   Young man, this bottle is shameless. Please bring another with a cork that is not rotten.

kishkes   guts

la partouse   orgy
le mot juste   the perfect word
l'homme moyen sensuel   an average man

madre del diablo   mother of the devil
mais oui   of course
malgré lui   despite him
mañana   tomorrow
Marxismo es mierda.   Marxism is shit.
Marxismo es odioso.   Marxism is disgusting.

mayombero   practitioner of *palo mayombe,* or black magic
mein Schatz, liebster Schatz   my sweetheart, my beloved
mille baisers   a thousand kisses
Monsieur, il y a des mauvaises nouvelles. Des nouvelles étonnants. Votre President Kennedy a été frappé par un assassin à Dallas, Texas.   Sir, there is very bad news. Shocking news. Your President Kennedy has been shot by an assassin in Dallas, Texas.
muy jocoso   very funny

nichts   nothing
novio   fiancé

Oberhofmeister   top boss
On ne sait de plus, monsieur, sauf qu'il y avait un grand bouleversement.   One doesn't know any more, sir, than that there's been a terrible disruption.

perdiz   partridge
pistolero   a man who carries a handgun
poco   a little
por fortuna   by chance
pourboire   tip, gratuity
precioso   rare, wonderful
prestidigitación   sleight of hand
privar   to deprive
pronto   immediately
pundonor   masculine honor, noblesse oblige
punkt   exactly, precisely

residentura   leading KGB man in a Russian embassy

Salud!   Health!
sans façons   without artifice, straight
Santería   Afro-Cuban magical religion that combines Yoruba gods with Catholic saints
shtup   fuck, i.e., a stuffing
shvartzer   black man
siestero   one who takes a midday nap
sub cauda   under the tail
Suerte   Good luck.
sui generis   unique

tapas   appetizers
todas las noches   every night

un hermafrodito   hermaphrodite
un juego de manos   a trick of the hands
un tour de drôle   a farce
una enormidad   an enormity, a catastrophe
una mujer sin alma   a woman without scruples
und so weiter   and so forth
Uno, dos, tres, quatro, viva Fidel Castro Ruz!   One, two, three, four, long live Fidel Castro Ruz!

vaquero   cowboy
verboten   forbidden
Verdad?   True? Is that so?
verwundbar   vulnerable, sore, tender
Vous-êtes américain?   Are you American?

Yanqui, fuera.   Yankee, go home.

NORMAN MAILER was born in Long Branch, New Jersey, in 1923 and grew up in Brooklyn, New York. After graduation from Harvard, he served in the South Pacific during World War II. *Harlot's Ghost* is his twenty-seventh book to be published since *The Naked and the Dead* in 1948. He won the National Book Award and the Pulitzer Prize in 1968 for *Armies of the Night* and won the Pulitzer Prize again in 1980 for *The Executioner's Song*. He has directed four feature-length films, was a co-founder of *The Village Voice* in 1955, and was president of American PEN from 1984 to 1986.